Behind the Scenes
of the Old Testament

Behind the Scenes
of the Old Testament

CULTURAL, SOCIAL, AND HISTORICAL CONTEXTS

EDITED BY

Jonathan S. Greer, John W. Hilber, and John H. Walton

Baker Academic
a division of Baker Publishing Group
Grand Rapids, Michigan

Published by Baker Academic
a division of Baker Publishing Group
PO Box 6287, Grand Rapids, MI 49516-6287
www.bakeracademic.com

Printed in the United States of America

Library of Congress Cataloging-in-Publication Data
Names: Greer, Jonathan S., editor. | Hilber, John W. (John Walter), editor. | Walton, John H.,
    1952– editor.
Title: Behind the scenes of the Old Testament : cultural, social, and historical contexts / edited by
    Jonathan S. Greer, John W. Hilber, and John H. Walton.
Description: Grand Rapids, MI : Baker Academic, a division of Baker Publishing Group, [2018] |
    Includes bibliographical references and index.
Identifiers: LCCN 2018020594 | ISBN 9780801097751 (cloth : alk. paper)
Subjects: LCSH: Bible. Old Testament—History of contemporary events. | Middle East—
    History—To 622. | Middle East—Civilization—To 622.
Classification: LCC DS62.23 .B45 2018 | DDC 221.9/5—dc23
LC record available at https://lccn.loc.gov/2018020594

Figure 19.7 included courtesy of The Eretz Israel Museum.

Figure 22.1 included courtesy of the Israel Museum. Collection of the Israel Museum, Jerusalem, and courtesy of the Israel Antiquities Authority, exhibited at the Israel Museum, Jerusalem.

Cover art
Top register: Painted lion hunt scene from Til Barsip (Fort Shalmaneser) dating to the reign of Tiglath-Pileser III (r. 745–727 BCE).
Bottom register: *Monleon y Torres*, Rafael (1835–1900). Watercolor. Navy Museum, Madrid. The painting is apparently based on Phoenician vessels depicted in an Assyrian wall relief from the southern palace of Sennacherib (r. 704–681 BCE).

22 23 24 25   8 7 6 5 4 3

green press
INITIATIVE

Contents

List of Illustrations   viii

Contributors   x

Abbreviations   xiv

Introduction   *Jonathan S. Greer, John W. Hilber, and John H. Walton*   xvii

PART ONE
Elements of the Drama

I. The Stage: Historical Geography

1. Introduction to Historical Geography
   Paul H. Wright   5

2. Regions and Routes in the Levant
   Carl G. Rasmussen   12

3. Climate and Environment of the
   Levant   *Elizabeth Arnold*   21

4. Plants and Animals of the Land of
   Israel   *Daniel Fuks and Nimrod
   Marom*   28

II. The Sets and Props: Archaeology

5. Introduction to Biblical Archaeology
   Seymour Gitin   39

6. Archaeology of the Late Bronze Age
   Joe Uziel   47

7. Archaeology of the Iron Age I
   Aren M. Maeir   54

8. Archaeology of the Iron Age II
   Amihai Mazar   62

9. Archaeology of the Neo-Babylonian
   and Persian Periods   *Constance E.
   Gane*   70

10. Archaeology of the Hellenistic Period
    Jordan Ryan   78

III. The Scripts: Ancient Near Eastern Literature

11. Introduction to Ancient Near Eastern
    Literature   *Adam E. Miglio*   91

12. Mesopotamian Literature   *David C.
    Deuel*   97

13. Egyptian Literature   *Nili
    Shupak*   104

14. Hittite Literature   *Alice
    Mouton*   112

15. Ugaritic Literature   *William D.
    Barker*   120

16. Northwest Semitic Inscriptions
    Margaret E. Cohen   126

17. Hebrew Inscriptions   *Judith M.
    Hadley*   135

18. Early Jewish Literature   *Ryan E.
    Stokes*   142

IV. The Frames: Ancient Near Eastern Iconography

19. Introduction to Ancient Near Eastern Iconography *Izak Cornelius* 151

20. Egyptian Iconography *Laura Wright* 159

21. Mesopotamian and Anatolian Iconography *Daniel Bodi* 165

22. Canaanite/Israelite Iconography *Brent A. Strawn* 172

PART TWO
Acts and Scenes of the Drama

V. Acts: Integrated Approaches to Broad Historical Contexts

23. The Ancestral Period *Richard S. Hess* 187

24. The Egyptian Sojourn and the Exodus *David A. Falk* 194

25. The Settlement Period *Pekka Pitkänen* 201

26. The United Monarchy *Steven M. Ortiz* 208

27. The Divided Monarchy: Israel *Jens Bruun Kofoed* 216

28. The Divided Monarchy: Judah *Eric L. Welch* 223

29. The Exile and the Exilic Communities *Deirdre N. Fulton* 230

30. The Achaemenid Persian Empire in the West and Persian-Period Yehud *Kenneth A. Ristau* 236

31. The Maccabean Revolt and Hasmonean Statecraft *Joel Willitts* 244

VI. Scenes: Integrated Approaches to Event-Based Historical Contexts

32. Akhenaten and the Amarna Period *Mark D. Janzen* 253

33. The Late Bronze Age Collapse and the Sea Peoples' Migrations *Gregory D. Mumford* 260

34. Sheshonq's Levantine Conquest and Biblical History *Yigal Levin* 272

35. The Battle of Qarqar and Assyrian Aspirations *Mark W. Chavalas* 279

36. The Mesha Inscription and Relations with Moab and Edom *Juan Manuel Tebes* 286

37. The Tel Dan Inscription and the Deaths of Joram of Israel and Ahaziah of Judah *K. Lawson Younger Jr.* 293

38. Sennacherib's Invasion of Judah and Neo-Assyrian Expansion *Kyle H. Keimer* 299

39. Eighth-Century Levantine Earthquakes and Natural Disasters *Ryan N. Roberts* 306

40. The Battle of Carchemish and Seventh/Sixth-Century Regional Politics *Sara L. Hoffman* 313

41. Alexander the Great and Hellenism *D. Brent Sandy* 320

PART THREE
Themes of the Drama

VII. God: Integrated Approaches to Themes in Israelite Religion

42. Interactions in the Ancient Cognitive Environment *John H. Walton* 333

43. Monotheism in Ancient Israel *Matthew J. Lynch* 340

44. The Temple in Context   *John H. Walton*   349

45. Priests in the Ancient Near East   *Gerald A. Klingbeil*   355

46. Worship, Sacrifice, and Festivals in the Ancient Near East   *Roy E. Gane*   361

47. Prophecy, Divination, and Magic in the Ancient Near East   *John W. Hilber*   368

48. Family Religion in Ancient Israel   *Andrew R. Davis*   375

49. Death and Burial in the Iron Age Levant   *Christopher B. Hays*   381

VIII. Family: Integrated Approaches to Themes in Family Networks

50. Tribes and Nomads in the Iron Age Levant   *Thomas D. Petter*   391

51. Women in Ancient Israel   *Carol Meyers*   396

52. Family, Children, and Inheritance in the Biblical World   *Victor H. Matthews*   403

IX. Sustenance: Integrated Approaches to Themes in Economic Contexts

53. Seasons, Crops, and Water in the Land of the Bible   *Oded Borowski*   411

54. Trade in the Late Bronze and Iron Age Levant   *Joshua T. Walton*   416

55. Slavery in the World of the Bible   *Richard E. Averbeck*   423

56. The Local Economies of Ancient Israel   *Peter Altmann*   431

57. Metallurgy in the World of the Bible   *Brady Liss and Thomas E. Levy*   438

58. Ancient Technologies of Everyday Life   *Gloria London*   446

59. Food Preparation in Iron Age Israel   *Cynthia Shafer-Elliott*   456

60. Feasting in the Biblical World   *Janling Fu*   464

61. Music and Dance in the World of the Bible   *Annie F. Caubet*   468

X. Governance: Integrated Approaches to Themes in Social Organization

62. Kingship and the State in Ancient Israel   *Nili S. Fox*   475

63. Social Stratification in the Iron Age Levant   *Avraham Faust*   482

64. Law and Legal Systems in Ancient Israel   *David W. Baker*   492

65. Wisdom Traditions in Ancient Israel   *Paul Overland*   499

66. Warfare in the World of the Bible   *Mark Schwartz*   506

Reference List   515

Scripture Index   594

Ancient Text Index   602

Author Index   606

Illustrations

2.1. Key Trade Routes of the Ancient Near East   13

2.2. Map of the Southern Levant   14

2.3. Southern Regions of the Levant   17

4.1. Phytogeographic regions of the southern Levant and rainfall isohyets   29

4.2. Rock outcrops as a runoff source in the Judean foothills   30

4.3. Runoff farms in the Negev Highlands   31

5.1. Sir Flinders Petrie and Lady Petrie in Jerusalem in 1938   40

5.2. Tell Beit Mirsim excavation staff, "Class of 1932"   41

5.3. Nelson Glueck on survey in Transjordan   42

5.4. Yigael Yadin   43

5.5. Yohanan Aharoni   43

5.6. Ekron Royal Dedicatory Inscription   44

5.7. The Tel Dan Inscription   45

10.1. Classical orders of columns   79

10.2. Fortress-palace of Iraq al-Amir, Jordan   80

10.3. Monumental stone-cut tombs in the Kidron Valley in Jerusalem   81

10.4. The stamped handle of a Rhodian amphora   82

10.5. A miqvah discovered at Magdala   83

10.6. Bronze prutah of Alexander Jannaeus   83

10.7. The Givati parking lot excavations   84

10.8. The synagogue at Gamla in the Golan Heights   85

10.9. A street in Magdala in Galilee   86

10.10. Synagogue ruins in New Testament Jericho   87

14.1. Map of Anatolia   113

16.1. Example of a "tree" model   127

16.2. Example of the dialect continuum model   128

19.1. Pharaoh as giant smiting the enemy   152

19.2. Siege of the city of Lachish   154

19.3. Replica of the Et-Tel/Bethsaida Stela   155

19.4. Cylinder seal and modern impression   156

19.5. Scarab seal and modern impression   156

19.6. Judean Pillar Figurines   157

19.7. Yehud coin   158

21.1. Winged composite creature   166

21.2. The Stele of the Vultures   167

21.3. Sargon's Victory Stele   167

21.4. The façade of the Ištar temple at Uruk 169

21.5. Painting of the investiture of the king of Mari 169

21.6. Statue of a goddess with a flowing vase 170

21.7. Statue of King Gudea of Lagaš 170

21.8. Seal impression from an Akkadian cylinder-seal 171

21.9. Orthostat reliefs 171

22.1. Bronze figurine 174

22.2. Judean Pillar Figurines 175

22.3. Pithos A 177

22.4. Projection drawing of Pithos A 178

22.5. Projection drawing of Pithos B 179

22.6. Detail of Pithos A 180

22.7. Limestone scaraboid 180

22.8. Bone scaraboid 181

22.9. Scaraboid from Beth-Shemesh 181

22.10. Scaraboid from Tell en-Nasbeh 181

33.1. Illustration of captive Sea Peoples 263

33.2. Map of settlements destroyed, attacked, or abandoned in the East Mediterranean 265

33.3. Illustration of the Sea Peoples' fleet destroyed at the eastern delta river mouth 268

34.1. Sheshonq conquest list on the Bubastite Portal of the Karnak temple 273

34.2. Partial Egyptian victory stele with cartouche of Sheshonq I 274

34.3. Possible itinerary for the Levantine campaign of Sheshonq I 275

36.1. The Mesha Inscription 287

43.1. A spectrum of biblical representations of Yhwh's categorical supremacy 342

57.1. Aerial photograph of Khirbat en-Nahas 443

57.2. A shaft mine in the Wadi Khalid in Faynan 444

58.1. A traditional potter in her courtyard 447

58.2. People pounding clay with a bent tree branch 448

58.3. Traditional potters in Cyprus 449

58.4. Communal Kornos Pottery Cooperative kiln 449

58.5. Traditional kiln, with a permanent roof 450

58.6. Ovens, jars, cooking pots, and flowerpots stacked in the Cooperative kiln 450

58.7. A traditional potter creates a temporary kiln door from factory-made bricks 451

58.8. Reconstruction of a two-story late-thirteenth-century house 452

59.1. An Iraqi woman baking with a *tannur* 458

59.2. Experimental archaeology at Tel Halif, Israel 459

59.3. Ninth-century traditional-style cooking pots 460

63.1. Plan of Tell el-Farʿa (North) 485

63.2. Graph representing (weighted) inequality at Tell el-Farʿa (North) 486

63.3. Graph representing (weighted) inequality at Beersheba II 486

63.4. Plan of the village of Khirbet Jemein 488

63.5. Graph representing (weighted) inequality at Khirbet Jemein 489

63.6. Graph representing (weighted) inequality at Beit Aryeh 489

Contributors

Editors

Jonathan S. Greer (PhD, The Pennsylvania State University), Associate Professor of Old Testament, Grand Rapids Theological Seminary, Grand Rapids, Michigan

John W. Hilber (PhD, University of Cambridge), Professor of Old Testament, Grand Rapids Theological Seminary, Grand Rapids, Michigan

John H. Walton (PhD, Hebrew Union College), Professor of Old Testament, Wheaton College and Graduate School, Wheaton, Illinois

Authors

Peter Altmann (PhD, Princeton Theological Seminary), Research Associate and Instructor in Old Testament, University of Zurich, Zurich, Switzerland

Elizabeth Arnold (PhD, University of Calgary), Associate Professor of Archaeology, Grand Valley State University, Grand Rapids, Michigan

Richard E. Averbeck (PhD, Dropsie College), Professor of Old Testament and Semitic Languages, Trinity Evangelical Divinity School, Deerfield, Illinois

David W. Baker (PhD, University of London), Professor of Old Testament and Semitic Languages, Ashland Theological Seminary, Ashland, Ohio

William D. Barker (PhD, University of Cambridge), Professor of Biblical Studies and Director of the Center for Faith and Inquiry, Gordon College, Wenham, Massachusetts

Daniel Bodi (PhD, Union Theological Seminary), Professor of History of Religions of Antiquity, University of Paris–Sorbonne, Paris, France

Oded Borowski (PhD, University of Michigan), Professor of Biblical Archaeology and Hebrew, Emory University, Atlanta, Georgia

Annie F. Caubet (PhD, University of Paris–Sorbonne), Louvre Museum, Department of Oriental Antiquities, Paris, France

Mark W. Chavalas (PhD, University of California–Los Angeles), Professor of History, University of Wisconsin–La Crosse, La Crosse, Wisconsin

Margaret E. Cohen (PhD, The Pennsylvania State University), Associate Fellow, W.F. Albright Institute of Archaeological Research, Jerusalem, Israel

Izak Cornelius (DLitt, Stellenbosch University), Professor, Department of Ancient

Studies, Stellenbosch University, Stellenbosch, South Africa

Andrew R. Davis (PhD, Johns Hopkins University), Associate Professor of Old Testament, Boston College, Chestnut Hill, Massachusetts

David C. Deuel (PhD, University of Liverpool), Academic Dean Emeritus, The Master's Academy International and Senior Research Fellow for the Christian Institute on Disability, Los Angeles, California

David A. Falk (PhD, University of Liverpool), Sessional Instructor, Department of Classical, Near Eastern, and Religious Studies, University of British Columbia, Vancouver, British Columbia

Avraham Faust (PhD, Bar-Ilan University), Professor of Archaeology, Bar-Ilan University, Tel Aviv, Israel

Nili S. Fox (PhD, University of Pennsylvania), Professor of Bible, Hebrew Union College, Cincinnati, Ohio

Janling Fu (PhD candidate, Harvard University), Harvard University, Cambridge, Massachusetts

Daniel Fuks (PhD candidate, Bar-Ilan University), Bar-Ilan University, Tel Aviv, Israel

Deirdre N. Fulton (PhD, The Pennsylvania State University), Assistant Professor of Religion, Baylor University, Waco, Texas

Constance E. Gane (PhD, University of California–Berkeley), Associate Professor of Archaeology and Old Testament, Andrews University, Berrien Springs, Michigan

Roy E. Gane (PhD, University of California–Berkeley), Professor of Hebrew Bible and Ancient Near Eastern Languages, Andrews University, Berrien Springs, Michigan

Seymour Gitin (PhD, Hebrew Union College), Dorot Director and Professor of Archaeology Emeritus, W.F. Albright Institute of Archaeological Research, Jerusalem, Israel

Judith M. Hadley (PhD, University of Cambridge), Associate Professor of Religious Studies, Villanova University, Villanova, Pennsylvania

Christopher B. Hays (PhD, Emory University), D. Wilson Moore Associate Professor of Ancient Near Eastern Studies, Fuller Theological Seminary, Irvine, California

Richard S. Hess (PhD, Hebrew Union College), Distinguished Professor of Old Testament, Denver Seminary, Denver, Colorado

Sara L. Hoffman (PhD, The Pennsylvania State University), Lecturer for the Applied Liberal Arts Division, University of Michigan, Ann Arbor, Michigan

Mark D. Janzen (PhD, University of Memphis), Assistant Professor of History and Archaeology, Southwestern Baptist Theological Seminary, Fort Worth, Texas

Kyle H. Keimer (PhD, University of California–Los Angeles), Lecturer in the Archaeology and History of Ancient Israel, Macquarie University, Sydney, Australia

Gerald A. Klingbeil (DLitt, University of Stellenbosch), Research Professor of Old Testament and Ancient Near Eastern Studies, Andrews University, Berrien Springs, Michigan

Jens Bruun Kofoed (PhD, University of Aarhus), Professor of Old Testament, Copenhagen Lutheran School of Theology, Copenhagen, Denmark

Yigal Levin (PhD, Bar-Ilan University), Associate Professor of Jewish History, Bar-Ilan University, Ramat Gan, Israel

Thomas E. Levy (PhD, University of Sheffield), Distinguished Professor of Anthropology and Norma Kershaw Chair in the Archaeology of Ancient Israel and Neighboring Lands, University of California–San Diego, La Jolla, California

Brady Liss (PhD candidate, University of California–San Diego), University of California–San Diego, La Jolla, California

Gloria London (PhD, University of Arizona)

Matthew J. Lynch (PhD, Emory University), Academic Dean and Lecturer in Old Testament, Westminster Theological Centre, Cheltenham, United Kingdom

Aren M. Maeir (PhD, Hebrew University), Professor of Archaeology, Bar-Ilan University, Ramat-Gan, Israel

Nimrod Marom (PhD, University of Haifa), Research Fellow, Institute of Archaeology, University of Haifa, Haifa, Israel

Victor H. Matthews (PhD, Brandeis University), Dean and Professor of Religious Studies, Missouri State University, Springfield, Missouri

Amihai Mazar (PhD, Hebrew University), Eleazer Sukenik Chair of Archaeology Emeritus, Hebrew University of Jerusalem, Jerusalem, Israel

Carol Meyers (PhD, Brandeis University), Mary Grace Wilson Professor Emerita of Religion, Duke University, Durham, North Carolina

Adam E. Miglio (PhD, University of Chicago), Associate Professor of Archaeology, Wheaton College, Wheaton, Illinois

Alice Mouton (PhD, Ecole Pratique des Hautes Etudes, Sorbonne, and Leiden University), Research Professor, The French National Center for Scientific Research, Paris, France

Gregory D. Mumford (PhD, University of Toronto), Associate Professor of Anthropology, University of Alabama at Birmingham, Birmingham, Alabama

Steven M. Ortiz (PhD, University of Arizona), Professor of Archaeology and Biblical Backgrounds, Southwestern Baptist Theological Seminary, Fort Worth, Texas

Paul Overland (PhD, Brandeis University), Professor of Old Testament and Semitic Languages, Ashland Theological Seminary, Ashland, Ohio

Thomas D. Petter (PhD, University of Toronto), Associate Professor of Old Testament, Gordon-Conwell Theological Seminary, Boston, Massachusetts

Pekka Pitkänen (PhD, University of Gloucestershire), Senior Lecturer in Liberal and Performing Arts, University of Gloucestershire, Gloucester, United Kingdom

Carl G. Rasmussen (PhD, Dropsie University), Professor Emeritus, Bethel University, St. Paul, Minnesota

Kenneth A. Ristau (PhD, The Pennsylvania State University), Instructor, Department of Classics, MacEwan University, Edmonton, Alberta

Ryan N. Roberts (PhD, University of California–Los Angeles), Associate Professor of Old Testament, Cornerstone University, Grand Rapids, Michigan

Jordan Ryan (PhD, McMaster University), Assistant Professor of New Testament, University of Dubuque, Dubuque, Iowa

D. Brent Sandy (PhD, Duke University), Adjunct Professor of New Testament, Wheaton College, Wheaton, Illinois

Mark Schwartz (PhD, Northwestern University), Associate Professor of Archaeology, Grand Valley State University, Grand Rapids, Michigan

Cynthia Shafer-Elliott (PhD, University of Sheffield), Associate Professor of Hebrew Bible and Archaeology, William Jessup University, Rocklin, California

Nili Shupak (PhD, Hebrew University), Professor of Biblical Studies and Ancient Egypt, University of Haifa, Haifa, Israel

Ryan E. Stokes (PhD, Yale University), Associate Professor of Old Testament, Southwestern Baptist Theological Seminary, Fort Worth, Texas

Brent A. Strawn (PhD, Princeton Theological Seminary), Professor of Old Testament, Emory University, Atlanta, Georgia

Juan Manuel Tebes (PhD, University of Buenos Aires), IMHICIHU-CONICET, Pontifical Catholic University of Argentina, University of Buenos Aires, Argentina

Joe Uziel (PhD, Bar Ilan University), Israel Antiquities Authority, Jerusalem, Israel

Joshua T. Walton (PhD, Harvard University), Lecturer, Capital University, Columbus, Ohio

Eric L. Welch (PhD, The Pennsylvania State University), Senior Lecturer, Lewis Honors College, University of Kansas, Lawrence, Kansas

Joel Willitts (PhD, University of Cambridge), Professor of Biblical and Theological Studies, North Park University, Chicago, Illinois

Laura Wright (PhD, Johns Hopkins University), Visiting Assistant Professor of Religion, Luther College, Decorah, Iowa

Paul H. Wright (PhD, Hebrew Union College), President, Jerusalem University College, Jerusalem, Israel

K. Lawson Younger Jr. (PhD, University of Sheffield), Professor of Old Testament, Semitic Languages, and Ancient Near Eastern History, Trinity Evangelical Divinity School, Deerfield, Illinois

Abbreviations

AASOR   Annual of the American Schools of Oriental Research
AB   Anchor Bible
ABD   *Anchor Bible Dictionary*. Edited by David Noel Freedman. 6 vols. New York: Doubleday, 1992.
ABS   Archaeology and Biblical Studies
AIL   Ancient Israel and Its Literature
AJA   *American Journal of Archaeology*
ÄL   *Ägypten und Levante / Egypt and the Levant*
AMD   Ancient Magic and Divination
ANEM   Ancient Near East Monographs
ANESSup   Ancient Near Eastern Studies Supplement Series
Ant.   Josephus, *Jewish Antiquities*
AO   Der Alte Orient
AOAT   Alter Orient und Altes Testament
AoF   *Altorientalische Forschungen*
AOS   American Oriental Series
APAAME   Aerial Photographic Archive of Archaeology in the Middle East. http://www .humanities.uwa.edu.au/research/cah /aerial-archaeology.
Apion   Josephus, *Against Apion*
AUSS   *Andrews University Seminary Studies*
BA   *Biblical Archaeologist*
BAR   *Biblical Archaeology Review*
BASOR   *Bulletin of the American Schools of Oriental Research*
BBR   *Bulletin for Biblical Research*
BBRSup   Bulletin for Biblical Research Supplements
BCE   before the Common Era (= BC)
BDB   Francis Brown, S. R. Driver, and Charles A. Briggs. *A Hebrew and English Lexicon of the Old Testament.*

Reprint, Peabody, MA: Hendrickson, 2016.
Bib   *Biblica*
BibOr   Biblica et Orientalia
BJS   Brown Judaic Studies
BJSUCSD   Biblical and Judaic Studies from the University of California, San Diego
BO   *Bibliotheca Orientalis*
BP   before the present
BWANT   Beiträge zur Wissenschaft vom Alten und Neuen Testament
BZAW   Beihefte zur Zeitschrift für die alttestamentliche Wissenschaft
CAD   *The Assyrian Dictionary of the Oriental Institute of the University of Chicago*. Chicago: Oriental Institute of the University of Chicago, 1956–2006.
CANE   *Civilizations of the Ancient Near East*. Edited by Jack M. Sasson et al. 4 vols. New York: Scribner, 1995.
CBET   Contributions to Biblical Exegesis and Theology
CBQ   *Catholic Biblical Quarterly*
CBQMS   Catholic Biblical Quarterly Monograph Series
CE   Common Era (= AD)
CEB   Common English Bible
CHANE   Culture and History of the Ancient Near East
CIJ   *Corpus inscriptionum judaicarum*. Edited by Jean-Baptiste Frey. 2 vols. Rome: Pontifical Biblical Institute, 1936–52.
COS   *The Context of Scripture*. Edited by W. W. Hallo and K. L. Younger Jr. 4 vols. Leiden: Brill, 1997–2016.
CPJ   *Corpus papyrorum judaicarum*. Edited by Victor A. Tcherikover. 3 vols.

	Cambridge, MA: Harvard University Press, 1957–64.
CUSAS	Cornell University Studies in Assyriology and Sumerology
DCH	*Dictionary of Classical Hebrew*. Edited by David J. A. Clines. 9 vols. Sheffield: Phoenix Press, 1993–2014.
DJD	Discoveries in the Judaean Desert
DMOA	Documenta et Monumenta Orientis Antiqui
EA	El-Amarna tablets
EC	*Early Christianity*
ErIsr	*Eretz-Israel*
ESV	English Standard Version
FAT	Forschungen zum Alten Testament
FRLANT	Forschungen zur Religion und Literatur des Alten und Neuen Testaments
HALOT	Ludwig Koehler, Walter Baumgartner, and Johann J. Stamm. *Hebrew and Aramaic Lexicon of the Old Testament*. Translated and edited by Mervyn E. J. Richardson et al. 4 vols. Leiden: Brill, 1994–96.
HdO	Handbuch der Orientalistik
HSM	Harvard Semitic Monographs
HSS	Harvard Semitic Studies
HUCA	*Hebrew Union College Annual*
IEJ	*Israel Exploration Journal*
JANER	*Journal of Ancient Near Eastern Religions*
JANES	*Journal of the Ancient Near Eastern Society*
JAOS	*Journal of the American Oriental Society*
JARCE	*Journal of the American Research Center in Egypt*
JAS	*Journal of Archaeological Science*
JBL	*Journal of Biblical Literature*
JCS	*Journal of Cuneiform Studies*
JEA	*Journal of Egyptian Archaeology*
JESHO	*Journal of the Economic and Social History of the Orient*
JISMOR	*Journal of the Interdisciplinary Study of Monotheistic Religions*
JNES	*Journal of Near Eastern Studies*
JNSL	*Journal of Northwest Semitic Languages*
JPOS	*Journal of the Palestine Oriental Society*
JPS	Jewish Publication Society Version
JSJ	*Journal for the Study of Judaism in the Persian, Hellenistic, and Roman Periods*
JSJSup	Journal for the Study of Judaism Supplement Series
JSOT	*Journal for the Study of the Old Testament*
JSOTSup	Journal for the Study of the Old Testament Supplement Series
JSSEA	*Journal of the Society for the Study of Egyptian Antiquities*
KAI	*Kanaanäische und aramäische Inschriften*. Edited by Herbert Donner and Wolfgang Röllig. 3 vols. 2nd ed. Wiesbaden: Harrassowitz, 1966–69.
KJV	King James Version
KRI	Kenneth A. Kitchen, *Ramesside Inscriptions: Historical and Biographical*. 8 vols. Malden, MA: Blackwell, 1968–90.
KTU	*Die keilalphabetischen Texte aus Ugarit*. Edited by Manfried Dietrich, Oswald Loretz, and Joaquin Sanmartin-Münster: Ugarit-Verlag, 2013.
kya	thousand years ago
LAI	Library of Ancient Israel
LHB/OTS	The Library of Hebrew Bible/Old Testament Studies
Life	Josephus, *Life of Josephus*
LNTS	The Library of New Testament Studies
MC	Mesopotamian Civilizations
NEA	*Near Eastern Archaeology*
NEAEHL	*The New Encyclopedia of Archaeological Excavations in the Holy Land*. Edited by Ephraim Stern, Ayelet Lewinson-Gilboa, and Joseph Aviram. 5 vols. Jerusalem: Israel Exploration Society, 1993, 2008.
NEASB	*Near Eastern Archaeological Society Bulletin*
NIV	New International Version
NJPS	New Jewish Publication Society Version
NKJV	New King James Version
NRSV	New Revised Standard Version
OBO	Orbis Biblicus et Orientalis
OBOSA	Orbis Biblicus et Orientalis, Series Archaeologica
OEAE	*The Oxford Encyclopedia of Ancient Egypt*. Edited by F. L. Cross and E. A. Livingstone. 3rd ed. Oxford: Oxford University Press, 2001.
OEANE	*The Oxford Encyclopedia of Archaeology in the Near East*. Edited by Eric M. Meyers. 5 vols. New York: Oxford University Press, 1997.
OEBA	*Oxford Encyclopedia of the Bible and Archaeology*. Edited by Daniel Master et al. Oxford: Oxford University Press, 2013.

OIP	Oriental Institute Publications		A. Yardeni. 4 vols. Jerusalem: Hebrew
OIS	Oriental Institute Seminars		University; Winona Lake, IN: Eisen-
OLA	Orientalia Lovaniensia Analecta		brauns, 1986–99.
OTL	Old Testament Library	UBL	Ugaritisch-biblische Literatur
OtSt	Oudtestamentische Studiën	UCOP	University of Cambridge Oriental
PÄ	Probleme der Ägyptologie		Publications
Pap.	Papyrus	*UF*	*Ugarit-Forschungen*
PEQ	*Palestine Exploration Quarterly*	UMM	University Museum Monograph
RAI	*Rencontre assyriologique internationale*	*VT*	*Vetus Testamentum*
RB	*Revue biblique*	VTSup	Supplements to Vetus Testamentum
RBS	Resources for Biblical Study	*War*	Josephus, *The Jewish War*
RC	*Religion Compass*	WAW	Writings from the Ancient World
REG	*Revue des études grecques*	*WD*	*Wadi Daliyeh I: The Wadi Daliyeh Seal*
RGRW	Religions in the Graeco-Roman World		*Impressions.* Edited by M. J. W. Leith.
RSV	Revised Standard Version		DJD 24. Oxford: Clarendon, 1997.
SAA	State Archives of Assyria	*WDSP*	*Wadi Daliyeh II: The Samaria Papyri*
SAAB	*State Archives of Assyria Bulletin*		*from Wadi Daliyeh.* Edited by M. J. W.
SAOC	Studies in Ancient Oriental Civilization		Leith. DJD 28/2. Oxford: Clarendon,
SBL	Studies in Biblical Literature		1997.
SHANE	Studies in the History (and Culture) of	YNER	Yale Near Eastern Researches
	the Ancient Near East	*ZAW*	*Zeitschrift für die alttestamentliche*
SJLA	Studies in Judaism in Late Antiquity		*Wissenschaft*
SymS	Symposium Series	*ZDPV*	*Zeitschrift des deutschen*
TA	*Tel Aviv*		*Palästina-Vereins*
TAD	*Textbook of Aramaic Documents*		
	from Ancient Egypt. By B. Porten and		

Introduction

JONATHAN S. GREER, JOHN W. HILBER, AND JOHN H. WALTON

The Old Testament, or Hebrew Bible, is an ancient collection of books written to ancient peoples. Yet it is also a book revered in contemporary communities of faith as God's Word and appreciated by believers and unbelievers alike for its enduring impact on many civilizations today. Though it is not written to us, generations of confessional communities have believed that it is written for us. Nevertheless, these two contexts, the ancient world on the one hand and the modern world on the other, are separated from each other by vast chasms of time, space, culture, and language, and this reality often limits our understanding of what was being communicated by those ancient scribes to their early hearers. Thus, for those who seek to understand the message of the Bible in its context, some understanding of the ancient world—its geography, archaeology, literature, iconography, history, and culture—is an essential starting point. As true as this may be, many readers of the Bible do not recognize this reality or, if they do, they often do not have easy access to information about the ancient world. In fact, typical Bible classes in confessional and nonconfessional institutions frequently consist of detailed, literature-based canonical surveys with little reference to the ancient world. The result is that we subconsciously impose our own cultural understandings on the text, at the same time missing the point of the ancient communicators.

This volume aims to provide an entry point to this ancient world, in general, and to illuminate the historical, cultural, and social contexts of the world behind the Old Testament, in particular. As such, it introduces students to "background studies" and "comparative studies." Background studies examine the literature, history, and material culture of the ancient world in order to understand the behavior, beliefs, culture, values, and worldview of the people. Comparative studies seek to juxtapose the data from two or more cultures, most often the Israelite culture compared to one or more of the ancient Near Eastern cultures. Such comparison offers the opportunity to observe both similarities and differences and helps readers to grasp the level of cultural embeddedness. These two disciplines together can be referred to as "cognitive environment criticism" and seek to help readers of the Old Testament recover the cultural layers from the world behind the text that were implicitly understood by the ancient audience but have been long lost to our modern world.

This book is designed for classroom use alongside traditional literature-based, canonical surveys and, we hope, will fill a gap in typical "Introduction to the Old Testament/ Hebrew Bible" courses. We also hope that it will serve as an accessible resource that will introduce readers—be they students, clergy, interested lay readers, or scholars from other subdisciplines within biblical and ancient Near Eastern studies—to a wide range of background materials relevant for understanding the Old Testament, including Levantine geography, archaeology, ancient Near Eastern texts and iconography, history, and a selection of religious, social, and economic topics. The concise treatments permit unparalleled breadth in the coverage of relevant subjects, thus allowing instructors flexibility in selecting chapters that may be best suited to meet their course objectives and offering all readers a handy, single-volume reference work.

We have assembled a panel of experts in the relevant fields from leading research institutions, confessional and nonconfessional, public and private universities and colleges, and seminaries in North America, Israel, Europe, Australia, South America, and Africa. As such, though we editors are confessional scholars working in Protestant institutions, our contributors represent a variety of perspectives about the theological nature of the text; for some it is Scripture understood within Jewish, Roman Catholic, or Protestant faith communities, yet for others, it is not. Different perspectives are also represented in the relationship of the text to history (and even the way one defines "biblical history"); for some the connection between the text and our understanding of history is close, and for others the gap is wider. Thus, a careful reader of this book will observe different opinions represented among these chapters, as not all of our authors represent the same perspectives as others or of the editors. We have left these tensions intact with the hope that they will enhance the pedagogical value

of the volume in serving diverse readers in different settings and allowing instructors the opportunity to identify, discuss, and evaluate these different perspectives. Regardless, all of our contributors agree that understanding the ancient world illuminates our understanding of those early contexts of the Old Testament and are committed to sharing their expertise to that end with a broad audience. Indeed, these men and women represent some of the best scholars currently working on many of these topics, and we are honored to include their contributions in this work.

The design of the book is based upon viewing the history of ancient Israel through the lens of a "drama," thus drawing a metaphor from the growing appreciation for the narrative art of the Israelite historians and the larger "story" framework in which the various genres of the Old Testament are embedded. As with any drama, much goes on "behind the scenes," and we have organized this work to "pull back the curtain," as it were, and illuminate the drama.

The first part, "Elements of the Drama," is comprised of introductory chapters addressing the essential methods utilized in background studies along with regional and chronological surveys. The sections are delineated within the larger paradigm of "drama" and are grouped as follows:

I. *The Stage*: These chapters introduce the field of historical geography and provide information on the history of the field, the geological regions of the Levant and related lands, and their climates, flora, and fauna.

II. *The Sets and Props*: In this section the field of Levantine archaeology is introduced, and the material and biological remains of the region are described according to the standard archaeological time periods: Late Bronze Age, Iron Age I, Iron Age II, the Neo-Babylonian and Persian periods, and the Hellenistic period.

III. *The Scripts*: These chapters introduce the field of the comparative study of ancient Near Eastern literature with introductions to Mesopotamian, Egyptian, Hittite, Ugaritic, and Hellenistic corpora as well as extrabiblical Hebrew and other Northwest Semitic inscriptions.

IV. *The Frames*: Ancient Near Eastern iconography is addressed in its own section with chapters introducing the field and specific treatments of Egyptian, Assyrian, and Canaanite/Israelite repertoires.

The second part, "Acts and Scenes of the Drama," contains synthetic historical surveys, drawing upon the geographical, archaeological, textual, and iconographic methodologies described in the preceding section. It is divided into two sections: "Acts" and "Scenes." This division is loosely based on the recognition that "history" functions at various levels of time.

V. *Acts*: This section deals with longer periods of time and is arranged according to the traditional stages of history from the perspective of the biblical story line in order to be most suitable for classroom use: the stories of the Ancestral period, the Egyptian sojourn, exodus and settlement, the Israelite kingdoms, exilic communities, Persian Yehud, and the Hasmonean kingdom.

VI. *Scenes*: In this section each chapter is based on a single event—often an event only alluded to, if mentioned at all, in the Bible—and the ramifications of that event for the biblical world either conceptually or historically. Such events include the reign of Akhenaten, the migration of the Sea Peoples, Sheshonq's campaign, the Battle of Qarqar, the Moabite wars, the Jehu revolt, the invasion of Sennacherib, an eighth-century earthquake, the Battle

of Carchemish, and the conquest of Alexander the Great. These episodic "scenes" demonstrate for students how major events shape the course of history and illustrate the sort of sociopolitical dynamics at work throughout Israel's history.

The third and final part, "Themes of the Drama," shifts from historical reconstructions to thematic treatments of important religious, social, and economic institutions (and the interaction among them), again drawing upon geographical, archaeological, textual, and iconographic materials across the breadth of the time periods and geographical regions in the section above. It is divided into four sections:

VII. *God*: This section focuses on Israelite religion and includes chapters on monotheism, polemics, the temple, the priesthood, sacrifice, "family" religion, prophetism-divination, and death and burial.

VIII. *Family*: The second section is centered on the topic of family with chapters on tribes, women, and children and inheritance.

IX. *Sustenance*: The third section focuses on the economy with chapters on seasons and crops, trade, slavery, local economies, technology (metallurgy, ceramics, and textiles), food preparation, feasting, and music and dance.

X. *Governance*: The fourth and final section is centered on social organization and includes chapters on kingship, social stratification, legal systems, wisdom traditions, and warfare.

It is our hope that readers will find this book accessible to all students of the Old Testament, comprehensive in range and scope, and practical for improving understanding. Ultimately, we trust that it will serve an important role in fostering a better understanding of the Hebrew Bible in its world to better equip readers to grapple with its message.

PART ONE

Elements
of the Drama

The Stage

Historical Geography

1

Introduction to Historical Geography

PAUL H. WRIGHT

The What and Why

There is truth to the adage that although history doesn't repeat itself, it does rhyme.[1] That it does so is probably due in part to the persistence of human nature, but also to facts on the ground—that is, realities of geography that prompt (and then reprompt) the nature of events. The discipline of historical geography is particularly helpful in our attempt to search out the how and why of the past in that, while it appreciates the uniqueness of individual moments in time, it especially notices patterns within regional contexts of place. A primary goal of historical geography is to understand the functionality and actual use of landscapes over time. A working appreciation of this "dynamic of the land" in turn reinforms, broadens, and deepens our understanding of events that are otherwise known primarily from texts.

As a discipline, historical geography looks at events within the context of the place and time in which they occurred. That it is *geog-*

raphy places it in the realm of the sciences (both material and social). That it is *historical*, especially as it concerns itself with the conditions of ancient life that can be reconstructed from texts, places it in the humanities. This task, both by nature and practice, is multidisciplinary, drawing on the fields of physical geography, philology (textual studies), archaeology, and cultural and anthropological studies, among others. And, depending on the interests of the scholar or the particular task at hand, historical geography is subordinate to either one or more of these disciplines or the umbrella under which they might all be placed. In the process, the historical geographer asks a wide variety of questions, some event-related, others text-related. This human-land dimension includes things specific not just to individual events (what happened where and why) but to larger phenomena as well, such as settlement patterns, the use of natural resources, methods of adaptation to the environment, strategic locations and networks of natural routes, and the development of social, economic, and political units that live on, exploit,

1. The maxim is often attributed to Mark Twain although it does not appear in any of his published writings.

or otherwise make use of natural regions. Note that our awareness of many of these factors comes from archaeology, and much of that derives, quite intentionally for many archaeologists, independently of texts (especially sacred texts). In any case, whether the history at hand is derived from texts or archaeology or both, an effective historical geographer must by nature be not only a wide-ranging collector of data but also a skilled synthesizer; a specialist as well as a generalist.

In making a case for students of the Old Testament to ground themselves in the world of the Bible, the biblical geographer Denis Baly passed on to his readers the words of his teacher, Percy Maude Roxby, that "geography, being concerned with everything upon the surface of the earth, is not one of the segments in the circle of sciences, but the center" (Baly 2005, 11). I do not wish to enter into a discussion about the relationship between geography (or, more specifically, its relevant subfield, *historical* geography) and theology, the latter long regarded (though for most no longer) as the queen of the sciences, but Roxby's words do offer a necessary prompt. Its sacred and literary contexts notwithstanding, the Old Testament is a text about people living in real places (i.e., geography) over time (i.e., history). These are realities that impact our understandings of the meaning(s) of the text, and it is from them that points of relevance for modern readers, including theologians, arise.

Within the parameters of this volume, historical geography has as its goal the task of revealing the historical and geographical contexts of situations in life from the world of the Bible, including specific events recorded in the Old Testament. The discipline assumes that certain ways of life, or facts on the ground, informed the authors of the Old Testament, and that information about many of these facts can, to a reasonable extent, be recovered and analyzed. The fields explored are broad and anything but uniform. In the world of the Bible we find, for instance, shepherds and farmers, hill-country dwellers and flatlanders, drylanders and seafarers, urban sophisticates and rural peasants, task-specialists and task-generalists, among many others, all of whom cross ethnic and national identities and each of whom exploited diverse parts of the land in ways best suited to their own place and time. Each also viewed the natural (and spiritual) world in ways that were consistent with the horizon line they knew best: Is the sea scary or useful? Is a frontier town a crossroads of opportunity or an open sieve of threat? Can an invader be leveraged for mutual economic gain? Is the cosmos better understood as a city (Rev. 21:1–2), a tent (Isa. 40:22), or the arch of the bent-over Egyptian goddess *Nwt*? "Their gods are gods of the mountains," while ours are gods of the plains (1 Kings 20:23); and so forth. And so a historical geographer has his or her feelers out for patterns of events but also for patterns of perception and thought, all of which are grounded in significant ways in realia of the landscapes of the past.

Historical geography is all about connectedness—one site to another, one region to another, one issue to another, one discipline to another. This is its strength. Still, core to the discipline is the idea that its relevance comes not only by studying the geographical setting of the events that shaped the world of the Old Testament but also by actually experiencing the land firsthand. Here we are reminded of the mandate of no less a scholar of the world of the Bible than Jerome: "Just as those who have seen Athens understand Greek history better, and just as those who have seen Troy understand the words of the poet Virgil, thus one will comprehend the Holy Scriptures with a clearer understanding who has seen the land of Judah with his own eyes" (*Preface to Chronicles*, cited in Freeman-Grenville, Chapman, and Taylor 2003, 2–3).

To this we can add the directive of the American geographer Carl Ortwin Sauer, also a fierce advocate of fieldwork, who speaks more broadly of cultural landscapes than of specific events: "The reconstruction of critical cultural landscapes of the past requires . . . the most intimate familiarity with the terrain which the given culture occupied. . . . One might say that [the historical geographer] needs the ability to see the land with the eyes of its former occupants, from the standpoint of their needs and capacities. This is about the most difficult task in all human geography" (Sauer 1963b, 362). So the land is not just the setting of events of the past but a laboratory, an arena for discovery and thought. Here, according to Sauer, "locomotion should be slow, the slower the better, and be often interrupted by leisurely halts to sit on vantage points and stop at question marks" (Sauer 1963a, 400). We should speak of field historical geographers just as readily as we speak of field archaeologists, in distinction to those of the lectern- or armchair-only variety, and encourage such activity in every way possible. When the stage and its settings are encountered personally, something transformative happens in the way that events are understood.

Development of the Discipline

Although historical geography as a scientific discipline traces its origins to the pioneering work of Edward Robinson and Eli Smith, who, on trips to Ottoman Palestine in 1838 and 1852, identified biblical places through names that were preserved as Arabic toponyms (Robinson and Smith 1841; 1856a), its roots are much older. The earliest written sources for biblical geography, both Jewish and Christian, attest to an interest in identifying places and describing characteristics of the land of ancient Israel that were part of the biblical story. This is only natural, given the essential connection to that land that is presupposed by the legal material, narrative line, and poetic expressions of the Bible (e.g., Exod. 12:25; 1 Kings 4:33; Matt.

6:26). Foremost among these sources is the *Onomasticon* of Eusebius, an annotated list of biblical place-names in Greek, together with comments identifying their locations as they were known in the early fourth century CE. In compiling his work, Eusebius, who was bishop of Caesarea, used both Jewish and Christian sources, some of which focused on the sacred character of the land while others seem to have been interested in the land for its own sake (Notley and Safrai 2005, xi–xxxvii; Freeman-Grenville, Chapman, and Taylor 2003). The *Onomasticon* was translated into Latin by Jerome in the late fourth century. In the mid-sixth century, mosaic artisans in Madaba, northeast of the Dead Sea in Transjordan, created a map on the floor of a church depicting the sacred geography of the Holy Land (Avi-Yonah 1954; Piccirillo and Alliata 1999) and based in part, it seems, on data from the *Onomasticon*. These, and a number of additional sources of various genre such as the *Geography of Strabo*, the medieval *Tabula Peutingeriana* (which was based on a map of the Roman Empire from the second century CE), and rabbinic writings including the Mishnah and Talmud are invaluable as primary sources to help historical geographers recover ways that biblical landscapes and place-names were preserved during and after the time of the New Testament. To these we can add later works in Arabic by Eutychius, patriarch of Alexandria (877–940 CE), and in Hebrew by Jewish scholars such as Estori ha-Parḥi (fourteenth century), who wrote geographical treatises with the familiarity of insiders (Rainey and Notley 2014, 13). Numerous accounts of Jewish and Christian pilgrims to the Holy Land from the Byzantine period through Ottoman times can also be helpful, although they naturally emphasize the spiritual geography of pious pilgrims (Wilkin 1992).

Exploration of the Holy Land took on a new phase in the nineteenth century as Western powers became interested in the lands of the

Ottoman Empire for political and economic reasons. Most also claimed to want to protect the holy sites, though whether from genuine concern or as a pretext to gain a foothold in the region is a matter of debate (Silberman 1982). This coincided with a rise in critical methodologies of the Bible, in comparative approaches of texts from the ancient Near East generally, and in the development of earth and human sciences such as geology, archaeology, and anthropology. What followed were attempts to uncover contexts of the Bible that were wrapped not in sacred traditions but rather in discovering the land for its own sake, as well as efforts to reveal the physicality of the context of the Bible and contemporary texts. Though not the first to search out the location of biblical place-names, Robinson and Smith were able to establish a methodology of site identification through toponymy that was to dominate the field for the next century (Rainey 1978).

Historical geography by definition presupposes a recorded history and with it a record of place-names, and so quite naturally has focused on identifying as many toponyms as possible. In this, Robinson's main contribution was one of method. He began by compiling, in the original languages, all the geographic information found in the primary sources available to him (i.e., from the classical world, since in his day cuneiform, hieroglyphic, and West Semitic alphabetic texts were just coming to light). This gave him a textual map of geographic data that he reasonably expected to coincide with actual facts on the ground. Once in the land, Robinson compared the data gleaned from these texts with the landscapes that he visited with the idea—correctly supposed, given his rigorous use of linguistics and Semitic philology—that many of the biblical place-names had indeed been preserved by Arabic toponyms (e.g., Beisan for Beth Shean, Mukhmas for Michmash, er-Raḥia for Jericho). Robinson also found that the geographic

data contained in ancient texts, including the Bible, by and large actually did coincide with what he encountered on the ground, and it was this that directed his search for individual sites. It is important to note that Robinson's success predated archaeology, although archaeology quickly became the primary tool to corroborate and refine site identifications when a recorded name was preserved and to suggest identifications when it wasn't. In any case, the philology-geography-toponymy-archaeology sequence has proved to be an invaluable tool for identifying ancient sites ever since.

A host of scholars (and pseudoscholar explorers) followed in Robinson's wake (Y. Ben-Arieh 1983). Most important was the work of the Palestine Exploration Fund's Survey of Western Palestine (1871–77), headed primarily by Lieutenants Claude Conder and Horatio Kitchener of the British Royal Engineers. This survey produced the first scientific map of the southern Levant, mapping 6,000 square miles west of the Jordan River from Tyre and Banias in the north to Gaza and Beersheba in the south. A vast amount of detailed geographical, archaeological, linguistic, and cultural data, including over ten thousand place-names, was collected and recorded in three hefty volumes and twenty-six map sheets (Conder and Kitchener 1881–83). Subsequent surveys in northern Transjordan by Gottlieb Schumacher (on behalf of the Deutsche Verein zur Erforschung Palästinas) and of the region between Gilead and Moab by Conder (of the Palestine Exploration Fund) provided additional important data. Perhaps the most far-reaching work of the late nineteenth century, however, was that of George Adam Smith, whose *Historical Geography of the Holy Land* (1894) remains the classic erudite template for combining scholarly insight regarding the land with biblical devotion in the field.

The twentieth century saw equal doses of geographical exploration and textual analysis, with fast-rising contributions of archaeology.

Notable are the works of Albrecht Alt on the history and character of territorial divisions within the land of ancient Israel (Alt 1925); William Foxwell Albright, whose annual trips into the field enriched his already magisterial efforts in collecting and synthesizing every aspect of the fast-emerging world of the Bible; Fr. F.-M. Abel (1933, 1938), whose work represented the wide-ranging interests of the École Biblique in Jerusalem; and Nelson Glueck (1970), who explored regions east of the Jordan. Denis Baly's *The Geography of the Bible* (1974) remains unsurpassed for its sensitive synthesis of geographical and biblical data. Israeli scholarship of the age is perhaps best represented by the insightful and comprehensive works of Yohanan Aharoni (1979), Michael Avi-Yonah (1966), and, most recently, Anson Rainey (Rainey and Notley 2014), all of whom have argued forcefully for a text-based methodology that is grounded first and foremost in philology.

By the latter third of the twentieth century most sites that could be identified in the land of ancient Israel had been identified, and the role of toponymy as the prime factor within the methodology of historical geography began to wane—this even though plenty of work tracking down the history of place-names remains to be done.[2] The completion of this initial task of historical geography coincided with an exponential growth in archaeological data and a tendency to prioritize archaeology over textual data, especially that of the Bible, for understanding the world of ancient Israel. Indeed, as the "biblical" of biblical archaeology has become eclipsed in the last few decades by approaches that are more expansively based, so has the "historical" of historical geography, and largely for the same reasons (Dever 2001, 1–157; Rainey 2001b). That is, to the extent that the Bible has been disfavored as a source

2. Note, for instance, Elitzur's exhaustive treatment of the history of sixty place-names mentioned in the *Onomasticon* (Elitzur 2004).

of historical data, *historical* geography has given way to a more broad-based human geography of the past, with archaeology rather than texts the main source of historical data. It is important to keep in mind that archaeology is very good at revealing living environments of the past, but much less often does it expose specific events (Sennacherib's siege of Lachish in 701 BCE and the destruction of Jerusalem by Titus in 70 CE are notable exceptions), and virtually never can it do so independently of texts, biblical or otherwise. For this reason, an archaeological geography is not historical geography per se, although it does probe many of the same issues (e.g., the use of available resources by local populations, demographic and economic connections between regions or sites, means and lines of defense, etc.). And in the process, the results of archaeology are brought to bear on texts, thus closing the historical-geographical circle.

Methodologies and Trends

Scholars who use the discipline of historical geography to better understand the world of the Bible generally favor one of three basic approaches: diachronic geography, regional geography, and literary geography.

Diachronic Geography

Diachronic approaches use historical geography to understand the ebb and flow of events over long periods of time. Here time, or history, is the organizing principle. These are primarily event-based efforts and focus on the movement of peoples or the rise and fall of political entities on large tracks of real estate. This is the general approach of historical atlases (e.g., *The Carta Bible Atlas*). Diachronic approaches have the advantage of establishing chronology and focusing on individual events but tend to be static in that single-event maps that jump from here to there geographically can give the impression that events (or series of events) are isolated occurrences in time or place.

Regional Geography

Regional approaches to historical geography focus on regions or groups of regions and attempt to define their character over time. Here geography is the organizing principle. We must again first mention Alt, for whom the defining criteria of a region were based primarily on official records found in texts (Alt 1989, 137). Relevant textual data tends to be of two types: either that reflecting administrative structures (political divisions, tax districts, conquered territories, and the like) or that reflecting demographics and ethnicity. The former presupposes some level of formal governmental jurisdiction (e.g., the city and boundary lists of Josh. 13–19, Solomon's administrative districts preserved in 1 Kings 4:7–19, or the districts of Galilee, Perea, Samaria, and Judea in the first century CE as delineated in *War* 3.51–56). The latter reflects social patterns irrespective of formal borders (e.g., the genealogical material in 1 Chron. 1–8). Some texts likely preserve both, under the reasonable assumption that formal boundaries tended to respect ethnic and tribal realities on the ground. Specifics as to context are debated, including whether the recorded data reflects real or idealized situations (Rainey and Notley 2014, 174–85; Kaufmann 1953; Y. Ben-Arieh 1989).

Regional approaches also can be based on realities of geography itself rather than the historical development of boundaries over time. Here historical geographers define regions based on natural factors such as geology, topography, climate, soils, and natural resources. Only after determining actual living environments do they examine demographics, settlement patterns, or events over time, and that within the context of natural regions. Notable examples are works on the Shephelah and biblical Negev by Rainey (1983; 1984), in which applied data was drawn from texts, and on the Shephelah in the Iron Age and on the Sharon Plain and Yarqon Basin in the tenth century BCE by Faust (2007; 2013), in which applied data was drawn from archaeology. There is often some correspondence between a natural region and a cultural or ethnic region, and this needs to be defined in every case. Approaches based on geographical regions are generally more powerful than those based on political divisions, simply because geographical conditions are much more stable over time. Here archaeological excavations, regional archaeological projects, and broad-based surveys are particularly helpful in that they provide an ever-growing body of comprehensive and comparative data over long periods of time.

In either case, a regional approach to historical geography can provide a more holistic context in which to reexamine individual events recorded in texts such as the Old Testament than a diachronic approach can. As a case in point we might consider the Judean Shephelah, a place that, in the words of George Adam Smith (1894, 201), is the "debatable ground" between highlands and coast. The Philistine incursions through the Shephelah in Iron I (the time of the judges and emergent Israel) are attested both textually and archaeologically. How might it be possible to track Philistine expansion eastward through the Shephelah? And what were its effects on the indigenous Canaanites or the people who were becoming Israel up in the hills? Or, what was the relationship between Rehoboam's western line of fortifications, which ran on a diagonal through the Shephelah (2 Chron. 11:5–10), and Shishak's line of march through Judah and Israel (1 Kings 14:25; 2 Chron. 12:1–12; Rainey and Notley 2014, 185–89)? Or, what conditions prompted Gezer to function as the primary junction point between the Shephelah and the coast for Solomon and Pharaoh (likely Siamun; 1 Kings 9:15–17), while for Hezekiah the key Shephelah city facing the coast was

Lachish (2 Kings 18:13–14)? And so on, even more so when the Shephelah is divided into its constituent natural subregions for a more nuanced study. For traditional readers of the Old Testament who are peering into the landed context of the biblical text for the first time, the horizon suddenly becomes alive with options. As we seek to understand the data before us, asking what the Philistines or Rehoboam or Hezekiah *could* have done in any given event-based context is as valid a historical question as what they actually *did* do, as it helps us understand the grounded reality of the actual choices made.

Literary Geography

Literary approaches are not traditionally part of historical geography, but they do offer a helpful rubric under which to consider yet other intersections of text and land (J. Beck 2015, 11–13). On the one hand, a comprehensive understanding of the dynamic of a region, including all the ways that human interaction takes place within that region and the regions to which it connects, helps the reader of a narrative understand the intent, motives, and actions of the characters within the story line (or those of the author of the story), and thus whether the story is properly historical or not. The Bible's geographic data is too realistic and too precise to be dismissed otherwise. The historicity of the Bible's conquest accounts, for instance, has been widely rejected by most historians of ancient Israel. What is much more difficult to dismiss is that the narrative line of Joshua's march, and the response to it by the Canaanite kings (Josh. 6–11), makes perfect geographical sense when one considers the natural routes, strategic points, and resources of the land of ancient Israel. So too the Samson story (Judg. 13–16), which presents a detailed back-and-forth dynamic of the Shephelah that is timeless in its essence. Explanatory power derives from patterns as well as from individual events, whether the locus of study is the

particulars of history or of literature. In both cases the danger of reductionism must be balanced against the danger of particularism, and a regional approach to historical geography tempers both.

An appreciation of literary geography will also help readers of ancient texts grasp ways that authors used the rich language of geography to inform the messages that they were trying to tell. This is perhaps most significant for the Bible, in which geographical images fill the narrative line but also the language of individual actors within the story line itself. A study of historical geography would be lacking if it did not look at ways that a people group shaped their self-awareness through the realities of their homeland, as revealed in their own texts. If we add to this a people's encounters in their homeland with the world of the divine, the land itself provides a host of rich, geographically oriented theological images. For this reason, scholars of historical geography recognize a close relationship between *reality* and *type*: a rock can be studied as an object of geology or as a building material, but also as an image of God (Ps. 18:1; 31:2; 71:3) or of Peter (Matt. 16:18). The *historical* part of historical geography pays attention not just to events described but also to the processes by which those events were remembered, recorded, and made relevant for readers then and today.

Historical geography, then, is a multifaceted discipline. Specialists from its many subfields take turns drawing water from its rich well, and often drink together. Historical geography opens new avenues for understanding the Bible and places constraints on others. It helps readers determine which hermeneutical options are viable based on realities of the actual context of the world of the Bible, and which are less so. To use another geographic image, historical geography grounds interpretations but also allows them to spring to life out of the deep soil in which the actual events of the text itself find their roots.

2

Regions and Routes in the Levant

CARL G. RASMUSSEN

Mesopotamia—the Far Eastern Levant

The term "Mesopotamia" comes from the Septuagint translation of Genesis 24:10, which states that Isaac set out for "Aram Naharaim"—"Aram of the two rivers." This probably referred to the land between the Upper Euphrates and the Balik or Habur Rivers. It now refers to the relatively flat area through which the Euphrates and Tigris Rivers flow. In the drama of the Old Testament, this is the area from which Abraham and Sarah originated and to which first the northern (Israel) and then the southern (Judah) kingdoms were exiled, and from which the Judeans eventually returned.

This area is bounded on the west by the Amanus Mountains and Jebel Zawiyeh, on the north by the Malatya Mountains, on the east by the Zagros Mountains, and on the south by the great Syrian/Arabian Desert. Life in this area is dominated by the Euphrates and Tigris Rivers. Along their banks irrigation canals brought water to the fields, especially in the area south of Hit and Samarra (fig. 2.1).

Throughout the area the annual rainfall is eight inches or more, and some grain crops could be grown and sheep and goats could be pastured. This was especially the case in the region of the Upper Euphrates near Carchemish and Haran. This was the ancestral home of the Aramaean tribes and the area where the patriarchs had their roots.

Along the northern Tigris dry farming and pasturage were more common than irrigation. This was the area where the great Assyrian cities of Nineveh, Nimrud, and Asshur flourished. Although stone from the mountains could be used as a building material, the usual building material was mud brick—the material that formed the core of houses, palaces, temples, and walls.

Both the Tigris and the Euphrates were used as "lines of communication." The Euphrates in particular was used to transport timber and other goods from the northwest to the southeast. Timbers were floated downstream and other goods placed on wooden barges that were supported by inflated animal skins. Because of the currents and prevailing winds, it was very difficult to sail upstream. Thus, land routes developed that followed the paths of the

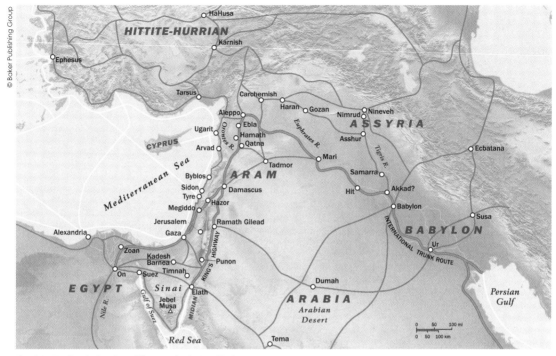

© Baker Publishing Group

Fig. 2.1. Key Trade Routes of the Ancient Near East

rivers. One such route led northward toward Nineveh and from there northwest through the Malatya Mountains into Anatolia. Another route led from Ur northwest along the bank of the Euphrates toward Mari. From there one continued northwest to the region of Haran and Carchemish. From both places, one could continue northwest into Anatolia, west to the Mediterranean Sea, or south-southwest toward Damascus and eventually into Israel and Egypt. Once the camel was domesticated, a path connected Mari with the desert oasis of Tadmor that shortened the trip to Damascus and provided easier access to the Mediterranean Sea.

Egypt—the Southwestern Levant

The African country of Egypt lies along the southwest portion of the "Levant" as broadly defined. It is bounded on the north by the Mediterranean Sea, on the south by the first cataract, on the west by a series of oases that lie about 120 miles from the Nile River, and on the east by the Suez Canal and the Gulf of Suez (see fig. 2.1). As Herodotus wrote, "Egypt is the gift of the Nile." Indeed, about 95 percent of the population lives on the fertile 5 percent of the land that is irrigated by the Nile.

Egypt is divided into two main regions. Upper Egypt is the southern portion that stretches from the first cataract in the south to Cairo in the north. In this area the habitable lands are the narrow fertile strips that are irrigated along both sides of the Nile. Apart from the few areas where limestone cliffs come down to the river's edge, the land is inundated during the months of July, August, and September. Grain is grown, as are many other crops. Fish are abundant. Travel in the area is via the Nile. The current carries boats and barges northward, and it is possible to sail south using the prevailing north wind.

Lower Egypt, in the north, is the triangular area north of Cairo through which branches of the Nile flow toward the Mediterranean Sea.

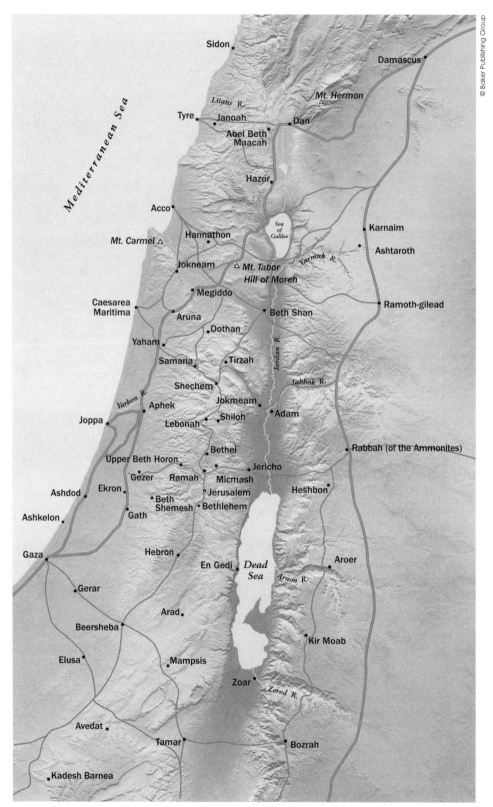

Fig. 2.2. Map of the Southern Levant

Traditionally, seven branches flowed through this area, and numerous canals and channels irrigated the fields. All kinds of crops could be grown here, and fish, fowl, and herds were abundant. Residents constructed their houses, palaces, and temples out of mud brick. Travel in the area was usually by small boats and barges.

Because of the fertility of the area, the bedouin from Sinai to the east often attempted to bring their flocks and herds into this lush area for pasturage. When droughts occurred in Canaan/Israel to the northeast, people from that area would attempt to enter the eastern delta in order to survive. Note the movements of Abraham and especially Jacob and his sons into the delta area.

The sandy northern reaches of the Sinai Peninsula formed the land bridge that troops would cross as they marched north (out of Egypt) or south (from, e.g., Assyria, Babylon, or Persia). The journey typically took ten days as armies and caravans proceeded from oasis to oasis. Central Sinai is a barren rocky territory that is mainly drained to the Mediterranean Sea by the Wadi el-Arish (the Wadi/Brook of Egypt of Num. 34:5; Rainey and Notley 2006, 283, 35). An interregional route ran through this area connecting Aqaba (modern city name, in Jordan next to Elath) with Suez. In ancient times shepherds and caravans coming from and going to Midian and Arabia used it. High granite mountain peaks cover the southern portion of Sinai. According to tradition it was in this area, at Jebel Musa, that the law was given to Moses—although there are many alternative suggestions for the location of this event.

The Eastern Mediterranean Regions of the Levant

In modern times the term "Levant" is often used to refer to the eastern end of the Mediterranean stretching from its northeast corner south to Gaza (fig. 2.2). This landmass is typically within 75 to 100 miles of the coastline.

As one proceeds from the coast eastward, the following "zones" are encountered: coastal plains, a central mountain chain, the rift valley, and the eastern mountain chain, followed by the Syrian steppe land or desert (fig. 2.3).

Southern Region of the Levant

The majority of events described in the Old Testament occurred in the area now occupied by Israel and Jordan. This area is bounded on the east by the Mediterranean Sea, on the north by the Litani River (in southern Lebanon) and Mount Hermon, on the east by the Syrian Desert, and on the south by the Nahal Besor. In this area the five zones are basically oriented north to south (figs. 2.2 and 2.3).

Southern Region of the Levant: Coastal Plain

The coastal plain of this region stretches from Gaza in the south to the Rosh HaNiqra/Litani region in the north (see fig. 2.2). It can be divided into four sections. The southern section, the Philistine Plain, stretches from Gaza in the south to the Yarkon River in the north. It is relatively flat. Wadis from the mountains to the east drain through it into the Mediterranean Sea. Alluvial (water-borne) soils predominate. Because of the lack of stones, most of the structures were built of mud brick. Everywhere annual rainfall is above twelve inches, and wheat and barley can be grown. After the grain harvest in the late spring, the sheep and goats were brought in from their winter pasturage on the east side of the central mountain chain to feed on the stubble and fertilize the fields. Springs, wells, and cisterns supplied local drinking water.

The sandy shore of the coast is devoid of coves, islands, or inlets that could safely harbor ships—except in the north at Joppa, where a promontory protected the harbor. However, seafaring boats could anchor offshore at Gaza, Ashkelon, and Ashdod and load and offload their cargos via smaller tenders.

This is the area where the Philistines settled the five cities of Gaza, Ashkelon, Ashdod, Gath, and Ekron. It has always been open to outside influences. The Great International Trunk Route, which ran northeast from Egypt through Damascus and Mari down to Ur in Mesopotamia, passed through this area.[1] Beginning in Egypt, armies or caravans would arrive at Gaza after crossing northern Sinai. Gaza served as a staging area, and from there one branch of the route proceeded north-northeast, near but not on the coast, avoiding the sand dunes, to Aphek. In the north, the Yarkon River formed a significant barrier, so the route turned east to Aphek to go around it. The inland branch of the International Route went by cities such as Gerar, Gath, and Ekron before arriving at Aphek. People living in the region provided caravans with food, lodging, and security. On the other hand, the armies of the great powers often brought death, destruction, disease, and oppression as they traversed this area.

Immediately to the north is the Sharon Plain, which is bounded on the north by Mount Carmel. Here a series of three kurkar (fossilized dune sandstone) ridges, parallel to the coast, prevent wadis from draining into the Mediterranean Sea. Because of this, much of the Sharon Plain was swampland good only for grazing cattle (1 Chron. 27:29). Because of the rough kurkar ridges the flat coastline was not hospitable for anchoring ships, and only in New Testament times did Herod the Great establish the port of Caesarea Maritima. In Old Testament times the Great International Trunk Route ran north from Aphek along the eastern edge of the plain, avoiding the swamps to the west.

Mount Carmel projecting northwest into the Mediterranean Sea interrupts the coastal plain. This 1,500-foot mountain ridge has three chalk passes that lead through it into the Jezreel Valley. The most important of these passes was the one that connected the city of Yaham in the Sharon Plain with Megiddo in the Jezreel Valley.

North of Mount Carmel a small plain continues north to Rosh HaNiqra. At the midpoint of this plain was Acco (New Testament Ptolemais), the main port of the southern region of the Levant.

Southern Region of the Levant: Central Mountain Range

The Central Mountain Range begins near the Litani River in Upper Galilee where elevations approach 4,000 feet (see fig. 2.2). It is composed of hard limestone that has weathered into deep V-shaped valleys that are difficult to cross or to travel through. Because of the dissected character of the region, most north-south traffic was diverted around Upper Galilee. The most interesting east-west road was the one that connected the oasis of Damascus with the port city of Tyre—this was possibly "the way of the Sea" mentioned in Isaiah 9:1 (Rainey and Notley 2006, 250–51). The area receives considerable rainfall due to its elevation and northern location, and the soil is fertile. Thus, those living in the area could grow good crops.

To the south of Upper Galilee is Lower Galilee, where elevations are about half as high. Here the valleys are broad and are amenable for roads. Thus it was much more open to outside influences. The Israelite tribes of Asher, Naphtali, Zebulun, and Issachar were allotted land in Galilee.

To the south of Galilee is the most important east-west connection in the southern Levant—the Jezreel Valley. It is "arrow-shaped," bounded on the north by the hills of Lower Galilee, on the southwest by Mount Carmel, and on the east by Mount Tabor and the Hill of Moreh. It is drained to the west and northwest by the Kishon River. A "shaft" of the arrow stretches southeast down to Beth Shan in the Harod Valley. Both valleys receive good amounts of rainfall, and grain crops were grown in them.

---

1. This route is sometimes, wrongly, called the Via Maris (the Way of the Sea). For a detailed discussion, see Rainey and Notley 2006, 250–51.

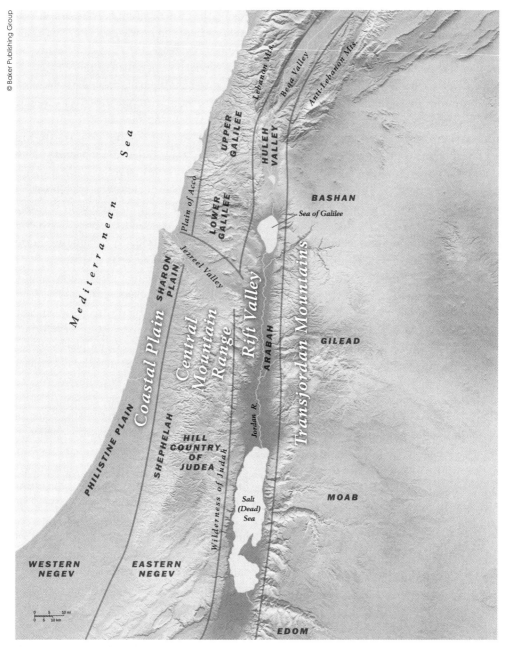

Fig. 2.3. Southern Regions of the Levant

A major road ran through these valleys from the southeast to the northwest. It connected the Transjordan Trunk Route (often called the "King's Highway"; see below) with the Mediterranean port of Acco. In addition, the major branches of the Great International Trunk Route ran through the Jezreel Valley—from Megiddo northeast to the Sea of Galilee, another southeast to Beth Shan and on to Transjordan, and another north-northwest to Acco and then northward up the Phoenician coast. Because of its strategic location the valley has often been a battleground—from the days of Thutmose III (1457 BCE) to General Allenby (1917 CE).

South of the Jezreel Valley the Central Mountain Range continues. Moving south, the first subregion is the hill country of Manasseh. Here there are plateaus and broad valleys that provide access to the elevated central mountain spine. From the Sharon Plain to the west, the Nahal Shechem leads up past Samaria to the natural center of the area—Shechem. Roads from Shechem lead northeast to Beth Shan, and along the way a branch turns southeast and goes down the Wadi Farah to the Jordan River. This was the old path through which the patriarchs entered and exited the country. From Shechem a major interregional road led south to Shiloh, Bethel, Ramah, Jerusalem, Bethlehem, Hebron, and Beersheba. This road "tiptoed" along the watershed ridge and figured very prominently in the biblical narrative.

Farther south the hill country of Ephraim is composed of hard limestone that weathers into deep V-shaped valleys. Its dissected character makes entry either from the west or from the east difficult. This "closed area" provided natural protection for its inhabitants—note the positioning of the tabernacle at Shiloh.

South of the hill country of Ephraim is the tribal area of Benjamin, where the central Benjamin plateau provides fertile soil where crops are grown. In this plateau area a number of roads meet. From the coastal plain on the west an important route led east past Gezer up to Ramah via the Aijalon Valley and the Beth Horon Ridge. From Ramah, one could turn north and travel to Shechem, east and descend to Jericho, or south and head to Jerusalem. The Gezer-Ramah connection was the most important approach to Jerusalem.

South of the central Benjamin plateau was the hill country of Judah, whose natural center was at Hebron. The ridge route from the north led into Hebron, and from there a branch headed due south toward Arad while another headed southwest to Beersheba. The hill country of Judah is composed of hard limestones. The fertile *terra rossa* soil and abundant rainfall

ensure the growth of grains, olives, and grapes on the terraced hillsides. On the east there is a 4,000-foot descent through the twenty-mile-wide wilderness of Judah to the Salt Sea. This barren and chalky wilderness was "home" for brigands and the place where flocks were pastured in the winter months.

To the west of the hill country of Judah is a buffer zone called the lowland (Hebrew *shephelah*). These low rolling hills and broad valleys form a zone that "buffers" those living in the hill country from peoples of the coastal plain. It was here that conflicts between the Philistines, Assyrians, Babylonians—among others—and the Judeans occurred.

To the south of the hill country of Judah is the biblical Negev—*negev* means "south" or "dry," which aptly describes the region. Its two basins, one to the east and the other to the west of Beersheba, are drained by the Wadi Beersheba flowing west into the Nahal Besor. It is composed of a fine windblown soil called loess. It receives ten inches or less of rainfall each year. Those living in the area attempted to grow grain crops and pasture their herds. Like the Jezreel Valley in the north, the Negev provided an east-west corridor for caravans as they brought luxury goods from southern Arabia to Mediterranean ports such as Gaza.

South of the biblical Negev are the Negev Highlands, which are composed of a series of ridges punctuated by four moonlike craters called *makhteshim*. This uplifted, rocky, and dry region was known as the Wilderness of Zin and the Wilderness of Paran in the biblical text.

Southern Region of the Levant: Rift Valley

East of the central mountain spine is a huge north-south depression that is part of the great Syro-African Rift Valley system. This portion begins at Dan in the north where the headwaters of the Jordan River originate. In its natural state, the Jordan flows through a marshy lake area, today called the Huleh Valley, before deeply cutting its way through a volcanic outflow on its way to the Sea of Galilee (see fig. 2.2). Because of the marshy nature of the region, the Great International Trunk Route ran around the west side of the swamp, up to Hazor, and then continued on to Dan as it headed toward Damascus and Mesopotamia.

The Sea of Galilee, mentioned frequently in the New Testament, is mentioned only four times in the Old Testament, where it is called the "Sea of Kinnereth." Its surface is 690 feet below sea level, and the climate is hot and humid in the summer and mild in the winter. Fish are abundant, and there are three small plains where agriculture is possible.

The Jordan River exits the Sea of Galilee at its southwest corner into the biblical "Arabah." The Jordan meanders 135 miles down to the Salt Sea, dropping 700 feet along the way. In the Arabah there is more rainfall in the north, where crops can be grown, but the amount decreases to only four inches annually where the Jordan enters the Salt Sea. In the spring of the year the river often floods its banks due to the melting snow and rain in the north.

The level of the Salt Sea has varied considerably throughout history. Today it is approximately 1,400 feet below sea level and continues to drop at a rate of 3 feet per year. The sea is mentioned twenty-three times in the Old Testament and is also called "the Sea of the Arabah" and "the eastern sea." It serves primarily as a boundary marker for the east side of the land of Canaan/Israel.

The Rift Valley continues 110 miles south to the Red Sea. This is a very barren area with little precipitation. It was sometimes used as a north-south passageway, but there are very few springs along its path. However, there are several places were copper was mined—namely, at Punon in the north and Timnah in the south.

Southern Region of the Levant: Transjordan Mountains

East of the Rift Valley are the Transjordanian mountains (see fig. 2.3). East of the Huleh Valley is the region of Old Testament Bashan, which is dotted with volcanoes and has well-watered and rich soil. It was known for its grain, hardwood forests, and well-fed cattle. However, it was difficult to travel through the area during the winter months because of very muddy conditions.

South of the Yarmuk River, Mount Gilead stretches to Heshbon. This area is composed of limestones that have weathered into deep, terraced, V-shaped valleys, along which olives, grains, and grapes are grown. The Jabbok River divides Gilead into two parts. Along its banks crops were grown, and a road followed it down to the Jordan. From Adam near the Jordan, one could ascend into the hill country via the Wadi Farah and arrive at Shechem.

To the south of Heshbon lies the *Mishor* or Madaba plateau. This area was farmed extensively and used for grazing flocks. In ancient times the Amorites, Ammonites, and especially the Moabites contested Israelite occupation of the plateau.

South of the massive Arnon Canyon the heartland of Moab stretches to the Zered Canyon. Along the mountain crest there is sufficient rainfall to grow crops and maintain herds.

South of the Zered Canyon are the high sandstone and granite mountains that border the Rift Valley on the east. This is the old Edomite heartland. Grain crops could be grown along the northern crest of this mountain chain.

About twenty miles east of the Transjordanian mountains the foreboding Syrian/Arabian Desert begins, and desert conditions prevail until one reaches the Euphrates River—some 400 miles to the east.

In this region east of the Rift Valley an important north-south road, often called "the King's Highway," led from southern Arabia (modern Yemen) to Damascus and additionally on to Mesopotamia. Caravans plying this route transported frankincense, myrrh, and gold from the Horn of Africa, Yemen, and elsewhere. Along the way, routes branched off to the west. Near modern Maan one route led to Egypt, while at the ancient Edomite capitol at Bozrah an important connection led northwest to Gaza on the Mediterranean Sea. At Ramoth-gilead a very important branch headed northwest via Beth Shan, the Harod and Jezreel Valleys, and Lower Galilee to Acco on the Mediterranean Sea.

Central and Northern Regions of the Levant

The central region of the Levant stretches from the Litani River in the south to the Nahr Kabir in the north. The lines of relief are basically southwest to northeast. The coastal "plain" is narrow, and at some points the mountains reach the sea. Thus, north-south traffic along the coast is difficult, and there is not much space to grow crops. However, the islands, promontories, and coves provided places where ships could find protective docking. Throughout the ages the major economic driver of the area was the shipping industry, for which the Phoenicians were famous.

Inland were the classic mountains of Mount Lebanon and the Anti-Lebanon ranges, with the Rift Valley between them—here called the Beqa Valley. These are the highest mountains in the area and are snow covered for almost half of the year. It is difficult to grow crops on the mountains due to the cold climate and tree cover. Here the prized cedar trees were grown. They provided long-lasting, straight timbers for boat masts and planking and for columns, roof timbers, and paneling for palaces and temples—note how these were secured for Judean building projects (2 Chron. 2:16).

The Litani River drains the well-cultivated Beqa Valley to the southwest. Because of the high double mountain ranges, east-west travel is difficult. While southwest to northeast travel in the Beqa is possible, the southern end of the Beqa ends in a jumble of mountains, and these throttled traffic into and out of the Beqa. In the northern portion of the Beqa, the Orontes River begins its course northward. To the east

of the southern end of the Anti-Lebanon range lies the oasis city of Damascus. Damascus was hemmed in by the high mountains to the west, by the Syrian Desert to the east, and by basalt outflows to the south.

To the north of the Nahr Kabir the pattern is: narrow coastal plain, mountain ridge, Rift Valley with the Orontes flowing north, and another north-south mountain range. At the north end of the Rift Valley the Orontes makes a great turn to the southwest and drains into the Mediterranean Sea.

It is difficult to travel along the coast and through the mountains, so the Great International Trunk Route ran to the east of the Anti-Lebanon range as it connected the great power centers of Mesopotamia to the northeast with Egypt to the southwest. Along the way a branch headed west at the oasis city of Tadmor to ports on the Mediterranean—for example, Sumur and Arvad. The branch that headed southwest from Tadmor had an important stopping point at Damascus, before heading into the southern region of the Levant (see above) and on to Egypt.

Conclusion

From the foregoing description, it is evident that when Israel settled in the "southern region of the Levant," they were living in "the land between" the great superpowers of antiquity—those in Egypt and in Mesopotamia. Indeed, God had placed Israel in his "testing ground of faith,"[2] and part of the drama of the biblical text is to trace how the Israelites reacted to the challenges that they faced—whether through political alliances and expediency or by placing their trust in the true and living God.[3]

2. For this terminology, see Monson with Lancaster 2009.

3. For more detailed information on the topics of "Regions and Routes," see the works of Rainey and Notley 2006 and 2014, Rasmussen 2010, Monson with Lancaster 2009, Dorsey 1989, Beitzel 2009, Baly 1974, and Aharoni 1979 noted in the reference list.

3

Climate and Environment of the Levant

ELIZABETH ARNOLD

Introduction

Interactions between humans and their environment have shaped societies and cultures throughout human history and continue to do so in modern times. Researchers from a variety of disciplines—including biology, geology, and archaeology—gather many types of data that are used to reconstruct environments and climatic conditions of the past. The strength of any reconstruction is improved when several types of data are combined. Debate over reconstructions of past environments and their influences on human cultures and societies occurs frequently as new evidence comes to light. This chapter examines several key sources of data that are utilized for environmental reconstruction and provides an outline of the environment of the Levant as the setting of the Old Testament, with a focus on the impacts of climate on the Late Bronze Age collapse.

Climate and Environment

The geographical location of the Levant between the Eurasian continent, the Saharan-Arabian Desert, and the Mediterranean Sea has significant impact on its environment. The Levant is influenced by the climatic patterns of Europe and the adjacent countries of North Africa and Asia (Bar-Matthews et al. 1999). Rainfall patterns originate in the northeastern Atlantic Ocean and pass over Europe and the Mediterranean Sea into the Levant. In addition, weather patterns pass over northeastern Africa and bring their influence to the region (Almogi-Labin et al. 2009). The modern Middle East is characterized by a subtropical climate, warm and dry with long hot summers and mild, wet winters. This strong pattern of two seasons is clearly recognized within the biblical narrative:

> As long as the earth endures,
>> seedtime and harvest, cold and heat,
> summer and winter, day and night,
>> shall not cease. (Gen. 8:22)

The proximity of several large bodies of water—including the Mediterranean and Red Seas, the Persian Gulf, and the Black Sea—offers a moderating influence with a more temperate climate in coastal areas. In addition, the varied topography throughout the Levant affects climate, with the plains and valleys experiencing warmer and drier conditions than the hills and the mountains. Both the Sinai and the deserts of the Negev present further climatic extremes.

The current environment of the Levant can be divided into four major environments based on the mean annual rainfall. The Mediterranean area is divided into two zones, the mesic Mediterranean zone (including the Galilee), which receives approximately 700 mm per year of rainfall, and the xeric Mediterranean zone (of the Judean and Samarian hills), which receives between 700 and 350 mm per year. In biblical times, wheat was cultivated in the wetter north, while areas to the south focused on barley as agricultural productivity decreased as one moves south due to decreasing rainfall. The Galilee, the Samarian hills, and the Judean hills were fertile areas suitable for agriculture, although the slopes were susceptible to erosion. In the Iron Age, this was controlled through terracing, and these areas were often devoted to olive and vine cultivation. The steppe environment receives between 350 and 150 mm per year, and the desert region (of Judea and the Negev) less than 150 mm per year (Hartman et al. 2013; N. MacDonald 2008b). The more arid areas of the south would have favored the shepherd, the nomadic bedouin, over a sedentary agricultural population (Issar and Zohar 2004; Marx 1970). This interaction between farmers (agriculture) and herders (pastoralism) is often portrayed in the Bible as adversarial (Borowski 1999). However, these groups would have had clear economic connections as plant and animal products were produced and exchanged (N. MacDonald 2008b).

While the climate of the Levant has not changed significantly since biblical times (King and Stager 2001; Har-El 2005), the annual rainfall amounts enumerated above can be misleading. Minor climatic variations can greatly impact the amount of precipitation

that communities receive in any given year (N. MacDonald 2008b). Sharon's (1965) analysis of rainfall variation in the Levant over a hundred-year period found that the Galilean highlands have a standard deviation of average rainfall of 20 to 25 percent. The Samarian and Judean highlands have an even higher standard deviation of 35 to 40 percent, and in the Negev Desert this variation is over 40 percent. Hopkins (1985, 89) translates this into the personal experience of ancient farmers: "that three years of ten will experience accumulation of rainfall about 16 percent less than the mean and that one or two of these years will experience more than 25 percent less." In marginal agricultural areas such as the Negev highlands, this could be devastating for agricultural production (N. MacDonald 2008b).

The timing of the rain could be as important as the amount of rain (King and Stager 2001; N. MacDonald 2008b).

> Let us fear the LORD our God,
> who gives the rain *in its season*,
>   the autumn rain and the spring rain,
> and keeps for us
>   *the weeks appointed for the harvest.*
> (Jer. 5:24, emphasis added)

N. MacDonald (2008b) highlights a common misconception about rainfall patterns as discussed in the passage above and also in Deuteronomy 11. The phrases "early rains" and "later rains" may be understood as two winter rainy seasons with a dry period between. However, the "early rains" mark the beginning of the wet season, and rainfall gradually increases through to the middle of the season and then declines. The "early rains" signal the time for plowing and sowing, while the "later rains" are the continuation of the rainy winter season until April. If the rains come later in the season, the crops do not have time to fully mature before harvest. Crops may be stunted if the rains end too early in the season. Historical data tell us that this was a fairly common occurrence and could have disastrous effects (N. MacDonald 2008b, 56). Shortfalls in precipitation could not be made up from surface water, which tends to be seasonal and unreliable in the Levant (B. Weiss 1982).

The Gezer Calendar, an inscribed limestone plaque dated to the tenth century BCE, recovered from excavations at Gezer, gives further details of the agricultural year subdivided by seasonal farming activities:

> Two months gathering
> [September-October]
> two months planting
> [November-December]
> two months late sowing
> [January-February]
> (one) month cutting flax [March]
> (one) month reaping barley [April]
> (one) month reaping and measuring
> (grain) [May]
> two months pruning [June-July]
> (one) month summer fruit [August].
> (Coogan 2009, 119)

While some debate exists on the purpose of the calendar, it illustrates the seasonal agricultural round. It begins in the fall with the olive harvest. The "early rains" follow in October-November and the planting begins. Harvest and feasting follow the "late rains" in April (King and Stager 2001).

Reconstruction of Past Environments

To reconstruct past climatic and environmental conditions, scholars may examine the distribution of major landmasses, volcanic and earthquake zones, and topography as well as the chemical and physical properties of soils. Scientists are unable to observe directly the climatic conditions of the past, so they use what is known as proxy data. Proxies are the preserved physical characteristics of the environment of the past that indirectly relate to what scientists wish to study. We are able to observe the proxy data, such as the presence of mammoth bones or pollen from a spruce tree, and are then able to infer the climatic and/or environmental conditions we are interested in studying. For example, the presence of mammoth bones may indicate a colder climate than what is present today (Dincauze 2000). Past climates are reconstructed from proxy data (such as microscopic plant and animal remains, ash, or dust) recovered from ice cores, deep-water marine sediments, and lake and cave deposits. The recovery of plant and animal remains from archaeological sites adds to these reconstructions. Historical documents from the Bronze Age onward can also provide observations and records of environmental conditions to complement reconstructions of past environments.

Ice cores are a key source of proxy data for environmental reconstructions. Ice accumulates in high mountain areas and near the poles from snowfall over many millennia. Researchers drill into the ice to collect cores that have distinct layers and that may contain dust, ash, air bubbles, and human pollutants based on the surrounding environment. The columns, or ice cores, represent a long timescale of environmental conditions. The inclusions can be analyzed to interpret the past climate of an area including temperature, precipitation, atmospheric composition, volcanic activity, and even wind patterns and pollution. For example, the Greenland ice core contains lead and silver from Greek and Roman periods, indicating that atmospheric pollution from smelting activities traveled as far as the Arctic over two millennia ago (Hong et al. 1994). A similar process of coring is carried out in oceans and lakes to examine the sediment that has accumulated in these basins over many years.

Speleothems are the mineral deposits in underground caverns, commonly known as stalagmites and stalactites. They are formed from groundwater and can provide climatic information (Bar-Matthews and Ayalon 2004). This water is impacted by a number of larger global climatic factors such as atmospheric composition and rainfall patterns. This enables both large-scale and local reconstructions. Key techniques utilized in reconstructing past environments from speleothems are isotopic analyses, primarily using carbon and oxygen isotopes. Isotopes are elements that have the same number of electrons and protons but differ in the number of neutrons (DeNiro 1987). These differences mean that isotopes will react chemically in the same ways but at different rates. For example, carbon has three isotopes (^{12}C, ^{13}C, and ^{14}C). The first two are stable, whereas ^{14}C disintegrates radioactively over time and is the basis for radiocarbon dating. ^{12}C and ^{13}C have been widely used for environmental reconstructions. Terrestrial plants are divided into different groups based on their differential means of fixing atmospheric CO_2. These different photosynthetic pathways result in distinct carbon isotope values. C_3 plants have carbon isotope values that range from -33 (‰) per mil (one part in every thousand) to -22 (‰) per mil, while C_4 plants range from -16 (‰) per mil to -9 (‰) per mil and therefore do not overlap. C_3 plants tend to grow in moister conditions than C_4 plants, so the carbon isotope values in speleothems reflect the plant communities in the vicinity of the caves during formation and can distinguish between C_3 (moister conditions) and C_4 (drier conditions) plant communities (Van der Merwe 1982). Oxygen isotopes from speleothems document rainfall as well as temperature. In the Levant, the lowest oxygen isotope values are seen in the coldest and wettest months (N. Roberts et al. 2011) and the highest values during the summer (Dansgaard 1964). The oxygen isotope values from the speleothems directly reflect the temperature during formation and the oxygen isotope value of the water from which it was formed. In marine sediments, the oxygen isotope values of microscopic plant remains can be used to calculate sea surface temperature (Bar-Matthews et al. 1999).

In addition, microscopic plant and animal remains may be recovered and identified from ice and sediment cores. Many animals and plants survive only under very specific conditions (i.e., temperature, water availability) and can be helpful for environmental reconstructions (Reitz and Wing 1999). Plant and animal remains are identified through the comparison of the unknown samples to known, comparative materials. Palaeobotanists and zooarchaeologists specialize in these identifications. Plant and animal remains are also recovered from archaeological excavations. The geographical distribution of plants (and by extension the animals and humans that utilize these resources) is related to climatic conditions. Scientists can also analyze isotopes from animal bones and teeth, plant material, and land snail shells (Goodfriend 1990) for further information. For example, the isotope values of the plants are reflected in the tissues of the animals that consume them (DeNiro and Epstein 1978; Vogel 1978). As a result, isotope analyses of bones and teeth can provide data on conditions of the environments within which the animals lived (Balasse and Ambrose 2005).

Pollen is commonly recovered from speleothems, archaeological sediments, and lake and ice cores. Pollen falls as "pollen rain" onto the land and water as it is released by plants and mixed by air currents. This rain can reflect the vegetation that produced it, and the buildup of this record through time will allow a reconstruction of past vegetation in that area—what agricultural crops, forest vegetation, or ground cover was present. This reconstruction is not a perfect reflection of the vegetation of an area as not all pollen is distributed by wind, and wind conditions may be variable. Wind-pollenating plants will produce large quantities of pollen, while plants that disperse their pollen through animal vectors or through water or are self-pollinating produce less pollen to be incorporated into the soils and recovered by palynologists. The vegetation that may be reconstructed from pollen evidence is also affected by preservation of pollen in the soil. Soil chemistry may be destructive to pollen (i.e., a high soil pH is destructive), and fungi, bacteria, and earthworms can all destroy pollen in the soil (Pearsall 2000).

The study of tree rings (dendrochronology) is often useful in reconstructing past environments. In temperate regions where there is a distinct growing season, trees generally produce one ring a year, thus recording the climate conditions of the year. In good years, with abundant water and sunlight, these rings will be relatively wide, and they will be narrower in years with less ideal conditions (Dincauze 2000). Trees can contain annual records of climate for centuries to millennia.

When available, historical documents can also contain information about past environments. Observations of weather and climate conditions may be found in administrative accounts, ship and farmers' logs, travelers' diaries, and other written records. While these must be carefully evaluated, historical documents can yield both qualitative and quantitative information about past climate.

Proxy data collected for environmental reconstructions may be either inorganic or organic and can provide information on a variety of scales that must also be considered. Environments (and changes in environments) can be studied not only on the global scale but also on smaller regional or local scales. One must consider the geographical extent of any environmental fluctuations. For example, did droughts impact only the southern arid areas or the entire region? In addition, the temporal scale must be determined, as environments may display change or stability on a long timescale (centuries or more) or with short-term fluctuations (over the course of only a generation). Proxy data must be dated to connect the different sources of data and to present an accurate picture of past environments through time. How old are the samples? What length of

time do they represent? The answers to these questions vary depending on the material being analyzed. For example, sediments may represent the single occupation of a house over just a few years or may have accumulated over millennia. Varieties of dating techniques are utilized and may be either relative or absolute. Relative dating methods do not provide a calendar date for materials but rather provide an ordering from oldest to youngest. Linkages may be made based on the assumption that strata containing similar fossil assemblages are of similar age. Archaeological sites might be linked by similarities in pottery and/or lithic assemblages. Absolute dating methods provide the age of a sample in an absolute timescale. The most common absolute dating techniques utilized in paleoenvironmental reconstructions are radiocarbon or C^{14} dating, uranium-thorium (U/Th), thermoluminescence (TL), and electron spin resonance (ESR). Radiocarbon dating is useful for organic material only and can date material up to about 50,000 years old. The other dating techniques can date inorganic material and have variable ranges of accuracy. Uranium-thorium has an upper limit of about 500,000 years and is used extensively for the dating of speleothems (Thomas and Kelly 2006; Schwarcz 1989). Accurate dating of proxy data is important not only for accurate environmental reconstructions but also for our consideration of the impact of these environmental conditions. One source of data may indicate a severe drought, but if we do not know when or for how long these conditions existed, we cannot accurately evaluate their impact on human societies and cultures.

Human Influences on the Environment

Accuracy requires that we also consider human impacts on the environment and not simply environmental impacts on human communities. Human-induced changes to the environment at this time would include forest clearance

25

and resulting soil erosion, the cultivation of agricultural crops, and animal husbandry and grazing. These human activities directly influence the proxy data that archaeologists and other researchers recover. There must be an effort to distinguish between natural factors and cultural impacts that are the result of human activity. The isotope data from sea cores and speleothems may be considered the most reliable proxies because these are the least affected by human activity (Bar-Matthews and Ayalon 2004).

Environmental Factors in the Late Bronze Age Collapse

Civilizations throughout the eastern Mediterranean region experienced significant decline and turmoil during the Late Bronze Age (ca. 1200 BCE) as settlement patterns shifted and many urban centers were destroyed or abandoned throughout the area, including Egypt, Anatolia, and the Aegean. This widespread collapse in the eastern Mediterranean areas was followed with a remarkable recovery only two centuries later. While aspects of this collapse and revival period are still debated, it is widely accepted that these regional events are connected, and climatic change has been suggested as a significant factor in this period, often labeled the "Late Bronze Age collapse" (Carpenter 1966; B. Weiss 1982).

Several types of proxy data support the idea that the Late Bronze Age collapse and subsequent recovery are the result of climatic shifts through the Late Bronze Age and into the Iron Age. Speleothems in Soreq Cave of Israel provide a long-term, continuous record of environmental change with small climatic fluctuations from warm to cool and wet to dry conditions and are a particularly important source of a variety of proxy data. The isotopic record of the speleothems at Soreq Cave recorded paleoclimatic conditions continuously through the past 185,000 years (Bar-Matthews

and Ayalon 2004). The cave is located approximately forty kilometers inland and 400 meters above sea level in the Judean hills. Oxygen isotope data from the cave indicates not only low annual precipitation during the Late Bronze Age to Early Iron Age transition (ca. 1150 BCE) but also a severe decline in precipitation from previous periods. As discussed above, this extreme fluctuation of precipitation would have been particularly impactful. Further evidence for a dry period is provided by pollen evidence from lake cores from the Sea of Galilee. The data show a significant decrease in tree pollen, indicating a major reduction in the Mediterranean forest cover and the driest period of the Bronze and Iron Ages, occurring ca. 1250–1100 BCE. This pollen record from the Sea of Galilee is particularly strong proxy data due to the high resolution of not only sampling, approximately one sample for every forty years, but also intensive radiocarbon dating (Langgut, Finkelstein, and Litt 2013). Other studies of pollen as a proxy to reconstruct environment in this region at this critical time period indicate a period of drought. Bernhardt, Horton, and Stanley (2012) focus on the Nile delta, Kaniewski et al. (2010) provide evidence from northern Syria, and Langgut et al. (2014) analyzed cores from the Dead Sea to reconstruct the environment of the Judean highlands. In addition, the historical record chronicles evidence for droughts and resulting famines at the end of the Late Bronze Age on tablets recovered from the archaeological sites of Hattusha, the former capital of the Hittite Empire, from Ugarit in northern Syria, from Emar on the Euphrates, and from Aphek in Israel.

The existence of widespread and extensive climatic change at the end of the Late Bronze Age is documented in several lines of evidence. Impacts of these climatic events include the collapse of the complex societies in the eastern Mediterranean, the end of international economic networks, regional crop failures and famine (Kaniewski et al. 2010), economic and political instability, destruction of cities, and economic and demographic decline (Langgut, Finkelstein, and Litt 2013). In addition, increased migration and population movements resulted, and it is not unexpected that people would be more mobile during times of drought as they leave unproductive areas in search of better agricultural possibilities (Kaniewski et al. 2013). These large population movements occurred throughout the Mediterranean, the Levant, and the Nile delta and are closely connected with the Sea Peoples and are viewed as wide-ranging and destructive (Drake 2012). As wetter conditions return at the beginning of the Iron Age, a period of recovery and resettlement begins. These new settlements are able to fill the economic and political power vacuum and give rise to the Hebrew kingdoms of Israel and Judah as well as other biblical nations, including the Aramaeans in Syria and the Ammonites and Moabites in Transjordan, territorial kingdoms known from the Hebrew Bible (Langgut, Finkelstein, and Litt 2013).

Conclusions

Any attempt to reconstruct the environment, either on the local level or more broadly, is greatly strengthened by using a variety of sources of data. Many lines of evidence are necessary to provide a strong evaluation of past environmental conditions. While researchers may debate the finer points of these reconstructions, all are in agreement that the environment has a degree of impact on human societies and human societies have an impact on the environment.

4

Plants and Animals of the Land of Israel

Daniel Fuks and Nimrod Marom

Introduction

The diversity of plants and animals in the land of Israel[1] resonates deeply with the Bible's imagery, commandments, and depictions of daily life. In this short chapter we will attempt to provide a basic background to the flora and fauna of ancient Israel from an archaeological perspective. Our aim is to set the stage for discussion of human cultural and economic relationships with plants and animals in this region (addressed in future chapters) by focusing on the rise of ancient agropastoral systems and the changing natural landscape. We will begin with a snapshot of the natural landscape as it appears today, focusing on a few of the major vegetation and faunal types in Israel, before attempting a brief history of human-landscape interaction.

A Synchronic Portrait of the Natural Landscape

At this crossroads of continents, the land of Israel's unique geography gives rise to its diverse flora and fauna. Israel is home to nearly three thousand plant species and over three hundred mammal, reptile, and bird species. This makes for a particularly high species-to-area ratio for the Mediterranean climate zone, which is characterized by long, hot, and dry summers and short, mild, and rainy winters. By comparison, California, also Mediterranean in climate, is over ten times the size of Israel but has less than twice as many plant species and the same number of mammal species. Israel's species richness results from habitat diversity, caused by several factors: the steep gradient of rainfall and temperature on a north-south axis (from around 1,200 mm mean annual precipitation in the north to less than 25 mm in the south, within 500 km); sharp altitudinal shifts (ranging from 2,200 meters atop Mount Hermon to -420 meters at the Dead Sea); variegated topography and soil structure; and increasing distance from the Mediterranean Sea on an east-west axis, coupled with the prominent central mountain range, which creates a rain shadow over the central Jordan Valley. In addition, Israel's enduring land bridge position between Asia and Africa results in the presence of taxa from several biogeographic regions. Species richness decreases—as a rule—from north

1. Here defined as the area between the Jordan Valley and the Mediterranean Sea, along with the Golan Heights, in accord with the disputed borders of the present-day State of Israel.

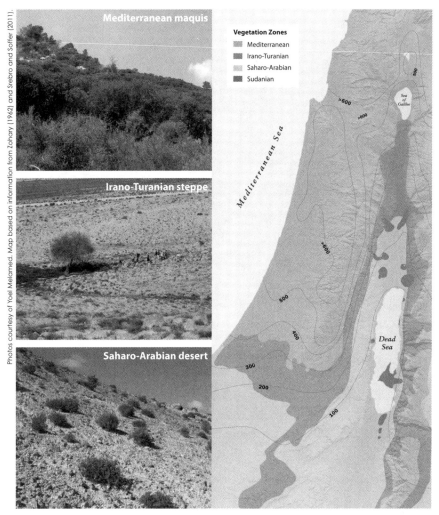

Fig. 4.1. Phytogeographic regions of the southern Levant and rainfall isohyets showing average annual precipitation in millimeters

to south with precipitation and is increased by the mosaic of microhabitats ultimately deriving from the diverse topography and geography. More species are likely to appear on the borders between climate zones (Zohary 1973; 1982b, 13–24; Danin 1992, 18–19; 1998, 24; Mendelssohn and Yom-Tov 1999).

Flora

Three major vegetation zones, or phytogeographic regions, meet at this continental junction, represented by Mediterranean, Irano-Turanian, and Saharo-Arabian territories (see fig. 4.1). In Israel, Mediterranean vegetation is typical of those areas receiving 400–1,200 mm of rainfall a year. Irano-Turanian vegetation inhabits the Asian steppes of Anatolia and Iran as well as the Syrian and Gobi Deserts, generally occupying Israel's 100–300 mm zone. Saharo-Arabian vegetation is associated with the desert belt of the Sahara, Sinai, and Arabia, surviving on an annual 100 mm or less. In addition, enclaves of Sudanian flora, typical of subtropical African savanna, abound along the southern Jordan Rift Valley, particularly in riverbeds receiving an effective 100–550 mm

Photos courtesy of Oren Ackermann

Fig. 4.2. Rock outcrops as a runoff source in the Judean foothills: (a) throughflow on nari outcrops, a week after a heavy rainfall; (b) human-made micro-catchment terraces; (c) olive trees planted in soil pockets to maximize rainwater runoff collection on a rocky slope. Note some small terraces and catchment walls for further enhancement of runoff collection.

of precipitation. Similarly, a number of Euro-Siberian species may be found in wet coastal parts, while Mount Hermon is home to some two hundred species characterized as sub-alpine or oro-Mediterranean vegetation (Zohary 1982b, 31–34; Danin and Plitmann 1987, 48; Danin 1998, 25–26; Danin and Orshan 1999, 15).

Mediterranean habitats contain the majority of plant species in Israel, spanning the greater part of those regions traditionally settled by sedentary people. Until the last century or so, Mediterranean forests and woodlands covered much of the hills of Judea, Samaria, the Carmel, the Galilee, and lower Mount Hermon. Depending on the soil type and topography, most of these woodlands were dominated

by kermes oaks (*Quercus calliprinos*), tabor oaks (*Q. ithaburensis*), or carob (*Ceratonia siliqua*) and lentisk (also called mastic, *Pistacia lentiscus*). Savanna-like vegetation abounds in the Philistean Plain, parts of the Rift Valley, and the valleys of Beth Shean, Jezreel, and Elah. It is also found in garrigue shrublands of the Judean foothills (Shephelah) at the edge of the Mediterranean zone (300–400 mm precipitation), where Mediterranean flora grows alongside a large number of Irano-Turanian species (Danin 1998, 30–32). In disturbed parts of this region, prickly burnet (*Sarcopoterium spinosum*) thrives between nari[2] outcrops on

2. "Nari is a local name for hard, pedogenic calcrete crust that ususally forms on chalk" (Ackermann 2007, 88n1).

Courtesy of Oren Ackermann

Fig. 4.3. Runoff farms in the Negev Highlands. Installations on the slope increase and divert runoff water to the wadi bed where check-dam terraces facilitate water harvesting.

low hillsides, exemplifying microenvironments enhanced by runoff (in this case over the rocks) absorbed into soil pockets (fig. 4.2a). Natural phenomena of this type have been utilized and mimicked by humans in various ways, including serving as a site for terrace installation (fig. 4.2b) or the planting of trees in soil pockets (fig. 4.2c), to maximize runoff collection (Ackermann 2007, 88–95; and see below).

In several of the above habitats, wild progenitors of traditional local cultigens are found. Wild olive trees (*Olea europaea* var. *sylvestris*) inhabit the Carmel woodlands dominated by carob and lentisk trees (also cultivated genera with local roots). Almonds (*Amygdalus communis*) as well as olives cover much of the former Mediterranean forests and woodlands. Wild ancestors of the major cereal crops of the Fertile Crescent—emmer wheat (*Triticum dicoccoides*), wild barley (*Hordeum spontanum*), and wild oats (*Avena sterilis*)—thrive in kermes oak woodlands of the Golan Heights and in several local Mediterranean grassland habitats (Danin 1992, 22; 1998, 30–32).

Irano-Turanian steppe vegetation along the borders of the Judean and Negev deserts is marked by low semi-shrubs. In parts of the Negev Highlands, outcrops of limestone in ephemeral streams (wadis) provide homes for trees of atlantic pistachio (also called Mount Atlas mastic tree, *Pistacia atlantica*) and to a lesser extent local almonds (*Amygdalus ramonensis*) and buckthorn (*Rhamnus disperma*). The stone outcrops provide a sheltered microenvironment for germination, while the riverbeds channel rainwater runoff for the plants' survival. These conditions have also been mimicked by humans in terraced wadis and rainwater collection conduits that enabled cultivation in the desert (fig. 4.3; Ackermann 2007; Danin 1998, 33–34; Evenari, Shanan, and Tadmor 1982).

Saharo-Arabian vegetation abounds in southern Israel, extending over the southern Negev and large parts of the Arabah Valley and Judean Desert. Toward the northern border of this arid zone, semi-shrubs are frequently scattered in uniform distribution patterns. Farther south, shrubs and trees, mostly of Sudanian

31

origin, such as acacia (*Acacia radiana*, *A. tortilis*, and *A. pachyceras*), grow only in wadis. Wadi vegetation varies according to the amount of (opportunistic) water flow in different sections of the banks and riverbed. The date palm (*Phoenix dactylifera*) is one of several inhabitants of the Rift Valley oases (Danin 1998, 34).

Fauna

The fauna of the land of Israel is as impressively diverse as its flora, including 33 families of mammals and 65 families of birds. This compares with the 28 extant families of mammals and 65 families of birds in all of Europe (Yom-Tov 2013, 79). Such diversity is attributed to the land's geological history; variegated climatic, topographic, and edaphic conditions; and also to human intervention. The many habitats available along steep ecological gradients accompanied by many topographical barriers create numerous niches for animals, as they do for plants. Diversity, often mediated by changes between related taxa and character displacement along these ecological gradients, is augmented by the location of the land of Israel at the edge of the Palearctic zoogeographical subkingdom, and in the vicinity of the Afrotropical and Oriental subkingdoms. Since the Miocene (ca. 65 million years ago), shifting sea levels have opened the way to animal migrations from proximate zoogeographical elements, resulting in a complex mélange of species representing Oriental (e.g., porcupine, *Hystrix indicus*), Palearctic (e.g., wolf, *Canis lupus*), and Paleotropical (e.g., mountain gazelle, *Gazella gazella*) taxa.

The most visible—and utilized—animals of the land of Israel were the large ungulates (Tsahar et al. 2009). These include the mountain gazelle, dweller of open landscapes and by far the most common prey taxon for early Holocene hunter-gatherers; fallow deer (*Dama dama*) and red deer (*Cervus elaphus*), browsers of open forest environments; wild boar (*Sus scrofa*) and cattle (*Bos taurus*), which favor water-rich habitats; and sheep (*Ovis aries*) and goats (*Capra hircus*), the most common livestock animals from the Neolithic period to the mid-twentieth century.

A Brief History of Human-Landscape Interaction in the Land of Israel

Having provided a snapshot of Israel's current natural landscape, we will now address some of the changes it has undergone, with a focus on human influence. The interplay of human activity and nonanthropogenic environmental factors influencing the changing terrain is a major theme of recent archaeological research (e.g., A. Rosen and S. Rosen 2001; Coombes and Barber 2005; A. Rosen 2007; Hunt, Gilbertson, and El-Rishi 2007; S. Rosen 2016). All organisms—especially humans—influence the environments they inhabit, and increasingly so since the development of agriculture and pastoralism (see B. Smith 2007; 2011a; 2016; Zeder 2016 and references there). For example, increasing hunting pressure resulting from the need to sustain human communities economically and ideologically has led on several occasions to marked changes in biodiversity, including extinctions (Tsahar et al. 2009). It is widely recognized that the physical and natural environment provides certain constraints, within which human activities aimed at increasing resource extraction and buffering against climatic instabilities have altered the natural landscape.

The evolution and diffusion of domesticates and synanthropes (i.e., species benefiting from human activity), as well as human-induced introductions and extinctions, are profound examples of humankind's influence on the natural environment. A dozen millennia before the Neolithic origins of agriculture (23 kya),[3] utilization of what would become the first do-

---

3. All dates in this section are approximate, rounded, in kya (= thousand years ago) calibrated BP (= before the present).

mesticated plants is attested to at Ohalo II on the Sea of Galilee (Weiss et al. 2004; Piperno et al. 2004; Nadel et al. 2004; 2012; see also Weiss, Kislev, and Hartmann 2008; Weiss et al. 2008; Snir et al. 2015). These include wild grass seeds (among them wild wheat, barley, and oats), wild pulses (including peas and lentils), and wild fruits and nuts (figs, grapes, olives, almonds, pistachios, and more). In addition to such protodomesticates, a significant number of "proto-weeds" provide evidence for the earliest effects of cultivation on biodiversity (Snir, Nadel, and Weiss 2015).

The potency of human resource extraction abilities, together with climate change, exacerbated a global wave of late Pleistocene mass extinctions (Braje and Erlandson 2013). The warmer and more humid early Holocene climate (beginning ca. 14 kya) increased carrying capacity in the Mediterranean region, leading to a phase transition in human resource management (e.g., Zeder 2011). While in marginal areas of the country itinerant hunter-gatherer societies persisted with broadly Pleistocene lifeways, the Mediterranean zone saw the rise of complex hunter-gatherer societies. The sites of the Natufian archaeological complex (15.5–11.5 kya), which extended from the Euphrates to the Negev, were often year-round settlements made possible by the higher primary production of Holocene ecosystems (Bar-Yosef 1998). These introduced, on the one hand, severe hunting pressure on game animals (Stiner, Munro, and Surovell 2000; Munro 2004), but on the other hand provided a new opportunity for animals to live and forage alongside people. This niche was utilized by house mice, house sparrows, and probably wolves/dogs and cats drawn to the human orbit (S. Davis and Valla 1978; Tchernov 1991; Weissbrod et al. 2012). Overhunting may also have played a role in pushing local wild cattle (*Bos primigenius*) and boar populations to domestication by Neolithic societies (11–7 kya), which competed with these taxa over alluvial habitats (Marom and Bar-Oz 2009; 2013).

The demographic growth and concomitant intensification of resource production brought about by Natufian sedentarization involved a strong emphasis on cereal cultivation (including grain storage). This was coupled with depletion of large, slow-breeding game animals such as wild cattle and fallow deer, and increased consumption of smaller, more demographically resilient prey such as gazelles and hares. Active propagation of cereal growth through burning natural woodland, known historically and ethnographically from Europe and America, may have begun at this phase. This durable form of human landscape modification intensified the conversion of woodland to grassland caused by the first grazing/browsing domesticated ungulates—sheep, goats, and cattle (B. Smith 2011b). The earliest cultivated plant of the Neolithic may have been the fig, apparently propagated from at least 11 kya through cuttings and complementing a diet of acorns, wild grains, and game in the lower Jordan Valley (Kislev, Hartmann, and Bar-Yosef 2006a; but see Lev-Yadun et al. 2006; Kislev, Hartmann, and Bar-Yosef 2006b). The domesticated dogs of the Natufians, used perhaps as hunting animals, emerged even earlier (S. Davis and Valla 1978; Skoglund et al. 2015).

As cultivation and husbandry evolved, humans selected traits in plants and animals that enhanced or eased their utilization. One example is the retention of seed dispersal units on the mother plant, a prerequisite for harvesting that is archaeologically traceable in disarticulation scars of cereal spikelets; another is increased grain size (Zohary, Hopf, and Weiss 2012, 21–22). The process through which genetic changes of this sort are brought about by human activity is known as domestication (B. Simpson and Ogorzaly 2001, 40; see also Harris 1989; 1996; Hancock 2006, 151–71).

Among the earliest and most economically significant plant species domesticated in southwest Asia are the cereals wheat and barley; the pulses lentil, pea, chickpea, fava bean, and bitter vetch; and flax as a fiber and oil source (Zohary, Hopf, and Weiss 2012, 75–95, 103–6). These founder crops formed the basis of systematic agriculture in the region. Some two thousand years after the Neolithic advent of sowing and one thousand years after the onset of domestication proper, the earliest evidence for weeds (i.e., plants that had evolved to agricultural environments) is found at Atlit-Yam on the northern coast of Israel, accompanied by infestations of six-legged crop pests (Hartmann-Shenkman et al. 2015; see also Wilcox 2012). The major fruit crops, including olives, grapes, figs, pomegranates, dates, and almonds, were fully domesticated during the Chalcolithic period (Zohary and Spiegel-Roy 1975; E. Weiss 2015).

The domestication of plants and animals drastically altered biodiversity and human settlement. From the later Neolithic period, a significant portion of the animals in human-inhabited sites belonged to four species: sheep, goats, cattle, and pigs. These domesticates were employed, in turn, to bind more landscapes into human-managed ecosystems. Cattle were means to intensify agricultural production by tilling more extensively in the valleys (Halstead 1995), which were planted with cereal, legume, and fruit crops. Meanwhile, sheep and goats accelerated human exploitation of marginal steppes and hilly forests, respectively. Their browsing and grazing in these habitats effectively converted natural vegetation into food products (meat, fat, milk) and commodities (live animals, wool) (Payne 1973; Redding 1984).

The ability to extract resource surpluses from a landscape full of villages was a precondition to the rise of the first city-states of the Early Bronze Age. This involved surplus-oriented legume and cereal cultivation as well as full-fledged arboriculture. Facing the need to provide for communities engaged in craft production and religio-political specialization, villages now yielded part of their animal and plant production to settlements higher up the social hierarchy.

Environmental determinants of carrying capacity and economic efficiency, combined with demographic growth that rendered these issues relevant, brought about geographic separation of agricultural and pastoral activities. In time, this caused nomadic pastoralist groups to diverge culturally, leading to the development of distinct agricultural and pastoral societies throughout the Levant and beyond. However, pastoral nomads were not, as was perceived until the early twentieth century, routinely in conflict with the urban/agricultural communities (Reifenberg 1955; Borowski 1999). Quite the opposite: they were part and parcel of the same economic system, wherein livestock products were transferred to agricultural communities in exchange for agricultural produce and craft goods (Rowton 1973; 1974; Cribb 1991; Khazanov 1994). Therefore, whenever urban systems declined, nomads tended to settle and to resort to the basic production mode of the self-sufficient village described above, *mutatis mutandis* (Salzman 1980). The trade and exchange networks, in which urban centers served as hubs, were connected by caravans, comprised initially of donkeys and later of camels. Breeding these animals became a part of pastoral-nomadic life and livelihood—in addition to securing (and preying on) long-distance overland trade.

In the long run and in broad strokes, the trend of floral and faunal resource extraction is marked by cycles of successively intensified exploitation. Initial domestication began in the Neolithic and continued through the Chalcolithic period, such that by the Early Bronze Age the major biblical plant and animal domesticates, including the components of the "Mediterranean diet," were well established in the southern Levant.[4] These include the major cereal, legume, fruit, and nut species utilized by local populations throughout history. As Bronze Age city-states gave way to Iron Age kingdoms

---

4. For a relatively recent treatment of the "biblical" or "Mediterranean" diet, see MacDonald 2008b.

(e.g., Israelite and Philistine) and subsequent empires (e.g., Persian and Assyrian), plant and animal exploitation intensified thanks to improved varieties, technologies, techniques, and organization of labor. At the same time, crop and livestock diffusion became more extensive as larger geographic areas were consolidated under central authorities, facilitating travel, trade, and rapid movement of plant and animal species (e.g., Perry-Gal et al. 2015).

Climate, Culture, and Economy in the Changing Historical Landscape

Several noteworthy examples of limitations on the distribution of agricultural and pastoral landscapes imposed by the physical environment have been discovered in Israel over the past few decades (summarized in Ackermann 2007). In the Golan and Upper Galilee, the distribution of olive oil and wine presses has been shown to follow geological fault lines. In general, oil presses have been found on rockier terrain, while the olive trees themselves were cultivated in soil pockets (vestiges of which are still found today; see fig. 4.2c). In the Maʿalot environs, nearly all the wine presses were quarried into limestone, with viticulture conducted on rendzina soil of the adjacent chalk formation. In the Judean hills, terraces are twice as common on soft chalk and marl as on hard dolomite and limestone. They are also one-and-a-half times as frequent on north-facing hillsides as on south-facing slopes, due to reduced solar radiation in the north and hence greater water availability. In the Judean foothills, the Negev, and Sinai, runoff farming systems are limited to drainage basins whose characteristics make them favorable for runoff generation and collection. These include a small collection-to-drainage-area ratio, favorable slope incline, and soil with low permeability (rocky and loessial surfaces).

However, the influence of environmental and climatic forces is not always so clear-cut.

To use the example of the Negev Desert, despite the aforementioned physical characteristics affecting runoff cultivation (practiced from at least the Iron Age and probably much earlier), the extent of its adoption has by no means been static (Evenari, Shanan, and Tadmor 1982; Bruins 2007; Bruins and van der Plicht 2014; but see Shahack-Gross et al. 2014; Shahack-Gross and Finkelstein 2015). Historical settlement peaks in the Negev include the Early Bronze II, the Intermediate Bronze, Iron II, Byzantine/Early Islamic periods, and the latter half of the twentieth century, with each peak representing increased levels of intensity (S. Rosen 2009). Some of these periods saw favorable climates, but others did not, suggesting a strong cultural component (S. Rosen 2016; see also Hunt, Gilbertson, and El-Rishi 2007). This included increased investment in runoff collection techniques and manure fertilizer to create and enhance agricultural landscapes (Evenari, Shanan, and Tadmor 1982; Tepper 2007).

An interesting test case of the interplay between climate and culture lies in Late Bronze to Iron Age Philistia and the (Israelite or "proto-Israelite") hill country. Several new introductions have been attributed to cultural influences of Philistine/Aegean "Sea Peoples." These include transportation and rearing of pigs from Europe (Meiri et al. 2013);[5] cultivation (as opposed to gathering) of cumin (*Cuminum cyminum*), sycomore (*Ficus sycomorus*),[6] opium

---

5. The case of the pig is especially illuminating of the difficulty with untangling environmental and cultural factors. Pigs are potentially markers of Philistine identity (Finkelstein 1996b; J. Lev-Tov 2010), but direct use of pigs as "ethnic markers" in the Iron Age is complicated by political, economic, and environmental variables (Zeder 1998; Hesse 1990; Hesse and Wapnish 1998; Sapir-Hen et al. 2013; Sapir-Hen, Meieri, and Finkelstein 2015).

6. The "sycomore" here refers to *Ficus sycomorus*, a species of fig identified with the biblical *shikma*, and is not to be confused with various other "sycamores" such as *Acer pseudoplatanus* and members of the *Platanus* and *Ceratopetalum* genera.

poppy (*Papaver somniferum*), and grass/red pea (*Lathyrus sativus/cicero*);[7] consumption of coriander (*Coriandrum sativum*) and bay leaf (*Laurus nobilis*); and the introduction of several weed/useful plant species that point to changes in land use (Frumin et al. 2015; Mahler-Slasky and Kislev 2010; see also Yasur-Landau 2010, 295–300). Meanwhile, there is strong evidence for a major warm and dry spell sometime between 1250 and 1100 BCE (Langgut, Finkelstein, and Litt 2013), which has been evoked to explain an archaeologically visible shift from mesic to xeric flora and fauna (Olsvig-Whittaker et al. 2015).

Conclusion

The land of Israel has been a meeting point not only for various cultures and civilizations but also for a plethora of floral and faunal types, creating a rich and variegated landscape. These include three main vegetation types (Mediterranean, Irano-Turanian, and Saharo-Arabian), and flora from additional vegetation zones (Euro-Siberian, oro-Mediterranean, and Sudanian). Similarly, the diverse fauna represent Oriental, Palearctic, and Afrotropical zoogeographic zones. This species richness is partially the result of the land of Israel's unique position as a crossroads of continents, as well as its climatic, topographic, and edaphic variation. However, the landscape was not determined solely by geographic and environmental conditions. Over the millennia, and especially since the origins of agriculture and pastoralism, humans have exerted an increasing impact on their environment. While this observation is borne out by Near Eastern archaeology, much future archaeological and historical research is needed to unravel the specifics of human and nonhuman influence on the changing landscape. Some major themes include the historical limits and effectiveness of cultural survival strategies in buffering against climatic instabilities and the workings of agropastoral intensification.

7. Grass pea (*Lathyrus sativus*) and red pea (*Lathyrus cicero*) are generally indistinguishable in archaeobotanical samples, hence the uncertainty.

The Sets and Props

Archaeology

5

Introduction to Biblical Archaeology

SEYMOUR GITIN

The beginnings of biblical archaeology can be traced to the surveys of biblical sites in the Holy Land conducted in 1838 and 1852 by the founder of Palestinology, Edward Robinson of Union Theological Seminary, New York (Robinson and Smith 1856a), and the subsequent major surveys undertaken by the British Palestine Exploration Fund and the Deutsche Orient-Gesellschaft over the next fifty years (King 1983, 7–10).[1] Another important stimulus was the British diplomat and archaeologist Austen Henry Layard's discovery in Mesopotamia of Neo-Assyrian monuments recording the names of Israelite kings known from the Bible. Examples include the Black Obelisk found at Nimrud in 1846 depicting Shalmaneser III receiving tribute from Jehu, king of Israel, in 841 BCE, and the reliefs found at Nineveh in 1845–47 that mention Judean king Hezekiah and depict the siege of Lachish by Neo-Assyrian king Sennacherib in 701 BCE (Layard 1849a; Hincks 1851).

The first "scientific" excavations in Palestine were conducted at Tell el-Hesi by W. M. Flinders Petrie under the auspices of the Palestine Exploration Fund in 1890 (Petrie 1891) (fig. 5.1). By applying the principle of sequence dating to a tell—a mound artificially created by layers of civilizations built upon one another—he established a rough ceramic chronology for Palestine based on the principle that "pottery is the essential alphabet of archaeology" (Petrie 1904, 16). Although Petrie incorrectly identified Hesi as biblical Lachish, his work at the site was the first step in the development of the discipline of biblical archaeology, which was soon to become the handmaiden of biblical studies.

The first American excavation was conducted at the biblical site of Samaria in 1908–10 by George A. Reisner of Harvard University (Reisner 1924), with the help of the American School of Oriental Research (ASOR).[2] It

---

1. For a detailed review, see ch. 1 above, "Introduction to Historical Geography."

2. Renamed the American Schools of Oriental Research in 1922, when a school in Baghdad was added to the school in Jerusalem. Two other schools were subsequently added: the American Center of Oriental Research (ACOR) in Amman, Jordan, and the Cyprus American

Fig. 5.1. Sir Flinders Petrie and Lady Petrie in Jerusalem in 1938
C. C. Steinback, courtesy of the American Schools of Oriental Research

marked the beginnings of advanced excavation methods, in which Reisner employed the debris layer method adopted decades later by British archaeologist Kathleen Kenyon (G. Wright 1969, 124). It was not, however, until William Foxwell Albright became ASOR director in 1920 and forged a new agenda for biblical studies that the discipline of biblical archaeology was created (D. Freedman 1989, 38; Gitin 1997, 62). He redefined biblical research as "the systematic analysis or synthesis of any phase of biblical scholarship, which can be clarified by archaeological discovery" (Albright 1969, 8–9). For the Bible to be understood, he maintained, it had to be seen within its historical *Sitz im Leben*—that is, within the larger context of oriental or ancient Near Eastern culture as determined by archaeological discovery and the tradition of comparative philology (Machinist 1996, 392). Together with John Garstang, W. J. Phythian-Adams, and L. H. Vincent of the British and French schools of archaeology, at a historic meeting in Jerusalem in 1922, Albright formulated a classification system of terms capable of specifying the phases of historical and archaeological evolution from the Paleolithic through the Hellenistic period (Palestine Exploration Fund 1923). Building on

this foundation, in his excavations at Tell Beit Mirsim in the 1920s and 1930s, Albright standardized excavation methodology by introducing the locus-to-stratum method linked to ceramic typology (Cross 1989, 22), chronologically subdividing the main periods of the Early, Middle, and Late Bronze Ages and the Iron Age (e.g., with Iron Age I starting at 1200 BCE and Iron Age IIA at 900 BCE and Iron Age III dated 600–300 BCE [Albright 1932, 10]). This represented a significant step forward in building the structure necessary to establish biblical archaeology as a discipline and became the basis in concept and detail of the chronology used by archaeologists today. Albright further advanced the discipline by creating the supportive subfields of research in West Semitic epigraphy and palaeography (J. Sasson 1993, 3). The net effect of Albright's work was to create order out of chaos by means of a systematic approach to archaeological research. Although scholars and research institutes of other nationalities conducted excavations in Palestine that contributed to the development of biblical archaeology,[3] the Americans came to dominate the field prior to World War II. And because of Albright's innovative contributions to archaeological research and the associated field of biblical studies, he is credited as being the father of biblical archaeology.

What drew Albright and others to archaeology was the firm conviction that biblical studies needed to develop beyond the dead end it had reached in the 1920s, when the dry and tedious nineteenth-century Wellhausen school of criticism had seemingly exhausted itself. Albright did not contest the Graf-Wellhausen hypothesis, which dominated most of biblical scholarship by the beginning of the twentieth century; rather, he accepted its argument that the first six books of the Bible were based on four major documents. What he rejected was

---

Archaeological Research Institute (CAARI) in Nicosia, Cyprus. The school in Jerusalem was renamed the W. F. Albright Institute of Archaeological Research in 1970.

3. For example, the British excavations at Lachish and Samaria and the German excavations in Jerusalem and at Megiddo.

Fig. 5.2. Tell Beit Mirsim excavation staff, "Class of 1932." Standing (l–r): William Gad (surveyor), Cyrus Gordon (ASOR Baghdad), Henry Detweiler (architect), John Bright (Union Seminary), W. F. Stinespring (Yale University), Rev. Eugene Liggit (Pittsburgh-Xenia Seminary), Rev. Vernon Broyles (Union Seminary), Aage Schmidt (Danish Shiloh Expedition); seated (l–r): James L. Kelso (Pittsburgh-Xenia Seminary), W. F. Albright (Johns Hopkins University), Melvin G. Kyle (Pittsburgh-Xenia Seminary), Nelson Glueck (ASOR).

the conclusion that these documents were of no historical value since they were centuries removed from the events they described. For Albright, the biblical text provided authentic testimony to real events and people and was not, as the Wellhausen school claimed, merely the reflection of the historical world of those who wrote the text (Machinist 1996, 395); for if the latter were true, then nothing could be known of early Israelite history and religion. Albright also held that the universal appeal and objective truth of historical criticism was not in conflict with religious faith. For him, it was an intellectual position that could be isolated from sectarian bias (Long 1997, 88).

The new interest in biblical archaeology, much of it generated by Albright's work, resulted in an intensive period of excavation, often called the "golden age of archaeology." It was at this time, between the two world wars, that some of the major biblical sites were excavated by all nationalities: Bethel,

Beth Shemesh, Beth Shean, Hazor, Jericho, and Lachish. Among the most important of these excavations was that conducted at Megiddo, which soon became one of the major type sites for biblical archaeology.[4]

The development of biblical archaeology from the 1930s through the 1970s and beyond was furthered by Albright's students—trained in both biblical scholarship and biblical archaeology, they were considered Albright's "children" and "grandchildren" (Van Beek 1989, 14; D. Freedman 1975, 221–26), some of whom are in the photo of the 1932 Tell Beit Mirsim excavation staff (fig. 5.2).

4. James Henry Breasted, an Egyptologist and the major orientalist of his generation, was the mastermind behind this project. The support he received from John D. Rockefeller Jr. produced Chicago House in Luxor in 1924 (the work base for the Oriental Institute in Egypt), the funding for the Megiddo excavations in 1925, and, working together with Albright, the establishment of the Rockefeller Museum in Jerusalem in 1938, as well as an endowment for ASOR in the 1930s.

Fig. 5.3. Nelson Glueck on survey in Transjordan

Among Albright's most renowned students were Nelson Glueck and G. Ernest Wright (D. Freedman 1989, 38).[5] Glueck was ASOR director in 1932–33, 1936–40, and 1942–47. He identified more than 1,000 sites in his survey of Transjordan and produced the first scientific demographic synthesis of Moab, Ammon, and Edom (fig. 5.3).[6] In his subsequent survey of the Negev he identified 1,500 sites from the Chalcolithic through the Byzantine periods, including many known from the Bible (Glueck 1959a; 1969). Glueck's approach to the Bible was typical of the Albright school: "No one can prove the Bible, for it is primarily a theological document. Those people are essentially of little faith who seek through archaeological corroboration of historical source materials in the Bible to validate its religious teachings and spiritual insights" (G. Wright 1959, 106).

Wright, who was influenced by Kathleen Kenyon's excavation at Jericho in the late 1930s and her use of the baulk debris method, directed the excavation at Shechem in 1950, the first major American excavation in the Levant after World War II (G. Wright 1965). It became the early training ground for his students and their exposure to the excavation methods used at Jericho. This method was adopted by Wright's students in the Gezer excavation, which began in 1964 and was the first American excavation conducted in the State of Israel. The Gezer excavation was the watershed experience for American archaeologists working in the eastern Mediterranean basin and for training the next generation of American dig directors and staff (Shanks 1990, 27, 29). Some of the sites they excavated in Israel include Tell el-Hesi, Merion, Sepphoris, Jebel Qaʿaqir, Khirbet el-Qom, Lahav-Tell Halif, Tel Miqne-Ekron, and Ashkelon.[7] This tradition continues into the current generation of American scholars, as seen, for example, in the renewed excavations at Gezer, Tell Keisan, Jaffa, and Acco, and the new excavations at Khirbet Summeily and Tel Rehov, many of which are joint American-Israeli projects.

5. Special mention should also be given to Frank M. Cross, David Noel Freedman, and John Bright.

6. His publication of this survey in four volumes (Glueck 1934a; 1935; 1939; 1951) still represents a primary textbook for the archaeology of Jordan, as is his volume on the Nabateans (Glueck 1965), based on his excavation at Khirbet et-Tannur (J. McKenzie et al. 2013).

7. Sites outside Israel include Tell el-Maskhuta in Egypt, Idalion on Cyprus, and Tall Hisban, Tall al-ʿUmayri, and Jalul in Jordan.

Fig. 5.4. Yigael Yadin

Fig. 5.5. Yohanan Aharoni

The Albright school and his approach to biblical archaeology were adopted by the first generation of Israeli archaeologists beginning in the 1950s, such as Yigael Yadin at Hazor (fig. 5.4), Nahman Avigad in Jerusalem, and Yohanan Aharoni at Arad and Beersheba (fig. 5.5). From these beginnings, the Israeli school of archaeology became the dominant force in advancing the field of biblical archaeology and developing it into a multidisciplinary field of research.[8]

By the last quarter of the twentieth century, biblical archaeology, whether defined as the archaeology of Palestine or the archaeology of ancient Israel, entered a new phase of development as it took on the double challenge of responding to questions regarding the validity of the archaeological record as a source for writing the history of the biblical period raised by members of the Copenhagen school of revisionists or minimalists and the challenge to the traditional chronology generated by Israel Finkelstein's proposed low

chronology. While nineteenth-century German scholarship had questioned the historical value of biblical texts written in the postexilic period about events that had occurred hundreds of years earlier, the more recent Copenhagen school raised the same question but pushed the writing of the texts much later into the Hellenistic period (Thompson 1999, 105). And when archaeology yielded documentation like the Ekron Royal Dedicatory Inscription (fig. 5.6) and the Tel Dan Inscription (fig. 5.7), the revisionists questioned their authenticity (Lemche *apud* Shanks 1997, 36–37, 43). For the revisionists, the "so-called" historical parts of the Bible represent a social construct that reflects the period in which they were written, not the time of the events they describe. Consequently, accepting this approach would mean that virtually no history of the biblical period could be written.

Lawrence E. Stager, among the many scholars who have challenged the revisionists, has asked: If the Bible was composed in the Hellenistic period by a Jewish storyteller, how could he have been so accurate in recording facts about the Philistines, if, as we know, there were no Philistines in the Hellenistic period (Stager

8. For a brief overview of the history of research including the main sites excavated from 1948 to 1988, see A. Mazar 1990a, 10–20; for the main sites up to 2015, see the chapters in Gitin 2015.

2006, 377)?[9] The most consistent and outspoken opponent of the revisionists, and the one who has taken the lead in responding to them, is W. G. Dever. He has described them as "a very small minority of biblical scholars, who have provoked the present historiographical crisis only by being the most extreme, the most vocal, the best strategists and easily the most effective propagandists" (Dever 2001, 24). Dever's

Photo by Zev. Radovan, Tel Miqne-Ekron Excavation and Publication Project

Fig. 5.6. Ekron Royal Dedicatory Inscription

> chief complaint is that the revisionists tend to distort or even ignore what many now see as our primary source for writing a history of ancient Israel, namely modern archaeology. At the same time, they approach the only source of data, the texts of the Hebrew Bible, with such overwhelming suspicion that they end up seeing the Hebrew Bible's narrative and ancient Israel largely as "fictions." . . . That is why I say that they are practically speaking nihilists. . . . They read the entire Hebrew Bible . . . as a "social construct" of Hellenistic Judaism. (Dever 2001, 296)

The revisionists' attack on the essence of biblical archaeology has not succeeded in diminishing either its importance or its development. Although a large number of those who describe themselves as biblical archaeologists no longer accept many of the basic tenets and significant historical conclusions established by Albright and his students, they still employ Albright's approach of studying the ancient Near Eastern background of the Bible to analyze the issue of the historicity of the biblical text. Many of these scholars, including historians, philologians, and archaeologists, have also followed Albright in correlating archaeological data and biblical and nonbiblical texts for the same purpose. This is the true measure of the durability of Albright's approach, a phenomenon highlighted by the fact that even some of Albright's severest critics—W. G. Dever and Israel Finkelstein—employ his approach to support their own interpretations of biblical history.

Dever, who has challenged a number of Albright's historical conclusions, such as the dating of the patriarchal period to the Middle Bronze Age (Dever 1977, 93–102), has come to appreciate the ancient Near Eastern background of the patriarchal epoch, which he now uses to establish its cultural context (Dever 2002). Although he rejects Albright's model of the conquest of Canaan by the Israelites (Dever 1993, 33), he nonetheless follows

9. For example, how could a Hellenistic writer have known about the Aegean origins of the Philistines, their gods, their armor, and best of all, that they charged a *pim* for sharpening the Israelites' metal tools, as recorded in 1 Sam. 13:21? The ancient Greek and Latin translators of the Bible did not know what a *pim* was; only in the twentieth century did archaeology reveal that a *pim* is a weight equaling two-thirds of a shekel that disappeared at the end of the Iron Age, by 586 BCE (Stager 2006, 381–82).

Albright's approach to several other major issues of biblical history (Dever 1999, 92–93, 96–97, 100–101). He has also challenged Finkelstein's rejection of the traditional treatment of the United Monarchy and its floruit under Solomon in the tenth century BCE (Balter 2000, 32).

As for Finkelstein, who is also deeply involved in the issue of what constitutes biblical history, while he rejects

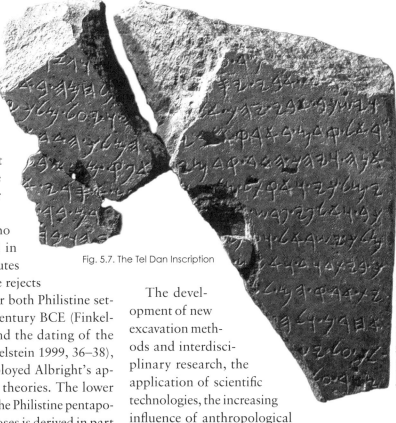

Fig. 5.7. The Tel Dan Inscription

Albright's paradigms for both Philistine settlement in the twelfth century BCE (Finkelstein 1998b, 140–41) and the dating of the Solomonic period (Finkelstein 1999, 36–38), he nevertheless has employed Albright's approach to produce new theories. The lower date for the founding of the Philistine pentapolis that Finkelstein proposes is derived in part from the Near Eastern background associated with the dynamic of Philistine settlement (Finkelstein 1999, 37). He bases his lower date for the strata traditionally associated with the Solomonic period and the tenth century on the typological analysis of a pottery assemblage from Jezreel that he equates with the pottery from Megiddo Stratum VA/IVB, both of which he assigns to the ninth century (Finkelstein 1998a, 170; 1999, 38–39; A. Mazar 2012, 6n1),[10] following the dating of a biblical text (Na'aman 1997a, 122, 125, 127). Like Dever, Finkelstein has begun to come full circle regarding the use of biblical text, and both of them now refer to their discipline as the "new-new" biblical archaeology (Finkelstein and Silberman 2001; Dever 2002).

10. Finkelstein's dating both of the Philistine settlement and of the Solomonic period is not accepted by most archaeologists.

The development of new excavation methods and interdisciplinary research, the application of scientific technologies, the increasing influence of anthropological concepts, and, most importantly, the enormous growth of the archaeological database have brought radical changes to our approach to archaeology and the history of the ancient Near East, including biblical history and biblical archaeology. Yet the possibility of establishing the historicity of parts of the biblical text based on the correlation of archaeological and Near Eastern textual data has been maintained, as has the basic value of Albright's pioneering work in fashioning the structure and tools of the discipline of biblical archaeology. The latter, which include the principles of stratigraphic definition, ceramic typology, and chronological periodization, have remained constants, even though new data have produced significant modifications in the historical conclusions and interpretations of the material culture that form a basis of the discipline of biblical archaeology.

What, then, can biblical archaeology contribute to this discussion and to our understanding of the history of the biblical period? Contrary to the revisionists' claims, a significant assemblage of written documents exists from the biblical period—including the Samaria and Arad ostraca, the Lachish Letters, the Siloam Inscription, the Moabite Stone, numerous seals and miscellaneous ostraca, the Dan and Ekron inscriptions, and Egyptian and Neo-Assyrian documents. Taken together with well-stratified archaeological data and contextualized within the broad range of scientific technologies applied in interdisciplinary research, biblical archaeology is a valuable and useful discipline in writing the history of ancient Israel.[11]

11. For an appreciation of the value of interdisciplinary research for biblical studies, see Maeir 2015b.

6

Archaeology of the Late Bronze Age

JOE UZIEL

The period of the Late Bronze Age can be defined as a bridge between the peak of the Canaanite urban culture of the Middle Bronze Age (see, e.g., Dever 1987; Ilan 1995) and the new ethnic groups that would eventually populate the southern Levant in the subsequent Iron Age (ch. 7 below). From a historical perspective, the period's onset has been intertwined with the rise of the Egyptian New Kingdom, although many have argued that the downfall of the Canaanite urban entities of the Middle Bronze Age was not related to the expulsion of the Hyksos and the conquest of Canaan by New Kingdom armies (e.g., Weinstein 1981; 1991; Hoffmeier 1989; 1990; 1991; Dever 1990a; Finkelstein 1992, 212; Na'aman 1994). Regardless of whether the Middle Bronze Age cities saw their downfall as a result of Egyptian destruction, the Late Bronze Age period is witness to intensive interaction between an Egyptian regime that desired control of the southern Levant and the local urban entities, who aimed at maintaining and expanding their control locally (see, e.g., Goren, Finkelstein, and Na'aman 2004). This is most clearly manifested in the ca. fourteenth century BCE Amarna Letters describing, with the loosened involvement of the Eighteenth-Dynasty king Akhenaten, the local rulers' violent interactions, alliances, and, most of all, desire to control territories (e.g., Finkelstein 1996c). Regardless, the Egyptian intervention in the territory of the southern Levant is of great influence on the material culture, settlement patterns, and overall understanding of the period. Roughly, this intervention can be understood in three stages (e.g., Rainey 2006):

- initial control through military conquest, as documented in the Egyptian campaign of Thutmosis III and others;
- distant control leading to a certain extent of upheaval, as seen in the Amarna correspondence; and
- reinstituted power through the establishment of locally placed governing bodies, for example at Jaffa, Beth Shean, and Aphek.

Archaeologically, the period of the Late Bronze Age can be defined as one of continuity and change in relation to the preceding Middle Bronze Age (Bunimovitz 1995). On the one hand, many aspects of material culture, such as local pottery styles, can be directly linked to the earlier period. Many of the urban centers of the Middle Bronze Age are reestablished—albeit on a smaller scale. On the other hand, there are also many differences between the two periods, notably in the scope of urban complexity as well as in local production. In turn, the Late Bronze Age is most clearly defined by the intensive integration of Late Bronze Age Canaan into the Mediterranean koine, focused on sea trade. This is most felt through the discovery of Mycenaean and most prominently Cypriot products found in excavations in Israel. While such interactions are also noted in the Middle Bronze Age, the scale of their appearance in the subsequent period is much greater. The following survey will examine several aspects of Late Bronze Age culture and settlement patterns, particularly in light of the preceding period, in order to summarize the character of the period.

Settlement Patterns and Demographics

Initial study of the Late Bronze Age set out to find a very well-developed urban culture. Z. Herzog (1997a, 164) notes, "That a prosperous urban culture existed was taken for granted." However, this perception is no longer valid, and after many years of excavation and survey a different picture arises. Following the collapse of the Middle Bronze, the rebirth of urban society in the Late Bronze follows a completely different pattern than that of its predecessor. Many settlements from the Middle Bronze II that had been destroyed were not resettled during the Late Bronze. The settlements clustered around the coastal plain, the Judean lowlands, and the Jezreel and Beth Shean Valleys. Fringe areas seem to be almost completely abandoned (e.g., the Beersheba Valley). In contrast, ports (e.g., Tell Abu-Hawam,

Tall Nami) thrived during the Late Bronze as a result of the very active maritime trade. The period is also witness to the general disappearance of most rural settlements until the final stages of the period, when it seems that the hinterland began to recover (e.g., A. Mazar 1990a, 239–40). The reduction of hinterland settlements in the Late Bronze seems to have been over 50 percent (see, e.g., Gonen 1984, 68).

While some of the urban entities of the Middle Bronze Age continued to exist, they seem to have shrunk considerably in many cases. One of the most notable features of Late Bronze Age constructions is the lack of fortifications. Some have explained this, at least partially, as the reuse of Middle Bronze Age fortifications (A. Mazar 1990a, 243), while others claim that Egyptian rule in the Late Bronze Age prevented their construction (e.g., Gonen 1984, 70). Whatever the reason, this is in contrast to the Middle Bronze Age system, where fortifications are found not only in the largest centers but also even at smaller entities (e.g., Burke 2008, 228–319; Uziel 2010).

In light of the information on settlement patterns, Bunimovitz (1994) pointed out that one of the most distinct differences between the Middle and Late Bronze Ages is that of population. While it is now well accepted that the reconstruction of exact demographic figures is quite difficult and not very reliable (see, e.g., Zorn 1994; Uziel and Maeir 2005), the decrease in the number of settlements and the size of urban entities clearly indicates a decrease in population.

Pottery

One of the main traits that have been used to show cultural continuity between the Middle Bronze Age and the Late Bronze is local pottery. The forms continue from one period to the next virtually unchanged (see, e.g., Bunimovitz 1995, 330). Carinated bowls, cooking pots, storage jars, dipper juglets, lamps, and other forms find their origins in the Middle Bronze but continue well into the Late Bronze. However, upon closer examination, three main differences between the ceramic corpora can be discerned. The first is the infiltration of imports. While imported pottery from Cyprus, Crete, and elsewhere reached the southern Levant from the early stages of the Middle Bronze Age, the quantity of imports—primarily from Cyprus—is nowhere near that of the Late Bronze Age, beginning in the Late Bronze I (Epstein 1966) and continually increased throughout the period (e.g., Amiran 1969). This is important because it reflects a social attitude toward imports that was not present beforehand, as well as a new economic order, in which trade was clearly very important (e.g., Serpico et al. 2003).

No less important are the differences in local pottery. The typological forms are very similar, but the process by which vessels were produced was quite different. In a study of ceramics from Tel Batash, Panitz-Cohen (2006, 274–313) showed that there were significant differences between the *châine opératoire* of the Middle Bronze and that of the Late Bronze, even in the choice of clays used. Panitz-Cohen (2006, 280) points out that the social "weight" of the production process can be more significant than the typological form. The lack of exactness and quality in the Late Bronze Age seems to reflect the socioeconomic conditions of the period. Similar results regarding the forming of vessels were obtained when studying the ceramics from Tell es-Safi. During the Middle Bronze Age, much more care was taken in both the preparation of clay and the finishing of vessels. While it is difficult to determine whether vessels were wheel-thrown or only wheel-finished, the finishing was so fine that in most cases it was impossible to tell if the vessel had been coil-built. In the Late Bronze Age, the choice of raw materials and sifting was poor, the coiling was not completely smoothed out, the smoothing of the vessels

was very sloppy, and more vessels seem to have been dissymmetrical (Ben-Shlomo, Uziel, and Maeir 2009). While there is no doubt that the persistence of vessel shapes indicates the continuation of the same culture, much can be learned from the way in which the vessels were formed. Panitz-Cohen (2006, 291–93) points to the differences as an indication of a switch from more to less centralized production. The "sloppiness" of local Late Bronze pottery also reflects the rising importance of imports as the fine ware ceramics.

The third change from Middle to Late Bronze Age pottery is the widespread use of decoration. Ceramic assemblages of the former period—save for specific wares (e.g., chocolate-on-white ware; red, white, and blue ware [e.g., Maeir 2002])—are generally finely made yet lack painted decoration. This may be due to the clay recipes, which were adapted for the use of the fast wheel (Franken and London 1995). In the subsequent period, painted decoration becomes very common. It is usually red and black (bichrome) or only red (monochrome), particularly in the later portion of the period (Gadot, Uziel, and Yasur-Landau 2012). The decorations—often appearing on the interior of bowls or on the shoulders of jugs (particularly biconical jugs)—are typically divided with triglyphs and metopes and display geometric, vegetal, and animal motifs. One of the most common of these motifs is the "palm tree and ibex" motif often appearing on bowls (sometimes called Gezer bowls because of their common appearance at the site [Gitin 1990]).

Unique vessels also reflect on the social and cultic nature of the period. One such vessel is the cup-and-saucer vessel composed of a bowl with a smaller bowl inside it, usually placed at the center of the vessel. These were discovered in excavations in the southern Levant as early as the late nineteenth century (e.g., Bliss and Macalister 1902, plate 46:6–7). Although made in other periods, its distribution is much greater in the Late Bronze, when the form is quite standardized, with just a few small variations. The outer bowl is hemispheric, with no base and an outfolded rim. The inner bowl is generally higher than the outer one and flares outward. Some of the vessels have a small hole connecting the two bowls. Another variation is a pinch on the rim of the outer bowl.

While the cup-and-saucer vessel appears from the Early Bronze Age onward, it seems that it gains importance in the southern Levant during the period of Egyptian influence in the Late Bronze IIB and later, with its popularity declining after the Iron Age I. It appears that the primary use of these objects is cultic, both for light and for the spread of scents. Examples from noncultic contexts—such as those originating at Megiddo—are indications that cultic activity was not restricted to specific locales (Uziel and Gadot 2010).

Cultic Practices

Ritual and cult also reflect the continuity and change between the two periods. For example, the location of certain cultic sites continues from the Middle Bronze Age through to the Late Bronze Age (e.g., Temple 2048 at Megiddo, the temple at Shechem, and the temples in Areas H and A at Hazor [see, e.g., A. Mazar 1992, 162–69]). Yet, as opposed to the Middle Bronze Age, the Late Bronze Age is witness to a nonuniform construction of temples, with many different styles. While the "Syrian temples" at Hazor, Shechem, and Megiddo continue to be in use, a great variety of types are built (e.g., compare the plans of the temples at Shechem, the Fosse Temple at Lachish, and Beth Shean Stratum VI [A. Mazar 1992, 163]).

Metal figurines are a fine example of the continuity and change between periods. On the one hand, certain deities continue from one period to the next, yet on the other, new deities are introduced, and it seems that worship of multiple deities in a single temple is undertaken

in the Late Bronze Age (Negbi 1976, 141). Iconography is also different, yet similar, between the periods. Middle Bronze Age themes depict scenes of loyalty, while those of the Late Bronze Age depict military scenes (Keel and Uehlinger 1998, 60). There is also a general trend over time toward increased worship of male deities and lowered status of women (Keel and Uehlinger 1998, 65, 88–97). Yet certain aspects remain the same, such as figurines of a fertility goddess (Keel and Uehlinger 1998, 54).

Of the most striking differences is the use of clay figurines. These figurines are very rare in the southern Levant during the Middle Bronze Age, yet are abundant in the Late Bronze Age, found in almost every excavation dating to the period (e.g., M. Fowler 1985, 334; Keel and Uehlinger 1998, 54; Cornelius 2004a, 62, 72). The few Middle Bronze Age examples known to date are from cultic contexts at Nahariya (S. Zuckerman, personal communication) and possibly Tel Haror (Katz 2009) and not from domestic contexts, where they become commonplace in the Late Bronze Age.

Clay figurines similar to those of the Late Bronze Age first appear in Mesopotamia during the Early Bronze Age (Pritchard 1943, 49; Fowler 1985, 343; Spycket 2000, 24). These figurines spread to Syria, where they appear from the Middle Bronze Age (Badre 1980; Marchetti and Nigro 1995, 22–24; Spycket 2000, 25) and continue to be common in the Late Bronze Age (Badre 1980; Maeir 2003b, 202). When these artifacts appear in Canaan in the Late Bronze Age, they show traces of Egyptian and Mesopotamian influence (Pritchard 1943, 83; Keel and Uehlinger 1998, 84), although they are most similar to the Syrian figurines (Tadmor 1982, 157).

It appears that the best explanation for the use of ceramic female figurines is cultic. Whether representing a specific goddess or not, the items had some sort of religious value to their owners. Cornelius (2004b) contends that the find context of the clay figurines is not useful in understanding their function since they are found in cultic, burial, and domestic contexts alike. Yet it may be that the varying contexts are what best reflect the functions of these figurines. The presence of these figurines in all aspects of life may reflect the use of these objects in the realm of what may be termed "popular religion." The use of these objects in small cultic corners in the home (Keel and Uehlinger 1998, 97) or simply as symbols of one's religious beliefs seems likely.

This returns us to the question of why these items were not used in the Middle Bronze Age southern Levant. In essence, if these objects are a form of pluralistic religious behavior, then it is likely that their scarcity was due to religious uniformity—not in the sense of monotheism, as various deities were worshiped in Middle Bronze Age Canaan. Rather, it seems that religious practice was more controlled. Cultic items seem to be more limited in this period to cultic sites. Temple form was also more uniform than in the Late Bronze and Iron Ages (e.g., A. Mazar 1992). Maeir (2003a, 63–64) has pointed out that distribution and similarity in cultic frameworks was intentional, used by governing forces to create a "sacred landscape" in order to promote elite dominance. Whether or not elite dominance was being promoted, the religious powers that be were dictating the form of worship. By the Late Bronze Age, such uniformity disappears. This is most likely related to both a general weakening of local authority within the realm of Egyptian hegemony and the entrance into the world markets, with exposure to and desires for new and diverse materials.

Writing

Scholarly research of writing in this and the preceding period has primarily focused on dating the introduction/invention/innovation of alphabetic script and not on discovering the extent to which that script was used, and in what

circles (Naveh 1982; Sass 1988; 2005; G. Hamilton 2006; see Millard 1999a for an exception). There is a sharp increase in written finds from Canaan dating to the Late Bronze Age. In fact, more than 50 percent of the Akkadian tablets that have been found in the southern Levant date to this period. Within this corpus, one can add the Amarna archive, which includes many letters from Canaan (Goren, Finkelstein, and Na'aman 2004). Excavations at Syrian sites including Emar, Alalakh, and Ugarit have revealed several rich archives, and it is tempting to assume that large Canaanite urban centers to the south of these sites had similar bureaucratic systems that included administrative archives. Nevertheless, written finds from Late Bronze Age Canaan are scarce, and it seems that documents were mostly limited to administrative needs. This differs from the situation in Syria, where writing was also used for literary purposes (Schniedewind 2004, 40–41).

The alphabetic script may have initially appeared in this period (Sass 2005; cf. Trigger 2004, 56; G. Hamilton 2006). Sass (2005, 153–54) even argues for a boom in alphabetic writing toward the end of the period, although this does not appear to be the case. Indeed, alphabetic writing dating to this period is scarce, with only several examples of such script found.[1] This is in contrast to cuneiform documents, of which a relatively large number have been found thus far (Horowitz, Oshima, and Sanders 2006, table 1). In this sense, the southern Levant is not unique, as Akkadian served the entire region as the international and administrative script (Gianto 1999, 123; S. Sanders 2004, 49). Egypt also used this script for international correspondence, even when it corresponded with Canaanite rulers, as evidenced in the Amarna archive. The need for an international script is easily understood, considering the global

1. Sass (2005, 154) claims that the dozen or so documents that have been found attest to a much wider use of script on papyrus. However, Akkadian was much more frequently used during this period, and it seems that this was the common script for all official purposes.

economic environment that existed in the Near East in the Late Bronze Age.

However, what is unique is the presence of alphabetic script alongside cuneiform. If Akkadian was used for international relations and administrative purposes, when was alphabetic script used, and whom did it serve? Why does there not appear to be any writing for purposes other than administration—for example, religious or mythological literature—such as those that have been found in Ugarit, Emar, and Allalah (Gianto 1999, 125–26)?

Regarding the question of when alphabetic script was used and by whom, it is important to point out that there are very few known alphabetic documents from this time, even according to Sass (2005). Moreover, because many of these are single letters, their content has not been deciphered, making it difficult to classify the texts. It is clear therefore that alphabetic script was not utilized for official purposes (S. Sanders 2004, 33; contra G. Hamilton 2006, 293). Millard (1999a, 321) suggests that both hieratic and alphabetic scripts were written on papyrus and used for administration, though this seems unlikely. Alphabetic script at this stage is very enigmatic and heterogeneous; the direction was not established, and the character of the texts discovered seems more like graffiti and less like formal writing (S. Sanders 2004, 44; Goldwasser 2006a, 133).

The official written language of Canaan in the Late Bronze Age was Akkadian, and possibly hieratic on a lesser scale (Millard 1999a, 319–21). Alongside this, a limited number of alphabetic documents have been discovered. The source and content of these documents suggest that this script was used by a marginal group, indicating the existence of an alternative way of life. The existence of numerous marginal groups during this period is attested by other aspects of culture, as well as historical sources (Shai and Uziel 2010).

To summarize, in the Late Bronze Age, a number of writing systems (cuneiform, hieratic, and alphabetic) appear. The scope of writing is more limited than in other societies, although governing forces did write. Akkadian cuneiform was used for international communication and administration, while alphabetic script was adopted by a small and marginal portion of society.

Discussion

The southern Levantine Late Bronze Age can be defined culturally, socially, and economically by several intertwined aspects. These are clearly defined when we compare the period to its predecessor—the Middle Bronze Age. First, there is no doubt that there were major demographic changes between the two periods. These changes are often linked to the Egyptian attitude to the region. There is no doubt that the onset of the period, brought about by Egyptian campaigns such as the defeat of Sharuhen and Thutmose III's conquest of the Canaanite coalition at Megiddo, hindered the regeneration of settlements, population, and economy on a whole. Within this situation, there is no doubt that some (particularly a small elite) thrived, as seen in the construction of palaces and the discovery of items of wealth, such as the Megiddo ivories. However, on a whole, the flourishing settlements of the Middle Bronze Age do not revive after their collapse at the end of the period. Small rural settlements are fewer, and urban centers are smaller and lack certain features such as fortifications. While many aspects of the material culture are clear continuations of their Middle Bronze predecessors, they lose much of their quality. It has been suggested that, beyond the limitations placed by the Egyptian overseers on the construction of fortifications, there were also limitations to technological developments. Whereas in the Middle Bronze Age technological advancement seems to have been a cornerstone of the Canaanite cultural sphere, in the Late Bronze Age, the Egyptians limited technological development, possibly in order to keep the local communities from gaining strength and wealth (for further discussion, see Uziel 2011b). The reawakening of Late Bronze society does occur toward the end of the period, when it appears that the number of settlements grows drastically. It may be the result of a change in Egypt's approach toward the southern Levant, as indicated by the establishment of more Egyptian local administrative centers.

Despite its relative paucity in local production and the decrease in settlements and fortifications, the Late Bronze Age culture of the southern Levant was quite pluralistic. This is apparent in many aspects of daily life of the period. Temple architecture was far from uniform (A. Mazar 1992). While pottery forms are common throughout the region, much of this is a continuation of the previous period. Within the ceramic corpus, diversity can be seen in the mass introduction of imports and the widespread use of decoration on pottery. Language also exhibits pluralism, as three forms of script are used in this period: cuneiform (Horowitz, Oshima, and Sanders 2006), hieratic (Millard 1999a), and the appearance of the alphabet (Sass 2005).[2] Names of rulers in this period exhibit pluralism, with Indo-European, Semitic, and Hurrian components. While only indicative of the upper rank, the appearance of non-Semitic personal names in the Amarna archive shows diversity within this class (Hess 1993a).

The figurines represent the religious side of this diversity. While temples still stood, the Late Bronze Age population had other—cheaper—methods of worship available to them in the form of plaque figurines. Furthermore, burial practices vary widely during this period (Gonen 1992a). Whether explained through differences in ethnicity or in socioeconomic status (Bunimovitz 1995), this points to diverse groups within Canaanite society.

There is no doubt that much of this cultural diversity must have been a function of the exposure to foreign cultures, mostly through the trade routes running so vibrantly along the Mediterranean. This trade koine has been understood as what would also lead to the collapse of these societies that were so dependent upon it for strong economies. With the slow collapse of empires and trading networks, the Late Bronze Age draws to a close. This is indicated not only by the slow process of Egyptian withdrawal from the region but also by the complete disappearance of imported pottery forms. The subsequent Iron Age sees the void left by the collapsing Canaanite culture filled with new ethnic groups. Although some may have had local origins while others were foreign to the region, there is no doubt that the onset of the Iron Age is witness to a change in settlement patterns, material culture, and systems of rule (and see, e.g., ch. 7 below).

2. Although the alphabet may have appeared already in the Middle Bronze period, there is no doubt that its use in the earlier period was minimal, and it only becomes "widespread" in the Late Bronze.

7

Archaeology of the Iron Age I

Aren M. Maeir

The Late Bronze / Iron Age Transition

Starting from the mid-to-late thirteenth century BCE and well into the mid-to-late twelfth century BCE, the eastern Mediterranean in general and the Levant in particular witnessed major changes in social, political, and economic makeup (in general, see Cline 2014). During most of the preceding Late Bronze Age (ca. 1500–1200 BCE), the socioeconomic structure in the eastern Mediterranean was of a "club" of "superpowers," including New Kingdom Egypt, the Hittite Empire, and the Assyrian Kingdom, along with regional and local kingdoms of varying influence and additional cultural and ethnic groups of varying character. All these entities were players in a web of intense diplomatic, cultural, and economic connections. Starting in the late thirteenth century, but more so in the twelfth, many of the basic building blocks of the Late Bronze Age world order disappear. The Hittite Empire collapses, the Egyptian Empire loses its control of Canaan by the mid-to-late twelfth century, the Mycenaean palace polities break down, the volume of international trade is significantly reduced, many of the Canaanite cities in Canaan are abandoned or destroyed, and new cultural and ethnic groups seem to appear throughout the region. This includes the so-called Sea Peoples, the Israelites, the Aramaeans, and various other groups. And while during the Late Bronze Age there are diverse written sources from throughout the ancient Near East, from the early twelfth century until well into the late eleventh and early tenth centuries there are few contemporaneous written sources relating to the historical situation in the southern Levant. Due to this, this period is very much a "dark age," and to reconstruct the underlying mechanisms that lead up to this period and what happens during it scholars are very much dependent on archaeological remains. The biblical text, while seemingly relating to this period, is really of tangential utility as a historical source for dealing with it, as the various narratives regarding the formation of Israel and related issues appear, by and large, to be based on later understandings, and some memories, of this period.

Chronological Framework

Traditionally, the Iron Age I usually is dated between 1200 and 1000 BCE, more or less between the end of the Nineteenth Egyptian Dynasty and the traditional dates of the beginning of the so-called biblical United Kingdom. This, though, should be regarded as only a very rough chronological framework.

To start with, various processes and mechanisms that are connected to the Late Bronze / Iron Age transition start before 1200 BCE. This includes some sites (such as Hazor) that appear to have been destroyed before 1200 BCE, evidence of the existence of the Israelites prior to 1200 BCE (such as in the Merneptah Stela), and possible indications of the first hints of the "Sea Peoples" phenomenon, yet in the thirteenth century BCE.

On the other hand, there are many who argue that most of the primary processes marking the collapse of the Late Bronze Age system did not occur until the early, mid-, or in some cases late twelfth century BCE. For example, major Late Bronze Age sites such as Boğazkale and Ugarit were not destroyed or abandoned before the second decade of the twelfth century; similarly, most, if not all, of the evidence for the Sea Peoples and the Philistines does not date before the first and perhaps even the second quarter of the twelfth century; and finally, at various sites (such as Megiddo) the Canaanite culture continues well into the eleventh century.

As to the end of the Iron Age I, it is almost universally accepted nowadays that the material culture typical of the Iron Age I continues into the tenth century BCE; the question is whether it ends in the first decades of the century (e.g., A. Mazar 2011) or perhaps around the mid-to-late tenth century (e.g., Finkelstein and Piasetzky 2011).[1]

1. Suggestions to date the appearance of the Israelites and other related phenomena to earlier periods, such as the transition between the Middle and Late Bronze Ages (ca. 1500 BCE), as propounded by, for example,

The Israelites

The vibrant biblical description of the Israelite conquest and settlement in Canaan and its cardinal role in biblical and postbiblical traditions have made the search for evidence of the initial stages of the Israelite culture of much interest in the study of the early Iron Age Levant. The biblical text, and in particular many parts of the book of Joshua, appear to portray a military conquest of the land by the Israelites. On the other hand, in the book of Judges, a more gradual process of settlement is implied. For many years, research on the appearance of the Israelites[2] was divided into several distinct schools of thought: (1) those who believed that archaeological evidence of the Israelite conquest could be found, such as Albright (e.g., 1949b) and Yadin (e.g., 1963); (2) those who preferred to see a process of gradual settlement by peoples coming from outside Canaan, such as Alt (1925) and Aharoni (1957); and (3) those who believed that the appearance of the early Israelites should be explained primarily as an internal phenomenon, mostly made up of peoples originating in Canaan, who during the early Iron Age realigned their identity, such as Mendenhall (1973) and Gottwald (1979).

Recent research has, to all intents and purposes, negated the "conquest view."[3] While there are a few sites at which evidence of destructions dating to the late Late Bronze or the early Iron Age can be found (such as Hazor [e.g., A. Ben-Tor 2016]), by and large, at most sites of this period, including several

B. G. Wood regarding the finds at Khirbet Maqatir (Wood 2009), are hard to accept. On this, see Maeir 2011, 100.

2. In most research, the term "Israelites" refers to the peoples of both the northern (later the kingdom of Israel) and the southern (later the kingdom of Judah) groups. And while there is much in common, the distinct differences between these groups should be taken into account, including during the Iron Age (see, e.g., Fleming 2012; Maeir 2013a).

3. There are still some attempts in recent literature (e.g., Hawkins 2013; Provan, Long, and Longman 2015) to adhere to the conquest model, but I do not believe they are convincing. See, e.g., Maeir 2016.

that play a central role in the biblical narratives of the Israelite conquest (such as Jericho, Ai, and Arad), there is no evidence of large-scale destructions at the majority of the sites mentioned in the biblical texts regarding the supposed conquest. Similarly, while there does seem to be a gradual process of settlement in many parts of the central hills and Upper Galilee throughout the early Iron Age, some regions are hardly settled (such as the Judean mountains), and for the most part, there is much similarity between the material culture of these new settlements in the central hills and the previous Canaanite culture. So much so that most scholars nowadays would agree that the early Israelites were comprised of a substantial amount of local Canaanite elements (mostly rural and nomadic elements who were already in the central hills region), some people deriving from the lowlands Canaanite urban matrix, along with some groups that entered the region in a gradual manner, perhaps from areas to the east and northeast of Canaan (such as Zertal's claims regarding the early Iron Age sites in Samaria; e.g., Zertal 2004). In other words, there is only marginal evidence of each of the three major schools noted above: conquest, slow but steady infiltration from the east, and dislocation from the Canaanite lowland cities. Rather, it appears that aspects of these three processes, and others, occurred at varying degrees during this time of change.

During the early Iron Age (perhaps even starting in the late thirteenth century BCE), there is substantial archaeological evidence of the appearance of many new sites in the central hills region, particularly in the region between Jerusalem in the south and the Jezreel Valley in the north (more or less, the region known as Samaria). Additional sites are known on the western foothills of Samaria (such as the well-known site of Izbet Zarta), in the hills in the eastern fringes of Samaria (above the Jordan Valley), and in northern Galilee (sites such as Saʿsaʿ and Har Adir). Interestingly, very few of

these sites are found in the region of Judah, from Jerusalem and southward (outstanding examples are Giloh and Tel Rumeida).[4] Most of these "settlement" sites can be characterized as small, enclosed villages with very simple, mainly domestic, architecture, primarily utilitarian pottery (storage jars, such as the well-known "collared rim jars," and cooking vessels), and almost no prestige or imported items. The majority of these "settlement" sites are built at new locations, but in some cases (such as at Hazor and Ai) they are built on sites that were occupied in earlier periods. In addition, a few sites with cultic remains are known, such as Shiloh (Finkelstein, Bunimovitz, and Lederman 1993), Mount Ebal (which can be identified as cultic even if one does not accept its identification as the "Altar of Joshua" [Zertal 1986–87; Hawkins 2012]), and the so-called Bull Site (A. Mazar 1982a). The late Adam Zertal, excavator of the Mount Ebal site, also suggested identifying a set of sites in eastern Samaria, which he claimed had a unique "sandal-shaped" form (Zertal and Ben-Yosef 2009). He believed that these were sites of the early Israelite settlers deriving from the regions east of the Jordan River and that the shape of the site was meant to mark occupation of the land. This interpretation has not been accepted by most scholars (e.g., Maeir 2014).

While the overall character of the "settlement sites" is quite different from that of the Late Bronze Age Canaanite cultural "assemblage" (e.g., Dever 2003; Faust 2007), many aspects, such as some of the pottery types, ritual objects, and subsistence patterns, are quite reminiscent of Canaanite traditions. This is one of the primary arguments for a connection between the inhabitants of these sites and

4. While somewhat outdated, Finkelstein 1988, Finkelstein and Na'aman 1994, and A. Mazar 1990a, 295–367, still provide overviews and discussions of many of the issues and sites relevant to the early Israelite settlement. For a more recent survey of the relevant literature on the Israelite settlement (although with a different understanding than suggested here), see Hawkins 2013.

the indigenous population of Canaan. Nevertheless, even if there is much continuity and similarity with cultures in Late Bronze Age Canaan, the overall "package" seen in these "settlement sites" in the hill country indicates the formation of new cultural identities in rather defined geographic zones. Many aspects of the early Iron Age "Israelite" sites do continue into the Iron II–III Israelite and Judahite cultures. This includes the "four-room house," which becomes very common in Iron II Israel and Judah, and an apparent lack of consumption of pig, at least in Judah but not necessarily in Israel (but note that both aspects should be related to with caution and cannot be used, per se, as definite identification of Israelite/Judahite sites; see, e.g., Faust 2007; 2012a; as opposed to, e.g., Maeir 2013c; Sapir-Hen et al. 2013; Kletter 2014).

All told, the processes that occurred in the central hills and Galilee regions during the Iron Age do point to the formation of new identity groups during the Iron I period. Without a doubt, these processes were of complex nature and cannot be boiled down to this or that monolithic trajectory. Rather, one should see a complex interplay of local and nonlocal groups, of various backgrounds and traditions, and the effects of various transformations, on local and regional scales, occurring during this period. It appears that many of these people, by the end of the Iron Age I, did in fact become what are later known in the biblical and nonbiblical sources as the Israelite and Judahite tribes and, subsequently, kingdoms. That said, a simplistic and linear relationship between all the Iron I settlement sites and later Judah/Israel should not be assumed (e.g., Nestor 2010). The situation on the ground undoubtedly was more complex. Similarly, shifting meta-identities should be acknowledged as well, where certain groups may have had fluid, fluctuating identities. They may very well have phased in and out of identification with the Israelite and Judahite

cultures, both during and after the Iron Age I, depending on specific political, economic, and social circumstances. This would be the case for groups in the regions bordering other "major" cultures (e.g., Philistines, Canaanites, Phoenicians, Transjordanian peoples). And some probably shifted between the internal Israelite and Judahite identities. Nevertheless, during the transition between Iron I and Iron II (somewhere in the tenth century BCE), many of the peoples in the various regions noted above coalesced into larger groups that served the basis for the kingdoms of Israel and Judah.

The Philistines

During the transition between the Late Bronze and Iron Ages, there is substantial evidence for movements of peoples, of different origins and sociopolitical character, throughout the eastern Mediterranean. Mainly from the Egyptian, but also from Hittite and Ugaritic written sources, there is evidence for groups of peoples originating from diverse regions in the eastern, central, and northern Mediterranean who reach the southern Levant. Some of these are termed in modern research as the "Sea Peoples" (e.g., Killebrew and Lehmann 2013). While in past research it was common to neatly divide the Sea Peoples into different groups of very specific origins and the areas they settled in the Levant in the early Iron Age (e.g., Shardanu, Sikil, Dananu, Philistine), it is now quite clear that the very definition of these groups, their origins, makeup, cohesiveness, and process of arrival, settlement, and transformation are much more complex. And in fact, the archaeological identification of other Sea Peoples groups besides the Philistines is highly contested at best.[5]

5. Recent suggestions to identify a "Northern Philistine" group in the Amuq Valley in Southern Turkey (e.g., Janeway 2017) are not without problems. While it is clear that this is a phenomenon connected to the Late Bronze / Iron Age transformation, and includes ample

For the current discussion, we will focus on the Philistines (Yasur-Landau 2010; Maeir and Hitchcock 2017a; 2017b), one of the groups included among the Sea Peoples (referred to in the Egyptian sources as the Peleset) and, according to the biblical sources and the archaeological remains, one of the main cultural groups in Canaan during the Iron I (and Iron II–III). Without a doubt, the Philistines were a major player, and opponent, in relation to the Israelite/Judahite elements. The Philistines were located in the southern coastal plain of modern-day Israel (biblical Philistia), more or less between the Yarkon River in the north and Gaza in the south and from the Mediterranean in the west to the Shephelah (Judean foothills) in the east. The actual size of the region dominated by the Philistine culture fluctuated during the Iron Age.

Although the biblical texts often discuss the relations between the Philistines and the Israelites/Judahites prior to the period of David and Solomon, in fact, when comparing the extensive archaeological evidence from Iron I Philistia, it appears that the biblical depictions mostly reflect later Iron Age realia.

On the other hand, archaeological evidence of the early Iron Age Philistine culture is extensive. Current research on the Philistines, based on ongoing excavations at various major Philistine sites, enables us to re-create a clear picture of who they were, where they came from, and how their culture developed, transformed, and eventually disappeared in the Late Iron Age. Earlier research (e.g., Dothan 1982) portrayed the Philistines as primarily deriving from Mycenaean Bronze Age Greeks who arrived in Canaan in the early twelfth century, captured and destroyed the Canaanite cities

in the southern coastal plain, settled in these cities with a unique, foreign influenced culture, and then, over a process of several hundred years, were slowly more and more influenced by the local cultures, until the last Philistine cities were destroyed in the late seventh century BCE by the Babylonians.

As opposed to this, current research (e.g., Maeir and Hitchcock 2017a and 2017b) suggests the following: The Philistine culture of the early Iron Age does not derive from one nonlocal region (e.g., the Mycenaean culture), but rather consists of various groups of diverse nonlocal origins (e.g., mainland Greece, Crete, western and southern Anatolia, Cyprus) that settled in Philistia during the Iron I. These groups were of varied socioeconomic character and may have included some that originally were of pirate-like nature. There is little evidence of destructions in the Late Bronze cities in the region, and if so, only in limited parts of the sites, perhaps the elite zones. Simultaneously, it appears that these nonlocal elements settled side by side with Canaanite elements, who continued living in these sites. Together, they formed what has been termed a "transcultural" or "entangled" culture. This complex culture had rich and diverse traditions and shows a high level of ceramic technology, architecture, metallurgy, and other aspects. Side by side with this, there are major differences between the culture of early Iron Age Philistia and that of the surrounding regions. Many of the foreign originating facets (pottery, urbanism, architecture, cult, diet, burial, etc.) are quite different from those of other cultural groups in the region, but as stated above, they are related not to a specific, uniform origin but rather to a broad range of roots.

The Philistine material culture includes an impressive pottery tradition, including unique decorated vessels, cultic and other objects, a unique diet (including the consumption of pig and dog meat at most sites, and new types of plants being consumed), differences in food

---

evidence of Aegean-oriented material culture, there are issues with associating this with the Philistines. First, it appears that the Aegean style pottery is later than that of the early Philistine pottery from Philistia and, second, the suggested association of local ethnonym "Palasitin/ Walasitin" with the ethnonym "Philistine" is contested (see Younger 2016, 127–34).

preparation (such as the use of hearths and specific cooking vessels), new agronomic traditions, specific cult practices, and many other aspects.

Archaeological excavations at Ashdod, Ashkelon, Ekron, and Gath (Tell es-Safi) have revealed significant remains of the Philistine culture, while the fifth city of the Philistine pentapolis, Gaza, has yet to be excavated. Other Philistine Iron I sites are known as well, and the sites of Tel Qasile and Nahal Patish, both with temples with rich remains, are of particular note.

The early Iron Age socioeconomic and political structure of the Philistines appears much more developed than that of the Iron I highland settlements. The Philistine culture was an urban-oriented, relatively complex culture, while the Israelite culture was much less hierarchical, complex, and technologically advanced. This appears to be reflected in the biblical texts, in which the Philistine polities and their military and social complexity pose a threat to the Israelites, before and during the early monarchy. The archaeological remains very likely indicate that the Philistines were socially, economically, and perhaps militarily dominant throughout the Iron Age I (and perhaps well into the Iron IIA as well). That said, at present there is no evidence of complex bureaucratic structures in the Philistine culture, and claims of the existence of an Aegean-inspired writing system have not been corroborated. Similarly, while the biblical portrait of the Philistines would seem to indicate a very martial character of this culture, in fact, archaeologically, there is very little evidence of Philistine weaponry (Maeir in press).

During the late Iron I and the transition to the Iron II, the Philistine culture becomes more and more similar to the surrounding cultures, but still it retains (in fact until the end of the Iron Age) unique identifying characteristics. Archaeological evidence of intense bidirectional contacts and influences between the Philistines and these neighboring cultures

is known, and perhaps also hinted at in the Samson narratives, in which many levels of Israelite-Philistine interaction are depicted.

The Phoenicians

The Phoenicians are, by and large, the continuation of the Late Bronze Age Canaanite culture and population along the coastal regions of the central and northern Levant, from the Carmel coast in Israel up through the coast of Lebanon to the southern part of the Syrian coast (in general, see, e.g., Markoe 2006). Much of the turbulence of the transition between the Late Bronze and Iron Ages is not felt in this coastal region, and, as opposed to many other regions in Canaan, it appears that international trade, particularly with Cyprus, continued to flourish during this period, except perhaps during the very beginning of the Iron I. The site of Dor serves as an example of this pattern. While it was often assumed that Dor should be seen as a site of the Sikil Sea Peoples, recent excavations have quite clearly demonstrated that the Late Bronze Canaanite culture continues at the site, and evidence of flourishing connections with Cyprus, and even with Egypt, can be seen (Waiman-Barak, Gilboa, and Goren 2014; Gilboa and Goren 2015). Already during the late Iron I, the Phoenicians, particularly in the cities along the Lebanese coast, develop vibrant polities with complex socioeconomic structures and lay the foundations for the far-ranging trading activities of the Phoenicians during the Iron II–III and later.

Canaanites

In other regions of Canaan, such as the Jezreel Valley, and according to some views in the Shephelah between the Philistines and the Israelites, some sites present evidence of a continuity of Canaanite culture during the Iron I. At sites such as Megiddo (e.g., Sass and Finkelstein 2016) and Rehov (A. Mazar 2016) in the north and perhaps Beth Shemesh (e.g., Bunimovitz and Lederman 2011) and Azekah (Kleiman, Gadot, and Lipschits 2016) in the south, there is a continuity of Canaanite elements during most of the Iron I, but eventually these sites are incorporated into the surrounding sociopolitical entities and the unique Canaanite aspects are lost (but see Maeir and Hitchcock 2016 for reservations on this). This is opposed to the Phoenicians on the one hand, who developed into a vibrant and cosmopolitan culture during the Iron I, and to the Philistines and the Israelites on the other, who incorporated into their cultures certain Canaanite features, but nevertheless developed more unique cultural facets at an earlier phase of the Iron Age.

Aramaeans

Early evidence of the Aramaeans in northern Syria is documented in the Assyrian texts from the eleventh century BCE and onward (see, e.g., Lipiński 2000; Younger 2016). In northern Canaan, in the area of the present-day northeast of Israel and southern Syria, archaeological finds from several sites (such as Kinrot and Hadar [see studies in Sergi, Oeming, and de Hulster 2016]) indicate that already in the Iron I, groups that are later identified with the various Aramaean groups in this region during the Iron II–III (such as the Geshurites) have a physical presence in this region. This said, the lack of sufficient comparative archaeological data from southern Syria makes it difficult to assess the character of these sites and the culture(s) they represent, and one should take into account the possibility that they represent other local groups in various stages of societal development during this formative stage in Canaan.

Transjordanian Groups

The early Iron Age is represented throughout Transjordan (see, e.g., Fischer and Bürge 2013;

Gass 2009; Levy, Najjar, and Ben-Yosef 2014; B. W. Porter 2013; Routledge 2008; Tyson 2014; van der Steen 2004), but it appears to be quite different from the areas to the west of the Jordan. During the early Iron Age, sites in the eastern Jordan Valley seem to be more connected to the west. This includes several sites with cultic structures (Pella, Deir Alla) as well as some with possible connections with the Sea Peoples (Saidiyeh, Abu Kharaz). In central Jordan, there is evidence of several fortified sites during the early Iron Age, including Tall al-'Umayri, Hesban, and Lahun. In southern Jordan, in the area later defined as Edom, there is evidence of nomadic groups (see, e.g., in the cemetery near Faynan), most likely evidence of the Shasu nomads mentioned in contemporary Egyptian sources. During the Iron I, a few sites seem to have been destroyed (Pella, Deir Alla, Umayri), but for the most part, many new sites are founded. Interestingly, at quite a few sites in central Jordan structures of the "four-room house" type have been reported, which are among the various reasons some scholars have suggested one can find evidence of the Israelite tribes in Transjordan (Reuben, Gad, Manasseh) as depicted in the Bible. This, though, would seem to require more substantial evidence than presently available.

All told, the Iron I finds from Transjordan present the early stages of the formation of the cultures and polities known in the region during the Iron II–III—for example, Ammon, Moab, and Edom.

Summary

The early Iron Age, commencing during the transition from the Late Bronze Age and continuing into the early Iron II, is a drawn-out period of more than two centuries in which the southern Levant transformed from a region under imperial Egyptian domination during the Late Bronze Age to that of a mosaic of ethnic kingdoms in the Iron II–III. While the processes of the appearance and crystalliza-tion of the Israelite tribes are probably the best-known motifs during this period, a broad range of groups were going through a complex variety of dynamic processes at the time. As this is a period with very few written sources, and the biblical narratives most likely reflect only vague memories of the events during this period, the picture that we can paint is somewhat limited. Thus, although the con-quest, settlement, and period of the judges play a central role in the formative narratives of the Israelite/Judahite biblical texts, there is very little concrete archaeological evidence to corroborate much of what is mentioned in these texts. That said, it is clear that during the two hundred or so years of the Iron I in the regions of the central hills, rural, tribal elements existed, which in a broad manner fit in well with the biblical depiction of tribal sociopolitical structures.

As noted above, these processes that the early Israelites and the other cultural groups were going through cannot be explained in monolithic, simplistic terms, but rather must be seen as multipronged and long-term processes. Likewise, while it is convenient to pigeonhole the archaeological evidence into neat packages of cultural and other identities (much of it based on groups and identities known from later periods), the on-the-ground situation was most likely much more complex. Never-theless, these processes are the background for the formation of the better-known cultural and political entities of the Iron Age II–III.

8

Archaeology of the Iron Age II

Amihai Mazar

Introduction

The Iron Age II is the name of the archaeological period that corresponds more or less with the time of the Israelite and Judean monarchies and the periods of Assyrian domination and Babylonian conquests. The period starts following the end of the Iron Age I, ca. 1000–980 BCE.[1] The traditional date for the end of the period is the Babylonian conquest of Judah in 586 BCE, though this date relates specifically to Judah. Some scholars would include the Babylonian period (until 530 BCE) in the Iron Age. Various inner divisions of the period

have been suggested. The most acceptable one is Iron Age IIA (tenth to ninth centuries BCE), Iron Age IIB (the end of the ninth century until the Assyrian conquests between 732 and 701 BCE), and Iron Age IIC (from the Assyrian conquest of northern Israel until the Babylonian conquests).

Late Bronze Age	1550–1200 BCE
Iron Age	1200–586 BCE
Iron IA (LB III)[a]	1200–1140/1130
Iron IB	1140/1130–ca. 980[b]
Iron IIA	ca. 980–ca. 800
Iron IIB	ca. 800–732/701[c]
Iron IIC	732/701–586 BCE
Babylonian Period	586–539 BCE
Persian Period	539–332 BCE

a. The time of the Twentieth Egyptian Dynasty rule in Canaan is called by some Iron IA and by others Late Bronze III.

b. The end of Iron I is debated within the range 1000–950 BCE.

c. Iron IIB ends with the Assyrian conquests of the northern kingdom between the years 732 BCE and 722 BCE and with Sennacherib's invasion of Judah in 701 BCE.

During this time of about four hundred years, the country was divided between several

---

1. The conventional date was ca. 1000 BCE. A low chronology by Finklestein and others since 1996 suggests that the transition occurred ca. 920–900 BCE. Yet more recent studies based on radiocarbon dating appear to support a transition date somewhere between these two dates, during the first half of the tenth century BCE. Thus the great destruction of Megiddo VI (end of Iron Age I at this site) was dated to ca. 1000 BCE while Khirbet Qeiyafa, which is attributed to the transition of Iron I–Iron II or early Iron II was dated to the first half of the tenth century BCE. For the latest summaries, see Finkelstein and Piasetzky 2011; A. Mazar 2011 with references to previous studies.

new political entities: the territorial states of Israel, Judah, Ammon, Moab, and Edom; the southern Aramaean states; and the Philistine and Phoenician city-states. Each of these units had its own identity, language, political leadership, religious beliefs, cultural traditions, and economic interests.

Wide-scale archaeological research related to this period has revealed many aspects of temporal and spatial developments of the material culture (for general surveys of the period, see A. Mazar 1980, 368–555; Barkay 1992; Herr 1997; E. Stern 2001; M. Steiner and Killebrew 2014, 677–840; for articles on sites and selected subjects, see E. Stern 1993a; 2008; Master et al. 2013). The settlement pattern and hierarchy of settlement—from capital cities through small towns, farms, fortresses, and small hamlets—is a source for the study of demographic changes and social structure. Studies of Iron Age architecture include palace plans, temples and other cult places, urban planning, fortification systems, dwellings, storage structures, stables, fortresses, water systems, and architectural decoration (Kempinski and Reich 1992, 191–301; Z. Herzog 1997a, 211–58). Pottery studies are a major tool for establishing relative chronology as well as defining regions (Gitin 2015, chs. 2.1–3.6, 4.1–4.4). The economy and aspects of daily life included metallurgy, agricultural technology (terraces, irrigation systems, production installations such as wine presses, oil presses, and beehives), domestic industries (such as textile production), and inland and international trade, including imported pottery, amulets, and even food—such as dried fish from Egypt. Iron Age art and iconography are studied based on ivory carvings, seals, clay figurines, and paintings on pottery vessels and plastered walls. Religious life can be reconstructed from studies of temples and cult places combined with study of cult objects, iconography, and textual evidence, both biblical and extrabiblical (Zevit 2001; Albertz and Schmitt 2012; see

also chs. 42–49 below). Burial customs and beliefs related to death can be learned from vast cemeteries, particularly those excavated in Judah (Bloch-Smith 1992a; 1992b; see also ch. 49 below).

Inscriptions, such as ostraca, inscribed seals, inscriptions on pottery vessels and plastered walls, and a few formal/royal inscriptions incised on stone, are an invaluable source for studying the spread of literacy, the development of the alphabet, the types of private names used, and historical, religious, and social issues.

The following discussion briefly outlines some results of this extensive and dynamic research, arranged by the main geopolitical units of this period.

The Question of the United Monarchy of David and Solomon

According to the biblical narrative and its inner chronology, toward the end of the eleventh century BCE, the tribal society of Israel, centered in the central hill country, established a kingdom. According to this narrative, the first king, Saul from the tribe of Benjamin, ruled over large parts of the country. David founded a new dynasty in Hebron and then moved to Jerusalem, which continued to be the capital of Judah, ruled by the house of David until its fall in 586 BCE. David is said to have conquered large parts of the land (excluding Philistia) and was an ally of Toi, king of Hamath in Syria. David's son Solomon is said to have built the temple and palace on the Temple Mount of Jerusalem, as well as several administrative and military centers throughout the country. The historicity of a "United Monarchy" that ruled both Israel and Judah as well as parts of Transjordan in the tenth century BCE is a debated subject: conservative views accept the biblical narrative as is, while more critical views suggest that the stories are a saga retaining only kernels of historical truth, while more radical views claim that the biblical description is totally unreliable as a historical source.

The only extrabiblical source is the mention of "the House of David" (*bytdwd*) as the name of the kingdom of Judah in the Tel Dan Inscription, several fragments of a commemorative stele attributed to Hazael, king of Damascus. Though later than David by almost 150 years, the mere occurrence of the name indicates the historical reality behind this ruler, who was considered even among the neighbors of Israel as the founder of the dynasty and state of Judah.

Archaeology could be an essential source for resolving this issue, yet there are serious disagreements among archaeologists as to the interpretation of the data. The debate concerns questions such as these: Could Jerusalem have been a capital of a substantial state? Was the population in the hill country sufficient for establishing such a state? Are there remains of monumental architecture that could be attributed to the days of David and Solomon? The answers to these questions are not agreed upon. Jerusalem was no more than 5 hectares (12.5 acres) in area during the time of David, but could have been 12 hectares (30 acres) in area when the Temple Mount was added. The "stepped stone structure" and "large building" to its west comprise a large monumental structure, which could be the largest structure in the southern Levant in the tenth century BCE (A. Mazar 2010). City gates and public architecture at Hazor, Megiddo, and Gezer were identified with those built by Solomon according to 1 Kings 9:15–17. The fortified site of Khirbet Qeiyafa in the Shephelah was identified by its excavator as a fortified city built by David against the Philistines. All these issues raised severe debates among archaeologists: there are those (like the present author) who accept the United Monarchy as a historical reality, though its scope can be questioned, while others (mainly Israel Finkelstein) deny the historicity of the United Monarchy altogether,

claiming that the structures mentioned above are later than the tenth century and that the earliest Israelite kingdom was northern Israel. This issue remains unresolved (see also ch. 26 below).[2]

The Northern Kingdom of Israel

The northern kingdom of Israel was the largest and richest political entity in the southern Levant for about two hundred years, from the last quarter of the tenth century until 732/722 BCE, when it was conquered by the Assyrian Empire. This kingdom enjoyed both the hilly terrain of the Samaria hills and the Galilee and also the fertile plains of Jezreel, the middle and upper Jordan Valley, and parts of the coastal plain. Trade routes connected it with Phoenicia and Cyprus on the one side and with Transjordan and Syria on the other; at times, it ruled the Gilead and northern Moab in Transjordan. It was dominant over Judah in the mid-ninth century BCE (Finkelstein 2013). The kingdom was in close political and economic relations with the Phoenician city-states of Tyre and Sidon, but it rivaled Aram Damascus, which at times conquered parts of the kingdom. The history of this state is known mainly from the biblical narratives in 1–2 Kings but also from several Assyrian royal inscriptions and local inscriptions. Two royal inscriptions from the ninth century BCE are of particular importance: Mesha's stele commemorating the liberation of territories north of the Arnon River from the yoke of the Omride dynasty of Israel (see ch. 36 below), and the Tel Dan Inscription (mentioned above) commemorating a war between an Aramaean king, most

---

2. Vast literature was published on this subject. For the conservative view, see summary in A. Mazar 1990a, 368–402; for deconstruction of this view, see Finkelstein 1996a; Finkelstein and Silberman 2001; the debate is presented in Finkelstein and Mazar 2007, 99–140. For Khirbet Qeiyafa debate, see Garfinkel, Kreimerman, and Zilberg 2016 with earlier literature.

probably Hazael, and a king of Israel and a king of the house of David (see ch. 37 below). Assyrian royal inscriptions mention Ahab as a member in a coalition of rulers who fought Shalmaneser III in 853 BCE (see ch. 35 below) and show Jehu, king of Israel, surrendering to the same Assyrian king.

The capital of Israel from the time of Omri was Samaria, located in the Samaria hills, while a second royal palace was at Jezreel. Excavations of both palaces revealed well-planned and fortified rectangular enclosures, encompassing royal architecture including ashlar masonry and stone capitals curved in the so-called proto-Aeolic style. The main excavated cities in the north (Dan, Hazor, Beth Shean, Rehov, Megiddo, Yoqneam, Dor, and Mizpah [Tell en-Nasbeh]) provide evidence of a thriving urban life in the kingdom: massive fortifications with typical city gates with six or four chambers defended most of these cities, underground water supply projects were cut (at Hazor, Megiddo, Yibleam), local palaces and forts were sometimes decorated with proto-Aeolic stone capitals, and royal stables and storage buildings were constructed as rectangular structures divided by two rows of monolithic pillars. A temple discovered at Tel Dan may be identified with the temple mentioned in the Bible as built by Jeroboam. Outside the main cities a network of smaller towns, villages, farms, and forts created a rather dense settlement in many parts of the state. Rich collections of finds such as cult objects, clay figurines, stone seals, and imported Phoenician, Cypriot, and Greek pottery are evidence for a thriving local culture and religious beliefs influenced by local Canaanite, Phoenician, and Egyptian traditions. A collection of carved ivories in Phoenician style found in Samaria reflects the close connections between the royal dynasties of Israel and the Phoenician cities of Tyre and Sidon. Inscribed seals (starting to appear in the eighth century BCE), ostraca from Samaria, as well as the inscriptions from Kuntillet ʿAjrud in eastern Sinai (though far away, probably operated by people who came from this kingdom), are evidence for scribal schools and administration. The kingdom flourished mainly during the days of Ahab in the ninth century and Jeroboam II in the eighth century, but internal strife weakened the kingdom and the Assyrian conquest put an end to it: much of its population was slaughtered or exiled or fled, and most of the cities and other settlements abandoned.

Judah

The kingdom of Judah was located in a much less hospitable environment than its northern sibling. The Judean hills are poor in natural resources and enclosed by deserts on the east and south. The Shephelah foothills—the most convenient area for settlement—formed a border zone toward the Philistine cities of Gath and Ekron. Scholars debate whether Judah was an independent state already during the late tenth and ninth centuries, or whether it was only a small and weak vassal of Israel in the ninth century, developing into a substantial state only in the eighth century, particularly after the fall of Israel. The answer to this question depends to a large degree on the dating of certain structures in Jerusalem and certain sites outside the capital, and this dating is still controversial. The present author thinks that the archaeological evidence from the City of David and the "Ophel" ridge, combined with new discoveries at Lachich and the mention of Judah in the Tel Dan Inscription as an independent state, supports the former possibility.

The heart of Judah was its capital, Jerusalem, which gradually grew from a small 4-hectare town in the early tenth century to a large city of 70 hectares in the eighth and seventh centuries BCE, when it became the largest city in the southern Levant. Monumental architecture discovered in the Ophel area south of the Temple Mount, including a huge tower (the "Warren Tower"), inner gate structure, city wall, and magazines, was built most probably during the Iron Age IIA, perhaps in the late tenth or ninth centuries BCE (E. Mazar 2015). This was possibly the southern edge of the royal enclosure of Jerusalem, which continued toward the Temple Mount, where the temple and royal palace stood. During the eighth century, Jerusalem expanded to the western hill (today's Mount Zion, Jewish Quarter, and Armenian Quarter of the Old City), where massive fortifications have been revealed. The Siloam tunnel, a unique water tunnel that brought water from the Gihon Spring into the fortified city, probably was cut by Hezekiah in the late eighth century BCE as part of the king's preparations for a revolt against Assyria, which ended in the siege by Sennacherib in 701 BCE, during which Lachish and many towns in the Shephelah and northern Negev were destroyed and devastated. The Assyrians failed to conquer the city, and it continued to flourish during the seventh century. In that century, when the northern kingdom no longer existed, Jerusalem became an outstanding capital, as reflected in many biblical passages. It became the scene of thriving spiritual creativity, the home of prophets such as Isaiah and Jeremiah, and the stage where Jewish monotheism developed and the early versions of many parts of the Bible were written. Jerusalem's size during this time reflects an unusual proportion between the capital and the rest of the state, where the largest city (Lachish) was 8 hectares in area and all others were less than 3 hectares in area. Few remains of monumental and public buildings in Jerusalem were preserved, such as the structures south of the Temple Mount mentioned above and parts of a palace with ashlar masonry, decorated with proto-Aeolic stone capitals, found in a collapsed layer in the upper part of the City of David.

A seventh-century royal palace was also excavated at Ramat Rahel south of Jerusalem. It was inspired in its plan, building techniques (ashlar masonry), and architectural decoration (proto-Aeolic capitals) by the palace of Samaria, though the latter was already in ruins. A stone window balustrade from this palace recalls Phoenician ivories showing a woman in a window. The periphery of Jerusalem was strewn with farms and agricultural terraces and installations, evidence for a thriving agricultural periphery of this large city.

Many of Judah's towns, not including Jerusalem, were destroyed during Sennacherib's attack in 701 BCE, which devastated Judah (see ch. 38 below). Following this campaign, large parts of the Shephelah were torn from Judah and abandoned, while areas in the northern Negev and the Judean Desert (in sites such as ʿAroʿer, Tel ʿIra, Beersheba [in the modern city], and ʿEn Gedi) developed and managed to play parts in an international trade system with Arabia, Transjordan, and the Mediterranean coast in the framework of wider Assyrian imperialistic activity. Fortresses like those at Arad, Hurvat ʿUza, and ʿEn Hazevah indicate central administration and a well-organized military system in the kingdom.

Judean royal administration can be deduced from a system of royal seal impressions used to stamp jar handles. These are inscribed with the word *lmlk* ("belonging to the king") followed by one of four city names. The jars certainly were produced and stamped during the time of Hezekiah in the eighth century and perhaps continued to be produced or just used through the eighth century until they were replaced by a new type of seal with a rosette sign. Other seals and seal impressions from Judah carry names of officials, and a few of them include the names of kings and officials known from the Old Testament.

Intensive archaeological research in Judah has revealed much data on settlement hierarchy, social structure, popular religion, trade relations, agriculture, burial customs, and more. Notable are hundreds of clay figurines showing a female with a "pillar-like" body (tree trunk?). These figurines must have been used in domestic cult practices related to the fertility of women, yet it is disputed whether they represented a certain goddess (Astarte? Asherah?) or whether they served just as fertility talismans (for the various views, see Kletter 1996; Zevit 2001; Darby 2014). Inscriptions from the eighth to seventh centuries BCE indicate that literacy was widespread in Judah. Most writing probably was made on perishable materials like papyri and parchment, but collections of ostraca (inscribed pottery shards) found at Lachish, Arad, and other sites are evidence for this literacy. They are important sources relating to the last decades of this kingdom (Ahituv 2008; Rollston 2010). Few formal lapidary inscriptions have been preserved, among them the famous Siloam Inscription describing the cutting of Hezekiah's tunnel.

Philistia

The Philistine city-states of Gaza, Ashkelon, Ashdod, Gath, and Ekron (see ch. 9 below) continued to thrive during the Iron Age II, though they passed through a gradual process of "acculturation": Philistine culture now lost many of its Aegean traits, and the population probably intermingled with the local population (Maeir 2013a). Yet these cities continued to maintain their autonomy and a local variant of material culture, which probably reflected their self-definition as independent entities, flourished. Gath (Tel es-Safi), one of the most important Philistine cities, was severely destroyed during the second half of the ninth century BCE, in accord with the biblical account of its conquest by Hazael, king of Aram Damascus (2 Kings 12:17). Ashdod continued to survive in the ninth and eighth centuries BCE until it was destroyed by Sargon II, king of Assyria, while Ekron and Ashkelon flourished as industrial and commercial centers throughout the seventh century BCE until they were

severely destroyed by Nebuchadnezzar in the years 605–604 BCE. An inscription found in a unique seventh-century temple at Ekron mentions five generations of local kings, among them Padi, known also from Assyrian inscriptions, and Achish, possibly an Indo-European name, known from the Bible as the name of the king of Gath during David's time.

The Transjordanian States

Of the three Transjordanian states Ammon, Moab, and Edom, the first is less known (Herr and Najjar 2008). Few remains date prior to the seventh century BCE, though excavations in the site of the capital Rabbath Ammon (modern Amman) revealed evidence for continuous occupation during the Iron Age. Seventh-century finds from Ammon include circular fortresses in the vicinity of the capital, several inscriptions and seals, and an exceptional group of stone statues representing male and female figures. Excavations in the Madaba plain, at the sites of Heshbon (Tall Hisban), Tall al-'Umayri, and Tall Jalul, provide the best archaeological evidence for the development of material culture in the Iron Age II in this border area between Ammon and Moab.

The earliest evidence for a Moabite entity is in the form of fortified settlements along the Arnon River (Wadi Mujib) tentatively dated to the eleventh century BCE. The area north of the Arnon was under Israelite control during the first half of the ninth century, when it was conquered by the Moabite king Mesha, who built Dibon as the capital of Moab; his commemorative stele found at Dibon is the longest Iron Age inscription from the southern Levant yet discovered. The town of 'Atarot, west of Dibon, yielded a temple that may have been founded during the Israelite regime and rebuilt during Mesha's time, and the town at Khirbat al-Mudayna ath-Thamad (perhaps biblical Yahaz) yielded evidence of town planning, fortifications, and a local shrine in the Iron Age II.

In Edom, the earliest Iron Age remains are the extensive copper mines and smelting production complex at Faynan, located in the western foothills of the Edom mountains, which operated from the late eleventh century until the ninth century BCE (see ch. 57 below). The main smelting site was at Khirbat en-Nahas, where a large fortress provides evidence for some central administration, perhaps a kernel of a tribal state. The highland of Edom was settled only later, during the eighth and seventh centuries, when the copper mines at Faynan were almost abandoned. At the capital, Buseirah (biblical Bozrah), palaces were inspired by Assyrian palace architecture. During the seventh century, many sites in Edom were founded on remote rock scarps, perhaps as a means of defense. Edom played an important role in the trade between southern Arabia and the Mediterranean coast in the framework of the Assyrian and Babylonian Empires.

Tell el-Kheleifah, on the shore of the Red Sea, once identified as Etzyon Geber, was perhaps the southernmost Edomite stronghold during the eighth to seventh centuries, serving and guarding the international trade routes toward Arabia. Some Edomite presence in the Beersheba Valley probably was related to this trade, and was a forerunner of the massive Edomite settlement of southern Judah in the Persian and Hellenistic periods.

Two shrines built along the trade routes (outside the fortress of 'En Hazevah in the Arabah Valley and at Hurvat Qitmit in the northern Negev) probably served camel caravans participating in the Arabian trade; richly decorated cult objects were found in these shrines, perhaps representing a specific style that developed among the Edomites or nomadic caravaneers during this period.

The Assyrian, Egyptian, and Babylonian Domination

From the mid-ninth century until the third quarter of the seventh century BCE, the Assyrian Empire left its impact on the entire Near East, including the southern Levant (for an extensive survey of the period, see E. Stern 2001, 3–300). The first military clashes occurred in Syria during the time of Shalmaneser III (the Battle of Qarqar, 853 BCE [see ch. 35 below]). Between 732 and 701 BCE, the northern kingdom of Israel, the Philistine cities, and Judah were all attacked by Assyria. The result was the total devastation of northern Israel (in two stages, 732 and 722 BCE), exile of much of its population, and replacement by new population brought from outside. Many of the cities and other settlements remained abandoned after the conquest. The Philistine city-states of Ashdod, Ashkelon, Gaza, and Ekron surrendered in the years 714–712 BCE. The last three continued to survive as vassals, enjoying economic prosperity during the seventh century BCE, thus securing the route to Egypt and serving Assyrian economic interests. Jerusalem survived the disaster of Sennacherib's attack on Judah in 701 BCE following the revolt initiated by King Hezekiah. But Sennacherib conquered Lachish and many other Judean towns, an event well recorded by archaeology, biblical sources, Assyrian texts, and the famous Lachish reliefs found in Sennacherib's palace at Nineveh. At Lachish, the only Assyrian siege ramp known today was found (see ch. 66 below). Following this event, large parts of the Shephelah were submitted to the Philistine city Ekron.

The Assyrian domination finds expression in numerous archaeological finds. Several palaces were designed after an Assyrian model, notably at Megiddo, which became the center of an Assyrian administrative district. In the northwestern Negev and along the southern coast, Assyrian forts and trade posts were related to the road to Egypt, the final goal of Assyrian expansion. Assyrian finds such as Assyrian "palace ware," seals, and administrative texts on clay tablets are evidence for the Assyrian domination of the country until between 640 and 630 BCE, when the empire retreated from the region.

Following the end of the Assyrian regime, a short period of Egyptian intervention in the coastal plain was followed by the Babylonian conquest of the southern Levant (E. Stern 2001, 303–50). The Babylonians had no interest in maintaining Judah and the independent Philistine states. In 605 BCE Nebuchadnezzar devastated Ekron and Ashkelon, in 597 BCE he attacked Jerusalem and exiled its king and nobles, and in 586 BCE he destroyed Jerusalem and most of Judah and exiled the upper classes to Mesopotamia. Archaeological excavations in all these cities and towns revealed violent destructions followed by occupation gaps. During the Babylonian occupation, which lasted until the area became part of the Persian Empire (538 BCE), most of these areas remained devastated, though settlement continuity has been observed in certain parts of the northern coastal plain, in a small region north of Jerusalem, and in Transjordan.

As noted above, the limited framework of this survey does not permit discussion of essential subjects in archaeological research of the Iron Age, such as economy, technology, religion, warfare, and burial customs discussed in other sections of this book.

9

Archaeology of the Neo-Babylonian and Persian Periods

Constance E. Gane

Introduction

Levantine archaeology of the Neo-Babylonian and Persian periods exposes destruction remains of the Iron Age territorial states under Assyrian domination. Recent research suggests that during Neo-Assyrian domination of the region, the populace enjoyed relative prosperity. However, following the violent expansion of the Babylonian Empire by Nebuchadnezzar II into the Levant, much of the region plummeted into a post-collapse society that did not fully recover until the late Hellenistic period of the Seleucids (Faust 2012c, 147).

The ancient Near East was under Neo-Babylonian sovereignty from 586 to 539 BCE, followed by Persian domination from 539 to 332 BCE. However, Babylonian dominance of Yehud (Judah) can be dated as early as 604 BCE (E. Stern 2001, 309). With a few regional exceptions, nearly every site in Palestine features massive destruction levels dating to the Babylonian invasions of the sixth century BCE (E. Stern 2001, 307; Faust 2012c, 31; B. W. Porter 2016, 400–401).[1] Sites that were

not destroyed in warfare appear to have been deserted, as evidenced by abandonment layers, an indication of an occupational gap that continues in some areas into the Achaemenid period.[2] The destruction of administrative centers and associated rural settlements resulted in the disintegration of society (P. Ray 2014, 40). The remaining inhabitants within the urban and rural sites subsisted in squatter settlements, continuing Iron Age traditions that eventually were lost (P. Ray 2014, 42).

Though the degeneration of the central sites began after 586 BCE, the Babylonians did not destroy the main sites in the land of Benjamin (e.g., Bethel, Gibeon, Tell el-Ful/Gibeah, and Tell en-Nasbeh) as they did in the rest of Palestine; the region prospered to some extent during Babylonian domination. However,

---

1. For example, destruction layers dating to this period have been found at Ashkelon, Ekron, Jerusalem, and Lachish. Benjamin Porter notes, "Destruction levels in the northern Levant have not been as readily identified, a possible sign that the region transitioned more easily to Babylonian rule compared to the southern Levant, where Egyptian political influence had come to replace the Assyrians in the final decades of the seventh century" (B. W. Porter 2016, 401).

2. The Persian period may also be referred to as the Achaemenid period. Achaemenes was thought to be the ancestor of the Persian royal family.

outlying rural settlements, including those within Benjamin, did not escape Babylonian devastation. By the beginning of the Persian period, both urban and rural areas were in a state of neglect (Faust 2012c, 228–29; Lipschits 2006, 24). The region gradually revived under the expanding imperial power of the Achaemenid Empire (B. W. Porter 2016, 401).[3]

Small farmsteads in western Samaria escaped destruction and continued to be in use from their establishment in the eighth century BCE through the Persian period. Due to the absence of the traditional Israelite "four-room house," it has been argued that the residents were non-Israelite deportees from the Assyrian takeover (Faust 2006a, 494, 499–501).

Despite the tumultuous political environment surrounding it, Ammon reached the height of its power during the seventh through fifth centuries BCE (Younker 2014, 764). Even after King Nebuchadnezzar II embarked on a campaign against Ammon and Moab following the rebellion of the vassal states (which included murdering Gedaliah, governor of Yehud), Ammonite settlements recovered and flourished through the Neo-Babylonian, Persian, and later Hellenistic periods (Younker 2014, 765). Neighboring Moab, however, did not recover for some time; the region lacks archaeological remains from both the Neo-Babylonian and Persian periods (M. Steiner 2014, 779).

The tribal kingdom of Edom also became subject to the Babylonians. Archaeological evidence suggests that a number of sites were occupied throughout both the Babylonian and Persian periods (Bienkowski 2014, 792; B. W. Porter 2016, 401). It seems that Edom eventu-

ally was subsumed into the greater Babylonian and later Persian Empires and never regained its status as an independent tribal kingdom. A relief of a king near Busayra, likely the Neo-Babylonian Nabonidus, attests to Babylonian rule over the region (Bienkowski 2014, 792).

Architecture

The discontinuity of society and culture is seen in both the architecture of private dwellings and the linguistic terminology used to describe the family unit. The four-room house emerged in the early Iron Age and dominated the architectural landscape of Iron Age II, but was phased out during the sixth century, following the Babylonian exile (Faust 2012c, 100–101). This change in architectural design occurred throughout the region, but is especially notable in Yehud, suggesting a major cultural break (Faust 2012c, 102, 104, 105). However, Zorn (2014a, 829) points out an exception at Tell en-Nasbeh (biblical Mizpah), where four-room houses have been "securely dated" to the sixth century and the material remains strongly suggest a Babylonian administrative presence.

Persian period buildings in Yehud present an entirely different plan known as the "open-court house" (E. Stern 2001, 468). This design was used in both private and public spheres and consisted of a number of rooms completely or partially surrounding a central open courtyard (E. Stern 2001, 468). This architectural style reflects a modification of the form of Assyrian administrative public buildings, as exemplified by the "residency" building at Lachish (Lehmann 2014, 845).

The contrast between the architectural plans of the Iron Age and Persian periods is paralleled in the linguistic terminology of the times. During the Iron Age, the term denoting kinship was *bet 'ab* (literally, "house of father") and referred to the extended family, which was reasonably small (González-Ruibal and Ruiz-Gálvez 2016, 397). The kinship term

---

3. Extrabiblical textual evidence for Jewish life in exile can be found in the Murashu archives, tablets written in Standard Babylonian from a highly successful Jewish merchant family in Nippur, and the Aramaic texts from the Jewish colony on the island of Elephantine in Egypt (Moore and Kelle 2011, 345–46). For an excellent discussion on the significance of onomastica in the Murashu archives, see Pearce 2006, 399–411.

bet 'abot (literally, "house of fathers") used in the Persian period, however, designated a more substantial demographic (Faust 2012c, 106).

In contrast to the dearth of organized settlements in Yehud, architectural remains in the Ammonite hinterlands during the Babylonian period attest to a well-established economy supported by agriculture. Agricultural complexes feature "enclosure walls, cisterns, wine presses, cup-holes, terraces, small fields, towers, and other elements associated with food production" (Younker 2014, 764–65). Recent archaeology in Transjordan has revealed substantial occupational layers dating to the Persian period as well. The vibrant Ammonite settlement, with residential and administrative complexes, uncovered at Jalul is one of several examples (C. Gane, Younker, and Ray 2010, 223).

Economy and Administration

Benjamin Porter succinctly notes, "Archaic empires often had transformative economic effects on their peripheries, disrupting local subsistence economies, reorienting old or stimulating new regional commercial routes, and demanding new levels of output of raw and finished products for consumption in the imperial core" (B. W. Porter 2016, 399). This can be seen in the flourishing of the Levant during the Neo-Assyrian period, the destruction of its sites in the Neo-Babylonian period, and the transformation of the region from desolation to reconstruction in the Persian period. In contrast to the preceding Neo-Assyrian imperial policy of mass deportation and cross-deportation that resulted in the repopulation of decimated regions, the Babylonians did not transfer other populations into conquered territories following deportations. In addition, they did not establish adequate provincial administration outside Babylonia (Vanderhooft 2003, 247).

There is little archaeological evidence of Babylonian imperial administration providing continuity after the fall of the Neo-Assyrian

Empire. The Assyrian administrative center at Megiddo was destroyed in the seventh century and left in ruins during the Neo-Babylonian period, after which the Persians built a fort on top of the rubble. Assyrian forts[4] were either destroyed and abandoned until Persian restoration, or abandoned without destruction until Persian reuse (Faust 2012c, 197–200).

According to Jeremiah 40:5–6, Nebuchadnezzar appointed Gedaliah governor over Yehud at Mizpah, the new administrative center for the region. This is one of the few examples of a possible imperial presence in Judah. Zorn, in his archaeological reexamination of Tell en-Nasbeh, notes significant architectural remains of administrative buildings and official residences dating to the Babylonian-Persian stratum, which support the concept of Mizpah as an administrative center (Zorn 2003, 444; 2014a, 829). In addition, material remains such as fragments of three coffins (Zorn 2003, 433), an ostracon with a Mesopotamian name written in Old Hebrew script (Zorn 2003, 439), and a bronze circlet with a cuneiform inscription[5] reflect Mesopotamian influence.[6]

Seals, Inscriptions, and Writing

Aramaic was the primary language in Yehud during the Neo-Babylonian and Achaemenid periods (Schniedewind 2013, 79; Kuhrt 1995, 393, 650, 699; 2007, 827; Polak 2006, 592).[7] Though Old Hebrew inscriptions are less frequent following 586 BCE, a number of seal

---

4. Such as those excavated at Kabri, Ayyelet HaShahar, Hazor, and Reishon Leziyon.

5. For translation and interpretation, see Vanderhooft and Horowitz 2002.

6. It must be noted that interpretation of the archaeological data at Tell en-Nasbeh and other Levantine sites with sixth- and fifth-century remains varies greatly with opposing views regarding population and settlement in Yehud (see Moore and Kelle 2011, 370–83).

7. For a sociolinguistic perspective and how it contributes to understanding the history of the biblical text, see Polak 2006, 589–628.

impressions and paleographic materials dating to the Babylonian era have been found in the land of Benjamin (E. Stern 2001, 335; Faust 2012c, 230).[8]

During the late Persian period, the wide variety of seals—particularly bullae—and sealings bearing nonepigraphic iconography testify to a rising elite involved in administration, trade, and commerce. The iconography reflects a local, Persian, Greek, or mixed style. Numerous bullae (more than 170), which secured papyrus documents, were excavated by P. L. Lapp in the Wadi ed-Daliyeh cave near Samaria, including a bulla with the name "Sanballat the governor of Samaria" (cf. Neh. 2:10) (E. Stern 2001, 540). A sixth-century BCE black scaraboid seal inscribed with "Shelomit, maidservant of Elnatan the governor" was found "in the vicinity of Jerusalem" and must have belonged to a woman of influence who was engaged in transactions that required the authorization of a seal (Avigad 1976a, 11–13, fig. 14).

Seventy-five Ammonite seal impressions or seals dating to the Babylonian period have been found at the Transjordanian site of Umayri, including a seal impression bearing the inscription "belonging to Milkom-ʾur, servant of Baʿal-yahsa" (Zorn 2014a, 832; Younker 2014, 765). This is likely the same Baalis, king of Ammon, whom Jeremiah implicated in the assassination plot against Gedaliah in Jeremiah 40:14 (Herr and Clark 2014, 126; Younker 2014, 765).

Tribute

Tax or tribute rendered to the state during the preexilic period was generally in the form of agrarian products, manual labor, and silver

(Chadwick 2015, 77). Imported materials, often secured through tribute, were needed to sustain Babylonia, which lacked natural resources such as timber, stone, produce, and other commodities (Barstad 2003, 9). An inscription by Nebuchadnezzar indicates that "heavy tribute," along with precious metals, gems, "the produce of all countries, goods from all inhabited regions," were collected and deposited at Esagil and Ezida (Fried 2003, 40). Thus, resources were pulled from all across the empire and centralized in Babylon itself (Barstad 2003, 9).

Taxes collected from Idumea during the Persian period are detailed in ostraca, which refer to grains, oil, wine, and livestock (Lemaire 2007, 56). The Achaemenid imperial organization was supported by a complex system of taxation and management of imperial resources. Royal, satrapal, urban, and private resources were treated diversely. Provincial regions were taxed according to products and specialists specific to their region, including trade, flocks, and land (Kurht 2007, 669). In all regions—including the postexilic Levant, the Persian satrapy known as "Beyond the River" (Rainey and Notley 2006, 278)—precious metals were an important form of tribute, particularly silver (Lemaire 2007, 58–60). Over time, coins took the place of in-kind exchanges (Lemaire 2007, 60; C. Carter 1999, 281). Nehemiah writes of mortgaging the land and vineyards of Yehud to pay taxes (Neh. 5:4–5).[9] He also speaks of establishing a yearly obligatory temple tax of one-third of a shekel (Neh. 10:32).

Coins

Coins, which were first minted in Lydia during the seventh century BCE (Lehmann 2014,

---

8. Sixth-century BCE jar handles from Gibeon (Ahituv 2008, 216–20) and Babylonian period seal impressions from Tell en-Nasbeh (Mizpah) (Zorn 2003, 437; Stern 2001, 335; Avigad 1972, 7). Persian-period *yehud* seals are found across a wide geographical range (E. Stern 2001, 545–49).

9. As the governor of the land of Yehud, Nehemiah could have demanded "the governor's bread" and forty shekels of silver, his due as representative of the Persian government, but he does not (Neh. 5:14–18).

848), were used on an occasional basis in the Levant during the Neo-Babylonian period, but it was not until the late Persian period (especially the late fifth and early fourth centuries BCE) that small silver and bronze coins began to be minted in large quantities in the Levant (E. Stern 2001, 555).[10]

The Philistine cities of Ashdod, Ashkelon, and Gaza created the "first indigenous coins of Palestine" during the Persian period. These cities were strategic for the Achaemenid army; the coins were thus made to facilitate trade and transactions and granted the local population a certain amount of economic autonomy (Tal 2005, 91). Some of these coins, sometimes called "Philisto-Arabian silver coins," feature an inscription that may refer to the city of Gaza, Ashkelon, or Antheodon (Lehmann 2014, 848–49). The coins initially copied the Athenian style, but later mints featured iconography unique to the region (Altmann 2016, 144).

In Yehud, coins bear the same iconographic motifs found on bullae (E. Stern 2001, 540), including the name *yehud*, which usually is inscribed in Aramaic rather than paleo-Hebrew (Lehmann 2014, 849). Seventeen such coins have been found in Yehud, both in Jerusalem and surrounding areas and in Beth Zur. These coins can be divided into three types coming from imperial, local, and provincial mints (including Yehud and Samarian coins) (C. Carter 2016, 230). Samaritans also minted coins during the mid-fourth century BCE, although their production likely ceased after the Greek invasion (Lehmann 2014, 849).

The first mention of coins in the biblical account is the reference to gold *darkemon*, most likely the Persian daric (E. Stern 2001, 558), that Ezra and Nehemiah collected for the reconstruction of the temple (Ezra 2:68–69; Neh. 7:70–71).[11]

Trade and Commerce

Trade and commerce gradually improved during the Persian period, but the financial stability of the province of Yehud remained dependent on Persia until the Greek city-states became the dominant source of economic stability (Berquist 1995, 109, 115). The Persians developed a route network, running down the Palestinian coast toward Egypt with branches extending to the east and north and connecting with the Arabian trade routes, which brought luxury items from southern Arabia, eastern Africa, and India (Tal 2005, 72, 74). Water routes—through the Indus River, the Indian Ocean, the Persian Gulf, and the Euphrates and Tigris Rivers—were used in addition to roads. This increase in trade explains the higher concentration of settlements along the Levantine coast. Spices, which were used cosmetically and in religious rituals, were some of the main luxury goods transported throughout the Persian Empire. Spices were also given as tribute; 2.7 tons of frankincense were given to Darius I as annual tribute from the Arabs (Ben-Yehoshua, Borowitz, and Hanuš 2012, 12).

Although Yehud persisted as an agrarian society relying primarily on the produce of the land (grain, wine, figs, and grapes) and livestock (Grabbe 2004, 204), material remains from Persian-period tombs and occupation levels provide a wide assortment of imported luxury goods—particularly from Persia, Phoenicia, Egypt, and Greece—indicating renewed trade but an apparent lack of local production (E. Stern 2001, 523). Among the categories of significant remains are Phoenician, Persian, and Greek coins (E. Stern 2001, 556); Greek ceramics (C. Carter 2003, 403); Greek, Phoenician, and Achaemenid furniture;[12] domestic

---

10. The earliest coin found in Yehud, a silver Attic coin, dates to the end of the sixth century. The coin was found at Ketef Hinnom and may have been used during the Neo-Babylonian period (C. Carter 2016, 230).

11. The weight standard for provincial *yehud* coins of the fourth century remains unresolved because a variety

of fractional denominations were used. *Yehud* coins from this period have been classified into eight groups. Root suggests that groups I and II follow the Persian shekel (Root 2005, 133).

12. These include a Greek-inspired Phoenician bronze couch and stool (tomb at Tell el-Farʿa [South]),

utensils such as Persian-style metal bowls, jugs, and other kitchen tools that often incorporate Assyrian, Babylonian, Persian, and Egyptian motifs (Noonan 2011, 289); and Egyptian-style cosmetic utensils of bronze, alabaster, bone, and paste (E. Stern 2001, 528). Achaemenid jewelry—such as earrings, rings, bracelets, and anklets—has been found in Persian-period tombs and occupational levels.[13]

Archaeological evidence suggests that Palestine had trade connections with Phoenicia through the Neo-Babylonian and possibly Achaemenid periods. Phoenician cylindrical jars, which were used for shipping measured items such as food, have been found across northern Palestine, in addition to carved ivories (Noonan 2011, 288–89). Late Iron Age and early Persian-period Palestinian ceramic bowls, cooking pots, jars, and jugs have also been found in Egypt—evidence of trade and/or the migration of Levantine inhabitants (Maeir 2002, 240–41).

In addition to indicating trade patterns, ceramics provide one of the most reliable sources for dating. In Transjordan, Attic ware—along with other items—found at Umayri and Jalul has enabled archaeologists to securely date Persian remains found in the region, thus establishing occupation at sites such as Hisban, Umayri, Jawa, Jalul, and Dreijat during the Persian period (Younker 2014, 767).

Military

There was no provincial standing army in the Levant during the Neo-Babylonian and Persian periods. The "army of Samaria" (*hel shomeron*) mentioned by Nehemiah (4:2) may refer to an actual foreign army or to powerful

individuals who carried military weight. A late sixth- to early fifth-century BCE fortress and military camp at Tel Michal (Makmish), on the Mediterranean coast, may have served Persian interests (Grabbe 2004, 38). A military presence, including Edomite soldiers, in the Persian district of Idumaea (located in southern Palestine) is referenced by ostraca from the fortress of Arad (E. Stern 2001, 531; Betlyon 2005, 17). Arrowheads provide the majority of definitively dated Persian weapon remains (E. Stern 2001, 531). Persian bronze horse bits (from Gezer) and helmets of Greek mercenaries (mostly underwater finds off Dor, Ashdod, and Ashkelon) are among the more significant finds (E. Stern 2001, 532–33). Locally produced iron arrowheads, daggers, and swords have also been uncovered at Levantine sites (E. Stern 2001, 534).

Cult

Cultic Centers

Some cultic centers are known with varying degrees of extant evidence. The cultic center at Dan in the north continued in use from the preexilic period into the Roman period (Biran 1994, 214, 228). A structure at Bethel, which may be a continuation of a previous cultic installation, appears to date to this period (E. Stern 2001, 347). A complex similar to the Jerusalem temple has been found at Mount Gerizim, but no confirmed architectural remains have been found of Solomon's temple (Lehmann 2014, 844). However, small artifacts dating to the eighth through sixth centuries BCE have recently been uncovered on the Temple Mount. These are the first artifacts resulting from an excavation on the Temple Mount that can be dated to the First Temple and include olive pits and animal bones as well as diagnostic ceramic fragments of bowls, juglets, and a storage jar.[14]

Achaemenid-style thrones (at Samaria and a shipwreck near ʿAtlit harbor), and Phoenician-style bronze candelabra (at numerous Persian-period sites including Samaria and Shechem) (Noonan 2011, 289; E. Stern 2001, 524–25).

13. These items generally have animal features rendered with composite elements from Assyria, Urartu, and Luristan (E. Stern 2001, 529–30).

14. These finds were presented at the 2016 annual conference of New Studies in the Archaeology of Jerusalem

A temple found at the Edomite city of Busayra may have been in use through the Babylonian and Persian periods. At the forts at ʿEn Hazevah, a shrine and figurines were found. Cultic figurines were also found at a shrine at Hurvat Qitmit (Zorn 2014a, 834).

From an architectural perspective, sanctuaries in the Levant built during the Iron III/Persian period emulate a "long-room plan," which had already been used throughout the Iron Age. Phoenician sanctuaries utilized Greek architectural elements (Lehmann 2014, 844).

Cultic Assemblages and Figurines

A dramatic break is seen in the religious life of those left in the Levant after the Babylonian destruction of the urban and rural areas. Whereas the preceding Levantine Iron Age was replete with a wide variety of cultic high places, shrines, altars, sacred stones (*matsebot*), and innumerable figurines[15]—especially female figurines—the following exilic and postexilic periods show an apparent absence of polytheism[16] in the heartland of Yehud and Samaria (Faust 2012c, 109–10; E. Stern 2001, 347; Dever 2005, 299).

Figurines continued to be produced and sacred stones set up in surrounding non-Jewish regions, including Galilee, Idumea, Philistia, and the coastal plain as well as in Byblos and Nabatean Petra (Faust 2012c, 109). Ammonite male and female ceramic figurines, including the "horse and rider figurines," are commonly found at Ammonite sites, including Hisban, Umayri, and Jalul, during the Neo-Babylonian and Persian periods (Younker 2014, 765–66).

Other Cultural Practices

The Evolving Calendar

The second- and first-millennium BCE Levantine calendars of Ugarit, Phoenicia, and Canaan designated months by names or words, some of which reflect Hurrian influence (M. Cohen 2015, 359). On the other hand, the preexilic calendar of ancient Israel used ordinal numbers to identify months—for example, "first month" (M. Cohen 2015, 371). Babylonia adopted the standard Mesopotamian calendar ca. 1740 BCE.[17] It began spreading to western Mesopotamia around 1400 BCE and by 1100 BCE was in use in Assyria, later spreading to the Nabateans and Palmyrans. The Judean exiles in Babylonia also adopted the standard Mesopotamian calendar and continued using it when they returned from exile in the sixth century BCE (M. Cohen 2015, 383–84).

Burial Practices

Yehudean bench tombs of the preexilic period ceased to be constructed during the Neo-Babylonian and Achaemenid periods (P. Ray 2014, 41). Burials of commoners are rare, but some of the remaining elite continued traditional Iron Age burial practices, as found in the tombs at Ketef Hinnom in Jerusalem (Zorn 2014a, 829). Burial caves, pit, cist, and shaft graves became the norm (Tal 2005, 87), with jar burials and cairns (tumuli) being used only occasionally (Tal 2003, 293).

Cave tombs have a long history and were used for both primary and secondary burial. Pit graves, used for primary burials,[18] were

---

and Its Region, held at the Hebrew University. They are the result of cooperative work over a number of years between the Muslim authorities and Israeli archaeologists. See reports by J. Greene (2016) and Ben Zion (2016) and presentation by Baruch, Reich, and Sandhaus (2016).

15. For a discussion of Iron Age terra cotta figurines, see Meyers 2017, 116–33.

16. This has been debated by de Hulster 2014, 16–24. See also Darby 2014, 250n200.

17. The standard Babylonian calendar may have been developed by Hammurabi (ca. 1792–1750 BCE) or his son Samsu-iluna (1750–1712 BCE) to facilitate unification in international commerce and spread through military conquest (M. Cohen 2015, 386). This calendar begins with *Nisannu* (standard Babylonian) or *nsyn* (Hebrew), equivalent to our March-April.

18. A primary burial is one in which an individual is buried as a whole corpse. A secondary burial involves moving the exhumed remains from their first resting place

dug into the soil to accommodate bodies laid horizontally. Found mainly in the coastal plain, Jezreel Valley, and Jordan Valley, Persian-style cist graves were used for both primary and secondary burials. These are similar to pit graves but are lined and covered with stone slabs and often contain elaborate burial goods (Tal 2003, 289). Some contain clay—or rarely, wooden—coffins that are oriented on an east-west axis (Tal 2003, 290; E. Stern 2001, 471–72). Ceramic coffins have been found at Tell en-Nasbeh 2 and may have been associated with the administration of the Babylonian occupiers (Zorn 2014a, 829). Shaft graves, which reflect Phoenician and Greek influence (E. Stern 2001, 474), are rock-cut caves approached through a vertical shaft. They may have one or two rooms and are found primarily on the coastal plain and in the Shephelah (Tal 2003, 290).[19] Two such

---

to another location as into a jar or ossuary. Primary burials were preferred during this time period (Tal 2005, 87).

19. Examples are ʿAtlit in the coastal region and Ha-Gosherim in the Galilee (Tal 2003, 291n8).

tombs, one at Gaza and another at Shavei Zion, contained stone anthropoid coffins (E. Stern 2001, 474). Palestine is unique in that shaft tombs from the west (Phoenicia and Greece) and cist graves from the east (Persia) are found in the same period and regional culture (Betlyon 2005, 45).

The less common cairn burials (tumuli) were used for primary burials and are pit or cist tombs covered with a heap of stones that create a mound (Tal 2003, 290). Jar burials were used for secondary burial (or primary burial for infants) in which the bones of the deceased were stored after decomposition had taken place (Tal 2003, 289).

Burial placement, usually outside the walls or near the outskirts of a settlement, indicates that the ancients viewed the dead as defiling. The position of the body—lying face up, with the head pointing eastward—suggests that at least some may have considered death to be an "eternal sleep" (Tal 2005, 88).

10

Archaeology of the Hellenistic Period

JORDAN RYAN

Introduction

The region of Palestine and, with it, the Persian province of Yehud (Judea) came under the control of Alexander the Great around 332/331 BCE. The transition from Persian to Macedonian rule is remembered by the author of 1 Maccabees, who writes, "After Alexander son of Philip, the Macedonian, who came from the land of Kittim, had defeated King Darius of the Persians and the Medes, he succeeded him as king" (1 Macc. 1:1).

When Alexander died in 323 BCE, his empire was divided among his generals. Two of these generals, Ptolemy and Seleucus, received the greatest portions and would found kingdoms that would endure until the dawn of the Roman period in the first century BCE. The region of Palestine, including Judea, was a strategic location with harbors and port cities located between Egypt, seat of the Ptolemaic Empire, and Syria, which was ruled by the Seleucids. As a result, Palestine was a contested region and the site of major conflicts during the six wars between the Ptolemaic and Seleucid Empires. Palestine was mostly controlled by the Ptolemies until 198 BCE, when it was conquered by the Seleucid ruler Antiochus III. Seleucid control lasted until the outbreak of the Maccabean Revolt (167 BCE), which resulted in the emergence of an independent Jewish state ruled by a new Jewish dynasty, the Hasmoneans.

Alexander and his successors brought Greek culture, learning, language, and religion to Palestine. The presence and impact of Greek culture is called "Hellenism." The "Hellenistic period" is used by archaeologists of Israel/Palestine to refer to the period beginning with Alexander's conquest of the region in 332 BCE until the period of Roman domination beginning in 63 BCE.

The archaeology of the Hellenistic period reflects the Hellenization of Palestine. It also reflects the emergence of certain distinctive Jewish identity markers. Both Hellenism and the emergence of Jewish material identity endured into the Roman period and beyond, showing the lasting influence of the developments of the Hellenistic period on Palestinian Judaism. As we will see, these two elements, Hellenism on the one hand and Jewish identity

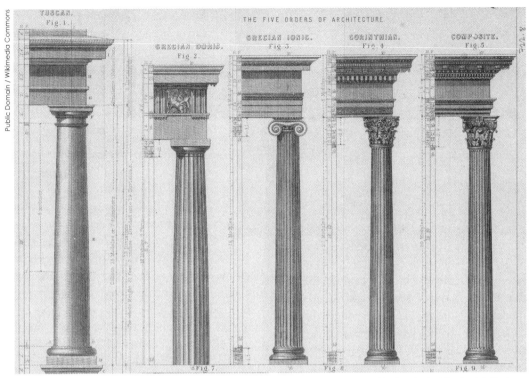

Fig. 10.1. Classical orders of columns including, from left to right, the Tuscan (a simplified variant of the Doric), Doric, Ionic, Corinthian, and the Composite (a combination of the Ionic and Corinthian orders)

and culture on the other, did not necessarily exclude each other. Rather, the two intermingled and combined in unexpected and interesting ways, producing some distinctive blends of Greek and Semitic conventions and traditions.

The Early Hellenistic Period

Classical Greek architecture entered Palestine in the Hellenistic period. The classical style would continue to influence and characterize the architecture of Palestine into the Roman and Byzantine periods. One of the most common signatures of Greek architecture is its trabeated or "post and lintel" design (see Klein 2016, 113–17). Vertical columns, set upon a level platform called a "stylobate," supported horizontal lintels. The area between the columns and the sloped roof eaves of Greek temples is called the "entablature." The entablature is divided into two areas. The upper

area is called the "frieze," while the lower area is called the "architrave." Three distinct styles of architecture, called "orders," were used in classical Greek architecture (see Marquand 1909, 280–84). These are the Doric, Ionic, and Corinthian orders. Each order can be identified by the type of column employed. The Doric order is the simplest, featuring columns with no base and round capitals. The Ionic order features carved bases and capitals featuring a design that looks like a rolled scroll called a "volute." The Corinthian order is not properly an order in itself but is really a variant of the Ionic order featuring a more ornate column capital with carved acanthus leaves and scrolls. Courtyards marked by columns surrounding a building, called "peristyle" courts, were also common features of this period.

A dramatic instance of the fusion of Hellenistic and Semitic styles can be found in the fortress-palace of Iraq al-Amir (see Lapp and

Public Domain / Wikimedia Commons

Fig. 10.2. Fortress-palace of Iraq al-Amir, Jordan

Lapp 1993). Iraq al-Amir is located in the Jordan Valley between Jericho and Amman in modern-day Jordan. The site includes a fortress called Qasr al-Abd, which translates to "Fortress of the Servant." This fortress belonged to the powerful Jewish Tobiad family. This is attested by two inscriptions of the name "Tobiah" on the facade. Moreover, its name probably refers to the Tobiah called "the servant, the Ammonite" in Nehemiah 2:10 (RSV) (Lapp and Lapp 1993, 646), who probably was the governor of Ammon appointed by the Persians and whose family apparently was left in the post by the Ptolemies (Berlin 1997, 11). Josephus mentions that during the reign of Seleucus IV Philopater (ca. 187–175 BCE), a certain Tobiad named Hyrcanus withdrew to the Transjordan and built a "strong fortress" that he called "Tyros" there (*Ant*. 12.230–33). It is quite likely that the building now called Qasr al-Abd is the Tyros fortress-palace built by Hyrcanus.

Although still resembling eastern monumental buildings of Syria and Palestine, Qasr al-Abd features Corinthian columns, indicative of the prevalence of the Hellenistic architectural style in this period. It also boasts a number of carved feline figures (lions and leopards) on its facade, along with a fountain featuring a similar carved feline. These carved figures are curious and instructive of Greek influence, because the palace was built by a member of the Jewish ruling class, and Jewish art in this period is typically aniconic, shying away from representation of living creatures.

Other examples of the influence of Hellenism on local architectural style can be found in the monumental Jerusalemite tombs of the period. While there are some points of continuity between the tombs of the Hellenistic period and the earlier First Temple period rock-cut bench tombs, there are also some significant differences. Hellenistic period tombs featured exterior decoration, whereas First Temple period rock-cut tombs did not. Moreover, burial chambers featured niches called "loculi" (Hebrew *kokhim*) rather than the pit-and-bench style of earlier periods. The tomb of Bene Hezir (second century BCE) makes use of Greek orders in its exterior decor. It features a porch leading into the rock-cut tombs, with two columns in the Doric style and a decorated frieze. The burial chamber itself is typical of the Jewish rock-cut style and contains loculi. Similarly, another tomb in Jerusalem called Jason's Tomb (early first century BCE) is topped with a pyramid structure and features a porch with a Doric column and architrave. The porch features two inscriptions, one in Aramaic and one in Greek.

The inspiration for these tombs seems to have been the monumental tomb of the Hasmonean family built by the Hasmonean Simon at Modein (Berlin 2002, 143–44). No archaeological remains of this tomb are extant, but it is described in vivid detail in 1 Maccabees 13:27–30:

And Simon built a monument over the tomb of his father and his brothers; he made it high so that it might be seen, with polished stone at the front and back. He also erected

Fig. 10.3. Monumental stone-cut tombs in the Kidron Valley in Jerusalem

seven pyramids, opposite one another, for his father and mother and four brothers. For the pyramids he devised an elaborate setting, erecting about them great columns, and on the columns he put suits of armor for a permanent memorial, and beside the suits of armor he carved ships, so that they could be seen by all who sail the sea. This is the tomb that he built in Modein; it remains to this day.

Simon's inspiration, in turn, seems to have come from the Hellenistic world. The description of the Hasmonean tomb bears some notable similarities to the tomb of Mausolus, also known as the Mausoleum, at Halicarnassus (fourth century BCE) and to the Belevi Mausoleum (third century BCE), which was the burial place of the Seleucid ruler Antiochus II (cf. Berlin 2002, 144–45). Both tombs are located in Turkey. Although only some fragments of the architecture have survived, Pliny describes the Mausoleum at Halicarnassus as surrounded by a colonnade and capped with a pyramid, with a marble carving of a four-horse chariot on top (*Natural History* 36.30). We are led to conclude that the monumental Jerusalemite tombs are best

understood as blends of local Jewish traditions and Hellenistic architecture.

Hellenism also had an impact on the non-Jewish residents of Palestine. Maresha is an Idumean city that had a substantial Sidonian (Phoenician) colony in the Hellenistic period. It is organized in typical Hellenistic fashion along an orthogonal grid pattern called a "Hippodamian grid" (Magness 2012, 76). It also contains two public spaces typical of Hellenistic cities, a marketplace called an "agora" and a temple complex. The Phoenician coastal city of Tel Dor is another example of a non-Jewish city from this period with similar Hellenistic features (see Stewart and Martin 2003).

Greek religion also made its mark on Palestine in the Hellenistic period. The worship of the Greek deity Pan was established in the early third century BCE at a place in the north of Palestine that would come to be called "Panias" (or "Banias") after the deity (Berlin 1999, 27). This cult site later would be expanded and renamed "Caearea Philippi" in the Roman period. Another striking example of the presence of Greek religion and culture in Palestine came to light at Hippos in the Golan, where a life-size stucco relief of Hercules measuring almost six feet in height was found (Segal and Eisenberg 2011, 50).

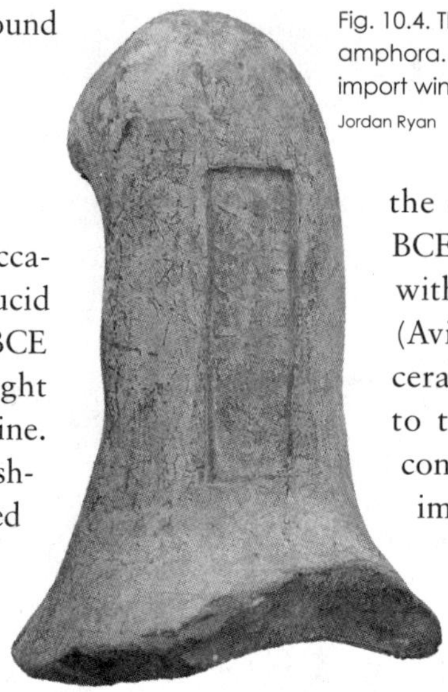

The Late Hellenistic Period

The success of the Jewish Macca-bean Revolt against their Seleucid overlords, which began in 167 BCE and ended in 134 BCE, brought about major changes in Palestine. Chief among these is the establish-ment of a Jewish kingdom headed by the Hasmonean dynasty. In this era, we see the widespread emergence of a distinct Jew-ish identity in material cul-ture throughout the Hasmo-nean kingdom.

The expansionism of the Maccabees is seen in campaigns during the revolt in the regions of Idumea, including Hebron and Maresha (1 Macc. 5:1–8, 65–66), Galilee (vv. 9–23), the Transjordan, including Gilead (vv. 24–44), and the coast, including Azotus/Ashdod (v. 68). It was continued by the later Hasmonean rulers John Hyrcanus I (reigned 135–104 BCE), Aris-tobulus (reigned 104–103 BCE), and Alexander Jannaeus (reigned 103–76 BCE). At its height under Alexander Jannaeus the Hasmonean kingdom encompassed Galilee, Samaria, Idu-mea, and much of the coastal region, and grew to an extent comparable to the territory of the biblical united Israelite monarchy under David and Solomon.

The dramatic shift in Galilee from gentile to Hasmonean control in the late second century BCE can be seen in the archaeological record. First of all, there is a notable shift in the ce-ramic profile of Galilee, indicating a culture shift. In the early Hellenistic period, a type of pottery called "Galilean coarse ware," which was produced by Galilee's pagan population, was ubiquitous in Galilee (Aviam 2013, 6–7). However, at many Galilean sites the use of Galilean coarse ware did not continue past

Fig. 10.4. The stamped handle of a Rhodian amphora. Amphorae like these were used to import wine from the Aegean to Palestine. Jordan Ryan

the end of the second century BCE, which probably corresponds with the Hasmonean expansion (Aviam 2013, 6). Moreover, the ceramic profile of Galilee prior to the Hasmonean expansion contains a significant amount of imported ware, such as ampho-rae, for carrying wine, with stamped handles indicating their origin from Aegean cities such as Rhodes and Knidos and a type of red-slipped tableware called "Eastern Sigillata A," which came from Phoenician cities (Berlin 2005, 442–44). However, during the first cen-tury BCE new local pottery began to replace the old types. According to Andrea Berlin, what differentiated this new local pottery from other types was not its form but its makers—that is, Jewish potters (Berlin 2005, 424).

There is some abandonment and destruc-tion of gentile sites in the Galilee, such as Mizpe Yamim, Yodefat, and Esh-Shuhara, around this time (Aviam 2013, 6–10, 12). This happens to correspond with the emergence of new settlements in Galilee that exhibit features of Jewish culture (Liebner 2009, 319–29). One such Jewish settlement is Magdala (Bauckham and De Luca 2015, 95), which was organized in an orthogonal "Hippodamian grid" in the Hellenistic style, much like non-Jewish cities such as Maresha and Tel Dor. Its economy was driven by fishery, and it features a harbor quay dated first to the Hasmonean period. De-spite being a Jewish town, Magdala also had a public bath in the Hellenistic style that was founded in the Hasmonean period (Bauckham and De Luca 2015, 100).

A key marker of Jewish ethnic identity that appears in the Hasmonean period is the ritual

Fig. 10.5. A miqvah discovered at Magdala. This miqvah is filled by groundwater.

bath, the miqvah. The Hebrew Bible prescribes bathing or washing in order to rid oneself of ritual impurity. Miqvahs typically are stepped baths or pools used for restoring ritual purity. Some were for public use, such as the large miqvah discovered at Gamla, while others were private, such as the miqvahs discovered in residential settings in the Herodian Quarter in Jerusalem. The discovery of miqvahs at Galilean sites is indicative of Torah observance and thus of the Jewish religio-ethnic identity of the inhabitants. One instructive example is the fortress at Qeren Naftaly, which originally was controlled by gentiles, but in the latter half of the second century BCE a miqvah was built into its foundation, indicating a change in control (Aviam 2013, 10). By the height of the early Roman period, miqvahs would be ubiquitous in Palestine.

The first true Jewish coins appear in the late Hellenistic period. From John Hyrcanus I on, the Hasmonean rulers minted bronze coins in the style of Hellenistic kings. The coins included inscriptions in both Greek and Hebrew of the names and titles of the ruler who minted them. However, unlike the coins of the Hellenistic kings, Hasmonean coins followed Jewish convention and did not depict animals, humans, or deities on their coins, preferring symbols such as anchors, wreaths, and cornucopias.

As a dynasty that claimed both the title of Jewish high priest and, from Aristobulus on, the title of "king" (Greek *basileus*), as the Hellenistic kings did, the Hasmoneans themselves combined both Greek and Jewish traditions and ideals. Their palaces at Jericho demonstrate this. The first palace was built by John Hyrcanus I, and renovations and additions were made by Alexander Jannaeus and Alexandra Salome. The original luxurious palatial complex had a multi-winged main building, along with a swimming-pool complex. Alexander rebuilt and fortified it. His wife, Alexandra Salome, later added two twin villas after Alexander's death. The palace complex features Hellenistic architectural elements, including Doric columns as well as some Corinthian capitals in an Alexandrian style (Peleg-Barkat 2013, 236). The pool complex from the time of Alexander Jannaeus has a colonnade with a complete Doric order with a carved frieze. The choice of the Doric order, the unusual Alexandrian style of the Corinthian capitals, along with some of the frescoes that decorate the palace walls, probably are the result of Alexandrian influence (Peleg-Barkat 2013, 239).

Fig. 10.6. Bronze prutah of Alexander Jannaeus, first century BCE
© Baker Publishing Group and Dr. James C. Martin

Fig. 10.7. The Givati parking lot excavations, where archaeologists may have found the remains of the Akra

The Jewish identity of the palace's inhabitants is strongly indicated by the presence of miqvahs. Moreover, the excavator Ehud Netzer discovered a building that he identified as a synagogue on the fringes of the palace grounds. Although some have questioned this identification of the building because its location in the palace complex precludes its public use, Anders Runesson has persuasively argued that it could have been a synagogue of the semipublic "association" type (see discussion below), serving the staff of the palace (Runesson, Binder, and Olsson 2008, 42). The Hasmonean palace complex thus features both Greek and Jewish elements, exemplifying the intermingling of Jewish tradition and Greek culture that characterized the late Hellenistic period.

Another structure that is relevant to the Maccabean rebels and their descendants is the Akra, a Seleucid fortress built in Jerusalem (1 Macc. 1:35–38; *Ant.* 12.252) that finally was taken by Simon Maccabee some years after the rest of the city had been seized by the rebels

(1 Macc. 13:49–52). A monumental building with a massive wall, tower, and glacis dating to the reign of Antiochus IV has recently been discovered in the area known as the City of David in Jerusalem. The excavators found lead shot, bronze arrowheads, and ballista stones on the site that were stamped with a trident, which was a heraldic symbol of Antiochus IV (Israel Antiquities Authority 2015). This led them to suggest that the building is the Akra mentioned by 1 Maccabees and Josephus. However, there is a difficulty with this identification. Josephus states that the Akra was built on a high place and "overlooked the temple" (*Ant.* 12.252). Because of its location, the building in the City of David area identified as the Akra would need to have been over 400 feet tall (Ritmeyer 2015), which is unreasonable. While it is likely that this discovery is part of the Hellenistic fortifications of Jerusalem, its identification as the Akra will need to be settled in future publications.

One of the most significant developments of the Hellenistic period for Jewish identity, religion, culture, and life is the emergence of synagogue buildings. The term "synagogue" refers to both Jewish assemblies and the places where they assembled (Catto 2007, 199–201; Runesson 2001, 232). While the genesis of the synagogue as an institution properly belongs to the Persian period (Runesson 2003), the emergence of distinct synagogue architecture in Palestine is first attested in the late Hellenistic period.

In earlier research, two distinct sets of evidence led to two competing definitions of the "synagogue." Some schol-

Fig. 10.8. The synagogue at Gamla in the Golan Heights. Note the arrangement of the stepped benches and the columns.

ars argued that the synagogue was a public institution derived from the city-gate assemblies that developed in the late Second Temple period, while others held that the synagogue was a type of Greco-Roman association (or *collegium*), similar to a club or guild. Each hypothesis was strongly supported by a different set of evidence, which led to the conclusion, first proposed by Anders Runesson, that there were in fact two types of synagogues: public synagogues, which were local official assemblies that developed from the earlier gate assemblies, and association synagogues, which were semipublic Jewish "associations" (Runesson 2001).

Public synagogues were political institutions. They were local assemblies in which decisions would be made for the town as a whole. Synagogues in the Diaspora were mostly association synagogues for which membership was based on Jewish ethnicity, though association synagogues belonging to specific Jewish groups could also exist in Palestine. Public synagogues, however, could exist in Palestine only in locales that were under Jewish control, because of their political function. The signature function

of both association and public synagogues was the communal reading and interpretation of Jewish Scripture.

In the Diaspora, evidence for the emergence of association synagogue buildings in Egypt is found as early as the third century BCE (e.g., *CIJ* 2:1440; *CPJ* 1:129; 3:1532a). Association synagogues were influenced in their architecture by that of Greco-Roman association meeting places. In addition to a benched meeting hall (similar to public synagogue architecture described below), they included additional rooms, such as *triclinia* (dining halls), for typical association purposes such as communal eating (P. Richardson 2003).

In the Hebrew Bible, the city gates are the place of local official assembly where trials took place and legal decisions were made (Deut. 17:5; 21:19; 22:15, 24; 25:7; 2 Sam. 15:2; Ruth 4:1–12; Amos 5:15; Zech. 8:16). The origin of the public synagogue, however, is found in the Persian period, when the first public reading of Scripture outside the temple took place in the Water Gate (Neh. 8:1–8). The combination of the gate assembly with the public reading of Scripture is the genesis of what came to be the public synagogue.

Jordan Ryan

Fig. 10.9. A street in Magdala in Galilee. The synagogue building is visible to the left.

Public synagogue buildings—that is, buildings constructed specifically for public synagogue functions—emerged in the Hellenistic period when defense architecture evolved. The multi-chambered gate construction of early periods, which typically had adjoining public squares, was replaced in the Hellenistic period by a simple passageway between two towers (L. I. Levine 2005, 34–35). The gates of the Hellenistic and Roman periods did not have adjoining public squares. As a result, the meetings that traditionally had taken place in the gate complexes eventually moved into buildings constructed specifically for the purposes of local Jewish assembly and Scripture reading. Lee Levine has suggested that the location of the synagogue building at Gamla next to the town entrance may reflect the earlier tradition of assembly for synagogue functions in the gates (L. I. Levine 2005, 27–38).

Eight buildings typically identified as synagogues dating to the period before the destruction of the Second Temple have been discovered in Israel-Palestine. These are located at Capernaum, Gamla, Herodium, Jericho, Magdala, Masada, Modein (Umm el-Umdan), and Qiryat Sefer. Of these, the synagogue at Jericho

is the only one likely to be an association synagogue. This identification is based on its location (see above) and is supported by its complex architecture, which includes a kitchen and a *triclinium*, a usual feature of an association building (P. Richardson 2003, 96, 112). The rest are most likely public. The synagogues at Modein and Jericho are dated with some confidence to the late Hellenistic period. The rest are more securely dated to the early Roman period. Other likely early synagogue buildings have recently been identified at Diab, Et-Tawani, Khirbet Majdouliya, Kefar Shikhin, and Tel Rechesh.

Early public synagogue buildings share a general architectural form. They are centered on a main meeting hall, which is quadrilateral in shape with stepped benches lining three or four of the walls. Columns supporting a windowed clerestory wall are located in the central floor area. The buildings are designed for communal discussion. The quadrilateral seating arrangement facilitated discussion, especially with those seated across the way from one another. Active public discussion and debate over the interpretation of the law or other local official matters was one of the characteristic elements of early synagogue gatherings (Binder 1999, 403; Mosser 2013, 550; Ryan 2017, 47). The stakes in discussion of the law could be quite high. By the Hellenistic period, we see the Torah being applied to situations that are beyond what we might categorize as "religious" (Watts 2013). It is applied to the performance of marriage contracts (Tob. 1:8; 7:12–13), battle plans (1 Macc. 3:48), Sabbath observance (1 Macc. 2:34–41), and criminal justice (Sus. 62). Thus, the outcome

Fig. 10.10. Synagogue ruins in New Testament Jericho

of discussion and debate in public synagogues could impact life and practice in Jewish locales in very real ways.

Public synagogues were also meeting places for the local council, called the *boulē* (*Life* 277–303). The *boulē* was a typical feature of the local government system of a Hellenistic city. It is no wonder, then, that synagogue architecture has a parallel in the Hellenistic *bouleutērion*, the civic building where the *boulē* gathered. Like synagogues, *bouleutēria* also featured stepped benches in quadrilateral arrangement and open space in the center. Thus, it seems as though Hellenistic influence is present even in the synagogue, one of early Palestinian Judaism's signature institutions.

Conclusion

The Hellenstic period saw the rise of Greek culture in Palestine, as well as the emergence of a distinct Jewish identity in material culture. As our review of the evidence shows, Hellenism and Judaism were not mutually exclusive categories. Judaism in Palestine was Hellenized, even following the Maccabean Revolt. The Hellenization of Palestine and the emergence of early Judaism and Jewish identity formation would pave the way for the practical and theological issues faced both by the rabbis and by the New Testament authors in the Roman period.

SECTION III

The Scripts

Ancient Near Eastern Literature

11

Introduction to Ancient Near Eastern Literature

ADAM E. MIGLIO

Recovery of Ancient Near Eastern Sources

The civilizations of the ancient Near East were almost entirely forgotten some time after the first centuries of the Common Era. Thousands of years of history were nearly lost. The ancient traditions of Greece and Rome had been preserved in monasteries and universities throughout Europe down through the Middle Ages, but the millennia of human history that had been recorded in the ancient Near East were known only from a few selective memories preserved in classical sources and the Hebrew Bible. And even then, many of these recollections were only shadowy memories, as is illustrated by Edgar Degas's painting of a fictitious queen of Babylon named Semiramis, or by Eugène Delacroix's depiction of an alleged Assyrian monarch, Sardanapalus. In both cases, the muses for these works of art were inventions or misrepresentations of the Greek historians Herodotus and Ctesias of Cnidus, among others. Yet these trace memories of the "lands and peoples of the Bible" were enough to prompt travelers down to the early modern period to visit the dusty mounds of Ur, Babylon, or Nineveh in Iraq or the monumental ruins of Egypt, despite the fact that little was actually known about the former inhabitants of these places.

The recovery of the ancient Near East, however, was energized during the late eighteenth and early nineteenth centuries in no small part by an amalgam of European biblicism and nationalist impulses. Biblicism, or a naive and reductionist understanding of the text of the Bible, compelled popular interest in the history of the "lands of the Bible." At the same time, the drumbeat of nationalism reverberated across Europe, and states marched to collect antiquities from the ancient Near East. For example, Napoleon arrived in Egypt in 1778 with more than two thousand non-military personnel to document Egypt's geography and history as well as to help bring back thousands of Egyptian antiquities to France. And in ancient Iraq, British, French, Italian, and German explorers angled to excavate ancient ruins (i.e., tells) in hopes of unearthing treasures that could be crated and shipped back to Europe.

As a result of the exploration of the ancient Near East during the late eighteenth and early nineteenth centuries, thousands of written sources were made available for scholarly study. Increased European awareness of the ancient Near East led in turn to decipherment of the important languages and scripts of Akkadian cuneiform and Egyptian hieroglyphs by the middle of the nineteenth century. The recovery of the ancient Near East, however, extended well into the twentieth century. In Anatolia at the site of Boğazkale, for example, a hitherto unknown language written in cuneiform was deciphered in 1915—the language of the Hittites. The discovery of the Hittites' language and traditions was particularly remarkable, since they had only been previously known from brief mentions in the Hebrew Bible (and not at all in classical sources). And similarly, not long after the excavations at Boğazkale, tablets written in an alphabetic cuneiform script were discovered at the site of Ras Shamra, located along the coast of modern-day Syria (1930). Today, roughly two thousand alphabetic cuneiform tablets, which preserve a Northwest Semitic language known as Ugaritic, have been excavated from this site. Ugaritic was written using a cuneiform alphabet of thirty signs and is linguistically akin to classical Hebrew. Lastly, in addition to the discovery of new languages and literatures, archaeological excavations have also unearthed many new textual artifacts from the land of Israel-Palestine that contribute to our understanding of the biblical world, including the well-known Dead Sea Scrolls from early Roman times and hundreds of inscriptions from earlier periods.

Introduction to Ancient Near Eastern Textual Sources

Many of the chapters included in this section entitled "The Scripts" focus on written sources recovered from the ancient Near East—from Egypt and Israel-Palestine to Anatolia and Syro-Mesopotamia. At times, these chapters treat sources from the ancient Near East that may be termed "literature" or sources that shared a cultural status as a sort of *belles lettres*. In other instances, the sources discussed are of a more quotidian nature, which may be described as archival documents or nonliterary sources. While these two broadly defined categories by no means exhaust the variety of textual sources that have been found across the civilizations of the ancient Near East, they nevertheless provide helpful heuristics for understanding the rich corpora from the ancient Near East.

Literary Sources

The literary sources from the ancient Near East include epics, mythologies, incantations, rituals, hymns, prayers, lamentations, sapiential (or wisdom) literature, humorous compositions, and monumental or display inscriptions, among others. Literary sources provide unique insight into the cultural, philosophical, and religious thought of the civilizations of the ancient Near East. And while the majority of textual sources from the ancient Near East are nonliterary in nature, it is not at all surprising that literary sources have attracted the greatest attention. It was royal inscriptions, after all, that played the central role in deciphering both Akkadian cuneiform and Egyptian hieroglyphs.

Moreover, the interest in the literary traditions of the newly deciphered languages of the ancient Near East was reinforced in part by chance discoveries during the early years of archaeology in the ancient Near East. For example, George Smith's lecture to the Society of Biblical Archaeology in 1872 serves as an example of both the enchanting quality of literary sources from the ancient Near East and the chance recoveries that added to the interest in literary sources. In his lecture, Smith, a British Assyriologist, presented his research to a distinguished audience, which included the Prime Minister William Gladstone. He lectured on what has come to be known as the eleventh tablet of the standard Babylonian version of the *Epic of Gilgamesh*. This tablet contains narrative poetry that tells the fascinating story of Mesopotamian gods who sent a flood to punish humanity. The protagonist is a man named Uta-napishti, who, like Noah, was given instructions to build a boat so that he would be spared from the divine wrath of a flood. Smith captivated his audience with this long-lost tradition from the ancient Near East and with the striking similarities between this cuneiform source and the Hebrew Bible (cf. Gen. 6–9). In fact, the sensational nature of Smith's research elicited strong support in the form of renewed British archaeological investigations at Nineveh in Iraq in hopes of finding additional literary compositions that would shed further light on Old Testament traditions. And as far as the chance recovery of the early British excavations at Nineveh (Kouyunjik), the sources found at this site serendipitously came to constitute the largest single collection of literary sources from ancient Mesopotamia.

Nonliterary Sources

As for nonliterary sources, documents such as letters, legal documents, scribal exercises, administrative sources, and several others are to be included in this category. As noted above, nonliterary sources constitute the majority of sources from the ancient Near East, by comparison with literary sources. For example, there are less than 200 literary sources known from the Ugaritic corpus, whereas nearly 1,800 nonliterary sources have been excavated. Likewise, even in the vast "library" recovered at Kouyunjik, mentioned above, only a small fraction of the 30,000 tablets constitute what might be called literary sources.[1]

1. It has been observed that according to one ancient inventory from the "library" at Nineveh, "[an] incidental place [was] occupied by 'belles lettres' (myths, epics, and so on), since only ten tablets [of the 2,300 documented texts] belonged to that genre" (Charpin 2011, 196).

Both the quantity of nonliterary sources and the information they contain make them extremely valuable for understanding the civilizations of the ancient Near East. In particular, the study of nonliterary sources often provides a distinctive perspective on life and society in the ancient Near East. For example, the Hebrew Bible provides a detailed description of the ritual calendar for ancient Israel—the celebration of Pesach or Yom Kippur. Yet the so-called Gezer "calendar," a Phoenician inscription from about the tenth century BCE (Pardee 2013, 226–46), offers a different perspective on the seasons of the year. The Gezer "calendar," which may be a scribal exercise, documents the agricultural rhythms in the land of Canaan, such as when specific crops were planted, harvested, or processed. Likewise, hundreds of papyri found at el-Lahun, near the entrance to the Faiyum in Egypt, help to round out our understanding of the social and civic aspects of life among farmers, metalworkers, fishermen, and others from this pyramid town. In particular, the administrative sources indicate some of the conditions under which these inhabitants worked as well as the organization of households within the town. Legal documents at the site further reveal social practices, such as matters of inheritance and the nature of other various commercial transactions. These nonliterary sources, of which only two examples have been noted, help to connect us with the daily experiences and practices that structured life in the ancient Near East.

Toward an Integrated Reading of Ancient Near Eastern and Biblical Sources

The literary sources that document the intellectual and cultural achievements of ancient Near Eastern civilizations as well as the nonliterary sources that tend to document the more conventional realities of life represent rich corpora for comparative study with biblical literature. At the same time, there are numerous challenges to integrating biblical and ancient Near Eastern sources. One well-remembered moment in the history of scholarship that has served as a catalyst for discussions regarding the relationship between Near Eastern and biblical literatures is a suite of three lectures given by Professor Friedrich Delitzsch to the Deutsche Orient-Gesellschaft (German Oriental Society) in 1902. In these lectures, Delitzsch provoked what has come to be known as the Babel-Bibel-Streit (Babel and Bible Debate). What prompted the debate, in part, was Delitzsch's provocative argument that the parallels between the literature of Mesopotamia and the Bible were the result of Israelite borrowings from their Babylonian counterparts. While this idea itself was not entirely novel, Delitzsch further insisted that Israelite literature, especially in its ethical vision, was intellectually derivative and inferior to that which is found in Mesopotamian sources. Delitzsch's lectures provoked diverse responses, ranging from polemical rejoinders, to more-nuanced critiques, to hearty affirmations. Yet what made Delitzsch's lectures a milestone in discussions of comparative studies was not merely his provocative claims but also the fact that he touched upon pointed methodological issues regarding the relationship between biblical and ancient Near Eastern literature (see further Larsen 1996).

Debates continue to the present about how to describe the relationship between the sources from the ancient Near East and the Bible and how these two corpora should be read in tandem. And answers to the questions raised by Delitzsch's lectures are not simple. Therefore, what is presented here is not intended to solve these challenges but rather to serve as a prolegomenon of sorts. That is, what follows are preliminary guidelines that may serve as a starting place for integrating ancient Near Eastern and biblical sources. A comparative reading of ancient Near Eastern and biblical sources requires rigor and care, yet the rewards of this task are many. At times it may be determined that biblical sources were influenced by traditions from the ancient Near East. For example, Isaiah 27:1 seems to show an awareness of a Canaanite tradition quite similar to that preserved in the Ugaritic *Ba'lu Myth*. In other instances, however, a more modest conclusion may be arrived at, in which ancient Near Eastern sources provide milieus for more skillfully interpreting the texts of the Bible, or vice versa. The Bible and ancient Near Eastern civilizations share common features, having been fashioned in adjacent geographies and during the same time periods. In other words, because biblical literature and the textual traditions of the ancient Near East are homologous, each may be brought into clearer relief by comparison against the backdrop of the other.

For practical purposes, at least three orienting considerations will help to constrain attempts at an integrated reading of ancient Near Eastern and biblical sources. These observations are in no way intended to be an exhaustive set of hermeneutic principles. Furthermore, the issues that are raised should not be thought of as entirely disconnected from one another; in fact, at times these considerations imbricate. They are, however, heuristics that can help to guide the complex task of relating ancient Near Eastern and biblical sources to one another. The first of these considerations specifically pertains to sources from the ancient Near East. The second arises from the distinct qualities of biblical texts, whereas the final issue is relevant to both ancient Near Eastern and biblical sources.

First, the study of ancient Near Eastern sources must take into account what we might call the artifactuality of these sources. Again, while most classical sources (e.g., Plato, Aristotle, Hesiod, and Homer) have come down to us via streams of traditions, nearly every ancient Near Eastern source has been recovered via explorations of the ruins in the region.[2] Ideally, ancient Near Eastern sources, then, were uncovered by proper archaeological excavations. For the science of archaeology a concern *sine qua non* is the role of context. Artifacts are excavated from specific places—from specific regions, cities, buildings, rooms, and so on—and originate from particular times.

The spatial and temporal contexts in which textual artifacts are recovered are crucial for helping to shape and guide understandings of these ancient sources. For example, some compositions are known only from a single extant copy and were not widely distributed across the ancient Near Eastern landscape. A case in point is the Akkadian composition known as the *Poor Man of Nippur*. This story is about an impoverished inhabitant of Nippur who is disrespected by the city's governor only to cleverly exact his revenge, and it is known only from a copy at the peripheral site of Sultantepe and one small fragment from Nineveh. For this reason, it cannot be assumed that this literary source was widely known throughout the ancient Near East. Moreover, because this source is only attested in the seventh century BCE, it would be quite difficult to determine its influence on textual sources, either ancient Near Eastern or biblical, that were written prior to this. By comparison, the so-called Law Code of Hammurabi is attested by numerous exemplars. In addition to the famous stele in the Louvre, which contains these well-known legal stipulations, portions of these laws have also been recovered on many tablets from Mesopotamia and perhaps even as far as Canaan. Moreover, the Law Code was also copied and

recopied over a time span of nearly a millennium. Likewise, a similar situation exists for the *Epic of Gilgamesh*, which is known from numerous exemplars that span roughly a millennium and is attested from Mesopotamia to Hatti and Ugarit to Megiddo. The distribution of these sources across a wide geographic distance and over an extended time frame anticipates their influences upon other traditions from the ancient Near East, including the text of the Bible.

In addition to their spatial and temporal contexts, epigraphic artifacts may be explored with regard to their physicality. Ancient Near Eastern texts are written on various media and have numerous physical characteristics that may be analyzed from the study of their geological compositions, their shapes, and their sizes. For example, the shape of a source or the media on which a text was written can significantly inform interpretation of it. In Mesopotamia, texts inscribed on clay plaques of a particular shape with a single piercing were often used for apotropaic or amuletic purposes. Thus portions of the myth about the gods Erra and Ishum, gods of pestilence and destruction, could be written on such a plaque in order to ward off plagues (see, e.g., Reiner 1960). Likewise, writing etched into metal among Northwest Semitic inscriptions may have served a similar function. Therefore, the existence of the Aaronic blessing (Num. 6:22–27) on two silver scrolls found in a tomb in Jerusalem points to magical uses for these artifacts that preserve some of the earliest extant portions known from the Hebrew Bible (Smoak 2016).

The second matter to consider when integrating biblical and ancient Near Eastern sources concerns the various modes of critical investigation of the Bible. Because the Hebrew Bible is primarily the product of transmission via various streams of traditions, the final formation of biblical texts is a matter of significant debates among specialists. Study of

---

2. Many textual sources from the ancient Near East were recovered prior to the advent of rigorous, scientific standards for archaeology, and as a result these sources are not well understood with respect to their artifactuality. Likewise, the looting of cultural heritage that persists today in many places in the modern Middle East, reflected most notably in news headlines concerning Iraq and Syria, presents similar challenges for interpreting ancient Near Eastern texts with respect to their artifactuality.

the formation of the Hebrew Bible involves numerous methods, from text-critical analyses to historical-critical approaches. These various forms of criticism can help to address both the content and the historical contexts of biblical literature. Every effort to integrate the reading of ancient Near Eastern and biblical sources must seriously consider issues of textual transmission, including the roles of the editors and tradents that helped to give biblical texts their final forms.

Lastly, both ancient Near Eastern and biblical sources must be thoroughly examined with respect to their textuality. While the term "textuality" is not unproblematic, in this chapter it is used to refer to the seemingly endless array of elements that characterize the linguistic properties of texts. That is, ancient Near Eastern texts may be considered at numerous levels—from their genres, to their themes, to their countless stylistic features, to their vocabulary, syntax, and morphology or phonology—and each of these features, among many others, helps to constitute textuality. And both ancient Near Eastern and biblical sources must be thoroughly investigated with regard to their textuality in order for them to be compared and contrasted.

Genres and themes are among the most commonly considered aspects of textuality in discussions of ancient Near Eastern and biblical texts. For example, several stories about origins are known from ancient Egypt, such as those found in pyramid texts, or a later account preserved on the Shabaka stone (not to mention accounts from other ancient Near Eastern civilizations). While the Egyptian accounts of origins are significantly different in many key details, the texts help to provide a sense of the formal and thematic elements that shaped the genre of "creation myth," both in Egypt and in biblical literature (e.g., Gen. 1).[3] Similarly, extant Hittite treaties and Assyrian loyalty oaths, along with the biblical idea of covenant delineated in Exodus-Leviticus or Deuteronomy, help to clarify the stipulations that framed suzerain-vassal relations. And the Mesopotamian compositions of Atra-Hasis, Etana, and Adapa testify to an interest in the theme of human mortality, again a subject also addressed in Genesis 2–3 and elsewhere in the Hebrew Bible.

Nonliterary sources, too, contribute to important issues associated with textuality. For example, the letters from ancient Mari (Tell Hariri) provide a glimpse into the rhetorical strategies used in narratives. Close attention to the texts of these letters reveals the linguistic tactics of persuasion and argumentation used by those who dispatched them. Likewise, administrative sources from Ugarit provide crucial philological and lexical data about Northwest Semitic languages. And Hebrew inscriptional evidence provides information for better understanding the spelling conventions in both classical and Biblical Hebrew.

Conclusion

In sum, an integrated reading of ancient Near Eastern and biblical sources requires thoughtful attention to the many characteristics of these sources. At the same time, this interdisciplinary undertaking promises to be intellectually rewarding. The study of both the Bible and the ancient Near East holds the potential to catalyze new and creative interpretations of sources that provide important perspectives on history, contain enduring humanistic insights, and preserve significant theological traditions.

3. For an introduction to ancient Near Eastern origin stories and the Hebrew Bible, see Walton 2009a.

12

Mesopotamian Literature

David C. Deuel

Introduction

The term "Mesopotamian literature" describes the textual remains from the region between the Tigris and Euphrates Rivers, the northeastern end of the Fertile Crescent. The corpus includes texts that originated in Mesopotamia but that messengers, merchants, peddlers, or other traveling officials carried to other regions—for example, diplomatic letters addressed to foreign kings. Mesopotamian scribes learned to build their texts skillfully and engage in rich and complex systems of text use.

Text-Building

Background for Text-Building

Why did ancient Near Eastern people generate texts? The Mesopotamians produced texts for many reasons, including documenting transactions; facilitating memory of lists, maps, and historical and mythological accounts; transferring administrative authority to a text bearer; and maintaining written records of rituals, procedures, and transactions in all spheres of society. Judging from the quantity and variety of texts that archaeologists have discovered in ancient archives, dossiers, and unclassifiable find spots, we can see that one of the greatest needs that texts met was for administrators to authorize agents to conduct their work over distances. Texts made it possible to respond to administrative needs from afar with effective surrogate presence.

Who wrote and used the texts? Generally speaking, trained scribes composed the texts, for "literacy was always highly restricted in the ancient Near East, and only an elite—scribes as well as government and temple officials—could read and write" (Michalowski 1995, 2279). Scribes were trained not only in the cuneiform script but also in literary conventions, including genre form and function (Postgate 2013, 48). Students wrote texts as practice exercises; accomplished scribes generated texts to meet the needs of the literati. Within this range of expertise, text quality reflects degrees of scribal proficiency. Shared text features may be traced to the scribes, their training, and ongoing interaction within their social contexts (van der

Toorn 2007, 1–3). Literacy among the general population is still not understood (Rollston 2010, 94–95). For example, professional but illiterate cooks utilizing written recipes and cooking procedures probably relied on literate persons to read them (Bottéro 1995b, 6). With these and other commonalities as well as variables in mind, how should one understand authorship?

Authorship is a complex matter. Texts were primarily state-sponsored, but that does not mean that kings and other high political and religious officials simply dictated the texts to the scribes who wrote them (S. Sanders 2015a, 114). Conspicuously, kings varied their speech levels when addressing different spheres in society (Liverani 2014b). Was this a scribal convention or the king's own pragmatic response to levels of language competence? It could be both. What is more, texts often served as propaganda in the form of polemics or apologies. Were the literary conventions of these potentially subtle political tools the work of kings or of their more literarily sophisticated scribal assistants? Most early myths were anonymous as we find them, although administrative texts such as letters used complex conventions of identity. Outside Mesopotamia, however, archived Hittite ritual and festival texts bear authors' names, ostensibly so that members of scribal circles could retrieve them in a manner resembling modern-day professors' library reserve reading lists (Gordin 2015, 115).

What languages are used in the texts from ancient Mesopotamia? The primary Mesopotamian languages in 2000 BCE include Akkadian, Amorite, Hurrian, and Sumerian. Arabic and Aramaic came into use after 2000 BCE (Postgate 2007, 1). Texts under consideration in this study appear in cuneiform and alphabetic scripts. Not surprisingly, the oldest archival records originate from the ancient Near East, but we "know surprisingly little about the purpose, functioning, and management of these archives" (Brosius 2003, 1). As expected, texts in languages other than those native to Mesopotamia are found in Mesopotamian archives but in most cases did not originate in the region.

How are the texts grouped and categorized for treatment? A standard method for treating texts begins when archaeologists unearth archives where tablets were systematically stored as dossiers or assemblages for further use. Some are found where they were discarded. Philologists then treat the texts by translating and categorizing them.

The entire corpus of available Mesopotamian texts may be broken down in several ways. First, texts may be understood on the basis of the places where they were displayed or stored. Monumental texts appear in reliefs and on obelisks or other objects. Archival materials are found in collections from official sites, such as temples or palaces, or in private locations, such as homes or workplaces. Canonical texts, characteristically composite documents, typically are found in royal or religious archives and in some contexts may have served as scribal curricula (van der Toorn 2007, 244–47; Rochberg 1984, 127–44). As noted above, Mesopotamian archives may contain texts written in languages and framed in genres from regions outside Mesopotamia. Texts also may be categorized on the basis of location of use, such as temple, palace, school, court, trade sites, or private space. Finally, the texts may be described within a broad functional framework such as the spheres of activity for which they were written, including ideological, martial, economical, or political (E. Morris 2013, 60). Some texts are titled on the basis of words used in the text, particularly at the text's beginning, such as *Enuma Elish*, "When on high."

A king's reputation strongly influenced the purposes behind texts. Although rule was administered by a system of officials, the king bore responsibility for wielding control. Consequently, a king's reputation for fortuity or calamity often overrode other interests in the texts they generated. A king's reign was measured by his standard of care for his people (Arnold 1994, 138–39; Millard 2012, 199). Each new scribal generation enhanced and preserved, damaged, or even erased the memory of kings based on perceptions of the kings' collective successes or failures. Propaganda could correct or create perspective on a current or former king's reign. Therefore, when considering matters of categorization, we must be aware that texts sometimes served purposes other than their ostensive messages.

Procedures of Text-Building

When were the texts written and where do they come from? The earliest written Sumerian texts date to ca. 3150 BCE from the ancient city of Uruk, level IVB. The most recent texts come from ca. 100 CE. Probably because the Sumerian language experienced a renaissance (ca. 2100–2000 BCE), most Sumerian literary texts date from the subsequent Old Babylonian period (ca. 2000–1600 BCE). The Akkadian language, consisting of Old Akkadian (ca. 2400–2000 BCE) and subsequent dialects of Babylonian and Assyrian, had a life span of 2,500 years (Black 2007, 6), with flourishes of text production in the late second and first millennia. Although it is possible to date administrative and other texts on the basis of archaeological remains in which they are found, most ancient literary works cannot be dated so easily (Michalowski 1995, 2279).

What do we know about the texts that ancient Mesopotamian peoples produced and used? The accident of discovery plays a role in finding and treating texts. Unfortunately, only a small portion of texts discovered in tells of the ancient Near East have been archaeologically excavated, treated, and published. Estimates run at around 1 percent. Treated and published texts serve as a basis for reconstructing a literary output of 2,500 years using many languages and dialects. What is more, the textual distribution at sites is often uneven, with the heaviest concentration in palace and temple archives. Somewhat predictably, administrative missions and related documentation increase exponentially when economic systems fail and enemies exploit or attack. Textual disruption occurs when peoples rebel internally (Millard 2005a, 302–5). In addition to destruction at the hands of enemy attackers, texts were often crushed after serving their intended purposes, due partially to their potential for abuse. Many texts gave their bearer authorization, a form of administrative power.

How were the texts produced? In general, "text production and transmission was driven by genre and participant" (S. Sanders 2015a, 119). Specific need determined the genre of text that a scribe would design. Materials used in Mesopotamian text production include rock surfaces and objects, soft clay, wax boards, ivory, wood, metal, parchment or leather, and forms of paper. Cuneiform wedge-shaped symbols were written on soft clay tablets with a stylus made from a reed shaped into a triangular tip (Pearce 1995, 2266–67). Even in texts from the early period (ca. 2500 BCE), shorter compositions were compiled as they were copied onto multiple tablets (Visicato 1995, 3). Although recording messages offered advantages, many contracts and other legal arrangements remained oral and committed to memory. Some of these eventually were recorded in texts (Millard 1999b, 238). Upon completion, tablets sometimes were wrapped in clay envelopes for protection and privacy, with participant names and other important details written on the envelope.

Scribal cultures shared ideas and practices but allowed for innovation. The *Epic of Gilgamesh* evolved over a period of several thousand years. At one phase, it was written on twelve tablets, making it one of the longest extant ancient Near Eastern compositions.[1]

1. Following Crisostomo, this study uses "the term 'text' to refer to an individual object and 'composition'

The epic's compositional history reflects some of the scribes' editorial conventions (Tigay 1982, 1–3), the patterns of which have been used in understanding the composition of the Hebrew Scriptures (Tigay 1985), although the results have been challenged (Person and Rezetko 2016). That said, recent studies of Hittite texts, although external to Mesopotamia, suggest that redaction was not always the result of conscious editing but also came from incorrect memorization (Marcuson and van den Hout 2015, 143).

Not only did individual scribal cultures employ idiosyncratic scribal practices but they also embraced distinct theological ideas. On the other side, shared scribal knowledge may help to explain why "Mesopotamian understandings of the universe remained remarkably constant over 2,500 years" (Horowitz 2011, xiii). Additionally, scribes often promoted the political agendas of ambitious rulers but censored out rebellions that could embarrass rulers or damage their reputations. In short, scribal cultures did not ensure shared content and practices; many factors shaped text content as well as text production and transmission.

Scribal practices were not linear and do not support sweeping generalizations about authorship. It is not clear that the scribes saw text creation as separate from text reproduction or that editing was clearly distinguishable from production (S. Sanders 2015a, 114). This is true not only in the ways that texts were composed but also in how they were copied, transmitted, compiled, and redacted (Crisostomo 2015, 122). It even applies to how they were collected and stored. The assumption that an author wrote an original text that was then copied word for word by subsequent generations of scribes is an oversimplification of a complex process. What is more, "The basic unstated assumption that the scribes intended

to refer to a loosely standardized and recognizable work, such as [a] literary composition" (Crisostomo 2015, 122).

always to reproduce as faithfully as possible an original is demonstrably incorrect" (Civil 2011, 229). Text-building employed a variety of practices—such as visual copying, memorization, and conscious innovation (S. Sanders 2015a, 114–15; Crisostomo 2015, 138).

Texts' genres could be fluid in form and adaptable in function. In fact, genres could undergo substantial transformations in form or function. Variables for genre transformation include "the purpose for which [a text] was produced and ways in which it was used" (Damrosch 1987, 38–39). Texts may even experience a second life after they have served their originally intended purposes (Maidman 1979). For example, a letter describing a piece of property that was sold could be used as documentary evidence of land ownership—much like a deed—for generations after the transaction. In addition, one administrative document could trigger a sequence of other documents (Deuel 2002). Interestingly, documents treating smaller-scale contracts such as marriage or adoption bear amazing similarities to large-scale international treaties. Both are contracts (Millard 1999b, 238).

Given all these factors, defining and classifying Mesopotamian literature is a work in progress. To date, no clear distinction can be made between prose and poetry. Furthermore, entire systems and categories of texts such as wisdom literature are constantly being refined (W. Lambert 1960, 1–2; Y. Cohen 2013, 8–9). Any unified theory of Mesopotamian text classification must be held tentatively.

Where did the texts go after scribes wrote them? Because kings relied on intricate systems of administration, scribes wrote many texts to be read and used outside the royal court. In short, "the king used both force and able administration to maintain order in his realm" (Millard 1999b, 238). Texts served both methods of rule, but administration required a disproportionate amount of documentation. Kingship "in reality was dominated by a network of interdependence" (Pongratz-Leisten 2013, 286). The king's reign required texts because kingship engaged "an elaborate system of advisors and administrators" (Fleming 2004a, 237). This also meant that kings relied on agents and missions of all sorts to administer the different spheres of their kingdoms (Deuel 2015, 355–68). Some texts were preserved in the royal archives as records of administrative decisions; others were dispatched and carried by messengers to officials who would perform the actions commanded therein.

Agents on missions delivered texts to their intended destinations in a variety of ways: foot runners traversed primarily short distances; caravans, boats, and donkeys, although somewhat slower, could carry correspondence on longer journeys; and chariot-riding messengers were probably one of the swiftest means of text delivery (Meier 1988, 82–89). Eventually the chariot was surpassed when the horse-riding messenger became a primary means of text delivery. During the period of Persian domination, perhaps earlier, kings built sophisticated networks of roads and relay stations, in essence a postal system, to accommodate the movement of correspondence (Westermann 1928, 375–76). With a communication infrastructure in place, kings were able to enlarge their economies and expand their borders using documents and delivery systems.

Textual conventions moved and languages spread for a variety of reasons. At all times, texts and their languages expanded with the currents of scholarship, diplomacy, commerce, and religion, as well as with deportees and military colonists. Others on the move, particularly immigrants arriving from peripheral locations (Bagg 2013, 122), also contributed to the dispersion of texts and the expansion of languages, usually in places where "the state's role was unfinished or unaccomplished" (S. Richardson 2010a, xxviii). Border areas not only were places of unrest but also served as sources for language change and text innovation (S. Rich-

ardson 2010b, 12–13). The movements of people, their languages, and systems of text production and use constantly introduced new ideas and practices. Not surprisingly, genres and literary conventions moved with them.

Types of Texts

A wide variety of texts and uses were available at the king's beck and call. The various administrative spheres required specific genres and functions of texts, many of which originated and were used outside the royal court in temples, even with private occupational and family use. The following text names, broader categories, and descriptions are self-explanatory. These data are based on rough approximations of form and content, and of function where they are known.

Archival texts. Because administrators relied on archives to preserve records of transactions, archival documents are far and away the most voluminous, and to ancient bureaucrats probably the most important written records. These include administrative lists and inventories, receipts, disbursements, accounts, business letters and memoranda, and private letters. Among the potentially limitless uses, letters authorized agents sent out from the royal court, the city gate, or wherever the king happened to be. Memoranda recorded administrative decisions, some awaiting further action, or, in a second text life, were saved as legal evidence for real property acquisition.

Legal documents. Contracts, title deeds, and wills served as documentary evidence for property transfer (Maidman 1979). Texts, although important, were not essential to recording contracts (Wilcke 2007, 12). Juridical documents such as lawsuits, witness lists, oaths, decisions, appeals, court declarations, and court memoranda all served the needs of the court (Hayden 1962, v–x). Law collections, although still not fully understood, appear to have provided legal guidelines, but often they served as monumental propaganda supporting the strategies and ultimately the reputation of the king and his administration.

Royal documents. Building inscriptions supported ritual processes such as consecration, purification, and dedication of public buildings, particularly temples, which served as terrestrial houses for the deities and the primary loci of human service (Hundley 2013a, 69). Many texts depicted the virtuous king as a master builder and in doing so eternalized the monarch's name and reputation. Composed at the original construction or repair of buildings, they usually were placed within the buildings of which they spoke (Hurowitz 1992, 27). Sometimes they were accompanied by drawings or figurines portraying the king hard at work building the temple. Figurines were made of bronze, gold, silver, stone, or clay, as was the case with inscribed cones, prisms, or cylinders, and could be accompanied by beads or other types of jewelry. Clay figurines protecting the home were buried beneath domestic buildings in services accompanied by rituals. Royal annals chronicled the exploits of kings. Royal land grants not only demonstrated property ownership with the authority of treaties but also provided propagandistic opportunities for the king. Decrees and edicts served as announcements with the force of law. Treaties at all levels of relationship resembled large-scale contracts. Diplomatic correspondence usually followed standard letter formats but included special greetings and identification formulas and required delivery by high-level official agents.

Chronological and related texts. Kings recorded their mighty acts, for example, major construction projects and military campaigns. These often serve as a relative dating schema and often functioned as royal propaganda. Date lists, king lists, and name lists also serve as chronological markers. Chronicles preserved the king's fortuitous ventures in self-laudatory terms intended to establish the king's reputation for posterity. The *Weidner Chronicle*, one of the oldest documents of its kind, reveals interests in the king's reputation for fortuity or calamity within a predictive framework (Arnold 1994, 138–42). Other historiographic documents served similar purposes.

Commemorative and monumental inscriptions. Though strange to modern notions of worship, votive statues served as representative worshipers in a temple adoring a god. Votive inscriptions were prayers that devotees offered through their votives. Funerary inscriptions served similarly as vicarious prayers to the god on behalf of the dead.

Liturgical and religious texts. Many types of texts played roles in ancient Near Eastern religion. Some of these were intended to facilitate worship in the form of music. Musical instruments used in Mesopotamian worship included strings, such as harps, lutes, and lyres; wind, such as flutes, double pipes, and panpipes; percussion, such as drums and cymbals; and various horns. Cult songs, hymns, and laments might be accompanied by musical instruments and sung by vocalists during worship services. Religious texts also included temple rituals and prayers.

Divination literature. Mesopotamians believed that a knowledge of the past enabled them to explain the present and better prepare for the future (Glassner 2004, xix). Deciding whether or not to take a particular action, such as go to war, was crucial for kings and other officials (W. Lambert 2007, vii). The need to consult the gods on important matters led to the use of procedures and devices. These revealed the gods' will through a variety of phenomena. Queries to know the future took on many forms. Prophecy, essentially abnormal human communication, took the form of messenger speech or letters. Using compendia of omens based on examination of animal entrails or the birth features of a fetus, kings could manipulate the gods for good outcomes in military, administrative, and even personal ventures and avoid bad outcomes (Leichty 1970, 7–20).

Rituals, oracle questions, and reports all supplied the inquirer with valuable counsel. Liver models served as compendia for interpreting animal entrails.

The Mesopotamian quest for future knowledge also entailed astrological and astronomical literature. Astronomical phenomena interpreted by specialists helped to manipulate the gods and secure good future outcomes. Omen compendia served as cataloged collections. To make decisions leading to fortuitous results, astrological reports, astronomical diaries, and astronomical tables and almanacs were employed, providing messages from the gods. To access the gods' powers, priests and other functionaries used exorcists' lore. They attempted to control the future through apotropaic and prophylactic rituals, charms, spells, and incantations. They also used prognostic and diagnostic omens, medical recipes and compendia, and calendrical omens, hemerologies, and almanacs. All these techniques promised to enhance fortuity and decrease calamity.

Texts supporting occupations. Many texts helped administrative officials and others to perform their work. For tasks requiring calculations, such as surveying, there were mathematical problem texts, numerical tables, and maps and plans. Specialists wrote technical manuals for craft-related activities and horse-training texts. Pedagogical texts, sometimes referred to as school texts, include sign lists, vocabularies, encyclopedic lists, glossaries, grammatical tables, commentaries and other scholia, and scribal exercises. Many of these texts made up curricula aimed to train scribes for roles within the administrative system.

Fine literature (belles lettres) includes mythological, epic, and narrative poetry. Some of the better-known texts are the *Epic of Gilgamesh* and the creation accounts, *Enuma Elish*, *Atra-Hasis*, and *Enki and Ninmach*. These stories did not exist only to satisfy interest in origins. They also served theological functions, such as explaining how Marduk became king of the gods, how the various temple communities gained their prestige, and what the pecking order between city-states should then be (Clifford 1994, 200–202). *Atra-Hasis* places humanity's participation in the cosmos in terms of human nature and function. The *Eridu Genesis*, a compilation of texts treating cosmology, attempts to explain how humanity became civilized and describes the creation of people and animals as well as the origins of cities, rituals, and kingship. The tale of *Enki and Ninmach* explains that people are sick and disabled and become elderly because of a dispute between two deities. Other forms of fine literature include literary hymns and devotional poetry, lyric and didactic poetry and prose, and wisdom literature. One theme in the *Epic of Gilgamesh* is the human concern for death and immortality, including the human desire for eternal life. Folk literature, including proverbs and fables as well as folk tales, often served utilitarian purposes. For example, the *Poor Man of Nippur* calls for a form of social justice by addressing the plight of the needy in the face of uninterested bureaucracy.[2]

2. This study is indebted for its text titles, classifications, and descriptions to the work of Andrew George (2007).

13

Egyptian Literature

Nili Shupak

U nlike the Hebrew Bible, no canon or defined corpus of ancient Egyptian literature exists.[1] Some scholars include within its scope all the texts discovered in archaeological excavations, including formulaic medical, mathematical, and magic texts.[2] The present discussion encompasses as broad a scope as possible of all the Egyptian literary material, discussing all those of a minimal length and coherent subject matter that reflect a measure of creativity, classified on the basis of literary form, content, style, and terminology.[3]

1. An abbreviated updated version of Shupak 2011 (in Hebrew), translated by Liat Keren; this material is used with the kind permission of Yad Ben-Zvi Press.
2. For the divergent approaches to the definition of Egyptian literature, see Baines 2003.
3. For a different categorization, based solely on literary form, see Posener 1951; 1952; cf. Lichtheim 1973–80, 1:3–12, 2:5–8, 3:3–10. The majority of the Egyptian literary corpus having survived only in later copies, no scholarly consensus exists regarding the composition date of many of the texts. Herein, I shall relate to the accepted view. For texts and translations, see Caminos 1954; Gardiner 1937; COS; Kitchen 1968–90; 1999; Lichtheim 1973–80; Sandman 1938; W. Simpson 2003. For commentary and general discussion, see Assmann 1992; Brunner

Religious Literature

The Mortuary Literature

This type of literature is designed to enable the deceased to make the transition to the world to come, warding off the dangers and calamities that might befall him or her. Its earliest example is the Pyramid Texts, inscribed on pyramid walls from the Fifth Dynasty onward (ca. 2300 BCE) to enable the king to reach the world to come safely and share Osiris's fate by dying and rising (Faulkner 1969). During the Middle Kingdom, such magic spells were extended to ordinary people, inscribed on their coffins, thus becoming known as the Coffin Texts (Faulkner 1977–78). Written on papyri buried in graves in the Eighteenth Dynasty (1550–1290 BCE), the *Book of the Dead* maintained the earlier tradition, also relating to people of nonroyal lineage (Faulkner 1985).

During the New Kingdom period, various works dealing with the world to come were

1966; Burkard and Thissen 2003; 2008; Loprieno 1996; Parkinson 1991a; 1991b; 2002; Posener 1951; 1952; Quack 2003; Quirke 2004. Unless otherwise noted, the quotations from Egyptian texts are my translation.

composed. Inscribed on tomb walls in the Valley of the Kings in Thebes, the most important are *That Which Is in the Underworld*, an account of the sun's journey through the netherworld; and the *Book of Gates* and the *Book of Caverns*, both of which outline the geography of the world to come, its occupants, and their deeds.

Theological Texts

An inscription belonging to Pharaoh Shabaka (Twenty-Fifth Dynasty, seventh century BCE; probably deriving from an earlier period, however) preserves the theology of Memphis, an important center for the worship of the god Ptah. Herein, Ptah creates the world by means of the "thoughts of his heart and the words of his mouth," resting afterward. This and other parts of Memphite theology closely correspond to the account of "creation by the word" in Genesis 1. In contrast to other Egyptian creation traditions, this is not a mythical account.[4]

Magic and Oracular-Apocalyptic Literature

Magic governed all areas of ancient Egyptian life. Usually performed by professionals—*ḥry-ḥb* (known as *ḥarṭummîm* in the Bible)—magic rituals were accompanied by various types of incantations. The best-known Egyptian magic books are Pap. Salt, which contains hymns and oaths, Pap. Chester Beatty VII, which includes spells against diseases and disasters, and Pap. Sallier IV, which details good and bad omen days.

Dreams were a means of communication with the realm of the gods, divining and predicting the future through dreams being common practice in Egypt. Two types of documents were prevalent: stories about dreams (see below) and collections of dreams and their interpretations. The most prominent of

the latter are Pap. Chester Beatty III (the Ramesside period, thirteenth century BCE) and Carlsberg Papyri XIII and XIV (second century CE). These contain hundreds of dream omens and their interpretation, written in brief and succinct style (Shupak 2006).

Another means of communicating with the gods was via oracles. These feature the apocalyptic literature that emerged in the Hellenistic-Roman period. Works such as the *Demotic Chronicle* and the *Potter's Prophecy*, composed under the yoke of a foreign regime, reflect political conflict and prophesy the disasters that would befall Egypt and its subsequent eschatological redemption (Blasius and Schipper 2002).[5]

Myths

Myths played a central role in ancient Egyptian daily life. That of creation was frequently cited in Egyptian literature, all its various versions being based on a common tradition according to which the world was formed by a single creator god out of primeval water or *nun*, which comprised all the elements of the world—both positive and negative. Creation was thus primarily an act of separation—light from darkness, fertile from infertile, the valley of the Nile from the wilderness, and so forth.

The Heliopolitan cosmogony held that the creator god was Atum, who fertilized himself and begot (spat out) the first pair of gods, who produced a long chain ending in the first ennead (Atum and four divine couples) (Faulkner 1969, 198, 246 [§§527 and 600]). The Hermopolis version maintains that the primeval waters were the abode of eight gods—the Ogdoad—who formed four divine couples, the males having frogs' heads, the females heads of serpents,

---

4. See "Myths" below.

5. Some wisdom texts from the Middle Kingdom period utilize the motif of foretelling but are not "prophecy" (cf. speculative wisdom literature below; for further discussion, see Shupak 1989–90). Conversely, priests spoke on behalf of the deity in direct address to the king in the royal cult, but such divine speech was not predictive (see Hilber 2011).

symbolizing the negative features of the primeval waters.

In a Roman period creation account found in the temple of Esna, Neith, the war goddess, forms the world in seven "creation by the word" acts, again recalling Genesis 1.[6]

In contrast to these creation myths that center around gods rather than human beings, the *Destruction of Mankind*—inscribed on royal tombs from the Ramesside period—deals with human fate. In response to their wish to rebel, the aged god Re decides to wipe out humanity by means of his eye—the sun—which assumes the bovine guise of Hathor for this purpose. Ultimately repenting of his decision, however, he saves the rest of humankind (cf. the stories of Adam and Eve of Eden and the flood; Gen. 3; 6:5–7; 7:23; 8:21–22).

The most seminal Egyptian myth was that of Osiris. It is not recorded in full in any extant Egyptian source, but Plutarch (first century CE) preserves the complete version. The good god Osiris and his evil brother Seth compete for the throne. Although Osiris is murdered by Seth, Isis, his loyal wife and sister, impregnates herself from his corpse and gives birth to Horus, who continues his father's struggle and wins.

Astarte and the Insatiable Sea (mid–Eighteenth Dynasty) recounts the combat between the gods and the covetous sea and has affinities with Mesopotamian, Canaanite, and Asia Minor myths. Allusions to this cosmic battle with the sea also occur in the Bible (Shupak 2006–7).

Historical Texts

Autobiographies

Autobiographical accounts, which help us reconstruct historical events and provide information regarding Egyptian ideas and beliefs, were inscribed on tomb walls and gravestones from the third millennium BCE through to the first centuries CE.[7] During the Old Kingdom period, they focused primarily on the deceased's professional career. In the New Kingdom period, following the emergence of a personal piety ideology that stressed the direct relationship between god and human beings, the autobiographies espoused the view that success and prosperity were totally dependent on the gods. Later on, the principal subject of the tomb inscriptions became the finality of death and the goal of finding pleasure in life (e.g., Taimhotep's inscription [Lichtheim 1973–80, 3:62–63]). In Hellenistic period autobiographies, wisdom ideology is prominent, a good example being the tomb inscriptions of the Petosiris family, whose head served as Thoth's high priest in Hermopolis (e.g., Sishu's inscription [Lichtheim 1973–80, 3:50]).

Royal Inscriptions

From the Middle Kingdom period onward, we find inscriptions commemorating the king's feats (Lichtheim 1973–80, 1:115–18; 2:12–13, 29–35, 57–78; 3:66–84). The "royal novel" lauds the monarch for his wisdom, reporting the decisions he took—many of which were of historical significance—and his achievements, such as construction (particularly of temples), military campaigns, and expeditions. The genre follows a fixed pattern: the king persuades his ministers to accept his plan, which is then approved by the gods via a dream or oracle and implemented. The earliest extant example (from the Middle Kingdom) depicts the erection of the Atum temple in Heliopolis by Sesostris I.

During the New Kingdom period, reports of wars and military campaigns became popular, as with the expulsion of the Hyksos by Ahmose (ca. 1550 BCE), preserved in the autobiography of one of his officials, and Thutmose III's military expedition to Asia and defeat of his enemies at Megiddo (ca. 1450 BCE). These

---

6. For creation myths, see Tobin 2001.

7. For autobiographies, see further Lichtheim 1988.

royal reports assumed three principal literary forms: annals based on the diaries of scribes who accompanied the king's expeditions, toponymic lists of conquered places, and poetic accounts of the events (e.g., Thutmose III's Gebel Barkal stele in Nubia).

The inscriptions from the El-Amarna period onward (fourteenth century BCE) reflect the close relationship of the king with the gods. The poetic account of Rameses II's battle at Qadesh, for example, attributes his victory to the assistance he received from Amun.

The stele of Merneptah, dated to the fifth year of Merneptah's reign (1208 BCE), commemorating the king's victory over the Libyans and their allies the Sea Peoples, is well known because it is the earliest extrabiblical source to refer to "Israel." The short poem at the end of the inscription lists Israel alongside the traditional adversaries of Egypt—the Hittites, Hurrians, Canaanites, and Libyans:

> All the princes lie prostrate, saying:
> "Shalom!" ("Peace!")
> No one among the Nine Bows [a traditional designation of Egypt's enemies] lifts his head.
> Libya is captured, Hatti is at peace,
> Canaan is plundered in all misfortune.
> Ashkelon is carried off, Gezer seized,
> Yanoam made nonexistent.
> Israel is wasted, bared of seed,
> Syria is become a widow because of Egypt. (Kitchen 1968–90, 4.19:2–8 [text])

Rameses III's inscriptions, in which he declares his faithfulness to Amun-Re, epitomize the trend of clothing historical events in religious garb, recalling the similar motif in the Bible of God's hand as the orchestrator of human activities. The stele of King Piye (Twenty-Fifth Dynasty, ca. 750 BCE), which recounts his defeat of Tefnacht of Sais, is particularly important for reconstructing the history of the Third Intermediate Period.

Accounts with a Historical Core

Exaggerated and imaginary stories frequently contain details of events undocumented in official historical sources. The *Story of Sinuhe* (Middle Kingdom period) tells the tale of a high official in the court of Amenemhet I who flees to Upper Retenu in the Biqaʿa (Bekaa) Valley following the king's assassination. It thus sheds light on second millennium Canaan; the description of the place in which Sinuhe makes his residence recalls the depiction of the Promised Land in Deuteronomy 8:7–8:

> Figs were in it and grapes,
> And more wine than water.
> Its honey was abundant,
> And its oil plentiful,
> All varieties of fruits on its trees,
> Barley was there and emmer. (B1 81–84)

In his autobiography, Thutmose III's commander-in-chief, Djehuty, recounts the capture of Joppa via a fraudulent trick (fifteenth century BCE). The report of Wenamun—a priest of Amun sent to Byblos during the reign of Rameses XI to bring back timber for Amun's boat—reflects Egypt's precarious position in Asia in the eleventh century BCE.

Folktales and Legends

Folktales were also popular in ancient Egypt. The tales of wonders performed by various magicians in *King Cheops and the Magicians* (Hyksos period, mid-second millennium BCE) may have inspired the biblical accounts of Moses and Aaron's contest with the Egyptian magicians (Exod. 7–8) and the dividing of the Reed Sea (Exod. 14:21–31).

The *Shipwrecked Sailor* (Middle Kingdom) tells the story of a seaman cast up on the shores of an exotic island, where he encounters a serpent god. Like the *Story of Sinuhe*, this tale is characterized by the protagonist's desire to return to his homeland and be buried there.

The *Tale of Two Brothers* (Nineteenth Dynasty) employs a motif found in many other texts from across the world, including the Joseph narrative (Potiphar's wife)—a young man's attempted seduction by another man's wife. The *Doomed Prince* (Ramesside period) treats the theme of human fate, recounting how a barren royal couple was granted a son cursed to die at the hands of a crocodile, serpent, or dog.

The *Dream of the Ethiopian Prince Tanutamun* (Twenty-Fifth Dynasty, 664–656 BCE) predicts his rule over all Egypt; the Sehel Stele (Ptolemaic period) recounts how Djoser (Third Dynasty, ca. 2700 BCE) brought to an end a seven-year drought by consulting a sage by the name of Imhotep (cf. Pharaoh's dreams and their interpretation in the Joseph story; Gen. 41).

A number of Ptolemaic-Roman tales (third and second centuries BCE) also recount wonders and miracle workings. These differ from their predecessors in forming a cycle pertaining to a specific figure rather than independent stories and in making use of motifs borrowed from Greek literature. The best-known tales from this period are the stories about Prince Setne Khamwas, the son of Rameses II, high priest of Ptah in Memphis and an exceptionally powerful magician.

Fables and Allegories

The genre of fables and allegories that began to emerge in the New Kingdom period revolves around a conflict between two protagonists—such as the *Dispute between the Head and Stomach*, and *Truth and Falsehood*. A unique group of hundreds of ostraca and a handful of papyri decorated with animal figures acting like human beings—most prevalent during the Ramesside period—depicts fables that probably were originally transmitted orally, some having been preserved in writing (Demotic and Greek), however (Shupak 1999).

Poetry

Egyptian poetry followed a standard meter and was accompanied by musical instruments. Written in high literary language, its stylistic features (repetitions, parallelisms, wordplay, assonance, images, etc.) resemble those of biblical poetry. It falls into two principal categories: poems of praise (hymns to the gods or the king) and poems for banquets and entertainment (harpers' songs and love songs).

Hymns to the gods began to emerge in the Middle Kingdom period, the genre reaching its peak during in New Kingdom Egypt. Accompanying the temple cult and festival rites, they are prefaced by a short introduction identifying the author, then proceed to portray the god and list his attributes, titles, and worship centers, then conclude with a laudation.[8]

The most popular was the hymn to the Nile flood god Hapy, who irrigated the fields and desert, providing people with wheat and barley. The hymn to the creator-god Re in the *Instruction Addressed to Merikare* (second millennium BCE) is exceptional in Egyptian creation traditions because it sets human beings center stage, everything being formed for their sake (cf. lines 131–38 [Lichtheim 1973–80, 1:106]). This is conceptually similar to the creation story in Genesis 2.

During the New Kingdom period, numerous hymns were penned to Osiris as lord of the underworld who died and rose. As Amun's status rose during this era, he merged with the head of the pantheon, Re. Hymns to Amun-Re were thence engraved on the walls of tombs—some extolling and lauding the god, others recording personal wishes. The best-known of these—engraved on the tombstone of the two twin brothers, Suti and Hor, during the reign of Amenhotep III (Lichtheim 1973–80, 2:86–89)—links Amarna period tenets with the preceding form of religion, the traits ascribed to Amun-Re here later being associated with Aten.

8. For hymns and prayers, see further Assmann 1975.

The *Great Hymn to Aten* is of great significance for understanding the religion of Aten introduced by Amenhotep IV, Akhenaten (1551–1334 BCE) (Lichtheim 1973–80, 2:96–99). Although based on traditional notions found in earlier hymns, it portrays Aten as a universal god worshiped by all people who acts alone without the aid or cooperation of other gods. Its presentation of the king as the sole teacher of the new religion is also revolutionary, the previous direct relationship between the individual and god now being mediated exclusively through the royal family: "You are in my heart, there is no other who knows you, except your son . . . whom you taught your ways and your power" (Sandman 1938, 95, lines 16–17).

Hymns to the kings extolling their deeds and qualities occasionally occur in stories or wisdom texts. The *Story of Sinuhe*, for example, contains an encomium to Sesostris I that almost certainly belongs to the propaganda produced by the royal court. Alongside hymns to the kings inserted into other genres, some also existed independently. The Kahun papyrus from Faiyum, for example, includes six hymns in praise of Sesostris III's victories in Nubia. A famous victory ode in honor of Thutmose III engraved on a tombstone in the temple of Amun in Karnak presents the god as responsible for defeating Pharaoh's enemies (Lichtheim 1973–80, 2:36–37).

Banquet and entertainment songs include Egyptian love songs, the majority of which date to the New Kingdom period. The words, spoken antiphonally by the young lovers, are erotic and at times also naive. Imbued with a sense of humor, they convey the here and now and hope of an eternal relationship.[9]

The harpers' songs—so called because they were engraved on tomb walls and tombstones alongside pictures of a harper—were particularly popular during the New Kingdom period. Forming part of the rites of the dead, they were sung at banquets and funerals, their principal message—*carpe diem*—being grounded in the belief that life is transitory and there is no afterlife. One of the most prominent examples of this genre is the song from the tomb of King Intef (Lichtheim 1973–80, 1:196–97).

The personal piety poems—customarily appeals for divine aid that reflect the spirit of individualism and humility that emerged in the New Kingdom period—closely correspond to the individual complaints or repentance psalms in the Bible. The prayer of Nebre to Amun-Re, for example, contains an encomium to the gracious and merciful god "who comes at the voice of the poor in distress" (Lichtheim 1973–80, 2:105–7).

Wisdom Literature

Like the autobiographical genre, the Egyptian wisdom corpus stretches from the Old Kingdom through to the first centuries BCE. In line with its biblical counterpart, it falls into two principal groups: didactic wisdom, designed for teaching and educational purposes; and speculative wisdom, addressing philosophical-moral issues (Brunner 1988; Vernus 2010; *COS* 1:61–68, 93–125; 3:321–26; Shupak 2016).

The wisdom instructions (*Lebenslehre*), known in Egyptian as *sb3yt* (comparable to Hebrew *musar*), form part of the first class. Usually taking the form of a father's advice to his son, they served as a type of textbook for the use of high-ranking courtiers. They are distinctive for their identification of their author—a king, vizier, or scribe—writers generally being anonymous in ancient Egypt.

The most complete early instruction to have survived is the *Instruction of Ptahhotep*, a vizier of the Fifth Dynasty who gave advice to his son/heir in relation to diverse fields—various types of relationships, behavior in diverse situations, and ethics.

---

9. For an encompassing investigation of the Egyptian love songs and their affinities with Song of Songs, see M. Fox 1985.

The majority of the Middle Kingdom period books of instructions are imbued with a political tone, two being attributed to kings and two lauding the monarch. The *Instruction Addressed to Merikare*, probably composed by Khety III of the house of Herakleopis (second millennium BCE), largely consists of advice based on the pharaoh's royal experience. Its reference to the judgment of the dead and the significance it attributes to offering sacrifices to the gods and burial preparations exemplify its religious tone, however. Two passages are particularly noteworthy: (1) the statement "The character (or 'loaf of bread') of the righteous-hearted is more acceptable (or 'better') than the ox of the evildoer" (line 129) is exceptional in Egyptian literature, recalling the classical prophets' belief that ethics is more important than ritual (cf. Isa. 1:11–17; Amos 5:21–25; Mic. 6:6–8); and (2) the hymn to the creator-god Re, who created the world for the sake of the human race, which evokes the account of the formation of man in Genesis 2. The *Instruction of Amenemhat I*, the founder of the Twelfth Dynasty, also addresses his son, but it is imbued with bitterness resulting from the attempt made on his life.

Some special books of instructions from this period—the *Instruction of the Loyalist* and the *Instruction of a Man to His Son*—encourage the king's subjects to serve and obey him. Both are pieces of royal propaganda.

The New Kingdom period instructions include the *Instruction of Any*, a collection of sayings relating to proper behavior. The conclusion contains a unique dispute between Any and his son over the possibility of attaining knowledge, the son arguing that a person who lacks the necessary talents can never be educated. Any contends that everyone is capable of learning, students merely needing to be trained like animals (B22,17–23,7; Shupak 2014, 260–62).

The *Instruction of Amenemope* (Twentieth and Twenty-First Dynasties, 1100–1000 BCE) is now well known because of its affinities with Proverbs. Like the *Instruction of Any*, it is a scribe's advice to his son. Although it resembles previous instructions in both form and content, it is distinctively divided into thirty chapters, each headed by a number. Amenemope is imbued by a spirit of personal piety that finds expression in an ethical tone and its representation of god as sovereignly responsible for human fate.

In later instructions the Ramesside language is replaced by Demotic, and their structure is also changed. The *Instruction of Onchsheshonqy* (fourth to third centuries BCE) is composed of two parts, a narrative frame and a collection of short sayings. The narrative, which recalls the *Story of Ahiqar*, recounts how Onchsheshonqy was thrown into jail due to his ostensible involvement in a plot to assassinate the king, whence he writes instructions to his son relating to everyday life. The work is infused with a religious tone, yet it is cynical and utilitarian. A deep religious sense and recognition that the gods govern human fate also occurs in the Demotic instruction known as Papyrus Insinger.

Most of the Egyptian speculative wisdom texts were composed in the Middle Kingdom period, which brought to an end the anarchy that erupted in Egypt in the wake of the collapse of the Old Kingdom. The imprint of these events is evidenced by a series of common motifs: a description of the vicissitudes of the times, socioethical and sometimes also religious reproof of the generation, and a depiction of future redemption by a king-deliverer. All these are addressed in the six poems that comprise the *Admonitions of the Egyptian Sage* (or the *Admonitions of Ipuwer*). The *Prophecies of Neferti*, given by a priest-magician of that name to King Snefru, climax in an account of the salvation to come through the hands of a king called Ameni (Amenemhat I), who will right all the wrongs detailed in the initial description.

The best known of these sources is the *Dialogue of a Man with His Soul* (Ba), in which a man—who closely corresponds to Job—seeks to end his life, struggling with his *ba*, which endeavors to dissuade him from committing this act.

In the *Eloquent Peasant*, the protagonist directs nine complaints to Rensi, the high steward, from whom he demands a fair trial. Addressing contemporary social corruption, this is written in a high literary language and is laced with proverbs and similes from daily life (e.g., B1 lines 92–99, 247–50; Lichtheim 1973–80, 1:173, 179).

Grievances also form a central feature of the *Complaints of Khakheperre-Sonb*, composed by a priest in Heliopolis. Although Khakheperre-Sonb seeks to be original and innovative rather than traditional and repetitive ("Would I had unknown phrases, Maxims that are strange, Novel untried words, Free of repetitions, Not maxims of past speech, Spoken by the ancestors" [recto 1–3]), his account of the present day exhibits the customary insights.

Textbooks

In the Middle Kingdom, the ancient Egyptian school system began to expand, educational institutions opening their doors to children of the middle class as well as the scions of the upper class. This led to increasing need for didactic literature, with two works being written expressly for this purpose. *Kemit* (*The Complete*), one of the earliest textbooks in the world, is written in hieratic and adduces examples of diverse writing styles. The *Instruction of Khety*, who was a scribe, contains the words of a father to his son in traditional form. Its opening part is unusual, however. Known as the *Satire of the Trades* and composed in a high literary language and graceful humor, this exalts and extols the scribal profession by comparing its light working conditions with the burdensome nature of others. Becoming hugely popular, it even left its stamp on Ben Sira (Sir. 38:24–39:15).

A group of Ramesside school textbooks comprises letters from teachers to pupils,

correspondence between scribes, various instructions and admonitions for students, and material serving as school exercises (Gardiner 1937 [text]; Caminos 1954 [translation]). The best-known letter in this collection is that of a scribe named Hori to a colleague (Pap. Anastasi I). Seeking to expose his colleague's boorishness, he employs typical Ramesside rhetoric, using images, wordplay, scorn, and irony:

> You have come (to me) loaded with
>   great secrets;
> You told me a wisdom-saying of
>   Djedefhor;
> (But) you do not know whether it is
>   good (positive) or bad (negative),
> What chapter comes before it or after it.
>   (11, 1–2) (Fischer-Elfert 1983, 97)

Djedefhor, known as the author of a wisdom instruction (Lichtheim 1973–80, 1:58–59), belongs to a circle of eight prominent Egyptian scribes whose works formed the school "canon" during the Ramesside period. Gaining a worldwide repute, their names are immortalized in Pap. Chester Beatty IV (from the same era):

> As for the learned scribes . . .
> Their names remain forever. . . .
> They did not make for themselves pyra-
>   mids of copper and steles of iron,
> They were not able to leave heirs in chil-
>   dren. . . .
> The instructions are their pyramids,
> The reed-pen their child,
> And the surface of the stone their wife.
>   (verso 2, 5–9) (Shupak 2001)

The great Egyptian scribes of the past thus won fame and recognition, becoming cultural heroes on the strength of their spiritual legacy—their books, scrolls, instructions, and wisdom sayings. As we have seen, their compositions broadly attest to the subjects of interest and thought patterns of the ancient Egyptians across diverse areas of life.

14

Hittite Literature

Alice Mouton

Hittite Anatolia was a powerful kingdom that prospered between the seventeenth and the end of the twelfth centuries BCE (fig. 14.1). We know quite a lot about this kingdom thanks to the thirty thousand cuneiform tablet fragments uncovered in Hattuša/Boğazkale, the capital city (see fig. 14.1). The great majority of these tablets are written in the Hittite language, but other languages are also present: Akkadian, Sumerian, Luwian, Hattian, Palaic, and Hurrian. The first question we should ask ourselves is: What is Hittite literature and does it even exist? There are three main views on this question: (1) some scholars believe that anything written is basically literature (V. Haas 2006); (2) others consider any text with a narrative (Beckman 2009) or any text that has been duplicated (van den Hout 2002)[1]

literary in nature; (3) a third group of scholars prefer a more restricted definition that includes only texts resulting from an expressive elaboration—namely, mythological compositions, prayers, and historical texts (Güterbock 1978; Archi 1995).

Thus the very definition of Hittite literature is still largely debated, and there is no consensus about it. This can be easily explained by the fact that the Hittites themselves did not have a word for "literature." The categories that they considered were royal annals (Hittite *pešnatar*, "manly deeds"), prayers (*arkuwar*, "pleas"), invocations (*mugawar*), songs (SÌR), rituals (SISKUR), and cultic festivals (EZEN₄) (Hutter 2011). If "literature" is taken as synonymous with *belles lettres*, only the very specific category of Hurrian songs can be unequivocally called "literary," as it is the only genre without any immediate practical use in the Hittite cultural context. However, not only

---

1. Thus literature would also include divination treatises, scholarly texts (such as lexical lists), laws and diplomatic texts, and festival and ritual texts. The structure of Hittite treaties has been compared to biblical formulas such as are found in the Decalogue or the Holiness Code (see, e.g., Fensham 1963; Matthews and Benjamin 2006), but this structure itself could have been at least partly

inherited from older models (see, e.g., the Old Assyrian treaties [Veenhof 2013]). Concerning possible religious links between Hittite Anatolia—through the Hurrians—and the biblical world, see, for example, Janowski, Koch, and Wilhelm 1993; Schwemer 1995.

Fig. 14.1. Map of Anatolia

the Anatolian mythological compositions but also the prayers and the historical records do show some expressive elaboration. They will, therefore, also be included in this overview.

In Hittite Anatolia, literature was produced by scribes eager to demonstrate their talents in cuneiform writing as well as their knowledge of Mesopotamian models. The prestige of Mesopotamian literature haunts the land of Hatti, as it is deeply rooted in Hittite scribal education. Some Mesopotamian literary texts were imported to the Hittite capital city to serve as models for the Hittite scribes who copied and translated them into Hittite (Klinger 2012), other Syro-Mesopotamian literary compositions were transmitted orally to the Hittite scribes (Archi 2007), and even Hittite historiography started with Akkado-Hittite bilingual tablets. This being said, Hittite scribes managed to develop literary models of their own, and many Hittite literary texts denote a subtle mixture of non-Anatolian and Anatolian features (Singer 1995).

Historical and Pseudohistorical Records

"Historical" records include several rhetorical and stylistic figures that can be viewed as literary (de Roos 2001; Hoffner 2013; Andrew Knapp 2015). They do not present objective facts but adopt, on the contrary, the king's viewpoint. Furthermore, several of these texts combine historical events with legends. For instance, it is generally admitted that the so-called *Tale of Zalpa* (Hoffner 1998, 81–82; Holland and Zorman 2007) is a subtle combination of mythological and even folkloric motifs with historical events. The tale narrates the birth in the same year of thirty baby boys by the same mother, the queen of Kaneš (the archaeological site of Kültepe; see fig. 14.1). Dismayed by this unnatural event, the queen decides to abandon the newborns on containers that she launches on the river. This is a very widespread literary motif in the ancient Near

East that appears not only in the Old Testament (Moses) but also already in Mesopotamian literature (Sargon of Akkad). As with Moses and Sargon, in this Hittite narrative the abandoned children will not die but will be protected by the gods and even raised by them. They spend their childhood in the city of Zalpa in northern Anatolia (see fig. 14.1).

Sometime after she gives birth to her sons, the same queen of Kaneš gives birth to thirty baby girls in the same year. This time, she decides to keep the babies and to rear them herself. When the thirty brothers grow up, they decide to look for their mother. They travel through the city of Tamarmara, where someone tells them that the queen of Kaneš has given birth to thirty girls at once. They immediately understand that such an extraordinary birth, so similar to their own, has occurred from the same mother. When they arrive at Kaneš, their mother does not recognize them because the gods have changed their appearance. The queen plans to marry her daughters to the thirty brothers, and several of the brothers are about to accept this union, but the youngest brother recognizes the thirty girls as his sisters and warns his brothers that they are about to commit incest. This myth is generally viewed as a narrative of the origins of the Hittite royal dynasties. The motif of abandoning the boys to rear only the girls reminds us of the Greek myth of the Amazons, who were described as Anatolian.

The *Apology of Hattušili III* is a self-justification of Hattušili's coup d'état. Starting the narration from the time of his birth, the great king demonstrates in detail how his personal goddess Šaušga of the city of Šamuha chose him to rule on the throne of Hatti. A passage states, for example, "The goddess Šaušga (of) the city of Šamuha claimed me to my father, (while I was) still a little child, so that my father offered me at the goddess's service. As I started to experience the goddess's favor, thanks to the goddess, (it) was going better and better for me." As a boy, Hattušili's health is very fragile. Šaušga claims Hattušili to his father through a dream of his, promising a long life for his son in exchange for his serving her.

Myths and Legendary Narratives

In the libraries of the temples or of the royal palace of Hattuša, several mythological texts were uncovered. Hittite scribes collected Hattian narratives as well as foreign compositions. Syrian, Mesopotamian, and Hurrian myths were translated into Hittite. We know Akkadian, Hittite, and Hurrian versions of the *Epic of Gilgamesh* and Akkadian and Hittite versions of *Atra-Hasis*. Mythological texts of the Hittite corpus can be divided into two main groups, as follows.

The Anatolian Myths[2]

These compositions come from the Hattian cultural background. Most if not all of them were recited as invocations in ceremonial contexts. For instance, the myth of the moon god who fell from the sky was recited during a ceremony to perform "when the storm god thunders frightfully."

The *Myth of Illuyanka* belongs to this group. It is documented by several tablets dating to the Imperial period (thirteenth century BCE), but its Hittite language is older. The beginning of the composition states that this myth—at least in its first version—was recited during the great *purulli* festival of the city of Nerik. This cultic festival was celebrated in honor of the storm god. The composition is subdivided into two narratives separated by a double paragraph line. These two narratives most probably have a distinct origin, but they were written together because they both deal with the monstrous serpent called Illuyanka. The scribe Pihaziti compiled them on the same tablet, thus reporting the words of Kella, an anointed priest of the storm god of Nerik.

2. See Hoffner 1998, 9–39.

This differentiated origin explains the discrepancies that can be observed between the two narratives. For instance, in the first version Illuyanka lives in a hole in the ground, whereas in the second version he lives in the sea. However, these two narratives share a common motif: the gods manage to defeat the monstrous snake only thanks to human help. The *Myth of Illuyanka* describes the battle between the Hattian storm god and the serpent Illuyanka. One might realize that through this battle, it is a battle opposing heaven to the underworld that is taking place. For this reason, some scholars thought that this battle symbolized the seasonal cycle, but other hypotheses have also been put forward. The serpent subjugates the storm god a first time, and the storm god plans his revenge. In order to help him, his daughter the goddess Inara organizes a feast to which she invites Illuyanka and his children. During the feast, the snake becomes drunk, thus allowing Inara and her human lover Hūpašiya to bind his limbs. Then the storm god can easily kill him.

The continuation of the first narrative focuses on the goddess Inara and the mortal Hūpašiya. After their common fight against Illuyanka, Inara wants to keep her human lover for herself. She forbids him to contact his wife and children. The close relationship that the mortal entertains with the goddess makes him a special being who is irremediably segregated from the rest of humanity. In this way, Hūpašiya represents the archetype of the Hittite great king. The fact that Hūpašiya is not authorized to look through the window symbolizes a strict separation between the world of the gods (the goddess's house where he is coerced to stay) and that of humans (what he sees through the window).

The second narrative relating to Illuyanka describes the victory of Illuyanka over the storm god. During the fight, the storm god loses his heart and his eyes. Too weak for recovering his organs on his own, he asks for help from one of his sons, that son being conveniently married to Illuyanka's daughter. As his son-in-law, the storm god's son goes and asks Illuyanka for his father's heart and eyes. As Illuyanka is bound to his son-in-law by the system of dowry and bride wealth, he agrees to give back the storm god's organs. As soon as he gets his heart and eyes back, the storm god goes to battle against Illuyanka. A similar motif occurs in the ancient Greek myth of the great serpent Typhon. At that point of the narrative, an unexpected incident happens: the storm god's own son takes Illuyanka's side, refusing to betray his father-in-law. The storm god is further confronted with the tragic choice of killing his own son or letting his enemy live.

The *Myth of Telepinu* belongs to a group of compositions narrating the disappearance of various deities after an anomaly has occurred. The identity of the vanishing deity varies: it could be the sun deity, the storm god, the tutelary deity, the mother goddess, or Telepinu, who is an agrarian god and the son of the storm god. The myth of Telepinu is known in three different versions. They describe the departure of the agrarian god after he becomes angry. His departure provokes fog that enters every house. As the god takes with him the prosperity of the land, all living creatures become barren.

On the occasion of a feast organized by the sun deity, the storm god notices the absence of his son and supervises searches to find him. The sun deity first sends the eagle, whose acute glance is legendary, but the eagle cannot find Telepinu. The storm god goes and looks for his son in person, but he is unsuccessful as well. The mother goddess comes up with the solution: in spite of the storm god's mockery, she sends the bee after Telepinu. The bee exhausts itself in looking for Telepinu but finally manages to find him. The bee stings Telepinu's hands and feet to wake him up.

In one version of the myth, the composition includes ritual incantations of analogical magic, as well as invocations. The goddess of magic, Kamrušepa, intervenes in the ritual process; she tries to placate Telepinu. Finally, Telepinu agrees to go back home and to resume his protection of the land. The game bag that Telepinu used to transport all the sources of the land's prosperity is described at the end of the composition. It is comparable in some aspects to the aegis of ancient Greek mythology.

The Hurrian Myths[3]

Unlike the Anatolian myths, the Hurrian myths do not seem to have any cultic or ritual usage. It is quite likely that these compositions were considered to be literary texts that contributed to the training of the Hittite scribes.

Although the Hurrian myths are known to us in their Hittite translations, traces of oral transmission are still perceptible. For instance, several sentences are repeated in the beginning of the first song of the *Cycle of Kumarbi* (called the *Song of Emergence*), and this repetition reminds us of a sort of refrain that the storyteller would use to help in remembering the story. The designation of all these myths as "songs" is significant in itself. Furthermore, some scholars have shown that a certain versification existed in these compositions.

The *Cycle of Kumarbi* is a group of mythological narratives revolving around the fight between the old netherworld god Kumarbi and the Hurrian storm god Tešub. Tešub manages to take the divine throne for himself, thus vanquishing Kumarbi. The latter develops several stratagems for getting his throne back. All these narratives probably originate from Hurrian Syria and were imported in Hittite Anatolia later on. The order of the songs composing the *Cycle of Kumarbi* could be as follows:

1. The *Song of Emergence*: this song narrates the time of the first divine kings, as well as the time when Tešub supplanted Kumarbi on the divine throne in the sky.

3. See Hoffner 1998, 40–80.

2. The *Song of the Tutelary God*: this god takes Tešub's throne by force but is himself overthrown and then killed.

3. The *Song of Silver*: Silver is a son of Kumarbi and a mortal woman who becomes the new king of the gods. He is overthrown later on for having perturbed the cosmic order.

4. The *Song of Hedammu*: Hedammu is a gigantic sea serpent born from the union between Kumarbi and the daughter of the sea god. Hedammu is sent by Kumarbi to overthrow Tešub. Šaušga, Tešub's sister, manages to seduce him and make him drunk so that her brother Tešub can kill him. Some patterns of this composition can be compared to the Illuyanka myth.

5. The *Song of Ullikummi*: this narrative describes the birth of an ever-growing stone monster[4] who is the offspring of Kumarbi and a rock. As it is blind and deaf, it is not seduced by Šaušga's charms, unlike Hedammu. Ea, the god of wisdom, finds the way to defeat him: as Ullikummi grows endlessly, thanks to his physical contact with the Atlas-like god Ubelluri who carries the sky, Ea cuts Ullikummi off Ubelluri, thus disabling his growth. Tešub can easily defeat Ullikummi after he has been so weakened.

In the *Song of Emergence*, the first Song of the *Cycle of Kumarbi*, the text describes the first divine kings who ruled in the sky. The netherworld god Alalu was the first king in the sky. His cupbearer was Anu, a celestial god who supplanted him and became the new king of the gods after him. Anu's cupbearer is the netherworld god Kumarbi, who challenges his master Anu, just like Anu had challenged his own master Alalu before him. Kumarbi becomes the next king. In this succession of

divine kings, one can notice the alternation of netherworld and celestial gods on the throne.

The fight between Kumarbi and Anu is fierce. During that battle, Kumarbi cuts off and swallows Anu's genitalia. But he is thus not as victorious as he thinks he is: he becomes pregnant with Anu's offspring. The song narrates the successive births, all very painful. Among the newborn deities are the storm god Tešub and his twin brother and vizier, Tašmišu. Thus, by mutilating Anu, Kumarbi seals his own doom without knowing it, as Tešub will be his challenger. Several literary motifs of this song are analogous to those found in ancient Greece in the *Theogony* of Hesiod. One of those motifs is the mode of Tešub's birth: just as the Greek goddess Athena gets out of Zeus's head after a long and painful process, Tešub also emerges from Kumarbi's head, whose skull has been cut open. The unbearable pain felt by Kumarbi was predicted by his enemy Anu, who told him, "In the end you will smash your own head into the Tašša mountain!" Once baby Tešub is out of his skull, Kumarbi attempts to devour him, but a third party replaces the newborn god with a stone, so that Kumarbi hurts his teeth while trying to eat Tešub. This reminds us of the Greek god Chronos, who also swallows a stone instead of his son Zeus.

The *Song of Kešši* is another Hurrian myth. It is known in both Hittite and Hurrian versions. We also know a fragment of a tablet in the Akkadian language belonging to this composition; this fragment was uncovered at the Egyptian site of Tell el-Amarna (the capital city of Pharaoh Akhenaten). The story narrates the misfortune of the hunter Kešši, who has committed a fault toward the gods by neglecting them for the benefit of his wife. Unable to find any game, Kešši becomes sick and then receives seven symbolic dreams expressing the gods' anger. The Hittite version ends with Kešši's mother interpreting his seven dreams. Several aspects of this episode of Kešši's dreams remind us of Mesopotamian literary compositions,

4. For comparison with Dan. 7–8, see R. Gane 2008a.

among which is the *Epic of Gilgamesh*. The *Song of Kešši* is a mixture of Hurrian and Syro-Mesopotamian literary motifs, and the scribes who translated it into Hittite might have added their own touch as well.

The *Song of Release* is a bilingual text (Hurrian-Hittite) that contains several mythological narratives and fables imported from the Hurrian world (Neu 1996). Each of the seven fables carries a pedagogic message, like the fables of Aesop. One of these fables deals with a coppersmith and his cup, which curses him, a motif that might have several echoes in the Old Testament (Chavalas 2011, 154).[5] Another of these fables is as follows:

> Leave that story! I will tell you another story. Listen to (its) message! I will tell you a wisdom-tale:
>
> A deer. It was grazing the grass that (was) beside a watercourse. (However), he was also coveting the grass that (was) on this side. (However), he could not approach the grass of (this other) side, he could not reach this (side)!
>
> It is not a deer: (it is) a person. That man that his lord had made district governor, they had made him governor of that district. (However), he was coveting a second district. The gods took a wise decision regarding that man: he could not approach that district, he could not reach (that) second district.

The *Song of Release* is most probably a poetic Hurrian composition that was secondarily translated into Hittite. Note that the scribes of Hattuša seem to have tried to render in the Hittite version the poetic traits of the Hurrian original composition (Francia 2010).

Prayers and Hymns

Prayers

Prayer texts are generally parts of ritual or cultic events. As the identity of an angry deity

is seldom known, many prayers are addressed to divine intercessors—namely, sun deities. The solar deities are the perfect intermediaries in such cases, as they are in the sky during the day but spend the night inside the earth, so that they meet the celestial, the terrestrial, and the netherworld deities. Furthermore, the solar deities generally officiate as supreme judges, as they can see everything from the sky. Prayers can be addressed to any god on many different occasions—to placate one or several deities, to prepare for war (one asks for the gods' protection or curses the enemy), in the context of a cultic festival (one asks for the god's benediction over the royal family), among other events.

Most of the prayers are royal in nature: they are addressed by the Hittite great king himself or, more rarely, by a close relative. Once written down, the prayer is sometimes read aloud on a regular basis by a scribe. Several allusions also indicate that these prayers often were uttered by the great king in the context of a public ritual.

Hittite texts designate prayers by three different terms:

1. The noun *arkuwar*, "plea," has a legal connotation. In such prayers, the supplicant is the defendant who tries to convince the gods that he has extenuating circumstances and should therefore be forgiven. He tries to move the gods who are his judges by embracing their viewpoint (as in Psalms [P. Sanders 2007]).

2. The term *mugawar* or *mukeššar*, "invocation, petition," is the designation of the myths of the disappearing deities such as Telepinu.

3. The noun *walliyatar*, "praise," is used of prayers that exalt the gods.

These three categories often are combined in one and the same composition.

Some texts of prayers go back to the Old Kingdom (seventeenth–sixteenth centuries

---

5. For another fable compared to Deut. 32, see Wikander 2013.

BCE), while others date to the sixteenth and fifteenth centuries or the end of the Imperial period (fourteenth–thirteenth centuries).

Hymns

Hymns often are translations of foreign compositions. Several compositions exalting the gods are translations from Mesopotamian models. Some have even been directly imported from Syria or Mesopotamia. We also know of a trilingual text (Sumerian-Akkadian-Hittite) that illustrates the great interest of the Hittite scribes in Mesopotamian literature.

Several Hittite translations of a Mesopotamian hymn to the sun god have been uncovered. Parts of it have been included in the *Prayer of Prince Kantuzzili*, as well as in the following passage: "Life is bound up with death for me and death is bound up with life for me. A mortal is not alive forever, the days of his life are counted. If a mortal were to live forever, it would not be a grievance to him even if illness, the bane of man, remained." This passage is a calque of an Old Babylonian hymn written in Sumerian (C. Metcalf 2011, 174).

Be it historical or pseudohistorical literature, myths, or prayers, several Hittite literary motifs seem to have their counterparts in biblical literature. The motif of looking through the window and thus witnessing an offense that is being perpetrated is one of them (Christiansen 2007), as well as that of placing a newborn child on his father's knees as a sign of official recognition (Hoffner 1968, 201n27), among others.

15

Ugaritic Literature

WILLIAM D. BARKER

Ugaritic is a Northwest Semitic language named after the ancient city of Ugarit. It uses a consonantal alphabet, but unlike other West Semitic alphabets, it is written on clay tablets in cuneiform (Huehnergard 2012, 1). Ugaritic is also distinct from other languages that use cuneiform scripts attested throughout the ancient Near East, which often use hundreds of signs, while Ugaritic employs only thirty signs in its alphabet. As Ugaritic texts continue to be translated, new research is conducted, and new commentaries on the Ugaritic literature are written, Ugaritic continues to be a language of vital importance for the study of both the ancient Near East and the Hebrew Bible. Its relevance for biblical studies is quite significant because of the rich resources Ugaritic provides in, among other fields, comparative studies. Some prime examples of the importance of Ugaritic literature for comparative studies can be found in linguistics, socioeconomic contexts, and religious texts.

Discovery, Decipherment, and Nature of the Texts

In 1928 a farmer, Mahmoud Mella az-Zir, was plowing his fields near the coastline of modern-day Syria. The tip of the farmer's plow struck a stone in the field, and he subsequently attempted to remove the stone from the field. In doing so, he found the entrance to an ancient tomb. Within the tomb he discovered a number of artifacts, and he proceeded to sell them to an antiquities dealer (Craigie 1983, 7; M. S. Smith 2001b, 14). Shortly thereafter, as word of the artifacts spread, the area was investigated and brought under the supervision and archaeological excavation of a team led by the prominent French archaeologist C. F. A. Schaeffer, from 1929 to 1939. As the site was expanded to include the nearby Tell Ras Shamra, a number of artifacts, including clay tablets with cuneiform writing, were discovered (M. S. Smith 2001b, 14). Some of these tablets have since been discovered with texts in "Akkadian, Sumerian, Hittite, Hieroglyphic Luwian, Hurrian, Egyptian, and Cypro-Minoan" (Huehnergard 2012, 2). However, most of the clay tablets discovered featured an otherwise unknown cuneiform script. By 1930, three scholars—H. Bauer, E. Dhorme, and C. Virolleaud—deciphered the cuneiform alphabet, which we now know as Ugaritic (C. Gordon 1965, 1). Then, in 1940, after ten years of research by some of the world's leading Semitic grammar scholars, Professor Cyrus H. Gordon produced a landmark publication: the first Ugaritic grammar. This ultimately launched decades of robust comparative research of the Ugaritic language and literature and biblical studies (M. S. Smith 2001b, 28–34). Additionally, the texts discovered at Ugarit are now recognized as comprising a variety of different types, or genres, which include (1) literary and religious texts (e.g., mythology, epics, ritual, hymns, medical texts, and incantations), (2) common letters and royal correspondence, (3) legal and juridical texts, (4) economic and trade texts, (5) scribal exercises, (6) inscriptions, and (7) unclassified and fragmentary texts. Additionally, a number of texts remain unpublished. All these genres, and others, form the basis for the numbering system employed to identify and reference the various clay tables (*KTU* ix–x).

Comparative Research in the Fields of Biblical and Ugaritic Studies

Early in the history of research into the Ugaritic language and literature, there was a tendency to maximize the use of Ugaritic for biblical studies. As a result, some of these earlier efforts have been criticized as overly enthusiastic, ultimately coming to be known as "parallelomania" (Sandmel 1962, 1–13). This was perhaps nowhere more prevalent than in the case of Mitchell Dahood and his study of the book of Psalms (Dahood 1965–70). Dahood perceived so many grammatical parallels between specific Ugaritic texts and Psalms that both his methodology and his conclusions remain highly debatable. As a result, he likely had a negative impact on the inclination of scholars in biblical studies to make use of Ugaritic (M. S. Smith 2001b, 159–65). At the same time, Dahood "showed a talent for identifying items in the Masoretic Text that require further examination, and at times he spurred other scholars to more judicious assessments" (M. S. Smith

2001b, 165). Since then, there has been a pronounced reticence among the scholarly community to risk engaging in "parallelomania." Unfortunately, this has resulted in a degree of minimizing valid parallels, refraining to present or explore potentially valid hypotheses, and ignoring "informative correlations" (*COS* 3:xxxvii). This reactionary strain of scholarship has thus been termed "parallelophobia" (Ratner and Zuckerman 1986, 52; *COS* 3:xxxvii). Hopefully, both of these problematic approaches will eventually result (or, are perhaps now beginning to result) in progress toward a more principled and methodological hermeneutic (e.g., see *COS* 1:xxiii–xxviii; *COS* 3:xxxv–xlii). Meanwhile, the current trends in Ugaritic studies are to value Ugaritic texts in their own right apart from contributions to biblical studies. Yet, across both disciplines, there is a simultaneous acknowledgment of the need for greater methodological caution than was present in the early days of Ugaritic studies, as well as a recognition that the various shared features of lexicon, grammar, and literature between Ugaritic and Hebrew will continue to have value and produce valuable scholarship.

Examples of Comparative Research between Ugaritic and Biblical Studies

As has already been noted, since the discovery and decipherment of Ugaritic, its inestimable value for biblical studies has been recognized. Major examples of this include comparative and contrastive research in grammar, poetry, philology, and cultic ritual studies. Each of these categories of study usually has included a sustained effort to correlate certain aspects of the Ugaritic texts with specific verses or chapters from the Hebrew Bible. As there are a significant number of these examples, which readily illustrate the value of this comparative research between Ugaritic and biblical studies, the ones presented here are limited to some of the most significant for linguistics, socioeconomic contexts, and religious texts.

Shared Linguistic Affinities

As both Ugaritic and Biblical Hebrew are Northwest Semitic languages, the vocabulary, semantic domain, syntax, and overarching grammatical structure of Ugaritic share a substantial amount of commonality with Biblical Hebrew. This, in turn, has helped to assist in the interpretation of a number of difficult passages in the Hebrew Bible (Greenstein 2010). As Professor Simon Parker once noted, "Ugaritic represents better than any other second millennium language or literature the antecedents of the language and literature of ancient Israel" (S. Parker 1989, 225). The impact upon scholarship resulting from the linguistic affinities between the two languages may be more specifically demonstrated in terms of uniquely shared grammatical features and parallel word pairs.

In terms of grammatical character and traits, John Huehnergard, a prominent Semitic language expert, offers a good introductory summary:

> Among many other BH [Biblical Hebrew] features elucidated by Ugaritic may be mentioned the following:
>
> - the enclitic particle *mem* . . . probably attested in several BH passages, such as . . . Ps 29:6;
> - the asseverative proclitic particle *l-* . . . [in] for example . . . Ps 119:91;
> - the use of the prepositions *bə-* and *lə-* in clauses in which they must be translated "from";
> - the tense–mood–aspect system of the Northwest Semitic verb, much of which was still in force in early Hebrew.

Ugaritic vocabulary has contributed in many ways to our understanding of the Hebrew lexicon. An example is the identification of a new BH root *ḥrš*, and the separation of the noun *ḥārāš* "craftsman" (original Semitic root √*ḥrs*) from the root *ḥrš* meaning "to plow, engrave" (originally √*ḥrθ*). . . . Among many biblical phrases that have been reinterpreted in the light of Ugaritic is [the description found in] . . . Ps 86:5, which has been compared with . . . "cloud-rider," an epithet of the Ugaritic storm-god Baal. (Huehnergard 2012, 10–11)

As the late Umberto Cassuto observed, "The vocabularies of two dialects belonging to the same linguistic group, like Hebrew and Ugaritic, naturally have many words in common" (U. Cassuto 1971, 20). While this is true, "What is less common, and therefore more important in establishing literary backgrounds and shared traditions, is the phenomenon of parallel word pairs" (W. Barker 2014, 177). W. G. E. Watson helpfully offers the accepted criteria for defining parallel word pairs and indicates the important connection to the Ugaritic literature:

> Parallel word pairs can be recognized as such if they fit the following requirements: 1) each must belong to the same grammatical class (verb, noun, etc.); 2) the components must occur in parallel lines; 3) such word-pairs must be relatively frequent. . . . Although it has long been known that Hebrew poets used a selection of stock word-pairs, it was not until scholars had studied Ugaritic literature that they became aware of the extent to which such word-pairs actually occurred . . . because Ugaritic poetry, too, used a whole range of parallel word-pairs; not only that: a high percentage of these pairs are identical with Hebrew word pairs. . . . Further, correct recognition of word-pairs can have consequences with respect to textual changes and meaning. (W. Watson 1984, 128–29, 141)

Such parallel word pairs have been instrumental in analyzing the common Semitic origins of various passages in the Hebrew Bible, such as Ecclesiastes 12:5–6 and Psalm 74:13 (W. Watson 1984, 130–44). The role of parallel word pairs has also contributed to understanding the background of texts such as Isaiah 24–27 and portions of the Ugaritic Baʿal Cycle. In this last case, strikingly, the Hebrew and Ugaritic texts also share an identical narrative progression, similar themes, and the same deities, spirits, and/or monsters (W. Barker 2014, 51–170, 177–97, 208–12).

Context and Socioeconomic Data

Among the hundreds of texts found written in Ugaritic (over 1,500 of them), many of the legal and economic texts are collectively referred to as "administrative texts." These many accounts and records offer insight into the everyday lives of the people of Ugarit during the late Bronze Age. The commercial transactions recorded in these texts offer examples of things such as the prices of goods, livestock, and services; the varying qualities of wine and oil; and the types of livestock kept and sold. Even the average prices of certain goods and livestock—and to whom they were sold—during particular time frames can be discerned as a result of these texts. There are also a handful of legal texts and approximately one hundred letters of correspondence (Huehnergard 2012, 5). As the city of Ugarit was located in close northern proximity to the land of ancient Canaan, these texts furnish us with comparative data for biblical studies. Additionally, the evidence of Ugarit as a politically autonomous commercial power is extensive, especially as it pertains to Ugarit-Egypt relations (e.g., Curtis 1985, 9–24; Giveon 1981, 55–58; Singer 1999, 627). Furthermore, there is also significant archaeological and textual evidence of Ugarit's relationships with various portions of Canaan (e.g., Owen 1981; Teissier 1990, 71; *KAI* 14, 2:23; *KAI* 26, 2:43; Keel and Uehlinger 1998, 177–282; Nocquet 2004, 289–330, 347–70; Köckert 2010). As Huehnergard observed, "The culture and society of the Ugaritians were similar in many respects to those of the Canaanites who inhabited Pal-

estine at the end of the Late Bronze Age and the early Iron Age, the period purportedly described in the biblical books of Joshua, Judges, and Samuel. . . . The Ugaritic letters and administrative texts present a vivid picture of life in a large Levantine city in the period just before the beginning of the kingdom of Israel" (Huehnergard 2012, 10). While one must be careful and principled in any effort to understand the interpretive impact of these various data points, there is ample evidence to suggest that many of these administrative, legal, and correspondence texts can inform our understanding of particular biblical words, phrases, and passages. This is best evidenced by many of the contemporary commentaries on the Scriptures, which take measured and careful account of the Ugaritic literature on a case-by-case basis.

Parallels between the Hebrew Bible and the Religious Literary Texts of Ugarit

Some of the most important texts found at Ugarit are classified as epic poems (or mythological epics). Other Ugaritic religious texts include deity lists, incantations, and rituals. Each of these provides meaningful data on the religion of Ugarit. Our limitations here preclude a fuller discussion of the deity lists, incantations, and ritual texts. However, it will suffice to say that these provide important information about Canaanite deities, as well as Ugaritian religious beliefs, cultic rites, and even "medical" practices interwoven with religious or cultic themes (e.g., one thinks of the [in]-famous recipe for a hangover in a tale about the god El's drunken stupor). Among the epic poems of Ugarit are the *Tale of Aqhat*, the *Legend of King Kirta*, and the Baʿal Cycle. Of particular importance for biblical studies is the Baʿal Cycle.

The Ugaritic texts provide the written accounts of the Baʿal myths. These formed the basis of the Baʿal cult, which persisted in the western half of the Fertile Crescent in one form or another from the kingdom of Ugarit, through the days of the kingdoms of Israel and Judah, and into syncretism with other religions in both the late Egyptian dynasties and the Talmudic period. Consequently, these texts are vital for understanding religion and ritual at Ugarit, as well as providing the cultural and religious background to a large number of texts in the Hebrew Bible. Chief among these are passages that discuss the god Baʿal or followers of the Baʿal cult in ancient Israel (e.g., Judg. 6:25, 28, 30–31; 1 Kings 18). There also appear to be a number of instances in the Hebrew Bible in which Baʿal imagery from the Ugaritic texts is creatively adapted to honor Yhwh instead of Baʿal (e.g., Ps. 29:10; 104:3) or to condemn the worship of Canaanite deities, including Baʿal, while extolling the supremacy of Yhwh (e.g., Isa. 24:21–23; 25:6–8; 26:13–19; 27:1). It would be quite difficult to fully state the importance of the Baʿal Cycle and other texts in the Ugaritic literature related to Baʿal for biblical studies.

In addition to those deities appearing in the Baʿal Cycle, throughout the Ugaritic literature there is a significant number of deities and figures who appear in biblical references, allusions, puns, or adaptations. Such possible parallels should be robustly investigated and debated, and, in fact, the majority of scholars in both Ugaritic and biblical studies recognize a spectrum of interpretive options. This spectrum ranges from possible but highly debatable parallels (e.g., Dan'el and Ezek. 14; 28) to the very probable direct quotation of the text in *KTU* 1.5 I 1–3 in Isaiah 27:1. Further, even the most skeptical scholars would acknowledge that there are a number of definite biblical references to the deities of the Ugaritic literature. A few of the most often cited Ugaritic deities, monsters, and figures, together with some common citations in the Hebrew Bible—whether definite, probable, plausible, or merely possible references (!)—are listed below (Michael Williams 2012, 14–22):

- ʾEl (cf. Ezek. 28:2; Ps. 48:1–2; Gen. 14:18–22; 33:20);
- Baʿal (e.g., Judg. 6; 1 Kings 16–18; 2 Kings 10–11, and passim; cf. Ps. 68:5; Isa. 26:13–19; and various theophoric place-names);
- Mot (e.g., Isa. 25:6–8; Job 18:12–13; cf. Prov. 27:20; Hab. 2:5);
- Athirat/Asherah (e.g., Deut. 7:5; 16:21; 1 Kings 15:13; 18:19; 2 Kings 21:7; 23:4, 7; cf. 1 Kings 16; 18–19);
- Litan ("Leviathan," e.g., Isa. 27:1; Ps. 74:13–15; 104:26; Job 3:8; 26:13; 41; cf. Gen. 3; Rev. 12:3);
- Rapaʾūma ("Rephaim," cf. Deut. 3:11; Isa. 14:9; 26:13–19);
- Shapshu ("Shapash," cf. Isa. 24:21–23);
- Yamm (e.g., Ps. 74:13–14; cf. Ps. 114:1–5; 1 Kings 7:23–26);
- Anat (e.g., theophoric personal and place-names in Judg. 3; Neh. 10; Josh. 19; 21; cf. 1 Sam. 31:8–10);
- Dan'el (cf. Ezek. 14:14, 20; 28:3).

Conclusions

The Ugaritic language and literature are of preeminent importance for the study of the Hebrew Bible. Inquiries into the Ugaritic tablets and texts and their relationship to biblical studies have also formed a significant portion of the field of comparative studies for nearly a century. The tension between "parallelomania" and "parallelophobia" has likely served as a catalyst fueling the current trend in seeking a more principled hermeneutic for comparative research. Because of the linguistic affinities and shared Canaanite literary traditions with Biblical Hebrew, Ugaritic has helped illuminate the understanding of several difficult lexemes and passages in the Hebrew Bible. Common stock phrases, parallel word pairs, and evidence of significant parallels (e.g., themes and motifs and narrative progression) between the Ugaritic literature and the Hebrew Bible continue to provide a wealth of linguistic and interpretive insight. The Ugaritic letters and administrative texts provide significant insight into life in ancient Canaan. This includes extensive textual resources for socioeconomic data concerning northern Canaan during the late Bronze Age and early Iron Age. Not least of all, the Ugaritic epic poems and religious literature serve as the most substantial source of textual information about Ba'al and the Ba'al cult. In conclusion, one must resoundingly agree with the assessment of the eminent W. F. Albright, who famously noted, "Every student of the Old Testament would do well to work on Ugaritic."

16

Northwest Semitic Inscriptions

MARGARET E. COHEN

What Is Northwest Semitic?

Northwest Semitic is part of the Semitic language family and includes the ancient languages of Ugaritic, Phoenician, and Hebrew. There are two main models for understanding the relationships among the members of the Semitic language family. In the standard "tree" model (the Stammbaum theory), from the precursor, Proto-Semitic, branches with their own history of evolution separated. The Stammbaum model was promoted by Robert Hetzron in the 1970s and has remained generally well regarded, though with various emendations in recent decades.

But languages develop both vertically and horizontally (Geisler and List 2013). Even though we speak of a sort of Semitic language tree with "branches" or "parents," it is important to remember that these languages interacted with one another. The second model, the "wave" or dialect geography model, is perhaps best exemplified by W. Randall Garr's 1985 work, *Dialect Geography of Syria-Palestine, 1000–586 BCE*. In this model, the horizontal relationships between the languages are

acknowledged, and the result is a continuum of various dialects rather than a vertical, genetic evolution.

Geographically, Semitic languages extend from Mesopotamia in the (north)east and the Arabian Peninsula and Ethiopia in the south(west). The Northwest Semitic languages belong to the region of the Levantine littoral and span a period from the third millennium BCE to the modern day. Students of more than one Northwest Semitic language will begin to see the relationships within this family immediately by the presence of numerous cognates, or words with shared origin. Sometimes cognates may come to have different meanings as their role in a particular language evolves, but their common etymology is usually discernible. So, for example, we find *bayit* in Hebrew, *bitu* in Akkadian, and *bet* in Phoenician, all meaning "house."

For the reader who is used to dealing with the biblical text in its familiar modern publication forms, a few points about the terminology of inscriptions and their study may prove useful. The writing system of Northwest Semitic

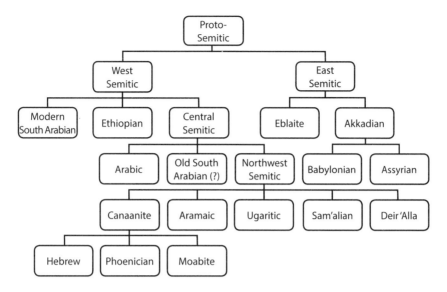

Fig. 16.1. Example of a "tree" model (after Rubin 2008, 62)

uses characters to denote phonemes (i.e., units of sound) and is therefore alphabetic. It is technically called an "abjad" since the graphemes (i.e., the written units) represent consonants and not vowels. The Northwest Semitic script is generally attributed to the Phoenicians, who standardized it, and this alphabet became the basis of adaptation for a number of other related scripts. The Northwest Semitic scripts were used, of course, in the writing of inscriptions of all sorts, and epigraphy is the study of the form and placement of letters written in ink or inscribed into clay, stone, or other materials. The epigrapher must decipher the form of the incisions or marks in order to identify the letters that they represent and so is the first to offer other scholars the physical reading of the letters and words of an ancient inscription. Closely related to the epigrapher's work is that of the paleographer, who studies the scripts in order to understand the diachronic development of the written language. In the absence of other chronological data, such as archaeological provenance, it is the paleographer's ability to identify the evolution of characters and their place in time that allows for dating. Other types of analyses also support the study

of inscriptions, including chemical and physical analyses, which can provide information about the actual material (clay, stone, metal, etc.) on which the text is written; onomastics, the study of proper names and the cultural information they encode; anthropologic theories on the nature of literacy and scribal traditions; comparative linguistics; and many others.

Thus far in this section, the reader has reviewed the literatures of various Near Eastern peoples, and these have included narrative prose, poetry, and other types of documents. While we are fortunate to have the array of Northwest Semitic inscriptions that we do, we also must recognize the challenges specific to working with inscriptional data. It is certainly the case that we have many examples of inscriptions with dozens of lines, from which we garner a good deal of textual data. But it is also true that many inscriptions are very short texts and may or may not have much surrounding context. Sometimes inscriptions are only a few letters or have only been partially recovered due to the fortunes of the archaeological record. Sometimes these inscriptions are of a known type or genre, such as a funerary dedication or a financial transaction, and knowledge of

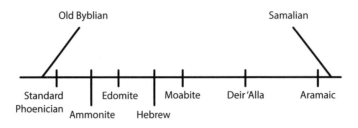

Fig. 16.2. Example of the dialect continuum model (after Garr 1985, 231)

these types sometimes allows for plausible reconstruction of missing words or lines. In many other cases, though, we have no hope of recovering missing lines. And though our corpus of inscriptions is always growing with new discoveries, we must recognize that Northwest Semitic scholars are working with a limited data set, both in terms of quantity: the total number of extant words and forms in known inscriptions; and in terms of quality: the range of topics and information from everyday life that known inscriptions cover. We are limited in many ways: by not having direct access to the spoken language; by not having access to the language of different classes, genders, and social locations; and by not knowing to what degree scribes who wrote inscriptions represent the "real life" language of nonscribes—that is, regular people. Though we have a number of inscriptions written in Northwest Semitic languages, and our understanding of the languages and their cultural contexts has grown considerably over the last two centuries, it is important to bear in mind what material we are still missing. The nature of inscriptions also, sadly, predisposes them to nefarious activity, and students of this discipline must continue to combat the damage caused by forgeries and other antiquities crimes.

Survey of Northwest Semitic Inscriptions

We turn now to representative examples of inscriptions in the major Northwest Semitic languages described above. Because they are addressed in detail in other chapters of this book, Ugaritic and Hebrew examples are not included here. By necessity, the selection here is brief, but even this limited set of examples will provide evidence of the geographic and chronological scope of Northwest Semitic, as well as highlight some inscriptions that are of particular interest to biblical scholars. First, we consider Canaanite examples in Phoenician and Moabite, then some Aramaic material, and finally inscriptions in the languages of the ancient kingdom of Sam'al, modern Zincirli in southeastern Turkey, and of Deir Alla, a site in Transjordan near the debouchment of the Zarqa (Jabbok) River. We treat these languages here as distinct branches of the Northwest Semitic family tree, even while acknowledging close linguistic overlap with both Canaanite and Aramaic features.

Phoenician

Ahiram. The Ahiram Coffin is an artifact on which we find the oldest connected and readable Phoenician inscription, dated to the tenth century BCE (Rollston 2016, 17). The relatively short, two-line inscription states that the sarcophagus was made for Ahiram by his son, Ittobaal, and that anyone who upsets the coffin will suffer—by losing his status, his power, his kingdom. While this inscription is rather basic, it provides important information for epigraphers due to some of the specific details of the letter shapes, and for historians it provides some insight into the treatment of the dead, and specifically the treatment of dead royalty. "[This is the] coffin which Ittobaal, son of Ahiram, king of Byblos, made for Ahiram, his father, when he placed him in the house of eternity"[1] (line 1). We learn something of the role of a son—that is, that he may be responsible for providing proper burial accoutrement—and, in the next line, something of the belief in what may befall those who tamper with the dead: "Now, if a king among kings, or a governor among governors or a commander of an army should come up against Byblos and uncover this coffin, may the scepter of his rule be torn away, may the throne of his kingdom by overturned and may peace flee from Byblos. And as for him, may his inscription be effaced" (line 2). The threat of losing one's political power and perhaps that of his family line is touted here as a devastating blow. Students of the biblical text will find the intense concern over losing the staff of one's judgment (*htr mshpth*) familiar, as well as the power of the threat of existential erasure. Compare the wiping out of his inscription here (*ymh sprh*) with the idea of wiping out one's name in the Hebrew Bible (e.g., *ymmhw mspr* in Ps. 69:28).

Arslan Tash. From Arslan Tash comes a small limestone plaque on which is carved several figures and an inscription written in an Aramaic-style script with mixed Aramaic and Phoenician forms (Garr 1985, 220; Gibson 1971–82, 3:79–80). The inscription is a kind of incantation directed against evil spirits, imploring the night demons to pass away from the house of the supplicant, and is dated to the seventh century BCE. This inscription has

caught the attention of some scholars because it contains a number of phrases and lexical pairs that are quite akin to examples in the biblical text, such as *bny 'lym* ("sons of gods") and *shmym/'rts* ("heaven/earth").

Further, the Arslan Tash inscription employs the style of poetic couplet commonly found in the Hebrew Bible, where two verses are paired in parallel lines of rhythm and meaning.

> The house I enter you shall not enter
> And the courtyard I tread you shall not tread. (lines 5–8)

Perhaps most provocatively, some have interpreted the relationship obligations between Assur and "us" in this inscription as a parallel to the covenant relationship language used in the Hebrew Bible (Ramos 2015; Zevit 1977). While this may seem an attractive parallel, caution is warranted as the term *'lt* in the incantation covers a more diverse semantic field than simply "covenant" (Brichto 1963, 22–71).

> Assur had made an eternal pact with us
> he has made (it) with us, and all the sons of the gods. (lines 9–11)

Certain details of the inscription do find parallel with biblical material. The language from this inscription, *krt ln 'lt lm 'shr krt ln* (lines 9–10), recalls the biblical "cut a covenant" (e.g., Gen. 15:18, *krt . . . brt*). Additionally, the parties of the agreement share similarities: Assur and "us" in the Arslan Tash inscription, and Yahweh and "us" in the biblical examples (e.g., Deut. 5:2). Divine witnesses are called, be they heaven and earth in Deuteronomy 30:19 or the "sons of the gods" in this inscription. And finally, like the injunction in Deuteronomy 6:6–9 to place these instructions (i.e., the terms of the covenant) on one's doorposts, the inscription here also understands doorposts to have a special, perhaps apotropaic function. The doorposts (*mzzt*) in the Arslan Tash inscription represent safety and the successful

---

1. All translations and line numbers of inscriptions are taken from Gibson 1971–82 unless otherwise noted. This handbook is an excellent starting point for English-speaking students of the ancient Near Eastern world who are looking for technical information on each inscription, as well as side-by-side original language and translation. Other important resources are *KAI*, whose identification numbers are still the standard way to refer to many inscriptions (e.g., the Ahiram Coffin is *KAI* 1); Hoftijzer and Jongeling 1995; Ahituv 2008; *COS*; and the West Semitic Research Project at the University of Southern California (http://wsrp.usc.edu/index.html).

passing over of any evil spirits in the dark of night.

> It has arrived at my door and has
> thrown light on the doorposts; the
> sun has risen! (lines 22–26)

Indeed, the small, pierced tablet itself may have hung on a doorjamb.

The inscription from Arslan Tash is clearly meant to record some sort of incantation against unwanted demons, but in doing so it also preserves a wealth of data on how its owner may have understood the nature of a divine covenant and the deity's obligation to protect his faithful from all manner of threats.

Yehaumilk. Yehaumilk dates to the middle of the fifth century BCE and is a long inscription on a limestone stele that also has images of two figures (Gibson 1971–82, 3:93–99). This inscription deals with changes made to the temple of the goddess of Byblos during the Persian period. Yehaumilk's dedication of his new architectural items reminds us of the intimate connection in the ancient world between the deity's sanctioning the ruler (e.g., "I . . . whom the lady, Mistress of Byblos, made ruler over Byblos" [lines 1–2]) and the ruler's reciprocating with building projects for the deity (examples in this inscription include an "altar," a "winged disk," a "gateway," a "portico," "pillars," "capitals," and a "roof" [lines 4–6]). Two gates are described in this inscription, one belonging to the lady and the other belonging to Yehaumilk, providing us with an indication of a sacred precinct that contains both royal and religious edifices.

> And I made for my lady, Mistress of Byblos
> . . . this gateway of gold which is opposite
> the gateway of mine. . . . (lines 3–5)

Such a spatial combination is familiar both in the biblical text and in the archaeological record of Bronze and Iron Age Levant (S. Johnston 2004, 551).

Moabite

Mesha. The Mesha Stela is detailed elsewhere in this book (see ch. 36 below), but it must be mentioned here as the preeminent example of Moabite language available to us at this time. It recounts the successes of the Moabite king against the Israelites. The style of the inscription is reminiscent of the historiographic accounts of kings in the biblical text and royal annals from across the ancient region.

Ataruz. Recent excavations at Khirbat Ataruz, near Dhiban in Jordan, have recovered a stone pedestal with an inscription of seven lines, which the excavator and epigrapher date to the ninth century BCE. That preliminary descriptions of the epigraphy and language indicate the inscription is written in Moabite and perhaps even in a "national script" means that the Ataruz pillar may support the claim in the Mesha Stela that Mesha took the city of Atarot (Khirbat Ataruz) from the king of Israel.[2]

Early interpretation of the inscription suggests that each of the first three lines contain this structure:

$$\text{numeric} + mn \text{ (“from”)} + \text{lexeme}$$

The numerals are in hieratic (an Egyptian script) and are large values. Since the pillar was recovered from a cultic space at the site, it is reasonable to conclude that the numerals refer to the amounts of various offerings.

If the Ataruz inscription can help corroborate the information in the Mesha Stela, we are forced to reconcile the seeming disparity between the Moabite version of events and that of the biblical text in 2 Kings 3. Here we

2. At the time of writing, publication of the *editio princeps* is imminent, but the inscription has until now only been preliminarily described for the Department of Antiquities in Jordan and presented at scholarly meetings. The best source of information currently is provided by the epigrapher at http://www.rollstonepigraphy.com/?s=Ataruz.

see a fine example of the complexity of ancient historiography accessed through both the biblical text and the archaeological record.

Aramaic

Tell Fekheriya. Discovered in the 1970s, this inscription preserves a bilingual text in Akkadian and Aramaic on a basalt statue of a dressed figure. The life-size statue dates to the ninth century BCE, and the two dedicatory inscriptions to Hadad are found on the front (Akkadian) and back (Aramaic) of its tunic skirt (Greenfield and Shaffer 1983; Gropp and Lewis 1985). The Akkadian seems to be the basis for the work, perhaps based on a previous dedicatory inscription from Guzan, and the Aramaic is offered as a kind of supplement, perhaps to adapt the inscription for this statue to be dedicated in Sikan (Gropp and Lewis 1985, 56).

> The statue of Hadd-yith'i king of Guzan, and of Sikan, and of 'Azran, for the . . . and dominion of his throne, . . . and for the lengthening of his life, and that the utterance of his mouth be pleasing to gods and to me, he made this image more splendid than before. Before Hadad, who resides in Sikan, lord of the Habur, he set up his statue. (lines 12–16, Gropp and Lewis 1985 translation)

Besides characteristics like the composite nature of this inscription and its historical implications, the prominent use of the terms *dmwt* and *tslm* typically draws scholarly attention. This pair, of course, is recognizable from its use in the biblical text (e.g., Gen. 1:26; 5:3). The two terms appear to be used in Tell Fekheriya interchangeably to refer to the statue—for example, in lines 1, 12, 15, and 16. The context and usage patterns in this inscription seem to suggest that the two terms can easily serve the same semantic fields, and this may be evidence against the suggestion that in the biblical text the two terms represent opposing aspects—that *dmwt* denotes some

sort of metaphysical, dynamic image while *tslm* refers to a concrete, static copy (Gropp and Lewis 1985, 47).

Zakkur. A stele erected by the king of Hamath, Zakkur, contains a badly preserved relief and an inscription of some forty-seven lines (Gibson 1971–82, 2:6–17). This stele likely was erected in the early to mid-eighth century BCE and records the success of Zakkur against a siege of his capital, Hadrach, by a coalition force of petty kings.

> Then Barhadad son of Hazael, king of Aram, organized against me an alliance of [six]teen kings . . . all these kings laid siege to Hadrach. (lines A.4–9)

The early eighth century BCE saw a wounded Damascus trying to recover from a defeat by the Assyrians and Assyrian occupation. During this same period, the biblical accounts of Jehoash of Israel (2 Kings 13:25) and Jeroboam II after him (2 Kings 14:25) claim this was a time of Israelite territorial acquisitions in the same region.

Beyond its historical circumstances, the Zakkur inscription is written with well-developed literary imagery. Particularly striking is the author's repeated use of a hand motif: "my hands to Baalshamayim" (line A.11); "by the hands of seers" (line A.12); "the tradition of my hands" (line B.15). He concludes with the perpetual concern for the "name of Zakkur" (line C.2). The combination of these literary tropes is evocative of the biblical turn of phrase *yd wshm* (e.g., Isa. 56:5), which also expresses the concern over memory and memorializing.

> I have set up this stele and written on it the tradition of my hands so that whoever effaces the tradition of my hands, of Zakkur king of Hamath. . . . (line B.14–17, my translation)

Tel Dan. This inscription is discussed in detail elsewhere in this book (see ch. 37 below), but its significance within the corpus of Northwest

Semitic inscriptions must be noted here as well. The discovery of the first piece of the Tel Dan Stele was immediately recognized as a critical datum in our understanding of the political history of ancient Israel. An Aramaic inscription, on several slabs found in secondary use, the incomplete stele was made famous because of its extrabiblical citation of the phrase "house of David" (*bytdwd* [line 9]). Further information offered in the inscription suggests that it was erected by Hazael in the late ninth century BCE, or possibly his son Bar Haddad II (Halpern 1994).

Sefire. From Sefire, in Syria, come three Aramaic inscriptions dated to the eighth century BCE. These inscriptions detail treaties between various petty kings of the ancient polity of Arpad (Fitzmyer 1967). The treaties are significant because they include numerous details concerning the characters, both human and divine, involved in the agreements, the terms of treaty, the consequences for violation, and the actions involved in ratification. The treaties share format and content with Hittite and Assyrian treaties, as well as with biblical material dealing with covenant agreements. There is a lengthy numeration of the humans and gods who witness the treaty.

> This treaty, which Barga'yah has concluded . . . in the presence of Marduk and Zarpanit . . . in the presence of Shamash and Nur, in the presence of Sin. . . . (I, lines 7–9)

Further, a series of curses is described as punishment for anyone who violates the treaty. The language is reminiscent of the curses included in Deuteronomy 28 for violation of Yahweh's commandments.

> Let him (Hadad) pour out upon Arpad hail[stones]; seven years let the locust devour; seven years let the worm devour; seven [years] let blight [come up] over the face of its land; let no grass sprout, nor anything green be seen. . . . (I, lines 25–28)

There is debate regarding the power dynamic between the parties of the agreement: Do they enjoy a parity? Is one a vassal? Regardless of the exact relationship, the language of the agreements and the vivid depiction of the curses are striking. The extent to which these treaties concern themselves with the relationship between the actions of a man and that of his son, grandson, and other descendants is substantial.

> Or to your son or to a descendant of yours or to any of the kings of Arpad, and speaks against me or against my son or against my grandson or against my descendant . . . (III, line 1)

We see in Sefire III almost every permutation of antagonism of one relation against another, and the description of the responsibility of each generation to the other is reminiscent of biblical iniquity punishments (e.g., Exod. 34:7; Deut. 5:9).

The Language of Sam'al

Panammu. Three monumental inscriptions from Zincirli in southeastern Turkey provide us with evidence for the place of the ancient Sam'alian language in the Northwest Semitic family (Garr 1985, 231). A large statue of Hadad from Zincirli contains a lengthy inscription commissioned by Panammu, seemingly connected to the erection of his tomb. The inscription is dated to the first half of the eighth century BCE.

> I am Panammu, son of QRL, king of Y'DY, who has raised this statue for Hadad . . . whatever I grasped with my hand . . . cultivated; and whatever I asked from the gods they used to give to me. . . . In my days command was given . . . to establish cities and establish towns; and to the inhabitants of the villages my authority extended. (lines 1–10)

This period of freedom and general prosperity is the same in which Jeroboam of Israel and Uzziah of Judah enjoyed their long and successful reigns. In this text Panammu is coming to the end of his life and reign, and he expresses concern over whether his successor will ascend to the throne peacefully and, perhaps most urgently, whether his memory will be preserved. In lines 15–18 he beseeches the god, if his son should sit on the throne and do proper sacrifice to this Hadad and remember the soul of Panammu and tend it properly, that the son should be looked upon favorably.

> If (however), [any] of my sons should grasp the scepter and sit on my throne as king over [Y'DY] and maintain power and do sacrifice [to this Hadad, and should not] remember the name of Panammu . . . with wrath may Hadad confound him . . . may he not allow him to eat because of rage, and sleep may he withhold from him in the night, and may terror be given to him. (lines 20–24)

Kuttamuwa. A finely crafted basalt stele from Zinjirli was recovered in 2008 with both text and iconography (Struble and Herrmann 2009). Dated to the late eighth century BCE, the inscription concerns a man named Kuttamuwa (KTMW) and his care in the afterlife. The stele was found in context with various vessel offerings paralleling the vessel offerings depicted in the iconographic representation.

Much scholarly interest in this inscription surrounds the use of the term "soul" and how the text demonstrates a belief in the existence of disembodied souls (R. Steiner 2015, 11–22).

> I am KTMW, servant of Panamuwa, who commissioned for myself (this) stele while still living. I placed it in an eternal chamber and established a feast (at) this chamber: a bull for Hadad Qarpatalli, a ram for NGD/R ṢWD/RN, a ram for Šamš, a ram for Hadad of the Vineyards, a ram for Kubaba, and a ram for my "soul" (NBŠ) that (will be) in this stele. (Pardee 2009 translation)

We see the typical reminder of the role of sons and descendants in caring for the father and other ancestors, as well as a description of the desired types of foods for offerings. All these motifs serve as points of comparison for similar concerns in the biblical text as well as other regional literatures.

> Henceforth, whoever of my sons or of the sons of anybody (else) should come into possession of this chamber, let him take from the best (produce) of this vine(yard) (as) a (presentation)-offering year by year. He is also to perform the slaughter (prescribed above) in (proximity to) my "soul" and is to apportion for me a leg-cut. (Pardee 2009 translation)

The Language of Deir Alla

Balaam Son of Beor. In 1967 an inscription was discovered at the site of Deir Alla in modern-day Jordan. The writing, dated to the eighth century BCE, was inked on the plaster surface of a wall, though the plaster fragments were recovered having already fallen (Hoftijzer and van der Kooij 1976). Groups of these fragments were combined to reveal a lengthy inscription that details the divine visions delivered to the seer Balaam, son of Beor, widely understood to be the prophet known from Numbers 22–24. When the inscription was first published—and indeed even now—the scholarly consensus was that the language must be some "mixed" form of Canaanite and Aramaic, and the predominant question is only whether it should be described as Canaanite with Aramaic features or Aramaic with Canaanite features. The better interpretation (Huehnergard 1989; Garr 1985; Rubin 2008) is that this language is its own category of Northwest Semitic and represents an otherwise unattested but distinct "branch."

In this inscription, we are introduced to Balaam, who is privy to divine knowledge delivered to him in visions:

> The sa]ying[s of Bala]am, [son of Be]or, the man who was a seer of the gods. Lo! Gods

came to him in the night [and spoke to] him according to these w[ord]s. Then they said to [Bala]am, son of Beor, thus: "Let someone make a [ ] hereafter, so that [what] you have hea[rd may be se]en!" (combination I, lines 1–2, McCarter 1980 translation)

The frightening vision leads Balaam to weep and fast and recount the disasters that await at the hands of the heavenly council. This council is described as "the Shaddayin" (combination I, line 6), which recalls one of the epithets of the deity in the Hebrew Bible, "El Shaddai" (e.g., Gen. 17:1; 35:11) or just "Shaddai" (e.g., Job 21:20; Isa. 13:6). The style and content of Balaam's pronouncements include a number of motifs that will be familiar to students of the Hebrew Bible and other related literatures, such as the rejection of the prophet (combination II, line 9) and the desolation of death (combination I, lines 6–14). Perhaps only an interesting coincidence, but students of the Bible will also recall the use of plaster-covered stones for the inscription of the law in Deuteronomy 27.

17

Hebrew Inscriptions

JUDITH M. HADLEY

Introduction

The steadily growing corpus of ancient Hebrew inscriptions (inscriptions written in the classic Hebrew script of the ninth through sixth centuries BCE) is a valuable resource for our understanding of ancient Israelite religion and the Hebrew Bible. Through these inscriptions we have a window into the already established milieu of religious thought and culture that gave rise to the biblical texts. The inscriptions are relatively few in number; we have no huge archives from Israel and Judah from the preexilic period as we do from earlier periods elsewhere in the Levant. Hebrew inscriptions come in many forms: incised in stone, metal, or pottery; impressions in clay (bullae) or on pottery made using incised seals; or writing with ink, most commonly on pottery pieces (ostraca) but also on plaster, papyrus, or walls. The content of the inscriptions also varies: tomb inscriptions, letters, prayers and poems, graffiti, narratives, or nonliterary weights, receipts, or names of people or places, mostly from seals and seal impressions (see Hadley 2005, 366).

Literacy

Opinions differ substantially on the significance of the quantity of inscriptions for the degree of literacy in Iron Age Israel and Judah, including the existence of scribal schools (see, e.g., Hess 2002; Rollston 2010, 127–35 and references there). Some see a widespread and high literacy, perhaps bolstered by the discovery of abecedaries at various sites. However, there is no evidence that literacy was spread beyond a scribal class—with perhaps others able to draw up receipts or sign their names (see, e.g., Whitt 1995, 2395). Abecedaries, the alphabet written on ostraca, pottery vessels, or stone, have been found at numerous sites in Israel and Judah, from as early as the eleventh century BCE on a shard from Izbet Zarta, about two miles east of Aphek (G. Davies 1991, 35.001). Other abecedaries have been discovered at Tel Zayit, which excavators date to the tenth century BCE (Tappy et al. 2006), several from ninth-century BCE Kuntillet ʿAjrud (Dobbs-Allsopp et al. 2005, 294), ninth- and eighth-century Lachish (G. Davies 1991, 1.105), and elsewhere.

Neither the number of inscriptions nor their genres would cast into doubt the view that Israel/Judah was like its neighbors and like all traditional societies in that literary activity was confined to a small professional class, mostly if not exclusively in the service of the state, with a possibility that some merchants/traders might have been able to keep their own records and a few able to sign their own names. Most of our examples are ostraca or official (including royal) seals stamped on pottery or bullae (see Millard 2005b, 1008–9). There is as yet no evidence of scribes attached to shrines, high places, temples, or "the temple" (in Jerusalem).

Epigraphic material is found all over the country, but in relatively little quantity. The capitals of Samaria and Jerusalem are rich in this material, but even remote sites like Tel Zayit and Kuntillet ʿAjrud had writing. We also know that a fair amount of material has been lost. The growing corpus of bullae, many of which have the imprint of the papyrus stamped on their backs, is evidence that other written documents once existed that have not been preserved.

The extended control by the state depends on writing, bringing bureaucracy to the village. The presence of writing probably enabled the centralization of worship also, and, to effect the normalization of the religious ideology, made the production of canonical literature, such as the Bible, possible.

The Problem of Forgeries

People are eager to part with a lot of money in order to own something from the biblical period. And if that object has an inscription, especially including a name that is also found in the biblical text, then the amount of money increases exponentially. Therefore, the forging of artifacts has become a big and lucrative business in recent years, to the extent that one must be particularly careful in dealing with any inscription that was not found in a secure archaeological context from a controlled excavation. This is particularly important for inscriptions from Israel and Judah. Apart from one seal from Megiddo, mentioned below, which reads "Shema, servant of Jeroboam," we have no seals from stratified excavations that have the name of any king. Some examples have come to light in private collections or on the antiquities market, and many of them have since proved to be forgeries (see Rollston 2010, 137–40, for techniques that forgers use and their motives).

Inscriptions

It is impossible in an introductory chapter to discuss or even list all of the Hebrew inscriptions that have been discovered to date. For more exhaustive lists, see G. Davies 1991 and Dobbs-Allsopp et al. 2005. Here will be discussed a handful of some of the most relevant inscriptions for our understanding of the Hebrew Bible.

The Siloam Tunnel Inscription

Underneath the ancient city of Jerusalem is a rock-hewn tunnel extending from the Gihon Spring to the Pool of Siloam. Engraved into the wall of the tunnel, about twenty feet in, was discovered a monumental inscription consisting of six lines, which has been dated to the end of the eighth century BCE. The tunnel is often called "Hezekiah's Tunnel" because of the account in 2 Kings 20:20, which talks about the deeds of Hezekiah, and "how he made the pool and the conduit and brought water into the city" (cf. 2 Chron. 32:4: in anticipation of the siege of Sennacherib; see Hadley 2012; V. Sasson 1982). But the inscription does not appear to be an official inscription and does not mention any king or impending invasion. It is solely an account from the workers' perspective about the joyous completion of the tunnel. This is unlike any other ancient Near Eastern monumental inscription.

The Ketef Hinnom Silver Scrolls

In 1979 Gabriel Barkay excavated several Iron Age burial caves along the shoulder of the Hinnom Valley in Jerusalem (Ketef Hinnom). Among the many artifacts discovered were two small silver plaques or scrolls. Based on the style of the writing and where the plaques were discovered (the larger of which I found *in situ*), Barkay dates the plaques to the late seventh to early sixth century BCE (Barkay et al. 2003, 170; see Smoak 2016 for a full discussion).

The larger scroll reads (Smoak 2016, 19):

> [1]. . .] YHW . . . [3] the grea[t . . . who keeps] [4] the covenant and [5] [G]raciousness toward those who love [him] and (*alt*: those who love [hi]m;) [6] those who keep [his commandments . . . [7] . .]. [8] the Eternal [. . .] [9] [the?] blessing more than any [10] [sna]re and more than Evil. [11] For redemption is in him. [12] For Yahweh [13] is our restorer [and] [14] rock. May Yahweh bles[s] [15] you and [16] [may he] guard you. [17] [May] Yahweh make [18] [his face] shine . . .

The smaller scroll reads (Smoak 2016, 31):

> [1] [For PN, (the son/daughter of) xxxx][1] h/hu. May h[e]/[2] sh[e] be blessed by Yahweh, [3] the Warrior and [4] the one who expels [5] [E]vil: May Yahweh bless you, [7] guard you. [8] May Yahweh make [9] his face shine [10] upon you and [11] give you [12] p[ea]ce.

The text of these two scrolls bears a striking similarity to Numbers 6:24–26 (cf. Ps. 67:1). Fragments of other phrases on the scrolls are also echoed in the biblical text. On the larger scroll Barkay et al. (2003, 170) restores the phrase "who maintains covenant loyalty with those who love him and keep his commandments" (Deut. 7:9). There are also parallels to Daniel 9:4 and Nehemiah 1:5, 9 (which also have other phrases in common). The smaller scroll contains the phrase "the one who expels evil," which is similar to Zechariah 3:2.

The Khirbet el-Qom Tomb Inscriptions

Khirbet el-Qom is located approximately 35 miles southwest of Jerusalem. Three tomb inscriptions have been found at the site, and salvage excavations were carried out under the direction of William Dever (Dever 1970, 139). The inscription of greatest interest is no. 3. The main part of the inscription consists of three lines engraved above a deeply incised image of a hand. It is dated to the mid-eighth century BCE (Dever 1970, 165). The inscription reads (Hadley 2000, 86):

1. Uriyahu the rich wrote it.
2. Blessed be Uriyahu by Yahweh
3. for from his enemies by his (YHWH's) asherah he (YHWH) has saved him
4. by Oniyahu
5. by his asherah
6. and by his a[she]rah

It will be noted that Yahweh and asherah appear together here in a positive context. This is extremely important for the study of Israelite religion. Asherah was a Northwest Semitic deity whom the ancient Israelites worshiped. The word *asherah* (including plurals and possessive forms) occurs forty times in the Hebrew Bible, usually in negative contexts. Most of the occurrences of the word refer to the wooden symbol of the goddess Asherah (known as an asherah), and very rarely to the goddess herself (Hadley 2000, 54–83).

From the context here it is not clear whether *asherah* refers to the goddess or her symbol. The word appears with the possessive pronominal suffix attached. Since suffixes are never attached to names in Biblical Hebrew, many scholars believe that the term in this inscription refers to the symbol of the goddess (Hadley 2000, 99 and references there).

Whether referring to the goddess herself or to her symbol, there still remains a positive association between Yahweh and "his asherah," a position that runs counter to the negative picture of the goddess and the asherah poles that we have from the Bible.

The Kuntillet ʿAjrud Inscriptions

Kuntillet ʿAjrud is located in northern Sinai, approximately 30 miles south of Kadesh-barnea, near several intersecting routes through the desert. The site, excavated under the directorship of Zeʾev Meshel, dates to the end of the ninth or the beginning of the eighth century BCE (Meshel 1978b; 2012). The site appears to be a desert way station used by a variety of people from both Israel and Judah and beyond, as some of the inscriptions appear to be in Phoenician script (Hadley 2000, 106–20).

The inscriptions discovered there are written in ink on pottery or wall plaster. Most of them are written on two large pithoi (large storage jars) and often overlap one another. Apart from the abecedaries mentioned above, the inscription of most interest is Inscription no. 1, written above the heads of two standing Bes figures (see Keel and Uehlinger 1998, 210–25; Hadley 2000, 136–52, for a discussion of the drawings). The inscription reads (Hadley 2000, 121): "X says: say to Yehal[lelʾel] and to Yoʿasah and [to Z]: I bless you by Yahweh of Samaria and by his asherah." The mention of "Yahweh of Samaria" has interesting implications. It may have a parallel in an inscribed tomb inscription from Khirbet Beit Lei. The reading is contested, but some scholars read it as mentioning "the God of Jerusalem" (see Dobbs-Allsopp et al. 2005, 128–30 and the references there). Other inscriptions from ʿAjrud on the pithoi and wall plaster mention "Yahweh of Teman," which is another geographical name generally indicating the southern region, mentioned in Habakkuk 3:3 and Zechariah 9:14. Since ʿAjrud is in the Sinai Peninsula and considering the connection of Yahweh with Teman in the Bible, one might expect a reference to the south. But to find "Yahweh of Samaria" at a site so far south is intriguing.

This may be evidence that people from Israel as well as Judah visited the site. The mention of "Yahweh of" various sites is interesting when one compares the fundamental statement of faith in Deuteronomy 6:4, literally: "Yahweh our-God Yahweh one." However, it is more likely that the writers of these inscriptions wanted to refer to Yahweh as worshiped in Samaria or Teman, rather than evidencing a belief in multiple deities, all called Yahweh (see Emerton 1982, 12–13). Other deities are mentioned on the wall plaster, including El and Baʿal. So it makes sense that a diversity of peoples with different forms of worship have left their mark here at this site.

As in the Khirbet el-Qom inscription, the form of the term *asherah* has the possessive pronominal suffix attached. That might mean that the wooden symbol of the goddess is indicated, but in this inscription Yahweh and Asherah are mentioned as joint agents of blessing. Usually only deities bless, so this may be a case for the term referring to the goddess here. And yet the mention of "Yahweh of Samaria" brings up an interesting possibility lacking in the Khirbet el-Qom inscription—namely, that "his asherah" may instead be "its asherah," or the asherah of Samaria. Second Kings 13:6 says that "the asherah [NRSV: sacred pole] also remained in Samaria." A reference to the asherah in Samaria during the reign of Jehoahaz would correspond well with the chronology of the site. There is thus the possibility that this inscription refers to the asherah statue in the temple of Yahweh in Samaria, perhaps including Asherah with Yahweh as a divine pair. The Khirbet el-Qom inscription did not need to specify Yahweh of any place, since only Judah remained.

The Tel Arad Ostraca

Tel Arad is located about twenty miles east-northeast of Beersheba, in the Judean Negev. The Iron Age citadel is comparatively large and has its own temple, so in addition to serving as a military outpost and regional administrative center, it may also have been a religious center. During the course of excavations under Yohanan Aharoni in the 1960s, over eighty ostraca were discovered. Most of these date to the eighth to sixth centuries BCE, with some possibly as early as the tenth century (Aharoni and Naveh 1981, 3).

Eighteen of the ostraca were discovered together in a destruction layer dating to the end of the seventh or beginning of the sixth century BCE (Aharoni and Naveh 1981, 9). All of these ostraca are letters addressed to the administrator/commander of the fortress, named Eliashib. Most of them appear to be vouchers authorizing the distribution of various foodstuffs. Another similar group of ostraca that are receipts for foodstuffs comes from Samaria and is dated to the eighth century BCE. They are the only major group of inscriptions from the Northern Kingdom apart from seals (see Dobbs-Allsopp et al. 2005, 423–97).

Perhaps the most interesting of these letters is one written to Eliashib by a subordinate who states that a certain person "is staying in the house (temple) of Yahweh" (see G. Davies 1991, 8.018). There has been much speculation concerning what the reference to "the house of Yahweh" means. There was a temple of Yahweh at Arad, but the excavators believe that it was dismantled before this ostracon was written, so the temple must be the one in Jerusalem (see Aharoni and Naveh 1981, 36–37). The Bible mentions that the temple in Jerusalem could serve as a place of sanctuary or refuge (1 Kings 1:50–51; 2:28; Neh. 6:10). Whether the temple is the one at Arad or in Jerusalem, this Arad ostracon 18 is the only genuine extrabiblical reference to any preexilic temple dedicated to Yahweh. A few other inscriptions have this claim, but they have been proved to be forgeries (see Ahituv 2008, 10).

The Lachish Ostraca

Lachish is about forty-five miles southwest of Jerusalem in the Shephelah. Among the collection of inscribed material discovered at Lachish is a group of eighteen ostraca discovered in 1935. They were in a gateroom that was destroyed by fire in 587 BCE by Nebuchadnezzar. At least ten of these are letters and are known as the Lachish Letters. Several of the letters contain hopes for good news. This is particularly poignant since the city was soon to be destroyed, as the letters were found in the destruction debris.

The letter of most interest here, and the one with the closest connection to the biblical text, is Lachish Letter 4 (G. Davies 1991, 1.004). The letter is thirteen lines long, with the biblical parallel occurring in the last four lines. They are,

10. And know that for the Lachish signals we
11. are watching, according to the code which my lord
12. gave, for we cannot see
13. Azekah.

Lines 10 and 11 mention fire signals. These evidently were some type of communication between cities when other normal means were unavailable. Jeremiah 6:1 mentions fire signals in a more general sense, and we have rising smoke in Judges 20:38, 40. There must have been an encoded message, since lines 11–12 refer to a code that the watchers were to follow.

Lines 12 and 13 state that the watchers cannot see Azekah. Azekah lies about 10 miles north of Lachish, but cannot be seen from there. So the writer must have been located at a point in the hill country where both Lachish and Azekah could be seen. From the context of the letter, it appears that as long as these sites were under Judean control, some sort of signal would be sent. Since the watchers could no longer see Azekah, presumably it had been destroyed. This mention of both Lachish and Azekah from the end of the Judean kingdom has a striking parallel with Jeremiah 34:7.

Before the discovery of the Ketef Hinnom scrolls mentioned above, this letter was the closest direct parallel to a text in the Hebrew Bible. These close comparisons happen rarely. I therefore think that this Lachish Letter 4 records an event from the last days of the Judean kingdom, which was written perhaps only a few days after the corresponding situation as related in the biblical text.

Seals

Almost all genuine Iron Age seals are stamp seals, which make an impression by pressing down on wet clay. They are generally ovoid in shape and rather small (with a diameter no larger than a quarter). They usually are made of stone, either local limestone or finer stone, but semiprecious gems occasionally are used. Most seals are pierced through lengthwise to be strung on a cord and worn on the body, as with the Ketef Hinnom scrolls discussed above. Seals were used for various purposes. They could indicate ownership of a vessel and its contents, seal a vessel before shipping to ensure that the contents remained intact and unaltered, or seal a document to indicate the sender and ensure that only the recipient would be able to read the contents.

Seals from the eighth century BCE mostly have decorations or images with little or no writing. As they progress into the seventh and sixth century, the decorations dwindle, and seals with only writing predominate. Most seals have a prefixed *lamed* ("belonging to") followed by the name of the owner, and then *bn* ("son of") or sometimes *bt* ("daughter of") with the name of the father on a second line, and sometimes a third line with another name, type of animal, or profession indicated (see Hestrin 1983).

No examples of seals of any of the kings of Israel or Judah have been found in stratified excavations, and a number of published royal seals have been proved to be forgeries. Recently, however, a bulla that reads "Belonging to Hezekiah [son of] Ahaz king of Judah" from the City of David excavations has been reported in various press releases.[1] Other examples include a handful of seals that belong to women, which means that a prominent woman would have been able to mark items as her own and speak on her own authority. There are also seals belonging to the "Governor of the City" and the "servant of the king." The only "servant of the king" seal that bears the king's name that has been discovered in a controlled excavation was found at Megiddo in the early 1900s, and dates to the early eighth century BCE. It is a fabulous seal, which says "Belonging to Shema, servant of Jeroboam" (see G. Davies 1991, 100.068). Between the two lines of the inscription is a marvelous image of a snarling lion. It appears that this seal belonged to an official in the court of Jeroboam II of Israel.

Often all that is discovered is the impression that the seal made and not the seal itself. There are two basic types of seal impressions: blobs of clay (bullae) that were used to seal objects such as documents or a vessel and impressions made directly onto the vessel (mostly on the handles) while the clay was still leather-hard.

Bullae

In recent years there has been an explosion in the number of bullae coming onto the market and from private collections. Many hundreds of bullae are not provenanced, and many of these have proved to be forgeries (Ahituv 2008, 10–11 has a few of these). Therefore, it is unwise to use any unprovenanced material to draw conclusions. As a result, many names that are also found in the biblical text (including Berekyahu son of Neryahu, thought to be Jeremiah's scribe) are of necessity removed from our discussion. And yet some real gems remain, including one bulla from Lachish that

1. For the official 2015 press release, see http://new.huji.ac.il/en/article/28173.

reads "Belonging to Gedaliah who is over the house" (in other words, the Royal Steward) (see G. Davies 1991, 100.149). There are also some with the title "son of the king," a term also found in the Bible.

Another valuable collection is from the City of David archive, discovered in 1982 in a clear seventh- to early sixth-century context. One of these bullae bears the name "Gemaryahu, son of Shaphan" (see G. Davies 1991, 100.82). Gemaryahu is a common name from the Bible (Jer. 36:10) as well as extrabiblical texts.

Continuing excavations by Eilat Mazar at the City of David have yielded two other bullae from the sixth century BCE with names similar to those from the book of Jeremiah. One of them reads "Belonging to Yehuchal son of Shelemyahu son of Shavi" (see E. Mazar 2009, 67; cf. Jer. 37:3). The other bulla reads "Belonging to Gedalyahu son of Pashhur" (see E. Mazar 2009, 68). Both of these names occur in Jeremiah 38:1, where the men so named conspire with two others against Jeremiah and throw him into a cistern. It cannot, of course, be proven that the bullae belong to the two men from the biblical text, but it does indicate that the author of Jeremiah knew and used names that were in use during the time of Zedekiah.

Seal Impressions on Jar Handles

There are two basic types of seal impressions on jar handles: "private seals" and "*lammelek*"

("belonging to the king") seal impressions, because most of them have *lmlk* on the top register. These are obviously royal seals, and they form the largest group of seal impressions that we have.

Since the 1800s about two thousand of these *lmlk*-stamped jar handles have been discovered from all over Judah. They all date to the late eighth century BCE, and more specifically to the reign of Hezekiah (see Vaughn 1999). Amazingly, all of these impressions can be traced to just twenty-two seals (Lemaire 1981). All of these jars probably were made at the same site and used by Hezekiah's administration to provide provisions to the various military garrisons and outposts, perhaps even as part of his extensive preparations for his revolt against Assyria.

Inscribed Weights

The last category of inscriptions under consideration is that of inscribed weights. We have many weights from excavations, and fortunately some of them are inscribed (see Kletter 1998; Dobbs-Allsopp et al. 2005, 623–33). From the weights with "shekel" inscribed on them we get an approximate picture of how much a shekel weighed (ca. 11.4 grams [see Ahituv 2008, 244]). Some of the weights are heavier than the average, and some lighter, which in some cases may provide archaeological attestation of false weights (cf. Amos 8:5).

18

Early Jewish Literature

RYAN E. STOKES

Over the past several decades, the literature of early Judaism has figured increasingly prominently in the study and interpretation of the Old Testament. The centuries between Alexander the Great and the rise of Christianity, once regarded by Christian scholars as a sort of Jewish "dark age" in which little of value was produced, are now recognized as a time of vibrant literary and theological productivity. This recognition is owed in large part to the discovery of the Dead Sea Scrolls in 1947, which revolutionized scholars' perception of Judaism in this period. In addition, a renewed interest among scholars in previously known Jewish documents from the centuries just prior to the turn of the era has contributed to a newfound appreciation of this period of Judaism. It is now evident that these centuries saw the composition of certain portions of the Old Testament (hence the label "intertestamental period" is somewhat of a misnomer), translation and editing of the Old Testament, and the production of many new works that creatively interpret and expand upon books of the Old Testament. Further, in these centuries the very

important notions of "Scripture" and "canon" began to develop, even if they did not yet become what they would eventually be in later Jewish and Christian tradition. Early Jewish literature reveals much about the composition of the Old Testament, the context of the Old Testament, and the early reception and interpretation of the Old Testament. For these reasons, it is difficult to overstate the importance of this literature for Old Testament studies. The present chapter introduces the reader to the various collections and kinds of literature of early Judaism, noting the relevance of this literature for Old Testament interpretation.[1]

Collections of Early Jewish Literature

The writings of early Judaism are quite diverse. They attest to a wide range of religious ideas, they represent a variety of literary genres, and they have been received in different ways

1. Numerous reference works pertaining to early Jewish literature have been published in recent decades. For students interested in learning more about specific topics or this literature in general, an excellent resource is Collins and Harlow 2010.

throughout their history by different religious communities. Traditionally, these writings have been classified as "apocrypha," "pseudepigrapha," or "intertestamental literature," labels that serve to distinguish these works from those deemed to be Scripture by later Jewish and Christian traditions. This sort of classification is problematic, however, since a work that is "apocryphal" to one religious community may be "canonical" to another. What is more, conceptions of "Scripture" and "canon" in the period under consideration, to the extent that one can even speak of such conceptions, appear to have been quite different from modern perspectives. Opinions among early Jews about which books qualified as divine revelation differed from one another, as well as from later Jewish and Christian tradition. No enumeration of authoritative books approaching what moderns would consider a "canon" is attested until the late first century CE.[2] Nevertheless, scholars continue to make use of such canonically based categories as a convenient, even if less than ideal, way of speaking of certain groups of writings.

Old Testament Apocrypha

"Apocrypha," or sometimes "Old Testament Apocrypha," is the common designation for those books that are not found in the Protestant Old Testament but are in the Old Testament of the Roman Catholic Church.[3]

2. Near the end of the first century CE, *4 Ezra* 14.44 speaks of ninety-four divinely revealed books. Twenty-four are said to be for the worthy and unworthy unlike. Although *4 Ezra* does not specify which books are included among these twenty-four books, they presumably correspond more or less to the Old Testament / Tanak, the number of which is twenty-four according to Jewish tradition. The other seventy books are said to be reserved exclusively for the wise to read. These very likely included books that, although considered revelatory by the author of *4 Ezra*, would be classified by later tradition as "apocrypha" or "pseudepigrapha." Josephus, writing in the early second century CE, would speak of twenty-two divinely inspired books (*Apion* 1.38).

3. Alternatively, "Apocrypha" may refer to those books that are not among the Jewish Scriptures (Tanak) but do appear in some copies of the Greek Old Testament. For

The word *apocrypha* (singular *apocryphon*) referred originally to the "secret" or "hidden" nature of these writings, as opposed to the more public and widely recognized status of the (other) books of the Bible. Over time, however, the label "apocrypha" has come to connote spuriousness or inauthenticity in comparison with more authentic, canonical texts. Understandably, "deuterocanonical Scriptures" is the preferred term of the Roman Catholic Church for these writings. This designation recognizes the books' canonical status but also acknowledges that this recognition was formalized more recently than for the other books of the Old Testament. The Apocrypha consist of an assortment of literature. They include historiographic works (1 and 2 Maccabees), wisdom books (Ecclesiasticus and Wisdom of Solomon), folktales (Tobit, Judith), an apocalyptic vision (2 Esdras), poetry (Psalm 151 and the Prayer of Manasseh), additions to the biblical books of Daniel and Esther, and other kinds of writings.[4]

Old Testament Pseudepigrapha

The word *pseudepigrapha* (singular *pseudepigraphon*), strictly speaking, refers to writings whose authorship is falsely attributed, usually to a significant figure from the distant past such as Enoch or Ezra. Pseudepigraphy appears to have been a relatively common practice in early Judaism and has been explained by scholars in various ways. One reason for ascribing one's composition to another author might have been to claim the respect and authority associated with that figure for one's

example, although *Psalms of Solomon* is not considered canonical by the Roman Catholic Church, it is among the "Apocrypha" in that it appears in some copies of the Greek Old Testament.

4. The Old Testament Apocrypha should not be confused with the New Testament Apocrypha, a designation that refers to a number of Christian writings related to the New Testament but not included in the New Testament (e.g., *Gospel of the Ebionites* and *Acts of Paul and Thecla*).

own composition. A book supposed to have been written by Enoch, who was believed to have ascended to heaven without dying, for instance, would have received a more favorable hearing from many Jews than a book written by one of their contemporaries. Pseudepigraphy also allowed authors to address current events in the form of prophecies uttered long ago by inspired persons of distinction.

As a collection of writings, however, the "Old Testament Pseudepigrapha" are defined much more broadly than as falsely attributed compositions. These books include just about any religious work that does not belong to the Bible or the Old Testament Apocrypha, whether it is formally pseudepigraphal or not. As a result, the Old Testament Pseudepigrapha constitute quite a diverse group of literature with regard to the genres and theologies represented, but also with regard to their dates and provenances.[5] Many of the Old Testament Pseudepigrapha were composed by Jews in the Second Temple era (e.g., *1 Enoch*, *Jubilees*, and *Letter of Aristeas*). Others were composed by Christians somewhat later (e.g., *Testament of Solomon* and *Ascension of Isaiah*). And others are more difficult to pin down with regard to their date and whether they should be regarded as primarily Christian or Jewish (e.g., *Testaments of the Twelve Patriarchs*). Those Old Testament Pseudepigrapha that are clearly the products of early Judaism are an important source of information about Jewish beliefs in the centuries with which we are concerned.

Dead Sea Scrolls

The Dead Sea Scrolls have been hailed as the greatest manuscript discovery of modern times, and understandably so. The designation "Dead Sea Scrolls" can refer to any number of ancient manuscripts that have been discovered in various locations in the region of the Dead Sea. More commonly, however, the designation refers specifically to the nearly nine hundred mostly fragmentary manuscripts discovered between 1947 and 1956 in eleven caves near Qumran. Most of these scrolls (or, more typically, scroll fragments) are written in Hebrew, though a number of them are in Aramaic, and a few of them in Greek. They date from the third century BCE to the early first century CE.[6]

There are different ways of categorizing the contents of the Dead Sea Scrolls, none of which is perfect. The scrolls may be distinguished on the basis of whether they contain works that would eventually be included in the Bible or not. Of the nine hundred manuscripts that were discovered, over two hundred of them are copies of books that would be included in the Old Testament and constitute the very oldest copies of many of these books in their original languages. The scrolls could also be divided into two groups based on whether they are "sectarian" or not. Most scholars believe that the scrolls belonged to a particular group of Jews, usually identified as Essenes. Some of the scrolls seem not to represent the ideas of Judaism as a whole but the ideas of a particular, idiosyncratic group within Judaism who believed they were living in the last days and held distinctive notions with regard to how they should conduct themselves so as to be faithful to God's laws. The Dead Sea Scrolls can also be distinguished on the basis of literary genre, comprising Scripture-based narratives, liturgical works, rule books, commentaries, wisdom writings, and many other sorts of literature. The Dead Sea Scrolls are invaluable for what they reveal about the state of the text of the Old Testament around the turn of the era, as well as its early reception and interpretation.[7]

---

5. The standard edition of the Old Testament Pseudepigrapha in English is Charlesworth 1983–85. This edition includes introductions to each work.

6. For English translations of the Dead Sea Scrolls, see García Martínez 1996 and Vermes 1997.

7. An excellent, student-friendly introduction to the Dead Sea Scrolls is VanderKam 2010.

Jewish Literature Written in Greek

Some early Jewish works were composed in Greek by Jews living in Egypt and elsewhere in the Greek-speaking world. This literature reflects the complex relationship that existed between Judaism and the Greek culture amid which many Jews found themselves after Alexander the Great's conquests in the fourth century BCE. It bears witness to how Jews adopted, adapted, and rejected aspects of Greek culture. "Hellenism," the adoption of elements of Greek culture, was not a phenomenon that was limited to those Jews who lived in the Diaspora and spoke Greek, but existed even among Jews who lived in Jerusalem and wrote in Hebrew and Aramaic. In a very real sense, then, all Jewish literature from the time of Alexander through the first century CE could be regarded as "Hellenistic." As with the categories Apocrypha and Pseudepigrapha, although "Jewish literature written in Greek" is an imperfect label from a historical standpoint, it is nonetheless a convenient category for speaking of these important early Jewish texts.

A wide range of Jewish literature was composed in Greek in numerous genres (e.g., history, poetry, wisdom, tragedy). Unfortunately, much of this material is preserved only in the form of excerpts quoted by later Christian authors. Two Jewish authors who wrote in Greek and a great deal of whose work has been preserved are Philo and Josephus. Philo of Alexandria wrote in the first part of the first century CE and is most noted for his allegorical exposition of the Jewish Scriptures and for the prominence of Hellenistic philosophy in his thinking. Josephus wrote in the late first and early second century CE, producing a history of the Jewish people from biblical times to the beginning of the Jewish revolt, a history of the revolt itself, and a defense of the Jews.

The Septuagint

The most influential collection of texts produced by Greek-speaking Judaism is in fact a collection not of Greek compositions but primarily of Greek translations of the Hebrew and Aramaic Jewish Scriptures. An account of the origin of the Septuagint is contained in the second-century BCE *Letter of Aristeas*. According to *Aristeas*, the translation of the Jewish law was commissioned by Ptolemy II (285–247 BCE) for the library of Alexandria. Approximately seventy Jewish men are said to have traveled from Jerusalem to Alexandria for the project, hence the designation "Septuagint" (from the Latin for "seventy") or "LXX" for this group of texts. Further, while *Aristeas* narrates only the translation of the Jewish law, the designation "Septuagint" came to be applied by association to Greek translations of all the books of the Old Testament. While much about the account in *Letter of Aristeas* is fantastic, it is likely that the Greek translations of the Jewish Scriptures had their origins in Alexandria in the third century BCE. The translation process does not appear to have been systematic, however. Rather, different Old Testament books (even within the Pentateuch itself) had different translators who held different translation philosophies. Moreover, it is unlikely that these translations were intended primarily for the intellectual pursuits of the Greeks. Rather, they were produced foremost in order to give Greek-speaking Jews access to their own sacred books.

Of particular interest to modern scholars are those passages for which the Septuagint contains a reading that differs from that of the Masoretic Text—the Hebrew and Aramaic textual tradition of the Old Testament that became the standard biblical text of Judaism. Hebrew manuscripts of biblical books discovered among the Dead Sea Scrolls, some of which agree with the Septuagint against the Masoretic Text, demonstrate that many of the differences between the Septuagint and the Masoretic Text are the result of variant Hebrew versions of the biblical texts existing prior to the translation of some of them into Greek. In some cases, the Hebrew of the Masoretic Text preserves the more original reading; in others, the Septuagint, though a translation, reflects a Hebrew text that is earlier than the one preserved by the Masoretic Text. There are also passages in the Septuagint that diverge from the reading of the Masoretic Text as a result of the concerns of their translators, who attempted to make sense of the Hebrew Scriptures in a new, Hellenistic context. The Septuagint tells us much about the origins and development of the biblical texts, as well as about the people who transmitted and translated these texts.

Types of Early Jewish Literature

The preceding section refers several times to the various genres or kinds of literature composed by Jews between the fourth century BCE and first century CE. While it is not possible here to discuss all of these, it will be helpful to highlight some of the more important types of Jewish writings from this period and how these writings inform Old Testament interpretation.

History

Several books that may be deemed historical to varying degrees were produced by Jews in the Second Temple period. We have already noted the work of Josephus in our discussion of Jewish literature composed in Greek above. Also among the historiographic writings of early Judaism are 1 and 2 Maccabees, which in many respects resemble the biblical historical books of Samuel, Kings, and Chronicles. First and Second Maccabees recount the persecution of Jews under the Greek (Seleucid) king Antiochus IV Epiphanes and the Jewish struggle for independence from the Greeks led by Judas Maccabeus and his brothers. It is this historical situation with which much of the book of Daniel (chs. 7–12) is concerned, and these books supply the context necessary for comprehending Daniel's prophecies.

Tales

Closely related to historical literature, "tales" are narratives set in the past. The objectives of a tale, however, have less to do with recounting historical events and more to do with telling a compelling story, albeit with varying degrees of historical verisimilitude, that promotes certain values among its readers. These stories typically feature an individual who exemplifies virtue in the face of life-threatening circumstances. It is not uncommon for these heroes to receive divine help in the form of angels who come to assist them in their time of desperation. Examples of this type of literature include Tobit, Judith, 3 and 4 Maccabees, as well as several of the narratives associated with Daniel and his friends (e.g., Dan. 3; 6, Susanna, Bel and the Dragon).

Apocalypses

The word "apocalypse" (Greek *apokalypsis*) means "revelation." As a genre of literature, however, "apocalypse" is difficult to define. The label is derived from the first verse of the book of Revelation ("The *revelation* of Jesus Christ, which God gave to him . . .") and is applied by scholars to writings that, very generally speaking, resemble this New Testament book. Those works that scholars agree belong in this category of literature are narratives of a divine revelation to a human being, often through angelic mediators. Apocalypses are also typically pseudepigraphal, in that the recipient of the revelation and purported author of the book is usually an esteemed figure from Israel's past. Apocalypses may tell of the travels of the visionary into heaven (e.g., *Apocalypse of Abraham*) or to mythical places on the earth, such as the Garden of Eden or the prison for fallen angels (e.g., *1 Enoch* 17–36). Alternatively, they may recount history in the form of a symbolic vision. The *Animal Apocalypse* (*1 Enoch* 85–90), for example, presents the history of Israel in the form of an allegory in which various animal species represent the different nations of the earth.[8]

In the Old Testament, chapters 7–12 of Daniel belong to this category of literature. They formally resemble the early Jewish apocalypses. Their revelatory visions are of the historical variety, similar to the *Animal Apocalypse*. The theology of this portion of Daniel, with its attention to angelology and its teaching regarding a postmortem judgment, to name just two facets of its theology, is also of the sort found in many early Jewish apocalypses. The subject matter, the Maccabean crisis of the mid-second century BCE, also situates these chapters of Daniel squarely among the early Jewish apocalypses. The interpretive value of studying Daniel among the apocalyptic writings of early Judaism is immense.[9]

Rewritten Scripture

Rewritten Scripture is a fascinating type of literature in which the author takes one of Israel's sacred texts as a starting point but rewrites it, making changes to the story to suit the author's purposes. Rewritten Scripture can omit material from its source text, add material, rearrange material, and otherwise creatively adapt the story, sometimes altering it significantly. This type of literature includes works such as *Jubilees*, the *Genesis Apocryphon*, the *Reworked Pentateuch*, and pseudo-Philo's *Biblical Antiquities*.[10] That writings of this type frequently take considerable liberties in their retellings of scriptural stories raises some very interesting questions about the status of Scripture in early Judaism.

An excellent example of this practice is the book of *Jubilees*, which was composed sometime in the second century BCE. This work presents itself as a law book revealed to Moses on Sinai and retells the story of Genesis and the first nineteen chapters of Exodus, from creation to Sinai. Intriguingly, although *Jubilees* is clearly indebted to the authoritative texts of Genesis and Exodus, it presents itself as an (equally?) authoritative version of Israel's origins and laws. Though *Jubilees* did not garner enough popularity in early Judaism to be included eventually in the Jewish canon of Scripture, it appears to have been received as divine revelation by some. It is cited as an authority by one of the sectarian Dead Sea Scrolls (Cairo Damascus 16.3–4). Among Christian traditions, the Ethiopian Orthodox Church includes *Jubilees* among its sacred literature.

Wisdom

Wisdom literature is concerned with the acquisition of knowledge, the ability to make prudent choices, and achievement of success in life. It offers practical instruction pertaining to mundane matters but also addresses right living in relation to God, without which one's success in life might be jeopardized. Biblical wisdom literature includes the books of Proverbs, Job, and Ecclesiastes. Early Jewish wisdom includes the Wisdom of Jesus ben Sira (Ecclesiasticus [= Sirach]) and the Wisdom of Solomon, both of which are part of the Old Testament Apocrypha / deuterocanonical Scriptures. Several fragmentary wisdom writings were also found among the Dead Sea Scrolls. In addition, many scholars date the biblical book of Ecclesiastes (Qoheleth) to the late third or even the second century BCE. Its discussion of the possibility of an afterlife for human beings (3:18–21) fits this period well, since the fate of humans after death was a popular and debated topic in early Judaism. Identifying a date for this

---

8. The standard introduction to Jewish apocalyptic literature is J. Collins 2016.

9. For critical scholars, that Daniel should be dated to the second century BCE and counted among the early Jewish apocalyptic texts is beyond question. Some conservative scholars, however, for theological reasons, maintain the traditional dating of Daniel to the sixth century BCE. As a result, many of these conservative scholars are reluctant to interpret Daniel in the context of early Jewish apocalypses.

10. For a short but very helpful piece on "Rewritten Scripture," see Crawford 2008.

work, however, is difficult, and no consensus exists among scholars.[11]

Poetry

A number of poetic works, including hymns, prayers, and psalms, were composed by Jews during the Second Temple period. Several copies of the collection *Thanksgiving Hymns* were found among the Dead Sea Scrolls. The hymns in this work, which are modeled on the biblical psalms, give thanks to or bless God for dealing so mercifully with lowly human

11. On these and other matters related to early Jewish wisdom literature, see J. Collins 1997.

beings. *Psalms of Solomon* is an important collection of eighteen psalms pseudonymously attributed to Solomon. This work was likely completed in the latter half of the second century BCE and reveals much about Jewish hope in this period for a messianic son of David who would defeat Israel's enemies. The Prayer of Manasseh, which is included in the Bible of the Slavonic Church, is a moving literary work that purports to be the prayer of repentance uttered by King Manasseh of Judah mentioned in 2 Chronicles 33:13. These are just a few examples of the many poetic works preserved from early Judaism.

The Frames

Ancient Near Eastern Iconography

Introduction to Ancient Near Eastern Iconography

IZAK CORNELIUS

Introduction

The Old Testament / Hebrew Bible is not a modern or contemporary text, but an ancient collection of writings. It breathes its ancient context: the physical world, way of life, and worldview of the ancient Near East. It is therefore best read in this ancient context. To come to grips with the context, one studies the geography of the land (see part one, section I), the material culture (e.g., by way of archaeology, see part one, section II), and ancient Near Eastern texts (see part one, section III). A unique type of source is the visual material or iconography, the visual imagery (note: whenever the term "imagery" is used in this chapter, it means visual imagery).[1]

In this chapter the following aspects of ancient Near Eastern iconography will be discussed:

1. What is it? (definition)
2. Where can it be found? (sources)
3. What does it include? (types)
4. How can it be studied? (approaches and methods)
5. How can it be used in Old Testament studies? (practice)

---

1. Artifacts are especially to be found in these museums (listed with their artifact database start pages):

British Museum, London: https://www.britishmuseum.org/research/collection_online/search.aspx

Louvre, Paris: http://cartelen.louvre.fr/cartelen/visite?srv=crt_frm_rs&langue=en&initCritere=true

Metropolitan Museum of Art, New York: http://www.metmuseum.org/art/collection

Israel Museum, Jerusalem: http://www.imj.org.il/Imagine/collections/index.asp?cat=Departments

Bibel+Orient Museum, Fribourg, Switzerland: http://www.bible-orient museum.ch/bodo/ for the artifact database

Important publications with different types of illustrations are Gressmann 1927; Pritchard 1969b; Keel 1978b; Keel and Uehlinger 1998. A new, more comprehensive systematic collection of images is IPIAO (Schroer and Keel 2005; Schroer 2008; 2011), with three volumes already published, covering the period from the Middle Stone Age to the Late Bronze Age (ca. 12,000–1100 BCE) and already including a total of 993 images. The *Zondervan Illustrated Bible Backgrounds Commentary* (Walton 2009b) includes various images in full color.

Fig. 19.1. Pharaoh as giant smiting the enemy

What Is Ancient Near Eastern Iconography?

"Ancient Near East" refers to the countries of the Near East including the Levant (Syria, Jordan, Palestine/Israel), Egypt and Kush, Anatolia, Mesopotamia, and Persia (see fig. 2.1). The time period extends from the Stone Age ca. 12,000 BCE to the advent of Islam in the seventh century CE.

"Iconography" (*eikōn* + *graphē*) literally means "image description" (Carile and Nagelsmit 2016). Sometimes iconography is differentiated from "iconology," which refers more to the *study* of visual images. Iconography does not deal with illustrations of the Bible in Christian art or the icons in certain churches, but rather with the visual material of the ancient Near East. However, it does not refer only to the study of the visual imagery and its meaning but also to the imagery and visual culture as such—the artifacts, the material objects.

This chapter therefore discusses the materials used to make these objects and the types of artifacts at hand.

In the ancient world there was little difference between art and artifact, or between artist and artisan, or between arts and crafts (Boertien and Steiner 2009; Cornelius 2013). This does not ignore the fact that some objects are beautifully made and have a certain aesthetic value. These objects are not "art" as such, as the visual material had a functional use and their creation was never a case of "art for art's sake." Statues were not placed in an art gallery or museum as they are today (out of their contexts), but (for example) rather played a role as substitutes for the deceased in the tomb or for the worshiper in the temple. Large reliefs or steles were intended for public display and served as propaganda for kings and deities, communicating a certain divine order.

The ancient Near Eastern material has unique characteristics, sometimes very foreign to what modern observers are used to. This can best be explained by looking at the Egyptian material, where the pharaoh is shown as a giant compared to his enemies (fig. 19.1). This is a different kind of perspective, if perspective at all, sometimes referred to as a-perspective (nonperspective) or aspective (Brunner-Traut 1986). In this case, attention is drawn to a certain *aspect* such as the pharaoh as a giant to make the statement that he is the greatest of beings. The ancient Near East created conceptual rather than perceptual images. It is not so much a matter of what is seen but of what the viewer is supposed to see or perceive—a notion or symbol that was communicated or was supposed to be communicated. Images are neither always realistic nor historical in the sense of representing reality. It is not a case of what some ruler or historical person really looked like or what really happened that matters, but rather, for example, the "idea" of kingship that is communicated. This is important, as it means that iconography provides information on the *world of ideas* of the ancient Near East.

Where Can Ancient Near Eastern Iconography Be Found?

The interest in imagery goes far back to the study of Jewish coins. However, the rediscovery of the ancient Near East following the expedition of Napoleon to Egypt (1798) and the consequent systematic excavations of the Near East (for the southern Levant, see part one, section II) provided a corpus of original imagery. There are now even more images than texts available, especially in the region of the southern Levant, where few texts have been found. The prohibition on images in Exodus 20 is directed against making a cultic statue of the deity and not against imagery as such. Ancient Israel and Judah were not without images or "art" (Schroer 1987), as was still the case in Persian Yehud (Frevel, Pyschny, and Cornelius 2014).

The imagery is found in various media (types), and the materials from which the artifacts were made range from cheap clay to stone, as well as animal ivory and bone, precious and semiprecious stones, and more expensive metals, such as gold. Stones such as lapis lazuli had to be imported from Afghanistan, and gold came from Kush (the Sudan). This indicates that iconography was linked to international trade. There are also social aspects involved, from the kings and the temple officials who commissioned the making of imagery, to the artists and artisans who produced it, to the ordinary people who observed and responded to it. In all the different types of imagery the way in which it was made (technique and style) and where it was made (workshops) also play a role (Uehlinger 2000; Suter and Uehlinger 2005).

Types of Imagery

The imagery of the ancient Near East can be found in different media, ranging in size from huge monuments, which includes architecture, to very small decorated seal amulets (see de Hulster, Strawn, and Bonfiglio 2015b, 32–34).

Monumental imagery. In addition to the gigantic Egyptian pyramids (ca. 140 meters tall) and Mesopotamian-Iranian ziggurats (ca. 50 meters tall), there are palaces, temples, and tombs that were decorated with imagery in the form of reliefs and wall paintings. Reliefs also occur on rock faces. Well known from Egypt are temple reliefs such as at Karnak, Luxor, and Medinet Habu (Robins 1997). In Mesopotamia the most impressive are the reliefs in the palaces of the Neo-Assyrian kings (ca. 900–600 BCE) at Nimrud, Chorsabad, and Nineveh depicting, among many other things, warfare and the lion hunt (P. Collins 2008). One relief shows the siege of the city of Lachish in Judah in 701 BCE (Usshishkin 1982; for its interpretation, see Uehlinger 2007) (fig. 19.2). In the Hittite Empire (ca. 1400–1200 BCE) there are

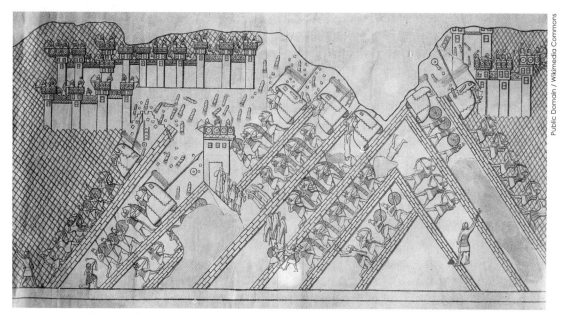

Public Domain / Wikimedia Commons

Fig. 19.2. Siege of the city of Lachish

reliefs at the sanctuary of Yazilikaya near the capital Hattuša depicting Hittite deities (Seeher 2011a). This tradition of monumental art lived on in the Syro-Hittite states of the first millennium BCE, and there are stone reliefs at Zincirli and Carchemish (Gilibert 2011). Some of the reliefs were painted, but over time their luster has disappeared. Paintings go very far back in history, with the best examples being from Egyptian tombs (Tiradritti 2008). The paintings often are fragmentary, and remains are found in the debris. No large reliefs are known from the southern Levant, although there are paintings from very early Teleilat Ghassul (4200 BCE) (Drabsch 2015) and fragments from Kuntillet ʿAjrud (830–750 BCE) in the Sinai (Meshel 2012). Egyptian obelisks (30 meters tall) and colossi of pharaohs are known, like that of Ramses II (20 meters). The Great Sphinx next to the Great Pyramid is 73 meters long.

Large imagery. These include steles (standing stones), orthostats (upright stones or slabs), and statues (standing or seated). Steles could be large images of great kings such as Esarhaddon (3.5 meters tall) or more private

Egyptian funeral steles of only 30 cm high. Steles are known from Ugarit (Yon 1991) and the Syro-Hittite world (Orthmann 1971), but, excluding the Late Bronze Age Egyptian statues and steles, there is very little material from the southern Levant. The Hebrew Bible describes the *matsebot* (standing stones). Mention should be made of the Bethsaida Stela, depicting a god (Bernett and Keel 1998) (fig. 19.3). Statues of rulers and deities are known from Egypt (Russmann 1989) and western Asia (Spycket 1981). For the Levant, there are statues of the kings Idrimi and Hadayithi and of the southern Levant Ammonite rulers (Zayadine 1991), but there is nothing comparable for Israel/Judah. Large metal statues are rare, but there are examples like that of Pharaoh Pepy I of 1.77 meters (Robins 1997, fig. 59).

Miniature imagery. In terms of quantity, imagery is found mostly on smaller objects. The most common types are the engraved seals (glyptic sources), which were used to seal documents as well as containers and doors by making an impression in clay. There are two types: the cylinder seal, which was rolled across the clay, and the stamp seal (Collon 1988; Keel

Fig. 19.3. Replica of the Et-Tel/Bethsaida Stela

1995; 1997; 2010a; 2010b; 2013; 2017). The most typical Egyptian form is the scarab or sacred beetle. Some were carried as amulets or talismans around the neck on a string inserted through a hole in the seal. These seals are small (5–10 cm), but they are decorated with images of deities and mythological beings, officials and rulers, fauna and flora, and so on, which is very informative (fig. 19.4, fig. 19.5). Some contain larger scenes such as cultic processions, but there are few mythological scenes. The seals are the most important visual medium, especially in the southern Levant, where there is an absence of larger visual material. There are many more stamp seals than cylinder seals.

Amulets were carried primarily to protect and bring good luck and are also fairly common. These could be in the form of deities or animals or symbols, and in Egypt there are amulets in the form of hieroglyphic signs. There are thousands from the southern Levant (C. Herrmann et al. 2010; C. Herrmann

2016). Jewelry is more than decoration because of its symbolism. Ivory objects were made of elephant and (mostly) hippopotamus ivory. Important finds come from Assyrian Nimrud, very early examples from Beersheba, Late Bronze Age material from Megiddo, and Iron Age ivories from Samaria (Barnett 1982). Motifs depicted are human figures, banquets, the woman-at-the-window, and Egyptian mythology and deities. To these ivories can be added objects of carved animal bone. Clay was used to make decorated cult stands (examples from Taanach and Rehov) and plaques and figurines of women (whether all of these are goddesses is debatable). There are animal figurines as well as horse-and-rider figurines typical of the Persian period. A unique type is the late eighth–seventh-century BCE Judean Pillar Figurine, ca. 15 cm tall with a pillar-shaped body depicting a woman with enormous breasts. About one thousand are known, with half coming from Jerusalem (fig. 19.6). These are sometimes linked to the cult of the goddess Asherah, but their interpretation is more complex than this (Darby 2014). Metal figurines have been found, but not all of these are deities (Negbi 1976).

Coins were the first true media of mass communication because they were carried by everyone who used them as payment. They appear only in the seventh century BCE in Anatolia. Darius I of Persia minted coins, and in Yehud and Samaria coins were used in the late Persian period (Wyssmann 2014). They are more than a medium of payment because of the imagery that appears on them (fig. 19.7).

How Can Ancient Near Eastern Iconography Be Studied?

Just as texts do not speak for themselves but have to be interpreted, so does arriving at an understanding of images entail a certain method. No theoretical reflection on images or art as, for example, occurs among the Greeks

Fig. 19.4. Cylinder seal and modern impression: royal worshiper before a deity on a throne; human-headed bulls below

is found in ancient Near Eastern texts. An Egyptian stele contains reflections by the artist himself (Barta 1970) in which some of the techniques used are described. In the eighteenth century J. Winckelmann pioneered the study of classical art, although he was skeptical of the value of Egyptian art as he had limited material and did not understand its concepts. H. Schäfer (1986 [German original 1919]) was the pioneer in developing a method to understand Egyptian art with its unique concepts (see now Hartwig 2015). I. Winter contributed to the study of the Mesopotamian material (2010) as did Z. Bahrani (2003; 2017) and the essays in M. Feldman and Brown (2013). P. Beck (2002) was a pioneer in understanding the southern Levantine (Israelite) material.

In the 1930s E. Panofsky (1970) laid the foundation of the "iconographical method" with three basic stages: (1) pre-iconographical description, (2) iconographical analysis, and (3) iconological interpretation. This method remains fundamental and is used in studies such as those by Bonatz (2000) and Ornan (2010), but has since been refined because it relied too heavily on texts to understand images (Keel 1992a; Weissenrieder and Wendt 2005). O. Keel (1992a) described "the right of images to be seen" and the way images should

be interpreted and provided case studies. He divided the iconographic interpretation scheme into the analysis of motifs, scenes/themes, and decorations and stressed that a motif can mean different things depending on the *Sitz im Leben* or context in which it is found. Contemporary approaches like that of W. Mitchell talk of "imagetext" (1994, 89n9) to explain the relation between images and texts and emphasize that pictures want "equal rights" with texts (2005, 47). Newer approaches use methods from disciplines such as semiotics (Weissenrieder and Wendt 2005), and R. Bonfiglio (2016) works with a "visual hermeneutics."

The visual record can provide primary information that is complementary to, or even dif-

Fig. 19.5. Scarab seal and modern impression: Osiris flanked by protective deities

Fig. 19.6. Judean Pillar Figurines

ferent from, what is known from textual sources (I. Winter 2010, 1:72). H. Gressmann (1927, viii) already wrote, "'Texts' and 'images,' philology and archaeology, are *equally* indispensable for a historian, both belong necessarily together. They presuppose one another, complement one another, assay one another, and provide for one another a *mutual* witness" (as translated in de Hulster and LeMon 2014b, xix). There still seems to be a sort of division among scholars with regard to the use of texts, on the one hand, and the use of artifacts (which include images), on the other, a split between philologists ("text people") and archaeologists ("image people").

With regard to ancient Israel, the imagery often complements and supplements what is described in the texts—for example, the role of the goddess. But there is no one-for-one relation between text and image or a "parallelism" between text and image. One should look not for matches but for a similar "mental background" (Suter 2000, 8). In this regard J. LeMon (2010) works with concepts such as "congruent iconography and texts," and I. de Hulster, B. Strawn, and R. Bonfilgio use the terms "congruence, correlation, and contiguity" (2015b, 22–26).

No superficial and overly hasty links should be made between text and image; one should not look for the "right" text to describe the image or the image that best illustrates the text. Text and image should be studied independently

and properly. First the visual source should be described, analyzed, and interpreted in the appropriate way. The same applies to the textual material. Only then can the two be compared, correlated, and interfaced (Cornelius 2016; 2017). Both sources are important and should be studied in conjunction, because "there is nothing better than more" (Berlejung 2010). The more sources one has from the lost cultures of the ancient Near East, the better one might be able to understand its world.

How Can Ancient Near Eastern Iconography Be Used in Old Testament Studies?

Earlier approaches used the visual material merely as illustrations. J. LeMon (2009, 143–45) describes an example, the "Adam and Eve" seal, which was related to Genesis 3. Sometimes images are used to illustrate historical events or persons, as in Pritchard 1969b, which has a section on "scenes from history." The figure on the Black Obelisk is described as Jehu in the accompanying text, but this is not a "historical portrait"; it is merely a typical subjugated ruler who looks very similar to the other subjugated figure on the obelisk. The depiction of the siege of Lachish is also stereotypical and cannot be used to reconstruct the city (Uehlinger 2007). Referring to the figure on a potsherd from Ramat Rahel, Gabriel Barkay wrote, "I believe it is likely a portrait of king Hezekiah, the king who built Ramat Rahel and its palace" (2006, 44). However, ancient Near Eastern iconography did not represent historical individual kings as portraits (Cornelius 2015).

A second approach uses iconography to illustrate customs and material culture such as clothing (e.g., Borowski 2003, 7). Usually these images are taken from the larger context, and in this way the whole point of the image is missed, ignoring the broader ideological-sociological context (Keel 1992b, 369).

A third approach, developed by O. Keel (1978b) and his followers, emphasizes the use of images in relation to the symbolic and conceptual world. There are studies on the image of nomads (Staubli 1991), the warrior and weather imagery of Yahweh (M. Klingbeil 1999), imagery of deities and their symbols (Keel and Uehlinger 1998), body symbolism (Schroer and Staubli 2001; Cornelius 2017), lion imagery (Strawn 2005), and the wings of Yahweh (LeMon 2010). Some biblical commentaries also incorporate the imagery of the ancient Near East (Keel 1994; Walton 2009b).

One should not speak of "biblical iconography" as if there is a direct link between the biblical text and iconography. "Iconographical exegesis" (de Hulster 2009) is described as "an

Fig. 19.7. Yehud coin

interpretive method that explains aspects of the Hebrew Bible with the help of ancient Near Eastern visual remains" (de Hulster, Strawn, and Bonfiglio 2015b, 20). However, this is not so much a type of "exegesis" as a perspective on the conceptual level. Images are also more than a "help" because these sources can make an independent contribution in their own right toward understanding the ancient Near East.

Conclusion

To understand the world of the ancient Near East, of which ancient Israel formed an integral part, one should study ancient Near Eastern texts as well as visual images. However, these are two different kinds of sources and should be studied independently. A vast array of visual sources is available that inform the contemporary student on the conceptual world of the Old Testament.

20

Egyptian Iconography

LAURA WRIGHT

Egypt has played a vital role in the iconography of the broader southern Levant. Its role in ancient Israel as part of that region is undisputable. Egypt's geographic proximity to the southern Levant has led to close economic and social ties between the two regions throughout their shared history. The iconography of the material culture of the southern Levant has reflected this close relationship with Egypt even in periods when trade with the wider Mediterranean waned. While patterns of Egyptian production and trade of objects bearing this iconography did not determine southern Levantine patterns of consumption of objects, the two are bound to each other. While often the history of these two regions is told as a succession of discrete events—*l'histoire evenementielle*—those events can be drawn together to recount the steady forces over the *longue durée* of centuries that drew these two regions together from the Middle Bronze Age through the Iron Age (Braudel 1958).

Egyptian Iconography and the Southern Levant

The Middle Bronze Age

Increasing urbanization and new technology permitted expanding trade networks in the southern Levant during the Middle Bronze Age. Egyptian power diminished at the close of this period, and a Semitic polity known as the Hyksos rose to power in Lower Egypt during the Second Intermediate Period. Monumental-sized art from the southern Levant is rarely extant from this period, yet small, portable objects tell the story of local Levantine consumption of Egyptian iconography. The southern Levant was one of the primary consumers of Egyptian amulets in the form of scarab beetles. These beetles were believed to have apotropaic powers because they were thought to be able to self-regenerate (Keel 1997, 21–22). After purchasing these amulets during the Middle Kingdom, local southern Levantine artists crafted their own scarab amulets for local use (D. Ben-Tor 1997; 2007). They appropriated contemporary Egyptian iconographic traditions and fundamentally altered the Egyptian tradition. At times, they even created pseudohieroglyphic writing in which glyphs appear to have been chosen because their shape filled the negative space available due to the tapering or expanding width of a column on the scarab's face (L. Wright 2016, 145–58). These amulets from the Second Intermediate Period continued to be placed in southern Levantine tombs for over a millennium. The Egyptianizing iconography of these amulets continued to be adapted and produced locally in successive centuries.

The Late Bronze Age

Local Levantine production of Egyptianizing motifs of the Second Intermediate Period continued in the Late Bronze I, as seen in the scarabs from the Beth Shean IX group (Ben-Tor and Keel 2012, 87–104; Keel 2010a, 158–59 [Beth Shean 136]; 2013, 436–37 [Gezer 628], 562–63 [Tel Harasim 22]; cf. Tufnell 1958, plates 37/38.308, 311; S. Ben-Arieh, Ben-Tor, and Godovitz 1993, 82, fig. 5; Sellin 1904, 28–29, fig. 23). The motifs on these amulets—such as the anthropomorphic figure holding a lotus bloom or the striding lion—were similar, though the shift in material created more schematic adaptions of the images from the Second Intermediate Period. While the rate of local Levantine production certainly was lower in the Late Bronze I than in the Second Intermediate Period, local adoption and adaptation of Egyptian motifs persisted as they became part of the local iconographic tradition. After centuries of use, it is unclear to what degree they would have even been viewed as foreign.

As Egyptian hegemony increased during the Eighteenth and Nineteenth Dynasties, a number of southern Levantine cities came under greater Egyptian influence and some even under direct Egyptian rule (Weinstein 1981; E. Morris 2005).[1] The material culture of cities in the southern coastal plain attested significant appropriation of Egyptian iconography; cities under direct Egyptian control, such as Beth Shean, imported even greater numbers of

1. See also Bryan 1996; Higginbotham 2000; M. Martin 2004 for more perspectives on the relationship between elite emulation and direct rule. Elite emulation of Egyptian iconography alone need not indicate one kind of Egyptian governance in a region. For New Kingdom examples of Egypto-Canaanite ceramic forms, see the discussion of ceramics at Beth Shean (e.g., Mullins 2002, 161–62, 291–94, 305–6; James and McGovern 1993, 78–79) and Tell es-Sa'idiyeh (J. Green 2006, 68, 192–207, 565–71).

objects from Egypt proper and produced their own appropriations of that iconography (see also Keel 1998, 49–97). Both imported Egyptian objects and locally produced amulets with Egyptianizing iconography were found in the same tombs from the Late Bronze IIB. Using other media such as ivory, local artisans crafted images of a local ruler wearing Canaanite attire, yet the ruler was situated in a typical New Kingdom scene of conquest (Giveon 1971, 201–2; Loud 1939, plates 4, 32; Liebowitz 1980; 1987). The iconographies of the two regions were bound up in one another.

Iron I

In the early Iron I, trade routes shifted and the import of ceramics from the Mediterranean dropped dramatically. Ties between southern coastal sites and the broader Mediterranean declined, as seen in the petrographic analysis of Ashkelon's storage jars, which transported commodities on these shipping routes.[2] When the routes reemerged in the later Iron I, they connected the southern Levantine coast with the Phoenician coast. As trade routes shifted during the Iron I, Egyptian influence on ceramic technology waned in the southern coastal plain (Master 2011, 261). Inland sites also experienced a steep decline in trade with the broader Mediterranean, with only rare connections with Egypt persisting (Wolff 1998, 453; Zertal 2012, 364). Despite declining Egyptian political hegemony and trade, the local iconographic traditions continued to produce images based on Egyptian iconography as in the Late Bronze IIB. As in the Beth Shean IX group, iconographic motifs once popular in southern Levantine iconography during the Second Intermediate Period reemerged at sites on the coast during the Late Bronze IIB (L. Wright 2016, 158–95). For example, the image of an anthropomorphic figure holding

2. See Daniel Master's data cited in Ben-Shlomo 2014a, 26.

a lotus blossom and the so-called *anra* motif[3] again came to the fore in the transition between the Late Bronze IIB and Iron I. Though production of these Egyptianizing motifs declined in the Late Bronze IIA, locally produced scarabs from the Second Intermediate Period remained in circulation for centuries, and the motifs reemerged after half a millennium. It is unlikely that they would even have been viewed as foreign by local artisans. The term "Egyptianizing" is likely questionable in discussion of these locally produced scarabs from the Iron I. Finally, local artisans at inland sites such as Ahwat continued to produce local imitations of Egyptian motifs and writing by engraving them into materials like bone—a material very rarely used for Egyptian scarabs (e.g., Brandl 2012a, 255–57). Conoid and pyramidal stamp seals were also made in the southern Levant of locally available limestones. Scenes that appeared on New Kingdom Egyptian scarabs now appeared alongside local Canaanite motifs of caprids on these local stamp seals (e.g., Keel 2010b, 414–15 [Tell el-Far'a South 924]; 2013, 142–43 [Tel Gerisa 7]). While historians note the retraction of the Egyptian imperial system during the Twentieth Dynasty at the end of the Iron I, the iconography attested an enduring relationship between the two regions. It would be simplistic to correlate mere Egyptian hegemony and emulation of Egyptian iconography.

Iron IIA

Local iconography continued to have motifs with an Egyptian origin in the Iron IIA despite the political fragmentation of Egypt during the continuation of the Third Intermediate Period. One glyptic group, the so-called mass-produced Ramesside scarabs, grew in popularity during this period (Münger 2005), though its production began in the Iron I as attested by a seal found in a certain Iron I context from stratum XII at Qasile (A. Mazar 1985, 18–20, fig. 6). This group depicted motifs from scarabs in Egypt, including the "master of crocodiles" motif and the chariot scene with a bound enemy (e.g., Petrie 1909, plate XXXIV, no. 92). In fact, the motif of the "master of crocodiles" was a new addition to the southern Levantine iconographic tradition. Other scarabs produced in this period also mention the Egyptian deity Amun-Re, indicating possible worship of this deity in the southern Levant (Keel 1998, 138). While worship of Amun-Re likely occurred through amulets, he and many Egyptian deities found among the amulets of the Iron II are conspicuously absent from onomastic evidence (Tigay 1987a, 164). In addition to these new appropriations of Egyptian motifs, Iron IIA seals also curiously altered motifs with an Egyptian origin. Local southern Levantine stamp seals once depicted dyads and triads of Egyptian deities with distinctively Egyptian headdresses and linked hands (e.g., Keel 2010b, 414–15 [Tell el-Far'a South 924]). The image seems to have been appropriated in the Iron IIA, but as generic stick figures with linked hands. Anthropomorphic figures were no longer shown with their distinctive Egyptian headdresses or attire (L. Wright 2016, 247–48). As Egyptian hegemony waned in the Iron IIA, Keel argues, there was an intentional distancing of the local traditions from Egypt in their portrayal of deities (Keel 1998, 138–40). Keel cites the Mesopotamian motifs of the "master of the scorpions" and the "master of the ostriches" as replacements of the "master of crocodiles" motif. While the shift toward Mesopotamian based images is broadly true, the shift was gradual. All three motifs came from primary archaeological contexts with similar dates in the Iron IIA and Iron IIA–B (e.g., Brandl in Keel 1997, 60–61 [Achsib 115]; Keel 2010a, 222–23, 232–33, 236–37 [Beth Shemesh 10, 36, 42]; Keel

---

3. This motif consists of a sequence of hieroglyphs that represent the phonemes *a-n-r-(a)*, perhaps comparable to the use of an Egyptian abbreviation of three different signs representing "life, health, and prosperity" associated with the pharaoh and here adapted as a good-luck formula for protection.

2013, 120–21, 204–5 [Gath 55; Gezer 83]; Keel and Mazar 2009, no. 17).

Iron IIB

Iconographic elements with an Egyptian origin were increasingly mediated through the Syro-Phoenician iconographic traditions during the Iron IIB, especially at sites located in the northern kingdom, Israel (Keel 1998, 195–98, 248–51). As such, Syro-Phoenician motifs on scarabs and ivories cannot be strictly identified as Egyptian or Egyptianizing when found on locally produced southern Levantine objects. In addition to scarabs, amulets depicted Egyptian divine beings—such as Bes, Pataikos, and Isis—during the Iron IIB (C. Herrmann 2006, 35–38). Onomastic evidence also confirmed the worship of Bes and Horus in the Iron IIB, yet the rarity of Egyptian deities in theophoric names indicates that worship of these deities was never likely to be the dominant tradition in the region (Tigay 1987a, 164–65). The southern kingdom, Judah, also emulated broad trends in Egyptian iconography, though as novices. In fact, one group of locally made bone scaraboids depicted cartouches with hieroglyphs that have been variously identified as the throne name of Thutmosis III or a phonetic spelling of Sheshonq, yet they were more likely pseudo-hieroglyphs (e.g., Keel 1997, 588–89, 666–67 [Akko 164, Ashdod 11]; 2010a, 310–11, 394–95 [Beth Shemesh 215, Dan 30]; 2010b, 126–27 [Tell el-Far'a South 231]).

Iron IIC

Assyria's ascendancy in the Iron IIC led to much greater Mesopotamian influence on the iconographic traditions of the southern Levant. Egyptian influence wanes but is still present among amulets of Thoth, Anubis, Sakhmet, the Horus-eye, and the dwarf-like *pataikoi* (C. Herrmann 2006, 15, 35–38).

While Egyptian hegemony over the southern Levant recedes and advances from the Middle Bronze to the Iron Ages, Egyptian influence is constant. New Egyptian motifs were added constantly to long-established motifs that once had an Egyptian origin. The social, political, and iconographic ties between these two regions were persistent over the *longue durée* of the history of the southern Levant and ancient Israel.

Egyptian Iconography and the Biblical Text

Often Egyptian influence on images in biblical texts has been explained by employing a version of the comparative method. However, identifying Egyptian influence within biblical texts has been a methodologically problematic endeavor for over a century.

In the early twentieth century, the Assyriologist Friedrich Delitzsch used a rudimentary comparative method to elucidate biblical iconography using Near Eastern images. He described Near Eastern material culture and literature "as 'interpreter and illustrator' of the Bible" (Delitzsch 1903, 71). In publications filled with images of newly discovered Near Eastern iconography, he popularized the work of a previous generation of biblical scholars by presenting Mesopotamian imagery as a simplistic, unmediated parallel of the biblical text (e.g., Delitzsch 1903, 11, 20–21, 48, 56, 64). Hermann Gunkel critiqued the imprecision of Delitzsch's appropriation of biblical scholarship. According to Gunkel, Delitzsch identified simplistic similarities between ancient Babylonian and Israelite religion. Gunkel advanced the comparative methodology of biblical studies, though its progress may appear slight after a century of southern Levantine excavation. Gunkel argued that scholars must examine the similarities between parallel phenomena, whether artistic or literary, and the mechanisms whereby the parallels were created (Gunkel 2009 [German original 1903]). Gunkel's methodological shift would be foundational for later study of iconography, though he himself did not often examine iconographic evidence, which undoubtedly was partial at the time.

In the last half of the twentieth century, the comparative method was increasingly used for the study of ancient Israelite iconography. Biblical scholars sought to understand infrequent biblical images through parallel iconography from Egypt, Mesopotamia, and the Levant. Those using the comparative method expected the parallels to create greater elucidation of the biblical text as the geographic and chronological proximity shrunk (e.g., Pardee 1985; S. Parker 2000). With the discovery of the Ugaritic corpora, iconographic parallels with the Hebrew Bible multiplied. A sea of comparanda surrounded images employed once or infrequently in the texts of the Hebrew Bible, but the parallels did not always produce better readings of the text.

An example will illustrate the methodological problem. An image of Yahweh's "outstretched arm" and "strong hand" is repeatedly used within Deuteronomic sources and elsewhere (e.g., Deut. 4:34; 1 Kings 8:42; Jer. 32:21). The image has been connected to a related Egyptian phrase (Hoffmeier 1986) and group of images (see Strawn 2015) that are attested within West Semitic sources as early as the Amarna Letters, when Egyptian influence on the southern Levant was robust. One Akkadian lexeme is found in three of the Amarna Letters from the southern Levant, and it was a cognate to the Hebrew word for "arm" (Hoffmeier 1986, 384–85). This Akkadian lexeme is conspicuously attested only in Amarna Letters from Jerusalem, demonstrating that the motif likely reflected a local Levantine dialect. However, despite this evidence, a genetic connection between the biblical image and Egyptian iconography cannot be established. In fact, the image could also be connected to similar Mesopotamian imagery (J. Roberts 1971). Congruence alone between the chronologically and geographically

proximate Egyptian iconographic tradition did not necessarily reflect influence (de Hulster, Strawn, and Bonfiglio 2015b, 23–26).

Congruence of images from Egypt and the Hebrew Bible may also reflect indirect Egyptian influence on the broader West Semitic world that would have no longer been identified as specifically Egyptian by ancient Israelites. As noted above, images once thought to be Egyptian likely became part of the southern Levantine iconography after centuries of use. Biblical scholars have at times pointed to congruence between the winged seraph of Isaiah 6 as a likely winged snake (see the poetic lines in Isa. 14:29; 30:6; see also the appositional substantive in Deut. 8:15) and the uraeus common in Egyptian iconography. Nevertheless, the uraeus was already attested on locally produced scarabs from the Second Intermediate Period (D. Ben-Tor 2007, 127–29, 161–62, plates 52, nos. 41–59, 53, nos. 1–22, 77, nos. 15–42). Winged uraei were found on scarabs in the southern Levant during the Late Bronze II (e.g., Keel 2010a, 278–79 [Beth Shemesh 145]; 2010b, 186–87, 370–71, 386–87 [Tell el-Farʿa South 368, 811, 852]). Would ancient Israelites have even identified Isaiah's image as Egyptian in character? Perhaps not.

As the parallels multiplied, calls for caution against "parallelomania" restrained the field (Sandmel 1962). Because definitive identification of Egyptian or Mesopotamian influence on the iconography of many biblical texts was often challenging, if not impossible, careful scholars like William Hallo advocated a contextual approach that sought to "silhouette the biblical text against its wider literary and cultural environment" (Hallo 1990, 3) to discover where the biblical corpora reflected and contrasted with the broader ancient Near Eastern context. Because the genetic connections were almost always elusive to the careful scholar, silhouettes would have to do.

The silhouette often is created by the performance of a broad survey of Egyptian,

Mesopotamian, and Levantine comparanda for one biblical image. This so-called ancient Near Eastern context is the product of the scholar's imagination and never precisely existed in the ancient world. Nevertheless, the process of establishing the Near Eastern context disciplines the interpreter's subjectivity. Disciplined subjectivity then ages the relationship with the self by distancing the interpreter from the self to create awareness of the nature and kind of distance that lies between the interpreter and the reception of a text or object. Though admittedly the process is still subjective, the interpreter nevertheless prizes highly geographic and chronological proximity where possible in order to better understand the distance that lies between the interpreter and the interpreted. This process of knowledge creation creates inevitable distortions, yet discipline, transparency, and self-awareness limit them. Interpreters will never be able to fully traverse the gap between them and ancient receptions of an object or text, yet we hope to narrow the gap.

21

Mesopotamian and Anatolian Iconography

Daniel Bodi

Introduction

In line with its Greek etymology, the term "iconography" (from *eikōn* ["image"] + *graphē* ["writing, drawing"]) refers to all forms of visual representation found on ancient Near Eastern artifacts, including any material means of artistic pictorial illustration: reliefs, statues, sculptures, amulets, drawings, and seals and seal impressions (Amiet 1972; 1992; Beyer 2001). Two centuries of archaeological excavations from Egypt to Mesopotamia have provided a wealth of iconographic material, which, once properly analyzed, sheds new light on various aspects of biblical texts. Studying ancient visual art contemporary with the documents of the Hebrew Bible provides valuable insights for the reconstruction of the historical context of the biblical text and facilitates better understanding of cultural attitudes, showing how the ancient authors and audiences saw, thought, and made sense of their world. Right from the beginning of comparative studies, iconography caught the attention of biblical scholars as another approach that can lead to a more nuanced and better understanding of biblical texts. The Scriptures represent the single most important influence in the artistic inspiration of Western art and literature. As Northrop Frye convincingly argued, the Bible represents the "great code" of Western art (Frye 1982). The Bible is encyclopedic in its character, stretching from the creation to the end of the world, offering references to history, various prophetic visions, and rich poetic perspectives on human life and destiny. One of the reasons for the monumental impact of the Bible on the development of Western art and civilization is that it is deeply steeped in the cultures that preceded it for several millennia, drawing roots in the images and narrative themes and motifs from ancient Near Eastern art and literature.

The excavations at Tell Kuyunjik, ancient Nineveh, in the mid-nineteenth century by Austen Layard brought about the discovery of the monumental and richly decorated palaces of the Assyrian kings. Layard immediately suggested that Ezekiel's vision of the cherubim in Ezekiel 1 and 10 might have been inspired by the Assyrian composite creatures, winged

Fig. 21.1. Winged composite creature

Illustration by Isabelle Duport-Lercher after Gressmann, 1909, 88–89, figs. 163–64. Used with permission from the illustrator.

human-headed lion-bull figures guarding the palace portals. "It will be observed that the four forms chosen by Ezekiel to illustrate his description—the man, the lion, the bull, and the eagle,—are precisely those which are constantly found on Assyrian monuments as religious types" (Layard 1849b, 2:464; see Ackerman 2010, 124–42; fig. 21.1). Further excavations carried out at other Mesopotamian sites revealed the monumental realizations of ancient Babylonian rulers, and the readers of the Bible were able to better assess the world in which some of the events described in it took place. It prompted the publication of collections of ancient Near Eastern pictures by Hugo Gressmann in 1909 (Gressmann 1927) and James Pritchard in 1954 (Pritchard 1969b). These compilations manifest a somewhat fragmented approach to iconography, having a very low threshold for what constitutes congruence between text and image. Strictly speaking, iconography would be a discipline within art history (I. Winter 2010). An image communicates differently than a text. It has its own codes and language that need to be read and interpreted properly. In view of its importance for biblical studies, however, biblical scholars increasingly

use iconography in their work, without always possessing the theoretical tools of art historians and ignoring art-historical discussion about interpreting images.

Iconography and the Bible

The Old Testament scholar Othmar Keel—founder of the so-called Fribourg School of Biblical Iconography, which includes, among others, Urs Winter (1987), Silvia Schroer (1987), Christoph Uehlinger (Keel and Uehlinger 1998), and Thomas Staubli (1991)—was among the first to systematically exploit iconographic data to elucidate Psalms and other books of the Hebrew Bible (Keel 1978b; 1998; 1995; 2010a; 2010b; 2013; see also ch. 19). The use of images and iconography in Bible exegesis is somewhat hampered, however, due in part to the predominance of traditional word-centered exegesis and, to a great measure, a lack of proper methodology. This lacuna has now been filled with Izaak de Hulster's publications on the use of iconographic material in biblical exegesis, offering methodological guidelines with many references to previous studies and suggestions for further readings with an abundant seventy-page bibliography (de Hulster 2009; see also de Hulster and Schmitt 2009; de Hulster and LeMeon 2014a; de Hulster, Strawn, and Bonfilgio 2015a).

Within the limited scope of this article, a few examples will be adduced showing the heuristic value of ancient Near Eastern iconography for elucidating aspects of biblical texts. Since biblical texts and ancient Near Eastern iconography represent two different genres, for comparisons to be pertinent scholars should strive to achieve the "congruence triangle" by combining, first, a biblical text; second, related ancient Near Eastern texts; and, third, relevant iconographic examples. One should also respect chronological correlation and avoid combining, for example, Sumerian iconography from the third or second millennium

BCE with late first-millennium BCE Persian or Hellenistic texts with no intermediary texts or iconography to connect the two.

The Net Motif—Biblical and Ancient Near Eastern Textual and Iconographic Evidence

A good illustration of the "congruence triangle" is found in the work of Jean-Georges Heintz, who combined the iconographic approach with a systematic, thematic study of the net motif as the divine weapon (Heintz 2015, 48; Bodi 2016). Starting from the term *ḥrm* ("net"), which occurs several times in the biblical text of Ezekiel in the context of punishing the breach of the covenant relationship, he traced the motif in Sumerian and Akkadian literary texts, in Mari texts with prophetic content, and combined it with iconography: the Stele of the Vultures in Sumerian iconography and Sargon's Victory Stele in the Akkadian, Semitic domain. The reproductions shown below in figures 21.2 and 21.3 indicate that the Semites have adopted the ancient Sumerian net motif (Parrot 1957, 15; Spycket 1945–46, 152). The "divine net" is the weapon with which the divinity captures and punishes those who break the covenant.

Fig. 21.2. The Stele of the Vultures

Illustration by Isabelle Duport-Lercher after Parrot 1957, 15, fig. 5. Used with permission from the illustrator.

Heintz established a methodological requirement and procedure followed by subsequent scholars. The Old Babylonian Mari texts from the Northwest Semitic domain (Durand 1988, 473–74 [no. 233, lines 37–38, *ARM* X 80:14–15]; 424 [no. 197; lines 14–15, *ARM* XIII 23:9–10]; 438–39 [no. 209]) anticipate Hebrew usage of the motif (Ezek. 12:13; 17:20; 19:8,

Fig. 21.3. Sargon's Victory Stele

Illustration drawn by Isabelle Duport-Lercher after Spycket 1945–46, 152, fig. 1. Used with permission from the illustrator.

9; 32:3), confirming numerous similarities not only in form but also in content (Bodi 1991, 162–82). A recently published cuneiform text (Veenhof 2003, 325), confirms the real presence of the net as a weapon of divine punishment on occasions of swearing oaths in conjunction with covenant making (British Museum 96998, lines 39 and 49), creating an almost physical awareness of the danger of perjury (see figs. 21.2 and 21.3).

Living Waters and Trees of Healing in Ezekiel 47:1–12 and in Ancient Near Eastern Texts and Iconography

The following case study respects the "congruence triangle" and offers an example where the three elements mentioned above are present. In Ezekiel 47:1–12 two major ancient Near Eastern literary, iconographic, and religious motifs have found their way into a vision of spectacular renewal, a desert turning into a fertile region: (1) the rivers of living waters or a double current flowing from the temple in Jerusalem and (2) the trees of healing growing on the river banks (Bodi 2015). Ezekiel is the only Hebrew prophet who uses both motifs combined in the way they are in ancient Near Eastern texts and iconography, which implies that the book of Ezekiel is where these motifs entered the biblical tradition. The Hebrew term used in Ezekiel 47:2 to designate the bursting forth of water (*mayim mepakkim*) under the podium of the temple is a hapax legomenon. The form *mepakkim* is a D-stem (piel) participle of the verb *pakah*, which means "to flow or gurgle from a vase" (*pak*, meaning "vase" or "jar").

The rabbis correctly understood this unusual feature. *Tosefta Sukkah* 3:10 comments on Ezekiel 47:1–12: "This teaches that all waters of creation (*mê bᵉrēʾšît*) have to come out as if from a bottleneck" (Lieberman 1969, 269). Moreover, the use of the dual *naḥᵃlayim* ("rivers") in Ezekiel 47:9a for the double current flowing from the Jerusalem temple probably is a reflex of the two rivers issuing from a flowing vase as attested in ancient Near Eastern iconography.

The Middle and Neo-Assyrian Healing Incantations

The motif of the tree of healing found in Ezekiel 47:12 seems to have a Mesopotamian background and appears to originate in the Babylonian literary tradition. It is found in a bilingual healing incantation with versions from Middle and Neo-Assyrian times. The latter copy was found in the library of the Assyrian king Ashurbanipal in Kuyunjik dating from the seventh century BCE (Campbell Thompson 1903, 1:200–202 [Part XVI, plates 46, 183–47, 198]). The use of two languages and particularly of Sumerian in such a late text is not surprising in view of the effective magical power that the ancient Mesopotamians attributed to cuneiform signs and to incantations (Glassner 1989, 1638–39). In this particular worldview, the word was capable of bringing into being the thing evoked. "The conviction that a name somewhat partakes of the reality of that which it denotes is a prominent feature of Sumerian, as of most other, mythopoeic thought" (Jacobsen 1946, 149).

In this bilingual Sumerian-Akkadian incantation (Widengren 1951, 5–7; Geller 1980, 34) a series of symbols is invoked: a particular tree, the dark *kiškanū*, possessing therapeutic virtues; the primordial waters of the *apsû*, which have creative, regenerative powers; several divinities are called upon, such as Nammu, active in the creation of human beings, as well as other gods who provide abundance, renewal, and fertility. The healing incantation mentions the tree called giš-kin in Sumerian and *kiškanū* in Akkadian, possessing particular therapeutic virtues. The incantation text here quoted is for a sick man, and the *kiškanū* tree is to afford the remedy for his disease. A medical text describes the concoction of a particular drug for medical usage from the bark of the *kiškanū* tree. In the Assyrian texts, *kiškanū* is a plant or tree appearing as *peṣû* ("white"), *ṣalmu* ("black, dark"), and *sāmu* ("red, brown"). The tree of healing mentioned in Ezekiel 47:12 would thus incorporate the therapeutic function of certain trees from the Babylonian literary and medical tradition. The Ezekiel passage mentions trees in plural. It heightens and multiplies the usefulness of the healing trees.

Moreover, in the incantation, the *kiškanū* tree growing at the mouth of two rivers plays the role of the tree of life. It provides the source of life and eternal youth, and its sap flows from the deep regions of the primordial waters, *abzu*. The conjunction of the *kiškanū* and the *abzu* is found already in the third-millennium BCE Sumerian Gudea Cylinder (A xxi 22): g i š—g a n á—a b z u—g i n ("like the giš-gana of the abzu"). In the context of this incantation, with its reinvigorating, regenerating, and healing powers, the *kiškanū* tree serves to readjust the troubled and distraught person, providing a central axis around which the sick person can regroup and reactivate his or her regenerative and self-healing forces. From an anthropological point of view, the incantation would be a form of a talking cure aiming at "stimulating an organic transformation which would consist essentially in a structural reorganization" (Lévi-Strauss 1963, 201; cf. 192). It also reveals the mythological and religious origins of ancient Babylonian medical practices. Even today, the caduceus, the symbol of the physicians and the medical trade, represents a tree around which one or two serpents are intertwined.

The Iconographic Motif of the "Streams Flowing from a Vase" at the Uruk Ishtar Temple

In the city of Uruk, the Kassite king Karaindaš in the fourteenth century BCE built a temple whose vestiges are still well preserved. The temple, dedicated to the goddess Ishtar, had a remarkable exterior decoration made out of multicolored glazed bricks with reliefs representing an entire row of different gods and goddesses holding in front of their breast or belly a vase out of which two rivers flowed. The flow of water was represented by a spiral going from one divinity to another, surrounding the entire facade of the temple in an imaginary flow (Andrae 1939, plate 152, fig. 1; Bodi 2009, 497; see fig. 21.4). The symbolism of water associated with Ishtar can be explained by the fact that she is the goddess not only of battle and war but also of sex and fertility, and there can be no fertility without water.

The Painting of the So-Called Investiture of the King at Mari

This color painting (2.5 meters long and 1.75 meters high), dating from the beginning of the second millennium BCE, was discovered on one of the walls decorating the court (designated room 106 by excavators) at the Mari Royal Palace (fig. 21.5). Its original colors are still well preserved (Parrot 1937b, 335–46; Bodi 2009, 498; Charpin and Ziegler 2003, 19). The painting is comprised of a central scene with upper and lower registers, framed on both sides with stylized tree representations. All of the drawn items are represented in twos and symmetrically placed: two palm-trees; two trees that are difficult to identify; four winged animals, probably griffins, guarding access to the trees; and two divinities. The goddess Ishtar in battle attire dominates the scene in the upper level. The present analysis focuses only on the lower register, where two goddesses hold a vase with rivers of flowing waters.

The two goddesses face each other, holding in their hands at the level of their breasts the vase from which flow the streams and from which a plant grows with stylized leaves depicted symmetrically. The living and fertilizing character of the waters is highlighted by the numerous fish that swim up and down the

Fig. 21.4. The façade of the Ištar temple at Uruk, built by the Kassite king Karaindaš in the fourteenth century BCE, representing a row of divinities holding a vase out of which streams flow connecting the entire temple with an uninterrupted spiral.

Illustration drawn by Isabelle Duport-Lercher after Andrae 1939, plate 152.1. Used with permission from the illustrator.

Fig. 21.5. Painting of the investiture of the king of Mari dating from the eighteenth century BCE

Illustration drawn by Isabelle Duport-Lercher after Parrot 1937b, 325–54 (335–46), plate 39. Used with permission from the illustrator.

rivers, recalling the fish in Ezekiel 47:9–10 ("its fish [i.e., of the Dead Sea] will be of a great many kinds, like the fish of the Great Sea [i.e., of the Mediterranean]"). Some scholars have identified the rivers of flowing waters with the Tigris and the Euphrates (Heuzey 1891–1915, 169), the major sources of food and prosperity for Mesopotamia, providing abundant fish and transportation of goods. From each vase emerges a plant, maybe an ear of grain, again standing for fertility and abundance. In this Mari pictorial representation the dominant theme is that of fertility as symbolized by the streams of flowing waters. The entire painting is encircled by an uninterrupted spiral representing the flowing waters. In her interpretation of this painting, Marie-Thérèse Barrelet (1950, 19) suggested that we see in it a material and graphic representation of a temple following ancient Mesopotamian conventions. If her interpretation is correct, the temple aspect makes the comparison with Ezekiel's temple even more pertinent.

The Statue of the Goddess with a Flowing Vase at Mari, Lagaš, and Hatti and in Syria

During the third campaign of excavations at the Mari palace, at the feet of a podium in room 64, André Parrot (1937a, 78–80, plate XII; van Buren 1933) unearthed a statue of a goddess with a flowing vase decorated with spirals symbolizing water (fig. 21.6). The vase that the goddess holds with both hands at the level of her belly is hollow and is connected with an exterior conduit going vertically through the statue. The water comes from an external reservoir, placed at a higher level, and flows from the inclined vase,

Fig. 21.6. Statue of a goddess with a flowing vase found at Mari from the eighteenth century BCE

Illustration drawn by Isabelle Duport-Lercher after Parrot 1937a, 54–84 (78–80), plate 12. Used with permission from the illustrator.

Fig. 21.7. Statue of King Gudea of Lagaš (ca. 2200 BCE) with streams flowing from a vase

Illustration drawn by Isabelle Duport-Lercher after the statue at the Louvre Museum in Paris. Used with permission from the illustrator.

offering a striking spectacle to people who came to the inner court in the Mari palace. The visitors of the king were witnessing a "miracle," devised in such a way as to impress them, with the refreshing and fertilizing waters dispensed by the goddess to her worshipers. This iconographic motif is very ancient, found already in Sumer. In Lagaš, King Gudea (ca. 2200 BCE) had a statue of himself carrying a vase with flowing waters (fig. 21.7).

The iconographic motif of a vase with flowing streams found in Sumerian Lagaš and later at Mari is also found on a Hittite cylinder seal published by André Parrot (1951, 182) and dated to the middle of the second millennium BCE. The hematite cylinder depicts a female divinity holding a vase from which four streams flow, and one stream fills a goblet. Another hematite cylinder from northern Syria dating from 1850–1720 BCE represents a water divinity with streams issuing from his shoulders and holding a flowing vase.[1]

The Hittite Cylinder Seal Impression and the Sacred Space

In the field of iconography, the seal impressions from numerous ancient Near Eastern cylinder seals are often used to shed some light on biblical motifs (Keel 1977, figs. 183–85; see fig. 21.8).

1. The cylinder seal can be seen online at http://www .bible-orient-museum.ch/bodo/details.php?bomid=580. It is provided by the Bibel+Orient Museum in Fribourg, Switzerland, which offers a helpful database called Bibel+Orient Datenbank Online, or BODO (http:// www.bible-orient-museum.ch/bodo/).

Fig. 21.8. Seal impression from an Akkadian cylinder-seal showing a divinity with a flowing vase in the middle of a sacred space guarded by two similar looking beings

Illustration drawn by Isabelle Duport-Lercher after Porada 1948, plate 31, no. 202E. Used with permission from the illustrator.

Othmar Keel interprets the presence of guardians on such a cylinder-seal impression as having a role to uphold the skies and to mark the separation between the sacred and the profane domains, ensuring that the soiled and impure field remains separated from what is pure and holy. In Ezekiel 10:1 the prophet sees above the heads of the cherubim the firmament or the skies. This function of the guardians of the sacred space is further illustrated with orthostat reliefs from Ain Dara (see fig. 21.9).

Such representations of guardians on both sides of a divinity imply an iconographic code that requires interpretation in order to be understood. In this case, comparative ancient Near Eastern iconography brings a corrective and tempers the enthusiasm of some commentators who spoke of the revolutionary aspect of Yhwh's theophany in the impure land of Babylonia. On the contrary, the presence of the cherubim with lion, human, bull, and eagle heads in the visions of Yhwh's throne in the land of Babylonia as described in Ezekiel 1 and 10 underlines the radical separation between the holiness of Yhwh and the impure land of Babylon, polluted by idolatry.

A new generation of scholars, realizing that ancient Near Eastern iconography provides a window into the cultural, social, religious, and political world behind the Hebrew Bible, are increasingly practicing iconographic exegesis, striving to refine its methodology and elaborate precise interpretative codes. One of the pitfalls of which this type of research should be aware, however, is the increased presence of fake archaeological objects on the market, of unknown provenance, which calls for circumspection and vigilance.

Fig. 21.9. Orthostat reliefs from Ain Dara showing a divinity guarded by winged creatures with a lion, human, and eagle heads

Illustration drawn by Isabelle Duport-Lercher after Keel 1977, figs. 183–85. Used with permission from the illustrator.

22

Canaanite/Israelite Iconography

BRENT A. STRAWN

Introduction

In light of the Second Commandment of the Decalogue, which prohibits the making of images (Exod. 20:4–6; Deut. 5:8–10), readers of the Bible who are unfamiliar with the artifactual record might suspect that the presence of artistic remains in ancient Israel/Palestine would be slim to nonexistent. But, as those who are familiar with the archaeology of the land know well, nothing could be further from the truth. To borrow from the title of Silvia Schroer's important monograph on the subject, *In Israel gab es Bilder* (1987), "there were pictures in Israel." As Schroer observes, the Old Testament itself mentions a good bit of representational art—the decorative elements in Solomon's temple, for example, or the bronze serpent, or the ephod (see Schroer 1987, 46–66, 104–15, 155–58, respectively). Such items are not at odds with the Second Commandment since that command does not prohibit *all* representation, but speaks only of *divine* representations, including, perhaps, representation of Israel's own God, Yhwh.[1]

1. It may even be the case that the prohibition is less about figural art per se and more about the nature of

Be that as it may, the Second Commandment has been generously interpreted for millennia so as to encompass not only aniconism (lacking visual images) with reference to the divine realm (both God and the gods) but also aniconism in many other arenas of religious experience. The various iconoclastic moments in the history of Christianity, Judaism, Islam, and beyond are instructive examples of this interpretive tendency (see Latour and Weibel 2002), with the Reformed tradition of Protestant Christianity particularly noteworthy for the great significance it places on the prohibition of images (writ large) in Christian worship (see Dyrness 2004). It is no doubt due to these much later controversies over "the image" that the aniconic tendency of ancient Israelite religion (and elsewhere) has often been overstated and overestimated. Even those who are new to the Bible or who do not practice Christianity or Judaism are likely to know—if they know nothing else about

divine images and image-making since, in the ancient world, images were a primary way that divine presence was thought to become real (see, e.g., Dick 1998; Walker and Dick 2001; Bahrani 2003). Prohibiting such images and image-making is thus a rejection of rival deities as well as a way to halt their ability to become manifest.

worship, in ancient Israel—something about its supposed aniconism.

But, according to David Freedberg, aniconism is a widespread myth (Freedberg 1989, 54–81), and this judgment holds true not only for Israel in its earliest stages (cf. Mettinger 1995). Much later than that, well after the establishment of the Torah and the Decalogue therein, various groups within early Judaism made extensive use of artistic images, employing, for example, zodiacal representations in synagogue mosaics (Avi-Yonah 1981; L. I. Levine 2012; Goodenough 1953–68). To this one might add, *inter alia*, the artistic use of the Hebrew script in the beautiful carpet pages of medieval manuscripts of the Hebrew Bible such as Codex Leningradensis (D. Freedman et al. 1998). Still further, even the strictest interpretation of the Second Commandment did not prohibit the authors of Scripture from figuring Yhwh in a vast range of images, symbols, and metaphors—even if these are limited to instances of figural language rather than figural art (e.g., Korpel 1990; cf. LeMon 2010).

The present chapter focuses on the ancient periods, and its title, "Canaanite/Israelite Iconography," requires some explanation. First, "iconography" may be defined as the study of artistic/visual remains and is also a shorthand term for those remains themselves. An orientation to iconographic study and method with reference to ancient Israelite history and religion, as well as to the exegesis of the Hebrew Bible, is found in chapter 19 above (see further de Hulster 2009; de Hulster, Strawn, and Bonfiglio 2015a). As for "Canaanite/Israelite," the combined term in this instance is quite important, not a matter of confusion as to the proper category. It is not always clear, that is, when a particular artifact is specifically "Israelite" as opposed to more generally "Canaanite." Periodization, while helpful, is not foolproof. Obviously, something from the Middle Bronze period (2000–1550 BCE) should be characterized as "Canaanite" since there was no Israelite

nation-group yet established in the land. But, even in periods after the traditional date of such establishment (after, i.e., the Late Bronze to Iron Age transition, ca. 1200 BCE), it is still possible that various finds might reflect *non-*Israelite practice and belief. Alternatively, seen from a different vantage point, some scholars have opined that the Israelites themselves were Canaanites (Finkelstein and Silverman 2001; Dever 2003), and so, again, the combination "Canaanite/Israelite" is instructive. If it seems noncommittal, that is not without good reason, especially as the combined term is an attempt to remain descriptive without importing too many assumptions about (later) developments in religious beliefs and practices into the earliest periods.

Even if the combined term is helpful in some ways, it is problematic in others, particularly insofar as it potentially (even exponentially) expands the range of what could and should be treated in an article devoted to this topic. Given space limitations, specificity is in order, and so in what follows I explore some well-known and/or well-attested iconographic pieces from ancient Israel/Palestine, which afford access to important aspects of Cananite/Israelite iconography and the question of representation of God and the gods. The presentation here is a truly infinitesimal sample and so cannot claim to be representative, though I hope it is informative and generative for further thinking on these subjects nonetheless.[2]

The Bull Statue . . . and El/Yhwh (?)

We begin with the famous bronze figurine of a bull (17.5 cm long, 12.4 cm tall) that was found east of Dothan in what might be an

---

2. The most important repositories of images for the study of iconography, ancient Israelite religion, and the Hebrew Bible are Keel 1978b; 1995; 1997; 2010a; 2010b; 2013; Keel and Uehlinger 1998; Eggler and Keel 2006; Schroer and Keel 2005; Schroer 1987; 2008; 2011; U. Winter 1987.

open-air shrine dating to the twelfth century BCE (fig. 22.1). Such a figurine is unique in the archaeology of Israel/Palestine and quite rare among the many bronze figurines that have been recovered from the Levant (A. Mazar 1982a, 29); the uniqueness of the piece complicates its analysis. The excavator of the site, Amihai Mazar, observed that "the importance of the bull motif in Syro-Palestinian iconography from the Middle Bronze Age onward is illustrated by numerous examples," noting that it "appears as an object of cult, both by itself and as an attribute of the storm god Hadad (Baʿal)" (1982a, 30). Indeed, on the basis of several bull representations that he amassed, Mazar asserted that "the worship of the bull as a symbol of a deity was well known in the Levant during the second millennium B.C." (1982a, 32). Most scholars would agree with such a statement, but the key question in this particular case is: *Which* deity is evoked here (if any)? The high quality of the figurine, coupled with the fact that it was cast in bronze, not made of terra cotta, suggests that it was quite important, which suits a piece designed for cultic use (Schroer 1987, 93–94). But again, worship of *exactly what or whom*? And how, exactly, might the bull figurine have been used?

Unfortunately, we simply cannot answer these crucial questions given the paucity of evidence recovered from the site (A. Mazar 1982a, 1983; Zevit 2001, 176–80). That has not stopped scholars from identifying this bull as a representation of the weather god Hadad-Baʿal (per Mazar), or El, or even Yhwh (see Coogan 1987; Keel and Uehlinger 1998, 118). In point of fact, while bull imagery is

Fig. 22.1. Bronze figurine (17.5 cm long, 12.4 cm high), east of Dothan, ca. twelfth century BCE. See also A. Mazar 1982a, 30–31, figs. 2–3; cf. Keel and Uehlinger 1998, 119, fig. 142; Schroer 1987, 524, fig. 43.
© Baker Publishing Group and Dr. James C. Martin

not infrequently used of the first two gods, most especially El (particularly at Ugarit; see Curtis 1990; Pope 1955), it is quite rare with reference to Yhwh (see Korpel 1990, 532–38; Schroer 1987, 95–104; far more frequent is the lion: see Strawn 2005). It seems rather unlikely, therefore, to identify this bronze figure with Yhwh, but—and this is the point—it seems equally speculative to associate this bull with *any* specific deity since we have no corroborating evidence to establish the claim. "Like every other important natural entity," Keel and Uehlinger write, "the bull's significance is complex," so "only context can show which of the possible meanings was most important in that particular culture" (1998, 118) or in a given instance of the image(ry). The presence of additional context for a proper interpretation is thus as crucial for iconography as it is in the study of words (philology) and literature. But, as Keel and Uehlinger go on to note, such context "is not available when a bronze figure is found all by itself [as in the Bull Site] . . . [in which case] even the simplest two-dimensional picture generally furnishes more contextual elements" (1998, 118).

One can, of course, look at other iconographic representations of bulls; such comparative analysis demonstrates that the animal's power is typically what is emphasized as opposed to, say, its fertility (see Keel and Uehlinger 1998, 118–20). Images of the bull not infrequently associate the animal with deities, especially the weather god, and can serve as the mount or familiar—even the emblem—of such divinities (see, e.g., Pritchard 1969a, 170, figs. 500–501).[3] But insofar as the various comparable pieces were not found at the Bull Site, it is difficult to know if and/or how far they may obtain for a proper interpretation of this famous figurine. In the end, then, the bronze bull from the Bull Site remains a curious enigma. Its workmanship and medium suggest that it is an important object, probably one used in worship, but beyond that little more can be said. Even association with El is not foolproof since there is little *textual* attestation of El's bovine profile in the Levant outside the earlier Ugaritic texts (Pope 1955). Finally, we should observe that it is not certain that the Bull Site is Israelite, and some scholars have challenged the dating, positing that it is much earlier than the twelfth century (see Hess 2007, 236).

The Judean Pillar Figurines . . . and Asherah (?)

The Judean Pillar Figurines are particularly well known in discussions of ancient Israelite religion (fig. 22.2), if only because a vast number have been found in Jerusalem (Darby 2014, 98, 143). There are actually several different types of such figurines, but, in the main, they can be described as "small clay figurines with pillar bases and arms either supporting or

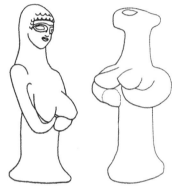

Fig. 22.2. Judean Pillar Figurines
After Keel and Uehlinger 1998, 326, figs. 321a–c, used with permission.

holding the breasts; a small number hold a disk or a child" (Darby 2014, 2). Apart from, perhaps, references to *teraphim* (NRSV: "household gods"; NJPS: "household idols"; CEB: "household's divine images"), especially in a text like Genesis 31, which says that Rachel stole (√*gnb*, v. 19) such items and indicates they were small enough to hide in a saddle and sit on (v. 34), we probably would not know what to call objects like the Pillar Figurines. But even the texts that employ the word *teraphim* (or various other words for "idols") do not necessarily lead one to expect the particular form of the Pillar Figurines; nor should one simply assume that the Pillar Figurines are *teraphim*. Hence, the crucially important question is: Are the Judean Pillar Figurines idols? If so, idols of what or of whom?

Many scholars have believed that the Pillar Figurines do represent a deity—especially a mother goddess, since the often enlarged breasts

3. The use of the bull as an emblem or symbol means that the animal may "stand in" for the deity even when the god in question is not present. Such could be the case with the bull figurine from the Bull Site, and the kinds of usage described above have often been taken to bear on the discussion of the golden calf (Exod. 32:4) and Jeroboam's calves at Bethel and Dan (1 Kings 12:28–29). The biblical calves, no less than the bull from the Bull Site, could, that is, be seen as animal mounts, in which case they would not represent the object of worship proper but instead somehow "carry" the divine presence on their backs, even if the divine "image" in question is present only aniconically: by means of empty space (see Mettinger 1995). Once again, the data at hand permit no firm conclusions on these matters with reference to the bull figurine or the calves mentioned in the Old Testament. It should also be noted that there are other animals (realistic and otherwise) that are used as divine mounts and emblems.

on the figurines seem to imply fertility—with not a few positing the specific goddess in question to be Asherah (see, e.g., Dever 2005; for a review of this interpretive trend, see Darby 2014, 34–60, esp. 34–46). The problems besetting such an interpretation are several, however. For one thing, there is no clear epigraphic indication on any of these pieces that the female figure is (1) a goddess, let alone (2) the specific goddess Asherah. Barring such an identifying tag, one must look to other details for confirmation: Do the Pillar Figurines contain iconography that is identifiable as Asherah? Most iconographers would reply in the negative because it is hard to speak of a distinctive Asherah iconography (Cornelius 2004a; 2009; Merlo 2010). Moreover—and this is not unlike the situation with the bull figurine—apart from the Ugaritic texts, there is little *textual* data from ancient Israel/Palestine that would confirm an association of Asherah with fertility. If the Judean Pillar Figurines represent a deity, then it is very difficult to say which deity it is, especially given the overlapping presentations of several goddess profiles (Cornelius 2004a). So, if the figurines represent a goddess, it is at least possible that they represent different goddesses, not just (and maybe not at all) Asherah. If there is a divine connection, moreover, it probably is not with a major goddess but rather with an unnamed associate—in part due to the cheap quality of the media (clay, not often used for idol construction) and the often crude craftsmanship. So, in Erin Darby's judgment, "the extended search for the figurines' identity is misguided" (2014, 366), while others wonder if the Pillar Figurines are depictions, not of the worshiped deity, but of the worshipers themselves: they are "prayers in clay," as it were (Zevit 2001, 274; Cornelius 2009, 84).

Another interpretation has posited that the Judean Pillar Figurines have some sort of erotic function or that they were used somehow to encourage reproduction (Byrne 2004). This line of interpretation also suffers a number of problems, most especially the fact that the pudendum proper is not depicted on the figurines, which are, to the contrary, rather modest below the waist. Such modesty can be contrasted with other examples of far more explicit art from the ancient Near East (see Keel 1994; U. Winter 1987, figs. 340–66), whatever the purpose of this latter may have been.

After Darby's comprehensive review of the media used, the archaeological distribution (most of the figurines are found "as random trash in domestic structures without any evidence for specialized deposition" [2014, 31]), the cognate evidence, the iconography, and so forth, she concludes that the Judean Pillar Figurines do *not* represent main deities, nor are they "recipients of accompanying supplications" (2014, 399). The Pillar Figurines were not, that is, objects of veneration. The find spots simply will not allow one to say that the figurines were elite cult objects; the fact that apparently they were not used in formal shrine spaces, but were instead recovered in domestic contexts, suggests that any rituals associated with these figurines "must have been performed in or near the home" (2014, 400). Still further, the chronological distribution of the figurines will not permit their easy association with reform (or counter-reform) movements: they "arise prior to the supposed reforms of Hezekiah, remain popular through the end of the eighth century, and continue to be produced through the supposed Josianic reform and until the destruction of Jerusalem. Thus, they appear to have been totally unaffected by reforms associated with Yahwistic orthodoxy" (2014, 400). On the basis of figurine rituals from elsewhere in the ancient Near East, where it was the main deities who inflicted and cured disease, with lower-level supernatural beings serving as intermediaries, Darby argues that the Pillar Figurines "would not have threatened the belief in Yahweh, whether Yahweh was considered the head deity above others or the only deity" (2014, 401). Finally, Darby opines that the archaeological evidence does not support any particular connection between the Pillar Figurines and specifically female petitioners or concerns (2014, 402).

In the end, then, it seems that the best understanding of the Judean Pillar Figurines is that they played some sort of role in protection and healing; they are thus best attributed some sort of apotropaic function. Darby notes that their pillar-shaped body and base allowed for easy placement around a house "in open and liminal areas," or perhaps allowed their being "stationed around the body of a sick individual," even as they might also "be wielded by hand during a ritual" (2014, 394). While these conclusions are less exciting, perhaps, than identifying such a figurine *as* the goddess Asherah, they nevertheless are quite significant. In Darby's opinion, "far from being relegated to heterodoxy or base instinct, apotropaic figurine rituals were probably an important aspect of the Iron II ritual complex" (2014, 404–5). This is an important observation that affords significant insight onto Israelite religion in the Iron Age II, even if it is less spectacular or controversial than those interpretations that (wrongly) identify the figurines with Asherah and use them to assert widespread heterodox worship of the goddess(es).

Kuntillet ʿAjrud . . . and Yhwh (?) and A/asherah (?)

There is probably no more famous image and inscription related to Canaanite/Israelite iconography than Pithos A from Kuntillet ʿAjrud, which dates to the first half of the eighth century (fig. 22.3). The find was a blockbuster as soon as it was announced, though it took almost forty years for the final excavation report to appear (Meshel 2012). What was so exciting about the find was that, in contrast to the bull figurine from the Bull Site or the Judean Pillar

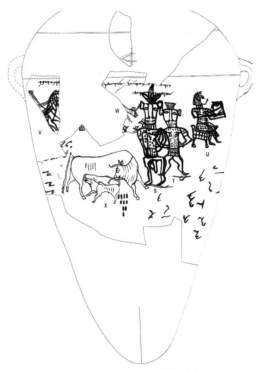

Fig. 22.3. Pithos A; partial, drawing of the right side; Kuntillet ʿAjrud (L6); eighth century BCE. See also LeMon and Strawn 2013, 97, fig. 3.

After Meshel 2012, 147, fig. 6.4a, used with permission.

Figurines, here was an image accompanied by an inscription (or so it seemed). Although Pithos A contains quite a number of images (fig. 22.4), the figures that were of most interest were the two bovine-like figures, one (S) larger than the other (T), with a lyre-player (U) apparently belonging to the same iconographic constellation. Across the top, making contact with the headdress of figure S, is an inscription that reads (Meshel 2012, 87):

1 ʾmr.ʾ[-]°°[-]m̊[-]k.ʾmr.lyhl̊ẙ.wlyw°šh.wl[——
——] brkt.ʾtkm.

2 lyhwh.šmrn.wlʾšrth.

1 Message of ʾ[-]°°[-]M[-]K: "Speak to Yāhēlî, and to Yôʿāśāh, and to [. . .] I have blessed you

2 to Yhwh of Shōmrōn (Samaria) and to His *asherah*.

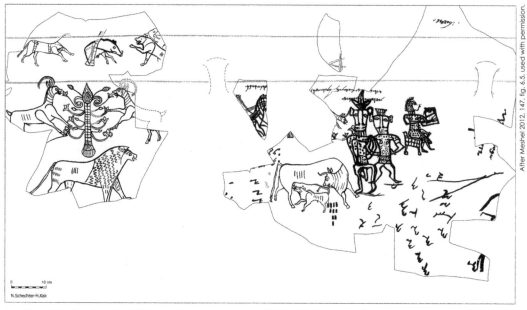

After Meshel 2012, 147, fig. 6.5. used with permission.

Fig. 22.4. Projection drawing of Pithos A. See also Strawn and LeMon forthcoming, fig. 5.

Several scholars were quick to see in this inscription a description of or caption for the images: the inscription must identify the figures as Yhwh and Asherah (*lyhwh šmrn wl'šrth*). But here again things proved to be not quite so straightforward. Problems beset the interpretation of the inscription, the images, and their interrelation (see Strawn and LeMon forthcoming).

First, with regard to the inscription: according to most scholars, the Hebrew language does not permit a suffix on a proper noun (see, e.g., Emerton 1999; but contrast Xella 1995; 2001). One can write "his *house*" but not "his *David*." If this grammatical rule is correct and universal, the word *'šrth* cannot be "his Asherah"—the proper name of a goddess, presumed by some to be Yhwh's consort—as this would break the rule. Instead, the word must mean "his *asherah*," whatever *asherah* might mean here, with the main possibilities being some sort of religious object (a wooden pole that perhaps symbolized the goddess?) or a word designating a place ("his sanctuary"?).

Second, with regard to the iconography: Why are there two bovine-like figures, and which, if either (or both!), represents Yhwh?

Some scholars argued that the smaller figure was female, perhaps a goddess (again, Asherah?), with still others positing that the seated lyre player was the goddess in question. Most iconographers now think the bovine figures are representations of the Egyptian god Bes (Keel and Uehlinger 1998, 220–23; cf. Zevit 2001, 387–88). Pirhiya Beck (1982) authored the definitive article on the iconography at Kuntillet 'Ajrud,[4] in which she determined that not all of the images on Pithos A were drawn at the same time, and so the present configuration is the work of more than one artist. Bes figure T and the lyre-player U were drawn before Bes figure S. An enduring question is whether the two Bes figures are different genders: in some drawings of the pithos (e.g., Keel and Uehlinger 1998, 213, fig. 220), there is an object between the legs of *both* Bes figures, which some have identified as a phallus. If that is

4. Reprinted in P. Beck 2002, 94–170. Beck's essay was also republished, but with a few important differences, in Meshel 2012, 143–203 (for a discussion, see LeMon and Strawn 2013, 85n7). Beck has been followed closely by Keel and Uehlinger 1998, 210–48; see also LeMon and Strawn 2013; Strawn and LeMon forthcoming.

After Meshel 2012, 148, fig. 6.6, used with permission.

Fig. 22.5. Projection drawing of Pithos B; Kuntillet ʿAjrud (L19), eighth century BCE. See also Strawn and LeMon forthcoming, fig. 6.

correct, it is difficult indeed to identify one figure as male and the other female. Most recently, however, Ze'ev Meshel has expressed the opinion that there is no object between figure T's legs: Meshel believes it to have been a soot smudge that faded over time (2012, 65). Still others have posited that the object in question, on either or both figures, is not a phallus at all but a tail loop of sorts, not uncommon with Bes iconography (see Keel and Uehlinger 1998, 219n49).

And third, with regard to the interrelation of the images and the inscription: according to Pirhiya Beck's diachronic, stratigraphic analysis, the inscription was added later as the third and last stage in the composition of this particular tableau, and by a different hand than the one that drew figure S (stage 2) and figures T and U (stage 1). If Beck is correct, the inscription may not be an integral part of

the scene at all but little more than a graffito that someone wrote after the fact and that may have nothing whatsoever to do with the images. Pithos A contains a decent number of different images, after all—and the same is true for Pithos B (fig. 22.5)—and it is very hard to "read" them all as one coherent scene (see P. Beck 1982). Furthermore, even if the inscription did mean to identify two of the various figures as Yhwh and his consort, which image is which deity, especially given the third figure (the lyre player), not to mention the other options on Pithos A? According to Keel and Uehlinger (1998, 241), the best candidate for a representation of "A/asherah" is not the lyre player or either of the Bes figures, but rather the stylized tree that apparently is riding on the back of a lion mount (fig. 22.6).

In sum, even when an image is accompanied—and in the case of Pithos A this may

Fig. 22.6. Detail of Pithos A, left side. See also LeMon and Strawn 2013, 100, fig. 6.

After Meshel 2012, 147, fig. 6.4, used with permission.

be the wrong word—by an inscription, interpretation is seldom an easy matter. Early interpreters were overly excited; Beck's careful treatment tempers all that. And yet, even if Beck is correct, with the (later) inscription having no necessary relationship with the images, it is still the case that the pithos now does contain *both* an inscription mentioning Yhwh and asherah along with a number of images on the same object. The current composition, that is, suggests that at least one person—the scribe responsible for adding the inscription perhaps—may have seen in the two Bes figures and lyre player (if not also other images on the pithos) a representation (or evocation?) of Yhwh and his A/asherah. The same judgment may have also held true for other viewers who came along after the inscription was added, assuming that they could read the inscription. But even if they could not read the inscription, if they had some measure of visual literacy (far more common, it would seem, in antiquity than skill in reading and writing), later viewers may well have "seen" in the Kuntillet ʿAjrud figures a divine pair (or couple), with a third divine figure (or worshiper). It is equally possible that Yahwists viewing the pithos may have identified Yhwh with one or more of the Bes figures (see LeMon and Strawn 2013, 102–12; Strawn and LeMon forthcoming; more fully Bonfiglio

2016, 227–310). In the case of iconography, no less than with literature, authorial or artistic intention is only one factor in interpretation—and not always the most important one. Alongside questions of production and intention are the equally important issues of interpretation on the part of the viewer/reader and the reception of the art at hand.

Seals . . . and Plentiful Images of Yhwh?

If viewer reception is indeed a crucial matter in iconographic interpretation, it is possible that a vast number of images from the archaeological record may well have been "seen" (i.e., received) as depictions of Yhwh. Whether such images or such seeing would violate the Second Commandment is a question that cannot be answered here. Much would depend on dating of the command, its promulgation in Israel, and so forth; other important issues that would need to be addressed would include what, exactly, is forbidden by the commandment and if certain media (e.g., clay) may have been exempt. Whatever the case, it is quite possible that Yhwh might have been "seen" by Yahwists in any number of images—even Canaanite ones—not unlike how, in contemporary times, people "see" Jesus in various images or find Mary on various objects (see Morgan 1998; 2005; see also Bonfiglio 2016).

Fig. 22.7. Limestone scaraboid (15 mm long × 12 mm wide × 7 mm high), Jerusalem, IA II. See also Strawn 2016, 97, fig. 6.11.

After Ornan et al., 2012, 5*, fig. 1. Drawing by Dalit Weinblatt Krauz; figure by Benjamin Sass, used with permission, courtesy of the Israel Antiquities Authority.

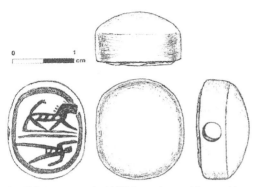

Fig. 22.8. Bone scaraboid (15.5 mm long × 14 mm wide × 8.5 mm high), City of David, eighth or ninth century. See also Strawn 2016, 97 fig. 6.12.

After Brandl 2012b, 384, fig. 13.7, used with permission, courtesy of the Institute of Archaeology, the Hebrew University of Jerusalem.

If this is accurate, perhaps the best place to look for images of Yhwh or other deities is not in famous but uncertain objects like the bull figurine, the Judean Pillar Figurines, or Pithos A from Kuntillet 'Ajrud, but rather in the thousands of seals that have been recovered from ancient Israel/Palestine and Jordan (see Keel 1995; 1997; 2010a; 2010b; 2013; Eggler and Keel 2006; cf. Avigad and Sass 1997). Many of these depict what can only be divine figures. Not all of these seals are imports; many are apparently local products from Israelite sites that date to Israelite periods. Perhaps such seals represent foreign gods and are thus testimony to heterodox or syncretistic, non-Yahwistic tendencies on the part of certain Israelite populations. But another possibility is that in some instances such divine figures were stand-ins, as it were, for Yhwh—ways, that is, that Yhwh was figured even if such figuration was quite malleable, varied, and not standardized. Such "flexibility" in divine presentation is, in fact, precisely what one finds in the pages of the Old Testament and in the literary profile of Yhwh, who could be portrayed as a lion roaring from Mount Zion or trammeling humans (Amos 1:2; 3:12; cf. figs. 22.7 and 22.8; see further

Strawn 2005; 2016) or depicted as master of the animal kingdom, including the unusual ostrich (Job 39:13–18; cf. figs. 22.9 and 22.10; see further Keel 1978a, 64–68). Regardless of whether such seals definitively portray Yhwh—at the level of production and/or reception—they nevertheless comprise important data that should be assessed in any analysis of various images and texts from the Hebrew Bible (see Strawn 2016). The seals are plentiful, for one thing, and are highly mobile, for another. They represent a kind of premodern mass communication media (Keel and Uehlinger 1996) and are by far the most extensively attested image-bearing object from ancient Israel/Palestine. And if Yhwh was indeed found or "findable" in such images, then there are a vast number of objects to consider on this point.

In his famous book *Ways of Seeing*, John Berger wrote that "no other kind of relic or text from the past can offer such a direct testimony about the world which surrounded other people at other times [as art]. In this respect images are more precise and richer than literature" (1990, 10). If this judgment is true, then study of Canaanite/Israelite iconography is essential, and, given the nature of the archaeological record of ancient Israel/Palestine, such study must begin, if not also end, with the seals.

Fig. 22.9. Scaraboid (14.2 mm long × 10.2 mm wide × 5 mm high). Beth-Shemesh, Iron Age IIA (980–940).

After Keel and Uehlinger 1998, 139, fig. 162c, used with permission.

Fig. 22.10. Scaraboid. Tell en-Nasbeh, Iron Age IIA (980–940).

After Keel and Uehlinger 1998, 139, fig. 162d, used with permission.

PART TWO

Acts and Scenes
of the Drama

SECTION V

Acts

*Integrated Approaches
to Broad Historical Contexts*

23

The Ancestral Period

RICHARD S. HESS

This chapter reviews what we know about the Old Testament ancestors and their culture and history. By "ancestors" we refer to those significant characters whose lives appear in Genesis 12–50 (see Meyers 2014c).

A second definition has to do with the term "period." As has long been observed, the chronology described by the Hebrew Bible suggests a Middle Bronze Age context for the period outlined in Genesis 12–50.[1] If one assumes a historical exodus that took place in the thirteenth century BCE, and a settlement of Israel in Egypt about four centuries prior (cf. Gen. 15:13 but note v. 16 where this period is defined more generally as four generations), then a ca. 1700 BCE context for the Israelite settlement in Egypt would position figures such as Abraham, Sarah, Isaac, Rebekah, and Jacob in the preceding two or three centuries. This would coincide with Egypt's Middle Kingdom until the mid-eighteenth century BCE and the rise of the Hyksos.

1. Private communication from Kenneth A. Kitchen, April 29, 2013; for the general aspects of the late-date scheme, see Kitchen 2003b, 359.

The larger question in terms of chronology is that of the cultural context as described in these chapters of Genesis. This has been the subject of controversy. We will consider some of the salient features. Overall the thesis of this chapter will argue that the Middle Bronze Age remains the most reasonable context for the origins of the traditions that lay behind much of Genesis 12–50.

Historical Interpretations

Israel's ancestors are thought to have descended from the "Amorites," a term used of peoples in the third and second millennia BCE. This does not necessarily refer to the Amorites mentioned in the Bible, who generally are enemies of Israel found in inland Palestine (Liverani 1973; Ahlström 1993a, 152–54, 174–80). Amorites appear in Mesopotamian cuneiform texts as early as 2600 BCE, where they come from a mountainous region northwest of Babylon (Gelb 1961). These peoples gradually permeated all levels of society in Mesopotamia. By the early second millennium BCE, cities such as Mari and Babylon preserve Amorite personal names of their citizens (e.g., Hammurabi), composed in a language with similarities to later Hebrew and Aramaic. Amorite is a West Semitic language (or multiple West Semitic languages). West Semites later included both Israelites and Canaanites.

William Albright (1924a) posited an invasion of Amorites from outside the Middle East ca. 2000 BCE; although the evidence for an invasion remains ambiguous (McCarter 2011, 12),[2] an external origin is likely[3] (Rainey and Notley 2006, 46–47).[4] They were pastoralists driven by ecological and social circumstances. In Syria, Amorite pastoralists spread across the region and intermarried with urban populations (Buccellati 1992).

By the 1960s, scholars identified these pastoralists as enclosed, dimorphic, and transhumant nomads (Rowton 1967; 1973). They were enclosed because they lived in regions that included towns and cities. They were dimorphic because they participated in these settled societies. They were transhumant because they wandered between summer and winter pastures. Mari, situated at the bend of the Euphrates River where it flows out of modern Syria and into Iraq, provided the evidence for this in its cuneiform archive. This type of nomadism was compared with that of Abraham in Genesis (Finkelstein 1988–89, 143).

In the 1970s scholars challenged this application of Mari to Genesis (Thompson 1974; Van Seters 1975). They argued that the stories of Abraham, Isaac, and Jacob have little to do with nomadism. The Genesis stories were an amalgam of later views regarding nomads.

Meanwhile, new Mari texts were published. Daniel Fleming (1998b; 2004b; 2008; cf. Arnold 2014) revitalized Mari and its application to the study of Genesis. At Mari most letters attest to a state ruled by a sovereign, Zimri-Lim,

who had separate administrative systems, one for the city of Mari and another for the tribal confederations in the surrounding region. The nomadic groups had kin in the cities. They traveled long distances in all directions, far beyond the immediate vicinity of Mari. Fleming (2008, 84–86) compares this with Genesis 37, where the sons of Jacob travel more than sixty miles from Hebron in their quest for pastureland for their flocks. They are absent for a long period of time, while other members of their family remain at home in Hebron. Compare Mari: the herders and the citizens of the town were parts of larger families; these herders also traveled long distances from home and maintained family ties that stretched hundreds of miles and crossed the city-state borders of that early period. Not only is this true of Jacob and his sons in Genesis 37, but also it describes something of Jacob's earlier life: (1) his connections with his father Isaac in southern Palestine and (2) his relationship to his "uncle" Laban in Harran, hundreds of miles to the north. This separation of families was common at Mari (Fleming 2008, 90–92). One letter (Boyer, Parrott, and Dossin 1958, 11) describes thirteen sons of Awin, of whom eight were on the move with their flocks while the remaining five stayed at home. They held their property in common. Compare the twelve sons of Jacob and the texts noted above.

The Mari tablets reveal that, in the eighteenth century BCE, there were two major tribal confederations, the Binu-Yamina—that is, the "sons of the right" (also the biblical name of Benjamin)—and the Binu-Sim'al, the "sons of the left."[5] Contrary to the criticism of earlier scholars (e.g., Van Seters 1975), it is possible to use the urban archives found at Mari to study a pastoralist people. The urban and pastoralist peoples were of the same kin, and their king retained his tribal ties with his Binu-Sim'al nomadic tribal confederation. Contrary to the view of Thomas Thompson

2. Thompson 1992, 7–8, attributes this to a drought.
3. Finkelstein 1988–89, 139, 144 (see also Finkelstein 1993, 45).
4. See A. Mazar 1990a, 176–91.

5. For this and what follows, see Fleming 2004b; 2016.

(1974), "Binu-Yamina" is a proper name (as is "Benjamin"), not just a reference to "southerners." There are too many references to them and to the Binu-Sim'al to read them as other than proper names.

From the textual record of contemporary Egypt come the Execration Texts. These three groups of clay documents (ca. 1800 BCE) name towns in Canaan. The personal names indicate that tribal/clan groups existed alongside urban leaders. In the Egyptian story of Sinuhe (ca. 1920 BCE) we read of a loyal Egyptian who visited southern Canaan and lived there for many years. Sinuhe lived among West Semitic pastoralists with cattle. This was similar to Abraham and Isaac, clan chiefs with cattle who fit the Egyptian term "chiefs of tribes."

As noted by Kenneth Kitchen (2003b, 334–35), both the Execration Texts and the *Story of Sinuhe* describe a Palestine different from any time later than the Middle Bronze Age. These texts identify inhabitants of Palestine and Syria with West Semitic names, not unlike the Mari texts and almost all the figures from this region in the biblical accounts of Genesis 12–50. The warriors or heroes (*nḫt*) are given first place in the Execration Texts. This is the same word used in the Sinuhe tale to describe "a military figure having a following who is the head of his own family" (Rainey and Notley 2006, 53). Some *nḫt* boasted that they were the "sole hero" of their land. Compare the figure of Abram as a warrior in Genesis 14.

Comparative Notes between Middle Bronze Culture and the Ancestors

Many contemporary approaches tend to accept a middle first-millennium BCE date for the Genesis 12–50 accounts and to argue that the stories were written to encourage or to instruct Israelites in their faithfulness to God in various situations, especially during the exile that followed Jerusalem's destruction by the Babylonians in 587/586 BCE. There are additional cultural features, however, that lend an authenticity to the accounts behind the narratives and to an earlier cultural setting.

Personal, Place, Divine, and People Names

Personal names are a unique source for examining the authenticity of narratives. This is due to their frequency (tens of thousands are attested in the ancient world) and the fact that name forms change with time. For example, a form known as *y*-prefix names (e.g., "Jacob" and "Isaac") fits best the early second millennium BCE, when this form occurs most frequently. Y-prefix names occur less frequently in the late second millennium, and only occasionally in the first-millennium BCE world of West Semitic personal names.[6] As already noted, various names of the ancestors are found in similar forms among West Semites in this period. After this period they become rare. Further, "Jacob" appears on scarabs attributed to at least one "Hyksos" king in Egypt, ca. 1750–1550 BCE.

"Abram" is a common name known from Ugarit, Egypt, Cyprus, and Mari (Ahlström 1993a, 181). Abraham has been related to a people mentioned as *rhm* on a thirteenth-century BCE stele from Beth Shean.[7] Ronald Hendel (1995) argues that "the Fort (or Fortified Town) of Abram" conquered by Pharaoh Shishak in the Negev in 925 BCE was a fort built by David or Solomon and named in honor

---

6. Kitchen 1993b, 45–46, estimates 16 percent as *y*-prefix among early second millennium BCE Amorite personal names, 2 percent for late second millennium BCE names from Ugarit, and 6 percent of all Phoenician names from the first millennium BCE. Akkadian and Aramaic names of the first millennium BCE have less than 1 percent. Contra Hendel 1995, 57, statistics remain significant.

7. Cf. Liverani 1979b and Ahlström 1993a, 187n1. Liverani argues that Abraham, "father of the *rhm* people," would then be an eponym for a clan later incorporated into Israel. However, it could also be that the *rhm* themselves are descendants of an earlier Abraham.

of the Genesis ancestor. Kenneth Kitchen (1998, 49; 2003b, 313) concurs.[8]

"Terah," "Serug," and "Nahor" resemble place-names in the region of Harran. Haran and Nahor are mentioned in the eighteenth-century BCE Mari archives (Albright 1924a, 385–88; Hendel 1995, 59; Kitchen 1998, 49; 2003b, 317; Hess 2009b, 85–89).

The name "Benjamin" may be related to the Binu-Yamina tribal confederation at Mari. "Binu-Yamina" means "sons of the right hand"—that is, of the south. This tribal group reached into southwestern Syria, close to Palestine. Benjamin itself has been explained as the southernmost of the "Rachel tribes."[9] The identification of Harran with the Binu-Yamina (Durand 1988, 24) and with Abraham, Jacob, and their family (including Benjamin) "shows an unconscious link" (Fleming 2004b, 219).[10]

The name "Canaan" occurs in early second-millennium BCE Mari (Malamat 1989, 55).

The frequent connections with Aram and Aramaean,[11] as parts of place-names, as people groups, and as names of the region in which Abraham's servant and Jacob traveled, connect the traditions of Mari and inland Syria with Genesis before the Aramaean migrations of the twelfth century BCE (Fleming 2004b, 227–32). This coincides with the observations of Anson Rainey (2007) that Hebrew has a closer affinity with the inland languages Moabite and Ammonite than with the coastal tongues of Phoenician and Ugaritic. Thus the heritage was connected with Mari and the inland Syrian traditions. Indeed, Aramaeans in inland Syria appear to have been mentioned in Egyptian sources as early as the beginning of the fourteenth century BCE. Further, the equation of the Ahlamu and Aramaeans move attestations

of this tribal group back to the Mari period (Younger 2007, 131–36; 2016).[12]

The Aramaeans may illustrate the identification of an early group of people by a name commonly associated with a later group of people from the same area or otherwise associated with them. We find another illustration of this phenomenon in the appearance of Philistines in Genesis. Here the name may apply to people living in the regions where the Philistines would later settle (Kitchen 2003b, 340–41).[13] More generally, one cannot date the original composition of texts on the basis of isolated "late" words, such as "Philistine" and "Chaldees" (with reference to Ur), in Genesis. The Tale of Sinuhe (ca. 1900 BCE) also appears, in part, on a thirteenth-century BCE ostracon from Cairo. On this updated version of the account, the earlier Egyptian word for "sea," *nwy*, is replaced with the "modern" Semitic loanword, *yam*. Further, the older location of Qedem is replaced by Qadesh, a site popularly connected with the Levant at the time (Kitchen 2003b, 483). In Genesis as well, updating may have replaced earlier names of people groups with those of the Philistines, a more familiar entity by the twelfth century and one from the same region as the earlier non-Semitic people.[14]

Customs from Other West Semitic (and Related) Archives

Some Nuzi (fifteenth and fourteenth centuries BCE) and Alalakh (eighteenth century BCE)

---

8. He notes that the translation "enclosure of Abram" would be more accurate.

9. For example, those born to Rachel: Manasseh, Ephraim, and Benjamin.

10. Cf. further parallels, Fleming 2004b, 222.

11. Gen. 24:10; 25:20; 28:2, 5, 6, 7; 31:18, 20, 24; 33:18; 35:9, 26, and its preservation in Deut. 26:5.

12. Perhaps where the Ahlamu were a tribe within the larger Aramaean group.

13. Further, the odd location of the Philistines at Gerar may suggest an earlier non-Canaanite group with Aegean connections. From the early second millennium BCE, Middle Minoan II pottery (from the Aegean region, where the Philistines are normally seen as originating) occurs at Hazor. At Tel Kabri in Israel, we find a contemporary palace with frescoes of Cretan style. Sixteenth-century BCE Avaris, a site in the region of Goshen in Egypt, contained Minoan paintings (from the Aegean world). Elsewhere in Israel from this time, Megiddo possessed Cypriot pottery (also Aegean), as did Tel Haror and Tell Jemmeh.

14. Cf. "Phicol," a non-Semitic name associated with Philistines at Gerar (Gen. 21:22, 32; 26:26).

customs (C. Gordon 1940; Selman 1980; Walton 1989, 45–65) are found in the Genesis accounts. Van Seters (1975), Thompson (1974), and others have argued against these comparisons between Genesis 12–50 and second-millennium BCE ancient Near Eastern culture. They note that the customs are common to the lives of those living in the early second millennium, but that they are also found in other periods. The nature of family law suggests that it would be traditional and conservative and therefore not useful as a means of dating (Eichler 1989). This is true in some cases. However, in other cases there are distinctive parallels whose number and similarity are found only in the early second millennium BCE, not later. Here are four examples.

First, a barren wife shall provide her husband with a handmaid to bear children (Gen. 16:1–2; Chiera 1929, 67, lines 19–21). Kitchen (1993a) disputes Van Seters's (1975) evidence that it occurs later. The twelfth-century BCE Egyptian text that Van Seters finds as a parallel is a list of unusual adoptions, not normal ones. The seventh-century BCE Assyrian marriage document says nothing about inheritance. The female slave may be sold off at will. For Thompson (1974), the Nuzi parallel (Chiera 1929, 67, lines 19–21)[15] does not mention barrenness and is a legal contract, contra Genesis. However, the parallel is a husband having a child by another woman when his wife is unable to bear children. Further, Late Bronze Age Alalakh text no. 93 exemplifies a condition where barrenness establishes a legal requirement to conceive by another woman. Behind such laws lies the importance attached to families and to inheritance rights.

Second, there is the *Erebu* marriage of Jacob in which the heir is adopted and marries the daughter of the adopter (Gen. 29:13–19). The arguments that (1) no bride price was paid in such situations at Nuzi, (2) nor is Jacob ever recorded as adopted by Laban, fail to recognize that (1) the parallel does not depend on a bride price, and that (2) Laban describes Jacob as "my bone and my flesh" (Gen. 29:14), implying a family member. Perhaps there was no adoption because a kinship already existed.[16]

Third, a daughter or sister could be sold into "adoption" with a proviso that the woman be married. Abraham and Isaac had a "tendency" to call their wives sisters (Gen. 12:13, 19; 20:2, 5, 12; 26:7, 9). This has been compared with the institution of *ahatūtu* (sisterhood adoption) at Nuzi. It did not create a sister-wife or confer a high status. It was a business arrangement for women in need of familial protection. It transferred rights to negotiate a marriage for the woman (and so to receive the bride price) from the natural brother (or the woman herself) to the adopted brother (Greengus 1975; Eichler 1989). However, there remains the parallel in which someone who is not a "sister" by kinship becomes designated as a "sister."

Fourth, at Alalakh an early second-millennium text has a parallel to Genesis 15 in the act of killing an animal while taking an oath concerning the gift of land (Gen. 15:9–11, 17–18) (Hess 1993b; 2007, 162). Evidence for a covenant-making ceremony in the early second-millennium BCE West Semitic culture of Alalakh (Wiseman 1958; Draffkorn 1959; *COS* 2:137) includes lines 39b–42:

> Abba-AN
> swore an oath of the gods to Yarimlim
> and he cut the neck of one lamb
> (saying):

---

15. The translation by T. J. Meek in Pritchard 1969a, 220, provides the relevant lines: "Furthermore, Kelim-ninu has been given in marriage to Shennima. If Kelim-ninu bears (children), Shennima shall not take another wife; but if Kelim-ninu does not bear, Kelim-ninu shall acquire a woman of the land of Lullu as wife for Shennima, and Kelim-ninu may not send the offspring away."

16. We should not expect that the Genesis narratives would contain the same wording as legal documents from Nuzi and elsewhere. All "approved" marriages in the ancestral line are endogamous—that is, within the tribe whose forefather is Terah (Steinberg 1991). This would preserve the family's wealth within the family (Steinberg 1993). In this sense it might also be possible for Abram to refer to Sarah as his "sister."

(May I be cursed) if I take what I have
given to you.

The sacrificial aspect is demonstrated by Alalakh text 54, where the Akkadian contains a
description of the lamb as *asakku*—that is,
"set apart" (lines 16–18):

> The neck of the sacrificial lamb
> in the presence of Niqmepa
> was cut.

Van Seters (1975) has argued that the oath
text is fragmentary. Better comparisons exist
in the first millennium BCE with Jeremiah and
Assyrian and Aramaic treaties. However, the
first-millennium comparisons all have as part
of their oath the implication that what happened to the animals should also happen to the
oath-taker if the oath-taker breaks the treaty.
This is not explicit in Genesis 15 and doubtful since the oath-taker is God. The same is
true in the texts from Mari and Alalakh.[17] The
text from Alalakh is clear in these points, and
the comparison remains closest to the Genesis
account (Hess 1993b).

While it is true that many customs originally
assumed to be only of a second-millennium
BCE date are now found in the first millennium
as well, they come to a focus in the period of
the Genesis ancestors and of Nuzi and the
other cuneiform cultures from the middle and
early second millennium BCE (Kitchen 1993b,
46).[18]

Ancestor Wanderings and the World of Genesis 14

The best times for Abraham-type nomads
wandering across the Fertile Crescent remains
the Middle Bronze Age, during the nonurban
period (Kitchen 1995, 56–57; 1998, 51–54;

2003b, 316). At no other period were these
regions uncontrolled by major powers such as
Egypt, Hatti, Babylonia, and Assyria. Thus,
the Mari tribal confederation of Binu-Yamina
moved back and forth over the same region as
the Genesis ancestors (Malamat 1989, 44, 53).
The view that domesticated camels could not
have existed this early (Finkelstein and Silberman 2001, 37) is contradicted by evidence from
the early second millennium BCE and earlier
(Kitchen 2003b, 338–39; Heide 2010).

Regarding the international armies of Genesis 14, Kitchen (1993b, 47; 2003b, 319–20) asserts that only in the period between 2000 and
1700 BCE, and at no other time, does Mesopotamia possess groups of rival kings who could
form the sort of alliance conceived of in this
chapter. He also observes how the names of
the kings match Mesopotamian (Amraphel
and Arioch), Elamite (Chedorlaomer), and
Hittite (Tidal) personal names.[19]

Alliances between Elam and West Semitic
groups occur in this period only, and they are
attested in the Mari letters.[20] Note the superiority of Elam over Syro-Mesopotamian rulers in
the Mari texts and in Genesis 14:4–5.[21]

The Joseph Story

Various details of Genesis 37; 39–50 fit Egypt
of the early and mid-second millennium BCE in
a unique manner (Kitchen 1993a; 1993b; 1995,

---

17. This includes the more recently published ones
from Mari (Malamat 1995).

18. That this is unique is never addressed by McCarter
2011, 11–14.

19. For comparisons, see Kitchen 2003b, 320. Hendel
(1995, 56–57) argues that there is no evidence for Elamite
rule in Palestine at any time and that shifting alliances
in Mesopotamia and Palestine occurred throughout the
biblical period. However, as Kitchen notes, this is not true
of alliances with Mesopotamia and the east. Further, it
does not address the agreement of the name elements
of the kings of Gen. 14 with their suggested places of
origin. Finally, alliances of four or more kings are well attested in the eighteenth-century BCE Mari letters (Kitchen
2003b, 320–21).

20. See Heimpel (2003, 609) and the Mari letters that
discuss Elam and relations: Durand 1988, 75, 228, 305,
306; Parrot and Dossin 1950, 71.

21. States as far west as Qatna became vassals of Elam,
demonstrating connections and control across the Fertile
Crescent (Fleming 2004b, 226).

52–53; Halpern 1992, 92–99).[22] The eighteenth-century BCE slave price averaged twenty silver shekels.[23] The rise of Joseph may reflect connection with the Hyksos, West Semitic rulers in the Egyptian delta, ca. 1750–1550 BCE.[24] The Hyksos culture, as identified in the eastern delta and Sinai, has cultural affinities with contemporary Syro-Palestinian ceramic culture (Redmount 1995) and the architecture at Tell el-Dabʿa, a major Egyptian Hyksos center in the delta region where the Bible relates that the family of Jacob settled.

The Religion of the Genesis Ancestors

Setting aside the various ways (e.g., open and inclusive, association of trees and pillars, no special priests) in which the religion of the ancestors differed from that of later Israel (Moberly 1992, 84–87), we consider an important, but often overlooked, discovery. An economic cuneiform text from early or middle second-millennium BCE Hebron includes Hurrian and Amorite personal names, references to sheep and male-goat offerings, and a king, perhaps of Hebron. It is important for the Genesis stories of the ancestors living there and in nearby Beersheba because: (1) like Genesis 14, the Hurrian name indicates an international world; (2) sacrifices to divinity are made with animals from flocks; (3) like the Egyptian Execration Texts of the same period, kings govern cities (so Abimelek and Melchizedek); and (4) cuneiform-trained scribes in Hebron were available to someone such as Abraham (Anbar and Naʾaman 1986–87).[25]

Conclusion

On multiple levels, from a wealth of archaeological and textual evidence, the world of the ancestors as described in Genesis 12–50 is identical to the world of the Middle Bronze Age in the region of the Levant, ca. 2200–1600 BCE. Better understanding this world provides invaluable insights into the interpretation of these crucial texts.

---

22. It is unfortunate that a scholar writes concerning the Joseph story of Genesis, "All that can be said for sure is that certain elements in the Joseph saga cannot be proven to be older than the Persian period" (Lemche 1998b, 43), without citing any evidence for his statement and without addressing the evidence presented here and found in published scholarly sources.

23. Hendel (1995, 56) attempts to dispute this by arguing that the same price appears in the early first millennium BCE. However, the only text he presents as evidence is Lev. 27:5. This begs the question since the date of this text is disputed. As Kitchen (1998, 49–50; 2003b, 344–45) observes, periods before and after the early second millennium BCE attest to different prices for slaves, but never to 20 shekels.

24. The Egyptian priest Manetho from the third century BCE uses the term "Hyksos" and connects Joseph's entry and rise to power with the Hyksos king Apophis (Ahlström 1993a, 187–96).

25. Hess 2017, 261, 271–73. Note that from this same period fragments of administrative and other texts have been discovered at Hazor. These link it with the Amorite cultures to the north, especially Mari, on the basis of script, grammar, names, and forms. See Malamat 1989; A. Ben-Tor 1992; Horowitz and Shaffer 1992a; 1992b; 1993; Horowitz and Oshima 2007; 2010; Horowitz, Oshima, and Winitzer 2010; Horowitz, Oshima, and Vukosavovic 2018.

24

The Egyptian Sojourn and the Exodus

David A. Falk

The Archaeological Background

The exodus is the one event that defines the ancient Israelites more than any other, becoming an overarching theme in the nation's literature and national identity. Yet for the modern scholar and Bible reader, the exodus presents challenges regarding not only the nature of evidence but also what is often a Western understanding of the ancient texts. While maximalist scholars had to contend with evidence that shed new light upon early Israelite identity, culture, and history, biblical "minimalist" scholars like Ahlström (2002, 12–13), Thompson (1992, 403–4), Van Seters (2003, 45–46), and Philip Davies (2006, 26) have argued that the events described in the exodus were "mythological fiction" unsuitable for use as historical data.[1]

The Egyptian sojourn account begins in the book of Genesis by recounting that the land of Canaan had a severe famine (Gen. 42:1–2) that caused the sons of Jacob to relocate to the land of Goshen (Gen. 45:10), an area probably along the now extinct Pelusiac branch of the Nile, which was the easternmost branch and ended in an estuary located in the Sinai (Hoffmeier 1996, 165–66). Given that the Israelites most likely lived in the Nile delta (Lower Egypt), an important consideration is that the preservation of the archaeological record in this particular region presents difficulties. Few archaeological remains have survived the harsh conditions of Lower Egypt. In ancient times, Lower Egypt was known for its marshes, and even today the ground is saturated with water containing salt that can destroy papyrus and stone alike. Few records exist from Lower Egypt from any time period—less than a dozen to date. For example, excavation of the scriptorium at Avaris (Tell el-Dabᶜa) discovered the existence of 470 bullae (seal impressions), but all the documents had rotted away because of the wet conditions (Reali 2014, 67–68). Expecting documents to survive from the period in question is doubtful given the poor state of preservation of this location.

The earliest Egyptian (or any other kind of) document that explicitly mentions the Israelites is the Victory Stele (the so-called

1. See Geraty 2015, 55–63, for a detailed survey of exodus views and theories.

Israel Stela), which documented the victory of Merneptah (ca. 1213–1203 BCE) over Libyan invaders. The stele has a brief mention in passing of Merneptah destroying the seed—that is, the posterity—of Israel (*KRI* IV 19.7) in a list of nations that he supposedly overthrew. Regardless of Merneptah's claims, the Victory Stele suggests that the Israelites had already left Egypt by the time of Merneptah's victory (Habichi 2001, 120), thus limiting the date of the exodus and the national identity of Israel to no later than Merneptah's fifth regnal year (ca. 1208 BCE).

In an attempt to establish the historicity of the Israelites, other groups of Semites have been identified with the ancient Israelites but are no longer generally seen as viable options. One early proposal was the Hyksos, who inhabited the Nile delta from the early Twelfth Dynasty (O'Conner 1997, 48; Mourad 2015, 12) and filled the power vacuum when it was no longer clear who ruled Egypt, seizing control over the wealth of Egypt and Avaris, Egypt's largest city at the time. Josephus identified the Israelites with the Hyksos (*Apion* 1.73–91), but that identification usually is no longer considered viable since the Hyksos were chased out of Egypt at the beginning of the Eighteenth Dynasty (ca. 1530 BCE), much earlier than most modern authorities are comfortable accepting for Israel's exodus. A few (e.g., D. Redford 1992a, 412–13) still accept that the Hyksos exit from Egypt became a type of cultural memory while at the same time recognizing that no direct link existed between the Hyksos and the Israelites of later periods, although such theories depend largely upon a late date for the writing of the biblical texts and the demythologization of vaguely similar "exodus" traditions scattered across the Levant.[2]

Furthermore, Josephus's *Against Apion* was driven not so much by history as by an ideological debate in Hellenistic discourse over whose culture was superior by virtue of its antiquity (Barclay 2007, lxxi).

Another problematic identification with the ancient Israelites is the Hapiru/Apiru (*ʿprw*), which was proposed to be a corruption of the ethnonym "Hebrew" (*ʿibri*) (Fritz 2012, 129). The Hapiru occur in a variety of ancient sources dating from 1800 BCE to 1100 BCE and appear in regions from Egypt to Mesopotamia contemporaneously with the Egyptian sojourn. Their activities earned them a reputation as nomadic raiders more than sojourners (Bryce 2005, 167–68). The Hittite king Hattušili I (ca. 1650–1620 BCE) recruited bands of Hapiru to help him raid important trade centers in Syria (Hoffner 2009, 76), and they assisted the Amorite king Abdi-Ashirta and his sons in their conquest of Byblos during the fifteenth century (EA 82, 85, 103). Donald Wiseman (1980, 143–44) noted that "Hapiru" appears to be more a sociological designation than a term of ethnicity, as "Hebrew" is used in the biblical texts (Gen. 39:14; Exod. 1:15–19).[3] Any connection between the Levantine Habiru (or Hebrews) and the Hapiru may then hearken to a common Semitic ancestry, but the two groups appear to be isolated by geography and history. Nevertheless, William Dever (2003, 181–82) included the Hapiru among the many diverse groups that inculcated the cultural memory of the early Israelites (Dever 2015, 399–405).

---

2. D. Redford 1992a dates all the toponymic evidence to the fifth and sixth centuries BCE (p. 410), neglecting more comprehensive sources that date to the late thirteenth century. He lumps together the writing of Exod. 1–14 with Ps. 78:12, 43, to being contemporaneous with Dynasty 26 (p. 409). The logic that Redford uses appears to be that since Ps. 78 identified the source city of the exodus as Tanis, then this must be what the writer of the exodus also intended, and thus the two documents must have been written contemporaneously—a circular argument the present author does not find convincing.

3. Rainey (1987, 540–41), from his study of the Amarna Letters, agrees with Wiseman that the term "Hapiru" represents a "social class" rather than an ethnicity and has demonstrated that there is no etymological relationship between "Hapiru" and "Hebrew." Rainey (2008, 54) nevertheless believes that the Israelites originated from the Shasu; however, this hypothesis would need further evidence before it could be properly engaged.

The Israelites, then, appear to have originated as one of the sojourning groups of Semites that emerged possibly out of the Amorite people groups, an ethnic origin suggested by Ezekiel 16:45. The use of Amoritic imperfective names—that is, an imperfective form of a verb followed by a deity name—as used by the Israelites, as well as other cultural similarities, suggests that there may be a connection with the Amorites (J. Sasson 2015, 19–20). As far as the ancient Egyptians were concerned, the Israelites were just one of several groups of Semitic (ʿmw) people groups that had lived in their land.

The Nature of the Evidence

By this point it should be apparent that the evidence being considered is indirect—that is, a consideration of whether the exodus account is consistent with what is known of ancient Egypt and the late Bronze Age (Kitchen 2003b, 4). While not as satisfying as direct evidence, indirect evidence is often the best available to the ancient historian and valid when built into a properly structured induction. Fortunately, much of the material culture that remains from Egypt allows us to say definitive things about the Egyptian sojourn and the exodus. The sometimes-cited "negative evidence"—that is, lack of evidence taken as proof that the exodus did not occur—besides being logically fallacious, is insufficient for doubting the historicity of a person or event (D. Fischer 1970, 47–48, 62–63).

Prima facie, the date of the exodus lands sometime in the Egyptian New Kingdom (ca. 1530–1069 BCE), whether one adheres to the early date of 1446 BCE or the late date of ca. 1260 BCE.[4] Kitchen's low chronology correlates the reigns of the kings Amenhotep III, Akhenaten, and Tutankhamun with the reigns of Kadashman-Enlil I (EA 1–5) and Burna-

Buriash II (EA 6, 9) of Babylon and Ashur-Ubalit I (EA 15) of Assyria, which have pegged much of the dating of the New Kingdom. Given the solidity of Mesopotamian chronology from the fifteenth century onward (Pruzsinszky 2009, 17),[5] little leeway exists as to which Egyptian kings ruled at any stage of New Kingdom history, with only a few exceptions, such as Horemheb (Thomas Schneider 2010, 393). Even though the low chronology has yet to gain traction with the majority of North American scholars (Ashton 2013, 297), the low chronology allows us to date the kings of the Egyptian New Kingdom with reasonable assurance.

Pi-Ramesses and the Egyptian Sojourn

The toponyms used in Exodus not only are specific as to their location but also fixed in historical context. In the Pentateuch, five passages mention "Rames(s)es" as a toponym (Bietak 2000, 186). The first passage is Genesis 47:11, where the text speaks of Joseph and his kin being given possession of territory "in the land of Rameses, as Pharaoh had instructed." The name "Ramesses" makes its first appearance in the archaeological record with Ramesses I (ca. 1295–1294 BCE). The title "pharaoh" comes from the Egyptian pr-ʿꜣ, "Great House," and first appears in the archaeological record during the reign of Thutmose III (ca. 1479–1425 BCE). While everyone agrees that Ramesses was not contemporary with Joseph, this text gives strong indication as to when Genesis was written, as both "Rames(s)es" and "pharaoh" are retrojective terms to the events in the text. The ancient Israelites wrote toward a living audience and were comfortable introducing retrojection if it helped the reader relate to

---

4. See Walton 2003, 258–72, for a summary of the arguments surrounding the proposed dates for the exodus.

5. This is especially true for the dating of the Neo-Assyrian and Neo-Babylonian Kingdoms, which have king lists considered accurate to the year and against which the Egyptian Eighteenth Dynasty can be synchronized. When synchronized with what is known of the regional powers of the ancient Near East, the dates derived are accurate within five to ten years (Pruzsinszky 2009, 21).

events and places that were unfamiliar.[6] For example, the psalmist Asaph ascribed the place of Israelite captivity in Egypt to Zoan (Tanis) in Psalm 78:43. Asaph chose the closest living city at the time.

The other four appearances of the name "Rames(s)es" occur in references to the hardship of the Israelites and the exodus itinerary. Exodus 1:11 mentions that the Israelites built the "supply cites" of Pithom/Etham[7] and Rameses. "Pithom" comes from the Egyptian *pr-tm*, "house of Atum" (G. Davies 2004, 28). Pithom was located in the Wadi Tumilat and was occupied by semi-nomadic Asiatics during the Hyksos period. A recent excavation of Tell el-Retabah showed that the site generally was unoccupied during the early New Kingdom (Rzepka et al. 2013, 270) and eventually fell into disuse during the Saite period (D. Redford 1982, 1055). The area generally was known in Egyptian as *ḥtm ṯkw* but gained the epithet *pr-tm ṯkw* when a temple and fortifications were built by Ramesses II (ca. 1279–1213 BCE) (Rzepka et al. 2013, 273; Bertha Porter and Moss 1934, 53; Petrie 1906, 28).

The purpose of these storage cities was to store food for the offerings made within temple and royal cults. The mass storage of food was the endowment that a king would leave to ensure the perpetuation of offerings after his death and was predicated upon the belief that the soul needed to be fed offerings to be sustained in the afterlife. The storage cities were a series of magazines made of mud brick (Exod. 5:7–8), which the Israelites were tasked to make (Exod. 1:14). Several of these cities remain surrounding the temples of Egypt to

this date (e.g., surrounding the Ramesseum). The use of mud brick for the storage magazines was common because mud brick kept the food cool in the heat of the day and warm at night, prolonging preservation.

The manufacture of mud brick was recorded as a task performed by foreign slaves starting from the beginning of the New Kingdom, and the lack of straw (Exod. 5:7) as a problem for brickmakers was recorded in Pap. Anastasi IV (Caminos 1954, 188). Likewise, the Egyptians were known to set quotas for the brickmaker according to Pap. Anastasi III (Caminos 1954, 106; Exod. 5:13–14). The tomb of Rekhmire (Theban Tomb 100) shows Asiatic slaves making mud bricks (N. Davies 1943, 54 and plate 58; Kemp 2000, 83). Generally, the role of slaves in Egypt was to perform skilled labor since Egypt had a surplus of unskilled peasant farmers.

The other three biblical instances of the "Rames(s)es" toponym in the Pentateuch are as the first point of reference for the journey of the exodus (Exod. 12:37; Num. 33:3, 5) and invariably refer to the same city mentioned in Exodus 1:11. The only city in antiquity known by this name was Pi-Ramesses, "House of Ramesses." Pierre Montet thought he had discovered Pi-Ramesses at Tanis (Montet 1936, 200), but the Ramesside blocks arranged in orientations other than in their original plane of writing indicated that the blocks were not original to the site but had been transported from another site (Bietak 1987, 164). The source of those blocks was identified by Habachi (2001, 23) at the archaeological site of Tell Qantir located 2 kilometers east of the site of Avaris/Tell el-Dabᶜa. Pi-Ramesses, being situated on an island in the midst of the Pelsiac branch of the Nile (Bietak and Forstner-Müller 2011, 50, fig. 1), was geographically distinct from Avaris, and existed contemporaneously with the former Hyksos capital into the early Nineteenth Dynasty and during the reign of Seti I (ca. 1294–1279 BCE) (Bietak, Marinatos,

---

6. Modern writers follow the same practice. For example, historians talk about the archaic Mayans (ca. 250–900 CE) living in the "Americas" when America was not a named entity until the publication of Waldseemüller's world map in 1507 CE.

7. "Etham" is a synonym for "Pithom" with the *pi/pr* ("house/estate of") prefix omitted, similar to how the "Rames(s)es" toponym mentioned in Exodus also probably drops its prefix.

and Palivou 2007, 14)[8] until Avaris was abandoned later during the Nineteenth Dynasty (Bietak, Math, and Müller 2013, 45) followed by the abandonment of Pi-Ramesses at the end of the Twentieth Dynasty.

The site of Tell Qantir was first occupied as a royal residence of Seti I (Nineteenth Dynasty) and was later expanded to become the capital of Egypt under Ramesses II. Caesium magnetometry surveys done in 1996, 2003, and 2008 have revealed no remains beneath the Ramesside foundations of the city (Forstner-Müller et al. 2008, 97–99). This presents a problem for any fifteenth-century dating of the exodus based upon a modern Western reading of 1 Kings 6:1 in contrast to the way such numbers would have been read by the ancient reader (Gray 1970, 3–4, 160; J. Robinson 1972, 70).[9]

Given that the Ramesside ancestral home and capital city was in the midst of the Israelite landholdings on the Pelusiac branch of the Nile, this makes events such as those found in Exodus 2:1–10 plausible. It is also plausible that a "daughter of Pharaoh"[10] could have adopted on her own initiative, as women in ancient Egypt had the right to adopt children and often did so (Watterson 1991, 27–28).

8. While evidence exists for limited occupation of Avaris during the early Ramesside period, the full extent of this occupation will never be known because of agricultural leveling at the site.

9. The use of the 480 years in 1 Kings 6:1 presents possibilities as either a literal or symbolic figure, but reading it together with texts mentioning Ramesses as literal at the same time is untenable. The majority of scholars today regard 1 Kings 6:1 as symbolic because of precedents found in ancient Near Eastern literature; e.g., the Mesha Stela (COS 2:137) ascribes forty years to Omri, who reigned no more than twelve years (Thiele 1965, 24–25). Also see Kitchen 2005, 181–83, for a complete discussion of the issue of the 480 years.

10. It is plausible that this too is retrojective writing; that is, she was not a daughter of a king at the time of the adoption but became such when her father, possibly Ramesses I or Seti I, took the throne. The retrojective use of titles occurs elsewhere in the Egyptian corpus. For example, Taharqo calls himself by the kingly title "his majesty" in his autobiographical account of his military campaign when at the time he was only a prince. The practice similarly occurs in Assyrian texts (Millard 1980, 53).

Likewise, given the proximity of a large Semitic population to Pi-Ramesses, Moses having direct contact with the household of Ramesses II would have been plausible, as opposed to the Theban dynastic court of the Eighteenth Dynasty, which was located in Upper Egypt, far from Semitic population concentrations.

The Route of the Exodus

The identification of the ancient city of Pi-Ramesses is important for modern analysis of the exodus because it is the starting point of the journey (Exod. 12:37; Num. 33:3). The number of Israelites who left Egypt is estimated to be "six hundred thousand men" (Exod. 12:37) plus women and children, boosting the total to two or three million people. However, when the men and women of Israel over the age of twenty paid the redemption fee of a *beka* (a half-shekel of silver in weight) to the tabernacle, the entire weight was recorded and the number of individuals was calculated to be 603,550 people (Exod. 38:26).

While the Israelites made few preparations for the journey, they were given objects of precious metals and fine materials from the Egyptians that would become the raw materials for the construction of the tabernacle at Mount Sinai. Also, the mummy of Joseph was recovered for burial in Canaan (Exod. 13:19). That such a recovery was possible implies the existence of a Second Intermediate Period necropolis above the water table. The only major Second Intermediate Period necropolis found in Lower Egypt that is currently known surrounds Avaris and has a curious range of burials from peasants to army officers (Bietak 1979, 240–45; 1996, 45).[11] Yet, the Avaris cemetery is an unlikely candidate as the original burial site of Joseph because the saturated ground water would have made Joseph's mummified

11. The paucity of priestly and royal burials has led to speculation that the Hyksos were a "warrior aristocracy" (Karageorghis 1995, 74).

body (Gen 50:26) impractical for disinterment and transport.

When the children of Israel left the land of Egypt, the people took the bread in its kneading bowls bound up in clothes on their shoulders (Exod. 12:34). While later Israelite and Levantine kneading bowls were low, wide, and hemispherical in shape, Egyptian bread bowls were tall, narrow, and cylindrical. And Egyptian custom was to carry large cylindrical items such as scrolls upright wrapped in their garments over their shoulders (Oriental Institute, Epigraphic Survey 1932, plate 55).

The exodus began at (1) Pi-Ramesses on the fifteenth day of the first month (Num. 33:3). The Israelites' first destination was (2) Succoth (Exod. 12:37), and then they traveled to (3) Pithom (Exod. 13:20). They then turned back to (4) Pi-Hahiroth (Exod. 14:2), *pr-ḥwt-ḥrt* in Egyptian,[12] which faced Baʿal-zephon, and there they camped before the fortress of Migdol (Num. 33:7). Migdol (*mktr*) was one of the fortresses shown on the map of Seti I at

Karnak (Gardiner 1920, plate 11) and was mentioned by Ramesses III (ca. 1184–1153 BCE) at Medinet Habu (Cavillier 2004, 65–67). This map lists the fortresses on the Way of Horus, which was the road that hugged the northern coast of the Sinai and went from Tjaru and extended to the Philistine pentapolis. They traveled from Pi-Hahiroth, passing through (5) the Reed Sea (*yam suf*), and camped at (6) Marah.

The translation of *yam suf* as "Red Sea" is a traditional reading that entered into English Bibles through the Greek Septuagint (ca. 250 BCE) translation *erythra thalassa*. The problem with the traditional translation is that during the Hellenistic period there appears to be disagreement among ancient geographers as to the location of what they called the Red Sea. Regardless, the literal translation from the Hebrew *yam suf* is "Sea of Reeds," which almost certainly is not the Gulf of Arabia (the modern Red Sea).

In fact, *yam suf* most likely comes from the Semitic-Egyptian etymology *p3 ṯwfy*, "the reeds" (Moshier and Hoffmeier 2015, 106–7). The *p3 ṯwfy* was known to Egyptians to be one of the lakes (possibly Lake Ballah or Lake Timsah) that were part of the swampy area along what is now the Suez Canal and is mentioned in Pap. Anastasi III, 2.11–12 (Gardiner 1937, 22). Pap. Anastasi III dates to the third year of Merneptah (ca. 1210 BCE) and reflects the geographical understanding of the period. The document mentions that nearby is the "foliage and greenery" of Pi-Hahiroth (Pap. Anastasi III, 3.3 [Gardiner 1937, 23]). The text also mentions the arrival of the king to Pi-Ramesses spelled out with the birth name of Ramesses II (Ramesses Meriamun) (Pap. Anastasi III, 1.12 [Gardiner 1937, 21]), leaving no doubt after whom Pi-Ramesses was named. The fact that the three toponyms mentioned in Pap. Anastasi III are placed in a geographic sequence similar to what is found in Exodus leaves little doubt as to their identity.

---

12. The translation of "Pi-Hahiroth" is debated. While early Egyptologists suggested that it might mean "House of Hathor," Albright (1948, 16) suggested that it might mean "the mouth of the canals," perhaps derived from the name of an Egyptian goddess, "Heret." D. Redford (1987, 142–43) suggested that *ḥrt* was the name of a Semitic goddess known as "Heret" but eventually conceded to the possibility of a Semitic root as an etymology (D. Redford 1992b, 371) because it was apparent not only that the etymology did not support the assertion but also that no goddess of that name had been identified in either Egyptian or Levantine mythologies. Hoffmeier (1996, 170) held a view similar to Albright's but rejected his etymology. However, where Pi-Hahiroth is mentioned in the Egyptian corpus (e.g., Pap. Anastasi III, 3.3), the orthography is clear. The toponym follows Egyptian convention beginning with the hieroglyphic *pr-ḥwt*, "estate of the temple" (F. Friedman 2015, 21–24), and ends with the goddess determinative, indicating that the toponym is theophoric. I would suggest that the *ḥrt* may be a variant spelling of *ḥry(t)-tp*, "the one who is on top," with the *tp* (Gardiner Sign D1) abbreviated to a *t* (Gardiner Sign X1), and is one of the epithets of the Uraeus goddess. Compare this spelling with the orthography found on the Karnak Rhetorical Stela (*KRI* V 89.10); Buhen, Lesser Stela, Year 1 (*KRI* I 101.10); Serapeum Stele, Apis-Burial, Year 30 (*KRI* II 370.9); Battle of Qadesh (*KRI* II 89.7–9); and Pap. Harris I, 50.2.

Conclusion

After crossing the Reed Sea, the Israelites traveled three days into the wilderness of Shur and to Marah (Exod. 15:22; Num. 33:8). They arrived at Elim, and then they departed on the fifteenth day of the second month (Exod. 16:1) and progressed into the Wadi Feiran to Mount Sinai. At Mount Sinai, the Israelites camped at the foot of the mount and constructed the tabernacle and its ritual furnishings, including the Ark of the Covenant (Exod. 25).

The state of the evidence points toward the plausibility of the exodus narrative. The cultural and geographic references point to an ancient writer who was intimately familiar with the area of the Nile delta and the customs of Egypt as they existed in the late New Kingdom, strongly suggesting the reliability of the exodus account as a historical event.

25

The Settlement Period

PEKKA PITKÄNEN

Introduction: The Period and Its Sources

From the perspective of the biblical sources, the settlement period can be considered to have started when the ancient Israelites entered the so-called Promised Land. This takes place in the book of Numbers for the east side of the river Jordan and subsequently in the book of Joshua for the west side, the main Promised Land (cf. Num. 32). The book of Judges then describes how the Israelites fared in the land after the death of Joshua, and the judges period essentially draws to a close when the Israelites ask for a king and a monarchy is established at the time of Samuel, Saul, David, and Solomon (1 Sam.–1 Kings 10, with parallels in 1 Chron.–2 Chron. 9), at which time the settlement can also be classified as having been completed (cf. 1 Kings 9:20–22 and see below). In addition, the legal materials in Exodus–Numbers and Deuteronomy include explicit indication that they are meant for the new land, itself already promised to the forefathers Abraham, Isaac, and Jacob in the book of Genesis (cf. Gen. 12:1–3, 7; 26:2–5; 28:10–15; Deut. 1:8; 12:1; Lev. 18:1–5). All in all, then,

it is appropriate to include the biblical materials from Genesis–1 Kings 10 (with parallels in Chronicles) when considering the Israelite settlement. In fact, it is this wider context that is important in understanding the settlement process. A narrow focus on texts that describe actual conquests and direct appropriation of land (such as Num. 21; 27; 31–34; 36; Joshua; Judg. 1–2) will result in an incomplete evaluation of the period (see below).

Except for the biblical texts, archaeological evidence from the area provides a major source for interpretation and historical reconstruction. Such evidence has been accumulating since the end of the nineteenth century (see, e.g., Moorey 1991; Hawkins 2013; M. Steiner and Killebrew 2014). It is not the intention here to survey the archaeological evidence, as that is done elsewhere in this book. However, a few salient remarks are in order. The Merneptah Stela does mention Israel ca. 1208 BCE, indicating that a people group with that name was in existence in the land at the time. On the other hand, the Amarna Letters from the fourteenth century do give a clear impression that ancient Israel as a society had not yet appeared on the scene in the southern Levantine area. In addition, archaeological data does indicate clear changes in settlement patterns in the Palestinian (and Transjordanian) highlands in the Iron I period (see, e.g., Finkelstein 1988; Faust 2006b). Such changes give clear reason for suspecting that a new entity arose there at the time. Accordingly, then, from an archaeological perspective, it is quite natural to link the settlement period with the Late Bronze to Early Iron Age transition in the area. This does broadly fit with the biblical chronology, even if the texts, when read literally, would imply a date for the conquest and settlement in the fifteenth century BCE (see 1 Kings 6:1; Judg. 11:26).[1]

Main Previous Interpretations

The above comments about archaeological evidence already reveal tensions between textual and archaeological data. It is important to have an idea of the main issues in that respect, as the tensions are real and should not be ignored. In addition, there is the issue of how one should read the biblical texts in themselves. From a chronological perspective, until the Enlightenment period and rise of biblical criticism, the historical information contained in the biblical books was largely taken at face value. This included the Mosaic origin of the Pentateuch and a literal reading of the Israelite conquest and settlement. A closer scrutiny of the Pentateuch in the eighteenth and nineteenth centuries led to dividing it into a variety of sources, labeled as J, E, D, and P, with J and E narrative sources using the divine names "Yahweh" and "Elohim," respectively, P consisting of priestly narratives and legal materials, and D of Deuteronomy (see, e.g., Wenham 2002,

160–70). Accompanying the source division, W. M. L. de Wette's work on Deuteronomy in the early nineteenth century (see Harvey and Halpern 2008) resulted in anchoring this source to the seventh century BCE, and Julius Wellhausen's work in the latter part of the century can be seen as having fixed the P source to the exilic to postexilic time, in contrast to its early dating previously (see Wellhausen 1927 [first published 1878]). A separate Holiness Code, abbreviated as H, was also distinguished within the P source at the time and was seen as slightly earlier than P, but later than Ezekiel by Wellhausen (see Wellhausen 1927 [first published 1878], 378). The J and E materials were dated to the tenth to ninth centuries BCE (see, e.g., Wenham 2002, 176–83). In the nineteenth century, the book of Joshua was seen together with the Pentateuch (as a Hexateuch) and was dated with it. The late datings of the materials, especially by Wellhausen, were accompanied by skepticism about their historical value. Form-critical scholarship, associated with Hermann Gunkel in the early twentieth century, did, however, postulate oral traditions behind the sources that could go back to an earlier time (see, e.g., Wenham 2002, 171–72).

Another watershed in the interpretation of these materials, and also of Judges–Kings, was the publication of Martin Noth's theory about the Deuteronomistic History (Noth 1991). According to Noth, Deuteronomy–Kings were composed in the Babylonian exile as a unified history based on sources that were available to the so-called Deuteronomistic historian. This essentially changed one's view about the composition of the books in question and also implied that, for example, both Joshua and Judges, which directly describe the period of the Israelite conquest and settlement, were composed more than half a millennium later than the events they portrayed, even if the sources behind them could go back to an earlier time. The idea of a Deuteronomistic History was prominent in the latter part of

1. It should be noted, however, that Exod. 1:11 may be read as more naturally suggesting a thirteenth-century date. See Hoffmeier 1996, 116–26, for a related discussion; see also ch. 24 above on the Egyptian sojourn and the exodus.

the twentieth century, but scholarship has now been returning to the concept of a Hexateuch (see, e.g., E. Otto 2012, 62–256).

All in all, later scholarship has challenged the delimitation and dating of the sources and books on the whole, but the dating of Deuteronomy to the seventh century BCE and the late dating of the priestly materials have still essentially held in mainstream scholarship (see, e.g., E. Otto 2012, esp. 62–185). In addition to that scholarship, the so-called maximalists tend to interpret these materials based on a Mosaic date or an early date (e.g., Kitchen and Lawrence 2012). There are also minimalists, particularly since the late twentieth century, who largely tend to see the documents and their portrayal of preexilic Israel as late postexilic scribal invention (e.g., Whitelam 1996; P. Davies 1992). But ultimately these three basic strands of interpretation have existed since the rise of biblical criticism (see E. Otto 2012, 62–185). One should also keep in mind that there is variation in details between individual academics.

As for archaeology, it arose initially in the nineteenth century as an attempt to enlighten the context of the biblical materials (see, e.g., Moorey 1991; cf., e.g., Levy 2010a). However, as data started to accumulate, a number of problems were identified in relation to interpreting them with the biblical materials. The period of the conquest and settlement turned out to be particularly problematic. It became clear that the conquest could not be dated to the fifteenth century, given what is known about the area at the time (see above). The only alternative possibility would be the thirteenth and twelfth centuries and the Late Bronze to Early Iron Age transition. However, important problems remained. In particular, it became clear that the archaeological record did not and does not provide positive evidence for a conquest at sites that are most crucial to the biblical narrative. Jericho and Ai are the most difficult sites in this respect. In particu-

lar, the site of Ai does not seem to have been occupied at all when the Israelites are supposed to have conquered it. Accordingly (see, e.g., Pitkänen 2010, 31; Lenski 2005, 148–52; Hawkins 2013, 29–48), alternative conquest models were sought, such as that advocated by William Albright and his disciples in the early twentieth century, which attempted to match thirteenth-century destructions in Canaan with a unified conquest under Joshua. The peaceful-infiltration model proposed by Albrecht Alt with Martin Noth in the mid-twentieth century suggested that the Israelites were nomads who immigrated into the land peacefully. The peasant-revolt model proposed by George Mendenhall and Norman Gottwald in the late twentieth century suggested that the Israelites were Canaanites who revolted against their Canaanite overlords. Scholarship has shown problems with all these models; however, many, especially within mainstream scholarship, continue to maintain a position that ancient Israel had indigenous origins, or at the very least included a large indigenous component (see Hawkins 2013, 43–48).

A Social Scientific Perspective: Frontier Societies, Migration, and Settler Colonialism

The above survey has indicated that both biblical and extrabiblical evidence should be taken into account when one tries to reconstruct the period of early Israelite settlement. Certainly, we can see that some kind of transformation took place in the area, since a system of Canaanite small political units as attested in the Amarna Letters is found as an Israelite entity at least by the time of the divided monarchies. Exactly what the transformation was in its details is, however, less certain, and this includes the question about the character of the United Monarchy, a period specifically covered elsewhere in this book (see ch. 26 below). The following discussion offers a plausible new reconstruction as proposed recently by the present author. It looks at ancient Israel as a society and then, based on interpreting biblical and archaeological data within a social scientific framework and recent advances in the social sciences, considers how that society could have come into being (see esp. Pitkänen 2016a).[2]

Escaping Oppressive Social Structures

Social scientific scholarship can provide an interesting backdrop to the early Israelite society. The ancient Near East on the whole can be seen in the context of agrarian societies and related social stratification. These are a development from hunter-gatherer societies, in which people could not develop a surplus and therefore social stratification was limited (see Nolan and Lenski 2015). In stratified agrarian societies, a tiny elite is in control of most of the societal resources, with the rest of the population generally living in poverty. The ancient Israelite law codes, particularly Deuteronomy, speak for a relatively egalitarian society, and an express motif for egalitarianism is Israel's past experience of slavery in Egypt (see, e.g., J. Berman 2008). Archaeological evidence fits with an idea of egalitarianism, with dwellings from Iron Age I in the highlands being of similar size (see Dever 2003, 169, 193). As Gerhard Lenski suggests, throughout history sometimes people have been able to escape the constraints of standard agrarian social structures and establish a new, at least relatively egalitarian order. This would, however, usually be only a temporary development; after some time the older order would reestablish itself (see Lenski 2005, 159–63; Nolan and Lenski

2015, 199–200). Such reestablishment can be considered as having happened in ancient Israel from the onset of the monarchy on, with both the biblical texts (see, e.g., 1 Sam. 8:10–18; 1 Kings 12:1–4) and archaeological evidence, particularly in terms of relative size of dwellings, suggesting increasing social stratification (see Dever 2003, 169, 193). Interestingly, the new egalitarian order would tend to be possible as long as so-called frontier conditions held, where the new society would be able to expand territorially and acquire new resources (see Lenski 2005, 159–60; Nolan and Lenski 2015, 199–200). This fits well with early Israel, as the closing of the frontier for them essentially coincided with the establishment of kingship according to the biblical texts (see 1 Kings 9:20–22), and this also fits with the pattern of expansion of highland material culture (see below).

Migration and Settler Colonialism

The idea of a frontier society is in many ways compatible with the peasant-revolt model (see above). However, as Lenski points out, such revolts have not been successful in history, at least in the sense of changing the social order into a more egalitarian one (Lenski 2005, 153–54). When one combines this with the fact that elites usually do not relinquish power voluntarily (see Lenski 2005, 153), it seems difficult to see how the system of more-or-less independent small entities as attested in the Amarna Letters for the fourteenth century could have changed into a new egalitarian order, even if such units might have found a way to unify politically. Postulating an external element can, however, provide a plausible cause and mechanism for a transformation. Lenski himself suggested a source of people from the lowlands, with an elite arriving from Egypt and able to establish its narrative of liberation from Egypt for the society as a whole (Lenski 2005, 163–66). It would seem that this is close

2. Social sciences generally involve comparing human societies across time and space and determining common features in them, at the same time acknowledging the possibility of unique features in each society. This can then lead to an enhanced understanding of the society/societies in question.

to what may have happened. That the biblical texts speak of a mixed multitude (*'ereb rab* [Exod. 12:38]) departing Egypt with the Israelites would seem to allow for a variety of origins for the early Israelites, especially as the new society was in its initial formative stages, even if this term could represent immigrants from places other than Egypt itself. But recent migration studies indicate that people migrating into new areas can increase even phenomenally in their destination (see Bellwood 2013, 247). Accordingly, an Egyptian component, even if initially small, could have become dominant in terms of numbers also.[3] The mechanism of how the new society was established and expanded from any initial areas it might have managed to take and hold can be understood in terms of a social scientific model of settler colonialism. In settler-colonial theory, settlers are colonizing migrants who move into a new land to establish a new society (Veracini 2010, 3–8; cf. P. Manning 2013, 5–7). They are different from ordinary migrants in that they bring a claim of sovereignty with them, as opposed to cross-community migrants, who are suppliants, ready to adapt to the existing social and political order at their destination (see Veracini 2010, 3). With enough people with a claim of sovereignty at the destination, a settler collective is established, and this collective may then reproduce and expand. As part of expansion, any indigenous peoples existing in the areas the new society spreads into are eliminated through killing, expulsion, and assimilation (see Veracini 2010, 16–52 for details). The new society typically legitimates its hold in the land in a variety of means and also conceptualizes and establishes its new social and political order in place of that of the indigenous societies (see D. Day 2008; Wolfe 2008). All in all, settler colonialism is a specific complex social

formation and a structure, rather than an event, in which an initial invasion gives rise to a prolonged process of eliminating the indigenous population (Wolfe 1999, 2, 163; 2006, 402).

As regards ancient Israel, the initial invasion was an entry into Canaan of a group of refugees from Egypt, where most likely they were held as slaves, in line with the aftermath of the expulsion of the Hyksos and a subsequent likely deteriorating status of Asiatics in Egypt (see ch. 24 above), also given that slavery was a usual institution in agrarian societies. The initial group did increase at destination and started to expand in the highlands, and may have been accompanied by further return migration of Semites from Egypt and others who might have joined the new Israelite society (again, note the mixed multitude in Exod. 12:38).[4] The expansion of the society eventually reached the lowlands by about the end of Iron Age I, as also suggested by archaeological evidence. The new society legitimated its hold to the land based on a belief that it had been promised to their ancestors, the patriarchs Abraham, Isaac, and Jacob.[5] They established law codes, attributed to Yahweh himself in the biblical texts, to act as a foundation of life in the new land, drawing from existing ancient Near Eastern legal and treaty traditions (see Kitchen and Lawrence 2012). Naturally, the exodus narrative would serve as a powerful legitimation for the new egalitarian order, including in the law codes themselves. The settlers also put in place a program of elimination of indigenous peoples (Exod. 23:27–33; 34:11–16; Lev. 18:24–30; Deut. 7).[6] In practice, the biblical

---

3. The large numbers in the book of Numbers should in my view be taken as intentional exaggeration. For a variety of positions on the issue, see e.g., Wenham 1981, 60–66; Achenbach 2003, 470–71.

4. Compare the concept of exogenous others who can (usually relatively easily) assimilate into the settler collective (Veracini 2010, esp. 26–27), leading to the concept of a tripartite division of a settler colonial situation into the settler collective, exogenous others, and indigenous others (Veracini 2010, 16–32). For further details in this respect in relation to ancient Israel, see Pitkänen 2017a.

5. On issues that relate to the historicity of the patriarchs, see ch. 23 above on the Ancestral period.

6. The texts describe such elimination as Yahweh's judgment on them (and cf. Gen. 9:18–28).

texts themselves already indicate that some of the indigenous people were assimilated (e.g., Josh. 6:22–25; 9), and it may also be that the Israelite ethnogenesis in the hill country involved a wider program of assimilation by at least partially eponymizing the names of territories (see Pitkänen 2016b).[7] The design and building of the tent sanctuary at Mount Sinai (Exod. 25–40) and its erection at Shiloh were seen as a kind of restoration of creation in the new land where Yahweh was again present with his people Israel (see Pitkänen 2014, esp. 245, for details), fitting with idylls that settler societies may have, even when their conquests are not complete (see Veracini 2010, 88; see also below).

A settler-colonial interpretation then emphasizes that the Israelite settlement was a long process. It was not a blitzkrieg in which everything was taken over in an instant, as suggested by some readings of the book of Joshua, then pitted against the book of Judges, which indicates that the conquest was not a simple matter, with this creating an apparent discrepancy between the books. It is correct that the book of Joshua describes a conquest, but a closer reading indicates that things were not as simple as that, with swathes of land not immediately under Israelite control (e.g., Josh. 13:1–7). A social-scientific interpretation can also highlight that the societal elites were not able to achieve their program fully even inside Israelite society. They did not have the means to enforce their ideals, as the book of Judges reflects (cf. the concepts of centrifugal ideologization and cumulative bureaucratization of coercion in Malešević 2010). An expressly settler-colonial interpretation also notes that not all settlement needs to be associated with violence, even when aspects of it naturally would be, given that another society is being replaced.[8] As for the conquests depicted in Joshua, at least some of them can be seen as a telescoping of events that took place over a longer time into a continuous narrative, with Joshua standing for Israel as a whole (cf. Josh. 12:7, which names Joshua *and* the Israelites). The narratives can also be seen to be in a stylized, exaggerated form, in line with other ancient Near Eastern conquest accounts (see esp. Younger 1990 for further details). Not all conquered sites were destroyed, even according to the biblical narrative itself (Josh. 11:12–13); one should not necessarily expect such acts of conquest to be attested in the archaeological record. Hazor itself does attest destruction that potentially fits with the biblical record (cf. Josh. 11:10–11). Jericho is badly eroded, including for any Late Bronze remains, and if one reads the narrative about its conquest as embellished, an Israelite foray of some kind against it is not excluded (see Kitchen 2003b, 187–88; Pitkänen 2010, 162–69). This leaves only Ai as a real problem, but except for possible explanations that can be offered (e.g., Hawkins 2013, 105–8; Pitkänen 2010, 182–84), one may keep in mind that all theories include anomalies (see, e.g., Kuhn 1962), and any theory construction needs to consider the pros and cons of possible alternatives, and this should be done on the basis of a total picture that a model can give.

Conclusion: Interpreting the Ancient Israelite Settlement

The above reconstruction of the Israelite settlement reads Genesis–Joshua as a unified doc-

7. Note that the name "Asher" seems to be attested in extrabiblical documents before the time of the Israelites for the corresponding area (see, e.g., *ABD* 1:482). This would seem to suggest that the patriarch's name is based on an area of settlement within the territory that was seen as part of early Israel (note also the at least relative lack of traditions about Asher; cf. also, e.g., the name "Gilead" in Num. 26:29; 27:1). Even if so, it does not necessarily follow that the same has to be the case for all the patriarchs and tribes.

8. Compare this with Lenski's concept of intersocietal selection (see Nolan and Lenski 2015, esp. 63–66) that can at least conceptually be compared with natural selection.

ument that legitimates ancient Israelite settler colonialism and that also provides broad, even if embellished, information about early Israel. Such a unified reading does not need to ignore diachronic source-critical considerations. For example, the usual Pentateuchal sources can in essence be acknowledged to exist, but their ordering and overall social context and meaning are reconstituted. In this, as also argued recently in detail based on source and redaction-critical considerations themselves, Deuteronomy can be seen as building on the Covenant Code in Exodus and the Priestly and Holiness materials in Exodus–Numbers (see Kilchör 2015). To account for a change of style and yet narrative continuity between Numbers and Deuteronomy, one may comfortably postulate that two authors wrote Genesis–Joshua, in line with the two covenants, in Exodus–Numbers and in Deuteronomy (see Pitkänen 2015; cf. Kitchen and Lawrence 2012, 3:127–31). In this way, one may arrive at a new interpretation of the settlement period that nicely intermeshes biblical and archaeological considerations.[9]

Such a reading does have religious and political implications. Above all, this interpretation can have linkages to postcolonial readings, many of which already exist, as it takes into account the problem of violence and societal replacement implemented by stronger societies against weaker ones. Comparable processes in the modern world include the British and US conquest of the Northern American continent (see, e.g., Hixson 2013), the birth of Australia and New Zealand, South Africa and the resulting apartheid, and the continuing expansion of modern Israel into Palestinian areas, which traces back to European nationalism and colonialism and the birth of Zionism in the nineteenth century (see, e.g., Pappe 2004; cf. Pitkänen 2010, 89–99; cf. also Cavanagh and Veracini 2017).

---

9. That is, the biblical texts in Numbers–Joshua reflect actual history, even if that history need not be taken entirely literally and includes programmatic and idealized features in terms of their present and future. The book of Judges shows how the idealism of Numbers–Joshua is to be tempered when we consider what actually happened during the period in question, even if such tempering is already implied in the book of Joshua if one reads it carefully. And the archaeological evidence ultimately contributes toward seeing broad patterns within which events and transformations take place. For further details, see esp. Pitkänen 2010; 2017b.

26

The United Monarchy

STEVEN M. ORTIZ

Introduction

The biblical texts about the events of the United Monarchy contain many images, from battle exploits to palace intrigue, from the great leadership and life of David to the wealth and wisdom of Solomon. The biblical authors are not necessarily focused on writing a systematic history of ancient Israel. The term "United Monarchy" is not even used by the biblical authors. In fact, for the period of Solomon most of the text involves the construction of the temple. Hence, one of the issues for the historian is to remove the layers of tradition associated with these two kings. In addition, there is not much extrabiblical historical evidence for the United Monarchy. Historians tend to assume that David and Solomon would leave an imprint in other historical sources. That they have not is easily understood since historical and archaeological records from prior to the Iron Age II rarely reveal names or inscriptions of kings of ancient Palestine (this is true for Philistia, Edom, Ammon, Moab, Aramaean states, etc.).

The facts that the texts were written after the events and that historical references are lacking have prompted various approaches to reconstructing the United Monarchy.[1] Some scholars abandon any attempt to reconstruct the history of the United Monarchy,[2] while others propose that we can discern historical events from later tradition.[3]

With the discovery of the Tel Dan Inscription, the historicity of David is no longer questioned. Biblical scholars and archaeologists are debating how much of the biblical account of the United Monarchy is historical and how much has undergone editing by the biblical authors. This chapter focuses on a historical reconstruction based on the biblical text and archaeological data.[4]

1. See Kitchen 2003b, 88–91, for a fuller discussion of the straw-man argument for the lack of references to David and Solomon in Egyptian and Assyrian sources.
2. It appears that "minimalist" has become the best term, possibly by default; it will be the term used here (see, e.g., P. Davies 1992; Thompson 1992; Lemche 1998a).
3. For example, S. McKenzie 2000; Halpern 2001; Finkelstein and Silberman 2001.
4. In addition, the Mesha Inscription might also refer to David (see ch. 36 below).

The Biblical Account

The accounts of David and Solomon are found in three major sources: the books of Samuel, Kings, and Chronicles. The accounts in the books of Samuel and Kings belong to a larger source—the so-called Deuteronomistic History. Scholars have identified "sources" within the corpus, such as a succession narrative, the account of the temple construction, the Ark narrative, Saul's rise and fall, the rise of David, Nathan's oracle, and the court history of David. In addition to original source material, the United Monarchy became a template for various theological motifs, such as messianism, kingship, God's kingdom, Zion, and the centrality of the Jerusalem temple. These motifs had naturally grown into major concepts through the life of the community so that they have influenced the recording of the actual events during this period.

The biblical accounts about David tend to focus on various military exploits and private interactions (e.g., the battle with Goliath, David's private conversations with his wives, and events in the king's court). These types of accounts have led several scholars to equate these stories with legends. Naturally, these specific stories would have developed into their own literary tradition and eventually were woven into the larger account of the founding of the Israelite state. There is no way to separate the traditions or verify the historicity of these accounts, except in broad strokes.

The biblical account of Solomon (1 Kings 1–11) focuses on the administration of the monarchy versus establishing the concept of the king and the social transformation from a confederacy of chiefdoms. A summary of the biblical accounts of Solomon describes his wisdom, wealth, marriage to foreigners, and building projects—most importantly, the temple. The biblical author summarizes Solomon's reign by saying that he "excelled all the kings of the earth in riches and in wisdom. The whole earth sought the presence of Solomon to hear his wisdom, which God had put into his mind" (1 Kings 10:23–24).

Geopolitical Context

During the Iron Age I–II transition (ca. 1100–900 BCE) the Levant experienced the growth of various secondary states. Although this development was not unilateral or caused by a single variable, historians can reconstruct the political gamesmanship that occurred as various polities grew into secondary states and vied for control of the two major north-south routes. The United Monarchy occurred during these major shifts in the eastern Mediterranean and specifically the southern Levant. The collapse of major states (e.g., Egypt, Mitanni, Hittite, Mycenae) created a power vacuum commonly referred to as the thirteenth-century (or Late Bronze Age) collapse, which produced major destruction and displacement. The biblical account of the rise of Saul and the diminishment of the prophet Samuel illustrates this period. As the Philistines were becoming a dominant entity, the subjugated people of Israel wanted a "king" to organize the tribes into a similar polity. Saul, though not able to develop a state, was able to organize the Israelite tribes into a larger polity. It was not until David that the political transformation could take place, but even then it was still a fragile social organization based on tribal allegiances.

In addition to shifts in political and social organization, the geographical location of the southern Levant influenced the rise of the United Monarchy. The southern Levant consists of two major north-south routes, the traditional Via Maris (International Coastal Highway) and the highway along the Transjordan plateau, which were major thoroughfares in the ancient Near East. In addition, there were two major east-west routes, the broad Jezreel Valley linking the two north-south highways in the north and the Negev desert linking them between Gaza and the Edomite territory.

These four routes and the topography of the southern Levant created interaction spheres, where the intersections became valuable points of power control that states wanted to possess.

The Philistines were the first polity to capitalize on control of the major routes, especially since they already occupied an important section of the major north-south coastal route. Although the biblical texts of Samuel focus solely on the expansionist policies of the Philistines to the west of the Israelite tribes, archaeology is able to provide a larger window into this period. By the eleventh century BCE, the Philistines already had major urban centers throughout the southern coastal plain (e.g., Ashdod, Gath, Ekron, Ashkelon, and perhaps Gaza) (Dothan 1998). Although the biblical text does not mention it, they were also expanding into the western Negev with several smaller occupation sites, allowing them to control the southern trade route from Arabia to the coast (Singer 1994; Z. Herzog 1994).

While there are biblical references to the "King's Highway" (Num. 20:17; 21:22) in Transjordan as an important route from Elat to Damascus, references to state polities do not occur until later historical periods. Recent archaeological work in Edom has shown that there was a major copper mining industry at Khirbat en-Nahas in the Faynan region, east of Wadi Arabah in Jordan (see ch. 57 below). A large citadel and administrative buildings are dated by the excavators to the tenth century BCE. Thomas Levy has postulated that Edom was a centralized polity in the tenth century BCE with an intensive trade network (Levy et al. 2004).

State Formation

The United Monarchy is best viewed as a secondary state within the southern Levant.[5] This

is typical for the Iron Age II period, as many other secondary states were formed during this period (e.g., Aramaean, Philistia, Ammonites, Moabites, Edomites). Hence, the small states of the southern Levant, of which the United Monarchy was one, were formed in the vacuum as the large primary states of the Late Bronze Age collapsed (e.g., the Egyptian New Kingdom, Mitanni, Mycenae, Hittites). One of the catalysts for state formation in the history of the Middle East is the underlying tribal organization that still underpins the states of this region. Several scholars have noted that the rise of the Davidic state fits the pattern found in many Middle Eastern cultures.[6] Lawrence Stager has presented a model that incorporates the kinship model of a patrimonial kingdom (Stager 2003a). This is supported by biblical texts in which David and Solomon organize the kingdom on the basis of the already established tribal structures of the earlier period (e.g., the Solomonic administrative districts [1 Kings 4:7–19]).

The territory of the United Monarchy was geographically diverse. The southern tribe of Judah was confined to the central hill country and bordered by desert regions to its south and east. It competed with the Philistines for control of the fertile Shephelah between the hill country and the coast. The northern tribes were intermingled with various cultural and political influences (e.g., Phoenicians, Aramaeans) as they occupied Galilee and the hill country of Samaria. It was no small task to unite the people of both the northern and southern regions into a common polity.

David first established his support among the southern tribes by protecting them from the Amalekites to the south. He also subdued Phi-

5. A "secondary state" refers to a state that develops within the context of a "primary/dominant state." It usually emerges from the collapse of a preexisting state or forms in the interaction between various complex

societies (Master 2001; Joffe 2002; Kletter 2004). For a contrary position on state formation in the southern Levant, Finkelstein 2010 proposes that the state started in the ninth century BCE with the catalyst being the westward expansion of the Assyrian Empire.

6. Joffe 2002 has presented the most comprehensive model incorporating anthropological theory. See also Younker 1999 and B. W. Porter 2013.

listine hostility by cunningly establishing a base of fighting men at Ziklag in Philistine territory. It was a natural step to establish his first capital at Hebron, where he won the support of this region. He had a harder time gaining support from the north. That did not happen until after the civil war between the house of David and the house of Saul, when the northern leadership fell apart (2 Sam. 2:12–4:12). He quickly gained support by reclaiming Michal, Saul's daughter, as his wife (2 Sam. 3:13) and showing kindness to Mephibosheth of the house of Saul (2 Sam. 9).

David's domestic policy was twofold: security for the tribes from the Philistines (2 Sam. 5:17–25) and uniting the tribes by creating new images of unity. David chose a neutral capital in the center of the country, Jerusalem, which belonged to neither the southern nor the northern tribes. After the capture of Jebusite Jerusalem, he moved the Ark of the Covenant there (2 Sam. 6) and publicly stated his desire to build a temple (2 Sam. 7) as a central place of worship belonging to the state and not to any particular tribe.

David's foreign policy was also twofold: either conquering or subduing as vassals neighboring polities or those that controlled important communication and trade routes. We have a summary of this in Chronicles from the west to the east: Philistines (1 Chron. 18:1), Aram-Zobah and Moab (vv. 2–3), the northern Transjordan plateau, Hammath (v. 10) and Aram Damascus (vv. 5–6), Edom (vv. 12–13), and Ammon (19:10–19). The United Monarchy had conquered kingdoms that provided tribute (Edom, Moab, Ammon, Aram Damascus, Aram Zobah; some had Israelite governors appointed over them [2 Sam. 8:6, 14]), and vassal kings who were then forced to accept David's hegemony.

Political and Social Organization

The United Monarchy corresponds chronologically with the Twenty-First and Twenty-Second Dynasties of Egypt. While Egypt was weak during this period, two of its kings were able to

mount campaigns: Siamun of the Twenty-First Dynasty and Sheshonq I of the Twenty-Second (Kitchen 1986; Mysliwiec 2000). The texts that provide the most enigmatic references to the interaction of Egypt and the United Monarchy come during Solomon's reign. Some concern the conquest of Gezer by the pharaoh and its gift to Solomon as a dowry, his building of a place for the princess, and her move from the "city of David" to her house (1 Kings 3:1; 7:8; 9:16, 24; 11:1; 2 Chron. 8:11). The others refer to trade relations between Solomon and Egypt, specifically horses and chariots from Egypt (1 Kings 10:28; 2 Chron. 1:16; 9:28). On the surface, these texts present conflicting accounts on the relation between the United Monarchy and Egypt.[7] It appears that a weakened Egypt had a foreign policy that still wanted to control the southern Levant, as Egypt had during the New Kingdom, but had to adapt to the reality of secondary states emerging in what was once their northern frontier. One of these adaptations was to form alliances with these states.[8]

Political Organization

There is no reference in the Bible to David's political organization beyond his military and the unification of the tribes under the capital of Jerusalem. There was a rational plan to secure the major trade routes of the coastal highway and the Transjordanian plateau. It is during Solomon's reign that we get an idea of an organizational structure to the kingdom. We have two kinds of references to planned administration. The first are to Solomon's districts (Hess 1997; Rainey 2006). The second is a small reference tucked away in a summary statement regarding Solomon's building projects: 1 Kings 9:15 mentions that he rebuilt Jerusalem and

---

7. See Schniedewind 2010 for a discussion of the history of interpretation of these texts reflecting editing and later redactions.

8. See Malamat 1982; Kitchen 2003a; for an alternative view, see Ash 1999.

the cities of Hazor, Megiddo, and Gezer. No explanation as to why he rebuilt these cities, but it is easy to see that Solomon was placing key cities to guard the major communication routes, and Gezer now served as the forward guard in the Aijalon Valley, even farther west than the fortress at Khirbet Qeiyafa.[9] In addition to these three cities, the text (vv. 15–19) mentions several other cities (e.g., Beth Horon, Baalath, Tadmor) as well as store cities and towns for his chariots (v. 19). In spite of these texts, any evidence to reconstruct the political and social organization comes from the archaeological record. This only provides a reconstruction of the basic framework (for further detail on the archaeology of this time period, see ch. 8 above).

Settlement Hierarchy

One feature of a state is a settlement hierarchy in which a tiered distribution system is imposed on the landscape. The biblical text hints at such a system, whether it is in districts (1 Kings 4:7–19), Levitical cities (Num. 35:1–8; Josh. 21; 1 Chron. 6:54–81), or fortified cities (such as Rehoboam's [2 Chron. 11:5–10]). A recent study has shown that in the tenth century there was a drastic change of urbanization as rural settlements ceased to exist and cities sprang up (Faust 2015). There are four types or tiers of cities during the Iron Age: (1) capital cities (e.g., Jerusalem, Samaria), (2) major administrative centers, cities in which a majority of the settlement plan is devoted to public complexes, (3) secondary administrative cities or royal fortresses, and (4) provincial towns that have no or few public structures (Z. Herzog 1992).

Naturally, when we discuss the kingdom of David and Solomon we must address the capital city of Jerusalem. It is accurate to note that not much archaeological data excavated in Jerusalem can be associated with the United Monarchy. The archaeology of Iron Age Jerusalem presents several difficulties. The Iron Age (and Bronze Age) city was built on the crest of the eastern hill (the City of David), where, unlike classic tells with built-up layers of cities, each successive period of Jerusalem removed the earlier city to build on bedrock, thus removing the stratigraphy of earlier occupation. The only evidence left would be material culture found in fills, dumps, and erosion. Excavations have found pottery and artifacts that date to the tenth century BCE. Recent excavations have shown that there is an area of public buildings and structures that probably represent the palace of David.[10]

Joe Uziel and Itzhaq Shai have noted that one of the problems in reconstructing the development of Jerusalem is a modern paradigm, or perception, that ancient Jerusalem should be a large city. They posit that first the center appears (e.g., temple and palace) and then urban development. Hence we should see a trajectory from a nucleus to urbanization instead of the other way, and this is what we see as Jerusalem grows from a centralized capital and religious center in the tenth century BCE to a large urban city in the eighth century (Uziel and Shai 2007). This fits the archaeological record of the expansion of Jerusalem from the tenth century to the eighth.

Military

The biblical account contains many references to battles, particularly David's. David had a standing army and his "mighty men" (NRSV: "warriors" [2 Sam. 20:7; 23:8–39; 1 Chron. 11:11, 19]). Solomon created a force of 1,400

9. Khirbet Qeiyafa is a fortified center overlooking the Elah Valley from the Judean hills where the traditional battle between the Israelites and Philistines took place as recounted in the David and Goliath military account. The site dates to the tenth century and appears to have been a forward post during the United Monarchy (Garfinkel and Ganor 2009; Garfinkel, Ganor, and Hasel 2014).

10. E. Mazar (2009) posits that she has uncovered a monumental building that she identifies with David's palace. Others (e.g., Faust 2012b) note that the building dates to an earlier period, yet was reused by David when he conquered the city from the Jebusites.

chariots, which were stationed at Jerusalem and at various "chariot cities" (1 Kings 9:19; 10:26). Archaeologists have found tenth-century remains of stables at Megiddo, Lachish, and Jezreel. A monograph by Deborah Cantrell (2011) has demonstrated that ancient Israel had a robust equestrian component to its military and state. She defines the various compounds throughout Iron Age cities as "horse-related architecture." She notes that "training facilities, such as Megiddo, with stables for 450 horses; the Jezreel fortress with its huge enclosed courtyard; and Lachish with its courtyard, chambered gates, and stables were in fact processing thousands of horses, only some of which required stabling at any given time" (Cantrell 2011, 9).

In addition to fortified and chariot cities, a series of forts developed starting in the Iron Age I and fully developing during the Iron Age II. Forts have been found in the vicinity of Jerusalem (A. Mazar 1981; 1982b; 1990b; Finkelstein 1990) and in the Negev (Faust 2006c; Hairman 2012). Adam Zertal has surveyed the territory of Ephraim and Manasseh and found a pattern where a major city is surrounded by forts in its hinterland. For example, the city of Samaria was guarded by fourteen forts (Zertal 2001). While this provides evidence for the situation in the northern kingdom during the divided monarchy, it probably illustrates a similar pattern for the United Monarchy.

Urbanization

Evidence of urbanization includes the size of a settlement and of the structures found in it. Demographic studies have shown that there were seven thousand to twenty thousand people living in Judah (Ofer 1994; Lehmann 2003). Amihai Mazar (2003) notes that with the added territories of the north and some from Transjordan added to Judah, this is more than enough for a basis for a territorial state. This demographic data is reasonable for social

scientists working with ancient cultures but usually is seen as too low by biblical scholars, who assume that it should be larger, probably based on modern estimates of territorial states (Jamison-Drake 1991).

Large public works have been typical identifying features of a state-level society. Evidence of monumental architecture dating to the tenth century BCE is found throughout ancient Palestine in the form of large public buildings, fortifications, palaces, water systems, and monumental ornamentation. A typical Israelite city consisted of public and domestic quarters. It would contain a fortification system with a city wall connected to a gate complex. There would also be several large multiuse buildings with magazines consisting of a series of long rows of rooms used for storage, collecting taxes, barracks, and even stables.

The Territorial Extent of the Monarchy

The biblical report that Solomon "ruled over all the kingdoms from the Euphrates River . . . as far as the border of Egypt" (1 Kings 4:21 NIV) implies that the territory extended all the way from modern-day Iraq to Egypt. This is an idiom that refers to controlling the land bridge between Egypt and Mesopotamia and not necessarily a statement of complete territorial control or expansion. The Brook of Egypt is at Nahal Besor, which is located in the western Negev as the border between Sinai and the coastal plain. Another biblical idiom, "from Dan to Beersheba" (1 Kings 4:25), refers to the whole of Israel and reflects a more accurate picture of the territorial boundary of the United Monarchy from the Huleh basin in the north (with the conquered Canaanite cities of Hazor and Tel Dan) to the Negev (Beersheba).

Economics

The biblical text refers to Solomon's wealth, particularly the descriptions of the temple with gold-plated walls and gold furniture and vessels (1 Kings 6:21; 7:48–51). In addition, there are several descriptions of items of trade, caravans, and gifts and tribute (1 Kings 9:11, 28; 10:2, 10, 14). Later Pharaoh Shishak (Sheshonq I) also "took away the treasures of the house of the LORD and the treasures of the king's house; he took everything. He also took away all the shields of gold that Solomon had made" (1 Kings 14:26). Alan Millard has noted that the descriptions and comparisons are comparable to other descriptions and finds from the ancient Near East, particularly the New Kingdom of Egypt (fifteenth to thirteenth centuries BCE) and the Neo-Assyrian Empire (ninth to seventh centuries) (Millard 2007).[11] Granted that a small territorial state in the southern Levant cannot be compared to large empires such as Assyria and Egypt, many scholars assume that the descriptions are a small kingdom's attempt to use hyperbole or later writers' attempts to copy royal descriptions of wealth from the Neo-Assyrian or Babylonian period.

John Holladay has addressed the royal economy of ancient Israel, particularly of the eighth century BCE, and has compared Hezekiah's tribute in relation to the Neo-Assyrian typology and history of tribute extraction (Holladay 2006). He notes that Judah was particularly positioned to take advantage of the various trade spheres (e.g., Phoenicia in the north and the south Arabian caravans in the south). He analyzed texts from the archives of royal inscriptions of Mesopotamia and concluded that tolls levied on ninth-century camel caravans from the south were a major economic source of the wealth for eastern Africa, Arabia, and the Indian Ocean economies.[12] Although the analysis was of a period after the United Monarchy, it is easy to reconstruct a trajectory of the economy based on control of these trade routes.

11. For a popular account, see Millard 1989.
12. Holladay 2006, 326–27. See Master 2014 for an updated view.

Temple and Cult

Associated with the difficulties with the archaeology of Jerusalem is Solomon's temple. Some biblical scholars are quick to point out that there is no archaeological evidence for the temple of Solomon. This is a straw-man argument, or a naive assumption of the nature of archaeological data. We do not have archaeological evidence of Herod's temple, but no scholar seriously doubts its existence (Galil 2012). Many temples have been discovered in the Levant, and we are able to trace the evolution of temple design. The tripartite temple described in the biblical text fits the era of the United Monarchy (John M. Monson 2004). One of the features of the landscape of the tenth century is that there are no major cultic sites. During the second millennium, temples and sacred buildings are found everywhere and in most cities, but in the tenth century this changes for the western highlands where Iron Age I temples and cult sites are abandoned, giving credence to the centralization of worship in Jerusalem (Mierse 2012, 100; Faust 2010).

Writing, Scribes, and Literacy

From the biblical texts we see much statecraft—diplomacy, districts, taxation, military lists, and so forth—that should provide evidence for a robust documentation system for the state. Chance finds from later Iron Age II periods show that ostraca were commonly used for documentation. The excavations at the City of David in Jerusalem have found a room full of bullae, hinting that a majority of the documentation was written on perishable materials and that the likelihood of finding writing dating to the tenth century would be slim. The question of literacy is debated. Abecedaries provide evidence of students of writing. It is clear that during the divided monarchy there were functional scribal schools. The question is how early these schools appeared in ancient Israel (Hess 2009a).

Conclusion

The United Monarchy was short-lived. The region continued to contain geographically centered territorial states that continued to form alliances and fight for control over the southern Levant. The house of David's control over the northern polity survived for only two generations. Future Judahite kings would continue to be counted from this era, and the theology of Zion, Jerusalem, and election would continue to develop through the divided monarchy up to the exile and return.

27

The Divided Monarchy

Israel

JENS BRUUN KOFOED

The Sources

The relevant sources for the reconstruction of Israel's history are various nontextual archaeological remains and textual evidence from monumental inscriptions and canonical compositions from Assyria, Egypt, Aram, and Moab; administrative and graffiti-like notes on walls, pots, and sherds from Palestine; and the biblical texts of 1–2 Kings, 2 Chronicles, Amos, Hosea, Micah, and Isaiah 1–33.

The monumental inscriptions differ from the canonical compositions of Assyria and the Bible by being contemporary with the events or persons they purport to describe. Since the biblical texts' information on Israel is embedded in considerably later compositions, many historians tend to exclude the biblical sources or to include them as primary sources only if they can be corroborated by nonbiblical evidence. However, wherever we can check it, the author(s)/editor(s), irrespective of when the book of Kings was written or edited, must have based the account on reliable sources (Kofoed 2005).

This does not mean, however, that the biblical information should be used uncritically.

Just as the monumental inscriptions are written with obvious royal interest, the biblical texts are written from an equally biased perspective. What we have in 1–2 Kings—and even more so in 2 Chronicles—is what Daniel Fleming has described recently as "the legacy of Israel in Judah's Bible" (Fleming 2012), and since the author(s) or editor(s) responsible for the final compositions were theologically critical toward Israel, we should expect that the narratives are more or less deprived of positive information on Israelite kings who receive a theologically bad evaluation. The nontextual archaeological remains are also subject to interpretation, not least as far as stratigraphic chronology is concerned. The discussion is beyond the scope of this chapter. I have followed A. Mazar (2011).

Overview

In the broader context of Egyptian and Levantine history, the tenth century was a period when both Egypt and Assyria were weak, allowing small territorial polities such as Israel,

Judah, Edom, Moab, Ammon, Aram Damascus, and others to appear and grow into fully developed territorial kingdoms in the geographical buffer zone between Assyria and Egypt. Except for a limited campaign under Sheshonq I (943–922), Egypt did not reassert control over the Levantine coast until a brief period in the seventh century under Necho II (610–595); and except for a resurgence of Assyrian power under Shalmaneser III (859–824) and Adad-nirari III (811–783) in the late ninth century, it was not until the reign of Tiglath-Pileser III (745–727) that Assyria was able to gain imperial control over the aforementioned territorial polities. In the meantime, Aram Damascus and Israel became the strongest and most prosperous kingdoms in the region.

At the end of the tenth century, the region dominated by Israel saw the beginning of an urbanization process that culminated in the eighth century (A. Mazar 2007, 155). Avraham Faust, in a comprehensive analysis of the archaeological data, has demonstrated that whereas Judah in the ninth and eighth centuries was a "simple agrarian society" with two main social strata, Israel—at least in the eighth century—developed into "an advanced agrarian society" with a relatively large number of social strata and a varied settlement hierarchy (Faust 2012a, 205–6). Faust's interpretation of the nontextual archaeological data is supported by the description of Israel as a full-blown state in the royal inscriptions from Assyria, Aram, and Moab.

People, Politics, and Events

Israel Divided

The only textual source for the early history of monarchic Israel is the biblical text, which provides us with two explanations for the collapse of the United Monarchy following the death of Solomon: Solomon's apostasy (1 Kings 11:1–13) and his successor Rehoboam's politically suicidal decision to reject the request from "all the assembly of Israel" to lighten the hard service put on them by Solomon (1 Kings 12:1–15; 2 Chron. 10:1–15). The fact that Rehoboam had to leave his Judahite power base in Jerusalem and go to the old ancestral and tribal gathering place in Shechem to meet "all the assembly of Israel" adds to the impression that his power was crumbling and that other factors such as suppression of corporate decision strategies, political nepotism, taxation inequities, and lack of defense measures against the rising Aramaean power of Damascus may have played a role as well.

The Houses of Jeroboam and Baasha

The collapse of the Israelite United Monarchy and the ensuing civil war between the two resulting kingdoms allowed the Aramaeans in Damascus to consolidate their power just as the Egyptian pharaoh Sheshonq I (943–922)—the Shishak mentioned in 1 Kings 14:25–26—found opportunity ca. 925 to campaign in the territories of Judah and Israel.

In the investiture scene painted in 1 Kings 11:29–39, Jeroboam is elected and dynastically rewarded by the prophet Ahijah with unmistakable reference to David's election in 2 Samuel 7. Jeroboam is told that he must emulate David, but he does not, and though initially blessed, and after being warned twice (1 Kings 13–14), the same Ahijah announces that Jeroboam's line will be terminated (1 Kings 14:14).

The reason was the cultic reform described in 1 Kings 12:26–33: rival shrines replacing Jerusalem as the sole cultic center were established at Dan and Bethel, with golden calves to replace the Ark of the Covenant. Non-Levites were appointed to serve as priests, and a new cultic calendar was enforced. Theologically, we should understand the cult not as syncretistic but as an expression of unorthodox Yahwism. "The very fact that Jeroboam apparently maintained Yahwistic pilgrim festivals," Jonathan Greer remarks, "is significant as an indicator of continuity and his commitment to the religious traditions in Israel" (Greer 2013, 41). At Tel Dan evidence of a podium and a large four-horned altar has been found, as well as various religious paraphernalia such as three iron shovels, a small horned altar, and an iron incense holder.

Jeroboam's son Nadab, having reigned only two years (911–910),[1] was assassinated by Baasha the son of Ahijah of the house of Issachar (1 Kings 15:27). Baasha moved the capital to Tirzah and reigned for twenty-four years (1 Kings 15:33). He was at constant war with Judah's king Asa, and in order to avert an attack from Baasha, the weaker Asa bribed the Aramaean king Ben-Hadad in Damascus to intervene. Ben-Hadad attacked the northern territory of Israel, and, being attacked on two flanks, Baasha had to retreat to his capital, Tirza (1 Kings 15:16–22).

Baasha receives a bad evaluation by the Deuteronomistic author, and at the very end of his reign another prophet, Jehu the son of Hanani, announces to Baasha that his house will perish (1 Kings 15:34–16:4, 13–14). This was fulfilled after Baasha's son Elah had reigned for just two years and his commander Zimri killed him and "struck down all the house of Baasha" (1 Kings 16:11). Zimri's own reign, however, turned out to be the shortest of all, since another commander, Omri, forced Zimri to commit suicide after only seven days on the throne (1 Kings 16:15–20).

The House of Omri

Having assassinated Zimri, the commander Omri (1 Kings 16:21–22) had to remove another rival, Tibni the son of Ginath, before he could begin his twelve-year reign as king of Israel. Omri's dynasty, which lasted from his accession in 886 to the death of his great grandson J(eh)oram[2] in 841, is remarkable in more than one way. First, we finally come to a period where

---

1. The chronology of Kitchen 2003b is followed.
2. The name is spelled both "Joram" and "Jehoram" in the biblical texts.

---

the biblical texts can be supplemented by other sources. Second, the period of the Omride dynasty is the golden age of the kingdom of Israel. In the middle decades of the eighth century, Israel exercised great influence in the region, and though this was a time of stability and expansion for the southern Levant as a whole, it nevertheless testifies to the strategic and political flair of the Omrides. Omri's decision to transfer the capital from Tirza to Samaria was a clever strategic move. Logistically and economically, the capital was placed much nearer to the primary north-south trade route, the Via Maris, with access to Phoenicia, Anatolia, and Mesopotamia, just as it was placed astride one of the main routes from the Transjordanian territories to the coastal plain and the harbor at Dor.

The relative strength of the first Omrides is also clear from the fact that Ahab was a leading partner in a coalition of twelve regional polities that succeeded in warding off an attack from the resurgent Assyrian power of Shalmaneser III (858–824) in the battle at Qarqar in 853. In the Kurkh Monolith inscription Shalmaneser informs us, however, that Ahab contributed with 2,000 chariots and 10,000 soldiers. As for Moab, the Mesha Stela from the late ninth century informs us that "Omri was the king of Israel," that he "oppressed Moab for many days," and that his son or descendant still oppressed Moab in king Mesha's own time, that is, during the entire Omride period (COS 2:137). That not only Moab but also Judah was in a vassal-like relation to Israel during the Omrides is hinted at in 1 Kings 22:4, where Judah's king Jehoshaphat seems forced to join Ahab in his attempt to recover Ramoth-gilead from the Aramaeans.

Monumental architecture at Samaria, Jezreel, Hazor, and Megiddo can be dated to the time of Omri and (primarily) Ahab (A. Mazar 2007, 159–60).

Another important characteristic of the Omride period is the Phoenician connection. Prominent is, of course, Ahab's diplomatic marriage to Jezebel, daughter of the Sidonian king Ethbaal (1 Kings 16:31), but the most dramatic influence was the introduction of Baʿal and his consort Asherah into Israelite worship. Jeroboam's unorthodox Yahwism was devolving into syncretism, and this is why Ahab (with Jezebel) receives a harsher evaluation and is given more space than any other Israelite king by the Deuteronomistic author (1 Kings 16:30, 33). Ahab and Jezebel figure prominently in the Elijah narratives, where the royal couple is made responsible for the consequences of replacing Yahwism with Baʿalism as exemplified in the Naboth incident (1 Kings 21:1–16), where the abuse of royal power leads to violation of Deuteronomistic laws about possession and use of land, false testimony, murder, and theft. For the same reason, Elijah announces the same condemnation against Ahab that his prophetic predecessors had issued against Jeroboam and Baasha (1 Kings 21:17–24). Ahab's line was terminated in the next generation when the army commander Jehu assassinated his son J(eh)oram (852–841), who had succeeded his childless brother Ahaziah (853–852).

As for the Aramaeans, Israel's relationship with Damascus seems to have been governed by a swinging-door policy. In times of pressure on the small states of the southern Levant by the far mightier Assyria, they cooperated and formed alliances like the above-mentioned coalition in the Battle of Qarqar, but as soon as the external threat was warded off, regional conflicts resurfaced. The many conflicts mean that parts of Israel's northern territories frequently changed hands, and since Ahab, following his retrieval of territories described in 1 Kings 20:34, launched another campaign to retrieve Ramoth-gilead (1 Kings 22), we must assume that the city, despite the covenant mentioned in 1 Kings 20:34, had been retaken by Ben-hadad II in the meantime. The campaign was unsuccessful, however, and Ahab died from his wounds in the battle (1 Kings 22:29–40).

Ahab's son Ahaziah (853–852) "walked in the way of his father" (1 Kings 22:52) and died childless after only two years on the throne (2 Kings 1:2). Though his brother J(eh)oram (852–841) also "clung to the sin of Jeroboam," he receives a slightly better evaluation because he put away the pillar of Baʿal that his grandfather Ahab had made (2 Kings 3:2–3) and had a better relationship with the prophet Elijah (2 Kings 3:13–14). From 2 Kings 3 we learn that King Mesha of Moab rebelled, and that J(eh)oram led an indecisive campaign against Moab in coalition with Judah's king Jehoshaphat and an unnamed Edomite king. The event is in all likelihood the same as described in the Mesha Inscription, in which Mesha states that he rebelled successfully against Israel after Omri and his son had oppressed Moab for forty years. In that case "his son" must be understood to refer not to Omri's eldest biological child, Ahab, but more loosely to his grandson J(eh)oram.[3]

In 2 Kings 5 it appears that there are fairly good relations between Aram and Israel, since the Aramaean commander Naʾaman consults both the Israelite king and the prophet Elijah to be cured of leprosy. In 2 Kings 6–7 we find the Aramaean king Ben-hadad II warring against the Israelites again, however, and though his attack on Samaria was miraculously averted, we are reminded again of how often and suddenly the tables could turn. In 2 Kings 8:28–29 J(eh)oram—with (his vassal?) King Ahaziah of Judah—fights the Aramaean king Hazael, who had recently usurped the throne. J(eh)oram probably lost the war, since it is reported that he was wounded and had to retreat to Jezreel. Although the battle seems to have taken place around Ramoth-gilead (2 Kings 9:14–15), it is likely that the Israelites also lost the city of Dan in the process and that it was Hazael who set up the victory stele found there in 1993–94

3. For a recent and more detailed discussion of the relationship of 2 Kings 2 with the Mesha Inscription, see Greenwood 2014.

(*COS* 2:161–62). The broken and fragmentary inscription commemorates the victory of an Aramaean king over the king of Israel and the king of the house of David, and there is general agreement that the names of the two kings should be restored as J(eh)oram, king of Israel, and Ahaziah, king of the house of David.[4] In the inscription Hazael claims to have killed both kings, and though this, on the face of it, seems to contradict the information in 2 Kings 9:14–28 that it was J(eh)oram's commander Jehu who killed them, it is quite possible that both Jehu and Hazael were responsible. The key to this is the prophet Elisha, who instigated both Hazael to usurp the Damascene throne by killing his predecessor Ben-hadad II (2 Kings 8:7–15) and Jehu to do the same in Israel (9:9–13). It makes perfect political sense that Jehu, in order to usurp the throne of J(eh)oram, sought support from J(eh)oram's enemy, the king of Damascus, and that he more or less acted on Hazael's behalf in killing the kings. In any event, the commander Jehu not only became king but also terminated the Omride dynasty decisively by executing Queen Jezebel (9:30–37) and slaughtering Ahab's descendants (10:1–17).

The House of Jehu

Though Jehu (841–814) initially struck down the prophets of Ba'al (2 Kings 10:11–28), both he and his dynastic successors Jehoahaz (814–806), Jehoash (806–791), Jeroboam II (791–750), and Zechariah (750) receive the same negative evaluation by the Deuteronomistic author.

The second half of the ninth century and the beginning of the eighth were dominated by strong Damascene kings (Hazael and Ben-hadad III) and the aforementioned resurgence of Assyrian power under Shalmaneser III (859–824) and Adad-nirari III (811–783). "In those

4. For a recent discussion of possible reconstructions, see Greenwood 2014, 296 and the literature listed there.

days," we learn from 2 Kings 10:32, "the LORD began to trim off parts of Israel. Hazael defeated them throughout the territory of Israel." In the same period, the region as a whole was under pressure from the Assyrians. According to the description of Shalmaneser III's campaigns on the Black Obelisk, Jehu had to pay tribute in 841 (*COS* 2:269–70).

Following the death of Jehu in 814, Hazael renewed his attacks on Israel, and though Jehu's son Jehoahaz momentarily "entreated the LORD" and was promised "a savior," Israel in reality became a vassal of Hazael (2 Kings 13:1–9, 22). The "savior" is probably to be identified with the Assyrian king Adad-nirari III, who relieved the Israelites of Aramaean pressure by attacking Damascus. During the Damascene crisis, Israel, now under Jehoahaz's son Jehoash (806–791), revolted and decided to pay tribute to the Assyrians. On the Calah Orthostat Slab Adad-nirari III tells that he subdued Israel (*COS* 2:276–77), and in the Tell Al Rimah inscription that he received tribute from "Joash the Samarian" (*COS* 2:275–76). After the death of Hazael around 800, Jehoash retook from Ben-hadad III the cities that his father, Hazael, had taken from Jehoahaz (2 Kings 13:24–25).

After the death of Adad-nirari III in 783, Assyrian campaigns in the west were limited, and Israel—under the long reign of Jehoash's son Jeroboam II (791–750)—was to experience its second and last period of economic and national restoration. He restored Israel's ancient borders "from Lebo-hamath as far as the Sea of the Arabah" (2 Kings 14:25), and though it is unlikely that Israel exercised direct rule as far as Lebo-hamath, north of Damascus, it is even more unlikely that the Deuteronomistic author would thus boast of an Israelite king who otherwise receives the same negative theological evaluation as his predecessors if there was no reality behind it.

The critique of Amos, Hosea, Micah, and to a certain extent also Isaiah belongs to this period and demonstrates that the relative peace and prosperity under Jeroboam II led to extravagance, moral decay, and idolatry "financed" by corruption, social injustice, and oppression of the poor. The declaration of Amos is probably a direct reference to the ivory house in Samaria and the royal residence at Jezreel (Amos 3:15).

Three mid-eighth-century inscriptions on storage jars found at Kuntillet ʿAjrud, a remote caravansary on the trade route between the Arabian Peninsula and the Mediterranean, demonstrate that the mixture of Baʿalism and Yahwism so characteristic of the Omride period continued to dominate both official and popular religion in Israel (Lipiński 2006, 373–81). The inscriptions mention "Yahweh of Samaria and his Asherah" and thus testify to the belief that Yahweh, like the Canaanite high god El, had a consort. Short of mentioning a consort of Yahweh, Hosea's condemnation of "the calf of Samaria" (Hosea 8:5–6) demonstrates that the next generation of prophets had to continue the struggle against the syncretistic Baʿalism of their predecessors Elijah and Elisha.

The Fall of Samaria

Peace and prosperity came to an end when Tiglath-Pileser III (745–727)—the biblical Pul—ascended the Assyrian throne, began a new imperialistic policy, and focused his campaigns in the west. In Israel the instability was marked by the very short reigns of Jeroboam II's son Zechariah (750) and his assassin, Shallum (749), who reigned for only six months (2 Kings 15:8–12) and one month (15:13–16), respectively. And though Menahem (749–739), who also executed his predecessor, ruled for ten years (2 Kings 15:17–22), it was the beginning of the end. From Tiglath-Pileser III's Iran Stela from around 738 we learn that he imposed tribute on "Menahem the Samarian" (COS 2:287–88), "a thousand talents of silver," according to 2 Kings 15:19–21. Menahem's son

and successor, Pekaiah (739–737), followed by Pekah (737–732), who usurped the throne by assassinating Pekaiah, continued to pay tribute to the Assyrian king. An alliance between King Rezin of Damascus and King Pekah of Israel turned out, however, to be disastrous for both kingdoms. The coalition, we learn from 2 Kings 15:37 and 16:5–6, "came up to wage war on Jerusalem," probably to force Judah into a coalition that would be able to withstand the pressure from Assyria. And though the prophet Isaiah tried to persuade King Ahaz to trust in Yahweh (Isa. 7–8), Ahaz eventually chose to pay the Assyrians off to rescue him from the alliance. In 732 Tiglath-Pileser conquered Damascus and killed Rezin (2 Kings 16:9). Subsequently, 2 Kings 15:29 reports, he annexed the northern part of Israel to the Assyrian Empire and carried its people captive to Assyria. In one of the so-called Summary Inscriptions, Tiglath-Pileser III reports that he removed Pekah and installed Hoshea in his place (COS 2:288). Hoshea's assassination of Pekah (2 Kings 15:30) thus seems to have been orchestrated or at least supported by the Assyrians, who installed him as their puppet king.

Hoshea (732–722) turned out to be a turncoat, however, and "therefore," the Deuteronomistic author continues, Tiglath-Pileser III's successor, Shalmaneser V, "confined him and imprisoned him" (2 Kings 17:3–4). The prison, according to the biblical text, was Samaria itself. Having invaded "all the land," Shalmaneser besieged the capital for three years, and "in the ninth year of Hoshea the king of Assyria captured Samaria; he carried the Israelites away to Assyria" (17:5–6). In line with Assyrian warfare policy, foreign groups were settled in the territories of the fallen kingdom, which was placed under direct Assyrian rule (17:24).

The Assyrian sources are divided as to who conquered Samaria in 722/721. The Babylonian Chronicle describes the reign of Shalmaneser V and notes that "he shattered Samaria" (COS 1:467). Shalmaneser died in 722, and his successor, Sargon II (722–705), several times claims that *he* conquered Samaria (*COS* 2:293). One possibility is that Shalmaneser V actually conquered the city, whereas Sargon II was responsible for the deportation.[5] In any event, the kingdom of Israel disappeared and became the new and directly ruled Assyrian province of Sāmerīna. Deportation of the Israelite elite and repopulation of the region with elitist foreigners created an even more diverse population, and since many of the Israelites who had not been deported probably fled to their kin in the south, the fall of Samaria also had significant consequences for Judah.

5. For a more detailed discussion of the possibilities, see Becking 1992, 21–56.

28

The Divided Monarchy

Judah

ERIC L. WELCH

Introduction

The historical fate of the biblical kingdom of Judah is a central component of the larger narrative of the Old Testament. During the time in which Judah outlasted the northern kingdom of Israel by 136 years, the Old Testament portrays Judah as the sole manifestation of God's chosen people living within the Promised Land. As the home of Jerusalem, both a religious and a political capital, Judah was a direct contributor to the theologies and ideologies that helped shape the Old Testament. Its ability to survive the dynamic political landscape of the Late Iron Age helped elevate its status, and the status of its rulers, to an idealized standard—a standard no northern king was capable of attaining. In many ways Judah was directly responsible for much of the biblical text of the Old Testament.

Apart from its religious significance, the history of Judah offers a number of avenues for exploration and study. Judah's position in the regional landscape placed small secondary states on each of its borders. Beyond the kingdom of Israel on the north, Judah's territory bordered on that of the Philistines, Moabites, and Edomites. This constant contact made for a lively political experience. Subject to the same fate as the rest of the region, Judah also encountered the wrath of the Neo-Assyrian Empire as Sennacherib campaigned through the region.

Discussing the history of Judah is made significantly easier by the quantity of evidence. To date, Judah has been one of the most intensely excavated areas in the southern Levant. As a result, archaeologists are capable of reconstructing settlement patterns, economic trends, and even ways of daily life from a high-resolution dataset. In addition to archaeological evidence, Judah benefits from a strong epigraphic record from outside its borders, especially from the Neo-Assyrian Empire. For events like the Neo-Assyrian campaign to Judah in 701 BCE, scholars can make use of the biblical text, archaeological data, Neo-Assyrian royal annals, and graphic representations such as Sennacherib's palace reliefs at Nineveh to reconstruct a vivid depiction of this turning point in Judah's history.

These many things combine to make Judah a unique case study in biblical history. While Judah may represent the heartland of the biblical narrative, in many ways Judah's unique contributions to the political and theological narrative supply the heartbeat of the Old Testament.

The Foundation of Judah

Judah did not always exist as an independent kingdom. With the foundation of the monarchy, the land of Israel was united under a single king—Saul and later his successors, David and Solomon—who ruled from Dan to Beersheba (2 Sam. 3:10; 1 Kings 4:25). However, following the death of Solomon, his son Rehoboam was not received by all, and the tribes of Israel separated themselves from Judah, forming a separate kingdom. With the addition of the tribe of Benjamin, Judah as an independent kingdom was born.

Geographic Extent

Because Judah began as the tribal allotment of Judah and then Benjamin, its territory is located in central Israel. Judah was topographically diverse with its capital, Jerusalem, in the hill country, its western periphery in the Shephelah, its southern frontier the Negev, and its boundary on the east the Dead Sea. As a landlocked state in the Iron II, Judah was surrounded by neighboring polities. To the west, the Philistines dominated the coastal plain, holding key cities such as Ashdod, Ashkelon, and Gaza. To the south, Edom was a neighbor, while across the Jordan was the territory of Moab. At its maximum extent, the Old Testament claims, Judah extended its reach from Jerusalem south to Eilat. However, its western border with the Philistines was firm, with the most significant advance coming with the possession of the former Philistine city of Gath (Tell es-Safi) by King Uzziah, some decades following its defeat at the hands of Hazael of Damascus (2 Kings 12:17; 2 Chron. 26:6).

Neither the size of its allotment nor the variety of terrain found within Judah should be seen as a weakness of the kingdom. The Shephelah was among the most fertile regions in the entire land, and well suited to cultivating grain, olives, and grapes. The wide ranges of the Negev were profitable for pastoral activities, especially those related to raising sheep and goats. The Judean wilderness, or that hot, dry area immediately east of the hill country, was perfectly suited to host an enormous date palm industry. Furthermore, the deposits of salt and bitumen made this seemingly dead land an invaluable resource. The hill country, with its seasonally abundant rainfall in topographically isolated valleys near Jerusalem, created opportunities for the kings to implement royal estate farms.

Not to be overlooked when considering Judah's resources is its position in the land. While material resources in crops and minerals could supply Judah's consumption, its role as the crossroads of ancient Near Eastern trade filled its coffers with bullion. Arabian trade across the desert, exotics coming up from Egypt, had to go through Judah (Holladay 2006). All things considered, "little Judah" was an abundant land with bountiful resources.

Early Judah's History

Judah's political history begins in the tenth century with the division of the kingdom of Israel into northern and southern kingdoms. Under the reign of Rehoboam, Judah began its trajectory as a separate entity from the northern kingdom. During the early years of Judah's independence, its territory probably was limited to the hill country (J. M. Miller and Hayes 2006, 94–96).

The early history of the independent kingdom of Judah was marked by numerous wars as the newly separated kingdom sought to establish control over its northern neighbor. The reigns of Kings Rehoboam, Abijam, and

Asa were marked by their constant devotion of energies and resources to engaging Israel in battle (1 Kings 14:21–15:24). The kingdom also suffered a considerable blow at the hands of the Egyptian pharaoh Shishak (Sheshonq), who is said to have sacked Jerusalem during the fifth year of Rehoboam's reign, around the year 922 (1 Kings 14:25–26; 2 Chron. 12).

With the reign of Jehoshaphat, the narrative depicts a change in administrative policy. Rather than fighting against Israel, the kings of Judah sought ways to enter into alliances. A common way of achieving such alliances in the ancient Near East was through diplomatic marriage. Both Jehoshaphat and Jehoram aligned themselves with Ahab of Israel through strategic marriages. Although Jehoshaphat's bride is unnamed (2 Chron. 18:1), we know that Jehoram married Ahab's daughter Athaliah (2 Chron. 21:6). Outside of marriages, Judah also found ways to cooperate with Israel on larger ventures such as international trade or military campaigns. Jehoshaphat partnered with Ahaziah of Israel to construct ships and launch a maritime expedition to Ophir, an unfortunate investment that eventually ended in disaster (2 Chron. 20:35–37). Jehoshaphat also aligns with Israel in 2 Kings 3 to fight against the king of Moab. In this account, the book of Kings demonstrates its preference for Judah over Israel by casting Jehoshaphat as the righteous king who seeks out a prophet of Yahweh, who happens to be Elisha.

The Eighth Century

The early eighth century was a time of relative peace for the kingdom of Judah, with only one substantial military event early in the century. Archaeological excavations have produced very few signs of military destruction at this time. On the whole, it was a time of prosperity for Judah, and very likely a time during which Judah's influence as a regional player came to fruition. In part this is due to the stability

of the Judahite crown. Each monarch of the early eighth century reigns between fifteen and twenty-five years. This type of continuity is markedly different from the rapid succession seen at times in the preceding centuries.

During the first half of the eighth century the achievements of the kings of Judah were primarily in improvements in the kingdom's infrastructure and territorial extent. Following a victory over ten thousand Edomites (2 Kings 14:7), Amaziah enters into conflict with Jehoash of Israel. In the only significant military event of the early eighth century, a confrontation at Beth Shemesh results in Amaziah's capture, Jerusalem being besieged, and the temple looted of its gold and silver (2 Kings 14:13–14). The reign of Uzziah, however, would remedy this. Under Uzziah, Chronicles indicates, Jerusalem is improved and fortified (2 Chron. 26:9–15). Territories that have been lost are restored as Judah expands its influence in the south as far as Eilath and deep into Philistine territory on the west (2 Chron. 26:2, 6). The reign of Uzziah is summarized as a time of economic prosperity and political stability. The book of Kings reports only in summary on the reign of Jotham, but indicates a reign consistent with that of his father, Uzziah, and notes improvements to the temple (2 Kings 15:35).

The stability of the first half of the eighth century was not permanent. As the Neo-Assyrian Empire increased its territorial expanse, the secondary states of the southern Levant were drawn into a dynamic political world in which neighboring states joined together in regional coalitions to resist the advances of the empire. Year after year, the Neo-Assyrian kings launched campaigns into the Levant, beating those states into submission and imposing annual tribute. The looming threat of the Neo-Assyrian Empire would have lasting effects on the kingdom of Judah, shaping its political and economic history, but especially its religious history.

Syro-Ephraimite Conflict

The Late Iron Age was a difficult time for small states in the ancient Near East. With the Neo-Assyrian Empire gaining momentum, the various kingdoms of the Levant were faced with a decision: band together and fight Assyria or become Assyrian provinces. This dilemma forms the backdrop of an event often referred to as the Syro-Ephraimite Conflict. Around 734 BCE the kingdoms of the Levant recognized their impending doom and began to organize a coalition to fight the Assyrians. Israel, along with Aram, the Philistines, and Moab, agreed that a coalition was in the region's best interest. Judah, however, wanted no part in the coalition. As a punishment and a misguided attempt to gain Judah's allegiance to the coalition, the other members levied assaults on Judah's various borders. Finally, King Ahaz surreptitiously approached Tiglath-Pileser III and pledged his allegiance to the Neo-Assyrian Empire on the condition that those neighboring territories harassing Judah would be dealt with. In the coming year, the northern kingdom of Israel would be attacked by Assyria and reduced to a fragment of its former territory. Likewise, the surrounding territories were assaulted and forced to pay heavy annual tributes until Samaria's eventual downfall in 722.

A Growing Jerusalem

As a part of the fallout from the defeat of the northern kingdom, Jerusalem experienced a time of growth. Formerly a city constrained to the spine of a single hill descending from Mount Moriah, Jerusalem expanded westward, incorporating Mount Zion. As Jerusalem's population expanded, so did the need for its protection. According to 2 Chronicles 32:5, Hezekiah was responsible for the construction of a wall to incorporate this new western neighborhood into Jerusalem. Today, this wall is visible in the Jewish Quarter of Jerusalem's Old City.

Around this time, Hezekiah also undertook an effort to move the traditional water source of Jerusalem, the Gihon Spring, within the city (2 Kings 20:20). In a marvelous feat of engineering, Hezekiah's workers excavated a shaft through the bedrock of Jerusalem designed to move water from the Gihon toward a collection pool, the Pool of Siloam. Contributing to the amazing nature of this feat is the fact that the workers began excavating from two directions and joined their tunnels in the middle. Workers then inscribed an account of joining the two tunnels and allowing the water to flow from its source to the pool.

In order to feed its growing population, Jerusalem looked to the surrounding valleys to produce food for its inhabitants. State-run farming operations cultivated and harvested crops, which were then collected and distributed in officially sealed jars. On the handles of these jars a stamp bearing the phrase "belonging to the king" (*lmlk*) designated the contents as royal products. This estate farming system and the system of administrative stamps began a long tradition in the valleys around Jerusalem (Gadot 2015).

This system of estate farming may also have been understood in the light of the growing need to generate surplus crops in order to meet the tribute demands imposed by the Neo-Assyrian Empire. In this way, Jerusalem became increasingly significant as an economic center in the late eighth century.

701 BCE

One of the critical turning points in Judah's history came in the year 701 BCE when its relationship with Assyria deteriorated and Assyria besieged the Judean landscape. No single historical event until the exile would have such lasting effects on various aspects of Judean life, such as the economy, religion, and even family structure.

Stemming from the events of the 730s, Judah remained a vassal state of the Neo-Assyrian Empire. As a paying vassal, Judah enjoyed peace under the reigns of Ahaz and Hezekiah in Jerusalem, while Tiglath-Pileser III and Sargon II were on the throne in Nineveh. However, with the death of Sargon, Hezekiah seized the opportunity to end the contract with Assyria, revolting against Sargon's successor, Sennacherib.

Sennacherib did not respond kindly to this rebellion. In the year 701 he advanced his armies throughout Judah, laying siege to cities such as Lachish and Jerusalem, while devastating numerous others. Altogether, Sennacherib claims in his annals to have destroyed forty-six of Hezekiah's cities, while shutting him up in Jerusalem "like a bird in a cage." Beyond the destruction of the land, Sennacherib claims to have redistributed some of the conquered territory to Padi, Şillibel, and Mitinti, the Philistine kings to Judah's west (COS 2:302–3, no. 119B).

The archaeological record of 701 demonstrates a consistent and widespread pattern of destruction (Dagan 1992; Vaughn 1999). Extensive survey and excavation in the Shephelah reveals a traumatic event happening at the end of the eighth century BCE. Smashed and broken pottery, burnt beams, and thick layers of dark ash are all signs of the destruction associated with 701.

The fallout from 701 for Judah was widespread. For the first time in Judah's history the land was lost to the hand of a foreign enemy. While battles had been fought and cities on the periphery had been subdued, the reassignment of lands to the Philistines was a devastating blow to Judah's inheritance. Economically, the impact of 701 is best demonstrated in the production of olive oil. Following 701, what was at one time a regional cottage industry of Judah ceased to exist in Judean hands. Major Judean sites producing olive oil such as Beth Shemesh were abandoned, never again to engage in olive oil production. Instead, the Philistine city of Ekron (Tel Miqne) began producing olive oil for the first time and did so on an industrial scale. Around the perimeter of the site, nearly two hundred presses were found, capable of producing 245,000 liters of olive oil each fall during the seven-week olive harvest season (Eitam 1996). This entire industry was very likely supplied by the olives of the Judean heartland; however, due to the subjugation of Judean lands as a consequence of 701, the agricultural products were not to the benefit of Judah, but instead its Philistine neighbors at Ekron.

The events of 701 contributed greatly to Jerusalem's prominence in Judean ideology. With the looming threat of Assyria, much of the Judean countryside was abandoned as Judah adopted a "hedgehog" defense (Halpern 1991). Threatened by the advances of Assyria, Judah's natural reaction was to contract into its urban centers, natural safe havens in light of the raiding bands. This new movement toward the cities likely aided in streamlining a number of practices in daily life, especially religion.

Hezekiah is lauded by the author of Kings for his religious reforms in Jerusalem. In the summary introduction of his reign, Hezekiah is said to have removed the high places, smashed the sacred stones, and cut down the Asherah poles (2 Kings 18:4). Furthermore, Kings supplies the detail that Hezekiah was responsible for removing Nehushtan, the bronze serpent fabricated by Moses. This artifact apparently was a lingering component of former cultic practices, as the text indicates, in which the Israelites used to burn incense to the image. Because of this purge, the author of Kings holds Hezekiah highest among the kings of Judah, saying that there was no one like him before him or after him (2 Kings 18:5). Chronicles reinforces this idea, showing Hezekiah's reforms as a foil to the practices of Ahaz, whose reign is viewed as an unmitigated disaster (2 Chron. 28:1–4, 22–25). For the Chronicler, Hezekiah fixes the many sins of Ahaz by reopening the temple (2 Chron. 29:3), organizing and reconsecrating the priests (vv. 4–18), restoring sacrifices (vv. 18–36), and celebrating the Passover (2 Chron. 30).

The threat of an Assyrian military presence in the countryside likely facilitated many of the reforms that Hezekiah brought about (Halpern 1991; Bloch-Smith 2009). The so-called hedgehog defense enacted by Hezekiah in 701 had the added benefit of severing rural ties to the land and probably to many of the traditional folk religious practices related to agriculture and fertility. Since Judah's rural populations were forced into the urban centers, they became citizens and were likely brought in line with the royal standards for religious practices.

The Seventh Century and the *Pax Assyriaca*

Following the devastation of 701, Judah was left to reinvent itself—a feat accomplished remarkably well. While in its early days Judah could have been described as an agricultural economy, the seventh century BCE witnessed Judah's transformation into an industrial economy. Given the continued reality of tribute demands originating from Assyria, the estate-farming model initiated in the eighth century was perfected in the seventh. In the valleys outside Jerusalem, intensive operations focused on wine and grain production. Along the Dead Sea, rich mineral deposits were exploited, and date palms were grown as they are today. During this time Judah also expanded its agricultural reach into the Judean desert, making use of innovative irrigation techniques that transformed barren land into Judah's breadbasket (Stager 1976). Despite having faced one of the most critical blows in its history, Judah used the seventh century to remake its economy, transitioning toward surplus-oriented industrial agriculture.

A significant part of Judah's prosperity in the seventh century was due to the very force that brought about its devastation in 701—the Neo-Assyrian Empire. Following Assyria's domination of the region in 701, order was restored. Rebellious kings were brought back in line, sometimes being replaced with more pro-Assyrian alternatives. With stability restored and Assyria's control firmly established over the region, a period of relative peace in the southern Levant began. The so-called *Pax Assyriaca*, or Assyrian Peace, refers to the time during the seventh century when the region became immensely productive because of stability brought about by Assyrian domination. This homeostasis, combined with the need to generate economic returns sufficient to keep Assyria at bay, resulted in a time of unprecedented economic growth for the Levant. From the port city of Ashkelon, olive oil from Ekron was shipped as far as the Iberian Peninsula; grain from the Judean desert was discovered in a marketplace in Ashkelon, probably also a commodity that was largely exported around the Mediterranean (Faust and Weiss 2005).

Following the long rule of Manasseh (2 Kings 21:1), under which most of the economic prosperity was initially gained, Judah experienced further revitalization under the reign of Josiah (2 Kings 22–23:30). As Assyria's imperial power in the west began to wane, many of its former vassal states entered into a period of newfound independence. During the reign of Josiah, Judah capitalized on these political dynamics and began to regain some of its former territory. Perhaps most significantly, it is under Josiah's reign that Jerusalem was renovated as the most holy place. Josiah is portrayed as a righteous king who is responsible for renovating the temple and instituting religious reforms that realigned Judah's national religion with the instructions given by Yahweh in Deuteronomy (2 Kings 22). As part of his reforms Josiah purged the countryside of its illicit shrines, sanctified Jerusalem by desecrating any semblances of paganism, and rededicated the country to the right worship of Yahweh.

The End of Judah

The Iron Age culminated for Judah with the forced relocation of its populations and the destruction of the temple in Jerusalem by the Babylonians in the year 587 BCE. This event, known as the exile, ended the existence of Judah as an independent kingdom.

Judah's final years leading up to the exile were complicated. Following the reign of Josiah, Judah witnessed the reign of four different kings, two exiled out of the country and two others installed separately by Egypt and by Babylon. Not only is the political history itself dynamic but the sources for the period are also difficult. Within the Hebrew Bible, the books of 2 Kings, Jeremiah, Ezekiel, and Habakkuk make up the written testimony. Extrabiblical evidence includes a number of inscriptions, such as ostraca collections from Lachish and Arad (see ch. 17 above), as well as the independent political records of both Egypt and the Neo-Babylonian Empire (e.g., the "Nebuchadnezzar Chronicle" [Wiseman 1956]). The history of this dynamic royal succession and a review of relevant sources can be found in the next chapter.

Although Judah was only a small territory within the larger kingdom of Israel, its central place in the narrative of the Old Testament cannot be overlooked. As the home of Jerusalem and the lone survivor in a dynamic political landscape that brought about the early demise of Israel, Judah and its inhabitants were key actors in the events and ideas that helped shape the Old Testament. From its inception as the castoff from a fractured kingdom to its eventual exile, the story of Judah is the story of the Old Testament—the story of kings and their people seeking right standing with their God in the face of an uncertain world operating around them.

29

The Exile and the Exilic Communities

Deirdre N. Fulton

Introduction

The Babylonian exile marks the period when many Judeans were deported from the kingdom of Judah in both the first siege of Jerusalem by Babylon in 597 BCE and in the later conquest and destruction in 587 BCE. A third deportation may have taken place around 582 BCE. The traditional dates for the exile coincide with the collapse of the kingdom of Judah (587 BCE) to the destruction of the Babylonian Empire (539 BCE).

The Babylonian exile is difficult to reconstruct because the Bible does not contain one narrative dedicated to the events of the exile, and Babylonian sources are limited. In the biblical texts, one must examine 2 Kings (24–25), Jeremiah (39–43), and 2 Chronicles (36) to try to piece together how the exile arose, and Ezra to see how it concluded. As Rainer Albertz succinctly states, "The exilic period thus represents a huge lacuna in the historical narrative of the Hebrew Bible. It stands as a murky, gaping hole in the history of Yahweh and his people, illuminated only briefly by isolated beams of light" (Albertz 2003, 3–4). Even though it is a "murky" period of history, the exile stands as one of the most significant periods of biblical history, reforming and reshaping the political and theological boundaries of the people of Judah.

The Collapse of Judah

The exile occurred as a result of the disintegration and eventual collapse of the kingdom of Judah. During the reign of Jehoiakim (608–597 BCE), Judah was in an alliance with Egypt against the Babylonian Empire because of Egyptian control over the southern Levant, specifically focused on the coastal roadway (Via Maris) during the latter half of the seventh century BCE (Vanderhooft 1999, 69–72). Egypt's domination was severely crippled at the Battle of Carchemish in 605 BCE by Nebuchadnezzar II's Babylonian forces. Destruction layers at sites such as Ashkelon (dated to 604 BCE) point to the shifting tide of political control in the southern Levant with the accession of Nebuchadnezzar II (Stager 1996b; Vanderhooft 1999, 69–72). Indeed, during the first twelve years of Nebuchadnezzar II's reign, he spent nine years campaigning in the west against powers such as Hattu, Egypt, and Judah (Grayson 1975, 100–102).

Jehoiakim's decision to ally with Egypt probably was a response to Nebuchadnezzar's indecisive battle with Pharaoh Neco at the borders of Egypt in 601 BCE. After Babylonian forces returned home, Jehoiakim revoked the vassal treaty he had made with Babylon to side with Egypt. Nebuchadnezzar rebuilt his forces in 598/97 BCE and, in answer to Jehoiakim's rebellion, marched to Jerusalem. Before the arrival of Nebuchadnezzar, Jehoiakim died, leaving his son Jehoiachin to rule. When Nebuchadnezzar arrived in Judah, he laid siege to Jerusalem in 597 BCE, which only lasted for a short time because Jehoiachin surrendered (2 Kings 24:10–12). As punishment for Judah's alliance with Egypt, Jehoiachin was taken into exile, along with elites, servants, and many other Judeans (v. 12). Nebuchadnezzar also took the treasures from the temple and the king's house in Jerusalem (v. 13).

The Babylonian Chronicles (British Museum no. 21946; Wiseman 1956), dating to the reign of Nebuchadnezzar, also records this siege. It states that Nehbuchadnezzar "encamped against the city of Judah and on the second day of the month of Adar he captured the land (and) seized (its) king. A king of his own choosing he appointed in the city (and) taking vast tribute he brought it into Babylon" (Grayson 1975, 102). According to the Weidner ration tablets—a set of cuneiform tablets recording ration lists for Jehoiachin's family— Jehoiachin and his sons were provided food rations throughout their lifetime (Weidner 1939). The narrative in 2 Kings 25:27–30 also relates that Evil-merodach of Babylon (Amel-Marduk) released Jehoiachin from prison and provided him with a place among the other kings who were in exile in Babylon.

After the removal of Jehoiachin, his uncle, the pro-Babylonian Judean elite Mattaniah,

renamed Zekediah, became king (2 Kings 24:17). Zedekiah remained a loyal vassal to Babylon until his eventual rebellion (Ezek. 17:13–15). According to Jeremiah 27–28, an anti-Babylonian faction arose in Jerusalem. Zedekiah rebelled against Babylon, seeking an alliance with Egypt. This rebellion triggered the destruction of the kingdom of Judah, beginning with the siege in 588 BCE and defeat of Jerusalem in 587. Babylon's punitive expedition brought about the end of the monarchy, the destruction of the temple and walls in Jerusalem, and the exile of many Judeans. Zedekiah fled but was caught and punished for his rebellion when he was taken to Riblah in Hamath (2 Kings 25:20–21), located 150 miles from Jerusalem. Zedekiah's sons were slaughtered while he was forced to witness the events; he was subsequently blinded and taken in chains to Babylon. The high priest and second-in-command were also slaughtered at Riblah. A third exile is mentioned in Jeremiah 52:30, dated to 582 BCE. Another anti-Babylonian movement may have brought about this exile, but little is known concerning these events (Albertz 2003, 56).

The Impact of the Babylonian Exile

Scholars have debated the exact impact of the exile on the population and subsequent administration of Judah. Originally, many argued that a large percentage of the Judeans were taken into captivity as a result of Nebuchadnezzar's campaigns and later conquest of Judah (see Albright 1949b). Second Kings 24:12, 15–16, record that Jehoiachin's mother, wives, eunuchs, officials, "the elite of the land," "the artisans and the smiths," and "all the men of valor . . . all of them strong and fit for war" also accompanied him into exile.[1] While the text tends to focus on the elites, mention of "the artisans and

---

1. For a brief overview of the text-critical issues concerning the lists of exiles in 2 Kings 24:12, 15, and Jer. 29:2, see Lipschits 2005, 56–57.

the smiths" reveals that skilled laborers were also part of the exile (Smith-Christopher 2002). Estimates of the exact number of people exiled to Babylon range from 10,000 (Lipschits 2005) to 250,000 (Albright 1949b).[2] The biblical texts are unclear but never provide a large number for the exiles. Only "the poorest people of the land" remained after this first exile (2 Kings 24:14). In the 587 BCE conquest of Judah, 2 Kings 25:11–12 records that Nebuzaradan, the captain of the guard, came to Jerusalem and took the people who were left in Jerusalem as well as the deserters to Babylon. Only the poorest people were left to be "vinedressers and tillers of the soil." This is in contrast to Jeremiah 52:28–30, which records that in the first exile (597 BCE) 3,023 people were exiled, in the second exile (587 BCE) 832, and in the third exile (582 BCE) 745.

Unlike the earlier Assyrian exile of the kingdom of Israel (722 BCE), which deported much of Israel's citizenry and settled people from the Assyrian heartland or other deportees in Israel's territory, Babylon did not resettle people in Judah. Indeed, the evidence in Judah points to modest activity on the part of Babylon (Vanderhooft 1999; Betlyon 2003; Lipschits 2003; 2005). Earlier, the Assyrians had set up border fortresses, roads, and way stations throughout their empire. The Assyrians also encouraged economic development and growth in the southern Levant. This policy did not continue into the Babylonian period, which led to a decline in the economy of the southern Levant. While there is archaeological evidence for the presence of the Assyrians, particularly along the Philistine coast, the Babylonians left little evidence of their period of dominance over Judah and the southern Levant. This lack of presence and biblical texts related to the deportation of many Judeans gave rise to the notion of the "empty land."[3] Though the population did decrease, the land was never "empty," but rather economically depressed.

The Babylonian campaigns against Judah in both 597 and 587 BCE concluded with the destruction and sack of Jerusalem. One of the areas of scholarly debate is how much the Babylonian damage extended to the northern areas of Judah, in the territory of Benjamin (see Magen and Finkelstein 1993; Milviski 1997; C. Carter 1999; Lipschits 2005; Faust 2012c). In the area of Judah, it is widely agreed that the city of Jerusalem shows signs of destruction. Most scholars agree that in both Judah and Benjamin settlement patterns point to the continuation of only a few urban centers, all of which suffer a diminished population.

Babylonian Administration of Judah

After the destruction of Jerusalem and the exile of Zedekiah, Nebuchadnezzar did not appoint another king. Instead, he appointed Gedaliah, son of Ahikam, as the governor over the towns and people in Judah (2 Kings 25:22). Gedaliah's administrative center was in Mizpah—presumed to be Tell en-Nasbeh located twelve miles north of Jerusalem—in the area of Benjamin (Zorn 1993; 2003). Since Nebuchadnezzar's armies destroyed Jerusalem, moving the administration to another location was logical. Other important people were also with Gedaliah at Mizpah, including Jeremiah the prophet (Jer. 40:5–6), Chaldean soldiers (Jer. 41:3), the "king's daughters," eunuchs, and other Judeans (41:10). Gedaliah's tenure was short-lived because a member of the Davidic royal family, Ishmael, killed him.

The story of Gedaliah indicates that initially the Babylonians appointed locals to positions of power. After the death of Gedaliah, however, there is no textual material that outlines who was appointed next. Unlike earlier Assyrian

2. Albright's number is untenable, due to more recent demographic studies.

3. See Barstad 1996 for a discussion of the "myth of the empty land." For differing views on the impact of the Babylonian conquest of Judah, see Lipschits 2005; Faust 2012c.

control of the southern Levant, there is no clear evidence that Judah became part of a Babylonian province (Vanderhooft 2003). If Babylon's goal was to transform Judah into a province, both the biblical texts and the material culture do not reveal this to be the case. As Vanderhooft has argued, "The archaeological data point to a minimalist reconstruction of the Babylonian imperial bureaucracy" (Vanderhooft 1999, 110).

One noteworthy example of Babylonian bureaucracy is found at Ramat Rahel, where continued activity from the late Iron II through the Babylonian period is evident (Lipschits et al. 2011), albeit on a smaller scale. Ramat Rahel continued to function as an economic center for the Babylonian crown to collect payment in goods. The evidence for a presence there in the Babylonian period is based on continuity in the administrative stamp seal evidence (Lipschits and Vanderhooft 2011) as well as continuity in occupation (Lipschits et al. 2011). But Ramat Rahel and Tell en-Nasbeh are the exceptions to the larger picture of economic disruption from the Assyrian to the Neo-Babylonian periods.

Exilic Communities

The biblical texts indicate that the deportees were taken out of their land and into exile. Exiling recalcitrant kingdoms was not a Babylonian invention. The earlier Assyrian Empire also practiced exiling rebellious vassal kingdoms. There were several noteworthy differences, however, in the deportation policies of the Assyrians and the Babylonians. Most noteworthy of these policies is that the Assyrians practiced bidirectional deportation whereas the Babylonians practiced unidirectional deportation. When Shalmaneser V of Assyria annexed Israel in 722/721 BCE, he deported much of the population into the heartland of Assyria and imported peoples to resettle Israel, particularly the area of Samaria. The populations exiled to the Assyrian heartland

were settled in several cities. The strategy of scattering exiled populations throughout the Assyrian Empire indicates that "any who would challenge Assyrian rule faced utter ruin and obliteration" (Pearce and Wunsch 2014, 3). The Babylonians practiced deportation, but they did not resettle people back into the land of Judah. Also, the exiled Judean populations were not scattered but rather remained as communities within specific towns and cities in Babylon.

Several sites are named in the biblical texts as places in Babylonia where Judeans were settled, including Tel-abib (Ezek. 3:15), Tel-melah, Tel-harsha, Cherub, Addan, Immer (Ezra 2:59), and Casiphia (Ezra 8:17).[4] There were also Judeans living in Egypt, specifically at Migdol, Tahpanhes, Memphis, and Pathros (Jer. 44:1).

Our knowledge of the exilic community has grown over the past few decades based on the analysis of important Babylonian-era texts. As these legal and administrative documents reveal, the Babylonians resettled deported populations and named towns after the ethnic names or toponyms of the populations settled in them (Zadok 1979; Vanderhooft 1999; Pearce 2011). The Babylonians chose to keep exiled communities together, moving them to settlements in agricultural regions that had been devastated during the late seventh-century wars between the Assyrians and Babylonians (Pearce and Wunsch 2014, 3). In return for the land, the deportees provided taxes and military assistance for the monarchy. This policy allowed Nebuchadnezzar II to implement an impressive building program in the city of Babylon. This strengthening of the Babylonian heartland was essential to Nebuchadnezzar's model of governance, seemingly not focusing on the peripheral parts of the empire. This is in

4. In Ezekiel, the prophet is among the exiles in Tel-abib ("mound of the deluge") near the Chebar River. For possible locations of the Chebar River, see Zadok 1996, 727; Vanderhooft 1999, 110.

direct contrast to earlier Assyrian policies that focused on economic growth in the peripheral zones of the empire in order to build the central economy (Beaulieu 1989). But due to the areas near Babylon that had been devastated by the late seventh-century wars, Babylon's focus on their interior appears to have been a wise administrative and economic choice.

The āl-Yāḫūdu ("town of the Judeans") texts provide information on the deportees from Judah. Āl-Yāḫūdu was a settlement mentioned in a series of Neo-Babylonian and Persian-period cuneiform texts. Unfortunately, the texts are unprovenanced, but Laurie Pearce argues from evidence in the texts that "āl-Yāḫūdu was located in the Nippur-Keš-Kakara triangle" (Pearce 2011, 270). Scholars such as Pearce (Pearce 2011; Pearce and Wunsch 2014) argue that the texts from āl-Yāḫūdu preserve the activities of the exiled Judeans because (1) the name of the town follows the Babylonian practice of naming a place after the origin of its settlers; and (2) the appearance of names with a Yahwistic theophoric element (i.e., a shortened form of the name of Judah's exclusive God, Yahweh) in the documents is evidence for the presence of a Judean population (Zadok 1979; Pearce 2006; Pearce and Wunsch 2014). As Pearce and Wunsch note, "The archives from āl-Yāḫūdu and neighboring towns, along with those from Babylon, provide the framework for reconstructing a more complete picture of the experiences of the lives of the lowly as well as the high-born Judean and West Semitic exiles as lived in the urban and rural landscapes of Neo-Babylonian Mesopotamia" (2014, 4). The documents focus on economic matters but also provide names and genealogies spanning up to four generations. The documents continue for several generations, indicating the gradual promotion and success of certain families in Babylonian exile.

Another exilic community was located in Egypt. According to Jeremiah, when Gedaliah son of Ahikam was killed, several people fled to Egypt. There is little information concerning this community except for Jeremiah 43:7–44:30. Jeremiah 43:7 narrates that a group of Judeans who feared Babylonian punishment for the death of Gedaliah emigrated to Tahpanhes in Lower Egypt. Jeremiah 44:1 makes clear that there were Judeans already living in Egypt, specifically in Migdol and Noph (i.e., Memphis). Daniel Smith-Christopher observes that the community in Egypt is very different from the community in Babylon because one is a chosen exile and the other is a "forcible relocation" (1997).

The End of the Exilic Period

After the death of Nebuchadnezzar II in 562 BCE, his son Amel-Marduk (Evil-merodach in 2 Kings 25) came to the throne but reigned for only two years. Neriglissar, the son-in-law of Nebuchadnezzar II, murdered Amel-Marduk and reigned in his place. Neriglissar had a short reign (560–556 BCE) and was succeeded by his young son Labashi-Marduk (556 BCE), who was killed in a palace conspiracy soon after his accession.

Nabonidus (556–539 BCE) was the final king of the Neo-Babylonian Empire. He was a usurper to the throne and not part of the royal family (Beaulieu 1989). Nabonidus did not follow in the earlier patterns of the Babylonian kings, specifically Nebuchadnezzar, who generally eschewed Assyrian imperial practices. Nabonidus used Assyrian-style propaganda to establish a connection between his reign and the earlier Assyrian reign, specifically Ashurbanipal (Vanderhooft 1999, 52). He also switched focus away from Marduk—the chief god of the Babylonian pantheon since the time of Nebuchadnezzar I—to the moon god Sîn. Nabonidus left the administration of the city of Babylon to his son and coregent Belshazzar while he sought better control of the southern region of his borders.[5] After securing control

5. This same Belshazzar is mentioned in Dan. 5.

for Belshazzar, Nabonidus moved to the oasis of Taima, located in Arabia (553 BCE).

During the reign of Nabonidus, Cyrus the Great came to power in Persia (559 BCE) and soon after conquered the Median Empire (550 BCE). After Cyrus's conquest of other territories, including Lydia in western Asia Minor, Persia became the dominant power in the Near East. As Pierre Briant asserts, "The Neo-Babylonian kingdom now remained Cyrus's most formidable adversary and rival in the Near East" (2002, 40). According to the Nabonidus Chronicle (British Museum 35382, 3.12–13), at the battle at Opis on the Tigris River the Persians and "the army of Akkad" (i.e., the Babylonians) fought and the Babylonians were defeated and retreated (Grayson 1975, 109). Cyrus was victorious and soon after the victory at Opis also took the nearby city of Sippar. After the defeat at Opis, the Nabonidus Chronicles (3.14–15) record that Nabonidus fled to his capital city of Babylon. The Persian army followed and was soon victorious, capturing Nabonidus in Babylon.

The Nabonidus Chronicles are silent concerning how Cyrus was able to conquer the city of Babylon. According to Herodotus, when Cyrus approached the city, he kept most of his army a distance from the city and sent a small part of his army to dig a channel to divert the Euphrates River, which ran through the middle of the city. Herodotus states, "When the Euphrates had subsided until the water reached more or less the middle of a man's thigh, they entered Babylon along the river-bed" (1.191). The small army was able to walk into the heart of Babylon and defeat the city. Indeed, on the day of the Persian conquest, Herodotus reports that the Babylonians were celebrating a festival in the middle of the city and were "unaware of the capture of their compatriots from the edges of the city" (1.191). Later, when Cyrus entered Babylon, "there was peace in the city while Cyrus spoke his greeting to all of Babylon" (Nabonidus Chronicles 3.19–20 [Grayson 1975, 110]).

The exact fate of Nabonidus is unknown since no extant source records what Cyrus did with the captured king. With the defeat of Nabonidus and his son Belshazzar, the Babylonian Empire came to an end, and with accession of Cyrus and the Persian Empire, the Babylonian exile of Judah ended as well. By that time, diasporic communities from Judah and Israel were located throughout Mesopotamia and Egypt.

Conclusion

The Babylonian exile (597/587–539 BCE) was an era of significant change for Judah and the Judeans. New communities, specifically in Babylon and Egypt, either appeared or grew in number during the period of the exile. The exile as a discrete historical period came to an end, but the memory of exile continues throughout the narratives and poems in the Old and New Testaments.[6] The demise of the Davidic monarchy and the forced relocation of Judeans forever changed the theological landscape of the biblical texts. While the Persian defeat of Babylon brought about the end of the exile, this new era did not bring about the end of the exilic communities. The exiles from Judah (and earlier Israel) changed the landscape of where those who worshiped the God of Israel (Yahweh) resided.

6. For a discussion of the theological implications of exile for the ancient Judeans, see Smith-Christopher 1997; 2002.

30

The Achaemenid Persian Empire in the West and Persian-Period Yehud

Kenneth A. Ristau

The disruption and caesura caused by the destruction of Jerusalem in 587 BCE are not easily overstated. In addition to precipitating severe ideological tremors that undermined the traditional political and religious claims of Jerusalem's inviolability and Yahweh's perpetual support for the house of David, the architectonic and demographic evisceration of the city and its environs as well as the concomitant collapse of the kingdom of Judah were undeniably dramatic. In the wake of destruction and collapse, Judean society splintered. On the one hand, the Babylonian campaigns in 597 and 587 produced exiles and refugees, which created or added to Diaspora communities throughout the greater Near East that had been growing and developing since the Neo-Assyrian period (ca. 732–604 BCE). On the other hand, the remnants left in the land coalesced into two distinct enclaves: one in Benjamin, centered on Mizpah, and a second in the highlands south of Jerusalem. These enclaves consisted of a few landholding families, an impoverished populace, and disenfranchised refugees with tribal sheikhs, clan chiefs, and family heads as the local leadership.

While these dispersed communities and enclaves shared a regional history and mostly reflected the ethnic milieu of earlier periods, Nebuchadnezzar destroyed the Judean state, its supratribal monarchy and socioeconomic systems, and the central sanctuary in Jerusalem, which had bound the inhabitants of the larger territory together.

The Babylonians did not develop a provincial system of the same efficiency as the Assyrians did before them (Beaulieu 1989; Vanderhooft 1999). Rather than utilizing a network of provinces and client kingdoms in the Levantine corridor to facilitate trade, as the Assyrians had, the Babylonian kings pursued mainly bilateral trade with the coastal regions and maintained a territorial, rather than provincial, system of direct rule in the Levant. The emergence of the Achaemenid Persian Empire, however, changed the geopolitics of the Near East by bringing the east into greater military conflict, economic interdependence, and dialogue with the west and thereby reactivated the historical importance of the Levant as a major transit corridor for cultural, political, and economic interaction and exchange. Amid these great events, a new polity emerged to rebuild Jerusalem as a political and spiritual capital for Judeans in the region and abroad.

The Rise of the Achaemenid Empire

The incipient event in the renewed engagement between the east and the west was the conquest of Lydia by the Persian king Cyrus. Crossing the Halys River into western Anatolia, Cyrus captured Sardis and thus positioned the Persian Empire in geographical proximity to the Greek colonies of Ionia. Already under Cyrus a new imperial model, or a revived Assyrian imperial model, is evident. In contrast to Babylonian policy, Cyrus not only deported groups out of Anatolia but also encouraged colonization and Iranization in the conquered territories (Sekunda 1985; 1988; 1991). Persian colonists, typically nobles or soldiers, settled in newly conquered territories, especially cities such as Sardis and Ephesus, while Lydian nobility adopted Iranian names and other aspects of the empire's culture and religion (Sekunda 1985; Dusinberre 2003). Colonization and Iranization in Anatolia, which the Greeks characterized as Medism, quickly reached the regions of Caria, Phrygia, and Lycia (Sekunda 1988; 1991).

In 539 Cyrus moved against the Babylonian Empire, securing a decisive victory at Opis. Once in control of the capital, Cyrus demonstrated remarkable perspicacity by, in this case, appropriating Babylonian political and religious rhetoric rather than encouraging Iranization. Casting himself as an agent of the Babylonian gods, he granted limited rights of return to exiles previously deported from the northern and eastern parts of Mesopotamia and restored previously confiscated sacred idols and vessels. An edict attributed to Cyrus in biblical texts (2 Chron. 36:22–23; Ezra 1:1–4; 6:2–5) is consistent with these measures. Likewise, considerable evidence points to the reinstatement of elites in the east in Sogdiana and Bactriana and the west in Phoenicia,

Cyprus, and Cilicia (Briant 1982; Bianchi 1994; Lemaire 1996). Rather than being an act of altruism, the granting of such rights almost certainly was a calculated measure to establish loyalists in the peripheral regions of the empire, including the Levant, in which Cyrus did not immediately campaign (Kuhrt 1983). Gifts, such as the return of sacred gods and cultic vessels, as well as other subventions were essential to ensuring that the repatriates had the necessary advantages to assume or resume, and maintain, their leadership.

The consolidation of Persian power in the Levant occurred under Cambyses, the son and successor of Cyrus, who cultivated Phoenician, Cypriot, and Qedarite support to aid in his campaign against Egypt (Briant 2002, 50–55). Notably, archaeological evidence points to dramatic urban expansion and a revitalization of the rural sector in the coastal Levant, likely owing to the local autonomy and imperial support granted to the Phoenicians by Cambyses (Stern 2001, 379–412). Through this relationship, Cambyses established a royal navy—a feat unparalleled by the Assyrians or Babylonians and notable for intensifying engagement between east and west and escalating the Greco-Persian wars. In 525, Cambyses employed this naval power to conquer Egypt, bringing together (for the first time) Iran, Anatolia, Mesopotamia, and Egypt under a single imperial regime. Echoing Cyrus's policies in Babylon, Cambyses adopted pharaonic protocols, supported the indigenous cult centers in Egypt, and may have even supported the Yahwistic temple at Elephantine (Briant 2002, 55–61).

During the first part of the fifth century, Darius I consolidated the new empire, carrying out an ambitious program of administrative and fiscal reorganization and reform. Darius's controversial ascendancy, his reign, and his policies are well known through the Behistun Inscription, archival evidence, and the work of Herodotus. His attention to the organization, administration, and taxation of the empire, as suggested by these textual sources, likely resulted in a more efficient and productive tributary economy (Briant 2002, 388–471). Notably, Darius's role as a benefactor of temples throughout the empire, especially in Egypt, is well attested and unmatched by his successors and may account for the support the biblical text claims Darius ordered for the reconstruction of a temple in Jerusalem (Ezra 6:1–13) (contra Edelman 2005).[1] The reorganization and reforms under Darius formed the basis of the imperial regime for the next 150 years, though not without variation, modifications, and reforms by subsequent kings.

The Creation of Transeuphrates

One of the significant steps undertaken after Darius's reign was the partitioning of the Babylonian satrapy to create Transeuphrates, probably sometime in Xerxes's reign and almost certainly no later than 420 (Stolper 1989). Before this, the Babylonian satrapy encompassed roughly the whole of the former Neo-Babylonian Empire, reflecting the simple absorption and appropriation of that regime within the new Persian Empire. The fundamental administrative relationship between the principalities in the Levant and the central authorities in Babylonia persisted with only limited modifications and reforms to suit the interests of the new imperial masters. Local dynasts, such as the Sanballat family in Samaria,[2] the Sidonian dynasty of Eshmunazor,[3] the Tobiads in Ammon,[4] the house of Geshem in the Qedarite Kingdom,[5] and perhaps the Saulides in Benjamin and Davidides in the Judean highlands,[6] exerted authority in a divided regional landscape. The (arguably inefficient) exploitation of the region to the benefit of Babylonia likely remained de facto policy.

This condition could not have represented a wholly ideal situation for the Achaemenid kings, but the reorganization of the region must have been a low priority so long as the Persians pursued a policy of aggression and expansion against the Greeks. At that point, the chief interest of the Persians in the Levant was maintaining their alliances with the Phoenicians, who provided critical maritime assets. They secured this support not through direct imperial control of the apparently semi-autonomous Phoenician kingdoms but rather through traditional patron-client relationships with local dynasts who aided the Persian crown in return for concessions and gifts. Primary evidence for this policy is provided by the Eshmunazor Sarcophagus Inscription (*KAI* 2:19–23; *COS* 2:182–83), in which Eshmunazor describes his annexation of much of the Sharon plain from Dor to Joppa as a concession from the Achaemenid king, likely Xerxes I.

After significant setbacks in the Greek wars, however, the Persians, probably by the force

---

1. On the temple as an instrument of fiscal policy, see Schaper 1995; 1997; Trotter 2001. In Egypt, Darius I likely authorized temple-related projects at El Khargah, El Kab, Busiris, and the House of Life at Sais; donated to the temple at Edfu; and took up the duties of the pharaoh in relation to the Apis Cult. For relevant commentary, see Bresciani 1985, 508–9; Blenkinsopp 1987; Dandamaev and Lukonin 1989, 141–46; Tuplin 1991, 264–79; Briant 2002, 472–84.

2. For extrabiblical references to the Sanballat family, see *WDSP* 11r3; *WD* 22; *TAD* A4.7–9. For critical discussions, see esp. Cross 1975a; 1975b; Gropp 2000; Mittmann 2000.

3. For the Sarcophagus Inscription of Eshmunazor, see *KAI* 2:19–23; *COS* 2:182–83. For that of his father Tabnit, see *KAI* 2:17–19; *COS* 2:181–82. On the chronology of the dynasty, see the differing views of and the literature cited by Peckham 1968; Kelly 1987; Elayi 2007.

4. The Tobiad dynasty is attested in several extrabiblical sources, including *Ant.* 12.160; the Zeno papyri (*CPJ* 1.118–130); and inscriptions from 'Araq el-Emir. For critical discussions of the dynasty, see B. Mazar 1957; McCown 1957; Mittmann 2000; Hengel 1974, 39–43, 47–56, 267–77.

5. On the house of Geshem in extrabiblical sources, see Winnett 1937, 50–51; Albright 1953; Rabinowitz 1956; Dumbrell 1971.

6. On this contentious line of thought regarding the Saulides and the Davidides, see esp. Edelman 2001 and Sacchi 2000, 51–68, respectively.

of their losses or at least the lack of permanent success, evidently decided to alter their military posture toward the Greeks, which marked the start of notable changes in the organization and administration of the Levant. Rather than continue their attempts to conquer the Greek city-states, the Persians chose to solidify their control of Asia Minor, the Levant, and the eastern Mediterranean, keep conflicts contained at local and regional levels, and weaken the Greeks through political manipulation and regional intrigues. Because of its historic trade routes, Phoenician maritime assets, and strategic coastline on the Mediterranean, the Transeuphrates naturally served as a crucial commercial and military staging point and a key transit corridor in support of the change in imperial policy. As a corollary to the change, the principal theater of conflict in the Greek wars, which continued through most of the latter early fifth century, shifted from the Balkans and Asia Minor to Cyprus. Cyprus was a critical forward staging area and commercial hub in the eastern Mediterranean over which Athens and Persia fought for control and influence.

Indeed, the classical evidence, especially Thucydides and Diodorus, testifies to exactly this type of change in Persian policy toward Greece and the vital role of the governors and satrap of Transeuphrates to respond to crisis in Asia Minor and Egypt. Exploiting the advantages of the region for this change undoubtedly required a responsive regional administration to facilitate new investment, stimulate economic productivity, increase the efficiency of tax and resource collection, mobilize regional armies to contain uprisings and local/regional conflicts, and engage in limited conflicts to expand Persian interests and influence. Furthermore, this administration would have needed to be driven by local and regional interests with a military and economic orientation toward the Mediterranean world and not toward Babylonia.

From Apex to Nadir

In the middle of the fifth century BCE, approximately 462, the Libyan Inaros, aided by an Egyptian chieftain Amyrtaeus and the Athenian navy, attacked and laid siege to the citadel at Memphis in a bid to overthrow Persian hegemony in Egypt.[7] The Athenians supported the revolt in order to open a second front in the war with Persia over Cyprus. The Persians, occupied principally with Cyprus, responded slowly. The siege lasted for nearly six years before being lifted by Megabyzus, the satrap of Transeuphrates, in 456. Fortunately for the Persians, the revolt did not gain popular support among either commoners or most of the Egyptian elite. Otherwise, it might have achieved its ultimate purpose. Insofar as the coalition could not even take the citadel at Memphis, however, Persian imperial control was never really threatened. Indeed, soon after the suppression of the Inaros revolt in Egypt, Artaxerxes I concluded a peace with Athens, which had suffered significant naval losses in support of that revolt.[8]

Artaxerxes I subsequently oversaw a relatively peaceful and largely prosperous period in the history of the Persian Empire. The major extrabiblical sources for the period after the Greek wars are primarily economic and administrative texts. Important collections are the Persepolis Fortification and Treasury Tablets (Cameron 1948; Hallock 1969),[9] the "Kasr" (Stolper 1988; 1990) and Murashu (Stolper 1985; 1992) archives,[10] the Elephantine papyri (Porten and Yardeni 1986; 1989; 1993; 1999;

---

7. On this revolt, see Hoglund 1992, 97–164.

8. On the Peace of Callias, see Meiggs 1972, 129–51, 487–95; Briant 2002, 557, 579–80, 582, 591, 967–68, 971, 974–76, 1008.

9. Refer also to the "Persepolis Fortification Archive Project" at https://oi.uchicago.edu/research/projects/persepolis-fortification-archive.

10. The archives of the houses of Ea-iluta-bani at Borsippa, Iddin-Nabu at Babylon, and Egibi at Babylon are also relevant, though they end with the reign of Darius I. For quick reference, see Joannès 1995, 1475–85.

Porten 1996), and the Arsham (Cowley 1923, AP 26; Driver 1965, AD 1–13) and Bactrian (Naveh and Shaked 2012) correspondence. These sources show that the Persian Empire inherited many traits from its Assyrian and Babylonian imperial predecessors and permitted variation in the local economies of the empire, and that the imperial economy of this period, under Darius I and afterward under Xerxes I, Artaxerxes I, and Darius II, developed on an unparalleled scale, enjoying the benefits of a new *Pax Persica*.[11]

Still, the inability of the Persians to quickly suppress the Inaros revolt exposed a clear weakness in their military deployment and strategy—a weakness the Egyptians would use to achieve their independence at the end of the fifth century and to make further attempts to exploit by leading or supporting revolts in the Levant and Asia Minor throughout the fourth century until they were subjugated again by Artaxerxes III in 343. The emphasis on small, more responsive regional armies and the rejection of an overtly offensive military posture made the Persian Empire more susceptible to attack by Mediterranean coalitions. The Persian strategy depended on the disunity of its enemies and the fidelity of the regions under its control. If conflicts arose in too many places, the regional armies would be stretched too thin and could not respond as quickly or as decisively as required. Furthermore, if a larger coalition attacked and a conflict could not be contained, the Persians had to raise an imperial army, which apparently deployed only from Babylon or even as far away as the Iranian plateau. Mustering an imperial army took time and left the Persians vulnerable in the interim, as dramatically revealed by the campaigns of Cyrus the Younger and finally and fatally by Alexander the Great.

11. This period also marks the apex of the Athenian Empire under the leadership of Pericles. The "peace" with Persia and a peace with Sparta allowed Athens to expand its cultural, economic, and political influence across the Greek and Mediterranean world.

The Regional Landscape in the Restoration Period

Relative to the imperial and even regional developments of the era, the Judean story is a minor one. Samaria was the most prominent political and cultural center in the hill country through the Babylonian and early Persian periods (Zertal 1990; 2003; Knoppers 2006a), while reconstruction in Jerusalem and its environs was gradual and in the geopolitics of the era largely inconsequential (Ristau 2016). Nevertheless, surveys, excavations, and material evidence in the Judean hills suggest that Jerusalem did benefit from Achaemenid Persian hegemony and did reemerge as an administrative center in the fifth century as a part of broader trends toward administrative consolidation occurring at that time (Lipschits 2006; Lipschits and Tal 2007; Lipschits and Vanderhooft 2007). In the Persian period, there are noteworthy changes in Benjamin's urban settlement patterns and a relatively significant recovery in the rural sector of the north-central Judean highlands. The epigraphic evidence suggests that these developments are related to the provincialization of Yehud and the reemergence of Jerusalem as its provincial capital, superseding the Babylonian territorial administration that had been centered in Mizpah.

Settlement Patterns in Benjamin and the North-Central Judean Highlands

Although there is significant evidence for continuity of settlement in much of the Benjamin region, there is a remarkable, though gradual, decline and, in some cases, possibly cessation of settlement at sites such as Gibeon, Mozah, and Gibeah by the fifth century and a concomitant rise in activity at sites such as Nebi Samwil and Ramat Rahel (Lipschits 2005, 248; Gadot 2015, 19). The marked contrast in the fortunes of these sites is further elucidated by the systems and distribution of stamp impressions (see below), likely related to change in the economic, viticultural production centers associated with the weakened status of Mizpah and the rise in status of Jerusalem (Lipschits 2005, 248).

In the north-central Judean highlands, there is a significant recovery in the rural sector, such that the total settled area ultimately returns to pre-destruction levels. Most of the settlement activity in the Persian period, however, occurs in a more concentrated area than in the earlier periods, near "fortresses" at Khirbet Umm el-Qala, Khirbet Kabbar, Khirbet Abu Twain, Khirbet el-Qatt, Khirbet Zawiyye, and Beth Zur. This settlement pattern is imitated outside the province, in the Shephelah, near Khirbet er-Rasm, Khirbet Rasm Shuʻliya, and Lachish. Given that most of the virgin sites are located in these clusters and occupy less than five dunams (ca. 1.24 acres), the settlement patterns may be the archaeological reflex of *hatru*-administered lands (Edelman 2005; 2007).[12]

This interpretation can be strengthened by epigraphic and biblical evidence relating to the administrative organization of the region, the most striking of which is the coetaneous and analogous use of the title *saknu* ("chief"), the highest administrative official of the *hatru*, in its Hebrew and Aramaic cognate form, *segen* (see note 12). The *segen* is attested in the Wadi ed-Daliyeh and Elephantine papyri, and exclusively in the Bible in the exilic and postexilic texts of Isaiah 40–66, Jeremiah,

Ezekiel, Daniel, Ezra, and Nehemiah (Lemaire 2007, 55–56). Additionally, the Idumean Ostraca point to mechanisms of taxation and redistribution in the region common to *hatru*-administered lands, while the registers in Ezra 2 and Nehemiah 7 attest compatible sociopolitical organization by toponyms and (cultic) sodalities, the register in Nehemiah 11 evinces relevant martial overtones, and, though ubiquitous in tribal cultures, the narratives in Ezra-Nehemiah prominently mention the ethnic assembly, all expected reflexes of *hatru*-administration.[13] To support this population, new, likely Greek-inspired, pottery techniques gradually moved inland and supplanted local traditions (Franken 2005, 200).

The new settlements, functioning according to an imported political and economic model, likely precipitated tensions, disrupting political and economic interests of the local dynasts and sheikhs who had established themselves in Mizpah, Samaria, and Ammon during the Babylonian and early Persian period (cf. Ezra-Nehemiah).

The Creation and Administration of Yehud

Significantly, a substantial corpus of epigraphic evidence, including stamp impressions and coins from Yehud and archival evidence from Elephantine, paints a complementary portrait to the changing settlement patterns and administrative developments in Yehud.

The Yehud stamp impressions, found on storage jar handles, are particularly instructive for tracing administrative changes in the region. The attestation of the toponym "Yehud" is evidence for an administrative unit of that name and contrasts sharply with the earlier practices reflected by *lmlk*, zoomorphic, and

---

12. The *hatru* was a type of cooperative that received land allotments to fund men at arms for the imperial armies. The three categories of allotments were bow land (*bit qashti*), horse land (*bit sisi*), and chariot land (*bit narkabti*), each successively larger plots commensurate with the cost required to provide a fully armed and maintained bowman, horseman, or charioteer. The *hatru*, overseen by an elder assembly and a *saknu* ("chief"), distributed plots of land to their members and ensured that the military obligations were fulfilled. The earliest reference to the *hatru* appears in a Babylonian text dated to 529, the ascension year of Cambyses (Dandamaev and Lukonin 1989, 149). From that point on, references to the *hatru* or comparable institutions indicate that it constitutes an essential and distinctive organizational unit in the Persian Empire (Stolper 1985, 71–72).

13. See note 12 above. Interestingly, this may have repercussions for understanding Ezra's commission. Perhaps, he was appointed to conduct a review of the Judean cooperatives in the Transeuphrates, not to a provincial position in Yehud.

geomorphic stamp impressions and the *gbn* and *mwṣh* stamp impressions. The earlier types identify the jars and produce in them as property of tribal or supratribal sheikhs and their estates, while the Yehud stamp impressions identify the jars and contents as property of a province. Although there is arguably very little practical significance in this distinction—sheikhs, in either case, administered the territory—the ideological contrast is potent, especially as proof of provincialization.

There is evidence from the sixth century for three roughly coeval systems: the *gbn* stamp impression system centered in Gibeon, the *mwṣh* stamp impression system centered in Mizpah, and the lion stamp impression centered in Ramat Rahel and Jerusalem. The Yehud stamp impression system superseded these, succeeding the lion stamp impression and supplanting both the *mwṣh* and Gibeon systems, perhaps even transferring administration of the latter system to Nebi Samwil.[14] The geographical distribution of Yehud stamped handles points to production centers in the Rephaim Valley, a primary collection and administrative center at Ramat Rahel, and distribution to various ancillary sites, especially Jerusalem, Mizpah, Nebi Samwil, Jericho, and ʿEn Gedi (Lipschits and Vanderhooft 2011, 31–59).[15]

Yehud coins from the Persian period similarly reflect the growth and development of the provincial administration. The coins are a distinct subgroup of the Palestinian coin types, based on the Philisto-Arabian issues and employing Greek, Persian, and Phoenician motifs.[16] They bear legends with the provincial name "Yehud" or personal names inscribed nearly exclusively in paleo-Hebrew script, with two extant exceptions that have the provincial name written in Aramaic script. The coins are conventionally dated to the fourth century BCE and have been discovered primarily in Jerusalem or its environs, though Tell Jemmeh in Philistia and Mount Gerizim in Samaria are notable exceptions. Whereas the stamp impression system is unique to Judah, the Yehud coin issues are parallel to Samarian coin issues that were discovered in the cities and environs of Samaria, Shechem, and the caves of Wadi ed-Daliyeh.[17] The Samarian coins share the same weights as and similar motifs to the Yehud coins. Given this parallel, it is possible to posit a similar status for Samaria as for Yehud in the Persian period, at least insofar as these coins attest to the right to mint coinage and, in that respect, a provincial status within the Fifth Satrapy of the Persian Empire, the Transeuphrates.

A letter (of which two drafts are preserved) and a memorandum of the Yedaniah archive from Elephantine confirm an active cultic administration in Jerusalem and a civil administration on par with Samaria. The letter, dating to 407 BCE, petitions the governor of Yehud, Bagavahya, for support to rebuild a temple to Yahweh in Elephantine. It refers to previous correspondence with "Jehohanan, the high priest, and his colleagues the priests who are in Jerusalem," the governor, and "Avastana, brother of Anani, and the nobles of Judah" as well as parallel correspondence with "Delaiah and Shelemiah, sons of Sanballat, governor of Samaria" (*TAD* A4.8; cf. A4.7 [Porten 1996, 139–47]). A reply came as a joint recommendation from Delaiah and Bagavahya (*TAD* A4.9 [Porten 1996, 148–49]). By the end of the fifth century, therefore, a civil and cultic administration is unequivocally attested in Yehud, with at least a cadre of priests operating in Jerusalem.

---

14. This economic shift may have a polemical reflex in the biblical portrait of Saul and David and their patrimony, and in the relationship between Benjamin and Judah. In this vein, see Edelman 2001; 2003; Amit 2003; 2006; Blenkinsopp 2006; Knoppers 2006b, 25–27.

15. On the importance of Ramat Rachel, see esp. Lipschits, Gadot, and Langgut 2012; Gadot 2015.

16. Surveys of the finds include Mildenberg 1979; Meshorer 1982, 13–34; E. Stern 1982, 224–27; Betlyon 1986; Machinist 1994; C. Carter 1999, 259–85; E. Stern 2001, 562–69.

17. For a survey of the Samaria coins, see Meshorer and Qedar 1991.

The leadership and garrison in Elephantine regard this administration as comparable to that of Samaria and as possessing sufficient influence or authority in the region as to be of assistance in an appeal to the Persian administration in Egypt, or alternatively as having legal standing in the case.

The Territorial and Theological Significance of Restored Jerusalem

The biblical texts that reflect on the Persian period convey aspirations and hopes for restoration and reconstruction but also acknowledge the destitution and impoverishment of the restoration community (e.g., Isa. 49; Haggai; Zech. 1:8–17). The texts point to insecurity in the Judean highlands, marked by injustice and violence, recurrent regional conflicts, and internal dissension (e.g., Isa. 58:1–59:8, Zech. 9–14; Malachi). The texts also point to a much larger Yahwistic milieu spread throughout the Near Eastern and Mediterranean world (see, e.g., Ezra 2:59; 8:17; Ezek. 3:15).[18] Amid the promotion of Jerusalem in Persian-period biblical texts, prevailing neglect is the constant, explicit and implicit refrain (Ristau 2016). A careful reading of the texts, informed by the historical and archaeological evidence, suggests the continuation of a very counterintuitive, yet human, story—a story of struggle and

hardship, even failure, though also of resilience and endurance, with a cast that regularly vacillates between imprudent and inspired, impotent and indomitable.

Ultimately, the reconstruction of Jerusalem occurred, but not as a great and singular momentous event. Instead, it was the culmination of a relentless movement overcoming a succession of trials and tribulations, attributable either to the dogged determination of the Judean people (often in spite of themselves) or, in the language of faith, to Yahweh. The accomplishment was at once inconsequential and insignificant and also profound and perduring. The reconstruction of a small and encumbered Jerusalem meant very little to the Persians or nearly anyone else in the period, but interpreted as the reenthronement of Yahweh and the restoration and validation of a faithful remnant, it is the central accomplishment of the biblical story of this era and helped to create a political and spiritual capital for Judeans living in Yehud, Transeuphrates, and throughout the Near Eastern world, which in turn lent authority to the textual tradition and religious interpretation emanating from there and ultimately unified much of the Judean world around it (Ristau 2016). With the majority of Judeans living outside Jerusalem and Yehud, the historical and especially sociological impact of this and of the Persian period more generally in preserving, if not forging, the Jewish nation out of defeat and exile should not be understated or underappreciated.

---

18. On the international dimension of Persian-period Yahwism/Judaism, see esp. Knoppers 2009; 2011.

31

The Maccabean Revolt and Hasmonean Statecraft

Joel Willitts

Zealous faithfulness to God in the midst of religious persecution, murder, double-cross, and treachery, heroic protagonists and maniacal villains, reversals of fortune and poetic justice—these are just some of the reasons the story of the Hasmoneans has captured the imagination of so many for two millennia. The Hasmonean story, coupled with the related annexation of Judea by the Roman Empire in 63 BCE, is arguably the most formative historical stage of the late Second Temple period, into which Jesus was born and from which both Christianity and Rabbinic Judaism eventually originated (Efron 1987). Early Judaism emerged into its late adulthood in the early first century as a result of the tumultuous political, cultural, social, and religious changes experienced during the Hasmonean story.

The name "Maccabee" is actually the nickname for the third son of Mattathias, Judas, who distinguished himself militarily and administratively as the successor of his father (1 Macc. 2:4). The religious rebels whom he led in revolt against the Hellenization of the land of Israel came to be known as the "Maccabees." The most likely explanation is that "Maccabee" means "hammer" in light of the Aramaic word *maqāby*, though one cannot be certain.

"Hasmonean," on the other hand, is the name of the priestly family of which Mattathias was the elderly father. Mattathias had five sons, of whom three became leaders of the rebellion and two eventually high priests. It is commonplace to refer to this period and to the family with either "Maccabean" or "Hasmonean," and so the terms must be treated as interchangeable.

The story of the Maccabean Revolt and the Hasmonean state can easily be divided into a beginning, middle, and end. The religious-turned-political phenomenon lasted from 167 BCE, with the emergence of Mattathias of the priestly family of Asmonaios and his five sons leading a rebellion against Jewish Hellenizers and the Seleucid kingdom, to about 35 BCE, with the death of Aristobulus III. The latter was murdered by the command of Herod the Great after Herod had appointed him high priest at the age of only seventeen (*Ant.* 15.56).

What is more, the movement of the story from religious rebels to priest-kings was not a straightforward triumphal march. The future was never guaranteed. And the Hasmonean state disappeared from history faster than it appeared with the abrupt and surprising annexation of Judea by Pompey the Great in 63 BCE. Many times the prospects looked bleak and the outcome could have easily gone another way. While the propaganda of 1 and 2 Maccabees, the chief sources for the beginning of the story (Harrington 1988; Sievers 1990, 1–15), is overly positive about God's support and intervention through the course of events of the early Hasmonean family, it is still correct in a more general sense: much of the success the Hasmoneans experienced was the result of things over which they had little to no control.

From the Ascension of Antiochus IV to the Death of Judas Maccabeus (175–160 BCE)

In 175 BCE Antiochus IV Epiphanes ascended to the Seleucid throne with political and military ambition. The Seleucid kingdom, one of the four kingdoms created in the aftermath of Alexander the Great's death, was centered in Syria. Antiochus III had grasped control of the Levant after his victory over the Ptolemies at Panias in the northern part of Palestine in 198 BCE. By the time of his ascendency, the seeds of Hellenism had already been planted and were bearing fruit in the region of Judea. In the nearly two centuries since Alexander's arrival in the Levant, the appeal of the Greek culture and manner of life had grown especially among Jerusalem's priestly aristocracy.

The story of controversy among members of the temple priesthood in Jerusalem in 2 Maccabees 3–4 suggests that the real force behind Hellenization was not an outside power exercising an oppressive hand on Judea, but instead elements inside the Jewish aristocracy

that were interested in adopting a Hellenistic pattern of life (Regev 2013, 15; Sievers 1990, 16, 20–26; VanderKam 2004, 188–226). The Zaddokite priest Onias III was ousted by his own brother Jason when Jason bribed the newly installed Seleucid king Antiochus to make him high priest in his brother's place. Not only did the financial contribution seem attractive to Antiochus, but Jason also pledged to make Jerusalem a Greek city by establishing a gymnasium (2 Macc. 4:7–17; cf. 1 Macc. 1:14; *War* 1.32; *Ant.* 12:237–41) and registering the people of Jerusalem as citizens of a renamed "city of Antioch." Then, after only three years, Jason was beat at his own game when a non-Zadokite, Menelaus, an even more radical pro-Hellenistic Jew, outbid Jason and was granted the position of high priest by Antiochus IV in his place.

Meanwhile, Antiochus IV Epiphanes, seeking to expand his kingdom, set his sights on Egypt. Upon his return from an initial campaign against Egypt, he plundered the Jewish temple. Josephus says that Antiochus became "master of Jerusalem" (*Ant.* 12.246). Later a false rumor reached Jerusalem that Antiochus had been killed in battle. Seizing what appeared to be a golden opportunity to reestablish his authority, the ousted Jason attempted to grasp the high priesthood again from Menelaus and led a rebellion. The still quite alive Antiochus, hearing of the coup, attacked Jerusalem. He again plundered the temple and built a citadel called "the Akra" (1 Macc. 1:29–33; 2 Macc. 5; *War* 1.32; *Ant.* 12.248–52) (Sievers 1990, 17–20).

In addition, in 167 BCE Antiochus IV ordered the cessation of traditional Jewish practice, forbidding the reading of Torah, circumcision, and the celebration of festivals. What is more, he ordered that the temple be profaned and turned into a temple for the worship of the Greek gods, notably Zeus. He required all the inhabitants of Judea to sacrifice to idols and eat food forbidden by the Torah. While

Antiochus's true motive is impossible to know, the author of 1 Maccabees attributes it to his desire to make "his whole kingdom . . . one people" (1 Macc. 1:41). The edict was to be enforced on the pain of death (1 Macc. 1:50). We are told that on the twenty-fifth day of the month of Chislev in the year 167, an idolatrous sacrifice was offered on a newly erected altar in the temple. Also the books of the law were torn and burned, and women were put to death "who had their children circumcised . . . they hung the infants from their mothers' necks" (1 Macc. 1:60–61).

Jewish responses to Antiochus IV's decree, not surprisingly, were divided, given the already pro-Hellenistic tendency of some. The author of 1 Maccabees tells us, "Many even from Israel gladly adopted his [Antiochus IV's] religion; they sacrificed to idols and profaned the sabbath" (1 Macc. 1:43). But we are also told, foreshadowing the story of the Maccabeans, that "many in Israel stood firm and were resolved in their hearts not to eat unclean food. They chose to die rather than to be defiled by food or to profane the holy covenant; and they did die" (1 Macc. 1:62–63 [see also 2 Macc. 6–7; *War* 1.34–35; *Ant.* 12.253–56]). Enter the Maccabees.

The Maccabean story begins when royal officials come to the village of Modein, a small hamlet in Israel's Shephalah, to enforce Antiochus IV's edict. The officials, aware of the high status of the elderly Mattathias in the town, commanded him to be the first to sacrifice on the altar to an idol. He refused to do so. Upon seeing a fellow Jew step forward to offer the first sacrifice, Mattathias, full of the zeal of his forefather Phinehas (Num. 25:7–13; 1 Macc. 2:26), took lethal action against the Jew and the royal officials (1 Macc. 2:19–30), initiating the Maccabean Revolt. Within the year of this event, Mattathias died and Judas Maccabeus took his place as the leader of the Jewish rebellion (1 Macc. 3:1; cf. 2 Macc. 8:1; *War* 1.36–37; *Ant.* 12.285).

After several early victories using guerrilla tactics, the Maccabean Revolt grew in strength (Sievers 1990, 42–46). These early victories emboldened the rebels to continue their fight until finally, three years to the day after the temple had been desecrated in 167 BCE, Judas recaptured Jerusalem and the temple, although he was unable to take the citadel erected by Antiochus IV. On the twenty-fifth of Chislev in the year 164 the temple was rededicated. The rededication of the temple is commemorated annually in the festival of Hanukkah (1 Macc. 4:36–59; 2 Macc. 10:1–8; *War* 1.39; *Ant.* 12.316–22) (Regev 2013, 37–57).

The revolt continued under Judas's leadership after the rededication of the temple. We are told that Judas sent envoys to establish a treaty with the Roman senate (1 Macc. 8; *War* 1.38; *Ant.* 12.414–19). In 160 BCE he was killed in a battle against the Seleucid general Bacchides, and his brother Jonathan assumed the mantle of leadership (1 Macc. 9; *War* 1.47; *Ant.* 12.426–34) (Sievers 1990, 62–67).

From the Ascension of Jonathan to the Annexation of Judea by Rome (160 BCE–63 BCE)

With the ascension of Jonathan and then his brother Simon, the last remaining son of Mattathias, the story of the Maccabees continued, but the future of the rebellion looked bleak at the time of the transition (Harrington 1988, 90). Having achieved a victory over Judas, Bacchides pursued Jonathan and the Hasmonean faction. The strength of the Seleucid military was too much for the forces loyal to the Maccabees. Jonathan and his brother Simon, along with the rest of the leadership of the revolt, fled to the wilderness, leaving Jerusalem. In this exile, a two-year peace ensued because of the death of the king's appointed high priest Alcimus, a pro-Hellenist (1 Macc. 9:56–57) (VanderKam 2004, 226–39). The high priesthood, consequently, was left vacant for seven years (159–152 BCE) (VanderKam 2004, 244–50). Instigated by the pro-Hellenistic Jews in Jerusalem, fighting flared up again. The Hasmonean faction had sufficiently strengthened militarily in the interim, and a victory forced the Seleucid general Bacchides to sue for peace and the end of hostilities (*Ant.* 13.22).

The stage was now set for one of the significant developments in the middle part of the story. In 152 BCE Jonathan was appointed high priest by Alexander Balas, a claimant for the Seleucid throne (1 Macc. 10:20). Jonathan's brilliance as a politician and strategist was evident in his ability to leverage the political weaknesses of the Seleucid kingdom to his benefit (Harrington 1988, 80). A significant transformation took place (Regev 2013, 18). The Maccabees, once enemies of the Seleucid king, were now counted on as allies whose support was necessary to secure power in the Seleucid kingdom.

What is more, the Maccabees shifted their aim from living freely under Seleucid authority to being freed from Seleucid authority altogether, from revolt to "Hasmonean statecraft." Jonathan took steps toward independence, and this was a development beyond the initial focus of religious freedom pursued by his father, Mattathias, and brother Judas (Dabrowa 2010, 42–56; Sievers 1990, 73–103).

In addition to the high priesthood, Alexander Balas bestowed honors on Jonathan, naming him a "friend of the king" and giving him a purple robe and a golden crown (1 Macc. 10:20) (VanderKam 2004, 251–70). Josephus, perhaps too positively stating it, wrote that Jonathan "was appointed high priest and liberated the Jews from Macedonian supremacy" (*War* 1.53). Jonathan reentered Jerusalem and repaired and fortified its walls, although the citadel remained a bastion of Seleucid and pro-Hellenistic power in the middle of Jerusalem (1 Macc. 11:74; *Ant.* 13.163, 181–83). Jonathan also renewed his alliance with the Romans, reaching out as well to Sparta (1 Macc. 12:1–23; *Ant.* 13.163–70).

It is noteworthy that at this point in the story Josephus first makes mention of the political-religious parties: "Now at this time there were three schools of thought among the Jews . . . the first being that of the Pharisees, the second that of the Sadducees, and the third that of the Essenes" (*Ant.* 13.171–72). These parties represent a diverse set of reactions to Hasmonean statecraft and to the assumption of the high priesthood. Early scholarship believed that the figure called the "Wicked Priest" / "Man of Lies," who opposed the Teacher of Righteousness in the Qumran literature, was in fact Jonathan. While that theory has received criticism, the emergence of the Qumran community on the shores of the Dead Sea corresponds to the time of Hasmonean statecraft (Dabrowa 2010, 50–51; Eshel 2008, 29–61; Magness 2002; Sievers 1990, 88–92; VanderKam 2004, 264–70).

In 142 BCE Jonathan was killed in a double-cross by a certain Tryphon, and Simon, the last remaining son of Mattathias, took his place (1 Macc. 12:39–13:24; *War* 1.49; *Ant.* 13.187–93). Although in most respects he merely continued the statecraft begun by Jonathan, Simon's reign is noteworthy. The Seleucid king Demetrius II granted Simon and the Jewish people further independence by ending taxation, granting an imperial pardon for all previous state offenses, and allowing Jews to be enrolled in the king's military forces. As confirmation of this significant change of status for the Jews, the symbolic siege of the citadel in 141 BCE successfully removed the presence of the Seleucid power and pro-Hellenistic Jews from the center of Jerusalem (1 Macc. 13:49–51; *Ant.* 13.214) (Harrington 1988, 91; Sievers 1990, 105–34; VanderKam 2004, 270–85).

First Maccabees interprets these developments significantly: "The yoke of the Gentiles was removed from Israel, and the people began to write in their documents and contracts, 'In the first year of Simon the great high priest and commander and leader of the Jews'"

(13:41–42). This statement forms a proleptic summary of the recognition and proclamation of the "great assembly" recorded in 1 Maccabees 14:41–45: "that Simon should be their leader and high priest forever, until a trustworthy prophet should arise, and that he should be governor over them and that he should take charge of the sanctuary . . . and that he should be clothed in purple and wear gold."

With the recognition of the "great assembly," Simon became both the religious and royal authority over Israel. For the first time in the story of Israel, both biblical and extrabiblical, one person was both high priest and ruler. While Simon remained a client of the Seleucid kingdom, he had managed to lead the Jewish people into independence through political machinations. It was to be his grandson Aristobulus I (104–103 BCE), three decades later, who would first use the title "king." But for all intents and purposes there was little difference in the structure of power between Simon and Aristobulus I. In 134 BCE Simon was killed through the treachery of his son-in-law Ptolemy, and his son John Hyrcanus I ascended to his position.

Hyrcanus I had the longest and most productive reign of any of the Hasmoneans, ruling three decades, from 134 to 104 BCE (Sievers 1990, 135–56; VanderKam 2004, 285–312). His major contribution was the territorial expansion of the Hasmonean state. The Hasmonean heads of state from Hyrcanus I to Alexander Jannaeus (103–76 BCE) attempted to recapture the territory of the biblical kingdom of David and Solomon during their combined forty-two years of rule. Perhaps ironically influenced by the earlier reforms of Antiochus IV, the Hasmonean heads of state forced the inhabitants of conquered territory to convert to Judaism. Hyrcanus I forced the Idumeans and the Samaritans to become Jewish, destroying the rival Samaritan temple in the process. The conversion of the Idumeans is especially important because one of these converts was

Antipas, who was the father of Antipater and the grandfather of Herod the Great. Hyrcanus again renewed his alliance with Rome (*Ant.* 13.259–66).

While his reign was not without internal opposition, especially that of the Pharisees (*Ant.* 13.288–98), Hyrcanus I died peacefully of natural causes and was acclaimed by Josephus as one who possessed "three of the greatest privileges": "the rule of the nation, the office of high priest, and the gift of prophecy" (*Ant.* 13.299–300). Emil Schürer rightly summed up Hyrcanus I's contribution as having "created a Jewish state" (Schürer 1973, 215).

Hyrcanus I was succeeded by his eldest son, Aristobulus I, whose brief, one-year reign was significant (VanderKam 2004, 312–18). As previously mentioned, he was the first Hasmonean ruler to assume the title "king." While nothing structurally changed since the time of Simon in his taking of the title, his willingness to be called "king" shows how far the story had come since the first uprising led by his great-grandfather Mattathias.

A full-fledged political state had materialized from a revolt for religious freedom. Josephus states that Aristobulus "transformed the government into a monarchy and was the first to assume the diadem" (*War* 1.70). While debates may continue as to whether it is more accurate to call the Hasmoneans a "royal priesthood" or a "priestly monarchy" (Dabrowa 2010, 106), there is no doubt that a new category of office had been embedded into the Jewish tradition that had not previously existed, with the combination of both high priestly and royal authority in one office and person.

Aristobulus I continued the territorial expansion policy of his father, conquering the northern districts of Israel and forcing the conversion of the inhabitants. His short-lived reign was productive, but controversial, and his rule brutal. He usurped the civil authority from his mother, to whom it was left by Hyrcanus I. He had her imprisoned along with all of his five brothers save one, Antigonus, who eventually was murdered (*War* 1.77; *Ant.* 13.304–10). His mother starved to death in prison. Upon his surprising death from disease, his widow, Alexandra Salome, released his brothers from prison and appointed one of them, Alexander Jannaeus, as king and high priest in his place.

Alexander Jannaeus not only continued the cruelty of Aristobulus I's rule but also intensified it significantly in his long reign of twenty-seven years (103–76 BCE) (VanderKam 2004, 318–36). While continuing the territorial expansion policy of his predecessors, he found himself embroiled in conflicts both external and internal. Josephus reports that Jannaeus engaged in a civil war against insurrectionists for six years and in the process killed fifty thousand Jews (*War* 1.91; *Ant.* 13.376). Similarly, Josephus reports that during one Festival of Tabernacles Jannaeus had six thousand pilgrims killed because they pelted him with citrons (*Ant.* 13.372–73). His strongest opposition, however, came from the Pharisees. At one point, they sought the support of the Seleucid king Demetrius against Alexander Jannaeus. Having quelled the uprising, Jannaeus had eight hundred Pharisees crucified while banqueting on the roof of his palace and watching them (*War* 1.92–98; *Ant.* 13.377–87; 4QNahum Pesher 3–4 1:3, 6–8).

Alexander Jannaeus died from an illness that Josephus attributes to heavy drinking (*Ant.* 13.398), and his widow, Alexandra Salome, assumed his royal position and granted their firstborn son, Hyrcanus II, the high priesthood, since women were forbidden to serve as priest by biblical law (VanderKam 2004, 337–39). Alexandra ruled for nine years (76–67 BCE) until her death and, according to Josephus, "kept the nation at peace" (*Ant.* 13.432).

Most notably, during her reign she sided with the Pharisees, bringing them back into the center of political life after they had been exiled by Alexander Jannaeus. On his deathbed, Alexander had advised Alexandra to reconcile

with them and include them in her government in order to secure it; so she did (*Ant.* 13.401–4). So powerful did the Pharisees become in her government that Josephus quipped, "If she ruled the nation, the Pharisees ruled her" (*War* 1.112). The Pharisees used the opportunity for political revenge against their enemies.

The unchecked influence of the Pharisees created resentment, and her younger son, Aristobulus II, called by Josephus "hot-headed" (*War* 1.109), "a man of action," and "high of spirit" (*Ant.* 13.407), led a coup against her and Hyrcanus II, whom she had by now appointed coruler as well as high priest. Before Alexandra died at the age of seventy-nine, Aristobulus had taken the government and high priesthood away from Hyrcanus II (*War* 1.118–19; *Ant.* 13.422–29) (VanderKam 2004, 340–45).

Hyrcanus II, who is characterized in less-than-glowing terms by Josephus as lacking energy and "incompetent to govern" (*Ant.* 13.407), conceded initially to Aristobulus, preferring a "quiet life." The peace between the two brothers and claimants for the Hasmonean throne did not last long because of Antipater, the father of Herod the Great. Antipater convinced Hyrcanus II that he had been mistreated and his position usurped by his brother. Emboldened and perhaps propped up by Antipater, Hyrcanus rose up against Aristobulus with the help of the Nabatean king Aretas, and he took Jerusalem and reinstalled himself as king and high priest (*War* 1.123–26).

Meanwhile, the Roman Empire was expanding eastward and Pompey the Great was in the region. In 63 BCE both Aristobulus II and Hyrcanus II appeared before Pompey in Damascus seeking support for their claims to the Hasmonean throne. Along with them a third party of "the Jewish people" also appeared whose intent was freedom from Hasmonean authority altogether (*Ant.* 15.37–45). The outcome of the meeting was surprising to all parties and disappointing in some way to all. After the dust settled, Pompey sided with

Hyrcanus II and affirmed his high priesthood, and Aristobulus was banished to Rome with his sons (VanderKam 2004, 345–46).

However, Pompey stripped Hyrcanus II of his royal authority, reducing him to a client of Rome; he dismantled the territorial kingdom, freeing the peoples conquered by Hasmonean armies since John Hyrcanus I to their original ethnic places and traditions; he reduced the territory over which Hyrcanus II ruled to only the regions with large Jewish populations, those being Galilee, Samaria, Judea, and Idumea; he created the Decapolis; and he established a new Roman province called Syria, appointing a governor to administrate the province from Antioch (*War* 1.153–57).

With Pompey's reorganization of the region, the experiment of Jewish statecraft in the hands of the Hasmoneans came to its sudden end; the independent Jewish state ceased to exist. Its influence, however, would continue well beyond its material demise. The story of the Hasmoneans would continue through the Herodian period. Herod the Great is singly responsible for snuffing out the Hasmonean line with the murders of his own beloved wife, the Hasmonean princess Mariamme, Alexandra Salome's daughter (49 BCE), Alexandra's sons Aristobulus III (35 BCE) and Hycanus II (30 BCE), Alexandra herself (28 BCE), and his own two sons by Mariamme, Alexander and Aristobulus (7 BCE). By the time of Herod's death in 4 BCE, the Hasmonean line had been completely co-opted by the Herodians.

SECTION VI

Scenes

*Integrated Approaches
to Event-Based Historical Contexts*

32

Akhenaten and the Amarna Period

MARK D. JANZEN

Introduction: Akhenaten's Remarkable "Cultural Afterlife"

Within five years of ascending the throne ca. 1352/53 BCE,[1] Amenhotep IV ("Amun is satisfied") changed his name to Akhenaten ("effective for the Aten"); instituted sweeping religious changes toward worship of the sun disk, the Aten; and began building a new capital city, Akhetaten (Tell el-Amarna). His religious revolution was short-lived, as his successors—Tutankhamen, Ay, and Horemheb—attempted to remove all traces of Atenism and Akhenaten.[2] However, in the past approximately one hundred and fifty years, Akhenaten has had an extraordinary "cultural after-life" (Montserrat

2003, 1), and the volume of excellent articles and books on Akhenaten from prominent Egyptologists is unrivaled.[3] No doubt, his successors would be displeased to find that their efforts at erasing his memory and name have failed in such grand fashion.

In many respects, Egyptologists have been fighting a losing battle in attempting to recover the factual Akhenaten. Though there is a substantial wealth of data from his reign, much of it is fragmentary, inconclusive, or heavily biased. Additionally, his successors were embarrassed by his reforms and diligently sought to erase his name and monuments and memory of him to the extent that later Egyptians were too ashamed of the Amarna period to even mention the king by name (Hoffmeier 2015, 243–45). Despite this, many facts regarding his reign emerge from a variety of sources—textual, iconographic, archaeological, and architectural.

---

1. There is considerable debate about when his reign began and whether there was a coregency with Amenhotep III. For a useful review of the evidence and the debate itself, curious readers should consult Hoffmeier 2015, 68–69, 87–90; Dodson 2009; Shaw, 2000; Murnane 1995.

2. There is perhaps no time in all of ancient history that was been written about with greater frequency than the Amarna period. As Geoffrey Martin put it, "Scarcely a month passes without a publication appearing on the Amarna period" (G. Martin 1991, 1).

3. For recent summaries of scholarship relating to Akhenaten and the Amarna period, see Williamson 2015, 1–4; Hoffmeier 2015; Kemp 2012; Montserrat 2003.

The Early Years: Iconography, Architecture, and the Rise of Atenism in Thebes

After many successful campaigns in Nubia and the Levant, Eighteenth-Dynasty pharaohs carved out a large empire, crediting the god Amun-Re for their victories and building a plethora of monuments honoring him.[4] No pharaoh more clearly enjoyed the blessings of peace and prosperity than Akhenaten's father, Amenhotep III. Indeed, no king except perhaps Ramesses II left "more monuments, more tangible proof of his greatness, than Amenhotep III" (L. Berman 2001, 1). However, some changes in the relationship between the king and the gods were already taking place during his reign (H. Smith 1994, 80).[5] The use of the epithet "the Dazzling Aten" occurs at this time, and there is a considerable increase in the use of the term "Aten" and associated sun disk iconography (Hoffmeier 2015, 76–82). When the king died in his thirty-eighth year, Akhenaten, then known simply as Amenhotep IV, succeeded him.[6]

The Initial Building Program

Prior to changing his name and moving the capital to Akhetaten, the young king was an active builder at Thebes, dedicating temples and chapels to "Re-Horakhty who rejoices in his horizon in his name of light which is the sun-disc (Aten)."[7] This is the first so-called "didactic"

name of the Aten, which underwent two additional changes during Akhenaten's reign, reflecting the evolution of the pharaoh's thought (more below). This name is unusually restrictive for an Egyptian deity, links the Aten to a physical manifestation (Laboury 2010, 126), and sets defined parameters for its domain. As Jacquelyn Williamson observes, "It appears Akhenaten already understood the Aten as different from other Egyptian gods" (Williamson 2015, 5).

Yet, surviving depictions on these earliest monuments use orthodox imagery and the standard artistic canon, such as depicting Ra-Horakhty with a falcon head (D. Redford 1984, 64; Darnell and Manassa 2007, 26), which will soon give way to an entirely new depiction of the sun disk itself, frequently shown with rays ending in life-giving anthropomorphic hands (D. Redford 1976, 47–61; 2013, 28–29).[8] During the first two years of his reign, Akhenaten finished his father's projects at Soleb in Nubia and the third pylon at Karnak using traditional artistic style (Williamson 2015, 5; D. Redford 2013, 13–14).

Because Akhenaten's successors dismantled his monuments, none of the temples devoted to this new god have survived intact. Later pharaohs reused many of the blocks in their own building projects. In fact, thousands of small, inscribed blocks (52 × 26 × 24 cm) were found in the late nineteenth century. Dubbed *talatat*, these badly broken blocks are all that remains of Akhenaten's temples at Thebes. Approximately forty-seven thousand *talatat* have been cataloged and photographed (see D. Redford 1973; 1975; 1988; Redford and Smith 1976; Lauffrey 1979), revealing that there were at least four named temples in the "Domain of Aten" at Karnak, meaning that initially Akhenaten was content to honor his new god alongside the traditional gods at Thebes.[9] He

---

4. On the conquests and building activities of the Eighteenth Dynasty, see Bryan 2000, 218–71; Hoffmeier 2015, 32–61.

5. For an extensive treatment on Amenhotep III, see Kozloff and Bryan 1992.

6. This happened despite Amenhotep IV not being the initial heir apparent. The throne was supposed to pass to another son, Thutmose, who died in his youth. For more, see Dodson 1990, 88; Reeves 2001, 61; Hoffmeier 2015, 62–64. On a possible coregency, see note 1 above.

7. Akhenaten made clear his intent to build a great Benben temple to this new god on a stele from Gebel el-Silsila, the main sandstone quarry south of Karnak, erected early in his reign (Williamson 2015, 5; Caminos 1992, 54–55n13; Sandman 1938, 143–44, plate cxxxviii).

8. These depictions are in fact ubiquitous from Amarna. For examples, see N. Davies 1903–8, plates xxix–xxx; Hoffmeier 2015, 149, fig. 5.3, 150, fig. 5.4a–b.

9. See Hoffmeier 2015, 107–17.

showed little aversion to the gods; he and others are seen venerating Amun, Atum, Osiris, and other deities (D. Redford 2013, 13). In fact, two of his titles pay homage to Karnak and southern Heliopolis/Thebes (Von Beckerath 1999, 143; D. Redford 2013, 13), so clearly the young king was comfortable residing in the territory of Amun even if he saw the Aten as unique. When he set out to construct the aforementioned "Domain of Aten," he deliberately chose unoccupied ground, rather than infringing upon preexisting sacred space, nor did his initial building program deface or otherwise harm the monuments of Amun or other gods (D. Redford 2013, 13–14).

The Colossi and Akhenaten's Bizarre Appearance

During the building of a drainage canal in the 1920s, bizarre statues of Akhenaten were found, providing the first clues to the location of the Domain of Aten in Thebes. These colossal statues portray the king in a manner wholly foreign to Egyptian artistic sensibilities. Gone is the militaristic, broad-shouldered, and muscular pharaoh; instead, the king has a long, narrow face, pointed jaw, slender shoulders, and, most puzzling, wide hips. One of these statues even appears to be androgynous (Hoffmeier 2015, 95–96, fig. 4.4; Manniche 2010). Iconography from later in Akhenaten's reign at Amarna portrays him in a similar fashion, yet this shocking style is otherwise utterly unique to the Amarna period (Freed 1999, 112). Some scholars believe that the statues could even depict Nefertiti (Reeves 2001, 165–66), others that they were originally carved for Amenhotep III (Kozloff 2012, 242) or that the androgynous nature of some of them is intended to reflect the notion that the Aten creates without the aid of a female consort (Robins 1993, 38).

Scholars have also sought a wide range of genetic reasons for Akhenaten's strange appearance—such as adolescent gynecomastia, Fragile X syndrome, Marfan syndrome—while some simply believe that the king's odd appearance can be explained on stylistic grounds alone.[10] Because one of the purposes of Egyptian art was to express religious ideals visually, it is likely that such unique representations of Akhenaten relate to his religious ideas (D. Redford 1984, 175; Robins 1993; Hoffmeier 2015, 133–34).

The Jubilee Festival, the Name Change, and Initial Iconoclasm

A major turning point in Akhenaten's reforms took place when the young king celebrated the Sed festival, a jubilee, during year four or five of his reign, before he moved the capital in year six. Typically, such jubilees were enacted at the thirtieth anniversary of a king's reign for the purpose of revitalizing an aged king and renewing his rule, so it is puzzling that such a young ruler would celebrate one.[11] This Sed festival might have served a dual purpose in establishing the Aten as the supreme deity and Akhenaten as his sole representative on earth (Hornung 1999, 42; Hoffmeier 2015, 122–23). That Akhenaten offered sacrifices only to the Aten and not multiple deities, as tradition would have demanded, is indicative of the elevated status of the Aten. Regardless of the motivation for this festival, its impact on the king's reign is clear. Donald Redford notes, "All the evidence militates in favor of the kaleidoscope of revolutionary changes associated with Akhenaten's program having taken place at his jubilee, or in anticipation thereof. This includes the new style of art, the new, outlandish representation of the king, the first steps in overt iconoclasm, and the introduction of

10. Many of these, enticing though they be, cannot be sustained following extensive DNA analysis of the royal mummies from Akhenaten's family. Unfortunately, the identification of his mummy remains a mystery. For more, see Hoffmeier 2015, 130–34; Hawass et al. 2010, 34–60; Burridge 1993, 63–74.

11. For more, see Hoffmeier 2015, 117–25; Hodge 1981, 17–26; Reeves 2001, 96; Johnson 1998, 90–93; van Dijk 2004, 268; Hornung 1999, 42.

the Disc (Aten) as an icon, and the enclosing of the didactic name in cartouches" (D. Redford 2013, 19). The enclosing of the didactic name of the Aten in cartouches is considered by Egyptologists to mark the second form of Aten's didactic name and endowed "the Aten with all the royal prerogatives of an Egyptian king" (Williamson 2015, 5 [see also Laboury 2010, 129]).

Scholars remain unsure precisely when Akhenaten married Nefertiti, but it may have occurred in conjunction with his Sed festival (Gabolde 2005, 34–35). The queen, popular today due to the famous bust on display in Berlin (see Williamson 2015, fig. 2), had enormous influence on Akhenaten's reign. She is depicted numerous times in Amarna art and was used as the substitute for female goddesses, such as Hathor, whom Akhenaten's religion considered anathema (Williamson 2015, 4–5). She might even have been considered part of a new trinity with the Aten and Akhenaten.

It is likely that Akhenaten dropped his birth name, "Amenhotep IV," at this point (or possibly earlier). When Aten temples were built in Karnak, the name "Amenhotep" was used, but shortly after the name was erased and replaced with "Akhenaten" (D. Redford 1984, 140–41). At this time too the young ruler likely began his program of iconoclasm (van Dijk 2004, 270), his intention made clear with the unprecedented claim on a stele from Karnak that the gods, besides the Aten, had "died" (Murnane 1995, 31; D. Redford 2013, 14–15). Thus, in year five the king began to attack the names and images of other gods, especially the Theban triad Amun, Mut, and Khonsu (Williamson 2015, 6). This endeavor was rather sloppily done (Laboury 2010, 199–200), perhaps indicating haste. Redford theorizes that the iconoclasm accompanied the move to Akhetaten, one last vindictive act before the king moved the capital (D. Redford 2013, 23–26). The connections between the Sed festival, the name change, iconoclasm, and construction of

Akhetaten are reasonably certain, and overall the "signs of iconoclasm at Karnak point to the final years before the move to Amarna" (Hoffmeier 2015, 194).

The Amarna Revolution in Full Bloom: Atenism, Akhetaten, and Monotheism

The move to Akhetaten was announced in year five on the thirteenth day of the fourth month, Peret (Williamson 2015, 6). Sixteen border steles were set up at the site of modern Amarna, and Akhetaten ("The Horizon of the Aten") was founded. The new capital was established on a desert plain defined by the Nile River and amphitheater-forming cliff faces (Williamson 2015, 6; Kemp 2012). Barry Kemp estimates that perhaps twenty thousand Egyptians accompanied the king (Kemp 2012, 17), and many Theban elites made the journey and built their tombs at Amarna (Williamson 2015, 6–7; N. Davies 1903–8). Within twenty years the city was abandoned, and its stone blocks were reused elsewhere, although it remains the "largest area of readily accessible domestic occupation from ancient Egypt" (Kemp 2012, 17).

By this time Akhenaten's religious revolution had undergone several steps before reaching its final and most theologically advanced form. William Murnane understands the progression as occurring in three phases: Aten coexisted with the traditional gods, who were (1) neglected, then (2) abandoned, and ultimately (3) persecuted (Murnane 1999, 303–12). Such a progression is clear in the treatment of Theban monuments, but this still does not explain the impetus for the revolution. Theories once again abound, most connected in some way to political power or the priesthood of Amun (e.g., Steindorff and Seele 1957, 80). John Wilson believed a struggle arose between the priests and the pharaoh over the king's alleged pacifism, which may have led him to neglect the empire, consequently limiting the riches of the priesthood (J. Wilson 1951, 207). More generally, David Silverman believes Akhenaten simply wanted to diminish the power of the Amun priesthood (Silverman 1991, 4–75).

Certainly, there would have been obvious political benefits for Akhenaten's religious program if the power of the priests of Amun were reduced in some fashion,[12] but this does not fully account for the radicalness of his reforms. One of the key aspects of Atenist theology is revelation through nature, as the sun disk by its very existence reveals "its practical effects on the world and man" (Tobin 1985, 265). Using an approach based on the phenomenon of religion as well as linguistic analyses, James Hoffmeier has recently made the intriguing suggestion that Akhenaten experienced what the king himself believed to be a genuine hierophany which necessitated the revolution while retaining the solar element of Egyptian religion (Hoffmeier 2015, 139–49). Such an understanding of Amarna religion fits well with Akhenaten's personal statements on the highly fragmentary border steles from Amarna. Dated to his fifth year, one text recounts Akhenaten's discovery of Akhetaten, the Aten's "place of the primeval event" (Murnane 1995, 74; Murnane and Van Siclen 1993). For Akhenaten, here is where the Aten first revealed himself, establishing a holy place (Hoffmeier 2015, 147–48). There need be little doubt that Akhenaten was a genuine convert to his religion, which was much more to the king than political gamesmanship, but his move to Akhetaten could have served both religious and political purposes.

Atenism and Monotheism

The new religion doubtless concentrated on the Aten's physical manifestation and thus was more concerned with the real and visible than the esoteric cult of Amun, whose name means "Hidden One" (Williamson 2015, 7; D. Redford 2013, 27; Kemp 2012, 26–29; Gabolde 2005, 45). Atenism taught that Akhenaten was the Aten's son and only prophet and served as a mediator between god and humans (D. Redford 2013, 26–29; Assmann 2012; Laboury 2010; Ikram 1989).

No question regarding the revolution and reign of Akhenaten has spilled more ink than "Was Akhenaten a monotheist?"[13] The current consensus among Egyptologists is that he was, though this is far from unanimous. Siegfried Morentz believed that Akhenaten was not an advocate of simple monotheism, but rather, given the inclusion of Re-Horakhty and Shu in the initial didactic name, a trinitarian (Morentz 1973, 147). Others speak of a trinity involving the Aten, Akhenaten, and Nefertiti (Hornung 1999, 57). Nicholas Reeves opined that Akhenaten's much celebrated monotheism was nothing of the sort but rather a form of particularly determined ancestor worship designed to celebrate kingship (Reeves 2001, 118).[14] Furthermore, great care must be taken to distinguish between official Atenism as practiced by Akhenaten (dogma) and the practices of common people during his reign. Many residents retained traditional household gods such as Taweret and Bes, and it is impossible to determine the extent to which Akhenaten's exclusive form of Atenism extended beyond the royal family and inner circle (Stevens 2012, 92–97; Williamson 2015, 7).

It is important to understand the changes that took place in Akhenaten's religious thought in order to properly determine the extent of *his* monotheism. Early in Akhenaten's reign, while the Aten was worshiped and the traditional

---

12. Akhenaten himself appears to admit as much on boundary steles K, M, and X, in which he "denounces elite-generated aspirations on his kingship" (Williamson 2015, 6 [see also Murnane and Van Siclen 1993, 26–27, 41–42; Reeves 2001, 110–11]).

13. For a useful recent survey of scholars who hold varying views about the degree of Akhenaten's monotheism, see Yamauchi 2010, 1–15.

14. This requires Reeves (2001, 73–75) to adapt a modified view of Raymond Johnson's co-regency theory (cf. Johnson 1998, 91).

gods were at least tolerated, Akhenaten appears to be a henotheist (worshiping one god while believing in the existence of others). However, the final years at Thebes and the iconoclasm there demonstrate a step toward monotheism (Assmann 2008, 29). After the move to Akhetaten came a final change to the didactic name of the Aten, "Living Re, Ruler of the Horizon, Rejoicing in the Horizon in His Name of Re, the Father, who has come as the Sun-disc [Aten]" (D. Redford 1984, 186).[15] The most important change in this final form of the didactic name is the removal of "Horakhty" and "Shu," "a deletion that was meant to remove any doubt that Aten is connected to these gods" (Hoffmeier 2015, 206). Thus, only the Aten can be considered a god, despite the previously strong connections to earlier solar theology. Redford points out that this removal of solar theology can be seen in the iconography as well in the absence of the Re-Horakhty falcon, the scarab beetle symbolizing the act of creation, the winged sun disk, the solar boat, and the like (D. Redford 2013, 27). At this point, it is reasonable to assert that Akhenaten's reforms culminate in a form of monotheism.

Additionally, orthographic considerations point toward the uniqueness of the Aten, for the divine determinatives are not used of the Aten, nor is it/he ever called a god (Zabkar 1954, 87–101). Orly Goldwasser offers an excellent interpretation of these phenomena: putting a god-determinative on the writing of the Aten would mean that, though the chosen god, Aten is still but one among many (Goldwasser 2006b, 267–79).

If it is reasonably certain that Akhenaten was a monotheist, the follow-up question is "What effect did his monotheism have on the ancient Israel?"[16] There are a staggering amount of complications in attempting to answer this question.[17] Scholars who maintain that there was a historical exodus event place it in either the mid-fifteenth or mid-thirteenth century.[18] If the early date is preferred, then Akhenaten had not even been born. If one opts for the later date, the exodus was roughly one hundred and twenty-five years after the Amarna period. Akhenaten's successors, particularly Horemheb, had already dismantled Aten temples, carried out their program to erase the memory of Akhenaten, and restored Egyptian religion. Thus, the issue becomes one of transmission: How exactly would Moses have been exposed to Atenism? Unlike other founders of monotheistic faiths, Akhenaten had no disciples to propagate the message (Hoffmeier 2015, 264); quite the opposite happened!

Then there is the simple issue of content, despite attempts to link Psalm 104 to the Great Hymn to the Aten.[19] Yahweh is not purely a solar deity; nor is he to be depicted.

---

15. Similar translations are offered in Aldred 1988, 278; Hornung 1999, 76, to name but two.

16. It was this question that Sigmund Freud sought to answer in his final book, *Moses and Monotheism*, where he gives the fanciful theory that Moses was a vizier or priest of Akhenaten and was exposed to monotheism in that role (Freud 1939, 33). Egyptologists and biblical scholars alike have wholly dismissed this suggestion, but it is emblematic of Amarna-mania as an otherwise brilliant author with no academic training in either ancient Egyptian or Israelite culture cannot resist the allure.

17. This brief treatment is but an introduction to the issues from the Egyptian perspective, to say nothing of issues such as the composition of the Pentateuch, the nature of Israelite religion, the name of Yahweh, and Israelite origins in Canaan. For more on those issues, see Kitchen 1979; Olyan 1988; M. S. Smith 1990; 2001a; Cook 2004; Dozeman and Schmidt 2006; Sherwin 2008; Hoffmeier 2015, 257–64. Cook's work is an especially useful critique of the use of an evolutionary model to account for the origins of Israelite monotheism, while Sherwin's article is a good analysis of the problems with the notion of the late development of Israelite monotheism.

18. For discussion on the Israelite sojourn in Egypt, its date, and other historical issues, see Hoffmeier 1996; 2005; Rendsburg 1992; Kitchen 2003b, 299–312.

19. See Hoffmeier 2015, 247–51, for a summary and critique of this view. Many excellent translations and analyses of the Great Hymn and the lesser hymns are available: Breasted 1921, 371; Sandman 1938, 93–96; J. Wilson, 1951, 222–29; Roland Williams 1958, 145; W. Simpson 1973; Lichtheim 1976, 89; Tobin 1985; J. Foster 1995, 1754; Murnane 1995; Kitchen 1999; Hoffmeier 2015, 211–29. For transcriptions of the hieroglyphs, see Davies 1903–8, plate XXXVII; Sandman 1938, 93–96.

Jan Assmann notes, "The rejection of other gods is the sole element that the two monotheisms, Akhenaten's and Moses's, have in common" (Assmann 2014, 68). Perhaps Atenism's greatest contribution to the understanding of Israelite religion is simply that it illustrates Winfred Corduan's accurate observation that religions do not evolve in a series of traceable steps from animism to monotheism (Corduan 2012, 29–46); thus, one need not necessarily view Israelite monotheism as late development on those grounds.

Foreign Policy in the Amarna Age

Akhenaten is often accused of letting the empire fall to ruin as if his religious reforms kept him from focusing on political issues. While the king was not as active militarily as his predecessors, recent finds at frontier sites such as Tell el-Hebua and Tell el-Borg are challenging the assumption that Akhenaten allowed the empire to decay in the Levant (see Hoffmeier 2015, 177–92). He is also accused of not being the diplomat that his father was, possibly because foreigners were deemed less deserving of his attention and the Aten's protections (Murnane 2000, 106–7), despite the year-twelve visit of international ambassadors bringing lavish gifts to the king, as recorded in tombs at Amarna (N. Davies 1905a, plate XXXVII; 1905b, plate XIV).

Cuneiform tablets from Tell el-Amarna, the so-called Amarna Letters, are a treasure trove of diplomatic correspondence from both those considered to be Akhenaten's equals—rulers of Babylon, Mittani, Hatti, Arzawa, and Alashiya—and his vassals (Williamson 2015, 7; Moran 1992). It is possible that many of these letters went unanswered, or, since the archive comes from Egypt, Akhenaten's replies might be lost in the various regions to which they went. The Amarna Letters, though incredibly useful for historical reconstructions, are heavily biased and must be used with great caution.

Conclusion

Given the complexities of the Amarna period, it is unsurprising that interpretations of Akhenaten and his religious revolution have changed over time. For James Henry Breasted, Akhenaten was the "first individual" in history, and his religion was the "gospel of beauty" (Breasted 1933, 294). To Cyril Aldred, Akhenaten's presentation of himself as a family man strikes a "humane and sympathetic" chord (Aldred 1988, 303–6). Quite the opposite, Redford refers to him as a "misshapen individual" and an "iconoclastic freak" ruling over a "tiresome regime" (D. Redford 1984, 4, 158, 204). One could go on *ad infinitum* citing the influence of Akhenaten on various groups or attempting to identify with him on racial, religious, or even sexual grounds (Montserrat 2003).

All of this paints a picture of a pharaoh more mysterious and controversial than any of his contemporaries. His long "cultural afterlife" is explained both by the wide range of interpretations that his reign enables and by his radical religious reforms. No other pharaoh attempted something so grand, and though ultimately the sun would set on his religion of light, many scholars acknowledge Akhenaten as one of history's first monotheists, a legacy of which even his most vengeful successors cannot rob him.

33

The Late Bronze Age Collapse and the Sea Peoples' Migrations

GREGORY D. MUMFORD

Introduction

The study of the Late Bronze Age collapse and the Sea Peoples' migrations is exceedingly complex and contentious regarding diverse and often contradictory evidence and interpretations. Its scope spans multiple regions in the eastern Mediterranean, Egypt, and Near East; it covers several centuries straddling the Late Bronze Age (1550–1200 BCE) to the Iron Age (1200–586 BCE); it entails diverse disciplines and specialists, including the archaeology, art, languages, and the history of the Aegean, Western Anatolia, the Hittites, Cyprus, Syria-Palestine, Mesopotamia, Egypt, Libya, and elsewhere (for a suggested historical framework of periods by region, see table 33.1, "Late Bronze Age to Iron Age I Chronologies"). The topic also incorporates a continuous influx of new data and reassessments.[1] The textual-pictorial account from Ramesses III's memorial temple at Medinet Habu has long dominated more popular and simplified perceptions and misconceptions regarding a "single" event ca. 1200 BCE (elsewhere 1190–1177 BCE):[2] this pivotal event is applied to mark the "collapse" of Late Bronze Age empires, kingdoms, city-states, and their affiliated cultures throughout the eastern Mediterranean and the Near East, followed by their integration and/or partial replacement during the early Iron Age, with hybrid populations, societies, material culture, and polities. In contrast, the extant and emerging patchwork of evidence suggests that the foundation of a new geopolitical and socio-cultural landscape of the biblical Philistines, Israelites, and their neighbors reflects far more complex, multifaceted, obscure, and long-term factors. Such data also imply a continuity and merging of the Canaanites and other indigenous cultures with various Sea Peoples (e.g., Philistines), the Israelites, and other peoples and influences (Bachhuber 2013).

1. See Sandars 1985; Ward and Joukowsky 1992; Drews 1993; Stager 1995; Oren 2000; Leahy 2001; Bachhuber and Roberts 2009; Yassur-Landau 2010; Haider, Weinstein, Cline, and O'Connor 2012; Bachhuber 2013; Cline 2014; D'Amato and Salimbeti 2015.

2. Absolute dates vary according to high, middle, or low chronologies and cross-cultural synchronisms (Dodson 2013; Kotsonas 2013).

Table 33.1. Late Bronze Age to Iron Age I Chronologies

Levantine Periods (dates and terminology in flux)		Egyptian Dynasties	Egyptian Rulers	Mycenaean Pottery
Late Bronze IA (1550–1450)	Transitional Middle Bronze–Late Bronze or Middle Bronze IIC–Late Bronze IA (1550–1459+)	Eighteenth (Early New Kingdom)	Ahmose (1550–1525) Amenhotep I (1525–1504) Thutmose I (1504–1492) Thutmose II (1492–1479) Thutmose III (1479–1425) Hatshepsut (1473–1458)	Late Helladic I Late Helladic IIA
Late Bronze IB (1450–1400)	Late Bronze IB (1459–1390)	Eighteenth (consolidation of the empire)	Thutmose III (1479–1425) Amenhotep II (1427–1400) Thutmose IV (1400–1390)	Late Helladic IIB
Late Bronze IIA (1400–1300)	Late Bronze IIA (1390–1295; Late Bronze IB–IIA transition is sometimes dated ca. 1352)	Eighteenth (Amarna period)	Amenhotep III (1390–1352) Amenhotep IV (Akhenaten, 1352–1336) Neferneferuaten (Smenkhara, 1338–1336) Tutankhamun (1336–1327) Ay (1327–1323) Horemheb (1323–1295)	Late Helladic IIIA1 Late Helladic IIIA2
Late Bronze IIB (1300–1200)	Late Bronze IIB (1295–1177)	Nineteenth (early Ramesside period)	Ramesses I (1295–1186) Seti I (1294–1279) Ramesses II (1279–1213) Merenptah (1213–1203) Amenmessu (1203–1200?) Seti II (1200–1194) Siptah (1194–1188) Tausret (1188–1186)	Late Helladic IIIB
Late Bronze III or Iron IA (1200–1150)	Early Iron	Twentieth (Ramesside Empire retains Canaan)	Sethnakht (1186–1184) Ramesses III (1184–1153) Ramesses IV (1153–1147) Ramesses V (1147–1143) Ramesses VI (1143–1136)	Late Helladic IIIC
Iron IB (1150–1000)	Late Iron	Twentieth (Late Ramesside Egypt retains Nubia)	Ramesses VII (1136–1129) Ramesses VIII (1129–1126) Ramesses IX (1126–1108) Ramesses X (1108–1099) Ramesses XI (1099–1069)	Late Helladic IIIC
		Twenty-First (Third Intermediate Period)	Smendes (1069–945) Amenemnisu (1043–1039) Psusennes I (1039–991)	Submycenaean

After A. Mazar 1990a, 238; Shaw 2000, 481; Shelmerdine 2008, 4–5, figs. 1.1–2; see also Mumford 2001a, 361, table 1; A. Sherratt in Steiner and Killebrew 2014, 499, table 33.1.

Sources

Although the Medinet Habu account plays a major role in clarifying the Sea Peoples' migrations and the end of the Late Bronze Age (Murnane 1980, 11–18), other significant historical sources exist from Ramesses III's reign (Pap. Harris I and other texts) (Kitchen 2008). In addition, many pertinent texts predate and postdate this event including the Amarna Letters (Moran 1992), records from Ramesses II's reign (Kitchen 1968–90, vols. 2, 3), Linear B texts (Deger-Jalkotzy 2008, 387–92), the Hittite archives from Hattuša (Hoffner 2009), Ugarit's archives (Yon 2006), the onomasticon of Amenemope (Gardiner 1947), the *Journey of Wenamon* (W. Simpson 2003, 116–24), and many other sources (Wente and Meltzer 1990, 268 [Meshwesh], 269 [Sherden]; Peden 2001, 182–237). For instance, the Amarna Letters (mid-fourteenth century BCE) and the Battle of Kadesh (year five of Ramesses II) attest to the presence of the Sherden/Shardana (who appear later in the Sea Peoples' confederation) as auxiliaries in the Egyptian army (Moran 1992; Kitchen 1982, 55, fig. 18). The Sherden and other (sea) peoples (i.e., Lukka, Shekelesh, Teresh, and Ekwesh) are also listed among the Libyan (Libu) force attacking Egypt during the reign of Merenptah (late thirteenth century BCE) (Kitchen 2003b, 4). Furthermore, the archaeological record furnishes much supplementary, albeit often contradictory, information regarding the Sea Peoples and other events leading to the Late Bronze Age's collapse. This includes paleo-environmental data (e.g., climate change), settlements, burials, and shipwrecks (e.g., Cape Gelidonya, Point Iria), and affiliated ecofacts (Broodbank 2013, 445–505; P. Walsh 2014, 170, 178, 286; Renfrew and Bahn 2016, 50).

Background

During the Late Bronze Age, New Kingdom Egypt expanded its empire over many Ca-naanite city-states in Syria-Palestine (M. Hasel 1998; Mumford 1998; E. Morris 2005; Spalinger 2005; Steiner and Killebrew 2014). During Late Bronze Age IA (1550–1450 BCE), Egypt initially dispatched periodic military campaigns and exacted annual tribute under threat of retaliatory attacks. Thutmose III intensified Egypt's domination of the Levant, starting with the Battle of Megiddo and continuing with attacks and inspection tours to the north (D. Redford 2003). In Late Bronze Age IB–IIA (1450–1300 BCE) his successors consolidated this new imperial infrastructure (e.g., provincial capitals and garrisons), formalized borders (with Mitanni), and expanded interactions with neighboring kingdoms via treaties and diplomatic marriages.[3] Egypt's relations with the Hittite Empire declined sharply in the late fourteenth century BCE (the Amarna period), following the Hittite expansion and incursion into Mitanni; the defeat, defection, and loss of some northern Egyptian vassals (in Amurru); and an Egyptian escort's alleged murder of a Hittite prince dispatched to Egypt (Dodson 2009, 89–94; 2014, 76–81, 135–38; Stavi 2015). Under Ramesses II (Late Bronze IIB, 1300–1200 BCE) Egypt fought with Hatti, restoring order in its Canaanite Empire and eventually establishing peace and a stable border with the Hittites. However, during this period Egypt and adjacent regions faced natural disasters (climatic change, low Niles, drought, famine), unrest in Canaan, Nubia, and marginal regions (vassal rebellions, Shasu Bedu attacks, Israelite stirrings), Libyan incursions into the Nile Valley (Ramesses II fortified the western delta), fights over the succession (Amenmesse versus Seti II), internal strife (Queen Tawosret, Siptah, and Chancellor Bay in the late Nineteenth Dynasty), gold depletion in Nubia's mines, other economic problems (inability to pay tomb workers, workmen's strikes), and

3. See Der Manuelian 1987; O'Connor and Cline 1998; Cohen and Westbrook 2000; Bryan 1991; Cline and O'Connor 2006; Dodson 2009.

Fig. 33.1. Illustration of captive Sea Peoples from the Medinet Habu reliefs of Ramesses III

other factors affecting Egypt and its empire (Dodson 2010; N. Spencer 2014; Goelet 2016).

The Iron Age IA–B period (1200–1000 BCE) witnessed a relatively rapid decline in Egypt and its imperial territories (Dodson 2012), with increasing Libyan incursions at home and further population movements and settlement by indigenous refugees, bedouin, and others. For instance, a confederation of Philistines arose in southwest Canaan, the Tjeker, Sherden, and other Sea Peoples are attested in various parts of the Levant (e.g., Phoenicia, Transjordan), while the Israelites emerge in the southern hill country (Kitchen 1995, 243–54; Killebrew 2005).

The Sea Peoples' Migrations

Medinet Habu portrays the Sea Peoples' migrations as a "single event" dating to year eight of Ramesses III, who claims, "The foreign countries, they made a conspiracy in their isles. Removed and scattered in battle, were the lands at one time. No land could stand up against ('before') their arms, beginning from Hatti (Anatolia);—Qode (Syria), Carchemish (Syria), Arzawa (southern Anatolia), and Alashiya (Cyprus), cut off (all) at once in one [place]" (Kitchen 2008, 34). These foes represent three newcomers—the Peleset, Tjeker, and Weshwesh—and familiar enemies: the Sheklesh, the Denyen/Danuna (the Danaoi of the *Iliad*?), and a captured enemy labeled "Sherden of the Sea" (Bachhuber 2013, 6098). This group is described as establishing a camp in the Hittite controlled region of Amurru (southwest Syria), devastating this region, and moving southward overland to Egypt's imperial frontier in Djahi (i.e., northern Palestine to southern Syria), perhaps as far south as Tell el-Borg and the Pelusiac branch of the Nile delta (Hoffmeier 2014a). In the land battle scenes, the Sea Peoples are shown advancing in chariots and as infantry with clean-shaven faces, flaring (feathered?) helmets, upper-body armor, tasseled kilts, circular shields, spears, axes, and long swords; they utilize three-person crews (i.e., characteristic of Anatolian chariotry) and are identified as Peleset, Denyen, and Tjekel. The chariots are followed by identical warriors driving wagons carrying women and children, drawn by "humped" oxen typical of Zebu cattle from Syria and Anatolia (O'Connor 2000, 95–97). Ramesses III also mentions securing Egypt's delta with warships and troops along the riverbanks (Wachsmann 2000). The Sea Peoples' fleet is represented by five ships with bird-headed ends. Three ships contain warriors with flaring helmets (identified as Peleset, Denyen, and Tjekel), and two boats have crew members wearing horned helmets (often equated with the Sherden) (Haider et al. 2012, 198). Ramesses III claims victory against both the land and the sea invasions, while affiliated texts mention the presence of the Sherden and Teresh. However, the Teresh and Denyen are attested a few decades before as foes during the reign of Merenptah, while the Denyen and Sherden appear even earlier as troublesome peoples in the fourteenth century BCE. The frequency of hostile sea raiders is attested by other Late Bronze Age accounts of piracy by the Lukka (from Lycia in southwest Anatolia) and Ekwesh (from western Anatolia?), who are otherwise absent from Ramesses III's list of enemies.

The Late Bronze Age Collapse

The Aegean

The decline of the Mycenaeans and the Aegean in general is complicated, remains unclear, and is widely debated. It involves multiple factors (e.g., droughts, famines, earthquakes, warfare, palace system collapse), varies in nature and intensity between polities and regions, and ranges from gradual to more rapid developments (Deger-Jalkotzy 2008, 387). Earlier attacks and earthquake destructions appear at some Mycenaean palace centers toward the

end of Late Helladic IIIB1 (1300–1250 BCE), including Mycenae, Tiryns, and Thebes, while the remainder of the thirteenth century BCE (Late Helladic IIIB2, 1250–1190 BCE) is characterized by increasing instability and decline. Mycenaean palace citadels and Aegean settlements experience diverse problems, such as an apparent overexploitation of agricultural lands, soils, and other resources (evident in several regions), natural disasters (earthquakes, flooding, droughts, disease), declining populations (e.g., northern Rhodes), some potential population influxes (foreign migrants), gradual impoverishment and abandonment (Grotta on Naxos), the strengthening and expansion of fortifications (Mycenae, Tiryns, Midea, Athens, Ayios Andreas on Siphnos, Phylakopi on Melos), some augmentation of coastal watch systems (e.g., Pylos), attacks and destructions (Mycenae, Tiryns, Midea, Thebes, Orchomenos, Dimini, Gla), and other circumstances (civil strife). Despite such long-term developments, many Mycenaean palace-citadels, including Linear B tablets, reveal indications for a "final disaster" with little to no warning at the end of Late Helladic IIIB2, ca. 1200/1190 BCE (e.g., a conflagration at Thebes baked some wet Linear B tablets), disrupting an otherwise functioning society, administration, economy, and lifestyle (Deger-Jalkotzy 2008, 390–92). The potential culprits vary widely: indigenous uprisings, warring neighbors (Mycenaean Big Men, chiefdoms, and city-states), and external raiders (Sea Peoples? northern "Dorian" invasion [refuted]? "barbarians"?). However, while individual sites and circumstances fit some of these scenarios, it seems that multiple and varying factors contributed to the gradual and ultimate collapse of Mycenaean and Aegean societies (Tartaron 2013, 17–20).

Anatolia

Despite the popular assignment of the "Sea Peoples" as the main cause behind the ca. 1200 BCE collapse of Hatti, Arzawa, Kizuwadna,

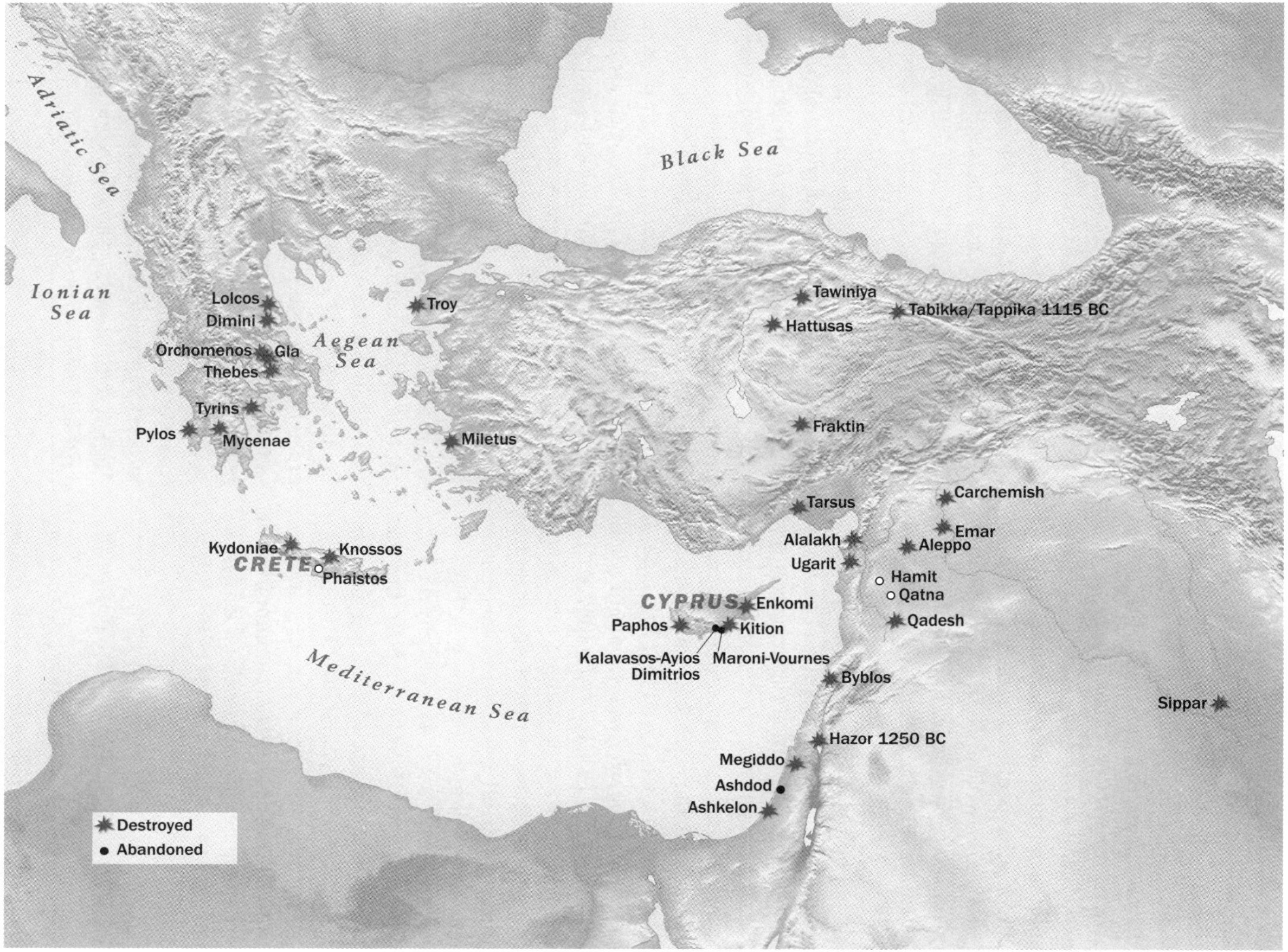

Fig. 33.2. Some settlements destroyed, attacked, or abandoned ca. 1250–1150 BCE in the East Mediterranean, contemporary with the Sea Peoples and other peoples and factors

265

Willusa (Troy?), Alashiya, and the Levantine states, the underlying mechanisms and factors are complex, unclear, and debated (Bryce 2005, 327–51; Beckman, Bryce, and Cline 2011, 267–82). At a superficial level, the complex sociopolitical landscape across Anatolia did encounter tumultuous disturbances, destructions, abandonments, and other socioeconomic, political, and cultural changes at the end of the Late Bronze Age. The Hittite Empire faced increasing pressures along its frontiers, including vassal rebellions in western and southern Anatolia, Kaska tribal raids from northern Anatolia, and the expansion of and conflict with the Assyrian Empire to the southeast. During the late thirteenth century BCE, the Hittites' heartland struggled increasingly with issues over the succession to the throne, shortages in agricultural laborers, and a declining economy, plus widespread natural disasters such as prolonged droughts, famine, disease, and earthquakes (e.g., Hisarlik/Troy) (see van den Hout 2013, 41–43; Bryce 2014, 86–94). Hence, the Sea Peoples, many of whom appear to have originated from western and southern Anatolia, including a few groups that had been active in this region for a few centuries, probably reflect only one of many components aiding in and emerging from the fall of Late Bronze Age Anatolia. By the early twelfth century BCE, many polities and sites are destroyed and abandoned in Hatti and adjacent regions, including the Hittite capital at Hattuša, while other sites have squatter occupation, reduced village communities, or resettlement nearby (Sagona and Zimansky 2009, 287, 291–92; Gates 2011, 405; Seeher 2011b, 384).

Cyprus

Cyprus experienced similar site destructions (e.g., Kition, Enkomi), abandonments (e.g., Maroni-Vournes, Kalavasos-Ayios Dimitrios), and turmoil around 1200 BCE (A. Bernard Knapp 2013, 447–48), but the island yields closer links to the Sea Peoples and related activities (Tatton-Brown 1987, 15). For much of the preceding fourteenth through thirteenth centuries BCE, the Hittites may have dominated or controlled key portions of Cyprus: King Šuppiluliuma II refers to naval activity against maritime pirates in this region and a subsequent land battle on Alashiya (Cyprus). Correspondence between the Hittite vassal ruler of Ugarit and the king of Alashiya reveals hostile Sea Peoples' fleets, coastal raids, plus other maritime marauders in this region immediately prior to ca. 1200 BCE (Karageorghis 1982, 82–84; A. Bernard Knapp 2013, 448). One probable Sea Peoples–affiliated group, the Mycenaeans, displays close links with Cyprus, especially during the thirteenth century BCE (Late Cypriot IIC) and later: imported and locally copied Mycenaean (Late Helladic) IIIB pottery and motifs, bronze equipment, and weaponry (Enkomi Tomb 18: greaves and a Naue II–type sword), and other items in settlements and burials; other Cypriot artifacts display typical Sea Peoples–type warriors with flaring helmets, circular shields, and tasseled kilts (e.g., Enkomi stamp seal and ivory game box) (Mee 2008, 375–77; Karageorghis 1982, 84–85, fig. 68). Cyprus also contains some imported "Trojan ware" ("Grey ware") at Kition, Enkomi, and elsewhere, suggesting additional links with northwest Anatolia and the Aegean (Karageorghis 1982, 86). However, the archaeological and historical data enable a broad range of interpretations concerning the significance of Aegean and west Anatolian imported items, influences, and local copies such as indirect Aegean trade, Mycenaean traders, transitory migrants (emissaries, mercenaries, raiders), captives/booty, and potential limited Aegean settlement (i.e., colonization) within a predominant Cypriot population.

Syria-Palestine

Canaan exhibits a variety of destruction levels, decline, impoverishment, and abandonment at different sites during the thirteenth century BCE through the early Iron Age that can be attributed to different scenarios: local nomadic raids (e.g., Shasu, Apiru), Sea Peoples' attacks (e.g., Ugarit), Egypt's subjugation of the Israelites and others (attested in Merenptah's "Israel" stele), an Israelite conquest (described in later biblical texts), warring city-states (especially in the northern Levant), Egyptian conflict with and suppression of rebellious vassal city-states (e.g., Ashkelon), potential civil uprisings (1250 BCE destruction of Hazor's Stratum XIII citadel), earthquakes (Deir Alla, Lachish), and more obscure socioeconomic, political, and other factors (e.g., depopulation: Jericho remained unoccupied for much of the Late Bronze Age). Although northern Syria fell under Hittite control during much of Late Bronze Age IIA–B (Bryce 2014), this region experienced fluctuating conflict with Egypt, Mitanni, Assyria, and Hatti, while the stabilization of a frontier between Egypt and Hatti (in year twenty-one of Ramesses II) did not end the internal strife and regional warfare during the remainder of the Late Bronze Age (Spalinger 2005).

The Israelites' emergence, their influx, and their precise role(s) in the Late Bronze Age and its collapse and transition to the Iron Age are equally obscure and debated (Hoffmeier 1996; 2005). Although the Israelites are attested in Palestine during Merenptah's reign and perhaps earlier (Ramesses II? Berlin Stela 21687), the Egyptian and Near Eastern textual and archaeological evidence does not corroborate later biblical accounts of a sojourn and exodus during the Ramesside period (Frerichs and Lesko 1997). The biblical conquest account is problematic in view of some of the archaeological record from Canaan, where excavations have yielded a mixture of contradictory and corroborative data for occupation strata, settlements, and ethnic populations affiliated with the Israelite conquest account (Levy, Schneider, and Propp 2015). In contrast, the archaeological evidence to date supports a more gradual emergence of small, agrarian settlements in the hill country during the early Iron Age, which draw upon Canaanite traditions and may reflect a combination of semi-nomadic pastoralists, deurbanized Canaanites (refugees), and others (Killebrew 2005; Faust 2006b).

Egypt

Aside from the failed Sea Peoples' attacks around 1200 BCE, Egypt also experienced increasing turmoil throughout the Nineteenth and Twentieth Dynasties (1300–1069 BCE): declining climatic conditions (droughts, low Niles, famines), vassal revolts in Canaan and Nubia (Seti I, Ramesses II, Merenptah, Ramesses III and IV), campaigns abroad (Seti I's and Ramesses II's attempts to regain Amurru and Kadesh from Hatti), bedouin hostilities (Libyan and Meshwesh incursions from the Western Desert, Shasu raids across north Sinai, subjugation of the Seir Bedu [Negev?]), Egypt's militarization of key frontier regions and imperial territories (fortifying the western delta, north Sinai, and Canaan), economic hardship (depletion of Nubian gold mines, growing inflation, royal-tomb workmen's strikes, increasing tomb robberies), an evident rise in corruption (theft of temple wealth, widespread involvement in Theban tomb robberies), civil strife (fights over the royal succession, the assassination of Ramesses III [slit throat], power struggles between the king and the Amun cult), and the eventual dissolution of Egypt into a southern Theban theocracy and a northern Tanite kingdom under the nominal leadership of Ramesses XI (van Dijk 2000, 295–313; S. Redford 2002; Vernus 2003; D. Redford 2006, 157–204; Bietak 2007, 438–48).

Aftermath

During the Iron Age IA–IB aftermath following the 1250–1200 BCE coastal and inland

Fig. 33.3. Illustration of the Sea Peoples' fleet destroyed at the eastern delta river mouth, from the Medinet Habu reliefs of Ramesses III

conflicts, migrations, flight, and settlement, new peoples integrated variously into the indigenous populations of the east Mediterranean: the Phrygians, the kingdom of Urartu, and others emerge in Anatolia (Sagona and Zimansky 2009, 291–370); some Aegeans appear in Cyprus (A. Bernard Knapp 2013, 449); the neo-Syro-Hittites forge new states in northern Syria (Sader 2014, 618); Aramaeans shift into southeast Syria (forming Aram Damascus); the Israelites (and others) coalesce in the hill country (Gilboa 2014); Ramesses III–VI control an increasingly reduced area of Canaan during Iron Age IA (Mumford 2001b, 343; 2014, 78–81); the Peleset (Philistines) merge with Canaanites in the southern coastal plain of Philistia (Dothan and Dothan 1992); other Sea Peoples may have settled elsewhere in the Levant (e.g., Phoenicia), including the Tjeker at Dor, Sherden at Akko, and perhaps others inland (e.g., Sherden [?] at Tell es-Saidiyeh in the Jordan Valley) (Tubb 2000, 189; Sader 2014). Leading up to and during the Iron Age, tribal societies established chiefdoms and subsequent kingdoms in Ammon, Moab, and Edom in Transjordan and the Negev (Bienkowski 1992;

Herr and Najjar 2008; Levy, Najjar, and Ben-Yosef 2014).

Iron Age Syria-Palestine

Following ca. 1200/1177 BCE, Ramesses III–VI retained political control of Canaan in Iron Age IA, while the specific relationship with the Sea People captives, migrants, and other peoples remains less clear. It is uncertain whether captured warriors (e.g., Peleset) served as auxiliaries in Egyptian garrisons within Canaan or mainly in Egypt: some Iron Age IA ceramic anthropoid coffins bearing striped headdresses appear in Egyptian garrison cemeteries at Deir el-Balah (which also has Late Bronze Age IIB coffins [Mumford 1998, 1604–1743]), Tell el-Far'a South, Beth Shean, and perhaps elsewhere (e.g., a body fragment occurs at Lachish). These examples have often been equated with the flaring helmets sported by some Sea People mercenaries (i.e., Peleset, Tjeker, Denyen), but this equation remains speculative and contested (Killebrew 2005, 65–67, 218; T. Dothan 2008, 94–95). Of note, a pottery deposit associated with the Deir el-Balah residence/fort may reflect a Philistine practice.[4] Regardless of individual areas and circumstances, Iron Age I displays a major shift in the political and cultural landscape of the Levant (and beyond) (Mumford 2007), witnessing the influx and blending of the Philistines, Tjeker, Sherden, Israelites, and other peoples with the former Canaanites and other ethnic groups (Apiru, Shasu, Seir Bedu). This includes the consolidation of powerful Phoenician city-states to the north (e.g., Byblos, Tyre, Sidon), and new polities to the east (Aram Damascus, Ammon, Moab, Edom).

The Sea Peoples and Canaanites in the Levant

The archaeological and historical records suggest that the Peleset and other Sea Peoples (Tjeker, Sherden) settled among the Canaanite population (Killebrew and Lehmann 2013), probably via Cyprus (which yields much locally made Mycenaean IIIC1b pottery). The Peleset initially concentrated at and around the towns of Ashkelon, Gaza, and Ashdod in the Plain of Philistia during Iron Age IA: an emerging hybrid Peleset, Tjeker, Sherden, and Canaanite population replace some Late Bronze IIB Canaanite towns (e.g., Ashdod), abandon other sites (e.g., Ugarit; a hiatus occurs at Lachish in Iron IB), establish new towns (Iron IB Tel Qasile), and continue occupying other towns (e.g., Tell el-Farʿa South, Gezer). The onomasticon of Amenemope confirms the presence of the Sherden, Tjeker, and Peleset in Canaan, plus the importance of Ashkelon (150 acres), Ashdod (20 acres), and Gaza (mostly unexcavated). These settlements are associated with the biblical Philistines, implying that these migrants had become quite settled by 1150–1100 BCE (A. Mazar 1990a; Lipiński 2006, 49–57). The *Journey of Wenamon* (ca. 1069 BCE [W. Simpson 2003]) mentions an

---

4. Personal communication with John S. Holladay Jr.; see Dothan and Nahmias-Lotan 2010, 111–13.

Egyptian emissary stopping at a Tjeker port town of Dor (Plain of Sharon). Wenamon also relates that the Tjeker operated many ships along the Levantine coast, while the prince of Byblos is called Tjeker-Baʿal. The Sherden also may have occupied the northern valleys and plains of Canaan, including Tell es-Saidiyeh (Tubb 2000). Regarding Aegean links, northern Palestine and coastal Lebanon and Syria have produced locally made Mycenaean IIIC1b pottery (e.g., Acre, Beth Shean), albeit in much smaller amounts than Philistia (Mee 2008, 378, 382).

The Peleset, who are best equated with the biblical Philistines, may have roots from Crete (biblical Caphtor [Amos 9:7; Jer. 47:4]) but also display strong ties with the Ionian coast (western Anatolia) and the Aegean in general: the Plain of Philistia yields Mycenaean pottery forms (Late Helladic IIIC bell-shaped bowls and kraters, stirrup jars, strainer jugs, pyxides), Mycenaean-style art and motifs (e.g., birds), figurines (e.g., seated and standing human figures), seals with glyptic art (resembling Cypro-Minoan script), architecture (megera, bench-shrines), and other components (T. Dothan 1982; A. Mazar 1990a). A flaring headdress similar to the style associated with the Peleset is found on the Phaistos Disk from Late Bronze Age Crete (Gardiner 1947, 203*: *kftyw*). The Bible has some Philistine names and designations with apparent, albeit contested, links to Luwian languages from western Anatolia (Singer 1988, 243). Anatolian parallels to the Sherden (?) and Tjeker (?) may be reflected by the introduction of many double pithos burials at Tell es-Saidiyeh (in the Jordan Valley) and some double pithos and cremation burials at Azor (near Tel Qasile).

During Iron Age IB, after Egypt lost control of Canaan, the characteristic Philistine material culture expands farther north and inland, including the settlements of Ekron (Tel Miqne) and Gath (Tel Safi), which biblical texts (Judg. 16) ascribe to a Philistine confederacy of five towns (Younker 2003, 372; Yasur-Landau 2010, 282–97). This autonomy enabled the Philistines to fortify their growing cities (Ashdod increased to 100 acres). Some elite housing includes Mycenaean-style buildings with a central hearth and four pillars (Miqne-Ekron); a few homes adopted a "four-room house" plan, which becomes typical for mainly Iron Age Israel and Judah (Holladay 1997, 337). Philistine temples, exemplified at Tel Qasile and partly exposed at Tel es-Safi (Gath), exhibit Aegean-style roots (e.g., Kition, Phylakopi) with rectilinear structural plans, two central pillars, interior benches for votive offerings, an altar, treasury, outer courtyard, and other features. They contained ritual equipment such as Aegean-derived Ashdoda female figurines, mourning female figurines (hands-to-head), pottery stands, rhyta, and kernoi, plus triton shells (possibly a horn for ritual calls), alabaster vessels, jewelry, seals, and other votives (A. Mazar 1980; 1985; 1990a). One popular misperception concerning the Philistines introducing and having a monopoly on iron production and superior weaponry (see 1 Sam. 13:19–22) is misplaced: iron items appear earlier in the Levant and are manufactured and dispersed widely during the Iron Age, including in Israelite territory (Dever 1990b, 80). In addition to the continuation and dominance of typical Canaanite pottery forms in Iron Age IB Philistia, Philistine pottery shifts to a hybrid bichrome ware with a more stylized bird motif, painted spirals, frames, rarely fish, and sometimes an Egyptian-style lotus blossom. Although other Aegean-derived items continue in Iron IB and likewise merge with Canaanite material culture (e.g., a hybrid "Orpheus" jug from Megiddo stratum VIA), bichrome pottery characterizes Philistine culture. It is also exported to settlements along the borders of Philistia and reaches the foothills of the Israelite hill country. The Philistine heartland contains multiple burial types, from the common indigenous simple pit graves and rectilinear cist graves to foreign-derived pithos burials (Azor, Tell Zeror), some Aegean (?)-derived rock-cut bench tombs (Tell el-Far'a South), and sporadic cremation burials (e.g., Azor) (M. Dothan 1993, 128, 129; Kochavi 1993, 1525; Yisraeli 1993, 442–43).

Israelites

In contrast to the coastal concentration of foreign influences, the southern hill country region is associated particularly with the emergence and foundation of the early Israelites (and other groups), who display roots from indigenous semi-nomadic pastoralists—Canaanites and other peoples (Faust 2006b). The early Israelites develop into an agrarian population comprised mainly of small egalitarian communities (extended households and villages), clearing trees, creating terraces for farming, storing water in cisterns, and maintaining small herds (Gilboa 2014, 640–44). Most sites contain a few houses within an ovoid enclosure that closely reflects semi-nomadic pastoralist camps, while the material culture is utilitarian and simple, drawing upon Canaanite pottery, arts, crafts, and architecture. Hence, the early Israelites likely formed from multiple peoples, perhaps encompassing Canaanite refugees from coastal towns, other nomadic groups (Shasu, Apiru, Seir Bedu?), and possibly some Levantine persons returning from Egypt (e.g., perhaps reflecting the earlier Hyksos flight from Egypt? other fugitives? [see Caminos 1954, 255: the "Exodus Papyrus"]) (Dever 2003; J. M. Miller and Hayes 2006; Maeir 2013a; Levy, Schneider, and Propp 2015).

Conclusions

Although the Sea Peoples and other ethnic groups (especially Philistines) remained politically and culturally separate from Israel by the Iron Age IIA (1000–925 BCE), much of their preserved material culture becomes less distinct or disappears, being submerged within the predominant Canaanite-derived cultures (including Phoenician influence). For instance, red-slipped and burnished pottery, which is popular in Phoenicia, appears alongside Philistine bichrome ware in the eleventh century BCE (Qasile strata XI–X), some containers share red-slip surface treatment and bichrome decoration (e.g., black-painted spirals), while Philistine bichrome ware disappears by 1000 BCE (Ben-Shlomo 2014b, 723). During the Iron Age II we become more reliant upon biblical, Egyptian, and Syro-Mesopotamian textual-pictorial records to clarify the nature of the various Sea Peoples' descendants (particularly the Philistines) and other ethnic groupings in the Levant (Maeir 2013b, 241–42).

34

Sheshonq's Levantine Conquest and Biblical History

Yigal Levin

The invasion of Judah and Israel by Sheshonq I, known in the Bible as Shishak, is arguably one of the most important episodes in the study of biblical history. Despite the significant differences in details between 1 Kings and Sheshonq's own description on the Bubastite Portal of the Karnak temple, the two definitely refer to the same event. Shishak is the earliest biblical figure to be mentioned in contemporary sources, and his campaign is the first event in biblical narrative to be attested in a clear, dated, extrabiblical context. This, together with the available archaeological evidence, makes the Sheshonq campaign a key factor in the study of biblical historiography and chronology and their relationship with the "real" history, archaeology, and historical geography of the southern Levant in the Iron Age IIA.

The Biblical Account

According to 1 Kings 14:25–26, "In the fifth year of King Rehoboam, King Shishak of Egypt came up against Jerusalem; he took away the treasures of the house of the LORD

and the treasures of the king's house; he took everything. He also took away all the shields of gold that Solomon had made." Second Chronicles 12:2–9 adds a theological justification for the invasion, including a prophetic exposition and an account of the princes' and the king's repentance, but also a number of additional details: Shishak came "with twelve hundred chariots and sixty thousand cavalry. A countless army came with him from Egypt—Libyans, Sukkiim, and Ethiopians. He took the fortified cities of Judah and came as far as Jerusalem." Shishak himself is mentioned once before, in 1 Kings 11:40, as the king of Egypt to whom Jeroboam fled after "lifting up his hand" against Solomon. The incident itself, and indeed Shishak's very name, are never again mentioned in the Bible.

Within the context of biblical narrative, the story itself is not extraordinary. The Kings version fits well within the Deuteronomistic account of the fall of Solomon's empire, with 1 Kings 11 as part of the "setting up" for the kingdom's fall as a divine reaction to Solomon's sins, and 1 Kings 14 being just one of a series of events that show how far Judah had

Fig. 34.1. Sheshonq conquest list on the Bubastite Portal of the Karnak temple. The "name-rings" on the lower left portion of the wall are just a few of the 156 rings on the wall, containing the names or symbols of various conquered peoples.

fallen under the foolish and rude Rehoboam. Chronicles, in its typical manner, accentuates Rehoboam's own sins, adding a prophetic messenger and the king's repentance. It also cites rather large numbers of enemy troops.[1] In any case, had this been all the information available, the story of Shishak's invasion would have been just one more biblical war story.

The Sheshonq I Inscriptions and Their Interpretation

At some point in the 1820s Jean-François Champollion, then-recent decipherer of Egyptian hieroglyphs, realized that the monumental inscription on the Bubastite Portal of the Karnak temple at Luxor describes a campaign of a king named "Sheshonq" to the Levant (fig. 34.1), and that this Sheshonq and the biblical Shishak must be one and the same.[2] As more of

Egyptian history became known to scholars, it was learned that this Sheshonq I was the founding monarch of the Twenty-Second Dynasty, was of Lybian descent, and that his twenty-one-year reign, which lasted approximately from 945 to 925 BCE, was one of the high points of Egypt's Third Intermediate Period.[3]

The inscription itself includes three elements: a scene showing the king smiting Asiatic enemies, with the gods, especially Amun, supporting him; a speech by Amun in support of the king; and a topographical list of over 150 individual "name-rings," each placed within a depiction of a bound prisoner.[4] In this, the inscription was created in a style emulating that of the New Kingdom inscriptions carved on the older sections of the Karnak complex. It was also noticed that the list is divided into an "upper register" in which many of the names seemed to be those of towns in the central and northern parts of Israel (easily identified are Aijalon, Gibeon, Beth Shean, Rehob, Shunem, Taanach, and Megiddo; other readings have been debated) and a "lower register" in which

1. Whether the "factual" information about the composition of Shishak's army and the devastation of Judah's fortified cities has any historical value is debated. For a recent assessment, see Sagrillo 2012.

2. The Egyptian form of the king's name, *ššnq*, is vocalized as either "Sheshonq" or "Shoshenq" by Egyptologists. Of the six references to this king in the Bible, 1 Kings 11:40 and all four mentions in 2 Chron. 12 have "Shishak" and 1 Kings 14:25 actually has "Shoshak," but traditionally this is vocalized as "Shishak" as well. In Hebrew, the letter *nun* is a "weak" letter that often "falls out" of names. The difference between the *q* and the *k* at the end of the name is actually a matter of convention

in English spelling—it would have been more "correct" to spell the biblical form "Shishaq."

3. For the background of Sheshonq's reign, see D. Redford 1973; Kitchen 1986, 287–302; Currid 1997, 174–80; K. Wilson 2005.

4. For an analysis and interpretation of the relief as a whole and of its significance within the context of Third Intermediate Period Egypt, see Ben-Dor Evian 2011.

those names that could be read seemed to be in the Negev, such as two places named "Arad." Many of the names are so badly preserved that they are unreadable.

At first, many scholars were skeptical as to the value of the topographic list as a historical source, especially since Jerusalem, which is the focus of the biblical account, seems not to be mentioned in the list at all. It was also pointed out that many of the places listed in the inscription seem to be in the northern kingdom of Israel, which not only is not mentioned in the biblical account but also seems to contradict 1 Kings 11:40, which indicates that Jeroboam was some sort of a protégé or ally of Shishak. These scholars assumed that Sheshonq had simply copied most of the northern place-names from older lists in order to present himself as a great conqueror like the kings of old.[5]

However, in 1925 American archaeologists preparing their excavation of Megiddo came across a fragmentary stele of Sheshonq I in the dump heaps of previous excavations at the site (fig. 34.2). Since Megiddo does appear on the Karnak list, this discovery lent credibility to Sheshonq's account of the events.

In 1938 the German scholar Martin Noth showed that many of the names included in the list had not been listed in earlier inscriptions, and that even those that had were now written differently. In his view, such differences proved that the place-names were not simply copied from the older lists, thus showing contemporary knowledge of the sites. Noth also criticized the priority given by scholars to the biblical account, which was written centuries after the events by writers with a clear theological agenda.

Noth's article paved the way for most modern treatments of the campaign, especially in their focus on the topographical list as the primary source for the events. A long list of scholars

Courtesy of the Oriental Institute of the University of Chicago

Fig. 34.2. Partial Egyptian victory stele with cartouche of Sheshonq I, as found by the Chicago Expedition in 1925

have followed Noth's basic methodology, each adding their own specific readings of place-names, their proposed itinerary for Sheshonq's forces, and their suggested interpretation of the events in light of the inscriptions, the biblical accounts, and the archaeological evidence (for the present author's proposed itinerary, see fig. 34.3).[6] Some of these scholars attempted to "harmonize" the inscription with the biblical account by explaining why Jerusalem does not seem to be mentioned in the inscription (e.g., because Rehoboam bribed off Shishak before the latter actually arrived at Jerusalem [thus Aharoni 1979, 329; Na'aman 1992, 84], or because recognizing a foreign capital was contrary to "Egyptian practice" [so Edelman 1995, 190]) and why the biblical account does not mention anything else (e.g., because of the Bible's focus on Jerusalem and its temple or on Solomon's golden shields, or because all

5. So, for example, Albright 1924b, 145—although he actually considered the Negev names to be authentic.

6. Some of the most prominent of these are B. Mazar 1986; S. Herrmann 1964; Aharoni 1979, 323–30; Kitchen 1986, 294–300, 432–47; Ahlström 1993b; Na'aman 1992; K. Wilson 2005.

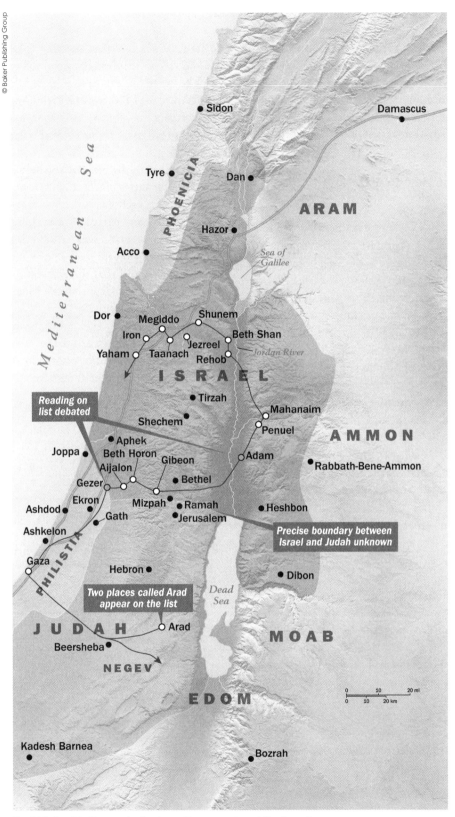

Fig. 34.3. Possible itinerary for the Levantine campaign of Sheshonq I

Labels on map:
Sidon
Damascus
Tyre
Dan
ARAM
Hazor
Acco
Sea of Galilee
Mediterranean Sea
PHOENICIA
Dor
Megiddo
Shunem
Iron
Beth Shan
Yaham
Jezreel
Taanach
Rehob
Jordan River
ISRAEL
Tirzah
Mahanaim
Reading on list debated
Shechem
Penuel
Aphek
AMMON
Joppa
Beth Horon
Gibeon
Adam
Aijalon
Bethel
Rabbath-Bene-Ammon
Gezer
Mizpah
Ramah
Heshbon
Ekron
Ashdod
Gath
Jerusalem
Precise boundary between Israel and Judah unknown
Ashkelon
Gaza
PHILISTIA
Hebron
Dibon
Dead Sea
Two places called Arad appear on the list
JUDAH
Arad
Beersheba
NEGEV
MOAB
EDOM
Kadesh Barnea
Bozrah

0   10   20 mi
0   10   20 km

the information the author had was from a short chronicle that only mentioned the tribute paid by Rehoboam). Others assumed that the biblical account was totally unreliable, and that only the Karnak inscription contains actual historical information (e.g., Clancy 1999).

The Chronological Debate

All in all, the Sheshonq inscriptions are widely accepted as the earliest known reference to a "biblical" event in a contemporaneous epigraphic source, with Sheshonq/Shishak himself being the earliest historical figure to appear both in the Bible and in contemporary inscriptions. The campaign has come to be seen as an "anchor" or "external control" for the entire chronology of the early Israelite monarchy: if Sheshonq reigned until 925 BCE, and if we assume that the campaign must have occurred toward the end of his reign (most of which was spent consolidating his power over Egypt itself), then the biblical date of Rehoboam's fifth year must have been between 930 and 925. This then allows us to calculate the dates for the reigns of David, Solomon, and the kings of the divided monarchy, using the dates given in the Bible itself.[7] Throughout most of the second half of the twentieth century, archaeologists assumed that what they identified as the "Solomonic" fortifications at Megiddo and Gezer (see 1 Kings 9:15) were in fact destroyed by Shishak (although the reading of Gezer in the Karnak list is not at all clear), and this became an "anchor" in the archaeological stratigraphy of the early monarchy as well.

However, despite all this, things are not as clear-cut as they may seem. Because of the nature of the Egyptian sources for the Third Intermediate Period, the internal chronology of its rulers is far from certain.[8] Not a few scholars have criticized the assumed synchronism between Sheshonq's reign and the biblical "fifth year of Rehoboam," claiming that it was actually the biblical dates that influenced the Egyptologists. Others, on the fringes of scholarship, have denied the very equation of Sheshonq I with the biblical Shishak, offering various alternative chronologies; even within "conventional" scholarship, dates for the campaign itself have varied by decades.[9] Some scholars have even suggested that Sheshonq actually undertook more than one campaign to the Levant, and that the Karnak list is actually a summary rather than an itinerary (so Niemann 1997; Knauf 2001).

Cross-referencing the campaign with archaeological evidence from the mentioned sites and others has proven even more difficult. Had the above-mentioned stele from Megiddo been found in its original context, it could have shown us which of the thirty layers of this mound was the one visited by Sheshonq, but since it was overlooked by the original excavators and only found later in the dump, it is of no use for this purpose. In the case of Arad, the only site on the lower register that is both securely identified and intensively excavated, there is still a debate on just which stratum is that visited by Sheshonq or his army (for which, see Z. Herzog 2002, 92–93).

The issue of chronology has become even more acute since the beginning of the debate on the "low chronology" for the beginning of the Israelite monarchy first proposed by Israel Finkelstein (1996a). As the "Solomonic" Iron IIA strata at Arad, Megiddo, Taanach, and so on, together with the very rise of the Israelite state, were "down-dated" by some scholars from the tenth century BCE to the ninth, Sheshonq was

---

7. The next possibility for such cross-referencing of biblical dates with external chronology is in the invasion of Tiglath-Pileser III of Assyria in 733 BCE, two centuries later.

8. For example, nearly half of Kitchen's book on the period is devoted to chronological issues. See Kitchen 1986, 3–239.

9. For an example of the former, see Bimson 1986; for some of the latter, see D. Redford 1973, 10; Currid 1997, 182; Dodson 2000.

now seen as destroying the previous, late Iron I strata instead. In Finkelstein's view, Sheshonq did not attack the kingdom of Judah at all, since such a kingdom did not yet exist. Rather, he attacked a local Negev "chiefdom" and the still-Canaanite cities of the Jezreel Valley. Indeed, it was Sheshonq's destruction of these cities that eventually paved the way for the emergence of Omride Israel and later of Judah as territorial states that spread into the lowlands (Finkelstein 2002; for a slightly more updated iteration see Finkelstein 2013, 41–44, 76–77). This radical departure from the "conventional" history of early Israel became a part of the "minimalist-maximalist" debate, much of which is not based purely on the archaeological evidence. On the other side of this debate are the many archaeologists and historians who have not accepted the "low chronology" and who continue to assume that there was some sort of "United Monarchy," even if in a somewhat "downgraded" form. Here, the Sheshonq campaign is at the center of the debate: Did Sheshonq destroy previously existing "Solomonic" Israelite cities at Megiddo and Gezer, or were the cities that he destroyed actually Canaanite, "proving" that the United Monarchy of David and Solomon was more myth than history? Did Sheshonq not mention Israel, Judah, Jerusalem, Rehoboam, and Jeroboam in his account because of Egyptian hubris that refused to recognize the very existence of other sovereign kingdoms, or was it because they really did not exist (or were too insignificant to mention)? Shishak thus lies at the very heart of the ongoing debate on the history of the early monarchy. In fact, even as the two sides have grown closer in recent years, the question of which strata can be identified as those visited by Shishak remains a point of contention (for which, see, e.g., Ussishkin 2008).

Shishak and the Study of Biblical History

Despite this debate, the Shishak campaign remains one of the most significant episodes for the study of the history of the early Israelite monarchy. It is, after all, the very first specific event mentioned both in the Bible and in a contemporary epigraphic source, and Shishak himself is the earliest "biblical" character to be mentioned in a contemporary inscription. In fact, Shishak is the first Egyptian monarch whom the Bible calls by name rather than by the generic title "pharaoh" used of all earlier kings. But beyond the mere mention of Shishak and his invasion of the land of Israel, the inscription and its biblical "counterpart" can contribute to our knowledge of the history of the period in the following ways.

Historicity. The very fact that the author of Kings, living and writing centuries after the events, even knew about this invasion and could refer to Shishak by name shows that that author must have had access to some sort of records that reached back to the late tenth century BCE. This fact must be taken into account in any discussion on the sources and historicity of the biblical account of this period. The same is true for any discussion of the additional details given in the even later book of Chronicles.

Historiography. Conversely, the very significant differences between the way the campaign is depicted in the two biblical sources (Kings and Chronicles) and in the Karnak account can serve as a lesson in ancient historiography: none of the three accounts was written simply for the sake of recording "history"; each of them was written by an author who had a theological and political agenda (we should remember that Karnak is a temple and the god Amun plays a prominent part in the Sheshonq inscription). We should be aware of this when we read other episodes in biblical historiography as well.

Archaeology. As mentioned above, the Sheshonq campaign plays a prominent role in the archaeological reconstruction of the Iron Age IIA—the time of the early Israelite monarchy. Different archaeologists have identified different strata at sites such as Arad, Gezer, Beth Shean, and Megiddo as having been destroyed by Sheshonq and have based their reconstructions of the period accordingly.

History. In the history of Egypt, the reign of Sheshonq I is a passing incident, a short period of unity and grandeur during the Third Intermediate Period that had no lasting effect. His influence on the history of Israel is debated, with some scholars asserting that his campaign was a major factor in the rise of the Israelite monarchy, and others insisting that it was responsible for the destruction of the achievements of the kingdom of Solomon and the weakening of the divided kingdoms. In any case, the appearance of Egyptian troops in the Negev, the central hills, and the Jezreel Valley must have left a lasting impression on the local inhabitants.

Historical Geography. The very existence at Karnak of a list of 150 places in the land of Israel, securely dated to the late tenth century BCE and arranged in some sort of geographical order, is a major asset to the study of biblical historical geography. Even if many of the names are unreadable, those that can be read are an important source of data on the toponomy of the land. Sites that are mentioned only rarely in other sources can be located using the information provided in this list. This is especially true of the "lower register" with dozens of place-names in the Negev region, including some that are actually called "Negev of . . . ," which can be compared to similar names in the Bible such as the Negev of Judah, the Negev of the Jerahmeelites, and the Negev of the Kenites (1 Sam. 27:10) and the Negev of the Cherethites and the Negev of Caleb (1 Sam. 30:14), as well as the Negev near Arad (Judg. 1:16). Arad itself is listed as two sites, an "Arad the greater" and an "Arad of Bet-Yeroham." Seven of the sites are listed with the title *p³-ḥgr*, which has been understood as either "fort," "field," or "enclosure" and compared with the biblical term "Hazer" or "Hazar," very common in the lists of Negev towns in Joshua 15:20–32; 19:1–8, Nehemiah 11:25–28; 1 Chronicles 4:28–33.[10]

Linguistics. The existence of a list of Western Semitic (Canaanite/Hebrew) names transcribed into Egyptian hieroglyphs is an invaluable aid to the study of the actual pronunciation of both languages. Just as an example, the city called "Megiddo" in Biblical Hebrew is spelled *ma-k-ta* in the conquest list that was inscribed in the Karnak temple by Thutmose III in the fifteenth century BCE, and *ma-k-d-û* in the Sheshonq I list, on a different wall of the same temple (Rainey and Notley 2006, 72, 186). The difference reflects the changes that took place in the pronunciation of both languages over the 550 years that separate the two lists.

Despite all the differences between the sources and between scholars' readings of those sources, the campaign of Sheshonq I—the Bible's Shishak—to the land of Israel, is a perfect case study for the way external sources, when cross-referenced with archaeological and geographical data, enhance and enrich our understanding of both the history of the biblical period and the way that history is presented by the writers of the Bible.

10. For an analysis of these names, see Levin 2010.

35

The Battle of Qarqar and Assyrian Aspirations

Mark W. Chavalas

Prospect

Though not mentioned in the Bible, the Battle of Qarqar in 853 BCE lurks behind the events of the reigns of the kings of Israel, Judah, and Aram Damascus in the mid-ninth century BCE (1 Kings 16–2 Kings 10) (see Hallo 1960, 34–61; Astour 1971). The protagonists were the newly resurgent Assyrian Empire, ruled by Shalmaneser III (ruled 859–824 BCE) and the newly formed Damascus (or southern) coalition, a group of smaller states in Syria-Palestine. As the sources for the battle are exclusively Assyrian, it comes as no surprise that the Assyrians viewed it as a great victory. However, a closer examination of the narratives concerning the battle shows that the outcome was not so clear.

Background

Evidence of Assyrian economic interest in the west is known from the Assyrian mercantile texts from Kanesh in Anatolia (early second millennium BCE). Moreover, a number of the Middle Assyrian period monarchs were involved militarily with the west, either against the state of Mittani or the Hittites. By the time of Tiglath-Pileser I (ruled 1114–1076 BCE), the Assyrian army had crossed the Euphrates River on multiple occasions, bringing them in direct contact with Aramaean tribes. However, a generation later, Ashur-bel-kala (ruled 1073–1056 BCE) was unable to restrain the Aramaeans from blocking communication routes to Phoenicia in the west and Egypt in the south.

After the collapse of the Mitanni and Hittite states, the regions of northern Syria and southeastern Anatolia were governed by Luwian, or Neo-Hittite successor states, as evidenced by scattered memorial royal inscriptions at Carchemish, Tell Ahmar, Zincirli, Hama, and elsewhere. Moreover, Phoenician states began to compete for power farther south along the Mediterranean coast, Aramaean enclaves were making their presence known in inland Syria, and, of course, the Israelite and Judahite states were being formed. A number of these smaller states were in fact a mix of these groups, often called "Sryo-Hittite." The writer of 1 Kings

(10:29) mentions that Solomon traded with the kings of the Hittites (i.e., Neo-Hittites) and the kings of Aram, perhaps showing that these groups were still somewhat distinct in the early tenth century BCE.

We do not again hear of a strong Assyrian presence in the region west of the Euphrates River until the late tenth century during the reigns of Ashur-Dan (ruled 934–912 BCE), Adad-nirari (ruled 911–891 BCE), and Tukulti-Ninurta II (ruled 890–884 BCE), all of whom campaigned extensively against the Aramaeans, claiming to push the tribes farther west. However, the strongest intrusion into the region began with the reign of Ashurnasirpal II (ruled 884–859 BCE). A number of contemporary local inscriptions have been uncovered in Syria and southeastern Anatolia; rarely do they mention Assyrian presence in the region, however. Ashurnasirpal II was the first Assyrian monarch to march to the Mediterranean Sea in over three centuries. He claims in his annals to have attacked polities in Syria (e.g., Bit Adini [probably biblical Beth-Aden] and Carchemish on the Euphrates) on at least three separate occasions. However, the annals do not mention the Aramaean stronghold of Damascus, perhaps implying that this Assyrian monarch did not venture that far south. Ashurnasirpal II also claims to have received tribute from the Phoenician cities. His success against the west may be interpreted as the result of a surprise attack; there may have been no time for the smaller states to prepare a coalition. At any rate, a generation later the western states were well prepared for an invasion by the Assyrian monarch's son and successor, Shalmaneser III (ruled 859–824) (see W. Lambert 1974).

Battle of Qarqar

Sources for the Battle of Qarqar

A few words need to be said about the nature of our sources (for Assyrian annals, see Grayson 1991; 1996). Compared to those of his father, Shalmaneser III's annals are in a much better state of preservation. However, Assyrian annals must be viewed with great caution. The purpose of the annals was not simply to compile a list of military events that occurred during the year; they were highly self-congratulatory and served to glorify the exploits of the monarch. Military encounters that were not successful were either overlooked or interpreted as great victories. Thus, they cannot be taken at face value.

The Battle of Qarqar occurred during Shalmaneser III's sixth military campaign. Thus far, there are at least six mentions of the sixth campaign (dated to 853 BCE) in the monarch's royal inscriptions. The earliest extant source is the Kurkh Monolith, probably composed during the seventh-year campaign and deposited near the source of the Tigris River in southeastern Anatolia (Na'aman 1976). Each edition of the annals recapped previous campaigns, often updating and revising details. The historian has the task of making sense of the composite yet often contradictory information. For example, the editions differ as to the number of allies involved in the war; between eleven and fourteen are listed. To hazard a guess: when a former enemy had subsequently become an ally, perhaps the historical record had to be modified in later editions to account for this transformation. For instance, Ahab is listed in the earlier editions of the sixth campaign, but his name (or the name of his successor) was suppressed in the third edition. In this case, Israel was no longer an enemy but rather a tribute-bearing ally (under the leadership of Jehu). Moreover, the number of slain troops in the different editions ranges between 14,000 and 29,000. Though these numbers vary in different Assyrian recensions of the war, they are most likely not greatly exaggerated. There are perhaps both literary and mathematical reasons for the variations, all of which had propagandistic purposes of calling attention to the exploits of the deeds of the Assyrian king.

Here is an excerpt of the Assyrian account from the Kurkh monolith:

> With the supreme forces which Aššur, my lord, had given me and with the mighty weapons which the divine standard, which goes before me, had granted me, I fought with them. I decisively defeated them from the city of Qarqar to the city of Gilzau. I felled with the sword 14,000 troops, their fighting men. Like Adad, I rained down upon them a devastating flood. I spread out their corpses and I filled the plain. I felled with the sword their extensive troops. I made their blood flow in the wadis. The field was too small for laying flat their bodies; the broad countryside had been consumed in burying them. I blocked the Orontes river with their corpses as with a causeway. In the midst of the battle I took away from them chariots, cavalry, and teams of horses. (Grayson 1996, 23)

The Northern Coalition

Military campaigns were carried out in each of Shalmaneser III's thirty-four years, over twenty of which were against Urartu in the north (biblical Ararat) and the Syro-Hittite states in the west (see Yamada 2000; Tammi Schneider 1993). From the annals, it can be ascertained that there were at least two coalitions against the Assyrian menace; one was in the north, where several small states such as Sam'al, Patinu, Carchemish, and Bit Adini formed an alliance (for inland Syria, see Chavalas 1997). In fact, the earliest edition of the annals portrays the Assyrian monarch crossing the Orontes River from the Amanus mountain range, soundly defeating this northern coalition at Lutibu near Sam'al in modern-day south central Turkey (ca. 857–56 BCE) (see Grayson 2001, 185–87). Til-Barsip (present-day Tell Ahmar, about 20 km south of Carchemish along the Euphrates River in modern-day Syria), the seat of Bit Adini, was occupied and annexed to Assyria, and renamed Kar-Shalmaneser (fortress or trading station

of Shalmaneser) (Liverani 1988; Ikeda 1999). Moreover, the Assyrian king occupied three other cities, also giving them Assyrian names and settling Assyrians in them. It is uncertain, however, exactly how intrusive the Assyrian presence was west of the Euphrates after this. However, Til-Barsip no doubt was the economic and political center of these territories, perhaps as a base in which to control the iron and silver trade into Anatolia. The city was supplied with a local governor and feudal responsibilities. Furthermore, the Assyrians probably mined these territories for corvée labor to help in the myriad building projects in northern Iraq, the heart of the Assyrian state. Many of these deportees were conscripted into the Assyrian military. During his sixth campaign, Shalmaneser claims to have visited the renamed city and received tribute from the previously mentioned northern Syrian states (minus Bit-Adini, which no longer existed—an event perhaps alluded to in Amos 1:5) as well as the Syro-Hittite states of Bit-Agusi, Kummuh, Melid, and Gurgum. After this, it appears that the Assyrian forces traveled south, capturing cities in the kingdom of Hama, burning Qarqar with fire. It is at this point that Shalmaneser faced the southern coalition, perhaps with the support of his new northern allies.

The Southern Coalition

The southern coalition, often called the "Damascus coalition," was composed of about a dozen allies (depending upon the edition of the annals that is studied; see Elat 1975; Dion 1995, 487–89). There were three major role players: Adad-idri (biblical Hadad-ezer) of Aram Damascus, Irhuleni of Hamath, and Ahab of Israel. In addition, there was a Phoenician contingent, consisting of Irqanatu, Usanatu, Adunu-Ba'al of Shianu, Matinu-Ba'al of Arvad, and Byblos, along with Egypt (perhaps as an ally of Byblos). Other allies were Gindibu the Arab, and Ba'asa of Bit-Ruhubi, described as an "Ammonite." The fact that 1,000 soldiers came from Egypt and 1,000 camels from Arabia shows the underlying economic and military concerns of the allies. The Assyrian annals tell us nothing about how this confederation was formed (although it certainly was in response to the Assyrian threat). Ahab of Israel certainly was a major role player, as he had perhaps just defeated Aram Damascus (cf. 1 Kings 20:23–34), causing the Israelite king to be an ally of equal rank with trade privileges (Kelle 2002).

As one can see, the annalistic scribe was not consistent in his list, sometimes listing the leaders' names without the state in question. He summarized that there were twelve allies but listed only eleven, at least in the first edition. Interestingly, Ahab offered a significant number of forces (2,000 chariots and 10,000 troops), which may have included forces from his own allies. After all, Judah under Jehoshaphat certainly was dependent upon Israel (1 Kings 22:4; 2 Kings 3:7). Perhaps other subordinate territories sent troops (e.g., Moab and Edom). A generation later, Jehoahaz of Israel could only muster 50 chariots against Aram Damascus (2 Kings 13:7).

The Damascus coalition made its first stand at Qarqar on the Orontes River (for Qarqar, see Dornemann 2003). The precise location of Qarqar on the Orontes River is still questionable. The most plausible identification of the site is Tell Qarqur, which is just south of where the main road between Aleppo and Latakia crosses the Orontes River. Indeed, the excavations at Tell Qarqur have exposed extensive remains of a long occupational history from the Bronze and Iron Ages. The Iron Age settlement shows that the site played a significant role in the northern Orontes area. Though there is no definitive proof, Tell Qarqur certainly is the best candidate to be considered the site of ancient Qarqar, which is called a "royal city" in Shalmaneser's inscriptions.

Naturally, Shalmaneser boasted of a great victory for himself. He had led his army from Aleppo up the Orontes to Qarqar on the northern border of the kingdom of Hamath with little opposition. But at Qarqar he was faced with the coalition, which, according to the Kurkh Monolith (written shortly after the event), consisted of nearly 4,000 chariots, 2,000 cavalry, over 40,000 infantry, and 1,000 camels.

Against these chariot forces was probably a much smaller Assyrian force. Although not mentioned in the Qarqar account, this can be deduced from later annals, which produce Assyrian numbers about half the size of enemy forces. For example, the annals of Shalmaneser's twentieth year appear to have totaled about 2,000 chariots and over 5,000 "cavalry horses." There is no reason to think that during the Qarqar campaign Assyrian numbers were any larger. It is probable that the Assyrian army fell far below the strength of the southern coalition, which had approximately twice as many chariots as the Assyrians (nearly 4,000), although it can be assumed that the Assyrian cavalry force was greater than that of the allies, who had less than 2,000.

At the Battle of Qarqar, the kingdoms of Hamath and Israel provided more than two-thirds of the allied forces ranged against Shalmaneser, and Israel's chariot force alone was equal to our proposed Assyrian force. The revealing figures relating to the size of the coalition and Assyrian forces given in Shalmaneser III's inscriptions provide an argument that Shalmaneser did not win a major victory.

Post-Qarqar

Shalmaneser, however, claims to have beaten the southern coalition and to have slaughtered and plundered as the enemy fled the scene of battle (Yamada 1998). One must be skeptical of Assyrian claims; the real outcome of the battle is debatable. The only clear indication that the Assyrian boast is justified is that after the battle the Assyrian army proceeded on to the Mediterranean Sea. Interestingly, the Assyrians did not mention invading any of the territories of the coalition or receiving any tribute from them. Further, there was no Assyrian activity in the region recorded until year ten of Shalmaneser (849 BCE). In that year, Shalmaneser had to attack Carchemish and Bit-Agusi in the north, perhaps implying an Assyrian breakdown in that region. If Ahab of Israel and the coalition had been soundly defeated, the biblical writer of Kings would not have hesitated to mention Ahab's defeat; it would have served the didactic purposes of the writer. This is reinforced by the fact that Ahab broke with Aram Damascus soon after this war and fought against them at Ramoth-gilead, where he met his death (1 Kings 22).

On the other hand, three more pitched battles were fought with the Damascus coalition (849, 848, and 845 BCE). Details about the 849 battle are not given; the annalist simply duplicates the stereotypical language of the sixth-year annals. This is essentially repeated for year eleven (848). Year fourteen is even less clear, although 120,000 soldiers were conscripted to fight for Assyria. Thus, if the coalition forces had suffered a setback at Qarqar, they had not been decisively beaten, as they were able to contend with Assyria at least three more times.

After 845, the annals do not describe any major military encounters in this region. By this time, the states immediately west of the Euphrates seem to have been thoroughly subdued. By 841, the coalition apparently had disappeared. But there had been a change of ruler at Damascus: Adad-idri was replaced by Hazael, known in Assyrian annals as a "son of a nobody" (i.e., a usurper). The writer of 2 Kings 8:7–15 also viewed him in this way. Perhaps the coalition dissolved with the death of Adad-idri.

Certainly the Assyrians did not push farther into Syria immediately after the battle of 845. There is, then, no proof for or against the Assyrian claim to victory in 845; the dissolution of the Damascus coalition may have been an independent development. Whatever the reason, by 841 the coalition was no more and the main obstacle to Shalmaneser's expansion into southern Syria had vanished. In 841 Hazael of Damascus, in the face of the Assyrian advance, took up a position on a summit in the foothills of the Lebanon range. The Assyrians gained the fortified position, but Hazael escaped and was pursued and besieged in Damascus. Shalmaneser cut down the orchards and burned the surrounding country, but the annalistic source does not record that Hazael yielded. Thus, although Damascus had not fallen, Shalmaneser could proceed to ravage cities by Mount Hauran and then erect a stele by the Mediterranean Sea at Mount Ba'li-ra'si (perhaps Mount Carmel). He received tribute from Tyre, Sidon, and Jehu (Yaua) king of Israel. The Bible, once again, is silent on the Assyrian involvement; perhaps it was because of the unsettled conditions with new rulers in Aram, Israel (Jehu), and Judah (Athaliah) (2 Kings 8:7–15, 25–29). Jehu is actually called a king of the house of Omri, the customary name for Israelite kings in the annals. We surmise that Jehu was happy to get Assyrian "protection" as he had perhaps broken away from the southern coalition. It is clear that Israel volunteered submission to Shalmaneser III, presumably in 841, since Jehu (Yaua), as is well known, is mentioned in the text and likely portrayed in the iconography on the Black Obelisk kneeling before the king. But there is no evidence that Shalmaneser entered central Israel, let alone Samaria, at any time. Nor is there any evidence of contact with Judah (Lipiński 1973).

Even Shalmaneser's next invasion in 838 BCE did not deter Hazael, who was able to defeat Jehu and become the most powerful ruler in the south once again. Interestingly, an Aramaic inscription was published in 1988 that shows Hazael providing an offering of a horse harness to the temple of Hera on the island of Samos and states "year when our Lord crossed the River" (perhaps meaning the

Euphrates). Perhaps this was war booty dedicated to Hadad, which may imply an offensive against the Assyrians. On the Tel Dan Inscription, found on the northern border of Israel, it is likely Hazael who boasts of killing seventy kings, including Jehoram of Israel and Ahaziah of Judah. In 838–837 he once again turned his attention to southern Syria, plundering the cities of Damascus and receiving tribute from Tyre, Sidon, and Byblos.

The Assyrian Decline

At this point, Assyrian internal issues play a role in international affairs. Perhaps the constant military campaigns in the west contributed to Assyria's decline. Late during the reign of Shalmaneser III campaigns were led not only by the king but also by the *turtanu* (biblical Tartan), a high official. In fact, several powerful provincial governments emerged and their leaders acted as virtual monarchs in their own districts, although professing allegiance to the Assyrian crown. The concentration of wealth and power in the hands of a small number of dignitaries appears to have weakened the monarchy, eventually leading to an insurrection, eroding the power of the monarchy. Some Assyrian nobles actually left their own records of campaigns and deeds. This problem continued during the reign of Shalmaneser's successor, Shamshi-Adad IV (ruled 823–810 BCE), who faced a succession struggle that lasted for four years.

The Political Background of the Bible

It is against the background of the Assyrian domination that we can see the local events mentioned in 1–2 Kings (see Na'aman 1999; H. Tadmor 1975). Sometime before the Qarqar campaign, Ben-Hadad invaded Israel and besieged Samaria with "thirty-two kings" (or allies), taking the spoils of Samaria and forcing Ahab to become "his servant" (1 Kings 20:1–4). But Ahab was able to defeat Ben-Hadad soundly at Aphek (20:27–31), forcing the Aramaean king to restore cities that had been annexed from Israel in previous years: "Ben-hadad said to him, 'I will restore the towns that my father took from your father'" (20:34). We are next told that there were three years of peace between Aram Damascus and Israel (22:1). This certainly fits well chronologically during the Assyrian invasion of 853 BCE. Perhaps soon after Qarqar, Ahab (and his Judahite ally Jehoshaphat) attacked Ramoth-gilead, claiming that the men of Aram had not restored the cities and pointing out to his officers, "Do you know that Ramoth-gilead belongs to us, yet we are doing nothing to take it out of the hand of the king of Aram?" (22:3). However, the attempt to restore Ramoth-gilead to the territory of Israel failed, and Ahab met his death in this battle (ca. 852 BCE).

Perhaps the fall of the ruling dynasty in Damascus encouraged Ahab's son Jehoram to repeat his father's unsuccessful efforts to restore Israel's lost territories. He also set out to do battle against Hazael's forces at Ramoth-gilead (2 Kings 8:28–29; 2 Chron. 22:5–6). The Syrian-Israelite alliance was shaken by Jehu's revolt in 842–841 BCE. It appears that Jehu was not satisfied with the mere dissolution of the alliance with Aram Damascus, but went even further and asked for the support of the alliance's enemy, King Shalmaneser of Assyria. Of course, it is also possible that Jehu operated in concert with Hazael of Damascus while presenting tribute to the Assyrian king, but this is not certain. Shalmaneser set up an image of himself on the Mediterranean Sea coast, perhaps implying that he actually led his army into Israel. The book of Hosea perhaps hints at this (Hosea 10:14; this depends upon where the city of Beth-Arbel is located). In light of this, Hazael of Damascus was able to conquer the Israelite Transjordan (2 Kings 10:32–33) and then proceed against Judah, capturing Gath and marching upon Jerusalem, where he received massive tribute.

Summary

Though obviously a major event, the Battle of Qarqar is not hinted at in the Bible. This should come as no surprise, as previously stated, since the battle did not fit the didactic purposes of the writer of Kings. Since the battle did not appear to have a decisive outcome, it did not serve an immediate theological purpose to explain the success (or more likely a failure) of an Israelite or Judahite king. Thus, international affairs are mentioned in Kings only when they made a difference in the nature and status of the Israelite or Judahite monarchy. The writer of Chronicles had perhaps an even a more precise perspective, as the events described therein are related to the temple. Thus, the Chronicler was perhaps even more hesitant than the writer of Kings to discuss international affairs.

36

The Mesha Inscription
and Relations with Moab and Edom

Juan Manuel Tebes

The Mesha Inscription and Its Background

The Mesha Inscription, or Moabite Stone, is an inscribed black basalt stone (a stele) dating to the ninth century BCE and now exhibited in the Musée du Louvre, Paris (fig. 36.1). It was found in 1868 in Dhiban (ancient Dibon), a village located in central Transjordan east of the Dead Sea, an area known in biblical times as the land of Moab. The surviving fragments of the stele, some original and others reconstructed from a squeeze made at the time of the discovery, contain at least thirty-four lines written in Moabite, a language very close to Biblical Hebrew, using the Phoenician alphabetic script. According to the inscription, the stele was commissioned by the Moabite king Mesha (ca. 850 BCE) for the purpose of recording his reign's accomplishments, such as erecting a temple, rebuilding cities, and, most particularly, the defeat of the Israelites occupying part of Moab. As an external witness to the Hebrew Bible, the Mesha Inscription constitutes one of the most important textual sources for studying the history of the ancient Israelite kingdoms and their relationships with their Transjordanian neighbors. It provides the earliest extrabiblical attestation of Yahweh as Israel's god and mentions for the first time the kingdom of Israel's house of Omri and probably Judah's house of David. Also, twelve of the seventeen place-names present in the inscription are also mentioned in the biblical text, which makes it a good source for biblical geography.

The kingdom of Moab was one of the three main polities that existed in Transjordan during the Iron Age, the others being Ammon, to the north in the region of modern Amman, and Edom, to the south. Like most of the small local political entities of this period, Moab did not have fixed boundaries but rather established areas of political hegemony or kinship relationships that fluctuated episodically, sometimes expanding and sometimes contracting. The land upon which Moab could claim supremacy of territory comprised the plateau east of the Dead Sea between the Wadi al-Hasa (the biblical Zered) in the south and the territory north of the Wadi Mujib (the biblical Arnon).

Fig. 36.1. The Mesha Inscription, Musée du Louvre, Paris

The earliest sources that refer to Moab date back to the thirteenth century BCE, when the ancient Egyptians carried out several military campaigns in the region and recorded the name of the land (*mu'a-bu*) and of a few of its settlements, among which was probably Dibon. According to the archaeological evidence, during the eleventh and tenth centuries BCE numerous sites were founded—most of which were clustered along the wadis (dry river beds) that flood to the Dead Sea—either as a result of the immigration of new people or because of local nomadic inhabitants adopting a new, settled way of life (Dearman 1989a, 155; Routledge 2004, 58–113; B. W. Porter 2013, 57–68).

Although we are not completely certain how this society transformed into what is known as the "kingdom" of Moab, during the last decades in scholarship there has been a shift in paradigm toward viewing Moab, and to a large extent all the Iron Age Transjordanian polities, as based on tribal or "segmentary" identities that at certain times coalesced into larger political units. The Mesha Inscription is one of the main sources for recognizing these local identities, as it mentions several territorial units within Moab, forming a clear hierarchy of segments. In the upper level stand larger territorial units denoted with the phrase "land of [location]," such as the "land of ʿAtarot" and the "land of Madaba," while lower-level segments were identified with the expression "men of [location]"—for example, "men of Sharon" and "men of Maharoth" (see Routledge 2004, 133–53). The answers to certain questions are still not clear, such as how many levels of hierarchy existed, whether these segments were blood-related or based only in the territory, and, relatedly, what is the precise relationship between these segments and the idealistic tribe/ clan/family social organization presented in the Hebrew Bible.

The tribal nature of these societies, coupled with the lack of the classical features attributed to ancient states—such as large urban centers, three-tiered settlement patterns, and monumental architecture—and the predominance of nomadic pastoralism as the main economic activity have led some scholars to avoid the use of the term "state" for these polities. Alternative terms such as "tribal kingdom," "segmentary state," and "chiefdom" are nowadays preferred (Routledge 2004; Bienkowski 2009; Tebes 2014).

The Hebrew Bible and the Moabite War

The biblical account of the Moabite War is only one record of a series of conflicts between Israelites, Moabites, and other Transjordanian polities that go back to the times of the exodus. In the story of the exodus, Moab is already presented as a fully formed kingdom: the children of Israel pass through southern Transjordan not engaging with Edom and circumventing Moab (Num. 21:11–24:25; cf. Deut. 2:8b–36). There is a suspicious insistence in noting Moab's northern boundary in the Arnon, north of which lay the territory of King Sihon of the Amorites, conquered militarily by the Israelites. This probably betrays the Israelite claim to the rights of the lands north of the Arnon, which some biblical texts attribute to the tribes of Gad and Reuben. In the Mesha Inscription the area north of the Arnon is precisely the center of Mesha's operations. The book of Judges recounts how the Moabite king Eglon subdued Israel for eighteen years before being murdered by Ehud (Judg. 3:12–30). It was King David who finally defeated the Moabites and subjected them to tribute (2 Sam. 8:2).

But this situation did not last long. Second Kings 3:4–27 records the rebellion of Moab against the northern kingdom of Israel: "Now King Mesha of Moab was a sheep breeder, who used to deliver to the king of Israel one hundred thousand lambs, and the wool of one hundred thousand rams. But when Ahab died, the king of Moab rebelled against the king of Israel" (vv. 4–5). King Jehoram of Israel (Ahab's son), allied with King Jehoshaphat of Judah and an unnamed king of Edom, attacked Moab in its southern flank by entering "by the way of the wilderness of Edom" (v. 8). But after seven days in the desert, the army was short of water, so Jehoshaphat decided to ask the prophet Elisha, who was in the area, for help. The prophet, showing only scorn to Jehoram but respecting the king of Judah, transmitted Yahweh's order that they should dig ditches because the valley would be full of water with no wind and no rain, and also predicted that Yahweh would put Moab under their power. The next morning, "water began to flow from the direction of Edom" and the valley was flooded with water (vv. 16–20). The Moabites, viewing the water as red as blood and believing that the kings

were fighting one another, rapidly approached the camp only to be defeated by the coalition army. After destroying towns, ruining fields, blocking water holes, and cutting down trees, the three kings finally besieged Mesha at his capital, Kir Hareseth. The story ends abruptly recounting how a desperate Mesha offered in sacrifice his firstborn son on the city wall, an action after which "great wrath came upon Israel" (v. 27) and they abandoned the siege and left for their homeland.

As can be easily perceived, this chapter in 2 Kings has many problems of interpretation, most of which revolve around the discrepancy with the events and chronology as recorded on the Mesha Inscription (see J. M. Miller 1989, 34–40; Dearman 1989a, 197–201; P. Stern 1993). Events: while the biblical account paints a picture of the march of an undefeated Israelite-Judaean-Edomite army until they retreat without losses, the war in the Mesha Inscription is one of a series of undisputed Moabite victories against Israel. Chronology: in 2 Kings 3 Moab's revolt occurs *after* Ahab's death; in the inscription Mesha rebels *during* Omri's son's (Ahab's) reign. Geography: the three kings invade Moab from the south via Edom, whereas in the inscription the core of Mesha's activities occurs north of the Wadi Mujib. Another problem is the identification of Mesha's capital as Kir Hareseth, traditionally identified as Kerak because of the similarity of names and its localization in southern Moab, thus fitting the geography of 2 Kings 3. However, in the Mesha Inscription Mesha's capital is clearly Dibon in northern Moab. Characters: none of the three allied kings nor Elisha is referred to by name in the inscription.

In fact, in regard to the third player in the anti-Moabite coalition, not only is the anonymous king of Edom a shadowy figure in the biblical narrative but also his mention contradicts the statement in 1 Kings 22:47 that during Jehoshaphat's reign "there was no king in Edom; a deputy was king." The land of Edom was the southernmost and most arid of the territories of Iron Age Transjordan, and the local inhabitants resorted to nomadic pastoralism as their main economic activity. During the Late Bronze Age the area probably was occupied by nomadic tribes known as "Shasu" in contemporary Egyptian sources. During the tenth and ninth centuries BCE the earliest sedentary settlements were established in the rich copper-mining lowland area of Wadi Faynan, forming a short-lived chiefdom that lasted until the end of the ninth century BCE (Tebes 2014, 7–10). If one takes the narrative of 2 Kings 3 at face value, the Edomite king could be just a local chief of this desert polity or the "deputy" appointed by the Israelites in Edom. But it could also be a product of a later interpolation, when the "classical" kingdom of Edom was flourishing.

Predictably, the prophet Elisha's intervention goes unnoticed in the Mesha Inscription, while his miracle and (unfulfilled?) prophecy follow the usual lines of the relationship between prophets and monarchs in the biblical narrative. Last but not least, mention should be made of the unexpected conclusion after Mesha's sacrifice of his own son. Although the reason for the allied army's flight is not altogether clear, it seems clear that the writer(s) was (were) aware of the significance of the child-sacrifice. This would be a rare case of recognition in the Bible of other people's god's effectiveness in their own homeland, a view that is common in the religious world of the ancient Near East (Mattingly 1989, 230).

Mesha's Account: War with Israel and Moabite Society

The Mesha Inscription is a memorial inscription intended to celebrate King Mesha's main accomplishments, and we can conjecture that it probably was displayed in a temple. As such, it shares many features with contemporary inscriptions of the same genre, such as the king's

constant self-reference demonstrated in the use of the first person, a summary of his achievements, the role of the homeland's god, the use of hyperbolic language, and the strong sentiment of identity. The inscription's main theme is the "holy war" against the Israelites and their god, Yahweh, and as such it follows the usual lines of "holy war" texts that are customary in ancient Near Eastern royal inscriptions and in the Hebrew Bible: angry deity and consequent punishment, divine command, divine intervention, ritual consecration to deity (*herem*), victory of our god against yours, and construction of a temple. It has long been debated whether the inscription recounts, in line with 2 Kings 3:4–27, only one conflict in a restricted period of time or a series of military campaigns over a period of several years. It was typical for ancient Near Eastern kings to record their building activities, and Mesha is no exception to the rule. He concentrated special efforts in Qarhoh, where he built or rebuilt walls, gates, towers, a palace, and a reservoir.

The content of the inscription can be roughly divided into five main parts (following Routledge 2004, 142):

1. Introduction: Mesha and Moab (lines 1–4)
2. Campaigns in northern Moab (lines 5–21a)
3. Kingly construction in northern Moab (lines 21b–31a)
4. Campaigns in southern Moab (lines 31b–34)
5. Kingly construction in southern Moab (lines 34–broken) (missing)

"I am Mesha' son of Kmsh[yt], king of Moab, the Dibonite" (line 1).[1] Echoing analogous

1. I follow the translation of Jackson 1989. Many other translations exist of the inscription including Pritchard 1969a, 320–21; Routledge 2004, 135–36. For the transcription, see *KAI* 181. The most extensive study is still Dearman 1989b.

memorial inscriptions, the inscription starts by indicating the king's name, his father's name, and his place of origin. His father is traditionally identified as Kemoshyat, a name also known from a short inscription found at Kerak that probably should also be ascribed to Mesha. Given its central role in the inscription, Dibon was most likely the capital of Mesha's kingdom, if not his (and his father's) homeland. This can be ascertained from several biblical verses that clearly associate Dibon with Moab (Num. 21:30; Isa. 15:2; Jer. 48:18, 22), but also from verses describing the land allotted to the tribe of Reuben or Gad (Num. 32:3, 34; 33:45–46; Josh. 13:17). The remains of ancient Dibon probably are located in the modern village of Dhiban (Dearman 1989a, 171–74), where archaeological excavations in the 1950–60s and in the 2000s unearthed remains of a town dated to the ninth century BCE with a palace, a wall, and a gate (Routledge 2004, 162–68).

The stele most likely was made to be displayed in a temple, the "high place" (*bmt*) of the god Kemosh in Qarhoh (line 3). The reference to Qarhoh is still enigmatic, although it has been suggested that it refers to the royal quarter of Dibon or, based on the similarity of the name, modern Kerak, identified by some scholars as the Kir Hareseth of 2 Kings 3:25.

Apparently, Mesha's radius of operation was circumscribed to the area north of the Wadi al Mujib (the biblical Arnon, e.g., Num. 21:13; Isa. 16:2; also mentioned in the inscription's line 26), which is the region where Dibon was located and where most of his military and building activities occurred. It is noteworthy that Mesha portrays himself as a "Dibonite" and not as a "Moabite," while similar references to local identities inside Moab proliferate in the text. Although Mesha apparently intended to transcend those identities through allusion to a larger pan-Moabite polity, the tribal system continued to be the central framework of the central Transjordanian identities (Routledge 2004, 114–32).

It has been suggested that in Mesha's time Dibon was the name of Mesha's tribe, the leading tribe in the Moabite confederation, while the "seat" of the Dibonite tribe was known as Qarhoh, modern Dhiban. Sometime after Mesha's death the name of the tribe was transferred to Qarqoh, and the Moabite capital began to be known as Dibon. If this identification is correct, then a major riddle is solved. In the biblical account of Mesha's war, the name of the Moabite capital is Kir Hasereth, not Dibon. Kir Hasereth would then be Qarhoh, the old name of Dibon, an identification that would fit well on philological and historical grounds (van der Steen and Smelik 2007).

Line 5 reads, "Omri was king of Israel, and he oppressed Moab for many days because Kemosh was angry with his country." This is the earliest extrabiblical attestation to the northern kingdom of Israel as a political entity. Although Omri, king of Israel (885–874 BCE) after several years of internal strife, was not the founder of this kingdom and he and his dynasty were seen by the biblical writers in a very negative light, he certainly was one of Israel's most important monarchs, establishing a four-reign dynasty and building a new capital at Samaria (1 Kings 16:16–28). In fact, five Neo-Assyrian inscriptions refer to the kingdom of Israel as the "land of Omri" (*Māt Ḫumrî*) or "the house of Omri" (*Bīt Ḫumrî*).[2]

The inscription continues by recounting that Omri was succeeded by "his son, and he also said, 'I will oppress Moab'" (line 6). Omri's son was Ahab (874–853 BCE) (1 Kings 16:29–22:40), known in the Neo-Assyrian sources as one of the Levantine kings who fought against Shalmaneser III in the Battle of Qarqar (853 BCE) (Pritchard 1969a, 278–79). But Mesha "prevailed over him and over his house, and Israel utterly perished forever" (line 7).

2. See, for example, the Black Obelisk of Shalmaneser III (*COS* 2:269–70).

According to the inscription, Omri had taken the land of Madaba (modern Medeba) and "he lived in it during his days and half of the days of his son(s)-forty years; but Kemosh returned it in my days" (lines 7–8). The inscription is pointing to an unnamed successor of Omri, but there is a difficulty here because *bnh* can be read as either "his son" or "his sons," so it can be referring to Ahab or to his successors and sons Ahaziah (853–852 BCE) and Jehoram (852–841 BCE) (1 Kings 22:51–2 Kings 1:18; 2 Kings 3; 9:14–24). Although potentially useful, the reference to "forty years" can be a figurative number, something like "many years."

Although the stele is badly preserved, the important historical connotations of the Mesha Inscription for the history of the ancient Israelites are amplified by new readings of the fourth section, of which survives only an allusion to events taking place in Horonen (biblical Horonaim [Isa. 15:5; Jer. 48:3, 5, 34]) in southern Moab. In 1994 epigraphist André Lemaire proposed to restore in line 31 the word *btdwd*, thus reading the phrase as "and the [house of Dav]id dwelt in Horonen" (Lemaire 1994). If this reading is correct, which is not certain, then it is one of the earliest extrabiblical attestations to the name by which the kingdom of Judah was probably known, paralleled by the reference to *bytdwd*, read by most scholars as "house of David," in the contemporary Aramaic stele of Tel Dan discovered in 1993. However, there are some historical and philological problems with this reading. Not only had no king of Judah ever "dwelt" in Horonen, but in Jerusalem; further, he is identified not by his name but by a collective designation. There is the additional fact that we would expect to read the justification for the conquest of southern Moab, as in the case of the war against Omri, in the first part of the inscription (Na'aman 1997b, 89).

The Mesha Inscription contains several place-names that are paralleled in the Bible. While some texts—mostly of poetic or pro-

phetic nature—attribute these sites to the Moabites, other texts dealing with the distribution of territory taken from the Amorite king Sihon assign them to the Israelite tribes Reuben and Gad. Sites that can be identified reasonably well include Madaba/Medeba (Num. 21:30; Josh. 13:9, 16; Isa. 15:2), 'Ataroth/Ataroth (Num. 32:3, 34; Josh. 16:2, 7), Nebo (Num. 32:38; Deut. 32:49; 34:1; Isa. 15:2; Jer. 48:1, 22), and Jahaz (Isa. 15:4; Jer. 48:21, 34//Josh. 13:18) (see Dearman 1989a, 170–96; B. MacDonald 2000, 101–55).

Mesha turned his attention toward the land of 'Ataroth (modern Khirbat Ataruz), where "the Gadites had lived . . . forever, and the king of Israel had rebuilt 'Ataroth for himself" (lines 10–11). The allusion to the Gadites is clearly reminiscent of Gad, one of the twelve tribes of Israel, but whose references in the biblical text are in short supply. However, here the Gadites seem to have a distant, if any, relationship with the Israelites; in fact, they are said to have lived there "forever." This reference does not necessarily contradict the biblical account, because we know that in ancient societies genealogical links were fluid and in constant change owing to diverse social, political, and geographical reasons. It is obvious that this was a frontier zone with borders and alliances of political and kinship nature in constant flux. The Gadites could have had shifting loyalties between Israel and Moab, while the biblical author(s) could have incorporated them into their own genealogies, as well, in order to reaffirm the Israelite claims to the lands east of the Jordan.

Lines 12–13 contain one of the most troublesome readings of the stele. After taking the city of 'Ataroth and killing its entire population, Mesha "brought back from there the *'r'l dwdh* and [dr]agged it before Kemosh in Qiryat." That some sort of cultic equipment is meant here is clear because in lines 17–18 we have a parallel allusion to the "[ves]sels of Yahweh" that Mesha dragged before Kemosh. What does *'r'l dwdh* mean? Following some biblical verses, translators usually translate the word ʾrʾl as "altar hearth," well within the lines of the implied cultic connotation (Jackson 1989, 112–13). As for *dwdh*, some have suggested it is a reference to a certain god "Dod," or, if we follow its meaning in Biblical Hebrew ("beloved"), it could have been used as an epithet for Yahweh (Barstad 1995, 493–94). It may also represent the name "David," as was proposed for line 31, but *dwdh* carries a final possessive *h*. Personal names in Hebrew usually do not carry possessive endings, so either *dwd* does not mean "David" and is something else (Philip Davies 2008, 97), or the possessive *h* is intended for the preceding word, ʾrʾl, the entire phrase thus being translated as "its Davidic altar hearth" (Rainey 2001a, 300).

Two more towns were taken by Mesha from Israel: Nebo (Khirbet al Muḥaiyat?) and Jahaz (lines 14–21a). Lines 17–18 narrate that, after taking the city of Nebo and devoting its inhabitants to Kemosh, Mesha "took from there th[e ves]sels of Yahweh (ʾ[t k]ly yhwh) and dragged them before Kemosh." This is almost unmistakably the earliest reference to the name "Yahweh" as a deity outside the Hebrew Bible.[3] This allusion is usually seen as Moabite

recognition of Yahweh as "the official god of the Israelites" (van der Toorn 1995b, 1713), and although the text seems to imply a high status of Yahweh in the Israelite cult, this does not necessarily mean that Yahweh was the only deity worshiped at that time in Israel.

What about the god Kemosh? Kemosh was the national deity of Moab, or at least of Moab's reigning dynasties, and as such is present as a theophoric element in the name "Kemoshyat" and in other Moabite kings' names known from Neo-Assyrian sources. Little is known about Kemosh and his characteristics. He was already known in Ebla and Ugarit, while he is referred to in a few biblical passages with the usual diatribes against foreign gods (Mattingly 1989; Müller 1995). Although he is clearly identified as Moab's god (Num. 21:29; Jer. 48:7, 13, 46; see Judg. 11:24 for his incorrect attribution to the Ammonites), the cult of "Kemosh, the abomination of Moab" was introduced in Israel by Solomon (1 Kings 11:7 [NRSV: "Chemosh"]) and terminated by Josiah (2 Kings 23:13).

In sum, despite the many problems in translation and interpretation, the Mesha Inscription is still a gold mine of information about the history of Israel and its Transjordanian neighbors. New, innovative approaches drawing from anthropology and ethnography are certainly helping to place this inscription within the larger tribal framework of Iron Age Moab.

---

3. Earlier possible references to Yahweh appear in Egyptian inscriptions dating to the fourteenth and thirteenth centuries BCE (van der Toorn 1995b, 1714), but these are most likely toponym or tribal names in Edom and Midian, probably related to the deity's name but not direct references to him.

37

The Tel Dan Inscription and the Deaths of Joram of Israel and Ahaziah of Judah

K. Lawson Younger Jr.

New discoveries of ancient texts play important roles in the ongoing work of historical reconstruction of the histories of ancient Israel and Judah. In concert with the biblical material, each of these new texts can clarify certain things, cloud others, or contradict the biblical texts (i.e., offer a very different account of the past).[1] Furthermore, when these inscriptions are fragmentary—as often is the case with West Semitic inscriptions—they present their own special challenges, which can, in turn, complicate the reconstruction.

The discovery of the Tel Dan Inscription is a good example of this. It is comprised of three fragments, uncovered in excavations at the site of Tel Dan, although in secondary use (Biran and Naveh 1993; 1995). It is clearly a royal inscription written in Aramaic. But since the opening lines of the text are lost,[2] the name of the author of the inscription is not preserved. Additionally, the names of the kings of the other entities mentioned in the inscription, Israel and Judah, are not fully preserved. Nevertheless, the king of Israel's name ends with the letters *rm*, and this can only refer to [*yw*]*rm*, "[Jo]ram" (i.e., Jehoram), the son of Ahab, since he is the only king of Israel whose name ends thus.[3] The king of Judah (in the inscription referenced as "Bēt-David"), whose name ends with the letters *yhw*, must refer to [*'ḥz*]*yhw*, "[Ahaz]iah." Thus, on the basis of these assuredly reconstructed names, it can be deduced that Hazael, the king of Aram Damascus, is the most likely author of the inscription. These three individuals are, of course, known from the Hebrew Bible.

---

1. For example, the different main thrust of Sennacherib's account of his 701 invasion of Judah and the biblical accounts in 2 Kings 18–19; Isa. 36–37; 2 Chron. 32. Each account is tied to its ideological perspective. For discussion, see Younger 2003, 245–63.

2. While different arrangements of the fragments have been proposed (Galil 2001; Athas 2003, 178–89), these have not been accepted (see Hafþórsson 2006, 49–65; Ghantous 2013, 43; see the recent comments of Blum 2016, 37–38).

3. Biran and Naveh 1995, 9; Schniedewind 1996, 80.

To facilitate further discussion, the translation of the Tel Dan inscription is given.[4]

> [*Some lines are missing at the beginning*]
> [1][s]aid [ ]
> and cut [ ]
> [2][ ]*l* my father;
> he went up [against him when] he fought at Ab[el?].[5]
> [3]And my father lay down;
> he went to his [fathe]rs.
>
> Now the king of I[s][4]rael earlier invaded the land of my "father";
> [but] Hadad made me, [5]myself, [4]king.
> [5]And Hadad went before me;
> [and] I departed from seven [ ] [6]of my kingdom/kings.
> And I killed [power]ful ki[ng]s, who harnessed thou[sands of ch]ari[7]ots and thousands of horsemen;
> and [I killed Jo]ram, son of [Ahab], [8] king of Israel.
> And [I] killed [Ahaz]yahu, son of [Joram];
> [and I overthr][9]ew Bēt-David (Judah).
>
> And I set [ ]
> [10] their land [ ]
> [11] another and [ ]
> [and Jehu, son of Nimshi] [12]ruled over Is[rael]
> [And I] [13]besieged [ ]

There are numerous problems and issues in the text, and it is impossible to address them all

here. Only a few select ones can be discussed for the purpose of this chapter.

Who Was Hazael's Father?

The most obvious question is the identity of the person whom Hazael is referencing as his father (*'by*). The Assyrian and biblical texts declare that Hazael was a usurper. But if Hazael was a usurper on the throne of Damascus, and if he was the author of the Tel Dan Stele, why does he talk about his "father" at the beginning of the inscription (*'by* is used three times in lines 2, 3, and 4)?

Some scholars have suggested that this brings into question the biblical and Assyrian assertions that Hazael was a usurper (Dion 1999, 153–54; 1997, 192–94).[6] However, methodologically, such an approach is problematic. It uses the fragmentary and difficult passages in the Tel Dan Stele to evaluate passages from two different sources that are much clearer. From a hermeneutical and historiographic standpoint, it is far sounder to reconstruct the historical events based on the clear claims preserved in multiple different sources from different parts of the ancient Near East than to reconstruct the historical events on the basis of an interpretation of a fragmentary inscription (an interpretation that may or may not be correct) and then make the multiple sources fit that reconstruction.[7]

---

4. For a full discussion of the numerous textual and interpretive matters, see Younger 2016, 593–613.

5. For discussion of the restoration, see Younger 2016, 594n172. Erhard Blum (2016, 41–42) proposes a restoration of *shin* and *resh* after the *aleph*, yielding *'šr* = Aššur (Assyria). In addition, he suggests a restoration of the sentence as ". . . my father was injured when he fought against Assyria" (either *'by ysq[b . . . b ']tlḥmh b 'šr* or *ysq[b 'by b ']tlḥmh b 'šr*), although he admits that "my father went up to fight against Assyria" (*'by ysq[. . . l ']tlḥmh b 'šr* or *ysq['by l ']tlḥmh b 'šr*) would also be possible. However, in the photographs, the bottom of the tail of the final preserved letter in line 2 does not appear to have the left upward turn necessary for a *shin*.

6. See 2 Kings 8:7–15 and Shalmaneser III's Assur Basalt Statue, which states, "Hadad-ezer (Adad-idri) passed away. Hazael, son of a nobody (DUMU *la ma-ma-na*), took the throne. He mustered his numerous troops; (and) he moved against me to do war and battle. I fought with him. I decisively defeated him. I took away from him his walled camp. In order to save his life he ran away. I pursued (him) as far as Damascus, his royal city. I cut down his orchards" (Royal Inscriptions of Mesopotamia, Assyrian Periods 3:118, A.0.102.40, i.25–ii.6). The phrase "son of a nobody" (*mār lā mammāna*) refers to a usurper or upstart. This strongly suggests that Hazael was not first in the line of succession and had seized the throne in an unusual manner. See Yamada 2000, 189; Younger 2005, 245–57; Stith 2008, 51–53; Niehr 2011, 340; Blum 2016, 45.

7. Younger 2016, 598–99.

There are a number of possible ways that the Tel Dan Inscription could be using 'by.[8] The inscription might be using it (1) figuratively or (2) literally. If it is literal, there are three possibilities: (2a) it could refer to Hadad-ezer himself (i.e., the Aramaean king known to have preceded Hazael); (2b1) it could refer to a different father who was part of the royal family; or (2b2) it could refer to a different father who was not part of the royal family but leader of another tribe. Each of these will be discussed in more detail.

(1) If the term 'by is figurative, then Hazael is referring not to his literal "father" but rather to the previous ruler (most likely Hadad-ezer) as "father" in order to establish his legitimacy. André Lemaire (1998, 6) suggests that in calling Hadad-ezer (Assyrian: Adad-idri) his "father," Hazael was following an ancient Near Eastern historiographic tradition: kings of a new dynasty might refer to the previous king as "father." Thus, Lemaire concludes, "One should not be surprised that Hazael, whose father is not known, could call Hadad-ezer: 'my father.' It was a traditional way to present oneself as a legitimate successor."[9]

(2a) This interpretation sees 'by ("my father") as literal: Hazael was a biological son of the previous king (Hadad-ezer), but he was not the first in line for succession, or perhaps he was a younger brother or illegitimate half brother. Possibly the legitimate heir was sickly, and this provided the basis for the 2 Kings 8 tradition. Wayne Pitard (1987, 133) suggested that the Ben-Hadad (Bar-Hadad) of 2 Kings 8 may have been a son of Hadad-ezer whom Hazael murdered.[10] However, this remains as specula-

tive as when it was first proposed, even since the Tel Dan Inscription's discovery.[11] Nevertheless, it is possible to understand Hazael as a minor son of Hadadezer who assassinated his father and eliminated his rival siblings.[12]

(2b1) This view also sees 'by as literal: it is a reference to Hazael's father, who was not Hadad-ezer but belonged to a subsidiary royal branch (Yamada 2000, 312; Na'aman 2002, 207). In this view, Hazael was the assassin of the legitimate heir but could refer to himself as a true son in "a broad sense" (Yamada 2000, 312).

(2b2) The term 'by is used literally as a reference to Hazael's actual father, who was not a member of the dynasty of Hadad-ezer of Aram Damascus but was the leader of an Aramaean tribe during the time of Hadad-ezer (Suriano 2007, 165), an important Aramaean sheikh (Niehr 2011, 341). H. Ghantous (2013, 51, 60, 111, 136) has suggested that Hazael was the son of the king of the Aramaean kingdom of Bēt-Reḥob who succeeded his father on the throne of that kingdom and then was successful in becoming king of Aram Damascus by uniting the two kingdoms to create a greater Aramaean kingdom of Damascus.[13]

---

for the confusion that led to the insertion of the later Ben-Hadad stories in their present context. In my opinion, both options manifest methodological weaknesses, having to rely on the historian's intuition to discern "additions" to various texts and to speculate about them, when there is no actual textual evidence in any of these passages that relates to this question.

11. It also appears to be contradicted by Shalmaneser III's text quoted above in note 6 (the Assur Basalt Statue), which has a succession of Hadad-ezer (Adad-idri) to Hazael, without a Bar-Hadad.

12. In other words, similar to the apparent intentions of Esarhaddon's brothers in the murder of Sennacherib, though thwarted by Esarhaddon. See Andrew Knapp 2015, 301–35.

13. This is too speculative, in my opinion. Ghantous bases this on Na'aman's (1995, 386) understanding of Shalmaneser III's Kurkh Monolith in ii.95: ᵐba-'a-sa DUMU ru-ḫu-bi KUR a-ma-na-a-a; "Ba'asa of Beth-Rehob and of Mount Amana (the Ammanite)." This is a doubtful interpretation. But Ghantous then couples it with his assumption that Hazael is the son of this Ba'asa, for which there is no actual evidence.

---

8. The following discussion is based on Younger 2016, 601–6.

9. For further discussion, see Younger 2016, 600–601.

10. Following the earlier suggestion of Jepsen 1941–44, 158–59. While some scholars have argued that the name "Ben-Hadad" has been added to the story in 2 Kings 8:7–15 (e.g., Lipiński 2000, 373; 1969, 172–73; Noth 1960, 245n1), Pitard 1987, 134, emphasizes that this is not necessarily correct, since the name may have originally appeared in the story and have been partially responsible

To a certain extent, each of these options is possible. At this point, pivotal to the understanding of the use of *'by* in the Tel Dan Stele is a recognition of the inscription's use of the genre of apology (cogently argued by Suriano 2007; Andrew Knapp 2012, 223; 2015, 277–300). It is manifest that Hazael was in all respects not the expected successor. Therefore, the repeated references to "my father," whether literal or not, clearly result from a need to convince the audience that his kingship is legitimate.

Of course, the Tel Dan Inscription may be using the term *'by* figuratively as suggested by Lemaire; at the same time, the actual literal father of Hazael may have been an Aramaean tribal leader. The only thing that is actually known—and this is from 2 Kings 8—is that Hazael was in the service of the previous king (named Ben-Hadad[14] according to the biblical narrative). On the other hand, the fact that Aram Damascus will be designated in the Assyrian inscriptions after the death of Hazael as Bīt-Ḫaza'ili may well indicate that they considered Damascus an entity based on a tribal system.[15] If correct, Matthew Suriano's remarks are very germane: "The fluidity of seminomadic tribal elements within a patrimonial society fits well with the aggressive and mobile character of Hazael, who may have conquered various tribal groups before he eventually seized control of Aram-Damascus" (Suriano 2007, 174). So Hazael was in the service of the previous king, but, being from another tribal entity within the Damascene tribal network, he seized upon his opportunity.

If the Tel Dan Inscription manifests the rhetoric of an apology (Suriano 2007), then the use of the term *'by* must be an important element in a planned rhetorical strategy (Andrew Knapp 2012, 223–33; 2015, 290–93).

14. "Ben-Hadad" (Aramaic "Bar-Hadad") may be a royal title or epithet (see Younger 2016, 583–91).

15. See Postgate 1974, 234; Younger 2016, 43.

Therefore, it should be treated accordingly. It explains the rather odd way that Hazael narrates his succession in the stele:

> [3]And my father lay down;
> he went to his [fathe]rs.
>
> Now the king of I[s][4]rael earlier invaded the land of my father;
> [but] Hadad made me, [5]myself, [4]king.

If Hazael had been the legitimate successor, one would have expected immediately following the statement about his father's death a statement of his enthronement, just as one sees, for example, in the Mesha Stela and the Bar-Rakib Inscription.[16] In other words, there is no natural succession here.[17] Instead, there are statements about the Israelite invasion and the emphatic attribution of the work of the god Hadad in making Hazael king. The parallel way in which the usurper Zakkur credited the god Ba'lšamayn with having made him king (*whmlkny . b'lšm[yn . 'l / b][4][ḫ]z⌈r⌉k*)[18] demonstrates that Hazael's words are functioning apologetically. In this case, an assertion that there was a military crisis and that in such a crisis the chief deity of the nation himself raised Hazael to the throne makes perfect sense.[19] Hazael forcefully claims that the god Hadad utilized a special divine election of him as king. Thus, who can debate such a selection by divinity? Furthermore, Hazael asserts that this divine support is validated through

16. See *KAI* 181, lines 2–3; *KAI* 216, lines 4–7.

17. Some might object based on the clauses in line 3, "And my father lay down; he went to his [fathe]rs," assuming that such wording automatically implies a natural death. However, this is not the case. In the Hebrew Bible, "the phrase relates to inheritance, specifically succession rights" and "signified dynastic integrity" (Suriano 2010, 42). See further Suriano 2010, 32–50, 71–72; 2007, 164–66.

18. *KAI* 202, lines 3b–4a.

19. Dion 1999, 154. If this is sequential (the father dies, the invasion happens), the question should be asked: If one wanted to say "my predecessor died, and the king of Israel invaded the land of my predecessor . . . ," how would you say it? Especially if one was a usurper attempting to legitimate oneself?

his ensuing achievements in battle. Hazael relates that "Hadad went before me" into battle (line 5), and the justice of his cause is further highlighted by the contrast of his rise with the demise of Joram and Ahaziah. In sum, Hazael uses the term *'by* in the inscription to reference his royal predecessor as part of his claim to legitimacy as king of Aram Damascus.

Who Killed Joram and Ahaziah?

The final problem in the Tel Dan Inscription to be discussed here is the contradiction between Hazael's claim to have killed "[Jo]ram, son of [Ahab], king of Israel," and "[Ahaz]iah, son of [Joram],"[20] king of Judah, and the assertion in 2 Kings 9:14–28 that Jehu killed both kings on the same day. Once again, the fragmentary nature of the inscription means that caution is essential. Some scholars have argued for the historical reliability of the inscription's report over against the pro-Jehu account in 2 Kings 9.[21] Thus, a fragmentary and very difficult to interpret text is declared historically more reliable than the biblical text.[22] Both texts (Tel Dan and 2 Kings 9) are ideological and require close critical reading. One text should not a priori be deemed historically more reliable than the other.

Other scholars have explained this by noting the similarity to the claims made by various kings of the ancient Near East to involvement in regime changes in their enemies' kingdoms.[23] In this case, it is probable that Hazael and Jehu conspired together. Since Hazael was the superior partner, he could claim that he "killed" the two kings because Jehu, who actually carried out the "killings," was acting as his agent.[24] Thus, this claim is another component of Hazael's apology.

Interestingly, then, the answer to the question "Who killed the two kings?"—as it appears that the ancients would have perceived it—is not Hazael versus Jehu, but Hadad versus Yahweh. Hazael is unquestionably claiming divine empowerment from Hadad himself in his slaying of the two kings. This is in total concert with the theology and royal ideology found in his other inscriptions.[25]

Yet, the biblical text in 2 Kings 8:7–15 credits Yahweh with predicting Hazael's ascension to the throne, thus trumping any claim that Hadad put Hazael there. In addition, the later text of 2 Chronicles 22:1–9 contains a variant Yahwistic tradition of the death of Ahaziah, crediting God specifically in his death (see esp. v. 7a). Just as Yahweh was credited directly in bringing about the death of Joram of Israel through the anointing of Jehu (with the coincidental killing of Ahaziah), so he is credited by the Chronicler directly with "the downfall" of Ahaziah (yielding a corresponding narrative to 2 Kings 9).[26] Regardless of the historicity of the details and their dates of composition,[27] these passages reflect "a tradition that

---

20. Once again, due to the fragmentary nature of the Tel Dan Inscription in lines 7–9, the text must be restored. The various proposals cannot be rehearsed again here. For discussion, see Younger 2016, 606–12.

21. For example, Na'aman 1999, 10–11; Irvine 2001.

22. Recently, Blum has assessed the evidence this way: "Apparently, the royal chronicles were used also by the author of the Jehu narrative in 2 Kings 9–10 (cf. 9:15a, 16b) which reports the killing of Joram son of Ahab and Ahaziah son of Jehoram by Jehu in contradiction to Hazael's claim. For several reasons, it is the Jehu-narrative which seems more reliable in this respect, although it was composed later than the Tel Dan Stele, probably in the first half of the 8th century BCE" (2016, 47). For dating the pre-Deuteronomistic material about Jehu's revolt to the reign of Jeroboam II as a legitimation of the Jehuite dynasty, see S. Otto 2001, 97–104.

23. For example, see Lemaire 1998, 10–11; Schniedewind 1996; Younger 2016, 610–13.

24. Schniedewind 1996, 84–85; Stith 2008, 90–99; Andrew Knapp 2015, 287n35.

25. See Hazael's booty inscriptions (Younger 2005, 257–61).

26. Jehu's treatment of Ahaziah in 2 Chron. 22:9a is in contrast to Ahab's treatment of Ben-Hadad in 1 Kings 20:30b–34. The term תְּבוּסָה "downfall" (see *HALOT*, 1680–81) in 2 Chron. 22:7a is a *hapax legomenon*. Intriguingly, the Peshitta has *həpīktā*, "the destruction/ruin/overthrow of (Ahaziah)" (from the root *hpk*).

27. For different opinions on pre-Deuteronomistic or post-Deuteronomistic composition, see, respectively, Schniedewind 1996, 84; S. McKenzie 1991, 81–100.

considered the Hazael and Jehu revolts as parts of one overarching whole" (Andrew Knapp 2015, 280). Therefore, it seems that there was some type of political interlinkage to the events in Aram Damascus, Israel, and Judah.

Conclusion

This short chapter has attempted to demonstrate how ancient Near Eastern royal inscriptions present new data that stimulate new reconstructions of the events. The ancient Near Eastern and biblical texts demonstrate their religious and ideological originations, which must be brought into consideration by the modern historian. Although these texts often pose challenges for the interpreter, with the hard work of interpretation they ultimately yield improved historical accounts that benefit the modern reader.

38

Sennacherib's Invasion of Judah and Neo-Assyrian Expansion

KYLE H. KEIMER

Introduction

In 701 BCE Sennacherib (704–681 BCE), king of Assyria, campaigned against rebellious vassals in Phoenicia, Philistia, and Judah. The most organized and staunch of the rebellious polities was the kingdom of Judah. This Levantine campaign was Sennacherib's third. He had already put down rebellions in Babylon and Elam (first campaign) and in the Zagros Mountains (second campaign).

Many specific details of Sennacherib's third campaign are preserved in Assyrian and biblical sources, but unfortunately these sources do not provide the entire picture. Archaeological remains and artistic sources help us to more fully understand the course of the campaign, its outcome, and even the local preparations in Judah for Assyrian aggression in the region. Sennacherib's campaign, and Assyrian imperialism in general, influenced biblical authors and had major impacts on Israelite religion and self-perceptions.

Sennacherib's Invasion of Judah

Sennacherib's third campaign has been the source of much debate (see the articles and summary in Grabbe 2003). Questions about the specific sequence of events within the campaign to the nature and interpretation of the biblical and Neo-Assyrian sources abound, and no scholarly consensus has been reached for these issues. Despite differing interpretations, the general progression of Sennacherib's campaign can be reconstructed as follows. The Assyrian army crossed the Euphrates River and began a systematic (re-)subjugation of Phoenician cities throughout the Levant. Some cities, such as Arwad, Byblos, and Samsimuruna, submitted and offered tribute upon the Assyrian army's arrival, but others, such as Sidon (Great and Lesser Sidon) and the cities under its authority—Bit-Zitti, Sarepta, Mahalliba, Ushu, Akzib, Acco, and other unnamed fortified cities and fortresses—required more punitive action. Luli, the king of Sidon, was deposed, and Sennacherib installed a pro-Assyrian king, Tu-Ba'lu, in his stead.

Additional local rulers quickly submitted and sent tribute: Mitinti of Ashdod, Budi-il of Bit-Ammon, Kammusu-nadbi of Moab, and Aya-ramu of Edom. Tsidqa, the king of Ashkelon, resisted Sennacherib, requiring the Assyrians to "surround, conquer, and plunder" (Grayson and Novotny 2012, 64) not only Ashkelon but also other cities that were under Tsidqa's control: Bit-Daganna, Joppa, Banay-abaraq, and Azuru. Upon Tsidqa's defeat, he and his royal family were deported and the son of the former pro-Assyrian king was placed on the throne. The specific sequence and military actions taken against Tsidqa's cities are unclear due to the formulaic language of the Assyrian inscriptions.

Sennacherib's annals relate that he next turned against the nobles and citizens of Ekron, who not only had deposed their king, Padi, sending him to Hezekiah of Judah but also had called upon the Egyptians and Nubians for help. In the only clear open-field battle of the campaign, the Assyrians engaged and defeated the alliance of Egyptians and Nubians on the plain of Eltekeh before surrounding, conquering, and plundering the city of Eltekeh itself along with the nearby site of Timna. Ekron was captured and its leaders impaled around the city as retribution. Sennacherib reinstated Padi, though this specific action likely happened after Sennacherib's subsequent conquest of Judahite territory in the Shephelah.

The last rebellious leader, and the one who receives the longest description in Sennacherib's inscriptions, is Hezekiah of Judah. Sennacherib's annals state that he surrounded and conquered forty-six of Hezekiah's fortified walled cities and innumerable smaller settlements by means of "ramps trodden down and battering rams brought up, the assault of foot soldiers, sapping, breaching, and siege engines" (Grayson and Novotny 2012, 65). Blockades and fortresses were set up against

Jerusalem (or merely on roads up to Jerusalem) until Hezekiah paid tribute and Sennacherib returned to Nineveh. Neither the biblical nor the Assyrian sources claim that the Assyrians conquered Jerusalem. In fact, the biblical sources highlight the city's deliverance by Yahweh, and the Assyrian sources simply say that Sennacherib enclosed Hezekiah in Jerusalem "like a bird in a cage."

The forty-six cities besieged by the Assyrian army are not named in the Assyrian sources, though 2 Kings 18:14 and 19:8 mention the sites of Lachish and Libnah, respectively.[1] Archaeologists have attempted to attribute destruction layers at sites throughout Judah to Sennacherib's campaign; at present there are some nineteen sites that have destruction layers ascribed to Sennacherib (see Bloch-Smith 2009 for site-specific discussions and bibliography).[2] Most of the sites are in the Shephelah and the Negev with no clear archaeological evidence that the Assyrians moved farther into the hill country of Judah, conquering any sites there. The only indication that the Assyrians sent even a contingent of their army into the mountains to Jerusalem is in 2 Kings 18:17 where it mentions that the Tartan, Rab-saris, and Rab-shaqe—Assyrian officials—along with "a great army" went up from Lachish to Jerusalem.

The sources by which this sketch of Sennacherib's third campaign is reconstructed include Assyrian annals (the Rassam Cylinder

---

1. Outside the Assyrian annals, Lachish is mentioned by name in the reliefs found in Sennacherib's throne room in Nineveh, and the site of Azekah is referred to in the so-called Letter to God, which dates to the reign of either Sargon II or Sennacherib. In biblical sources, it may be that the sites listed in Mic. 1 and/or Isa. 10:28–32 were some of the sites destroyed by Sennacherib, though there is no consensus on this matter.

2. These sites include Lachish Stratum III, Tell Beit Mirsim A2*, Beersheba II, Kh. Rabud B-II, Tel Halif VIB, Arad VIII, Tell es-Safi Temporary Str. 3, Tel Batash III, Beth Shemesh IIc (Level 2), Tel 'Erani VI, Hebron*, Tel Malhata IV, Tel 'Eton, Tel Judeideh, Ramat Rahel VB*, Mareshah*, Tel Miqne II, Tell el-Hesi VIIIa*, and Ter Sera VI*. Asterisks (*) indicate that the nature of a destruction layer is unclear.

[700 BCE], Cylinder C [697 BCE], the Chicago Prism [691–689 BCE], and the Taylor Prism [691–689 BCE], and numerous other clay cylinders [see Grayson and Novotny 2012; 2014]), the biblical texts (2 Kings 18:13–19:37; 2 Chron. 32:1–22; Isa. 36–37), archaeological remains (Bloch-Smith 2009), and iconographic materials from Sennacherib's palace at Nineveh (J. M. Russell 1991). Later written versions also appear in Herodotus (2.141–42) and in Josephus (*Ant.* 10.1–23).

While there are interesting parallels in particular between the Assyrian and the biblical sources (e.g., the amount of gold paid in tribute by Hezekiah, the nonconquest of Jerusalem), it is the differences not only between these sources but also within these sources— the biblical sources in particular—that make a decisive reconstruction of Sennacherib's campaign problematic. The version of Sennacherib's campaign preserved in 2 Kings 18–19 is generally divided into two or three sources in an attempt to understand why there are conflicting details and an unclear sequence of events. Second Kings 18:13–16 is referred to as Source A (the annalistic account), while 2 Kings 18:17–19:37 is referred to as Source B (the prophetic account). Often Source B is further divided into B1 (2 Kings 18:17–19:9a, 36–37) and B2 (2 Kings 19:9b–35). There is no consensus on how these sources have been integrated (see Evans 2009, 3–15, for a recent survey of these issues) or how they relate to Isaiah 36–39 and 2 Chronicles 32, which are parallel versions of the same events (Young 2012, 123–50).[3] Source A ends with Hezekiah paying tribute, while source B ends with the destruction of the Assyrian army by the angel of the Lord and the subsequent murder of Sennacherib by his own sons (which did not happen until 681 BCE, despite the telescoping of 2 Kings 19:37). The Assyrian versions of the

campaign do not include major variations but become more condensed over time as writing space was dedicated to more recent activities (Grayson and Novotny 2012).

Assyrian Imperialism

Assyrian imperial expansion in the ninth to seventh centuries BCE was not uniform and attests to multiple control strategies, from direct territorial control, which at its fullest entailed no autonomy from imperial power; to hegemonic control, which allowed for varying levels of local autonomy; to the use of buffer zones, which were regions where imperial control was either limited or nonexistent. The degree of control over a given region depended on a region's political, economic, and military benefit(s) (B. Parker 2013, 136), and the manifestation of Assyrian control appeared as either a network of strategic "islands" or as an "oil stain" (Liverani 1988; S. Parpola 2003). In the former, Assyrian rule expanded from strategic points, creating a web of communication and transport hubs and a system of agricultural colonization and settlement (Liverani 1988, 88; B. Parker 2001; M. L. Smith 2005). Over time Assyrian rule expanded from these islands, thickening the web until all intervening territories also fell under Assyrian hegemony. In the latter, Assyrian control expanded continuously from the core of the empire to the periphery (Liverani 1988, 84–86). Rigid borders expanded and contracted with the waxing and waning of the empire. In either case, implementing Assyrian control was done either directly, through annexation or military control, or indirectly, through subjugation or collaboration with local proxies (Thareani 2016, 79–80; B. Parker 2001).

The Assyrians did not set out to conquer the entire Near East; rather, such a result was the culmination of a lengthy ideological evolution related to political machinations and economic aspirations (see below). Neo-Assyrian ideology

---

3. Additional passages from Isaiah have also been adduced to reconstruct aspects of Sennacherib's third campaign (Gallagher 1999).

finds its roots in the Middle Assyrian kingdom of Assur, which extended control from the heartland of Assyria west to the Euphrates River and south to Babylonia. Following the collapse of the Middle Assyrian kingdom there was a period of internal struggle, but beginning with Ashur-dan in 934 BCE the kingdom of Assur reestablished its authority over its own heartland and took back land to the north, east, and south that it considered its own, as it had been during the Middle Assyrian period. It was not, however, until Shalmaneser III in the ninth century that Assyria began expanding its borders beyond those traditionally held in the Middle Assyrian period.

After the reign of Shalmaneser III, another subsequent lull in internal organization ended with the ascension of Tiglath-Pileser III to the throne; his reign marks the beginning of the pinnacle of the Neo-Assyrian Empire and really the first true empire. Subsequent kings—Shalmaneser V, Sargon II, Sennacherib, Esarhaddon, and Ashurbanipal—continued the expansionist policies implemented by Tiglath-Pileser, ultimately extending the Assyrian border to Nubia.

Royal Ideology and Imperial Motivations

The Assyrian king was portrayed both as a king among equal kings and as a king without rival elsewhere in the world (K. Radner 2010, 28; Holloway 2002; Perdue, Carter, and Baker 2015, 40–44). In religious/royal ideology, the patron god Assur chose the king to rule on earth and charged him to bring order (and creation) wherever there was chaos. The king accomplished this charge by conquest and exploitation. Surrounding territories needed the order of Assur for their own good as their inhabitants needed enlightening (see Liverani 1979a). This royal ideology grew (or was maintained) by the use of verbal and visual propaganda, including victory steles, reliefs,

ballads, hymns, iconography, and imagery (see S. Parpola 2010, 37–39 for a list of the images and icons used), and it was propagated by the imperial court, which was comprised of scholars (scribes, craftsmen, sculptors, etc.), temples, and mystery cults (S. Parpola 2010, 40–41).

While religious ideology certainly fueled Assyrian expansion, so did political necessity and economic considerations. In the ninth and eighth centuries external pressures by Aramaeans, Babylonians, and Urartians prompted Assyrian response. Internally, Assyria suffered from inefficient farming techniques, a dearth of labor, and a lack of resources because of disrupted trade routes (B. Parker 2013, 129). Military campaigns addressed the external pressures and brought money and resources to Assyria. Methods of breaking an enemy's will were imposed, including the division of annexed kingdoms into multiple administrative units, and the use of large-scale deportations (see Oded 1979) and resettling of conquered peoples created opportunities to exploit and expand agricultural lands across the empire.

Beginning at least with Ashurnasirpal II (883–859 BCE), the Assyrians used multiple strategies of control throughout their realm, strategies related to the location and economic cost of campaigning in a given region (Baudains et al. 2015; B. Parker 2013, 136; Thareani 2016). Punitive actions against nearer and weaker neighbors allowed the Neo-Assyrian Empire to rise. Over time the Assyrian economy was strengthened and the administrative structure refined, though the Assyrians still had to weigh the cost of a campaign in time, personnel, and economic payoff. Economic considerations were a key component that dictated the way in which the Assyrian Empire expanded and established its presence, particularly along the borders of its realm. Buffer zones occasionally were established that allowed for Assyrian control without extensive interaction; the best evidence comes from Philistia and southeast Anatolia (see Ben-Shlomo 2014c, 82–85; Thareani 2016; B. Parker 2003). Assyrian interest in Philistia, especially the region around Gaza, the Negev, and even Edom, attests to economic interest in controlling the lucrative incense trade coming from Arabia (Ben-Shlomo 2014c, 83; Na'aman 2001, 263; 2004a; Cogan 1993, 407; Thareani 2007; 2009).

Ramifications for Judah

Historical Ramifications

After witnessing two unsuccessful rebellions against the Assyrians in 720 and 712 BCE, not to mention the Assyrian destruction of the northern kingdom of Israel in 722 BCE, it stands to reason that Hezekiah understood that any chance of successfully rebelling against Assyria would require pragmatic and extensive preparations. Archaeological remains indicate that Judah had a coherent defensive network by the end of the eighth century, no doubt initiated in light of Assyrian aggression in the area. King Hezekiah in particular would appear to be the instigator of this network, which utilized the natural geography of Judah to its advantage.[4] A combination of fortified cities, fortresses, and watchtowers protected Judean interests in the Shephelah, Negev, central Benjamin plateau, Judean wilderness, and central hill country of Judah.

Further, Hezekiah developed or appropriated a system for collecting and exploiting the

4. The biblical texts do not record that Hezekiah himself built any new fortified sites (except for Jerusalem), but rather that he had the means to man and operate such sites (cf. 2 Kings 20:13; 2 Chron. 32:6, 27–29). Second Chronicles 32:29 reads, "He made cities for himself." It may be possible to infer the construction of fortifications from the verb *'sh* ("to make"), but that is not clear. Bloch-Smith 2009, 35, citing Borowski 1995, notes that Hezekiah's religious reforms and the centralization of the cult in Jerusalem are good indicators of his plans for rebellion against Assyria, as centralization of the cult would concentrate resources in Jerusalem and refill the temple coffers.

agricultural resources of Judah. Traces of this system are preserved in the *lmlk* ("belonging to the king") impressed jars. When the distribution of the over two thousand *lmlk* impressions is juxtaposed with the topographical context of the fortified sites and fortresses, the brilliance of Judah's defensive network comes into focus. Topographical variation led to regional defense networks; in more open areas and/or in more populated areas fortified cities were predominant (e.g., the Shephelah), whereas in more geographically isolated or challenging regions there was less investment in architectural defenses than in reliance upon the natural topography of the region (e.g., the western Judean hills and Judean wilderness) (Keimer 2011, 169–73).

The maintenance, if not the actual creation, of this defensive network had a dramatic impact on the economy and society of Judah; the economy flourished as Judah appropriated and/or exploited new agricultural lands in the Shephelah and Negev in particular, but the traditional social structure of Judah was eroded in favor of the rise of the individual and the bureaucracy necessary to organize and operate the mechanisms of revolt against the Assyrians—namely, the defensive network and the stockpiling of its constituent sites with supplies (Keimer 2011, 244–51).

Following Sennacherib's campaign, Judah's borders shrank and some sites were abandoned. Yet, at the same time the region around Jerusalem flourished (Gadot 2015); it could be that the economy grew even more in the days of the pro-Assyrian Manasseh, following Hezekiah's death. Stating more than this is difficult, as more evidence and better archaeological anchors are necessary to articulate the archaeological picture in the first half of the seventh century.

The breakdown in family structure that is evident in the archaeological record—in the individual titles and names on seals (which move from patronymics to "bureaucratic" titles), the standardization of ceramic forms, a quantitative shift from a presumed family distribution (more cooking pots and fewer bowls and jugs) to a nonfamilial distribution (more bowls, storage jars, and fewer cooking pots), and the smaller and more uniform size of houses—is mirrored in the broader conceptual worldview of ancient Israel (see Halpern 1991). The rise of the "individual" as a concept opposed to the family or community appears in various eighth-century prophetic texts (Holladay 1970) and perhaps leads to a greater understanding of the uniqueness of Israel's God as the one true God. When the family is no longer *the* defining category of social identification, and responsibility shifts from the family to the individual, so too a family of deities gives way to the conceptualization of an individual deity who is responsible for everything (M. S. Smith 2016, 287; 2001a, 164–65).

There is also a perceived shift in the way that prophets operated. Prior to the mid-eighth century their oracles were given to the king, but from the mid-eighth century on they were directed to the people of Israel/Judah as a whole. John Holladay (1970) has argued that this shift is a direct result of Assyrian diplomatic methods, by which royal messengers/heralds started conveying the message(s) of their suzerain—the Assyrian king—to the general population of a kingdom and not to the vassal king of that kingdom. This method of psychological warfare put the onus on the people to decide what Assyrian military action would subsequently happen.

Conceptual Ramifications

Judah's interaction with Assyria sent the kingdom to its highest highs, according to the biblical author/s and his/their concern with salvation history (i.e., the preservation of Jerusalem [2 Kings 19:29–36]), and to the lowest lows, as portrayed in God's wrath against Judah in the days of Jeremiah (Jer. 7:1–8:3), a wrath that had been building from an Assyrian-to-Babylonian-controlled Near East.

An array of similarities and differences can be observed between Assyrian and more broadly Mesopotamian genres, conventions, and literary works, and, while there are debates about literary indebtedness versus cultural embeddedness, many scholars draw connections between Mesopotamian influences that began with the Assyrian deportations and campaigns in the southern Levant and many features of biblical literature.

More explicit are the parallels between Neo-Assyrian royal inscriptions and the book of Isaiah. It appears that Isaiah depicts the Assyrian army as "an overwhelming military machine, destroying all resistance in its path, devastating the lands of its enemies, hauling away huge numbers of spoils and captives to its capital or elsewhere in its realm, and rearranging by this devastation and deportation the political physiognomy of the entire region" (Machinist 1983, 722). This is the image of the Assyrian king and his army as portrayed in the Assyrian royal inscriptions as well. Yet Isaiah is using Assyrian phrases and terminology polemically to show that Yahweh, not the king(s) of Assyria, is mighty and worthy of praise. Less overt linguistically, but espousing a similar message shortly before the days of Isaiah, is the prophet Hosea (Perdue, Carter, and Baker 2015, 49–63; cf. Yee 1992).

That familiarity with Assyrian propagandistic terminology and texts was likely in Judah is bolstered not only by the internal evidence from the book of Isaiah but also by the presence of Assyrian victory inscriptions set up as near as Ashdod and Samaria (L. D. Levine 1972). The prophet Nahum subsequently also adopted Assyrian terminology as filtered through Isaiah (Nah. 1:8, 13; 2:11–13). Interestingly, the prophet Hosea alludes to Assyria in many of his oracles to the northern kingdom of Israel, possibly even mentioning Shalmaneser V (Hosea 10:14).

Zion Theology and the Place of God

The idea of Jerusalem's inviolability flourishes after the city survives Sennacherib's campaign. Whether one accepts the Assyrian or the biblical account of the events that led to Sennacherib's withdrawal from Judah, both agree that Jerusalem was not conquered or destroyed. The origin of the so-called Zion theology, which claims inviolability for Jerusalem, has been posited from the days of David to post-701 BCE, though a date in the days of the United Monarchy appears warranted. J. Roberts (2003, 169) notes that Isaiah presupposes this theology. Jerusalem, it was understood, would be saved—in this instance from the Assyrians—because (1) Yahweh is the great king over all nations and other gods; (2) Yahweh made a covenant with David and his descendants that they would rule in perpetuity (2 Sam. 7; 23:1–5; 2 Kings 8:19; Pss. 78:67–70; 89; 132); and (3) Yahweh has chosen Zion as his dwelling place (Pss. 2:6; 48:2; Isa. 8:18; cf. 2:3) and as the location for David's dynastic rule (cf. 1 Kings 20:34; Pss. 78:68–69; 132:13–14).

What was required of the Judahites and Hezekiah was faith in God's promises. Yet faith is not passive, nor does it preclude pragmatic military preparations as were undertaken by Hezekiah and attested to in the archaeological record. In fact, the idea that the prophet Isaiah was a proponent of a passive Zion theology has been criticized, instead highlighting Isaiah's call to be brave in the face of aggression and trust in Yahweh (cf. the portrayal of faith in various chapters of Isaiah; see P. Johnston 2009; Wong 2001).

The nonconquest of Jerusalem by Sennacherib only fueled the royal ideology and theology of the biblical authors. Jerusalem clearly was inviolable. The so-called Deuteronomistic historian writes that God will preserve the city (2 Kings 19:34; 20:6) and his temple (21:7). Yet, covenant promises that were perceived unconditional were called into question as moral decay grew in Judah over the next 120 years (Ps. 125; Jer. 7). The Babylonian exile, wherein Jerusalem was lost, the temple destroyed, and the line of David dethroned, ended Zion theology.

39

Eighth-Century Levantine Earthquakes and Natural Disasters

Ryan N. Roberts

Introduction

The eighth century BCE witnessed a large number of social changes from natural disasters, military incursions, forced migrations, and refugee crises. These events are drawing increasing study from interdisciplinary approaches that are able to propose newer models and methods to investigate further the implications of these historical episodes. As our understanding of ancient Levantine earthquakes is more advanced in comparison to other natural disasters, the predominant focus of this chapter is on earthquakes. There is, however, overlap in the social scientific study of disaster that is germane not only to natural disasters but also to anthropogenic communal disasters such as forced migrations, refugee crises, and other similar events.

The study of earthquakes in the biblical period has progressed quite rapidly over the last several decades due primarily to scientific advances in the study of ancient earthquakes. This chapter proceeds by first outlining the main functions of earthquake language in the Hebrew Bible. It next traces the scientific and archaeological undergirding for identifying and studying earthquakes in the ancient Levant. It then highlights several realities of disasters by reconstructing how an earthquake may have affected the ancient Levantine population. Last, it examines the issue of social justice in light of disaster study.

Earthquake Language in the Hebrew Bible

Literary Functions of Earthquake Imagery

Earthquake imagery is most often employed in language describing ancient Israel's account of God intervening in human history. These texts often have, in addition to "quaking" language, other phenomena, such as wind, storm, and fire, and are more technically labeled as storm-theophanic texts describing the divine warrior (Cross 1973, 156–77). This type of language has a shared background with Ugaritic and Mesopotamian texts (Loewenstamm 1984) that are employed to announce the appearance of a god. Within the Hebrew Bible, a number of these theophanic texts (Judg. 5:4–5; 2 Sam.

22:8–16 = Ps. 18:8–16; Ps. 68:7–10; Hab. 3:3–15) have commonly been understood as representing some of Israel's oldest hymns. Later prophetic texts tie earthquake imagery into pronouncements of the future eschatological day of reckoning (Isa. 29:5–6; Joel 2:10; Nah. 1:5) (F. Spencer 2007). This eschatological theme will continue into the New Testament. It is found in the context of a triple tradition regarding Jesus's eschatological pronouncements (Matt. 24:7; Mark 13:8; Luke 21:11) and in the apocalyptic language of Revelation (Rev. 6:12; 8:5; 11:13, 16:18–19).

Beyond the common motif of Yhwh appearing in traditional theophanic texts or in eschatological passages, various texts have been posited as reflecting real earthquakes. These include stories such as Sodom and Gomorrah (Gen. 19:24–29), the Korahite rebellion (Num. 16:31–33), and the battle at Jericho (Josh. 6:20–21). It is difficult to speculate if some or all texts do indeed describe an earthquake that is then interpreted through a lens of divine judgment. One is on much more sound footing, however, when reading the superscription in Amos as referring to an earthquake (1:1: "two years before the earthquake").

The Earthquake in Amos

Indeed, there is broad scholarly agreement that the reference in Amos to an earthquake describes a real event. Further, this quake also finds support in the archaeological and geological records. Various dates have been posited for this quake, but a date between 760 and 750 BCE is a reasonable approximation. The superscription is comparably longer than most other prophetic superscriptions, as it includes the title of the book ("The words of Amos") and then a lengthy elaboration of the title via a series of appended relative clauses (Tucker 1977, 60). The superscription also contains a double synchronistic royal date linking the prophet with both the southern kingdom ("in the days of King Uzziah of Judah") and the northern

kingdom ("and in the days of King Jeroboam son of Joash of Israel").[1] Superscriptions were added later to prophetic texts to confirm the divine origin of the prophetic messages. For the book of Amos, the reference to an earthquake in the superscription suggests that later editors viewed Amos's prophetic activity as divinely given (Mays 1969, 20; D. Freedman and Welch 1994). It may also suggest that he was seen as predicting the earthquake as a sign of God's judgment on his people (Amos 2:13; 3:14–15; 6:11; 9:1).

A few hundred years after the prophetic activity of Amos, language in Zechariah 14:5, "and you shall flee as you fled from the earthquake in the days of King Uzziah of Judah," appears to allude to the same earthquake. This reference is couched in Yhwh's future judgment on Jerusalem and his appearance as a divine warrior setting foot on top of the Mount of Olives (Zech. 14:4). While it is common to interpret this verse as referring to widespread seismic destruction of both the northern and southern kingdoms (Boda 2016, 759), the fleeing may be better understood as escape from adobe mud brick homes in light of the *threat* of collapse following an earthquake (R. Roberts 2015, 194–95).[2]

Given earlier tendencies of "biblical archaeology" to uncritically correlate archaeological material finds with biblical texts or to link any potential seismic damage in eighth-century strata with the earthquake mentioned in Amos, a host of sites have been suggested as containing

---

1. Scholars commonly view the double synchronistic reference to the kings of Judah and Israel as a later Deuteronomistic addition, in which the pre-Deuteronomistic superscription would have read, "The words of Amos of Tekoa, which he saw concerning Israel, two years before the earthquake" (W. Schmidt 1965, 168–70).

2. The latter interpretation distinguishes between shaking and seismic destruction. In other words, though shaking may have been widespread throughout the land, the location of severe damage was much more limited to the northern kingdom. Regardless, it is plausible that people throughout the land would have fled their homes, as they lacked a modern understanding of plate tectonics.

seismic evidence. Newer methodologies discussed below have begun to apply better controls to assess the purported evidence. And newer research on historic earthquakes is drawing attention to two earthquakes in the eighth century rather than one (Agnon 2011; Kagen et al. 2011, 23–27).

Earthquake Science

The geological environment of Israel makes it a natural host for earthquakes. The Dead Sea Transform Fault is approximately 1,000 km long and is usually divided into three segments: the southern section from the Gulf of Aqaba to the Jordan Valley; the central section, including Mount Lebanon and the Anti-Lebanon ranges; and the northern section, which runs parallel to the eastern side of the Syrian coastal mountains and joins with the East Anatolian Fault in southern Turkey (Masson et al. 2015, 161). As a strike-slip fault, it slides laterally and forms the boundary between the Sinai subplate west of the Jordan and the Arabian plate to the east (Kottmeier et al. 2016, 1055). The positive aspect of this fault type—relatively speaking—is that large-magnitude events are rare and less intense than in subduction zones such as the fault systems found, for example, in the Zagros Nountains (Masson et al. 2015, 167; Kottmeier et al. 2016, 1055). In fact, the last large earthquake to affect broad areas of Israel occurred on July 11, 1927. As the transform consists of a number of pull-apart basins on its southern end, this geologically explains the low depressions of the Galilee and the Dead Sea.

The study of ancient earthquakes has progressed quite noticeably in the last thirty years due to advances in new and emerging interdisciplinary fields. The most noteworthy areas include paleoseismology (the pre-instrumental study of earthquakes, especially their location, timing, and size), historical seismology (the study of written sources that mention earthquakes), archaeoseismology (the study of seismic damage in the archaeological record), and social scientific / natural disaster studies.

Advances in paleoseismology are indebted to the analysis of sediment layer cores from the Dead Sea. These layers are first made as sedimentary deposits are formed in the Dead Sea lake bed. During an earthquake the layer is then deformed; through counting layers in the core and by using radiocarbon dating, researchers can correlate disturbed sections of the core with a number of historic earthquakes (Ken-Tor et al. 2001; Migowski et al. 2014). The cores provide data from more than one hundred millennia and can also provide insight into the climate history of the region. As several cores have now been drilled and studied in the last decade, the research has seen immense strides in its ability to differentiate between different types of fault behavior within the Dead Sea Transform as well as to help fine-tune the study of historic quakes.

In light of these studies, earthquakes within the period of the Iron Age and the Persian period have been correlated around the eleventh to twelfth centuries BCE, two mid-eighth-century quakes, and quakes in 525 and 331 BCE (Agnon 2011, 235).[3] While the epicenter of the eleventh- or twelfth-century quake has been suggested close to the Gulf of Aqaba and the 525 BCE epicenter in the Mediterranean northwest of modern Haifa, most scholars place the epicenter of at least one of the mid-eighth-century quakes north of the Galilee or even into Syria (see below for fuller discussion on why only one of the two epicenters is given a probable location; Migowski et al. 2014, 311). The felt-shaking pattern of more modern quakes with similarly suggested epicenter locations include the 1759 and 1837 CE quakes. These felt-shaking patterns suggest that most inhabitants of ancient Israel would

3. The Roman and Byzantine eras, by comparison, report quakes in 31 BCE, 33 CE, 115 CE, 303/306 CE, 363 CE, 419 CE, and 526 CE. See Ambraseys 2009; Agnon 2011, 235.

have felt shaking during the quake, but the area that suffered structural damage would have been more limited, broadly speaking, to areas associated with the northern kingdom.

Archaeoseismology

Sufficient methodological controls to properly assess seismic damage are difficult for the Iron II and earlier periods in the Levant. Aegean specialists have pioneered the archaeoseismic methodology; thus, these later time periods have different building materials and techniques, and consequently different diagnostics can be used to identify seismic damage. For example, methodology centered on relevant damage in stonework would limit its relevance to the Iron II period. Other effects of seismic damage, including toppled columns or slipped keystones in archways and doorways, are also nearly impossible to find in this time period. Other criteria may be desired but unlikely; these include crushed skeletons or unretrieved bodies under walls and widespread fires (Stiros 1996, appendix 2). Indeed, one of the challenges with Levantine archaeoseismology is the small-scale nature of what archaeologists unearth. For example, a single tilted wall a few meters long may be the best and only evidence at an archaeological site to suggest an earthquake. However, a number of other factors such as fill pressure, poor building technique, or foundation collapse and differential settling must also be considered.

Some type of seismic damage related to the quake mentioned in Amos has been suggested at close to twenty Levantine sites, diffused throughout the region. On the one hand, in light of very recent paleoseismic research, two mid-eighth-century earthquakes may help explain such widespread seismic damage (Agnon 2011, 236). In this view, the epicenters would plausibly be at different locations on the fault system to account for such widespread damage. Prior to this advance in paleoseismology,

however, there has been an uncritical acceptance of almost all purported seismic damage in eighth-century strata (S. Austin, Franz, and Frost 2000). On the other hand, the geomorphology of the Levant as well as the specific type of fault argue against an earthquake that could decimate sites from Dan to Eliat and from the Shephelah to the Transjordanian plateau. As Nicolas Ambraseys has argued, an event this large would have obliterated Jerusalem, yet neither textual nor archaeological data support such a claim (Ambraseys 2005). In sum, the suggested sites with mid-eighth-century seismic damage are spread too far apart for any single earthquake to cause so much widespread damage (Ambraseys 2009, 70). Rather, in light of the scientific work, sites in the north are more proximate to the probable location of the epicenter of at least one of the quakes. Thus, Abel-Beth-Maacah, Dan, Hazor, Tel Kinrot, Bethsaida, En Gev, Jezreel, Beth Shean, Deir Alla, and Rehov are strong candidates to contain seismic damage. Whether sites in the south may reflect a second eighth-century quake or may be victim to falsely assuming a cause and effect relationship—damage in an eighth-century strata is unexplained, we know an earthquake occurred in the eighth century, therefore this damage is due to an earthquake—is a current research question in need of further clarification.

The Social Scientific Study of Earthquakes

Health Effects of Earthquakes

Using findings from earthquake epidemiology, we can describe health effects resulting from an earthquake as follows. Common injuries are to the head and back, with broken bones a very widespread injury (Alexander 1996, 237). Population estimates are difficult to approximate for this time period, but a number in the low hundreds of thousands is a reasonable estimate for those in an affected location of a mid-eighth-century quake (R. Roberts 2012, 2; Broshi and Finkelstein 1992). The elderly are almost three times more likely to suffer injury, and women had more than twice the risk of injury than men (Peek-Asa et al. 2003). Statistically, the next-to-youngest child was most susceptible to injury because the youngest child often was closer to its mother while older children are physically and developmental stronger (Glass et al. 1977). Higher casualties and injuries occur at night due to a greater number of occupants being inside the home.

In the immediate aftermath of a quake, the quest to find survivors unites communities, and social connections often are strengthened while race or class distinctions are overlooked (Clarke 2002; Kaniastry and Norris 2004). In conjunction with the search for survivors, availability of water is of immediate concern. Storage jugs inside affected homes have suffered damage, and water levels in water tables, springs, and wells can go up or down following an earthquake (Nir and Eldar-Nir 1988). Cisterns with cracks in the plaster are affected, as are wells where rough fieldstone has fallen in the shaft and blocked access. Agricultural terracing, which helps with cultivation on steep slopes, is susceptible to landslides (Keefer 2002). As nightfall comes, temporary housing is set up and the population will stay away from permanent structures due to the risk of aftershocks.

Earthquake Effects on Structures

Homes made of adobe mud brick, the most common type of building material in the ancient Levant, are structurally prone to collapse during an earthquake. As shear waves hit these homes, the motion can momentarily separate bricks from one another and from their stone foundations, negating friction and causing collapse. In addition, the brushwood roof is prone to collapse. The heavy weight of the roof, as it was coated in plaster to protect against the elements, will further cause injury or death (Herr and Clark 2001). A comparative study of Guatemalan villagers found that all deaths and serious injuries affected those who lived in mud brick homes (Glass et al. 1977, 640). As a point of comparison, the 2003 Bam earthquake in Iran caused the deaths of twenty-five thousand people. Similar to ancient Israel, they mainly lived in mud brick homes. One cause of death was suffocation due to dust following the quake as well as asphyxiation where roofs collapsed.

Social Vulnerability in Disaster

Research continues to emphasize the human side of disaster. Hence, disasters are as much or more social events as they are physical events (Oliver-Smith 2002, 27). Thus, rather than viewing vulnerability as a passive concept outside the control of the affected actors, we should see that social vulnerability contributes to hazard and disaster. This can be seen, for example, in the quality of construction or construction materials in a home and the ability to access clean water, food, or medical care after a disaster (Macabuag 2010).

Religious Revival

Frequent areas of impact that often follow disaster include religious revival, political unrest, and socioeconomic injustice (Fretheim 2010; Robertson 2010). The Lisbon quake of 1755 provides one case study in religious revival. An estimated fifty thousand to sixty thousand people died as the quake struck at 9:30 a.m. on All Saints' Day. High ceilings and unreinforced masonry arches and vaults caused parish churches and cathedrals to collapse. This exacerbated the number of deaths, along with hundreds of fires that spread throughout the city. Since so many people died in churches, a common view of the day was that the earthquake was a punishment by God. The quake also virtually annihilated the philosophical view of Optimism, which saw everything in the world working toward the general good.

Instead, intellectuals such as Voltaire went on the offensive, using the earthquake as intellectual leverage to contest the idea of an all-loving God (Nur 2008, 248–59).

In the same way, one reason for the staying power of Amos's message may have been the openness of a disaster-afflicted population to receive the harsh message of condemnation. This was even truer if one of the quakes struck the north. In this way, it validated the theological judgment against the north, while largely sparing the south. At the same time, the quake may have engendered the northern population to reevaluate their cultic practices and fidelity to Yahweh.

Social Justice

The theme of social justice in the eighth-century prophets is well known (Houston 2008). The genesis of these calls for justice often has been connected to the growing prosperity of those living in cities and their elites (priests, judges, rich landowners), whereas a contrast is drawn with the poor dwelling in the countryside (Nardoni 2004, 101). Other views, however, downplay the urban-rural divide and focus on the urban environment as the locus for disparity. Yet, regardless of the location behind calls for justice, women, elderly, and minorities often suffer disproportionately from disaster (Kreps 2006, 64–66). This underscores again the social dimensions of disaster, where disaster proneness often is linked with famine potential, low income, and chronic malnutrition (Oliver-Smith 2002).

In outlining the theme of vulnerability and disaster, one may read anew the social justice texts found in the book of Amos. Though often they have been read in light of a rich-poor divide generated by a time of wealth and divorced from notions of disaster, an alternative reading shows how disaster can highlight the rich-poor divide. At the same time, these texts need not be cast in an either-or scenario. Thus Amos 2:6b–7a is one passage that may be read in light

of a disaster. Here, one may envision the rich quickly moving on with their lives following a disaster while the poor struggle to rebuild their lives: "because they sell the righteous for silver, and the needy for a pair of sandals—they who trample the head of the poor into the dust of the earth, and push the afflicted out of the way." The words of Amos 6:3–6 may also carry extra weight about the ability of the rich to put off disaster as they lay on their beds of ivory. Though this passage traditionally has been understood as reversing the meaning of the expected "day of Yahweh"—when Israel expected their God to right wrongs but are in fact visited by the judgment of God—there is irony in the ability of those with the means to put off disaster. In light of a disaster, this pronouncement would have carried even greater religious judgment as the rich would have been tossed from their beds of ivory, all the while being able to more quickly return to their extravagant way of life.

Conclusion

The study of earthquakes in the ancient Levant is a fascinating topic to explore.

A number of intersecting fields help inform a more balanced and insightful picture of the type and scope of disasters that the eighth century BCE witnessed. Archaeoseismic study continues to refine methodology that is germane to the Iron II period. This is needed to provide further scrutiny of Iron II sites with purported seismic damage. In turn, this will help to untangle probable evidence of seismic damage from wrongly attributing observed damage to seismic cause. Two of the most pressing research questions for Levantine paleoseismology include the following: What more may be said about the location or size of the two mid-eighth-century quakes? And how many more earthquakes occurred during the Iron Age and Persian period beyond the four quakes that can be corroborated in sedimentary cores?

In addition to earthquakes, other natural disasters include volcanoes, tsunamis, floods, drought, and destructive weather patterns. Volcano activity in the Sinai Peninsula has been connected with the origins of Yahweh (Dunn 2014), though the lack of volcanic activity in the Levant also is reflected in its paucity within biblical tradition. A recently produced tsunami catalog for the Eastern Mediterranean suggests that strong tsunamis strike about every 1,200 years but low or moderate tsunamis occur every few years (Fokaefs and Papadopoulos 2007). A number of these tsunamis can be associated with earthquake activity of the Dead Sea Transform, but current models do not connect significant tsunami activity with the biblical period. More recent studies in ancient climate change present promising vistas for understanding drought and destructive weather patterns (Langgut, Finkelstein, and Litt 2013; Langgut et al. 2015).

As more scholars integrate research from disaster studies, our reading of social justice texts will continue to expand. At the same time, contemporary challenges such as climate change or income inequality exacerbated by disasters find a rich lexicon of prophetic voices that continue to cause reflection and provide a voice to those in need.

40

The Battle of Carchemish and Seventh/Sixth-Century Regional Politics

SARA L. HOFFMAN

In 605 BCE Egyptian and Babylonian forces collided on the banks of the Euphrates River at the city of Carchemish. The battle is remarkably well attested in both textual and archaeological records, and by all accounts the Twenty-Sixth Dynasty suffered a major defeat that opened the door to the expansion of the Babylonian Empire as far south as Egypt's own border. The Deuteronomist characterizes Nebuchadnezzar's victory at Carchemish and his subsequent campaigns through the Levant as a total transfer of power in the region (2 Kings 24:7), and Jeremiah's oracles against the nations cast Egypt's downfall in explicitly theological terms (Jer. 46:10):

> And that day belongs to the Lord GOD
>   of Hosts,
> a day of vengeance, to take vengeance
>   on his enemies.
> And the sword will consume but will
>   not be sated,
> and it will drink of their blood,
> for it is a sacrifice to the Lord GOD of
>   Hosts

in the land of the north, at the Euphrates River.[1]

However, even as the Hebrew Bible celebrates Egypt's defeat, these perspectives on Carchemish obscure Egypt's ongoing role in the Levant. Although its power and territory were diminished, the Twenty-Sixth Dynasty continued to influence Judah's political calculations for years to come.

Historical Backdrop of the Battle of Carchemish

At its height, the Assyrian Empire not only controlled the entire Levant but also expanded into Egypt. Assyrian forces conquered Memphis under Esarhaddon (Leichty 2011, 185–86, no. 98 reverse, lines 37b–50a; Grayson 1975, 85–86, Chronicle 1, iv, lines 23–28) and reached Thebes under Ashurbanipal (Borger 1996, 17–26, column ii, lines 28–48). However, such power proved difficult to maintain so far from

---

1. All Scripture quotations in this chapter are the author's translation.

the Assyrian heartland, despite the presence of Assyrian officials in Egypt to oversee local vassal rulers and despite repeated military campaigns to suppress rebellion. During the second half of the seventh century BCE, Egypt's status shifted in two crucial ways.

First, having reunited under the leadership of Psammetichus I and having gained independence from Assyria, Egypt now served as the dying empire's ally against the Babylonians. By 616 BCE, the Twenty-Sixth Dynasty was fighting alongside the Assyrian army in the northern Levant (Grayson 1975, 91–96, Chronicle 3, lines 10–11, 61–69). Ultimately, this coalition was unable to preserve Assyria. Its capital at Nineveh fell in 612 BCE, and after Ashur-uballit's failed attempt to fall back to Harran, Assyrian forces simply fade out of the Babylonian Chronicle. However, the Twenty-Sixth Dynasty continued to campaign in Syria. In the year before the Battle of Carchemish, the Chronicle reports that Egypt was on the offensive, successfully besieging the Babylonian garrison at Kimuhu and forcing Babylonian troops camped at Quramatu to withdraw from the region (Grayson 1975, 97–98, Chronicle 4, lines 16–26).

Second, as the Assyrian Empire contracted, the Twenty-Sixth Dynasty also seized the opportunity to reassert Egypt's political and economic interests in the Levant.[2] By the late seventh century BCE, the Twenty-Sixth Dynasty had successfully established an administrative presence in Phoenicia. In its description of an Apis bull burial in 612 BCE, the Serapeum Stele refers to the provision of wood for the coffin

by foreign kings, and it designates these rulers the "tenant-farmers of the palace" (nḏt ḥ'), noting that they were under the supervision of an Egyptian official and subject to taxes "just like the land of Egypt."[3] The Saqqarah Papyrus also suggests established relationships with client states closer to home, in Philistia.[4] In this letter, Adon, the ruler of Ekron (Porten 1981, 42–45), pleads for Egyptian reinforcements to protect his city from Babylonian aggression. As a justification for this request, he specifically states, "Your servant has preserved his good relations." This Aramaic expression parallels the Akkadian technical treaty term ṭābta naṣār, and it implies that Adon's appeal is based on the obligations and expectations of a formal agreement (Porten 1981, 39; Fitzmyer 1979, 239–40).

Egypt also looked farther inland to Judah, which offered access to lucrative overland trade routes through the Negev. In 2 Kings 23, the account of the death of Josiah and the tumultuous succession process that followed points to Judah's status as an Egyptian vassal by the last decade of the seventh century BCE.[5] When, in the wake of Josiah's death, Judean elites placed Jehoahaz on the throne in Jerusalem, Egyptian officials intervened within just a few months, installing a successor whom Necho apparently considered more amenable to Egyptian interests, collecting a substantial payment from Judah, and putting its deposed king in chains at Riblah in the land of Hamath.

3. For the most recent edition, see Perdu 2002, 40–41.
4. Alongside the Saqqarah Papyrus, there are several other scattered references to Saite military action in Philistia. Jeremiah 47:1, the superscription to the book's oracles against the Philistines, specifically mentions the Egyptian conquest of Gaza, and Herodotus 2.157 also includes a garbled historical tradition about a 29-year siege of Ashdod under Psammetichus I. See also the more ambiguous reference to being sent to "smite Asia" in a statue inscription of the Twenty-Sixth Dynasty general Amasis that dates to the reign of Necho II (D. Redford 2000, 187–88).
5. For the argument that Judah was already an Egyptian vassal prior to Josiah's death, see Na'aman 1991, 51–54; Schipper 2010.

2. The timing of Egypt's initial expansion into the Levant is unclear. The earliest reconstructions of these events assume that Assyria's grip on its periphery had already begun to loosen during the lifetime of Ashurbanipal and that there may have been an opening for Egyptian expansion as early as ca. 640 BCE (Vanderhooft 1999, 64–81). The latest reconstructions suggest that rebellion in Babylonia after the death of Ashurbanipal marked the empire's true crisis point and that Egypt likely did not move into the Levant until the late 620s BCE (Na'aman 1991, 35–40).

In comparison to this Egyptian expansion, Assyrian and Babylonian imperialism left a more significant imprint on the southern Levant. While their destructive campaigns in the late eighth and late seventh to early sixth centuries BCE sparked significant demographic changes in several regions (Faust 2008, 172–73; Lipschits 2005, 323–65),[6] Egyptian hegemony under the early Twenty-Sixth Dynasty was relatively short-lived and is largely invisible in the material record.[7] However, by the end of the seventh century BCE, Egypt controlled a network of Levantine vassals and had maintained the upper hand against Babylonian incursions in Syria in recent military campaigns far from its own borders. On the eve of the Battle of Carchemish, the Twenty-Sixth Dynasty was in a position of strength.

The Battle of Carchemish in Texts and Archaeology

Carchemish, a site on the Euphrates River along the modern border of Turkey and Syria near Jerablus, was a major base for the northern military operations of the Twenty-Sixth Dynasty. In his twenty-first year, Nabopolassar, king of Babylon, stayed home, and the crown prince, Nebuchadnezzar, led the Babylonian assault on the town. According to the Babylonian Chronicle (Grayson 1975, 99, Chronicle 5, obverse, lines 1–8), Egyptian forces could not hold off the attack on Carchemish itself, attempted to retreat, and were finished off when Nebuchadnezzar pursued them. Although terse, the report stresses the lopsidedness of the battle, hyperbolically claiming a defeat so decisive that not a single Egyptian soldier

survived. The account concludes with a statement on the significance of Carchemish for control of the broader region: "At that time Nebuchadnezzar conquered all of Hamath."

Alongside the Babylonian Chronicle, Jeremiah's oracles against the nations also contain a poetic account of the events at Carchemish with a theological interpretation (Jer. 46:2–12). The picturesque comparison of Egypt's political rise with the rise of the Nile in verses 7–8 acknowledges Necho's imperial ambitions: "I will rise. I will cover the earth. I will destroy each city and its inhabitants."[8] However, this imagery also implicitly diminishes the significance of the Twenty-Sixth Dynasty's political achievements in the Levant. In the annual inundation cycle, the counterpart to the rise of the Nile is, of course, its inevitable fall. In contrast to a parallel text in Amos 9:5 that explicitly refers to both the rising (*'lh*) and falling (*shq'*) of the Nile, Jeremiah 46 plays on this image more subtly with references to the fall (*npl*) of Egyptian soldiers in verses 6 and 12. Like the Babylonian Chronicle, Jeremiah 46 also depicts the battle as a crushing defeat for Egyptian forces: "Let not the swift flee, nor the warrior escape. In the North, beside the Euphrates River, they stumble and fall" (v. 12).

The textual picture is complemented by archaeological evidence from House D at Carchemish, which was excavated by Leonard Woolley in the early twentieth century (Woolley 1921, 126–29). Two rare circumstances allow the finds to be dated with unusual precision. First, in contrast to other excavated structures at the site, House D had only one construction phase. Second, the destruction layer that marked the end of the building's use covered over floors on which excavators found items inscribed with the names of the early

---

6. For Assyrian-style architecture in the southern Levant, see also Van Beek 1993 on Tell Jemmeh and Kogan-Zehavi 2008 on the Assyrian palace locus near Ashdod.

7. Schipper 2010 provides a useful overview of Egyptian material culture in the Levant during this period. However, the sample size is too small to draw meaningful conclusions about Twenty-Sixth Dynasty imperialism on archaeological grounds.

8. For a more nuanced discussion of the Nile imagery here and its intersection with biblical traditions about Yahweh's subjugation of the waters of chaos and Mesopotamian representations of the king as a destructive flood, see Huddlestun 1996, 236–47.

Twenty-Sixth Dynasty pharaohs Psammetichus I and Necho II, anchoring the building and its contents to the late seventh century BCE.

House D contained not only evidence of a battle but also signs of Egyptian presence at the site. Beneath the burned rubble and ashy debris that covered over House D's floors, human skeletons were found in two rooms, and excavators found hundreds of metal arrowheads scattered throughout the building, alongside lanceheads, a sword, and a Greek shield. Even more surprising, though Egyptian material culture is rare in the Iron IIC Levant, Egyptian objects were found throughout House D, including a ring with the cartouche of Psammetichus I on its bezel, scarabs of Necho II, fragments of an alabaster vessel with a hieroglyphic inscription, a fragmentary inscribed faience New Year's vessel, and a series of Egyptian statuettes.

Thus, the Battle of Carchemish represents an unusual degree of convergence of texts and archaeology for the reconstruction of the events of 605 BCE. The outcome is not really in doubt. However, the impact of the battle on regional politics in the Late Iron Age is more complex.

Aftermath of the Battle of Carchemish

Babylonian Campaigns in the Southern Levant

The defeat of Egyptian forces at Carchemish opened the door to the Babylonian conquest of the southern Levant soon after (Grayson 1975, 100, Chronicle 5, obverse, lines 15–23). Nebuchadnezzar's early campaigns in Hattu are best attested by the destruction of Ashkelon, a large port on the southern coast of Philistia and a hub for Mediterranean trade throughout the region (Master 2003; Faust and Weiss 2005). The Babylonian Chronicle reports that, in addition to capturing Ashkelon's king and plundering the city, Nebuchadnezzar and his forces turned the site into "a tell" (*ana tilli*) (Grayson 1975, 100,

Chronicle 5, obverse, lines 15–20).[9] Archaeological evidence from Ashkelon itself supports this picture. Late seventh-century BCE material from the site includes a seaside marketplace and a large winery in the center of the city (Stager 2011, 5–8). In both areas, an ashy destruction layer filled with vitrified building materials and shattered pottery created a snapshot of the city's final days, and the skeleton of a female resident of Ashkelon found amid the rubble on the floor of Room 406 in the marketplace reflects the city's violent end (Stager 1996a, 69*). The fact that there were no signs of reoccupation in either the marketplace or the winery until Persian-period reconstruction (Stager 2011, 11) reinforces the Babylonian Chronicle's claim that Nebuchadnezzar left the city in ruins.

Although Egyptian material culture is rare at seventh-century Levantine sites, concentrations of Egyptian objects were found in both major excavation areas.[10] The rooms of the winery contained a bronze model offering tray, seven bronze situlae, and a bronze Osiris statuette, along with scarabs and amulets. On the corner of South Street in the port's seaside marketplace, excavators also uncovered a group of artifacts that included a bronze balance scale for weighing cut silver and a cache of Egyptian scarabs and amulets. Ashkelon's excavators (Stager and Master 2011, 740; Stager, Master, and Schloen 2011, 706–8) argue that these clusters of Egyptian objects reflect the presence of Egyptian agents overseeing the city's commercial transactions.

From this perspective, Nebuchadnezzar's interest in rooting out Egyptian influence at

9. On the confirmation of the reading "Ashkelon" in BM 21946 lines 18–20, see the discussion of the tablet's collation in Fantalkin 2011, 87n1.

10. Fantalkin 2011 argues that the significant quantity of Greek pottery at Ashkelon also marked the presence of an Egyptian-sponsored Greek mercenary garrison at the site, which provoked the Babylonian attack. However, Waldbaum 2011 convincingly refutes this interpretation of Greek pottery at Ashkelon and identifies this material as further evidence of the city's extensive commercial activity.

Ashkelon outweighed the Babylonian Empire's interest in exploiting the city's extensive Mediterranean trade connections. Ashkelon's neighbor Ekron, a major olive oil production center in Philistia (Gitin 1989) and an Egyptian vassal in the late seventh century BCE, was also destroyed and abandoned during this period.[11] Together, the destruction of these city-states may point to Nebuchadnezzar's attempt to maintain a buffer zone along the empire's southern border and to disrupt Egypt's access to markets in Philistia.

At least initially, Judah's allegiance also shifted to Babylon following the Battle of Carchemish (2 Kings 24:1). The Deuteronomist does not spell out the circumstances of this transition during the reign of Jehoiakim, focusing instead on offering a theological explanation for Judah's subjugation that traces blame back to the sins of Manasseh. However, the summary statement in 2 Kings 24:7 suggests a total transformation of the status quo in the region: "The king of Egypt did not come out from his land again because the king of Babylon had taken, from the Brook of Egypt to the Euphrates River, all that had belonged to the king of Egypt." Nevertheless, while Babylon's victory at Carchemish sparked a major shift in the balance of power in the Levant, it by no means marked the end of Egypt's role in Late Iron Age regional politics.

The Failed Babylonian Campaign against Egypt

Although the Babylonians had outmatched Twenty-Sixth Dynasty forces abroad, Egypt maintained its own borders. Alongside the oracles related to Egypt's defeat at Carchemish, Jeremiah 46 also includes dire predictions of a successful Babylonian attack on Egypt itself, anticipating not just incursions against border fortresses in the eastern Nile delta, such as Migdol and Tahpanhes (Defenneh), but rather a campaign deep into Egypt, leading to the fall of Memphis (Jer. 46:14, 19). They further predict that Egyptian leadership will be captured, that Egypt's hired foreign mercenaries will desert their employer (v. 21), and that inhabitants of Egypt will be deported (v. 19).

While much of the language of these oracles is stereotypical, the events that they anticipate are in touch with the historical realities of the Saite period. Although evidence for Greeks is best known, Levantine soldiers also were incorporated into the Egyptian military.[12] These foreign mercenaries played important roles under the Twenty-Sixth Dynasty (Kaplan 2010), fighting alongside Egyptian troops on campaigns (Bernand and Masson 1957; Schmitz 2010; Leahy 1988) and manning Egyptian border fortresses (Oren 1984; Breasted 1906–7, vol. 4, §994). Moreover, though Babylonian sources never explicitly discuss Nebuchadnezzar's imperial strategies, evidence from Philistia and Judah demonstrates his willingness to employ scorched-earth tactics and to deport large segments of local populations.[13] Alongside Ashkelon, Ekron was also destroyed in the Iron IIC and apparently not reoccupied during the Babylonian period, and Nebuchadnezzar conducted three distinctive rounds of deportations in Judah in 597, 586, and 582 BCE.

11. Ekron's excavators assume that it was also destroyed in conjunction with Ashkelon during the 604 BCE campaign (Gitin 1998, 276n2). Note, however, that there is no concrete textual evidence for the precise timing of the city's destruction. For an overview of proposed late seventh- and early sixth-century dates for its fall, see Fantalkin 2011, 88n2.

12. The longest Greek inscription at Abu Simbel, from a campaign of Psammetichus II against Kush, identifies a twofold division of troops: a corps of native Egyptians and a corps of "foreign speakers." However, Egyptian military titles make somewhat more precise distinctions among those supervising Greeks (ḥ3w nbw), Libyans (ṯmḥw and ṯḥnw), and Asiatics ('3mw), alongside more vague references to foreigners (ḫ3styw). See Chevereau 1985.

13. Alongside evidence for the destruction of urban sites and the depopulation of the southern Levant at the hands of the Babylonians, however, see also Lipschits 2011 on the evidence for continuity in Judah, particularly around Naṣbeh and Ramat Raḥel, and ongoing Babylonian interest in the region's agricultural products.

However, though the oracles' expectations were at least reasonable in the midst of the geopolitical struggle between Egypt and Babylon, these prophecies never came to fruition. In reality, Nebuchadnezzar's attempts to conquer Egypt failed. The Chronicle describes his first invasion of Egypt in 601/600 BCE in terms of heavy casualties for both sides, but it nevertheless admits that Nebuchadnezzar's troops ultimately were forced to return home (Grayson 1975, 101, Chronicle 5, reverse, lines 5–7). A close reading of Chronicle entries for subsequent years also suggests that this defeat had a significant impact on Babylonian forces, since Nebuchadnezzar and his troops remained in Babylon the next year and engaged in minimal campaigning in the year after that (Eph'al 2003, 180–83; Kahn 2008, 142–43). Expansion of the empire into Egypt would remain elusive throughout Nebuchadnezzar's reign.[14]

Egyptian Involvement in the Levant Post-605 BCE

Even if Egypt never regained the upper hand in the Levant, Twenty-Sixth Dynasty pharaohs continued to meddle in the affairs of Babylonian vassal states and foment resistance to Babylonian control. During this struggle for influence, Judah's loyalty to Babylon proved tenuous at best. Although Jehoiakim, who originally had been installed on the Judean throne by Necho II in 609 BCE, was briefly a Babylonian vassal, his allegiance shifted back to the Twenty-Sixth Dynasty after just three years (2 Kings 24:1), and Nebuchadnezzar's recent failed attempt to invade Egypt likely factored into Judah's confidence in resisting Babylonian rule.

Similarly, Zedekiah, who had been installed on Judah's throne by Nebuchadnezzar himself after Jehoiachin's surrender in 597 BCE, wavered in his loyalty to Babylon and pursued a pro-Egyptian foreign policy. In an attempt to organize neighboring polities into a coalition against Babylon, he hosted envoys from Ammon, Moab, Edom, Tyre, and Sidon in Jerusalem (Jer. 27), and he also sent Judean ambassadors to Egypt to seek military reinforcements for his rebellion (Ezek. 17:11–15).[15]

Further, despite the statement in 2 Kings 24:7 that "the king of Egypt did not come out again from his land," the Twenty-Sixth Dynasty also conducted additional military expeditions in the Levant alongside its diplomatic efforts. In 592 BCE Psammetichus II led an Egyptian contingent up the Mediterranean coast (Pap. Rylands 9, 14.16–19). While commentators waver on whether to characterize this event as a full campaign, all agree that it served Egypt's geopolitical interests by raising anti-Babylonian sentiments and cementing Egypt's alliances with city-states in the region (Kahn 2008, 148–53; Schipper 1999, 243–44).

Psammetichus II's successor, Apries (biblical Hophra), also sent troops to Jerusalem's aid and at least temporarily broke the final Babylonian siege of Jerusalem (Jer. 37:5, 11). Given its failure, the significance of this intervention can easily be missed in hindsight. However, on the ground in the early sixth century BCE, Judean officials still considered an alliance with Egypt a viable alternative to submission to Babylon. Ultimately, this confidence had devastating consequences, leading to the decimation of Jerusalem and other major Judean cities and the deportation of many of the Judean elite.

---

14. A royal Egyptian stele from Elephantine that dates to the reign of Amasis refers to a dual land and sea attack by the Sttyw ("Asiatics") (Leahy 1988, 190–93). See also the fragmentary cuneiform tablet BM 33041 from 568 BCE, which includes references to a military campaign and mentions "the Egyptian king and the totality of his troops" (Spalinger 1977, 236–37).

15. Lachish Letter III also includes a terse report of the Judean military commander Coniah ben Elnathan crossing over the Egyptian border and sending for Judean troops. It is unclear whether this letter ought to be regarded as evidence of a diplomatic mission seeking Egyptian support or a defection of Judean soldiers seeking asylum in Egypt. For further discussion and references, see Schipper 1999, 245–46.

Biblical Perspectives on Late Iron Age Politics

Thus, although Nebuchadnezzar's victory at Carchemish was a watershed moment in Iron Age history, the question of whether a Babylonian or an Egyptian alliance better served Judah's interests remained open long after 605 BCE. For the next two decades, Judah's kings vacillated between these two options as they attempted to better position themselves for survival in a dynamic geopolitical landscape. The book of Jeremiah, in particular, reflects the divide between pro-Babylonian and pro-Egyptian factions among the Judean elite.

In Jeremiah's narrative, the prophet is consistently depicted as an advocate for acceptance of subjugation to Babylon,[16] which he presents as the will of Yahweh himself (Jer. 27). Prior to the conquest of Jerusalem, he regards Babylonian victory as inevitable (e.g., 21:1–10; 32:2–5; 37:17) and surrender as the only means of survival (e.g., 21:8–10; 38:2, 17–23). He sternly warns royal officials hoping for the success of the Egyptian military intervention against deceiving themselves by believing that the Babylonians will abandon their campaign against Jerusalem (37:6–10). Even after Jerusalem's fall, Jeremiah, like Gedaliah ben Ahikam, the Babylonian-appointed leader at Mizpah, repeats the same basic message to the Judean remnant: the only way forward for the community is to put aside its fear of Nebuchadnezzar and remain in the land in submission to Babylon (42:10–12; cf. 40:9–10).

Conflicting voices are woven into the text. The anti-Babylonian position is also represented by its own prophetic spokesmen, such as Hananiah, who proclaims that Yahweh has "broken the yoke of the king of Babylon" (Jer. 28:2) and anticipates the swift reversal of the

597 BCE deportations. Alongside Jeremiah's prophetic opponents, royal officials who favor Zedekiah's rebellion accuse Jeremiah of harming Judah by weakening the resolve of the people to withstand the Babylonian siege: "This man is not seeking peace for this people but rather calamity" (Jer. 38:4). However, the editors' incorporation of these views focuses on their illegitimacy.

Opposition to Egypt is the natural counterpart to Jeremiah's pro-Babylonian perspective. The celebration of Egypt's defeat at Carchemish in Jeremiah 46 fits into a much broader trend of anti-Egyptian rhetoric that crosses the boundaries of literary genres, redactional stages, and Masoretic and Septuagint readings.[17] In the early stages of the tradition's development, the need for such a systematically negative characterization of Egypt is an implicit acknowledgment of the strength of pro-Egyptian voices who regarded the Twenty-Sixth Dynasty as a legitimate ally against the Babylonian threat and considered seeking asylum in Egypt a viable alternative to life in the land. As the Jeremiah tradition evolved, pro-Babylonian and anti-Egyptian perspectives remained relevant but were appropriated and expanded to meet new needs, most notably by members of the Babylonian *golah* (i.e., exiles) as they sought to claim exclusive status as the people of Yahweh and to dismiss Judean exilic communities in the land of Judah and in Egypt.[18]

---

16. This characterization is underscored by repeated accusations that Jeremiah and his scribe Baruch intend to collaborate with the Babylonians (Jer. 37:13–14; 43:2–3).

17. Egypt appears as the nation that enslaved Israel's ancestors in the past (Jer. 2:6; 7:21–26; 11:1–8; 16:14; 23:7; 31:31–32; 32:20–22; 34:13) and is repeatedly characterized as an unreliable political ally in the present (2:16–18, 36–37; 37:1–10). The prophet rejects Egypt as a legitimate place of refuge, condemns those who emigrate, and offers no hope for this community's future (24:8–10; 42:1–43:7; 44). Multiple oracles anticipate Egypt's downfall at Yahweh's hands (9:25–26; 25:15–26; 43:8–13; 46).

18. On the literary development of the book of Jeremiah and conflicts between exilic Judean groups, see esp. Rom-Shiloni 2013, 198–252. Note, however, that Rom-Shiloni does not account for the practical political implications of this rhetoric in the tradition's earliest stages.

41

Alexander the Great and Hellenism

D. BRENT SANDY

lexander the Great was a dark horse in the ancient world and accomplished a feat few thought possible. For centuries the empires and royal rulers of much of the Mesopotamian and eastern Mediterranean world were champions of the east. But Alexander and his generals were intruders from the west, and their conquest of Darius III and the Persian Empire in the fourth century BCE brought an abrupt end to the succession of eastern superpowers. Apart from Alexander and his successors, it is unlikely that the subsequent western empire (the Romans) would have become a world-class superpower in its own right.

Be that as it may, it is an oversimplification to paint the pictures of east and west as if the distinctions were black and white. Greek civilization had made significant advances, and the Persians were progressive in their own ways, just differently. No boundary marker clearly divided the two, and some mingling of cultures had gone on long before Alexander. But the earlier cultural interplay was not nearly at the same level or scope as it was after Alexander conquered and wrested control of the entire area that had been the Persian Empire. For many people, especially in urban areas and among upper classes—whether in the west or the east—it was no longer possible to continue in the comforts of the former homeland and traditional culture. The new world order necessitated adopting and adapting to a mixture of ways of thinking and living.[1] This was true for the Jews as much as for everyone else.

The Drama[2]

We might never have heard of Alexander the Great were it not for his father, Philip.[3] The

1. On the inbreeding of cultures, see Peters 1970, 22. Regarding the creativity of the Hellenistic period, see Rostovtzeff 1941, 1:v. See also Burstein 2003 on "new ways of being Greek in the Hellenistic period."
2. For the primary ancient sources, see Diodorus Siculus (first century BCE), Quintus Curtius Rufus (first century CE), Strabo (first century CE), Plutarch (second century CE), Arrian (second century CE), and an epitome of the lost history of Pompeius Trogus preserved by Justin (third century CE). A quick synopsis can be found in 1 Macc 1:1–10. All of these—not being contemporaries of the events they recorded—were dependent on earlier sources now lost (except for occasional fragments), such as by Ptolemy and Aristobulus. For detailed discussion of the lost sources, see Bosworth 1988, 295–300; Bosworth and Baynham 2000; Bosworth 2002. (See note 19 below on the lack of Persian sources.)
3. It is common to give too much credit to Alexander when it was largely Philip who fashioned a Macedonian/

year was 359 BCE, when, upon the death of his brother, Philip—at the age of twenty-two—became regent over Macedonia, a small region on the Balkan Peninsula north of ancient Greece.

In the course of only eight years of diplomacy and opportunistic seizure of weak tribal areas and city-states, Philip gained control of almost the entire region north of Greece. It helped that Philip was a mastermind of fighting techniques. The most important element was an innovative form of the phalanx. Wielding uncommonly long spears, the infantry formation was especially imposing and could be more effective than previous heavily armed contingents.[4]

For the next decade, Philip turned his attention to his neighbors to the south. Gradually and methodically he gained control of one Greek city-state after another. Eventually Athens was forced to declare war and seek to build a coalition to defend the heart of Greece. But it was too little too late. In 338 BCE at the decisive Battle of Chaeronea, Philip and his armies defeated the best forces that the Greeks could muster.[5]

At a subsequent council convened at Corinth, Philip announced a "universal peace," which would be on his terms. Three things were evident:

- Macedonia, once an inconsequential neighbor to the north, was now more powerful than all of Greece put together.
- The freedom of the long-established Greek city-states to act independently was over.
- Persia was next on Philip's agenda.

Yet in reality Philip's kingdom was little more than a blip on the radar relative to the vast Persian Empire, stretching across mountains

and valleys and deserts from the eastern shores of the Mediterranean to the Indus River valley.

Alexander[6]

Eighteen years earlier, one of Philip's wives by political alliance, Olympias, had given birth. Though there were other sons, Philip favored the new one, Alexander III, and began shaping him to follow in his footsteps. He even arranged for the philosopher Aristotle to come to Macedonia and give Alexander the best Greek education of the day.

The potential and prowess of the young Alexander soon became evident, especially at the Battle of Chaeronea, while still a teenager. The charge of Alexander's cavalry brigade broke the Greek resistance, giving him credit for the victory. With Philip and Alexander working together, it seemed that the Macedonian army was ready for anything. But it was not to be.

Just eighteen months later Philip was dead, unexpectedly assassinated, as possibly arranged by Alexander's distraught mother or, worst of all, some suppose, even by Alexander himself.[7] The question now was: Could the now twenty-year-old Alexander successfully succeed his father?

Astoundingly, in little more than a year, with the assistance of the Macedonian generals, Alexander proved to the army and to the Greeks that he too was a master of diplomacy and military competence. He boldly announced that war on Persia would begin the next year, with serious preparations beginning immediately. Alexander's reasons for attacking Persia

---

Greek kingdom and an army capable of defeating the Persians; see Gabriel 2010; Worthington 2014.

4. On Macedonian fighting techniques, see Snodgrass 1999, 114–30.

5. For this important battle, see Diodorus, *Library of History* 16.84.1–16.88.2.

6. Ancient and modern studies of Alexander are voluminous (second only, probably, to Jesus of Nazareth); some are balanced, while others tend to view Alexander too heroically. Good places to begin are Bosworth 1988; P. Green 1992; O'Brien 1992; Bosworth and Baynham 2000; Roisman 2002; Anson 2013; and the seminal papers of Ernst Badian, now collected and republished in Badian 2012.

7. For an account of how the assassination was carried out, see Diodorus, *Library of History* 16.91.1–16.95.1.

included repaying the Persians for what they had done to the Greeks 150 years earlier (Diodorus, *Library of History* 16.89.2) and freeing the Greek cities in Asia from Persian domination. Nevertheless, in his wildest dreams, Alexander could hardly have anticipated the extent of the exploits and achievements that lay ahead. (With Philip passing from the scene, it needs to be emphasized that without the shoulders of his father to stand on, it is unlikely that Alexander's accomplishments would have been anywhere near the same.[8])

The Invasion

The invasion of Persia took place in the spring of 334 BCE. Remarkably, the army that Alexander led across the Hellespont into Asia was less than one-third Macedonian; the rest were recruits from Greece and elsewhere.[9] Yet victories came easily, the first being at the Granicus River in the northwest corner of what is today Turkey, with the ancient city of Troy nearby.[10] Of the Greek mercenary soldiers employed to fight on the Persians' side, approximately half were killed in battle and the rest were captured by Alexander and sent back to Greece as slaves.

With Alexander's resolve and his army's confidence inflated, they forged ahead, charging south and east, laying siege to key cities, seizing treasuries, and moving ever closer toward another inevitable engagement with better-prepared Persian forces. Along the way Alexander removed various provincial governors and replaced them with his own officials. In some cases, he established democratic government in cities formerly under Persian control.

Meanwhile the Persian king, Darius III, had mustered an army intended to far outnumber Alexander's and marched up from Babylon. The battle was engaged at the town of Issus, more than five hundred miles southeast of where the first battle had been fought, which was half the distance to Babylon.[11] Once again the Greek sources report that it was a quick and resounding triumph. It put Darius himself on the run, with Alexander in hot pursuit. Surprisingly, Alexander captured the wife, mother, and children of Darius along with various harems of the Persian nobles, plus stunning amounts of booty.[12] Yet Darius escaped.

A Diversion

In the course of just eighteen months (it was now the fall of 333 BCE), Alexander had become so powerful that he could have marched into the heart of the Persian Empire probably with little resistance. But he saw an opportunity that had greater appeal: to proceed down the coast of the Mediterranean to Egypt. Except that two cities in particular stood in his way: Tyre and Gaza.

Tyre was essentially a fortress on an island off the coast, with walls erected right on the water's edge. Previously the city had been on the mainland, but the Babylonians under Nebuchadnezzar had demolished the old city, and the inhabitants rebuilt on the island.[13] In order to lay siege to the seemingly impregnable fortress, Alexander devised a scheme: he would use debris left from the old city and build a causeway out to the island. It was measured at 200 feet wide and 900 yards long extending

---

8. "This king [Philip], known for having the smallest of resources to acquire a monarchy, actually gained the greatest monarchy in Greece" (Diodorus, *Library of History* 16.95.2). See Worthington 2014.

9. See Diodorus, *Library of History* 17.17.3–4; Arrian, *History of Alexander* 1.2.3.

10. For the battle at the Granicus River, see Diodorus, *Library of History* 17.19.1–17.21.7; Arrian, *History of Alexander* 1.12.6–1.16.7.

11. For the battle at Issus, see Diodorus, *Library of History* 17.32.1–17.38.7; Arrian, *History of Alexander* 2.8.5–2.11.10.

12. For an example of the apparent bias evident in Greek sources, see Diodorus, *Library of History* 17.37.3–7; Arrian, *History of Alexander* 2.12.3–8.

13. Tyre is mentioned more than fifty times in the Bible; representative examples are 2 Sam. 5:11; 1 Kings 5:1–12; 2 Chron. 2:3–16; Isa. 23:1–18; Ezek. 26–28; Mark 7:24.

into the Mediterranean. Though it took seven months, the plan worked, and Tyre was destroyed.[14] Any male captives capable of fighting were cruelly crucified; the women and children who survived were callously sold into slavery. (Alexander's causeway, in the centuries since, has withstood the test of time; the island has never been an island again.)

After another extended siege in order to capture Gaza, Alexander led his army into Egypt. But there was no need for military engagement; confronted with the Macedonian/Greek military machine, Egypt acquiesced.[15] After founding a city on the coast of Egypt to be named "Alexandria," Alexander led his troops back north and then east, well aware that another battle with Darius lay ahead.[16]

The Last Battle

It was September of 331 BCE, and in the two years since the battle at Issus, Darius had made every preparation possible to stop the advancing Alexander, including a special force of chariots with long blades attached to the yokes and axles (designed to be driven directly into enemy ranks).[17] Darius chose the battleground that would be most advantageous for his strategy.[18]

But all the preparations went for naught. It was another rout by Alexander's forces, and he marched on to the great city of Babylon unopposed. He remained there "more than thirty days because there was an abundance of provisions, and the inhabitants were friendly" (Diodorus, *Library of History* 17.64.4).[19]

This intriguing story could go on for many more pages, providing endless details behind the headline news of Alexander's exploits as he led his army farther and farther into the recesses of the Persian Empire. Only when his tired troops at long last gave up and mutinied, having trudged all the way to India—more than 2,000 miles since crossing into Asia—did Alexander finally turn toward home. Unfortunately (though some consider it fortunate),[20] Alexander's adventures were to come to an end upon arriving back in Babylon. In the midst of indulging in massive celebrations—while contemplating yet additional expeditions (in spite of it being more than a decade since he left Macedonia)—Alexander suddenly fell ill. He died eleven days later, some of his contemporaries suspicious that he had been poisoned.[21] It was 323 BCE.

The Sequel

Drop a pebble in a pond, and the ripples do not amount to much. But if it is a boulder, the impact will be substantial. So Alexander. He was a boulder, and what he accomplished was huge, if not heroic.[22] However, he was soon

---

14. For detailed description of the capture of Tyre, see Diodorus, *Library of History* 17.40.2–17.46.6; Arrian, *History of Alexander* 2.21.1–2.24.6.

15. Alexander "took possession of all its cities without use of force" (Diodorus, *Library of History* 17.49.1). A possible explanation is that "Egypt's tormented history of relations with the Persian empire may explain its quiet surrender" (Kuhrt 2007, 1:421).

16. Alexandria would become one of the greatest cities of the ancient world, with the largest population of Jews of any city outside Judea. For an assessment of the claim that Alexander visited Jerusalem and of other supposed contacts between Alexander and the Jews, see Noy 2010.

17. For more detailed description of these specially designed chariots, see Quintus Curtius, *History of Alexander the Great* 4.9.5; Diodorus, *Library of History* 17.53.1–2; for scholarly assessment, see Heckel, Willekes, and Wrightson 2010.

18. For this battle, which took place at Gaugamela, see Diodorus, *Library of History* 17.53.1–17.61.3; Arrian, *History of Alexander* 3.9.1–3.15.6.

19. It is perplexing that there are almost no Persian records of the defeat of Darius by Alexander; Kuhrt 2007 (ch. 10) must rely almost entirely on Greek sources to describe the fall of the Achaemenid Empire. As a result, it is difficult to assess possible distortion created by the one-sided Greek sources. See Briant 2002.

20. Alexander had already ruthlessly conquered more territory than he was prepared to administer, and one wonders what the point was in continuing to do more of the same.

21. For scholarly discussion, see Heckel 2007; Schep 2009.

22. Some recent scholars, instead of idealizing Alexander as a hero of peace and prosperity, use adjectives like "ruthless" and nouns like "destroyer" or "butcher,"

gone. But not the ripples. The rest of the story is about the ripple effect: the consequences superseded the force of the impact itself.

There are varied aspects to the sequel, many of them complex. Upon Alexander's death, his army, generals, and kingdom were at a loss. Alexander had not prepared to die, and no one was in position to lay claim as his successor. The upshot was that the conquered territories became battlegrounds, as the former generals fought numerous wars across fifty years, each seeking a piece of the pie, if not the whole pie. Alexander's kingdom, once stretching from Macedonia to India, was fragmented—irretrievably.[23] When the dust of the civil wars settled, three primary successors had established major kingdoms and dynasties, though there were smaller ones.[24]

- Antigonus came closest to uniting and ruling the disparate parts of what Alexander had conquered, even claiming to have done so.[25] But that was his downfall. Other former generals banded together against him. His offspring continued the Antigonid dynasty, mostly ruling Macedonia and sometimes Greece, until conquered by Rome in 168 BCE.
- Ptolemy quickly seized Egypt and, though challenged, was able to defend his claim. It helped his status that he had made off with Alexander's corpse. In 305 BCE he took the title "king" and ruled—in addition

to Egypt—Cyprus, Phoenicia, and Palestine.[26] The famous Cleopatra was the last of the Ptolemaic dynasty. Egypt was annexed as a province of Rome in 30 BCE.

- Seleucus laid claim to Babylonia. He then successfully enlarged his domain to the east and west.[27] The subsequent Seleucid king, Antiochus III, defeated the Ptolemies and added Phoenicia and Palestine to the Seleucid kingdom. Under Antiochus IV (Epiphanes), the expression of Jewish faith was suppressed, and the temple in Jerusalem defiled. Eventually the Jews revolted in the famous Maccabean Revolt beginning in 166 BCE. Syria was annexed as a province of Rome in 64 BCE.

Hellenization

More important than the fragmentation of Alexander's kingdom was its amalgamation of various ethnicities and cultures. The blending varied from place to place, with numerous factors contributing to the process.

- The armies of Alexander and the successors—and to a lesser extent the armies of Darius—became melting pots. Alexander's army initially included soldiers from Macedonia, from Balkan tribes, and from various Greek city-states. As he went along, he enlisted additional warriors from regions he conquered.
- The battles between Alexander and Darius and the wars between the successors dislodged many locals from their native villages and homelands (including Jews), forcing them to take refuge with other peoples and cultures.

with one even stating that there was as much tragedy as triumph and that "killing is what he did best" (Bosworth 1996, v). See also O'Brien 1992; Burstein 1997.

23. "The Macedonian enterprise . . . dug the grave of the political unity the Great [Persian] kings had been able to establish and safeguard through the preceding two and a half centuries" (Briant 2002, 876); see Bosworth 1996; Heckel 2003.

24. Smaller kingdoms included Pergamum, Bithynia, Pontus, and Galatia. For Alexander's generals and successors, see Bosworth 2002; Anson 2014; Heckel 2016. For discussion of the number of kingdoms vis-à-vis the book of Daniel's four kingdoms, see Sandy 2002, 114–16.

25. For a history of Macedonia incorporating archaeological finds, see Borza 1990. For a biography of Antigonus, see Billows 1997.

26. For a biography of Ptolemy I, see W. Ellis 1994. For assessment of Ptolemaic ideology and administration and relationships between the Greco-Macedonians and the Egyptians, see Samuel 1989; Sandy 2000.

27. For discussion of the beginnings of the Seleucid kingdom, see Grainger 1990.

- Alexander and his successors established military colonies at strategic points, primarily designed to safeguard the regions from revolts and insurrection. The settlements, though small, interacted with local people, especially for supplies.

- Alexander and his successors founded new cities and reconstituted others (the Seleucids, for example, are credited with creating sixty new settlements). The cities were given considerable independence, though, in many cases, their constitutions and administrations were modeled after those of Greek city-states. Colonists (many of whom had come to the east in response to the successors' invitations) lived and worked side by side with local peoples.

- The successors established elaborate administrative structures with many openings to fill. Though they welcomed Macedonians and Greeks to serve in various roles (thrusting foreigners into ruling people they knew little about), in many cases locals who had proved themselves well under previous administrations were granted roles in the successors' governments.

- Enterprising people from the west moved into the regions that had come under Macedonian/Greek control, searching for economic opportunities.

It has been common to refer to this integration of ethnicities and cultures as Hellenization, which can imply that the people of the west were evangelistic with their Hellenism, seeking to spread a "superior" message as far as possible.[28] That was a hard form of Hellenization

and may have been present in some cases, but it is more accurate to speak of soft Hellenization, more of a coexistence of cultures with influences in all directions, not only the west impacting the east.[29] The Ptolemies, for example, were pictured in Egyptian temples as if they were pharaohs. The Greeks and Macedonians ruling Egypt adopted the long-standing organization of Egypt's territory rather than imposing a Greek model.

The clearest example of soft Hellenization, which happened by default more than intent, was the development of Koine (common) Greek. It was the by-product of many non-native Greeks learning to speak Greek, leading to a simpler language, which became the *lingua franca* of the Hellenistic world (and subsequently of the Roman world).

Beyond language, the cross-fertilization of cultures impacted many aspects of life: economy and trade, religion, philosophy, literature, art, rhetoric, law, architecture, and so forth. Greek culture may have had the upper hand in the confluence of cultures, but in most cases the combination happened intuitively, not by deliberate scheme.

The Jews

Discussions of the Hellenization of the Jews have ranged far and wide, some contending that the Greek influence was very significant, others that it was insignificant.[30] There is little

---

28. The Greeks referred to their land as Hellas and their culture as Hellenism. The process of Hellenization "used to be seen through rose-tinted spectacles as the innocent gift of civilization to the benighted barbarians" (Price 1988, 321). Along the same line, "The dominant theme of recent Hellenistic scholarship is skepticism concerning their predecessors' optimistic picture of Greco-Macedonian invaders and their Near Eastern subjects

harmoniously living together and cooperating in the creation of a brilliant new mixed civilization" (Burstein 1997, 40).

29. The Hellenistic age is probably best defined as the period beginning with Alexander's death and ending with Cleopatra's death, when Rome annexed the last of the Hellenistic kingdoms. While this period is sometimes overlooked because of interest in Classical Greece or the Roman Republic or Empire, it may be considered one of "the four great areas of ancient history" (Welles 1970, 3). For insights into this period, see esp. Walbank 1993; Burstein 1997; Erskine 2005; M. Austin 2006; Bugh 2006.

30. L. I. Levine 1998; the best representative for those who find significant Hellenization of the Jews is Hengel

doubt that Jewish religion and culture underwent considerable change during the period, aside from whether it was directly under the influence of Greek culture.[31]

An example of the openness of Jews to Hellenism was Greek institutions in Jewish cities, especially Jerusalem. A gymnasium was a particularly obvious expression of Greek ideals, but some Jews, rather than resisting what was in opposition to Jewish culture, welcomed the customs, even to the point of abandoning the covenant of circumcision (1 Macc. 1:11–15). Though that example may be an exception rather than the rule, the passage probably is representative of conservative Jews' concern about such trends.

An undisputed example of the Jews adopting Greek culture is language. All across the Mediterranean world Jews were speaking and writing Greek, composing history, philosophy, fiction, and so forth. Most notable of all is the translation of the Jewish Scriptures into Koine, beginning as early as the third century BCE.[32] Many adopted it as being as authoritative as the Hebrew version itself.

The Book of Daniel

The book of Daniel may surprise readers by its repeated references to the Persian, Greek, and successor kingdoms. Actually, there was good reason. Going back to the Assyrian and Babylonian destructions of Samaria and Jerusalem, this was the dark ages of the history of Israel. God was using a series of gentile kingdoms to wield a brutal sword of judgment, because the crimes of his chosen people against him had become intolerable: idolatry, empty worship,

and injustices—sins that the prophets had been pointing out for centuries (e.g., Ezek. 21:1–32). Not only did gentile armies destroy the principal cities, temples, palaces, and treasuries but also most of the population was killed or deported, with only a small portion ever to return. It meant that the nation of Israel lived with a sense of desperation, dispersed far and wide, with a preponderance eking out an existence among the gentiles rather than living in the Promised Land.[33]

In this context the book of Daniel spoke poignantly. The court tales of the first six chapters challenged the chosen people that they could live true to their religion, even though in exile and in conflict with the values of the gentile kingdoms. The apocalyptic visions in the second part of the book offered a message of hope in the midst of crisis: all was not lost even when they were faced with threats of persecution and death. God would ultimately defeat the evil forces.

The first reference to the kingdoms is in Nebuchadnezzar's dream of a large statue, which represented four successive empires (Dan. 2:27–45). One of the four was Persia and one Alexander's.[34] In the second part of the book, Daniel's vision of four fierce animals again pictured four kingdoms, the last being an unnamed but terrifying beast with iron teeth and ten horns (7:1–27). The fourth beast was symbolic of Alexander's kingdom, for out of the ten horns another horn appeared, which waged war against the saints—almost certainly alluding to the Seleucid king Antiochus Epiphanes.

Yet another of Daniel's visions described a goat with a prominent horn attacking and defeating a ram with two horns (Dan. 8:1–14).

1974 (also Hengel 1980); for the opposing viewpoint, see esp. L. Feldman 1993; for assessment, see J. Collins 2005; J. Collins and Sterling 2001; Hengel 1989.

31. Gruen 1998; for change in religious practices, see Grabbe 2000.

32. For general introductions to the Septuagint, see Dines 2004; Fernández Marcos 2000; Jobes and Silva 2015. For a deeper investigation, see Aitken 2015; Rajak 2009.

33. For studies of the Jews in the dispersion, see Gruen 2002; 2010; Pucci Ben Zeev 2010; for ancient sources regarding Jews outside Palestine, see Margaret Williams 1998.

34. The allusiveness of the dream's apocalyptic imagery leads to differences of opinion over which part of the statue represents Persia and which Greece; for discussion, see Walton 1986; Lucas 2012, 115–17; Newsom 2014, 80–97.

The goat's single horn is broken off and four horns replace it. While Daniel was rightfully distraught (v. 27), the angel Gabriel identified the ram and the goat as the kings of Media and Persia and the king of Greece (vv. 20–21).[35]

The longest and most detailed discourse on the kingdoms focused on "the king of the north" and "the king of the south," signifying the Seleucids and the Ptolemies (Dan. 11:2–45). Many battles between the kingdoms took place in Palestine, resulting in much destruction and many deaths. The detail is remarkably specific yet sometimes difficult to match up with historical events. Nevertheless, the point is clear: the Jews were pinballs, bounced back and forth as the gentile nations engaged in ferocious conflicts.

Fortunately, the book of Daniel ends on a high note, with energizing words for the faithful in spite of what kingdom oppressed them. The promise was that they would shine with the brightness of the heavens and be made spotless (Dan. 12:2–3, 10).

Conclusion

Sizing up the unprecedented events of his day, the Athenian orator Aeschines—having received news that Alexander had defeated the best army the Persians could amass—stated in an oration (in the summer of 330 BCE):

> What unexpected and astonishing thing hasn't happened in our lifetime?! We certainly have not lived a normal human life but were born to be a phenomenon to future generations. Is not the Persian king . . . the one who dared to write in his letters that he was master of all people from the rising to the setting of the sun, struggling at this very moment—not to have mastery over others—but to save his own life? (*Against Ctesiphon* 132)[36]

While it is clear that a little-known Macedonian conqueror came out of nowhere—like David against Goliath—and unexpectedly and abruptly slew the mighty Persian superpower, the question is: How much did the drama impact subsequent generations? And more specifically: How much were the Jews affected? Alexander's contemporaries predicted that the consequences would be substantial. Only those who were part of the sequel could fully grasp the impact.

---

35. For a discussion of the lack of precise historical referents for the symbolism in the vision, see Sandy 2002, 111–20.

36. Demetrius offered a similar assessment, noting that the formerly unknown Macedonians had mastered the Persians and effectively made the Persians' name unknown; cited in Polybius, *Histories* 29.21.1–6.

PART THREE

Themes
of the Drama

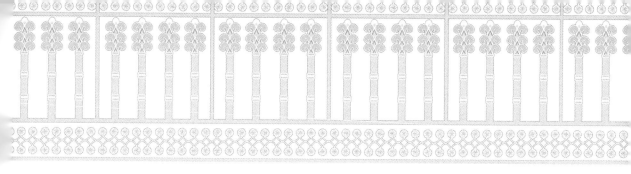

SECTION VII

God

*Integrated Approaches
to Themes in Israelite Religion*

Interactions in the Ancient Cognitive Environment

JOHN H. WALTON

The discipline that discusses the relationship between the Old Testament and its cultural milieu may be called "cognitive environment criticism." The goal of this discipline is to recover the cultural layers from the world behind the text that were inherently understood by the ancient audience but have been long lost to our modern world. Texts, along with iconography, serve as windows to the cognitive environment of the ancient world.

One of the important difficulties in this task is discerning exactly how the Israelites were aware of this broader culture and how they used it in composing the Old Testament. Several models can be identified that propose to provide a foundation for understanding the interrelationships between the Old Testament and the rest of the ancient Near Eastern literatures.

Models for the Relationship

Borrowing

The first model suggests that Israelite scribes had direct access to literary pieces that circulated among the scribal schools of the ancient world and adapted material directly from those literary pieces to shape their own traditions. Evidence supporting this model would include the find of a fragment of the *Epic of Gilgamesh* at Megiddo dated to Iron Age I. Most commonly, however, this model assumes that the Israelites encountered this literature beginning with the Assyrian incursions into the west in the ninth and eighth centuries, but primarily as exiles in Babylon in the sixth century. Problems encountered by this model include the wide range of literature from other cultures—and as early as the mid-second millennium—to which parallels can be identified and the fact that there are very few cases where the Old Testament literature and its putative ancient Near Eastern source are actually similar enough to make a persuasive case for borrowing. This model also faces the challenge that if borrowing is to be suggested, probable cause must be established. Evidence required would include proximity in time and space such that Israelites could plausibly have encountered the literature from which they are suspected of borrowing.

Polemics

A common approach that modern scholars take toward the similarities between the Old Testament and other ancient literatures is to consider the Israelite scribes as conducting an aggressive polemic against the literature and views of their neighbors. A focus on the Old Testament polemics would describe passages that showed awareness of a particular ancient Near Eastern text (or texts) and are constructed to refute what that text (or texts) affirms (Currid 2013, 26–32).

Convenient examples such as the caricatures of images in Isaiah 44 and Jeremiah 10 demonstrate that the Hebrew Bible does indeed at times engage in polemics. The methodological question is whether polemics can be used as an explanation when the putative target of the polemic is not referred to. Can choice of words ("great lights" in Gen. 1:16 instead of "sun" and "moon," whose cognates are also used as the names of the sun god and the moon god) or promotion of an alternative view (Yahweh riding on the clouds or chaos creatures under Yahweh's control) be construed as polemic? Arguably, for something to be considered seriously as polemic it cannot be tacit; the target must either be identified (rather than left to the imagination) or be demonstrably so well known that general recognition by the audience could be assumed. If we use a criterion requiring polemic either to refute directly or at least to undermine an alternative by insinuation, we might be surprised to discover that the literature of the Old Testament never forthrightly refutes or undermines an ancient myth—it only lampoons or denies the power of the gods.

Counter-texts

Eckart Frahm utilizes the descriptor "counter-texts" to describe works from the ancient Near East that he concludes have been composed as reactions to earlier texts (e.g.,

Erra and Ishum as a reaction to *Enuma Elish* [Frahm 2011, 347–64]). In that sense, they take their place in the reception history of the earlier work. The difference between this and polemics is in the intention: Is the writer trying to disprove his counterpart's claims (polemics) or simply presenting his own alternate perspective (counter-texts)? In counter-texts, one form of reaction would be to reverse the plots of earlier works. Less obviously, "small but significant manipulations of older works were another way to adapt texts to the needs of a later era and produce new meanings" (Frahm, 2011, 345). Frahm proceeds to suggest that passages in the Hebrew Bible such as the P account of creation (Gen. 1:1–2:3) and the Tower of Babel narrative show enough similarity to works from ancient Near Eastern literature (and therefore arguably awareness of them) to conclude that they are adopting a counterpoint position, offering their own view rather than refuting the views of others (Frahm, 2011, 364–68). In such a case, the views can be meaningfully juxtaposed to interpretive advantage.

Echoes

A fourth model understands similarities as reflecting an even lower threshold as a form of intertextuality. In this view, the biblical tradents or composers are broadly familiar with the literature of the ancient Near East and make faint allusions to it that echo its themes or content at the minimalist end of the spectrum. Alternatively, at the maximalist end, they are actually using the tropes or motifs of specific literature to craft a new work. In the latter case, there is no intention of parodying, arguing against, or even countering the subject text. Examples can be found in the way that Ezekiel makes use of *Erra and Ishum* (Bodi 1991).[1]

1. Another example is the way that Dan. 4 or Ezek. 31 uses the motif of the world tree.

Diffusion

A final model differs from the rest in that it does not require that specific pieces of literature were known by the Israelite scribes (whether they actually were or not). In this view, what we know as literary traditions circulated around in informal ways and often in oral form. A diffusion model does not deny that whatever scribal schools there were in Israel may have had access to the literary works that comprised a scribal curriculum. It recognizes, however, that archival texts may not have been the most prominent forms in which the traditions circulated. One of the advantages of the diffusion model is that it can also account for many of the fundamental aspects of ancient culture that are evident in the Hebrew Bible but are not tied specifically to literary traditions, even though they may surface in one or several specific pieces.

Conclusions

These approaches are not mutually exclusive. Theoretically, we might find examples of texts scattered throughout the Hebrew Bible where each approach is useful. They share some common ground in that in all but the last the Hebrew writer shows an awareness of the cognate literature. He is a protagonist in a conversation, whether engaged in borrowing and reworking, debate (polemic), reflection (counter-text), or casual intertextuality, or simply characterized by general awareness of the way ideas were framed or approached in the ancient world. Each, therefore, requires the modern scholar to present evidence that the Hebrew writer would have plausibly been aware of either the specific piece of literature or the tradition, whichever the case may be.

To think about the ancient world using these models we can use the metaphor of a cultural river that flows through the societies and thoughts of the peoples and nations of the ancient Near East. Israel was immersed in that cultural river, embedded in that conceptual world. Sometimes God gave revelation that drew them out, as Moses from the Nile, and distinguished them, but we should generally think of them in this cultural river. Sometimes they are simply floating on its currents (facilitating echoes or diffusion); sometimes they veer out of the currents and stand apart (perhaps leading to counter-texts); other times they swim resolutely upstream against those currents (as would be reflected in polemics). Consequently, Israel's relationship to those currents varies case by case. Importantly, however, as modern readers, we have no familiarity with that river at all. Our cultural river is very different. Whether Israel is floating or swimming, we must recognize that they are in a different river than we are. To interpret the Old Testament well, we must try to dip into their cultural river.

Sample Texts

We now proceed to the consideration of several key texts in the Hebrew Bible that often have been the subject of comparative analysis to consider what methodology or approach proves defensible.

Genesis 1

The creation account in Genesis 1:1–2:4 has been mined often for its similarities to cosmologies of the ancient Near East (G. Hasel 1972; 1974). In Mesopotamian traditions *Enuma Elish* is the most commonly identified correlate, while others have promoted Egyptian connections (Hoffmeier 1983). Points of contact with *Enuma Elish*, however, are few and far between. Often suggested similarities include the syntax of the respective opening lines (but only when Gen. 1 is modified), the cognate relationship between *tehom* ("sea" in Gen. 1:2) and Tiamat (the antagonist representing the sea in *Enuma Elish*), and the relationship between the creative spirits, *mummu* in *Enuma*

Elish and the spirit of God in Genesis 1:2. Numerous other lines of connection or contrast are drawn between Genesis and ancient Near Eastern traditions, including the avoidance of "sun" and "moon" in Genesis, the reference to the great sea creatures (Gen. 1:21), and the idea of the creation of humans followed by divine rest.

None of these purported connections are close enough to suggest borrowing, and in fact a number of them have been mitigated based on further analysis. The opening line of Genesis must be emended in order to have any correspondence with the opening line of *Enuma Elish*. The passing reference to *tehom* in Genesis neither adopts nor contests anything about Tiamat in *Enuma Elish*. Tiamat's name is a variation of the normal Akkadian word for "sea" (*tamtu*), which finds its cognate in Hebrew *tehom*. *Enuma Elish* need not be brought into the picture. The role of *mummu* or even the identification of her as spirit is questionable. The reference to the sun and moon as "lights" rather than using the words "sun" and "moon" can hardly be considered polemical. Genesis does not make a case that they are not gods. In fact, though the names for the gods associated with the sun and moon in West Semitic are variations of the names of the sun and the moon themselves, sun and moon are not considered gods themselves but rather manifestations chosen by the gods. The Hebrew text uses "lights" because that is what they are. Any attempt at polemic would have to be more specific and more nuanced to have any effect.

In Genesis 1, then, we find the evidence supporting a case for borrowing to be nonexistent or contrived, the evidence for polemic to be overstated, and the evidence for serving as a counter-text as too sporadic and vague to build a case. If there are intertextual echoes of any specific ancient Near Eastern texts, they are so faint that only the most informed ancient reader would catch them. In contrast, the case

for diffusion is fairly strong in that the ways of thinking about cosmology in Genesis 1 are deeply rooted in the ancient world rather than our own. Ordering by means of naming and separating, establishing the functioning cosmos, and God taking up his residence in this temple-like environment all betray the cosmological conversations of the world in which ancient Israel was situated.

Psalm 29

This psalm is comprised of lines that echo Ugaritic hymnic literature—so much so that some scholars have considered it to be an Israelite adaptation modified for Yahwism (Avishur 1994, 39–110; Kloos 1986, 94–124; A. Green 2003, 261–64).[2] Verses 6–8 locate Yahweh's activities in relation to geographical locations north of Israel. The vocabulary and the concepts are considered more at home in Ugaritic than in Hebrew, though they are not absent from Hebrew. It is difficult to claim borrowing when the piece of literature that is purportedly borrowed from is only hypothetical. It is difficult to claim that it is adapted and modified to serve as a polemic when it does not make its case against Baʿal explicitly. We could identify it as a counter-text if we believed that the composer intentionally alludes to Baʿal's typical profile and the Israelite audience would have recognized the language and motifs as characteristic of hymns to Baʿal. But again, diffusion would be the most defensible option, as the Israelites would be expected to praise Yahweh using styles and phrases commonplace in their time and cultural setting, for Yahweh and Baʿal were considered to have some overlapping traits.

Psalm 74 (Chaoskampf)

The literature on this topic is extensive, including a number of dissertations (Ballentine

2. Accepted in the classic formulation by Cross 1973, 151–56, on the basis of the seminal Hebrew book by H. L. Ginsberg of 1936.

2015; Batto 1992; J. Day 1985; Gunkel 2006; Kloos 1986; Scurlock and Beal 2013; Tsumura 2005; Wakeman 1973; Walton 2008; R. S. Watson 2005). Psalm 74 is generally considered the clearest example in the Bible of creation through conflict, in which the creator God defeats the chaos enemies to establish order and security. It is likened especially to Marduk's defeat of Tiamat in *Enuma Elish*. Once Psalm 74 is considered as asserting that tradition, allusions in other texts, opaque on their own, are then added to the list of supporting passages. In a recent analysis, however, David Tsumura has suggested that the defeat of the chaos creatures alluded to in Psalm 74 pertains not to creation (motifs of creation entirely lacking in the psalm) but to Yahweh's defeat of Israel's enemies in history. Furthermore, Tsumura asserts that "in all the cosmological myths of the ancient Near East, only in Enuma Elish do the conflict motif and the creation motif exist together" (Tsumura 2015, 554). Recent discussions suggest that *Chaoskampf* (divine war against chaos) ought to be considered within the larger category of theomachy—battle involving the divine realm (Walton 2008). This concept of divine battle is diffused throughout the literature of the ancient Near East for a variety of rhetorical purposes. *Chaoskampf* should be limited to referring to conflict focused on attempts to contain macrocosmic disorder and can pertain to the initial establishment of order, dealing with a one-time threat from a chaos monster, or with renewal on a seasonal basis.

Isaiah 24–27

Isaiah 27:1 has long been considered an indisputable example of literary dependence of a biblical passage on ancient Near Eastern literature since two lines are quoted verbatim from an Ugaritic text (*KTU* 1.5 i.1–3). Regardless of the overlap, questions remain concerning the likelihood that Isaiah in eighth-century Judah should be aware of a Late Bronze Age Ugaritic text circulating half a millennium earlier. Also worthy of note and the subject of frequent comment is the fact that what was part of the Ba'al myth in Ugaritic has been transformed in Isaiah to a metaphor for historical parties. This passage therefore provides the parade example for suggesting the comparative paradigm for the Old Testament use of myth—a retasking of familiar imagery to a new locution.

William Barker's groundbreaking work has suggested that this verse is only one small part of a larger kingship polemic that stretches across Isaiah 24–27 (W. Barker 2014). The most notable additional parallels that he identifies between Isaiah and Ugaritic are *mawet* in Isaiah 25:6–8 and Mot in the Ba'al myth (W. Barker 2014, 209–10) and the banqueting motif found in connection with those (though he sees Isaiah as inverting the *marzeaḥ* Northwest Semitic feast). He concludes that the Ugaritic perception of Litan (= Leviathan in Isa. 27:1) is that it is one of Mot's functionaries. This observation pulls all the parallels together to lead to the conclusion that Isaiah 24–27 is a "polemic against Mot, in which Yhwh's secure and unlimited kingship is proclaimed over every enemy, including Death [*mawet*] and its allies" (W. Barker 2014, 212). This conclusion is further supported by the nearly identical narrative progression observed in Isaiah 24:17–25:8 and the Ba'al Myth (*KTU* 1.4 vii–1.5 ii.20) in comparable discussions of divine kingship. He concludes, "The general message of Isa. 24–27 concerning Yhwh's sovereignty is that his kingship is eternal, immutable, mutually exclusive, and enforced against all challengers. Isaiah 24–27, then, is primarily a polemic against challenges to Yhwh's rule and a polemic in favour of Yhwh's firmly established and unlimited kingship" (W. Barker 2014, 212). Isaiah need not have been familiar with the distinct Ugaritic textual tradition that expressed these ideas. He may simply have drawn from the "cultural river" in which such ideas were commonly known in the Levant.

This passage stands as the most persuasive example of such polemic in the biblical text, and as such it exemplifies the phenomenon of diffusion and demonstrates the method of intertextual retasking.

The Tower of Babel

Frahm considers the Tower of Babel account the hallmark example of a counter-text (Frahm 2011, 364–68). He compares the account to *Enuma Elish* 6.59–73, in which the Anunna gods work for a year making bricks to "raise the head" of Esagil, the temple at Babylon, and its ziggurat, Etemenanki. At its completion its name, Babylon, is proclaimed. He views the Tower of Babel account in Genesis 11 as an ideological reversal that gives a negative reading of the founding of Babylon and its ziggurat through its polemical tone. "In Genesis, Babylon and its tower, instead of being symbols of unification, are presented as archetypal monuments of a human arrogance that is punished by God with the dissipation of the people and the confusion of their tongues" (Frahm 2011, 367).

This interpretation of the Tower of Babel as a counter-text is weakened by its presupposition that it should be located in an exilic context as a reflection of Israel's animosity toward its captors. However, one need not posit an exilic context for the composition of this text. An alternative interpretation suggests a different mechanism of interaction between text and culture.

The key to such an alternative interpretation is to be found in an understanding of the function of a ziggurat in the ancient world. Rather than viewing the building project as a symbol of political arrogance (as per Frahm) or theological arrogance (in traditional Christian and Jewish interpretation), a study of the names of the ziggurats in ancient texts indicates that they were seen as cosmic portals constructed as part of sacred space. They were not designed so that humans, in their arrogance, could ascend to heaven, but rather so that the gods could be invited to descend and take up their residence in the temples that adjoined the ziggurats in sacred space.[3] Temples, as the palaces of deity, became the focal point for people to meet the needs of the gods who descended to receive offerings. Ziggurat construction, then, represented human effort to induce divine blessing in a symbiotic exchange.[4] The people would "make a name for themselves" in that they would be remembered always as those who had succeeded in reestablishing the presence of God on earth, and they would become great as the god blessed them. This interpretation of the account fits the literary context in that it shows the account to be an inclusio with Genesis 1–3, where the presence of God took up residence in Eden and then was lost in what we call the fall. The initiative taken by the builders of Babel, however, was rejected because it was motivated by their desire to make a name for themselves instead of making a name for God—the ideal purpose for sacred space.

The chronological context is likewise respected in that this human initiative precedes the establishment of the covenant with Abram, which represents God's counter-initiative to reestablish relationship and sacred space (relationship through the covenant and sacred space in the eventual construction of the tabernacle).

This interpretation reflects the diffusion of ideas and does not require that the authors had access to texts or that they argue against particular pieces of literature. Rather, it simply presupposes the common understanding in the ancient Near East of sacred space and the function of ziggurats. Other texts also reflect related aspects of the cultural river:[5]

3. The *gigunu* at the top of the ziggurat also provided residential quarters apart from the throne room and audience chamber of the temple. In that, the *gigunu* would be like a modern "break room" or "green room" or could be equated to the residential quarters of the White House.

4. See ch. 44 below, "The Temple in Context."

5. I am not suggesting that Israel had access to any of these texts or that the texts should be understood as

1. Numerous pieces of literature reflect the motif of the irreverent king who incurred the anger of a god and could not get permission to build a temple.[6] In the Amar-Suen texts, the king even expresses his desire to build the temple and ziggurat in Eridu (the first city, often interchanged with Babylon) in order to make a name for himself (Espak 2015, 61).

2. In *Nergal and Ereshkigal* the messenger of the gods, Namtar, uses the *simmiltu*, the stairway that serves as a portal between the cosmic realms, to descend from the heavens. One of the names given to a ziggurat is "sacred space [Sum. É] of the pure *simmiltu*" (George 1993, 115).[7]

3. In *Enmerkar and the Lord of Aratta*, in a controversial section identified as the spell of Nudimmud, a situation is envisioned in which "the whole world of well-ruled people will be able to speak to Enlil in one language" (Vanstiphout 2003, 64–65, lines 145–46).[8] However this might be interpreted, it demonstrates

that the question of multiple languages was an issue in the ancient world.

4. A comment in a broken line of Amar-Suen suggests that communication was confusing and lacking wisdom.[9]

5. The omen series *šumma alu* offers a negative interpretation of a city that is built up high (S. Freedman 1998, 1:26–27, line 1).

Due to limitations of space we will need to pass briefly over other very intriguing examples. Much discussion has focused on the proposal that the book of Deuteronomy is composed as a polemic against the vassal treaty of Esarhaddon. This view has been soundly critiqued and rejected in some recent studies and therefore will not be treated here (Crouch 2014).

Conclusion

To return to the questions raised at the beginning of the chapter: we do not need to know how much the Israelites knew of the literature of the wider ancient world. The approach suggested here does not assume either knowledge or lack of it and does not depend on that decision. How much do they make use of that literature and in what ways? I have suggested that they may make use of the literature in any number of ways but that for the most part the similarities we observe can be accounted for by diffusion. Polemical passages exist in the Hebrew Bible, but not every touchpoint with the ancient Near East should be considered polemical, and most can be understood in other ways.

---

related to the Tower of Babel account. But texts like these show us the sorts of issues that were in what I have called the cultural river. The Tower of Babel account reflects some of the same motifs but in a very different context. Interpreters should see it as neither a borrowed piece of literature nor a counter-text to Neo-Babylonian building texts. Yet we dare not interpret it without consulting the ancient Near Eastern context.

6. Examples range from Naram-Suen and Amar-Suen in the Ur III period, to Nabonidus in the Neo-Babylonian period, and even include the assessment of David (not given permission to build the temple). See treatment of the motif in Michalowski 1977.

7. #672 (*simmiltu* = Sumerian KUN₄) (see *CAD* S:273–75).

8. In his notes on pp. 93–94, Vanstiphout acknowledges that other interpreters translate the spell as referring to the primordial past and admits that the grammar could support such an interpretation.

9. See the translation at http://etcsl.orinst.ox.ac.uk /cgi-bin/etcsl.cgi?text=t.2.4.3.1#.

43

Monotheism in Ancient Israel

Matthew J. Lynch

Framing Monotheism

At the heart of Jewish and Christian claims about God, rooted in the pages of the Hebrew Bible / Old Testament, is the claim that there is only *one* God (Deut. 4:35, 39). Yet the nature of this claim and its presence or pervasiveness in the Old Testament is a matter of considerable debate.

Scholars of ancient Israel differ by about eight hundred years on when they place the "origins," or emergence, of monotheism. They differ further on which and whether cultural influences may have played a role in the formation of Israelite monotheism. Whereas the focus on "origins" assumes that monotheism came from one or a few causes, Israel's history attests instead to a range of cultural and religious cross-cultural interactions, each of which provoked a range of responses within Israelite religion that contributed to the emergence of various monotheistic expressions. While monotheism's origins may be unclear and more complicated than often assumed, the emergence of Yhwh's sole divinity as a critical dimension of Israelite religion is undoubtable.

In this chapter, we will look at monotheism as a diffuse and diverse phenomenon.

What Do We Know about the Origins of Monotheism, and When Do We Know It?

Finding the birthdate of monotheism ranks as a high priority for many historians of Israelite monotheism. Some place it in the time of Moses (fourteenth to thirteenth centuries [e.g., Kaufmann 1960, 137]) and draw on the possible influence of Atenism to strengthen the case. One might go back even further to the Sumerian "Babel of Tongues" poem, in which the poet recalls a time when *all* the nations worshiped the same (conveniently Sumerian) deity, Enlil (Kramer 1968, 109).[1] Others place the origins of monotheism in the seventh or sixth centuries BCE (M. S. Smith 2001a) or even later.

---

1. While not deriving from an "actively" monotheistic culture, the Sumerian poem attests to the conception of a time when at least *worship* was directed toward one deity (monolatry) and "in one tongue." That this would have included the recognition of only one deity (monotheism) is also likely.

The scholarly emphasis on origins has shaped the discussion around Israelite monotheism in two significant ways. First, it has generated a great deal of theorizing about the cultural influences contributing to the particular configuration of monotheism in Israel. Second, it has deflected attention from understanding the broad and diverse phenomenon of Israelite monotheism in order to probe the few early poetic texts (Deut. 32:8–9; Ps. 82) in hopes of discerning the premonotheistic "stage" of Israelite religion. This chapter addresses both origins and the rich diversity of ancient Israelite monotheism and explores the benefits and limits of using extrabiblical evidence for making claims about Israel's monotheistic beliefs. The challenges facing this task are numerous, but they begin with a lack of clarity on what we mean by "monotheism."

The Meaning and Appropriateness of "Monotheism"

The term "monotheism" is anachronistic, deriving among the seventeenth-century Cambridge Platonists as part of a larger project aimed at systematizing religions according to belief systems (N. MacDonald 2012, 16). However, the problem of anachronism besets any attempt to describe ancient Israelite religion and is no *more* present when speaking of monotheism than when speaking of monolatry, henotheism, polytheism, or atheism. The best we can do is allow the biblical and extrabiblical material to shape and refine what we mean by monotheism rather than abandon the term's usefulness.

"Monotheism" is a useful term insofar as it captures Israel's insistence that its deity Yhwh is categorically supreme (Lynch 2014a). The term proves inadequate when restricted to numerical oneness in the divine realm (usually "heaven") or to texts that ostensibly deny the "existence" of other deities.[2] For instance, some biblical

2. I use the term here in an ontological sense, referring to the metaphysical being of other divinities and not just the experience thereof.

texts make claims like "the LORD is God in heaven above and on the earth beneath; there is no other" (Deut. 4:39). This appears to be an absolute expression of monotheism. However, texts that date later than Deuteronomy make similar assertions while simultaneously affirming a "host of heaven" that worships Yhwh: "You are the LORD, you alone . . . and the host of heaven [*tseba' hashamayim*] worships you" (Neh. 9:6). Even in very late extrabiblical texts like the *Songs of the Sabbath Sacrifice* the worshiper summons all ranks of heavenly beings (*'elim*) to give praise to Yhwh (e.g., 4QSongs of the Sabbath Sacrifice[d] fragment 1, column 1, 30–37). Those divine beings simply enhance Yhwh's supremacy and worthiness in worship. So the question "How many deities did Israel recognize?" is far less fruitful and precise than "In what terms did Israel distinguish Yhwh and configure Yhwh's relationship to reality?" The latter question will lead us closer to an indigenous conception of monotheism in ancient Israel.

In an earlier work (Lynch 2014b, 31) I depicted the spectrum of biblical representations of Yhwh's categorical supremacy as shown in fig. 43.1. On the left side we might plot texts like Nehemiah 9:6 and passages from *Songs of the Sabbath Sacrifice* where divine beings appear, and on the right texts like Deuteronomy 4:39 and passages from Deutero-Isaiah that explicitly deny other divine beings. Biblical writers are capable of expressing Yhwh's supreme uniqueness within *either* system. In other words, widely varying types of monotheistic rhetoric exist in the Old Testament, and they are not all intrinsically connected. "Monotheism" nonetheless provides a useful analytic category for explaining that varied insistence among most biblical writers that Yhwh is categorically supreme, even if not all texts self-consciously point to that category.

However, some texts describe Yhwh's present existence as categorically *similar* to that of other deities. For instance, Israel's judge

Fig. 43.1. A spectrum of biblical representations of Yhwh's categorical supremacy
Lynch 2014b, 31

Jepthah recognizes the mutual territorial claim of Yhwh and Chemosh: "Should you not possess what your god Chemosh gives you to possess? And should we not be the ones to possess everything that the LORD our God has conquered for our benefit?" (Judg. 11:24). We should not be surprised that some ancient Israelite writers and characters espouse such views. The idea that one's deity is not alone, and is akin to other national deities, was a common view among Israel's neighbors, who even exhibited aniconic tendencies like those in early Israel (Mettinger 1995). Micah 4:5 states that "all the peoples walk, each in the name of its god, but we will walk in the name of the LORD our God." In other cases, biblical texts *allow for* the possibility of other deities, without commenting on their relative status (e.g., Exod. 20:3).

In short, some biblical texts *assume*, but do not necessarily *argue for*, equivalence in the relationships between other deities and their respective nations on the one hand and Yhwh and Israel on the other.[3] Others assert variously Yhwh's categorical supremacy, whether or not a plurality of divine beings exists. Still others, like Exodus 20:3, are so underdetermined that they can function easily within *either* a henotheistic or monotheistic system.[4]

3. We cannot be certain from such brief texts how far a given biblical writer or character might go in describing the parity between Yhwh and other deities. From the data available, however, we can at least state that each nation was viewed as owing its allegiance to its own god, without any comment on the relative supremacy of one deity over another.
4. Henotheism refers to the recognition that only one deity should be *worshiped*, even if others exist.

The foregoing discussion should at least problematize the possibility of charting the history of Israelite monotheism in a linear fashion. One cannot deduce a shift in religious *belief* on the basis of intensified monotheistic *rhetoric*. Israelite "monotheizing"—understood as the robust assertion of Yhwh's categorical supremacy (in praise or polemic)—was a possibility to which Israelites could turn, and did turn, at various points in their history. As they did so, the Yahwistic monotheism that emerged took on different shapes. In what follows, I will outline a *sampling* of relevant data on the subject of Israelite monotheism, while remaining sensitive to the diverse forms and expressions of monotheism that emerged. Along the way we will consider what extrabiblical evidence can and cannot tell us about Israelite monotheism.

Ancient Israel and Egyptian Atenism

In the fourteenth century BCE, Pharaoh Akhenaten of Egypt engaged in a thoroughgoing religious revolution in which he moved the capital from Thebes to Amarna and prohibited worship of any deity except the Aten—a sun deity known from the much earlier Old Kingdom period (see ch. 32 above). The significance of Atenism for understanding Israelite monotheism is debated. On the one hand, Atenism provides a brief instance of belief in one supreme divinity within the orbit of earliest Israel. Atenism is also unique in that it was not simply an assertion or belief but also a practice. The fact that some dating schemes situate Israel in Egypt during the time of the Akhenaten revolution suggests to some an indirect religious influence of Atenistic solar religion.[5]

Evidence for direct monotheistic influence upon Israel is difficult to detect. Some argue that the Great Hymn to Aten influenced Psalm 104, which employs solar imagery to describe Yhwh's supremacy as creator. Nevertheless, the connections are generic, and evidence for direct influence is tenuous at best (Hoffmeier 2015, 249; M. S. Smith 2008, 70). More likely, the motifs expressed in the hymn were part of a wider set of cultural influences, along with other West Semitic material, on the writer of Psalm 104. Moreover, while Psalm 104 certainly offers an exalted portrait of the creator God, it does not demand a monotheistic reading, except perhaps by the psalm's omission of any reference to other deities.

The possibility of even indirect monotheistic influence from Egypt upon earliest Israel will remain unlikely for those who date the first unambiguously monotheistic formulations to the eighth to sixth centuries (M. S. Smith 2001a). For others, the example of Psalm 104 suggests that Aten-inflected solar religion was one stream contributing to Israelite monotheism, though with significant differences. For instance, while Israelite Yahwistic religion typically was aniconic, the Atenistic emphasis on one supreme deity represented by the sun disk made clear impressions on ancient Israelite iconography (cf. Mal. 4:2) (Uehlinger 1993; Hess 2007, 165).[6]

In terms of our thinking about the *development* of monotheism in Israel, the case of Atenism proves most remarkable. For many, the march toward monotheism was irreversible and somewhat late in Israel. Yet, Atenism shows the (rather obvious) possibility of reversal from monotheism. Even those who date monotheism's emergence to the late monarchic period must also reckon with the concurrence of henotheistic and polytheistic beliefs and practices in Israel, and thus a mixed religious system. The biblical story itself attests to spiralistic patterns of henotheism and polytheism, and, as I discuss below, iconic tendencies emerge in early *and* late periods in Israel.

Wherever one lands on the question of whether earliest Israel was influenced by Atenism, it is notable that apart from Deuteronomy 4:35, 39, and 32:39, there is little *explicit* monotheistic rhetoric in the Pentateuch. If Moses came into contact with the vestiges of Atenism, as James Hoffmeier maintains, it is surprising that Yhwh's *uniqueness*, and not necessarily his *sole divinity*, so absorbs the author(s) of the Pentateuch. Granted, those expressions of uniqueness are uncompromising. There are universal claims to Yhwh's uniqueness found in the exodus story, where Yhwh dismantles what was then considered the most powerful nation on earth (Exod. 9:16–17, 29). One might rightfully consider such claims monotheistic by implication, but not by direct assertion (as in the "denial clause" statements in Deut. 4; 32). Nevertheless, consistent messaging around Yhwh's sole divinity, of the sort expressed in the Great Hymn to Aten, is not forthcoming in biblical sources that historical maximalists ascribe to Moses.

The Canaanite Matrix of Monotheism: El, Ba'al, and Asherah

One prominent question confronting historians of Israelite religion is whether Israel was monotheistic in origin. Was there a monotheistic core to Israelite religion from its earliest days (the fourteenth century)? Yehezkel

5. The presence of a temple of Aten on the Sinai Peninsula provides a possible point of historical connection with early Yahwism. The Bible itself claims that Yhwh came from Seir, Teman, Sinai, and other regions in the south (e.g., Deut. 33:2; Hab. 3:3), and some external evidence appears to corroborate this claim (Astour 1979). This, combined with evidence for a possible fourteenth-century cult to Yhwh somewhere in the region of Edom, lends further credibility to this suggestion (Giveon 1978, 21).

6. For instance, on the Taanach cult stand, which some suggest had aniconic *and* sun-disk representations of Israel's deity.

Kaufmann believed so and argued the point consistently in his eight-volume *Religion of Israel* (1937–56). For Kaufmann, Israel knew nothing of the polytheism, magic, or idolatry of its Canaanite neighbors (Kaufmann 1960). In a similar vein, William Albright argues in his landmark book *Yahweh and the Gods of Canaan* (1968, 1994) that while early Israel was influenced by conceptions of other deities, it was at its core monolatrous (i.e., adhering to only one deity, Yahweh). Israel stood in sharp contrast to the polytheistic Canaanite "other."

Since Kaufmann and Albright (and many others), scholarly opinion has shifted away from the theory of early Israelite monotheism. The predominant perspective is that Israel emerged out of a shared polytheistic Canaanite culture. It did not just "borrow" from it (Niehr 2010; Anderson 2015, 72). Among the most articulate proponents of this view is Mark Smith. In *The Early History of God* (2002), Smith highlights the problematic division between internal and external religious influences, suggesting that the worship of gods like Baʿal, El, and Asherah formed part of *Israel's* earliest story, and that we see vestiges of this in the Old Testament (M. S. Smith 2002, 3). Even the name "Yisra-el," not "Yisra-Yah," bears witness to a common West Semitic divine name (S. Sanders 2015b, 73; M. S. Smith 2001a, 142–43) that Israel shared.

Smith's response is helpful, but it does not address the difficult question of how widely and when monolatrous or monotheistic beliefs took hold, or whether those beliefs developed in a linear fashion. Apart from the biblical witnesses, and depending on one's view of the composition of the Old Testament, the data are unclear. For instance, the fact that the Kuntillet ʿAjrud inscription refers to "Yhwh and his Asherah" tells us little about what the vast majority of Israelites believed, and is itself unclear on whether its writer refers to Yhwh's consort *or* to Yhwh's cultic symbol.

In an attempt to gain a clearer picture of *popular* commitment to Yahweh as the one

God, some turn to onomastic evidence (i.e., the examination of personal names in ancient sources). For some, Iron Age onomastic evidence shows a clear shift toward *nearly* exclusive devotion to Yhwh as Israel emerged as a nation in the land of Canaan. Jeffrey Tigay argued (1987a) that the overwhelming majority of preexilic Judahite and Israelite names found outside the Bible use Yhwh (94.1%), with only about 6% using any other divine name.[7] This represents a shift from Canaan in the fourteenth century, when the names "Baʿal" and "Asherah" (and "El") occurred with greater frequency (Hess 2007, 270–71).

Others present a different picture, however. Seth Sanders, following the more recent study by Albertz and Schmitt (2012, 245–386) and correcting several methodological flaws in Tigay's study, suggests less remarkable numbers, with names deriving from "Yahweh" (like "Yah" or "Yaw") comprising only 67.7% of the Hebrew names (cf. Golub 2014).[8] According to Sanders, the Ammonites, by contrast, use the name of their high god El 81.8% of the time. Israelite onomastics nevertheless stand out, not because of the tendency to use one deity in names (other nations in the region did as well), but because of the unique preference for "a single god who is also the royal dynastic god" (S. Sanders 2015b, 80). For the Ammonites, by contrast, the dynastic god Milcom was not the popular god, occurring in only 1–2% of names. Nor was the Aramean dynastic god Baʿalshamayn the popular god. In other words, while "pantheon

7. Richard Hess points out that Samaria is an exception, where the name "Baʿal" occurs with higher frequency, though still in "a minority of names" (Hess 2007, 270). Strikingly, within the Bible itself, the "yahweh-related elements only slightly outnumber El-names in the Bible (about 130/120), as opposed to the 7/1 ratio (outside the Bible)" (Pardee 1988a, 129, quoted in Sanders 2015b, 77).

8. Tigay excluded instances of El from his study. Mitka Golub (2014, 630) calculates that the theophoric elements *yh*, *yw*, and *ywh* occur 53% for material from the tenth through eighth centuries and 68% in the seventh through sixth centuries. She also observes a decrease in the occurrence of the theophoric *bʿl* in the latter centuries.

reduction" is unexceptional within the region, the equation of the dynastic deity with the popular deity is exceptional (S. Sanders 2015b, 67). Yhwh's status as "high" or even "sole" deity in the Iron IIA and Iron IIB–C periods likely obtained for as many elites as common folk.

Related to the question of theophoric names is the phenomenon of Israelite aniconism (the avoidance of divine representation in images). Some scholars draw a close connection between Israelite aniconism and emergent Israelite monotheism. Aniconism does not mean that no representation took place, but rather that representation took place through objects that were non-imagistic, like the ubiquitous *matsebot* ("standing stones") (Bloch-Smith 2006; 2014).[9] Aniconism also characterized nations around Israel (Doak 2015), yet its shift from "de facto" to "programmatic" aniconism in the eighth and seventh centuries was distinct (Mettinger 1997). While debate exists around the precise nature and extent of aniconism (e.g., the Nehushtan image in the temple [2 Kings 18:4]),[10] it is worth asking whether the demolition of divine images and worship places necessarily entails a particular claim about divinity, as some assume (Becking 2001, 163; cf. M. S. Smith 2001a, 89).[11] Need the rationale for programmatic aniconism be theological (N. MacDonald 2007, 27)? Conversely, did monotheism ever exist in a form that tolerated images or aniconic representation? I will return to these questions when discussing Persian-period Yehud.

9. *Matsebot* are stone markers of divinity, also called "standing stones." On the similar Hittite *huwashi* and *sikkanu* stones, see Fleming 2000.

10. I leave aside here the complex debates about how wide this aniconic impulse spread and the various exceptions to the aniconic "rule" in ancient Israel.

11. Doak 2015, 36–37, cites William Robertson Smith's view, preserved in his classic *Religion of the Semites* (1894) and shared by anthropologists of his time, that religion progressed from "nature worship to idols to something more sublime (and probably aniconic)." Ludwig Feuerbach also recognized a "natural" shift from idol worship to monotheism.

Babylonian Reflexes

A key dimension of Israelite monotheism in the exilic period is its engagement with Babylonian *imperial* reality. Israel had already confronted Assyrian political claims to universal supremacy (Aster 2007) in ways that were stridently monotheistic (Lynch 2013). Israel would now confront even more directly Babylonian imperial claims, mediated through a state-focused cult to Marduk. Monotheism in the Babylonian period was decidedly political (M. S. Smith 2004). When in Isaiah 46:9 and elsewhere Yhwh states, "I am God, and there is no one like me," he does so in contrast to the rival claim of *Babylon* (and its associated cult) that "I am, and there is no one besides me" (47:8, 10). Similar rhetoric appears in Zephaniah 2:15 in regard to Nineveh as well.

Accordingly, Israel encountered Babylonian political theologies advancing Marduk's claim to universal supremacy (Halpern 2009, 404), which the prophets vigorously contest (M. S. Smith 2001a, 194; Halpern 2009, 404). The Babylonian myth *Enuma Elish* offers a configuration of divine supremacy that is different from that of Akhenaten's solar religion. Whereas the latter eradicated the gods and elevated the Aten, the Babylonian myth portrays the emergence of Marduk as the bearer of fifty divine names, where each deity is still the recipient of worship, but as a local manifestation of Marduk (6.119–20). Smith calls this "summodeism," or a belief that the many deities who formerly made up a pantheon are "aspects or functions of a chief god" (M. S. Smith 2008, 169). Set in the wider context of the myth, it is clear that belief in, and worship of, other deities continued to be assumed. Yet, certain portions of *Enuma Elish* sound monotheistic on their own: "Over all things that your hands have created, who has [authority, but you]? Over the earth that you have created, who has [authority, but] you?" (5.133–36).

The significance of Israel's engagement with Babylonian religion and politics cannot be understated and seems to have provoked several varied responses. On the one hand, one might point to the pugnacious assertions of Yhwh's sole divinity in Isaiah 40–55. On the other hand, the (potentially) exilic Genesis 1 can be seen to counteract Marduk's claims to supremacy via omission (e.g., the *tehom*-Tiamat connection in Gen. 1:2 [Jacobsen 1968, 108]).[12] Ezekiel offers yet another response to Babylonian religion by deliberately avoiding the term *'elohim* when referring to other deities. Ezekiel preferred the dysphemistic *gillulim* or *'elilim* (Kutsko 2000). Apparently other deities did not even deserve the dignity of the term *'elohim*. Thus both Genesis 1 and Ezekiel (both priestly) engage in varied forms of monotheizing by omission, while Deutero-Isaiah monotheized by assertion.

Several reflections follow from this brief look at Israel's engagement with Babylonian politics and religion. First, the polemical monotheizing of Deutero-Isaiah should not be mapped simplistically onto a larger narrative of slowly emerging monotheism (i.e., as a religious self-designation). Instead, Deutero-Isaiah exists as one rhetorical moment (restricted to Isa. 43–47) in which Yhwh's political claim over Israel was maintained, specifically toward the hopes of deliverance from Babylonian power (Hartmann 1960, 229–35). Nathan MacDonald appropriately labels Deutero-Isaiah's rhetoric "soteriological" (N. MacDonald 2009, 51), a term that also applies to other instances of the "denial clause" in the Old Testament (e.g., 2 Sam. 7:22; 1 Kings 8:60; Ps. 18:31; Hosea 13:4). The concern in these texts is not with ontological existence but rather with soteriological ability. Yhwh is the only one who can *save* Israel. There was none other. Second, Israelite writers responded variously to Babylonian politics and religion. We should not be surprised if that reality is

matched by a similarly broad range of reflexes in earlier and later periods of Israel's religious life. Our ability to trace a clear line of religious development through these varied responses is significantly compromised by this diversity. Third, nevertheless, the distinguishing feature of this period is the consistent and pervasive portrayal of Yhwh's categorical supremacy (see M. S. Smith 2001a, 167–78). Exilic portraits of Yhwh exhibit a shift in either belief or rhetorical needs.

Persian-Period Yehud

Life in Judah among the returnees from Babylon was difficult. Economic conditions were poor; the people had no king or standing army; the land and temple were dim reflections of a grander past. However, from the evidence available, the Jewish returnees and those who remained in the land had embraced Yhwh, not only as *their* deity but also as *the* deity. While most would agree that monotheism had "won the day," questions linger around the degree to which an anti-iconic impulse had merged with monotheistic beliefs. Did the latter imply the former?

For many scholars, the "absence" of images or figurines in Persian-period Yehud and Samaria proves that the exile had purified Israel of its polytheistic past (E. Stern 2001, 488–513). Adi Erlich believes the same holds true for the Hellenistic period: "Monotheistic populations living in the Judean hill country—the Jews and Samaritans—can be defined as decidedly anti-art in this [Hellenistic] period. They have left no art of the Hellenistic period dating to prior to the second century. . . . The differences of the monotheistic peoples are readily distinguishable" (Erlich 2009, 112). The aniconic archaeological record seems to prove that monotheism had emerged victorious.

Nevertheless, there are several problems with such views, requiring us to reconsider how to speak of the relationship between

---

12. J. Day 1985, 49–56, contests any direct influence from the *Enuma Elish* on Genesis 1. But see M. S. Smith 2010, 69, 239.

monotheism and material culture. The evidence for this particular mix of monotheism and iconic representation in the Persian period is more complex than some archaeologists admit. For instance, Bes, Ptah, and Pataikos figurines in Samaria date from the Persian period (E. Stern 1976, 183–87; 2001, 507–10). Ephraim Stern dismisses these as vestiges of "popular" and not "official" worship, though this division is artificial. Similarly, incense altars and figurines exist from the same period at Lachish. The same altars and figurines were in use in Iron Age Judah, suggesting their possible use by the returnees.[13]

Moreover, among the rubble and *yhd* seals of Stratum 9 (Persian) in the City of David were some Judean Pillar Figurine fragments. While they are not typologically unlike the Iron Age figurines, Isaac de Hulster makes a strong case that they indicate continuity in use, and possibly even production (de Hulster 2015, 132; cf. Darby 2014).

Further, Persian and Hellenistic coins with the goddess Athena and an earlier "Yehud drachm" with a possible image of Yhwh suggest at least that the Judeans were not categorically anti-image (Tal 2011, 548–49; de Hulster 2015). These examples, combined with the presence of Judean Pillar Figurines in Persian remains, urge us toward caution when forging links between monotheism and all forms of aniconism (Lynch 2014b, 56; de Hulster 2015). Moreover, depending on the significance of the Pillar Figurines, one cannot rule out the possibility of some heterodox worship.

Finally, the diversity of Judaism during the Persian and Hellenistic periods should give us pause before fitting the material and cultic realities of early Judaism into a homogenous monotheistic mold. For example, we know of at least four Jewish temples during these times, and at least six if we include the later temples at Leontopolis (Tell el-Yahudiyeh) and possibly at

Dan[14]: (1) the Jerusalem temple, (2) the "House of YHWH" on Mount Gerezim, (3) the temple of the God YHW (i.e., Yhwh) in Elephantine, Egypt, and (4) the "BYT YWH" in Idumea (Lemaire 2004). These temples bear witness not only to diversity within Judaism but also to a diverse range of religious convictions. At Elephantine, for instance, some Jews appear to have embraced a highly syncretistic form of Yahwism (Bright 2000, 376; Porten and Yardeni 1986).[15]

In sum, while the Persian and early Hellenistic periods attest to an impressive array of monotheistic expressions in the Hebrew Bible / Old Testament, material cultural remains cast doubt on the idea that iconoclasm was linked inextricably to that monotheism. The cultural and cultic configurations of Yahwistic monotheism were not uniform, and questions remain over the degree to which *all* Persian and Hellenistic Jewish practices were monotheistic.

Conclusions

This chapter highlights the need for clarity regarding the meaning of monotheism. If "monotheism" is to describe the three monotheistic religions derived from ancient Israelite Yahwism, the term cannot only mean that Yhwh was the only divine being who exists. I suggested that the term is helpful for explaining the diverse biblical rhetoric about Yhwh's supreme uniqueness.

This chapter also raises questions around monotheism's entailments. First, monotheism does not involve by necessity the explicit denial of other deities. Some monotheistic texts simply *ignore* other deities (e.g., Gen. 1).

---

13. Andrea Berlin, personal conversation, 2012.

14. Alluded to in the Zilas inscription, which refers to "the god who is at Dan," but whose name remains unidentified. It likely refers to Yhwh (Biran 1994, 221–23).

15. Note the reference to "Horus-Yaho" in a prayer by an Aramean community from Syene, Southern Egypt (near Elephantine), around the fourth century BCE, preserved in Papyrus Amherst 63 (R. Steiner 1991; S. Russell 2009, 44).

That diversity in monotheistic expression reflects the varying cultural influences that gave shape to Israelite monotheism in its early days and on through the Persian and Hellenistic periods.

Second, that diversity in rhetorical expression also problematizes efforts to pinpoint *the* single causal factor that gave rise to monotheism. Instead, monotheism was a variegated response to external political and religious forces and, internally, a response to Israel's own experience of God. Even when monotheistic rhetoric became self-consciously explicit about Yhwh's sole agency in the Babylonian period (Isa. 40–55), not all traditions followed suit.

Third, iconic representation, and even Israel's radical iconoclastic and cult-centralizing movements, related variously to claims about Yhwh's sole divinity. Archaeologically speaking, absence of images or cult altars is not proof of monotheism. Nor is their presence evidence against monotheism. That one God would necessarily have one cult and no images does not square with the complex picture of religious life in ancient Israel.

Fourth, biblical and extrabiblical evidence suggests that one cannot assume a simple pathway from polytheism to monotheism any more than from nature worship to idols to iconoclastic monotheism. While Jews eventually self-identified as monotheists, ancient Israel's journey toward that identity was not one of slow but steady progress, but rather one of varied fits and starts.

44

The Temple in Context

JOHN H. WALTON

The Idea of a Temple

The temple was the central and fundamental component of the cosmos, the centerpiece of the function and identity of the community and the principal mechanism for the interface between humans and the divine. As the god sat enthroned in the temple, the order established through creation was maintained, the forces threatening that order were held at bay, and the viability of the human community was maintained.

Temples were places of divine residence, not just places where worship took place. Worship was only one part of a much larger enterprise represented in the idea that a god had made his or her dwelling in the midst of a human community. As people engaged in the various worship activities, they provided for the gods, provided for the stability of their lives and communities, and played their part in the functioning of the cosmos.

Temples are at the center of sacred space and delineate its zones. Space is made sacred because of the divine presence that inhabits it, but at times is chosen by the deity beforehand as a place for his dwelling with instructions that it be prepared for his presence. Once the temple is built, zones of diminishing sacredness radiate out from the center, where the divine presence is located. Each of the resulting zones has its own required levels of purity and its own sacred activities.[1]

Cosmic Role

Because of the deity's residence in the temple, it was the center of order in the cosmos. Different cultures had different ways of portraying the temple as cosmic nexus, but because of this role, if the temple was not maintained and its god sustained, the cosmos would be in jeopardy and subject to collapse (Hundley 2013a,

---

1. The literature on temples is extensive and growing. Key resources for further reading include Averbeck 2002; Beale 2004; Bloch-Smith 1994; 2002b; Boda and Novotny 2010; Davey 1980; J. Day 2005; Dietrich 2001; George 1993; Hundley 2011; 2013b; Hurowitz 1992; Jacobsen 1989; Janowski 2001; Kamlah 2012; Levenson 1984; Lundquist 1982; 1983; Mettinger 1995; Mierse 2012; Postgate 1972; Shafer 1997; Van Seters 1997; Walton 1995; Wenham 1986; Woods 2004.

48). In this way the threat of temple dissolution would be considered as having a similar impact to that which we connect today with nuclear devastation, radical climate change, or the worst imaginable effects of pollution (i.e., the apocalypse). In much conversation today advocates of "greener" living emphasize how each person's commitment to and practice of something like recycling can join with the efforts of others to have a lasting positive impact on the planet. In the ancient world, the same sort of logic was applied to the responsibilities that each person, each clan, and each city had in maintaining stability in the cosmos by being actively involved in maintaining the temple. Each one played their role in contributing to continuing cosmic stability.

Role in Divine-Human Relationships: The Great Symbiosis

Besides their cosmic role, temples served as the focal point for divine-human relationships. The premise of this relationship in the ancient world can be understood within the framework of what we could call the "Great Symbiosis." People in the ancient world believed that the gods had created humans as an afterthought. The cosmos had been made by the gods for the gods. But the gods were sufficiently like humans that they had needs; they had to sustain their own survival.

Food was the most pressing need, and everyone knew the work that it took to provide sufficient food on a regular basis. Beyond agriculture, the activities of caring for herd animals were also part of the provision that was needed on an ongoing basis. The gods also needed drink, whether the purest of water, the finest of wine, or a hearty beer. As gods, they not only desired the finest provisions but also expected to partake of them in sumptuous feasts accompanied by the most accomplished musicians and dancers.

Beyond the basic need for food and drink, the gods needed housing, and only the most luxurious would be suitable. The more gold, silver, gems, lapis lazuli, fine woods, carved stonework, and glorious tapestries, the more honor would accrue to the god. The gods eventually tired of providing all of these for themselves. Like any human lord, they expected things to be done for them. So it was in accordance with the entitlement of the gods that humans were created to care for the needs of the gods.

As the gods were therefore dependent upon the human creatures that they had brought into existence to serve them, it became clear that they would need to ensure the continuing existence of these humans if the gods' needs were to continue to be met. Consequently, people were dependent on the provision and protection of the gods, and the gods, in turn, were dependent on what the people provided for their upkeep. This codependence eventuated in the Great Symbiosis of the ancient world, in which the gods could acquire all their entitlements and could receive what was appropriate to their station.

This Great Symbiosis framed the religious system and practice of the ancient world and was centered in the temple. The ritual meeting of a god's needs was conscientiously carried out so that the god would continue dwelling among the people. The people were diligent in performance of their ritual responsibilities because in that way they could enjoy divine favor.[2] If the god became angry (and this could happen for any number of reasons, whether petty or serious, whether the cause was known, unknown, or even unknowable), stability of the community or the individual would be in jeopardy. In many instances the king was expected to maintain justice within the community so that the gods could be served and in

---

2. See Pongratz-Leisten 2012, especially the quote from an Assyrian text: "He who performed this banquet and gave bread and water to the gods—give (them) back to him long, copious and wide" (298). For Hittite parallels, see the introduction to text 20 in J. L. Miller 2013.

turn would bring safety, security, stability, and prosperity for the people. This *is* the religious world of the ancient Near East.

In the temples the gods were pampered. No expense was spared to ensure that the gods would not become angry and strike out at the people, become offended and abandon the people to demonic forces or to their enemies, or, worst of all, become so dissatisfied that they would leave altogether. The god's presence was essential, and thus the temple became the locus for divine-human interrelationship, a fragile and often unpredictable relationship of mutual need and dependence.

Supporting Components: Personnel and Procedures, Images and Ziggurats

In Mesopotamian cultures, a variety of supporting components played a role in the successful functioning of the temple. The rituals were designed to meet the needs of the gods and to affirm the greatness of the gods by giving gifts. Worship consisted of rituals, and they took place in the temple to assure the god's comfort and favor. The priests were the appointed guardians of sacred space, making sure the system was working the way that it should. Proper offerings needed to be brought at the proper times and offered in proper ways. The ritual status of the person bringing the offering must be ascertained. Sacred times, whether for daily offerings or annual festivals, all had to be observed, and this was the duty of the priests. It was a dangerous role because they could most easily be the ones responsible for offending the gods. It was also a role that had great significance in the community because these specialists were responsible for making sure that the needs of the gods were supplied and that the gods were thereby kept content.

All the rituals conducted in the temple were dependent on the established presence of the god, represented by the image of the deity. Without the image, there was no assurance that the deity was present, in which case the temple was of no consequence. Rituals developed over time that were designed to acquire the deity's blessing on the manufacture of an image so that the image might be deemed a suitable receptacle for the essence of the deity. The image then became the focal point for the care given to the deity: food and drink were offered before the image, beautiful clothing was provided, offerings from divination were presented in its presence for divine guidance, and (as deemed appropriate) the image was carried forth in procession for major festivals.

If the inner sanctum of the temple was the most sacred space associated with the temple, the ziggurats arguably ranked only a little lower. Ziggurats were positioned next to temples and were intended to provide a convenience for the gods as they descended to the temples to be worshiped—one of many ways to entice a deity to take up residence among the people. The ziggurats had names that designated them as sacred space and that can at times give us a sense of their cosmic role (e.g., "sacred space that links heaven and earth" and "sacred foundation of heaven and earth").

The significance of the ziggurat is to be found in the ramps or stairways that are the most prominent physical feature and in the shrine that graced the peak of the structure, the *gigunu*.[3] The *gigunu* is not like the temple adjoining the ziggurat in that it does not house the image of the deity. Furthermore, it appears that sacrificial rituals did not take place there, though at times food gifts were provided there for the deity. The *gigunu* provides the god's living quarters (distinguished from the throne in the temple itself; compare the distinction in the American White House, where there are private residential quarters for the president and his family as well as the Oval Office, in which business is conducted). A bed was maintained in the *gigunu* in addition to a table where

---

3. Jacobsen 1990, 41*, identifies it as the upper temple (at the top of the ziggurat) in the temple complex.

food was supplied, and vessels for bathing and anointing the statue. Perhaps the image of the deity would be brought there when it was not "at work" in the temple. There the god could be bathed and refreshed while "off duty."

Given all this information, it is clear that the ziggurats were generally off limits to people. This was the property of the gods, and it provided divine prerogatives and sacred privacy.

Distinctions of Israel's Temple

The ideology of the temple in Israel shared many features with that of the peoples around. The temple had cosmic identity and was thought of as the center of the cosmos. It represented the link between the realms and was considered heaven on earth (e.g., Ps. 78:69; Isa. 66:1). The temple was where Yahweh sat enthroned and continually maintained order in the cosmos and on the earth. It was his palace and his base of operations.

The temple in Jerusalem also represented God's presence among his people and therefore established sacred space. It was a boon granted to the people of Israel and stood as one of the major objectives of the covenant. As Yahweh dwelt in their midst, his presence brought blessing to Israel and gave Israel a means of being in relationship with Yahweh.

Despite the similarities of the general outline of temple ideology, once we shift our attention to the deeper issues, we find noteworthy contrasts. Six aspects can be identified in brief summary.

Relationship to Eden. In Israelite thinking, the first sacred space was in the Garden of Eden, where God dwelt among the people he had created and was in relationship with them. In the rest of the ancient world there is no parallel to anything like the Garden of Eden playing this particular role. This connection provides the setting for Israel's understanding of sacred space because it occurs in a setting where there is no sin to be cared for and no

rituals designated; God is simply enjoying relationship as he lives with his people. This is lost in Genesis 3, and all the ideology of sacred space going forward is related to restoring God's presence among his people.

Great Symbiosis / Covenant Symbiosis. The most fundamental distinction between the temple ideology in the ancient Near East and that in Israel concerns what was labeled above as the "Great Symbiosis." In Israelite thinking, people are not an afterthought created with the purpose of meeting divine needs. Yahweh has no needs. People are created for relationship. This contrast represents a revolutionary ideology that could hardly be imagined in the rest of the ancient world. If Yahweh had no needs for the people to meet, then the rituals in Israel served a very different function. He did not dwell among his people because they took care of him; he dwelt there because he desired relationship with them. Since the covenant is the means by which Yahweh structured this relationship, we could say that in Israel the Great Symbiosis was replaced by a "Covenant Symbiosis." This Covenant Symbiosis provided the same sorts of benefits to the Israelites that the Great Symbiosis provided to others: promises of blessing in forms such as protection and provision (covenant blessings and curses). The difference is apparent in what the symbiosis provides for the deity. Instead of meeting divine needs, the temple and its rituals were designed to ensure that Israel was maintaining the holiness of sacred space by attending to breaches or lapses in their adherence to the covenant stipulations. With this transformation, the religion of Israel could not be comprised of the care and feeding of the gods but rather would entail the much broader range of behavior that characterized covenant faithfulness (see Ps. 50, esp. vv. 5, 12–16). Relationship with Yahweh in Israel likewise centered on the temple but was not needs-based. Yahweh loved his people and expected them to love him. Love entailed loyalty to the covenant and Israel's exclusive worship of Yahweh. It is captured in the refrain "I will be your God and you will be my people." In the ancient Near East, both gods and humans were self-serving; in Israel, the ideal was that God's presence was an act of grace to his people and Israel's responses (rarely manifested) were to reflect wholehearted service to God, who was worthy.

Significance of purity. Purity in the ancient Near East is associated with the elitist attitudes of the gods and the prerogatives to which they felt entitled. They deserved the very best and could easily grow offended at any carelessness in performance or at any lapse in quality of what was provided for them.[4] They were persnickety and petty. Purity was designed to meet their exacting demands so that they would not express their inherently temperamental nature. In Israel, Yahweh is unarguably exacting, but a different rationale stands behind that understanding. Rather than reflecting divine pettiness and entitlement, the purity requirements in Israel are protection from the inherent hazards of the presence of a holy God—a concept unparalleled in the ancient Near East. Such purity is required so that Yahweh will continue to dwell among his people.

Holiness. Even though *purity* is a concept well known in the ancient Near East and is essential for participation in the rituals that are at the core of their religious practice, the *holiness* that is a staple of Old Testament theology has no immediate parallel of any significance. Holiness is not a quality to be achieved but rather a status that incorporates Israel into Yahweh's identity. Israel *is* holy as God is holy; that is, God has designated Israel as holy, his holy people. Aside from a few vague references in Ugaritic, perhaps the closest parallel that exists in the ancient Near East is to be found in the way that Akkadian indicates the status of someone or something by attaching the

"dingir" sign to it.[5] This indicated that the object or person existed in the divine realm with all the privileges and responsibilities associated with that status. Gods and temples were so designated, as well as celestial bodies, occasionally kings, and a wide assortment of sacred objects. In the ancient Near East, this classification designated prerogatives; in Israel, holy status identified Israel's relationship with their God.

Law. In Israel, the Torah contains both ritual and societal responsibilities, all designed to define cosmic order and give shape to holiness. As such, it gives direction concerning how to maintain access to God's presence and the relationship that God's presence facilitates and how to preserve God's favor so that his identity is well reflected in the people. Torah can then be seen as the foundation for Yahweh's presence as it gave Israel guidelines for living in the presence of a holy God. The Torah is contingent on the temple, not the other way around. The Torah was incumbent upon each Israelite because, in theory, any individual's neglect or violation of the Torah could potentially result in God's presence being removed from his people.[6] In this sense, each person had a role in maintaining God's presence, and God's presence brought order to the cosmos and to Israel. Blood rituals such as those that were part of the sin offering and guilt offering were designed to cleanse sacred space of impurity that, if left to build up, could result in Yahweh's departure. Such blood rituals with this particular function are found rarely if ever anywhere else in the ancient Near East, but they play a major role in Israel's temple ideology.[7]

---

4. For a good example, see the instructions for the priests and temple personnel in J. L. Miller 2013, 249.

5. B. N. Porter 2009, 153–94; Hundley 2013b.

6. This principle is illustrated in Josh. 7, where all Israel suffers divine disfavor because of Achan's violation of the command.

7. Scattered blood rituals do exist in the rest of the ancient Near East, but not for the cleansing of sacred space as in Israel. For Hittite blood rituals, particularly the *zurki* ritual, in which blood is used to cleanse a temple

Image. Israel is known for being aniconic; that is, no crafted cult image served as a receptacle for the divine essence or mediated divine presence. People are the only image that Yahweh tolerates. That means that all the functions of the cult statue that were so central to temple ideology in the ancient Near East, if retained at all, had to be reassigned in Israel. In the ancient Near East, the temple lost its significance if the image was not installed. In Israel, the Ark of the Covenant stood in the center of sacred space representing a part of God's throne, but was not a receptacle for the divine essence.[8] It represented God's presence, but did not mediate it. Thus, no parallel to the cult image is present in Israelite theology. Much controversy has centered on Israelite aniconism—when it began and how it was reflected—but exclusive aniconism in the ancient Near East outside Israel is unknown.[9] The significance of this is far-reaching and cannot be overstated.

Conclusion

Nothing was of greater importance in the ancient world than sustaining the presence of deity in the temple, though a variety of different strategies are evident. From architecture and function to use and ideology, different cultures achieved the objectives of divine presence in different ways. Securing divine favor was paramount; therefore, temple practices and ideology are key to understanding the perceptions about deity that characterized the individual societies of the ancient Near East.

---

icon, see Feder 2011, 20–23. As early as Sumerian narratives, Lugalbanda pours the blood of a sacrificed bull into a pit for the gods to smell, but that does not pertain to the preservation of sacred space (see Vanstiphout 2003, 123, lines 358–59).

8. Egyptian portable shrines, which sometimes house divine statues, can be compared to the Ark but cannot be used to determine characteristics of the Ark not referred to in the biblical text.

9. Punic examples are ruled out due to their late date. In referring to "exclusive aniconism," I am reflecting sensitivity to the distinction that Mettinger draws between "de facto aniconism" and "programmatic aniconism" and giving tacit recognition to the fact that examples of aniconism and trends in that direction can be observed in a variety of cultures. For discussion, see the articles (including especially Mettinger's) in van der Toorn 1997 as well as Mettinger's 1995 monograph, and more recently Doak 2015.

45

Priests in the Ancient Near East

GERALD A. KLINGBEIL

Priests and other religious specialists were part of an elite in ancient Near Eastern cultures whose services were to secure the well-being of king, people, and land by representing them before the deity. Unlike in the context of the Old Testament, priests in the ancient Near East were in most cases closely associated with royalty or local leadership, even though this varied among distinct religious traditions, regions, time periods, and sociopolitical realities. This chapter briefly introduces the different sources that are available to understand the nature of ancient Near Eastern priesthood, followed by succinct descriptions of the characteristics and roles of priests in Egypt, Mesopotamia, Syria-Palestine, and the Hittite region. Finally, we will attempt a closer look at the distinct functions of ancient Near Eastern priesthood.

Sources

Understanding ancient realities from a twenty-first-century Western perch is not an easy task. Texts written in ancient languages require translations and involve technical terminology that can be difficult to grasp; the pictorial evidence is often inconclusive since, as noted by Dominque Collon (1999, 17–25, esp. 25), it tends to lack clear context or a direct correlation between depiction and inscription; archaeological data is frequently tentative (Klingbeil 2008, 134–41), and distinctions between public and private, cultic and religious activities are not always easily recognizable (see Y. Cohen 2007; van der Toorn 1995a).[1] These real limitations, however, should not discourage those seeking to understand ancient Near Eastern priesthood, but rather should lead to a realistic humility that recognizes the complexity of the task at hand.

Priesthood in Ancient Egypt

Egyptian religion was dominated by the figure of the pharaoh, considered to be the man-god (particularly in earlier periods) able to connect the human and the divine realms (te Velde 1995, 1731). In many images, only the pharaoh is shown carrying out cultic activities associated

---

1. The notion of personal piety and official religion in relationship to Israel's and Babylon's religious practice was introduced by Albertz 1978.

with temples, and, until the New Kingdom (ca. 1550–1100 BCE), most priests served on a part-time basis while also holding civil administrative positions (Doxey 2001, 68). Priests were appointed by the pharaoh (or a person he delegated), even though in later periods it seems as if there were also hereditary lines (Pernigotti 1997, 129). Early on in Egypt's long history, the priesthood was reserved for local leaders and administrators, suggesting no clear distinction between temple and palace (or, in more modern terms, religion and state). Priestly offices varied locally and according to temple ritual. Some of the better-known priestly categories included the *hmw-ntr*, "god's servants"; the lower-ranked *w'bw*, "pure (or *wab*-) priests"; the *hntiw-š*, "secular officials associated with the temple"; the *hry-hbt*, "lector priests"; and the *smw*, "*sem*-priests" who were associated with the important "opening-of-the-mouth" funeral ritual (Doxey 2001, 69), which, in the mind of Egyptian faithful, determined the deceased's transition into the realm of eternity.

Priests were involved in various ritual activities and had to live according to strict purity rules. These purity rules apparently also involved moral dimensions, as can be seen from an inscription in the temple of Edfu admonishing the priests serving in the temple: "Turn your faces toward this domain in which His Majesty has placed you. When he sails across the sky, he looks below: and he is satisfied if his law is observed! Do not present yourselves in a state of sin! Do not enter in a state of filth! Do not tell lies in his house! Divert none of his provisions; do not levy taxes injuring the little person in favor of the powerful!" (Dunand and Zivie-Coche 2004, 101).

Other responsibilities included carrying the god's image in processions (done by the *wab*-priests), while others would recite spells and incantations (often done by the lector priests). Not all priestly classes could enter the most sacred innermost court of an Egyptian temple. Only the *hmw-ntr* priest could directly serve the image of the deity in the sanctum, suggesting a clear hierarchical structure with the pharaoh at its head. Administrative tasks, including the reception and administration of offerings, were handled by *wab*-priests. Egyptian priests wore mostly white linen and white sandals, and are often shown with shaved heads. *Sem*-priests sometimes wore leopard skins in the New Kingdom period (te Velde 1995, 1733). Generally, priests served the well-being of the deity in his or her "house" (or temple), including dressing, feeding, cleansing, anointing, and protecting the deity's statue. The opening-of-the-mouth ritual was one of the most important rituals because it enabled the deity to act through his or her statue (see A. Roth 2001a, 575–80; 2001b, 605–9).

In light of the close connection between administrative leadership and the priesthood, Joseph's marriage to Asenath, the daughter of Poti-Pherah, priest of On, in Genesis 41:45 makes perfect sense and seems to reflect historical realities.

Women carried priestly titles during the Old Kingdom in Egypt, including "god's servant," and often were associated with the goddess Hathor, the deity of women, dance, drunkenness, and sexual licentiousness. When the priesthood became a full-time occupation during the New Kingdom, women served mostly as musicians and singers (Doxey 2001, 69–70).

Priesthood in Ancient Mesopotamia

Similar to the situation in Egypt, the history of the priesthood in Mesopotamia covers nearly three thousand years and reflects widely different political, social, and religious realities. In other words, while religious institutions are inherently conservative, conceptual development and geographical variations can be easily documented, as noted by Johannes Renger (1966, 111).

As in Egypt, Mesopotamian priesthood was closely associated with royalty in the early

Sumerian city-states. The priest-kings (*en*) combined political and religious leadership. Later, the *en* became the person taking care of the priestly temple routine while the term *ensi* designated the ruler (Saggs 1962, 345), whose participation in many festivals (including the *Akītu* New Year feast) was paramount for the successful completion of the ritual. The influence of the king in cult and ritual changed over time and also developed distinctly in Babylon and Assyria. In the New Babylonian period, for example, there was a clear distinction between priests and kings, as their roles as provider and protector (king) and servant (priest) differed significantly (Waerzeggers 2011, 733–37). Ultimately, however, kings, priests, and gods were closely tied together, each deriving and offering legitimacy for the other members of this triangle (Waerzeggers 2011, 746).

Renger's (1966; 1969) useful division of the Mesopotamian priesthood (based mainly on Old Babylonian data) into three categories includes cult priests, incantation priests, and divining priests, with numerous technical terms included in each category. The sheer volume of distinct priestly terminology suggests complexity and strict organization. Both male and female priests served in Mesopotamian temples. The chief priest of a temple was considered the spouse of the deity and could be either male or female, depending on the gender of the city deity (Wiggermann 1995, 1864). The temple (or "house") of the main city deity was a center of religious, administrative, and judicial activities and was organized along the lines of a regular household. Priests offered daily provisions for the deity on a table (or altar), often located before the statue of the deity, in the *cella* (or central room). Besides the feeding of the gods, priests also had to daily wash, bathe, perfume, and dress the statue of the deity. A series of festival processions and other outings of the statue for specific events guaranteed the loyalty and continued support of the people of the town or region to the deity and often were associated with significant events in the life rhythm of an agrarian society.

All this reflected the theocentric focus of Mesopotamian cult, which was mainly concerned with the well-being of the gods and is also reflected in cuneiform literary works (Bottéro 1995a, 225–26). In later periods, the layout of temple complexes became more involved and included divine sleeping rooms, side rooms for the god's servants and family, water basins for cleansing visitors, and stables for the deity's chariot and draft animals (Wiggermann 1995, 1861; cf. Jursa 2011, 184–90). These temple "households" and their associated holdings represented a significant socioeconomic factor in Mesopotamian city life and included also craftsmen (e.g., millers, fullers, oil pressers, barbers, weavers, smiths) and servants (e.g., cupbearers, mat makers, water pourers, water carriers, stewards) beyond the strictly cultic personnel.[2]

The presence of musicians and lamentation priests in Mesopotamian temple personnel lists underlines the importance of vocal and instrumental sound as part of Mesopotamian religious ritual. Fertility rites (including the sacred marriage festival) in Mesopotamian religion are clearly present, even though the exact nature of the sacred marriage rituals is still debated.[3] In the past, naked female figures on Mesopotamian art have been interpreted as priestesses, but there is little supporting evidence, even though there seems to be a clear link to fertility rites (Collon 1999, 21).

Priests depicted on Old Babylonian seals wear a short, wrap-over garment with an ornamental border, draped over one shoulder and, like Egyptian priests, are beardless and shaven-headed except for a forehead ornament (Collon 1999, 22), which may possibly be a lock of hair left unshaved. Besides bloody sacrifices and

2. For an example of a list of temple personnel (at Ninurta's temple at Lagash), see Nemet-Nejat 1998, 190–91.

3. See here the collection of helpful studies in Nissinen and Uro 2008.

vegetal offerings, Mesopotamian priests are also depicted in many distinct libation rites—sometimes carrying a bucket and tall, flaring cup with a pouring lip (Collon 1999, 22; W. Lambert 1993). In first-millennium BCE Assyrian contexts, priests are depicted as beardless and distinguished by tall, cone-shaped headdresses (Collon 1999, 24). Individuals wearing fish cloaks are often identified in texts as *apkallu*-priests or sages and are associated with protective rituals. A recently published medical text from a private collection in Japan and possibly originating from Emar includes the following colophon: "By the hand of Madi-Dagan, son of Abi-kapi, scribe (and) *apkallu*-priest," underlining the wide variety of priestly functions in Mesopotamian culture, including also an overlap between magic and medicine (Tsukimoto 1999).

Priesthood in Ancient Syria-Palestine

The region of Syria-Palestine includes a number of important city-states producing significant textual material during the third to first millennia BCE (including Ebla, Mari, Emar, and Ugarit).[4] While most of the third-millennium BCE epigraphic material from Tell Mardikh (Ebla) is administrative in nature, scholars were surprised to see clear differences from Mesopotamian Sumerian city-states, particularly noting the sharp distinction between royal and religious powers that seemed to have functioned side by side but independently at Ebla (Pettinato 1991, 176–81). The Middle Bronze II (2000–1800 BCE) archaeological data includes not only a temple but also a sanctuary for deified royal ancestors and a stone cult terrace that may have housed the sacred lions of Ishtar, one of the main deities of Ebla, as well as minor cultic places spread throughout the city (Matthiae 2006). It appears that distinct from the evidence

found in Egypt and Mesopotamia, the economic impact of the temple was limited to sacrificial activities and the disbursing of sacrificial meat (Milano 1995, 1224–26). Ebla's pantheon was clearly West Semitic, with Dagan at its head. Most information about the priesthood comes from sacrificial or other administrative lists. Based on this data, there is evidence for male and female priests (Archi 1998), in line with other ancient Near Eastern practices, in which the priestly leadership of a temple depended on the gender of the temple's deity. G. M. Urciuoli (1995) has distinguished between two classes of midlevel priests: the *šeš-Il-ib kéšda* and the *šeš-Il-ib* priests. It seems that the first group had been contracted specifically (considering the possible meaning of *kéšda* as a reference to somebody contractually bound), enabling them to serve at specific Eblaite festivals and locations. Is it possible that the *šeš-Il-ib kéšda* priest had passed the equivalent of a priestly state board exam and was thus qualified to preside at specific events requiring this board exam?

The early second-millennium BCE cuneiform texts found in the ancient city of Tell Hariri, or ancient Mari, have generated many comparative studies focusing upon the prophetic office at Mari and in the Hebrew Bible.[5] The unique titles of *nābû* and *munabbiātu*, for example, appearing both at Mari and at Emar, have been associated with temple personnel who pronounced messages on behalf of the temple's deity (Fleming 1993; 2004a). Furthermore, texts from Mari have highlighted the importance of the *bārû*-priest, associated with divination, but not with the temple. The field of expertise of the *bārû* (seer or diviner) included omens, extispicy, and lecanomancy (Koch 2011, 455). The office is well known from Mesopotamian sources and underlines Mari's unique location connecting Syria-Palestine to Mesopotamia. Some religious professionals at Mari (such as the *āpilu* or *āpiltu*) must have

---

4. The texts found at Tell Mishrifeh (ancient Qaṭna) seem to include mostly administrative texts (Richter and Lange 2012).

5. See, for example, the helpful syntheses in Malamat 1989 and more recently in Huffmon 1997; 2000; Stökl 2012.

been involved in divination, but apparently were not considered part of the temple personnel. Mari's tribal organization and the roles of the "elders" within that organization echo the reality of early Israel and are distinct from other city-states (Fleming 2004a). In Mari, city and tribal hinterland connect to form a unique sociopolitical mix distinct from the focus on royal power in Mesopotamia and Egypt.

This unique Syrian (or West Semitic) perspective is even more recognizable in the Late Bronze Age (1550–1200 BCE) cuneiform texts found at Tell Meskene, or ancient Emar. Situated 90 km (ca. 55 miles) east of modern Aleppo on the banks of the Euphrates, the extensive archive included hundreds of important religious texts, including a detailed prescriptive ordination ritual of a NIN.DIN-GIR of ᵈIM, or high priestess of Baʿal (see Fleming 1992a; G. Klingbeil 1998). This 94-line text, Emar 369, offers a unique window into Syro-Palestinian religion and ritual during the Late Bronze Age and has been extensively discussed in conversation with the ordination ritual in Leviticus 8 (G. Klingbeil 1998).[6] The ritual mentions eight different deities that are linked to the ordination ritual, even though the high priestess is most closely associated with the storm god Baʿal. Based on this text, the *entu* (Dietrich 1989) or *ittu* (Fleming 1992a, 80–84) is selected by sacred lot, but can be "the daughter of any son of Emar" (line 3), even though the list of expensive gifts to be provided from her father's house would require an elevated socioeconomic level. Other important participants associated with this ritual include the ˡᵘ‌ḪAL, "diviner"; the *zamaru*, "singers"; the enigmatic "men of the *qidašu*" (possibly referring to an overarching group including the king of Emar, the diviner, and the singers); the *Ḥamša'u* men (associated with mourning); the *bēl bīti*, "lord of the house" (who may have been in charge of all the provisions

and sacrifices); the elders of Emar (offering gifts to the new high priestess and recognizing her selection); the *nugagtu* woman, "wailing woman"; as well as the larger family of the high priestess. Not all of these participants were exclusively associated with the temple and priesthood though. The unique texts from Emar witness to local Syrian religious traditions and institutions (Fleming 1992b) that show less dependence on Mesopotamia and Egypt. An example of the contribution of the Emar ritual for the study of the Hebrew Bible can be found in the oil-based anointing rite forming part of the larger ordination ritual (cf. Lev. 8:12 [G. Klingbeil 1996; Fleming 1998a]), which prior to the discovery of the Emar text had been associated with Greek rituals.

The data regarding priesthood in the Late Bronze Age texts from Ras Shamra, or ancient Ugarit, is quite complex as the texts list a significant number of officials associated with the cult, but the ritual texts do not specify their roles.[7] The *khn* in Ugaritic texts seems to be a cognate of the Hebrew *kohen* for "priest," and the *rb khnm* could be understood as the "high priest" or "chief priest." Unfortunately, the absence of the *khn* from the ritual texts leaves us in the dark about their actual role in ritual and religious activities. It is clear, however, that the king played an important role in some rituals, particularly in monthly royal dynastic rituals involving ancestor worship (Tsumura 1999). As already noted by Lester Grabbe, "The Ugaritic material probably presents more problems than solutions" (Grabbe 1995, 56).

Priesthood in Hittite Religion

The Hittite Empire, centered on Anatolia, reached its greatest extension during the Late

---

6. A helpful translation of this important text is in *COS* 1:427–31.

7. The term *khn*, "priest" (del Olmo Lete and Sanmartín 1996, 1:212), appears repeatedly in texts from Ras Shamra, but does not appear in the index of the most up-to-date publication of Ugarit's ritual texts (Pardee 2000, 2:898–935).

Bronze Age. At that time, it controlled Asia Minor (Anatolia) as well as a number of buffer vassal states on the periphery (including Ugarit, Aleppo, Karchemish, and Emar). Hittite religion was ultimately controlled by the royal family, whose care of the local cult guaranteed divine blessings. This close link between pantheon, deity, and royal leadership follows a similar evolution as already noted in Egypt and Mesopotamia (V. Haas 1994, 33, 181–84). Ritual activities played a significant role in Hittite religion, as can be noted by the sheer number of extant ritual texts (e.g., B. Collins 1995; Taggar-Cohen 2006; D. Wright 1993; Bawanypeck and Görke 2001; Feder 2011). Humans communicated with the gods through sacrifice, libations, prayer, and divination, and each of these important worship activities required the intervention of the priesthood (B. Collins 2007).

The Hittite pantheon was immense—more than a thousand gods according to Hittite texts—and represented a mix of national and local deities (Hoffner 1997b, 87). So far, more than thirty temples have been identified in Boğazkale, the site of ancient Hattuša, the capital of the Hittite Empire (B. Collins 2007, 840), with the storm god [d]IM (the Syrian and Canaanite equivalents were Hadad and Ba'al, respectively) as the head of the pantheon (V. Haas 1994, 619; A. Green 2003, 134–52). The official cult included a sequence of important festivals and seasonal rituals and was served by two types of male priests and one female type (Hoffner 1997b). A female member of the royal family (and later the wife of the king) held the title of *tawananna*, the high priestess associated with the sun deity Arinna (V. Haas 1994, 204).

Depictions of Hittite priests from the fourteenth century BCE onward show priests wearing masks in some instances. They are also shown as attendants to the king, carrying jugs and food. The Inandik Vase (ca. 1600 BCE), the most complete and representative of the Hittite relief vases, depicts priests and priestesses participating in ritual sex and shows altar offerings and the pouring of libations on an altar before a seated female deity. Other scenes include the sacrifice of a bull, preparations for a sacred banquet, and musicians with instruments (Collon 1999, 23).

Functions of Ancient Near Eastern Priesthood

Priests functioned as mediators between the human and divine spheres and were generally considered attendants of the deity. Their service (including feeding, cleaning, clothing, anointing, protecting, honoring, and other rites) to the deity, represented by the statue, determined future blessings or curses for the people and the royal house. Except for city-states in northern Syria, where a limited kingship was complemented by the leadership of tribal elders, royalty was generally closely associated with the priesthood, and the king or queen often was involved in a high-priestly role. When the relationship between the deity and the city, state, or people was strained, priests had to reestablish the link through sacrifices and offerings. Another highly specialized function of ancient Near Eastern priesthood involved divination, the attempt to anticipate the outcome of future events through magic rituals. Since most of the extant literature is archival, monumental, or canonical, our view of the ancient Near East is dominated by the elite and official leadership and often lacks the nitty-gritty of village and personal piety and their relationship to the priesthood.[8] Since writing was often associated with temples, priests (or at least some) wielded a powerful influence because writing (and the preservation of names) meant a future in the worldview of the ancient Near East (E. Radner 2005). Their function as teachers is not easily documented, but may have been part of their official portfolio.

---

8. For a brief view of village religion in the Hittite context, see Macqueen 1986, 111–15.

46

Worship, Sacrifice, and Festivals in the Ancient Near East

Roy E. Gane

Definitions

"Worship" is activity that honors a deity, which can include sacrifices and festivals. Ancient Near Eastern worship usually was directed toward deities that were represented by anthropomorphic images or other kinds of symbols. Biblical Israelite worship was oriented toward Yhwh in heaven (ascending smoke [Lev. 1:9]) or toward his resident personal presence in his sanctuary (Lev. 16:12–16), without the need for material representations.

A "ritual" is a fixed system of activities that is believed to interact with someone (e.g., deity or demon) or something (e.g., sin or ritual impurity) that ordinarily is inaccessible to humans in the material domain (R. Gane 2004, 61). Rituals can be used for worship, but some rituals, such as magical rituals or nonsacrificial elimination of impurity, are not worship.

A "ritual complex" is a group of individual rituals, usually of different kinds, that function together for a higher-level goal.

A "(religious) ritual system" is comprised of all rituals performed by or on behalf of a given religious community, such as Israel, that affect its relationships with the divine and subdivine members of the cosmic community.

The word "cultic" is basically synonymous with "ritual." A "cult" or "cultic system" consists of a ritual system and the infrastructure associated with it.

A "sacrifice" is a ritual offering that transfers something to a deity for his or her utilization. If an animal is offered, it is slaughtered to provide meat for the deity. However, sacrifice of other materials, such as grain items (Lev. 2), does not involve slaughter.

A "festival" is a special sacred occasion that recurs at one or more times of the year and calls for celebration or other special activity, usually including rituals. Although the uniquely Israelite weekly Sabbath, requiring cessation of work, is a cyclical sacred occasion that forms the basis for sacred time (Lev. 23:3), we do not refer to it as a festival.

Worship

Worship in the ancient Near East, including Israel, took many forms, including sacrifices and nonsacrificial rituals, daily service to deities, celebrations on special sacred occasions, such as festivals, as well as prayers, hymns/music, and practicing physical self-denial. Many iconographic representations of ancient Near Eastern worship have been preserved, but texts are our main sources of precise information.

Daily "care and feeding" of deities involved both offerings/sacrifices of food and drink and nonsacrificial ritual activities. For instance, the regular morning liturgy in an Egyptian temple included "spells of prostration, praise and offerings, after which the cult statue is removed, salved, clothed, adorned, and provided with unguent and eyepaint . . . fresh sand is strewn on the chapel floor, and the god is purified by water and natron" (COS 1:55). Similarly, daily service to a Mesopotamian god, represented by his or her idol, entailed elements such as fumigations and purifications with water at mealtimes, when various foods (grain products, fruit, meat) and beverages (beer, wine, milk) were served. Other regular, but not necessarily daily, care included ritual washing of the image and arraying it in magnificent clothing with jewelry (Hundley 2013a, 273–76).

Every morning and evening, Israelite priests performed a complex of rituals for the deity Yhwh at his sanctuary that consisted of offering food and drink (Num. 28:1–8), along with burning incense and tending and lighting the lamps (Exod. 27:20–21; 30:7–8) (see Haran 1985, 205–29). However, unlike other ancient Near Eastern meals for deities, Yhwh's food was burned up on the altar in the courtyard and ascended to him in the form of smoke, thereby avoiding the impression that he was dependent on human sustenance.

People prayed to their deities throughout the ancient Near East. Some texts record prescribed prayers in ritual contexts (Pritchard 1969a, 331–34 [Mesopotamian]; COS 1:164 [Hittite], 283–85 [Ugaritic]). Biblical prayers, however, generally were not prescribed for repeated use, with an exception in Deuteronomy 21:7–8, a declaration of innocence and supplication for corporate absolution concerning an unsolved murder. Moshe Greenberg has demonstrated that several kinds of biblical prayers expressing petition, confession, and gratitude were patterned after similar expressions in speech between humans because Yhwh was a personal being and the Israelites could communicate with him only analogously to ways in which they communicated with one another (Greenberg 1983, 20–37).

Music in the ancient Near East employed a wide variety of string, wind, and percussion instruments (Braun 2002; King and Stager 2001, 285–98), especially to accompany singing. Worship could include music, as in a Neo-Assyrian hymn to the goddess Nanaya: "Musicians of wide repertoire are seated before her, performers on the lyre, the harpsichord, the clappers, the flute, the oboe, the long pipes" (COS 1:472). Somewhat similarly, Psalm 150, an Israelite hymn, speaks of praising Yhwh by means of trumpet, lute, harp, tambourine, pipe, and cymbals (vv. 3–5), and praise and thanks to God by singing and instrumental music were an important part of worship at the temple in Jerusalem (1 Chron. 16:4–7; 2 Chron. 5:12–13). Hymns to deities are preserved in ancient Near Eastern texts, mainly from Egypt and Mesopotamia (COS 1:20–21, 37–46 [Egypt], 418–19, 470–74, 526–32 [Mesopotamia]), and in the Hebrew Bible, especially the book of Psalms.

Another kind of worship practice was physical self-denial, as described by Adad-Guppi (mother of the Neo-Babylonian king Nabonidus): "In order to appease the heart of my god and my goddess, I did not put on a garment of excellent wool, silver, gold, a fresh garment; I did not allow perfumes (or) fine oil to touch my body. I was clothed in a torn garment. My fabric was sackcloth. I proclaimed their praises. The fame of my god and goddess were set (firmly) in my heart. I stood their watch. I served them food" (COS 1:478). This resembles the self-denial of Daniel, her contemporary (Dan. 10:2–3, 12; cf. Lev. 16:29; Ps. 35:13).

Sacrifice

Sacrificial Procedures

Prescriptive or descriptive ritual texts can supply two levels of information: (1) specifications regarding performance of activities, and (2) indications of function or meaning attached to the activities. Here we focus on the former and in the next section on the latter.

There were various ways to offer sacrifices in the ancient Near East. Common in Mesopotamia, Egypt, and Hatti was the presentation offering of food that was simply placed on a table or stand before the image or symbol of a deity, along with drink that was poured out in front of the god (or goddess). The deity/idol was thought to need human sustenance and apparently was regarded as consuming food and drink in some immaterial sense (Hundley 2013a, 275; cf. Oppenheim 1964, 191–92). In Hatti, breaking bread could represent the god's consumption of it (Hoffner 1974, 217). However, the Hittite "Instructions to Priests and Temple Officials" acknowledge that the food and drink offered to a deity physically remained to be secondarily consumed by priests and in some cases also their family members (COS 1:218).

The only presentation offering in the Israelite ritual system was the "bread of the Presence," which was placed every Sabbath on the golden table in the sanctuary with drink offerings (Exod. 25:29–30; Lev. 24:5–8; cf. Num. 28:7b). Frankincense placed on the bread apparently was burned for Yhwh when the bread was changed and his priests could eat it (Lev. 24:7–9). Therefore, Yhwh utilized only the incense, indicating that he did not consume the bread at all because he did not need human food (e.g., Ps. 50:12–13) (R. Gane 1992; cf. Hundley 2011, 113–15).

Sacrifices in which offering materials were burned up and received by deities in the form of smoke were rare in Mesopotamia. In Egypt, sacrificial "meat was not burnt for the god, but eaten by the worshiper after the ritual had ended" (Willems 2004, 326). However, burnt offerings were more common in parts of Hatti (later Hurro-Luwian [Beckman 2004, 339]) and the Levant. Ugaritic literature attests some terms for different kinds of sacrifices, including burnt offerings and well-being (so-called "peace" or "fellowship") offerings, that parallel Hebrew terms (Pardee 2002, 225; Selman 1995, 97–99). All edible parts of an Israelite burnt offering were consumed by the altar fire and ascended to Yhwh as smoke like incense (Lev. 1). However, only the fat of a well-being offering was burned and the offerer(s) ate the meat after the priest received his portions as an "agent's commission" from Yhwh (Lev. 3; 7:11–36).

Ancient Near Eastern ritual texts show some specific similarities to Israelite sacrifices. For example, a Sumerian inscription reports that when the ruler Gudea (ca. 2100 BCE) sacrificed to his god Ningirsu, he arranged "perfect ox and perfect he-goat" (COS 2:419) just as an Israelite sacrifice required a victim without defect (e.g., Lev. 1:3; 22:17–25). In Hittite sacrifice, an individual was to place a hand on the offering material, apparently to signify that he or she was its owner and therefore the offerer, who would receive the benefit of the ritual (cf. Lev. 1:4) (D. Wright 1986, 443).

Most ancient Near Eastern sacrifices did not assign any special role to the blood of the victims. However, Hittites offered blood to netherworld gods and used it to purify things (Feder 2011, 209–15, 227–28; Beckman 2011, 100–101). Ritual purification of a new Anatolian temple for the Goddess of the Night involved putting blood on the image of the goddess, the temple wall, and all of the deity's implements (COS 1:176). Only the Israelite ritual system systematically included application of blood, representing ransom for the life of the offerer (Lev. 17:11), to altars and other parts of the sanctuary of a celestial deity as a significant part of animal sacrifices (esp. Lev. 1–7; 16).

Child sacrifice was practiced in some parts of the Levant (e.g., Phoenicia [Dever 2005, 218]; Moab [2 Kings 3:27]), but it was forbidden in the Israelite cultic system (Lev. 18:21; 20:1–5; Deut. 18:10).

Sacrificial Functions

Frank Gorman has distinguished between rituals of founding, which establish the normative state of a ritual system (e.g., Lev. 8–9); cyclical rituals of maintenance, which keep the system working properly once it is set up (e.g., Num. 28–29); and rituals of restoration, which return the system to its normative state (e.g., Lev. 16) (Gorman 1993). We can add rituals of enhancement, which contribute to improvement of relationships between individuals and the deity through voluntary homage (e.g., Lev. 2) or praise (Lev. 7:12–16). I will discuss functions of sacrifices under these four headings, keeping in mind that sacrifices often operated within ritual complexes.

Founding

Initiation of a new ancient Near Eastern temple or high-cultic official could include sacrifices to honor deities. When the idols of the god Ningirsu and his consort Baba were moved into a temple that Gudea had built, there were purification and divination procedures, gifts to the divine couple, a banquet, and animal sacrifices (COS 2:431–32). Installing a high priestess of the storm god at Emar (second-millennium BCE Syria) took nine days in which many activities were performed, including placement of oil on her head, shaving her, putting gold earrings on her ears and a gold ring on her right hand, wrapping her head with a red wool headdress, and offering sacrifices to the storm god and other deities (COS 1:427–31; cf. Fleming 1992a).

The one-time consecration of the new Israelite sanctuary and its priesthood (Lev. 8; cf. Exod. 29) lasted seven days. However, this did not include ritual installation of the deity. He was not represented by an image, but rather moved his real Presence into the sanctuary before the consecration ritual was performed (Exod. 40:34–35).

Maintenance

Once ancient Near Eastern gods were installed in their temples, it was crucial to feed and care for them so that they would remain happy and well disposed toward the community. Priests, who functioned like servants of monarchs, were responsible for this care. A number of texts from Mesopotamia, Egypt, and Hatti indicate that priests provided gods with presentation offerings of food (usually meat and grain products) and drink twice every day, morning and afternoon/evening, just as humans ate twice per day (e.g., Pritchard 1969a, 334, 343–45). Egyptian priests washed and clothed idols and applied makeup to them (COS 1:55).

Israelite priests also performed twice-daily regular ritual service for Yhwh at his sanctuary, consisting of morning and evening burnt offerings with accompanying grain and drink offerings (Num. 28:1–8) to make a full meal (cf. Num. 15:1–16; Gen. 18:6–8), a regular grain offering of the high priest (Lev. 6:19–23 [Heb. vv. 12–16]), and ritual activities in the outer sanctum that included a drink offering (Num. 28:7), burning incense (Exod. 30:7–8), and tending lamps (also Exod. 30:7–8). However, Yhwh was distanced from anthropomorphism by the facts that he received his animals as food (Num. 28:2) in the form of smoke and there was no daily presentation offering of food at the Israelite sanctuary; the "bread of the Presence" presentation offering was performed weekly (see above).

In addition to temple worship, many ancient Near Eastern nonpriests performed maintenance rituals on a smaller scale because they believed that their deceased ancestors had become divine spirits who required regular offerings of food and drink, lest they would become unhappy and cause harm (Selman 1995, 91–92 [Mesopotamia]; Stevens 2011, 736–37 [Egypt]). Archaeology of domestic contexts in Israel has exposed artifactual evidence for syncretism with non-Yahwistic worship, such as model shrines, incense stands and other cultic vessels, and figurines (Zevit 2001, 256, 267–343; King and Stager 2001, 345–50).

Restoration

Ancient Near Eastern individuals or groups could fall from favor with a deity and suffer negative consequences for various reasons, including failure to properly maintain the cult or violation of the god's norms. It appears fairly common for people to feel stress because they were unaware of the reasons for their suffering (*COS* 1:488; van der Toorn 1985, 94–97 [Mesopotamia]; *COS* 1:47 [Egypt]). Nevertheless, a wrongdoer could hope that the god would calm down and be merciful to forgive sin (*COS* 1:490).

Yhwh offered the Israelites far more certainty because they only needed to relate to him, he defined sin as violation of commandments that he communicated, and he specified just a few kinds of sacrifices to expiate/remove (*kipper*) sins (R. Gane 2009, 294). The purification offering (the so-called sin offering) was required to remove inadvertent and hidden (mostly due to forgetting) sins, prerequisite to divine forgiveness (Lev. 4:1–5:13); the reparation offering (the so-called guilt offering) was required to remedy sins of sacrilege involving misuse of something holy or fraud through a false oath in Yhwh's name (Lev. 5:14–6:7) (Milgrom 1976); and the voluntary burnt offering (Lev. 1) appears to have dealt with other kinds of sins, except those committed defiantly (Num. 15:30–31). No close parallels

to the mandatory purification and reparation offerings have been found in other ancient Near Eastern ritual systems.

Unique in the ancient Near East was a two-stage system of expiation through Israelite purification offerings that demonstrated the way in which the deity extended mercy with justice to human subjects (R. Gane 2005, 331–33). First, sins were removed from the persons who offered purification offerings throughout the year, as indicated by goal formulas of prescriptions for such sacrifices—for example, in Leviticus 4:26: "Thus the priest shall make expiation for him from [privative preposition *min*] his sin, and it shall be forgiven him" (my translation) (see R. Gane 2005, 106–62; R. Gane 2008b). Second, the same sins were then cleansed from God's sanctuary on the annual Day of Atonement (Lev. 16:16), representing vindication of Yhwh as judge when he forgave loyal people, and this vindication resulted in their final moral purification so that there were no remaining impediments to the divine-human relationship (Lev. 16:29–31) (see R. Gane, 2005, 273–84, 305–23).

The purification offering also contributed to removal of severe physical ritual impurities from persons (e.g., Lev. 12:6–8; 14:19) and then from the sanctuary on the Day of Atonement (Lev. 16:16, 19). These impurities, which originated with the humans, represented the birth-to-death cycle of mortality (Milgrom 1991, 766–68, 1000–1004; Maccoby 1999, 31–32, 48–50, 207–8). Because they interfered with the divine-human relationship, they had to be kept separate from Yhwh's sphere of holiness/life (e.g., Lev. 7:20–21; 15:31).

Whereas Israelites held that death was impure (esp. Num. 19), Egyptians regarded death as holy because it was merely a transition to continued life in another form. Mesopotamians and Hittites thought of impurities as evils coming from the underworld rather than from humans. Mesopotamians, but not Hittites, believed that impurities were caused by demons (D. Wright 1987, 248–71). Both groups used a variety of rituals to expel such evils (D. Wright 1987, 272), but not sacrifices because the impurities did not involve gods.

Enhancement

An ancient Near Eastern individual could spontaneously express praise or thanks to a deity, as when the Assyrian king Shalmaneser III recorded his praise for "the majesty of the great gods" on a stone stele (COS 2:262) and the grateful Phoenician king Yeḥawmilk gave works of art to his goddess (COS 2:151). Such expressions could plausibly be regarded as enhancing the divine-human relationship.

A person could also vow a gift to a deity as a form of praise, often on condition of receiving a benefit, in which case the gift also expressed thanks. Making a vow was voluntary, but fulfilling it was mandatory. A votive gift could be a valuable object, such as a statue of precious metal or a stele (COS 2:152–53; 3:66), but it could also be an animal sacrifice (COS 2:248).

Homage and praise to gods through sacrifices could occur in contexts where these were specified along with other ritual elements. Ritual texts from Emar concerning the installation of a new high priestess for the storm god (COS 1:428–29) and the Zukru Festival (COS 1:433–35, 437–38, 440–41) specify sacrificial homage that utilized mainly animals. Establishing a temple for the Goddess of the Night in Hatti called for animal sacrifices as rituals of praise (COS 1:174, 176). These rituals belonged to ritual complexes of "founding" (new high priestess and temple) and "maintenance" (Zukru Festival).

An Israelite could voluntarily offer several kinds of sacrifices to enhance his or her relationship with Yhwh, including grain offerings (Lev. 2; 6:19–23), which apparently expressed homage, and three kinds of well-being offerings: thanksgiving (Lev. 7:12–15), votive (v. 16), and "spontaneous gift" (v. 16 CEB) offerings.

Men or women could voluntarily take Nazirite vows, which came with the obligation to offer several kinds of sacrifices (Num. 6:1–21). As elsewhere in the ancient Near East, an Israelite could express devotion to Yhwh by dedicating (including through a vow) a valuable item to him at his sanctuary (Lev. 27).

Festivals

Ancient Near Eastern peoples observed many special sacred occasions at various times of the year, such as beginnings of months, one or both of the equinoxes, and seasons tied to the agricultural cycle (M. Cohen 2015; cf. Fleming 2000). Festivals could honor particular deities, commemorate mythic events, seek to ensure fertility, celebrate harvests, purify cults, and so on, or combinations of these. In the Canaanite area of the Levant, myth and fertility were joined when the death of Baʿal in the fall and his revival in the spring were viewed as causing the waning and renewal of the agricultural cycle.

The importance of festivals for ancient Near Eastern societies is indicated by, for example, the fact that we have more festival texts than texts of any other genre in the Hittite language. Furthermore, some festivals were exceedingly elaborate and lengthy. Some Hittite festivals lasted several weeks and seem to have been religious tours of cultic sites throughout the empire by the king, often with his queen (Ardzinba 1982, 16; Beckman 1989, 103). The annual spring Babylonian *Akītu* Festival lasted eleven days and featured magnificent processions of idols with reenactment of the first triumphal entrance into the city by its chief god (Marduk in this case), as in similar *akītu* festivals elsewhere in Mesopotamia (M. Cohen 2015, 389–92, 400–402; cf. 393–99, 403–8; van der Toorn 1991a, 3).

Festivals often carried political significance, especially when they involved participation of rulers. They expressed corporate religious solidarity and showed divine support for leaders of the social order at regional and national levels (e.g., Bidmead 2004).

Deities often received additional offerings on festival days to supplement their regular meals. However, temple religion, including many activities performed during festivals, was mostly accessible to elite persons (e.g., Egypt [Spalinger 1998, 241–60]). Nevertheless, some festival events, such as the processions in Babylon, brought otherwise hidden objects (such as idols) into view. This, combined with the perceived provision of corporate well-being, along with feasting and revelry, would tend to make festivals popular with common people.

Some festivals, including those that celebrated the New Year, enacted renewal through means such as assessment of persons dependent on a temple and renewal or termination of their contracts for the coming year (COS 1:528; R. Gane 2005, 355–62 [Mesopotamia]), and purification of sacred precincts and/or sacred objects contained in them (R. Gane 2004).

Israelite festivals (esp. Exod. 12; Lev. 23; Num. 28–29) were similar to other ancient Near Eastern festivals in that they revolved around the agricultural cycle, celebrated the sovereignty and beneficence of the deity and harvests that he provided, included special festival offerings, provided for renewal of the cult by purification of the sanctuary (Lev. 16), and in several cases involved feasting by the people. However, the Israelite festivals were simpler than many other ancient Near Eastern festivals, and some Israelite sacred occasions (esp. Festival of Passover / Unleavened Bread) were unique in that they explicitly commemorated the historical deliverance of the nation by their deity.

47

Prophecy, Divination, and Magic in the Ancient Near East

JOHN W. HILBER

Definitions

In the history of Old Testament studies there has traditionally been a clear differentiation between "prophecy" and "divination." This followed the distinction expressed in Deuteronomy 18:9–22. Prophecy referred to the proclamations of charismatic preachers who spoke for God, whereas divination was characterized as the illegitimate practices of those who invoked the gods to reveal their will through observation or manipulation of objects in the natural world. More recent discussion, particularly in the context of broader ancient Near Eastern religion, has nuanced the definitions differently. In contemporary discussion, "divination" simply refers to any means by which humans gain access to secret information known only from the divine realm (Grabbe 1995, 136–41; Hamori 2015, 4). According to this definition, "prophecy" is a subtype of "divination" in the sense that God discloses the secrets of his heavenly council to his prophets (e.g., Jer. 23:18, 22). In this usage of the term, "divination" is a neutral word to describe processes by which humans receive divine revelation, including prophecy.

In spite of this redefinition, it remains useful to differentiate between "prophecy" on the one hand and "technical divination" on the other. "Prophecy" is a divine message, *intuitively received* by a human agent with a commission to transmit it to a third party (Guinan 2002, 18; Nissinen 2004, 20; 2017, 20–21). This process involves direct divine intervention into a person's cognitive processes with the result that the person perceives reception of a divine message. If this divine communication is intended only for the immediate recipient (e.g., in a dream), then it is revelation, but it becomes "prophecy" only when it is a message intended for another party. "Technical divination" refers to practices in which people receive information from the gods *by ritual manipulation and/or observation of objects exterior to the human agent.* In the case of prophecy, the agent is a passive recipient of the message, and any individual might be qualified to receive such a message; with technical divination, the agent is more actively involved, employing a learned skill set (Nissinen 2017, 14–19). The line between the two sometimes is blurred, such as when an individual induces a dream experience in a temple or when a diviner interpretively expands upon a liver inspection. But even in these cases, one can differentiate the stages between mechanical inducement of the revelatory experience and the intuitive reception of an associated message. Whether by intuitive prophecy or by the exercise of technical skill, these human agents had *special access* to divine knowledge by divine call or by training (Hamori 2015, 6). This differentiates revelation that is received by "divination" from more common experiences of people, such as dreams, by which many in the ancient world claimed to receive information from the nonhuman world.

The term "magic" has traditionally carried a negative connotation in religious discussions. Contrasted with "religion," which is characterized as a truer expression of human devotion to God or gods, "magic" has had the connotation of a primitive and inferior art of manipulating the unseen world. From the viewpoint of general religious studies, it is more accurate simply to recognize magic as one component of religious expression (i.e., engaging the supernatural). Magic "aimed to achieve a desired effect by symbolic means, usually in the form of a verbal utterance (such as a spell) that could be accompanied by a ritualized action involving an object or a certain combination of ingredients" (Borghouts 1995, 1775). The words and actions were thought to harness an *impersonal force*, sometimes with the intent to coerce personal forces to action. However, the value placed upon magic might be negative or positive depending on the religious tradition. For religious systems in which one must only depend on the appropriate supernatural agent, then a theology of manipulating impersonal forces might indeed be illegitimate.

Technical Divination and Magic

Mesopotamia

Among people of Mesopotamia, the most important means of discerning the will of the gods or receiving information from the divine realm were through observation of astronomical phenomena (e.g., the color of celestial objects, an eclipse, a convergence of stars and planets) and through examination of the entrails (especially the liver) of sacrificial animals (called "extispicy"). The Babylonians and Assyrians believed that the sky was like a writing tablet upon which the gods "wrote" their intentions by the configuration of celestial objects (Rochberg 2004). The challenge for the ancient scholars who "read" these omens was to properly interpret their significance. An example: "On the 14th day the moon and the sun were seen together. . . . If on the 14th day the moon and the sun are seen together: reliable speech; the land will become happy; the gods will remember Akkad favourably."[1]

Observations were interpreted by reference to written collections of omens, handbooks for understanding messages written in the heavens. These omen series themselves were the work of the same specialists who drew a link between an observation and its significance. Some observations are actually impossible (e.g., the sun appearing in the middle of the night), and this shows how these manuals were often a matter of speculative exploration. Babylonian scholars began with the endless possibilities inherent in the nature of cuneiform text, such as the ambiguity of cuneiform sign values, homonyms between words, overlapping semantic domains, as well as similarities between the physical appearance of signs themselves (van de Mieroop 2016, 115–27, 188–90). Whether through empirical experience or through hermeneutical speculation, scholars interpreted celestial omens to anticipate the future.

While astronomy was the most authoritative form of divination and pertained mostly to official, royal affairs of state, another class of scholars (the *barû* priests) specialized in reading the "writing" of the gods on the entrails of animals. This was available for ordinary

---

1. Abbreviated from Hunger 1992, no. 110, pp. 67–68.

people. As part of the ritual, the priest asked the god a binary question (the answer to which is either "yes" or "no"). The condition of various parts of the liver was regarded as either "favorable" or "unfavorable" in response to this question. One example of such a query reads in part:

> Šamaš, great lord, give me a firm positive answer to what I am asking you! Should Esarhaddon, king of Assyria, appoint [the ma]n whose name is written in this papyrus and placed before your great divinity, [to the po]sition which is written in [th]is papyrus? . . . Be present in this ram, place (in it) a firm positive answer, favorable designs, favorable propitious omens . . . and may an oracle be given as an answer.[2]

Other examples of divination, both active solicitation of omens as well as passive observation, included practices such as dropping oil in water or noticing abnormal births.

Regardless of the omen, the results were not a fatalistic prediction of the future. Rather, the omens were viewed as warnings or confirmations from the gods; if an omen was ominous, apotropaic rituals might avert the calamity. These in themselves were part of a larger, elaborate system of magic and herb lore whereby specialists (the *āšipu*, the "magical expert," and the *asû*, the "physician") could propitiate an angry deity, ward off demon attacks, reverse spells by sorcerers, and so cure the accompanying illnesses (see Farber 1995).

Hatti

The Hittites of ancient Anatolia also practiced binary solicitation of oracles through extispicy or watching the behavior of animals such as sheep, snakes, and especially birds. The last appears to have been unique to the Hittites (Beal 2002).

2. Abbreviated from Starr, Aro, and Parpola 1990, no. 156, pp. 167–68.

Egypt

Aside from the proclamations of the pharaoh, who embodied deity and so spoke with divine authority, the most important means of inquiring of the gods in Egypt was during festivals when the god's statue was brought out of the temple into public on a portable shrine. Individuals were permitted to present binary questions regarding any matter of concern, whether it be for guidance in decision-making or resolution of legal disputes. The exact manner in which the god answered yes or no is unclear, but evidence points to the movements of the shrine as it was carried by the priests (perhaps dipping or moving backward) (Kruchten 2001).

The Levant

Religious custom in the Levant also looked to divination for divine guidance. Astronomical omens, models for reading livers, and interpretation of abnormal births are known from Ugarit, together with texts recording apotropaic incantations against snakebite, sexual dysfunction, and sorcery (Pardee 2002, 127–48, 157–66).

Conclusion

Peoples of the ancient Near East eagerly sought the will of their gods through a variety of means. In the Old Testament there is a complicated relationship between technical divination and the prophetic reaction against it (Kuemmerlin-McLean 1992, 469–70). Some passages suggest a positive role for technical divination in the lives of Israel's leaders. This is undeniable for the Urim and Thummim (Exod. 28:30; 1 Sam. 28:6), to which the "ephod" seems related as a means of inquiry (1 Sam. 2:28; 14:3; 21:9; 23:6, 9; 30:7–8) (see Grabbe 1995, 120–21). However, other texts denounce technical divination and magic (Exod. 22:18; Lev. 19:26; Deut. 18:9–12). It seems unlikely that the dominant prophetic viewpoint throughout the Old Testament and the orthodoxy of its tradents would permit such a contradictory presentation, unless they understood the Urim/ephod in a manner compatible with prophecy and distinguished them theologically from other forms of divination.[3]

Prophecy

The discovery in 1933 and subsequent publication of the royal archive at Mari greatly expanded our understanding of prophetism in the ancient Near East. In recent decades, scores of additional prophetic texts from the ancient Near East have come to attention, either through new discovery or, more often, through publication in accessible forms.[4] There are approximately 150 extant texts containing prophetic speech or describing prophetism from Ur, Uruk, Kish, Mari, Babylon, Eshnunna, Biblos, Hatti, Ugarit, Emar, Assyria, Amman, Hamath, Deir Alla, and Egypt. Not only is there wide geographical representation but also the dates for these texts range from the late third millennium to the third century BCE.

Mesopotamia

Letters and other administrative documents from the eighteenth-century BCE royal archive at Mari disclose much about prophecy in early Mesopotamia (Huffmon 2000; van der Toorn 2000b). Prophetic functionaries spoke their impressions from the deity, sometimes out of dream experiences and ecstatic visions, at times responding to sacrifices, and in one case after being induced by drink. A typical example of these prophetic words is the following, which contains commands to the king concerning the supply of furniture and a female servant for the temple: "Thus says Šamaš: '[I am] the lord of the lan[d]! Send quickly to Sippar, the city of life, a great throne for [my] enjoyable dwelling, and your daughter whom I desired from you!'"[5] One text describes a symbolic action that accompanied the prophetic oracle. A prophet devoured a lamb in the city gate to graphically illustrate the deity's threat against the city. The official sending the letter reports, "[I gave] him a lamb and he devoured it raw [in fr]ont of the city gate . . . and said 'A devouring will take place!'"[6]

Revelations came to variously titled functionaries, both male and female.[7] Some were vocationally attached to a temple: the *āpilum* (the "answerer," who perhaps responded to inquiries), the *qammatum* (meaning unclear), and the *assinnu* (possibly a eunuch). Others appear not to have been official cult personnel: the *muḫḫûm* (the "ecstatic"; the noun is related to a verb meaning "to be crazy," so perhaps they exhibited trance-like behavior). One of the titles, *nabû* ("called one"), is cognate to one of the Hebrew words for a prophet, *nabi'*. Along with the *muḫḫûm*, another name for prophets and prophetesses became dominant in the Neo-Assyrian period (particularly the seventh century BCE): the *raggimu* (related to a verb meaning "to shout").[8]

Prophecy often originated in temples, but records attest to prophetic words being delivered in private contexts as well as in public forums. The prophets most often addressed cultic duties of the king and his political affairs. While the extant records of prophecy from Mari are known only from *excerpts* of prophetic oracles embedded in royal correspondence, the records from Assurbanipal's

---

3. For prophetic attitudes toward divination and divine accommodation to the Urim, see Van Dam 2012, 160–62.

4. For a nearly exhaustive collection of texts with translation and commentary, see Nissinen with Seow and Ritner 2003. See the important treatment of prophecy by Nissinen 2017 for general discussion. For sources, see pp. 57–114.

5. Nissinen with Seow and Ritner 2003, no. 4, p. 24.

6. Nissinen with Seow and Ritner 2003, no. 16, p. 38.

7. The identity in both gender and roles of Mesopotamian prophets is a complex problem. See Stökl 2012.

8. For an overview of Neo-Assyrian prophecy, see Nissinen 2000.

library discovered in the Neo-Assyrian capital, Nineveh, report prophetic oracles recorded directly. Most of these divine speeches originated to encourage Esarhaddon during a civil war, when he was fighting to gain his right to the throne. An example reads, "I am the great Lady, I am Ištar of Arbela who throw [sic] your enemies before your feet. Have I spoken to you any words that you could not rely upon? I am Ištar of Arbela, I will flay your enemies and deliver them up to you. I am Ištar of Arbela, I go before you and behind you. Fear not!"[9]

These Mesopotamian prophets and prophetesses displayed behavior that was largely shared by their Israelite counterparts. Both were recognized by eccentric behavior, claimed access to the divine council, performed symbolic actions, found inspiration in part through music, responded to inquiry and lament, admonished kings concerning cultic infractions, utilized similar speech forms, relied on scribes for writing, and at times offered oracles that were contrary to the words of other prophets. The most distinguishing difference between Mesopotamian prophets and those whose words were preserved in the Hebrew Bible is their conception of God/gods. Mesopotamian prophets were committed polytheists, speaking on behalf of multiple deities and never against other deities. In contrast, the prophets of the Bible spoke exclusively in the name of their one God. Although evidence shows some concern for social justice by Mesopotamian prophets, the quantitative emphasis on this matter in biblical prophecy constitutes, in my opinion, a significant difference. Similarly, while Mesopotamian prophets on occasion admonished the king, the issue was always for cultic infractions. Only one text reports a serious threat by the deity toward the king, and this from a prophet whose location effectively placed him out of the king's reach. But the Bible reports Israelite prophets

confronting royal and cultic authority "face to face."[10]

Hatti

It is entirely possible that there were prophets among the Hittites, but no evidence remains. The "man of god" and "old woman" of Hittite texts most likely practiced some form of technical divination rather than speaking intuitively.[11]

Egypt

The consensus is that Egyptian texts containing prognostication of the future belong to the genre of wisdom, whereby sages spoke concerning the future either by reflection on past tradition or through magic. Divine messenger speech is absent (Shupak 1989–90). However, Egypt had the religious prerequisites for prophecy in its acceptance of divine revelation through other means (prognostication through magic and shrine processions noted above, dreams, and fortune-telling by the "wise woman"). In addition, divine speech was mediated by priests to the king in the royal cult, and numerous royal inscriptions record first-person divine speech framed with introductory speech formulas delivered in this setting (Hilber 2011).

The Levant

The Egyptian story of Wenamun as well as the "Prayer of the Righteous Sufferer" found at Ugarit both attest to ecstatic prophecy in the Levant in the second millennium.[12] Other texts from the first millennium record prophetic oracles among Israel's close neighbors. One contains a divine speech in a building dedication

9. Abbreviated from Nissinen with Seow and Ritner 2003, no. 68, p. 102.

10. For a more exhaustive comparison, see Nissinen 2010; Hilber 2012, 221–23.

11. This has been confirmed to me in personal communication with Hannah Marcuson (cf. Marcuson 2016, esp. 401–5).

12. For texts, see Nissinen with Seow and Ritner 2003, no. 142, p. 220, and no. 122, p. 184, respectively.

from the Ammonite capital, and another reports a salvation oracle to king Zakkur of Hamath (Syria): "Baalshamayn [said], 'F[e]ar not, for I have made [you] king . . . and I will deliver you from all [these kings who] have forced a siege against you!'"[13] Discovered in a sanctuary just across the Jordan River about fifty miles east of Jerusalem, a plaster inscription dated about 800 BCE records an apocalyptic-like oracle of "Balaam, son of Beor" (cf. Num. 22:5). Also important are three ostraca from the Judean city of Lachish reporting Israelite prophetic activity at the time of Nebuchanezzar's campaign against Judah.[14]

Prophecy and Writing

The plethora of prophetic oracles that became preserved in writing provides a window into the prophetic world outside the Bible. These texts also inform us about the relationship between prophecy and writing. In recent decades much doubt has been expressed regarding whether biblical prophecy preserves for us the actual words of Israel's prophets.[15] However, ancient Near Eastern prophecy and scribal culture support a more hopeful model (Hilber 2012).

Prophecy in Correspondence

Both Mari and Nineveh illustrate transcription of prophetic words. In correspondence, one might expect some paraphrase, hence not the *ipsissima verba* (exact words) of the prophet. The evidence shows a continuum of transmission practice from literal to paraphrase. However, divine messages were treated like diplomatic correspondence, so accuracy of the illocution if not the exact wording of the prophetic word was important. Tampering with divine speech would have been tantamount

to religious and political treason. Furthermore, the identity of the prophets was important in order to maintain the accountability of the human intermediary. Their veracity sometimes was tested by other means of divination.

Oracle Reports and Collections

In the Nineveh archive, the use of the quotation particle in these texts shows that scribes were recording the reported speech. However, the language of the oracles is pure Neo-Assyrian, the oral dialect of the prophetesses, not Standard Babylonian, which was used by scribes for composition and copying. This suggests that these tablets offer close access to the oral performance of prophets. Similar to the custom of correspondents from Mari, scribes were careful to preserve the name of the prophetess. They also recorded the city of origin and in one case the exact date of the oracle. In other words, the link between the prophet's identity and the recorded word was important.

Some Nineveh tablets consist of single oracle reports, but most oracles were copied from single reports into collections of oracles on archival tablets. The oracles seem to be chronologically and thematically related, like subunits within biblical prophetic books. But since none of the Assyrian collections exceeds the length of the book of Nahum, the comparison is limited.

Divine Letters

Written correspondence between the deity and the king is known from Old Babylonian and Neo-Assyrian periods. Most letters from deities are replies that simply echo campaign reports offered by the king to the god. However, several divine letters are form-critically indistinguishable from oral prophecy. This offers an illustration of *written composition of prophecy*. Bifurcation between scribe and prophet in these cases is an unnecessary distinction. These

13. Nissinen with Seow and Ritner 2003, no. 137, p. 206.

14. Nissinen with Seow and Ritner 2003, nos. 136–41, pp. 201–18.

15. The classic articulation of this is R. Carroll 1983.

texts are similar to Egyptian cultic prophecy in that they also likely originated in written form.[16]

Conclusion

Mesopotamian and Israelite prophets shared much in common; and all ancient Near Eastern societies held the divine word in high regard, carefully transmitting prophetic speech in a variety of written genres. On the one hand, there is no evidence that *prophets* ever wrote in the ancient Near East; rather, prophets worked in partnership with scribes (Nissinen 2014).[17] Like scribal support noted above from Neo-Assyrian practice, this is illustrated when one Mari prophet requested of his superior, "Send

me a discreet scribe!" The resulting oracle is preserved in the form of a divine letter to the king.[18]

The ancient Near Eastern evidence suggests a close link between prophetic books and the individual prophets whose oracles make up the literary masterpieces of the Bible (Hilber 2015, 173). These books are much more sophisticated in literary shape than any prophetic texts produced in the ancient Near East. One might conclude that prophetic books were the product of long redactional processes to achieve such shape. But the books of the Hebrew Bible in general find few literary parallels at the macro-level. The discussion hinges in some measure on the extent of literacy presupposed for preexilic Israel and the interest of the culture to record prophetic speech and produce prophetic literature. But if the people of preexilic Israel were capable of producing literature of any nature, then there is no inherent reason they could not have produced sophisticated prophetic compositions, literate prophets or not (Hilber 2015, 159).

16. Not discussed in this article are "literary-predictive texts" (so-called Akkadian Prophecies and Apocalypses [see M. Ellis 1989]). With only superficial similarity to prophecy (Nissinen 2003, 140; 2017, 111–15), they appear to be an application of omen interpretation for historiographical purposes, hence "mantic historiography" (Neujahr 2012). For a critique of their application to biblical prophecy, see Hilber 2015, 165–69.

17. Nissinen details the evidence of this conjunction; however, he would not necessarily agree with the extent of my deductions. For Nissinen, literary (scribal) prophecy offers only an opaque window into the historical phenomena (Nissinen 2017, 332–33).

18. Nissinen with Seow and Ritner 2003, no. 48, p. 75, and no. 4, p. 24 respectively.

48

Family Religion in Ancient Israel

Andrew R. Davis

Introduction

At one point in Saul Bellow's 1953 novel *The Adventures of Augie March*, the eponymous narrator describes Grandma Lausch's commemoration of her deceased husband: "Grandma, all the same, burned a candle on the anniversary of Mr. Lausch's death, threw a lump of dough on the coals when she was baking, as a kind of offering, had incantations over baby teeth and stunts against the evil eye. It was kitchen religion and had nothing to do with the giant God of the Creation, who turned back the waters and exploded Gomorrah, but it was on the side of religion at that" (Bellow 2003, 393). The kind of rites that Augie catalogs and terms as "kitchen religion" are not unique to twentieth-century Jewish grandmas, but rather have a long history in Judaism. Indeed, such "kitchen religion," or "family religion," has been an integral part of its cultic tradition since the beginnings of Israel.

Although Augie distinguishes between family religion and the *magnalia dei*, the distinction may not have been so sharp in ancient Israel. Admittedly, God's mighty deeds take center stage in the biblical narrative, and instances of family religion usually occur in marginal scenes of this main drama. Often family religion is mentioned in polemical passages, which are tricky sources to evaluate. On the one hand, a polemic against this or that cultic activity indicates its prevalence; if no one performed the cultic practice, there would be no need to censure it. On the other hand, interpreters must weigh this popularity against the polemical view of the biblical author/editor. Would all Israelites have viewed a denounced cultic practice as transgressive, or is the criticism unique to the author/editor describing it? To take a concrete example, a Deuteronomistic editor disapproves of Micah's teraphim (Judg. 17:5–6), but other passages mention them without condemnation (Gen. 31:19; 1 Sam. 19:13). These references agree that teraphim were part of family religion but depict the cult objects with varying degrees of censure.

The sometimes obscure biblical evidence for family religion makes recourse to nonbiblical sources an indispensable part of interpretation.

Besides expanding our view of family life in ancient Israel, encounters with family religion "behind the scenes" of the Old Testament shed new light on its biblical depictions. The best sources for such encounters are personal names found in the Hebrew Bible and in inscriptions and archaeological evidence from domestic and cultic contexts. This evidence reveals several points of contact with biblical tradition as well as practices that would have been unacceptable to biblical writers. This chapter explores these points of convergence and divergence by putting epigraphic and archaeological data in dialogue with the biblical evidence of family religion.

But first a word about terminology is in order. Over the last few decades, scholars have shown increasing interest in the religious beliefs and cultic practices under review here, but they have not always agreed on what to call this subdiscipline of Israelite religion. In my opinion, "family religion" is preferable to alternative designations. "Popular religion," for example, can imply cultic practice that is degenerate or derivative (Albertz 2008, 91; Stavrakopoulou 2010b), and "private religion" risks introducing modern conceptions of individuality that are ill-suited for the study of ancient culture (van der Toorn 1996, 3–4). Although "household religion" and "domestic religion" are valid for describing cult practices in and around the home, they are unable to account for families' worship at local and regional sanctuaries (A. Davis 2013, 95–107; Albertz and Schmitt 2012, 46). "Family religion" itself is not ideal, since some examples of official religion included familial elements (e.g., Lev. 16:6–14; Deut. 16:11), but the term is still the best appellation, not least because many of the beliefs and practices that it designates are related to the life cycles of a family—for example, rites of mourning, healing, and fertility as well as ancestor worship (Albertz 2008, 97–99). In this chapter "family" refers to the social unit denoted by the Hebrew phrase

bet ʾab, or "house of the father," which could include multiple generations of relatives as well as various dependents. Here I will follow the model proposed by J. David Schloen (2001, 154–55), who estimated that the average nuclear family consisted of five persons, the average joint-family *bet ʾab* ten persons, and the average *mishpahah* (i.e., clan) 120 persons.

Onomastic Evidence

Because Semitic personal names include a theophoric element, they are a valuable resource for reconstructing ancient Israelite religion. Examples of Hebrew personal names come from two main sources. The first is the Hebrew Bible, which includes around a thousand names,[1] and the second consists of names from epigraphic sources, such as ostraca, jar handles, seals, and seal impressions. A recent compilation of epigraphic names totaled 799 for Israel and Transjordan in the Iron II period, ca. 1000–586 BCE (Golub 2014). Together, the biblical and epigraphic sources combine for a total of over 2,000 personal names, which, according to David Clines (2016, 4), represent 6,761 individual Israelites.[2]

The importance of personal names for understanding family religion in ancient Israel has been highlighted by the work of Rainer Albertz. In an earlier monograph he argued that biblical names reflect the piety and interests of family life in ancient Israel (Albertz 1978, 49–77), and more recently he added epigraphic data to his investigation of personal names and family religion (Albertz

---

1. Martin Noth's (1928) compilation of names totaled 1,426, but Albertz and Schmitt (2012, 250) have revised the list to 957.

2. Clines arrived at this number by counting the individuals represented by each name. We should note that his counts of names differ from the numbers already mentioned; by Clines's reckoning, we have 1,465 Israelite names in the Hebrew Bible and 667 Israelite names from epigraphic sources up to 200 CE (Clines 2016, 2).

and Schmitt 2012, 245–386, 534–609). Albertz showed that names rarely refer to Israel's national story but instead use language found in individual psalms of lament and thanksgiving. This shared vocabulary suggests that personal names, like individual psalms, are windows into personal beliefs and piety.

Most Hebrew personal names are sentences that include a theophoric element as subject and a verb or noun as predicate (e.g., *'immanu* ["with us"] + *'el* ["God"] = *'immanu'el* ["God is with us"]). Attention to these theophorics and their predicates yields a glimpse of the beliefs and concerns that produced the names. For example, half the biblical and epigraphic names represent some kind of personal prayer, either giving thanks for what God has done (e.g., *yishma'e'l*, "God has heard"), identifying God with a divine characteristic (e.g., *'uriyahu*, "my light is Yhwh"), or praising God (e.g., *mikayahu*, "who is like Yhwh?") (Albertz and Schmitt 2012, 505).

Two aspects of these names indicate the familial context of their bestowal. First, many names identify God with kinship language. Over 40 percent of names from the biblical and epigraphic onomastica include a kinship term, especially brother (*'ah*) and father (*'ab*). Often the term is equated to a specific deity—mostly Yhwh, but over a dozen other deities are attested—but sometimes the kinship term itself is the theophoric element (Albertz and Schmitt 2012, 508). In the latter case, the kinship term may represent a deity, though others interpret them as divinized ancestors or personal gods. In any case, the prevalence of kinship language in personal names to designate divine beings shows how familial relationships shaped theological ideas in ancient Israel.

Second, about a third of the personal names in both corpora are related to childbirth (e.g., *mattanyahu*, "gift of Yhwh"). Given this prevalence, some scholars argue that the experience of childbirth underlies many prayer names even if they lack an explicit reference (Albertz and

Schmitt 2012, 253), but others take the prayer names as more general statements of faith (J. Fowler 1988, 18, 89, 97, 101, 104). However we understand the intentions behind these names, all agree that they offer a unique window into the language and practice of prayer among ancient Israelite families. While the biblical onomasticon provides a glimpse of this family religion, those names can be difficult to date and often represent select classes of Israelite society (royalty, priests, etc.). The ever-expanding corpus of epigraphic names is an indispensable supplement to the biblical evidence. Although this corpus also represents a select group, since the need for written names implies status and perhaps literacy, it nonetheless offers an invaluable look behind the scenes of the biblical corpus.

This familial piety may seem distant from the *Heilsgeschichte* that dominates the biblical narrative, but studies have demonstrated theological congruence between epigraphic and biblical names. Examining the epigraphic corpus from ancient Israel, scholars have analyzed the frequency of "Yhwh" as a theophoric element compared to other deities. This analysis has shown that unlike other ancient Near Eastern societies, where names feature a variety of deities, Yahwistic names predominate in ancient Israel (Tigay 1987b; J. Fowler 1988; Golub 2014). Names featuring other deities, especially Ba'al and El, are attested, but for the most part, the familial piety reflected in epigraphic names is consistent with the exclusive worship of Yhwh that is prescribed throughout the Hebrew Bible.

Archaeological Evidence

Archaeological evidence of family religion attests cultic activity both within individual households and at local and regional sanctuaries. Evidence from the former consists primarily of cultic objects, such as lamps, figurines, incense burners, ornate vessels and stands, amulets, and nonutilitarian pottery, which have been found in domestic contexts. The reconstruction of family religion from these objects faces several obstacles, however. For one thing, it is not always clear that the artifact was in fact a cultic object; many of the examples noted above could just as easily serve noncultic purposes (lamps give light, incense masks foul odors, pottery and vessels are containers, etc.). Moreover, because these objects are usually small and portable, we cannot be sure that their find spot represents the (only) site of their usage. With these caveats in mind, we will look at some examples of domestic cult as it is attested in individual objects, in clusters of objects, and in certain household activities.

Many of the cultic objects found in domestic contexts seem to have served apotropaic functions. Amulets often depict Egyptian protector deities (e.g., Isis, Bes, and Udjet [C. Herrmann 1993]), and recent studies of the so-called Judean Pillar Figurines, which flourished in Judah in the eighth and seventh centuries BCE, have emphasized their role in healing and protection (Darby 2014). It is tempting to specify further that these objects were used to provide protection from the dangers of childbirth. After all, Isis often is depicted in amulets with the infant Horus, Bes is associated with the protection of pregnant or birthing women, and the prominence of breasts on the Pillar Figurines suggest their significance for reproduction (Meyers 2010, 127).[3] This motivation would provide a link to the onomastic evidence, which also reflects familial concerns over the dangers of pregnancy and childbirth. While these concerns did likely underlie some of the apotropaic objects, the diversity of artifacts and archaeological contexts does not allow for such generalizations.

3. On this last point Carol Meyers (2013, 156) has revised her opinion and, following the work of Darby 2014, now associates the Pillar Figurines with healing rites by women and men.

Fluidity in purpose and meaning persists even when multiple cultic artifacts are found together. Usually the presence of more than one cultic object is taken to indicate a "cult corner," a space in a house or courtyard dedicated to cultic activity (Zevit 2001, 123). According to this criterion, the number of Israelite cult corners found could total as many as thirty-eight (Albertz and Schmitt 2012, 74–172), but identification of domestic cult spaces is beset by the challenges already noted. Cultic objects found in clusters usually are small and portable, and it is still possible to reconstruct noncultic uses for many of them. Indeed, when clusters of cultic objects are found alongside noncultic artifacts, we cannot be sure if the space was a dedicated cult corner or the site of sundry activities, some cultic and others not.

Despite these difficulties, some clear examples of domestic cult have been found. At Tell Halif, for example, excavators found cultic objects in different houses, and one in particular featured a cluster of objects that suggests a dedicated cultic space (Albertz and Schmitt 2012, 99–102; Zevit 2001, 313). One locus (G8005) within the four-room "northern house" included the head of a pillar figurine, a fenestrated stand, two limestone blocks, two jugs, and a juglet. The concentration of cultic objects and the separation of the space from the rest of the house are indicative of a cult corner, but even here the presence of common pottery suggests the space's mixed usage. This room in the "northern house" likely served as a cult corner but not, it seems, to the exclusion of other uses.

Likewise, at Beersheba there is evidence of cultic activity in several houses, but this evidence too is mixed with noncultic artifacts (Albertz and Schmitt 2012, 80–84; Zevit 2001, 175–76). One house had a locus (25) that featured a pillar figurine, a model chair, and a lamp or incense burner, but also included ordinary cooking pots and bowls. Another house (loci 430, 442, 443) near the city gate had a similar cultic assemblage—the head of a pillar figurine, a model chair, and two cuboid incense altars—but here there were no accompanying cooking vessels. If we assume that these artifacts were used where they were found, it is interesting to encounter a similar combination of cultic objects in two different contexts. These clusters of objects, along with other quite different cultic assemblages at Beersheba, demonstrate again the fluidity of family religion in ancient Israel. Even when we have clear evidence of domestic cult, it is difficult to determine the cultic practices and religious beliefs that they represent and how the domestic character of these finds is related to the life and concerns of the families who used them.

Thus the evidence of family religion in domestic spaces indicates that cultic activities took place within households in spaces not used exclusively for such activities. This mixed usage sheds light on various biblical passages that depict family religion within the household. Perhaps the best portrait of domestic cult comes from Judges 17–18, which describes the household shrine of Micah and his family. Parts of this story are consistent with the picture provided by archaeological data. The shrine, for example, is a dedicated space within the household of Micah, which contained a cultic garment and various figurines (17:4–5; 18:14, 18, 20), and at first it is a member of Micah's own family who presides over the cultic activity (17:5). On the other hand, there are other signs that Micah's shrine is exceptional: the dedicated space is not a "corner" but rather its own house; one of its cult images was made of precious metal; and eventually it was staffed by a religious professional (Ackerman 2008b). Despite its extraordinary features and its condemnation by Deuteronomistic editors, the domestic cult depicted in Judges 17–18 provides a key biblical example of family religion that complements the archaeological evidence.

In addition to the presence of cultic objects, certain household activities, such as food and textile production, seem to have had religious significance. The production, offering, and consumption of food were an important part of the worship at temples and sanctuaries, and scholars have shown that the same was likely true of domestic cult. Drawing on archaeological, biblical, and ethnographic data, Carol Meyers (2007) has demonstrated the importance of bread production within the household, and she has drawn particular attention to its significance in the lives of women. It was not only a source of social and familial power but also cultic. Evidence of bread's place in domestic cult comes from figurines of a woman kneading dough and from some cult corners that feature ovens among the cultic objects (e.g., Tell el-Farʿa North). These material remains are complemented by biblical depictions of women producing bread for cultic usage. The prophet Jeremiah, for example, describes the whole family involved in the production of cakes for the Queen of Heaven, with special emphasis on the mother's role (Jer. 7:18), and another passage links women's bread production to other cultic activities, such as incense-burning and libations (Jer. 44:17–19). Textile production is another activity mentioned in the Hebrew Bible as part of temple worship (2 Kings 23:7) and that may have had an analogue in domestic cult, though the evidence is meager. Although loom weights and spindle whorls have been found in domestic spaces (Meyers 2003b, 432–34) and the religious significance of textile production has been explored (Ackerman 2008a), our present data only allow us to speculate on its role in household cult.

Moving out of domestic spaces, we can also look at examples of family religion that took place in public settings. Although initial studies of the archaeology of family religion focused almost exclusively on cultic activity within domestic contexts, scholars have recently begun to look for traces of family religion within public cult places. Temples in the ancient Near East often included, in addition to their main sanctuaries, subsidiary chapels for smaller cultic ceremonies. The temple at Tel Dan in northern Israel, which featured a monumental altar and podium as well as side rooms for small-scale cultic activity, likely represents an Israelite example of this spatial arrangement (A. Davis 2013, 95–107). This interpretation of Tel Dan's temple is consistent with the biblical evidence for family worship at local and regional sanctuaries. One example is the sacrifice offered by Hannah and Elkanah at Shiloh (1 Sam. 1–2); although it is offered at a regional temple with its own cultic personnel, the sacrifice is performed by the couple themselves in fulfillment of a vow that Hannah made to dedicate her son to the temple (A. Davis 2013, 102–5). These biblical and extrabiblical examples of family religion show that it was not restricted to domestic space. Israelite households could and did worship as families at sanctuaries that until recently had only been associated with "official religion" (Olyan 2008, 114–15; Albertz and Schmitt 2012, 46; Stavrakopoulou 2010b, 41).

In conclusion, onomastic and archaeological data attest a tradition of family religion in ancient Israel that is at least as diverse as the rites undertaken by Grandma Lausch in *The Adventures of Augie March*. This tradition made its way into the Hebrew Bible, but the evidence is fragmentary and filtered through the theological bias of the biblical writers. Extrabiblical data take us behind the scenes of the biblical depictions and reveal various expressions of family religion in domestic and public contexts. Although some of this material is heterodox by biblical standards, the evidence also shows that family religion was not as contrary to the biblical tradition as Grandma Lausch supposed.

49

Death and Burial in the Iron Age Levant

CHRISTOPHER B. HAYS

Death and Burial in the Levantine Context

Death has long been a major focus of human cultural production, and burials have been one of the most important sources of data about ancient cultures, including those that surrounded ancient Israel and Judah in the Levant.

Some attention to the situation prior to the Iron Age is useful. Particularly important are the texts from Late Bronze Age Ugarit, on the coast of present-day Syria; these attest funerary and mortuary rituals for the care of the dead, invoking divinized royal ancestors and requesting their blessings. The tombs appear designed for the purpose of cults of the dead, with lamp niches, offerings, and unsealed doors. In the same time period, imperial Hatti practiced one of the most elaborate royal burial rituals known in the ancient Near East outside Egypt, lasting fourteen days and including food and drink offerings, a statue of the deceased, and cremation of the body. Other aspects of Hittite imperial mortuary religion were shared with Mesopotamia and Egypt: the role of the sun god as royal psychopomp, belief in an afterlife where food and drink are scarce, fear of the neglected dead, and the practice of necromancy.

From the ninth and eighth centuries BCE, there are a number of Neo-Hittite mortuary steles that attest to the expectation of care and enjoyment for the afterlife. In one, the Katumuwa Stele from Zincirli, the decedent calls for mortuary banquets "for my soul that is in this stele" (Pardee 2009, 53–54). The soul was believed not only to survive apart from the body—a belief of great antiquity in Anatolia—but also to somehow be resident in the monument. The archaeological context of the Katumuwa Stele has been interpreted as a mortuary chapel, one of perhaps a number in the Syro-Hittite sphere. Similar cultic sites have been tentatively identified in Moabite regions and hypothesized to have hosted feasting in cults of the dead. These mortuary chapels were not burial sites. No remains have been found with the Neo-Hittite steles; instead, large-scale cremation cemeteries have been found in cities such as Carchemish and Hamath.

There are many indications that supernatural beliefs about the afterlife endured in the Iron Age Levant. An inscription by Panamuwa, king of the Aramean state of Sam'al in the eighth century, instructs whichever of his sons inherits the throne to make sacrifices and say to Hadad, "May the soul of Panamuwa eat with you, and may the soul of Panamuwa drink with you" (COS 2:157). The tenth-century sarcophagus of Ahiram of Byblos, from the early tenth century BCE, portrays the deceased king sitting on a throne receiving funerary offerings, and the inscription warns against disturbing the burial, a common concern known also from eighth- and seventh-century Aramaic inscriptions. A text on the sarcophagus of Tabnit of Sidon from the fifth century also attests to the hope of a place among the divinized dead: "If you . . . open my cover and disturb me, may you have no . . . resting-place with the Rephaim" (COS 2:182). The same curse is invoked in the sarcophagus inscription of his son 'Eshmun'azor, and that text adds: "let [the one who disturbs the remains] not be buried in a grave" (COS 2:183).

These royal burials were somewhat exceptional; in general, cremation was the dominant type of burial in Phoenicia, with the remains buried in jars accompanied by food and drink offerings. Various cultural and even geological considerations determined decisions about burial types, in addition to religious ones. In her foundational study, Elizabeth Bloch-Smith found a very high correlation between burial types and cultural groups; for example, Egyptians used pit burials, cist graves, and anthropoid coffins; the Assyrians used bathtub coffins; Phoenicians cremated or buried their dead; and the people of the highlands used caves as tombs (Bloch-Smith 1992a, 63).

The recent discovery of a major Philistine cemetery at Ashkelon means that the history of Levantine burials will need to be rewritten again. Early reports state that the most common burial form was the simple pit interments, though cremation burials in jars and elite stone tombs were also in evidence.

Many were supplied with grave goods, as was common, but the burials were exceptional in being fully articulated rather than gathered after decomposition, as was common in the hill country (see below).

Such a brief overview helpfully calls attention to diversity, but it also is an oversimplification. The options were varied in all cultures, and particularly in later periods hybrid forms of burial increasingly emerged. For example, the aforementioned Phoenician use of sarcophagi suggests Egyptian influence, as does the fact that Tabnit's body was embalmed. Diversity was particularly notable in larger, cosmopolitan cities (Bloch-Smith 1992a, 55).

The rest of the present discussion focuses on Judah rather than the northern kingdom, Israel, because neither archaeology nor the (mostly southern) biblical text supplies much good information about the north.

The Archaeology of Death in Ancient Israel and Judah

The characteristic Judahite form of elite burial was the bench tomb, normally a man-made room cut into rock, about five meters square, with low benches protruding from the perimeter walls. Additional rooms could be added, but normally when a body decomposed it was brushed into a charnel pit to make room for the next burial. Early in the biblical period, cave tombs were more popular, but were phased out during the Iron II period.

It may have been less than five percent of the population that employed the bench tomb. Common people tended to bury their dead in simple pit graves, perhaps in a field owned by the family (2 Kings 23:6; Jer. 26:23; 31:40). Pit graves become nearly "invisible" to archaeology, although some have been excavated.

A family's tomb was a symbol of its endurance and hoped-for permanence, and it may even have been a marker of the family's property. It was not, however, viewed as an opportunity for artistic self-expression: Judahite burials generally showed little variation in style, except in their relative wealth and fineness.

Grave provisioning was practiced consistently by Judahites, most often by use of pottery jars and bowls intended to provide food and drink for the dead. Other goods included travel gear, food, jewelry and amulets, and assorted household items. Various clasps found among the remains indicate that the dead were clothed and wrapped in cloaks. Female figurines made of clay were also commonly placed in burials.

Tomb inscriptions tend to identify the tomb's owner and seek to ward off robbers, similar to those of the Phoenicians. For example, the Tomb of the Royal Steward inscription at the Silwan cemetery tells potential robbers that there is "no silver and no gold, only his bones and the bones of his slave-wife with him," adding, "Cursed be the man who will open this" (J. Roberts et al. 2003, 508).

History of Scholarship

To understand what ancient Israel and Judah did and thought about death requires a critical approach to the data. First, the biblical text as it comes to us includes a number of statements (e.g., about the finality of death and the powerlessness of the dead) that probably ran counter to commonly held beliefs. The biblical text largely reflects reforms that began under Hezekiah and Josiah, theological struggles that continued through the postexilic period.

Second, there would have been no single belief or praxis about death or most other matters. Religious diversity existed along various axes. We could, of course, point to regional variations, international influences, and diachronic change, but the diversity also reflected economic status, gender, and other social factors. Despite the unifying work of the aforementioned authors and redactors, ample

indication of this diversity remains in the Bible. It is quite possible to discern a society that, as a matter of course, worshiped chthonic gods, cared for its dead, practiced necromancy, knew very well about the religions and mythologies of its neighbors (at least at upper levels of society), and often was inclined to try them out, especially when Yhwh did not seem to answer to the usual means.

Because of the challenges of the data, there has been a long debate over cults of the dead in Israel and Judah, which I have reviewed in detail elsewhere (Hays 2011, 133–92).

Burial in the Hebrew Bible

The only instruction about burial in the Pentateuch is that anyone who is executed and hung on a tree must be buried the same day (Deut. 21:22–23). Nevertheless, the biblical narratives show a strong interest in burials.

In general, the biblical authors seem to have been aware of the diachronic shifts and cultural differences in customs. For example, Abraham's acquisition of a burial cave at Machpelah in Genesis 23 is compatible with premonarchic practice in the Levant, and the embalming process and mourning for Jacob and Joseph (Gen. 50:2–3, 26) accord well with Egyptian practices. Other details, such as the erection of a memorial for Rachel (Gen. 35:20), have not been corroborated by archaeology. The burial places of many prominent figures are recorded, including those of Miriam, Aaron, Joshua, Gideon, and all the judges after him. This makes it a curiosity that Deuteronomy 34:5–6 insists that "no one knows [Moses's] burial place to this day." The importance of proper burial is emphasized by the restoration of divine favor to Israel after Saul and Jonathan are buried (2 Sam. 21:14).

The burials of Israelite and Judahite kings are routinely recorded in the historical books; in 1–2 Kings the recurrent phrase "he slept with his ancestors" reflects a peaceful death and normal burial. Most kings are said to be buried in their capital cities (e.g., David and Solomon in the City of David [1 Kings 2:10; 11:43], Omri in Samaria [1 Kings 16:28]). Even kings slain in battle were returned by chariot to Jerusalem and buried there, if at all possible (e.g., Ahaziah in 2 Kings 9:28, Josiah in 2 Kings 23:30).

The royal tombs in Jerusalem have never been conclusively identified, and may have been quarried away and lost. Ezekiel 43 suggests that some Judahite kings were buried in or adjacent to the Jerusalem temple.

Most of the kings of Judah up to Ahaz are said to have been "buried in the city of David," but this formula abruptly disappears after that point. It may be that at this late period the original royal necropolis was full. This is consistent with Josiah's burial "in his own tomb" (2 Kings 23:30; the City of David is not mentioned).

Nadav Na'aman has argued that the place of the Judahite kings' burials moved for religious reasons. It is written in 2 Kings 21:18, 26 that Manasseh and his son Amon were buried in "the garden of Uzza." Na'aman asserts that this is the same as the "garden of the king" in 2 Kings 25:4; Jeremiah 39:4; 52:7; Nehemiah 3:15, and that it was established by Hezekiah as a royal burial grounds outside the City of David in contrast to the earlier royal tombs near the palace. He views this as part of Hezekiah's reform program (2 Kings 18:4, 22) and as a response to the priestly revulsion at the proximity of royal burials to the temple.

Chronicles is more selective and detailed about burial information and differs from Kings in its reports about several rulers, denying them placement in the royal tombs on the basis of impurity due to sickness (e.g., Jehoram in 2 Chron. 21:20; Uzziah in 26:23) or wrongdoing (Ahaz in 28:27). The account of Asa's burial says, "They laid him on a bier that had been filled with various kinds of spices prepared by the perfumer's art; and they made a very great fire in his honor" (2 Chron. 16:14), perhaps indicating that Asa was cremated.

Some aspects of Judahite royal burial remain mysterious. For a number of kings who were murdered, no burial information is noted. (Perhaps this is because the murdered were counted among the unhappy dead and so were not buried with the other kings.) And unlike the women of the Genesis narratives, it is not recorded that family members were buried with the kings of Israel or Judah, although a few nonroyal burials in other places are recorded (2 Sam. 3:32; 4:12; 17:23; 19:37; 1 Kings 2:34) (Bloch-Smith 1992a, 116).

Whereas there is little instruction about how to bury the dead in the Hebrew Bible, it is quite clear throughout that the lack of proper sepulture and mourning is viewed as a horrible fate, as in the curse of Deuteronomy 28:26: "Your corpses shall be food for every bird of the air and animal of the earth, and there shall be no one to frighten them away" (cf. 1 Kings 13:22; 14:11–13; 2 Kings 9:10; Ps. 79:3; Eccles. 6:3; Isa. 14:19–20; Ezek. 29:5). The threat of exposure is a particularly persistent theme in Jeremiah (Jer. 9:22; cf. 7:33; 8:1–2; 14:16; 16:4; 19:7; 22:18–19; 26:23; 36:30).

Beyond mere non-burial, there was "antiburial," or the abuse of the corpse. Exceptionally, there are references to burning kings, or their remains, in vengeance (Amos 2:1; Isa. 30:33). Other examples include hanging Saul's and Jonathan's corpses on a wall (1 Sam. 31:10), and the devouring of Jezebel's corpse by dogs (2 Kings 9:33–37).

I propose the following hierarchy of burial types, from most to least desirable, as a modification of Olyan 2005:

1. individual burial in a personal tomb
2. honorable burial in the family tomb
3. honorable interment in a substitute for the family tomb
4. dishonorable forms of interment
5. non-burial
6. anti-burial

Mourning

Israelite and Judahite customs of mourning and lamentation appear, from the biblical text, to have been very similar to those of their neighbors. At the death of a prominent person, a whole family (Zech. 12:12) or tribe (Num. 20:29) might gather. Indeed, allowing for hyperbole and the legendary character of certain texts, a whole nation might be said to gather (Gen. 50:7–12; Deut. 34:8; 1 Sam. 25:1; 1 Kings 14:18)—more likely a maximum turnout would have included *representatives* from the whole nation. Large numbers of mourners helped to mark a successful life, since lack of mourning was seen as a curse (Job 27:15; Ps. 78:64; Jer. 16:4; 25:33).

Loud weeping and wailing (e.g., Jer. 4:8) were central to mourning. Professional mourners seem to have been employed in some cases: "Call for the mourning women to come; send for the skilled women to come; let them quickly raise a dirge over us, so that our eyes may run down with tears" (Jer. 9:17–18 [cf. Amos 5:16]). A para-canonical written text of laments is referred to in 2 Chronicles 35:25, but no such text has survived.

Mourning was accompanied by physical manifestations, which included a bowed posture (Ps. 35:13), shaving the head or disheveling the hair (Ezek. 27:31; Amos 8:10), tearing garments (Gen. 37:34; 2 Sam. 1:11; Joel 2:13), donning sackcloth or other specific "mourning garments" (2 Sam. 14:2; Jer. 4:8; 6:26; Joel 1:8), and smearing ashes on one's body (Job 2:8; Jer. 6:26). However, gashing flesh is portrayed as a foreign practice in Jeremiah 49:3 and is specifically prohibited (Lev. 19:28; Deut. 14:1, which also forbids shaving the temples). Mourning might also be accompanied by fasting (2 Sam. 12:23; Ps. 35:13).

It is not clear what a traditional period of mourning would have been; many references do not specify a length of time (Gen. 27:41; 37:34; 2 Sam. 13:37; 14:2; 1 Chron. 7:22; Isa. 60:20; 1 Macc. 9:20; 13:26). When a length of time is specified, it may be one or two days (Sir. 38:17), seven days (Gen. 50:10; Sir. 22:12), or up to thirty days (Num. 20:29; Deut. 34:8).

Public mourning festivals are reported to have arisen in specific periods to honor certain people such as Josiah (2 Chron. 35:24–25) and Jephthah's daughter (Judg. 11:39–40). Zechariah 7:3–5 refers to a custom of mourning in the fifth and seventh months, almost certainly related to the destruction of Jerusalem in the fifth month.

Although the data are less than conclusive, it appears that there were some dedicated spaces for mourning and the cultic functions associated with burials. Ecclesiastes 7:2, 4, mention a "house of mourning," and Judah seems to have had venues in which funerary feasting could take place (Jer. 16:5–8; Amos 6:7). Since these are viewed negatively in both biblical attestations, it may well have been judged as heterodox at some point.

The Corpse

Corpses are perceived as ritually impure in various biblical texts, but also there are intimations that they were thought to have supernatural powers.

The priestly legislation is particularly concerned about defilement of the living by the dead. Any person is made ritually unclean for seven days by contact with a human corpse (Num. 19:11–16; 31:19), making it a very powerful impurity. Even the one who touches a person defiled by a corpse is unclean for a day (Num. 19:22)! And the impurity extends beyond human corpses to animal corpses; one who touches a dead lizard is also impure for a day (Lev. 11:31). In keeping with the phenomenon of gradations of holiness, priests are allowed to handle the corpses only of close relatives (Lev. 21:1–2), and the high priest is allowed no contact at all with the dead (Lev. 21:10–11). Ezekiel and Haggai also show awareness of defilement by dead bodies (Ezek.

6:5; 44:25; Hag. 2:13–14), but the theme is absent from the Covenant Code and the Deuteronomic Code.

The potential power of bones is seen most vividly in the resurrection miracle of Elisha's bones (2 Kings 13:21), but also in the desire of the prophet from Bethel to be buried with the bones of the unnamed man of God (1 Kings 13:31).

The Powers and Cult of the Dead

There are many examples in the biblical literature of polemic against the power of the dead. The dead, it is said, do not praise (e.g., Pss. 30:9; 88:10); instead, they "go down into silence" (Ps. 115:17). They know nothing (Eccles. 9:5, 10) and sit in darkness (Lam. 3:6).

Other texts, however, complicate the picture. The numerous references to the Rephaim attest that Israel clearly knew of the common Syro-Palestinian belief in a group of supernatural dead. The biblical Rephaim fall into two categories: sometimes they are reckoned as a mythic ancient tribe (Gen. 14:5; 15:20; Deut. 2:11) of giants (Deut. 3:11), and at other times the term refers to the assembled dead, whether royal (Isa. 14:9) or unspecified (Prov. 2:18; cf., e.g., Job 26:5; Ps. 88:10). The two usages probably are related. In any case, despite the biblical claims about the weakness of the Rephaim, the Hebrew etymology of their name suggests that originally they were seen as supernatural healers/protectors (Hays 2011, 167–68).

The idea that the dead are a source of divinatory knowledge is richly attested. Necromancy is banned or condemned in various places (Lev. 19:31; 20:6, 27; Deut. 18:11; 2 Kings 21:6; 1 Chron. 10:13–14). The story of Saul and the necromancer in 1 Samuel 28 has become a touchstone; despite the condemnation of Saul for employing necromancy, the story makes no effort to deny that it "worked." Samuel was summoned, and he was correct. The Hebrew term 'ob appears in relation to the female diviner and may denote both a spirit of the dead and a cultic object. This situation finds analogies in West Semitic *npsh/nbsh*, which came to mean both the soul and the funerary monument; and in Hebrew *'asherah*, typically thought to be both a goddess and the wooden pole that symbolized her.

Israelites did have figurines representing ancestors that were used for divination: in other contexts, these are called *teraphim* (Ezek. 21:21; Zech. 10:2). The *teraphim* clearly were physical objects of some sort (Gen. 31:19–35; Judg. 17:5; 18:14–20; 1 Sam. 19:11–17). There is reason to think that the *teraphim* were once an accepted part of Israelite family religion. They are never condemned in the legal codes, but only in 1 Samuel 15:23 and the report of their removal by Josiah in 2 Kings 23:24.

Ancestor cults may have been banned for several reasons. Most basically, necromancy had the potential to come into conflict with central forms of Yahwistic divination, especially prophecy. Changing social conditions in the Neo-Assyrian period that changed family patterns and strained the authority of elders may have given the condemnation additional momentum (Douglas 2004).

The Underworld and Its Deities

The underworld in Israelite thought is known primarily by the name "Sheol," which essentially is unique to Hebrew and of uncertain etymology. Sheol is characterized as deep (Deut. 32:22; Job 11:7), even as a pit deep underwater (Ezek. 28:8). It is dark (Job 17:13; 38:17; Pss. 23:4; 88:6; 143:3; Lam. 3:6) and dusty (Pss. 22:15, 29; 30:19; Job 17:16; Dan. 12:2). In the grave one finds forgetfulness (Eccles. 9:10) and is forgotten (Pss. 31:12; 88:5; Job 24:19–20). Sheol is also a symbol of sadness (Gen. 42:38; 44:29–31) and is nevertheless often described as the end of all people (Ps. 89:48; cf. Eccles. 8:8).

Other terms also are used for the underworld in the Hebrew Bible, such as "Abaddon," which occurs primarily in poetic contexts (Job 26:6; 28:22; 31:12; Ps. 88:11; Prov. 15:11; 27:20). More naturalistically, the underworld was known in Hebrew as "the pit" (e.g., Pss. 16:10; 28:1) and "the earth" (e.g., Pss. 22:29; 71:20; Jer. 17:13; Jon. 2:6). This is only a small example of the numerous poetic images that could be used for the underworld. Some texts have affinities with "foreign" ideas about the afterlife, such as the Egyptian image of weighing of the heart as a part of the judgment of the dead (Job 31:6; Prov. 21:2).

Death is personified quite clearly at times in the Bible. One of the most famous references to the swallowing of the god Death occurs in Isaiah 5:14 (see also Job 28:22; Ps. 49:14; Jer. 9:21; Hosea 13:14; Hab. 2:5). It is not likely, however, that Mot ("Death") had a cult in Judah or Israel or was commonly regarded as an active divine presence.

The chthonic god Malik/Molek was certainly known to the Israelites (Lev. 18:21; 20:2–5; 2 Kings 23:10; Jer. 32:35, Isa. 57:9 [emended]). Molek is repeatedly portrayed as a god who received child sacrifices (Ezek. 16:20–21; 23:37–39) (see Day 1989; Heider 1985). Child sacrifice is well attested in the ancient world, especially in times of crisis. King Mesha of Moab sacrifices his firstborn son (2 Kings 3:27) and a battle turns in his favor; similar child sacrifices are attested in Phoenician cities such as Carthage and those at Sicily, Sardinia, and Cyprus. The intrabiblical debate about child sacrifice is large and diachronically complex—too much so to survey in this venue (see Levenson 1993).

Historians of religion have sometimes proceeded as if Yhwh had been thought to have no commerce with death and the underworld in the mainstream preexilic religion. God's power over the underworld is expressed in different ways in Deuteronomy 32:39; 1 Samuel 2:6; Proverbs 15:11; and Amos 9:1–2. There were pessimistic traditions in which death was seen as final and the underworld as sealed, and Israelite thought about the restoration from death does seem to have become more elaborate and central over time, but from the early stages of biblical literature, Yhwh was always portrayed as a god who had the power to save from death, and who was quite able to access and control the underworld, even if such actions were seen as exceptional.

Family

*Integrated Approaches to Themes
in Family Networks*

Tribes and Nomads in the Iron Age Levant

THOMAS D. PETTER

Definition

Defining tribal dynamics is a complex task due to the inherently fluid nature of the context in which tribes evolve. However, there are certain characteristics that can be isolated and applied to the Old Testament context. Core traits include loyalties based on real or manipulated kinship ties, and flexibility in economic pursuits where tribal groups will shift back and forth between subsistence strategies associated with a sedentary lifestyle to ones connected to nomadic ways.[1] These shifts result in various degrees of territorial mobility, along with fluid interrelationships where alliances are routinely forged and broken (van der Steen 2004, 3–5).

The Frontier Setting: Sedentarization and Ruralization

The notion of *shifting frontier* is a key ecological factor without which we cannot fully grasp the tribal dynamics on the stage where the drama of the Bible is played out. Following in the footsteps of the pioneering work of Leon Marfoe in the Baqah valley of Lebanon (1979), students of the southern Levant have applied the principles to the landscape of both Cisjordan and Transjordan (Stager 1985; La-Bianca and Younker 1995).

The basic premise is grounded in the idea that the shifting frontier creates an environment where, depending on the circumstances, pastoral nomads[2] could and would adopt a sedentary lifestyle while inhabitants of permanent settlements (e.g., villages and towns) would turn to pastoral-nomadic lifeways. This twin process of sedentarization and ruralization has been documented in specific periods in the history of the region, particularly in explaining the phenomenon of the settlement of early Israel in Canaan (Finkelstein 1994; Stager 1998; 1985). However, the forces at work are also documented in periods preceding and following

---

1. Note Gertrude Bell's classic dichotomy between the "desert" and the "sown" (1907).

2. In the context of the southern Levant, pastoral nomads are herders of small, domesticated livestock (sheep and goats) that periodically migrate into a given range of territories to find food for their flocks.

the Late Bronze / Early Iron Age in the region (Harrison 1997). From a physical standpoint, as a passageway between the great powers of Egypt, Anatolia, and Greater Mesopotamia,[3] or what Anson Rainey called the "Sacred Bridge" (Rainey and Notley 2006), the tribal groups occupying the region find themselves in periodic phases of dislocation (Abraham [Gen. 12:10–13:1] and especially the Joseph story [Gen. 37–50]). Ecologically vulnerable (unlike the Nile Valley or the irrigation systems of Mesopotamia), the region depended on annual rainfalls for subsistence, which in turn gave a high ecostrategic value to water sources such as wadi systems, springs, and wells (cf. Num. 21:17). This overdependence on regular rainfall for agriculture, especially in the marginal zones of the Negev and parts of Transjordan,[4] made these regions particularly susceptible to changes in subsistence strategies. Sustained drought resulted in economic collapse because production of food supplies screeched to a halt (Gen. 41:53–57). This fragile ecosystem also explains the constant need to depend on other forces for rain (cf. 1 Kings 18).

From a theological viewpoint, under Yahweh's covenant administration, the prerequisite of obedience provided certain guarantees of agricultural production and national security for the settled "good life" (Deut. 28:4, 11–12). However, the Deuteronomic blessings of home and economic flourishing were never a given. At the height of the ideology of Zion and temple investiture as a permanent settlement in Jerusalem, Solomon did not take for granted the permanence of the erected sacred space (cf. 1 Kings 8:46). Jeremiah would put it far more bluntly to the ensconced powers of the late Judean monarchy: unless they returned to a pure form of Yahwism, the return to a figurative wilderness

and nomadic lifestyle through the dislocation of exile (586 BCE) would be a reality, whether they accepted it or not (Jer. 7:14–15).[5] Thus the physical tribal frontier setting also had deep social and theological ramifications.

This *longue durée* (= the long view) process of intensification of settlement buildup and abatement draw down (LaBianca and Younker 1995) provides a framework not only for Israelite tribes but also for the related tribal groups of Moab,[6] Ammon, and variegated Amorite and Canaanite subgroups that settled the region across time (van der Steen 2004, 3–5). The vicissitudes of life on the frontier and capricious weather patterns were the great equalizers among the occupants of the southern Levant. Nevertheless, in this "adapt or die" harsh social and ecopolitical environment, some tribes proved remarkably resilient. They may have "disappeared" from the face of history (in ancient Israel via exile), only to "reappear" later on (the return during the postexilic period). Such tribal dynamics in frontier zones have been documented in other settings as well, including the Roman frontier (Derks 2009).

Tribal Identity as Loyalty and Betrayal

At the core, Israel viewed itself in deeply kin-based tribal terms throughout its recorded history, from the "generations" (*toledot*) of Genesis (Gen. 2:4 and passim) to postexilic genealogies (1 Chron. 1–9; Ezra 2//Neh. 7). Primordial lineage mattered to ancient Israel (e.g., Gen. 15:4), so the primary identification marker for an Israelite inevitably was based on common ancestry and loyalty (Sparks 1998). This loyalty, *hesed* (Sakenfeld 2002), to the

5. See Neh. 9 for a succinct summary of how Israelite history played out.

6. Moab also experienced dislocation as a result of its perceived disobedience to the Moabite deity Chemosh (Num. 21:27–30). Note the statement in the Mesha Inscription that "Chemosh was angry against his land."

3. For example, the region drained by the Euphrates and the Tigris, including the Western Zagros and the Susiana plain.

4. Dry farming requires at least 200 mm of rainfall annually.

tribe, however, was also negotiated through instrumental means that extended beyond simple blood relationships. A tribal sense of "belonging" could be offered to the most unlikely candidates, such as Rahab (Josh. 2; 6), Jael (Judg. 4–5), and Ruth, who became members of the tribal confederation on the basis on their own loyalty to Israel (and ultimately to Yahweh, Israel's tribal patrimonial head [see below]). These manipulated kinship ties hark back to the very origins of the tribes since Yahweh "brought out of Ur" Abram (Gen. 15:7), an Amorite tribesman who came from a family with a past (Josh. 24:2), and entered into a covenant with him. Thus, from the outset, the relationship between kinship and covenant formed a powerful bond between the primordial realities of tribal bloodlines and instrumental opportunities for nontribal members to join the covenant community (Petter 2014).

Sociologists have recognized that identities are also defined over against other groups (S. Jones 1997). However, especially in tribal settings, while otherness can be defined in strictly primordial terms (i.e., "Canaanites"), otherness can also be created via betrayal among the groups. As ethnographers of tribal dynamics in the Hashemite Kingdom of Jordan both in the present and the past, Evelyn van der Steen and Andrew Shryock have documented regular internecine strife among varying tribal groups (Shryock 1997). This motif of betrayed loyalties between "brothers" runs the course of the larger narrative of Scripture as well ("am I my brother's keeper?" [Gen. 4:9]). This is especially illustrated in the Joseph story (Gen. 37:8, 19–20), but as the story unfolds, kin-based loyalty and betrayal become essentially two faces of the same coin (Gen. 50:21). The principle plays out throughout Israel's history: the fight among the tribes during the period of the judges; the dynastic contest between Saul's and David's claims to Israel's kingship (2 Sam. 3:1), even as David knows full well that the kingship will belong to him one day (1 Sam. 16:13); and on a larger scale, the divided kingdoms of Israel/Ephraim and Judah (1 Kings 12). Israelites are brothers, but they can also fight to the death (see Judg. 20:14; 21:11). However, the picture is also one of tender and genuine loyalty among the tribal groups ("The Israelites had compassion for Benjamin their kin" [Judg. 21:6]). David laments the deaths of Saul and Jonathan ("How the mighty have fallen!" [2 Sam. 1:19]) and that of his own son ("O my son Absalom, my son, my son Absalom!" [2 Sam. 18:33]). The prophets dream of a future when the north and the south will be one again (Ezek. 37:19–22). Isaiah can even envision a "day" when the "tribes" of nations, including Israel's historic enemies Egypt and Assyria, will be brothers with Israel ("Blessed be Egypt my people, and Assyria the work of my hands, and Israel my heritage" [Isa. 19:25]). Tribal loyalties (*hesed*) run deep and ultimately prevail.

Competing Territorial Claims

Tribal dynamics routinely involve competing territorial claims in both ancient and modern contexts (Shryock 1997). "To whom does the land belong and on what ground?" is the perennial question among tribal groups. The territory of each tribe is held sacred since it is part of a first-order priority for sustainability and life (especially wells and water sources [Glueck 1959b]). Thus, tribal groups will assert rights over territories from "time immemorial" (Mesha Inscription, line 10) and defend them fiercely (Weippert 1997; Petter 2014, 13) based on the rationale that their particular god has granted them access to the territory. From a biblical perspective, as the creator of the whole material realm, Yahweh owns the whole earth (Ps. 24:1), so that even Chemosh's land, Moab, despite claims to the contrary,[7] never falls outside Yahweh's control (Jer. 48).

7. According to Moabite ideology, Chemosh owns the land and Mesha's good stewardship of it will guarantee him the rights to stay there (see the text of the Mesha

Since Yahweh is holy, by implication the territorial boundaries are a sacred trust that must be looked after according to his dictates. Thus, apart from holiness, there are no guarantees that tribal members might be able to retain the rights to the land. A potent clue to this reality comes from Joshua 5:13–15, which suggests that Yahweh will side with whoever is holy before him.

The incident at Ai puts the principle into practice (Josh. 7:10). Rahab the Canaanite prostitute (who should be *herem*) becomes Yahweh's friend (Josh. 6:25), but Achan's house—of the tribe of Judah, no less—becomes Yahweh's enemy and is liable to *herem*, the same fate as Jericho (Josh. 7:25).[8] Territories will be gained and lost on precisely the same grounds throughout Israelite history (and Moabite history) until, like the Canaanite city of Jericho, which was *herem* (Josh. 6:17), Jerusalem, the "city of the Great King" (Ps. 48:2), ends up in flames under the Deuteronomic curse also because of its people's disobedience (586 BCE; see Jer. 52; Lamentations). Thus, *herem*, if such may be applied here, can be seen as a "two-way street" in the fashioning of Israelite tribal identities (Petter 2014; for a differing viewpoint, see Walton and Walton 2017, 184).

These realities remain true during the postexilic period. Even after Israel ceases to be a polity in the southern Levant, this theme of competing accounts of legitimacy continues to play an important role during the Persian period. While those in exile understand that the land now belongs to Persia as a Trans-Euphrates Province (Neh. 9:36: "we are slaves"), nevertheless Nehemiah refuses his tribal neighbors (including an "Ammonite" [Neh. 2:19–20]) the access and the right to participate in the restoration of the wall and worship in Jerusalem. Zion remains Yahweh's "holy city" (Neh. 11:18). Consequently, those who were not able to document their primordial ties to the tribes of Yahweh could not worship there.

Tribal Kingship

So how did the tribes govern themselves? Patrimonialism perhaps best captures tribal social organization in ancient Israel. Yahweh stands above the patrimonial social structure (tribe-clan-family-house [Josh. 7:16–19]). As the tribal head, he is also "king" (*melek*) and father to his son "Israel" (Hosea 11:1). Thus the "house of the father" (*bet 'ab*)[9] provides the foundation of the patrimonial social structure that governs Israel's tribal king and his kingdom (Schloen 2001), since it is based on Yahweh's own kingship over the king himself and Israel. This kingship, however, cannot be dislodged from its tribal moorings. Kings are also "shepherds" at heart. The obvious example is David, but there is also Mesha, the "shepherd-king" (*noqed*) of Moab who controls a flock so vast that it was a main textile supplier (or source of tribute) to the kingdom of Israel (2 Kings 3:4).[10]

In the same way, the time of the monarchy and its state-ordered traits (e.g., monumental architecture, enlisted army, redistributive economy, centralization, etc. [Holladay 1995]) cannot be viewed apart from its tribal moorings (Master 2001). To be sure, Israelites

Inscription and 2 Kings 3:4–27 for the Judean-Israelite retaliation).

8. The term *herem*, typically understood as "devoted to destruction," is found in the conquest texts of the Bible as well as in neighboring cultures (at Ugarit and in Moab as well as in Hittite contexts [see Kang 1989; Walton and Walton 2017]). Depending on the context, the term includes both the idea of "being set apart" (as a noun, "devoted things" [cf. Josh. 7:11 ESV]) and "devoted to destruction" (cf. Josh. 7:12). Scholars differ whether "destruction" is the primary meaning of *herem* and, if there was destruction, whether it was complete or partial (see Josh. 11:12–13 [Walton and Walton 2017, 170; see also Milgrom 2001, 2418]).

9. See Josh. 7 for a summary of Israel's segmented society.

10. In the context of the eighteenth-century BCE city-state of Mari in the middle Euphrates valley, Zimri-Lim was a nomad king who ruled "the land of the mobile herdsmen" (Fleming 2009, 230–31; see also Miglio 2014).

do settle in permanent "cities" (Hebrew ʿir/ ʿarim).[11] However, the option of reverting back to nonsedentary ways was never far from their minds, even if spoken in figurative ways ("To your tents, O Israel!" [1 Kings 12:16]).

The patrimonial framework expresses itself through the notion of blessing from the Father to the son. This free gift of "inheritance" is based on the inherent *goodness* and *faithfulness* of the Father. He is the sole provider, protector, and purveyor of blessings to his children.[12] Thus the connections between Yahweh's kingship, David's kingship, and inheritance (Israel as the firstborn) are all themes that take on lives of their own in the symposium of biblical theology (e.g., Gentry and Wellum 2012). In the New Testament, believers have all become firstborn "sons" (male and female) as recipients of the full blessing of the Father (Gal. 4:7).

Keeping Records

The enduring nature of tribal society in ancient Israel is founded on both oral tradition and written tribal records (Niditch 1996). Names and patronymics (the syntax of genealogies

11. The lexeme has some flexibility in meaning, so we should not always associate it with "fortified"—that is, "large" settlements (see Num. 13:19).

12. The prologue to the Code of Hammurabi illustrates the function of the king as protector and provider for his people. Ironically, since the Code was found in Elamite hands at Susa, Hammurabi failed to deliver on his promise to his people.

[Revell 1996]) are the obvious artifacts of tribal identity in a patrimonial context. Patronymics codify the reality of tribal historical memory, and when gathered in genealogies, they become a *recorded testimony*. In the ebb and flow (see above) of life in ancient Israel, the Persian period provides us with a remarkable testimony to the enduring importance of the tribal heads in ancient Israel. Without Levites who could claim their ancestry according to the records, the restoration of worship could not have happened (see Neh. 7 and esp. 11). Genealogies supply the framework within which the life of the tribes exists. The genealogies of 1 Chronicles (from the postexilic period) attest to the essentially tribal history of ancient Israel and provide a fitting bookend to the genealogies of Genesis: "these are the generations [*toledot*]." The underlying commentary to each of the names recorded over several chapters is that Yahweh's steadfast love (*ḥesed*) endures forever.

This commitment to patrimonial memory in the ancient context is also reflected in modern tribal history-writing, as Andrew Shryock's work with the modern tribes of Jordan attests (1997). Patrimonial history is important to tribes (also in tribal settings of Africa [Levy and Holl 2002]). Shryock's work in the tribes of Jordan documents the incredible genealogical memory of the tribal chiefs who can trace their ancestry (along with battle accounts) over several centuries. What the elders, the patrimonial heads, say is binding and authoritative.

51

Women in Ancient Israel

Carol Meyers

Introduction

Most women, like most men, lived in small agricultural settlements in ancient Israel.[1] Virtually every aspect of their daily lives took place in the family household, which was the smallest and most numerous unit of society. A household was not simply a domicile or a family; it was both and more, for it encompassed the activities that its members performed in order to survive in the rather harsh environment of the hill country of Palestine. Households, each of which probably consisted of an extended family,[2] were largely self-sufficient; thus their economic functions dominated the rhythms of everyday life. In addition, social, political, and even religious functions, along with childbearing and child rearing, were embedded in the

activities and interactions of household members. The Israelite household likely resembled the colonial-era American household, which has been compared to an "organizational Swiss army knife—many institutions in one convenient package" (Angier 2013). Women had important roles in this all-encompassing unit of society. Some women also had responsibilities beyond the household, in the service of the larger communities in which they lived.

To achieve as full and as balanced a view as possible of the lives of Israelite women of the Iron Age (ca. 1200–587 BCE) entails the use of multiple sources, especially biblical texts and archaeological materials. However, using these sources poses special problems (Meyers 2011, 62–72). For one thing, the Hebrew Bible is androcentric. Women account for about six percent of the named people in the Hebrew Bible (Bohmbach 2000, 34), and most are the relatively few exceptional or elite women, not the ordinary women who were the majority. Consequently, the Hebrew Bible provides little information about the daily experiences of most women. Moreover, because the authors

---

1. "Israel" and "Israelite" are used here in a general cultural sense, not as geographic or political designations, for the people of the preexilic period. For a discussion of women's lives in postexilic times, see Eskenazi 2014.

2. The household family likely corresponds to biblical *bet 'ab*, "father's household" (see, e.g., Stager 1985, 20–23), and the less common *bet 'em*, "mother's household" (see Meyers 1991).

were mainly elite urban males, biblical texts often preserve unreliable or biased perspectives (Meyers 2016, 119). Another problem is that many biblical texts originated or received their final form centuries after what they describe.

In contrast, the archaeological remains of households have not been subjected to centuries of editing or revision. But they too pose problems, for archaeologists dig up things, not people. The materials found in Israelite dwellings must be interpreted, often in several stages, in order to learn about women's activities.[3] Because ancient objects are not gender noisy, identifying objects used by women requires consulting ancient iconography, relevant texts (both the Bible and other ancient documents and inscriptions), and often ethnographic data. Even more important, the social context and meaning of women's activities can be ascertained mainly by consulting ethnographic analogies. In short, archaeological remains must be subjected to multidisciplinary interpretive processes.

Household Functions

Working Women: Economic Activities[4]

Food production, the most common and important household task, was gender-inclusive: men were largely responsible for growing basic foodstuffs, harvesting them probably was a family endeavor, and women converted crops that could not be consumed raw into edible form. Some of women's food-processing tasks, like spreading grapes out to dry in the sun so they would be available as raisins months later, were seasonal. But, because cereal crops provided about three-fourths of a person's daily caloric intake, transforming grains into bread was an everyday process in a world without grocery stores.

Making bread involved several steps, some of which are represented in the archaeological record. Grains had to be ground in order to produce flour. Grinding stones—an upper stone and a lower one, together probably denoted by the dual biblical term *rehayim* (e.g., "millstones" [Isa. 47:2])—are commonly found in Iron Age dwellings. Moreover, multiple sets are often recovered together in the main activity areas of dwellings, indicating that several women would be grinding at the same time (cf. Matt. 24:41). This would not be unusual, given that it could take several hours to produce enough flour for a nuclear family, which averaged six people. Time-consuming and monotonous procedures are surely more pleasant when shared. Baking the bread also brought women together, for the round, dome-shaped clay ovens of biblical antiquity (similar to ovens still in use in traditional Middle Eastern communities) are often found in outdoor spaces or courtyards accessible to several domiciles.[5] Sharing an oven, still a practice in isolated Mediterranean villages (B. Parker 2011, 611), helped conserve fuel. It also provided another opportunity for women to socialize as they gathered to bake their loaves and cook their stews of vegetables and beans or lentils (see Baadsgaard 2008).

Other food-processing activities cannot always be identified with archaeological materials, but biblical texts along with ethnographic data (Amiry and Tamari 1989) provide information about these activities and the gender of those who performed them. Making cheese, for example, surely was a woman's task (see Judg. 5:25), as was the seasonal drying of fruits and legumes. Women also collected and dried herbs and then ground them in the mortars and pestles typically found near the grinding stones mentioned above. Dried herbs not only flavored foods but also (see below) served medicinal purposes. As for beverages, vintners probably were men (see Isa. 5:1–3), but brewers likely were women, given that beer-making

---

3. For information about dwellings, see Meyers 2014a.

4. For additional information and references on this subject, see Meyers 2013, 125–39.

5. Outdoor ovens, probably used in dry, sunny months, typically were larger than indoor ones, used in cold, rainy months.

technology in the biblical world was linked to bread production (Ebeling and Homan 2008).

Food processing was a major but not the sole contribution of women to the household economy. The textiles used for clothing, containers, and coverings of various sorts were also produced by women. Wool, which was the predominant material used by ordinary Israelites, was shorn from sheep by men (e.g., Gen. 31:19) and then washed, spun into thread (e.g., Prov. 31:19), woven into fabric (2 Kings 23:7), and sewn into clothing or household items by women (cf. Prov. 31:22, 24).[6] Most of these processes are represented in the archaeological record: stone, bone, or ceramic spindle whorls; ceramic loom weights; bone weaving tools; and ivory, bone, or metal needles. Like grinding, many stages of textile production were time-consuming. Thus the presence of multiple spindle whorls or sets of loom weights (often near the tools of bread production) suggests that women worked together to produce fabrics for household use. In addition, ethnographic evidence shows that women probably were the ones who made the tools and installations of food and textile production, including many of the ceramic vessels found at all sites, and also baskets, which rarely survive. Moreover, the construction of looms or ovens or large ceramic vessels was often a collaborative project (for ovens, see McQuitty 1993–94, 57).

All told, women's economic activities were numerous and varied, and several features deserve emphasis. One is that many tasks were social in nature, with women working together in the same household space. Another is that many tasks, such as the construction of ovens or the weaving of fabrics, were technologically sophisticated; the necessary skills had to be transmitted from experienced women to their daughters, their younger neighbors, or both. Also, the economic tasks of both women and men were essential for household survival and

were complementary: women transformed the raw products produced by men into edible or wearable form.

Women and Children: Reproductive Activities[7]

Bearing children was also an essential female role. Children contributed much-needed household labor (e.g., Jer. 7:18), as adults they cared for elderly parents (e.g., Exod. 20:12a),[8] and male children (or females, if there were no sons [Num. 27:1–8]) inherited family property (e.g., Prov. 19:14). The survival of both household and community depended on biological reproduction (see Koepf-Taylor 2013). Yet, as in premodern and developing societies everywhere, many factors (inadequate prenatal nutrition, unsanitary parturition conditions, and pregnancy at or near puberty) endangered the lives of mothers. Women's average lifespans—as low as twenty to twenty-five years—were considerably shorter than men's. Also, infant mortality rates were high (see Isa. 65:20); common infectious diseases and other risks to newborns meant that only about half survived past the age of five. The common notion that Israelites had large families is therefore erroneous. The numerous offspring of kings and figures like Jacob are the result of polygyny. Note that Jacob's twelve sons are borne by four women, for an average of three each. Three was the average number of Israelite offspring (as determined by the size of domiciles [Stager 1985, 18]), but having three surviving children might mean six pregnancies.

Women's reproductive activities involved child rearing too; their parental role was an instrumental part of cultural as well as biological continuity. In societies lacking schools and formal education (except perhaps for elites),

---

6. See Barber 1994 for an overview of women's roles in textile production in the ancient world.

7. For additional information and references on this subject, see Meyers 2013, 97–102, 136–39.

8. "Honor" in the fifth commandment refers to the filial obligation to care for the elderly; see D. Lambert 2016, 330–31.

children learn technical and also social skills from those who raise them. Both life skills and social identities are reproduced in children through the instruction of parents (e.g., Prov. 1:8; 6:20). Mothers and fathers had complementary roles as educators, especially as children grew older and learned appropriate tasks and behaviors from the same-gender parent. However, because very young children of both genders were in their mothers' (or grandmothers') care, women arguably had a dominant role in teaching and socializing their offspring.

This instructional role was integrated into women's daily activities. As they carried out household tasks, they intuitively imparted both technical and behavioral skills to their children. Even ordinary food preparation activities were occasions for the transfer of skilled practices to the next generation (Sutton 2013, 305). This may be difficult to comprehend in our industrialized world, where we purchase bread at markets and give our children over to daycare or preschool at ever-younger ages (unless we homeschool them). Yet the very continuity of Israelite households depended on children learning, especially from their mothers, how to perform household tasks and how to interact with others. Indeed, the essential role of women in teaching and socializing their children may be reflected in the figure of the personified Woman Wisdom in Proverbs (see Camp 2000).

In addition to acquiring practical and social knowledge, children learned about their lineages from their parents (Deut. 4:9–10; Josh. 4:21–22) and also their grandparents, if the latter lived long enough. Moreover, in contemporary traditional societies grandmothers especially are the ones who tell stories, thereby transmitting family and community lore to their children's children (Connerton 1989, 39).

Women and Their Communities: Social and Political Activities

The many household tasks that women performed together meant the formation of informal social networks connecting women who lived in the same area of a settlement. The obvious benefit of joint work time was companionship; less obvious was its information-sharing function, which played an important role in household and community life. In spending hours together, women formed bonds that obligated them to help one another in difficult times. Their informal networks thus served as mutual-aid societies. Assistance from neighbors was the only mechanism for dealing with difficulties like a reduced food supply because of crop shortfalls or a loss of household labor because of inevitable illnesses or injuries. As an ethnographer reports about a premodern Mediterranean community, "Women are the typical channels of social communication. While they prepare dough and bake bread, they make X-rays of the town" (Counihan 1999, 33). Through their social interactions women become aware of a neighbor's problems and help resolve them by providing food, labor, or perhaps just comfort in a world without institutional social services. Perhaps the cohort of female neighbors (*shekenot*, "women of the neighborhood") attending the birth of Ruth's son (Ruth 4:14–17) reflects this kind of interaction, which often was critical for the survival of a household.

The information-sharing aspect of women's informal networks played a role in other areas of household and community life. Women share knowledge of technical household processes with one another as well as with their daughters, thereby enhancing everyone's ability to perform various household tasks. Older women in particular transmit their household skills or "wisdom" to younger members of their cohort, who in a sense become apprentices as they learn, for example, how to fashion storage jars or construct ovens (see B. Parker 2011).

The communicative aspect of women's networks also meant that women were privy to certain kinds of information that affected, albeit indirectly, the political dynamics of a community. The elders or leaders of a community had to resolve conflicts that inevitably arose in their settlement, and their decisions often depended upon information about the disputing parties and their disagreement. Women interacting regularly with other women were often privy to relevant information, which they conveyed to their spouses, who in turn transmitted it to the leaders. Another kind of information sharing facilitated the organization of work at communal agricultural installations (i.e., olive presses, threshing floors). Not every household could use these installations simultaneously, and the sequence of access to them depended on knowing when a household had completed its olive or wheat harvest and also how large the crop was. This knowledge, obtained readily by women working together, contributed to the efficient use of communal installations.

In addition, because they left their natal households (likely in another village) and moved to their spouse's households when they married, women had connections with households in other communities. These connections, typically maintained when families gather at regional festivals (see below), provide intercommunity contacts that might facilitate assistance to households in trouble in nearby communities (see Ortner 1996, 136) or even deter hostilities between feuding communities.

Women and the Supernatural: Religious Activities[9]

Because of the prominent attention given in the Hebrew Bible to the national cult and its male priests, household religious activities are barely visible and those of women even less so. Yet religious activities, no less than food production and childcare, were part of the fabric of their daily lives. Indeed, household religious practices, some of which have left traces in the archaeological record, were

the primary and most common aspects of the religious lives of most people.

Some practices were likely those of women, given that various apotropaic (protective) objects are often found in women's work areas in Israelite households (Willett 2001). Because the problems of pregnancy and childbirth (see above) were attributed to malevolent spirits, behaviors that we might consider magic were used to deflect those forces. For example, amulets in the shape of the Egyptian dwarf god Bes, a protector of pregnant women or their newborns, are found frequently at Iron Age sites;[10] several molds have also been discovered, indicating that the amulets were in such demand that they were manufactured locally. Even ordinary oil lamps could have religious meaning, for their light, if placed near a sleeping infant, was thought to protect the child from evil forces that lurked in the dark (see Job 29:2–3). Other similar apotropaic practices, including offerings (Feder 2016), helped women cope with reproductive problems that today would be treated by medical personnel. And because women were familiar with herbs (see above), they likely treated illnesses—which, like reproductive problems, were attributed to evil forces—with appropriate medicinal substances and accompanying incantations. Also, a woman's daily routine of preparing bread might be imbued with religious meaning; some bread or dough might be dedicated to God to secure a blessing on the household (Num. 15:19–21; cf. Ezek. 44:30b).

Other household religious activities were shared by all. These included sporadic life-cycle transitions, such as celebrations of births and marriages, and also the regular festivities that provided relief from the arduous daily life of most Israelites. The latter included the three annual agricultural festivals (Passover, Weeks,

---

9. For more information and references on women's religion, see Meyers 2005; 2012; 2013, 147–69. See also Albertz and Schmitt 2012.

10. Using Bes amulets—and also amuletic eyes of Horus, another Egyptian deity thought to protect women and infants—does not mean Israelite women worshiped these gods; powerful symbols can travel across cultures without their attendant theologies.

and Booths), in which everyone participated, whether at a national, regional, or local shrine.[11] Monthly new moon festivals likely originated as household and clan feasts (e.g., 1 Sam. 20:5–29), and weekly Sabbaths involved household observance (Exod. 20:8–10). What all the festivities, both sporadic and regular, have in common—besides the welcome respite from work and the enjoyment of gathering with kin and neighbors—is feasting, often with special foods and beverages. Women were responsible for most food preparation and surely contributed essential parts of religious feasts while also enjoying the social aspects. Cultic objects found in household eating areas suggest that even daily meals prepared by women had a sacral aspect, with small portions of food set aside for ancestors or deities, as among other Semitic peoples.

Community Roles[12]

Although the lives of most women were centered on household activities, some served the larger community. Nearly twenty such "professional" positions are mentioned in the Hebrew Bible. Some were held exclusively by women, but others were gender-inclusive. Some involved cultural creativity or community authority; others were simply manual labor. Some were performed alone, others in groups. Only one, prostitution, is viewed negatively (e.g., Prov. 23:27), but two prostitutes (Rahab and Judah's daughter-in-law Tamar) seem heroic.

Religious roles included prophecy,[13] prognostication, and divination (e.g., necromancy [1 Sam. 28]) (see Hamori 2015). The women

"weeping for Tammuz" had a ritual role in the temple (Zevit 2001, 558–59), and the women at the entrance to the tent of meeting (Exod. 38:8; 1 Sam. 2:22) likely had menial jobs. The term *qedeshah* (e.g., Deut. 23:17), sometimes translated "cult prostitute," probably refers to cultic personnel, not women performing sacral sex. Women were musicians—singers, dancers, and instrumentalists—who performed in both religious (e.g., Exod. 15:20–21; Ps. 68:24–25) and secular (e.g., 2 Sam. 19:35) contexts. As elsewhere in the ancient world, women were professional mourners who recited appropriate dirges and taught them to apprentices (Jer. 9:17–20). Even midwives (e.g., Gen. 35:17) were likely religious specialists, chanting appropriate prayers for the well-being of mothers and newborns, as well as health professionals. Like wet-nurses (e.g., 2 Kings 11:2), midwives were hired mainly by royal or wealthy families.

Some women practiced trades or crafts, like the production of sumptuous textiles (e.g., Exod. 35:25–26), related to their household tasks, and the bakers, cooks, and herbalists in the royal court were young women conscripted to perform those jobs (1 Sam. 8:13). The discovery of stamp seals, which were used for business or legal transactions, inscribed with women's names indicates the presence of Israelite businesswomen. At least some elite women could write (e.g., 1 Kings 21:8–9) and may have been scribes. Whether literate or not, female heralds (Isa. 40:9) and messengers (Prov. 9:3–4) worked in the communications realm.

Important community leaders are Deborah, as both military leader and judge (as well as prophet), and the wise women of Tekoa (2 Sam. 14:1–20) and, especially, of Abel of Beth-maacah (2 Sam. 20:16–20), who exhibit sagacity, psychological acumen, and the knowledge of traditional sayings. Other women sages are unmentioned but likely

11. Biblical texts imply that the annual feasts were celebrated only in Jerusalem, but those pilgrimage events did not preclude local or household observance (see, e.g., Exod. 12:3–7).

12. For additional information and references, see Meyers 2013, 171–79. See also Brenner 1985 and the relevant entries in Meyers, Craven, and Kraemer 2000.

13. Four named women (Miriam, Deborah, Huldah, and Noadiah) and several unnamed ones (e.g., Joel 2:8)

are prophets, and bands of prophets (e.g., 1 Sam. 10:5) likely included women (see Gafney 2008).

existed. Also on a national level are some queens who exercised political power (e.g., Jezebel and Athaliah) and several queen mothers (e.g., Solomon's mother, Bathsheba; Asa's mother, Maacah) who bear the title *gebirah* ("great lady") and presumably were court functionaries of some kind.

Discussion

Evaluating women's lives means refraining from reading current ideas about women's activities into the Israelite past. For example, unpaid housework tends to be trivialized in our industrialized world. However, in ancient Israel the household was the workplace for both genders, and most of life's necessities were produced there. Women's economic activities were as essential as men's for household survival. Carrying out those activities would have afforded senior women a measure of household power; they were the ones to organize daily tasks, supervise children, allocate resources, and determine the use of space (see D. Cassuto 2008, 77). In so doing, they exercised control over their offspring, including adult sons and daughters-in-law, and sometimes even their spouses. Several biblical narratives about elite women (e.g., Abigail and the Shunammite woman) show them managing household resources, making decisions, giving orders, and interacting effectively with outsiders. In short, senior women had managerial power in many aspects of household life, thus calling into question the common supposition

of women's general subordination.[14] Similarly, the idea that men dominated religious life is dubious when one looks at household religious activities, where women, no less than men, were important actors in household practices considered essential for maintaining household vitality and continuity.

Women's informal social networks, while far less visible than men's formal organizations, were also important for both household and community survival. In addition, they provided opportunities for women to exercise leadership in organizing assistance for other households or in teaching skills to younger women. Professional women, too, experienced the satisfaction of mentoring novices or apprentices as well as providing services to their communities. Informal hierarchies in women's neighborhood and professional groups operated independently of male-dominated ones in other areas of Israelite life, again challenging the notion of total male dominance.

Altogether, women's lives probably were more complex and more difficult than we might have supposed. Yet, in carrying out their many household activities, adult women had opportunities to experience gratification for contributing in essential ways to the well-being, if not the very survival, of their households and communities. The household roles of women and men were complementary, and although ancient Israel was hardly an egalitarian society, women did have agency in many aspects of their lives.

14. The patriarchy idea can also be contested; see Meyers 2014c.

52

Family, Children, and Inheritance in the Biblical World

Victor H. Matthews

If we were to look for the most important theme that guided the everyday activities of the ancient Israelites, it would be family. That is a clear indication that these ancient people cared about many of the same things we care about today, but their laws and social customs were predicated on a very different cultural context. So, for example, they wanted financial security for themselves and their children, and they took great pleasure in the religious and seasonal festivals that marked their lives; however, their emphasis on communal rather than individual identity, their strict sense of honor and shame, and their ritual and legal practices contain considerations that are quite foreign to the present social situation in today's Western culture.

In both the village and urban context, the drama of their lives focused on their social identity, their associations, their marriage practices, and their inheritance patterns. Each in turn is based on the smallest social unit, the household. For them, you are who your father is. Where your father lives, where your father works, and the social interactions initiated by your father will govern your behavior, your attitudes, and your future (Block 2003, 41–43). Although things will begin to change when the monarchy is established and previous patterns are modified to deal with the intrusive decrees or demands of the kings and their officials, ancient Israel, for the most part, remained a basically insulated and rural community.

In the communal society of ancient Israel, which for the majority of the people was dominated by life in small villages of 100 to 150 people, kinship ties and family relations were at the heart of every aspect of life. Even in the more complex setting of larger villages and cities, social interaction and customs remained much the same except in the houses of the elites. However, in urban settlements the village assembly of local elders was replaced by appointed officials, and the local high place (*bamah*) or house shrines were replaced by more elaborate cultic facilities. Here Levitical priests conducted the sacrifices and rituals that once had been the sole province of the head of each household. Only members of the elites had the opportunity to move up socially or to have an impact on events. With that in mind and given the sources of information on family, marriage, and inheritance law contained within the biblical text and other Near Eastern sources, the focus here will be more on the village setting with occasional references to variations among the elite population.

Basic Family Units

The household unit, or *bet 'ab*, was led by a dominant male, given the title of "father" (Matthews and Benjamin 1993, 7). It consisted of four or five generations, including the mother and children as well as the extended family of elderly parents and other related dependents who could not maintain an independent household of their own. Of course, there were other kinship connections with brothers, uncles, and cousins within the community, and that wider set of relationships comprised the clan, or *mishpahah* (Num. 1:18b) (Blenkinsopp 1997, 50–52). Within the village, these associated families often built their multistoried, pillared houses with from two to four rooms on adjoining lots in order to draw on the strength of the entire kinship group while working the fields together or in defense of their homes (Herr 2009). Tribal affiliation (*matteh* or *shebet*) was based on ties to a founding ancestor and an association with a particular geographic region (Gen. 49:1–28; Josh. 13–19). While of some political significance, especially after the monarchy was established, the ties to a particular tribe generally were secondary to the needs and personal associations with the smaller kinship units (Block 2003, 35–36).

In this tight-knit community, the father orchestrated most of the family's hard labor associated with farming, herding, and construction. He provided sage advice and basic technical instruction, invoked tradition to manage all social interactions, and strove to protect the honor and economic assets of the household. Women, whose efforts included

working in the fields, also managed household duties, nurtured the children, prepared and distributed food, and constituted a valued part of the family's total workforce (Meyers 1997, 24–26). It should be kept in mind, however, that the biblical account and legal statements generally address the activities of a basically self-sufficient household encountering the normal economic and political stresses (Blenkinsopp 1997, 54). Only occasionally are the rights and concerns of a failing household mentioned, as in the case of a father whose debts require him to sell his daughter into debt slavery (Exod. 21:7).

In all matters that involve the honor or interests of the family, it was the father's responsibility to represent the household. That would include when he and the other elders (heads of household) met to deal with a community issue (e.g., the "rebellious son" [Deut. 21:18–21]) or to hear a legal case dealing with the terms of a marriage contract (Deut. 22:13–19; Ruth 4:1–6). Within the household itself, he served as the arbiter of all of the household's dealings and had the right to administer summary justice (Gen. 38:24–26).

When a marriage contract was negotiated, it was the father who met with a representative from the other household and worked to create the most satisfactory covenant between them (Gen. 24:34–60). These Israelite marriage agreements, much like those negotiated in ancient Mesopotamia (Westbrook 1988a), were business transactions rather than love matches. The choice of a spouse often was based on status-related issues or economic factors that not only were part of the arrangement between families but also were multigenerational in their outcome. They would involve a prenuptial, public exchange of bridewealth (*mohar*) by the groom's family to the bride's father (Lemos 2010, 36–41, 59–61). Although less well documented, a dowry payment may have been provided by the bride's family as part of the exchange and an economic tie between the grandchildren (the ultimate inheritors of this gift) and the maternal household. These actions were intended to demonstrate to the community at large that these two families were engaging in a social transaction that reached well into the future. In this way traditions were upheld, the honor of the household was maintained, the potential for economic stability was strengthened, and life could progress in an orderly and familiar manner.

Role of Children

The birth of a child is an occasion for songs of praise and celebration (1 Sam. 2:1–5; Ps. 127:3–5) (Colijn 2004, 74). Within this world of close family interaction, children played a fundamental part and were a source of joy to their parents (Ps. 113:9). However, until puberty they represented a liminal group isolated from the adult world (Garroway 2014, 31). They were considered untrained and in need of strict discipline from their parents (Prov. 22:15; Isa. 3:4–5; Wis. 12:24–25). Mothers were essential teachers, preparing them to successfully traverse the stages of maturation in order to reach adulthood and the age of responsibility (Prov. 1:8; 6:20) (Benjamin 2015, 57–58). Children also served as potential economic assets when marriage contracts were arranged and, of course, served as the future of the household in terms of an orderly succession of leadership and a smooth transference of inherited property into the next generation. The legal requirement that children "honor your father and your mother" (Exod. 20:12) imposed an obligation not only to be attentive to parents but also to serve as their caregivers in later life (Lev. 19:32) and to provide them with a proper burial (Gen. 49:29–33) (J. Carroll 2001, 122).[1]

A wise and dutiful son made his parents content, while an uncaring, foolish son brought contempt on the household (Prov. 10:1). This principle often was extended by the biblical writers to depict the relationship between the Israelites and Yahweh, who was characterized as their caring parent (Deut. 1:30–31; Hosea 11:1).

Failure to produce children was one of the greatest catastrophes faced by any family, whether they be simple villagers or the wives of kings (2 Sam. 6:23). Wives obtained honor within their family and the community through producing children and were shamed when they proved to be infertile (1 Sam. 1:4–8). Rachel's plea to Jacob when she had remained barren after many years of marriage illustrates this point quite well: "Give me children, or I shall die!" (Gen. 30:1). Furthermore, childlessness was not just a personal tragedy. It could be interpreted as a sign of divine disfavor and the stark potential for the demise of the household. Contingency plans were formulated, such as the use of a surrogate mother (Gen. 16:1–2) or the adoption of an heir (Gen. 15:2–3) in order to ensure that land and property remained within the control of the household and to perpetuate the "name" of the household (Garroway 2014, 48–49). Having a second wife was not unusual in Israelite households (1 Sam. 1:2). It was more common, however, for tribal leaders or kings. Multiple wives provided political links to other leaders and insured the birth of a son and heir (Judg. 8:30; 2 Sam. 5:13; 1 Kings 11:3).

A solemn obligation required of the family was to educate their children (Ps. 34:11–14; Prov. 22:6). Therefore they were taught the basic tasks associated with the family's existence, whether it be herding sheep, various farming techniques, creating pottery, or repairing the house. Their lessons also included the history, the law and the covenant with God, and

---

1. The Ugaritic epic of Aqhat, which dates between 1600 and 1200 BCE, contains a prayer by King Danil, who pleads for a son who will "build a shrine for the household" and "chant beside his grave," "drive away" his enemies, "support him when he is full of spirits,"

"repair Danil's roof," and "purify his clothes from spells" (Matthews and Benjamin 2006, 71–72).

the traditions of the household and the larger social units with which they were affiliated. For example, among the strict admonitions given to the people is that they must teach their children about God's giving them the law (Deut. 4:9–10; 6:1–2; 11:19). That is echoed quite often in the book of Proverbs, which, like much of wisdom literature, contains the plea that children should both hear and accept the instructions of their fathers (Prov. 5:7; 7:1) (J. Carroll 2001, 123). Righteous behavior is thus defined in terms of a "love of discipline" (Prov. 13:1), for stupidity and a lack of attention to the needs of the household can result in its and its father's ruin (Prov. 10:5; 19:13).

Although there is a sense of the future inherent in nurturing, training, and making marriage plans for one's children, the everyday activities of Israelite families were focused on the tasks at hand. For example, the Gezer Calendar, a tenth-century BCE schoolboy exercise written on a small limestone tablet, details the life of a small agricultural community during the various seasons of the year. For, of course, the fields needed to be cleared, plowed, cultivated, and harvested. And, even then, they had to cope with the realities of weather and insects that could reduce their food supply (Deut. 28:38–40). So, in the end, the success of these tasks in terms of increasing herds and bountiful harvests of grains or fruits needed to be celebrated, for they represented the continuance of life for the household and of God's blessing (Exod. 22:29).

Though it may have seemed otherwise at times, life was not all hard work for these ancient people. The households living in the many small villages in the central highlands regularly joined together to feast, dance, sing, and give praise for what had been accomplished through hard work and the blessings of their God (Judg. 9:27; Eccles. 10:19). These seasonal festivals (Exod. 34:18–22; Num. 10:10), since they could involve more than one village within a clan's territory, marked the occasion for refreshing associations and kinship ties and served as opportunities to negotiate the exchange of goods and marriage contracts.

Inheritance Patterns

Because of the regularity of natural calamities or military invasions, the cultures in ancient Mesopotamia and ancient Israel could not count on long-term continuity for their societies. Thus, having children and establishing clear patterns of inheritance functioned as a means to tie generations together. Economic assets (land and property) of the household were held communally, and the covenantal promise of land given by God reinforced their sense of ownership. This coupling of covenant and land can be seen in Naboth's ability to deny King Ahab's request to sell him his vineyard by claiming that such an act would "give you [King Ahab] my ancestral inheritance" (1 Kings 21:2–3) and thus deny it to his sons. The king has no right to seize the land without legal justification, and it is only after Queen Jezebel engineers the deaths of Naboth and his sons that the land could finally revert into the ownership of the state (i.e., Ahab) (S. Russell 2014, 467–68).

It was supremely important that these land holdings be passed on through the successive generations (*toledot*) of the family. The commonest pattern of inheritance found in both Mesopotamian and biblical legal texts is an equal distribution to the heirs, most often males, and not necessarily according to birth order (Greenspahn 1996, 75–79). However, given the drama that often divides households when there is more than one wife, the legal instructions in Deuteronomy 21:15–17 indicate that a favored wife (one who has "negotiated a covenant" with the father) may have exercised greater influence in "the appointment of heirs for their household" (Benjamin 2015, 136).

Of course, there are always occasions when an orderly succession is not possible and old traditions must be reexamined. The lack of sons to inherit from their father comes up in the dramatic story of the five daughters of Zelophehad. In this case, the daughters successfully argue that they should inherit their father's portion in order to provide themselves with the means of survival and to preserve his name (i.e., his household's identity) (Sakenfeld 1988, 40–42). When consulted by Moses, God reaffirms their claim and a hierarchy of inheritance is then established by divine command (Num. 27:1–11). Interestingly, in a follow-up episode, the "brothers" (kinsmen) of Zelophehad call for an amendment to the case requiring the women to marry within their own clan so that their inheritance is not "taken from the inheritance of our ancestors" (Num. 36:1–12). What results is an affirmation of clan rights to apportioned lands with a temporary "fix" determined to deal with gaps in the normal inheritance pathway.

The law of levirate marriage also provides an example of stretching the laws of inheritance to fit a difficult situation and turn potential disaster into a return to normality. The drama arises when a father's oldest son, the inheritor of a significant share of his father's possessions, dies without producing a son of his own. While that could be a boon for the other brothers, it has the potential for extinguishing the name/household of the deceased brother, and if the widow is remarried outside the family, her dowry would be lost to them as well (Deut. 25:5). With that looming family tragedy in place, it becomes the obligation of the kinsman-redeemer or legal guardian (go'el, usually the brother of the dead man or a near relative) to marry and impregnate the widow and thereby produce an heir for the deceased man (Deut. 25:5–6).

Even such an orderly process, however, cannot cover every situation, since it involves human nature and personal desires that may not coincide with the honor and needs of the household. For that reason, an "escape clause" is written into the law, which allows the redeemer to refuse his duty at the expense of public shaming by the widow before the elders at the city gate (Deut. 25:7–10). In a similar case of interrupted legal procedures, when Judah's firstborn son, Er, dies and his second son, Onan, refuses to impregnate the widow Tamar (Gen. 38:8–9), Judah is left with only one surviving son. His reluctance to send him to this unlucky woman results in an unexpected subterfuge by Tamar in which Judah himself, unknowingly, gives her the child she craves (38:12–19). While the birth of their twins satisfies the needs of the family (38:27–30), it also demonstrates that some social customs can or must be violated, at least temporarily, to bring about the necessary outcome (Matthews 2008, 48–64).

Perhaps because the continuity of the family and of inheritance patterns is so engrained into Israelite culture, even in a time of national crisis, the legal necessities continued to operate. Thus during the siege of Jerusalem by the Babylonian army of Nebuchadnezzar in 588 BCE, Jeremiah was contacted by a kinsman to accept his "right of redemption" (ge'ullah) and redeem a piece of property from his cousin (Jer. 32:6–8).

Yet another difficult case involving inheritance is told about the widow Naomi. She is too old to produce a child to serve as her husband's heir. It then falls to her daughter-in-law, the Moabite Ruth, to plead with Naomi's male relative Boaz to serve as their legal guardian (Ruth 3:1–13). When he points out that technically there is a nearer kinsman, it becomes a matter for the village elders, who hear the case at the village gate and listen to the testimony and the refusal of the kinsman to serve in this capacity. His refusal is most likely based on the fact that he would otherwise be the ultimate inheritor of the property in question. In order to resolve the case and provide the needed support for Naomi and Ruth, Boaz steps forward and offers to take on the responsibility, and in the process he finalizes Ruth's identity as a member of the Bethlehem community (Matthews 2006, 50). He eventually provides Ruth and Naomi with the child needed to maintain the existence of the dead man's household, and once again a social gap is closed (Ruth 4:13–17) (Dearman 1998, 121).

Tied to the governance of inheritance was the maintenance of property rights (both spatial and physical). The Decalogue is clear in its prohibition of adultery, theft, and false witness as well as the emotional longing (coveting) that can result in all of these crimes (Exod. 20:14–17). For example, no one was to move a neighbor's boundary marker, encroaching on the rights of generations to that property (Deut. 19:14; 27:17). Family assets in terms of people, goods, and lands were to be respected and protected against the incursions of those willing to violate the covenantal mandate to love God and obey all the commandments he has given (Deut. 6:3–9). Expressions of right behavior under the law included acts of compassion for the weak segments of the community (widows, orphans, and strangers [Deut. 14:28–29]) by sharing a portion of the tithe with them and allowing them to glean the intentionally unharvested areas of the fields and orchards (Deut. 24:19–21). Not only did this form of charity reflect an extended sense of

family obligation for the entire community, it also recognized that people who treated others as family could expect to receive respect and honor from their fellows.

Conclusion

The rhythm of life in much of ancient Israel was governed by the seasons as they engaged in their agricultural and herding pursuits. While the elites also took note of seasons, their primary concerns had more to do with when to go to war (2 Sam. 11:1) or engage in trade. Regardless of whether they lived in villages or cities, the social glue that held these people together was kinship and family ties. Their identity was created and articulated in terms of a pyramid of relationships with its foundation in the household and expanding socially into clan, tribe, and nation. Their connection to one another was also formed by their ties to the land and their sense of a perpetual inheritance passing through the generations. The social customs, traditions, and laws that governed their interactions and attitudes were impressed on them as children by their parents and elders, and their sense of honor and shame as a sort of social calculator affected the success or failure of their households.

Sustenance

*Integrated Approaches to Themes
in Economic Contexts*

Seasons, Crops, and Water in the Land of the Bible

ODED BOROWSKI

The Bible is a story of a people in a particular place at a particular time. However, to understand the text one needs a context, which includes the land and the different forces that shaped it. The survival of the people depended heavily on their understanding of the available natural resources and the ability to adapt to and manipulate these resources. The text contains references to these activities, and with the help of archaeology and analyses of the finds it is possible to a certain degree to re-create the conditions that were extant in biblical times.

The Land

Biblical descriptions of the land stress its agricultural richness and availability of other natural resources. "For the LORD your God is bringing you into a good land, a land with flowing streams, with springs and underground waters welling up in valleys and hills, a land of wheat and barley, of vines and fig trees and pomegranates, a land of olive trees and honey, a land where you may eat bread without scarcity, where you will lack nothing, a land whose stones are iron and from whose hills you may mine copper" (Deut. 8:7–9 [see also Exod. 3:8]). Similar descriptions appear also in an Egyptian source from the Twelfth Dynasty (ca. 1800 BCE) known as the *Story of Sinuhe*, where the main character describes the land as "a goodly land named Yaa; figs were in it and grapes. It had more wine than water. Plentiful was its honey, abundant its olives. Every (kind of) fruit was on its trees. Barley was there, and emmer" (Pritchard 1969a, 19).[1] Although some of the biblical descriptions, especially those referring to water sources (see below) and minerals, are somewhat exaggerated, the basic descriptions fit very well with what is known from extrabiblical sources and archaeological evidence.

The landscape is also quite varied. The country lies along the eastern coast of the Mediterranean (the Great Sea) with the Syrian Desert in the east and the Jordan or Rift Valley running from north to south splitting

1. For more on the agricultural richness, see Borowski 1987, 3–30.

the hill country into the western ridge, which includes (from north to south) the Upper and Lower Galilee, the Ephraim hill country, the Judean hill country and the Negev highlands; and the eastern ridge, which includes (from north to south) the Bashan, Gilead, Moab, and Edom highlands (A. Curtis 2007, 13–28). The biblical text contains numerous references to these regions: *har* (hill country [Josh. 11:2; 12:8]), *har 'eprayim* (hill country of Ephraim [Josh. 17:15]), *har yehudah* (hill country of Judah [Josh. 11:21]), and more.

Between the mountainous block of the Galilee and the central hill country lies the Valley of Jezreel, the largest in this region, with several other smaller valleys where brooks flow toward the sea or the Jordan River. The coastal plain stretches from the north (modern Lebanon) to the northeastern edge of the Sinai Peninsula with Mount Carmel (Josh. 19:26) dividing the northern part, the Plain of Acco, from the central part, the Sharon (Isa. 33:9) and Philistia farther south. Between the Judean mountains and the coastal plain is the Shephelah (Josh. 9:1), the low hill country, an important part of the kingdom of Judah.

The geological and topographical conditions dictated the location of the roads, the main ones running north-south with secondary and local roads connecting them in a mostly east-west direction.[2] These conditions also determined the location of settlements.

The Climate

The climate prevalent in the region is referred to as Mediterranean climate, a subtropical climate that is characterized by its two main seasons, hot and dry summers and cool and wet winters, with transitional seasons, autumn and spring (A. Curtis 2007, 29–36). The idea of seasonality (Eccles. 3:1–8) was well embedded in the Israelite consciousness and is therefore

2. See also Borowski 2003, 1–14.

reflected in the blessings awarded for observing the covenant: "The LORD will open for you his rich storehouse, the heavens, to give the rain of your land in its season" (Deut. 28:12). The importance of rain for life sustenance can be surmised by the fact that rains were named: the early rains, usually in October, were named *yoreh*, while the late rains, in April, were named *malqosh* (Deut. 11:14; Jer. 5:24). The seasons and the climatic conditions, in addition to the types of soil available, determined the selection of plants grown and animals raised by the inhabitants of the land in biblical times (see below).

However, while rain was the primary source of water for agriculture and animal husbandry, there were other sources of water that contributed to the amount of precipitation, such as dew (*tal* [2 Sam. 1:21]) and snow (*sheleg* [Isa. 1:18]).[3]

Precipitation determines water availability in several other ways; runoff water creates rivers and brooks and fills pools and cisterns, and enriches groundwater, which results in springs and the supply for artificially created wells.

Land Use

Closely related to water availability is the matter of land use. Flat, fertile lands could be found in the large and small valleys where field crops could be cultivated. The hill slopes could be used for growing fruit trees; however, since much of the terrain is made of steep slopes not suited for agricultural purposes, a solution was introduced by the construction of terraces on the slopes, thus creating flat plots that could be used for growing both fruit trees and field crops (Ron 1966; Borowski 1987, 15–18). Terraces helped absorb precipitation and prevented soil erosion.[4]

3. For precipitation and its influence on vegetation, see A. Curtis 2007, maps on pp. 30, 33.

4. For more on terracing, see Edelstein and Gat 1980–81; Edelstein and Kislev 1981; Edelstein and Gibson 1982.

To gain land in the hill country so that they could build terraces, the Israelites had to clear the forested slopes. Echoes of this are well documented in Joshua 17:17–18: "Joshua said to the house of Joseph, to Ephraim and Manasseh, 'You are indeed a numerous people, and have great power; you shall not have one lot only, but the hill country shall be yours, for though it is a forest, you shall clear it and possess it to its farthest borders.'" The felled trees were used in the construction of houses and other structures.

Another way of extending agriculture into inhospitable areas is by employing runoff farming, which is practiced in arid areas. Its main principle is dependence on diversion of runoff rainwater to areas where there are no other water sources. Water diversion was accomplished by the construction of dams to stop the running water and channels to direct the runoff water to collection basins and from there to the fields. This approach enabled the extension of agriculture to areas that otherwise would be barren (Aharoni et al. 1960; Evenari, Shanan, and Tadmor 1971; Borowski 1987, 18–20).

Water Resources

While precipitation is a natural phenomenon, the resulting water can be manipulated. Rain, dew, and snow directly affect the growth of wild and cultivated vegetation by penetrating the soil and reaching the roots of the plants. However, not all the water penetrates the soil or is absorbed by the plants. The superfluous water flows over ground to lower elevations where brooks and rivers are flowing. Water fills up natural depressions and forms pools (*gebe'* [Isa. 30:14]),[5] which can be used to water plants and animals.

Other natural water sources include springs (*'ayin* [1 Sam. 29:1]) the strength of which depends on the amount of winter precipitation.

It is possible to manipulate runoff water before it reaches the natural waterways or when it flows down toward bodies of water such as lakes and the sea (see below). Water that is not absorbed by plants slowly penetrates the ground and finally reaches a hard layer of stone to form groundwater. If not too deep, this accumulation of underground water can be reached and used by digging wells (*be'er* [Gen. 21:25, 30]); in most cases the dirt walls of the shaft were supported with stone walls. Examples of wells from the period of the Hebrew Bible have been discovered in Arad, Beersheba, Lachish, and other sites. Water could be diverted from one location to another by the construction of dams and digging of channels or tunnels. An example of the latter is the so-called Hezekiah's Tunnel in Jerusalem, which was dug to convey the water of the Gihon Spring from a less fortified part of the city to a pool within the city fortifications. Another type of tunnel was dug to enable the inhabitants of a city to reach groundwater within the confines of the city. Examples of this water system were discovered in Hazor, Megiddo, Gibeon, Ible'am, and Gezer.[6]

Some cities built water systems that diverted and collected runoff water into large underground containers. Beth Shemesh had such a system that collected rainwater from the area surrounding the city gate; a similar system was recently discovered under the Arad temple; Beersheba had a system that diverted flash-flood water from a wadi running by the site into a large set of plastered cisterns. Single cisterns or groups of cisterns carved in bedrock and plastered to prevent the water from seepage have been discovered inside settlements and outside. Their openings were covered with

5. Both the Jewish Study Bible (2nd ed.) and the Revised English Bible translate this term as "puddle" or "pool"; the Revised Standard Version, New Revised Standard Version, and New American Bible translate it as "cistern." BDB translates it in Isa. 30:14 as "cistern" and in Ezek. 47:11 as "pool, marsh."

6. Recently, the excavators of the water system at Gezer have dated it to the Middle Bronze Age. For a discussion of water systems, see Borowski 2005.

large stones to prevent the water from evaporation and to protect against unauthorized use (Gen. 29:1–12). These cisterns were also fed with runoff water by channels.

Agriculture

Agriculture, which is the cultivation of plants for the benefit of their fruit and by-products, was the main occupation and source of livelihood for the Israelites, who grew field crops, fruit trees, vegetables, and herbs and spices.[7] The various agricultural activities are well known from the Bible, but the order in which they were performed is laid out in the so-called Gezer Calendar, an inscribed limestone slab discovered at ancient Gezer at the beginning of the twentieth century that in seven lines outlines the order and length of the main eight agricultural seasons (Albright 1943; M. Cassuto 1954). Four chores take two months to complete and the rest occupy one month, so the total months accounted for in the inscription is twelve. Although there still is some argument concerning the interpretation of certain terms, the importance of this document is without question.

The most common field crops were cereals (*dagan* [Gen. 27:28]), which include wheat, barley, and millet. The grain produced by these crops was used for baking bread and other goods and in gruel and similar dishes. Second in importance were legumes, which include broad beans, lentils, bitter vetch, chickpeas, and peas. These crops were used mostly in dishes like pottage (see Gen. 25:29–34). Cultivated herbs, including black cumin, cumin, and coriander (see Isa. 28:25, 27), were used to flavor these dishes.[8] Other field crops included flax (Zohary 1971) and sesame (Borowski 1987, 99).

The next important group of plants was fruit and nut producers. The two most important were grapes and olives (see below) followed by figs, pomegranates, dates, sycamore, and a variety of nuts, including almonds, pistachios, and walnuts. Vegetables were grown in a garden near the house, as suggested in the story of Ahab and Naboth (see esp. 1 Kings 21:2). Very little is known about vegetables grown in this period from biblical records and archaeological remains. Some of the native vegetables include cucumbers, melons, leeks, onions, and garlic (see Num. 11:5, though the reference is to Egypt). Vegetables are seasonal and could not be processed for long-term use. Their nature prevents most vegetables from being present in the archaeological record.

As mentioned above, grapes and olives were the most important fruits for the Israelite economy. Grapes were turned into different kinds of wine (C. Walsh 2000) that could be consumed by the producer's family and used for barter locally and for export. Another by-product of grapes is vinegar (Ruth 2:14). Olives were pressed to provide oil that was used locally for lighting, cooking, or medicinal purposes and also exported; but, unlike grapes, oil was the sole use of olives. Grapes, however, could also be boiled to make syrup or dried into raisins. The other fruits mentioned above had various uses, such as being dried for out of season use.

The amount and quality of the agricultural produce depended not only on the amount of water available but also on soil quality, appropriate practices, and the presence and absence of pests and diseases.

Animal Husbandry

Following in second place of importance for livelihood was animal husbandry, especially herding.[9] The two top herding animals were

---

7. For a detailed discussion of agriculture in the period of the Hebrew Bible, see Borowski 1987.

8. Wild plants were collected as well to be used as herbs. For detailed descriptions of biblical plants, see Zohary 1982a.

9. For a detailed description of herding in the period of the Hebrew Bible, see Borowski 1999, 39–85.

goats and sheep. These animals were very valuable not only for their meat, which was consumed mostly on special occasions such as festivals, but also for their by-products, which could be harvested again and again. The first by-product that comes to mind is milk, which could be processed for long-term use into yogurt, a variety of cheeses, and other products. Another by-product was the raw material for weaving textiles: hair (goats) and wool (sheep). When the animal was slaughtered, not only was its meat used but also its hide, bones, and horns. One by-product produced by all animals in the Israelite farmyard was dung, used to fertilize the soil and as fuel in ovens and kilns.

Other animals kept in small numbers by the Israelites were those used as draft and pack animals. The most common of these was the donkey; other animals included horses, mules, oxen, and camels, all in very small numbers (Borowski 1999, 87–131). It is interesting that while the Israelites were not allowed to cross-breed animals (Lev. 19:19), they used mules as working animals (2 Kings 5:17) and for riding, especially by nobility (2 Sam. 13:29; 1 Kings 1:33). It is possible that while the prohibition against crossbreeding was observed, mules were acquired from outside sources (1 Kings 10:25; 2 Chron. 9:24).

Conclusion

As it appears from the written and archaeological evidence, the Israelites and the other inhabitants of the land during the period of the Hebrew Bible recognized the potential embedded in the available natural resources and, most importantly, learned to manipulate these resources to their advantage and to employ the natural conditions of the land to their benefit. Thus, in spite of sometimes harsh conditions, such as drought and locust attacks, they managed not only to provide for their livelihood but also to produce surpluses that enabled them to trade locally and internationally. Extrabiblical records and archaeological remains testify to the fact that some products of the land, such as woolen textiles, wine, and olive oil, were highly prized beyond the borders of the land of Israel and were exported in trade or as tribute. It seems ironic that, because of its agricultural richness, the land of Israel was attractive to outside forces, a fact that partly explains the numerous attacks and conquests by these forces.

54

Trade in the Late Bronze and Iron Age Levant

Joshua T. Walton

Introduction

Economy and trade rarely play the role of the main character in biblical texts. Despite this, the economic structures of ancient Israel serve as a critical part of the background, setting the stage for the biblical narratives. Trade, broadly construed, can be defined as "the mutual appropriative movement of goods between hands" (Polanyi 1957, 266; Renfrew 1975, 4; Earle 1982, 2). Trade is most commonly associated with the buying and selling of commodities through the marketplace, and is thus an inherently social action, linking different individuals or social groups through the exchange of materials. From large-scale merchant ventures to small local village markets, trade takes place at different scales. The participants include royal state-sponsored trading ventures, private merchants or merchant collectives, and barter among neighbors in agricultural communities. This chapter is primarily concerned with the long-distance trade in nonstaples and precious and semiprecious luxury goods, despite the fact most of the population resided in agricultural communities where small-scale

barter and local village markets played a more significant role. Long-distance trade catered to the upper echelons of society, furnishing palaces, temples, and dwellings of the elite. The acquisition of luxury goods over distance was important for opulent displays of wealth and power throughout the Bronze and Iron Ages. While the details and intricacies of trading networks were in constant flux, the overarching patterns governing distribution of goods across the Mediterranean and the ancient Near East remained largely unchanged throughout the Bronze and Iron Ages. This chapter examines major aspects of long-distance trade, from the mechanisms of exchange (money and markets), to the participants (public and private merchants), and to the avenues of distribution (maritime and overland routes).

In the ancient Near East, long-distance trade was made profitable through value differentials, taking advantage of regional differences in demand to justify the costly and risky transport of goods over distance. Therefore, long-distance trade was built on flow of knowledge: informing traders of the best locations to acquire resources or materials and where to sell them for the highest profit (North 1990; Monroe 2009; Sommer 2007). In this sense, trade was inherently social and required vast networks and connections of information to be profitable. Better knowledge systems reduced risk, while at the same time increasing profit and efficiency.

Money and Markets

Many different goods functioned both as commodity (an item desired for exchange) and money (a form of payment, value standard, or storable wealth) in the ancient world, resulting in commodity money, long before the invention of coinage. Money, simply understood, is a mechanism for indirect exchange. Early monies took the form of commodities,[1] which served a variety of functions, including (1) a form of payment, (2) a standard for establishing the value of other goods, and (3) a means of storable, liquid wealth through hoarding. Money, as a standard of valuation against which all other goods could be measured, facilitated indirect exchange by systematizing exchange values and allowing for the storage of value between exchange events, thereby increasing the efficiency of trade (see Earle 1985, 374–75). Early forms of commodity money included grain, lead, copper, tin, bronze, silver, and gold (Powell 1996, 227; Monroe 2009, 39–40). However, by the seventh century BCE silver had risen to become the most common and widely accepted standard and form of indirect payment in the ancient Near East and Mediterranean (K. Radner 1999, 129; Fales 1996, 19–20; Gaspa 2014). Barley, copper, and bronze commonly functioned as money into the eighth century (K. Radner 1999, 128; Fales 1996, 17–19), and barley and silver served as the most common standards of valuation (Powell 1996, 228).[2]

Commodity money, especially as a standard and as easily convertible wealth, played an important role in making long-distance and market trade more accessible and facilitating transactions. Barter at local markets certainly continued to play an important role in the economic life of much of the population, but larger marketplaces and convertible, easily transportable wealth were essential for long-distance trade at commercial centers. The term "market" can refer to the marketplace—that is, a location where buying, selling, or barter takes place. The market as a location is a space where the social interaction of exchanging goods takes place. In a more modern sense, however, the term "market" has grown to mean a process, or mechanism, through which buying and selling take place, more than a physical location. The market as a process is governed by "market principles," such as self-regulating prices determined by supply and demand, largely impersonal exchange, and principles of profit maximization, as opposed to transactions that do not follow market principles, such as gift-giving or administered royal trade ventures governed by formal treaties. Market and non-market exchange are not mutually exclusive, and both were practiced simultaneously throughout the Bronze and Iron Age ancient Near East and are attested in the Hebrew Bible (see Nam 2012; Monroe 2009).

Silver is the most commonly attested form of payment in the Iron Age. Payments for goods in silver are well attested in Akkadian sources (Fales 1996; Gaspa 2014). Additionally, an ostracon found in the Ashkelon marketplace records a payment for grain (Cross 2008, 336). The Bible records the use of silver to purchase land (2 Sam. 24:24; 1 Kings 16:24), horses and

---

1. Broadly speaking, a commodity is understood, if not specifically defined, as an item that is traded and is thus defined by its use in exchange. For a more detailed discussion cf. I. Morris 1986.

2. For a short time in the Late Bronze Age, gold was the common standard in Babylonia and Egypt, due to the large influx of gold into the metal market in the Amarna period (Brinkman 1972).

chariots (1 Kings 10:29), slaves (Amos 2:6), and agricultural produce (2 Kings 6:25; 7:16).[3]

Transactions involving silver or other precious metals were carried out according to weight, measured with a balance pan and weight set, artifacts that are well attested in archaeological contexts associated with commerce, including the seventh-century BCE marketplace excavated at Ashkelon (Stager, Master, and Schloen 2011, 47) and the Ulu Burun Shipwreck (Pulak 1998).

The procedure of weighing out payments is attested in biblical accounts recording the purchase of land (Prov. 16:11; Jer. 32:9–10). This method of transacting is also reflected in the concern of the biblical authors for honest weights and scales (Amos 8:5; Mic. 6:11, cf. also Lev. 19:36; Deut. 25:13–15; Prov. 11:1; 20:23).

Maritime Trade

In the ancient world, there were two main avenues for transporting goods long distances: land routes and water routes. Water routes included travel across major bodies of water, such as the Mediterranean Sea, Red Sea, or Persian Gulf, as well as transport up or down major riverine systems such as the Nile, Tigris, or Euphrates. Scholars traditionally have considered water transport to have been faster, cheaper, and more efficient than overland transport (Weber 1976; A. Jones 1964, 841–44; Heltzer 1977, 208).[4] Water transport, however, was limited to locations adjacent to the coastline or along the banks of major rivers. Thus, some overland transport was always

necessary to transport goods to landlocked population centers. While the major riverine systems of Mesopotamia and Egypt were essential to the local economies of those regions, for the Bronze and Iron Age polities of the southern Levant (including Israel and Judah), the Mediterranean Sea served as the primary maritime route.

The presence of maritime trade on the Mediterranean Sea has been a constant factor in the development of the Near East from prehistoric until modern times (see Braudel 1972; Horden and Purcell 2000; Broodbank 2013) and was essential to the commercial networks of the Late Bronze and Iron Ages. In the Late Bronze Age, seafaring merchant ventures linked Egypt to the Levantine coast, Cyprus, and the Aegean. The wealth and the expanse of this trade are best illustrated through finds from shipwrecks off the coast of Turkey at Cape Geledoniyah and Ulu Burun. These ships preserve a snapshot of Late Bronze Age trade, while simultaneously serving as examples of larger trends, such as the cargos and routes of ships during this period. The Ulu Burun wreck, dating to ca. 1300 BCE, represents the richest find recording Bronze Age maritime shipping. The ship's cargo included some ten tons of variously shaped copper ingots, one ton of tin ingots, and almost 150 Canaanite storage jars (amphorae), occurring in three different sizes and typologically associated with northern regions of Syria-Palestine. These amphorae primarily contained terebinth resin (ca. one ton) but also olives and in one instance glass beads. Other finds included cobalt-blue glass ingots, ebony, cedar, raw ivory,[5] and worked ivory cosmetic boxes, alongside figurines, weapons, tortoise shells, ostrich egg shells, gold and silver jewelry, Egyptian scarabs, balance weights, and Cypriot-style pottery (Pulak 1997; 1998; 2008). While some of these objects undoubtedly belonged to crew members, the majority of objects on

---

3. Hosea pays for a woman with both silver and barley (Hosea 3:2).

4. This assertion can be complicated by a host of different issues, including the distance of sites from water, the dangers of certain areas of river or coast, the direction of travel (e.g., upstream or downstream, with or against seasonal winds), making it clear that under certain conditions and variables land transport could be preferred to water transport (see C. Adams 2007).

5. In the form of hippopotamus teeth and an elephant tusk.

the vessel reflect key trading stops along this ship's journey, including Egypt, Cyprus, and Syria-Palestine. A similar object assemblage is depicted in a fourteenth-century Egyptian wall painting from the Tomb of Kenamun, the mayor of Thebes, which illustrated the unloading of a Syrian merchant fleet at an Egyptian port (N. Davies and Faulkner 1947). The goods from Ulu Burun are also reminiscent of commodities mentioned among shipments of gifts and tribute between Egypt, its vassals, and other international powers in the Amarna Letters.

Sometime at the end of the twelfth century, however, the great commercial and political centers that comprised the Bronze Age commercial system collapsed (Cline 2014), ushering in a dark age marked by a supposed temporary cessation of maritime trade. Continuing research (E. Stern 1993b; Master 2009) challenges assumptions of this cessation, providing new archaeological evidence for the continuance of trade, which complements textual sources such as the Egyptian *Tale of Wenamun* (discussed more in-depth below), which suggest the persistence of maritime trade into the Iron Age. While it is clear that the collapse of the Late Bronze Age had widespread consequences in the world of Mediterranean trade, new evidence suggests that some portion of this trade continued through the Iron I, leading into a full revitalization of Mediterranean trade under the Phoenicians in the Iron II.

In the Iron Age II, maritime trade became primarily associated with the expansion and colonization efforts of the Phoenicians across the Mediterranean. The Phoenicians were the Iron Age inhabitants of the Canaanite cities along the northern Levantine coast, with major centers at Tyre, Sidon, and Byblos. Beginning in the tenth century, these city-states began a massive program of exploration and settlement across the Mediterranean from North Africa to the Aegean, to Italy, to Spain, and even along the Atlantic coast of Portugal (Neville 2007, 35). Phoenician expansion brought the polities

of the southern Levant easier access to the resources and wealth of these areas, especially metals and most notably silver (see Gitin 1995; 2012). The Phoenicians also found new markets for commodities from the Levant and Mesopotamia, delivering cargos of wine and olive oil to Egypt, North Africa, and Spain. Shipwrecks from the eighth through sixth centuries BCE found off the coast of Ashkelon (Stager 2003b), Turkey (Greene, Leidwanger, and Ozdas 2011), and Spain (Negueruela et al. 1995) show that amphorae, of the kind used to transport these agricultural semi-luxuries, were the primary cargo of many of these merchant ventures. The extensive trade networks of the Phoenicians have been documented archaeologically through the excavation of Phoenician overseas settlements across the Mediterranean (see Aubet 1993; Niemeyer 2000; 2006; Pappa 2013) but are best highlighted through Ezekiel's description of the trade of Tyre (Ezek. 27), which includes a detailed list of Tyre's trade partners, both maritime and overland, including Spain, Cyprus, Anatolia, the Aegean, Mesopotamia, Syria, Judah, and Arabia. According to Ezekiel, Phoenician trade included precious items, such as metals, spices, and ivory; semi-luxuries, such as fine textiles, wine, and olive oil; and even bulk products, such as wheat and livestock. Beginning in the seventh century, Greek traders rose in competition with the established Phoenician system, establishing their own colonies and trading posts, attested by increasing amounts of Greek pottery at sites around the Mediterranean (Tsetskhladze 2006; Waldbaum 1994; 1997).

Overland Trade

Overland trade, in the form of large caravans, was essential for transporting goods between water-based travel systems or to and from landlocked locales. In many cases, due to the location of natural resources, production centers, and consumption centers, the use of maritime or riverine systems was not an efficient possibility. In these cases goods were transported overland by beasts of burden. In the second and third millennium, donkeys were the most common caravan animal, well attested in the ancient records of the Old Assyrian caravan trade between Ashur and Karum Kanesh in Anatolia (see Barjamovic 2011; Larsen 1982; Veenhof 1972). Toward the end of the second millennium, the widespread domestication of the dromedary (Uerpmann and Uerpmann 2012) opened up new routes across previously inaccessible terrain. The resistance of dromedary to the harsh elements as well as its increased load-bearing capacity in comparison with the donkey led to its popularity in the first millennium, especially for the emerging caravan traders from the Arabian Peninsula. Much of the information on the logistics of overland trade comes from the Old Assyrian caravan documents; however, the most important overland route for long-distance trade of precious items in the Iron Age was the Old South Arabian caravan route, which brought aromatics from the Arabian Peninsula to markets across the Mediterranean and Mesopotamia (see Eph'al 1982; Byrne 2003).

The main products of the South Arabian trade were the aromatics of the kingdom of Saba', located in modern-day Yemen, primarily frankincense and myrrh (Groom 1981), but the Arabian Peninsula was also a well-known source of gold and precious stones. The exact date of the beginnings of the South Arabian trade is unclear. The earliest clear attestation of the Arabian caravans comes from a ninth-century cuneiform document from the province of Suhu, located in the Middle Euphrates region. The text records a successful raid by the governor of Suhu against a caravan from Tema and Saba'. Although the end of the text is broken, it is clear that the governor acquired a rich haul from the raid, including precious goods such as iron, precious stones, and rich purple textiles from the coast. The

goods found in the caravan suggest that they had already traded some of their spices for the luxury goods of Mesopotamia and northern Syria/Phoenicia and were returning to the Arabian Peninsula. Another possible early attestation comes from the biblical account of Solomon and the Queen of Sheba. Sheba is well known as ancient Saba', and the gifts that the queen presents to Solomon—camels, spices, gold, and precious stones (1 Kings 10:2)—are associated with the Arabian trade. Scholars have linked this meeting to a response by Saba' to protect their trade interests in the Red Sea following Solomon's construction of a fleet at Ezion-Geber with the Phoenicians (1 Kings 9) and his subsequent ventures to Ophir (Wiseman 1993, 129; Mulder 1998, 507).

John Holladay (2006; 2009; 2014) has suggested that the taxation of Arabian caravans would have been a source of great wealth for the United Monarchy of Israel and later for Judah, providing David and his successors with luxury goods for their palaces as well as ample supplies of precious metals. There is nothing in the archaeological or textual evidence that suggests exploitation of the transit trade to this degree (Tebes 2006; Faust and Weiss 2005), but the biblical authors certainly were aware of this lucrative trade. Isaiah speaks of those who "carry their riches on the backs of donkeys and their treasure on the humps of camels" (Isa. 30:6) and prophesies of a time when "all those from Sheba shall come. They will bring gold and frankincense" (Isa. 60:6). Ezekiel was also familiar with the South Arabian trade, identifying the merchants of Sheba and Raamah as the purveyors of spices, precious stones, and gold to Tyre (Ezek. 27:20–22). Certainly by the late Iron Age, the South Arabian trade and its merchandise had risen to prominence in the world of ancient Near Eastern and Mediterranean commerce, fueling Neo-Babylonian expansive interests into Arabia under the reign of Nabonidus (Beaulieu 1989; Hausleiter 2006). It is likely that Judah was able to profit to some degree (although not to the extent proposed by Holladay) from interacting with and taxing some of the trade that passed through Judahite territory on the way to Gaza and the broader Mediterranean world.

Trade Participants

Given the richness of the Ulu Burun find, the risks of long-distance trade, and the necessary capital required to invest in such a venture, scholars traditionally have associated long-distance trade with royal ventures sponsored by the palace, the only institution that could have afforded such an investment (Rainey 1963; Pulak 1997, 251; Heltzer 1996). However, more recent analysis suggests a more complicated picture that included both public and private trading ventures (Monroe 2009; 2010; Bongenaar 2000). Large merchant ventures took place under the aegis of the palace in the form of royally sponsored trade ventures or the activities of royally sponsored merchants. However, trade was also practiced privately by collectives of merchant entrepreneurs, sometimes through the sponsorship of wealthy elites (Monroe 2009, 181–89, 243–75; Manning and Hulin 2005, 273). The distinction between the public and private spheres was complicated because it was possible for royally commissioned or supported merchants to also function privately under their own commercial interests. The overlap between public and private trade is especially clear in documents from the Late Bronze Age Canaanite city of Ugarit (McGeough 2015; Monroe 2009).

Royal trade took many forms, including the exchange of gifts between palaces as a form of international diplomacy, trade treaties or agreements between kings, and sponsored long-distance expeditions to exotic lands. Gift-giving between kings[6] is well-attested in the Amarna Letters (Liverani 1979b; Cochavi-Rainey 1999) as part of Late Bronze Age diplomacy, conducted through a ceremonial language of bargaining (Zaccagnini 2000, 142–49; Avruch 2000).[7] Gift exchange was also part of the Mycenaean palace economy (Halstead 1992). Whereas gift-giving served an important diplomatic role, gift exchange was restricted to certain types of goods and settings, and thus could not have accounted for all, or even most, of Bronze Age exchange (Manning and Hulin 2005, 273).[8] The Queen of Sheba's gift to Solomon in 1 Kings 10 should be viewed in this context, as an attempt to establish international diplomatic trading relations through the presentation of a greeting gift, as should Solomon's reception of gifts "year after year" from all who visited his court (1 Kings 10:24–25).

An early Iron Age attestation of a sponsored trade venture is found in the Egyptian *Tale of Wenamun*, dating to the eleventh century BCE,[9] in which Wenamun sets off on a trading venture from Egypt to the northern Levantine coast to buy timbers from the ruler of Byblos. Sponsored trade missions could have been carried out by either palace agents or royal merchants, such as those employed by Solomon to buy horses from Egypt (1 Kings 10:28). Other examples of royal trade include Solomon's joint ventures with Tyre on the Red Sea to Ophir (1 Kings 9) and a later unsuccessful attempt by

---

6. These gifts are couched in familiar terms. The great kings refer to each other in a familial manner ("brothers"), and the metaphor extends to economic exchanges, which are given as signs of friendship or as "greetings" (Zaccagnini 2000, 142–45).

7. The language of gift-giving in transaction contexts is well attested throughout the patriarchal narratives in Genesis, most notably in Abraham's purchase of the cave at Machpelah in Gen. 23.

8. It is also worth noting that the language of gift exchange, especially in the Bible, encompasses a number of transactions, from the payment for services (1 Kings 15; 1 Sam. 9), to payments of tribute (2 Kings 16:8; Ps. 72:10), to bribe money (1 Kings 15:19).

9. The *Tale of Wenamun* is generally believed to be a fictionalized reworking of an official report, and thus, while the dialogue contained in it is the work of the author, the background events and the trade mission generally are regarded as historically appropriate (Lichtheim 1976, 197; Egberts 2001, 495–96).

the Judahite king Jehoshaphat to build a royal trade fleet of his own for a similar expedition (1 Kings 22:48). These exploration and trading missions parallel earlier Egyptian expeditions of the New Kingdom, such as Hatshepsut's mission to the land of Punt illustrated on the walls of her memorial temple at Deir el-Bahri.

An example of a royal trade agreement is found in Solomon's treaty with Hiram of Tyre (1 Kings 5:8–9), in which Hiram supplies Solomon with timber, gold, and skilled labor for the construction of his palace and the temple in exchange for land in the Galilee and a yearly provision of wheat and olive oil. Later in the Iron II, documents such as Esarhaddon's vassal treaty with Tyre demonstrate that the palace and the king still had a vested interest in trade, primarily its taxation and regulation. Instead of large royal trading ventures, the king, like other wealthy citizens, could invest with certain merchant venturers. The members of the Assyrian court are particularly noted for their trade interests, investing with Phoenician merchant houses (Luukko and Van Buylaere 2002, nos. 127, 128, pp. 113–15). Most merchants were part of private trading collectives or families. The best records for understanding the workings of merchants come from the earlier Old Assyrian period, and the vast documentation of their overland caravan trade between Assur and Kanesh. These trade collectives included foreign enclaves or colonies, a common feature of trading groups that is seen again in the Iron II with the expansion of the Phoenicians across the Mediterranean, and later the Greeks, establishing colonies and trading posts in strategic areas.

Conclusions

Trade permeated all aspects of life in the ancient Near East, and the biblical world was no exception. While the Bible rarely focuses on long-distance trade, it served as an important backdrop for biblical texts, from the narrative of Solomon and the Queen of Sheba to Ezekiel's oracle against Tyre. Control of major overland trade routes and maritime ports was an important motivating factor in the political endeavors of ancient Near Eastern polities and serves as a background to the political conflicts recorded in the book of Kings. Understanding the role in statecraft of trade in luxury items helps provide a framework for the persistent striving of ancient Near Eastern kings to acquire exotic foreign goods throughout the Bronze and Iron Ages.

55

Slavery in the World of the Bible

RICHARD E. AVERBECK

Scholars have given a good deal of attention to the subject of slavery in the ancient Near East and in the Bible (esp. beginning with Mendelsohn 1949). Slavery was an important institution in the ancient Near Eastern world, and so it was in ancient Israel as well. There certainly was a need for labor forces, especially at certain times of the year. Nevertheless, it is important to note up front that the kind of slavery known to New World studies, in which peoples were captured and taken en masse from their homeland specifically to supply and breed for labor in another country (or on another continent) is unknown in the ancient Near East, including the Bible. Foreign chattel labor consisted mostly of warfare refugees (Culbertson 2011c, 2–7, 11–12) or came from the slave trade carried on by merchants, who were also the main creditors in society. They would foreclose on insolvent families, forcing them to sell family members to the merchants in order to pay off debts (Neumann 2011, 25).

Israel's deliverance from slavery in Egypt, however, shaped how they were to view and manage slavery. Yahweh's main concern was that the Israelites belonged to him and to him alone, not to any other god and not to any other master. He was their Lord and Master. In conclusion to the slavery regulations in Leviticus 25:39–55, the Lord made the point clear: "For to *me* the people of Israel are servants; they are *my* servants whom *I* brought out from the land of Egypt: *I* am the LORD your God" (v. 55, emphasis added). The term for "servant" here is the regular term for "slave" used in the previous context. Slave terminology was also used metaphorically for the relationship that people and their leaders had with God or their gods, and sometimes relationships with people of honored status.

Sources and Definitions

The sources for slavery in the ancient Near Eastern world surrounding Israel are mostly in the cuneiform script, which was used to write various languages (and a few late Aramaic legal texts from Egypt). With regard to law collections in particular, they include, in Sumerian, the Laws of Ur-Namma (twenty-first century BCE) and the Laws of Lipit-Ishtar (twentieth century); in Akkadian, the Laws of Eshnunna (eighteenth century), the Law Code of Hammurabi (eighteenth century), the Middle Assyrian Laws (thirteenth century), and the Neo-Babylonian Laws (sixth century); and in Hittite, the Hittite Laws (fourteenth century).

With some exceptions, the principles and practices that applied to slavery were largely held in common across the ancient Near East. There are, however, complications. First, the terminology used is sometimes ambiguous, and second, the conditions that people served under varied in ways that were handled differently in the various legal regulations (Westbrook 2009b, 162–65; Allam 2001, 294; Larsen 2017; Magdalene 2014; P. Williams 2011 for terminology; see also, e.g., the treatment of the Law Code of Hammurabi below). Moreover, law collections usually do not provide the larger view of the "household" context of slavery. Workers had differing status among them whether they were slaves or nonslaves. Economic and administrative sources sometimes reflect these distinctions more clearly than the legal traditions (Culbertson 2011b).

The study of slaves in these household contexts in the ancient Near East suggests, for example, that slavery actually filled a "negligible role in labor spheres of Near Eastern societies" (Culbertson 2011c, 1, 7; Neumann 2011, 21). In ancient Mesopotamia the household concept extended to temples as households of the gods and palaces as households of the rulers (Neumann 2011, 26–27; Kleber 2011; Tenney 2011). Moreover, family households were not just places of residence but also places of production, which brings up the issue of child slaves, who could be either debt or chattel slaves (Garroway 2014, 113–55), among other considerations. "Households" often involved more than just the natal or extended family; they included those who worked in, with, and for the family. When treating slaves within a

household context, therefore, it is especially important to think of their status as situational and interactional, depending on their abilities and assignments within the household system (Culbertson 2011a, 35).

There was plenty of room for abuse, of course, but there was also real concern in society for humane treatment of both debt and chattel slaves, although more in regard to the former than the latter. In general, debt slavery can be differentiated from chattel slavery in that it honored the link that remained between slaves and their natal families. In chattel slavery, however, the slave actually belonged to the master and his household, whether that was a family household or the extended temple or palace household.

Debt Slavery

In Israel the two categories of slavery were temporary debt slavery and permanent chattel slavery. The terminology for both is the same, but we can distinguish between them in the biblical law collections. For example, there was no allowance for forcing Israelites into chattel slavery (Lev. 25:44–46), and the same seems to have been the case even with the Judeans in Babylonian captivity (Magdalene 2011). Nevertheless, Israelites who had been debt slaves could voluntarily enter into permanent slavery because they loved their masters and were doing well with them (Deut. 15:16–17), especially if they had gained a family through the master while in debt slavery (Exod. 21:5–6).

Debt Slavery in the Ancient Near East

It is sometimes unclear whether a particular Near Eastern slave law is dealing with debt or chattel slavery, both, or some other kind of institutional situation such as tenant farming. We will include here all slave regulations that may have a bearing on our understanding of debt slave regulations in the Bible, even if they are not clearly referring to debt slaves.

Who could be sold as debt slaves and for how long? We know from other kinds of legal documents, other than the law collections, that debt slavery was a well-known practice from back even into the third millennium BCE. Debtors could sell themselves, their children, or their slaves for debt service (Neumann 2011, 24).

We begin with one particularly pertinent regulation from the Laws of Hammurabi: "If an obligation is outstanding against a man and he sells or gives into debt service his wife, his son, or his daughter, they shall perform service in the house of their buyer or of the one who holds them in debt service for three years; their release shall be secured in the fourth year" (§117 [M. Roth 1997, 103]). The three years of service and fourth-year release are of special interest here, since the regulation for the debt slave in biblical law is six years of service and release in the seventh (see Exod. 21:2; Deut. 15:12). In both cases, the law seems to assume that the years of labor would pay off the debt and any interest on it (Greengus 2011, 89–91).

The next law is related but does not make the same assumption: "If he should give a male or female slave into debt service, the merchant may extend the term (beyond the three years), he may sell him; there are no grounds for a claim" (Law Code of Hammurabi §118). In this case, the debtor has given a male or female slave to the creditor for his debt service. If the debt is not paid off in the three years the creditor may sell the slave to make gain on his investment. The three years' labor on the part of the slave does not necessarily make full payment for the creditor's investment.

The regular term for "slave," however, does not appear here, but rather the term *kiššātu*, rendered "debt service" by Martha Roth. Raymond Westbrook considers it a term for a "ransom" that needed to be paid for some minor offense, not debt obtained through a loan (see the discussion in Westbrook 2009a, 150; 2009b, 169; see also Neumann 2011, 23). These laws, therefore, may not have anything to do with debt slavery but rather with two different ways one person could compensate another for a breach of law. This is a good example of how the ancient Near Eastern legal context and situation may not correspond precisely to biblical debt slavery but may offer useful comparative information in spite of that fact.

Slave marriages. Laws of Ur-Namma §4 gives the following regulation for slave marriages: "If a male servant marries a female slave, his beloved, and that male slave (later) is given his freedom, she/he will not leave (or 'be evicted from'?) the house" (M. Roth 1997, 17). Although the Sumerian verb in the last clause could be rendered with "he" or "she," it probably should be rendered "she shall not leave the house (of her owner)" (Greengus 2011, 90). If so, the law is parallel to what we find in Exodus 21:4: "If his [the debt slave's] master gives him a wife and she bears him sons or daughters, the wife and her children shall be her master's and he shall go out alone." The apparent reason is that the debt slave had not paid the bride price for the woman to be his wife, and, moreover, that she and her children had value to the master as slaves. They would need to be redeemed out of their slavery if the man decided to both go out of debt slavery and retain his family.

Signs of slave status. Laws of Hammurabi §§226–27 deal with issues of the slave-hairlock: "If a barber shaves off the slave-hairlock of a slave not belonging to him without the consent of the slave's owner, they shall cut off the barber's hand" (§226 [M. Roth 1997, 124]). Ancient Near Eastern treaties commonly included provisions for the return of runaway slaves. Generally, slave marks were used so that slaves could be identified and, therefore, captured and returned. According to Exodus 21:6 and Deuteronomy 15:16–17, the master of a debt slave who voluntarily committed himself to permanent slavery "shall pierce his ear with an awl; and he shall serve him for life" (Exod. 21:6). In this case, of course, it is not a matter of preventing the slave from running away, but rather a permanent mark that he belongs to the master and has permanent slave status.

Injury done to or by slaves. Laws of Hammurabi §§199, 205, 213–14, 217, 219–20, and 223 (M. Roth 1997, 121–24) and Hittite Laws 8, 12, 14, 16, 18 (Hoffner 1997a, 218–19) are concerned with injuries done to slaves by free men or other slaves, or injuries done by slaves to free men. Some of these regulations recall those in Exodus 21:20–21, 26–27, 32, but it is debated whether the latter refer to debt slaves or chattel slaves (Greengus 2011, 122–28; Westbrook 1988b, 89–109). Some may apply to one or the other, and others to both. For example, the regulation in Exodus 21:32 most likely applies to chattel slaves, since it reduces the payment for goring by an ox from the death of the ox's owner to thirty shekels of silver, presumably paid to the master of the slave (cf. Laws of Hammurabi §§229–31, 251–52). On the other hand, Exodus 22:3b says, "The thief must make good on what he stole. If he has nothing, he must be sold to pay for his theft" (CEB). This seems to assume that there would be a period of debt slavery until the theft has been paid off (see Westbrook 2009b, 177–78; Neumann 2011, 23; Allam 2001, 294 for slavery because of committing a crime).

Contesting slave status. According to Laws of Lipit-Ishtar §14, "If a man's slave contests his slave status against his master, and it is proven that his master has been compensated for his slavery two-fold, that slave shall be freed" (M. Roth 1997, 28–29). In this instance, the slave is a debt slave who should be released once the debt is paid with interest, apparently through his debt service. The "twofold" payment may somehow relate to Deuteronomy 15:18a: "Don't consider it a hardship to set these servants free from your service, because they worked for you for six years—at a value double that of a paid worker" (CEB). The last regulation in the Law Code of Hammurabi reads, "If a slave should declare to his master,

'You are not my master,' he (the master) shall bring charge and proof against him that he is indeed his slave, and his master shall cut off his ear" (§282 [M. Roth 1997, 132]). The two laws just before the end make a clear distinction between native and foreign slaves: "If a man should purchase another man's slave or slave woman in a foreign country, and while he is traveling about within the (i.e., his own) country the owner of the slave or slave woman identifies his slave or slave woman—if they, the slave and slave woman, are natives of the country, their release shall be secured without any payment" (§280). According to §281, "if they are natives of another country," the buyer makes known how much he paid for them so that their owner can "redeem his slave or slave woman." Thus, the distinction between native versus foreign slaves was maintained elsewhere in the ancient Near East, not just in Israel.

Debt Slavery in Ancient Israel

The previous section cross-references cuneiform laws to comparable passages in the Pentateuch. Here we turn our attention to similarities and differences between the biblical collections.[1] There are three primary units of debt slavery regulations, one in each of the three main units of law in the Torah: Exodus 21:2–11 in the Book of the Covenant (Exod. 21–23), Leviticus 25:39–43 in the Holiness Code (Lev. 17–27), and Deuteronomy 15:12–18 in the Deuteronomic Code (Deut. 12–26) (see Chirichigno 1993). Much scholarly discussion has been devoted to the relationships between these regulations. There are important similarities between those in Exodus and those in Deuteronomy. In both passages the debt slave is a Hebrew who works for six

---

1. For a helpful treatment of ancient writing conventions, a critique of source criticism as it is applied today, and the relationships between the biblical law collections, see Berman 2017, 148–98. See also the detailed discussion of the biblical slave laws in this regard in Averbeck forthcoming.

years and goes out in the seventh year (Exod. 21:2; Deut. 15:12). Similarly, in both cases the debt slave can elect to stay with the master as a perpetual slave because things are going well for the debt slave in the master's household (Exod. 21:5–6; Deut. 15:16–17). In Exodus 21 this may be due not only to the good treatment of the slave by his master in general but also because the master has given him a wife and she has borne him children. This latter possibility is not considered in Deuteronomy 15, but the debt slave may nevertheless choose perpetual slavery with his master "because he loves you and your household, since he is well off with you" (v. 16).

Another related difference is the status of the female debt slave. In Deuteronomy 15 there is no mention of marriage; she is treated as an independent woman (vv. 12, 17b). The second part of the Exodus 21 regulations, however, is concerned with the female debt slave who is a daughter from another family, whom the master has "designated for himself" (v. 8) or "for his son" (v. 9) as a slave wife. Some would say that this daughter becomes a concubine, since there is no clear indication of a marriage and the relationship is dissolved by the daughter being redeemed out of the relationship, not divorced (v. 8) (Westbrook 2009a, 150–56). Others argue that it refers to legal marriage (Averbeck forthcoming). Two points in the text support this view: first, if she is appointed to the master's son, she gains the status of a "daughter" (v. 9), and second, the verb "takes" (another woman) in verse 10 is the normal verb for marriage. In any case, the regulation makes it clear that there are protections for the daughter and her family. If the master defaults on these protections, the female debt slave goes out free like a male debt slave (v. 11b; cf. v. 2).

Leviticus 25:39–43 is very different and is unique to Israel in the ancient Near East (see also debt slavery to a non-Israelite in vv. 47–54). The context is the regulations for the

Sabbatical Year and Jubilee. The year of release for the debt slave is the fiftieth year, the Year of Jubilee (v. 40), not the seventh year of his service as in Exodus 21:2 and Deuteronomy 15:12. There are different views on the relationship between this set of regulations and those in Exodus 21 and Deuteronomy 15 (see Averbeck forthcoming; Garroway 2014, 134–37, and the literature cited there). Without going into all the historical-critical issues and other proposals, we can note that it seems that the landed estate (i.e., the inheritance) of the family has been lost to creditors (vv. 41b, 47). Therefore, not just the father but the whole family goes into debt slavery (see the children mentioned in v. 41a). This would become their means of support, since the master who owned the debt would be responsible to provide for them while they worked for him during these years. The person who sold himself with his family, whether to a fellow Israelite or a non-Israelite, was to be treated as a hired worker or resident alien, not as a debt slave and, therefore, not subject to harsh treatment (vv. 39–40a, 42b–43, 53). Since the release is in the fiftieth year, they could theoretically serve as hired workers for as many as forty-nine years, in which case the father and perhaps others in the family may have already passed on. Yet it would not make sense to release them any sooner, since their means of support (i.e., their landed estate) would not revert to them until the Jubilee. In the meantime, through their labor the family paid off the debt they owed to their master.

In summary, Exodus 21:2–11 and Deuteronomy 15:12–18 refer to those who went into debt slavery to cover family debt. Presumably, they would or could return to their families after their six years of service. In other words, the family has not lost its landed estate but is in financial trouble due to debt and needs relief. One way to gain relief was to give one or more of the family members over into debt slavery for six years. This actually served as a "safety net" to avoid destitution. Leviticus 25:39–43 (with vv. 47–54) deals with the family that has actually become so destitute that it has lost the family landed estate. Here the situation is so dire that the whole family goes into debt service, but the family members are treated as hired laborers rather than debt slaves.

Chattel Slavery

As noted above, we cannot always tell from the ancient Near Eastern sources whether a person was a debt slave or a chattel slave or had some other status in a household context. In ancient Israel, chattel slaves could be gained through purchase from the nations around them, from the resident aliens who lived among them, and as prisoners of war or warfare refugees. Israelite families could pass them down from generation to generation (Lev. 25:44–46; Deut. 21:10, 14 [see more on these passages below]). Even earlier, we know that Abraham, the father of the Jewish people, had chattel slaves, some of whom were born in his house and others purchased from foreigners (Gen. 12:16; 17:23, 27), as did Isaac (Gen. 26:19), and Jacob (Gen. 30:43) (G. Haas 2003, 779–81). This was a regular and expected practice in Israel and the ancient Near East.

Chattel Slaves in the Ancient Near East

Many of the regulations already discussed above, in fact, are about chattel slaves, but they have application to the debt slave regulations in the Bible and so were treated in that context. As reflected in Laws of Eshnunna §40, chattel slaves were regularly purchased and treated as property (cf. Laws of Hammurabi §7; Seri 2011, 49–51): "If a man buys a slave, a slave woman, an ox, or any other purchase, but cannot establish the identity of the seller, it is he who is a thief" (Laws of Eshnunna §40 [M. Roth 1997, 65]).

Laws of Eshnunna §§49–52 deal with the common problem of stolen or runaway slaves,

including the prevention through a mark of slave status and other strategies (see the full discussion in Westbrook 2009b, 209–14 and also the remarks on Laws of Hammurabi §§ 226–27 above): "If a man should be seized with a stolen slave or a stolen slave woman, a slave shall lead a slave, a slave woman shall lead a slave woman" (Laws of Eshnunna §49 [M. Roth 1997, 66]). Although it is not certain, the second clause of this law most likely means that the one who stole the slave or slave woman must return the stolen one, plus another slave of equal value (M. Roth 1997, 70n26).

Laws of Eshnunna §50 says that "any person in a position of authority" who captures a fugitive slave or a stray ox or donkey must return them. If they keep them in their house for more than a month, they are to be charged with theft. The following two laws (Laws of Eshnunna §§51–52 [M. Roth 1997, 67]) indicate that "fetters, shackles, or a slave hairlock" were used as means of preventing the theft or escape of slaves. More severe preventions or punishments for runaway slaves include, for example, engraving the face with the mark "Fugitive, seize!" (Westbrook 2009b, 210). According to Laws of Hammurabi §§15–16, anyone who helps a slave escape or harbors a fugitive slave will suffer the penalty of death. Laws of Ur-Namma §24 involves a slave woman as a payment for some kind of injury. Deuteronomy 23:15–16 is relevant here (cited below). The ancient Israelites were not willing to return slaves who ran away because they had been mistreated.

Slave women sometimes were used as surrogates to bear children for men whose wives (apparently) were infertile or whose status did not allow it (e.g., the Babylonian *nadītu*, "a female temple dedicate" [Laws of Hammurabi §§144–47]). In the Bible, Hagar is an example of a chattel slave woman whom Sarai gave to Abram for this purpose (Gen. 16) (see the discussion of this practice in Averbeck 2011). Laws of Hammurabi §146 offers a relatively close parallel to Hagar's pride before Sarai in Genesis 16, which led to Sarai's harsh treatment of Hagar and her eventual flight from the home: "If a man marries a *nadītu*, and she gives a slave woman to her husband, and she (the slave) then bears children, after which that slave woman aspires to equal status with her mistress—because she bore children, her mistress will not sell her; she shall place upon her the slave-hairlock, and she shall reckon her with the slave women" (Laws of Hammurabi §146 [M. Roth 1997, 109]). Laws of Hammurabi §§170–71 are concerned with the inheritance rights of a slave woman's children (cf. Laws of Lipit-Ishtar §25–26 [M. Roth 1997, 31]). It depended upon whether or not their father proclaimed them "my children." Abram considered Ishmael, the son of Hagar, to be his heir until the Lord made it clear to him otherwise (Gen. 17:17–22).

Chattel Slaves in Ancient Israel

As noted above, the debt slave regulations in Leviticus 25:39–43 tell us that if an Israelite became so poor and destitute that he even lost his family landed estate, then he and his family could enter into "debt slavery" until the Year of Jubilee, when his landed estate would revert back to him. Moreover, they must not make him and his family "serve as slaves." They were to be treated "as hired or bound laborers." Furthermore, if an Israelite family lost its family estate to a non-Israelite who lived in the land, "As a laborer hired by the year they shall be under the alien's authority, who shall not, however, rule with harshness over them in your sight" (Lev. 25:53). These regulations demonstrate that the Israelites differentiated between debt slaves (fellow Israelites) and chattel slaves (foreigners). The last clause of Leviticus 25:53 shows us that, in contrast to debt slavery, chattel slavery could become harsh.

In the meantime, Leviticus 25:44–46 turns directly to the issue of chattel slaves. There must be no Israelite chattel slaves in ancient Israel, but ownership of foreign chattel slaves was allowed. Even non-Israelite chattel slaves, however, had certain protections, as we can discern from the injury regulations in Exodus 21:20–21, 26–27, 32 (see the discussion above).

As already noted above, chattel slaves sometimes were refugees from war (cf., regarding Egypt, Allam 2001, 294–95). Deuteronomy 21:10–14 deals with the female war refugee whose parents were killed in war. If an Israelite man found her attractive and wanted to take her as a wife, he may bring her into his house, provide for her recovery from the war, and allow her to mourn her parents for a month. After that he may take her for a wife. The law concludes, "But if you are not satisfied with her, you shall let her go free and not sell her for money. You must not treat her as a slave, since you have dishonored her" (v. 14). Furthermore, according to Deuteronomy 23:15–16, "Slaves who have escaped to you from their owners shall not be given back to them. They shall reside with you, in your midst, in any place they choose in any one of your towns, wherever they please; you shall not oppress them." The assumption was that if they ran away, it was because they were being maltreated, and they must not be sent back for more of the same.

Conclusions

Given the collection of passages surveyed above, we can draw a number of important conclusions about slavery in the Bible and the ancient Near East:

1. Both chattel slavery and debt slavery existed in the ancient world, but they represent two very different kinds of slavery.
2. We do not know much about the extent that chattel slaves could be taken from among one's own people in the rest of the ancient Near East, but in Israel it was not permissible.

3. Chattel slaves were not granted full human dignity, though there is some debate as to the extent and nature of their degraded status.

4. Biblical slave laws differed in some degree from those of the rest of the ancient Near East, but institutionally they were very similar.

5. The institution of ancient slavery was not supplied the way that it was in the New World institution, though both could be characterized by dehumanization.

6. The biblical provisions are characterized by differences among themselves, and various explanations might be given for that. Suggestions range from different sources, to different social contexts over time, to different wisdom perspectives. The explanation of the biblical slave laws offered above contends that the regulations in the Pentateuch are consistent within and between one another.

7. The biblical provisions are not designed to provide for an ideal society, but rather to provide wisdom for Israel to live in covenant relationship to Yahweh in their time and place. The Old Testament law has fine ideals within it (e.g., the Ten Commandments, the two great commandments that Jesus drew upon, and much more), but the regulations discussed here, and many others, are meant to apply these ideals in realistic ways in the world of ancient Israel.

56

The Local Economies of Ancient Israel

Peter Altmann

Overview

Reflections on economics—the structure or conditions of the process or system by which goods and services are produced, sold, and bought in a country, area, or period—only emerged recently within biblical studies specifically and ancient Near Eastern studies as a whole. Frankly, the Bible and other records from the ancient world do not allow for precise measurement of gross national product, inflation, or savings rates—typically the type of indicators important for modern economists. This situation renders understanding of the economies of ancient Israel elusive. In any case, just as in modern society, general approaches to economics remain controversial because central philosophical, theological, and political questions about the nature of humans and societies undergird every attempt to understand the inner workings of any economy: Are individuals motivated, at their core, by profit and personal gain (capitalism [see, in biblical studies, Guillaume 2012)? Are economic conflicts the central struggle of human nature (Marxism [see Boer 2015])?

However, investigating *local economies* proves more straightforward for the ancient world as a whole and ancient Israel in particular. Generally speaking, regardless of the changes in religion and politics on the larger imperial and national stages, most people in ancient Israel existed in worlds defined primarily by their local environment: changes in empires and kings had less effect on the way these people carried out the day-to-day tasks required for providing the food and other basic necessities for existence.

The dominant way of viewing economics in modern society necessitates several initial framing observations for a look at ancient Israel. First, the notion of "economics" as a separate sphere of society did not exist during the biblical period. The lack of a separate economic sphere does not, however, indicate the absence of economic questions and concerns. Considerations of the family, agriculture, temple and religion, and politics all included aspects often seen as economic in the modern world. Second, except for the tail end of the Old Testament historical period, which is important for a small number of texts, the Old Testament reflects a time before the rise of coins. Individuals and societies hardly measured wealth in terms of countable pieces of money. Especially unique gifts laden with status allowed families and individuals to demonstrate their riches.

A third observation concerns the data available for talking about ancient Israel's economies. There are several very different kinds of data: (1) archaeological finds lay out the kinds of dwellings and possessions used by ancient Israel, (2) extrabiblical texts—especially contracts or records of economic transactions—can reveal actual economic dealings, and (3) biblical texts provide particular perspectives on the ways that *some* in the communities of ancient Israel and Judah experienced or imagined the handling of economic issues.

Fourth, while texts like Deuteronomy 8:7–10 depict the land of Israel as an idyllic place with a rich agricultural and mineral landscape in which the Israelites would thrive so long as they obeyed God's commandments, this description veils the stark diversity within the topography of Israel. Because the ancient Israelites and Judahites largely lived out their days in relatively small geographic settings, the topography and climate of their specific environments made all the difference in their economic realities. There was not *one* Israelite economy; rather, there was a variety of local *economies*.

The most prominent of these settings is the small village or homestead located in the hill country of Israel. The hill country regions offered terrain and climate suited to cultivation of the important products of wine and olive oil. Within this setting, sufficient grain production presented a recurring annual challenge. On the other hand, the cultivation of vineyards and olive tree groves required longer-term thinking because families were not able to benefit from the fruit of the harvest for at least several years (much longer in the case of olive trees). As a result, the quintessential Israelite household was necessarily bound up both in a yearly push for a sufficient grain harvest, while also maintaining strong practical ties with former and forthcoming generations in the cultivation of grapes, olives, and other products. The archaeological remains of these villages show that little difference in socioeconomic status existed: households depended greatly on one another for survival, and this spreading of the risk of failed crops regularly led to a strong communal dynamic (see Houston 2008, 21).

Another important kind of local economy was the more arid experience in the southern Negev, suitable mostly just for herding goats and sheep (cattle were kept more often for pulling plows). However, herders and more sedentary planters—in more amenable environments—tended to rely on one another to a considerable degree (and were often interrelated). Especially from the Neo-Assyrian period (eighth century BCE, the time of the divided monarchy in the biblical narrative) onward, Arabian trade caravans moved across this region to the Mediterranean coast. As a result, local settlements engaged in some trade with outside groups.

Very few places in ancient Israel can be considered "urban" in any sense, though Jerusalem and Samaria of the preexilic period highlands and some seaboard locations such as Ashkelon, Dor, or Gaza consisted of enough inhabitants and prominence to develop some urban dynamics. Each of these locations possessed some special dynamics that gave rise to its development: Samaria and Jerusalem were, of course, capital cities (Jerusalem with a very important sanctuary), while Ashkelon, Dor, and Gaza—Philistine cities—were among the leading ports and for this reason had a more metropolitan dynamic. Gaza even grew to such importance during the postexilic period as a center of trade with spices from Arabia and goods from Egypt (for which Gaza served as the gateway) and from the Mediterranean that the Greek historian Herodotus compares Gaza's size to the large city of Sardis (3.5).

The fertile lowlands, called the Shephelah, between the coast and the Judean and Ephraimite (i.e., northern "Israelite" during the divided monarchy) highlands as well as the Jezreel Valley in the north were the prime locations for growing grain and other crops. However, they were also borderlands, with the Philistines to the west or the Aramaeans to the north. This setting endangered their agricultural stability because of changing political affiliations, but their desirability also contributed to their flourishing. For example, the Shephelah close to Ashkelon could engage in trade of grain or other agricultural products for merchandise that came from elsewhere in the Mediterranean (Master 2003).

Finally, the economies of the exilic communities of Jews in Babylonia and Egypt exhibited some different dynamics, given their close interactions with foreign empires and peoples. After the destruction of Jerusalem by the Babylonians in 587/586 BCE, much of the more urban centers of Judah declined considerably. While there is debate over the extent of the decline of the more rural areas of Judah and the territory just to the north in Benjamin, there is no doubt that a considerable portion of Judahites, especially the elite, went into exile in both the city and the rural agricultural regions of Babylonia. Their existence in Babylonia was quite varied. Some Judean exiles worked as royal merchants (Astola 2017) and imperial bureaucrats in the sixth century (Y. Bloch 2014). This influence displays, at minimum, the kinds of economic experiences available to some of the Judean community in exile.

Other records (see Pearce 2006, 400) refer to a town in Babylonia called āl-Yāhūda, meaning "the city of Judah," reflecting many of its inhabitants' origin. These texts date no later than 572 BCE, within several decades of the conquest of Judah and destruction of Jerusalem. This evidence underscores "ethnic" communities for the Jews (cf. Ezra 8:17; Jer. 29:1, 25).

The largest number of Jewish names in Babylonia have arisen in connection with the archive of the Murashu "firm," a family-controlled commercial house in the region of Nippur, 100 miles (160 km) southeast of Baghdad from around 450 BCE (Stolper 1985). The Neo-Babylonian and especially later Persian authorities issued grants of land to ethnic and occupational groups; in return, these groups provided soldiers, labor, and taxes. The Jewish farmers in the records have small farms, and they contracted their grain to the Murashus in order to acquire silver to pay royal taxes or to pay for the expenses of a soldier. It appears that many of the farmers ended up heavily indebted. Therefore, the experiences of the Jews in exile proved quite diverse: some prospered, while others struggled considerably.[1]

Family/Household

As noted above, people in ancient Israel and most of the surrounding areas of the Old Testament period lived out the majority of their days in small, rural villages or homesteads, perhaps similar to the depiction in the book of Ruth. In terms of economic production and consumption, homesteads and villages were largely self-sufficient. They also would have delivered a portion of their agricultural produce to the regional and national rulers and sanctuaries.

In these rural settings, an economic premium existed on land and on children. Secure existence required owning one's own land, a concern appearing throughout the Old Testament. The Pentateuch contains laws regulating inheritance (also for daughters [see Num. 27]) and sale of land necessitated by poverty (Lev. 25).[2] Prophets rail against economic

---

1. One should also note the rise of some former royal and elite members of the exiles as reflected in 2 Kings 25:27–30.

2. Note the different approach taken to city dwellings in Lev. 25:29–30.

gain involving acquisition of large landholdings (Isa. 5:8–10; Mic. 2:2) because such arrangements made families dependent on these larger landowners as benefactors. The repeated concern for the widow, fatherless, and alien in Deuteronomy (esp. 14:28–29; 26:1–11) grows out of the lack of security inherent to the lives of these groups of people, given their tenuous connections to their own plot of land (not having either land or perhaps the ability to work their land).

In addition, small amounts of trade took place, mostly for luxury goods or perhaps some items that were specialties of certain households (e.g., pottery as seen in the mention of the "potter's house" in Jer. 18, and the mention of specific families of linen workers and potters in 1 Chron. 4:21–23). Thus, some exchange took place between households, most of it probably in reciprocity, exchanging with kin or neighbors based on the special abilities of each or particular needs for goods and help with tasks at various times during the year (e.g., helping to reap grain harvests in one another's plots).[3] Sometimes exchange occurred in a less symbiotic manner, such as cases mentioned in Amos 2:6–8.

Marriage and Dowries

Given the generally self-sufficient nature of families or households, the choice of marriage partners included significant economic aspects. Within the Bible, the economic factors for marriages are seen in an unnamed man's rejection of Ruth as a marriage partner in Ruth 4:6 because he fears damaging his inheritance. Furthermore, Genesis 24:30 reports that Laban notices his sister Rebekah's new gold nose ring and bracelets, as well as further costly jewelry given to the family (Gen. 24:53). These repeated mentions of valuables suggest the importance of demonstrating wealth when seeking a partner.

Furthermore, extrabiblical records of marriage contracts from the Jewish community of Elephantine in southern Egypt during the Persian period (fifth and fourth centuries) show how marriages were regulated such that a bride could bring wealth into the relationship, and that in the case of a divorce, she had the legal right to take her wealth with her (see S. Adams 2014, 29–39). The degree to which the same practices took place in preexilic Israel and Judah and postexilic Yehud is unknown, though this data on another Jewish community (which did have some interaction with the homeland) remains suggestive.

Wage Labor

Because the majority of the population lived and worked within local homestead and village settings, there was little labor conducted for wages. Beginning under the Neo-Assyrians (eighth century BCE), however, there are records in Mesopotamia of work being paid for in barley, dates, or silver. Most prominent are specialized occupations, such as sailors and smiths (K. Radner 2007, 189–91). Later, under the Babylonians in the sixth century, larger numbers of workers received payment for their work on large imperial and temple projects (e.g., Nebuchadnezzar's palace in Babylon [see Beaulieu 2005]).[4] Generally speaking, land was in abundance and labor scarce, which could have increased wages.[5]

In the Bible, hired laborers generally represent those who have lost their land. They are, therefore, in a precarious situation because they are dependent on others to reward them

---

3. M. Miller 2015, 6–7, terms such economic interaction dyadic exchange, which "consists of direct trade between equals and occurs where social stratification is minimal."

4. Some wages are even regulated much earlier—for instance, in the Law Code of Hammurabi.

5. One should be cautious before assuming such "free market" logic, however. Perhaps other concerns were more important for the determination of wages.

for their work. As a result, Deuteronomy 24:14–15 specifies that a laborer be paid by the end of the workday.

Debt

The Old Testament and texts from surrounding cultures indicate that various types of loans existed in the ancient Near East. Evidence from Babylonia shows that grain and silver were the primary forms taken by loans, with the "ideal" interest on silver loans at 20 percent and on grain at 33 percent, though rates could vary considerably (see Hudson 2000). Generally speaking, silver was loaned for merchant endeavors, while farmers whose harvest had failed required loans of grain (Jursa 2010, 628–29).

A number of biblical texts as well as the late seventh-century Mesad Hashavyahu Inscription from near Ashdod witness to labor for working off debts. Deuteronomy 24:10–13, 17 (cf. Exod. 22:25–27) comments on respecting the dire situation of the poor by giving them their wages each day and giving back items held as security, such as a coat, so that persons in this situation could cover themselves at night.

Deuteronomy 23:20 makes this difference between consumption and commercial loans explicit, naming the difference between "your brother" and "foreigners" (*nokri*). The permission to charge interest to the *nokri* likely arises from their character as those who did not reside in the region and who were present in the capacity of traveling merchants.

Also noteworthy are the numerous warnings against securing a loan for someone else in Proverbs 17:18; 20:16; 22:26; 27:13. Each of these verses underlines hazards associated with providing surety for someone else's loan. These wisdom sayings fit broadly into the ancient Israelite context by focusing on the security of one's household without taking any unnecessary risk. Commercial ventures or otherwise constructing deep economic ties outside the local homestead and village were not priorities.

However, as both Leviticus 25 and Nehemiah 5 demonstrate, one was to go to any lengths possible to secure the release of family members from debt and debt bondage. The narrative of Nehemiah 5:1–13 depicts a time when local family relations no longer sufficed to ensure the abilities of families to remain financially solvent. This text provides perhaps the deepest insight into the economic life of rural families in postexilic Yehud (the name for the Babylonian, then Persian, province). These families experienced pressure from poor harvests, the large number of children, and royal taxes, so they had to borrow from their richer local compatriots. Those borrowing then fell behind on repayment so that their children were sold into debt slavery. In the surrounding cultures, the sale of children into debt slavery was uncommon, taking place only under dire circumstances such as famine (as in Neh. 5) (see Oppenheim 1955).

Offerings, Tithes, and Sanctuaries

It is possible to overlook the important economic role played by the religious sphere in ancient Israel and Judah. Many religious practices included trips to a regional or national sanctuary (e.g., Jerusalem, Bethel, Shiloh, Dan). These pilgrimages consisted in large part of communal feasts, likely the most extravagant meals consumed by the majority of families the whole year. The considerable economic expenditures at these events gave rise to a focus of wealth at sanctuaries: priests and Levites could eat the wealth of the land on a more regular basis (cf. 1 Sam. 2:13–16; Lev. 1–7; but note also the precarious situation of the temple personnel described in Neh. 13:4–9). Given the focus on communal feasting, the ingredients of the meals constituted the primary gifts brought to the sanctuaries as offerings and tithes. While comparison with the depictions of the Second Temple at the time of Jesus (John 2:14) should not be overdone, some purchasing of desirable animals, wine, and other products for the feasts was envisioned (Deut. 14:24–26).

War as an Economic Theme

One of the primary avenues to economic progress in the ancient world consisted of conquering and taking booty from opposing polities. Such an endeavor appears in the biblical text in 1 Kings 14:25–26, where Pharaoh Shishak (Sheshonq in Egyptian texts) attacks Rehoboam and Judah, pillaging the royal treasury and gold shields (largely valuable in terms of the status they suggest). The details in Judges 5:29–30 on the dividing of spoils suggest how individual soldiers could profit from taking part in military campaigns. On the other hand, the Israelites complain in Judges 6:6 because the Midianites had impoverished them through repeated raids. Buying off an invading army could carry consequences for the dispersed villages and hamlets as well, seen in a case like 2 Kings 15:19–20, where King Menahem of Israel taxes every wealthy person fifty shekels to induce Tiglath-Pileser, king of Assyria, to withdraw his army.

Taxes and Tribute

In addition to war booty, taxes of some sort to local authorities and tribute to foreign empires were a regular part of Israelite life throughout most eras. At times this could be envisioned as a tithe of agricultural yields (cf. 1 Sam. 8:15, 17), but labor appears to have been an even more important commodity than harvests, especially when viewed in light of foreign empires (1 Sam. 8:12–13, 16–17) (see Guillaume 2012, 42, 79). For example, rulers desired workers to construct fortifications, canals as waterways, and palaces.

Money and Coinage

Coinage as a regular means of payment arose in Greek polities in the sixth century BCE. It did not dominate in ancient Israel in the same way that it did in Greece until after Alexander's conquests in 333 BCE. This absence does not mean that trade did not exist, nor that "money" was not used. Much of this is a matter of definition. Weighed silver and other goods functioned as "money." Furthermore, wages or prices could be given in silver (weighed in shekels) or in amounts of other products, often barley or dates in Babylonia. However, in Mesopotamia, beginning no later than the Neo-Babylonian and the early Achaemenid period, silver was used for quite small transactions. In Israel, silver appears as a form of money (*kesep*, meaning "silver," is in fact often translated as "money" in English translations [e.g., Gen. 17:12–13; 1 Kings 21], but this may lead to anachronistic conceptions) throughout the Old Testament, though only several small stashes of silver coins have been found dating prior to the slow rise of coins in Israel during the fifth and fourth centuries BCE.

While international trade was abundant along the Mediterranean coast in the Philistine cities (dominated by the Phoenicians in the postexilic period), there are only small hints of regional trade appearing in Jerusalem and in Yehud in the postexilic period. Nehemiah 13:15–22 tells of people of Judah bringing agricultural goods to Jerusalem to sell on the Sabbath, as well as Tyrians selling fish. These fish were from outside the local area, thus representing something of a delicacy, though widely available.

Conclusion

While no *single* Israelite economy existed, the baseline for the economic existence of Israelites in the Old Testament period was far and away agricultural subsistence in small farming homesteads or villages. Households generally provided for their own needs and wants, though some minimal trading occurred especially between neighbors. Economic change did come as a result of military conquest, such as the Assyrian and Babylonian invasions, which led to both decimation in Israel and the founding of exilic communities in Mesopotamia (and elsewhere). Through both these developments and the presence of trading centers along the Philistine coast, ancient Israel at first intermittently and then slowly became connected to the wider economies of the various empires (Egypt, Assyria, Babylon, Persia, Greece), which brought with them extra burdens in the form of tax and tributes as well as technologies and economic conceptions such as coinage.

57

Metallurgy in the World of the Bible

Brady Liss and Thomas E. Levy

Introduction

Since the inception of metallurgy, metals rapidly developed into a basic component of human experience and lifeway (C. S. Smith 1974), and this was no less true during biblical times. Metals, in all their applications, were fully integrated into the human cultural system, including but not limited to subsistence practices, economy, sociopolitical organization, and religion/ritual. This understanding is reiterated by the frequent references to metals and metallurgy in the Hebrew Bible (Old Testament). Moreover, the association of metals with prominent events in this holy text corroborates their significance (see below). However, as with any ancient text, one should evaluate the relationship between the narrative and archaeological records to achieve a deeper historical understanding (Levy 2010a). In other words, does the archaeological record of the biblical world reflect the depictions and uses of metals as they appear in the text, and how best do we test for this?

This short chapter explores the archaeological record of metallurgy in the Holy Land primarily from the perspective of ancient copper production based on the joint University of California, San Diego / Department of Antiquities of Jordan Iron Age excavations in the copper-abundant Faynan region of southern Jordan (Levy, Ben-Yosef, and Najjar 2014; Levy, Najjar, and Ben-Yosef 2014). For the purposes of this chapter, the "biblical world" is treated geographically as what is commonly referred to as the Holy Land (i.e., Israel, the Palestinian territories, Jordan, southern Syria and Lebanon, and the Sinai Peninsula), and it is chronologically focused on the Late Bronze and Iron Ages (ca. 1550–586 BCE). Through the pragmatic lens and cyber-archaeology methodology (the marriage of archaeology with the natural sciences, computer science, and engineering [see Levy 2013]), the excavation results from Khirbat en-Nahas (Levy et al. 2014), the largest Iron Age copper-smelting center in the southern Levant, provide an unparalleled view of metallurgy in the world of the Bible.

Metals in the Biblical Text

The Hebrew Bible contains numerous references to metals (including copper/bronze, iron, gold, silver, tin, and lead) in varying forms and contexts. Copper, the focus of this chapter, raises a translational issue because the Hebrew word *nehoshet* does not distinguish between copper and bronze (Hummel 2000, 278); however, both metals inherently require metallic copper (as bronze is an alloy of copper and typically tin). As such, mention of both copper and/or bronze in the biblical narrative should be considered when investigating the role and importance of copper; the only thing that is potentially lost in this formulation is a simplification of a society's technological engagement with bronze. Beyond simply mentioning metals, the textual context of these references can also be indicative of sociocultural perceptions toward the material, as will be seen. In what follows, a selection of lines from the biblical text dealing with copper/bronze that highlight the representation and significance of the metal are presented.

The importance of copper/bronze in the biblical sphere is made immediately apparent in the construction of the tabernacle and Moses's copper serpent (Exod. 26–36; Num. 21:9). In both contexts (typically dated to the end of the Late Bronze Age), copper is directly associated with emblematic symbols of the ancient Israelites. Moreover, in the case of the tabernacle, the ability and knowledge to produce metal is treated as a "divine spirit" endowed to its builder, Bezalel (Exod. 31:2–3). The significance of accessible copper (and other metals) is reiterated in the description of the Promised Land. In detailing the "good land," the author of Deuteronomy emphasizes the availability of raw metals, "a land whose stones are iron and from whose hills you may mine copper" (Deut. 8:7–9). Frequently cited mentions of copper and bronze in the biblical narrative are related to the construction of Solomon's temple in the Iron Age. Bronze plays a predominant role in the building process worthy of particular attention from skilled artisans. "King Solomon invited and received Hiram from Tyre . . . he was full of skill, intelligence,

and knowledge in working bronze" (1 Kings 7:13–14). The passage goes on to describe the numerous temple trappings created in bronze, including columns, capitals, tanks, and stands (7:15–51): "all these vessels that Hiram made for King Solomon for the house of the LORD were of burnished bronze" (7:45). Together, these mentions of copper and their association with paramount biblical places/features (the tabernacle, the Promised Land, and Solomon's temple) indicate the material's significance and availability in the biblical world. Recently, some scholars have suggested that during the Iron Age the Israelite god Yahweh was a god who evolved in relation to the control of pyro-technology and metallurgy, reiterating the intimacy between metals and the biblical narrative (Amzallag 2018, 127).

Some technological aspects of metallurgy including specific processes and knowledge are also addressed in the Hebrew Bible. The book of Job provides insight concerning mining activities and smelting where metals are listed among other "precious" materials extracted from the earth: "copper is smelted from ore. . . . They open shafts in a valley away from human habitation. . . . They put their hand to the flinty rock, and overturn mountains by the roots. They cut out channels in the rocks, and their eyes see every precious thing" (Job 28:2, 4, 9–10). The author of Job displays a clear familiarity with the early stages of copper production: the mining of ores and extraction of metal through smelting. In addition, the production of copper/bronze objects is briefly described during the furnishing of Solomon's temple: "In the plain of the Jordan the king cast them, in the clay ground between Succoth and Zarethan" (1 Kings 7:46). The casting process is also mentioned in the creation of the golden calf by Aaron, perhaps in this case using a clay mold (Exod. 32:3–4). Collectively, these lines provide a generalized overview of the copper production workflow: mining, smelting, and casting.

The technological practices and equipment of metal production are also frequently adopted for metaphorical purposes (see Amzallag 2018 and citations there for in-depth discussions). These metaphors are not always in direct reference to copper/bronze, and some date to the end of or slightly later than the Iron Age; however, their usage reiterates the important role of metallurgy in the biblical world. In one such example from Ezekiel, Israel is portrayed as a metal requiring purification by fire:

> the house of Israel has become dross [slag][1] to me; all of them, silver, bronze, tin, iron, and lead. In the smelter they have become dross. . . . As one gathers silver, bronze, iron, lead, and tin into a smelter, to blow the fire upon them in order to melt them; so I will gather you in my anger and in my wrath, and I will put you in [the fire] and melt you. I will gather you and blow upon you with the fire of my wrath, and you shall be melted within it. As silver is melted in a smelter, so you shall be melted in it. (Ezek. 22:18–22)

While metaphorical in nature, this selection also displays a technical knowledge of metallurgy by referring to smelting/refining metal and the need to blow air into the fire (see also the mention of bellows in Jer. 6:28–29). Isaiah also speaks of metal smelting and refining figuratively, again in reference to the purification of Israel: "I will turn my hand against you; I will smelt away your dross as with lye and remove all your alloy"; "See, I have refined you, but not like silver; I have tested you in the furnace of adversity" (Isa. 1:25; 48:10). In the latter case, a metallurgical furnace also serves a metaphorical purpose. Furnaces often appear in the text for this function, typically to indicate a transformation of the Israelites (McNutt 1990, 265).[2] For example, Egypt is repeatedly

likened to an iron furnace from which the Israelites were freed during the exodus (Deut. 4:20; 1 Kings 8:51; Jer. 11:4).

As shown, both metals and metallurgical tools/techniques are frequently referenced in the biblical narrative. From the above overview, it is apparent that metals and metallurgy play a substantial role in the world and text of the Hebrew Bible. Unfortunately, the discussed biblical symbols no longer exist in the archaeological record, or, in the case of Solomon's temple, potential archaeological investigations are restricted by current political and religious circumstances. However, archaeologists can still pursue the origins of this biblical copper. It is with starting points like this in mind that biblical archaeologists set out to discover confluences between the text and the archaeological record.

The "Golden Age" of Biblical Archaeology and the Early Explorations by Nelson Glueck

As director of the American School of Oriental Research (now the W. F. Albright Institute of Archaeological Research) during the "golden age" of biblical archaeology following World War I, Nelson Glueck (1934a; 1934b; 1935; 1939) headed extensive, systematic surveys of the Transjordan region in pursuit of archaeological substantiations of the biblical narrative (for a review of "biblical archaeology," see ch. 5 above). During his surveys of the Wadi Arabah (stretching between the southern tip of the Dead Sea and the Gulf of Aqaba) and the southern Negev desert of modern Israel, Glueck (1935) detailed the presence of significant archaeological remains in immediate proximity to abundant copper ores in two regions, Faynan and Timna.[3] In

---

1. Slag is a solidified waste by-product of the smelting process.

2. Also see McNutt 1990 for a thorough discussion of iron in the Hebrew Bible.

3. Due to the concise nature of this chapter, Timna will not be addressed, but recent research in the region makes a significant contribution to the discussion of copper production in the biblical world that should be considered. See Ben-Yosef et al. 2012; Ben-Yosef 2010.

both regions, the surface was populated with mining and smelting sites (identifiable by massive mounds of black copper slag) established to exploit the local ores. Faynan, located approximately 30 km south of the Dead Sea, is within the biblically recognized territory of the Edomites (Deut. 2:8; Num. 20:16; 34:3; Josh. 15:1). Glueck (1935, 20–35) investigated the major copper production sites of the area, including Khirbat en-Nahas, Khirbat al-Jariya, and Khirbat al-Ghuwayba, and based on ceramic typology, he attributed these sites to the Early Iron Age. Along with his chronological assessments, Glueck (1940, 50–88; 1935, 28, 50) posited that King Solomon (with an Edomite workforce) was the paramount controller of copper exports from Faynan, "the first great copper king," a point of scholarly intrigue and contention (cf. Muhly 1987). Glueck's conclusions directly positioned Faynan and its rich history of copper smelting in the biblical world. Yet, it would be over sixty years before his results could be properly tested through excavation.

Historical Biblical Archaeology

Before delving into modern excavations and their insight on biblical metallurgy, we must clarify the theoretical approach and perspective. In 2010, one of the present authors (Levy 2010a; 2010b, 9) made a call for a pragmatic approach in biblical archaeology to foster objectivity in investigating historical texts and the archaeological record (i.e., to help "bridge the gap" between biblical minimalists and maximalists). This "new pragmatism" is not burdened by ideology and proposes using innovative methods with cooperation between different scholarly communities to advance practical and action-oriented research concerned with solving concrete problems (Levy 2010b, 9). To accomplish this goal, the primary aim of the field should be theory- and model-testing based on the acquisition of robust data

sets (Levy 2010b, 11). Furthermore, modern advancements in methods and technologies (e.g., radiocarbon dating, geographic information systems, scientific techniques, etc.) must be harnessed in the exploration of the historical context concerning the biblical text (Levy 2010b, 11). In utilizing advanced methodologies to collect comprehensive data sets, the new pragmatism drives new theoretical approaches and models (e.g., see Levy and Higham 2005 for an example of using radiocarbon dating to develop new models/theories concerning historical biblical archaeology) (Levy 2010b, 11). In sum, a pragmatic approach to biblical archaeology employs innovative methods in archaeology to collect large data sets that can, in turn, enable theoretical and model development concerning the relationship between the textual and archaeological records, free of ideological encumbrances. This call for pragmatism has been largely taken up by the Edom Lowlands Regional Archaeology Project in its investigation of ancient copper production in Faynan using a pioneering cyber-archaeology workflow and on-site digital archaeology.

The Edom Lowlands Regional Archaeology Project

Following the paramount work of Glueck with his biblical assertions, Faynan secured a place in the scholarly discourse; however, the focus of archaeological research shifted to the hilltops above Faynan to the east—the Edomite plateau. In the 1960s, Crystal Bennett (1966; 1977; 1983) set out to test Glueck's identification of biblical sites in the highlands of Edom. Based on her excavations at Umm el-Biyara, Tawilan, and Buseirah, Faynan and its copper industry were chronologically shifted away from Glueck's conclusions to the Late Iron Age, the eighth to sixth centuries BCE, and attributed to Assyrian hegemony (primarily based on the correlation between the Qos-Gabr seal discovered at Umm el-Biyara and Assyrian annals)

(Bienkowski 1995, 44). However, Faynan and the copper-rich lowlands remained largely untouched by archaeological investigations. Beginning in the 1980s, Faynan and the surrounding areas were the subject of several surveys to build on Glueck's results (B. MacDonald 1992; B. MacDonald et al. 2004; Hauptmann 2007; G. Barker, Gilbertson, and Mattingly 2007). Together, these modern projects surveyed much of the Faynan landscape and emphasized the metallurgical nature of the archaeological record, but they lacked the deep time perspective of stratigraphic excavation.

In 1997 Thomas E. Levy, of the University of California, San Diego, initiated the Jabal Hamrat Fidan Project in partnership with Mohammad Najjar of the Department of Antiquities of Jordan and Russell Adams to facilitate archaeological research in Faynan (Levy, Adams, and Shafiq 1999). Using a combination of systematic survey and stratigraphic excavation, the project explored the relationship between copper metallurgy and social, economic, and political development (Levy, Adams, and Najjar 2001, 442). Initially focused on the pre-pottery Neolithic and Early Bronze Ages, the project transitioned toward an Iron Age concentration as the Edom Lowlands Regional Archaeology Project (ELRAP), which combines anthropological archaeology and cyber-archaeology methodologies to discern the nuances between technology (i.e., industrial-scale copper smelting) and sociopolitical evolutions in Faynan. Ongoing archaeological expeditions have excavated/surveyed major Iron Age copper smelting and mining sites throughout the region (see Ben-Yosef, Najjar, and Levy 2014 for a complete review). Previous excavations have amassed a substantial collection of thousands of georeferenced artifacts (over six tons of material culture stored at the University of California, San Diego—the largest archaeometallurgical assemblage for the Iron Age Levant) for reconstructing ancient technology (Ben-Yosef and Levy 2014, 887–92, 953).

From this data set, the ELRAP fostered the most complete understanding of the profound relationship between copper production and social transformations in Faynan.

Furthermore, through an intensive absolute dating methodology (including radiocarbon and geomagnetic archaeointensity) employed at all excavated sites, the ELRAP facilitated a paradigmatic shift in the accepted chronology by anchoring copper production in the early phases of the Iron Age in line with Glueck's ceramic analysis (see below) (Levy et al. 2008). Now, rather than an outgrowth of Assyrian hegemony in the Late Iron Age as previously believed, copper production could be considered an integral factor of the sociopolitical development of the biblical Edomites in the Early Iron Age (Levy et al. 2004, 877). The centerpiece for the ELRAP's reshaping of the significance of Early Iron Age copper production was Khirbat en-Nahas.

Khirbat en-Nahas and the Faynan Industrial Landscape

As mentioned above, Khirbat en-Nahas is the largest (ca. ten hectares or twenty-five acres) Iron Age copper-smelting center in the southern Levant, the "jewel in the crown" of the industrial landscape of Faynan (fig. 57.1) (Levy, Ben-Yosef, and Najjar 2012, 199). Among the architectural remains of over one hundred buildings, including a formidable 73 × 73 meter fortress, slag mounds cover much of the surface of the site (an estimated 50,000–60,000 tons of slag) (Levy et al. 2014, 89; Hauptmann 2007, 127). Between 2002 and 2009, the ELRAP led three excavation seasons at Khirbat en-Nahas (Levy et al. 2014). In total, seven excavation areas were opened, highlighting both architectural and metallurgical contexts (only two will be addressed below; see Levy et al. 2014 for a full discussion of all areas). Through employing a cyber-archaeological workflow, the excavations at Khirbat en-Nahas provide a cornerstone for

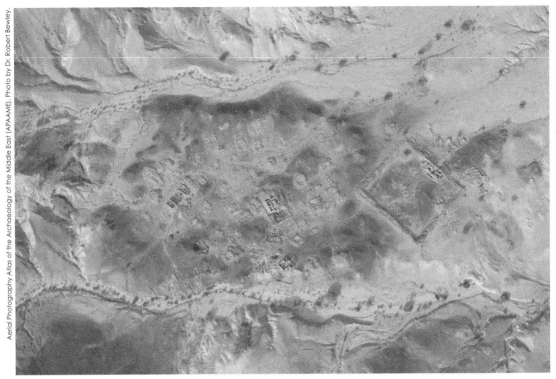

Aerial Photography Atlas of the Archaeology of the Middle East (APAAME). Photo by Dr. Robert Bewley.

Fig. 57.1. Aerial photograph of Khirbat en-Nahas. Note the 73 × 73 meter fortress on the right side of the photo and the distribution of black slag mounds across the site.

elucidating the chronology and context of ancient copper production in the Iron Age Levant.

During the 2002 and 2006 seasons, the four-chamber gatehouse (Area A) attached to the large fortress at Khirbat en-Nahas was the primary focus of excavations (Levy et al. 2014, 93–122). The perimeter of the gatehouse was initially discerned before excavating three of the four guardhouses and the alley running between them (Levy et al. 2014, 93–96). The excavations revealed three main occupation phases with varying functions; initially serving a military purpose, it subsequently transitioned to a domestic function with an associated architectural restructuring that was followed by a copper production phase (Levy et al. 2014, 119–20). A critical component of the excavation was the collection of stratigraphically controlled radiocarbon dates. In total, a suite of twenty-eight radiocarbon dates positioned the gatehouse construction chronologically.

Following further refinement through Bayesian statistics, the fortress was securely dated to the tenth through ninth centuries BCE (Levy et al. 2014, 113–20). These new absolute dates called for a reevaluation concerning the sociopolitical development of Faynan (as discussed above); however, the connection between the considerable architecture of the fortress and industrial copper smelting required further examination.

To explore the diachronic development of copper production at Khirbat en-Nahas, a systematic probe was excavated into one of the large slag mounds on the site's surface (Area M) over the course of the 2002 and 2006 seasons (Levy et al. 2014, 131–51; 2008). The project, the first of its kind in Jordan, excavated five major metallurgical horizons in the slag mound above the bedrock (Levy et al. 2014, 147). To temporally arrange production, excavations were supplemented with meticulous radiocarbon and archaeomagnetism sampling

Fig. 57.2. A shaft mine in the Wadi Khalid in Faynan. Two of these shafts date to the Iron Age, and the unique third shaft was built in Roman times—a prospection shaft (Hauptmann 2007, 121).

(Levy et al. 2014, 147–50). The main phases of copper production, identifiable by substantial accumulations of metallurgical debris (slag, furnace fragments, tuyere pipes, etc.), were assigned to the twelfth to eleventh centuries and tenth to ninth centuries BCE (Levy et al. 2014, 150–51; 2008). At the bottom of the sounding (approximately 6.5 meters in depth) and directly above bedrock, two installations and a thin accumulation of crushed slag represented the earliest occupation at Khirbat en-Nahas (Levy et al. 2014, 146, 151). Radiocarbon dates from this initial layer produced dates from the fourteenth and thirteenth centuries BCE of the Late Bronze Age (Levy et al. 2014, 151). Thus, the slag mound excavation yielded a complete history of copper production during the occupational history of Khirbat en-Nahas. The earliest metal production is associated with the last phases of the Late Bronze Age, and smelting reached an industrial scale in the Early Iron Age.

Mining sites throughout Faynan contribute another essential aspect of the Iron Age industrial landscape (Levy et al. 2003; Knabb et al. 2014; Hauptmann 2007; Weisgerber 2003). While methods and evidence of mining can take a variety of forms, deep mining in the Iron Age (to reach levels untouched by previous mining endeavors) often used a twin shaft methodology—one shaft for the miner and another for bringing the ore to the surface (fig. 57.2) (Weisgerber 2003, 84–85; Hauptmann 2007, 120–21). Several surveys of Faynan have discovered shaft-mining sites throughout the region, including locations in close proximity to major smelting sites such as Khirbat en-Nahas and Khirbat al-Jariya (supporting an Iron Age date for the mines) (Knabb et al. 2014; Hauptmann 2007, 112–21; Levy et al. 2003). In addition, camp sites discovered in association with mining site clusters indicate temporary settlement by the Iron Age miners who likely were mining and transporting copper ore to the smelting centers (Knabb et al. 2014, 616). Based on these excavations and surveys, Iron Age Faynan was characterized by large smelting sites producing copper at a significant scale supported by a system of shaft mining to exploit deep sources of raw ores.

Discussion—Connecting the Textual and Archaeological Records

Considering the results of the ELRAP (and previous research) in Faynan, it is possible to appropriately evaluate the question at hand: Does the archaeological record support the representations of copper in the Hebrew Bible? To recapitulate the text: copper in the biblical world is portrayed as an important material that is accessible in significant quantities. In addition, the authors of the biblical text possess familiarity with the copper production *chaîne opératoire*—including references to mining, smelting, and casting processes. Iron Age Faynan and its substantial copper industry fall in line with these descriptions from the Hebrew Bible. Excavations at Khirbat en-Nahas revealed large-scale copper production firmly dated to the Early Iron Age, chronologically consistent with events described in the Bible for the early monarchy. The massive slag heaps covering much of the site (as well as the roughly 6.5 meters of excavated slag in Area M) attest to industrial smelting exceeding local consumption. The excess copper likely was traded west (Yahalom-Mack et al. 2014; Martin and Finkelstein 2013, Martin et al. 2013) from Faynan to the greater Eastern Mediterranean, including possibly to the Israelites for projects involving copper/bronze such as Solomon's temple, assuming contemporaneous construction (cf. Finkelstein and Silberman 2001). Along with the scale of production, the fortress at Khirbat en-Nahas corroborates the value and significance of the metal. The size and early military function of the fort and gatehouse indicate a centralized control/organization and protection over production (most likely by the biblical Edomites that inhabited the region) further suggesting the importance of copper (Levy, Najjar, and Ben-Yosef 2014). Moreover, the smelting centers in Faynan were supported through a large network of mining sites and camps utilizing a sophisticated shaft mining technique to exploit the rich ore sources. These shaft mining practices associated with the Iron Age are accurately described in the book of Job (Weisgerber 2003, 85). To summarize, the archaeological record of copper production in Faynan, which is geographically and chronologically situated within the Iron Age biblical world, suggests copper was a valuable and abundantly available metal, affording archaeological substantiations for the metallurgy depicted in the biblical narrative. Thus, it is proposed that Iron Age Faynan provided some of the copper (and metallurgical technology) that is utilized and discussed in the synchronous world and text of the Hebrew Bible.

Conclusion

Through a pragmatic approach founded on cyber-archaeology methodologies, excavations by the ELRAP in the copper-rich Faynan region produced the most complete understanding to date of copper production in the Iron Age Levant. In doing so, these excavations provided a unique opportunity to evaluate the relationship between the biblical text and the archaeological record based on a robust archaeometallurgical data set. Excavations at the copper-smelting center Khirbat en-Nahas revealed industrial-scale production dated to the Early Iron Age (as originally suggested by Glueck), and surveys of Faynan discovered a system of shaft-mining sites providing the necessary ores. These archaeological data parallel the descriptions of copper in the Hebrew Bible—a valued and available metal. As such, Iron Age Faynan provides an ideal view into metallurgy in the world of the Bible.

58

Ancient Technologies of Everyday Life

Gloria London

Many of the ancient technologies used to create ordinary objects for everyday life required help from all family members, young and old, men and women. The work varied seasonally between the cool rainy winters and hot summers. During the dry summer months, people built new constructions, made repairs on existing structures and walls, and produced pottery, bronze, and iron. Herbs, dried branches, and straw collected by young people in the summer were woven into mats and baskets in the autumn and winter when there was less work to do outdoors. Cleaning practices for buildings and pottery varied to meet daily and seasonal needs.

Traditional technologies and practices that persist in a handful of Near Eastern and Mediterranean societies today mirror what life was like before the availability of mechanized equipment. The technologies described here rely in part on ethnoarchaeological research—that is, the study of living people by an archaeologist who searches for answers to specific questions about ancient lifestyles. Recent rural communities, where people made what they needed from local raw materials, can provide evidence of how ancient people lived and worked in similar preindustrial settings. This is especially true for how ancient clay pots were made, used, and cleaned. Because all pottery cracks easily, broken sherds are a prominent find at most archaeological sites. Broken pots that could not be mended were replaced. Because household pottery typically broke after a few months (although some pieces might last three to five years), gradual changes in their shape and surface treatment result in useful indicators of chronological and social changes. A pottery tradition might be stable for decades until subtle or more obvious alterations occur.

Ceramics

Clay pots were the primary containers for cooking, processing, and storing foods. Potters working in the courtyards of their homes, in workshops, and in factory settings (fig. 58.1) made cookware, bowls, plates, jugs, jars, incense burners, stands, decorative pieces, and

Fig. 58.1. A traditional potter in her courtyard works on a series of ovens in different stages of manufacture. The lower body of the oven is wrapped with strips of cloth to support the wet clay (left rear). After adding a flue, the initially flat base is scraped into a rounded form. Finished ovens stand upside down to dry. The oven is set on its side and encased in bricks and mud for use. (Agios Demetrios [Marathassa], Cyprus, May 2000)

more. The porous pottery had surfaces that were plain, incised, or painted in various patterns. Glazed ceramics were not used until early medieval times.

Clay Procurement and Preparation

The methods that traditional potters use to make pottery and prepare clay manually are comparable to the techniques of ancient potters. For example, traditional potters in Cyprus, an island in the eastern Mediterranean, produce jugs, jars, cooking pots, goat-milking pots, and so forth that resemble ancient forms in their manufacture, shape, and unglazed finish (London 2000; 2016, 53, figs. 4.4, 4.41, 17.1.1–3, 17.2.1–2, 19.3.4–7; London, Egoumenidou, and Karageorghis 1989). Cypriot potters work for six months, from April or May, after the rainy time of year. The work begins with digging locally available clay with a pick or axe.

Clay transported in baskets was spread on the ground in order to dry in the sun and to loosen the largest rocks that had been dug up with it. People pulled out the big rocks before the rest was pounded or trampled into powder. Children could trample it by foot, or men and women pounded it with the aid of a bent tree branch (figs. 58.2a, 58.2b). Until the 1960s, the clay was piled in the street to allow people and carts to crush it as they passed by.

With a basket or a piece of leather punctured with many small holes, potters sifted the powder before mixing it with water. Sometimes they altered the clay by combining it with another clay in order to benefit from the properties of each. An alternative was to add pulverized rocks, fired pottery (grog), or organic materials, such as fine chaff, straw, or dung. The additives ("grits" or tempering material) enhanced the quality of the clay. Organic material created a plastic, pliable clay body. Crushed calcite added

Fig. 58.2. People took turns pounding clay with a bent tree branch. They would swing it over their head before crashing it down on the clay. (Agios Demetrios [Marathassa], Cyprus, May 2000)

Photo by Gloria London.

dried slightly, for minutes, hours, or overnight, before it could support the weight of more coils, handles, and any additional work, such as thinning the lower body.

Once the handle(s) dried minimally, attention shifted to the flat base. The potter "turned" or scraped it into a rounded bottom. Pots with sharp wall-base angles are harder to shape. They crack more easily than rounded bases. Large stationary containers with rounded bases were embedded into the beaten earth floors and stood without problem. A large stationary jar can remain serviceable for decades or more than a century.

Large open platters and many round-bottomed pots initially were often shaped with the help of a mold. A coil or slab of clay was arranged in or on an old bowl that served as a mold. Small bowls, no larger than the palm, were made from a ball of clay as a pinch pot. A hole made in the clay was enlarged by pinching the clay between the fingers to create the bowl. Large jars, vats, and storage closets were built with rectangular slabs of clay, about the size of a hand, stacked edge to edge, on top of one another. The ancient oven, or *tabun* (plural *tawabin*), was made with slabs (Ebeling 2014).

Pots made of coils could be built with the aid of a slow-moving wooden or stone turntable that lacked momentum. It stopped rotating unless pressure was applied constantly, usually by hand and less often by foot. In contrast, pottery thrown on a fast, heavy wheel, capable of momentum, freed both hands to shape the clay as the feet kicked the wheel. To throw small bowls, lamps, cups, and juglets, potters centered a tall cone of clay on the wheel and shaped one piece after another from it. The potter used a pointed tool or piece of string to cut off each pot from the cone. Potters working

to cookware made pots that could withstand repeated heating. Grog was the preferred additive for painted wares. Unlike the rock additives, grog absorbed the paint, which enhanced its adhesion to the pot wall.

Manufacturing Techniques

Ancient handmade pots were made in the coiling, pinching, molds, slab, or turning techniques. Later, especially after the seventh century BCE, pots were thrown on a wheel. Handmade ceramics continued to be produced despite the availability of wheel-thrown pots, even until the twentieth century. The coarse handmade jugs, cookware, large jars and basins, served different purposes than wheel-thrown pottery.

Based on observations of traditional potters, we see that the process of making each pot involved an interrupted technique of manufacture that spanned several days or longer. First a potter placed a cylinder of clay on a turntable or work surface, known as a "bat," which was made of stone, bark, wood, or an old basket or mat. With a thumb, knuckle, and fist she opened a hole in the cylinder and enlarged it to create a bowl-like form. To heighten the wall she added coils (fig. 58.3). After applying each coil, the potter thinned and smoothed it so that no trace of the join remained. Afterward the pot

Fig. 58.3. Eleni, a traditional potter in Cyprus, rolls a coil in the air to attach to the pot under construction. Anthoulla scrapes away excess clay to make a round-bottomed pot. (September 1999)

with coils, molds, or a fast wheel can shape hundreds of pots per week.

Firing

To fire the fragile raw pots—either in pits lined and covered with dung or stacked in kilns with separate fuel boxes—was always risky, especially if the pots, kiln, and fuel were not fully dry. Clay pots harden if fired minimally to 600 degrees centigrade.

In Cyprus, the handmade pots were stacked in a kiln with a separate firebox for the fuel (fig. 58.4). Kilns had open or closed rooftops. Pots stacked in an open rooftop kiln were covered with broken pots or large sherds, roof tiles, metal sheeting, and wooden poles that burn away.

The fuel on the roof was in addition to wood placed in the firebox at a lower level, under the pots. Dark spots, or "fire clouds," resulted if pots had contact with the kiln wall or floor, which were the hottest parts of the kiln. For kilns with a closed roof, pots entered via a side door (figs. 58.5, 58.6), which was closed with a temporary door made of bricks and broken pots (fig. 58.7).

Kilns with an open roof are suitable for wheel-thrown pottery as at Zizia, an industrial

production center south of Amman. The Zizia kilns are fired with plastic bottles, bags, and all types of plastic trash.

Kiln firing in Cyprus begins with a small flame before 7:00 a.m. Potters would bless the kiln with an incense burner in which dried olive leaves burned. For the huge wine jars (pithoi or sing. pithos), it was customary to bless each one before it went into the kiln and again after firing. Each huge jar took two months to construct and three days to fire. It was normal to start with a very small fire on the ground. It was outside, in front of the kiln. The purpose was to thoroughly dry the pots and kiln.

For household pottery, the kiln burned for ten to eleven hours. A small flame fueled by

Fig. 58.4. Outside the firebox of the communal Kornos Pottery Cooperative kiln, branches burn following a smaller initial fire begun early in the morning. (1986)

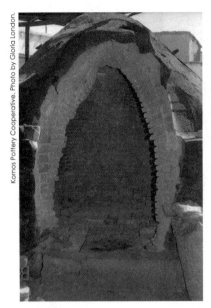

Fig. 58.5. A traditional kiln, with a permanent roof, stands empty before pots are stacked in the firing chamber. Heat generated from a firebox will rise through the grid-like floor of the firing chamber. (September 1999)

Fig. 58.6. Ovens, jars, cooking pots, and flowerpots stacked in the Cooperative kiln. Small pots fill the large pieces in order to maximize kiln space and fuel. Pots touched each other without damage. (1986)

twigs starts outside the firebox. It is moved closer to the kiln by early afternoon. Finally, wood branches and logs placed inside the fuel box resulted in huge flames by 6:00 p.m. Traditional potters burn bark, pinecones, old mats or baskets, and animal dung as fuel. Once the pots achieve the proper firing color, the remaining burning logs are pulled from the kiln and doused with water, later to be sold as charcoal. Pots, unloaded early the next morning while still hot, went directly into a cart pulled by a donkey or a truck to be sold to customers outside the village. Traditional potters in the eastern Mediterranean sold or bartered their wares at local markets or regional holiday fairs, especially in the autumn. They traded pottery for grains, beans, and other staples needed for the winter months.

Porous Unglazed Pottery

Clay jugs for carrying water were the original water coolers and purifiers. The unglazed walls kept the water cool through evaporation, in a process called "sweating," very similar to

what our bodies do to keep cool. At normal room temperature and atmospheric pressure, water is out of equilibrium. It wants to evaporate. Water slowly sweats through the porous walls and evaporates from the outside surface of the pot. This process takes five times as much energy as is needed to make water boil. The sweating or leaking is highly effective in slowing down any heating of the water. Water in a plastic or metal container warms up quickly because the absorbed heat from the environment cannot escape by evaporating. It remains trapped inside the plastic or metal receptacle and then heats the water. Water stays cooler much longer in a clay jug because of this efficient evaporation mechanism for carrying away most of the absorbed heat.

As water evaporated through the pot wall, the water channeled the bitter tasting minerals to the inside pot walls. They gradually coated the interior and created a dense white deposit that clogged the pot walls. After a few months of use, jugs were no longer able to sweat and cool the water. Instead the jugs were

Fig. 58.7. After stacking the pots, Anthoulla, a traditional potter in Cyprus, creates a temporary door from factory-made bricks. Broken bricks and large sherds minimize any shifting during the fire. (1986)

repurposed to store vinegar, oil, or cheeses held in oil or brine.

There are several methods to make traditional cooking pots watertight without the application of a glaze. Pots first were filled with water, to assure that they had no cracks, and then were filled with lard until the porous walls became fully saturated with it and impermeable. Another method involved coating vessel interiors with a mix of egg white and sugar. A combination of egg and ash was smeared on the exterior. People likely cooked meat, grains, and vegetables in very little water to minimize leakage. Boiling water could also be added at a later stage to make a soup or porridge.

Jars for fermenting and storing wine had linings made of resin and pitch collected from Aleppo pine, terebinth pistachio trees, or the

Dead Sea. The resin imparted a distinct flavor to the wine. Ancient jars rarely preserve evidence of a lining. Acids in the wine normally destroyed the resin. Jars were relined regularly to keep them from leaking (London 2016, 105–8).

Architecture

Domestic and Public Structures

Ancient houses were small. The limited interior space accommodated sleeping, food storage, clothes, bedding, and at times a household shrine. The few small windows kept out the heat or the cold. The rooftop and adjacent courtyard, which were larger than the interior sleeping and storage quarters, functioned much of the year for cooking, cleaning, eating, playing, and summertime sleeping. The courtyard was repurposed seasonally for making pottery and processing food in summer, or for daily cooking and sheltering animals in fall and winter.

Temples, palaces, and official residences included open public areas where people could gather. They were also used as storage facilities. The building materials, floor, and wall surfaces were more elaborate and better finished than in regular houses.

Construction Materials

Excavated buildings were made of handmade or molded sun-dried bricks, timber, field and quarried stones, bitumen, and plaster mortar, the same raw materials known from the biblical text (Gen. 11:3). The construction material selected depended on the location and building type. The soft limestone of the coastal area and lowlands was unsatisfactory for construction. As a result, handmade bricks were shaped from the plentiful clay deposits. In contrast, the harder limestone in the central hills of ancient Israel and basalt rock in the north were used for public and private houses.

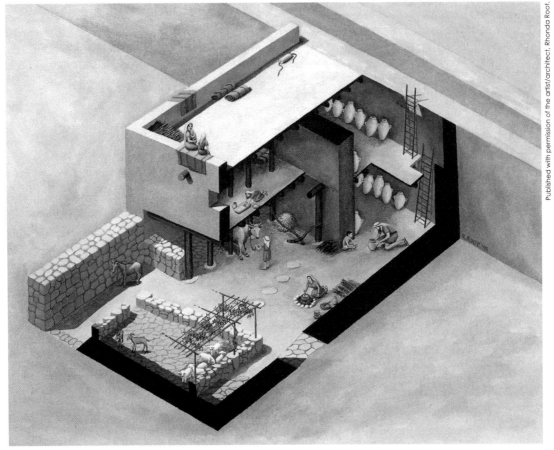

Published with permission of the artist/architect, Rhonda Root.

Fig. 58.8. Reconstruction of a two-story late-thirteenth-century house based on excavations at Tall al-'Umayri in Jordan. The structure had five rooms and measured 12 × 16 meters and was made of small stone boulders and mud bricks.

Clay bricks were incorporated into the upper walls of houses that had foundations made of stone. The stone foundation limited potential damages caused by water dripping from the roof or flowing down the hillsides in winter.

Raw, uncut fieldstones for houses contrasted to dressed, finely carved, and jointed ashlar masonry in the walls of temples or palaces. The fine masonry of ashlar stone was often limited to the exterior surface of walls that had rubble interior filler. Building and city walls were remarkably wide. The exterior walls of a two-story Late Bronze / Iron Age building at Tall al-'Umayri (fig. 58.8) measure 1.5 meters (Herr and Clark 2009, 77). Earthquake activity in the region might have induced people to overbuild walls, making them thicker than necessary in order to withstand powerful tremors and aftershocks.

Houses with floors of beaten earth or cobblestones contrast to the stone paving or plaster in public buildings, including temples. Limestone quarries and kilns provided the raw material for plaster. Soft limestone was crumbled in the hand and mixed with water to make ready-to-use plaster. Harder limestone was fired in a kiln. Seasonal whitewashing of walls and floors with plaster provided clean surfaces and eradicated insect infestations, according to rural residents of contemporary Cyprus. The thatch and wood rooftops, connected by mud plaster or clay, provided a constant source of dirt inside the house.

Textiles

Wool and Flax

Most clothing was made of sheep's wool (Lev. 13:47–48, 52, 59; 19:19; Isa. 51:8; Ezek. 34:3). Sheep and goat hairs were woven into wool to create bedding, sacks, and tents. The heaviest fabric for tents, made from black goat hair, was impervious to rain. Linen was a luxury woven fabric made from flax (Deut. 22:11; Prov. 31:13; Hosea 2:9). Sheepskins served as floor coverings (Judg. 6:37) or as outer clothing. Large pieces of plain or dyed fabrics that wrapped around the body provided warmth as well as a means to carry almost anything, including young children.

Wool preparation required multiple stages of work. After men sheared the animals following the winter rains, women and children washed the hair and rewashed it to remove dirt and grease. Then women and girls teased (spread out to dry) and carded (disentangled) it before it was spun. The spindle, or flywheel, was a small conical stone that fit over the end of a rod made of a long bone or a piece of wood. The yarn wrapped around the rod as it was spun.

Coloring Agents

Excavated grinding stones, of the type for crushing wheat and barley, preserve traces of crushed organic materials used to dye fabrics. It is assumed that they were coloring agents, rather than edible food, because the plants are lethal when ingested. The poisonous mullein (*Verbascum*) plant provided a light yellow-green dye. A purple or blue color came from a member of the spurge family known as turnsole (*Chrozophora tinctoria*) and from murex seashells. Red and brown colors derived from soaked pomegranate rinds. Dyes made of noxious material were also used for working leather (Crabtree 1986, 89).

Wood, bone, or stone spinning and weaving tools for yarn and thread created fabrics with the help of wooden vertical standing looms or parallel horizontal looms spread across the ground. The latter are depicted in Egyptian wall paintings and miniature models (Barber 1994, 80–81).

Basketry

Organic materials such as cloth and baskets are rarely preserved archaeologically due to the unfavorable humidity and soil conditions in the Levant. Indirect evidence of baskets and mats comes from the impressions on the bottom of clay pots worked on bats made from mats or baskets.

Materials

Dried date palm branches, rushes, reeds, grasses, twigs, bark, and pigments were collected in late spring and summer. To shape into baskets, they often required soaking prior to use. They also needed peeling, splitting, shredding, twisting, or dyeing before they were woven into open and closed forms, either colored or monochrome.

Uses of Baskets

Baskets were used to collect, harvest, serve, cook, or store food. Biblical texts refer to baskets of bread (Gen. 40:16; Exod. 29:3, 23; Lev. 8:2, 26, 31; Num. 6:15, 17, 19), grapes (Jer. 6:9), or figs (Jer. 24:1). A basket lined with tar and pitch hid the baby Moses in the Nile River (Exod. 2:3). Coatings of asphalt or bitumen from the Dead Sea created airtight baskets suitable for holding liquids. Baskets lined with pitch and filled with water were suitable for cooking food. Hot rocks dropped into a basket heated the water and cooked the food. Baskets were useful for making cheese. Until recently in rural Cyprus, milk curds, with extra salt added, were packed into an unlined, tightly woven basket and allowed to dry. It was hung outside as excess water drained from it. Then it was boiled in the basket and again dried for several days before it was ready to eat.

Basketry was made into homes for small animals, clothing and shoes, household furniture, pot stands, brooms, or decorations. Babies, fuel, and raw clay likely were transported in baskets attached to people or animals as in traditional Mediterranean societies until the twentieth century. With woven flat baskets women could separate chaff from grains and seeds or rocks from raw clay.

Cleaning and Fumigation Practices

In a region of limited water resources, people relied on natural cleaning abrasives and antiseptics for houses, pots, textiles, and more. The Bible refers to *neter*—possibly a mix of natron (salt) with lye (*borit*)—as a general cleaning agent (Jer. 2:22).

Buildings

One method to keep house interiors clean in traditional Mediterranean societies was to sprinkle salt on rooftops. This practice prevented weeds from sprouting in the earth and mud-plaster mortar that held the roof beams and thatch together. The annual plaster whitewashing of floors and walls served a similar purpose. Texts refer to cleaning houses, contaminated with illness, by scraping and entirely removing the stones, mortar, and plaster (Lev. 14:40–44).

Fumigation and Insecticide

Organic materials widely used in traditional Mediterranean societies until recently were likely available in antiquity. Burned sage (*Salvia* sp.) leaves are useful for fumigating buildings and other structures. Natural insecticides were made from the poisonous juices of the oleander tree (*Nerium*) and larkspur (*Delphinium*) in central Jordan until the late twentieth century. To deodorize beaten earthen floors, people in

the Madaba Plains area of Jordan collected and crushed edible savory (*Thymus*) and sweet clover (*Melilotus*) (Crabtree 1986, 80, 91–93).

Pottery

The scarcity of water made cleaning the unglazed pottery problematic. The porous walls absorbed the foods held or cooked in the pots. Roman era recipes specifically mention the need to clean clay pots (Bober 1999, 158). A medieval physician, Marwan Abd al-Malik ibn Zuhr (d. 1162), who believed that illness could result from food trapped in cookware, wrote that unglazed pots should be discarded after a single use! He concluded that glazed cookware could be used safely five times only (Zaouali 2007, 49).

Sand and water, with or without herbs, were suitable to scrub out any visible food stuck on pot interiors. The problem was that meat or dairy protein embedded in the pot walls could not be removed in this way. If allowed to accumulate, the residue would sour or spoil fresh foods. Unglazed pottery required daily and seasonal deep cleanings. Vinegar diluted with water and left standing in an unglazed cooking pot overnight could eliminate food residue. After the liquid was discarded the next morning and rinsed with water, the clean pot was ready for use.

Porous, unglazed clay pots also required periodic deep cleansing, especially those pots for processing dairy foods such as yogurt, milk, butter, and cheese. At the end of the goat-milking season, before the jugs, jars, and pots were stored away they were refired in a kiln to remove the residue embedded in the porous walls. If no kiln was available, the dirty pots were placed in a hot oven overnight in order to burn out whatever fats and protein remained.

Several plants in the mint family, known as effective for cleansing unhealthy skin (Lev. 14:4), provided convenient materials to clean handmade pottery. The antibacterial properties of thyme, a member of the mint family, provide old-fashioned disinfectants, antiseptics, and fungicides. Thyme contains a carbolic acid comparable to alcohol, but more acidic. Until the mid-twentieth century, Cypriot goat herders would swish a branch of dried or fresh thyme in a little water to clean clay milking pots daily. At the end of the summer, they refired the pots in a kiln for a deep cleansing.

The biblical kosher dietary laws hint at the problems in cleaning absorbent ceramic cookware. It is stated, "You shall not boil a kid in its mother's milk" (Exod. 23:19; 34:26; Deut. 14:21). If this implies that meat cannot be cooked in a pot used for milk, it acknowledges that dairy protein embedded in pot walls causes meat to sour. Before glazed cookware became common, it was dangerous to cook meat in a pot that once held milk. Instead, specific pots for milking, heating, fermenting, and storing dairy products differed from those reserved to cook meat (London 2016, 138–41).

59

Food Preparation in Iron Age Israel

CYNTHIA SHAFER-ELLIOTT

Introduction

Food is one of those subjects that most people find important—at least at mealtime, but what about food and cooking in ancient times? What did people eat? How did they prepare it? Examining the diet, cooking, and eating practices of an ancient society reveals much about it, including what daily life and meals were like and what food-related practices and behaviors were accepted and valued within the culture. The accepted behaviors, values, and norms of a society can be seen in that society's preparation and consumption of both everyday meals and special-occasion meals. This chapter introduces the current understandings of the cooking of everyday meals in Iron Age Israel (1200–586 BCE).

Many resources must be used in order to gain a full picture of food preparation in ancient Israel (Altmann and Fu 2014). The most obvious sources are texts, in particular the Hebrew Bible; however, pertinent texts from the ancient Near East, such as recipes from Babylonia, may also be helpful. Equally important is archaeological evidence that provides information about the physical reality of ancient cultures. Archaeological evidence related to cooking includes features (like ovens and grinding installations) and artifacts (such as cooking pots and bowls). Another resource that is essential to the study of ancient food preparation is ethnoarchaeology, which observes present-day traditional societies and how they prepare items related to food (such as cooking ovens and pots, to name just a few). The hope is that the traditional society's methods will provide insight into, and possible reconstruction of, food preparation techniques and technologies used by their ancient ancestors (Meyers 2003a, 185–97).

Diet

Before a survey of cooking in Iron Age Israel can be provided, the ancient Israelite diet must be summarized. Like many ancient societies, the Israelites were subsistence farmers; in other words, they focused on growing enough food to feed themselves and their families. Throughout the Iron Age, the average ancient Israelite household lived in a rural settlement such as a farm, hamlet, or village. The Israelites were agrarian and pastoral in nature and were preoccupied with surviving off the inhospitable land—often at a mere subsistence level. The fertility of the land, animals, and household members was essential to Israelite survival. Drought, famine, or war could devastate a household. The rise of the monarchy, followed by the dominating foreign powers of the Iron Age (mainly the Neo-Assyrian and Neo-Babylonian Empires), forced the people of the kingdoms of Israel and Judah to provide tribute and taxes. These extenuating factors, and others, increased the difficulty of the daily survival of the average ancient Israelite (Shafer-Elliott 2014).

The so-called Mediterranean triad—olives, grapes, and cereals—dominated the ancient Israelite diet. Furthermore, the essential products made from the triad crops—olive oil, wine, and bread—greatly overshadowed other goods (Deut. 7:12–13; 11:13–14; 2 Chron. 31:5–10; Neh. 13:12). Inscriptions also highlight the importance of the Mediterranean triad. For instance, the inscriptions written on broken pieces of pottery (ostraca) from Arad, a fortress on the southern border of Israel, direct the commander of the town to distribute grain, flour, bread, oil, and wine (Pace 2014, 188; Pritchard 2011, 291). The ancient Israelite diet was enhanced by seasonal fruits, vegetables, and nuts, including grapes, figs, pomegranates, dates, sycamore, legumes, vetch, pistachios, almonds, walnuts, pine nuts, and possibly cucumbers, leeks, onions, and garlic (Borowski 2004; 2002, 137–39; Altmann 2013, 288–91).

Daily sustenance was dependent upon cereals and the bread made from them. The Israelite diet relied on bread so heavily that the Hebrew word for it, *lehem*, is synonymous with food (Gen. 28:20; Exod. 2:20; Lev. 3:16; Num. 15:19; Ruth 1:6; 2 Sam. 9:10; Job 42:11; Ps. 132:15). It has been estimated that between half and three-fourths of the entire caloric intake by the average Israelite came from several kinds of grain, such as wheat, millet, and barley (Altmann 2013, 288; Borowski 2002, 88–92).

Another staple in the Israelite diet was dairy products. Sheep and goats were common herd animals that were a significant part of the household's economy. The household herds provided many essential secondary products, such as fleece, which was woven and made into clothes; dung, used as fuel for fire and as fertilizer; and milk, which was processed into a variety of dairy products such as butter, cheese, and curds (Gen. 18:8; Deut. 32:14; Judg. 4:19; 2 Sam. 17:27–29; Job 10:10).

The Israelite household seldom ate meat unless it was procured through the hunting of wild game, the household herd needed to be culled, the household needed ready cash, or there was a special occasion such as a wedding or agricultural or religious festival, or as a gesture of hospitality. It must be emphasized that the average ancient Israelite household was immensely dependent upon its herds for their secondary products, and as such the herds were a vital part of the household's economy; consequently, the slaughtering or selling of one of the herd was a financial decision more than a culinary one.

One major part of the ancient diet that is rarely included in discussions on Israelite food and cooking is the category of legumes. A legume is a type of plant with seeds that grow in long pods and the seeds are eaten as food. Types of legumes found in ancient Israel include lentils, peas, chickpeas, broad beans, and bitter vetch. Legumes are a good source of vegetable protein, which was imperative in a society that ate so little meat (Borowski 2002, 93–97). The daily diet of ancient Israel also included fermented beverages such as wine and beer (which was safer to drink than stagnant water), seasonings (such as salt, coriander, dill, and cumin), and sweeteners (such as honey or date syrup) (N. MacDonald 2008b, 39–40).

Daily chores centered on agriculture and animal husbandry. Certain times of year (such as planting and harvest) demanded all physically able members of the household to participate. The main cooked meal was eaten at the end of the workday. Breakfast and lunch were quick and would include bread, cheese, dried fruit, parched grain, water, and seasonal vegetables and fruit (Ruth 2:14) (Borowski 2003, 74).

Cooking Technology

Ovens

The average Israelite used a variety of cooking technologies to prepare meals. The most essential piece of technology was a thermal feature, or what we would call an oven today (Ebeling and Rogel 2015, 347). It is difficult to say precisely what an oven in ancient Israel looked like because those found in archaeological excavations usually are incomplete. Ethnoarchaeological studies in the Middle East illustrate several types of ovens, some of which may be the modern descendants of ovens used in ancient Israel. The most basic type of oven would not be described as an oven at all; food could be prepared on the embers of a fire or over hot rocks (Isa. 44:19). Another simple type of oven is a *saj*, which is a rounded metal disk placed over the fire or resting on the rocks. In the use of a *saj*, dough is thrown back and forth between the palms of the baker until it is a thin flap of dough and then placed on the *saj* to quickly bake on either side. The ancient Israelites would not have baked on a rounded metal disk, but this method of baking could indicate how bread was baked on hot rocks (1 Kings 19:6) or the coals of a fire (Isa. 44:19) (Shafer-Elliott 2013b, 119).

A third type of oven that ethnoarchaeologists have observed in the modern Middle East is the *tabun* (plural *tawabin*). A *tabun* is a low, truncated, dome-shaped oven made of clay between 25 and 50 cm tall. It has a large opening at its top through which the dough is placed on the floor to bake and the bread is removed. The oven is heated by placing fuel

Fig. 59.1. An Iraqi woman baking with a *tannur*

around the outside of the *tabun*. *Tawabin* in some geographic regions of the modern Middle East also have a second opening on the side that allows fuel to be inserted into the oven in order to raise the oven's temperature before baking began and for the ash to be discarded. But using the term *tabun* to describe ovens found in archaeological excavations in Israel is chronologically inconsistent, simply because this style of oven is not found in archaeological contexts any earlier that the seventh century CE; furthermore, the term *tabun* is not found in the Hebrew Bible or the Talmud (Ebeling and Rogel 2015, 328–30).

The ovens uncovered in archaeological excavations, although usually incomplete, resemble more of the *tannur* (plural *tannaneer*) type of oven used in the modern Middle East (figs. 59.1, 59.2).

A modern *tannur* is a conical or beehive-shaped clay oven that stands about 1 meter

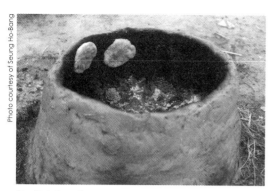

Fig. 59.2. Experimental archaeology at Tel Halif, Israel: making a *tannur* and cooking leavened bread in it

during the hot summer months. Ethnoarchaeological studies show that preparation of the household meal was performed primarily by women, largely because of their reproductive roles, which necessitated that they work near the home. The central location of ovens permitted women to conduct other household tasks while preparing food. Centralized ovens also allowed for the sharing of ovens (and fuel) with other women, which encouraged social relationships and cohesion among the group (Lev. 26:26) (B. Parker 2011, 603–27).

(3.2 feet) tall. It has a large opening at its top that allows access inside the oven and often is covered with a metal lid to retain heat. Like the *tabun*, many modern *tannaneer* also contain an opening at the bottom that serves as a flue. Unlike the *tabun*, the *tannur* is heated by starting a fire on the floor inside, and the dough is slapped onto the interior walls to bake. The term *tannur* is found in the Hebrew Bible fifteen times, seven of which refer to an oven used to bake bread (Exod. 8:3; Lev. 2:4; 7:9; 11:35; 26:26; Hosea 7:4, 6–7) (Shafer-Elliott 2013a, 219; Ebeling and Rogel 2015, 329). A lid is often placed over the top opening of both *tawabin* and *tannaneer* to retain heat and allow other items to be placed on top or even inside to cook (Shafer-Elliott 2013b, 120–21; Ebeling and Rogel 2015, 330).

Excavations of Iron Age houses in Israel typically find the remains of ovens in centralized locations both inside and outside the house. Ovens found inside the dwelling usually are located near an entryway, suggesting that houses lacked ventilation (Baadsgaard 2008, 21–22). Indoor ovens often are uncovered in the room that presumably was the main living area, where multiple household chores were performed. The outside oven typically is located in an adjacent courtyard. Ovens are regularly found in both locations, suggesting that food was prepared inside the house during the rainy winter months and outside

Cooking Pots

Meals were prepared in simple, but effective, cooking pots that evolved throughout the Bronze and Iron Ages (see, e.g., fig. 59.3). In the Hebrew Bible, words for cooking pots include *parur* (Num. 11:8; Judg. 6:19; 1 Sam. 2:14), *sir* (Exod. 16:3; 2 Kings 4:38–41; Jer. 1:13; Ezek. 11:3, 7, 11; Mic. 3:3; Zech. 14:20–21), *qallahat* (1 Sam. 2:14; Mic. 3:3), and *dud* (1 Sam. 2:14) (Shafer-Elliott 2013a, 220). To simplify matters, cooking vessels can be categorized into three basic forms: the Bronze Age pot or bowl, the Philistine jug, and the hybrid pot.

The cooking pots found within Bronze Age Canaan and later in Israel evolved from a simple and common bowl-shaped vessel. The typical pot was a large, handleless, open-mouthed pot with an everted rim, round base, and carinated body, which makes it look like a large bowl. As the pot evolved throughout the Bronze Age, it kept the traditional shape but with some variations in size, an increasingly carinated shape, and changes in the rim. The diameter of the bowl's mouth averaged 9.8 to 15.7 inches (25–40 cm), and its height averaged 5.9 to 7.8 inches (15–20 cm). Its open mouth, wide shape, and the special cooking ware the pot was made of allowed it to be used for several types of cooking, including steaming, frying, simmering, and boiling. The pot's open mouth and bowl shape supported cooking larger food items such as meat and serving larger groups of people. Bronze Age pots were placed inside the oven, over its upper opening, or against the stones of the hearth, while those with handles could be suspended over an open fire. This type of pot is familiar in Late Bronze Age Canaan and in Israel, with variations continuing to the end of the Iron Age (Killebrew 1999, 84, 92–95, 106–9).

In the Late Bronze and Early Iron I Ages the Philistines appeared and brought a new type of cooking vessel with them. This new type of pot resembled Cypriot and Aegean cooking jugs of the Late Cypriot IIC and IIIA and Late Helladic IIIC periods. The shape of the new pot was less like a bowl and more like a jug; it had a closed mouth, a globular to ovoid shape, and one or two loop handles from the rim to its shoulder. The typical cooking jug had a volume of about one-half to three-fourths of a gallon (2–3 liters), a maximum height of ca. 7.8 inches (20 cm), a maximum body diameter of ca. 7 inches (18 cm), and a diameter at the mouth of 3.5 to 4.7 inches (9–12 cm) (see Ben-Shlomo 2011). Like the Bronze Age pot, the cooking jug evolved throughout the Iron Age. The cooking jug is called the "Philistine jug" because it nearly replaced the traditional cooking pot at sites designated as Philistine on the southern coastal plain and is not found as much at sites outside Philistia. Unlike the traditional Bronze Age cooking pot, the size and shape of the cooking jug do not allow for different types of cooking. The primary mode of cooking with the jug was simmering; the jug's thin walls were useful for slow, low-heat cooking of liquid dishes, its flat base allowed it to rest directly on or near the heat source, and its

Fig. 59.3. Ninth-century traditional-style cooking pots

Photo courtesy of Aren Maeir, director, the Tell es-Safi/Gath Archaeological Project

handle assisted with easy removal. Soot marks on the bottom and sides of the jugs imply that they were placed directly over an open fire or leaned on a hearth. The Philistine jug's small size also regulated the amount of cereals or vegetables cooked within it, indicating smaller portions and consumption by fewer people (Ben-Shlomo et al. 2008, 225–46; Gur-Arieh, Maeir, and Shahack-Gross 2011, 349–55; Killebrew 1999, 93–95, 107).

During the end of the Iron Age I and into Iron Age II, the Bronze Age bowl and Philistine jug blended to create what is referred to as the "hybrid cooking pot." The most functional features of the pot and jug were combined, with slightly varying forms: the rounded body and open mouth of the Bronze Age pot married the handles and shape of the Philistine jug. Depending on the type of cooking ware used, the hybrid pot could be used for slow, low-heat cooking as well as for rapid, high-temperature cooking. The size of the pot determined whether it was used for small or large items or quantities of food. Hybrid pots did not replace the more traditional Bronze Age pot, which indicates that a variety of cooking methods were used. Even though the hybrid pot was more user-friendly than the jug, its size determined if it was used to cook large types or amounts of food; thus, the hybrid pot may have been used to cook liquid dishes, like soups, as well as heartier dishes, like stews and porridges. A traditional Bronze Age pot or larger hybrid pot would have been suitable if meat was included in a stew, depending on the size of the pieces of meat and the number of people to be fed. The smaller hybrid pots and even cooking jugs could have been used to process dairy products, especially in more rural communities (London 2016, 17.8). To cook using a hybrid pot, one could place the pot in a fire pit, next to or on top of a hearth, inside or covering the upper opening of a *tannur*, or suspend it over a fire if it had handles (Ben-Shlomo et al. 2008, 225–46; Killebrew 1999, 93–95, 107).

Every household within ancient Israel would have had some sort of thermal feature (i.e., oven) and cooking pots—possibly a few that included the different general styles of cooking pots. Everyday cooking was a necessity that dictated that simple yet multifunctional cooking technology be employed.

Meals

As in many societies in the ancient Near East, bread was essential to the everyday survival of the ancient Israelites—hence the popular biblical idiom "daily bread" (Prov. 30:8). Bread was baked almost daily from one of two types of bread dough: unleavened (*matsah*) and leavened (*hamets*). Grain was ground into flour by the use of stone vessels, such as a mortar and pestle set or a grinding slab and handstone. A mortar is a stone bowl in which small amounts of grain (or other items like spices) are placed; a pestle is a club-shaped implement used to grind the grain in the mortar. A grinding slab is a large, immobile stone or slab paired with a smaller handstone. The grain is placed on the large slab and the smaller handstone is ground back and forth against the grain to produce flour (Ebeling and Rowan 2004).

Unleavened bread is a mixture of flour, water, and a pinch of salt that is kneaded into dough. On the one hand, unleavened dough can be prepared quickly since it does not need time to rise; hence, it was often made when guests arrived unexpectedly (Gen. 18:6; Judg. 6:19; 1 Sam. 28:24). On the other hand, because it lacks yeast, the flat unleavened bread could not be stored for long. The same basic recipe is used to make leavened dough, but a yeast product is added to it, such as sourdough (dough left out to ferment) or brewer's yeast (used for brewing beer). Unlike unleavened bread, leavened bread is more satisfying and keeps longer.

Dough was kneaded on a trough or wooden board placed on a bench or on the floor close to the oven. Both types of bread could be baked on hot stones or griddles over an open fire, like a *saj* (Lev. 7:9; Isa. 44:19), or in a *tannur*-style oven (Lev. 26:26). Recipes and encyclopedias found in ancient Mesopotamia show that the baking of bread was quite diverse in the ancient Near East. These texts document two hundred to three hundred varieties of bread, depending upon the type, quality, and color of flour used; the type and amount of kneading; the additives and flavors; and the baking methods, presentation, geographic origin, and use. Ingredients added to dough include ghee, dates, milk, cheese, fruit, and sesame oil. Loaves of bread might accompany the meal or be served as part of the main dish. Dough was divided and arranged on platters to retain a particular shape, served with meat or stew, as bread cakes (*'ugot* in Gen. 18:6), or dumplings within the stew (*lebibot* in 2 Sam. 13:6, 8, 10) (Bottéro 2001a, 47; 1995b, 3).

Gruel made of cereals was an ideal morning meal since it was relatively fast and easy to make (Prov. 31:15). Gruel and porridge required small amounts of raw ingredients that stretched a long way, making them highly economical. In ancient Israel, porridge or gruel was made of spelt, emmer, barley, lentils, and chickpeas (Borowski 2003, 91–92, 95–96). In one Mesopotamian recipe, the cook is directed to take cooked birds out of the cauldron, put them on top of the porridge in a platter, and place the platter over the oven's upper opening to cook further (Bottéro 1995b, 14; Shafer-Elliott 2013b, 134).

The main hot meal was a soup or stew eaten at the end of the workday (Gen. 25:29–34;

2 Kings 4:38–41). The preference for stews in the ancient Near East is evident in Mesopotamian sources. One Assyrian source mentions at least one hundred different soups or stews. Babylonian recipes for stews are made from ingredients such as vegetables, legumes, and both fresh and not-so-fresh meats (Bottéro 1995b, 48; Shafer-Elliott 2013b, 132). Meat was not consumed on a regular basis by the average Israelite, so most stews were made from legumes and vegetables. The Hebrew word for "stew," *nazid*, is used to describe stews of vegetables or legumes (Gen. 25:29, 34; 2 Kings 4:38–40; Hag. 2:12). If these food items were scarce due to famine, war, drought, or economic difficulties, then porridge probably was served again as the main meal.

Meat was acquired by hunting wild game or when an animal from the herd was slaughtered (Gen. 18:7; 27:3–4; Judg. 6:19; 1 Sam. 28:24). When an animal was butchered, the entire animal was used, and nothing went to waste (P. Watson 1979, 108–9). The bones, cartilage, and meat were frequently turned into stews, the most economical of meat dishes (Mic. 3:3) (P. Watson 1979, 108–9). Meat could be roasted or braised and rinsed before adding it to the pot. Rinsing the meat could be done for several reasons: warm water was used to help pluck fowl; rinsing or soaking raw meat in cold water increased the firmness of the meat, which enhanced its texture; there may have been a concern with cleanliness; and rinsing may be related to the method of cooking. When meat was browned, juices from it were drawn out of the meat and into the vessel, leaving both with an undesirable residue or film that needed to be washed off. In Babylonian recipes, roasted grain seeds were soaked and preserved in bread that was crumbled on top of the stew to thicken it or provide it with a "burned" flavor (Bottéro 2004, 66–67; Shafer-Elliott 2013a, 223).

Special occasions such as hospitality, weddings, and festivals were observed with a feast that included meat. Often an entire animal was prepared for such occasions (Gen. 29:21–22; Deut. 14:22–27; 16:1–17; Exod. 12:3–9; 23:14–17; Lev. 23:4–25; Num. 28:11–15; 1 Sam. 20:5–6). The animal (usually a sheep or goat) was likely roasted over an open fire or in a pit (Isa. 44:16, 19). If the animal was butchered, small pieces of meat could be roasted on a plate, rack, skewers, or screen made of metal or clay placed on top of the upper opening of the oven (*tannur*) (Bottéro 2004, 45).

Food as Metaphor in the Hebrew Bible

Food is often used as a metaphor in the Hebrew Bible. Since bread was the mainstay of life in ancient Israel, it should come as no surprise that bread is the most widely used food metaphor in the Hebrew Bible. Bread frequently symbolizes God's provision for the Israelites. The twelve loaves of bread placed on the table of the bread of the Presence in the tabernacle, and later the temple, every Sabbath are seen as a token of gratitude for God's provision (Exod. 25:23–30; 35:13; 39:36; Lev. 24:5–9). The definitive example of bread as God's provision is the "bread from heaven" or manna. In the wilderness the Israelites were commanded to gather only enough manna for each day in order to help them learn to depend on God for their daily bread (Exod. 16:4–5). The metaphor of bread is also used in the phrase "eating the bread of idleness," which is interpreted to mean self-indulgence and ignoring one's household duty (Prov. 31:27); bread can symbolize diligence and financial investment (Eccles. 11:1).

A second example of food as a metaphor within the Hebrew Bible is the idiom "a land flowing with milk and honey" (Exod. 3:8, 17; 13:5; 33:3; Lev. 20:24; Num. 13:27; 14:8; 16:13–14; Deut. 6:3; 11:9; 26:9, 15; 27:3; 31:20; Josh. 5:6; Song 4:11; 5:1; Isa. 7:22; Jer. 11:5; 32:22; Ezek. 20:6, 15). The idiom is intended to highlight and exaggerate the abundance of the so-called Promised Land. Since honey specifically from bees (albeit wild bees) is mentioned only twice in the Hebrew Bible (Judg. 14:8; 1 Sam. 14:27), and no evidence of industrial bee-keeping had been found in either textual or archaeological evidence, scholars and archaeologists argued that the "honey" referred to in the idiom was syrup produced from dates and figs. However, the discovery of apiaries (or beehives) from the Iron IIA level (tenth to ninth centuries BCE) at Tel Rehov, Israel, in 2005 and 2007 demonstrates that bee-keeping was done on an industrial scale and that Israel was indeed a land of milk and bees' honey (A. Mazar and Panitz-Cohen 2007).

Conclusion

The ancient Israelites cooked meals that included seasonal ingredients mostly from their fields, orchards, and herds. These meals were prepared in simple yet multifunctional ovens and cooking pots. The archaeological remains of cooking technology, ancient Near Eastern texts, and ethnoarchaeological studies illustrate the daily life that is behind the scenes of the Hebrew Bible.

60

Feasting in the Biblical World

JANLING FU

The word "feast" calls to mind rich and abundant food and drink, often, as in the traditional American or Canadian Thanksgiving, to excess. Thanksgiving offers a good example of the possibility of a feast as, in its yearly ritual, its traditional celebration draws together family, however widely dispersed, and comes accompanied by a cluster of events—carving the turkey, sitting at the table, and watching sports events. In some families, the season partakes of a degree of formality, with established roles assigned for those who carve the meat and pull apart the wishbone.

One thinks naturally of traditional foods and a ritualized order of events, especially for those who prepare a feast. Memories may arise of how to plan a particular meal, acquire its ingredients, and of the many preliminary stages needed in setting it up—deciding on the menu, whom to invite, how the shopping will take place.[1] Indeed, the modern context often entails hectic last-minute preparatory stages, with failure to brine a turkey and/or overcooking or undercooking the meat as regrettable outcomes.

The festal table, of which Thanksgiving has served as an example, emblematizes much of the essence of family and partakes of seasonal rhythms that through time and repetition may be thought to bind individuals together. Through such gatherings, memories are created whose structures serve to coalesce, embody, and even help configure the identities of small groups of people, whether members of a family or, beyond the level of kinship relations, what might be thought as more tenuous ties of private and public groupings. Understood in this way, festal activity constitutes an important element of individual and group identity.[2]

A recent definition of the feast was offered by the present author and Peter Altmann. They suggested that the feast might be considered

---

1. For an idea of the steps necessary in preparing a feast, see M. L. Smith 2015. In a Polynesian context, see Kirch 2001. For a recent ethnographic example from Papua New Guinea, see Maeir 2015.

2. The argument could be made that the pivot between "ordinary" and "special," daily meal and feast, also relates to the understanding of time, of a ritualized, structured ordering of events and life. See Appadurai 1981; Pace 2014. In a modern context, many possibilities come to mind, including fraternities, sororities, and eating clubs.

"a central social event oriented toward abundant display and communal consumption with ritualizing tendencies. As localized in specific spaces and times, feasting differs in degree and kind from the daily intake of meals, though it overlaps with the quotidian routines of consumption. In addition, the focus on communal consumption sets feasting apart from individual consumption of food" (Fu and Altmann 2014, 16). In this definition, the feast stands as part of a continuum of eating and drinking. Daily meals stand on one side and special meals on the other, the latter possibly marked by the quantity of food, by special food and drink for the occasion, and in additional ways through which formality and ritual may help identify a feast. One might turn to the holiday season as an example, with the festive singing of carols, or similarly to the Pesach seder's ritual order and foods. The importance of dining together as opposed to alone is stressed with room to tack between the everyday and more pronounced festive times.

Feasting in the biblical world carries many of these thoughts: it suggests multiple parties who come together to eat and drink. In the Hebrew Bible, for instance, the term *mishteh* normally is used to designate a banquet or feast. These occasions seem to be one-time events hosted by an individual. Many involve a rite of passage such as a birthday (Gen. 40:20), weaning (Gen. 21:8), wedding (Judg. 14), or funeral (Jer. 16:5–8), although there are also occasional episodes of hospitality (Gen. 19:3; 26:30; 2 Sam. 3:20, the latter two with military purposes). Beyond these hosted events are also communal, religious (e.g., Exod. 10:9; 12:14; Deut. 16:1–8), seasonal, and agricultural festivals (Deut. 16:9–17, here using the Hebrew term *hag* ("festival"). An explicit focus on the clan is also attested (1 Sam. 20).

In the report of Solomon's encounter with the Queen of Sheba in 1 Kings 10, the climactic event convincing the queen of Solomon's wisdom lies in a summary in verses 4–5, quite literally leaving her "breathless" (NJPS). Prominently listed as reasons for Solomon's wisdom are "the food of his table, the seating of his officials, and the attendance of his servants, their clothing, his valets."[3] That so many of these involve something in the nature of table fellowship strongly alludes to the role that food and its service could play in the biblical world. Indeed, this ideal portrait points toward what the anthropologist Michael Dietler has termed the "micropolitics of daily life" (Dietler 2001, 66).

The usefulness of feasting considered from a political perspective can be easily imagined. For feasts hosted by an individual, the food and drink extended to guests may be considered in the context of hospitality as gifts (Mauss 1967). Although gifts seem to be free, upon closer inspection one realizes that gifts normally are repaid, although perhaps with a delay factor that may be considered as obscuring this literal *quid pro quo* (Appadurai 1986). When viewed from the perspective of this reciprocity, the gift may be thought of as lending status, with the giver viewed with a favorable lens. The exchange of food and drink carries with it an additional transformation: the conversion of economic capital (the food and drink themselves that are owned by the giver but are susceptible to being spoiled) to different types of capital, whether social, cultural, or political (Bourdieu 1977; 1986). These are different forms of wealth that are expressed in terms of friendship or closer social bonds (J. Friedman and Rowlands 1978; Joffe 1998).

The potential of political dynamics revolving around the feast can be integrated into existing models of Israelite social structure. J. David Schloen, drawing on Max Weber, has forcefully argued a model for Israelite society and much of the wider ancient Near East centered on the idea of a patrimonial household, or the "house of the father" (Schloen 2001; see also

---

3. Some debate has arisen over the dating of this passage, although in any case the familiar trope in this passage is clear.

Stager 1985; Master 2001). Individuals are located within a family, lineage, clan, and tribe, with the deity ultimately as the head of the house. Schloen sees an interplay between fact and symbol, between representation in material form and the conceptual idea, that together strengthen the effect of this metaphor. The examples that he discusses, which include architecture, demography, and the text of the Hebrew Bible, lack explicit attention toward food as a possible matrix expressing this dichotomy, and it may be argued that the table serves as a central point of connection between different household nodes (Fu and Altmann 2014, 20).

While the opening example showed how feasts can serve to draw a family together, in the light of Schloen's proposal royal banquets may be of special interest. Indeed, feasting like a king (1 Sam. 25:36) expressed the associated nature of feasting and kingship and surely referenced both the abundance and the elite nature of what kings ate (Meyers 2014b). But it may be useful here also to think through the possible intensifying effects of display that the feast could provide. The senses—sight, hearing, smell, taste, and touch—are all naturally present in the preparation and consumption of food (Sutton 2001). Taken a step further, feasts can involve a high level of pageantry and become performative spectacles, especially as additional elements of music, noise, multitudes of people, and so forth are added (see, e.g., Inomata and Coben 2006; T. Carter 2007; Mills 2007; I. Winter 2007). Under these conditions, feasts prove fitting examples of what DeMarrais, Castillo, and Earle (1996) consider "materializations of ideology"; that is, they enact in material form existing structures of authority and simultaneously also help make them into reality.

The importance of the senses may be more profound in ancient societies, with their proverbial, and possibly literal, bells and whistles accompanying feasts and processions. Indeed, a number of examples written in stone have been placed as monuments of these very events.

Out of northern Syria and the Neo-Hittite world can be seen a series of images carved out of stone that depict feasting (Bonatz 2000), sometimes centered on gateways (Gilibert 2011), where one visualizes a procession that culminates in a banquet. While they need not represent actual, physical events, their construction and placement surely signaled at least some reality—a message that was spoken in visual form that could proclaim and remind viewers of the largesse or abundance present under the reign of an individual monarch. As such, the importance of the feast as an iconic symbol—that is, as a representation of reality—cannot be underestimated as a tool used, one might say, as an ideological method to support, to suborn, and to instill a message about the role of the king in fertility, abundance, and the natural and divine order.

This message similarly is confirmed in the epigraphical texts available from the ancient Near East and the world of the eastern Mediterranean. As Douglas Green (2010) has shown, the importance of abundance and fertility was a major theme that West Semitic kings addressed (see, e.g., I. Winter 2007; Altmann 2014a). For instance, the Kilamuwa Inscription (*KAI* 24), from roughly 825 BCE and found at Zincirli in present-day southern Turkey, narrates the increased prosperity occurring under the king as the poor, who previously did not own flocks, had become wealthy (D. Green 2010, 152–54). The Panamuwa Inscription (*KAI* 215), also found at Zincirli, similarly highlights a transformation from impoverishment to plenty (cf. lines 5–6 to 9–10). Such rhetoric may also be reflected in the language of the Hebrew Bible (e.g., 1 Kings 4:20–25).

Indeed, such was the concern with feasting in these states that it may be surmised that the Neo-Assyrian state in its expansion westward adopted these same motifs, which then became part of its iconographic repertoire. In the ninth century BCE, the Neo-Assyrian king Ashurnasirpal II, who had spent time in the western periphery being feted by the kings of these small western states (Gilibert 2011), returned and founded the city of Kalhu/Nimrud, in which one major motif featured the king holding a cup to his mouth. Inscriptional evidence similarly shows a preoccupation with banqueting. The Banquet Stele commemorating the founding of this city narrates a large feast, for which nearly seventy thousand individuals (Wiseman 1952) were invited to a banquet of rich and exotic foods (see, e.g., Wiseman 1952; Ermidoro 2015, 200–207). The Black Obelisk of Shalmaneser III, the succeeding king, features processions of tribute bearers along its four sides. From epigraphic notes next to the images, we see that the monument cites five encounters with kings (Marcus 1987). The top two registers feature two different kings bowing in nearly the same pose. In one, Shalmaneser holds a bow, while in the other, whose caption indicates that this is Jehu, king of Israel, Shalmaneser appears to drink from a cup. The imagery fairly clearly points to the dichotomy of war and subsequent banquet that seem to hold center stage for Assyria.

A last, well-known scene serves to highlight this motif. The garden scene of Ashurbanipal shows the king reclining and the queen seated on a throne while at a private banquet surrounded by attendants and trees. Yet close scrutiny reveals a severed head hanging from a tree—that of the Elamite king Te'uman, recently defeated in a battle (Ziffer 2005).

The close relationship between war and peace, victory and post-victory banquet—essentially the association of the banquet with judgment—is repeatedly seen in these episodes and further reflected in the Hebrew Bible.[4] A motif of judgment appears prominently with the idea of a king with a cup (for the general motif, see I. Winter 1986; in Ps. 23, see Adam 2014). Indeed, prophetic notices that invoke drinking from the cup of God's wrath (see, e.g., Isa. 51:17;

Jer. 25:15) seem to employ this motif and suggest the role of God as king. The idea of judgment surrounding the cup, seen most clearly in the Assyrian examples, is even extended metaphorically to a future portentous day of judgment. A final eschatological banquet in Isaiah 25 involves a triumph over mythological or personified enemies, including death (Cho and Fu 2013).

The widespread presence of a motif of feasting that depends on the presence of abundance and the implied orderly and ideal world of a just king position the feast as an easily translatable motif within the apocalyptic imagination. Perhaps in response to a growing monolithic conception of empire and divinity originating in the rise of Neo-Assyria, the presence of a divine banquet and therefore of the implied ultimate judgment is asserted in conceptions of banquets, perhaps couched especially within seasons of pronounced austerity (Altmann 2011; 2014a; Magness 2014). The apocalyptic imagination seized upon the feast that displayed a different and divine template, thereby overturning the present temporal order. Thus, the latter part of Isaiah pictures the divine feast and procession in reflecting back Isaiah 2 and 25 and Micah 4. Such processions envisioned an overturning of the present material world with its injustices and provided hope for an awaiting future. In contrast to a legitimizing ideology grounded in material form, these texts portended a coming and not yet translated hope in the future, when the ideal could become real. Such visions may have provided the seeds of monotheistic zeal and proven a template of resistance in a world otherwise arrayed against a minority (for Dan. 5, see Fu and Cho forthcoming). The feast may thus be seen as a productive and useful metaphor in its application. Already present in the earliest stages of the biblical text and grounded in the world of the ancient Near East, it was subjected to the needs of its hearers, adapted and translated for a new generation.

---

4. Indeed, an argument could be made that the book of Esther as a whole is structured around these banquets, through which Haman ultimately receives judgment.

61

Music and Dance in the World of the Bible

ANNIE F. CAUBET

Music and dance are universal phenomena of humankind, basic and essential parts of world culture. Across time and space, a number of invariant elements are present in different civilizations, while individual aspects have changed with time in different regions, each people or culture evolving in their own ways. The musical data specific to the Old Testament are detailed and rich enough to serve as the base for the reconstruction of biblical and Jewish music undertaken by a number of major scholars in the field, such as Joachim Braun (2002) and Bathja Bayer (2014). Both were early proponents of a contextual approach to music in ancient Israel, examined against non-Israelite cultures, notably those of Mesopotamia. For the purpose of looking "behind the scenes" of the Old Testament, this chapter focuses on some of the invariants seen from a broad perspective of the ancient Near East and the Levant.

Music

Music is perceived to have been invented at the dawn of time: Yuval (or Jubal) was "the ancestor of all those who play the lyre and pipe" (Gen. 4:21). His brother Tubal-cain, "an instructer of every artificer in brass and iron" (4:22 KJV), produced sophisticated weapons for his father, Lamech. Rabbinic commentaries extrapolated on the association between music and metal. Yuval would have been inspired to invent rhythm and measure by listening to the cadence of Tubal's hammer resounding on the anvil (Rashi, *Commentary on Genesis 4*). A parallel legend in the classical world would have Pythagoras inventing the music of the spheres by walking past a smithy (Boethius, *De institutione musica* 1.10, quoting from earlier Platonic sources). In both legendary lineages, the biblical and the Greek, there is a double meaning to the story. One, on a plain level, associates music with the sound of metal and weapons (Caubet and Yon 2015). The other reading is placed on the moral plane: the harmony found in numbers, in nature, and in music is the symbol of measure, control, and balance, as taught by divine wisdom.

Music is an accomplishment that kings—Shulgi, king of Ur, or David, king of Israel—needed to master in order to become model rulers. Therefore, music was part of the education of the rulers and the elite. It was taught with the help of written annotations, as evidenced by the (much debated and still elusive) Babylonian "gamut" found at Ugarit, recording a hymn signed by Ammurapi, king of Ugarit, ca. 1200 (Vitale 1982; Bayer 2014, with bibliography).

Vocal Music

Vocal music—song, laments, chants, prayers, war chants, and so on—was and is nearly universal, though the designations of the different genres vary, as well as the circumstance of the performances. Deborah's war chant (Judg. 5) remains an exception as a female performance, while there are numerous textual examples documenting the existence of vocal ensembles involving several singers, but few details about the gender and age of the participants. While the existence of eunuchs may be implicitly inferred (N. Ziegler 2007, 23–24), there is not much indication for child singers; female choristers (using that term as a convenient anachronism) seem to be a general rule. Those performing in the palace of Mari received payments according to their respective accomplishment (N. Ziegler 2007, 24–26). Some of them are recorded as an ethnic group—the Amorites, the Subareans—perhaps an allusion either to their foreign origin or to the genre of their song, or both. The Mari singers often were recruited among secondary wives and placed under the authority of the queen or the "music master," a high-ranking official. Mesopotamian sources rarely specify whether the singers, solo or choir, accompanied themselves on instruments, as did the Greek bards of the Homeric age. While iconographic and archaeological evidence for singers is often by nature ambiguous, solo singers with a lyre appear on Iron Age figurines from Cyprus and the Levant: standing while they touch their instrument, they raise their faces to the sky, the better for the voice to soar out of their throat. Some are even depicted with open mouth (Fourrier et al. 1999, no. 360). Such figurines often are surrounded by a ring of dancers.

Musical Instruments

Most of the categories of instruments used in the Old World may be counted among the invariants, despite the many different improvements developed over the *longue durée*. Complex instruments such as the harp and the lyre, involving several different materials—gut, metal, wood—and built by highly specialized craftsmen, are observed to have been in use over a wide geographic area since the end of the fourth millennium. Bo Lawergren (1996) traces their various transformations over an immense space, extending from Mesopotamia and the Levant (notably Israel in the Iron Age) to Egypt, Iran, central Asia, and western China, and in the Mediterranean as early as the Cycladic culture (ca. 2500 BCE), and into the classical world. It is difficult to assign a precise origin for such complex instruments. The well-preserved harps and lyres from the Royal Tombs at Ur (ca. 2450) tend to tip the scale in favor of a Sumerian origin. However, textual sources from Mari ca. 1750 (N. Ziegler 2007, 39–50) refer to such instruments as being from Magan (in the Persian Gulf) or Marashi (eastern Iran or central Asia): they were sumptuous pieces, built of exotic wood and adorned with gold and lapis lazuli, a stone originating in modern Afghanistan.[1] They were played in great numbers together as "ensembles"; the Mari palace records an exceptional occasion when two hundred (female) lyre players performed on these instruments, an extremely high number for a specific ritual, the average being between seven and thirty.

The names of instruments listed in literary sources vary, of course, with the different

---

1. The use of lapis lazuli might be an indication that the Magan and Marashi instruments actually came from these faraway regions or were made to look as if they did.

cultures. Their identification with "real" instruments poses any number of problems. The precise definition of the *balag*, the *kinnaru*, or the *alû*, for instance, is still open to speculation, one reason being that ancient Near Eastern people did not classify musical instruments along the same criteria that we use nowadays, such as cordophones, membranophones, and so forth. It is not even clear whether the Sumerian BALAG, equated to the *kinnaru*, a stringed instrument, in the archives from Ebla (Gabbay 2014, 132) may not sometimes designate a drum (Mirelman 2014, 159). However, most of the names from the Old Testament have a counterpart in Late Bronze Age Ugarit (Caubet 2014); the word "oud," our modern lute, can be traced to Akkadian language, but it may have served to designate different variants of the instrument in the course of time. Iconographic dates for the musical instruments used in Iron Age Israel are listed in reference works (i.e., Braun 2002), such as the long-necked lute on a terra cotta relief from Tel Dan, the lyre painted on a pithos from Kuntillet ʿAjrud (Ornan 2016) and a Megiddo vase: they point to the existence of an instrumental repertoire very similar to the traditions of Bronze Age Mesopotamia and the Levant. The musical practices at Ugarit are well documented by texts, iconography, and actual remains of instruments (Caubet 2014). With additional evidence from contemporary images, such as the ivory lyre player from Kamid el Loz, the data from the Late Bronze age Levant shape an informative background to the situation in Iron Age Israel. Clappers and so-called magic wands in ivory from Ugarit indicate that part of the instrumental repertoire of the Levant was shared with Egypt. The "magic wand," named after its incised decoration of mythological demons, is shaped like a *harpē*, a type of curved scimitar or sword, and was associated with dancing performances. One such magic wand from Ugarit, ending in the shape of a hand, may have been half of a pair of clappers (Gachet-Bizollon 2007, nos. 393–94).

Dance

Dance mentioned in the Old Testament, among other episodes, includes the story of David dancing in front of the Ark of the Covenant (2 Sam. 6:14) and Miriam dancing as she sang the Song of the Sea (Exod. 15:20). In most ancient Near Eastern sources, it is not clear whether dancers were distinct from musicians, but dancers seemed to have been predominantly female and professional since dancing was the activity for which they were hired and attached to a temple or a palace. The Mari archives are exceptionally rich (N. Ziegler 1999, 70) on the number, training, salaries, social status, and so forth of the female musicians, some of whom probably were dancing girls ("petites musiciennes") in the harem. They were placed under the authority of the music master of the palace.

Iconographic sources are not so eloquent. Dance, like any movement, is especially difficult to translate on an inanimate medium. The artists are forced to employ visual devices that the spectator can read and understand. One such device is the depiction of aligned groups of human figures with their arms extended horizontally or letting their long hair float loose around their heads (Garfinkel 1998). The extended arms are a feature of ring dances, well documented by Cypriote terra cotta and stone groups where (female) dancers form a circle around a lyre player (Fourrier et al. 1999, 153–54, no. 202).

Another visual device used to express the movement of dance is the flexed knee, seen in profile, a depiction often used on Syrian cylinder seals (Matoušova-Rajmova 1979) and Cypriote vase paintings in association with music players. The flexed-knee motif was adopted by Greek artists to depict the action of running, especially for magic creatures like Medusa. Flexed knees may be depicted in frontal view, showing both knees flexed outward, thus revealing conspicuous genitalia. This visual device was reserved for images of magic creatures, notably the Mesopotamian Humbaba or the Egyptian Bes image. These demons share a challenging, snarling grimace, frowning eyebrows, and protruding tongue, as well as a semi-animal nature. The Bes-like figures on the Kuntillet ʿAjrud vase (Meshel 1978b, fig. 8; Ornan 2016) are local variations of the motif of the dancing demons depicted *en face*. Such seminal figures as the Humbaba and Bes images share powers over the underworld and its riches and are sometimes associated with mining and metallurgy (Caubet and Yon 2015). The proximity of Kuntillet ʿAjrud to the turquoise and copper mines of the Negev may provide a key to the understanding of these mysterious images. Similar Bes images, seen *en face* and dancing, are engraved on ivory magic wands, the curved *harpai* (swords) common in Egypt and the Levant.

There is iconographic evidence for sword and dance in ancient Mesopotamia: terra cotta plaques from Babylonia, ca. 1800–1700 BCE, depict two male figures going at each other with curved swords or clappers (Barrelet 1968, no. 289). Their dynamic élan seems directed by the rhythmic sound produced by the clashing of weapons, metal on metal. Greek literary and iconographic sources abound in examples of war dances, where rhythm is provided by the ringing of swords upon shields (W. Childs 2003). In that context, the dance of David introducing the Ark into Jerusalem is a war dance celebrating the triumphal entry of the Israelite tribe into the promised realm and leading the entourage of the divine warrior.

There are no clear boundaries between what we see as dance and other physical feats performed in the course of musical events (besides prostitution, which certainly was often correlated with music—but that question would call for a separate discussion). Acrobats are well attested in iconography, often a small, child-like or monkey figure (Pruzsinszky 2016). One is seen upside down among dancers holding hands on a cylinder seal from Ugarit (Amiet

1992, no. 265). Bull-leaping as a ritual is attested over a large geographic area extending from the Mediterranean to central Asia (Collon 1994; Staubli 2009; Francfort 2005).

It took 450 prophets of Baʿal to compete with Elijah (1 Kings 18:19–29). Their dance is a means to attain a state of ecstatic frenzy, a condition that allows them to reach out of themselves, get into contact with their gods, and predict the future. Prophets played an important role in ancient Syria (Durand et al. 2011). In the archives from Mari (ca. 1750 BCE) and Emar (ca. 1200 BCE), they represented the survival of the old nomadic and tribal ways of life before urbanization took place and kingship was established, and they remained a counterpower to the kings. As seers and magicians, they manifested their power by their dance, their speech, and their use of specific instruments: the clappers and magic wand from Ugarit were found together with clay liver models—the instruments of hepatoscopy—and a group of medico-magical texts written in Ugaritic cuneiform language (Pardee 1988b), evidence for the practice of divination and magic with musical accompaniment. Other instances of these combined practices include the Ritual of Ishtar, where an orchestra and prophets work in concert (Nissinen 2003, nos. 51, 52), and, in the Bible, in the story of Elisha and the harpist (2 Kings 3:15).

Setting the Scene

There are few actual descriptions of the settings where music and dance took place. One assumes that the rituals were held inside or outside the temple or the palace. On the occasion of the great Ishtar Festival in Mari (N. Ziegler 2007, 56), the pageant was organized on an impressive scale: hundreds of performers—singers, dancers, instrument players—interacted in a setting furnished with a large number of "props," cultic implements, altars and other tables, incense burners, tables, thrones and stools, and vessels. The description of participants and paraphernalia compares well with those described in the dedication of the temple by Solomon. Indeed, most of the implements present may have served for the ritualized consumption of food—that is, the banquets held in honor of gods, kings, and heroes. As in the feast of Belshazzar (Dan. 5), ancient Near Eastern banquets generally were accompanied by music and dance. Other performers, such as wrestlers, acrobats, and clowns, also took part (Mirelman 2014, 160). The scene may take place outdoors: in the famous garden relief from Nineveh in the British Museum (British Museum no. 124886–87), Assurbanipal (669–631 BCE) celebrates his victory over Elam with a banquet, relaxing on his couch to the sound of a harp. Tables, beds, chairs, and vessels are provided. The scene is framed by palm trees, and incense burners give the outdoor scene its religious atmosphere. Similar images occur in Iron Age Cyprus: banquet scenes and ring dance groups present similar implements framed by palm trees or centered around a dovecot tower, with a pithos and other vessels, associating music, dance, and drinking with the ominous presence of a deity (Karageorghis and des Gagniers 1974, 516–17; Fourrier et al. 1999, no. 202).

Music was by nature ambiguous morally and socially, as was the status of the musicians, as may be inferred by the uncertainty about gender and the existence of eunuchs. It is rarely clear whether female musicians and dancers were appreciated on the same level as their male counterparts. If, according to the Mari archives, the females' training was approximately similar and aimed at reaching the highest competence, some of them may have been little more than concubines, while royal spouses and secondary wives assumed high responsibilities in the performance of musical rituals. Some instruments seem to have been gender-oriented: the lyre *parahsitum* in Mari was played exclusively by women, and the vocal ensembles were female. In the iconography, notably the terra cotta plaques, the long-necked lute seems to have been played mostly by males, the hand tambourine by females.

Perhaps because it reaches beyond human nature, music is a world apart from reality, entailing an element of "otherness" on the part of the musicians and dancers, who are seen as "different" from regular humankind. This difference is expressed by a number of physical traits: the blind, the eunuch, the hybrid monster, and the animal as musicians are recurrent features in the artifacts from ancient civilizations.

SECTION

Governance

*Integrated Approaches to Themes
in Social Organization*

Kingship and the State in Ancient Israel

Nili S. Fox

In the ancient Near East, kingship was the normative form of government for a territorial state. For the great kingdoms of Egypt and Mesopotamia, kingship can be traced to the early third millennium and even earlier. Israel, however, was relatively late in emerging as a state, not until the end of the second millennium. The Bible traces Israel's history in Canaan from a group of loosely connected tribal entities led by chieftains to the formation of an independent kingdom. The transition to statehood involved the creation of a central government headed by a king. According to the biblical record, dissatisfaction with inefficient, petty rulers led Israel's elders to petition the prophet Samuel for a king: "appoint for us, then, a king to govern us, like other nations" (1 Sam. 8:5). Although displeased at the prospect of a human king in place of God as sovereign, Samuel heeded the people's request and with divine guidance anointed Saul as Israel's first king. Thus a monarchy was born in ancient Israel.

Kingship Ideology in the Ancient Near East

Although kingship was the normative form of government throughout the region, royal ideology surrounding the person and power of the king differed somewhat from state to state. In Egypt kingship was a divinely ordained institution with the king an earthly embodiment of the god Horus. Although not considered divine in life, the king's titulary (five names) included epithets like "son of Re," intimately connecting him to the gods. An exception, Rameses II (thirteenth century) actually claimed to be a living god (van de Mieroop 2011, 217). The king, or pharaoh, as he was called beginning in the New Kingdom (1540 BCE), was an absolute ruler: chief executive officer, chief justice, and supreme high priest. He was obligated to maintain a unified kingdom (Upper Egypt and Lower Egypt). As shepherd, he was expected to protect his subjects. Peace and prosperity depended on the maintenance of *ma'at*, cosmic harmony established by the creator deity. Chaos, which threatened *ma'at*, was attributed to enemies of the state, who had to be subdued. After death the king merged with Osiris, the underworld god, and indeed became a god for whom offerings and prayers were made at funerary temples.

Mesopotamia's long history of kingship began with the city-states of Sumer in the third millennium BCE and continued throughout the

475

first-millennium empires of Assyria and Babylonia. According to cuneiform literary texts, kingship was a divine gift, hence it can be said that kings ruled by divine authority as intermediaries between gods and humans (Stiebing 2009, 53–55, 284–86). As in Egypt, the king's administrative responsibilities encompassed the religious sphere, which meant that he was expected to build and maintain temples and propitiate the deities in his domain with food offerings. The welfare of the land and its inhabitants was dependent on the king's success in that regard. Rulers generally did not claim divinity in their lifetimes or in death. However, exceptions existed, such as Naram-Sin, king of Agade (twenty-third century), who adopted a divine title and pictorially portrayed himself with horns of divinity (Pritchard 1969a, no. 309). Loyalty to the crown, an expectation based on the belief that the royal line was legitimated by the state gods, was essential to the longevity of a dynasty.

The Hittite Empire, with its "great king," was another powerful player in the region (fourteenth and thirteenth centuries). Hittite kings as absolute rulers were army commanders, chief justices, administrators, and priests. Although not considered divine during their lifetimes, these kings assumed titles that reflected their close ties to the gods. Titles such as "My Sun" and "beloved of (a specific deity's name)" suggest that they too were agents of the divine (Stiebing 2009, 213). As powerful monarchs, they instituted binding vassal treaties within their extended empire and treaty relationships with kings of other great powers.

Kingship in the smaller states of the Levant during the Late Bronze Age (1540–1150 BCE) and Iron Age I (1150–1000 BCE) was manifested by city-state rulers. Written sources are generally limited, with the exception of material from Ugarit (mostly literary texts). For the city-states along the Mediterranean coast, such as Byblos and Tyre or the Syro-Palestinian kinglets further inland, the Amarna correspondence (fourteenth century) is our primary source. It testifies to Egyptian rule over the domains of the local princes (Moran 1992, xxii–xxxix). Not surprisingly, Levantine rulers whose positions were sponsored by their Egyptian overlords did not claim divine rights. As servants of pharaoh, they swore absolute allegiance to him. Still they held a measure of divine affiliation with local gods. With the coming of the Sea Peoples (late thirteenth century), Egyptian hegemony in the Levant weakened until finally Egypt withdrew from the region. By the eleventh century, opportunities arose for self-rule in various locales. The Phoenician city-states were fully independent; in Canaan the Sea Peoples were organized into a confederacy of five city-states, and the Israelites in the hill country, faced with inefficient local leadership and incursions by enemies from the east and the west, began the process of forming a centralized government.

Kingship Ideology in the Bible

Since the Bible is our only written source for the creation of kingship in Israel, our view of Israelite kingship ideology reflects biblical thought. Biblical writers, who likely authored their accounts centuries after the events, based on various source materials, presented kingship as a system of rule subservient to the will of God. Thus they were able to critique kings who according to their standards strayed from prescribed Yahwism. Biblical ideology held that the key to a flourishing kingdom was obedience to God's laws; in contrast, political failures are attributed to lapses of religious orthodoxy. One school of thought, that of Deuteronomy, advocated limiting royal prerogative (see the law of the king, Deut. 17:14–20). Notably, in evaluations of the reigns of Israelite kings, dynastic affiliation was key. Biblical ideology dictated that the house of David was the sole legitimate dynasty. Therefore, not a single king of the north receives a fully positive evaluation.

The Chronicler's records simply bypass these kings, mentioning only those whose acts were integral to accounts of the kings of Judah.

The United Monarchy

The inauguration of kingship in Israel—the anointing of Saul following the period of judges—is dated approximately to the end of the eleventh century BCE. Saul's kingship appears to have been limited, as Samuel in his role as priest and prophet sought to contain royal power (1 Sam. 15). The biblical writers painted Saul and his sons as failed tragic characters. In contrast, they depicted David and Solomon (ca. 1000–925 BCE) as Yahweh's anointed, the Davidic dynasty secured by divine covenant, with the relationship between God and king likened to that of father and son (2 Sam. 7; Pss. 2; 89; 132). David is credited with uniting all Israel into a recognizable territorial state (note the title *bet dawid*—"house of David" on the Aramean Tel Dan Inscription), while Solomon, building on his father's accomplishments, is credited with the construction of the Jerusalem temple as a house for Israel's national God. Notably, David and Solomon, unlike Saul, controlled all aspects of government: they appointed civil and military officials, served as chief justice, appointed priests while retaining some cultic roles, and removed from office those who fell into disfavor.

The Divided Kingdom

The United Monarchy was short-lived. Apparently, sectional differences, perhaps originating from the tribal period, were irreconcilable. Political and economic issues also played a role in fostering rebellion. According to the biblical account (1 Kings 11–12), Solomon's taxation policies favored Judahites and greatly alienated northerners. His son Rehoboam, who chose to continue his father's oppressive policies, kindled the rebellion. The revolution of the north was led by a royal official, Jeroboam, who later became the first king of the kingdom of Israel. Northern secession suggests that absolute kingship was not at home among Israelites and that loyalty to a Judahite king was not binding.

Kingship in Israel

The northern kingdom, Israel, was composed of ten of the twelve tribal territories; only the smaller territory of Benjamin and Judah remained under the rule of the house of David. During its existence, approximately two centuries (ca. 925–722 BCE), twenty kings representing ten dynasties sat on the throne of Israel. The lack of a stable dynasty no doubt facilitated the multiple palace conspiracies and changes of dynasty. Military officers especially, such as Zimri and Jehu, who secured the loyalty of the army, were in position to assassinate the reigning monarchs (1 Kings 16:9; 2 Kings 9). The location of the kingdom's capital was also subject to change (from Shechem to Tirzah to Samaria). The biblical writers maintained that these uprisings were the result of divine will; the frequent change in dynasty was attributed to the transgressions of individual kings, for example, "He did what was evil in the sight of the LORD, walking in the way of Jeroboam and in the sin that he caused Israel to commit" (1 Kings 15:34).

Although better situated geographically than Judah (sea access, natural resources), the proximity of Israel to unfriendly neighbors to the north made the kingdom more susceptible to foreign invasion, especially by Aramaeans and Assyrians. Judah to the south rarely served as an ally to its sibling kingdom. In 732 BCE Tiglath-Pileser III, king of Assyria, conquered most of Israel's territory and annexed it as an Assyrian province. As was Assyrian practice, he exiled a portion of the population and installed a puppet king, Hoshea, in Samaria. But Hoshea, like other vassal kings before him, did not remain loyal to his overlord. His revolt initiated the final destruction of the kingdom by Shalmaneser V and Sargon II in 722 to 720 BCE.

Kingship in Judah

The kingdom of Judah survived until 586 BCE, more than a century after the fall of Israel. With the exception of one usurper—Athaliah—the other nineteen rulers of Judah belonged to the Davidic dynasty and ruled from Jerusalem, the capital established by David. But although the kings of Judah belonged to the divinely chosen royal line, biblical writers are critical of more than half, whom they accuse of perverted religious practices. Furthermore, of those who receive positive evaluations, all except Hezekiah and Josiah are berated for maintaining functional shrines outside Jerusalem. In contrast, Hezekiah and Josiah, credited with sweeping religious reforms, were held as examples of model kings. Notably, both of these kings actually brought Judah to the brink of political disaster—Hezekiah when he revolted against his overlord, the Assyrian king Sennacherib (701 BCE), and Josiah when he attacked Pharaoh Necho at Megiddo (609 BCE). But the king ultimately blamed for the fall of Jerusalem was Manasseh, a cooperative vassal but one who instituted idolatrous worship in the temple of Yahweh.

The kings of Judah, like those of Israel, freely exercised royal power in a variety of spheres. Noticeably, however, they appear generally more receptive and respectful of the priests and prophets in Jerusalem. Priests such as Jehoiada at the court of Joash and Hilkiah at the court of Josiah were influential figures. Prophets such as Isaiah at the court of Hezekiah were involved in military and foreign policy decisions. Even Jeremiah, who had been jailed for his prophecies of doom, had the ear of King Zedekiah during the final days of Jerusalem. In contrast, kings of Israel rarely tolerated prophets who spoke against the crown (e.g., Elijah concerning Ahab).

State Officials[1]

The stability of the king's position as "paterfamilias," proprietor of the land and protector of the people (King and Stager 2001, 4–5), also depended on the loyalty and efficiency of the circle of officials and functionaries who comprised the bureaucratic organization. This included civil, military, and religious personnel who served at the royal court as central administrators or outside the capitals as local officials.

Reconstructing Israelite Officialdom

For the Israelite states, our primary source for information on officials comes from the historical books of the Hebrew Bible, especially Samuel, Kings, and Chronicles (and occasionally the Torah and the Prophets). Some scholars who question the historicity of the biblical data in general also question data relating to kingship and officials, especially if they consider the writing too far removed from the events, as that of Chronicles (N. Fox 2000, 14–23). However, before dismissing the historicity of a biblical text we should consider genre. Lists of officials (2 Sam. 8:16–18; 20:23–26; 1 Kings 4:1–19), for example, were more likely preserved in archives and are less tendentious than narratives conveying particular ideologies. In addition, comparable data from nonbiblical sources regarding the bureaucracies of neighboring states (e.g., Egypt, Assyria, Babylonia, Ammon, Moab, Edom) serve as useful models for reconstructing Israelite officialdom. Since Israel and Judah were also organized under a monarchical system, it is not surprising that their bureaucratic organization resembled these others, albeit on a smaller scale than those of the great empires.

1. This section is taken and adapted from my article "State Officials" in *Dictionary of the Old Testament: Historical Books*, edited by Bill T. Arnold and H. G. M. Williamson. Copyright © 2005 by InterVarsity Christian Fellowship/USA. Used by permission of InterVarsity Press, P.O. Box 1400, Downers Grove, IL 60515, USA. www.ivpress.com.

Important to the study of Israelite monarchic officials are the numerous inscribed finds uncovered in archaeological excavations in Israel and Jordan. The epigraphic corpus consists primarily of seals, seal impressions (bullae and jar handles), ostraca (inscribed pottery sherds), and marked weights. These often represent bureaucratic practices, as officials would have kept records, corresponded (on ostraca), and sealed documents with stamp seals displaying their names and positions. Thus, even these brief texts are invaluable in reconstructing Israelite officialdom and state organization. Still, we must exercise caution when identifying names in inscriptions with biblical characters or when utilizing unprovenanced finds, which may be forgeries (N. Fox 2000, 23–32, 36–42).

Officials of varying status, including high-ranking ministers, were essential for running the Israelite states. Notably, the biblical record indicates growth in complexity of the bureaucratic organization. For example, Saul, who had few officials, appointed family members to positions of power (1 Sam. 14:50–51). David continued this practice in his early reign, but he established a broader, more sophisticated administrative apparatus once his rule was secured in Jerusalem (the City of David). Solomon followed by creating a hierarchy of officials with new positions (1 Kings 4). Most officeholders were unrelated to the king. Instead, certain families of officials were prominent at court and remained so for generations. Royal scribes and priests, for example, can be traced by their patronymics to the families of Shaphan, Neriah, Hilkiah, and Achbor (2 Kings 22:3; 25:22; Jer. 32:12; 36:11; 51:59).

Civil Officials and Courtiers

Since most Near Eastern monarchies required the same basic administrators to fulfill the needs of statecraft, it is not surprising that many titles of functionaries are similar across

the region. In addition, because Semitic was the dominant language family in the Near East, linguistic similarities are prevalent in Akkadian, Ugaritic, and Hebrew titles of officials. Contrary to some scholarly opinion, however, no convincing evidence exists that either titles or offices were directly borrowed from one state to another (N. Fox 2000, 276–80).

The earliest officers were military personnel and priests. King David added to these a number of civil officials and courtiers: herald or crier (*mazkir*, 2 Sam. 8:16),[2] scribe (*soper*, 8:17), royal advisor (*yo'ets hammelek*, 15:12), overseer of corveé labor (*'al hammas*, 20:24),[3] and companion of the king (*re'a hammelek*, 1 Chron. 27:33), a confidant and/or bodyguard. Solomon's list of officials reflects further expansion of the bureaucratic organization of the central government and regional administration (1 Kings 4:2–19). Solomon appointed two scribes, the sons of his father's scribe, and added a royal house minister (*'al habbayit*)[4] whose authority encompassed royal property at court and probably nationwide. An administrative innovation under Solomon was his creation of twelve districts with a prefect to oversee taxation in each district. The chief prefect (*'al hannitsabim*) oversaw the regional prefects from Jerusalem.

The Bible does not preserve lists of officials for either Israel or Judah for the period of the divided monarchy, but these persons do appear within the context of narratives. As expected, many of the titles are those known from the Davidic and Solomonic lists. Importantly, archaeological evidence from Israel and Jordan in the form of stamp seals, bullae, ostraca, and a few brief inscriptions confirms the use

2. Some scholars define *mazkir* as "recorder," but that role would most likely have been subsumed in the position of scribe. Also, the position of herald is well attested in most ancient Near Eastern bureaucracies.
3. Labor obligations were a form of taxation in antiquity.
4. Semantically related titles for comparable offices are attested for officials in Mesopotamia, Ugarit, and Egypt.

of these titles for this period (eighth to early sixth century). While the bureaucracy seems similar to the earlier monarchy, it appears that the hierarchy of officials has shifted. When groups of three or more officials are mentioned in a biblical passage, the royal house minister is always listed first, probably indicating that this office was the highest (2 Kings 10:5; 18:18, 37; 19.2). Aside from overseeing the business of royal estates, his role included participation in diplomatic missions (Eliakim in 2 Kings 18–19). A second top-level official, the royal scribe, was responsible for correspondence, record-keeping, and accounting, all basic to a royal administration. Other functions of a scribe could entail control over the temple treasury (2 Kings 12:11) and participation in diplomatic missions (2 Kings 18–19). A third high-level official, the herald, also participated as a military and diplomatic agent (2 Kings 18–19) and in a late text served as financial officer (2 Chron. 34:8–13), perhaps indicating development of the role.

In addition to function-related titles, four titles denote status relationships, either ascribed to individuals by virtue of genealogy or acquired through membership in a special court circle. The two most widely attested in the Bible and inscriptions are "son of the king" (*ben hammelek*) and "servant of the king" (*'ebed hammelek*). "Son of the king" was reserved for a member of the royal family, either a prince or a close relative of the monarch. Seals bearing this title suggest that royals served in the state administration, as was the case in Egypt and Mesopotamia. In contrast, "servant of the king" was a generic, nondescript title for any minister regardless of family affiliation or office. Thus all the king's men—from the highest rank to the lowest—were labeled "servants" vis-à-vis the ruler. The title *'ebed hammelek* or *'ebed* + the king's name is found in both the biblical record and on seals and bullae.

Two other status-related titles are "elders" (*zeqenim*) and "children" (*yeladim*), the latter

appearing only opposite the former. Besides denoting the traditional elders, *zeqenim* also signified senior ranking within the bureaucracy. Like the title *'ebed*, the designation *zeqenim* (always plural) was not role-specific; rather, it referred to a group of senior palace functionaries, such as the group that King Rehoboam consulted when he ascended the throne (1 Kings 12). The term *yeladim* in that narrative seems to be a technical term for the junior functionaries, those who offered Rehoboam dangerous advice. The Bible mentions that Rehoboam grew up with these "children" at court (a comparable epithet is attested from the pharaonic court).

Military and Judicial Officials

Titles of military officers are already attested in the Bible for the early monarchy. Apparently, every political structure, regardless of how simply organized, required military leaders charged with securing the state.[5] Saul, the first king, relied heavily on his military officers: his uncle was army commander (*sar tsaba'*, 1 Sam. 14:50); an Edomite was "strongman" (*'abbir haro'im*, 1 Sam. 21:7); and David was "chief of thousands" (*sar 'alep*, 1 Sam. 18:13). When David ascended the throne, he appointed his nephew army commander. Loyalty was of utmost importance, and relatives usually were trusted more than others. Additional army officers are mentioned in the Bible for the reigns of David and Solomon.

Military leaders continued to play key roles in the kingdoms of Israel and Judah after the division of the monarchy. Names of officers of varying status are mentioned in the Bible: army commander (*sar tsaba'*, 1 Kings 16:16), chariot commander (*sar mahatsit harakeb*, 1 Kings 16:9), commanders of divisions of thousands and divisions of hundreds (2 Chron. 17:14–18; 23:1), and army scribe (2 Chron.

5. In the premonarchic period the judges functioned as generals or ruled jointly with them, as in the case of Deborah and Barak (Judg. 4).

26:11). Two officers entitled *shalish* (third man on the chariot, the armor bearer) appear in historical narratives (2 Kings 9:25; 15:25). Several military officers from Israel are notorious as usurpers of the throne: Zimri, who overthrew King Elah (1 Kings 16:9), and Pekah, who overthrew King Pekahiah (2 Kings 15:25). The term *na'ar* also appears in military contexts, where it refers to a squire or armor bearer (1 Sam. 26:22; 2 Sam. 2:14).

The judicial system in Israel was traditionally in the hands of local elders. In Deuteronomy Moses appoints "judges" (*shopetim*) from among his officers (Deut. 1:15–16; 16:19–20). It is unclear when judges became appointees of the central government, but we know that the king was actually chief justice of the land (2 Sam. 15:3–4). Based on what we know of judicial practices of Israel's neighbors, it seems that the legal system was jointly in the hands of government judges and local elders. According to 2 Chronicles 19:5–11, King Jehoshaphat assigned judges to the cities of his kingdom and established a high court in Jerusalem composed of lay judges and priests to deal with difficult cases. The latter would have situated the judiciary under the watchful eye of the king.

Religious Functionaries

Priests played key roles in the lives of Israelites from premonarchic times. Before the formation of the centralized state a powerful leader could exercise multiple functions, including that of cult officiant. Samuel, for example, served as military commander, judge, prophet, and priest. With the rise of kingship, the priesthood fell under the purview of certain families, sometimes in competition with one another, like the families of Abiathar and Zadok during David's reign (2 Sam. 20:23–26). Solomon banished Abiathar and eliminated that priestly house, demonstrating royal power over the priesthood.

Apparently, princes could also become priests (2 Sam. 8:18). Priestly roles consisted of all cult-related matters, including determining auspicious times for battle. Priests served at the Jerusalem temple and at local shrines throughout the kingdom. The influential role of priests continued during the divided monarchy. Most notable are the priests Jehoiadah and Hilkiah. Jehoiadah was instrumental in deposing the non-Davidic queen Athaliah, installing the child-king Joash, and instituting cult reforms in the temple (2 Kings 11–12). Hilkiah, in concert with King Josiah, conducted major cult reforms, removing the idolatrous cult established by Josiah's grandfather King Manasseh (2 Kings 21–23).

The Municipal Administration

Municipal administrators were also part of the state organization. The highest city official was the governor (*sar ha'ir* or *'asher 'al ha'ir*), whose jurisdiction extended to the regions surrounding the city. The title *sar ha'ir* is attached to governors of capital cities, Samaria and Jerusalem (1 Kings 22:26; 2 Chron. 34:8), but lesser urban centers and fortresses also were governed by this class of officials. The Chronicler records that princes, sons of Jehoshaphat, were appointed as municipal officials outside the capital (2 Chron. 21:1–3). Epigraphic finds such as seals and ostraca provide important evidence for this office. For example, a *sar* administered the fortress of Mesad Hashavyahu, and an officer named "Eliashib" was commander at Arad. The ostracon from Mesad Hashavyahu records the *sar*'s role as judge, while ostraca from Arad indicate that Eliashib oversaw the distribution of supplies. It is unclear whether these officials belonged to the category of civil or military, but perhaps these categories overlapped in small settlements. It is important to realize that during the monarchic period local governments were tied in a secure network to the central authority.

63

Social Stratification in the Iron Age Levant

Avraham Faust

Introduction

Was ancient Israel a stratified society, or were most Israelites fairly equal as far as their socio-economic standing was concerned? These two views, with a number of variants and intermediate positions, can be found in the scholarly literature (Bendor 1996; Neufeld 1960; Lang 1985; Schloen 2001; Houston 2004). Most discussions use the textual evidence—mainly the Bible—as their primary source, whereas the archaeological data has been used, if at all, as supplementary material or for illustrative purposes. It is the aim of this chapter to address the question of socio-economic stratification in the Iron Age Levant mainly from an archaeological perspective. The first part of the chapter outlines the rationale behind the approach and the methods for identifying social stratification through the archaeological record in general and for ancient Israel in particular; the second part briefly summarizes the results of an archaeological examination of the question of socioeconomic stratification in ancient Israel; and the third part briefly presents some of the implications of these results for study of the biblical texts.

The Method

While texts are, of course, invaluable to the study of any society, they tend to paint only a partial and biased portrait of the past. Thus, many texts present the perspectives of members of the urban, usually male, upper class. Not only are such texts biased in their presentation of information, but they also ignore some issues altogether. Rural life can serve as an example of a topic that is often not mentioned in texts, and the Bible is hardly an exception; life in small villages, hamlets, and farmsteads usually is not mentioned in the texts at all. Thus, although essential for many topics, the textual sources are sometimes insufficient for study of the entire fabric of ancient societies. Archaeology, however, despite its own shortcomings, does supply us with information on all segments of society, including the lower social strata, as well as women, children, and even the rural population. While the finds are not always straightforward and need interpretation, they do nevertheless offer us insights into all segments of society.

In the following, we will therefore review the methods for identifying socioeconomic stratification archaeologically. Naturally, social stratification can be identified through a number of mechanisms (Ames 2008; Faust 2012a; M. E. Smith 1987; Wason 1994). Small finds, for example, can direct us to the members of the upper classes via assessments of their economic or symbolic value, particular "style," or function (e.g., Mann and Loren 2001). Indeed, objects can be used to infer wealth or status when they were expensive and only the wealthy could afford them, or because they express a certain taste that is shared by members of a certain class and not by others who therefore do not use them (even if they are not very expensive) (see Bourdieu 1984). Additionally, there were sometimes sumptuary laws that prevented members of some classes or groups from using objects associated with higher classes. While we may use such objects to learn about class membership in the society in which we live (especially through the first two mechanisms, as the third is of less relevance), this is a much more difficult exercise when we attempt to study ancient societies, and, as much as such small objects are useful for identifying wealth and status in our society, their usefulness in the study of the past is hindered by a number of factors (e.g., Blanton 1994; Crocker 1985, 52; Kemp 1977, 137; cf. M. E. Smith 1987, 302). The issue has been discussed at length elsewhere (Faust 1999; 2012a, esp. 41–45, 117–27, with many references), but among the limitations or problems one can list the difficulty of identifying "added value" (e.g., brand names), the relatively inexpensive nature of small finds (even of metals and the like) when compared to houses and fields, the fact that such items are mobile and as a result of various mechanisms can be found outside their designated places of use (e.g., Hall 1992; Girourard 1980, 280; cf. Deetz 1996, 199), possible differences in curation behavior (e.g., Wason 1994, 111), and more. One should also remember that pottery, including imported pottery, which is often used to infer wealth in archaeological studies in the

Levant, probably was very cheap in antiquity (e.g., Vickers and Gill 1994) and therefore cannot serve as an indication of wealth in any straightforward manner.

Thus, while some objects were used mainly by the rich and can, when identified, serve as an indication of wealth, their identification is not a straightforward process. Most such items are not universally used only by the rich (unless the material is expensive), and their usage is culturally specific and can be identified only when we examine already identified high-class households. The main avenue to identify such households, in order to learn about their taste, is through architecture. Indeed, even scholars who believe that wealth can be identified on the basis of the small finds (and, despite the difficulties, it definitely can) usually agree that architecture is more reliable in this respect (e.g., Crocker 1985; M. E. Smith 1987, 301, 327; 1994, 151; 2015). Identifying rich households through architecture will allow us, at a later stage, to use the items associated with these households to identify status in other cases.[1] We must note, furthermore, that a detailed examination of various methods suggested to identify wealth in Iron Age Israel through objects shows that they are insufficient and do not explain the data (Faust 2012a, 117–27, and references there).

Many scholars have noted that architecture is usually regarded as the best tool we have for identifying economic and social differences (see, e.g., Blanton 1994; Crocker 1985, 52; Kemp 1977, 137; I. Morris 2005; M. E. Smith 1987, 301, 327; 2015; M. E. Smith et al. 1989; 2014). Studying architecture for such purposes, however, is also a complex endeavor, and some aspects probably are culture-specific.

1. Searches for those items should be conducted as part of a wide-scale attempt to learn about an ancient society—an attempt to learn not only about wealth but also about economy, organization, gender, ethnicity, and more, and in relation to various types of finds. Only in such a way can we hope to unearth the meaning of the various items used by members of the society examined.

It appears that, following previous detailed and contextual studies, we can use four major architectural components to study wealth and status specifically in the Iron Age Levant (Faust 2012a, 39–127, and references there).

1. **The area of the residential building:** This component could indicate the standard of living and status of the residents, as well as the number of inhabitants or the type of family living in the building. In many cases there is a correlation between these two factors—that is, rich families tend to be bigger.

2. **Construction quality:** The quality of the buildings can be expressed in the quantity and quality of the materials used, and, when exposure is wide, it is also easy to measure energetic investment as well as to assess whether the construction followed a plan by observing the extent of the use of corners and straight walls. Plan-based construction indicates an economic level above a certain threshold, and the ability to build while ignoring topographic features or the needs of other people in the area implies a degree of power. At least some elements in this category are easily identified (others require more work to measure).

3. **The use of shared walls:** Shared walls are a means of saving. Using them saves both building expenses, since there is no need to build a new wall, and space, since a double wall would take up twice the space of a shared wall. The use of a wall shared by more than one building, however, has limiting legal implications. An examination of the plans of buildings in the land of Israel during the Iron Age II shows that very few buildings were built without relying on shared walls, and that buildings without shared walls were usually larger and more nicely built. Thus, it appears that only the rich built

houses without shared walls, and that this criterion can also be used to infer wealth.

4. **Location:** Wherever possible, the previous components should be examined in light of the location of the building within the site and in relation to other buildings. A house's location close to a citadel or public complex may indicate that people connected to these buildings lived there, while houses in separate neighborhoods, which sometimes are identified archaeologically, may indicate clear social differentiation. Topographic location, air, light, visibility, and similar considerations should be taken into account.

The Results: Socioeconomic Stratification in the Kingdoms of Israel and Judah

The amount of archaeological data from Israel and Judah is unparalleled in any other part of the world (e.g., Faust and Safrai 2015). Many dozens of Iron Age sites have been excavated, sometimes on a very large scale, and hundreds of Iron Age houses have been exposed, presenting scholars with a uniquely large data set (e.g., Faust 2012a, with references). The scope of this brief review does not allow a presentation of the full results, but only a summary of the main conclusions. An examination of the area, quality of construction, use of shared walls, and location of residential houses unearthed in many towns in both Israel and Judah testifies to clear social stratification, and to the existence of a few distinct architectural/social groups, including:

1. palaces, which existed only in a number of cities (e.g., Jerusalem, Samaria, Lachish);

2. a limited number of wealthy residences, typically large four-room houses, built of

high quality, in sizes of 100–250 square meters;

3. a large group of middle-class houses, typically three- and four-room houses of some 60–100 square meters, built of medium quality; and

4. many houses of the lower classes, usually three-room houses along with some shapeless houses, built of low quality, in sizes of some 30–70 square meters.

Not in all sites were all four groups found, and commonly only groups 2–4, and even 2 and 4, were unearthed. Thus, in some of the cities (such as Hazor and Jerusalem) the entire socioeconomic spectrum existed, while in some towns (such as Mizpah [Tell en-Nasbeh] and Tell Beit Mirsim) there were probably only two main classes. We must stress, furthermore, that the groups themselves were not homogenous, and one can find differences within them. In at least some of the settlements—for example, at Tell el-Farʿa North (Tirzah) (fig. 63.1)—one can identify distinct neighborhoods that served the different social groups.

We can use Lorenz curves to present stratification. The Lorenz curve is a method used in economics to calculate inequality (for a sophisticated application, see M. E. Smith et al. 2014). The graphs present the degree of centralization of property or income in the hands of part of the population. The data to be calculated are arranged in an increasing order and presented on the graph with a cumulative calculation (e.g., if one is presenting income data, one starts with the lowest income). The X axis presents the number of elements calculated, while the Y axis presents the data calculated cumulatively. A graph with a straight diagonal line reflects an equal distribution of the resource under discussion, since each segment of the population possesses the same percentage of the resource. A concave graph indicates inequality, since as the level increases, so does the cumulative percentage

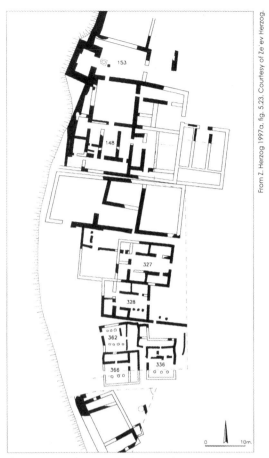

From Z. Herzog 1997a, fig. 5.23. Courtesy of Ze'ev Herzog.

Fig. 63.1. Plan of Tell el-Farʿa (North) / Tirzah. In the plan one can distinguish groups of small four-room houses, large four-room houses, and even larger four-room houses, which are almost palatial in nature. Walls separating the different groups can also be identified in the plan.

of the resource. Given the difficulty of combining the four different criteria, I used the Lorenz graphs freely, without an attempt at precise results, and the graphs are used here for comparative purposes only (for a broad discussion, see Faust 2012a, 39–127 and references there; for the formulation used in constructing these graphs, see pp. 42–45). Figures 63.2 and 63.3 present the results at Tell el-Farʿa North / Tirzah and Beersheba, both expressing significant stratification. The graphs help not only in identifying the socioeconomic gaps but also in observing differences in the nature of stratification (Faust 2012a).

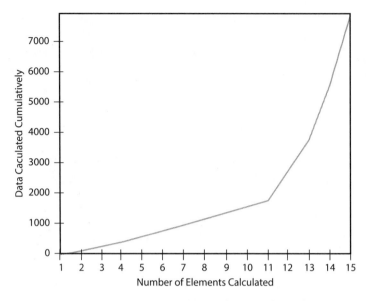

Fig. 63.2. Graph representing (weighted) inequality at Tell el-Far'a (North) / Tirzah. Note the concavity of the graph, indicating a large degree of socio-economic inequality and stratification (cf. 63.3, 63.5, and 63.6).

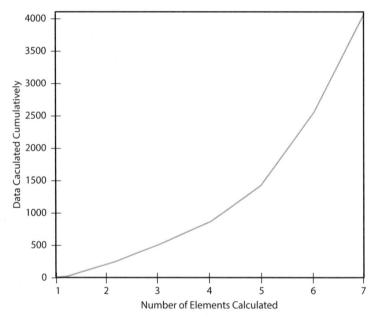

Fig. 63.3. Graph representing (weighted) inequality at Beersheba II. Note the concavity of the graph, indicating a large degree of socioeconomic inequality and stratification (cf. figs. 63.2, 63.5, and 63.6).

Interestingly, the evidence presented above for clear economic stratification pertains only to the urban sector in Israel and Judah (with some differences between the two kingdoms). As more and more data from the rural sector were published, it became apparent that no social and economic stratification could be observed there. Khirbet Jemein (figs. 63.4 and 63.5) and Beit Aryeh (fig. 63.6), for example, were excavated almost in their entirety, yet despite the wide exposure and the application of the same criteria to identify stratification, the data did not yield any significant differences.

The relative uniformity of the size of residential houses can be seen not only in an intra-site analysis, the main tool for examining such gaps, but usually also in an inter-site comparison. The typical rural house of this period was a large four-room house (almost always of the main type, with four clear spaces), whose area was usually 120–130 square meters (and rarely was outside the 100–160 square meters range), and whose quality and shape were similar in all the sites. The great similarity between the buildings indicates a high degree of equality in the rural society, especially since some of the sites are quite distant from one another. Since equivalent analyses of the period's cities showed clear socioeconomic stratification, it is clear that the gaps that probably did exist in the rural sector were small.

More importantly, the absence of evidence for stratification in the rural sector lends credence to the stratification identified in towns and cities and shows that the method identifies differences, when such exist. The data show, therefore, that the view that Iron Age towns and cities were only large villages (e.g., Holladay 1995, 392; and more below) is not well founded. It appears that state involvement in these towns led to, among other things, an increase in hired labor, which in turn led to the development of stratification (Faust 2012a, 169–70, with detailed discussion).

Finally, we should note the possible exceptions to the above rule. At very large rural sites such as Deir el-Mir and Khirbet Banat Barr in western Samaria, and in a few farmsteads near Jerusalem, there seem to be some differences in both quality and size among the various structures. Those differences, which were more extensive than those exposed at other rural settlements, might indicate that in the large villages as well as in the area around Jerusalem processes of social change were operating, probably as a result of their large size and exposure to the political and economic forces of the monarchy. While the architectural data is not complete, it allows us to identify the existence of socioeconomic stratification and to assess its degree and nature.

Before discussing the implications of the above for understanding Iron Age society at large, I would like to address another possible tool for examining social stratification: analysis of tombs, particularly in Judah. Tombs were often regarded as one of the best tools to study social structure (Binford 1972), but many scholars noted that this is not always the case (e.g., P. Metcalf and Huntington 1991; Parker Pearson 1999). The Iron Age Levant can serve as an additional example for the complexities involved in using burial data to infer social status. An examination of the type and nature of the many hundreds of Iron Age IIB–C tombs uncovered in Judah exposed the distinction between grand individual tombs of members of the ruling circle, grand family tombs, simple family tombs, poorly executed burial caves, individual trench graves, and sometimes even simple inhumations in the ground (e.g., Barkay 1999). Thus, in the eighth and seventh centuries in Judah, tombs can be used to identify socioeconomic stratification.

Still, we must be warned that this is not always the case, and tombs cannot be taken for granted as a source of information about status. Without elaborating on the problems inherent in using burials for such purposes, it

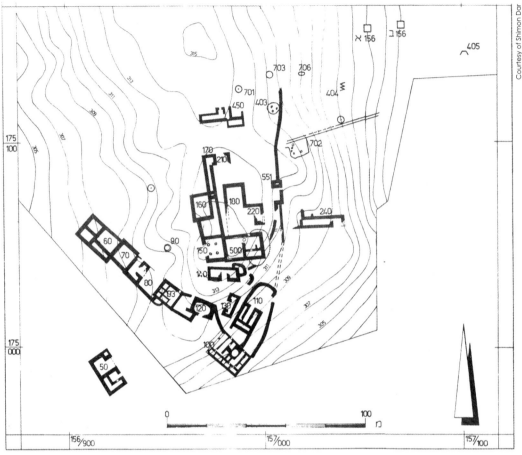

Fig. 63.4. Plan of the village of Khirbet Jemein. Note the large four-room houses that dominate the built environment of the village.

is sufficient to note that archaeologists do not always find burials. In the Iron Age I and IIA in Israel (especially in the highlands) hardly any burials have been found (Faust and Safrai 2015, 304–24). The first implication of this absence of evidence is that we are severely limited in what we can say. The second implication is perhaps more interesting: since we would all agree that the relative dearth of burials does not suggest that people did not die, we must ask ourselves why hardly any burials were found. The obvious answer is that people used simple inhumations in the ground outside their settlements, and those leave little for archaeologists to find (let alone date) and are typically located outside the areas

of archaeological inquiry (Kletter 2002; Faust 2004; 2011b). Whatever the reason behind this practice in the Iron Age I and IIA in Israel and Judah, the implications are that burials can be imbued with additional meanings, and cannot always teach about stratification because it might convey ideological messages about society and death (as is the situation today) and will not always reflect socioeconomic stratification (see Parker Pearson 1999; Faust 2004, with additional references). Moreover, even when burials are found, it does not mean that we witness the entire social spectrum, and it is more than likely that in tandem with the above-mentioned Judahite tombs, many of the poor were still buried in simple inhumations.

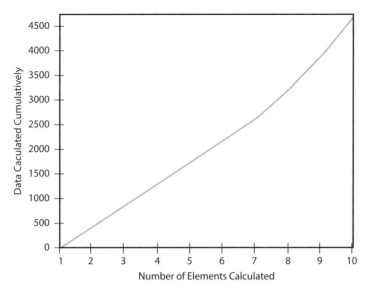

Fig. 63.5. Graph representing (weighted) inequality at Khirbet Jemein. The lack of significant concavity in the graph (cf. figs. 63.2 and 63.3) indicates the lack of clear socioeconomic stratification in this settlement.

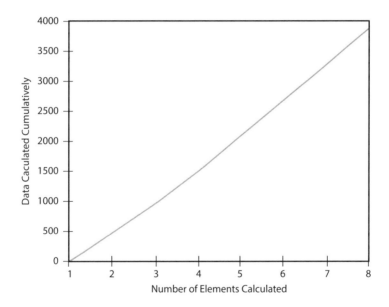

Fig. 63.6. Graph representing (weighted) inequality at Beit Aryeh. The lack of significant concavity in the graph (cf. figs. 63.2 and 63.3) indicates the lack of clear socioeconomic stratification in this settlement.

Moreover, one should remember that even for the Iron Age IIB–C, for which we do have hundreds of burials, the royal tombs (reported in the Bible) were not found. Thus, even for this period for which we have a wealth of data, the base of the social pyramid and even its tip are missing (see M. Bloch 1981, 144–46).

Implications for a Broad-Scale Understanding of Iron Age Israelite Society

Most biblical scholars dealing with Israelite society have stated that in the late Iron Age (late monarchic period, eighth and seventh centuries BCE) it became a very stratified society in which a small group of landlords controlled a mass of landless peasants (e.g., Neufeld 1960; Lang 1985; Chaney 1986). One of the main pieces of evidence for this situation is the prophets' references to social gaps, since they strongly denounce the oppression of the poor (e.g., Isa. 5:8–10; Mic. 2:2). This trend is apparent, to various degrees, in the prophecies of Amos, Isaiah, Micah, and the young Jeremiah (Hosea is probably the only exception). Other scholars have attempted to minimize the severity of the situation, and have interpreted the prophets' reproaches as relating to divisions and breaks within the traditional lineage structure (e.g., Bendor 1996). Archaeological evidence, like the finds at Tell el-Farʿa North / Tirzah, was brought to support the existence of stratification (e.g., De Vaux 1965, 72–73). But other scholars brushed this evidence aside, claiming that the differences observed in the examined sites (and reflected in the relevant verses) were quite small and did not denote real socioeconomic differences, and that the traditional social structure was relatively unharmed (e.g., De Geus 1982; Bendor 1996; Holladay 1995; Schloen 2001). None of them, however, systematically studied the available archaeological data, and all practically ignored the rural sector.

Thus, while the differences observed in the urban sector could be interpreted differently, and one may even claim that differences in the magnitude of three do not imply real stratification and can be found in fairly equal groups (e.g., Holladay 1995, 391–92), the almost total equality in the rural sector provides a good context that seems to disprove these suggestions. The results from the villages suggest that when there were no socioeconomic differences, they should be easily identified archaeologically, and thus when differences are identified (as in the cities), it means that differences did exist. The vast archaeological data set in our possession, from all sectors, clearly indicates that during the eighth and seventh centuries society in Israel and Judah was stratified (Faust 2012a; see also Dever 2012). The view that society was quite uniform and that the traditional kinship base prevailed unharmed is also contradicted by other studies concerning family structure (e.g., Faust 2012a, 159–66 and references there), as well as systems of production (Faust 2011a; 2011c), and even the economy at large (e.g., Moyal and Faust 2015).

This seems to indicate that the common interpretation of the prophets' criticism probably is correct (see also Houston 2004). Still, we have also learned that stratification did not exist in all the settlements, and that the reality was different in the rural sector. The prophets condemned what they saw in front of them. There were indeed social injustices, but these were far more prevalent in the cities. In the villages the situation was different. This picture is supported by B. Uffenheimer's (1968) analysis of the prophecy of Jeremiah. According to Uffenheimer, while Jeremiah resided at Anathoth, he did not mention social problems in his prophecies at all. Only when he moved to Jerusalem did such issues begin to appear in his prophecies (e.g., Jer. 5:27; 22:3). If this observation is correct, the change shows that, at least in seventh-century Judah, these problems existed mainly in the cities and not in the countryside, and we may extend this conclusion to the reality of the late Iron Age in general.

In the urban sector, too, the situation was not homogeneous. Although socioeconomic gaps probably existed in all cities, it seems that their severity varied from place to place. Thus, there were, for example, social differences between the cities in the highlands and the cities in the valleys, and even between Israel and Judah (Faust 2012a). All in all, however, we have clear evidence for socioeconomic stratification in the Iron Age.

64

Law and Legal Systems in Ancient Israel

DAVID W. BAKER

As human interrelationships become more complex, norms regulating such interrelationships develop in order to enable human flourishing and deter encroachment. Even at the simple level of the family are expectations that, when unmet, cause disruption, as when the first biblical family is fractured by fratricide (Gen. 4:1–8). Increasing social complexity leads to the necessity of some broader authority formalizing, and even codifying, expectations while attaching sanctions that may be brought if these expectations are ignored. This formalization is known as "law," which "comprises those rules that regulate relationships between humans who are the members of a society in the conduct of their everyday lives, protecting their economic, social, corporal, and psychological interests. Those rules establish rights and duties that can be enforced in a court of law" (Westbrook and Wells 2009, 1).

Additional complexity arises when societies, like those in the ancient Near East, are theocracies, with the highest authority level being the divine. Added to secular expectations are regulations regarding religious observance, another important part of family and national life. A sharp sacred-secular divide is, however, a modern construct, one not deriving from an ancient worldview, where life was unified, lived simultaneously in relations with both one's fellows and one's god(s). This is seen on the one hand by the common admixture of "sacred" and "secular" in the same collection, and on the other by the divine playing a role in "secular" law. Ritual legislation is treated elsewhere in the present volume (see ch. 46 above).

Law Types

Neither ancient Israel nor its neighbors had a single, overarching term for the abstract concept of "law" as jurisprudence. Even the Hebrew word commonly translated as "law" (*torah* and other words from the same root) is not restricted to legislation but extends more widely to guidance or advice (Gen. 46:28, "lead"; Exod. 15:25, "showed"; Job 36:22, "teacher"; *DCH* 8:612–16). Among legal texts, two general types of law in the ancient Near East have been proposed (Alt

1966, 101–71). First, apodictic or unconditional laws include at least three categories: "(1) unconditional imperatives, such as the Ten Commandments; (2) curses (e.g., Deut. 27:15–26); and (3) participial sentences concerning capital crimes (e.g., Exod. 21:17)" (Selman 2003, 504 [see also Frymer-Kensky 2003, 978]). Second, casuistic or case law is comprised of a protasis ("If . . .") and an apodosis ("then . . .") (e.g., Lev. 20:10–21). This type is much more common throughout the ancient Near East, as it is today, and it grows exponentially as new cases are encountered.

Sources

While material concerning legal practice is an important part of the Old Testament literature (e.g., the Pentateuch also being known as "the law" (Sir. prologue 1; Matt. 5:17; 7:12; 11:13; 22:40; Luke 16:16; 24:44; John 1:45; Acts 13:15), it is helpfully supplemented through ancient Near Eastern evidence, mainly from Mesopotamia. Some of this evidence will be adduced in this chapter.

Knowledge of laws and legal institutions is available from a spectrum of written sources ranging from primary records of legislation on one end to secondary references or simple allusions to legal practice on the other. In contemporary society, primary documentation on the national level is available.[1] For the ancient Near East, there are several records of royal edicts or decrees representing that primary end of the spectrum. Old Babylonian

1. For the United States it is at www.congress.gov, and in Great Britain at www.parliament.uk/business/bills-and -legislation/acts-of-parliament. These sources also provide "pre-legislation," the ability to track the development of a particular law from its original proposal through the amendment process to the form actually passed. Also available are records of actions leading to the passage of the legislation in the Congressional Record in the United States (www.congress.gov/congressional-record) and Hansard in the United Kingdom (www.parliament.uk /business/publications/hansard/).

kings issued "restoration edicts" (Charpin 2010, 82–90), called *mīsharum* (*CAD* M2:117), remedying economic injustices encountered at the beginnings of their reigns. People, including slaves, were returned to their original status and land restored to the original owners, an event called *deror* in Hebrew (Ezek. 46:17) and *andurārum* in Akkadian (*CAD* A2:115–17). Those of Samsu-iluna (1749–1712 BCE) and Ammisaduqa (ca. 1646–1626 BCE) have been discovered (Pritchard 1969a, 526–28; *COS* 2:362–64; see Sparks 2005, 423–24).

Moving along the spectrum are the more common Mesopotamian legal collections or "codes" in which disparate laws are gathered together into self-contained anthologies.

Sumerian	Laws of Ur-Nammu of Ur	2112–2095 BCE	M. Roth 1997, 13–22; Pritchard 1969a, 523–25; COS 2:408–10
	Laws of Lipit-Ishtar of Isin	1934–1924	M. Roth 1997, 23–35; Pritchard 1969a, 159–61; COS 2:410–14
Akkadian	Laws from Eshnunna, just northeast of Baghdad	ca. 1770	M. Roth 1997, 57–70; Pritchard 1969a, 161–63; COS 2:332–35
	Laws of King Hammurabi	1792–1750	M. Roth 1997, 70–142; Pritchard 1969a, 163–80; COS 2:335–53; M. Richardson 2000
	Middle Assyrian laws	eleventh-century copies of originals probably from the fourteenth century	M. Roth 1997, 153–94; Pritchard 1969a, 180–88; COS 2:353–60
	Neo-Babylonian laws	late eighth century	M. Roth 1997, 71–142; Pritchard 1969a, 197–98; COS 2:360–61; see Sparks 2005, 419–25

From Asia Minor, a Hittite law collection of the seventeenth to twelfth century has been found (Pritchard 1969a, 188–97; *COS* 2:100–113; see Sparks 2005, 426–27).

The law collections from Israel are a step further along the spectrum since they are secondarily embedded within narrative contexts. These include the Ten Commandments (Exod. 20:1–21; Deut. 5:1–22), the Covenant Code (Exod. 20:22–23:19), the laws enumerated in Leviticus through Numbers 11, and the Deuteronomic laws (Deut. 12–26). Included among them, and also in other places, are brief vignettes showing the historical background, narratives showing the circumstances giving rise to individual laws (Exod. 12:1–30; 27:20–21; 28:1–43; Lev. 10:1–11; 16; Num. 27:1–11; 36; 1 Sam. 30:22–25).

Even further along the spectrum are scribal texts that contain laws or legal terminology. These provide part of the education of scribes, who had to learn the legal forms and vocabulary rather than the actual workings of the laws themselves. A Sumerian law code is claimed to be such a school text (Pritchard 1969a, 525–56; also *COS* 3:307, 311–12). Some scholars consider the law codes further examples of academic scribal activity (Westbrook 1989), serving a propagandistic rather than practical function, lauding the king's justice before the gods in whose temples they are placed. A supporting argument is the paucity of references to specific law (particularly that within the Mesopotamian codes) used as precedent. Old Testament writers refer back to the law either generally, often in its breach (e.g., Josh. 1:7; 2 Kings 17:34, 37; 23:25), or specifically, mostly in ritual contexts (e.g., Lev. 5:10 referring to 1:14–17 [see Baker 1987, 194–97 for other examples]; Ezra 3:4 referring to the regulations in Lev. 1:3–17; 23:33–43), but not always so (e.g., Ezra 10:3). There are also cases setting legal precedent for future generations, even though no reference is later made back to them (Lev. 24:10–23; Num. 9:9–14; 27:1–11; 36) (Westbrook and Wells 2009, 13–14).

Kenneth Kitchen and Paul Lawrence suggest concerning the "codes": "They are, in fact, simply anthologies (selections) *from* the larger realm of legal *decisions* as formulated and used in practice by the ancient courts, and selected so as to illustrate the king's commitment to overall social justice" (2012, 24 [see also E. Otto 1993]). Finally, some suggest that the practical function of such law collections is to serve another educational function, as a "treatise," a model inspiring similar just actions (Bottéro 1995a, 167). There is no compelling reason why the collections cannot serve several functions—propagandistic, pedagogical, and practical—since they reflect situations known to exist from actual case documentation.

In a seventh-century extrabiblical Hebrew letter, a laborer petitions for the return of a confiscated garment (*COS* 3:77–78, showing some similarity with Exod. 22:25–26; Deut. 24:12–15, 17), and in an undated, unprovenanced letter a widow pleads to inherit the estate of her late husband, who left no male offspring (*COS* 3:86; see Num. 27:1–11; 36:1–12).

Further along the spectrum, records of actual cases and legal transactions show the law in practice, while they may not contain any of the language of the primary law itself. There are thousands of such ancient Near Eastern records concerning a range of civil and criminal cases (e.g., *COS* 3:21–32 [Egyptian], 57–60 [Hittite], 77–78, 86, 137–98 [West Semitic], 249–72, 283 [Akkadian], 299–312 [Sumerian]). In ancient Israel, these are found only in the narratives mentioned earlier (see below under "Procedures" for examples).

At the end of the spectrum are allusions to laws in nonlegal contexts. For example, dishonest measurements are forbidden by law (Lev. 19:35–36; Deut. 25:13–15), condemned by the prophets (Hosea 12:7–8; Amos 8:5; Mic. 6:11; cf. Ezek. 45:10), and viewed negatively in wisdom literature (Prov. 11:1; 20:23).[2] Also,

---

2. Egyptian wisdom instruction also condemns such practice (*Instruction of Amenemope*, Nineteenth and

the prophets condemn fiscal exploitation (e.g., Ezek. 18:18; 22:29; Amos 4:1; Mic. 2:2; Zech. 7:10; Mal. 3:5) without citing relevant law (Lev. 19:13; Deut. 24:14) specifically as precedent.

In sum, while there is much Old Testament material relating to law, it is for the most part secondary rather than primary.

Interrelationships among Collections

Old Testament law is at home among many other ancient Near Eastern, especially Mesopotamian, laws, as shown above. A matter of debate is the interrelationship, if any, between the laws of Israel and those of its neighbors. Views of this relationship range through another spectrum, from no correspondence at all on one end (e.g., Boecker 1980, 155, citing Preiser 1972, 243–44) to complete dependence on the other, with steps between ranging from simple resemblance with shared themes, similarity with a closer match of topic but not detail, correspondence with only minor differences, to identification both thematically and in detail (Wells 2006, 89–91). There is also discussion on whether any correspondence arises from a shared legal tradition throughout the area or from either oral or written sources, and also as to when any contact might have led to borrowing (D. Wright 2009, 16–24).

Strong similarities in wording and even the ordering of laws between those in the eighteenth-century collection of Hammurabi and the Covenant Code in Exodus 22:22–23:19 have led to the suggestion that the author of the latter had the former as a written source from which he borrowed directly during the Neo-Assyrian period (740–640 BCE) (D. Wright 2003; 2009). These similarities are also accompanied by significant differences between these collections, however, and also by the fact that other individual, and at times

even stronger, similarities are found between Exodus and other collections from both Mesopotamia (the eighteenth-century laws from Eshnunna and the fourteenth-century Middle Assyrian laws) and Asia Minor (the Hittite laws), suggesting that a direct literary borrowing by Exodus from Hammurabi is not proven as the only possible explanation of similarities (Wells 2006). The timing of any cross-cultural interaction is also open to question, since the Bible records contacts between Mesopotamia and Canaan/Israel all the way from the time of Abraham to the return from the exile. Since the use of Hammurabi's collection as part of scribal training lasted for generations, while this allows a Neo-Assyrian date of influence, it does not preclude an earlier date (see Lemaire 2012, 403). The actual composition of the Israelite legal texts and their relationships to the traditions of Israel's neighbors, while important and fascinating, is still undetermined and awaits further refinement.

Personnel

God(s) and Kings

In Israelite understanding, law originated from Yahweh, Israel's God, mediated through another, often Moses (e.g., Exod. 20:1, 22). This contrasts with Mesopotamian understanding, where the sun god, Shamash, the god of justice, brought injustice to light. Hammurabi credits Shamash with providing him as king the ability to promulgate just legislation, and the top of the stele on which his laws are inscribed depicts Shamash extending to Hammurabi a ring and a reed straightedge, representing either the god's authority passed to the king (de Hulster 2009, 213) or, rather than the actual written laws (as Yahweh gives Moses in Exod. 24:12), the means by which to determine whether a decision shows "justice and righteousness" (*kittum u mīsharum*). Hammurabi would thus be judged not only as to whether he was a wise legislator promulgating

Twentieth Dynasties, chs. 16–17 [COS 1:119–20]), as does Mesopotamian hymnic literature (Hymn to Shamash, first millennium BCE [COS 1:418]).

just laws but also as a just administrator of the laws. Israel's intermediaries' responsibilities focused on administration. This is exemplified in Moses judging the people in Exodus 18:13–26. He initiated no new law, but rather applied established law to individual cases. Similarly, when the daughters of Zelophehad brought questions of female inheritance and property rights before Moses and other Israelite leaders (Num. 27:2), Moses brought them before Yahweh for a ruling (Num. 27:5; 36:2, 6).

The general independence of law from the king is shown in several ways. Israel's foundational laws preceded the establishment of the monarchy (Exod. 20–24), and the king himself was subject to legal restrictions (Deut. 17:14–20). The latter point is particularly emphasized by repeated reminders by the prophets of royal breach of legal expectations, fulfilling one of their roles: confronting power (e.g., 2 Sam. 12:1–15; 2 Chron. 12:5; 21:12; 25:15) (Brueggemann 2001).

The king was able to establish new legal precedent in some cases, as in, for example, the distribution of spoil (1 Sam. 30:23–25). Like Moses, he was also able to adjudicate cases brought to him, as when Solomon determined legal motherhood (1 Kings 3:16–28). In that case, no reference was made to precedent law, and the incident was recorded to exemplify Solomon's wisdom in meting out justice (vv. 5–9, 28). Even more than Moses, kings were not able to hear all cases, needing other functionaries to fulfill this role, though not always doing so with integrity (1 Kings 21:11–16).

Priests

Priests had a responsibility for adjudicating as well as instructing in ritual affairs (Lev. 10:10–11). These are the subject of chapter 45 in the present volume. In at least one case, a priest engaged in an enigmatic civil case of a woman suspected of adultery (Num. 5:12–31), though still undertaking ritual rather than adjudicatory functions. Priests also are involved

in civil and criminal cases (Deut. 17:8–13) as "a superhuman agency of judicial decision-making" (Levinson and Sherman 2016, 403), though generally this was left to others.

Functionaries[3]

Several levels of adjudicatory functionaries served under the national leader. Moses appointed "officers," *sarim*, to decide minor cases (Exod. 18:25–26). *Sarim*, also translated as "rulers, governors" (Judg. 9:30; 1 Kings 22:26; 2 Kings 23:8; 2 Chron. 34:8; also mentioned outside the Bible in seventh-century Hebrew inscriptions [Avigad 1976b; Barkay 1994]),[4] continued to play judicial roles, among others, during the monarchy (Isa. 32:1; Jer. 26).

"Judges," *shopetim*, exercised governing authority prior to the monarchy (*HALOT* 1622–27; e.g., Judg. 4:4), including but going beyond the legal system. Premonarchic Israelites consulted them regarding complicated cases, and their rulings were ignored under penalty of death (Deut. 17:8–13). They could also supervise the meting out of penalties (Deut. 25:1–3). Their legal authority continued into the monarchy since in the ninth century Jehoshaphat ("Yahweh judged") appointed judges city by city in Judah (2 Chron. 19:4–7).

A more enigmatic category of "officers," *shoterim*, appears at times in conjunction with, and at times seemingly equivalent to, both of the preceding functionaries in legal contexts (Deut. 1:15; 16:18; Josh. 8:33; 1 Chron. 23:4). They perhaps served as legal "recorders" since the root of the word is cognate with an Akkadian word family related to "writing" (*HALOT* 1475–76; *CAD* 17:221–42).

Also involved in the legal process were the "elders," *zeqanim* (Num. 11:16; Deut. 19:12; 21:2; Josh. 24:1; (King and Stager 2001, 60–61), who functioned at a clan or even village level, though during the monarchy they could

---

3. See particularly Frymer-Kensky 2003, 986–90.
4. The laborer's petition mentioned above was directed to such a governor (*COS* 3:78n6).

also serve a wider constituency ("of the land" [1 Kings 20:7–8; Jer. 26:17]). They and the "fathers," 'abot (Num. 36:1–2), household heads, were concerned with local matters such as inheritance, forbidden sexual practices, and property transfer (Knight 2011, 73–75), matters often brought to them at the city gate (Josh. 20:4; Prov. 31:23). At this local level they mainly formulated case law, such as that regarding a goring ox (Exod. 21:28–32, 35–36; Knight 2011, 93).

Procedures

Several narratives show the practical application of law to Israelite life. They show two different kinds of legal procedure, informal and formal.

Dispute (rib)[5]

An initiating event is "a controversy between two parties on questions of law" (Bovati 1994, 30), with one bringing a charge against the other. Such a dispute can involve two individuals (unspecified cause [Deut. 19:17]; over insults [1 Sam. 25:39]), an individual and a group (over discrimination [Judg. 8:1]; over treason [Jer. 26]), two groups (over water rights [Gen. 26:20–22]), or even God and the pagans (Jer. 25:31) or his own people (Hosea 4:1; 12:2; Mic. 6:2). It can be resolved internally or informally, without recourse to court or judge. One party brings an accusation of a wrong against the other (e.g., Judg. 8:1; 2 Sam. 12:7–12) or a party feels self-recrimination (2 Sam. 24:10), the accused party rebuts the accusation (Judg. 8:2–3a) or makes a confession (2 Sam. 12:13a) and plea for pardon (1 Sam. 15:25; 2 Sam. 24:10), and the issue is resolved. Resolution could be through amicable reconciliation (Judg. 8:2b) or the necessity to take another route, either a penalty (2 Sam. 24:11–17), a legal tribunal (Deut. 25:1), or war.

5. See Bovati 1994, 29–166.

Litigation, Decision, Verdict (mishpat)

When outside resources were necessary to resolve the dispute, disputants turned to a formal tribunal (Bovati 1994, 167–387) involving impartial judges who, unswayed by undue influence such as bribery, brought judgment (Exod. 23:8; Deut. 16:19). Jeremiah 26:1–6 provides Jeremiah's sermon against Jerusalem and its temple. When "the priests and the prophets and all the people" heard this (v. 7), they accused him of treason (vv. 8–10). Judah's "officials" (sarim) established a tribunal at the gate (v. 10), and charges were brought by witnesses (v. 11). Jeremiah provided a defense (vv. 12–16), convincing some of his accusers (v. 17). Some elders brought forward a precedent to Jeremiah's message in the words of Micah (Mic. 3:12), pointing out that he had not been executed by the king to whom his message was directed (vv. 17–19), and the narrator inserts a tale of a prophet who had died for his message (vv. 20–23), possibly as a counterfoil to Jeremiah's situation. A highly placed friend in court, Ahikam (2 Kings 22:12; Jer. 39:14), also spoke in Jeremiah's support, so he was spared (Jer. 26:24). Another, frivolous, case is also recorded (1 Kings 21:11–16). They both follow the procedures spelled out in Deuteronomy 25:1–3.

Unbiased witnesses were an important part of the procedure (Exod. 23:2–3), and false statements were strictly forbidden (Exod. 20:16; Deut. 5:20). A malicious false witness could be tried and suffer the penalty intended for the original accused (Deut. 19:16–21). For help in preventing this, at least two witnesses were required to convict in a capital case (Num. 35:30; Deut. 17:6). In at least one instance, Solomon adjudicated a case without benefit of either external witnesses or evidence (1 Kings 3:16–18).

The judge heard the evidence, weighed it, and decided whether the charge was proven or not by issuing a verdict. The accused could be found innocent (Jer. 26:24) or guilty (Deut.

25:1–3). If the latter, the judge could determine the penalty (Exod. 21:22) unless it was a capital penalty mandated by law (e.g., Exod. 21:12, 14, 16). In one case, the king acting as judge commuted even a mandated death penalty (2 Sam. 14:4–11). The judge might also take part in meting out the actual punishment (Deut. 25:2), as would the witnesses in a capital case (Deut. 17:7).

Purview

Israelite law covered much that was relevant to the people's lives. Ritual prescriptions and other "religious" instructions are well represented and are applicable to both the local and national cult (e.g., Lev. 1–7; 22:16–23:44; Num. 6:1–21; 15:1–31; 28–29; Deut. 16:1–17, 21–17:7; 18:9–14). Since holiness was important, so too were instructions on how to maintain it within areas of daily life such as food (Lev. 11; 17; Deut. 14:1–21), personal injury (Exod. 21:12–36), making vows (Num. 30), waging war (Deut. 20), and sex and marriage (Exod. 22:16–17, 19; Lev. 18; Deut. 21:10–14). Even priests, the chief ritual officiants, were not exempt, also being carefully regulated (Lev. 21–22:16). Economic and business practices such as slavery (Exod. 21:1–11; Deut. 15:12–18), property ownership and theft (Exod. 22:1–15), inheritance (Deut. 21:15–17), child rearing (Deut. 21:18–21), and agriculture (e.g., Lev. 25) were regulated alongside "religious" regulations (e.g., Exod. 20:2–17; Deut. 5:6–21 [the Ten Commandments]; Lev. 19), showing the lack of a secular-sacred divide.

Care for the powerless and disenfranchised—widows, orphans, and resident aliens—was mandated by law (Exod. 22:22–24; 23:6, 9; Deut. 14:28–29; 24:17–21; 27:19), and their neglect was frequently chastised by the prophets (Isa. 1:23; 10:1–2; Ezek. 22:7; Zech. 7:10; Mal. 3:5) and also recognized as unacceptable by wisdom writers (Job 22:9; 24:3, 21). This deserved careful consideration by the Israelites since they are of concern to God (Deut. 10:17–18), who himself takes the place of the father and husband they lost (Ps. 68:5). In fact, economic crime and exploitation are targeted by the prophets for condemnation more than any other single type of crime or sin. If it is such a concern to Israel's God, so should it be to his people.

65

Wisdom Traditions in Ancient Israel

Paul Overland

It "surpassed the wisdom of all the people of the east, and all the wisdom of Egypt." Thus drawing on an international comparison, the biblical writer described the extent of an Israelite's wisdom (1 Kings 4:30). To better grasp traditions of wisdom[1] in the Hebrew Bible, a modern reader similarly will benefit from acquaintance with sapience among Israel's neighbors, ranging from Sumer and Babylonia to the Nile Valley. While content that qualifies as "wisdom" must necessarily vary from culture to culture, certain general observations may be useful.[2] Six questions help illuminate the world of sages in the ancient Near East:

1. How would sages have defined "wisdom"?
2. Who were the sages?
3. What characterized the worldview of the sages?
4. How did the sages approach their task?
5. What themes recur in teachings of the sages?
6. How were sages trained?

Concluding observations suggest connections linking the wisdom of Israel with that of its neighbors.

How Would Sages Define "Wisdom"?

Wisdom is the enterprise of making sense of life. Priorities and techniques reflected in sages' writings indicate that they may have defined wisdom thus: the observation of order in the natural, social, and divine realms, so as to discern by rational choice the path most effectively leading to the best life possible. Where order eluded observation, sages sought also to make sense of disorder (theodicy).

Who Were the Sages?

Sages and Kings

Early Mesopotamians regarded *nēmequ* (wisdom) as reserved for the gods Ea, El, and Marduk and for kings (Mack-Fisher 1990, 109;

---

1. Past assumptions of a singular, monolithic "Israelite wisdom tradition" now give way to more nuanced approaches (Sneed 2011).

2. Wilfried Lambert (1960, 1) was first to caution against equating Babylonian with Israelite wisdom categories (cf. Sneed 2015a, 52–53, 60–62).

Hurowitz 2008, 65–66). Endowed by Ea, the Sumerian king Šulgi boasted that all within his court sought out his eloquent, multilingual, peace-inspiring counsel (Kramer 1990, 43; Sweet 1990a, 51–57; for a Persian perspective, see J. R. Russell 1990, 82). Later Sumerian *abgal*s were sages renowned for introducing culture and civilization (Kramer 1990, 31). By the Ur III and Old Babylonian periods, sages were serving monarchs, sometimes assisting decision-making as diviners, *bārûs* (Sweet 1990b, 105). With the dawn of literacy (ca. 3400 BCE), scholar-sages began to preserve wisdom ranging from gnomic sayings to debate-like disputations to sharpen rhetorical prowess (Alster 2008, 47). As late as 700 BCE, the sage Ahiqar's composition reports him in the service of King Esarhaddon (Kottsieper 2008, 111).

Convinced that the gods governed both success and survival, Mesopotamian sages focused on exorcism and extispicy (interpreting a client's condition or future by examining entrails of sacrificial animals) to reconcile individuals with their personal deity (Sweet 1990b, 105). Toward the end of the Babylonian Empire in 539 BCE, the stature of royal advisors increased, as evidenced by Urad-Gula's confrontation of King Ashurbanipal (Beaulieu 2007, 11, 15–18; Hurowitz 2008, 76–87).

In the Nile Valley, the earliest mention of wisdom locates the *rḫ-(i)ḫt* (sage) in a royal setting (Ronald Williams 1990b, 27). Calling himself "king's son," Hardjedef counsels his son, Auibre, to invest in future security: "When you prosper, found your household" (Lichtheim 1973–80, 1:58–59). Dated to the Fifth Dynasty (ca. 2494–2345 BCE), the *Instruction of Prince Hardjedef* is the earliest example of Egyptian *sebayit* (instruction), a form spawned by the pharaoh's increased need for trained administrators during the Old Kingdom (2650–2135 BCE) (Clifford 1998, 35). Egyptian sages served as advisors, diplomats, physicians, and architects and to a lesser extent

as magicians, sorcerers, and interpreters of dreams (Ronald Williams 1990a, 95–98).

Sages and Scribes

The appetite in palace and temple for written epics, chronicles, hymns, liturgies, and taxation records produced considerable overlap between sage and scribe. In Sumer, for example, scribes trained in the *edubba* (tablet house) held a monopoly on learning (W. Lambert 1960, 7). Babylonian sages rose through the ranks as senior scribes, achieving the status of *ummânu*s (expert advisors, scholars) who offered counsel to monarchs such as Sargon (Kramer 1990, 31–32; Beaulieu 2007, 15; Hurowitz 2008, 66–67). In addition to divination texts and law codes, Mesopotamian scribes composed treatises on topics as varied as medicine, care of horses, and food preparation (Sneed 2015b, 90).

In Syria-Palestine scribes belonged to an elite class, enhanced by connection with the dominant culture of Babylonia. Some even adopted Babylonian *noms de plume* written with rare cuneiform signs. Syrian scribes might append brief postscripts to royal correspondence conveying personal greetings to fellow scribes in Babylonia, evidence of membership in a privileged international guild (Y. Cohen 2013, 24).

In Egypt literacy was an insufficient but often requisite skill to command respect. Prominent individuals commonly hired scribes as secretaries. Yet a search for Egyptian heroes regularly surfaces names of scribes with superlative administrative skills (Wente 1995, 2219).

As with other guilds, the role of scribe might pass from father to son. Four sons of Nu'me-Rašap of Ugarit (coastal Syria), copyist of the *Epic of Atra-Hasis*, became scribes, with Gamir-Addu advancing to the level of teacher (Y. Cohen 2013, 32). Highly literate Deir el-Medina, the craftsman village near Egypt's Valley of the Kings, also attests hereditary transmission of scribal skills (Wente 1995,

2219). Alternatively, "son" might designate an apprentice, not a literal descendant.

Mesopotamian scribal circles occasionally admitted females to the profession, such as Sargon's daughter Enheduanna (ca. 2300 BCE) and Ninshatapada, daughter of Sin-kashid of Uruk. Scribes during the Old Babylonian period (1792–1595 BCE) at Sippar and Mari also included several women (Alster 2008, 51).

Although generally associated with officials, Egyptian wisdom was not limited to the literate (Shupak 2015, 274–75). Thus the tale known as the *Eloquent Peasant* (Middle Kingdom, ca. 2055–1650 BCE) does not hesitate to attribute to a commoner (Khunanup of Salt-Field) a series of nine witty appeals before the high steward Rensi. So clever were his nine petitions that the king in this tale (Nebkaure, perhaps Ninth Dynasty) requested a written copy for his amusement (line 80 of the *Eloquent Peasant* [Lichtheim 1973–80, 1:173]).

blind faith evidenced by a resolve to praise a god until that god may relent (Beaulieu 2007, 8–9) (cf. the title of the late second-millennium BCE theodicy composition *Ludlul bēl nēmeqi*: "Let me praise the Lord of wisdom").

Egyptian wisdom similarly rested on a belief in divine order involving retribution, while rarely giving cultic instruction to secure remedy. The threat of divine retribution emerges from Amenemope's warning against land-grabbing in a widow's field: "he will be lassoed by the power of the Moon" (*Instruction of Amenemope*, column vii, line 19 [ca. twelfth century BCE]). The term *ma'at* designates both order and a deity embodying order (Shupak 2015, 270). As daughter of Re and goddess of truth, harmony, and justice, Ma'at served as patron deity of Egyptian sages, while the ibis-god Thot sustained knowledge and assisted scribes (J. Ray 1995, 20; Thomas Schneider 2008, 43).

What Characterized the Worldview of the Sages?

The worldview embraced by Mesopotamian sages rested on three principles. First, deities reigned supreme. Second, the rule of deities was characterized by justice, expressed through retribution. The late Assyrian *Advice to a Prince* cautions, "If [the king] does not heed the justice of his land, Ea, king of destinies, will alter his destiny and will not cease from hostilely pursuing him" (W. Lambert 1960, 113). Third, human misfortune resulted from offense against one or more deities. Wisdom served to minimize offense to deities, thereby minimizing misfortune. Sages employed wisdom received from the gods to mediate between deities and humans, a mediation rendered more effective if the sage was also an exorcist (W. Lambert 1960, 15; Beaulieu 2007, 17–18). By taking advantage of such wisdom, an individual could safeguard his or her future. But when misfortune descended, the sufferer was consigned to

How Did the Sages Approach Their Task?

Three traits characterize how sages approached their task. First, they were observers of the orderly, watching for repeatable cause-and-effect relationships. The Egyptian *Instruction of Onchsheshonqy*, a demotic work from the Ptolemaic era (332–30 BCE), cautions, "He who sends spittle up to the sky will have it fall on him" (Lichtheim 1973–80, 3:168).

Second, sages held the wisdom of antiquity in high regard: "The instructions of an old man are precious" (Sumerian *Instructions of Shuruppak* [Alster 2005, 58]). After overtaking the Sumerian culture, the Babylonians, in their respect for that culture, preserved Sumerian wisdom compositions in the original language, issuing an Akkadian translation in a parallel column on the same tablet (see plates 58–69 in W. Lambert 1960). At times, appreciation for legacy wisdom would lead sage-scholars such as Nabu-zuqup-kenu, a scribe in the palace of the Neo-Assyrian kings Sargon and Sennacherib, to journey to other cities to consult or copy another work, whether for the purposes of editing or to enrich one of his future compositions (Pearce 1995, 2273).[3]

Third, sages expressed their insights with both a variety of forms and a sophistication of style. Forms of Egyptian wisdom literature include cynical complaints (e.g., the *Admonitions of Ipuwer*, perhaps Twelfth Dynasty, 1991–1786 BCE), political propaganda (e.g., the *Prophecies of Neferti*, also Twelfth Dynasty), and *sebayit* (instructions) (e.g., the *Maxims of Ptahhotep*, Fifth Dynasty, ca. 2350 BCE; the *Instruction of Amenemope*, Twentieth Dynasty, ca. 1150 BCE). *Sebayit* compositions typically commenced with a heading: "The instruction (*sebayit*) which X made for Y." Instructions vary from highly pragmatic (the *Maxims of Ptahhotep*) to collections of advice mixed with piety (the *Instruction of Amenemope*). With the reunification of Egypt during the Middle Kingdom (Eleventh through Thirteenth Dynasties, ca. 2040–1633 BCE), a new genre arose called *kemyt*, meaning "completion" or "compendium" (see Thomas Schneider 2008 for a broader treatment of Egyptian genres).

Forms of Mesopotamian wisdom literature included Sumerian disputations, in which a commodity such as copper would make its case for superiority over silver. From copper many useful tools could be fashioned, while silver would benefit only palace and grave with its ornamentation (*Disputations between Silver and Mighty Copper* [Kramer 1990, 35]). Babylonian literature similarly included compositions comparing the value of two commodities, often taking the form of a debate between the personified materials (e.g., *The Tamarisk and the Palm*; *The Ox and the Horse* [W. Lambert 1960, 175–85]). A horse may serve in battle,

but it was the ox that supplied leather necessary for weapons. Mesopotamian collections also included shorter popular sayings, such as the father-to-son character advice of the *Instructions of Shuruppak* and the following example from Ashurbanipal's extensive library: "Last year I ate garlic; this year my inside burns" (W. Lambert 1960, 249). The topic of theodicy gave rise to longer Babylonian wisdom compositions, such as *Ludlul bēl nēmeqi* ("I will praise the Lord of wisdom") and the *Babylonian Theodicy*.

Sophistication of style in wisdom composition emerges most strikingly in an acrostic that binds together all twenty-seven stanzas of the *Babylonian Theodicy*. Line-initial letters spell out the following identification and expression of loyalty: "I, Saggil-kīnam-ubbib, the incantation priest, am adorant of the god and the king" (Pearce 1995, 2275). Sumerian scribes demonstrated their skill in *Enlil and Namzitarra* by employing sound- and sign-based puns so integral to the work that if overlooked, the omission would prevent a reader from grasping the composition's meaning (Y. Cohen 2013, 152). On a simpler level, shorter instructions may be motivated by incentives: "Do not jump over a wide canal! You will hurt yourself and you will have a wound" (from Late Bronze Age *Šimâ milka*, from Ugarit and Emar in Syria [Y. Cohen 2013, 89]).

What Themes Recur in Teachings of the Sages?

Three themes recur with regularity in the sages' teachings. First, the supremacy of the deity over human affairs often is expressed. James Crenshaw explains, "This notion of fear before the deity included the sense of dread in the presence of a potential threat as well as genuine submission in obedient love" (Crenshaw 1995, 2451).

Second, the dilemma of theodicy mingled with the insignificance of life appears frequently, particularly in Mesopotamia (W. Lambert

---

3. The reuse of legacy wisdom validates ethical instructions as contributing to a wisdom tradition, a tradition consisting of more than merely a modern scholar's construct (Fox 2015, 81).

1960, 10). Reminiscent of a broken contract, one might serve one's god devotedly yet fail to receive the customary retribution in the form of health and prosperity. This gave rise to compositions such as *Ludlul bēl nēmeqi* ("Let me praise the Lord of wisdom" [late second millennium BCE]), with its concern for manipulating the supernatural through exorcism, and also the *Babylonian Theodicy* (Kassite period, 1400–1200 BCE), with its debate between the sufferer who has lost hope in divine help and his friend who urges—successfully at last—that the suffering friend should cling resolutely to reverence.

The sentiment of life's insignificance appears in the Sumerian *Ballad of Early Rulers*: "All life is an illusion. Life onto which no light is shed, how can it be more valuable than death?" (Alster 2005, 303). Criticism of the status quo occurs in the *Advice of Shupe-awilum* (originating in Babylonia, extant only in Ugarit), where a son disputes his father's encouragement to amass wealth (Perdue 2008, 22; Rowe 2008, 101).

Third, since sapiential material served in part to develop courtiers, numerous wisdom compositions cultivated moral character, especially the sorts of responses suitable when serving a monarch. These included self-control, discernment needed for timely speech, and humility (Crenshaw 1995, 2453). In Sumer sages advised, "Don't buy an ass that brays; it will split your yoke," and "Don't act as a guarantor; that man will have a hold on you; and *you*, don't accept a pledge; (that man will be discredited)" (Alster 2005, 58 and 65). The Egyptian *Instruction of Amenemope* (ca. 1150 BCE) features thirty chapters that concentrate on character development. The Aramaic *Sayings of Ahiqar* (ca. 650 BCE) similarly deals with issues of decorum and moral conduct (Perdue 2008, 32–34).

How Were Sages Trained?

In Sumerian culture, scribes—together with sages—were trained in the *edubba* (tablet house), often located within a family's home (Michalowski 1995, 2283). This pattern continued through the Ur III and Old Babylonian periods, with a two-stage curriculum. In the first phase, pupils learned cuneiform signs through lexical lists, memorized four prescribed hymns, and were introduced to various Sumerian proverbs and short wisdom pieces. During the second phase they encountered advanced lexical lists, a set of ten literary works, and assorted other texts evidently selected to reflect a pupil's needs (Y. Cohen 2013, 26–27, 57). With the dawn of the Kassite period, schools that replaced the *edubba* focused on more basic training. Through more advanced training one might pursue additional skills of the *āšipūtu* ("craft of the exorcist"), the *kalûtu* ("craft of the lamentation singer"), or the *bārûtu* ("craft of the diviner") (Beaulieu 2007, 10–11; Hurowitz 2008, 69). Over fifty tablets include appended notes indicating specific educational use, ranging from instruction to dictation or reading aloud (Hurowitz 2008, 73). A letter of self-recommendation from a man named Marduk-šāpik-zēri gives a picture of the range of scribal skills that he mastered to qualify him for royal service (Hurowitz 2008, 68–71).

In ancient Emar, located along the Euphrates in northern Syria, one scribal school served multiple generations of students belonging to the Zū-Baʿla family and was run by the patriarch of that family. It was staffed by local scribal instructors together with the help of a foreigner, Kidin-Gula (likely a Babylonian), who lived not with the Zū-Baʿla family but rather in the merchant district of Emar. There, Kidin-Gula also assisted expatriates like himself with various scribal tasks (Y. Cohen 2013, 29–30; for a similar picture of schooling in Ugarit, see Rowe 2008, 106–7).

Hereditary transmission of skills and roles appears in Ugarit as well. Four sons of Nuʿme-Rašap (copyist of the *Epic of Atra-Hasis*) took up their father's scribal trade. One of them (Gamir-Addu) achieved the rank of teacher

(Y. Cohen 2013, 31). While not all scribes were sages, and while wisdom could not be passively inherited (Fontaine 1990, 156), the earliest stages of a sage's training often were scribal and family-oriented.

No independent schools have been found in the Old Kingdom of Egypt, leading to the inference that fathers taught sons (or quasi-sons) as apprentices (Sneed 2015b, 92). Schools do appear in the First Intermediate Period. By the time of the Middle Kingdom, the royal residence at Itjtawy (modern al-Lisht, near Memphis) housed the principal school. Civil administrators comprised its faculty. Enrollment included some worker-class pupils as well as children of the aristocracy. Future physicians, astronomers, magicians, and interpreters of dreams were trained along with priests in the "house of life," which was a temple scriptorium under royal patronage serving as Egypt's intellectual center (Wente 1995, 2215–16). There, pupils learned to compose and preserve texts, often through the discipline of making near-exact copies of earlier works (known as "schoolboy texts") (Ronald Williams 1990b, 22, 27; Clifford 1998, 37; Perdue 2007, 43–44).

Scribal training began at age ten and lasted four years during Egypt's New Kingdom. Pupils focused on *sebayit* (moral "instructions") compositions and *kemyt* (a compendium including epistolary greetings and customary phrases) (Ronald Williams 1990b, 21).

It is instructive to note that schooling materials have turned up in virtually every locale where cuneiform tablets have surfaced across ancient Syria. The appearance of lexical lists, liver model omens, a mathematical tablet fragment, and a fragment of the *Epic of Gilgamesh* in city-states of Canaan (Ashkelon, Aphek, Megiddo, and Hazor) leads Yoram Cohen to conclude that scribal schools must have been present during the Late Bronze Age (1500–1200 BCE) in Canaan as well, despite the lack of irrefutable evidence such as Mesopotamia's

*edubba*s or Egypt's house of life (Y. Cohen 2013, 23).

Conclusions

When wisdom traditions in ancient Israel are viewed against a backdrop of cognate cultures, several observations emerge. First, the definition of wisdom as consisting of insights that arise from the observation of order consequent on divine control—such a definition characterized wisdom both within and beyond Israel. However, manipulation of the divine through exorcism and magic commanded greater interest within wisdom of Babylonia than within that of Egypt or Israel.

Second, the identity of sages as gifted advisors who rose through the ranks of scribes, recipients of schooling, often serving in a court setting—this picture drawn from Mesopotamia and Egypt corresponds well with accounts of *hakamim* (the wise) in Israel (Whybray 1990, 134–36; Kynes 2015, 19–23). There are exceptions, however. As with the "eloquent peasant" of Egypt (known from a composition by the same name), Israel similarly included some who needed neither scribal training nor court status in order to merit classification as "wise." Among these are perhaps the clever woman of Tekoa (2 Sam. 14:2), a poor city-savior chronicled by Qohelet (Eccles. 9:13–16), and the female negotiator of Abel of Beth-maacah (2 Sam. 20:14–22).

Third, Israel's sages shared with comrades from cognate cultures a worldview grounded in the durability of truth, harmony, and justice—a dependability made possible by orderliness issuing from the divine realm.[4] While wisdom

4. Some question whether Israelite sages embraced a worldview distinct from that of prophets and priests (Sneed 2011, 53–54). A prophet may employ vocabulary and forms typical within wisdom literature, as does, for example, Ezekiel (M. Hamilton 2015, 246–56). Conversely, a sage may pray, as do Agur and Job. Yet the aims distinguishing prophetic application of sapience and sapiential application of piety are not of a single

gained personification within Israel's literature, this literary device did not extend to deification (in contrast to the theologies of neighboring nations) (Hadley 1995). As in neighboring nations, periodic disruption of order and an apparent breakdown of divine retribution in Israel gave rise to compositions (often dialogues) wrestling with the injustice of undeserved misfortune or lamenting the unfairness of life (Job, Ecclesiastes, and selected psalms; on wisdom psalms, see Saur 2015; Forti 2015, 213).

Fourth, sages of Israel approached their task much as did those of nearby nations. They employed powers of observation, mixed with high regard for legacy wisdom. Wisdom topics and skill in composition noted in Mesopotamia and Egypt often parallel those found in Israel (Overland 2008). Vocabulary and literary forms of biblical wisdom find close parallels in Egyptian material (Shupak 2015, 284–90). Mesopotamian compositions are distinguished by greater use of fables (but see Cathcart 1995) and the presence of magical compositions.

Fifth, themes within Israelite wisdom compositions include the confession of divine supremacy, concerns over theodicy, and an interest in the cultivation of character. Such themes were common in the wisdom literature of cognate nations as well, with the topic of life's futility engaging Sumerian sages' attention as early as ca. 1800–1600 BCE, in the *Ballad of Early Rulers* (W. Lambert 1995, 37–41; for an exploration of wisdom's influence in

biblical narrative, see Weinfeld 1972, 244–319; R. Gordon 1995; Lemaire 1995).

Sixth, as to training, circumstantial evidence leads to the conclusion that Israelite court sages obtained schooling, perhaps with curriculum supplied by wisdom literature (Crenshaw 1990, 212; Shupak 2015, 296; Sneed 2011, 71; but M. Fox 2015, 70, disagrees). That conclusion follows from (1) explicit information concerning schools and curricula in Egypt and Mesopotamia, (2) a growing need for trained scribes from the Solomonic era forward (Dell 2008), and (3) inscriptions recovered at various locations of Israel, inscriptions consistent with schooling exercises (Lemaire 1990; G. Davies 1995).

Given the transnational nature of wisdom literature (e.g., witness within biblical wisdom the evident contact with the Egyptian *Instruction of Amenemope* [Overland 1996], and Proverbs' indebtedness to the queen mother of Lemuel of Massa in the Transjordan), it is only natural that considerable similarity would emerge in a comparison of compositions from one nation with those of another (J. Day 1995; Sneed 2015a, 54–55). While one may observe regionally specific elements of topography (canals in Mesopotamian proverbs), fauna (water fowl in Egyptian sayings), or theology (e.g., Ea, Marduk, Ma'at, or Yahweh), the natural world and human communities observed by sages bore sufficient similarity as to yield analogous insights for making sense of life. Only, for the Israelite sage, nothing could make sense if ever one drifted from a foundational reverence for the creator, Yahweh (Clements 1995, 280–84).

---

sort. Thus the aims distinguishing wisdom traditions merit independent consideration to the degree that they vary from those of other voices in ancient Israel.

66

Warfare in the World of the Bible

Mark Schwartz

History and Geography

Wars pervade the biblical narrative, mentioned in all but two of the books of the Old Testament. This was due in part to the Levant's geographic position, making it the only viable route from southwest Asia to Africa. The strategic importance of this "land bridge" ensured that it would be of vital interest to growing empires in Mesopotamia and Egypt (King and Stager 2001). Besides geography, the topography of the land also played a large role in determining what tactics were possible there, the areas that were most likely to be in the path of invading armies, and the prominence of specific settlements (Cline 2000; Gabriel 2003; Ussishkin 1995).

In the twelfth century BCE, after the collapse of the Egyptian and Hittite Empires and before the expansion of the Assyrian, Babylonian, and Persian Empires, a power vacuum existed in the Levant that permitted several different ethnic groups to form their own nation-states (Postgate 1992; Liverani 2014a). From the late tenth to the early sixth century BCE, the ancient state of Judah in the south and the more powerful state of Israel in the north were engaged in conflict and diplomacy with each other and with their close neighbors—the Phoenicians, Moabites, Edomites, Ammonites, Aramaeans, and Philistines (Liverani 2014a; Park 2015; Rainey and Notley 2006). This era witnessed intervals of territorial expansion and military losses for all these emerging states (Isserlin 1998). The early ninth century BCE saw the height of the power of the northern kingdom of Israel under the reign of King Ahab (Finkelstein 2013). The ancient Israelites also resisted territorial expansion of the large empires of Mesopotamia (first Assyria, then Babylon) with varied success. For the most part, the coalitions that were formed with neighboring states to resist the armies of the ancient Assyrians and Babylonians were unsuccessful. Dire consequences resulted, especially for the general populace. Ultimately these events had a profound effect on the theological development of ancient Israel (Liverani 2014a).

The Nature of the Evidence

Many scholars have explored numerous aspects of warfare in the Old Testament from the viewpoints of archaeology, military history, and theology. The Hebrew Scriptures provide some descriptions of battles, larger campaigns, tactics, and the organization of armies, but these details may be representative of the time period of editorial redaction rather than the specific period described in the text (Liverani 2014a). Ancient texts outside the Old Testament also provide important historical details. Ostraca from sites such as Lachish and Arad provide some insight into state-organized provisioning of Israelite armies (Aharoni and Naveh 1981), while numerous archaeological remains of fortification systems provide a significant amount of information (Rocca 2012). While there are no contemporary artistic depictions of armies or large caches of weaponry in ancient Israel (Isserlin 1998), this kind of material does exist in the archaeological remains of other contemporaneous cultures, such as those of the Aramaeans, Neo-Hittites, and Assyrians (Yadin 1963).

The Nature of Warfare

The Late Bronze Age and Iron Age periods witnessed many military developments, including the decline in the dominance of chariots (Drews 1993; Fagan and Trundle 2010), the increase in the size of armies (Gabriel 2005), and the greater use of iron weapons versus bronze ones (Pleiner and Bjorkman 1974). Warfare in the ancient Near East involved great loss of life and trauma, to both soldiers and civilians, in addition to the destruction of infrastructure and agricultural land (Isserlin 1998; Zorn 2014b). The Old Testament makes reference to the kind of devastation wrought on a population by conquering armies (2 Kings 6:25–30) (Cogan 1983). However, there were tangible benefits to the victors of a battle, including wealth, land, and captive labor, which were motivations for leaders to initiate military campaigns (Zorn 2014b). A king's victory in battle was also seen as validation by the gods

of his right to rule (Liverani 1990; Melville 2016; J. Wright 2008).

Armies typically consisted of slingers, archers, heavy and light infantry, and chariots (Isserlin 1998). There is still debate as to how effective chariots were and in what capacity they served. Some scholars contend that the chariot had many advantages as a mobile launching platform and shock vehicle (Cantrell 2011; Scurlock 1997). In the open-field battles depicted by the Assyrians, it appears that chariots and cavalry were situated on the flanks of the army with infantry in the center to allow the mobile units the ability to encircle the enemy (Nadali 2010). Some scholars believe that ancient texts as well as archaeological evidence support the idea that chariots were an important force in the northern kingdom of Israel (Cantrell 2011). In the ninth century BCE, King Ahab was able to supply the largest number of both chariots and infantry in the Aramaean-led coalition against the Assyrians at Qarqar (Pritchard 1969a, 278–79). Interestingly, the texts of Sargon II from the eighth century BCE mention that two thousand Israelite chariots were incorporated into the Assyrian army after the conquest of Samaria, and that one of the principal horse trainers in the Assyrian army was from Samaria (Dalley 1985).

However, as the Assyrian Empire expanded into new kinds of terrain, they emphasized the use of cavalry over chariotry (Scurlock 1997). Mounted warfare developed first in the steppes of Eurasia, and cavalry first make its appearance in the Assyrian army in the ninth century BCE, but soldiers at that time lacked the skills necessary to maintain stability and control on horseback. Over the succeeding centuries, riding techniques improved dramatically in the Assyrian army, thereby relegating chariots to mainly ceremonial roles. Cavalry then became a significant part of the Persian Empire's military in the sixth through fourth centuries BCE (Drews 2004).

Likewise, the Levant witnessed changes in fortification systems from the Late Bronze Age to the Iron Age II period. In some regards, fortification of cities or towns was a measure of the level of complexity and political control of states in the region. In general, few new defensive walls were constructed in Canaan in the Late Bronze Age, and earlier fortifications were reused (Gonen 1992b; Z. Herzog 1997b), due in part to a reduced population and Egyptian imperial hegemony in the region (Bunimovitz 1994; Z. Herzog 1992; Na'aman 2005). As the kingdoms of Israel and Judah came to the fore in the Iron Age II period, new fortifications were constructed.

Weaponry

Artistic representations of soldiers and battles, as well as military artifacts, illustrate the kinds of weapons and armaments available from the twelfth to sixth centuries BCE in the ancient Near East, and are extensively documented in Yigael Yadin's compilation, *The Art of Warfare in Biblical Lands* (1963; for a comprehensive catalog of armies of the ancient Near East, see Stillman and Tallis 1984). Decorations on the chariot of Thutmose IV show Western Asiatic / Canaanite chariot warriors, or *mariyannu*, arrayed in bronze scale armor and helmets (Yadin 1963). Temple reliefs of Medinet Habu that show the Sea Peoples provide insight into the early weapons and armor of the Philistines (Yadin 1963). Orthostats from the Iron Age Aramaean site of Tel Halaf depict infantry, cavalry, archers, and slingers of the northern Levant, while Neo-Hittite stone carvings from the site of Carchemish provide excellent detail of chariots and heavy infantry in this region (Yadin 1963).

The only pictorial representation of an ancient Israelite army comes from the early eighth-century palace reliefs of Sennacherib depicting his successful siege of the Judahite city of Lachish (Ussishkin 2014b). Some Judahite soldiers depicted wear conical helmets similar to the ones worn by the Assyrian soldiers

in the reliefs. Others wear a fringed headcloth, which appears to be an ethnic marker for ancient Judahites (Ussishkin 2014b).

The majority of the armies of the Late Bronze Age and Iron Age would have been made up of infantry carrying spears and shields. The better-equipped armies would have had infantry units with helmets and perhaps body armor as well (Yadin 1963). The Assyrian army seems to have been especially well equipped (Dezső 2012; 2006), with armor made of iron or bronze scales that had a central rib for strength, laced together to form a corselet (Barron 2010; Cogan and Tadmor 1988; J. Curtis and Ponting 2012; De Backer 2013; Matney et al. 2007, fig. 21). Typical helmets of the time were similarly constructed from either iron or bronze and were conical in shape (J. Curtis and Ponting 2012; Dezső 2001). The iron helmets were heavier and more cumbersome than the bronze ones, but they offered better protection and seem to have been preferred by the Assyrians (Cogan and Tadmor 1988).

Siege Warfare

One of the most common forms of military engagement in the biblical period was the siege of a fortified city. Most of the descriptions in the Old Testament of successful attacks of cities by Joshua and the judges mention the use of subterfuge or intervention by Yahweh but not the employment of siege equipment (Kern 1999). Accounts from the period of the monarchy mention the use of siege ramps and battering rams by the Israelites, as in the siege of Abel Beth-maacah by Joab (2 Sam. 20:15), or the use of the tactic of attrition, as in the siege of the Moabite king Mesha by Israel and Judah (2 Kings 3:18–27).

Judging from the numerous accounts of successful sieges from the period, one might assume that the besieging army would have an advantage over its adversaries. On the contrary, archaeological evidence shows that sieges often were thwarted (Burke 2009). The two main strategies of those conducting a siege were either to starve a city into submission or to assault its fortifications. The outcome of a siege was dependent on the supplies available to each side, the size of the attacking army, and the impregnability of the city's defensive system (Kern 1999). Many of the sieges conducted by the peoples of the Levant employed a strategy of attrition because a frontal assault required a very large number of soldiers. The remains of the ninth-century BCE siege of Gath (Tell es-Safi) by Hazael of Aram Damascus may be the earliest archaeological evidence of a siege trench and berm, which were designed to prevent the escape of the city's inhabitants, disrupt its resupply from the outside, and protect the besieging army (Maeir and Gur-Arieh 2011). In sieges such as this, civilians usually suffered from starvation and disease, especially if people from the countryside took refuge inside the city walls (Zorn 2014b).

A large besieging force would allow an army to sustain the high number of casualties necessary to launch a frontal assault of the walls and not have to resort to a lengthy war of attrition (Eph'al 1997; 2009). No army excelled at this type of siege more than the ancient Assyrians, who successfully conquered a significant number of fortified cities in the farthest reaches of their empire. Many of the battles that the Assyrians fought were sieges, almost certainly because their enemies felt safer behind the walls of their city than facing the Assyrian army in open battle (Scurlock 1997). In response, the Assyrians developed improved strategies and technologies to master this type of warfare. The siege of the heavily fortified Judahite city of Lachish by King Sennacherib during his punitive campaign against King Hezekiah in 701 BCE is an excellent case to illustrate an ancient siege from the period of the Bible because evidence surrounding the event derives from (1) the biblical account, (2) the Neo-Assyrian annals, such as the Sennacherib Prism, (3) the

impressive carved stone reliefs from the palace of Nineveh, and (4) extensive archaeological excavations at the site of Lachish itself (Dever 2012; Ussishkin 1982).

In the siege of this Judahite city, the Assyrians chose to attack a corner of the fortification walls because corners are weak points in walls and because a concentrated assault on this area would limit the number of defenders able to engage directly with the Assyrians (Ussishkin 2014a). They constructed a large siege ramp consisting of tens of thousands of tons of stone, probably at night to lessen the chance of disruption from the city's defenders (Eph'al 2009). Typically, the defenders of a city would be continuously trying to impede the attackers' progress, which is another reason why covering fire provided by archers and slingers would be so crucial in a siege (Kern 1999; Nadali 2005a; Nossov 2005).

The palace reliefs from Nineveh also show Assyrian soldiers using siege ladders to scale the walls as archers and slingers provided some protection to them. More than fifteen sling-stones measuring 6 cm in diameter and 850 arrowheads were recovered from the debris of the destruction. Many of the arrowheads were iron, and 652 of them were bent and found in one area in front of the main city wall, the result of the concentrated firepower of Assyrian archers using powerful bows at a short distance to clear defenders from the tops of the battlements (Ussishkin 2014b).

The palace reliefs from Nineveh depict a battering ram covered with a protective structure attacking the city gate of Lachish, with five more of these mobile units deployed on the main siege ramp (De Backer 2006). Judahite defenders are shown hurling rocks, firing arrows, and throwing firebrands down on the Assyrian army, while the soldiers in the covered rams are using ladles of water to extinguish any conflagrations. Other Assyrian soldiers are shown operating the rams themselves, which were not used to smash through walls but rather to pry the walls' bricks loose (Campbell 2006). Defenders from Lachish appear to be trying to catch these rams with iron chains from the tops of the walls and snap off their ends (Ussishkin 2014a).

Archaeological evidence revealed a counter-ramp inside the town built against the wall being assaulted in an attempt to prevent the Assyrian rams from breaking through (Ussishkin 2014b). The wall was breached, however, and archaeologists found clear evidence of burning and destruction. The archaeological and artistic evidence likely indicates that many civilians of Lachish were killed. A nearby cave revealed 1,300 skeletons of men, women, and children (Ussishkin 2014b). The reliefs from Nineveh depict curved swords, chariots, and large incense stands carried off by Assyrian soldiers (Ussishkin 2014b). Looting, along with the removal or destruction of sacred objects, was a common practice throughout the ancient Near East (S. Richardson 2011).

Groups of Judahite men, women, and children are shown being led away by soldiers, while other captives were beheaded, flayed alive, and impaled (Ussishkin 2014b)—acts that were a standard tool of Assyrian imperialist policy (Nadali 2005a; S. Richardson 2015). The practice of mass deportation and population exchange was designed to break resistance to Assyrian imperialism and provide increased labor for agricultural production (Wilkinson et al. 2005), military campaigns, and craft activities (Nadali and Vidal 2014; Oates 2005; Oded 1979). The Assyrian army was a multi-ethnic military force, and many conquered peoples were integrated into the army to meet the demands of the empire (Nadali 2005b; S. Richardson 2011).

The use of public torture and executions and its depiction on the walls of Assyrian palaces were designed to dissuade foreigners from resisting imperial control (J. M. Russell 1991). Whether certain reliefs on palace walls were intended for the eyes of foreign dignitaries

as propaganda, or for members of the royal court itself, is a matter of some debate (Reade 1979), but the reliefs in the more public areas of palaces communicated the might of Assyria and the dire consequences of rebellion (J. M. Russell 1991).

Israelite Fortifications

As siege warfare became increasingly important in the ancient Near East, the kingdoms of Israel and Judah invested more labor in preparation for sieges, including construction of defensive walls, development of strategically placed fortresses, building of secure water systems, and organization and distribution of supplies (Dever 2012). Israelite fortified cities may go back as far as the United Monarchy (Garfinkel et al. 2012; for an alternative interpretation, see Finkelstein and Fantalkin 2012). Chambered gates such as those at Hazor, Megiddo, and Gezer (Dever 2012; Finkelstein 2013) were crucial elements in a fortification system because the entrance to a city was one of the weakest points in its defenses. Gates had to be wide enough for chariots to pass through, necessitating the use of double doors, which were naturally weak at the center (Kern 1999). Gates, therefore, usually were multi-chambered, and the approaches to cities often were set at an angle to make attack more difficult (Yadin 1963).

Casemate walls surrounding a city consisted of two parallel walls with subdivided chambers. These chambers could be used for storage or living space or filled with rubble for extra protection (Yadin 1963). Defensive walls had protruding towers or angular projections to create areas in which attackers could be assaulted from multiple directions (Bolin 2004; Rocca 2012). It appears that over time the Israelites shifted away from casemate walls to solid walls with recesses, in order to deal with the growing threat of Assyria (Kern 1999). The three-meter-thick walls from the eighth-century Judahite city of Lachish are the largest found in the Levant from this time period (Ussishkin 1980).

The kings of the divided monarchy such as Asa (2 Chron. 16:6), Uzziah (2 Chron. 26:9–15), and Hezekiah (2 Chron. 32:5) are recorded as having engaged in fortification projects and improvements to city walls (Kern 1999). Hezekiah had the solid "broad wall" (2 Chron. 32:5) and the Siloam water channel (2 Kings 20:20; 2 Chron. 32:30) constructed in anticipation of an Assyrian siege of Jerusalem (Dever 2012; Hom 2016). A water source was one of the most important elements in the ability of defenders to outlast a siege (Kern 1999), and many Israelite and Judahite cities were equipped with large cisterns in the Iron II period (Dever 2012). In addition, Hezekiah had springs outside the capital stopped up in order to deny the Assyrian army a source of water (2 Chron. 32:4).

Intelligence and Administration

Military expeditions were logistically complex affairs, requiring many individuals engaged in a wide range of activities. The Assyrian campaigns are an excellent example of how artisans, scribes, diviners, engineers, craftsmen, and food producers were vital for maintenance of the core retinue of officers, infantry, charioteers, cavalry, and siege specialists (Nadali and Vidal 2014). Communication networks and military outposts provided the means by which spies and informants could quickly relay information on enemy troop movements or other vital intelligence to the Assyrian capital (Cogan and Tadmor 1988; Dubovský 2006).

By at least the eighth century, the kingdom of Judah had the organization needed to prepare in advance for future Assyrian assaults, but most likely it had to fill the ranks of the army with members of the general population, given that only a few thousand people could have been full-time soldiers at that time (Zorn 2014b). Forts such as Arad and Kadesh Barnea were strategically located to protect communication lines, trade routes, and borders (Dever 2012; Faust and Ludlum 2012). Ostraca from Arad and Lachish also suggest the state administration of military installations (Dever 2012). Hundreds of official stamped *lmlk* ("belonging to the king") storage jars found in fortified cities like Lachish demonstrate centralized control and distribution of supplies (Ussishkin 2014b; Isserlin 1998). Surveillance and reconnaissance were also conducted by the ancient Israelites to determine the number, location, and movements of enemy soldiers (Dubovský 2006).

Accounts of Armies and Battles in the Scriptures

The Old Testament provides a good deal of information on the organization and structure of the Israelite army through time (Seevers 2013). Some scholars (Gabriel 2003; C. Herzog and Gichon 1997; Malamat 1978) have reinterpreted the descriptions of battles in the Old Testament through the lens of military history and proposed that the original pragmatic decisions of commanders have been lost in a theological reworking of the events by later redactors (Malamat 1978; Christopher Smith 2008). Some scholars take exception both with the reinterpretation of the texts in terms of military explanations of miraculous occurrences, and the acceptance of the accuracy of the texts in terms of historical events (Sheldon 2005; Christopher Smith 2008). While the descriptions of specific conflicts may not portray the battles as they occurred, and may be describing events from a different period (Grabbe 2007), many of the tactics outlined are sound military maneuvers and suggest that the ancient Israelites at least had knowledge of several important tactical principles (C. Herzog and Gichon 1997).

For example, Gideon's attack on the Midianites can be seen as an example of a guerrilla-style nighttime raid by a relatively small force, employing surprise and deception in order to appear to be a larger force. However, the idea that the real reason Gideon reduced his numbers of men was to select only the "elite" soldiers among them (Gabriel 2003) may be reading too much into the text (Christopher Smith 2008). In several biblical episodes, Yahweh requires that a smaller number of soldiers be used to fight an enemy in order to clearly demonstrate that the victory was a result of divine intervention (Christopher Smith 2008).

Likewise, Joshua's attack on the city of Ai can be interpreted as the use of a false retreat to draw an enemy out of a fortified position, nullify their defensive advantage, and attack them on open ground (Gabriel 2003; C. Herzog and Gichon 1997; Nossov 2005). This tactic must have been a common ruse in the ancient Near East because it is employed by the Israelites in another biblical account (Judg. 20:29–48) and was one that they themselves were fearful of falling victim to (2 Kings 7:12) (S. Parker 1997). Other tactics, such as night marches followed by early dawn attacks (Josh. 10:9), were used by contemporary cultures, as revealed in the royal inscription of the Moabite king Mesha in the ninth century BCE (Smelik 1992).

Divination, Augury, and Divine Aspects of Warfare

Divination was an important part of ancient warfare in the Near East, as exemplified by extispicy's prominent role in the military campaigns of the Assyrian Empire (Starr, Aro, and Parpola 1990 [SAA 4]). Matters such as whether to wage war against a specific enemy (SAA 4, no. 287, pp. 268–69), the future outcome of a campaign (SAA 4, no. 288, pp. 269–70), and the warlike intentions of another group (SAA 4, no. 281, pp. 264–65, and no. 289, p. 270) are some of the concerns recorded by Assyrian diviners. The ritual acts of receiving favor from the gods and consultation of oracles before a

battle were standard practices of many ancient Near Eastern cultures (Capomacchia and Rivaroli 2014; Melville 2016). Similar instances can be found in the Old Testament where war leaders employ priests and divination tools such as the ephod to inquire of Yahweh whether they should attack a certain enemy (Judg. 20:27–28; 1 Sam. 23).

In many of these societies, including that of ancient Israel, wars were divinely orchestrated, with the chief deity of each culture being an active participant in battle. Many of the national gods of the ancient Near East are described with warrior attributes (R. Carroll 1993; Kang 1989). Yahweh is also described in the Old Testament as a warrior (Exod. 15:3), the god of the armies of Israel (1 Sam. 17:45), fighting alongside them (Deut. 7:21; 9:3; 20:4; 31:3, 6, 8; Josh. 10:14, 42; 23:3, 10), but also using enemy armies to punish the Israelites for transgressions (2 Chron. 28:9; Jer. 5:15) (Bolin 2004).

Religious aspects of war can also be seen in the sections of Deuteronomy that contain the laws and commandments regarding war, including restrictions designed to ensure the ritual purity of an army camp (Deut. 23:10–14). Post-battle purification rituals are also mentioned in one instance (Num. 31:19–24). The concept of a "holy war" that many today associate with the Old Testament and that has been used by some to legitimize conflicts in the postbiblical period (J. Collins 2003) is held by some scholars to be an anachronistic interpretation of the Hebrew texts (Achenbach 2012; Bolin 2004; Crouch 2009), for a dichotomy between secular and holy wars did not exist in the ancient Near East (Weippert 1972). The phrase "holy war" never actually appears in the Bible but has been used by scholars to describe specific types of war in which Yahweh is present with the army (Von Rad 1952). Because these wars in the Bible are different from Islamic jihad or ancient Greek "holy war," some question the appropriateness of the term and have instead suggested "divine war" or "Yahweh war" (Rowlett 1996).

One aspect of warfare in the Old Testament that many modern readers find particularly disconcerting is the practice of *herem*, or "dedication," sometimes referred to as the "ban" and exemplified by the slaying of all living things in Jericho by the ancient Israelites (Josh. 6:21). Several passages in Deuteronomy (7:24; 13:15; 20:16–18) instruct the ancient Israelites to place the "ban" on the seven nations of Canaan and "utterly destroy them." *Herem* is also mentioned in several other instances in the Old Testament (Lev. 27:29; Num. 21:2 [the promise of the Israelites to Yahweh]; 1 Sam. 15:8 [Saul's destruction of the Amalekites]). There are numerous articles and monographs on theological, ethical, hermeneutic, and cross-cultural analyses of *herem* and the moral implications of its use by the Israelites. While the present précis is too brief to present a full picture of the scholarship to date, the discussion here will provide a basis for further study.

The practice of the "ban" likely predates the Israelites with parallels in Hittite and Sumerian texts (P. Stern 1991) and may have been an aspect of many Near Eastern cultures even if they did not have a specific term for it (Crouch 2009). The example that bears the closest similarity to the *herem* of the Old Testament is the total annihilation of the Israelite-occupied town of Nebo by Mesha, the king of the Moabites, upon the instruction of his god Chemosh, to whom he had dedicated it. The stele on which this event is described uses the term *herem* specifically. In the minds of the ancient Moabites and Israelites, their battles were as much between Yahweh and Chemosh as between the human servants of those gods. Thus the property of the conquered god belonged to the deity who ensured victory (Kang 1989). Some scholars identify two types of *herem* in the Old Testament, one being a sacrifice to Yahweh and the other an execution of Yahweh's justice (Niditch 2007).

Incidences of *herem* are rare in the Hebrew Bible, and in general the kings of Israel had the reputation of being merciful (1 Kings 20:31). Many biblical scholars argue that the war rhetoric of the books of Deuteronomy and Joshua may have served the specific biblical writers setting the text down hundreds of years later more than it reflects a historical reality (Bolin 2004; J. Collins 2003; Earl 2011; Hess 2008; Niditch 1995; 2007; Rofe 1985; Rowlett 1996; Trimm 2012). Some contend that the stories of *herem* in the text were designed as parables primarily addressing the principle of strict obedience to Yahweh rather than as factual accounts of annihilation of cities or groups (Earl 2011).

Other scholars hold that the texts are accurate reflections of historical events and see *herem* as the reaction of Yahweh against sin, not against a particular ethnic group (Copan 2011). Likewise, the "ban" was a necessary evil to prevent the greater evil of Israel turning away from Yahweh (Martens 2008), in addition to being a necessary precondition for the establishment of a kingdom of Israel in the region (Craigie 1978). Other scholars have taken a more holistic view of the text, stressing that the Hebrew Bible should be examined *in totum*, looking at the overall message and balancing portions that we might find troubling with texts that stress tolerance, peace, and coexistence with other peoples (Exod. 22:21; 23:9; Lev. 19:33–34; Deut. 23:7–8) (see E. Davies 2005). Interestingly, other sections of Deuteronomy discuss the offering of peace to cities before initiating hostilities (Deut. 20:10), leniency toward cities that have surrendered (Deut. 20:11), prevention of ecological destruction during a siege (Deut. 20:19–20 [M. Hasel 2005; J. Wright 2008]), prohibitions on the rape of female captives (Deut. 21:10–11), and required mourning periods for women captured in battle (Deut. 21:12–14).

In addition, the annihilation of Canaanite groups in the Israelite conquest is not continued in the period of the divided monarchy, and the prophets never compel Israelites to wage "holy war" (B. Childs 1985; E. Davies 2005). Other passages in the Hebrew Bible imply that *herem* was not executed completely by stating that Canaanites were still living in the land during the periods after Joshua (Hoffman 1999). Other scholars maintain that the Hebrew Scriptures clearly state that *herem* was to be employed only in regard to the specific peoples mentioned, and only in the context of the initial conquest of Canaan (Deut. 7:1–5), and therefore the text cannot be used as a general injunction to justify the use of the "ban" in future situations (Greenberg 1995).

Reference List

Abel, F.-M. 1933, 1938. *Géographie de la Palestine*. 2 vols. Paris: Librairie Lecoffre.

Achenbach, Reinhard. 2003. *Die Vollendung der Tora: Studien zur Redaktionsgeschichte des Numeribuches im Kontext von Hexateuch und Pentateuch*. Wiesbaden: Harrassowitz.

———. 2012. "Divine Warfare and Yhwh's Wars: Religious Ideologies of War in the Ancient Near East and in the Old Testament." Pp. 1–27 in *The Ancient Near East in the 12th–10th Centuries BCE; Culture and History: Proceedings of the International Conference Held at the University of Haifa, 2–5 May, 2010*, edited by Gershon Galil et al. AOAT 392. Münster: Ugarit-Verlag.

Ackerman, Susan. 2008a. "Asherah, The West Semitic Goddess of Spinning and Weaving?" *JNES* 67:1–29.

———. 2008b. "Household Religion, Family Religion, and Women's Religion in Ancient Israel." Pp. 127–58 in *Household and Family Religion in Antiquity*, edited by John Bodel and Saul M. Olyan. Malden, MA: Blackwell.

———. 2010. "Assyria and the Bible." Pp. 124–42 in *Assyrian Reliefs from the Palace of Ashurnasirpal II*, edited by Ada Cohen and Steven E. Kangas. Hanover, NH: Hood Museum of Art, Dartmouth College; University Press of New England.

Ackermann, Oren. 2007. "Reading the Field: Geoarchaeological Codes in the Israeli Landscape." *Israel Journal of Earth Science* 56:87–106.

Adam, Klaus-Peter. 2014. "Feasting and Foodways in Psalm 23 and the Contribution of Redaction Criticism to the Interpretation of Meals." Pp. 223–55 in *Feasting in the Archaeology and Texts of the Bible and the Ancient Near East*, edited by Peter Altmann and Janling Fu. Winona Lake, IN: Eisenbrauns.

Adams, Colin. 2007. *Land Transport in Roman Egypt: A Study of Economics and Administration in a Roman Province*. Oxford: Oxford University Press.

Adams, Samuel L. 2014. *Social and Economic Life in Second Temple Judea*. Louisville: Westminster John Knox.

Agnon, Amotz. 2011. "Pre-Instrumental Earthquakes along the Dead Sea Rift." Pp. 207–61 in *Dead Sea Transform Fault System: Reviews*, edited by Zvi Garfunkel, Avi Ben-Avraham, and Elisa Kagan. Modern Approaches in Solid Earth Sciences 6. Dordrecht: Springer.

Aharoni, Yohanan. 1957. *The Settlement of the Israelite Tribes in the Upper Galilee*. Jerusalem: Magnes. [In Hebrew.]

———. 1979. *The Land of the Bible*. Edited and translated by Anson F. Rainey. Rev. and enlarged ed. Philadelphia: Westminster.

Aharoni, Yohanan, et al. 1960. "The Ancient Desert Agriculture of the Negev, V: An Israelite Agricultural Settlement at Ramat Matred." *IEJ* 10:23–35, 97–111.

Aharoni, Yohanan, Michael Avi-Yonah, Anson F. Rainey, Ze'ev Safrai, and R. Steven Notley. 2011. *The Carta Bible Atlas*. 5th ed. Jerusalem: Carta.

Aharoni, Yohanan, and Joseph Naveh. 1981. *Arad Inscriptions*. Translated by Judith Ben-Or. Edited and revised by Anson F. Rainey. Jerusalem: Israel Exploration Society.

Ahituv, Shmuel. 2008. *Echoes from the Past: Hebrew and Cognate Inscriptions from the Biblical Period*. Translated by Anson F. Rainey. Jerusalem: Carta.

Ahlström, Gösta W. 1993a. *The History of Palestine from the Palaeolithic Period to Alexander's Conquest*. JSOTSup 146. Sheffield: Sheffield Academic Press.

———. 1993b. "Pharaoh Shoshenq's Campaign to Palestine." Pp. 1–16 in *History and Traditions of Early Israel: Studies Presented to Eduard Nielsen*, edited by André Lemaire and Benedikt Otzen. VTSup 50. Leiden: Brill.

———. 2002. *Ancient Palestine: A Historical Introduction*. Minneapolis: Fortress.

Aitken, James K., ed. 2015. *The T&T Clark Companion to the Septuagint*. London: Bloomsbury.

Albertz, Rainer. 1978. *Persönliche Frömmigkeit und offizielle Religion: Religionsinterner Pluralismus in Israel und Babylon*. Calwer Theologische Monographien, Reihe A: Bibelwissenschaft. Stuttgart: Calwer.

———. 2003. *Israel in Exile: The History and Literature of the Sixth Century B.C.E.* SBL 3. Atlanta: Society of Biblical Literature.

———. 2008. "Family Religion in Ancient Israel and Its Surroundings." Pp. 89–112 in *Household and Family Religion in Antiquity*, edited by John Bodel and Saul M. Olyan. Malden, MA: Blackwell.

Albertz, Rainer, and Rüdiger Schmitt. 2012. *Family and Household Religion in Ancient Israel and the Levant*. Winona Lake, IN: Eisenbrauns.

Albright, William F. 1924a. "Contributions to Biblical Archaeology and Philology." *JBL* 43:368–93.

———. 1924b. "Egypt and the Early History of the Negeb." *JPOS* 4:131–61.

———. 1932. *The Archaeology of Palestine and the Bible*. Cambridge, MA: American Schools of Oriental Research.

———. 1938. *The Excavations of Tell Beit Mirsim II: The Bronze Age*. AASOR 17. New Haven: American Schools of Oriental Research.

———. 1943. "The Gezer Calendar." *BASOR* 92:16–26.

———. 1948. "Exploring in Sinai with the University of California African Expedition." *BASOR* 109:5–20.

———. 1949a. *The Archaeology of Palestine*. Harmondsworth: Penguin.

———. 1949b. *The Biblical Period from Abraham to Ezra*. New York: Thomas Nelson.

———. 1953. "Dedan." Pp. 1–12 in *Geschichte und Altes Testament*, edited by Gerhard Ebeling and W. F. Albright. Beiträge zur historischen Theologie 16. Tübingen: Mohr Siebeck.

———. 1957. "The High Place in Ancient Palestine." Pp. 242–58 in *Volume du Congrès: Strasbourg 1956*, edited by G. W. Anderson. VTSup 4. Leiden: Brill.

———. 1968. *Yahweh and the Gods of Canaan: A Historical Analysis of Two Contrasting Faiths*. Garden City, NY: Doubleday.

———. 1969. The Impact of Archaeology on Biblical Research—1966. Pp. 1–14 in *New Directions in Biblical Archaeology*, edited by David Noel Freedman and Jonas C. Greenfield. Garden City, NY: Doubleday.

———. 1994. *Yahweh and the Gods of Canaan: A Historical Analysis of Two Contrasting Faiths*. Reprint, Winona Lake, IN: Eisenbrauns.

Aldred, Cyril. 1973. *Akhenaten and Nefertiti*. New York: Brooklyn Museum in association with the Viking Press.

———. 1976. "The Horizon of the Aten." *JEA* 62:184.

———. 1988. *Akhenaten: King of Egypt*. London: Thames & Hudson.

Alexander, David. 1996. "The Health Effects of Earthquakes in the Mid–1990s." *Disasters* 20:231–47.

Allam, S. 2001. "Slaves." *OEAE* 3:293–96.

Almogi-Labin, A., et al. 2009. "Climatic Variability during the Last ~ 90ka of the Southern and Northern Levantine Basin as Evident from Marine Records and Speleothems." *Quaternary Science Reviews* 28 (25): 2882–96.

Alster, Bendt. 2005. *Wisdom of Ancient Sumer*. Bethesda, MD: CDL Press.

———. 2008. "Scribes and Wisdom in Ancient Mesopotamia." Pp. 47–63 in *Scribes, Sages, and Seers: The Sage in the Eastern Mediterranean World*, edited by Leo G. Perdue. FRLANT 219. Göttingen: Vandenhoeck & Ruprecht.

Alt, Albrecht. 1925. *Die Landnahme der Israeliten in Palästina*. Leipzig: Reformations-programm der Universität Leipzig.

———. 1966. *Essays on Old Testament History and Religion*. Translated by R. A. Wilson. Oxford: Blackwell.

———. 1989. "The Settlement of the Israelites in Palestine." Pp. 133–69 in Albrecht Alt, *Essays on Old Testament History and Religion*. Translated by R. A. Wilson. Biblical Seminar. Sheffield: JSOT Press.

Altmann, Peter. 2011. *Festive Meals in Ancient Israel: Deuteronomy's Identity Politics in Their Ancient Near Eastern Context*. BZAW 424. Berlin: de Gruyter.

———. 2013. "Diet, Bronze and Iron Age." *OEBA* 1:286–96.

———. 2014a. "Feast and Famine: Theoretical and Comparative Perspectives on Lack as a Backdrop for Plenty in the Hebrew Bible." Pp. 149–78 in *Feasting in the Archaeology and Texts of the Bible and the Ancient Near East*, edited by Peter Altmann and Janling Fu. Winona Lake, IN: Eisenbrauns.

———. 2014b. "Tithes for the Clergy and Taxes for the King: State and Temple Contributions in Nehemiah." *CBQ* 76:215–29.

———. 2016. *Economics in the Persian-Period Biblical Texts: Their Interactions with Economic Developments in the Persian Period and Earlier Biblical Traditions*. FAT 2/109. Tübingen: Mohr Siebeck.

Altmann, Peter, and Janling Fu, eds. 2014. *Feasting in the Archaeology and Texts of the Hebrew Bible and Ancient Near East*. Winona Lake, IN: Eisenbrauns.

Ambraseys, Nicholas. 2005. "The Seismic Activity in Syria and Palestine during the Middle of the 8th Century; An Amalgamation of Historical Earthquakes." *Journal of Seismology* 9:115–25.

———. 2009. *Earthquakes in the Mediterranean and Middle East: A Multidisciplinary Study of Seismicity up to 1900*. Cambridge: Cambridge University Press.

Ames, K. M. 2008. "The Archaeology of Rank." Pp. 487–513 in *The Handbook of Archaeological Theories*, edited by R. A. Bentley et al. Walnut Creek, CA: AltaMira.

Amiet, Pierre. 1972. *Glyptique susienne des origines à l'époque des Perses achéménides: Cachets, sceaux-cylindres et empreintes antiques découverts à Suse de 1913 à 1967*. 2 vols. Mémoires de la délégation archéologique en Iran 43. Paris: Geuthner.

———. 1992. *Corpus des cylindres de Ras Shamra-Ougarit II: Sceaux-cylindres en hématite et pierre diverses*. Paris: Éditions Recherche sur les civilisations.

Amiran, R. 1969. *Ancient Pottery of the Holy Land*. Jerusalem: Bialik.

Amiry, Suad, and Vera Tamari. 1989. *The Palestinian Village Home*. London: British Museum.

Amit, Yairah. 2003. "Epoch and Genre: The Sixth Century and the Growth of Hidden Polemics." Pp. 135–51 in *Judah and the Judeans in the Neo-Babylonian Period*, edited by Oded Lipschits and Joseph Blenkinsopp. Winona Lake, IN: Eisenbrauns.

———. 2006. "The Saul Polemic in the Persian Period." Pp. 647–61 in *Judah and the Judeans in the Persian Period*, edited by Oded Lipschits and Manfred Oeming. Winona Lake, IN: Eisenbrauns.

Amzallag, Nissim. 2018. "Who Was the Diety Worshipped at the Tent-Sanctuary of Timna?" Pp. 127–36 in *Mining for Ancient Copper: Essays in Memory of Beno Rothenberg*, edited by E. Ben-Yosef. Sonia and Marco Nadler Institute of Archaeology Monograph. Tel Aviv: Tel Aviv University.

Anbar, Moshe, and Nadav Na'aman. 1986–87. "An Account Tablet of Sheep from Ancient Hebron." *Tel Aviv* 13–14:3–12.

Anderson, James S. 2015. *Monotheism and Yahweh's Appropriation of Baal*. LHB/OTS 617. London: Bloomsbury T&T Clark.

Andrae, E. Walter. 1939. *Handbuch der Archäologie*. Edited by Walter Otto. Abteilung 6. Munich: Beck.

Angier, Natalie. 2013. "The Changing American Family." *New York Times*, November 26, 2013. http://www.nytimes.com/2013/11/26/health/families.html.

Anson, Edward M. 2013. *Alexander the Great: Themes and Issues*. London: Bloomsbury Academic.

———. 2014. *Alexander's Heirs: The Age of the Successors*. Chichester: Wiley-Blackwell.

Appadurai, Arjun. 1981. "Gastro-Politics in Hindu South Asia." *American Ethnologist* 8:494–511.

———. 1986. "Commodities and the Politics of Value." Pp. 3–63 in *The Social Life of Things: Commodities in Cultural Perspective*, edited by Arjun Appadurai. Cambridge: Cambridge University Press.

Archi, Alfonso. 1995. "Hittite and Hurrian Literatures: An Overview." *CANE* 4:2367–77.

———. 1998. "The High Priestess, *dam ningir*, at Ebla." Pp. 43–53 in *"Und Mose schrieb dieses Lied auf": Studien zum Alten Testament und zum Alten Orient; Festschrift für Oswald Loretz zur Vollendung seines 70. Lebensjahres mit Beiträgen von Freunden, Schülern und Kollegen*, edited by Manfried Dietrich, Ingo Kottsieper, and Oswald Loretz. AOAT 250. Münster: Ugarit-Verlag.

———. 2007. "Transmission of Recitative Literature by the Hittites." *AoF* 34:185–203.

Ardzinba, Vladislav. 1982. "On the Structure and the Functions of Hittite Festivals." Pp. 11–16 in *Gesellschaft und Kultur im alten Vorderasien*, edited by Horst Klengel. Schriften zur Geschichte und Kultur des alten Orients 15. Berlin: Akademie.

Arnold, Bill T. 1994. "The Weidner Chronicle and the Idea of History in Israel and Mesopotamia." Pp. 129–48 in *Faith, Tradition, and History: Old Testament Historiography in Its Ancient Near Eastern Context*, edited by A. R. Millard, James K. Hoffmeier, and David W. Baker. Winona Lake, IN: Eisenbrauns.

———. 2014. "The Genesis Narratives." Pp. 23–45 in *Ancient Israel's History: An Introduction to Issues and Sources*, edited by Bill T. Arnold and Richard S. Hess. Grand Rapids: Baker Academic.

Ash, Paul S. 1999. *David, Solomon, and Egypt: A Reassessment*. JSOTSup 297. Sheffield: Sheffield Academic Press.

Ashton, David. 2013. "Radiocarbon, Wine Jars and New Kingdom Chronology." *ÄL* 22/23:289–319.

Assmann, Jan. 1975. *Ägyptische Hymnen und Gebete*. Zurich: Artemis.

———. 1992. "Egyptian Literature." *ABD* 2:378–90.

———. 2008. *Of God and Gods: Egypt, Israel, and the Rise of Monotheism*. Madison: University of Wisconsin Press.

———. 2012. "A New State Theology—The Religion of Light." Pp. 79–83 in *In the Light of Amarna: 100 Years of the Nefertiti Discovery*, edited by Friederike Seyfried. Berlin: Michael Imhof.

———. 2014. *From Akhenaten to Moses: Ancient Egypt and Religious Change*. Cairo: American University in Cairo Press.

Aster, Shawn Zelig. 2007. "The Image of Assyria in Isaiah 2:5–22: The Campaign Motif Reversed." *JAOS* 127:249–78.

Astola, Tero. 2017. "Judean Merchants in Babylonia and Their Participation in Long-Distance Trade." *WO* 47:25–51.

Astour, Michael C. 1971. "841 BC: The First Assyrian Invasion of Israel." *JAOS* 91:383–89.

———. 1979. "Yahweh in Egyptian Topographic Lists." Pp. 17–34 in *Festschrift Elmar Edel, 12 März*

1979, edited by Manfred Görg and Edgar Pusch. Ägypten und Altes Testament 1. Bamberg: Görg.

Athas, G. 2003. *The Tel Dan Inscription: A Reappraisal and a New Interpretation.* JSOTSup 360. Sheffield: Sheffield Academic Press.

Aubet, Maria. 1993. *The Phoenicians and the West: Politics, Colonies and Trade.* Cambridge: Cambridge University Press.

Austin, M. M. 2006. *The Hellenistic World from Alexander to the Roman Conquest: A Selection of Ancient Sources in Translation.* Cambridge: Cambridge University Press.

Austin, Steven A., Gordon W. Franz, and Eric G. Frost. 2000. "Amos's Earthquake: An Extraordinary Middle East Seismic Event of 750 B.C." *International Geology Review* 42:657–71.

Averbeck, Richard E. 2002. "Sumer, the Bible, and Comparative Method: Historiography and Temple Building." Pp. 88–125 in *Mesopotamia and the Bible*, edited by Mark W. Chavalas and K. Lawson Younger Jr. Grand Rapids: Baker Academic.

———. 2011. "Having a Baby the New-Fashioned Way: An Old Testament Perspective." Pp. 25–42 in *Why the Church Needs Bioethics: A Guide to Wise Engagement with Life's Challenges*, edited by John F. Kilner. Grand Rapids: Zondervan.

———. 2016. "The Egyptian Sojourn and Deliverance from Slavery in the Framing and Shaping of the Mosaic Law." Pp. 143–75 in *"Did I Not Bring Israel Out of Egypt?" Biblical, Archaeological, and Egyptological Perspectives on the Exodus Narratives*, edited by James Hoffmeier, Alan Millard, and Gary Rendsburg. Bulletin of Biblical Research Monograph Series. Winona Lake, IN: Eisenbrauns.

———. Forthcoming. "The Exodus, Debt Slavery, and the Composition of the Pentateuch." In *Exploring the Composition of the Pentateuch*, edited by L. S. Baker Jr. et al. Bulletin of Biblical Research Supplement. Winona Lake, IN: Eisenbrauns.

Aviam, Mordechai. 2013. "People, Land, Economy, and Belief in First-Century Galilee and Its Origins: A Comprehensive Archaeological Synthesis." Pp. 5–49 in *The Galilean Economy in the Time of Jesus*, edited by David A. Fiensy and Ralph K. Hawkins. Early Christianity and Its Literature 11. Atlanta: Society of Biblical Literature.

Avigad, Nahman. 1972. "Two Hebrew Inscriptions on Wine Jars." *IEJ* 22:1–9.

———. 1976a. "Bullae and Seals from a Post-Exilic Judean Archive." *Qedem* 4:1–36.

———. 1976b. "The Governor of the City." *IEJ* 26:178–82.

Avigad, Nahman, and Benjamin Sass. 1997. *Corpus of West Semitic Stamp Seals.* Jerusalem: Israel Academy of Sciences and Humanities, Israel Exploration Society, and Institute of Archaeology, the Hebrew University of Jerusalem.

Avishur, Yitzhak. 1994. *Studies in Hebrew and Ugaritic Psalms.* Jerusalem: Magnes.

Avi-Yonah, Michael. 1954. *The Madaba Mosaic Map.* Jerusalem: Israel Exploration Society.

———. 1966. *The Holy Land: A Historical Geography from the Persian to the Arab Conquest, 536 B.C. to A.D. 640.* Grand Rapids: Baker. Rev. ed., Jerusalem: Carta, 2002.

———. 1981. *Art in Ancient Palestine: Selected Studies.* Jerusalem: Magnes.

Avruch, Kevin. 2000. "Reciprocity, Equality, and Status-Anxiety in the Amarna Letters." Pp. 154–64 in *Amarna Diplomacy: The Beginning of International Relations*, edited by Raymond Cohen. Baltimore: Johns Hopkins University Press.

Baadsgaard, Aubrey. 2008. "A Taste of Women's Sociality: Cooking as Cooperative Labor in Iron Age Syro-Palestine." Pp. 13–44 in *The World of Women in the Ancient and Classical Near East*, edited by Beth Alpert Nakhai. Newcastle: Cambridge Scholars Publishing.

Bachhuber, Christoph. 2013. "Sea Peoples." Pp. 6098–99 in *The Encyclopedia of Ancient History*, vol. 11, *Ro-Te*, edited by Roger S. Bagnall et al. Oxford: Wiley-Blackwell.

Bachhuber, Christoph, and R. Gareth Roberts, eds. 2009. *Forces of Transformation: The End of the Bronze Age in the Mediterranean.* Banea Monograph Book 1. Oxford: Oxbow Books.

Badian, Ernst. 2012. *Collected Papers on Alexander the Great.* London: Routledge.

Badre, Leila. 1980. *Les figurines anthropomorphes en terre cuite à l'âge du Bronze en Syrie.* Paris: Geuthner.

Bagg, Ariel M. 2013. "Palestine under Assyrian Rule: A New Look at the Assyrian Imperial Policy in the West." *JAOS* 133:119–44.

Bahrani, Zainab. 2003. *The Graven Image: Representation in Babylonia and Assyria.* Philadelphia: University of Pennsylvania Press.

———. 2017. *Mesopotamia: Ancient Art and Architecture.* London: Thames & Hudson.

Baines, John. 2003. "Research on Egyptian Literature." Pp. 1–26 in *Egyptology at the Dawn of the Twenty-First Century*, edited by Zahi Hawass. Cairo: American University in Cairo Press.

Baker, David W. 1987. "Leviticus 1–7 and the Punic Tariffs: A Form-Critical Comparison." *ZAW* 99:188–97.

Balasse, M., and S. H. Ambrose. 2005. "Distinguishing Sheep and Goats Using Dental Morphology and Stable Carbon Isotopes in C4 Grassland Environments." *JAS* 32:691–702.

Ballentine, D. S. 2015. *The Conflict Myth and the Biblical Tradition.* Oxford: Oxford University Press.

Balter, M. 2000. "The Two Tels: Armageddon for Biblical Archaeology?" *Science* 287:31–32.

Baly, Denis. 1974. *The Geography of the Bible.* New and rev. ed. New York: Harper & Row.

———. 2005. "The Essentials of Biblical Geography: A Point of View." Pp. 11–16 in *Geography of the Holy Land: Perspectives,* edited by William A. Dando, Caroline Z. Dando, and Jonathan J. Lu. Kaohsiung, Taiwan: Holy Light Theological Seminary Press.

Baly, Denis, and A. D. Tushingham. 1971. *Atlas of the Biblical World.* New York: World.

Barber, Elizabeth Wayland. 1994. *Women's Work: The First 20,000 Years—Women, Cloth, and Society in Early Times.* New York: W. W. Norton.

Barclay, John M. G. 2007. *Against Apion.* Flavius Josephus: Translation and Commentary 10. Boston: Brill.

Barjamovic, Gojko. 2011. *A Historical Geography of Ancient Anatolia in the Assyrian Colony Period.* Copenhagen: Museum Tusculanum.

Barkay, Gabriel. 1990. "The Cemeteries of Jerusalem in the Days of the First Temple Period." Pp. 102–23 in *Jerusalem in the Days of the First Temple,* edited by D. Amit and R. Goren. Jerusalem: Yad Ben-Zvi. [In Hebrew.]

———. 1992. "The Iron Age I–II." Pp. 302–73 in *The Archaeology of Ancient Israel,* edited by Amnon Ben-Tor. New Haven: Yale University Press.

———. 1994. "A Second 'Governor of the City' Bulla." Pp. 141–44 in *Ancient Jerusalem Revealed,* ed. Hillel Geva. Jerusalem / Washington DC: Israel Exploration Society / Biblical Archaeological Society.

———. 1999. "Burial Caves and Dwellings in Judah during Iron Age II: Sociological Aspects." Pp. 96–102 in *Material Culture, Society and Ideology: New Directions in the Archaeology of the Land of Israel,* edited by Avraham Faust and Aharon Me'ir. Ramat-Gan: Bar-Ilan University. [In Hebrew.]

———. 2006. "Royal Palace, Royal Portrait? The Tantalizing Possibilities of Ramat Rahel." *BAR* 32 (5): 34–44.

Barkay, Gabriel, Marilyn J. Lundberg, Andrew G. Vaughn, Bruce Zuckerman, and Kenneth Zuckerman. 2003. "The Challenges of Ketef Hinnom: Using Advanced Technologies to Reclaim the Earliest Biblical Texts and Their Context." *NEA* 66:162–71.

Barker, Graeme, David Gilbertson, and David Mattingly. 2007. "The Wadi Faynan Landscape Survey: Research Themes and Project Development." Pp. 3–24 in *Archaeology and Desertification: The Wadi Faynan Landscape Survey, Southern Jordan,* edited by Graeme Barker, David Gilbertson, and David Mattingly. Oxford: Oxbow Books.

Barker, William D. 2014. *Isaiah's Kingship Polemic: An Exegetical Study in Isaiah 24–27.* FAT 2/70. Tübingen: Mohr Siebeck.

Bar-Matthews, M., and A. Ayalon. 2004. "Speleothems as Palaeoclimate Indicators: A Case Study from Soreq Cave Located in the Eastern Mediterranean Region, Israel." Pp. 363–91 in *Past Climate Variability through Europe and Africa,* edited by Richard W. Battarbee, Françoise Gasse, and Catherine E. Stickley. Dordrecht: Springer.

Bar-Matthews, M., A. Ayalon, A. Kaufman, and G. J. Wasserburg. 1999. "The Eastern Mediterranean Paleoclimate as a Reflection of Regional Events: Soreq Cave, Israel." *Earth and Planetary Science Letters* 166 (1): 85–95.

Barnett, Richard D. 1982. *Ancient Ivories in the Middle East.* Jerusalem: Hebrew University.

Barrelet, Marie-Thérèse. 1950. "Une peinture de la cour 106 du palais de Mari." Pp. 9–35 in *Studia Mariana,* edited by André Parrot. DMOA 4. Leiden: Brill.

———. 1968. *Figurines et reliefs de terre cuite de la Mésopotamie antique.* Vol. 1. Paris: Geuthner.

Barrick, W. Boyd. 1975. "The Funerary Character of 'High Places' in Ancient Palestine: A Reassessment." *VT* 25:265–95.

———. 2002. *The King and the Cemeteries: Toward a New Understanding of Josiah's Reform.* VTSup 88. Boston: Brill.

Barron, Amy E. 2010. "Late Assyrian Arms and Armour: Art versus Artifact." PhD dissertation, University of Toronto.

Barstad, Hans M. 1995. "Dod." Pp. 493–98 in *Dictionary of Deities and Demons in the Bible,* edited by Karel van der Toorn, Bob Becking, and Pieter W. van der Horst. Leiden: Brill.

———. 1996. *The Myth of the Empty Land: A Study in the History and Archaeology of Judah during the "Exilic" Period.* Oslo: Scandinavian University Press.

———. 2003. "After the 'Myth of the Empty Land': Major Challenges in the Study of Neo-Babylonian Judah." Pp. 3–20 in *Judah and the Judeans in the Neo-Babylonian Period,* edited by Oded Lipschits and Joseph Blenkinsopp. Winona Lake, IN: Eisenbrauns.

Barta, Winfried. 1970. *Das Selbstzeugnis eines altägyptischen Künstlers.* Berlin: Hessling.

Baruch, Yuval, Ronny Reich, and Débora Sandhaus. 2016. "The Temple Mount—Results of the Archaeological Research of the Past Decade." http://archaeology.tau.ac.il/?page_id=6160. [In Hebrew.]

Bar-Yosef, O. 1998. "The Natufian Culture in the Levant, Threshold to the Origins of Agriculture." *Evolutionary Anthropology: Issues, News, and Reviews* 6:159–77.

Batto, B. F. 1992. *Slaying the Dragon: Mythmaking in the Biblical Tradition.* Louisville: Westminster John Knox.

Bauckham, Richard, and Stefano De Luca. 2015. "Magdala as We Now Know It." *EC* 6:91–118.

Baudains, Peter, Silvie Zamazalová, Mark Altaweel, and Alan Wilson. 2015. "Modeling Strategic Decisions in the Formation of the Early Neo-Assyrian Empire." *Cliodynamics* 6:1–23.

Bawanypeck, Daliah, and Susanne Görke. 2001. "Das Festritual für den Wettergott der Wiese." Pp. 29–50 in *Kulturgeschichten: Altorientalische Studien für Volkert Haas zum 65. Geburtstag*, edited by Thomas Richter, Doris Prechel and Jörg Klinger. Saarbrücken: Saarbrücker Druckerei und Verlag.

Bayer, Bathja. 2014. "The Mesopotamian Theory of Music and the Ugarit Notation: A Reexamination." Pp. 15–91 in *Music in Antiquity: The Near East and the Mediterranean*, edited by Joan Goodnick Westenholz, Yossi Maurey, and Edwin Seroussi. Yuval 8. Berlin: de Gruyter; Jerusalem: Magnes.

Beal, Richard H. 2002. "Hittite Oracles." Pp. 57–81 in *Magic and Divination in the Ancient World*, edited by Leda Ciraolo and Jonathan Seidel. AMD 2. Leiden: Brill.

Beale, G. K. 2004. *The Temple and the Church's Mission*. Downers Grove, IL: InterVarsity.

Beaulieu, Paul-Alain. 1989. *The Reign of Nabonidus King of Babylon, 556–539 B.C.* YNER 10. New Haven: Yale University Press.

———. 2005. "Eanna's Contribution to the Construction of the North Palace at Babylon." Pp. 45–73 in *Approaching the Babylonian Economy: Proceedings of the START Project Symposium, Held in Vienna, 1–3 July 2004*, edited by Heather D. Baker and Michael Jursa. AOAT 330. Münster: Ugarit-Verlag.

———. 2007. "The Social and Intellectual Setting of Babylonian Wisdom Literature." Pp. 3–20 in *Wisdom Literature in Mesopotamia and Israel*, edited by Richard J. Clifford. SymS 36. Leiden: Brill.

Beck, John A. 2015. *Discovery House Bible Atlas*. Grand Rapids: Our Daily Bread Ministries.

Beck, Pirhiya. 1982. "The Drawings from Ḥorvat Teman (Kuntillet ʿAjrud)." *TA* 9:3–68.

———. 2002. *Imagery and Representation: Studies in the Art and Iconography of Ancient Palestine; Collected Articles*. Tel Aviv: Emery and Claire Yass Publications in Archaeology.

Becking, Bob. 1992. *The Fall of Samaria: An Historical and Archaeological Study*. SHANE 2. Leiden: Brill.

———. 2001. *Only One God? Monotheism in Ancient Israel and the Veneration of the Goddess Asherah*, edited by Bob Becking et al. Biblical Seminar 77. London / New York: Sheffield Academic Press.

Beckman, Gary. 1989. "The Religion of the Hittites." *BA* 52:98–108.

———. 2004. "Sacrifice, Offerings, and Votives: Anatolia." Pp. 336–39 in *Religions of the Ancient World: A Guide*, edited by Sarah Iles Johnston. Religions of the Ancient World. Cambridge, MA: Belknap Press of Harvard University Press.

———. 2009. "Hittite Literature." Pp. 215–54 in *From an Antique Land: An Introduction to Ancient Near Eastern Literature*, edited by Carl S. Ehrlich. Plymouth: Rowman & Littlefield.

———. 2011. "Blood in Hittite Ritual." *JCS* 63:95–102.

Beckman, Gary, T. R. Bryce, and E. H. Cline. 2011. *The Ahhiyawa Texts*. Society of Biblical Literature Writings from the Ancient World 28. Atlanta: Society of Biblical Literature.

Bedford, Peter R. 2007. "The Economic Role of the Jerusalem Temple in Achaemenid Judah: Comparative Perspectives." Pp. 3*–20* in *Shai le-Sara Japhet: Studies in the Bible, Its Exegesis, and Its Language*, edited by Mosheh Bar-Asher et al. Jerusalem: Bialik. [In Hebrew and English.]

Beitzel, Barry J. 2009. *The Moody Atlas of the Bible*. Chicago: Moody.

Bell, Gertrude Lowthian. 1907. *Syria: The Desert and the Sown*. London: Heinemann.

Bellow, Saul. 2003. *Novels 1944–1953: Dangling Man, The Victim, The Adventures of Augie March*. Library of America 141. New York: Literary Classics of the US.

Bellwood, Peter. 2013. *First Migrants: Ancient Migration in Global Perspective*. Chichester: Wiley-Blackwell.

Ben-Arieh, S., D. Ben-Tor, and S. Godovitz. 1993. "A Late Bronze Age Burial Cave at Qubeibeh, near Tel Lachish." *ʿAtiqot* 22:77–89.

Ben-Arieh, Yehoshua. 1983. *The Rediscovery of the Holy Land in the Nineteenth Century*. 2nd ed. Jerusalem: Magnes.

———. 1989. "Perceptions and Images of the Holy Land." Pp. 37–53 in *The Land That Became Israel: Studies in Historical Geography*, edited by Ruth Kark. New Haven: Yale University Press.

Bendor, S. 1996. *The Social Structure of Ancient Israel: The Institution of the Family (beit ʾab) from the Settlement to the End of the Monarchy*. Jerusalem: Simor.

Ben-Dor Evian, Shirly. 2011. "Shishak's Karnak Relief—More Than Just Name-Rings." Pp. 11–22 in *Egypt, Canaan and Israel: History, Imperialism, Ideology and Literature; Proceedings of a Conference at the University of Haifa, 3–7 May 2009*, edited by S. Bar, D. Kahn, and J. J. Shirley. CHANE 52. Leiden: Brill.

Benjamin, Don C. 2015. *The Social World of Deuteronomy: A New Feminist Commentary*. Eugene, OR: Cascade.

Bennett, Crystal M. 1966. "Fouilles d'Umm el-Biyara: Rapport preliminaire." *RB* 73:372–403.

———. 1977. "Excavations in Buseirah, Southern Jordan." *Levant* 9:1–10.

———. 1983. "Excavations at Buseirah (Biblical Bozrah)." Pp. 9–17 in *Midian, Moab and Edom: The*

History and Archaeology of Late Bronze and Iron Age Jordan and North-West Arabia, edited by John F. A. Sawyer and David J. A. Clines. JSOTSup 24. Sheffield: JSOT Press.

Ben-Shlomo, David. 2011. "Food Preparation Habits and Cultural Interaction during the Late Bronze and Iron Age in Southern Israel." Pp. 273–86 in *On Cooking Pots, Drinking Cups, Loomweights and Ethnicity in Bronze Age Cyprus and Neighbouring Regions: An International Archaeological Symposium Held in Nicosia, November 6th–7th 2010*, edited by Vassos Karageorghis and Ourania Kouka. Nicosia: A. G. Leventis Foundation.

———. 2014a. "Marked Jar Handles from Tel Miqne-Ekron." Pp. 17–32 in *Material Culture Matters: Essays on the Archaeology of the Southern Levant in Honor of Seymour Gitin*, edited by John R. Spencer, Robert A. Mullins, and Aaron J. Brody. Winona Lake, IN: Eisenbrauns.

———. 2014b. "Philistia during the Iron Age II Period." Pp. 717–42 in *The Oxford Handbook of the Archaeology of the Levant: C. 8000–332 BCE*, edited by Margreet L. Steiner and Ann E. Killebrew. Oxford: Oxford University Press.

———. 2014c. "Tell Jemmeh, Philistia and the Neo-Assyrian Empire during the Late Iron Age." *Levant* 46:58–88.

Ben-Shlomo, David, et al. 2008. "Cooking Identities: Aegean-Style Cooking Jugs and Cultural Interaction in Iron Age Philistia and Neighboring Regions." *AJA* 112:225–46.

Ben-Shlomo, David, J. Uziel, and A. M. Maeir. 2009. "Pottery Production at Tell es-Safi/Gath: A *Longue Durée* Perspective." *JAS* 36:2258–73.

Ben-Tor, Amnon. 1992. "The Hazor Tablet: Foreword." *IEJ* 42:17–20.

———. 2016. *Hazor: Canaanite Metropolis, Israelite City*. Jerusalem: Israel Exploration Society.

Ben-Tor, D. 1997. "The Relations between Egypt and Palestine in the Middle Kingdom as Reflected by Contemporary Canaanite Scarabs." *IEJ* 47:162–89.

———. 2007. *Scarabs, Chronology, and Interconnections: Egypt and Palestine in the Second Intermediate Period*. OBOSA 27. Göttingen: Vandenhoeck & Ruprecht.

Ben-Tor, D., and O. Keel. 2012. "The Beth-Shean Level IX Group: A Local Scarab Workshop of the Late Bronze Age I." Pp. 87–104 in *All the Wisdom of the East: Studies in Near Eastern Archaeology and History in Honor of Eliezer D. Oren*, edited by Mayer Gruber et al. OBO 255. Fribourg: Academic Press; Göttingen: Vandenhoeck & Ruprecht.

Ben-Yehoshua, Shimshon, Carole Borowitz, and Lumír Ondřej Hanuš. 2012. "Frankincense, Myrrh, and Balm of Gilead: Ancient Spices of Southern Arabia and Judea." Pp. 1–76 in *Horticultural Reviews*, vol. 39, edited by Jules Janick. Hoboken, NJ: Wiley-Blackwell.

Ben-Yosef, Erez. 2010. "Technology and Social Process: Oscillations in Iron Age Copper Production and Power in Southern Jordan." PhD dissertation, University of California, San Diego.

Ben-Yosef, Erez, et al. 2012. "A New Chronological Framework for Iron Age Copper Production at Timna (Israel)." *BASOR* 367:31–71.

Ben-Yosef, Erez, and Thomas E. Levy. 2014. "The Material Culture of Iron Age Copper Production in Faynan." Pp. 887–959 in *New Insights into the Iron Age Archaeology of Edom, Southern Jordan*, vol. 2, edited by Thomas E. Levy, Mohammad Najjar, and Erez Ben-Yosef. Los Angeles: UCLA Cotsen Institute of Archaeology Press.

Ben-Yosef, Erez, Mohammad Najjar, and Thomas E. Levy. 2014. "New Iron Age Excavations at Copper Production Sites, Mines, and Fortresses in Faynan." Pp. 767–886 in *New Insights into the Iron Age Archaeology of Edom, Southern Jordan*, vol. 2, edited by Thomas E. Levy, Mohammad Najjar, and Erez Ben-Yosef. Los Angeles: UCLA Cotsen Institute of Archaeology Press.

Ben Zion, Ilan. 2016. "Archaeologists Spotlight First Solomon's Temple-Era Artifacts Ever Found on Temple Mount." http://www.timesofisrael.com/archaeologists-reveal-first-solomons-temple-era-artifacts-ever-found-on-temple-mount/.

Berger, John. 1990. *Ways of Seeing*. Reprint, London: Penguin.

Berlejung, Angelika. 2010. "There Is Nothing Better Than More! Text and Images on Amulet 1 from Arslan Tash." *JNSL* 36:1–42.

Berlin, Andrea M. 1997. "Between Large Forces: Palestine in the Hellenistic Period." *BA* 60:3–51.

———. 1999. "The Archaeology of Ritual: The Sanctuary of Pan at Banias/Caesarea Philippi." *BASOR* 315:27–45.

———. 2002. "Power and Its Afterlife: Tombs in Hellenistic Palestine." *NEA* 65:138–48.

———. 2005. "Jewish Life before the Revolt: The Archaeological Evidence." *JSJ* 36:417–70.

Berman, Joshua. 2008. *Created Equal: How the Bible Broke with Ancient Political Thought*. New York: Oxford University Press.

———. 2017. *Inconsistency in the Torah: Ancient Literary Convention and the Limits of Source Criticism*. Oxford: Oxford University Press.

Berman, Lawrence. 2001. "Overview of Amenhotep III and His Reign." Pp. 1–26 in *Amenhotep III: Perspectives on His Reign*, edited by David O'Connor and Eric Cline. Ann Arbor: University of Michigan Press.

Bernand, A., and O. Masson. 1957. "Les inscriptions grecques d'Abou-Simbel." *REG* 70:3–20.

Bernett, Monika, and Othmar Keel. 1998. *Mond, Stier und Kult am Stadttor: Die Stele von Betsaida (et-Tell)*. OBO 161. Freiburg: Universitätsverlag; Göttingen: Vandenhoeck & Ruprecht.

Bernhardt, C. E., B. P. Horton, and J. D. Stanley. 2012. "Nile Delta Vegetation Response to Holocene Climate Variability." *Geology* 40 (7): 615–18.

Berquist, Jon L. 1995. *Judaism in Persia's Shadow: A Social and Historical Approach*. Minneapolis: Fortress.

Betlyon, John W. 1986. "The Provincial Government of Persian Period Judea and the Yehud Coins." *JBL* 105:633–42.

———. 2003. "Neo-Babylonian Military Operations Other Than War in Judah and Jerusalem." Pp. 263–83 in *Judah and the Judeans in the Neo-Babylonian Period*, edited by Oded Lipschits and Joseph Blenkinsopp. Winona Lake, IN: Eisenbrauns.

———. 2005. "A People Transformed: Palestine in the Persian Period." *NEA* 68:4–58.

Beyer, Dominique. 2001. *Emar IV: Les sceaux; Mission archéologique de Meskéné-Emar, recherches au pays d'Aštata*. OBOSA 20. Fribourg: Editions Universitaires; Göttingen: Vandenhoeck & Ruprecht.

Bianchi, Francesco. 1994. "Le rôle de Zorobabel et la dynastie davidique en Judée du VIe siècle au VIe siècle av. J.-C." *Transeuphratène* 7:153–65.

Bidmead, Julye. 2004. *The Akītū Festival: Religious Continuity and Royal Legitimation in Mesopotamia*. Gorgias Dissertations, Near East 2. Piscataway, NJ: Gorgias.

Bienkowski, Piotr, ed. 1992. *Early Edom and Moab: The Beginnings of the Iron Age in Southern Jordan*. Sheffield Archaeological Monographs 7. Oxford: Alden.

———. 1995. "The Edomites: The Archaeological Evidence from Transjordan." Pp. 41–92 in *You Shall Not Abhor an Edomite for He Is Your Brother: Edom and Seir in History and Tradition*, edited by Diana V. Edelman. ABS 3. Atlanta: Scholars Press.

———. 2009. "'Tribalism' and 'Segmentary Society' in Iron Age Transjordan." Pp. 7–26 in *Studies on Iron Age Moab and Neighbouring Areas in Honor of Michèle Daviau*, edited by Piotr Bienkowski. ANESSup 29. Leuven: Peeters.

———. 2014. "Edom during the Iron Age II Period." Pp. 782–94 in *The Oxford Handbook of the Archaeology of the Levant: C. 8000–332 BCE*, edited by Margreet L. Steiner and Ann E. Killebrew. Oxford: Oxford University Press.

Bietak, Manfred. 1975. *Tell el-Dabᶜa*. Vienna: Österreichische Akademie der Wissenschaften.

———. 1979. "Avaris and Piramesse: Archaeological Exploration in the Eastern Nile Delta." *Proceedings of the British Academy* 65:225–90.

———. 1987. "Comments on the Exodus." Pp. 163–71 in *Egypt, Israel, Sinai: Archaeological and Historical Relationships in the Biblical Period*, edited by Anson F. Rainey. Tel Aviv: Tel Aviv University Press.

———. 1996. *Avaris: The Capital of the Hyksos*. London: The Trustees of the British Museum.

———. 2000. "Der Aufenthalt 'Israels' in Ägypten und der Zeitpunkt der 'Landname' aus heutiger archäologischer Sicht." *ÄL* 10:179–86.

———. 2007. "Egypt and the Levant." Pp. 417–48 in *The Egyptian World*, edited by Toby A. Wilkinson. The Routledge Worlds. Abingdon: Routledge.

Bietak, Manfred, and Irene Forstner-Müller. 2011. "The Topography of New Kingdom Avaris and Per-Ramesses." Pp. 23–50 in *Ramesside Studies in Honour of K. A. Kitchen*, edited by Mark Collier and Steven R. Snape. Bolton: Rutherford.

Bietak, Manfred, Nannó Marinatos, and Clairy Palivou. 2007. *Taureador Scenes in Tell el-Dabᶜa (Avaris) and Knossos*. Vienna: Österreichische Akademie der Wissenschaften.

Bietak, Manfred, Nicola Math, and Vera Müller. 2013. "Report on the Excavations of a Hyksos Palace of Tell el Dabᶜa/Avaris." *ÄL* 22:17–53.

Billows, Richard A. 1997. *Antigonos the One-Eyed and the Creation of the Hellenistic State*. Berkeley: University of California Press.

Bimson, J. J. 1986. "Shoshenq and Shishak: A Case of Mistaken Identity." *Chronology and Catastrophism Review* 8:36–46.

Binder, Donald D. 1999. *Into the Temple Courts: The Place of the Synagogues in the Second Temple Period*. Society of Biblical Literature Dissertation Series 169. Atlanta: Society of Biblical Literature.

Binford, L. R. 1972. *An Archaeological Perspective*. New York: Seminar.

Biran, Avraham. 1994. *Biblical Dan*. Jerusalem: Israel Exploration Society.

Biran, Avraham, and J. Naveh. 1993. "An Aramaic Stele Fragment from Tel Dan." *IEJ* 43:81–98.

———. 1995. "The Tel Dan Inscription: A New Fragment." *IEJ* 45:1–18.

Black, Jeremy. 2007. "Sumerian." Pp. 4–30 in *Languages of Iraq, Ancient and Modern*, edited by J. N. Postgate. Cambridge: Cambridge University Press.

Blanton, R. E. 1994. *Houses and Households: A Comparative Study*. New York: Plenum.

Blasius, Andreas, and Bernd U. Schipper, eds. 2002. *Apokalyptik und Ägypten: Eine kritische Analyse der relevanten Texte aus dem griechisch-römischen Ägypten*. OLA 107. Leuven: Peeters.

Blenkinsopp, Joseph. 1987. "The Mission of Udjahorresnet and Those of Ezra and Nehemiah." *JBL* 106:409–21.

———. 1995. "Deuteronomy and the Politics of Post-Mortem Existence." *VT* 45:1–16.

———. 1997. "The Family in First Temple Israel." Pp. 48–103 in *Families in Ancient Israel*, edited by Leo G. Perdue et al. Louisville: Westminster John Knox.

———. 2006. "Benjamin Traditions Read in the Early Persian Period." Pp. 629–45 in *Judah and the Judeans in the Persian Period*, edited by Oded Lipschits and Manfred Oeming. Winona Lake, IN: Eisenbrauns.

Bliss, F. J., and R. A. S. Macalister. 1902. *Excavations in Palestine during the Years 1898–1900*. London: Palestine Exploration Fund.

Bloch, M. 1981. "Tombs and States." Pp. 137–47 in *Mortality and Immortality: The Anthropology and Archaeology of Death*, edited by S. C. Humphreys and H. King. London: Academic Press.

Bloch, Yigal. 2014. "Judeans in Sippar and Susa during the First Century of the Babylonian Exile: Assimilation and Perseverance under Neo-Babylonian and Achaemenid Rule." *Journal of Ancient Near Eastern History* 1:119–72.

Bloch-Smith, Elizabeth M. 1992a. *Judahite Burial Practices and Beliefs about the Dead*. JSOTSup 123. Sheffield: JSOT Press.

———. 1992b. "The Cult of the Dead in Judah: Interpreting the Material Remains." *JBL* 111:213–24.

———. 1994. "'Who Is the King of Glory?' Solomon's Temple and Symbolism." Pp. 18–31 in *Scripture and Other Artifacts: Essays on the Bible and Archaeology in Honor of Philip J. King*, edited by Michael D. Coogan, J. Cheryl Exum, and Lawrence E. Stager. Louisville: Westminster John Knox.

———. 2002a. "Death in the Life of Israel." Pp. 139–44 in *Sacred Time, Sacred Place: Archaeology and the Religion of Israel*, edited by Barry M. Gittlen. Winona Lake, IN: Eisenbrauns.

———. 2002b. "Solomon's Temple: The Politics of Ritual Space." Pp. 83–94 in *Sacred Time, Sacred Place: Archaeology and the Religion of Israel*, edited by Barry M. Gittlen. Winona Lake, IN: Eisenbrauns.

———. 2003. "Bronze and Iron Age Burials and Funerary Customs in the Southern Levant." Pp. 105–15 in *Near Eastern Archaeology: A Reader*, edited by Suzanne Richard. Winona Lake, IN: Eisenbrauns.

———. 2006. "Will the Real Masseboth Please Stand Up?: Cases of Real and Mistakenly Identified Standing Stones in Ancient Israel." Pp. 64–79 in *Text, Artifact, and Image: Revealing Ancient Israelite Religion*, edited by Gary Beckman and Theodore J. Lewis. Providence: Brown Judaic Studies.

———. 2009. "Assyrians Abet Israelite Cultic Reforms: Sennacherib and the Centralization of the Israelite Cult." Pp. 35–44 in *Exploring the Longue Durée: Essays in Honor of Lawrence E. Stager*, edited by J. David Schloen. Winona Lake, IN: Eisenbrauns.

———. 2014. "Questions about Monotheism in Ancient Israel: Between Archaeology and Texts." *JISMOR* 9:20–28.

Block, Daniel I. 2003. "Marriage and Family in Ancient Israel." Pp. 33–102 in *Marriage and Family in the Biblical World*, edited by Ken M. Campbell. Downers Grove, IL: InterVarsity.

Blum, Erhard. 2016. "The Relations between Aram and Israel in the 9th and 8th Centuries BCE." Pp. 37–56 in *In Search for Aram and Israel: Politics, Culture, and Identity*, edited by Omer Sergi, Manfred Oeming, and Izaak J. de Hulster. Oriental Religions in Antiquity 20. Tübingen: Mohr Siebeck.

Bober, P. B. 1999. *Art, Culture, and Cuisine: Ancient and Medieval Gastronomy*. Chicago: University of Chicago Press.

Boda, Mark J. 2016. *The Book of Zechariah*. New International Commentary on the Old Testament. Grand Rapids: Eerdmans.

Boda, Mark J., and Jamie Novotny, eds. 2010. *From the Foundations to the Crenellations: Essays on Temple Building in the Ancient Near East and Hebrew Bible*. AOAT 366. Münster: Ugarit-Verlag.

Bodi, Daniel. 1991. *The Book of Ezekiel and the Poem of Erra*. OBO 104. Freiburg: Universitätsverlag; Göttingen: Vandenhoeck & Ruprecht.

———. 2009. "Ezekiel." Pp. 400–517 in *Zondervan Illustrated Bible Backgrounds Commentary*, vol. 4, edited by John H. Walton. Grand Rapids: Zondervan.

———. 2015. "The Double Current and the Tree of Healing in Ezekiel 47:1–12 in Light of Babylonian Iconography and Texts." *Welt des Orients* 45:22–37.

———. 2016. Review of *Prophétisme et alliance*, by Jean-Georges Heintz. *CBQ* 78:796–806.

Boecker, Hans J. 1980. *Law and the Administration of Justice in the Old Testament and Ancient Near East*. Minneapolis: Augsburg.

Boer, Roland. 2015. *The Sacred Economy of Ancient Israel*. LAI. Louisville: Westminster John Knox.

Boertien, Jeannette H., and Margreet Steiner. 2009. "Arts and Crafts." Pp. 858–66 in *Encyclopedia of the Bible and Its Reception*, vol. 2, edited by Dale C. Allison et al. Berlin: de Gruyter.

Bohmbach, Karla G. 2000. "Names and Naming in the Biblical World." Pp. 33–39 in *Women in Scripture: A Dictionary of Named and Unnamed Women in the Hebrew Bible, the Apocryphal/Deuterocanonical Books, and the New Testament*, edited by Carol Meyers, Toni Craven, and Ross S. Kraemer. Boston: Houghton Mifflin.

Bolin, Thomas M. 2004. "Warfare." Pp. 33–52 in *The Biblical World*, vol. 2, edited by J. Barton. Abingdon: Routledge.

Bonatz, Dominik. 2000. *Das syro-hethitische Grab-denkmal: Untersuchungen zur Entstehung einer neuen Bildgattung in der Eisenzeit im nordsyrisch-südostanatolischen Raum*. Mainz: Zabern.

Bonfiglio, Ryan P. 2016. *Reading Images, Seeing Texts: Towards a Visual Hermeneutics for Biblical Studies*. OBO 280. Fribourg: Academic Press; Gottingen: Vandenhoeck & Ruprecht.

Bongenaar, A. C. V. M., ed. 2000. *Interdependency of Institutions and Private Entrepreneurs: Proceedings of the Second MOS Suymposium (Leiden 1998)*. Leiden: Nederlands Historisch-Archeologisch Instituut te Istanbul.

Borger, Rykle. 1996. *Beiträge zum Inschriftenwerk Assurbanipals*. Wiesbaden: Harrassowitz.

Borghouts, J. F. 1995. "Witchcraft, Magic, and Divination in Ancient Egypt." *CANE* 3:1775–85.

Borowski, Oded. 1987. *Agriculture in Iron Age Israel*. Winona Lake, IN, Eisenbrauns.

———. 1995. "Hezekiah's Reforms and the Revolt against Assyria." *BA* 58:148–55.

———. 1999. *Every Living Thing: Daily Use of Animals in Ancient Israel*. Walnut Creek, CA: Altamira.

———. 2002. *Agriculture in Iron Age Israel*. Boston: American Schools of Oriental Research.

———. 2003. *Daily Life in Biblical Times*. ABS 5. Atlanta: Society of Biblical Literature.

———. 2004. "Eat, Drink, and Be Merry: The Mediterranean Diet." *NEA* 67:96–107.

———. 2005. "Water and Water Systems." Pp. 980–84 in *Dictionary of the Old Testament: Historical Books*, edited by Bill T. Arnold and H. G. M. Williamson. Downer Grove, IL: InterVarsity.

Borza, Eugene. 1990. *In the Shadow of Olympus: The Emergence of Macedon*. Princeton: Princeton University Press.

Bosworth, A. B. 1988. *Conquest and Empire: The Reign of Alexander the Great*. Cambridge: Cambridge University Press.

———. 1996. *Alexander and the East: The Tragedy of Triumph*. Oxford: Oxford University Press.

———. 2002. *The Legacy of Alexander: Politics, Warfare and Propaganda under the Successors*. Oxford: Oxford University Press.

Bosworth, A. B., and E. Baynham, eds. 2000. *Alexander the Great in Fact and Fiction*. Oxford: Oxford University Press.

Bottéro, Jean. 1995a. *Mesopotamia: Writing, Reasoning, and the Gods*. Translated by Zainab Bahrani and Marc van de Mieroop. Chicago: University of Chicago Press.

———. 1995b. *Textes culinaires mésopotamiens / Mesopotamian Culinary Texts*. MC 6. Winona Lake, IN: Eisenbrauns.

———. 2001a. "The Oldest Cuisine in the World." Pp. 43–64 in *Everyday Life in Ancient Mesopotamia*, edited by Jean Bottéro. Baltimore: Johns Hopkins University Press.

———. 2001b. "The Oldest Feast." Pp. 65–83 in *Everyday Life in Ancient Mesopotamia*, edited by Jean Bottéro. Baltimore: Johns Hopkins University Press.

———. 2004. *The Oldest Cuisine in the World: Cooking in Mesopotamia*. Translated by T. Lavender Fagan. Chicago: University of Chicago Press.

Bourdieu, Pierre. 1977. *Outline of a Theory of Practice*. Translated by Richard Nice. New York: Cambridge University Press.

———. 1984. *Distinction: A Social Critique of the Judgement of Taste*. London: Routledge & Kegan Paul.

———. 1986. "The Forms of Capital." Pp. 241–58 in *Handbook of Theory and Research for the Sociology of Education*, edited by John G. Richardson. New York: Greenwood.

Bovati, Pietro. 1994. *Re-establishing Justice: Legal Terms, Concepts and Procedures in the Hebrew Bible*. Tanslated by Michael J. Smith. Sheffield: Sheffield Academic Press.

Boyer, Georges, André Parrot, and Georges Dossin. 1958. *Textes juridiques*. Archives royales de Mari 8. Paris: Geuthner.

Braje, Todd J., and Jon M. Erlandson. 2013. "Human Acceleration of Animal and Plant Extinctions: A Late Pleistocene, Holocene, and Anthropocene Continuum." *Anthropocene* 4:14–23.

Brandl, Baruch. 2012a. "Nine Scarabs, a Scaraboid, a Cylinder Seal, and a Bifacial Plaque from El-Ahwat." Pp. 233–63 in *El-Ahwat: A Fortified Site from the Early Iron Age near Nahal 'Iron, Israel; Excavations 1993–2000*, edited by Adam Zertal. CHANE 24. Leiden: Brill.

———. 2012b. "Scarabs, Scaraboids, Other Stamp Seals, and Seal Impressions." Pp. 377–96 in *Excavations at the City of David 1978–1985*, vol. 7B, *Area E: The Finds*, ed. Alon De Groot and Hannah Bernick-Greenberg. Qedem 54. Jerusalem: Hebrew University.

Braudel, Fernand. 1958. "Histoire et sciences sociales: La longue durée." *Annales: Économies, Sociétés, Civilisations* 13 (4): 725–53.

———. 1972. *The Mediterranean and the Mediterranean World in the Age of Philip II*. 2nd ed. Berkeley: University of California Press.

Braun, Joachim. 2002. *Music in Ancient Israel/Palestine: Archaeological, Written, and Comparative Sources*. Translated by Douglas W. Stott. The Bible in Its World. Grand Rapids: Eerdmans.

Breasted, James Henry, ed. 1906–7. *Ancient Records of Egypt*. 5 vols. Chicago: University of Chicago Press.

———. 1921. *A History of Egypt from the Earliest Times to the Persian Conquest*. 2nd ed. London: Hodder & Stoughton.

———. 1933. *The Dawn of Conscience*. New York: Scribner.

Brenner, Athalya. 1985. *The Israelite Woman: Social Role and Literary Type in Biblical Narrative*. Biblical Seminar. Sheffield: JSOT Press.

Bresciani, Eddia. 1985. "The Persian Occupation of Egypt." Pp. 502–28 in *The Cambridge History of Iran*, vol. 2, *The Median and Achaemenian Periods*, edited by Ilya Gershevitch. Cambridge: Cambridge University Press.

Briant, Pierre. 1982. "Contrainte militaire, dépendance rurale et exploitation des territoires en Asie aché-ménide." Pp. 199–225 in Pierre Briant, *Rois, tributs et paysans: Études sur les formations tributaires du Moyen-Orient ancient*. Annales littéraires de l'Université de Besançon 269. Paris: Les Belles Lettres.

———. 2002. *From Cyrus to Alexander: A History of the Persian Empire*. Translated by Peter T. Daniels. Winona Lake, IN: Eisenbrauns.

Brichto, Herbert Chanan. 1963. *The Problem of "Curse" in the Hebrew Bible*. Journal of Biblical Literature Monograph Series 13. Philadelphia: Society of Biblical Literature.

———. 1973. "Kin, Cult, Land and Afterlife—A Biblical Complex." *HUCA* 44:1–54.

Bright, John. 2000. *A History of Israel*. 4th ed. Louisville: Westminster John Knox.

Brinkman, J. A. 1972. "Foreign Relations of Babylonia from 1600 to 625 B.C.: The Documentary Evidence." *AJA* 76:271–81.

Broodbank, Cyprian. 2013. *The Making of the Middle Sea: A History of the Mediterranean from the Beginning to the Emergence of the Classical World*. New York: Oxford University Press.

Broshi, Magen, and Israel Finkelstein. 1992. "The Population of Palestine in Iron Age II." *BASOR* 287:47–60.

Brosius, Maria. 2003. "Ancient Archives and the Concept of Record-Keeping: An Introduction." Pp. 1–16 in *Ancient Archives and Archival Traditions: Concepts of Record-Keeping in the Ancient World*, edited by Maria Brosius. Oxford: Oxford University Press.

Brueggemann, Walter. 2001. *The Prophetic Imagination*. 2nd ed. Minneapolis: Fortress.

Bruins, Hendrik J. 2007. "Runoff Terraces in the Negev Highlands during the Iron Age: Nomads Settling Down or Farmers Living in the Desert?" Pp. 37–43 in *On the Fringe of Society: Archaeological and Ethnoarchaeological Perspectives on Pastoral and Agricultural Societies*, edited by Eveline J. van der Steen and Benjamin A. Saidel. British

Archaeological Reports International Series 1657. Oxford: Archaeopress.

Bruins, Hendrik J., and Johannes van der Plicht. 2014. "Desert Settlement through the Iron Age: Radiocarbon Dates from Sinai and the Negev Highlands." Pp. 349–66 in *The Bible and Radiocarbon Dating: Archaeology, Text and Science*, edited by Thomas E. Levy and Tom Higham. London: Equinox.

Brunner, Hellmut. 1966. *Grundzüge einer Geschichte der altägyptischen Literatur*. Darmstadt: Wissenschaftliche Buchgemeinschaft.

———. 1988. *Altägyptische Weisheit: Lehren für das Leben*. Zurich: Artemis.

Brunner-Traut, Emma. 1986. "Aspective." Pp. 421–48 in *Principles of Egyptian Art*, edited by Heinrich Schäfer. Oxford: Oxford University Press.

Bryan, Betsy M. 1991. *The Reign of Thutmose IV*. Baltimore: Johns Hopkins University Press.

———. 1996. "Art, Empire, and the End of the Late Bronze Age." Pp. 33–82 in *The Study of the Ancient Near East in the Twenty-First Century: The William Foxwell Albright Centennial Conference*, edited by Jerrold Cooper and Glenn Schwartz. Winona Lake, IN: Eisenbrauns.

———. 2000. "The Eighteenth Dynasty before the Amarna Period." Pp. 218–71 in *The Oxford History of Ancient Egypt*, edited by Ian Shaw. Oxford: Oxford University Press.

Bryce, Trevor. 2005. *The Kingdom of the Hittites*. New ed. New York: Oxford University Press.

———. 2014. *Ancient Syria: A Three Thousand Year History*. Oxford: Oxford University Press.

Buccellati, Georgio. 1992. "Ebla and the Amorites." *Eblaitica* 3:83–104.

Bugh, Glenn, ed. 2006. *The Cambridge Companion to the Hellenistic World*. Cambridge: Cambridge University Press.

Bunimovitz, Shlomo. 1994. "The Problem of Human Resources in Late Bronze Age Palestine and Its Socioeconomic Implications." *UF* 26:1–20.

———. 1995. "On the Edge of Empires—Late Bronze Age (1550–1200 BCE)." Pp. 320–31 in *The Archaeology of Society in the Holy Land*, edited by Thomas E. Levy. London: Leicester University Press.

Bunimovitz, Shlomo, and Z. Lederman. 2011. "Canaanite Resistance: The Philistines and Beth-Shemesh—A Case Study from the Iron Age I." *BASOR* 364:37–51.

Burkard, Günter, and Heinz J. Thissen. 2003. *Einführungen und Quellentexte zur Ägyptologie 1: Einführung in die altäyptische Literaturgeschichte I—Altes und Mittleresreich*. Münster: Lit.

———. 2008. *Einführungen und Quellentexte zur Ägyptologie 6: Einführung in die altäyptische Literaturgeschichte II—Neues Reich*. Münster: Lit.

Burke, A. A. 2008. *"Walled Up To Heaven": The Evolution of Middle Bronze Age Fortification Strategies in the Levant*. Studies in the Archaeology and History of the Levant. Winona Lake, IN: Eisenbrauns.

———. 2009. "More Light on Old Reliefs: New Kingdom Egyptian Siege Tactics and Asiatic Resistance." Pp. 57–68 in *Exploring the Longue Durée: Essays in Honor of Lawrence E. Stager*, edited by J. David Schloen. Winona Lake, IN: Eisenbrauns.

Burridge, Alwyn. 1993. "Akhenaten: A New Perspective; Evidence of a Genetic Disorder in the Royal Family of the 18th Dynasty Egypt." *JSSEA* 23:63–74.

Burstein, Stanley M. 1997. "The Hellenistic Age." Pp. 37–54 in *Ancient History: Recent Work and New Directions*, edited by Carol G. Thomas. Publications of the Association of Ancient Historians 5. Claremont, CA: Regina.

———. 2003. "The Legacy of Alexander: New Ways of Being Greek in the Hellenistic Period." Pp. 217–42 in *Crossroads of History: The Age of Alexander*, edited by Waldemar Heckel and Lawrence A. Tritle. Claremont, CA: Regina.

Byrne, Ryan. 2003. "Early Assyrian Contacts with Arabs and the Impact on Levantine Vassal Tribute." *BASOR* 331:11–25.

———. 2004. "Lie Back and Think of Judah: The Reproductive Politics of Pillar Figurines." *NEA* 67:137–51.

Cameron, George G. 1948. *Persepolis Treasury Tablets*. OIP 65. Chicago: University of Chicago Press.

Caminos, Ricardo A. 1954. *Late-Egyptian Miscellanies*. Brown Egyptological Studies 1. London: Oxford University Press.

———. 1992. "Phantom Architects at Gebel el-Silsila." Pp. 52–56 in *Studies in Pharaonic Religion and Society in Honor of J. Gwyn Griffths*, edited by Alan Lloyd. London: Egypt Exploration Society.

Camp, Claudia. 2000. "Woman Wisdom in the Hebrew Bible (Job 28:1–28; Prov. 1:20–33; 3:13–18; 7:1–5; 8:1–36; 9:1–6; 14:1)." Pp. 548–50 in *Women in Scripture: A Dictionary of the Named and Unnamed Women in the Hebrew Bible, the Apocryphal/Deuterocanonical Books, and the New Testament*, edited by Carol Meyers, Toni Craven, and Ross S. Kraemer. Boston: Houghton Mifflin.

Campbell, Duncan B. 2006. *Besieged: Siege Warfare in the Ancient World*. New York: Osprey.

Campbell Thompson, Reginald. 1903. *The Devils and Evil Spirits of Babylonia*. 2 vols. London: Luzac.

Cantrell, Deborah O. 2011. *The Horsemen of Israel: Horses and Chariotry in Monarchic Israel (Ninth-Eighth Centuries BCE)*. Winona Lake, IN: Eisenbrauns.

Capomacchia, Anna Maria G., and Marta Rivaroli. 2014. "Peace and War: A Ritual Question." Pp.

171–87 in *Krieg und Frieden im Alten Vorderasien: 52e RAI*, edited by Hans Neumann. AOAT 401. Münster: Ugarit-Verlag.

Carile, Maria C., and Eelco Nagelsmit. 2016. "Iconography, Iconology I: General." Pp. 777–83 in *Encyclopedia of the Bible and Its Reception*, vol. 12, edited by Dale C. Allison et al. Berlin: de Gruyter.

Carpenter, R. 1966. *Discontinuity in Greek Civilization*. Cambridge: Cambridge University Press.

Carroll, John T. 2001. "Children in the Bible." *Interpretation* 55:121–34.

Carroll, Robert. 1983. "Poets Not Prophets: A Response to 'Prophets through the Looking-Glass.'" *JSOT* 27:25–31.

———. 1993. "War in the Hebrew Bible." Pp. 25–44 in *War and Society in the Greek World*, edited by John Rich and Graham Shipley. London: Routledge.

Carter, Charles E. 1999. *The Emergence of Yehud in the Persian Period: A Social and Demographic Study*. JSOTSup 294. Sheffield: Sheffield Academic Press.

———. 2003. "Syria-Palestine in the Persian Period." Pp. 398–412 in *Near Eastern Archaeology: A Reader*, edited by Suzanne Richard. Winona Lake, IN: Eisenbrauns.

———. 2016. "(Re)Defining 'Israel': The Legacy of the Neo-Babylonian and Persian Periods." Pp. 215–40 in *The Wiley Blackwell Companion to Ancient Israel*, edited by Susan Niditch. Malden, MA: Wiley-Blackwell.

Carter, Tristan. 2007. "The Theatrics of Technology: Consuming Obsidian in the Early Cycladic Burial Area." Pp. 88–107 in *Rethinking Craft Specialization in Complex Societies: Archaeological Analyses of the Social Meaning of Production*, edited by Zachary X. Hruby and Rowan K. Flad. Arlington, VA: American Anthropological Association.

Cassuto, Deborah. 2008. "Bringing Home the Artifacts: A Social Interpretation of Loom Weights in Context." Pp. 63–77 in *The World of Women in the Ancient and Classical Near East*, edited by Beth Alpert Nakhai. Newcastle: Cambridge Scholars Publishing.

Cassuto, M. D. 1954. "Gezer, the Gezer Calendar." Pp. 471–74 in *Encyclopedia Biblica*, vol. 2, edited by E. L. Sukenik et al. Jerusalem: Mosad Byalik.

Cassuto, Umberto. 1971. *The Goddess Anath*. Jerusalem: Magnes.

Cathcart, Kevin J. 1995. "The Trees, the Beasts and the Birds: Fables, Parables and Allegories in the Old Testament." Pp. 212–21 in *Wisdom in Ancient Israel*, edited by John Day, Robert P. Gordon, and H. G. M. Williamson. Cambridge: Cambridge University Press.

Catto, Stephen K. 2007. *Reconstructing the First-Century Synagogue: A Critical Analysis of Current Research*. LNTS 363; London: T&T Clark.

Caubet, A. 2014. "Musical Practices and Instruments in Late Bronze Age Ugarit (Syria)." Pp. 172–84 in *Music in Antiquity: The Near East and the Mediterranean*, edited by Joan Goodnick Westenholz, Yossi Maurey, and Edwin Seroussi. Yuval 8. Berlin: de Gruyter; Jerusalem: Magnes.

Caubet, A., and M. Yon. 2015. "Dieux métallurgistes: Kothar, Tubal Caïn et l'image de Bès." *Semitica et Classica* 8:135–41.

Cavanagh, Edward, and Lorenzo Veracini, eds. 2017. *The Routledge Handbook of the History of Settler Colonialism*. Routledge History Handbooks. London: Routledge.

Cavillier, Giacoma. 2004. "Il 'Migdol' di Ramesse III a Medinet Habu fra originalità ed influssi asiatici." *Syria* 81:57–79.

Chadwick, Christie Goulart. 2015. "Archaeology and the Reality of Ancient Israel: Convergences between Biblical and Extra-Biblical Sources for the Monarchic Period." PhD dissertation, Andrews University.

Chaney, M. L. 1986. "Systematic Study of the Israelite Monarchy." Pp. 53–76 in *Social Scientific Criticism of the Hebrew Bible and Its Social World: The Israelite Monarchy*, edited by Norman K. Gottwald. Semeia 37. Atlanta: Society of Biblical Literature.

Charlesworth, James H., ed. 1983–85. *The Old Testament Pseudepigrapha*. 2 vols. Garden City, NY: Doubleday.

Charpin, Dominique. 2010. *Writing, Law, and Kingship in Old Babylonian Mesopotamia*. Translated by Jane Marie Todd. Chicago: University of Chicago Press.

———. 2011. *Reading and Writing in Babylon*. Translated by Jane Marie Todd. Cambridge, MA: Harvard University Press.

Charpin, Dominique, and Nele Ziegler. 2003. *Mari et le Proche-Orient à l'époque amorite: Essai d'histoire politique*. Mémoires de NABU 6; Florilegium marianum 5. Paris: Société pour l'Étude du Proche-Orient Ancien.

Chavalas, Mark W. 1997. "Inland Syria and the East-of-Jordan Region in the First Millennium BCE before the Assyrian Intrusions." Pp. 167–79 in *The Age of Solomon: Scholarship at the Turn of the Millennium*, edited by Lowell K. Handy. SHANE 11. Leiden: Brill.

———. 2011. "The Comparative Use of Ancient Near Eastern Texts in the Study of the Hebrew Bible." *Religion Compass* 5 (5): 150–65.

Chevereau, Pierre-Marie. 1985. *Prosopographie des cadres militaires égyptiens de la Basse Époque: Carrières militaires et carrières sacerdotales en Égypte du XIe au IIe siècle avant J.-C.* Paris: Cybèle.

Chiera, E. 1929. *Excavations at Nuzi*, vol. 1: *Texts of Varied Contents*. Harvard Semitic Series 5. Cambridge, MA: Harvard University Press.

Childs, Brevard S. 1985. *Old Testament Theology in a Canonical Context*. Philadelphia: Fortress.

———. 1987. "Death and Dying in Old Testament Theology." Pp. 89–91 in *Love and Death in the Ancient Near East: Essays in Honor of Marvin H. Pope,* edited by John H. Marks and Robert M. Good. Guilford, CT: Four Quarters.

Childs, William A. P. 2003. "The Human Animal: The Near East and Greece." Pp. 49–70 in *The Centaur's Smile: The Human Animal in Early Greek Art*, edited by J. Michael Padgett. Princeton: Princeton University Art Museum.

Chirichigno, Gregory C. 1993. *Debt-Slavery in Israel and the Ancient Near East*. JSOTSup 141. Sheffield: JSOT Press.

Cho, Paul Kang-Kul, and Janling Fu. 2013. "Feasting with Death in the Isaianic Apocalypse (Isaiah 25:6–8)." Pp. 117–42 in *Intertextuality and Formation of Isaiah 24–27*, edited by Todd Hibbard and Paul Kim. AIL. Atlanta: Scholars Press.

Christiansen, Birgit. 2007. "Der Blick aus dem Fenster: Bemerkungen zu einem literarischen Motiv in einigen Texten des hethitischen Schrifttums und des Alten Testaments." Pp. 143–52 in *Tabularia Hethaeorum: Hethitologische Beiträge; Silvin Košak zum 65. Geburtstag*, edited by Detlev Groddek and Marina Zorman. Dresdner Beiträge zur Hethitologie 25. Wiesbaden: Harrassowitz.

Civil, M. 2011. "The Law Collection of Ur-Namma." Pp. 221–88 in *Cuneiform Royal Inscriptions and Related Texts in the Schøyen Collection*, edited by A. R. George. CUSAS 17. Bethesda, MD: CDL Press.

Clancy, Frank. 1999. "Shishak/Shoshenq's Travels." *JSOT* 86:3–23.

Clarke, Lee. 2002. "Panic: Myth or Reality?" *Contexts* 1:21–26.

Clements, R. E. 1995. "Wisdom and Old Testament Theology." Pp. 269–86 in *Wisdom in Ancient Israel*, edited by John Day, Robert P. Gordon, and H. G. M. Williamson. Cambridge: Cambridge University Press.

Clifford, Richard J. 1994. *Creation Accounts in the Ancient Near East and in the Bible*. CBQMS 26. Washington, DC: Catholic Biblical Association of America.

———. 1998. *The Wisdom Literature*. Nashville: Abingdon.

Cline, Eric H. 2000. *The Battles of Armageddon: Megiddo and the Jezreel Valley from the Bronze Age to the Nuclear Age*. Ann Arbor: University of Michigan Press.

———. 2014. *1177 B.C.: The Year Civilization Collapsed.* Turning Points in Ancient History. Princeton: Princeton University Press.

Cline, Eric H., and David O'Connor, eds. 2006. *Thutmose III: A New Biography.* Ann Arbor: University of Michigan Press.

Clines, David J. A. 2016. "How Many Israelites Do We Know by Name? With a Proposal for a Hebrew Prosopography." Paper presented at the Annual Meeting of the Society of Biblical Literature, San Antonio. http://www.academia.edu/29734969/How _Many_Israelites_Do_We_Know_by_Name_With _a_Proposal_for_a_Hebrew_Prosopography.

Cochavi-Rainey, Zippora. 1999. *Royal Gifts in the Late Bronze Age, Fourteenth to Thirteenth Centuries BCE.* Beer-Sheva: Ben-Gurion University of the Negev Press.

Cogan, Mordechai. 1983. "'Ripping Open Pregnant Women' in Light of an Assyrian Analogue." *JAOS* 103 (4): 755–57.

———. 1993. "Judah under Assyrian Hegemony." *JBL* 112:403–14.

Cogan, Mordechai, and Hayim Tadmor. 1988. *II Kings.* AB 11. Garden City, NY: Doubleday.

Cohen, Mark E. 2015. *Festivals and Calendars of the Ancient Near East.* Bethesda, MD: CDL Press.

Cohen, Raymond, and Raymond Westbrook. 2000. *Amarna Diplomacy: The Beginnings of International Relations.* Baltimore: Johns Hopkins University Press.

Cohen, Yoram. 2007. "Public Religious Sentiment and Personal Piety in the Ancient Near Eastern City of Emar during the Late Bronze Age." *RC* 1:329–40.

———. 2013. *Wisdom from the Bronze Age.* Edited by Andrew R. George. WAW 19. Atlanta: Society of Biblical Literature.

Colijn, Brenda B. 2004. "Family in the Bible: A Brief Survey." *Ashland Theological Journal* 36:73–84.

Collins, Billie Jean. 1995. "Ritual Meals in the Hittite Cult." Pp. 77–92 in *Ancient Magic and Ritual Power*, edited by Marvin Meyer and Paul Mirecki. RGRW 129. Leiden: Brill.

———. 2007. "Hittites." Pp. 838–43 in *The New Interpreter's Dictionary of the Bible*, vol. 2, edited by Katharine Doob Sakenfeld. Nashville: Abingdon.

Collins, John J. 1997. *Jewish Wisdom in the Hellenistic Age.* OTL. Louisville: Westminster John Knox.

———. 2003. "The Zeal of Phinehas: The Bible and the Legitimation of Violence." *JBL* 122:3–21.

———. 2005. *Jewish Cult and Hellenistic Culture: Essays on the Jewish Encounter with Hellenism and Roman Rule.* JSJSup 100. Leiden: Brill.

———. 2016. *The Apocalyptic Imagination: An Introduction to Jewish Apocalyptic Literature.* 3rd ed. Grand Rapids: Eerdmans.

Collins, John J., and Daniel C. Harlow, eds. 2010. *The Eerdmans Dictionary of Early Judaism.* Grand Rapids: Eerdmans.

Collins, John J., and Gregory E. Sterling, eds. 2001. *Hellenism in the Land of Israel.* Notre Dame, IN: University of Notre Dame Press.

Collins, Paul. 2008. *Assyrian Palace Sculptures.* London: British Museum.

Collon, Dominique. 1988. *First Impressions: Cylinder Seals in the Ancient Near East.* Chicago: University of Chicago Press.

———. 1994. "Bull Leaping in Syria." *ÄL* 4:81–85.

———. 1999. "Depictions of Priests and Priestesses in the Ancient Near East." Pp. 17–46 in *Priest and Officials in the Ancient Near East: Papers of the Second Colloquium on the Ancient Near East*, edited by Kazuko Watanabe. Heidelberg: Universitätsverlag C. Winter.

———. 2008. "Playing in Concert in the Ancient Near East." Pp. 47–65 in *Proceedings of the International Conference of Near Eastern Archaeomusicology, ICONEA 2008: Held at the British Museum December 4, 5 and 6, 2008*, edited by Richard Dumbrill and Irving Finkel. Piscataway, NJ: Gorgias.

Conder, C. R., and H. H. Kitchener. 1881–83. *The Survey of Western Palestine: Memoirs of the Topography, Orography, Hydrology and Archaeology.* 3 vols. London: Committee of the Palestine Exploration Fund.

Connerton, Paul. 1989. *How Societies Remember.* Cambridge: Cambridge University Press.

Coogan, Michael D. 1987. "Of Cults and Cultures: Reflections on the Interpretation of Archaeological Evidence." *PEQ* 119:1–8.

———. 2009. *A Brief Introduction to the Old Testament: The Hebrew Bible in Its Context.* Oxford: Oxford University Press.

Cook, Stephen L. 2004. *The Social Roots of Biblical Yahwism.* SBL 8. Atlanta: Society of Biblical Literature.

———. 2007. "Funerary Practices and Afterlife Expectations in Ancient Israel." *RC* 1:1–24.

Coombes, Paul, and Keith Barber. 2005. "Environmental Determinism in Holocene Research: Causality or Coincidence?" *Area* 37:303–11.

Copan, Paul. 2011. *Is God a Moral Monster? Making Sense of the Old Testament God.* Grand Rapids: Baker Books.

Corduan, Winfried. 2012. *Neighboring Faiths: A Christian Introduction to World Religions.* 2nd ed. Downers Grove, IL: InterVarsity.

Cornelius, Izak. 2004a. *The Many Faces of the Goddess: The Iconography of the Syro-Palestinian Goddesses Anat, Astarte, Qedeshet, and Asherah c. 1500–1000 BCE.* OBO 204. Fribourg: Academic Press; Göttingen: Vandenhoeck & Ruprecht.

———. 2004b. "A Preliminary Typology for the Female Plaque Figurines and Their Value for the Religion of Ancient Palestine and Jordan." *JNSL* 30:21–39.

———. 2009. "In Search of the Goddess in Ancient Palestinian Iconography." Pp. 77–98 in *Israel zwischen den Mächten: Festschrift für Stefan Timm zum 65. Geburtstag*, edited by Michael Pietsch and Friedhelm Hartenstein. AOAT 364. Münster: Ugarit-Verlag.

———. 2013. "Art, Bronze and Iron Age." *OEBA* 1:49–57.

———. 2015. "Revisiting the Seated Figure from Ramat Rahel." *ZDPV* 131:29–43.

———. 2016. "Iconography, Iconology II: Hebrew Bible/Old Testament." Pp. 783–85 in *Encyclopedia of the Bible and Its Reception*, vol. 12, edited by Dale C. Allison et al. Berlin: de Gruyter.

———. 2017. "The Study of the Old Testament and the Material Imagery of the Ancient Near East, with a Focus on the Body Parts of the Deity." Pp. 195–227 in *IOSOT Congress Volume Stellenbosch 2016*, edited by Louis C. Jonker et al. Leiden: Brill.

Counihan, Carole. 1999. "Bread as World: Food Habits and Social Relations in Modernizing Sardinia." Pp. 25–42, 216–17 in *The Anthropology of Food, and the Body: Gender, Meaning, and Power*, edited by Carole Counihan. New York: Routledge.

Cowley, Arthur E. 1923. *Aramaic Papyri of the Fifth Century B.C.: Edited with Translation and Notes.* Oxford: Clarendon. Reprint, Osnabrück: Zeller, 1967.

Crabtree, P. 1986. "Flora of Tell Hesban and Area, Jordan." Pp. 75–98 in *Hesban 2: Environmental Foundations*, edited by Øystein S. LaBianca and L. Lacelle. Berrien Springs, MI: Andrews University Press.

Craigie, Peter C. 1978. *The Problem of War in the Old Testament.* Grand Rapids: Eerdmans.

———. 1983. *Ugarit and the Old Testament: The Story of a Remarkable Discovery and Its Impact on Old Testament Studies.* Grand Rapids: Eerdmans.

Crawford, Sidnie White. 2008. *Rewriting Scripture in Second Temple Times.* Grand Rapids: Eerdmans.

Crenshaw, James L. 1990. "The Sage in Proverbs." Pp. 205–16 in *The Sage in Israel and the Ancient Near East*, edited by John G. Gammie and Leo G. Perdue. Winona Lake, IN: Eisenbrauns.

———. 1995. "The Contemplative Life in the Ancient Near East." *CANE* 4:2445–57.

Cribb, Roger. 1991. *Nomads in Archaeology.* Cambridge: Cambridge University Press.

Crisostomo, C. Jay. 2015. "Writing Sumerian, Creating Texts: Reflections on Text-Building Practices in Old Babylonian Schools." *JANER* 15:121–42.

Crocker, P. T. 1985. "Status Symbols in the Architecture of El-ʿAmarna." *JEA* 71:52–65.

Cross, Frank Moore. 1973. *Canaanite Myth and Hebrew Epic.* Cambridge, MA: Harvard University Press.

———. 1975a. "A Reconstruction of the Judean Restoration." *JBL* 94:4–18.

———. 1975b. "Correction: A Reconstruction of the Judean Restoration." *JBL* 94:259.

———. 1989. "The Contributions of W. F. Albright to Semitic Epigraphy and Paleography." Pp. 17–31 in *The Scholarship of William Foxwell Albright: An Appraisal*, edited by Gus W. Van Beek. HSS 33. Atlanta: Scholars Press.

———. 2003. *Leaves from an Epigrapher's Notebook: Collected Papers in Hebrew and West Semitic Palaeography and Epigraphy.* Winona Lake, IN: Eisenbrauns.

———. 2008. "Inscriptions in Phoenician and Other Scripts." Pp. 333–72 in *Ashkelon 1: Introduction and Overview (1985–2006)*, edited by Lawrence E. Stager, J. David Schloen, and Daniel M. Master. Winona Lake, IN: Eisenbrauns.

Cross, Frank Moore, W. E. Lemke, and P. D. Miller, eds. 1976. *MAGNALIA DEI, the Mighty Acts of God: Essays on the Bible and Archaeology in Memory of G. Ernest Wright.* Garden City, NY: Doubleday.

Crouch, C. L. 2009. *War and Ethics in the Ancient Near East: Military Violence in Light of Cosmology and History.* BZAW 407. Berlin: de Gruyter.

———. 2014. *Israel and the Assyrians: Deuteronomy, the Succession Treaty of Esarhaddon, and the Nature of Subversion.* ANEM 8. Atlanta: Society of Biblical Literature.

Culbertson, Laura. 2011a. "A Life-Course Approach to Household Slaves in the Late Third Millennium B.C." Pp. 33–48 in *Slaves and Households in the Near East*, edited by Laura Culbertson. OIS 7. Chicago: University of Chicago Press.

———, ed. 2011b. *Slaves and Households in the Near East.* OIS 7. Chicago: University of Chicago Press.

———. 2011c. "Slaves and Households in the Near East." Pp. 1–17 in *Slaves and Households in the Near East*, edited by Laura Culbertson. OIS 7. Chicago: University of Chicago Press.

Currid, John D. 1997. *Ancient Egypt and the Old Testament.* Grand Rapids: Baker.

———. 2013. *Against the Gods: The Polemical Theology of the Old Testament.* Wheaton, IL: Crossway.

Curtis, Adrian. 1985. *Ugarit (Ras Shamra).* Grand Rapids: Eerdmans.

———. 1990. "Some Observations on 'Bull' Terminology in the Ugaritic Texts and the Old Testament." Pp. 17–31 in *In Quest of the Past: Studies on Israelite Religion, Literature and Prophetism; Papers Read at the Joint British-Dutch Old Testament Conference, Held at Elspeet, 1988*, edited by A. S. van der Woude. Old Testament Studies 26. Leiden: Brill.

———. 2007. *Oxford Bible Atlas*. New York: Oxford University Press.

Curtis, John, and Matthew Ponting. 2012. *An Examination of Late Assyrian Metalwork: With Special Reference to Nimrud*. Oxford: Oxbow Books.

Dabrowa, E. 2010. *The Hasmoneans and Their State: A Study in History, Ideology, and the Institutions*. Krakow: Jagiellonian University Press.

Dagan, Yehudah. 1992. "The Shephelah during the Period of the Monarchy in Light of Archaeological Excavations and Surveys." MA thesis, Tel Aviv University. [In Hebrew.]

Dahood, Mitchell. 1965–70. *Psalms: Introduction, Translation, and Notes*. 3 vols. AB 16, 17, 17A. Garden City, NY: Doubleday.

Dalley, Stephanie. 1985. "Foreign Chariotry and Cavalry in the Armies of Tiglath-Pileser III and Sargon II." *Iraq* 47:31–48.

D'Amato, Raffaele, and Andrea Salimbeti. 2015. *Sea Peoples of the Mediterranean c. 1400 BC–1000 BC*. Osprey Elite Series 204. Oxford: Osprey.

Damrosch, D. 1987. *The Narrative Covenant: Transformations of Genre in the Growth of Biblical Literature*. San Francisco: Harper & Row.

Dandamaev, Muhammad A., and Vladimir Lukonin. 1989. *The Culture and Social Institutions of Ancient Iran*. Translated by Philip L. Kohl and D. J. Dadson. Cambridge: Cambridge University Press.

Danin, Avinoam. 1992. "Flora and Vegetation of Israel and Adjacent Areas." *Bocconea* 3:18–42.

———. 1998. "Man and the Natural Environment." Pp. 24–39 in *The Bible and Radiocarbon Dating: Archaeology, Text and Science*, edited by Thomas E. Levy and Tom Higham. London: Equinox.

Danin, Avinoam, and Gideon Orshan, eds. 1999. *Vegetation of Israel*. Leiden: Backhuys.

Danin, Avinoam, and Uzi Plitmann. 1987. "Revision of the Plant Geographical Territories of Israel and Sinai." *Plant Systematics and Evolution* 156:43–53.

Dansgaard, W. 1964. "Stable Isotopes in Precipitation." *Tellus* 16:436–68.

Darby, Erin D. 2014. *Interpreting Judean Pillar Figurines: Gender and Empire in Judean Apotropaic Ritual*. FAT 2/69. Tübingen: Mohr Siebeck.

Darnell, John, and Colleen Manassa. 2007. *Tutankhamun's Armies: Battle and Conquest during Ancient Egypt's Late 18th Dynasty*. Hoboken, NJ: John Wiley.

Davey, Christopher J. 1980. "Temples of the Levant and the Buildings of Solomon." *Tyndale Bulletin* 31:107–46.

Davies, Eryl W. 2005. "The Morally Dubious Passages of the Hebrew Bible: An Examination of Some Proposed Solutions." *Currents in Research* 3 (2): 197–228.

Davies, Graham I. 1991. *Ancient Hebrew Inscriptions: Corpus and Concordance*. Cambridge: Cambridge University Press.

———. 1995. "Were There Schools in Ancient Israel?" Pp. 199–211 in *Wisdom in Ancient Israel*, edited by John Day, Robert P. Gordon, and H. G. M. Williamson. Cambridge: Cambridge University Press.

———. 2004. "Was There an Exodus?" Pp. 23–40 in *In Search of Pre-Exilic Israel: Proceedings of the Oxford Old Testament Seminar*, edited by John Day. New York: T&T Clark.

Davies, Norman de Garis. 1903–8. *The Rock Tombs of El-Amarna*. 6 vols. London: Egypt Exploration Society.

———. 1905a. *The Rock Tombs of El-Amarna II: The Tombs of Panehesy and Meryra II*. London: Egypt Exploration Society.

———. 1905b. *The Rock Tombs of El-Amarna III: The Tombs of Huya and Ahmes*. London: Egypt Exploration Society.

———. 1943. *The Tomb of Rekh-Mi-Rēʿ at Thebes*. New York: Metropolitan Museum of Art.

Davies, Norman de Garis, and R. O. Faulkner. 1947. "A Syrian Trading Venture to Egypt." *JEA* 33:40–46.

Davies, Philip R. 1992. *In Search of "Ancient Israel."* JSOTSup 148. Sheffield: JSOT Press.

———. 2006. *In Search of "Ancient Israel."* 2nd ed. New York: Continuum.

———. 2008. *Memories of Ancient Israel: An Introduction to Biblical History—Ancient and Modern*. Louisville: Westminster John Knox.

Davis, Andrew R. 2013. *Tel Dan in Its Northern Cultic Context*. ABS 20. Atlanta: Society of Biblical Literature.

Davis, Simon J., and François Valla. 1978. "Evidence for Domestication of the Dog 12,000 Years Ago in the Natufian of Israel." *Nature* 276:608–10.

Day, David. 2008. *Conquest: How Societies Overwhelm Others*. Oxford: Oxford University Press.

Day, John. 1985. *God's Conflict with the Dragon and the Sea: Echoes of a Canaanite Myth in the Old Testament*. UCOP 35. Cambridge: Cambridge University Press.

———. 1989. *Molech: A God of Human Sacrifice in the Old Testament*. Cambridge: Cambridge University Press.

———. 1995. "Foreign Semitic Influence on the Wisdom of Israel and Its Appropriation in the Book of Proverbs." Pp. 55–70 in *Wisdom in Ancient Israel: Essays in Honour of J. A. Emerton*, edited by John

Day, Robert P. Gordon, and H. G. M. Williamson. Cambridge: Cambridge University Press.

———. 1996. "The Development of Belief in Life after Death in Ancient Israel." Pp. 231–57 in *After the Exile: Essays in Honor of Rex Mason*, edited by John Barton and David J. Reimer. Macon, GA: Mercer University Press.

———, ed. 2005. *Temple and Worship in Biblical Israel*. New York: Continuum.

Dearman, J. Andrew. 1989a. "Historical Reconstruction and the Mesha Inscription." Pp. 155–210 in *Studies in the Mesha Inscription and Moab*, edited by J. Andrew Dearman. ABS 2. Atlanta: Scholars Press.

———, ed. 1989b. *Studies in the Mesha Inscription and Moab*. ABS 2. Atlanta: Scholars Press.

———. 1996. "The Tophet in Jerusalem: Archaeology and Cultural Profile." *JNSL* 22:59–71.

———. 1998. "The Family in the Old Testament." *Interpretation* 52:117–29.

De Backer, Fabrice. 2006. "Notes sur les machines de siège néo-assyriennes." Pp. 69–86 in *Krieg und Frieden im Alten Vorderasien: 52e RAI*, edited by Hans Neumann. AOAT 401. Münster: Ugarit-Verlag.

———. 2013. *Scale-Armour in the Neo-Assyrian Period: Manufacture and Maintenance*. Saarbrücken: Lambert Academic.

Deetz, J. 1996. *In Small Things Forgotten: An Archaeology of Early American Life*. New York: Doubleday.

Deger-Jalkotzy, Sigrid. 2008. "Decline, Destruction, Aftermath." Pp. 387–416 in *The Cambridge Companion to the Aegean Bronze Age*, edited by Cynthia W. Shelmerdine. Cambridge: Cambridge University Press.

De Geus, V. J. K. 1982. "Die Gesellschaftskritik der Propheten und die Archäologie." *ZDPV* 98:50–57.

de Hulster, Izaak J. 2009. *Iconographic Exegesis and Third Isaiah*. FAT 2/36. Tübingen: Mohr Siebeck.

———. 2014. "Ethnicity and 'the Myth of the Reborn Nation': Investigations in Collective Identity, Monotheism and the Use of Figurines in Yehud during the Achaemenid Period." *Approaching Religion* 4 (2): 16–24. https://ojs.abo.fi/ojs/index.php/ar/article/view/823.

———. 2015. "The Myth of the Reborn Nation." Pp. 123–38 in *Open-Mindedness in the Bible and Beyond: A Volume of Studies in Honour of Bob Becking*, edited by Mario C. A. Korpel and Lester L. Grabbe. London: Bloomsbury T&T Clark.

de Hulster, Izaak J., and Joel M. LeMon, eds. 2014a. *Image, Text, Exegesis: Iconographic Interpretation and the Hebrew Bible*. London: Bloomsbury T&T Clark.

———. 2014b. "Introduction: The Interpretive Nexus of Image and Text." Pp. xix–xxiv in *Image, Text, Exegesis: Iconographic Interpretation and the Hebrew Bible*, edited by Izaak J. de Hulster and Joel M. LeMon. London: Bloomsbury T&T Clark.

de Hulster, Izaak J., and Rüdiger Schmitt, eds. 2009. *Iconography and Biblical Studies: Proceedings of the Iconography Sessions at the Joint EABS/SBL Conference, 22–26 July 2007, Vienna, Austria*. AOAT 361. Münster: Ugarit-Verlag.

de Hulster, Izaak J., Brent A. Strawn, and Ryan P. Bonfiglio, eds. 2015a. *Iconographic Exegesis of the Hebrew Bible/Old Testament: An Introduction to Its Method and Practice*. Göttingen: Vandenhoeck & Ruprecht.

———. 2015b. "Introduction: Iconographic Exegesis: Method and Practice." Pp. 19–42 in *Iconographic Exegesis of the Hebrew Bible/Old Testament: An Introduction to Its Method and Practice*, edited by Izaak J. de Hulster, Brent A. Strawn, and Ryan P. Bonfiglio. Göttingen: Vandenhoeck & Ruprecht.

Delitzsch, F. 1903. *Babel and Bible: Two Lectures on the Significance of Assyriological Research for Religion*. Translated by Thomas J. McCormack, W. H. Carruth, and Lydia G. Robinson. Chicago: Open Court.

Dell, Katharine. 2008. "Scribes, Sages, and Seers in the First Temple." Pp. 125–44 in *Scribes, Sages, and Seers: The Sage in the Eastern Mediterranean World*, edited by Leo G. Perdue. FRLANT 219. Göttingen: Vandenhoeck & Ruprecht.

del Olmo Lete, G., and J. Sanmartín. 1996. *Diccionario de la lengua ugarítica*. 2 vols. Aula Orientalis Supplementa. Barcelona: Editorial Ausa.

DeMarrais, Elizabeth, Luis J. Castillo, and Timothy K. Earle. 1996. "Ideology, Materialization and Power Strategies." *Current Anthropology* 37:15–32.

DeNiro, M. J. 1987. "Stable Isotopy and Archaeology." *American Scientist* 75:182–91.

DeNiro, M. J., and S. Epstein. 1978. "Influence of Diet on the Distribution of Carbon Isotopes in Animals." *Geochimica et cosmochimica acta* 4 (5): 495–506.

Derks, Ton. 2009. "Ethnic Identity in the Roman Frontier: The Epigraphy of Batavi and Other Lower Rhine Tribes." Pp. 239–82 in *Ethnic Constructs in Antiquity: The Role of Power and Tradition*, edited by Ton Derks and Nico Roymans. Amsterdam: Amsterdam University Press.

Der Manuelian, Peter. 1987. *Studies in the Reign of Amenophis II*. Hildesheimer Ägyptologische Beiträge. Hildesheim: Gerstenberg.

———. 1999. "Administering Akhenaten's Egypt." Pp. 145–50 in *Pharaohs of the Sun: Akhenaten, Nefertiti, Tutankhamen*, edited by Rita Freed, Yvonne Markowitz, and Sue D'Auria. Boston: Museum of Fine Arts.

de Roos, Johan. 2001. "Rhetoric in the S.C. Testament of Hattusilis I." Pp. 401–6 in *Veenhof Anniversary*

Volume: Studies Presented to Klaas R. Veenhof on the Occasion of His Sixty-fifth Birthday, edited by W. H. van Soldt. Publications de l'Institut Historique-Archéologique de Stamboul 89. Leiden: Nederlands Instituut voor het Nabije Oosten.

Deuel, David C. 2002. "Apprehending Kidnappers by Correspondence at Provincial Arrapḫa." Pp. 191–208 in *Mesopotamia and the Bible: Comparative Explorations*, edited by Mark W. Chavalas and K. Lawson Younger Jr. JSOTSup 341. Sheffield: Sheffield Academic Press.

———. 2015. "Mission at Arrapḫa." Pp. 355–68 in *Tradition and Innovation in the Ancient Near East: Proceedings of the 57th RAI at Rome 4–8 July 2011*, edited by Alfonso Archi in collaboration with Armando Bramanti. Winona Lake, IN: Eisenbrauns.

Deutsch, Robert, ed. 2003. *Shlomo: Studies in Epigraphy, Iconography, History and Archaeology in Honor of Shlomo Moussaieff*, edited by Robert Deutsch. Tel Aviv: Archaeological Center Publications.

De Vaux, R. 1965. *Ancient Israel, Its Life and Institutions*. New York: McGraw Hill.

Dever, William G. 1970. "Iron Age Epigraphic Material from the Area of Khirbet el-Kôm." *HUCA* 40:139–204.

———. 1977. "The Patriarchal Traditions." Pp. 70–119 in *Israelite and Judean History*, edited by John H. Hayes and J. Maxwell Miller. OTL. London: SCM.

———. 1984. "Asherah, Consort of Yahveh: New Evidence from Kuntillet Ajrud." *BASOR* 255:21–37.

———. 1987. "The Middle Bronze Age: The Zenith of the Urban Canaanite Era." *BA* 50:149–77.

———. 1990a. "Hyksos, Egyptian Destructions, and the End of the Palestinian Middle Bronze Age." *Levant* 22:75–81.

———. 1990b. *Recent Archaeological Discoveries and Biblical Research*. Seattle: University of Washington Press.

———. 1993. "What Remains of the House That Albright Built?" *BA* 56:25–35.

———. 1999. "Histories and Nonhistories of Ancient Israel." *BASOR* 316:89–106.

———. 2001. *What Did the Biblical Writers Know and When Did They Know It? What Archaeology Can Tell Us about the Reality of Ancient Israel*. Grand Rapids: Eerdmans.

———. 2002. "Syro-Palestinian and Biblical Archaeology: Into the Next Millennium." Pp. 513–28 in *Symbiosis, Symbolism, and the Power of the Past: Canaan, Ancient Israel and Their Neighbors from the Late Bronze Age through Roman Palaestina*, edited by William G. Dever and Seymour Gitin. Winona Lake, IN: Eisenbrauns.

———. 2003. *Who Were the Early Israelites and Where Did They Come From?* Grand Rapids: Eerdmans.

———. 2005. *Did God Have a Wife? Archaeology and Folk Religion in Ancient Israel*. Grand Rapids: Eerdmans.

———. 2012. *The Lives of Ordinary People in Ancient Israel*. Grand Rapids: Eerdmans.

———. 2015. "The Exodus and the Bible: What Was Known, What Was Remembered, What Was Forgotten?" Pp. 399–408 in *Israel's Exodus in Transdisciplinary Perspective: Text, Archaeology, Culture, and Geoscience*, edited by Thomas E. Levy, Thomas Schneider, and William H. C. Propp. New York: Springer.

Dezső, Tamás. 2001. *Near Eastern Helmets of the Iron Age*. British Archaeological Reports 992. Oxford: J. and E. Hedges.

———. 2006. "The Reconstruction of the Neo-Assyrian Army: As Depicted on the Assyrian Palace Reliefs, 745–612 BC." *Acta Archaeologica* 57:87–130.

———. 2012. *The Assyrian Army 1: The Structure of the Neo-Assyrian Army as Reconstructed from the Assyrian Palace Reliefs and Cuneiform Sources*. 2 vols. Budapest: Eötvös Loránd University Press.

Dick, Michael B., ed. 1998. *Born in Heaven, Made on Earth: The Creation of the Cult Image in the Ancient Near East*. Winona Lake, IN: Eisenbrauns.

Dietler, Michael. 2001. "Theorizing the Feast: Rituals of Consumption, Commensal Politics, and Power in African Contexts." Pp. 65–114 in *Feasts: Archaeological and Ethnographic Perspectives on Food, Politics, and Power*, edited by Michael Dietler and Brian Hayden. Washington, DC: Smithsonian Institution.

Dietrich, Manfred. 1989. "Das Einsetzungsritual der Entu' von Emar (Emar VI/3, 369)." *UF* 21:47–100.

———. 2001. "Das biblische Paradies und der babylonische Tempelgarten: Überlegungen zur Lage des Gartens Eden." Pp. 281–323 in *Das biblische Weltbild und seine altorientalischen Kontexte*, edited by Bernd Janowski and Beate Ego. FAT 32. Tübingen: Mohr Siebeck.

Dincauze, D. F. 2000. *Environmental Archaeology: Principles and Practice*. Cambridge: Cambridge University Press.

Dines, Jennifer M. 2004. *The Septuagint*. Understanding the Bible and Its World. London: T&T Clark.

Dion, P.-E. 1995. "Syro-Palestinian Resistance to Shalmaneser III in the Light of New Documents." *ZAW* 107:482–89.

———. 1997. *Les Araméens à l'âge du fer: Histoire politique et structures sociales*. Etudes bibliques 34. Paris: Gabalda.

———. 1999. "The Tel Dan Stele and Its Historical Significance." Pp. 145–56 in *Michael: Historical, Epigraphical and Biblical Studies in Honor of Prof. Michael Heltzer*, edited by Yitzhak Avishur and Robert Deutsch. Tel Aviv: Archaeological Center Publications.

Doak, Brian R. 2015. *Phoenician Aniconism in Its Mediterranean and Ancient Near Eastern Contexts.* ABS 21. Atlanta: Society of Biblical Literature.

Dobbs-Allsopp, F. W., J. J. M. Roberts, C. L. Seow, and R. E. Whitaker. 2005. *Hebrew Inscriptions: Texts from the Biblical Period of the Monarchy with Concordance.* New Haven: Yale University Press.

Dodson, Aidan. 1990. "Crown Prince Djhotmose and the Royal Sons of the Eighteenth Dynasty." *JEA* 76:87–96.

———. 2000. "Towards a Minimum Chronology of the New Kingdom and Third Intermediate Period." *Bulletin of the Egyptological Seminar* 14:7–18.

———. 2009. *Amarna Sunset: Nefertiti, Tutankhamun, Ay, Horemheb, and the Egyptian Counter-Reformation.* Cairo: American University in Cairo Press.

———. 2010. *Poisoned Legacy: The Fall of the Nineteenth Egyptian Dynasty.* Cairo: American University in Cairo Press.

———. 2012. *Afterglow of Empire: Egypt from the Fall of the New Kingdom to the Saite Renaissance.* Cairo: American University in Cairo Press.

———. 2013. "Chronology, Pharaonic Egypt." Pp. 1485–87 in *The Encyclopedia of Ancient History*, vol. 3, edited by Roger S. Bagnall, Kai Brodersen, Craige B. Champion, Andrew Erskine, and Sabine R. Huebner. Oxford: Wiley-Blackwell.

———. 2014. *Amarna Sunrise: Egypt from Golden Age to Age of Heresy.* Cairo: American University in Cairo Press.

Dorman, Peter. 2009. "The Coregency Revisited: Architectural and Iconographic Conundra in the Tomb of Kheruef." Pp. 65–82 in *Causing His Name to Live: Studies in Egyptian Epigraphy and History in Memory of William J. Murnane*, edited by Peter J. Brand and Louise Cooper. CHANE 37. Leiden: Brill.

Dornemann, Rudolph H. 2003. "General Discussion and Historical References concerning Excavated Archaeological Sites in the Region around Tell Qarqur." Pp. 1–6 in *Preliminary Excavation Reports and other Archaeological Investigations: Tell Qarqur, Iron 1 Sites in the North-Central Highland of Palestine*, edited by Nancy Lapp. Boston: American Schools of Oriental Research.

Dorsey, David A. 1989. *The Roads and Highways of Ancient Israel.* Baltimore: Johns Hopkins University Press.

Dossin, Georges, and André Finet. 1946. *Correspondance féminine: Transcription et traduction.* Archives royales de Mari 10. Paris: Geuthner.

Dothan, Moshe. 1993. "Azor." *NEAEHL* 1:125–29.

Dothan, Trude. 1982. *The Philistines and Their Material Culture.* Jerusalem: Israel Exploration Society.

———. 1998. "Initial Philistine Settlement: From Migration to Coexistence." Pp. 148–61 in *Mediterranean Peoples in Transition: Thirteenth to Early Tenth Centuries BCE*, edited by Seymour Gitin, Amihai Mazar, and Ephraim Stern. Jerusalem: Israel Exploration Society.

———. 2008. *Deir el-Balah: Uncovering an Egyptian Outpost in Canaan from the Time of the Exodus.* Jerusalem: The Israel Museum.

Dothan, Trude, and Moshe Dothan. 1992. *People of the Sea: The Search for the Philistines.* New York: Macmillan.

Dothan, Trude, and Tamar Nahmias-Lotan. 2010. "A Lamp and Bowl Deposit." Pp. 111–13 in *Deir el-Balah: Excavations in 1977–1982 in the Cemetery and Settlement*, vol. 2, *The Finds*, edited by Trude Dothan and Baruch Brandl. QEDEM Monographs of the Institute of Archaeology 50. Jerusalem: Ahva.

Douglas, Mary. 2004. "One God, No Ancestors, in a World Renewed." Pp. 176–95 in Mary Douglas, *Jacob's Tears: The Priestly Work of Reconciliation.* Oxford: Oxford University Press.

Doxey, Denise M. 2001. "Priesthood." *OEAE* 3:68–73.

Dozeman, Thomas B., and Konrad Schmidt, eds. 2006. *A Farewell to the Yahwist? The Composition of the Pentateuch in Recent European Interpretation.* SymS 34. Atlanta: Society of Biblical Literature.

Drabsch, Bernadette A. 2015. *The Mysterious Wall Paintings of Teleilat Ghassul, Jordan: In Context.* Oxford: Archaeopress.

Draffkorn, A. 1959. "Was King Abba-An of Yamḫad a Vizier for the King of Ḫattuša?" *JCS* 13:94–97.

Drake, B. L. 2012. "The Influence of Climatic Change on the Late Bronze Age Collapse and the Greek Dark Ages." *JAS* 39 (6): 1862–70.

Drews, R. 1993. *The End of the Bronze Age: Changes in Warfare and the Catastrophe ca.1200 B.C.* Princeton: Princeton University Press.

———. 2004. *Early Riders: The Beginnings of Mounted Warfare in Asia and Europe.* Oxford: Taylor & Francis.

Driver, Godfrey R. 1965. *Aramaic Documents of the Fifth Century B.C.* Abridged and rev. ed. Oxford: Clarendon. Reprint, Eugene, OR: Wipf & Stock, 2005.

Dubovský, Peter. 2006. *Hezekiah and the Assyrian Spies: Reconstruction of the Neo-Assyrian Intelligence Services and Its Significance for 2 Kings 18–19.* BibOr 49. Rome: Biblical Institute Press.

Dumbrell, William J. 1971. "The Tell el-Maskhuta Bowls and the 'Kingdom' of Qedar in the Persian Period." *BASOR* 203:33–44.

Dunand, Françoise, and Christiane Zivie-Coche. 2004. *Gods and Men in Egypt 3000 BCE to 395 BCE.* Translated by David Lorton. Ithaca, NY: Cornell University Press.

Dunn, Jacob E. 2014. "A God of Volcanoes: Did Yahwism Take Root in Volcanic Ashes?" *JSOT* 38:387–424.

Durand, Jean-Marie. 1988. *Archives Épistolaires de Mari I/1.* Archives royales de Mari 26. Paris: Éditions Recherche sur les civilisations.

Durand, Jean-Marie, et al. 2011. "La fête au palais, banquets, parures et musique en Orient." *Journal asiatique* 299 (2): 601–13.

Dusinberre, Elspeth R. M. 2003. *Aspects of Empire in Achaemenid Sardis.* Cambridge: Cambridge University Press.

Dyrness, William A. 2004. *Reformed Theology and Visual Culture: The Protestant Imagination from Calvin to Edwards.* Cambridge: Cambridge University Press.

Earl, Douglas S. 2011 *The Joshua Delusion? Rethinking Genocide in the Bible.* Eugene, OR: Cascade.

Earle, Timothy. 1982. "Prehistoric Economics and the Archaeology of Exchange." Pp. 1–12 in *Contexts for Prehistoric Exchange,* edited by Jonathan Ericson and Timothy Earle. New York: Academic Press.

———. 1985. "Commodity Exchange and Markets in the Inca State: Recent Archaeological Evidence." Pp. 369–98 in *Market and Marketing,* edited by Stuart Plattner. Monographs in Economic Anthropology 4. Lanham, MD: University Press of America.

Ebeling, Jennie R. 2014. "Traditional Bread Baking in Northern Jordan, Part 2." https:www.youtube.com/watch?v=TaVca6KkMZQ.

Ebeling, Jennie R., and Michael M. Homan. 2008. "Baking and Brewing Beer in the Israelite Household: A Study of Women's Cooking Technology." Pp. 45–62 in *The World of Women in the Ancient and Classical Near East,* edited by Beth Alpert Nakhai. Newcastle: Cambridge Scholars Publishing.

Ebeling, Jennie R., and M. Rogel. 2015. "The Tabun and Its Misidentification in the Archaeological Record." *Levant* 47:328–49.

Ebeling, Jennie R., and York Rowan. 2004. "The Archaeology of The Daily Grind: Ground Stone Tools and Food Production in the Southern Levant." *NEA* 67:108–17.

Edelman, Diana V. 1995. "Solomon's Adversaries Hadad, Rezon and Jeroboam: A Trio of 'Bad Guy' Characters Illustrating the Theology of Immediate Retribution." Pp. 166–91 in *The Pitcher Is Broken: Memorial Essays for Gösta W. Ahlström,* edited by Steven W. Holloway and Lowell K. Handy. JSOTSup 190. Sheffield: Sheffield Academic Press.

———. 2001. "Did Saulide-Davidic Rivalry Resurface in Early Persian Yehud?" Pp. 70–92 in *The Land That I Will Show You: Essays in the History and Archaeology of the Ancient Near East in Honor of J. Maxwell Miller,* edited by J. Andrew Dearman and M. Patrick Graham. JSOTSup 343. Sheffield: Sheffield Academic Press.

———. 2003. "Gibeon and the Gibeonites Revisited." Pp. 153–67 in *Judah and the Judeans in the Neo-Babylonian Period,* edited by Oded Lipschits and Jospeh Blenkinsopp. Winona Lake, IN: Eisenbrauns.

———. 2005. *The Origins of the "Second" Temple: Persian Imperial Policy and the Rebuilding of Jerusalem.* London: Equinox.

———. 2007. "Settlement Patterns in Persian-Era Yehud." Pp. 52–64 in *A Time of Change: Judah and Its Neighbours in the Persian and Early Hellenistic Periods,* edited by Yigal Levin. Library of Second Temple Studies 65. London: T&T Clark.

Edelstein, G., and Y. Gat. 1980–81. "Terraces around Jerusalem." *Israel—Land and Nature* 6 (2): 72–78.

Edelstein, G., and S. Gibson. 1982. "Ancient Jerusalem's Rural Food Basket." *BAR* 8:46–54.

Edelstein, G., and M. Kislev. 1981. "Mevaseret Yerushalayim: Ancient Terraces Farming." *BA* 44:53–56.

Efron, J. 1987. *Studies on the Hasmonean Period.* SJLA 39. Leiden: Brill.

Egberts, Arno. 2001. "Wenamun." *OEAE* 3:495–96.

Eggler, Jürg, and Othmar Keel. 2006. *Corpus der Siegel-Amulette aus Jordanien: Von Neolithikum bis zur Perserzeit.* OBOSA 25. Fribourg: Academic Press; Göttingen: Vandenhoeck & Ruprecht.

Eggler, Jürg, and Christoph Uehlinger, eds. Forthcoming. *Iconography of Deities and Demons in the Ancient Near East.* Leiden: Brill.

Eichler, B. L. 1989. "Nuzi and the Bible: A Retrospective." Pp. 107–19 in *DUMU-E$_2$-DUB-BA-A: Studies in Honor of Ake W. Sjöberg,* edited by Hermann Behrens, Darlene Loding, and Martha T. Roth. Occasional Publications of the Samuel Noah Kramer Fund 11. Philadelphia: University Museum.

Eitam, David. 1996. "The Olive Oil Industry at Tel Miqne-Erkon during the Late Iron Age." Pp. 167–96 in *Olive Oil in Antiquity: Israel and Neighbouring Countries from the Neolithic to the Early Arab Period,* edited by David Eitam and Michael Heltzer. Padova: Sargon.

Elat, M. 1975. "The Campaigns of Shalmaneser III against Aram and Israel." *IEJ* 25:25–34.

Elayi, Josette. 2007. "An Updated Chronology of the Reigns of Phoenician Kings during the Persian Period (539–333 BCE)." *Transeuphratène* 32:11–42.

Elitzur, Yoel. 2004. *Ancient Place Names in the Holy Land: Preservation and History*. Jerusalem: Magnes.

Ellis, Maria de Jong. 1989. "Observations on Mesopotamian Oracles and Prophetic Texts: Literary and Historiographical Considerations." *JCS* 41:127–86.

Ellis, Walter M. 1994. *Ptolemy of Egypt*. London: Routledge.

Emerit S., ed. 2013. *Le statut du musicien dans la Méditerranée ancienne: Égypte, Mésopotamie, Grèce, Rome*. Lyon: Institut français d'archéologie orientale.

Emerton, J. A. 1982. "New Light on Israelite Religion: The Implications of the Inscriptions from Kuntillet ʿAjrud." *ZAW* 94:2–20.

———. 1999. "'Yahweh and His Asherah': The Goddess or Her Symbol?" *VT* 49:315–37.

Ephʿal, Israel. 1982. *The Ancient Arabs: Nomads on the Borders of the Fertile Crescent 9th–5th Centuries BC*. Jerusalem: Magnes.

———. 1997. "Ways and Means to Conquer a City, Based on Assyrian Queries to the Sungod." Pp. 49–53 in *Assyria 1995: Proceedings of the 10th Anniversary Symposium of the Neo-Assyrian Text Corpus Project, Helsinki, September 7–11, 1995*, edited by Simo Parpola and Robert McCray Whiting. Helsinki: Neo-Assyrian Text Corpus Project.

———. 2003. "Nebuchadnezzar the Warrior: Remarks on His Military Achievements." *IEJ* 53:178–91.

———. 2009. *The City Besieged: Siege and Its Manifestations in the Ancient Near East*. Leiden: Brill.

Epstein, C. 1966. *Palestinian Bichrome Ware*. DMOA 12. Leiden: Brill.

Erlich, Adi. 2009. *The Art of Hellenistic Palestine*. British Archaeological Reports International Series. Oxford: Archaeopress.

Ermidoro, Stefania. 2015. *Commensality and Ceremonial Meals in the Neo-Assyrian Period*. Antichistica 8. Studi Orientali 3. Venice: Edizioni Ca' Foscari—Digital Publishing.

Erskine, Andrew, ed. 2005. *A Companion to the Hellenistic World*. Chichester: Wiley-Blackwell.

Eshel, H. 2008. *The Dead Sea Scrolls and the Hasmonean State*. Studies in Dead Sea Scrolls and Related Literature. Grand Rapids: Eerdmans.

Eskenazi, Tamara. 2014. "The Lives of Women in the Postexilic Era." Pp. 11–31 in *The Bible and Women: An Encyclopaedia of Exegesis and Cultural History*, vol. 1.3, *The Writings and Later Wisdom Books*, edited by Christl M. Maier and Nuria Calduch-Benages. Atlanta: Society of Biblical Literature.

Espak, P. 2015. *The God Enki in Sumerian Royal Ideology and Mythology*. Wiesbaden: Harrassowitz.

Evans, Paul S. 2009. *The Invasion of Sennacherib in the Book of Kings: A Source-Critical and Rhetorical Study of 2 Kings 18–19*. VTSup 125. Leiden: Brill.

Evenari, Michael, Leslie Shanan, and Naphtali Tadmor. 1971, 1982. *The Negev: The Challenge of a Desert*. 1st and 2nd eds. Cambridge, MA: Harvard University Press.

Fagan, Garrett G., and Matthew Trundle, eds. 2010. *New Perspectives on Ancient Warfare*. History of Warfare 59. Leiden: Brill.

Fales, Frederick M. 1996. "Prices in Neo-Assyrian Sources." *SAAB* 10:11–53.

Fantalkin, Alexander. 2011. "Why Did Nebuchadnezzar II Destroy Ashkelon in 604 B.C.E.?" Pp. 87–100 in *The Fire Signals of Lachish: Studies in the Archaeology and History of Israel in the Late Bronze Age, Iron Age, and Persian Period in Honor of David Ussishkin*, edited by Israel Finkelstein and Nadav Naʾaman. Winona Lake, IN: Eisenbrauns.

Farber, Walter. 1995. "Witchcraft, Magic, and Diviniation in Ancient Mesopotamia." *CANE* 3:1896–1909.

Faulkner, Raymond O. 1969. *The Ancient Egyptian Pyramid Texts*. Oxford: Clarendon.

———. 1977–78. *The Ancient Egyptian Coffin Texts*. 3 vols. Warminster: Aris & Philips.

———. 1985. *The Ancient Egyptian Book of the Dead*. London: British Museum.

Faust, Avraham. 1999. "Socioeconomic Stratification in an Israelite City: Hazor VI as a Test-Case." *Levant* 31:179–90.

———. 2003. "Judah in the Sixth Century B.C.E.: A Rural Perspective." *PEQ* 135:37–53.

———. 2004. "Mortuary Practices, Society and Ideology: The Lack of Iron Age I Burials in Highlands in Context." *IEJ* 54:174–90.

———. 2006a. "Farmsteads in Western Samaria's Foothills: A Reexamination." Pp. 477–504 in *"I Will Speak the Riddles of Ancient Times": Archaeological and Historical Studies in Honor of Amihai Mazar on the Occasion of His Sixtieth Birthday*, vol. 1, edited by Aren. M. Maeir and Pierre de Miroschedji. Winona Lake, IN: Eisenbrauns.

———. 2006b. *Israel's Ethnogenesis: Settlement, Interaction, Expansion and Resistance*. Approaches to Anthropological Archaeology. London: Equinox.

———. 2006c. "The Negev 'Fortresses' in Context: Reexamining the 'Fortress' Phenomenon in Light of General Settlement Processes of the Eleventh–Tenth Centuries B.C.E." *JAOS* 126:135–60.

———. 2007. "The Sharon and the Yarkon Basin in the Tenth Century BCE: Ecology, Settlement Patterns and Political Involvement." *IEJ* 57:65–82.

———. 2008. "Settlement and Demography in Seventh-Century Judah and the Extent and Intensity of Sennacherib's Campaign." *PEQ* 140:168–94.

———. 2010. "The Archaeology of the Israelite Cult: Questioning the Consensus." *BASOR* 360:23–35.

————. 2011a. "Household Economies in the Kingdoms of Israel and Judah." Pp. 255–73 in *Household Archaeology in Ancient Israel and Beyond*, edited by Assaf Yasur-Landau, Jennie R. Ebeling, and Laura B. Mazow. CHANE 50. Leiden: Brill.

————. 2011b. "How Were the Israelites Buried? The Lack of Iron Age I Burials in the Highlands in Context." Pp. 13–32 in *In the Highland's Depth: Ephraim Range and Binyamin Research Studies*, edited by A. Tavgar, Z. Amar, and M. Billig. Ariel-Talmon: Gofna Seminar. [In Hebrew.]

————. 2011c. "The Interests of the Assyrian Empire in the West: Olive Oil Production as a Test-Case." *JESHO* 54:62–86.

————. 2012a. *The Archaeology of Israelite Society in the Iron Age II*. Winona Lake, IN: Eisenbrauns.

————. 2012b. "Did Eilat Mazar Find David's Palace?" *BAR* 38 (5): 47–52, 70.

————. 2012c. *Judah in the Neo-Babylonian Period: The Archaeology of Desolation*. ABS 18. Atlanta: Society of Biblical Literature.

————. 2013. "The Shephelah in the Iron Age: A New Look on the Settlement of Judah." *PEQ* 145:203–19.

————. 2015. "Chronological and Spatial Changes in the Rural Settlement Sector of Ancient Israel during the Iron Age: An Overview." *RB* 122:247–67.

Faust, Avraham, and Shlomo Bunimovitz. 2008. "The Judahite Rock-Cut Tomb: Family Response at a Time of Change." *IEJ* 58:150–70.

Faust, Avraham, and Ruth Ludlum. 2012. *The Archaeology of Israelite Society in Iron Age II*. Winona Lake, IN: Eisenbrauns.

Faust, Avraham, and Zeev Safrai. 2015. *The Settlement History of Ancient Israel: A Quantitative Analysis*. Ramat Gan: The Ingeborg Renner Center for Jerusalem Studies, Bar-Ilan University. [In Hebrew.]

Faust, Avraham, and Ehud Weiss. 2005. "Judah, Philistia, and the Mediterranean World: Reconstructing the Economic System of the Seventh Century B.C.E." *BASOR* 338:71–92.

Feder, Yitzhaq. 2011. *Blood Expiation in Hittite and Biblical Ritual: Origins, Context, and Meaning*. WAW Supplement Series 2. Atlanta: Society of Biblical Literature.

————. 2016. "A Sin Offering for Birth Anxiety." http://thetorah.com/a-sin-offering-for-birth-anxiety/.

Feldman, Louis H. 1993. *Jew and Gentile in the Ancient World*. Princeton: Princeton University Press.

Feldman, Marian, and Brian B. Brown, eds. 2013. *Critical Approaches to Ancient Near Eastern Art*. Berlin: de Gruyter.

Fensham, F. Charles. 1963. "Clauses of Protection in Hittite Vassal-Treaties and the Old Testament." *VT* 13:133–43.

Fernández Marcos, Natalio. 2000. *The Septuagint in Context: Introduction to the Greek Version of the Bible*. Translated by Wilfred G. E. Watson. Leiden: Brill.

Finkelstein, Israel. 1988. *The Archaeology of the Israelite Settlement*. Jerusalem: Israel Exploration Society.

————. 1988–89. "The Land of Ephraim Survey 1980–1987: Preliminary Report." *TA* 15–16:117–83.

————. 1990. "Excavations at Khirbet ed-Dawwara: An Iron Age Site Northeast of Jerusalem." *TA* 17:163–209.

————. 1992. Middle Bronze Age 'Fortifications': A Reflection of Social Organization and Political Formations." *TA* 19:201–20.

————. 1993. "The Central Hill Country in the Intermediate Bronze Age." *IEJ* 41:19–45.

————. 1994. "The Emergence of Israel: A Phase in the Cyclic History of Canaan in the Third and Second Millennium BCE." Pp. 150–78 in *From Nomadism to Monarchy: Archaeological and Historical Aspects of Early Israel*, edited by Israel Finkelstein and Nadav Na'aman. Jerusalem: Yad Ben-Zvi and Israel Exploration Society; Washington, DC: Biblical Archaeology Society.

————. 1996a. "The Archaeology of the United Monarchy: An Alternative View." *Levant* 28:177–87.

————. 1996b. "Ethnicity and Origin of the Iron I Settlers in the Highlands of Canaan: Can the Real Israel Stand Up?" *BA* 59:198–212.

————. 1996c. "The Territorial-Political System of Canaan in the Late Bronze Age." *UF* 28:221–55.

————. 1998a. "Bible Archaeology or Archaeology of Palestine in the Iron Age? A Rejoinder." *Levant* 30:167–74.

————. 1998b. "Philistine Chronology: High, Middle or Low?" Pp. 140–47 in *Mediterranean Peoples in Transition: Thirteenth to Early Tenth Centuries BCE*, edited by Seymour Gitin, Amihai Mazar, and Ephraim Stern. Jerusalem: Israel Exploration Society.

————. 1999. "State Formation in Israel and Judah." *NEA* 62:35–52.

————. 2002. "The Campaign of Shoshenq I to Palestine: A Guide to the 10th Century BCE Polity." *ZDPV* 118:109–35.

————. 2010. "A Great United Monarchy? Archaeological and Historical Perspectives." Pp. 3–28 in *One God—One Cult—One Nation: Archaeological and Biblical Perspectives*, edited by Reinhard G. Kratz and Hermann Spieckermann. BZAW 405. Berlin: de Gruyter.

————. 2013. *The Forgotten Kingdom: The Archaeology and History of Northern Israel*. ANEM 5. Atlanta: Society of Biblical Literature.

Finkelstein, Israel, Shlomoh Bunimovits, and Zvi Lederman. 1993. *Shiloh: The Archaeology of a*

Biblical Site. Monograph Series of the Institute of Archaeology 10. Tel Aviv: Tel Aviv University.

Finkelstein, Israel, and Alexander Fantalkin. 2012. "Khirbet Qeiyafa: An Unsensational Archaeological and Historical Interpretation." *TA* 39:38–63.

Finkelstein, Israel, and Amihai Mazar. 2007. *The Quest for the Historical Israel*, edited by Brian B. Schmidt. ABS 17. Atlanta: Society of Biblical Literature.

Finkelstein, Israel, and Nadav Na'aman, eds. 1994. *From Nomadism to Monarchy: Archaeological and Historical Aspects of Early Israel*. Jerusalem: Yad Izhaq Ben-Zvi.

Finkelstein, Israel, and Eli Piasetzky. 2011. "The Iron Age Chronology Debate: Is the Gap Narrowing?" *NEA* 74:50–54.

Finkelstein, Israel, and Neil Asher Silberman. 2001. *The Bible Unearthed: Archaeology's New Vision of Ancient Israel and the Origin of Its Sacred Texts*. New York: Free Press.

Fischer, David Hackett. 1970. *Historians' Fallacies: Toward a Logic of Historical Thought*. New York: Harper Perennial.

Fischer, P. M., and T. Bürge. 2013. "Cultural Influences of the Sea Peoples in Transjordan: The Early Iron Age at Tell Abū Ḥaraz." *ZDPV* 129:132–70.

Fischer-Elfert, Hans-Werner. 1983. *Die satirische Streitschrift des Papyrus Anastasi*, vol. 1, *Übersetzung und Kommentar*. Wiesbaden: Harrassowitz.

Fitzmyer, Joseph A. 1967. *The Aramaic Inscriptions of Sefire*. BibOr 19. Rome: Pontifical Biblical Institute.

———. 1979. "The Aramaic Letter of King Adon to the Egyptian Pharaoh." Pp. 231–42 in Joseph A. Fitzmyer, *A Wandering Aramean: Collected Aramaic Essays*. Society of Biblical Literature Monograph Series 25. Missoula, MT: Scholars Press.

Fleming, Daniel E. 1992a. *The Installation of Baal's High Priestess at Emar: A Window on Ancient Syrian Religion*. HSS 42. Atlanta: Scholars Press.

———. 1992b. "The Rituals from Emar: Evolution of an Indigenous Tradition in Second-Millennium Syria." Pp. 51–61 in *New Horizons in the Study of Ancient Syria*, edited by Mark W. Chavalas and John L. Hayes. Bibliotheca Mesopotamica 25. Malibu, CA: Undena.

———. 1993. "*Nābû* and *munabbiātu*: Two New Syrian Religious Personnel." *JAOS* 113:175–83.

———. 1998a. "The Biblical Tradition of Anointing Priests." *JBL* 117:401–14.

———. 1998b. "Mari and the Possibilities of Biblical Memory." *Revue d'assyriologie et d'archéologie orientale* 92:41–78.

———. 2000. *Time at Emar: The Cultic Calendar and the Rituals from the Diviner's Archive*. Mesopotamian Civilizations 11. Winona Lake, IN: Eisenbrauns.

———. 2004a. *Democracy's Ancient Ancestors: Mari and Early Collective Governance*. Cambridge: Cambridge University Press.

———. 2004b. "Genesis in History and Tradition: The Syrian Background of Israel's Ancestors, Reprise." Pp. 193–232 in *The Future of Biblical Archaeology: Reassessing Methodologies and Assumptions*, edited by James K. Hoffmeier and Alan R. Millard. Grand Rapids: Eerdmans.

———. 2006. "Prophets and Temple Personnel in the Mari Archives." Pp. 44–63 in *The Priests in the Prophets: The Portrayal of Priests, Prophets, and Other Religious Specialists in the Latter Prophets*. LHB/OTS 408. London: Bloomsbury T&T Clark.

———. 2008. "From Joseph to David: Mari and Israelite Pastoral Traditions." Pp. 78–96 in *Israel: Ancient Kingdom or Late Invention?*, edited by Daniel I. Block. Nashville: B & H Academic.

———. 2009. "Kingship of City and Tribe Conjoined: Zimri-Lim at Mari." Pp. 227–40 in *Nomads, Tribes, and the State in the Ancient Near East: Cross Disciplinary Perspectives*, edited by Jeffrey Szuchman. OIS 5. Chicago: University of Chicago Press.

———. 2012. *The Legacy of Israel in Judah's Bible: History, Politics, and the Reinscribing of Tradition*. Cambridge: Cambridge University Press.

———. 2016. "The Amorites." Pp. 1–30 in *The World around the Old Testament: The People and Places of the Ancient Near East*, edited by Bill T. Arnold and Brent A. Strawn. Grand Rapids: Baker Academic.

Fokaefs, Anna, and Gerassimos A. Papadopoulos. 2007. "Tsunami Hazard in the Eastern Mediterranean: Strong Earthquakes and Tsunamis in Cyprus and the Levantine Sea." *Natural Hazards* 40:503–26.

Fontaine, Carole R. 1990. "The Sage in Family and Tribe." Pp. 155–64 in *The Sage in Israel and the Ancient Near East*, edited by John G. Gammie and Leo G. Perdue. Winona Lake, IN: Eisenbrauns.

Forstner-Müller, Irene, et al. 2008. "Preliminary Report on the Geophysical Survey at Tell el-Dabᶜa/Qantir in Spring 2008." *ÄL* 18:87–106.

Forti, Tova. 2015. "Gattung and Sitz im Leben: Methodological Vagueness in Defining Wisdom Psalms." Pp. 205–20 in *Was There a Wisdom Tradition? New Prospects in Israelite Wisdom Studies*, edited by Mark R. Sneed. AIL 23. Atlanta: Society of Biblical Literature.

Foster, Benjamin R. 2005. *Before the Muses: An Anthology of Akkadian Literature*. 3rd ed. Bethesda, MD: CDL Press.

Foster, John L. 1995. *Hymns, Prayers, and Songs: An Anthology of Ancient Egyptian Lyric Poetry*. Edited by Susan Tower Hollis. WAW 8. Atlanta: Scholars Press.

Fourrier, S., et al. 1999. *L'art des modeleurs d'argile: Coroplastique de Chypre*. Paris: Réunion des musées nationaux.

Fowler, Jeaneane D. 1988. *Theophoric Personal Names in Ancient Hebrew: A Comparative Study*. JSOT-Sup 49. Sheffield: JSOT Press.

Fowler, M. D. 1985. "Excavated Figures: A Case for Identifying a Site as Sacred." *ZAW* 97:333–43.

Fox, Michael V. 1985. *The Song of Songs and the Ancient Egyptian Love Songs*. Madison: University of Wisconsin Press.

———. 2015. "Three Theses on Wisdom." Pp. 69–86 in *Was There a Wisdom Tradition? New Prospects in Israelite Wisdom Studies*, edited by Mark R. Sneed. AIL 23. Atlanta: Society of Biblical Literature.

Fox, Nili Sacher. 2000. *In the Service of the King: Officialdom in Ancient Israel and Judah*. Cincinnati: Hebrew Union College Press.

———. 2003. "State Officials." Pp. 941–49 in *Dictionary of the Old Testament: Historical Books*, edited by Bill T. Arnold and H. G. M. Williamson. Downers Grove, IL: InterVarsity.

Frahm, Eckart. 2011. *Babylonian and Assyrian Text Commentaries: Origins of Interpretation*. Guides to the Mesopotamian Textual Record 5. Münster: Ugarit-Verlag.

Francfort, Henri-Paul. 2005. "Note on the 'Acrobat and Bull' Motive in Central Asia." Pp. 711–16 in Центральная Азия: Источники, История, Культура, edited by E. A. Davidovich and B. A. Litvinsky. Moscow: Восточная литература. http://www.academia.edu/3322303/Note_on_the_acrobat_and_bull_motive_in_Central_Asia.

Francia, Rita. 2010. "The Poetic Style of the Direct Speeches in the Hittite 'Parables' of the 'Epos der Freilassung.'" Pp. 63–71 in *Investigationes Anatolicae: Gesdenkschrift für Erich Neu*, edited by Jörg Klinger, Elisabeth Rieken, and Christel Rüster. Studien zu den Boğazköy-Texten 52. Wiesbaden: Harrassowitz.

Franken, Hendricus J. 2005. *A History of Potters and Pottery in Ancient Jerusalem: Excavations by K. M. Kenyon in Jerusalem 1961–1967*. London: Equinox.

Franken, Hendricus J., and G. London. 1995. "Why Painted Pottery Disappeared at the End of the Second Millennium BCE." *BA* 58:214–22.

Freed, Rita. 1999. "Art in the Service of Religion and the State." Pp. 110–29 in *Pharaohs of the Sun: Akhenaten, Nefertiti, Tutankhamun*, edited by Rita Freed, Sue D'Auria, and Yvonne J. Markowitz. Boston: Museum of Fine Arts.

Freedberg, David. 1989. *The Power of Images: Studies in the History and Theory of Response*. Chicago: University of Chicago Press.

Freedman, David Noel. 1975. *The Published Works of William Foxwell Albright: A Comprehensive Bibliography*. Cambridge, MA: American Schools of Oriental Research.

———. 1989. "William F. Albright in Memoriam." Pp. 33–44 in *The Scholarship of William Foxwell Albright: An Appraisal*, edited by Gus W. Van Beek. HSS 33. Atlanta: Scholars Press.

Freedman, David Noel, et al., eds. 1998. *The Leningrad Codex: A Facsimile Edition*. Grand Rapids: Eerdmans; Leiden: Brill.

Freedman, David Noel, and Jonas C. Greenfield, eds. 1971. *New Directions in Biblical Archaeology*. New York: Doubleday.

Freedman, David Noel, and Andrew Welch. 1994. "Amos's Earthquake and Israelite Prophecy." Pp. 188–98 in *Scripture and Other Artifacts*, edited by Michael David Coogan, J. Cheryl Exum, and Lawrence E. Stager. Louisville: Westminster John Knox.

Freedman, S. M. 1998. *If a City Is Set on a Height: The Akkadian Omen Series Šumma Alu Ina Mēlê Šakin*. Occasional Publications of the Samuel Noah Kramer Fund 17. Philadelphia: University of Pennsylvania Press.

Freeman-Grenville, G. S. P., Rupert L. Chapman III, and Joan E. Taylor. 2003. *The Onomasticon by Eusebius of Caesarea*. Jerusalem: Carta.

Frerichs, Ernest S., and Leonard H. Lesko, eds. 1997. *Exodus: The Egyptian Evidence*. Winona Lake, IN: Eisenbrauns.

Fretheim, Terence E. 2010. *Creation Untamed: The Bible, God, and Natural Disasters*. Grand Rapids: Baker Academic.

Freud, Sigmund. 1939. *Moses and Monotheism*. New York: Knopf.

Frevel, Christian, Katharina Pyschny, and Izak Cornelius, eds. 2014. *A "Religious Revolution" in Yehûd? The Material Culture of the Persian Period as a Test Case*. OBO 267. Fribourg: Academic Press; Göttingen: Vandenhoeck & Ruprecht.

Fried, Lisbeth S. 2003. "The Land Lay Desolate: Conquest and Restoration in the Ancient Near East." Pp. 21–54 in *Judah and the Judeans in the Neo-Babylonian Period*, edited by Oded Lipschits and Joseph Blenkinsopp. Winona Lake, IN: Eisenbrauns.

Friedman, Florence Dunn. 2015. "Economic Implications of the Menkaure Triads." Pp. 18–59 in *Towards a New History for the Egyptian Old Kingdom: Perspectives on the Pyramid Age*, edited by Peter Der Manuelian and Thomas Schneider. Harvard Egyptological Studies 1. Boston: Brill.

Friedman, J., and M. J. Rowlands. 1978. "Notes toward an Epigenetic Model of the Evolution of 'Civilisation.'" Pp. 201–78 in *The Evolution of Social Systems*, edited by J. Friedman and M. J. Rowlands. London: Duckworth.

Fritz, Volkmar. 2012. *The Emergence of Israel in the Twelfth and Eleventh Centuries B.C.E.* Translated by James W. Barker. Biblische Enzyklopädie 2. Leiden: Brill.

Frumin, Suembikya, et al. 2015. "Studying Ancient An-thropogenic Impacts on Current Floral Biodiversity in the Southern Levant as Reflected by the Philistine Migration." *Scientific Reports* 5. http://www.nature.com/articles/srep13308.

Frye, Northrop. 1982. *The Great Code: The Bible and Literature*. New York: Harcourt Brace Jovanovich.

Frymer-Kensky, Tikva. 2003. "Israel." Pp. 975–1046 in *A History of Ancient Near Eastern Law*, edited by Raymond Westbrook. Handbook of Oriental Studies: Section One: The Near and Middle East. Leiden: Brill.

Fu, Janling, and Peter Altmann. 2014. "Feasting: Back-grounds, Theoretical Perspectives, and Introduc-tions." Pp. 1–31 in *Feasting in the Archaeology and Texts of the Hebrew Bible and Ancient Near East*, edited by Peter Altmann and Janling Fu. Winona Lake, IN: Eisenbrauns.

Fu, Janling, and Paul Kang-Kul Cho. Forthcoming. "Resistance and a Trope of Feasting in Daniel 5."

Gabbay, U. 2014. "The Balâg Instrument and Its Role in the Cult of Ancient Mesopotamia." Pp. 129–47 in *Music in Antiquity: The Near East and the Med-iterranean*, edited by Joan Goodnick Westenholz, Yossi Maurey, and Edwin Seroussi. Yuval 8. Berlin: de Gruyter; Jerusalem: Magnes.

Gabolde, Marc. 1998. *D'Akhénaton à Toutankhamon*. Lyon: Université Lumière-Lyon.

———. 2005. *Akhénaton: Du mystère à la lumiere*. Paris: Gallimard.

Gabriel, Richard A. 2003. *The Military History of An-cient Israel*. Westport, CT: Praeger.

———. 2005. *Empires at War: A Chronological Ency-clopedia*. Westport, CT: Greenwood.

———. 2010. *Philip II of Macedonia: Greater than Alexander*. Washington, DC: Potomac.

Gachet-Bizollon, J. 2007. *Les ivoires d'Ougarit et l'art des ivoiriers du Levant au Bronze Récent*. RasShamra-Ougarit 16. Paris: Éditions Recherche sur les civilisations.

Gadot, Yuval. 2015. "In the Valley of the King: Jeru-salem's Rural Hinterland in the 8th–4th Centuries BCE." *TA* 42:3–26.

Gadot, Yuval, J. Uziel, and A. Yassur-Landau. 2012. "The Late Bronze Age Pottery." Pp. 241–64 in *Tell es-Safi/Gath I: Report on the 1996–2005 Seasons*, edited by A. Maeir. Ägypten und Alten Testament. Wiesbaden: Harrassowitz.

Gafney, Wilda C. 2008. *Daughters of Miriam: Women Prophets in Ancient Israel*. Minneapolis: Fortress.

Galil, Gershon. 2001. "A Re-Arrangement of the Frag-ments of the Tel Dan Inscription and the Relations between Israel and Aram." *PEQ* 133:16–21.

———. 2012. "Solomon's Temple: Fiction or Reality." Pp. 137–48 in *The Ancient Near East in the 12th–10th Centuries BCE: Culture and History*, edited by

Gershon Galil, Ayelet Gilboa, Aren M. Maeir, and Dan'el Kahn. AOAT 392. Münster: Ugarit-Verlag.

Gallagher, William R. 1999. *Sennacherib's Campaign to Judah: New Studies*. CHANE 18. Boston: Brill.

Gane, Constance E., Randall W. Younker, and Paul Ray. 2010. "Madaba Plains Project: Tall Jalul 2009." *AUSS* 48:165–223.

Gane, Roy E. 1992. "'Bread of the Presence' and Creator-in-Residence." *VT* 42:179–203.

———. 2004. *Ritual Dynamic Structure*. Gorgias Dis-sertations 14, Religion 2. Piscataway, NJ: Gorgias.

———. 2005. *Cult and Character: Purification Offer-ings, Day of Atonement, and Theodicy*. Winona Lake, IN: Eisenbrauns.

———. 2008a. "Hurrian Ullikummi and Daniel's 'Lit-tle Horn.'" Pp. 485–98 in *Birkat Shalom: Studies in the Bible, Ancient Near Eastern Literature, and Postbiblical Judaism Presented to Shalom M. Paul on the Occasion of His Seventieth Birthday*, edited by Chaim Cohen. Winona Lake, IN: Eisenbrauns.

———. 2008b. "Privative Preposition *min* in Purifica-tion Offering Pericopes and the Changing Face of 'Dorian Gray.'" *JBL* 127:209–22.

———. 2009. "Leviticus." Pp. 284–337 in *Zonder-van Illustrated Bible Backgrounds Commentary*, vol. 1, edited by John H. Walton. Grand Rapids: Zondervan.

García Martínez, Florentino. 1996. *The Dead Sea Scrolls Translated: The Qumran Texts in English*. 2nd ed. Leiden: Brill; Grand Rapids: Eerdmans.

Gardiner, Alan H. 1920. "The Ancient Military Road between Egypt and Palestine." *JEA* 6:99–116.

———. 1937. *Late Egyptian Miscellanies*. Brussels: La Fondation Égyptologique.

———. 1947. *Ancient Egyptian Onomastica Text*. 2 vols. Oxford: Oxford University Press. Reprint, 1968.

Garfinkel, Yosef, 1998. "Dancing and the Beginning of Art Scenes in the Early Village Communities of the Near East and Southeast Europe." *Cambridge Archaeological Journal* 8:207–37.

Garfinkel, Yosef, et al. 2012. "State Formation in Judah: Biblical Tradition, Modern Historical Theo-ries, and Radiometric Dates at Khirbet Qeiyafa." *Radiocarbon* 54:359–69.

Garfinkel, Yosef, and Saar Ganor. 2009. *Khirbet Qei-yafa*, vol. 1, *Excavation Report 2007–2008*. Jeru-salem: Institute of Archaeology, Hebrew University.

Garfinkel, Yosef, Saar Ganor, and Michael G. Hasel. 2014. *Khirbet Qeiyafa*, vol. 2, *Excavation Report 2009–2013, Stratigraphy and Architecture (Areas B, C, D, E)*, edited by Martin G. Klingbeil. Jerusalem: Institute of Archaeology, Hebrew University.

Garfinkel, Yosef, I. Kreimerman, and P. Zilberg. 2016. *Debating Khirbet Qeiyafa*. Jerusalem: Israel Explo-ration Society.

Garr, W. Randall. 1985. *Dialect Geography of Syria-Palestine, 1000–586 BCE*. Philadelphia: University of Pennsylvania. Reprint, Winona Lake, IN: Eisenbrauns, 2004.

Garroway, Kristine H. 2014. *Children in the Ancient Near Eastern Household*. Winona Lake, IN: Eisenbrauns.

Gaspa, Salvatore. 2014. "Silver Circulation and the Development of the Private Economy in the Assyrian Empire (9th–7th Centuries BCE): Considerations on Private Investments, Prices and Property Levels of the Imperial *élite*." Pp. 85–136 in *Studia Mesopotamica: Jahrbuch für altorientalische Geschichte und Kultur*, vol. 1, edited by M. Dietrich, K. A. Metzler, and H. Neumann. Münster: Ugarit-Verlag. (Also in *Dynamics of Production in the Ancient Near East*, edited by Juan Carlos Moreno Garcia. Oxford: Oxbow, 2014.)

Gass, E. 2009. *Die Moabiter: Geschichte und Kultur eines ostjordanischen Volkes im 1. Jahrtausend v. Chr.* Abhandlungen des Deutschen Palästina-Vereins 21. Wiesbaden: Harrassowitz.

Gates, Marie-Henriette. 2011. "Southern and Southeastern Anatolia in the Late Bronze Age." Pp. 393–412 in *The Oxford Handbook of Ancient Anatolia*, edited by Sharon R. Steadman and Gregory McMahon. Oxford: Oxford University Press.

Geisler, Hans, and Johann-Mattis List. 2013. "Do Languages Grow on Trees? The Tree Metaphor in the History of Linguistics." Pp. 111–24 in *Classification and Evolution in Biology, Linguistics and the History of Science*, edited by Heiner Fangerau et al. Stuttgart: Franz Steiner.

Gelb, Ignace J. 1961. "The Early History of the West Semitic Peoples." *JCS* 15:27–47.

Geller, J. Mark. 1980. "A Middle Assyrian Tablet of *utukkū lemnūtu*, Tablet 12." *Iraq* 42:23–51.

Gentry, Peter J., and Stephen J. Wellum. 2012. *Kingdom through Covenant: A Biblical-Theological Understanding of the Covenants*. Wheaton: Crossway.

George, Andrew. 1993. *House Most High: The Temples of Ancient Mesopotamia*. Winona Lake, IN: Eisenbrauns.

———. 2007. "Babylonian and Assyrian: A History of Akkadian." Pp. 31–71 in *Languages of Iraq, Ancient and Modern*, edited by J. N. Postgate. Cambridge: Cambridge University Press.

Geraty, Lawrence T. 2015. "Exodus Dates and Theories." Pp. 55–64 in *Israel's Exodus in Transdisciplinary Perspective: Text, Archaeology, Culture, and Geoscience,* edited by Thomas E. Levy, Thomas Schneider, and William H. C. Propp. New York: Springer.

Ghantous, H. 2013. *The Elisha-Hazael Paradigm and the Kingdom of Israel: The Politics of God in Ancient Syria-Palestine*. Durham: Acumen.

Gianto, A. 1999. "Amarna Akkadian as a Contact Language." Pp. 123–32 in *Languages and Cultures in Contact: At the Crossroads of Civilizations in the Syro-Mesopotamian Realm; Proceedings of the 42nd RAI, 1995*, edited by Karel van Lerberghe and G. Voet. OLA 96. Leuven: Peeters.

Gibson, John. 1971–82. *Textbook of Syrian Semitic Inscriptions*. 3 vols. Oxford: Clarendon.

Gilboa, Ayelet. 2014. "The Southern Levant (Cisjordan) during the Iron Age I Period." Pp. 624–59 in *The Oxford Handbook of the Archaeology of the Levant: C. 8000–332 BCE*, edited by Margreet L. Steiner and Ann E. Killebrew. Oxford: Oxford University Press.

Gilboa, Ayelet, and Y. Goren. 2015. "Early Iron Age Phoenician Networks: An Optical Mineralogy Study of Phoenician Bichrome and Related Wares in Cyprus." *Ancient West and East* 14:73–110. http://dor.huji.ac.il/Download/Article/AWE14004.pdf.

Gilders, William K. 2004. *Blood Ritual in the Hebrew Bible: Meaning and Power*. Baltimore: Johns Hopkins University Press.

Gilibert, Alessandra. 2011. *Syro-Hittite Monumental Art and the Archaeology of Performance: The Stone Reliefs at Carchemish and Zincirli in the Earlier First Millennium BCE*. Topoi Berlin Studies of the Ancient World 2. Berlin: de Gruyter.

Ginsberg, H. L. 1936. *Ugaritic Texts*. Jerusalem: Bialik Foundation. [In Hebrew.]

Girouard, M. 1980. *Life in the English Country House*. Aylesbury: Penguin.

Gitin, Seymour. 1989. "Tel Miqne–Ekron: A Type-Site for the Inner Coastal Plain in the Iron Age II Period." Pp. 23–58 in *Recent Excavations in Israel: Studies in Iron Age Archaeology*, edited by Seymour Gitin and William G. Dever. AASOR 49. Winona Lake, IN: Eisenbrauns.

———. 1990. *Gezer III: A Ceramic Typology of the Late Iron II, Persian and Hellenistic Periods at Tell Gezer, Text and Database and Plates*, vol. 3. Annual of the Nelson Glueck School of Biblical Archaeology. Jerusalem: Hebrew Union College.

———. 1995. "Tel Miqne Ekron in the 7th Century BCE: The Impact of Economic Innovation and Foreign Culture on a Neo-Assyrian Vassal City-State." Pp. 61–79 in *Recent Excavations in Israel: A View to the West; Reports on Kabri, Nami, Miqne-Ekron, Dor and Ashkelon*, edited by Seymour Gitin. Archaeological Institute of America: Colloquia and Conference Papers 1. Dubuque, IA: Kendall/Hunt.

———. 1997. "Albright Institute of Archaeological Research." *OEANE* 1:62–63.

———. 1998. "The Philistines in the Prophetic Texts: An Archaeological Perspective." Pp. 273–90 in *Hesed ve-Emet: Studies in Honor of Ernest S.*

Frerichs, edited by Jodi Magness and Seymour Gitin. BJS 320. Atlanta: Scholars Press.

———. 2012. "Temple Complex 650: The Impact of Multi-Cultural Influences on Philistine Cult in the Late Iron Age." Pp. 223–58 in *Temple Building and Temple Cult: Architecture and Cultic Paraphernalia of Temples in the Levant (2.–1. Mill. B.C.E.)*, edited by Jens Kamlah. Abhandlungen des Deutschen Palästina-Vereins 41. Wiesbaden: Harassowitz.

Gitin, Seymour, ed. 2015. *The Ancient Pottery of Israel and Its Neighbors: From the Iron Age through the Hellenistic Period*, vol. 1. Jerusalem: Israel Exploration Society.

Giveon, Raphael. 1971. *Les Bédouins Shosou des documents égyptiens*. DMOA 18. Leiden: Brill.

———. 1978. *The Impact of Egypt on Canaan: Iconographical and Related Studies*. OBO 20. Freiburg: Universitätsverlag; Göttingen: Vandenhoeck & Ruprecht.

———. 1981. "Some Egyptological Considerations concerning Ugarit." Pp. 55–88 in *Ugarit in Retrospect: Fifty Years of Ugarit and Ugaritic*, edited by G. Douglas Young. Winona Lake, IN: Eisenbrauns.

Glass, Roger I., Juan J. Urrutia, Simon Sibony, Harry Smith, Bertha Garcia, and Luis Rizzo. 1977. "Earthquake Injuries Related to Housing in a Guatemalan Village." *Science* 197:638–43.

Glassner, Jean-Jacques. 1989. "La philosophie mésopotamienne." Pp. 1637–42 in *Encyclopédie philosophique universelle*, vol. 1, edited by André Jacob. Paris: Presses Universitaires de France.

———. 2004. *Mesopotamian Chronicles*. WAW 19. Atlanta: Society of Biblical Literature.

Glueck, Nelson. 1934a. *Explorations in Eastern Palestine, I*. AASOR 14. New Haven: American Schools of Oriental Research.

———. 1934b. "Explorations in Eastern Palestine and the Negeb." *BASOR* 55:3–21.

———. 1935. *Explorations in Eastern Palestine, II*. AASOR 15. New Haven: American Schools of Oriental Research.

———. 1939. *Explorations in Eastern Palestine, III*. AASOR 18–19. New Haven: American Schools of Oriental Research.

———. 1940. *The Other Side of the Jordan*. New Haven: American Schools of Oriental Research.

———. 1951. *Explorations in Eastern Palestine, IV*. AASOR 25–28. New Haven: American Schools of Oriental Research.

———. 1959a. "The Negev." *BA* 22:82–100.

———. 1959b. *Rivers in the Desert: A History of the Negeb*. New York: Farrar, Straus and Cudahy.

———. 1965. *Deities and Dolphins: The Story of the Nabataeans*. New York: Farrar, Straus and Giroux.

———. 1969. *Rivers in the Desert*. New York: Grove.

———. 1970. *The Other Side of the Jordan*. Cambridge, MA: American Schools of Oriental Research.

Goelet, Ogden. 2016. "Tomb Robberies in the Valley of the Kings." Pp. 448–66 in *The Oxford Handbook of the Valley of the Kings*, edited by Richard H. Wilkinson and Kent R. Weeks. Oxford: Oxford University Press.

Goldwasser, Orly. 2006a. "Canaanites Reading Hieroglyphs: Horus Is Hathor?—The Invention of the Alphabet in Sinai." *ÄL* 16:121–60.

———. 2006b. "The Essence of Amarna Monotheism." Pp. 267–79 in *Jn.t Dr.w: Festschrift für Friedrich Junge*, edited by Gerald Moers et al. Göttingen: Lingua Aegyptia, Seminar für Ägyptologie und Koptologie.

Golub, Mitka. 2014. "The Distribution of Personal Names in the Land of Israel and Transjordan during the Iron II Period." *JAOS* 134:621–42.

Gonen, Rivka. 1984. "Urban Canaan in the Late Bronze Period." *BASOR* 253:61–73.

———. 1992a. *Burial Patterns and Cultural Diversity in Late Bronze Age Canaan*. American Schools of Oriental Research Dissertation Series 7. Winona Lake, IN: Eisenbrauns.

———. 1992b. "The Late Bronze Age." Pp. 211–57 in *The Archaeology of Ancient Israel*, edited by Amnon Ben-Tor. New Haven: Yale University Press.

González-Ruibal, Alfredo, and Maria Luisa Ruiz-Gálvez. 2016. "House Societies in the Ancient Mediterranean (2000–500 BC)." *Journal of World Prehistory* 29:383–437.

Goodenough, E. R. 1953–68. *Jewish Symbols in the Greco-Roman Period*. 13 vols. New York: Pantheon; Princeton: Princeton University Press.

Goodfriend, G. A. 1990. "Rainfall in the Negev Desert during the Middle Holocene, Based on 13 C of Organic Matter in Land Snail Shells." *Quaternary Research* 34:186–97.

Goodnick Westenholz, Joan, Yossi Maurey, and Edwin Seroussi, eds. 2014. *Music in Antiquity. The Near East and the Mediterranean*. Yuval 8. Berlin: de Gruyter; Jerusalem: Magnes.

Gordin, Shai. 2015. *Hittite Scribal Circles: Scholarly Tradition and Writing Habits*. Studien zu den Bogazköy-Texten 59. Wiesbaden: Harrassowitz.

Gordon, Cyrus H. 1940. "Biblical Customs and the Nuzu Tablets." *BA* 3:1–12.

———. 1965. *Ugaritic Textbook: Grammar, Texts in Transliteration, Cuneiform Selections, Glossary, Indices*. AO 38. Rome: Pontifical Biblical Institute.

Gordon, Robert P. 1995. "A House Divided: Wisdom in Old Testament Narrative Traditions." Pp. 94–105 in *Wisdom in Ancient Israel: Essays in Honour of J. A. Emerton*, edited by John Day, Robert P. Gordon, and H. G. M. Williamson. Cambridge: Cambridge University Press.

Goren, Yuval, Israel Finkelstein, and Nadav Na'aman. 2004. *Inscribed in Clay: Provenance Study of the Amarna Tablets and Other Ancient Near Eastern Texts*. Monograph Series of the Institute of Archaeology 23. Tel Aviv: Emery and Claire Yass Publications in Archaeology.

Gorman, Frank H. 1993. "Priestly Rituals of Founding: Time, Space, and Status." Pp. 47–64 in *History and Interpretation: Essays in Honour of John H. Hayes*, edited by M. Patrick Graham, William P. Brown, and Jeffrey K. Kuan. JSOTSup 173. Sheffield: JSOT Press.

Gottwald, Norman K. 1979. *The Tribes of Yahweh: A Sociology of the Religion of Liberated Israel, 1250–1050 B.C.* Maryknoll, NY: Orbis.

Grabbe, Lester L. 1995. *Priests, Prophets, Diviners, Sages: A Socio-Historical Study of Religious Specialists in Ancient Israel*. Valley Forge, PA: Trinity Press International.

———. 2000. *Judaic Religion in the Second Temple Period: Belief and Practice from the Exile to Yavneh*. London: Routledge.

———, ed. 2003. *"Like a Bird in a Cage": The Invasion of Sennacherib in 701 BCE*. JSOTSup 363. Sheffield: Sheffield Academic Press.

———, ed. 2004. *A History of the Jews and Judaism in the Second Temple Period*, vol. 1, *Yehud: A History of the Persian Province of Judah*. London: T&T Clark.

———. 2007. *Ancient Israel: What Do We Know and How Do We Know It?* London: A&C Black.

———, ed. 2014. *Religious and Cultural Boundaries from Neo-Babylonian to the Early Greek Period: A Context for Iconographic Interpretation*. OBO 267. Fribourg: Academic Press; Göttingen: Vandenhoeck & Ruprecht.

Grainger, John D. 1990. *Seleukos Nikator: Constructing a Hellenistic Kingdom*. London: Routledge.

Gray, John. 1970. *I and II Kings: A Commentary*. 2nd rev. ed. Philadelphia: Westminster.

Grayson, A. Kirk. 1975. *Assyrian and Babylonian Chronicles*. Locust Valley, NY: J. J. Augustin. Reprint, Winona Lake, IN: Eisenbrauns, 2000.

———. 1991. *Assyrian Rulers of the Early First Millennium BC*, vol. 1, *(1114–859 BC)*. Toronto: University of Toronto Press.

———. 1996. *Assyrian Rulers of the Early First Millennium BC*, vol. 2, *(859–745 BC)*. Toronto: University of Toronto Press.

———. 2001. "Assyria and the Orontes Valley." *Bulletin of the Canadian Society for Mesopotamian Studies* 36:185–87.

———. 2004. "Shalmaneser III and the Levantine States: The 'Damascus Coalition.'" *Journal of Hebrew Scriptures* 5. http://www.jhsonline.org/Articles/article_34.pdf.

Grayson, A. Kirk, and Jamie Novotny. 2012. *The Royal Inscriptions of Sennacherib, King of Assyria (704–681 BC), Part 1*. Winona Lake, IN: Eisenbrauns.

———. 2014. *The Royal Inscriptions of Sennacherib, King of Assyria (704–681 BC), Part 2*. Winona Lake, IN: Eisenbrauns.

Green, Alberto R. W. 2003. *The Storm-God in the Ancient Near East*. BJSUCSD 8. Winona Lake, IN: Eisenbrauns.

Green, Douglas J. 2010. *"I Undertook Great Works": The Ideology of Domestic Achievements in West Semitic Royal Inscriptions*. FAT 2/41. Tübingen: Mohr Siebeck.

Green, John D. M. 2006. "Ritual and Social Structure in the Late Bronze and Early Iron Age Southern Levant: The Cemetery at Tell es-Sa'idiyeh, Jordan." PhD dissertation, University College, London.

Green, Peter. 1992. *Alexander of Macedon, 356–323 B.C.: A Historical Biography*. Berkeley: University of California Press.

Greenberg, Moshe. 1983. *Biblical Prose Prayer: As a Window to the Popular Religion of Ancient Israel*. The Taubman Lectures in Jewish Studies, Sixth Series. Berkeley: University of California Press. Reprint, Eugene, OR: Wipf & Stock, 2008.

———. 1995. "On the Political Use of the Bible in Modern Israel: An Engaged Critique." Pp. 461–71 in *Pomegranates and Golden Bells: Studies in Biblical, Jewish, and Near Eastern Ritual, Law, and Literature in Honor of Jacob Milgrom*, edited by David P. Wright, David Noel Freedman, and Avi Hurvitz. Winona Lake, IN: Eisenbrauns.

Greene, Elizabeth, Justin Leidwanger, and Harun Ozdas. 2011. "Two Early Archaic Shipwrecks at Kekova Adasi and Kepce Burnu, Turkey." *International Journal of Nautical Archaeology* 40:60–68.

Greene, Jennifer. 2016. "Thoughts on the Jerusalem Conference." http://tmsifting.org/en/2016/10/28/thoughts-on-the-jerusalem-conference/.

Greenfield, Jonas, and Aaron Shaffer. 1983. "Notes on the Akkadian-Aramaic Bilingual Statue from Tell Fekherye." *Iraq* 45:109–16.

Greengus, Samuel. 1975. "Sisterhood Adoption at Nuzi and the 'Wife-Sister' in Genesis." *HUCA* 46:5–31.

———. 2011. *Laws in the Bible and in Early Rabbinic Collections: The Legal Legacy of the Ancient Near East*. Eugene, OR: Cascade.

Greenspahn, Frederick E. 1996. "Primogeniture in Ancient Israel." Pp. 69–79 in *Go to the Land I Will Show You: Studies in Honor of Dwight W. Young*, edited by Joseph Coleson and Victor H. Matthews. Winona Lake, IN: Eisenbrauns.

Greenstein, Edward L. 2010. "Texts from Ugarit Solve Biblical Puzzles." *BAR* 36 (6): 44–53, 70.

Greenwood, Kyle. 2014. "Late Tenth- and Ninth-Century Issues." Pp. 286–318 In *Ancient Israel's*

History, edited by Bill T. Arnold and Richard S. Hess. Grand Rapids: Baker Academic.

Greer, Jonathan S. 2013. *Dinner at Dan: Biblical and Archaeological Evidence for Sacred Feasts at Iron Age II Tel Dan and Their Significance*. CHANE 66. Leiden: Brill.

Gressmann, Hugo. 1909. *Altorientalische Texte und Bilder zum Alten Testament*. Tübingen: Mohr Siebeck.

Gressmann, Hugo, in collaboration with A. Ungand and H. Ranke. 1927. *Altorientalische Texte und Bilder zum Alten Testament*. Rev. ed. Berlin: de Gruyter.

Grimal, Nicolas. 1988. *A History of Ancient Egypt*. Translated by Ian Shaw. Malden, MA: Blackwell.

Groom, Nigel. 1981. *Frankincense and Myrrh: A Study of the Arabian Incense Trade*. New York: Longman.

Gropp, Douglas M. 2000. "Sanballat." Pp. 823–25 in *Encyclopedia of the Dead Scrolls*, vol. 2, edited by L. H. Schiffman and J. C. VanderKam. Oxford: Oxford University Press.

Gropp, Douglas M., and Theodore J. Lewis. 1985. "Notes on Some Problems in the Aramaic Text of the Hadd-Yith'i Bilingual." *BASOR* 259:45–61.

Gruen, Erich S. 1998. *Heritage and Hellenism: The Re-invention of Jewish Tradition*. Berkeley: University of California Press.

———. 2002. *Diaspora: Jews amidst Greeks and Romans*. Cambridge, MA: Harvard University Press.

———. 2010. "Judaism in the Diaspora." Pp. 77–96 in *The Eerdmans Dictionary of Early Judaism*, edited by John J. Collins and Daniel C. Harlow. Grand Rapids: Eerdmans.

Guillaume, Philippe. 2012. *Land, Credit and Crisis: Agrarian Finance in the Hebrew Bible*. BibleWorld. London: Equinox.

Guinan, Ann K. 2002. "A Severed Head Laughed: Stories of Divinatory Interpretation." Pp. 7–40 in *Magic and Divination in the Ancient World*, edited by Leda Ciraolo and Jonathan Seidel. AMD 2. Leiden: Brill.

Gunkel, Hermann. 2006. *Creation and Chaos in the Primeval Era and the Eschaton*. Grand Rapids: Eerdmans. Translation of 1895/1921 original.

———. 2009. *Israel and Babylon: The Babylonian Influence on Israelite Religion*. Edited by K. C. Hanson. Translated by E. S. B. Hanson and K. C. Hanson. Eugene, OR: Cascade.

Gur-Arieh, Shira, Aren M. Maeir, and Ruth Shahack-Gross. 2011. "Soot Patterns on Cooking Vessels: A Short Note." Pp. 349–55 in *On Cooking Pots, Drinking Cups, Loom Weights and Ethnicity in Bronze Age Cyprus and Neighboring Regions: An International Archaeological Symposium Held in Nicosia, November 6th–7th 2010*, edited by Vassos Karageorghis and Ourania Kouka. Nicosia: A. G. Leventis Foundation.

Güterbock, Hans Gustav. 1938. "Die historische Tradition und ihre literarische Gestaltung bei Babyloniern und Hethitern bis 1200 II." *Zeitschrift für Assyriologie* 44 (10): 45–149.

———. 1978. "Hethitische Literatur." Pp. 211–53 in *Altorientalische Literaturen*, edited by Wolfgang Röllig. Neues Handbuch der Literaturwissenschaft 1. Wiesbaden: Athenaion.

Haas, G. H. 2003. "Slave, Slavery." Pp. 778–83 in *Dictionary of the Old Testament: Pentateuch*, edited by T. Desmond Alexander and David W. Baker. Downers Grove, IL: InterVarsity.

Haas, Volkert. 1994. *Geschichte der hethitischen Religion*. HdO 15. Leiden: Brill.

———. 2006. *Die hethitische Literatur: Texte, Stilistik, Motif*. Berlin: de Gruyter.

Habichi, Labib. 2001. *Tell el-Dabᶜa I*. Vienna: Österreichische Akademie der Wissenschaften.

Hackett, Jo Ann. 1980. *The Balaam Text from Deir ʿAlla*. HSM 31. Chico, CA: Scholars Press.

Hadley, Judith M. 1995. "Wisdom and the Goddess." Pp. 234–43 in *Wisdom in Ancient Israel*, edited by John Day, Robert P. Gordon, and H. G. M. Williamson. Cambridge: Cambridge University Press.

———. 2000. *The Cult of Asherah in Ancient Israel and Judah: Evidence for a Hebrew Goddess*. UCOP 57. Cambridge: Cambridge University Press.

———. 2005. "Hebrew Inscriptions." Pp. 366–80 in *Dictionary of the Old Testament: Historical Books*, edited by Bill T. Arnold and H. G. M. Williamson. Downers Grove, IL: InterVarsity.

———. 2012. "2 Chronicles 32:30 and the Water Systems of Pre-Exilic Jerusalem." Pp. 273–84 in *Let Us Go Up to Zion: Essays in Honour of H. G. M. Williamson on the Occasion of His Sixty-Fifth Birthday*, edited by Iain W. Provan and Mark J. Boda. VTSup 153. Leiden: Brill.

Hafþórsson, S. 2006. *A Passing Power: An Examination of the Sources for the History of Aram-Damascus in the Second Half of the Ninth Century B.C.* Coniectanea Biblica: Old Testament Series 54. Stockholm: Almqvist & Wiksell.

Haider, Peter W., James M. Weinstein, Eric H. Cline, and David O'Connor. 2012. "Nomads of Sea and Desert: An Integrated Approach to Ramesses III's Foreign Policy." Pp. 151–208 in *Ramesses III: The Life and Times of Egypt's Last Hero*, edited by Eric H. Cline and David O'Connor. Ann Arbor: University of Michigan Press.

Hairman, Moti. 2012. "Geopolitical Aspects of the Negev Desert in the 11th–10th Centuries BCE." Pp. 199–206 in *The Ancient Near East in the 12th–10th Centuries BCE: Culture and History*, edited by Gerson Galil, Ayelet Gilboa, Aren M. Maeir, and Dan'l Kahn. AOAT 392. Münster: Ugarit-Verlag.

Hall, M. 1992. "Small Things and the Mobile: Conflictual Fusion of Power, Fear and Desire." Pp. 373–99 in *The Art and Mystery of Historical Archaeology: Essays in Honor of James Deetz*, edited by A. E. Yentsch and M. C. Beaudry. Boca Raton, FL: CRC Press.

Hallo, William W. 1960. "From Qarqar to Carchemish: Assyria and Israel in the Light of New Discoveries." *BA* 23:34–61.

———. 1990. "Compare and Contrast: The Contextual Approach to Biblical Literature." Pp. 1–30 in *The Bible in Light of Cuneiform Literature*, edited by W. W. Hallo, B. W. Jones, and G. L. Mattingly. Ancient Near Eastern Texts and Studies 8. Lewiston, NY: Edwin Mellen.

Hallock, Richard T. 1969. *Persepolis Fortification Tablets*. OIP 92. Chicago: University of Chicago Press.

Hallote, Rachel S. 2001. *Death, Burial, and Afterlife in the Biblical World: How the Israelites and Their Neighbors Treated the Dead*. Chicago: Ivan R. Dee.

Halpern, Baruch. 1987. "'Brisker Pipes Than Poetry': The Development of Israelite Monotheism." Pp. 77–115 in *Judaic Perspectives on Ancient Israel*, edited by Jacob Neusner, Baruch A. Levine, and Ernest S. Frerichs. Philadelphia: Fortress Press. Reprint, pp. 13–56 in *From Gods to God: The Dynamics of Iron Age Cosmologies*, edited by M. J. Adams. FAT 1/63. Tübingen: Mohr Siebeck, 2009.

———. 1991. "Jerusalem and the Lineages in the 7th Century BCE: Kinship and the Rise of Individual Moral Liability." Pp. 11–107 in *Law and Ideology in Monarchic Israel*, edited by Baruch Halpern and Deborah W. Hobson. JSOTSup 124. Sheffield: Sheffield Academic Press. Reprint, pp. 339–424 in *From Gods to God: The Dynamics of Iron Age Cosmologies*, edited by M. J. Adams. FAT 1/63. Tübingen: Mohr Siebeck, 2009.

———. 1992. "The Exodus from Egypt: Myth or Reality?" Pp. 86–117 in *The Rise of Ancient Israel*, edited by Hershel Shanks et al. Washington, DC: Biblical Archaeology Society.

———. 1994. "The Stela from Dan: Epigraphic and Historical Considerations." *BASOR* 296:63–80.

———. 2001. *David's Secret Demons: Messiah, Murderer, Traitor, King*. Grand Rapids: Eerdmans.

———. 2009. "'Brisker Pipes Than Poetry': The Development of Israelite Monotheism." Pp. 77–115 in *Judaic Perspectives on Ancient Israel*, edited by J. Neusner, B. A. Levine, and E. S. Frerichs. Philadelphia: Fortress Press.

Halstead, Paul. 1992. "The Mycenaean Palatial Economy: Making the Most of the Gaps in the Evidence." *Proceedings of the Cambridge Philological Society* 38:57–86.

———. 1995. "Plough and Power: The Economic and Social Significance of Cultivation with the Ox-Drawn Ard in the Mediterranean." *Bulletin on Sumerian Agriculture* 8:11–22.

Hamilton, G. J. 2006. *The Origin of the West Semitic Alphabet in Egyptian Scripts*. Washington, DC: Catholic Biblical Association of America.

Hamilton, Mark W. 2015. "Riddles and Parables, Traditions and Texts: Ezekielian Perspectives on Israelite Wisdom Traditions." Pp. 241–64 in *Was There a Wisdom Tradition? New Prospects in Israelite Wisdom Studies*, edited by Mark R. Sneed. AIL 23. Atlanta: Society of Biblical Literature.

Hamori, Esther J. 2015. *Women's Divination in Biblical Literature: Prophecy, Necromancy, and Other Arts of Knowledge*. Anchor Yale Bible Reference Library. New Haven: Yale University Press.

Hancock, Jim F. 2006. *Plant Evolution and the Origin of Crop Species*. 2nd ed. Wallingford, UK: CABI Publishing.

Haran, Menahem. 1985. *Temples and Temple-Service in Ancient Israel: An Inquiry into Biblical Cult Phenomena and the Historical Setting of the Priestly School*. Winona Lake, IN: Eisenbrauns.

Har-El, M. 2005. *Understanding the Geography of the Bible: An Introductory Atlas*. Jerusalem: Carta.

Hari, Robert. 1985. *New Kingdom Amarna Period*. Iconography of Religions 16/6. Leiden: Brill.

Harrington, D. J. 1988. *The Maccabean Revolt: Anatomy of a Biblical Revolution*. Old Testament Studies. Wilmington, DE: Glazier.

Harris, David R. 1989. "An Evolutionary Continuum of People-Plant Interaction." Pp. 11–26 in *Foraging and Farming: The Evolution of Plant Exploitation*, edited by David R. Harris and Gordon C. Hillman. London: Unwin Hyman.

———. 1996. "Introduction: Themes and Concepts in the Study of Early Agriculture." Pp. 1–9 in *The Origins and Spread of Agriculture and Pastoralism in Eurasia*, edited by David R. Harris. London: UCL Press.

Harrison, Timothy P. 1997. "Shifting Patterns of Settlement in the Highlands of Central Jordan during the Early Bronze Age." *BASOR* 306:1–37.

Hartman, G., G. Bar-Oz, R. Bouchnick, and R. Reich. 2013. "The Pilgrimage Economy of Early Roman Jerusalem (1st century BCE–70 CE) Reconstructed from the δ 15 N and δ 13 C Values of Goat and Sheep Remains." *JAS* 40 (12): 4369–76.

Hartmann, Benedikt. 1960. "Es gibt keinen Gott außer Jahwe: Zur generellen Verneinung im Hebräischen." *Zeitschrift der deutschen morgenländischen Gesellschaft* 110:229–35.

Hartmann-Shenkman, Anat, Mordechai E. Kislev, Ehud Galili, Yoel Melamed, and Ehud Weiss. 2015. "Invading a New Niche: Obligatory Weeds at Neolithic Atlit-Yam, Israel." *Vegetation History and Archaeobotany* 24:9–18.

Hartwig, Melinda K., ed. 2015. *A Companion to Ancient Egyptian Art*. Chichester: Blackwell.

Harvey, Paul B., and Baruch Halpern. 2008. "W. M. L. de Wette's 'Dissertatio Critica . . .': Context and Translation." *Zeitschrift für alttestamentlische und biblische Rechtsgeschichte* 14:47–85.

Hasel, G. 1972. "The Significance of the Cosmology of Genesis 1 in Relation to Ancient Near Eastern Parallels." *AUSS* 10:1–20.

———. 1974. "The Polemic Nature of the Genesis Cosmology." *Evangelical Quarterly* 46:81–102.

Hasel, M. 1998. *Dominance and Resistance: Egyptian Military Activity in the Southern Levant, 1300–1185 BC*. PÄ 11. Leiden: Brill.

———. 2005. *Military Practice and Polemic: Israel's Laws of Warfare in Near Eastern Perspective*. Berrien Springs, MI: Andrews University Press.

Hauptmann, Andreas. 2007. *The Archaeometallurgy of Copper: Evidence from Faynan, Jordan*. Berlin: Springer.

Hausleiter, Arnulf. 2006. "Tayma, Northwest Arabia: The Context of Archaeological Research." Pp. 158–80 in *Collection of Papers on Ancient Civilizations of Western Asia, Asia Minor and North Africa*, edited by Yushu Gong and Yiyi Chen. Special Issue of *Oriental Studies*. Beijing: University of Beijing.

Hawass, Zahi, et al. 2010. "Ancestry and Pathology in King Tutankhamun's Family." *Journal of the American Medical Association* 303 (7): 638–47.

Hawkins, Ralph K. 2012. *The Iron Age I Structure on Mt. Ebal: Excavation and Interpretation*. BBRSup 6. Winona Lake, IN: Eisenbrauns.

———. 2013. *How Israel Became a People*. Nashville: Abingdon.

Hayden, Roy E. 1962. "Court Procedure at Nuzu." PhD dissertation, Brandeis University.

Hays, Christopher B. 2011. *Death in the Iron Age II and in First Isaiah*. FAT 79. Tübingen: Mohr Siebeck. Republished as *A Covenant With Death: Death in the Iron Age II and Its Rhetorical Uses in Proto-Isaiah*. Grand Rapids: Eerdmans, 2015.

Heckel, Waldemar. 2003. "Alexander the Great and the 'Limits of the Civilized World.'" Pp. 147–74 in *Crossroads of History: The Age of Alexander*, edited by Waldemar Heckel and Lawrence A. Tritle. Claremont, CA: Regina.

———. 2007. "The Earliest Evidence for the Plot to Poison Alexander." Pp. 265–75 in *Alexander's Empire: Formulation to Decay*, edited by Waldemar Heckel, Lawrence Tritle, and Pat Wheatley. Claremont, CA: Regina.

———. 2016. *Alexander's Marshals: A Study of the Makedonian Aristocracy and the Politics of Military Leadership*. 2nd ed. London: Routledge.

Heckel, Waldemar, Carolyn Willekes, and Graham Wrightson. 2010. "Scythed Chariots at Guagamela: A Case Study." Pp. 103–12 in *Philip II and Alexander the Great: Father and Son, Lives and Afterlives*, edited by Elizabeth Carney and Daniel Ogden. Oxford: Oxford University Press.

Heide, Martin. 2010. "The Domestication of the Camel: Biological, Archaeological and Inscriptional Evidence from Mesopotamia, Israel and Arabia, and Literary Evidence from the Bible." *UF* 42:331–83.

Heider, George C. 1985. *The Cult of Molek: A Reassessment*. JSOTSup 43. Sheffield: JSOT Press.

Heimpel, Wolfgang. 2003. *Letters to the King of Mari: A New Translation, with Historical Introduction, Notes, and Commentary*. Mesopotamian Civilizations 12. Winona Lake, IN: Eisenbrauns.

Heintz, Jean-Georges. 2015. *Prophétisme et alliance: Des Archives royales de Mari à la Bible hébraïque*. OBO 271. Fribourg: Academic Press; Göttingen: Vandenhoeck & Ruprecht.

Heltzer, Michael. 1977. "The Metal Trade of Ugarit and the Problem of Transportation of Commercial Goods." *Iraq* 39:203–11.

———. 1996. "The Symbiosis of the Public and Private Sector in Ugarit, Phoenicia and Palestine." Pp. 177–207 in *Privatization in the Ancient Near East and Classical World*, edited by Michael Hudson and Baruch Levine. Cambridge, MA: Peabody Museum of Archaeology and Ethnology, Harvard University.

Hendel, Ronald S. 1995. "Finding Historical Memories in the Patriarchal Narratives." *BAR* 21 (4): 52–59, 70–71.

Hengel, Martin. 1974. *Judaism and Hellenism: Studies in Their Encounter in Palestine during the Early Hellenistic Period*. Translated by John Bowden. 2 vols. Philadelphia: Fortress.

———. 1980. *Jews, Greeks, and Barbarians: Aspects of the Hellenization of Judaism in the Pre-Christian Period*. Translated by John Bowden. Philadelphia: Fortress.

———. 1989. *The "Hellenization" of Judea in the First Century after Christ*. London: SCM.

———. 2003. *Judaism and Hellenism: Studies in Their Encounter in Palestine during the Early Hellenistic Period*. Translated by John Bowden. 2 vols. Rev. ed. Eugene, OR: Wipf & Stock.

Herodotus. 1998. *The Histories*. Translated by R. Waterfield. Oxford: Oxford University Press.

Herr, Larry G. 1997. "Archaeological Sources for the History of Palestine: The Iron Age II Period: Emerging Nations." *BA* 60:114–83.

———. 2009. "The House of the Father at Iron I Tall al-'Umayri, Jordan." Pp. 191–205 in *Exploring the Longue Dureé: Essays in Honor of Lawrence E. Stager*, edited by J. David Schloen. Winona Lake, IN: Eisenbrauns.

Herr, Larry G., and Douglas R. Clark. 2001. "Excavating the Tribe of Reuben." *BAR* 27:36–47, 64, 66.

———. 2009. "From the Stone Age to the Middle Ages in Jordan: Digging up Tall al-'Umayri." *NEA* 72:68–97.

———. 2014. "Tall al-'Umayri through the Ages." Pp. 121–28 in *Crossing Jordan: North American Contributions to the Archaeology of Jordan*, edited by Thomas E. Levy, P.M. Michèle Daviau, Randall W. Younker, and May Shaer. New York: Routledge.

Herr, Larry G., and Mohammed Najjar. 2008. "The Iron Age." Pp. 311–34 in *Jordan: An Archaeological Reader*, edited by Russell B. Adams. London: Equinox.

Herrmann, Christian. 1993. *Ägyptische Amulette aus Palästina/Israel mit einem Ausblick auf ihre Rezeption durch das Alte Testament*. OBO 138. Fribourg: Universitätsverlag.

———. 2006. *Ägyptische Amulette aus Palästina/Israel*. Vol 3. OBOSA 24. Göttingen: Vandenhoeck & Ruprecht.

———. 2016. *Ägyptische Amulette aus Palästina/Israel*, vol. 4, *Von der Spätbronzezeit IIB bis in römische Zeit*. OBOSA 38. Fribourg: Universitätsverlag; Göttingen: Vandenhoeck & Ruprecht.

Herrmann, Christian, et al. 2010. *1001 Amulett: Altägyptischer Zauber, monotheisierte Talismane, säkulare Magie*. Stuttgart: Katholisches Bibelwerk.

Herrmann, Siegfried. 1964. "Operationen Pharao Schoschenks I. im östlichen Ephraim." *ZDPV* 80:55–79.

Herzog, Chaim, and Mordechai Gichon. 1997. *Battles of the Bible*. 2nd ed. London: Greenhill.

Herzog, Ze'ev. 1992. "Settlement and Fortification Planning in the Iron Age." Pp. 231–74 in *The Architecture of Ancient Israel: From the Prehistoric to the Persian Periods*, edited by Aharon Kempinski and Ronny Reich. Jerusalem: Israel Exploration Society.

———. 1994. "The Beer-Sheba Valley: From Nomadism to Monarchy." Pp. 122–49 in *From Nomadism to Monarchy: Archaeological and Historical Aspects of Early Israel*, edited by Israel Finkelstein and Nadav Na'aman. Jerusalem: Israel Exploration Society.

———. 1997a. *Archaeology of the City: Urban Planning in Ancient Israel and Its Social Implications*. Monograph Series of the Sonia and Marco Nadler Institute of Archaeology 13. Tel Aviv: Tel Aviv University.

———. 1997b. "Fortifications: An Overview." *OEANE* 2:319–21.

———. 2002. "The Fortress Mound at Tel Arad: An Interim Report." *TA* 29:3–109.

Hess, Richard S. 1993a. *Amarna Personal Names*. American Schools of Oriental Research Dissertation Series 9. Winona Lake, IN: Eisenbrauns.

———. 1993b. "The Slaughter of the Animals in Genesis 15:18–21 and Its Ancient Near Eastern Context." Pp. 55–65 in *He Swore an Oath: Biblical Themes from Genesis 12–50*, edited by Richard S. Hess, Gordon J. Wenham, and Philip E. Satterthwaite. 2nd ed. Grand Rapids: Baker; Carlisle: Paternoster.

———. 1997. "The Form and Structure of the Solomonic District List in 1 Kings 4:7–19." Pp. 279–92 in *Crossing Boundaries and Linking Horizons: Studies in Honor of Michael C. Astour*, edited by Gordon D. Young, Mark W. Chavalas, and Richard E. Averbeck. Bethesda, MD: CDL Press.

———. 2002. "Literacy in Iron Age Israel." Pp. 82–102 in *Windows into Old Testament History: Evidence, Argument, and the Crisis of "Biblical Israel,"* edited by V. Philips Long, David W. Baker, and Gordon J. Wenham. Grand Rapids: Eerdmans.

———. 2007. *Israelite Religions: An Archaeological and Biblical Survey*. Grand Rapids: Baker Academic.

———. 2008. "War in the Hebrew Bible: An Overview." Pp. 19–32 in *War in the Bible and Terrorism in the Twenty-First Century*, edited by Richard S. Hess and Elmer A. Martens. BBRSup 2. Winona Lake, IN: Eisenbrauns.

———. 2009a. "Questions of Reading and Writing in Ancient Israel." *BBR* 19:1–9.

———. 2009b. *Studies in the Personal Names of Genesis 1–11*. Winona Lake, IN: Eisenbrauns.

———. 2017. "Texts from Ancient Canaan." Pp. 259–73 in *The Context of Scripture*, vol. 4. *Supplements*, edited by K. Lawson Younger Jr. Leiden: Brill.

Hesse, Brian. 1990. "Pig Lovers and Pig Haters: Patterns of Palestinian Pork Production." *Journal of Ethnobiology* 10:195–225.

Hesse, Brian, and Paula Wapnish. 1998. "Pig Use and Abuse in the Ancient Levant: Ethnoreligious Boundary-Building with Swine." Pp. 123–36 in *Ancestors for the Pigs: Pigs in Prehistory*, edited by Sarah M. Nelson. MASCA Research Papers in Science and Archaeology 15. Philadelphia: University of Pennsylvania Museum of Archaeology and Anthropology.

Hestrin, Ruth. 1983. "Hebrew Seals of Officials." Pp. 50–54 in *Ancient Seals and the Bible*, edited by Leonard Gorelick and Elizabeth Williams-Forte. Malibu, CA: Undena.

Hetzron, Robert. 1974. "La division des langues sémitiques." Pp. 181–94 in *Actes du premier Congres international de linguistique semitique et chamito-semitique, Paris 16–19 juillet 1969*, edited by Andre Caquot and David Cohen. The Hague: Mouton.

———. 1976. "Two Principles of Genetic Reconstruction." *Lingua* 38:89–108.

Heuzey, A. Léon. 1891–1915. "Le bassin sculpté et le symbole du vase jaillissant." Pp. 149–70 in *Les origines orientales de l'art: Recueil de mémoires archéologiques et de monuments figurés*. Paris: E. Leroux.

Higginbotham, Carolyn R. 2000. *Egyptianization and Elite Emulation in Ramesside Palestine: Governance and Accommodation on the Imperial Periphery*. CHANE 2. Leiden: Brill.

Hilber, John W. 2011. "Prophetic Speech in the Egyptian Royal Cult." Pp. 39–53 in *On Stone and Scroll: Essays in Honour of Graham Ivor Davies*, edited by James K. Aitken, Katharine J. Dell, and Brian A. Mastin. BZAW 420. Berlin: de Gruyter.

———. 2012. "The Culture of Prophecy and Writing in the Ancient Near East." Pp. 219–41 in *Do Historical Matters Matter to Faith?*, edited by James K. Hoffmeier and Dennis Magary. Wheaton: Crossway.

———. 2015. "Isaiah as Prophet and Isaiah as Book in Their Ancient Near Eastern Context." Pp. 151–74 in *Bind Up the Testimony: Explorations in the Genesis of the Book of Isaiah*, edited by Daniel I. Block and Richard L. Schultz. Peabody, MA: Hendrickson.

Hincks, E. 1851. "Nimrud Obelisk." *Athenaeum* 1261:1384–85.

Hixson, Walter L. 2013. *American Settler Colonialism: A History*. New York: Palgrave Macmillan.

Hodge, Carleton. 1981. "Akhenaten: A Reject." *Scriptura Mediterranea* 2:17–26.

Hoffman, Yair. 1999. "The Deuteronomistic Concept of the Herem." *ZAW* 111:196–210.

Hoffmeier, James K. 1983. "Some Thoughts on Genesis 1 and 2 and Egyptian Cosmology." *JANES* 15:29–39.

———. 1986. "The Arm of God versus the Arm of Pharaoh in the Exodus Narratives." *Bib* 67:378–87.

———. 1989. "Reconsidering Egypt's Part in the Termination of the Middle Bronze Age in Palestine." *Levant* 21:181–93.

———. 1990. "Some Thoughts on William G. Dever's 'Hyksos, Egyptian Destructions, and the End of the Palestinian Middle Bronze Age.'" *Levant* 22:83–89.

———. 1991. "James Weinstein's 'Egypt and the Middle Bronze IIC/Late Bronze IA Transition': A Rejoinder." *Levant* 23:117–24.

———. 1996. *Israel in Egypt: The Evidence for the Authenticity of the Exodus Tradition*. New York: Oxford University Press.

———. 2005. *Ancient Israel in Sinai: The Evidence for the Authenticity of the Wilderness Tradition*. New York: Oxford University Press.

———, ed. 2014a. *Excavations in North Sinai: Tell el-Borg I: The "Dwelling of the Lion" on the Ways of Horus*. Winona Lake, IN: Eisenbrauns.

———. 2014b. "The Exodus and Wilderness Narratives." Pp. 46–90 in *Ancient Israel's History: An Introduction to Issues and Sources*, edited by Bill T. Arnold and Richard S. Hess. Grand Rapids: Baker Academic.

———. 2015. *Akhenaten and the Origins of Monotheism*. Oxford: Oxford University Press.

Hoffmeier, James K., Alan R. Millard, and Gary A. Rendsburg, eds. 2016. *"Did I Not Bring Israel Out of Egypt?" Biblical, Archaeological, and Egyptological Perspectives on the Exodus Narratives*. BBRSup 12. Winona Lake, IN: Eisenbrauns.

Hoffner, Harry A. 1968. "Birth and Name-Giving in Hittite Texts." *JNES* 27:198–203.

———. 1974. *Alimenta Hethaeorum: Food Production in Hittite Asia Minor*. AOS 55. New Haven: American Oriental Society.

———. 1997a. "Hittite Laws." Pp. 213–47 in *Law Collections from Mesopotamia and Asia Minor*, edited by Martha T. Roth. WAW 6. 2nd ed. Atlanta: Scholars Press.

———. 1997b. "Hittites." *OEANE* 3:84–88.

———. 1998. *Hittite Myths*. Edited by Gary M. Beckman. 2nd ed. WAW 2. Atlanta: Scholars Press.

———. 2009. *Letters from the Hittite Kingdom*. Edited by Gary M. Beckman. WAW 15. Atlanta: Society of Biblical Literature.

———. 2013. "'The King's Speech': Royal Rhetorical Language." Pp. 137–53 in *Beyond Hatti: A Tribute to Gary Beckman*, edited by Billie Jean Collins and Piotr Michalowski. Atlanta: Lockwood.

Hoftijzer, Jacob, and Karel Jongeling, eds. 1995. *Dictionary of the North-West Semitic Inscriptions*. HdO 1/21. Leiden: Brill.

Hoftijzer, Jacob, and G. van der Kooij. 1976. *Aramaic Texts from Deir 'Alla*. DMOA 19. Leiden: Brill.

Hoglund, Kenneth G. 1992. *Achaemenid Imperial Administration in Syria-Palestine and the Missions of Ezra and Nehemiah*. Society of Biblical Literature Dissertation Series 125. Atlanta: Scholars Press.

Holladay, John S. 1970. "Assyrian Statecraft and the Prophets of Israel." *Harvard Theological Review* 63:29–51.

———. 1995. "The Kingdoms of Israel and Judah: Political and Economic Centralization in the Iron IIA–B (CA. 1000–750 BCE). Pp. 368–98 in *The Archaeology of Society in the Holy Land*, edited by Thomas E. Levy. London: Leicester University Press.

———. 1997. "Four-Room House." *OEANE* 2:337–42.

———. 2006. "Hezekiah's Tribute, Long-Distance Trade, and the Wealth of Nations ca. 1000–600 BC: A New Perspective." Pp. 309–31 in *Confronting the Past: Archaeological and Historical Essays on Ancient Israel in Honor of William G. Dever*, edited by Seymour Gitin, J. Edward Wright, and J. P. Dessel. Winona Lake, IN: Eisenbrauns.

———. 2009. "How Much Is That in . . . ? Monetization, Money, and Royal States and Empires." Pp. 207–22 in *Exploring the Longue Durée: Essays in Honor of Lawrence E. Stager*, edited by J. David Schloen. Winona Lake, IN: Eisenbrauns.

———. 2014. "From Bandit to King: David's Time in the Negev and the Transformation of a Tribal Entity into a Nation State." Pp. 31–46 in *Unearthing the Wilderness: Studies on the History and Archaeology of the Negev and Edom in the Iron Age*, edited by Juan Manuel Tebes. ANESSup 45. Leuven: Peeters.

Holland, Gary, and Marina Zorman. 2007. *The Tale of Zalpa: Myth, Morality and Coherence in a Hittite Narrative*. Series Hethaea 6, Studia Mediterranea 19. Pavia: Italian University Press.

Holloway, S. W. 2002. *Aššur Is King! Aššur Is King! Religion in the Exercise of Power in the Neo-Assyrian Empire*. CHANE 10. Leiden: Brill.

Hom, Mary Katherine Yem Hing. 2016. "Where Art Thou, O Hezekiah's Tunnel? A Biblical Scholar Considers the Archaeological and Biblical Evidence concerning the Waterworks in 2 Chronicles 32:3–4, 30 and 2 Kings 20:20." *JBL* 135:493–503.

Hong, S., J. P. Candelone, C. C. Patterson, and C. F. Boutron. 1994. "Greenland Ice Evidence of Hemispheric Lead Pollution Two Millennia Ago by Greek and Roman Civilizations." *Science* 265 (5180): 1841–43.

Hopkins, D. C. 1985. *The Highlands of Canaan: Agriculture Life in the Early Iron Age*. Vol. 3. London: Burns & Oates.

Horden, Peregrine, and Nicholas Purcell. 2000. *The Corrupting Sea: A Study of Mediterranean History*. Malden, MA: Blackwell.

Hornung, Erik. 1992. "The Rediscovery of Akhenaten and His Place in Religion." *JARCE* 29:43–49.

———. 1999. *Akhenaten and the Religion of Light*. Translated by David Lorton. Ithaca, NY: Cornell University Press.

Horowitz, Wayne. 2011. *Mesopotamian Cosmic Geography*. MC 8. Winona Lake, IN: Eisenbrauns.

Horowitz, Wayne, and Takayoshi Oshima. 2007. "Hazor 15: A Letter Fragment from Hazor." *IEJ* 57:34–40.

———. 2010. "Hazor 16: Another Administrative Docket from Hazor." *IEJ* 60:129–32.

Horowitz, Wayne, Takayoshi Oshima, and Seth Sanders. 2006. *Cuneiform in Canaan: Cuneiform Sources from the Land of Israel in Ancient Times*. Jerusalem: Israel Exploration Society.

Horowitz, Wayne, Takayoshi Oshima, and A. Winitzer. 2010. "Hazor 17: Another Clay Liver Model." *IEJ* 60:133–45.

Horowitz, Wayne, Takayoshi Oshima, and Filip Yukosavovic. 2012. "Hazor 18: Fragments of a Cuneiform Law Collection from Hazor." *IEJ* 62:158–76.

Horowitz, Wayne, and Aaron Shaffer. 1992a. "An Administrative Tablet from Hazor: A Preliminary Edition." *IEJ* 42:21–33.

———. 1992b. "A Fragment of a Letter from Hazor." *IEJ* 42:165–66.

———. 1993. "Additions and Corrections to 'An Administrative Tablet from Hazor: A Preliminary Edition.'" *IEJ* 42:167.

Houston, Walter J. 2004. "Was There a Social Crisis in the Eighth Century?" Pp. 130–49 in *In Search of Pre-Exilic Israel*, edited by John Day. London: T&T Clark.

———. 2008. *Contending for Justice: Ideologies and Theologies of Social Justice in the Old Testament*. Rev. ed. London: T&T Clark.

Hübner, Ulrich. 2014. "The Development of Monetary Systems in Palestine during the Achaemenid and Hellenistic Era." Pp. 159–83 in *Money as God? The Monetization of the Market and the Impact on Religion, Politics, Law and Ethics*, edited by Jürgen von Hagen and Michael Welker. Cambridge: Cambridge University Press.

Huddlestun, John R. 1996. "'Who Is This That Rises Like the Nile?' A Comparative Study of the River Nile in Ancient Egypt and the Hebrew Bible." PhD dissertation, University of Michigan.

Hudson, Michael. 2000. "How Interest Rates Were Set, 2500 BC–1000 AD: Máš, Tokos and Fœnus as Metaphors for Interest Accruals." *JESHO* 43:132–61.

Huehnergard, John. 1989. "Remarks on the Classification of the Northwest Semitic Languages." Pp. 282–93 in *The Balaam Text from Deir 'Alla Reevaluated: Proceedings of the International Symposium Held at Leiden, 21–24 August 1989*, edited by J. Hoftijzer and G. van der Kooij. Leiden: Brill.

———. 2012. *An Introduction to Ugaritic*. Peabody, MA: Hendrickson.

Huffmon, Herbert B. 1997. "The Expansion of Prophecy in the Mari Archives: New Texts, New Readings, New Information." Pp. 7–22 in *Prophecy and Prophets: The Diversity of Contemporary Issues in Scholarship*, edited by Yehoshua Gitay. Semeia Studies 33. Atlanta: Scholars Press.

———. 2000. "A Company of Prophets: Mari, Assyria, Israel." Pp. 47–70 in *Prophecy in Its Ancient Near Eastern Context: Mesopotamian, Biblical, and Arabian Perspectives*, edited by Martti Nissinen. SymS 13. Atlanta: Society of Biblical Literature.

Hummel, Bradford S. 2000. "Copper." P. 278 in *Eerdmans Dictionary of the Bible*, edited by David Noel Freedman. Grand Rapids: Eerdmans.

Hundley, Michael B. 2011. *Keeping Heaven on Earth: Safeguarding the Divine Presence in the Priestly Tabernacle*. FAT 2/50. Tübingen: Mohr Siebeck.

———. 2013a. *God in Dwellings: Temples and Divine Presence in the Ancient Near East*. WAW Supplement Series 3. Atlanta: Society of Biblical Literature.

———. 2013b. "Here a God, There a God: An Examination of the Divine in Ancient Mesopotamia." *AoF* 40:68–107.

Hunger, Hermann. 1992. *Astrological Reports to Assyrian Kings*. SAA 8. Helsinki: Helsinki University Press.

Hunt, Chris O., David D. Gilbertson, and Hwedi A. El-Rishi. 2007. "An 8000-Year History of Landscape, Climate, and Copper Exploitation in the Middle East: The Wadi Faynan and the Wadi Dana National Reserve in Southern Jordan." *JAS* 34 (8): 1306–38.

Hurowitz, Victor. 1992. *I Have Built You an Exalted House: Temple Building in the Bible in Light of Mesopotamian and West Semitic Writings*. JSOTSup 115. Sheffield: JSOT Press.

———. 1994. "Inside Solomon's Temple." *Bible Review* 10:24–37, 50.

———. 2008. "Toward an Image of the 'Wise Man' in Akkadian Writings." Pp. 64–94 in *Scribes, Sages, and Seers: The Sage in the Eastern Mediterranean World*, edited by Leo G. Perdue. FRLANT 219. Göttingen: Vandenhoeck & Ruprecht.

Hutter, Manfred. 2011. "'Annalen,' 'Gebete,' 'Erzählungen,' 'Ritualtexte,' und anderes: Wie haben Hethiter ihre Literatur kategorisiert?" Pp. 111–34 in *Was sind Genres? Nicht-abendländische Kategorisierungen von Gattungen*, edited by Stephan Conermann and Amr El Hawary. Berlin: EB-Verlag.

Ikeda, Yutaka. 1999. "Looking from Til Barsip on the Euphrates: Assyria and the West in Ninth and Eighth Centuries B.C." Pp. 271–93 in *Priests and Officials in the Ancient Near East: Papers of the Second Colloquium on the Ancient Near East— the City and Its Life Held at the Middle Eastern Culture Center in Japan (Mitaka, Tokyo), March 22–24, 1996*, edited by Kazuko Watanabe. Heidelberg: Universitätsverlag C. Winter.

Ikram, Salima. 1989. "Domestic Shrines and the Cult of the Royal Family at el-ʿAmarna." *JEA* 75:89–101.

Ilan, D. 1995. "The Dawn of Internationalism: The Middle Bronze Age." Pp. 297–319 in *The Archaeology of Society in the Holy Land*, edited by Thomas E. Levy. London: Leicester University Press.

Inomata, Takeshi, and Lawrence S. Coben. 2006. "Overture: An Invitation to the Archaeological Theater." Pp. 11–44 in *Archaeology of Performance: Theaters of Power, Community, and Politics*, edited by Takeshi Inomata and Lawrence S. Coben. Lanham, MD: Altamira.

Irvine, S. A. 2001. "The Rise of the House of Jehu." Pp. 114–18 in *The Land That I Will Show You: Essays on the History and Archaeology of the Ancient Near East in Honor of J. Maxwell Miller*, edited by J. Andrew Dearman and M. Patrick Graham. JSOTSup 343. Sheffield: Sheffield Academic Press.

Israel Antiquities Authority. 2015. "Has the Acra from 2,000 Years Ago Been Found?" http://mfa.gov.il /MFA/IsraelExperience/History/Pages/Has-the -Acra-from-2000-years-ago-been-found-3-Nov -2015.aspx.

Issar, A., and M. Zohar. 2004. *Climate Change— Environment and Civilization in the Middle East*. Berlin: Springer.

Isserlin, B. S. J. 1998. *The Israelites*. New York: Thames & Hudson.

Jackson, Kent P. 1989. "The Language of the Mesha Inscription." Pp. 96–130 in *Studies in the Mesha Inscription and Moab*, edited by J. Andrew Dearman. ABS 2. Atlanta: Scholars Press.

Jacobsen, Thorkild. 1946. "Sumerian Mythology: A Review Article." *JNES* 5:128–52.

———. 1968. "The Battle between Marduk and Tiamat." *JAOS* 88 (1): 104–8.

———. 1989. "The Mesopotamian Temple Plan and the Kitîtum Temple." *ErIsr* 20:73*–91*.

———. 1990. "Notes on Ekur." *ErIsr* 21:40*–47*.

James, Frances W., and Patrick E. McGovern. 1993. *The Late Bronze Egyptian Garrison at Beth Shan: A Study of Levels VII and VIII*. Vol. 1. Philadelphia: The University Museum, University of Pennsylvania.

Jamison-Drake, David W. 1991. *Scribes and Schools in Monarchic Judah: A Socio-Archaeological Approach*. JSOTSup 109. Sheffield: Almond.

Janeway, Brian. 2017. *Sea Peoples of the Northern Levant? Aegean-Style Pottery from Early Iron Age Tell Tayinat*. Studies in the Archaeology and History of the Levant 7. Winona Lake, IN: Eisenbrauns.

Janowski, Bernd. 2001. "Der Himmel auf Erden: Zur kosmologischen Bedeutung des Tempels in der Umwelt Israels." Pp. 229–60 in *Das biblische Weltbild und seine altorientalischen Kontexte*, edited by Bernd Janowski and Beate Ego. FAT 32. Tübingen: Mohr Siebeck.

Janowski, Bernd, Klaus Koch, and Gernot Wilhelm, eds. 1993. *Religionsgeschichtliche Beziehungen zwischen Kleinasien, Nordsyrien und dem Alten Testament*. OBO 129. Freiburg: Universitätsverlag; Göttingen: Vandenhoeck & Ruprecht.

Janzen, Waldemar. 1972. *Mourning Cry and Woe-Oracle*. BZAW 125. Berlin: de Gruyter.

Jepsen, A. 1941–44. "Israel und Damaskus." *Archiv für Orientforschung* 14:153–72.

Joannès, Francis. 1995. "Private Commerce and Banking in Achaemenid Babylonia." *CANE* 3:1475–85.

Jobes, Karen H., and Moisés Silva. 2015. *Invitation to the Septuagint*. 2nd ed. Grand Rapids: Baker Academic.

Joffe, Alexander H. 1998. "Alcohol and Social Complexity in Ancient Western Asia." *Current Anthropology* 39:297–322.

———. 2002. "The Rise of Secondary States in the Iron Age Levant." *JESHO* 45:425–67.

Johnson, Raymond W. 1998. "Monuments and Monumental Art under Amenhotep III: Evolution and Meaning." Pp. 63–94 in *Amenhotep III: Perspectives on His Reign*, edited by David O'Connor and Eric Cline. Ann Arbor: University of Michigan Press.

Johnston, Philip S. 2002. *Shades of Sheol: Death and Afterlife in the Old Testament*. Downers Grove, IL: InterVarsity.

———. 2009. "Faith in Isaiah." Pp. 104–21 in *Interpreting Isaiah: Issues and Approaches*, edited by David G. Firth and H. G. M. Williamson. Downers Grove, IL: InterVarsity.

Johnston, Sarah. 2004. *Religions of the Ancient World: A Guide*. Cambridge, MA: Belknap Press of Harvard University Press.

Jones, A. H. M. 1964. *The Later Roman Empire 284–602*. 2 vols. Oxford: Oxford University Press.

Jones, Sian. 1997. *The Archaeology of Ethnicity*. London: Routledge.

Jursa, Michael. 2010. *Aspects of the Economic History of Babylonia in the First Millennium BC: Economic Geography, Economic Mentalities, Agriculture, the Use of Money and the Problem of Economic Growth*. AOAT 377. Münster: Ugarit-Verlag.

———. 2011. "Cuneiform Writing in Neo-Babylonian Temple Communities." Pp. 184–204 in *The Oxford Handbook of Cuneiform Culture*, edited by Karen Radner and Eleanor Robson. Oxford: Oxford University Press.

Kagen, Elisa, et al. 2011. "Intrabasin Paleoearthquake and Quiescence Correlation of the Late Holocene Dead Sea." *Journal of Geophysical Research* 116:1–27.

Kahn, Dan'el. 2008. "Some Remarks on the Foreign Policy of Psammetichus II in the Levant (595–589 BC)." *Journal of Egyptian History* 1:139–57.

Kamlah, Jens, ed. 2012. *Temple Building and Temple Cult: Architecture and Cultic Paraphernalia of Temples in the Levant (2.–1. Mill. B.C.E.)*. Wiesbaden: Harrassowitz.

Kang, Sa-Moon. 1989. *Divine War in the Old Testament and in the Ancient Near East*. BZAW 177. New York: de Gruyter.

Kaniastry, Krzysztof, and Fran H. Norris. 2004. "Social Support in the Aftermath of Disasters, Catastrophes, and Acts of Terrorism: Altruistic, Overwhelmed, Uncertain, Antagonistic, and Patriotic Communities." Pp. 200–229 in *Bioterrorism: Psychological and Public Health Interventions*, edited by Robert J. Ursano, Ann E. Norwood, and Carol S. Fullerton. Cambridge: Cambridge University Press.

Kaniewski, D., E. Paulissen, E. Van Campo, H. Weiss, T. Otto, J. Bretschneider, and K. Van Lerberghe. 2010. "Late Second–Early First Millennium BC Abrupt Climate Changes in Coastal Syria and Their Possible Significance for the History of the Eastern Mediterranean." *Quaternary Research* 74:207–15.

Kaniewski, D. E., E. Van Campo, J. Guiot, S. Le Burel, T. Otto, and C. Baeteman. 2013. "Environmental Roots of the Late Bronze Age Crisis." http://journals.plos.org/plosone/article?id=10.1371/journal.pone.0071004.

Kaplan, Philip. 2010. "Cross-Cultural Contacts among Mercenary Communities in Saite and Persian Egypt." *Mediterranean Historical Review* 18:1–31.

Karageorghis, Vassos. 1982. *Cyprus from the Stone Age to the Romans*. London: Thames & Hudson.

———. 1995. "Relations between Cyprus and Egypt, Second Intermediate Period and XVIIIth Dynasty." *ÄL* 5:73–79.

Karageorghis, Vassos, and Jean des Gagniers. 1974. *La céramique chypriote de style figuré: Age du fer (1050–500 a.v. J.-C.)*. Rome: Ateneo & Bizzarri.

Katz, J. 2009. *The Archaeology of Cult in Middle Bronze Age Canaan: The Sacred Area at Tel Haror, Israel*. Gorgias Dissertations, Near East 40. Piscataway, NJ: Gorgias.

Kaufmann, Yehezkel. 1953. *The Biblical Account of the Conquest of Canaan*. Jerusalem: Magnes.

———. 1960. *The Religion of Israel: From Its Beginnings to the Babylonian Exile*. Translated by Moshe Greenberg. Chicago: University of Chicago Press.

Keefer, Donald K. 2002. "Investigating Landslides Caused by Earthquakes: A Historical Review." *Surveys in Geophysics* 23:473–510.

Keel, Othmar. 1977. *Jahwe-Visionen und Siegelkunst*. Stuttgarter Bibelstudien 84. Stuttgart: Katholisches Bibelwerk.

———. 1978a. *Jahwes Entgegnung an Ijob: Eine Deutung von Ijob 38–41 vor dem Hintergrund der zeitgenössischen Bildkunst*. FRLANT 121. Göttingen: Vandenhoeck & Ruprecht.

———. 1978b. *The Symbolism of the Biblical World: Ancient Near Eastern Iconography and the Book of Psalms*. Translated by Timothy J. Hallett. New York: Seabury. Reprint, Winona Lake, IN: Eisenbrauns, 1997.

———. 1992a. *Das Recht der Bilder gesehen zu werden: Drei Fallstudien zur Methode der Interpretation altorientalischer Bilder*. OBO 122. Freiburg: Universitätsverlag; Göttingen: Vandenhoeck & Ruprecht.

———. 1992b. "Iconography and the Bible." *ABD* 3:358–74.

———. 1994. *Song of Songs: A Continental Commentary*. Translated by Frederick J. Gaiser. Minneapolis: Fortress.

———. 1995. *Corpus der Stempelsiegel-Amulette aus Palästina/Israel: Von den Anfängen bis zur Perserzeit: Einleitung*. OBOSA 10. Göttingen: Vandenhoeck & Ruprecht.

———. 1997. *Corpus der Stempelsiegel-Amulette aus Palästina/Israel: Von den Anfängen bis zur Perserzeit: Katalog Band I: Von Tell Abu Farağ bis ʿAtlit.* OBOSA 13. Göttingen: Vandenhoeck & Ruprecht.

———. 1998. *Goddesses and Trees, New Moon and Yahweh: Ancient Near Eastern Art and the Hebrew Bible.* JSOTSup 261. Sheffield: Sheffield Academic Press.

———. 2010a. *Corpus der Stempelsiegel-Amulette aus Palästina/Israel: Von den Anfängen bis zur Perserzeit: Katalog Band II: Von Bahan bis Tell Eton.* OBOSA 29. Göttingen: Vandenhoeck & Ruprecht.

———. 2010b. *Corpus der Stempelsiegel-Amulette aus Palästina/Israel: Von den Anfängen bis zur Perserzeit: Katalog Band III: Von Tell el-Farʿa Nord bis Tell el-Fir.* OBOSA 31. Göttingen: Vandenhoeck & Ruprecht.

———. 2013. *Corpus der Stempelsiegel-Amulette aus Palästina/Israel: Von den Anfängen bis zur Perserzeit: Katalog Band IV: Von Tel Gamma bis Chirbet Husche.* OBOSA 33. Göttingen: Vandenhoeck & Ruprecht.

———. 2017. *Corpus der Stempelsiegel-Amulette aus Palästina/Israel: Von den Anfängen bis zur Perserzeit: Katalog Band IV: Von Tel el-ʿIdham bis Tel Kitan.* OBOSA 35. Göttingen: Vandenhoeck & Ruprecht.

Keel, Othmar, and Max Küchler. 1982. *Orte und Landschaften der Bibel: Ein Handbuch und Studien-Reiseführer zum Heiligen Land*, vol. 2, *Der Süden.* Zurich: Benziger; Göttingen: Vandenhoeck & Ruprecht.

Keel, Othmar, and A. Mazar. 2009. "Iron Age Seals and Seal Impressions from Tel Reḥov." *ErIsr* 29:57*–69*.

Keel, Othmar, and Christoph Uehlinger. 1996. *Altorientalische Miniaturkunst: Die ältesten visuellen Massenkommunikationsmittel; Ein Blick in die Sammlungen des Biblischen Instituts der Universitat Freiburg Schweiz.* 2nd ed. Freiburg: Universitätsverlag; Gottingen: Vandenhoeck & Ruprecht.

———. 1998. *Gods, Goddesses, and Images of God in Ancient Israel.* Translated by Thomas H. Trapp. Minneapolis: Fortress.

———. 2010. *Göttinnen, Götter und Gottessymbole: Neue Erkenntnisse zur Religionsgeschichte Kanaans und Israels aufgrund bislang unerschlossener ikonographischer Quellen.* 7th ed. Fribourg: Universitätsverlag.

Keimer, Kyle H. 2011. "The Socioeconomic Impact of Hezekiah's Preparations for Rebellion." PhD dissertation, University of California, Los Angeles.

Kelle, Brad E. 2002. "What's in a Name? Neo-Assyrian Designations for the Northern Kingdom and Their Implications for Israelite History and Biblical Interpretation." *JBL* 121:639–66.

Kelly, Thomas. 1987. "Herodotus and the Chronology of the Kings of Sidon." *BASOR* 268:39–56.

Kemp, Barry J. 1977. "The City of El-Amarna as a Source for the Study of Urban Society in Ancient Egypt." *World Archaeology* 9 (2): 123–39.

———. 2000. "Soil (Including Mud-Brick Architecture)." Pp. 78–103 in *Ancient Egyptian Materials and Technology*, edited by Paul T. Nicholson and Ian Shaw. Cambridge: Cambridge University Press.

———. 2012. *The City of Akhenaten and Nefertiti: Amarna and Its People.* London: Thames & Hudson.

Kempinsky, Aharon, and Ronny Reich, eds. 1992. *The Architecture of Ancient Israel: From the Prehistoric to the Persian Periods.* Jerusalem: Israel Exploration Society.

Ken-Tor, Revital, et al. 2001. "High Resolution Geological Record of Historic Earthquakes in the Dead Sea Basin." *Journal of Geophysical Research* 106:2221–34.

Kern, Paul Bentley. 1999. *Ancient Siege Warfare.* Bloomington: Indiana University Press.

Kessler, Rainer. 2008. *The Social History of Ancient Israel: An Introduction.* Translated by Linda Maloney. Philadelphia: Fortress.

Khazanov, Anatoly. 1994. *Nomads and the Outside World.* 2nd ed. Translated by Julia Crookenden. Madison: University of Wisconsin Press.

Kilchör, Benjamin. 2015. *Mosetora und Jahwetora: Das Verhältnis von Deuteronomium 12–26 zu Exodus, Leviticus und Numeri.* Beihefte zur Zeitschrift für Altorientalische und Biblische Rechtsgeschichte 21. Wiesbaden: Harrassowitz.

Killebrew, Ann E. 1999. "Late Bronze and Iron I Cooking Pots in Canaan: A Typological, Technological, and Functional Study." Pp. 83–127 in *Archaeology, History and Culture in Palestine and the Near East: Essays in Memory of Albert E. Glock*, edited by Tomis Kapitan. ASOR Books 3. Atlanta: Scholars Press.

———. 2005. *Biblical Peoples and Ethnicity: An Archaeological Study of Egyptians, Canaanites, Philistines, and early Israel 1300–1100 B.C.E.* ABS 9. Atlanta: Society of Biblical Literature.

Killebrew, Ann E., and Gunnar Lehmann, eds. 2013. *The Philistines and Other "Sea Peoples" in Text and Archaeology.* ABS 15. Atlanta: Society of Biblical Literature.

King, Philip J. 1983. *American Archaeology in the Mideast: A History of the American Schools of Oriental Research.* Philadelphia: American Schools of Oriental Research.

King, Philip J., and Lawrence E. Stager. 2001. *Life in Biblical Israel.* Louisville: Westminster John Knox.

Kirch, Patrick V. 2001. "Polynesian Feasting in Ethnohistoric, Ethnographic, and Archaeological

Contexts: A Comparison of Three Societies." Pp. 168–84 in *Feasts: Archaeological and Ethnographic Perspectives on Food, Politics, and Power*, edited by Michael Dietler and Brian Hayden. Washington, DC: Smithsonian Institution Press.

Kislev, Mordechai E., Anat Hartmann, and Ofer Bar-Yosef. 2006a. "Early Domesticated Fig in the Jordan Valley." *Science* 312:1372–74.

———. 2006b. "Response to Comment on 'Early Domesticated Fig in the Jordan Valley.'" *Science* 314:1683b.

Kitchen, Kenneth A. 1968–90. *Ramesside Inscriptions: Historical and Biographical*. 8 vols. Malden, MA: Blackwell.

———. 1979. "Egypt, Ugarit, Qatna and Covenant." *UF* 11:453–64.

———. 1982. *Pharaoh Triumphant: The Life and Times of Ramesses II*. Monumenta Hannah Sheen Dedicata II. Mississauga, ON: Benben.

———. 1986. *The Third Intermediate Period in Egypt 1100–650 BC*. 2nd ed. Oxford: Aris & Phillips.

———. 1993a. "Genesis 12–50 in the Near Eastern World." Pp. 67–92 in *He Swore an Oath: Biblical Themes from Genesis 12–50*, edited by Richard S. Hess, Philip E. Satterthwaite, and Gordon J. Wenham. 2nd ed. Grand Rapids: Baker; Carlisle: Paternoster.

———. 1993b. "New Directions in Biblical Archaeology: Historical and Biblical Aspects." Pp. 34–52 in *Biblical Archaeology Today, 1990: Proceedings of the Second International Congress on Biblical Archaeology; Jerusalem, June–July 1990*, edited by Avraham Biran and Joseph Aviram. Jerusalem: Israel Exploration Society.

———. 1995. *The Third Intermediate Period (1100–650 B.C.)*. Reprint, Warminster: Aris & Phillips.

———. 1998. "The Patriarchs Revisited: A Reply to Dr. Ronald S. Hendel." *NEASB* 43:49–58.

———. 1999. *Poetry of Ancient Egypt*. Jorsered: Paul Åtröms Förlag.

———. 2003a. "Egyptian Interventions in the Levant in Iron Age II." Pp. 113–32 in *Symbiosis, Symbolism, and the Power of the Past: Canaan, Ancient Israel, and Their Neighbors from the Late Bronze Age through Roman Palaestina*, edited by William G. Dever and Seymour Gitin. Winona Lake, IN: Eisenbrauns.

———. 2003b. *On the Reliability of the Old Testament*. Grand Rapids: Eerdmans.

———. 2005. "Chronology." Pp. 181–88 in *Dictionary of the Old Testament: Historical Books*, edited by Bill T. Arnold and H. G. M. Williamson. Downers Grove, IL: InterVarsity.

———. 2008. *Ramesside Inscriptions: Translated and Annotated Translations*, vol. 5: *Setnakht, Ramesses III, and Contemporaries*. London: Blackwell.

Kitchen, Kenneth A., and Paul J. A. Lawrence. 2012. *Treaty, Law and Covenant in the Ancient Near East*. 3 vols. Wiesbaden: Harrassowitz.

Kleber, Kristin. 2011. "Neither Slave nor Truly Free: The Status of the Dependents of Babylonian Temple Households." Pp. 101–11 in *Slaves and Households in the Near East*, edited by Laura Culbertson. OIS 7. Chicago: University of Chicago Press.

Kleiman, S., Y. Gadot, and O. Lipschits. 2016. "A Snapshot of the Destruction Layer of Tell Zakarīye/Azekah Seen against the Backdrop of the Final Days of the Late Bronze Age." *ZDPV* 132:105–33.

Klein, Nancy L. 2016. "How Buildings Were Constructed." Pp. 105–20 in *A Companion to Greek Architecture*, edited by Margaret A. Miles. Chichester: Blackwell.

Klengel-Brandt, E., and N. Cholidis. 2006. *Die Terrakotten von Babylon im Vorderasiatischen Museum in Berlin. I. Die Anthropomorphen Figuren*. Wissenschaftliche Veröffentlichungen der deutschen Orient-Gesellschaft 115. Saarwellingen: Saarländische Druckerei.

Kletter, Raz. 1996. *The Judean Pillar-Figurines and the Archaeology of Asherah*. British Archaeological Reports International Series 636. Oxford: British Archaeological Reports.

———. 1998. *Economic Keystones: The Weight System of the Kingdom of Judah*. JSOTSup 276. Sheffield: Sheffield Academic Press.

———. 2002. "People without Burials? The Lack of Iron I Burials in the Central Highlands of Palestine." *IEJ* 52:28–48.

———. 2004. "Chronology and United Monarchy: A Methodological Review." *ZDPV* 120:13–54.

———. 2014. "In the Footsteps of Bagira: Ethnicity, Archaeology, and 'Iron Age I Ethnic Israel.'" *Approaching Religion* 4 (2): 2–15.

Klingbeil, Gerald A. 1996. "La unción de Aaron: Un estudio de Lev. 8:12 en su contexto veterotestamentario y antiguo cercano oriental." *Theologika* 11:64–83.

———. 1998. *A Comparative Study of the Ritual of Ordination as Found in Leviticus 8 and Emar 369*. Lewiston, NY: Edwin Mellen.

———. 2007. *Bridging the Gap: Ritual and Ritual Texts in the Bible*. BBRSup 1. Winona Lake, IN: Eisenbrauns.

———. 2008. "'Between North and South': The Archaeology of Religion in Late Bronze Age Palestine and the Period of the Settlement." Pp. 111–50 in *Critical Issues in Early Israelite History*, edited by Richard S. Hess, Gerald A. Klingbeil, and Paul J. Ray Jr. BBRSup 3. Winona Lake, IN: Eisenbrauns.

Klingbeil, Martin. 1999. *Yahweh Fighting from Heaven: God as Warrior and as God of Heaven in the Hebrew Psalter and Ancient Near Eastern*

Iconography. OBO 169. Fribourg: University Press; Göttingen: Vandenhoeck & Ruprecht.

Klinger, Jörg. 2012. "Literarische sumerische Texte aus den hethitischen Archiven aus überlieferungsgeschichtlicher Sicht I." Pp. 79–93 in *Palaeography and Scribal Practices in Syro-Palestine and Anatolia in the Late Bronze Age*, edited by Elena Devecchi. Publications de l'Institut Historique-Archéologique de Stamboul 119. Leiden: Nederlands Instituut voor het Nabije Oosten.

Kloner, Amos. 2004. "Iron Age Burial Caves in Jerusalem and Its Vicinity." *Bulletin of the Anglo-Israel Archeological Society* 19–20:95–118.

Kloos, Carola. 1986. *Yhwh's Combat with the Sea: A Canaanite Tradition in the Religion of Ancient Israel*. Amsterdam: van Oorschot; Leiden: Brill.

Knabb, Kyle, et al. 2014. "Patterns of Iron Age Mining and Settlement in Jordan's Faynan District: The Wadi al-Jariya Survey in Context." Pp. 577–625 in *New Insights into the Iron Age Archaeology of Edom, Southern Jordan*, vol. 2, edited by Thomas E. Levy, Mohammad Najjar, and Erez Ben-Yosef. Los Angeles: UCLA Cotsen Institute of Archaeology Press.

Knapp, A. Bernard. 2013. *The Archaeology of Cyprus: From Earliest Prehistory through the Bronze Age*. Cambridge World Archaeology. Cambridge: Cambridge University Press.

Knapp, Andrew. 2012. "Royal Apologetic in the Ancient Near East." PhD dissertation, Johns Hopkins University.

———. 2015. *Royal Apologetic in the Ancient Near East*. WAW Supplement Series 4. Atlanta: Society of Biblical Literature.

Knauf, Ernst Axel. 2001. "Shoshenq at Megiddo." *Biblische Notizen* 31:107–8.

Knight, Douglas A. 2011. *Law, Power, and Justice in Ancient Israel*. Library of Ancient Israel. Louisville: Westminster John Knox.

Knoppers, Gary N. 2006a. "Revisiting the Samarian Question in the Persian Period." Pp. 265–89 in *Judah and the Judeans in the Persian Period*, edited by Oded Lipschits and Manfred Oeming. Winona Lake, IN: Eisenbrauns.

———. 2006b. "The Demise of Jerusalem, the De-Urbanization of Judah, and the Ascent of Benjamin: Reflections on Oded Lipschits' *The Fall and Rise of Jerusalem*." Pp. 18–27 in "In Conversation with Oded Lipschits, *The Fall and Rise of Jerusalem*," edited by D. Vanderhooft. *Journal of Hebrew Scriptures* 7, article 2. http://www.jhsonline.org/Articles/article_63.pdf.

———. 2009. "Ethnicity, Genealogy, Geography, and Change: The Judean Communities of Babylon and Jerusalem in the Story of Ezra." Pp. 147–71 in *Community Identity in Judean Historiography: Biblical and Comparative Perspectives*, edited by Gary N. Knoppers and Kenneth A. Ristau. Winona Lake, IN: Eisenbrauns.

———. 2011. "Exile, Return and Diaspora: Expatriates and Repatriates in Late Biblical Literature." Pp. 29–61 in *Texts, Contexts and Readings in Postexilic Literature: Explorations into Historiography and Identity Negotiation in Hebrew Bible and Related Texts*, edited by Louis Jonker. FAT 2/53. Tübingen: Mohr Siebeck.

Koch, Ulla Susanne. 2011. "Sheep and Sky: Systems of Divinatory Interpretation." Pp. 447–69 in *The Oxford Handbook of Cuneiform Culture*, edited by Karen Radner and Eleanor Robson. Oxford: Oxford University Press.

Kochavi, Moshe. 1993. "Zeror, Tel." *NEAEHL* 4:1524–26.

Köckert, Matthias. 2010. "Yhwh in the Northern and Southern Kingdom." Pp. 357–97 in *One God—One Cult—One Nation: Archaeological and Biblical Perspectives*, edited by Reinhard G. Kratz and Hermann Spieckermann. BZAW 405. Berlin: de Gruyter.

Koepf-Taylor, Laurel W. 2013. *Give Me Children or I Shall Die: Children and Communal Survival in Biblical Literature*. Minneapolis: Fortress.

Kofoed, Jens Bruun. 2005. *Text and History: Historiography and the Study of the Biblical Text*. Winona Lake, IN: Eisenbrauns.

Kogan-Zehavi, Elena. 2008. "Ashdod." *NEAEHL* 5:1573–75.

Korpel, Marjo C. A. 1990. *A Rift in the Clouds: Ugaritic and Hebrew Descriptions of the Divine*. UBL 8. Münster: Ugarit-Verlag.

Kotsonas, Antonis. 2013. "Chronology, Bronze and Iron Age." P. 1485 in *The Encyclopedia of Ancient History*, vol. 3, *Be-Co*, edited by Roger S. Bagnall, Kai Brodersen, Craige B. Champion, Andrew Erskine, and Sabine R. Huebner. Oxford: Wiley-Blackwell.

Kottmeier, Christoph, et al. 2016. "New Perspectives on Interdisciplinary Earth Science at the Dead Sea: The DESERVE Project." *Science of the Total Environment* 544:1045–58.

Kottsieper, Ingo. 2008. "The Aramaic Tradition: Ahikar." Pp. 109–24 in *Scribes, Sages, and Seers: The Sage in the Eastern Mediterranean World*, edited by Leo G. Perdue. FRLANT 219. Göttingen: Vandenhoeck & Ruprecht.

Kozloff, Arielle P. 2012. *Amenhotep III: Egypt's Radiant Pharaoh*. Cambridge: Cambridge University Press.

Kozloff, Arielle P., and Betsy M. Bryan. 1992. *Egypt's Dazzling Sun: Amenhotep III and His World*. Cleveland: Cleveland Museum of Art.

Kramer, Samuel Noah. 1968. "The 'Babel of Tongues': A Sumerian Version." *JAOS* 88 (1): 108–11.

———. 1990. "The Sage in Sumerian Literature: A Composite Portrait." Pp. 31–44 in *The Sage in Israel and the Ancient Near East*, edited by John G. Gammie and Leo G. Perdue. Winona Lake, IN: Eisenbrauns.

Kreps, Gary A. 2006. *Facing Hazards and Disasters: Understanding Human Dimensions*. Washington DC: National Academies Press.

Kruchten, Jean-Marie. 2001. "Oracles." *OEAE* 2:609–12.

Kuemmerlin-McLean, Joanne K. 1992. "Magic (OT)." *ABD* 4:468–71.

Kuhn, Thomas S. 1962. *The Structure of Scientific Revolutions*. Chicago: University of Chicago Press. Rev. ed., 1970. 50th anniversary edition, 2012.

Kuhrt, Amélie. 1983. "The Cyrus Cylinder and Achaemenid Imperial Policy." *JSOT* 25:83–97.

———. 1995. *The Ancient Near East: c. 3000–330 BC*. Vol. 2. London: Routledge.

———. 2007. *The Persian Empire*. 2 vols. London: Routledge.

Kutsko, John F. 2000. *Between Heaven and Earth: Divine Presence and Absence in the Book of Ezekiel*. BJSUCSD 7. Winona Lake, IN: Eisenbrauns.

Kynes, Will. 2015. "The Modern Scholarly Wisdom Tradition and the Threat of Pan-Sapientialism: A Case Report." Pp. 11–38 in *Was There a Wisdom Tradition? New Prospects in Israelite Wisdom Studies*, edited by Mark R. Sneed. AIL 23. Atlanta: Society of Biblical Literature.

LaBianca, Øystein S., and Randall W. Younker. 1995. "The Kingdoms of Ammon, Moab and Edom: The Archaeology of Society in the Late Bronze/Iron Age Transjordan (ca. 1400–500 BCE)." Pp. 399–415 in *The Archaeology of Society in the Holy Land*, edited by Thomas E. Levy. New York: Facts on File.

Laboury, Dimitri. 2010. *Akhénaton*. Les grands Pharaons. Paris: Pygmalion.

Lambert, David. 2016. "Honor in the Hebrew Bible." Pp. 330–33 in *Encyclopedia of the Bible and Its Reception*, vol. 12, edited by Hans-Josef Klauck et al. New York: de Gruyter.

Lambert, Wilfried G. 1960. *Babylonian Wisdom Literature*. Oxford: Oxford University Press.

———. 1974. "The Reigns of Ashurnasirpal II and Shalmaneser III: An Interpretation." *Iraq* 36:103–9.

———. 1993. "Donations of Food and Drink to the Gods in Ancient Mesopotamia." Pp. 191–201 in *Ritual and Sacrifice in the Ancient Near East: Proceedings of the International Conference Organized by the Katholieke Universiteit Leuven from the 17th to the 20th April of 1991*, edited by J. Quaegebeur. OLA 55. Leuven: Peeters.

———. 1995. "Some New Babylonian Wisdom Literature." Pp. 30–43 in *Wisdom in Ancient Israel*, edited by John Day, Robert P. Gordon, and H. G. M. Williamson. Cambridge: Cambridge University Press.

———. 2003a. "Leviathan." Paper presented at the Senior Old Testament Seminar, Cambridge University, October 29.

———. 2003b. "Leviathan in Ancient Art." Pp. 147–54 in *Shlomo: Studies in Epigraphy, Iconography, History and Archaeology in Honor of Shlomo Moussaieff*, edited by Robert Deutsch. Tel Aviv: Archaeological Center Publications.

———. 2007. *Babylonian Oracle Questions*. MC 13. Winona Lake, IN: Eisenbrauns.

Lang, Bernhard. 1985. "The Social Organization of Peasant Poverty in Biblical Israel." Pp. 83–99 in *Anthropological Approaches to the Old Testament*, edited by Bernhard Lang. Philadelphia: Fortress.

Langgut, Dafna, Israel Finkelstein, and Thomas Litt. 2013. "Climate and the Late Bronze Collapse: New Evidence from the Southern Levant." *TA* 40:149–75.

Langgut, Dafna, F. H. Newmann, M. Stein, A. Wagner, E. J. Kagan, E. Boaretto, and I. Finkelstein. 2014. "Dead Sea Pollen Record and History of Human Activity in the Judean Highlands (Israel) from the Intermediate Bronze into the Iron Ages (~2500–500 BCE)." *Palynology* 38:280–302.

Langgut, Dafna, et al. 2015. "Vegetation and Climate Changes during the Bronze and Iron Ages (~3600–600 BCE) in the Southern Levant Based on Palynological Records." *Radiocarbon* 57:217–35.

Lapp, Paul W., and Nancy L. Lapp. 1993. "Iraq el-Emir." *NEAEHL* 2:646–49.

Larsen, Mogens Trolle. 1982. "Caravans and Trade in Ancient Mesopotamia and Asia Minor." *Bulletin of the Society of Mesopotamian Studies* 4:33–45.

———. 1996. *The Conquest of Assyria: Excavations in an Antique Land, 1840–1860*. London: Routledge.

———. 2017. "Between Slavery and Freedom." Pp. 289–99 in *At the Dawn of History: Ancient Near Eastern Studies in Honour of J. N. Postgate*, edited by Yagmur Heffron, Adam Stone, and Martin Worthington. Winona Lake, IN: Eisenbrauns.

Latour, Bruno, and Peter Weibel, eds. 2002. *Iconoclash: Beyond the Image Wars in Science, Religion, and Art*. Cambridge, MA: MIT Press; Karlsruhe: ZKM Center for Art and Media.

Lauffrey, Jean. 1979. *Karnak d'Égypte: Domaine du divin*. Paris: Éditions du Centre Nationale de la Recherche Scientifique.

Lawergren, Bo, 1996. "Harfen." Pp. 39–62 in *Die Musik in Geschichte und Gegenwart*, vol. 4, edited by Laurenz Lütteken et al. 2nd ed. Kassel: Bärenreiter; Stuttgart: Metzler.

———. 1997. Mesopotamien (Musikinstrumente)." Pp. 143–71 in *Die Musik in Geschichte und*

Gegenwart, vol. 6, edited by Laurenz Lütteken et al. 2nd ed. Kassel: Bärenreiter; Stuttgart: Metzler.

———. 2003. Review of *Music in Ancient Israel and Palestine*, by Joachim Braun. *BASOR* 332:100–102.

Layard, Austen Henry. 1849a. *The Monuments of Nineveh*. London: John Murray.

———. 1849b. *Nineveh and Its Remains*. 2 vols. London: John Murray.

Leahy, Anthony. 1988. "The Earliest Dated Monument of Amasis and the End of the Reign of Apries." *JEA* 74:183–99.

———. 2001. "Sea Peoples." *OEAE* 3:257–60.

Lehmann, Gunnar. 2003. "The United Monarchy in the Countryside: Jerusalem, Judah and the Shephelah during the 10th century BCE." Pp. 117–64 in *Jerusalem in Bible and Archaeology: The First Temple Period*, edited by Andrew G. Vaughn and Ann E. Killebrew. SymS 18. Atlanta: Scholars Press.

———. 2007. *The Persian Empire: A Corpus of Sources from the Achaemenid Period*. London: Routledge.

———. 2014. "The Levant during the Persian Period." Pp. 841–51 in *The Oxford Handbook of the Archaeology of the Levant: C. 8000–332 BCE*, edited by Margreet L. Steiner and Ann E. Killebrew. Oxford: Oxford University Press.

Leichty, Erle. 1970. *The Omen Series ∕umma Izbu*. Texts from Cuneiform Sources 4. Locust Valley, NY: Augustin.

———. 2011. *The Royal Inscriptions of Esarhaddon, King of Assyria (680–669 BC)*. Royal Inscriptions of the Neo-Assyrian Period 4. Winona Lake, IN: Eisenbrauns.

Lemaire, André. 1981. "Classification des Estampilles Royale Judéennes." *ErIsr* 15:54*–60*, plate VIII.

———. 1990. "The Sage in School and Temple." Pp. 165–81 in *The Sage in Israel and the Ancient Near East*, edited by John G. Gammie and Leo G. Perdue. Winona Lake, IN: Eisenbrauns.

———. 1994. "'House of David': Restored in Moabite Inscription." *BAR* 20 (3): 30–37.

———. 1995. "Wisdom in Solomonic Historiography." Pp. 106–18 in *Wisdom in Ancient Israel: Essays in Honour of J. A. Emerton*, edited by John Day, Robert P. Gordon, and H. G. M. Williamson. Cambridge: Cambridge University Press.

———. 1996. "Zorobabel et la Judée à la lumière de l'épigraphie (fin du VIᵉ s. av. J.-C.)." *RB* 103:48–57.

———. 1998. "The Tel Dan Stela as a Piece of Royal Historiography." *JSOT* 81:3–14.

———. 2004. "Nouveau Temple de Yahô (IVᵉ s. av. J.-C.)." Pp. 265–73 in *Basel und Bibel: Collected Communications to the XVIIth Congress of the International Organization for the Study of the Old Testament, Basel 2001*, edited by Matthias

Augustin and Hermann Michael Niemann. Frankfurt am Main: Peter Lang.

———. 2007. "Administration in the 4th Century BCE Judah in Light of Epigraphy and Numismatics." Pp. 53–74 in *Judah and the Judeans in the Fourth Century B.C.E.*, edited by Oded Lipschits, Gary N. Knoppers, and Rainer Albertz. Winona Lake, IN: Eisenbrauns.

———. 2011. "New Aramaic Ostraca from Idumea and Their Historical Interpretation." Pp. 413–56 in *Judah and Judeans in the Achaemenid Period*, edited by Oded Lipschits, Gary N. Knoppers, and Manfred Oeming. Winona Lake, IN: Eisenbrauns.

———. 2012. "A Reference to the Covenant Code in 2 Kings 17:24–41?" Pp. 395–405 in *Let Us Go Up to Zion: Essays in Honour of H. G. M. Williamson on the Occasion of His Sixty-Fifth Birthday*. VTSup 153. Leiden: Brill.

Lemche, Niels Peter. 1998a. *Ancient Israel: A New History of Israelite History*. Biblical Seminar 5. Sheffield: JSOT Press.

———. 1998b. *Prelude to Israel's Past: Background and Beginnings of Israelite History and Identity*. Translated by E. F. Maniscalco. Peabody, MA: Hendrickson.

LeMon, Joel M. 2009. "Iconographic Approaches: The Iconic Structure of Psalm 17." Pp. 143–68 in *Method Matters: Essays on the Interpretation of the Hebrew Bible in Honor of David L. Petersen*, edited by Joel M. LeMon and Kent H. Richards. RBS 56. Atlanta: Society of Biblical Literature.

———. 2010. *Yahweh's Winged Form in the Psalms: Exploring Congruent Iconography and Texts*. OBO 242. Fribourg: Academic Press; Göttingen: Vandenhoeck & Ruprecht.

LeMon, Joel M., and Brent A. Strawn. 2013. "Once More, Yhwh and Company at Kuntillet ʿAjrud." *Maarav* 20:83–114, plates VI–VII.

Lemos, T. M. 2010. *Marriage Gifts and Social Change in Ancient Palestine, 1200 BCE to 200 CE*. Cambridge: Cambridge University Press.

Lenski, Gerhard. 2005. *Ecological-Evolutionary Theory: Principles and Applications*. London: Paradigm.

Levenson, Jon D. 1984. "The Temple and the World." *Journal of Religion* 64:275–98.

———. 1993. *The Death and Resurrection of the Beloved Son: The Transformation of Child Sacrifice in Judaism and Christianity*. New Haven: Yale University Press.

———. 2006. *Resurrection and the Restoration of Israel*. New Haven: Yale University Press.

Levin, Yigal. 2010. "Sheshonq I and the Negev Ḥaṣerim." *Maarav* 17:189–215.

Levine, Lee I. 1998. *Judaism and Hellenism in Antiquity: Conflict or Confluence?* Peabody, MA: Hendrickson.

———. 2005. *The Ancient Synagogue: The First Thousand Years*. 2nd ed. New Haven: Yale University Press.

———. 2012. *Visual Judaism in Late Antiquity: Historical Contexts of Jewish Art*. New Haven: Yale University Press.

Levine, Louis D. 1972. *Two Neo-Assyrian Stelae from Iran*. Toronto: Royal Ontario Museum.

Levinson, Bernard M., and Tina M. Sherman. 2016. Pp. 396–414 in *The Wiley Blackwell Companion to Ancient Israel*, edited by Susan Niditch. Malden, MA: John Wiley & Sons.

Lévi-Strauss, Claude. 1963. "The Effectiveness of Symbols." Pp. 186–206 in Claude Lévi-Strauss, *Structural Anthropology*. Translated by Claire Jacobson and Brooke Grundfest Schoepf. New York: Basic Books.

Lev-Tov, Justin. 2010. "A Plebeian Perspective on Empire Economies: Faunal Remains from Tel Miqne-Ekron, Israel." Pp. 90–104 in *Anthropological Approaches to Zooarchaeology: Colonialism, Complexity, and Animal Transformations*, edited by Douglas V. Campana, Pam J. Crabtree, Susan D. deFrance, Justin Lev-Tov, and Alice Choyke. Oxford: Oxbow Books.

Levy, Thomas E., ed. 2010a. *Historical Biblical Archaeology and the Future: The New Pragmatism*. London: Equinox.

———. 2010b. "The New Pragmatism: Integrating Anthropological, Digital, and Historical Biblical Archaeologies." Pp. 3–42 in *Historical Biblical Archaeology and the Future: The New Pragmatism*, edited by Thomas E. Levy. London: Equinox.

———. 2013. "Cyber-Archaeology and World Cultural Heritage: Insights from the Holy Land." *Bulletin of the American Academy of Arts and Sciences* 66:26–33.

Levy, Thomas E., et al. 2003. "An Iron Age Landscape in the Edomite Lowlands: Archaeological Surveys along Wadi al-Ghuwayb and Wadi al-Jariya, Jabal Hamrat Fidan, Jordan, 2002." *Annual of the Department of Antiquities of Jordan* 47:247–77.

———. 2004. "Reassessing the Chronology of Biblical Edom: New Excavations and 14C dates from Khirbat en-Nahas (Jordan)." *Antiquity* 78:865–79.

———. 2008. "High-Precision Radiocarbon Dating and Historical Biblical Archaeology in Southern Jordan." *Proceedings of the National Academy of Sciences* 105:16460–65.

———. 2014. "Excavations at Khirbat en-Nahas, 2002–2009: An Iron Age Copper Production Center in the Lowlands of Edom." Pp. 89–245 in *New Insights into the Iron Age Archaeology of Edom, Southern Jordan*, vol. 1, edited by Thomas E. Levy, Mohammed Najjar, and Erez Ben-Yosef. Los Angeles: UCLA Cotsen Institute of Archaeology Press.

Levy, Thomas E., Russell B. Adams, and Mohammad Najjar. 2001 "Jabal Hamrat Fidan." *AJA* 105:442–43.

Levy, Thomas E., Russell B. Adams, and Rula Shafiq. 1999. "The Jabal Hamrat Fidan Project: Excavations at the Wadi Fidan 40 Cemetery, Jordan." *Levant* 31:293–308.

Levy, Thomas E., Erez Ben-Yosef, and Mohammad Najjar. 2012. "New Perspectives on Iron Age Copper Production and Society in the Faynan Region, Jordan." Pp. 197–214 in *Eastern Mediterranean Metallurgy and Metal Work in the Second Millennium BC: A Conference in Honour of James D. Muhly*, edited by Vasiliki Kassianidou and George Papasavvas. Oxford: Oxbow.

———. 2014. "The Iron Age Edom Lowlands Regional Archaeology Project: Research, Design, and Methodology." Pp. 1–87 in *New Insights into the Iron Age Archaeology of Edom, Southern Jordan*, vol. 1, edited by Thomas E. Levy, Mohammad Najjar, and Erez Ben-Yosef. Los Angeles: UCLA Cotsen Institute of Archaeology Press.

Levy, Thomas E., and Thomas Higham, eds. 2005. *The Bible and Radiocarbon Dating: Archaeology, Text and Science*. London: Equinox.

Levy, Thomas E., and Augustin F. C. Holl. 2002. "Migrations, Ethnogenesis, and Settlement Dynamics: Israelites in Iron Age Canaan and Shuwa-Arabs in the Chad Basin." *Journal of Anthropological Archaeology* 21:83–118.

Levy, Thomas E., Mohammed Najjar, and Erez Ben-Yosef. 2014. *New Insights into the Iron Age Archaeology of Edom, Southern Jordan*, vols. 1–2, *Surveys, Excavations, and Research from the University of California, San Diego – Department of Antiquities of Jordan, Edom Lowlands Regional Archaeology Project (ELRAP)*. Monumenta Archaeologica 35. Los Angeles: UCLA Cotsen Institute of Archaeology Press.

Levy, Thomas E., T. Schneider, and W. H. C. Propp, eds. 2015. *Israel's Exodus in Transdisciplinary Perspective: Text, Archaeology, Culture, and Geoscience*. Quantitative Methods in the Humanities and Social Sciences. New York: Springer.

Lev-Yadun, Simcha, Gidi Ne'eman, Shahal Abbo, and Moshe A. Flaishman. 2006. "Comment on 'Early Domesticated Fig in the Jordan Valley.'" *Science* 314:1683a.

Lewis, Theodore J. 1989. *Cults of the Dead in Ancient Israel and Ugarit*. HSM 39. Atlanta: Scholars Press.

———. 2002. "How Far Can Texts Take Us? Evaluating Textual Sources for Reconstructing Ancient Israelite Beliefs about the Dead." Pp. 169–217 in *Sacred Time, Sacred Place: Archaeology and the Religion of Israel*, edited by Barry M. Gittlen. Winona Lake, IN: Eisenbrauns.

Lichtheim, Miriam. 1973–80. *Ancient Egyptian Literature: A Book of Readings*. 3 vols. Berkeley: University of California Press.

———. 1976. *Ancient Egyptian Literature.* Vol. 2. Berkeley: University of California Press.

———. 1988. *Ancient Egyptian Autobiographies Chiefly of the Middle Kingdom: A Study and Anthology.* OBO 84. Fribourg: Universitätsverlag; Göttingen: Vandenhoeck & Ruprecht.

Lieberman, Saul. 1969. *The Tosefta (the Order of Mo'ed).* New York: Jewish Theological Seminary of America.

Liebner, Uzi. 2009. *Settlement and History in Hellenistic, Roman, and Byzantine Galilee.* Texte und Studien zum antiken Judentum 127. Tübingen: Mohr Siebeck.

Liebowitz, H. 1980. "Military and Feast Scenes on Late Bronze Palestinian Ivories." *IEJ* 30:162–69.

———. 1987. "Late Bronze II Bronze Ivory Work in Palestine: Evidence of a Cultural Highpoint." *BASOR* 265:3–24.

Lipiński, Edward. 1969. "Le Ben-hadad II de la bible et l'histoire." Pp. 157–73 in *Proceedings of the Fifth World Congress of Jewish Studies*, vol. 1, edited by Pinchas Peli. Jerusalem: World Union of Jewish Studies.

———. 1973. "An Assyro-Israelite Alliance in 841/841 B.C.E.?" Pp. 273–78 in *Proceedings of the Sixth World Congress of Jewish Studies*, vol. 1, edited by Avigdor Shin'an. Jerusalem: World Union of Jewish Studies.

———. 2000. *The Aramaeans: Their Ancient History, Culture, Religion.* OLA 100. Leuven: Peeters.

———. 2006. *On the Skirts of Canaan in the Iron Age: Historical and Topographical Researches.* OLA 153. Leuven: Peeters.

Lipschits, Oded. 2003. "Demographic Changes in Judah between the Seventh and the Fifth Centuries B.C.E." Pp. 323–76 in *Judah and the Judeans in the Neo-Babylonian Period*, edited by Oded Lipschits and Joseph Blenkinsopp. Winona Lake, IN: Eisenbrauns.

———. 2005. *The Fall and Rise of Jerusalem: Judah under Babylonian Rule.* Winona Lake, IN: Eisenbrauns.

———. 2006. "Achaemenid Imperial Policy, Settlement Processes in Palestine, and the Status of Jerusalem in the Middle of the Fifth Century BCE." Pp. 19–52 in *Judah and the Judeans in the Persian Period*, edited by Oded Lipschits and Manfred Oeming. Winona Lake, IN: Eisenbrauns.

———. 2011. "Shedding New Light on the Dark Years of the 'Exilic Period': New Studies, Further Elucidation, and Some Questions regarding the Archaeology of Judah as an 'Empty Land.'" Pp. 57–90 in *Interpreting Exile: Displacements and Deportation in Biblical and Modern Contexts*, edited by Brad Kelle, Frank R. Ames, and Jacob L. Wright. AIL 10. Atlanta: Society of Biblical Literature.

———. 2015. "The Rural Economy of Judah during the Persian Period and the Settlement History of the District System." Pp. 237–64 in *The Economy of Ancient Judah in Its Historical Context*, edited by Marvin L. Miller, Ehud Ben Zvi, and Gary N. Knoppers. Winona Lake, IN: Eisenbrauns.

Lipschits, Oded, Yuval Gadot, Benjamin Arubas, and Manfred Oeming. 2011. "Palace and Village, Paradise and Oblivion: Unraveling the Riddles of Ramat Raḥel." *NEA* 74:2–49.

Lipschits, Oded, Yuval Gadot, and D. Langgut. 2012. "The Riddle of Ramat Raḥel: The Archaeology of a Royal Persian Period Edifice." *Transeuphratène* 41:57–79.

Lipschits, Oded, and Oren Tal. 2007. "The Settlement Archaeology of the Province of Judah: A Case Study." Pp. 33–52 in *Judah and the Judeans in the Fourth Century B.C.E.*, edited by Oded Lipschits, Gary N. Knoppers, and Rainer Albertz. Winona Lake, IN: Eisenbrauns.

Lipschits, Oded, and David S. Vanderhooft. 2007. "Yehud Stamp Impressions in the Fourth Century B.C.E.: A Time of Administrative Consolidation?" Pp. 75–94 in *Judah and the Judeans in the Fourth Century B.C.E.*, edited by Oded Lipschits, Gary N. Knoppers, and Rainer Albertz. Winona Lake, IN: Eisenbrauns.

———. 2011. *Yehud Stamp Impressions: A Corpus of Inscribed Stamp Impressions from the Persian and Hellenistic Periods in Judah.* Winona Lake, IN: Eisenbrauns.

Liverani, Mario. 1973. "The Amorites." Pp. 100–133 in *Peoples of Old Testament Times*, edited by Donald J. Wiseman. Oxford: Oxford University Press.

———. 1979a. "The Ideology of the Assyrian Empire." Pp. 297–317 in *Power and Propaganda: A Symposium on Ancient Empires*, edited by Mogens Trolle Larsen. Copenhagen: Akademisk Forlag.

———. 1979b. *Three Amarna Essays.* Malibu, CA: Undena.

———. 1979c. "Un ipotesi sul nome di Abramo." *Henoch* 1:9–18.

———. 1988. "The Growth of the Assyrian Empire in the Habur/Middle Euphrates." *SAAB* 2:81–98.

———. 1990. *Prestige and Interest: International Relations in the Near East ca. 1600–1100 BC.* Vol. 1. Padova: Sargon.

———. 2014a. *Israel's History and the History of Israel.* London: Routledge.

———. 2014b. "The King and His Audience." Pp. 373–86 in *From Source to History: Studies on Ancient Near Eastern Worlds and Beyond, Dedicated to Giovanni Battista Lafranchi on the Occasion of His 65th Birthday, June 23, 2014*, edited by Salvatore Gaspa et al. AOAT 412. Münster: Ugarit-Verlag.

Loewenstamm, Samuel E. 1984. "The Trembling of Nature during the Theophany." Pp. 173–89 in

Comparative Studies in Biblical and Ancient Oriental Literatures. AOAT 204. Kevelaer: Bercker & Butzon; Neukirchen-Vluyn: Neukirchener Verlag.

London, Gloria. 2000. "Women Potters of Cyprus." https://www.youtube.com/watch?v=AZZZnUBw2Xs. https://www.youtube.com/watch?v=fEphWV1x5bA.

———. 2016. *Ancient Cookware from the Levant: An Ethnoarchaeological Perspective*. Sheffield: Equinox.

London, Gloria, Frosse Egoumenidou, and Vassos Karageorghis. 1989. *Traditional Pottery in Cyprus*. Mainz: Zabern.

Long, B. O. 1997. *Planting and Reaping Albright: Politics, Ideology, and Interpreting the Bible*. University Park: Pennsylvania State University Press.

Loprieno, Antonio, ed. 1996. *Ancient Egyptian Literature: History and Forms*. PÄ 10. Leiden: Brill.

Loud, G. 1939. *The Megiddo Ivories*. OIP 52. Chicago: University of Chicago Press.

Lucas, E. C. 2012. "Daniel: Book of." Pp. 110–23 in *Dictionary of the Old Testament: Prophets*, edited by Mark J. Boda and J. Gordon McConville. Downers Grove, IL: InterVarsity.

Lundquist, John M. 1982. "The Legitimizing Role of the Temple in the Origin of the State." *Society of Biblical Literature Seminar Papers* 21:271–97.

———. 1983. "What Is a Temple?" Pp. 208–9 in *The Quest for the Kingdom of God: Studies in Honor of George E. Mendenhall*, edited by H. B. Huffmon, F. A. Spina, and A. R. W. Green. Winona Lake, IN: Eisenbrauns.

Luukko, Mikko, and Greta Van Buylaere. 2002. *The Political Correspondence of Esarhaddon*. SAA 16. Helsinki: Helsinki University Press.

Lynch, Matthew J. 2013. "First Isaiah and the Disappearance of the Gods." Paper presented at the Annual Meeting of the Society of Biblical Literature, Baltimore.

———. 2014a. "Mapping Monotheism: Modes of Monotheistic Rhetoric in the Hebrew Bible." *VT* 64:47–68.

———. 2014b. *Monotheism and Institutions in the Book of Chronicles: Temple, Priesthood, and Kingship in Post-Exilic Perspective*. FAT 2/64. Tübingen: Mohr Siebeck.

Macabuag, J. 2010. "Dissemination of Seismic Retrofitting Techniques to Rural Communities." Paper presented at the EWB–UK National Research Conference 2010, "From Small Steps to Giant Leaps . . . Putting Research into Practice," hosted by The Royal Academy of Engineering, February 19.

Maccoby, Hyam. 1999. *Ritual and Morality: The Ritual Purity System and Its Place in Judaism*. Cambridge: Cambridge University Press.

MacDonald, Burton. 1992. *The Southern Ghors and Northeast ʿArabah Archaeological Survey*. Sheffield: J. R. Collis.

———. 2000. *"East of the Jordan": Territories and Sites of the Hebrew Scriptures*. ASOR Books 6. Boston: American Schools of Oriental Research.

MacDonald, Burton, et al. 2004. *The Tafila-Busayra Archaeological Survey 1999–2001, West-Central Jordan*. Boston: American Schools of Oriental Research.

MacDonald, Nathan. 2007. "Recasting the Golden Calf: The Imaginative Potential of the Old Testament's Portrayal of Idolatry." Pp. 22–39 in *Idolatry: False Worship in the Bible, Early Judaism, and Christianity*, edited by S. C. Barton. New York: T&T Clark International.

———. 2008a. *Not Bread Alone: The Uses of Food in the Old Testament*. New York: Oxford University Press.

———. 2008b. *What Did the Ancient Israelites Eat? Diet in Biblical Times*. Grand Rapids: Eerdmans.

———. 2009. "Monotheism and Isaiah." Pp. 43–61 in *Interpreting Isaiah: Issues and Approaches*, edited by David G. Firth and H. G. M. Williamson. Nottingham: Apollos; Downers Grove, IL: IVP Academic.

———. 2012. *Deuteronomy and the Meaning of "Monotheism."* 2nd ed. FAT 2/1. Tübingen: Mohr Siebeck.

Machinist, Peter. 1983. "Assyria and Its Image in the First Isaiah." *JAOS* 103:719–37.

———. 1994. "The First Coins of Judah and Samaria: Numismatics and History in the Achaemenid and Early Hellenistic Periods." Pp. 365–80 in *Continuity and Change: Proceedings of the Last Achaemenid History Workshop, April 6–8, 1990—Ann Arbor, Michigan*, edited by Heleen Sancisi-Weerdenburg, Amélie Kuhrt, and Margaret Cool Root. Achaemenid History 8. Leiden: Nederlands Instituut voor het Nabije Oosten.

———. 1996. "William Foxwell Albright: The Man and His Work." Pp. 385–403 in *The Study of the Ancient Near East in the Twenty-First Century*, edited by Jerrold S. Cooper and Glenn M. Schwartz. Winona Lake, IN: Eisenbrauns.

Mack-Fisher, Loren R. 1990. "The Scribe (and Sage) at the Royal Court in Ugarit." Pp. 109–15 in *The Sage in Israel and the Ancient Near East*, edited by John G. Gammie and Leo G. Perdue. Winona Lake, IN: Eisenbrauns.

Macqueen, J. G. 1986. *The Hittites and Their Contemporaries in Asia Minor*. Rev. and enlarged ed. New York: Thames & Hudson.

Maeir, Aren M. 2002. "The Relations between Egypt and the Southern Levant during the Late Iron Age: The Material Evidence from Egypt." *ÄL* 12:235–46.

———. 2003a. "Does Size Count? Urban and Cultic Perspectives on the Rural Landscape during the Middle Bronze Age II." Pp. 61–69 in *The Rural Landscape of Ancient Israel*, edited by Aren M. Maeir, Shimon Dar, and Ze'ev Safrai. British Archaeological Reports International Series 1121. Oxford: Archaeopress.

———. 2003b. "A Late Bronze Age, Syrian-Style Figurine from Tell es-Safi/Gath." Pp. 197–206 in *Shlomo: Studies in Epigraphy, Iconography, History and Archaeology in Honor of Shlomo Moussaieff*, edited by Robert Deutsch. Tel Aviv: Archaeological Center Publications.

———. 2011. Review of *Critical Issues in Early Israelite History*, edited by Richard S. Hess, Gerald A. Klingbeil, and Paul J. Ray Jr. *BASOR* 361:99–101.

———. 2013a. "Israel and Judah." Pp. 3523–27 in *The Encyclopedia of Ancient History*, vol. 7, *Io-Li*, edited by Roger S. Bagnall, Kai Brodersen, Craige B. Champion, Andrew Erskine, and Sabine R. Huebner. Oxford: Wiley-Blackwell.

———. 2013b. "Philistia Transforming: Fresh Evidence from Tell eṣ-Ṣafi/Gath on the Transformational Trajectory of the Philistine Culture." Pp. 191–242 in *The Philistines and Other "Sea Peoples" in Text and Archaeology*, edited by Ann E. Killebrew and Gunnar Lehmann. ABS 15. Atlanta: Society of Biblical Literature.

———. 2013c. Review of *The Archaeology of Israelite Society in Iron Age II*, by Avraham Faust. *Review of Biblical Literature*. www.bookreviews.org.

———. 2014. "Archaeology and the Hebrew Bible." Pp. 2124–36 in *The Jewish Study Bible*, edited by Adele Berlin and Marc Zvi Brettler. 2nd ed. Oxford: Oxford University Press.

———. 2015a. "A Feast in Papua New Guinea." *NEA* 78:36–34.

———. 2015b. "Many Voices Needed." Pp. 14–15 in *40 Futures: Experts Predict What's Next for Biblical Archaeology*. Washington, DC: Biblical Archaeology Society.

———. 2016. Review of *A Biblical History of Israel*, by Iain Provan, V. Philips Long, and Tremper Longman III. *Review of Biblical Literature*. www.bookreviews.org.

———. In press. "'The Philistines Be upon Thee, Samson' (Jud. 16:20): Reassessing the Martial Nature of the Philistines—Archaeological Evidence vs. Ideological Image." In *The Aegean and the Levant at the Turn of the Bronze Age and in the Early Iron Age*, edited by L. Niesiołowski-Spanò and M. Węcowski. Wiesbaden: Harrassowitz.

Maeir, Aren M., and Shira Gur-Arieh. 2011. "Comparative Aspects of the Aramean Siege System at Tell eṣ-Ṣāfī/Gath." Pp. 227–44 in *The Fire Signals of Lachish: Studies in the Archaeology and History of Israel in the Late Bronze Age, Iron Age, and Persian Period in Honor of David Ussishkin*. Winona Lake, IN: Eisenbrauns.

Maeir, Aren M., and L. A. Hitchcock. 2016. "'And the Canaanite Was Then in the Land'? A Critical View on the 'Canaanite Enclave' in Iron I Southern Canaan." Pp. 209–26 in *Alphabets, Texts and Artifacts in the Ancient Near East: Studies Presented to Benjamin Sass*, edited by Israel Finkelstein, Christian Robin, and Thomas Römer. Paris: Van Dieren.

———. 2017a. "The Appearance, Formation, and Transformation of Philistine Culture: New Perspectives and New Finds." Pp. 149–62 in *The Sea Peoples Up-To-Date: New Research on the Migration of Peoples in the 12th Century BCE*, edited by P. Fischer. Contributions to the Chronology of the Eastern Mediterranean. Vienna: Austrian Academy of Sciences.

———. 2017b. "Rethinking the Philistines: A 2017 Perspective." Pp. 249–67 in *Rethinking Israel: Studies in the History and Archaeology of Ancient Israel in Honor of Israel Finkelstein*, edited by O. Lipschits, Y. Gadot, and M. J. Adams. Winona Lake, IN: Eisenbrauns.

Magdalene, F. Rachel. 2011. "Slavery between Judah and Babylon: The Exilic Experience." Pp. 113–34 in *Slaves and Households in the Near East*, edited by Laura Culbertson. OIS 7. Chicago: University of Chicago Press.

———. 2014. "Freedom and Dependency: Neo-Babylonian Manumission Documents with Oblation and Sevice Obligation." Pp. 337–46 in *Extraction and Control: Studies in Honor of Matthew W. Stolper*, edited by Michael Kozuh. SAOC 68. Chicago: Oriental Institute of the University of Chicago.

Magen, Yitzhak, and Israel Finkelstein. 1993. *Archaeological Survey of the Hill Country of Benjamin*. Jerusalem: Israel Antiquities Authority.

Magness, Jodi. 2002. *The Archaeology of Qumran and the Dead Sea Scrolls*. Studies in the Dead Sea Scrolls and Related Literature. Grand Rapids: Eerdmans.

———. 2012. *The Archaeology of the Holy Land: From the Destruction of Solomon's Temple to the Muslim Conquest*. Cambridge: Cambridge University Press.

———. 2014. "Conspicuous Consumption: Dining on Meat in the Ancient Mediterranean World and Near East." Pp. 33–59 in *Feasting in the Archaeology and Texts of the Bible and the Ancient Near East*, edited by Peter Altmann and Janling Fu. Winona Lake, IN: Eisenbrauns.

Mahler-Slasky, Yael, and Mordechai E. Kislev. 2010. "Lathyrus Consumption in Late Bronze and Iron Age Sites in Israel: An Aegean Affinity." *JAS* 37:2477–85.

Maidman, Maynard P. 1979. "A Nuzi Private Archive: Morphological Considerations." *Assur* 1 (9): 179–86.

Malamat, Abraham. 1978. *Early Israelite Warfare and the Conquest of Canaan: The Fourth Sacks Lecture Delivered on 21st June 1977.* Vol. 4. Oxford: Oxford Centre for Postgraduate Hebrew Studies.

———. 1982. "A Political Look at the Kingdom of David and Solomon and Its Relation with Egypt." Pp. 189–204 in *Studies in the Period of David and Solomon and Other Essays,* edited by Tomoo Ishida. Winona Lake, IN: Eisenbrauns.

———. 1989. *Mari and the Early Israelite Experience.* The Schweich Lectures of the British Academy 1984. Oxford: Oxford University Press.

———. 1995. "A Note on the Ritual of Treaty Making in Mari and the Bible." *IEJ* 45:226–29.

Malešević, Siniša. 2010. *The Sociology of War and Violence.* Cambridge: Cambridge University Press.

Mann, R., and D. D. Loren. 2001. "Keeping Up Appearances: Dress, Architecture, Furniture, and Status at French Azilum." *International Journal of Historical Archaeology* 5:281–307.

Manniche, Lisa. 2010. *The Akhenaten Colossi of Karnak.* Cairo: American University in Cairo Press.

Manning, Patrick. 2013. *Migration in World History.* 2nd ed. Themes in World History. Abingdon: Routledge.

Manning, Stuart W., and Linda Hulin. 2005. "Maritime Commerce and Geographies of Mobility in the Late Bronze Age of the Eastern Mediterranean: Problematizations." Pp. 270–302 in *The Archaeology of Mediterranean Prehistory,* edited by Emma Blake and A. Bernard Knapp. Malden, MA: Blackwell.

Marchetti, N., and L. Nigro. 1995. "Cultic Activities in the Sacred Area of Ishtar at Ebla during the Old Syrian Period: The 'Favissae' F.5327 and F.5238." *JCS* 49:1–44.

Marcus, Michelle I. 1987. "Geography as an Organizing Principle in the Imperial Art of Shalmaneser III." *Iraq* 49:77–90.

Marcuson, Hannah. 2016. "'Word of the Old Woman': Studies in Female Ritual Practice in Hittite Anatolia." PhD dissertation, Department of Near Eastern Languages and Civilizations, University of Chicago.

Marcuson, Hannah, and Theo van den Hout. 2015. "Memorization and Hittite Ritual: New Perspectives on the Transmission of Hittite Ritual Texts." *JANER* 15:143–68.

Marfoe, Leon. 1979. "The Integrative Transformation: Patterns of Sociopolitical Organization in Southern Syria." *BASOR* 234:1–42.

Markoe, G. E. 2006. *The Phoenicians.* London: Folio Society.

Marom, Nimrod, and Guy Bar-Oz. 2009. "'Man-Made Oases': Neolithic Patterns of Wild Ungulate Exploitation and Their Consequences for the Domestication of Pigs and Cattle." *Before Farming* 1.

http://online.liverpooluniversitypress.co.uk/doi/pdf/10.3828/bfarm.2009.1.2.

———. 2013. "The Prey Pathway: A Regional History of Pig (Sus Scrofa) and Cattle (Bos Taurus) Domestication in the Northern Jordan Valley, Israel." *PLOS ONE* 8(2). http://dx.doi.org/10.1371/journal.pone.0055958.

Marquand, Allan. 1909. *Greek Architecture.* New York: MacMillan.

Martens, Elmer A. 2008. "Toward Shalom: Absorbing the Violence." Pp. 33–57 in *War in the Bible and Terrorism in the Twenty-First Century,* edited by Richard S. Hess and Elmer A. Martens. BBRSup 2. Winona Lake, IN: Eisenbrauns.

Martin, Geoffrey Thorndike. 1991. *A Bibliography of the Amarna Period and Its Aftermath.* London: Kegan Paul.

Martin, Mario A. S. 2004. "Egyptian and Egyptianized Pottery in the Late Bronze Age Canaan." *ÄL* 14:265–84.

Martin, Mario A. S., et al. 2013. "Iron IIA Slag-Tempered Pottery in the Negev Highlands, Israel." *JAS* 40:3777–92.

Martin, Mario A. S., and Israel Finkelstein. 2013. "Iron IIA Pottery from the Negev Highlands: Petrographic Investigation and Historical Implications." *TA* 40:6–45.

Marx, Emanuel. 1970. *Bedouin of the Negev.* Manchester: University of Manchester Press.

Masson, Frédéric, et al. 2015. "Variable Behavior of the Dead Sea Fault along the Southern Arava Segment from GPS Measurements." *Comptes Rendus Geoscience* 347:161–69.

Master, Daniel M. 2001. "State Formation Theory and the Kingdom of Ancient Israel." *JNES* 60:117–31.

———. 2003. "Trade and Politics: Ashkelon's Balancing Act in the Seventh Century B.C.E." *BASOR* 330:47–64.

———. 2009. "The Renewal of Trade at Iron Age I Ashkelon." *ErIsr* 29:111–22.

———. 2011. "Home Cooking at Ashkelon in the Bronze and Iron Ages." Pp. 257–72 in *On Cooking Pots, Drinking Cups, Loomweights and Ethnicity in Bronze Age Cyprus and Neighboring Regions: An International Archaeological Symposium Held in Nicosia, November 6th–7th 2010,* edited by Vassos Karageorghis and Ourania Kouka. Nicosia: A. G. Leventis Foundation.

———. 2014. "Economy and Exchange in the Iron Age Kingdoms of the Southern Levant." *BASOR* 372:81–97.

Master, Daniel M., Beth Alpert Nakhai, Avraham Faust. L. Michael White, and Jürgen K. Zangeberg, eds. 2013. *the Oxford Encyclopedia of Bible and Archaeology.* New York: Oxford University Press.

Master, Daniel M., and Lawrence E. Stager. 2014. "Buy Low, Sell High: The Marketplace at Ashkelon." *BAR* 40:36–47, 69.

Matney, Timothy, Lynn Rainville, Kemalettin Köroğlu, Azer Keskin, Tasha Vorderstrasse, Nursen Özkul Findik, and Ann Donkin. 2007. "Report on Excavations at Ziyaret Tepe, 2006 Season." *Anatolica* 33:23–74.

Matoušova-Rajmova, M. 1979. "La position à génuflexion inachevée: Activité et danse." *Archiv orientální* 47:57–66.

Matthews, Victor H. 2006. "The Determination of Social Identity in the Story of Ruth." *Biblical Theology Bulletin* 36:49–54.

———. 2008. *More Than Meets the Ear: Understanding the Hidden Contexts of Old Testament Conversations*. Grand Rapids: Baker Academic.

Matthews, Victor H., and Don C. Benjamin. 1993. *The Social World of Ancient Israel, 1250–587 BCE*. Peabody, MA: Hendrickson.

———. 2006. *Old Testament Parallels: Laws and Stories from the Ancient Near East*. 3rd ed. Mahwah, NJ: Paulist Press.

Matthiae, Paolo. 2006. "Middle Bronze Age II Minor Cult Places at Ebla?" Pp. 217–33 in *"I Will Speak the Riddles of Ancient Times": Archaeological and Historical Studies in Honor of Amihai Mazar on the Occasion of His Sixtieth Birthday*, vol. 1, edited by Aren M. Maeir and Pierre de Miroschedji. Winona Lake, IN: Eisenbrauns.

Mattingly, Gerald L. 1989. "Moabite Religion and the Mesha' Inscription." Pp. 211–38 in *Studies in the Mesha Inscription and Moab*, edited by J. Andrew Dearman. ABS 2. Atlanta: Scholars Press.

Mauss, Marcel. 1967. *The Gift: Forms and Functions of Exchange in Archaic Societies*. Translated by Ian Cunnison. New York: W. W. Norton.

Mays, James Luther. 1969. *Amos: A Commentary*. OTL. Philadelphia: Westminster.

Mazar, Amihai. 1980. *Excavations at Tell Qasile, Part One: The Philistine Sanctuary: Architecture and Cult Objects*. QEDEM Monographs of the Institute of Archaeology 12. Jerusalem: Ahva.

———. 1981. "Giloh: An Early Israelite Settlement Site Near Jerusalem." *IEJ* 31:1–36.

———. 1982a. "The 'Bull Site'—An Iron Age I Open Cult Place." *BASOR* 247:27–42.

———. 1982b. "Iron Age Fortresses in the Judean Hills." *PEQ* 114:87–109.

———. 1983. "Bronze Bull Found in Israelite 'High Place' from the Time of the Judges." *BAR* 9 (5): 34–40.

———. 1985. *Excavations at Tell Qasile, Part Two: The Philistine Sanctuary; Various Finds, the Pottery, Conclusions, Appendixes*. QEDEM Monographs of the Institute of Archaeology 20. Jerusalem: Ahva.

———. 1990a. *Archaeology of the Land of the Bible: 10,000–586 B.C.E.* The Anchor Bible Reference Library. New York: Doubleday.

———. 1990b. "Iron Age I and II Towers at Giloh and the Israelite Settlement." *IEJ* 40:77–101.

———. 1992. "Temples of the Middle and Late Bronze Ages and the Iron Age." Pp. 161–87 in *The Architecture of Ancient Israel: From the Prehistoric to the Persian Periods*, edited by Aharon Kempinski and Ronny Reich. Jerusalem: Israel Exploration Society.

———. 2003. "Remarks on Biblical Traditions and Archaeological Evidence Concerning Early Israel." Pp. 85–98 in *Symbiosis, Symbolism and the Power of the Past: Canaan, Ancient Israel and Their Neighbors from the Late Bronze Age through Roman Palestine*, edited by W. G. Dever and S. Gitin. Winona Lake, IN: Eisenbrauns.

———. 2007. "The Spade and the Text: The Interaction between Archaeology and Israelite History Relating to the 10–9th Centuries BCE." Pp. 143–71 in *Understanding the History of Ancient Israel*, edited by H. G. M. Williamson. Proceedings of the British Academy 143. London: British Academy.

———. 2010. "Archaeology and the Biblical Narrative: The Case of the United Monarchy." Pp. 29–58 in *One God—One Cult—One Nation: Archaeological and Biblical Perspectives*, edited by Reinhard G. Kratz and Hermann Spieckermann in collaboration with Björn Corzilius and Tanja Pilger. BZAW 405. Berlin: de Gruyter.

———. 2011. "The Iron Age Chronology Debate: Is the Gap Narrowing? Another Viewpoint." *NEA* 74:105–10.

———. 2012. "Iron Age I: Northern Coastal Plain, Galilee, Samaria, Jezreel Valley, Judah, and Negev." Pp. 5–70 in *The Ancient Pottery of Israel and Its Neighbors from the Iron Age through the Hellenistic Period*, edited by S. Gitin. Jerusalem: Israel Exploration Society.

———. 2016. "Identity and Politics Relating to Tel Reḥov in the 10th–9th Centuries BCE." Pp. 89–120 in *In Search of Aram and Israel: Politics, Culture and Identity*, edited by Omer Sergi, Manfred Oeming, and Izaak J. de Hulster. Orientalische Religionen in der Antike. Tübingen: Mohr Siebeck.

Mazar, Amihai, and Nava Panitz-Cohen. 2007. "It Is the Land of Honey: Beekeeping at Tel Rehov." *NEA* 70:202–19.

Mazar, Benjamin. 1957. "The Tobiads." *IEJ* 7:137–45, 229–38.

———. 1986. "Pharaoh Shishak's Campaign to the Land of Israel." Pp. 139–50 in *The Early Biblical Period: Historical Studies*, edited by Shmuel Aḥituv and Baruch A. Levine. Jerusalem: Israel Exploration Society. Originally published as "The Campaign of

Pharaoh Shishak to Palestine." Pp. 57–66 in *Volume du Congres: Strasbourg, 1956*, edited by Pieter Arie Hendrik de Boer. VTSup 4. Leiden: Brill, 1957.

Mazar, Eilat. 2009. *The Palace of King David: Excavations at the Summit of the City of David; Preliminary Report of Seasons 2005–2007*. Jerusalem: Shoham Academic Research and Publication.

———. 2015. *The Ophel Excavations to the South of the Temple Mount 2009–2013*. Jerusalem: Shoham Academic Research and Publication.

McCarter, P. Kyle, Jr. 1980. "The Balaam Texts from Deir ʿAllā: The First Combination." *BASOR* 239:49–60.

———. 2011. "The Patriarchal Age: Abraham, Isaac and Jacob." Pp. 1–34 in *Ancient Israel: From Abraham to the Roman Destruction of the Temple*, edited by Hershel Shanks. 3rd ed. Washington, DC: Biblical Archaeology Society.

McCown, C. C. 1957. "The ʿAraq el-Emir and the Tobiads." *BA* 20:63–76.

McGeough, Kevin. 2015. "'What Is Not in My House You Must Give Me.': Agents of Exchange according to the Textual Evidence from Ugarit." Pp. 85–96 in *Policies of Exchange: Political Systems and Modes of Interaction in the Aegean and the Near East in the 2nd Millennium BCE*, edited by Birgitta Eder and Regine Pruzsinszky. Vienna: Austrian Academy of Sciences.

McKenzie, J. S., J. A. Greene, A. T. Reyes, C. S. Alexander, and D. G. Barrett. 2013. *The Nabataean Temple at Khirbet et-Tannur*, edited by Judith McKenzie. 2 vols. Boston: American Schools of Oriental Research.

McKenzie, Steven L. 1991. *The Trouble with Kings: The Composition of the Book of Kings in the Deuteronomistic History*. VTSup 42. Leiden: Brill.

———. 2000. *King David: A Biography*. Oxford: Oxford University Press.

McLaughlin, John L. 2001. *The Marzēaḥ in the Prophetic Literature: References and Allusions in Light of the Extra-Biblical Evidence*. VTSup 86. Leiden: Brill.

McNutt, Paula M. 1990. *The Forging of Israel: Iron Technology, Symbolism, and Tradition in Ancient Society*. JSOTSup 108. Sheffield: Almond.

McQuitty, Alison. 1993–94. "Ovens in Town and Country." *Berytus Archaeological Studies* 41:53–76.

Mee, Christopher. 2008. "Mycenaean Greece, the Aegean, and Beyond." Pp. 362–86 in *The Cambridge Companion to the Aegean Bronze Age*, edited by Cynthia W. Shelmerdine. Cambridge: Cambridge University Press.

Meier, Samuel A. 1988. *The Messenger in the Ancient Semitic World*. HSM 45. Atlanta: Scholars Press.

Meiggs, Russell. 1972. *The Athenian Empire*. Oxford: Clarendon.

Meiri, Meirav, Dorothee Huchon, Guy Bar-Oz, Elisabetta Boaretto, Liora Kolska Horwitz, Aren Maeir, Lidar Sapir-Hen, Greger Larson, Steve Weiner, and Israel Finkelstein. 2013. "Ancient DNA and Population Turnover in Southern Levantine Pigs: Signature of the Sea Peoples Migration?" *Scientific Reports* 3, article no. 3035. doi:10.1038/srep03035.

Melville, Sarah C. 2016. "The Role of Rituals in Warfare during the Neo-Assyrian Period." *Religion Compass* 10 (9): 219–29.

Mendelsohn, Isaac. 1949. *Slavery in the Ancient Near East*. Westport, CT: Greenwoood.

Mendelssohn, Heinrich, and Yoram Yom-Tov. 1999. *Mammalia of Israel*. Jerusalem: Israel Academy of Sciences and Humanities.

Mendenhall, G. E. 1973. *The Tenth Generation: The Origins of the Biblical Tradition*. Baltimore: Johns Hopkins University Press.

Merlo, Paolo. 2010. "Ashera." In *Iconography of Deities and Demons in the Ancient Near East: An Iconographic Dictionary with Special Emphasis on First Millennium BCE Palestine/Israel*. http://www.religionswissenschaft.uzh.ch/idd/prepublications/e_idd _asherah.pdf and http://www.religionswissenschaft .uzh.ch/idd/prepublications/e_idd_illustrations _asherah.pdf.

Meshel, Ze'ev. 1978a. "Kuntillet ʿAjrud: An Israelite Religious Center in Northern Sinai." *Expedition* Summer 1978:50–84.

———. 1978b. *Kuntillet ʿAjrud: A Religious Centre from the Time of the Judaean Monarchy on the Border of Sinai*. Israel Museum Catalogue 175. Jerusalem: Israel Museum.

———, ed. 2012. *Kuntillet ʿAjrud (Horvat Teman): An Iron Age II Religious Site on the Judah-Sinai Border*. Jerusalem: Israel Exploration Society.

Meshorer, Ya'akov. 1982. *Ancient Jewish Coinage*, vol. 1, *Persian Period through Hasmonaeans*. Dix Hills, NY: Amphora.

Meshorer, Ya'akov, and Shraga Qedar. 1991. *The Coinage of Samaria in the Fourth Century BCE*. Jerusalem: Numismatic Fine Arts International.

Metcalf, Christopher. 2011. "New Parallels in Hittite and Sumerian Praise of the Sun." *Die Welt des Orients* 41:168–76.

Metcalf, Peter, and Richard Huntington. 1991. *Celebrations of Death: The Anthropology of Mortuary Ritual*. 2nd ed. Cambridge: Cambridge University Press.

Mettinger, Tryggve N. D. 1995. *No Graven Image? Israelite Aniconism in Its Ancient Near Eastern Context*. Coniectanea Biblica: Old Testament Series 42. Stockholm: Almqvist & Wiksell.

———. 1997. "Israelite Aniconism: Developments and Origins." Pp. 173–204 in *The Image and the Book: Iconic Cults, Aniconism, and the Rise of Book*

Religion in Israel and the Ancient Near East, edited by Karel van der Toorn. CBET 21. Leuven: Peeters.

Meyers, Carol. 1991. "'To Her Mother's House'—Considering a Counterpart to the Israelite *Bêt 'āb*." Pp. 39–52, 304–7 in *The Bible and the Politics of Exegesis: Essays in Honor of Norman K. Gottwald on His Sixty-Fifth Birthday*, edited by David Jobling, Peggy Day, and Gerald T. Sheppard. Cleveland: Pilgrim.

———. 1997. "The Family in Early Israel." Pp. 1–47 in *Families in Ancient Israel*, edited by Leo G. Perdue et al. Louisville: Westminster John Knox.

———. 2003a. "Engendering Syro-Palestinian Archaeology: Reasons and Resources." *NEA* 66:185–97.

———. 2003b. "Material Remains and Social Relations: Women's Culture in Agrarian Households of the Iron Age." Pp. 425–44 in *Symbiosis, Symbolism, and the Power of the Past: Canaan, Ancient Israel, and Their Neighbors from the Late Bronze Age through Roman Palaestina*, edited by William G. Dever and Seymour Gitin. Winona Lake, IN: Eisenbrauns.

———. 2005. *Households and Holiness: The Religious Culture of Israelite Women*. Facets Series. Minneapolis: Fortress.

———. 2007. "From Field Crops to Food: Attributing Gender and Meaning to Bread Production in Iron Age Israel." Pp. 67–84 in *The Archaeology of Difference: Gender, Ethnicity, Class and the "Other" in Antiquity, Studies in Honor of Eric M. Meyers*, edited by Douglas R. Edwards and C. Thomas McCollough. AASOR 60/61. Boston: American Schools of Oriental Research.

———. 2010. "Household Religion." Pp. 118–34 in *Religious Diversity in Ancient Israel and Judah*, edited by Francesca Stavrakopoulou and John Barton. London: T&T Clark.

———. 2011. "Archaeology—A Window to the Lives of Israelite Women." Pp. 61–108 in *The Bible and Women: An Encyclopaedia of Exegesis and Cultural History*, vol. 1.1, *Hebrew Bible / Old Testament: Torah*, edited by Irmtraud Fischer and Mercedes Navarro Puerto, with Andrea Taschl-Erbele. Atlanta: Society of Biblical Literature.

———. 2012. "Women's Religious Life in Ancient Israel." Pp. 354–61 in *Women's Bible Commentary*, edited by Carol A. Newsom, Sharon H. Ringe, and Jacqueline E. Lapsley. 3rd ed. Louisville: Westminster John Knox.

———. 2013. *Rediscovering Eve: Ancient Israelite Women in Context*. New York: Oxford University Press.

———. 2014a. "Domestic Architecture, Ancient Israel." *Oxford Bibliographies*, edited by Christopher R. Matthews et al. http://www.oxfordbibliographies.com/view/document/obo-9780195393361/obo-9780195393361-0096.xml.

———. 2014b. "Menu: Royal Repasts and Social Class in Biblical Israel." Pp. 129–46 in *Feasting in the Archaeology and Texts of the Bible and the Ancient Near East*, edited by Peter Altmann and Janling Fu. Winona Lake, IN: Eisenbrauns.

———. 2014c. "Was Ancient Israel a Patriarchal Society?" *JBL* 133:8–27.

———. 2016. "Double Vision: Textual and Archaeological Images of Women." *Hebrew Bible and Ancient Israel* 3:112–31.

———. 2017. "Disks and Deities: Images on Iron Age Terracotta Plaques." Pp. 116–33 in *Le-ma'an Ziony: Essays in Honor of Ziony Zevit*, edited by Frederick E. Greenspahn and Gary A. Rendsburg. Eugene, OR: Cascade.

Meyers, Carol, Toni Craven, and Ross S. Kraemer, eds. 2000. *Women in Scripture: A Dictionary of the Named and Unnamed Women in the Hebrew Bible, the Apocryphal/Deuterocanonical Books, and the New Testament*. Boston: Houghton Mifflin.

Michalowski, Piotr. 1977. "Amar-Su'ena and the Historical Tradition." Pp. 155–57 in *Essays on the Ancient Near East in Memory of Jacob Joel Finkelstein*, edited by Maria de Jong Ellis. Memoirs of the Connecticut Academy of Arts and Sciences 19. Hamden, CT: Archon.

———. 1995. "Sumerian Literature: An Overview." *CANE* 4:2279–91.

Mierse, William E. 2012. *Temples and Sanctuaries from the Early Iron Age Levant: Recovery after Collapse*. Winona Lake, IN: Eisenbrauns.

Miglio, Adam E. 2014. *Tribe and State: The Dynamics of International Politics and the Reign of Zimri-Lim*. Gorgias Studies in the Ancient Near East 8. Piscataway, NJ: Gorgias.

Migowski, Claudia, et al. 2014. "Recurrence Pattern of Holocene Earthquakes along the Dead Sea Transform Revealed by Varve-Counting and Radiocarbon Dating of Lacustrine Sediments." *Earth and Planetary Science Letters* 222:301–14.

Milano, Lucio. 1995. "Ebla: A Third-Millennium City-State in Ancient Syria." *CANE* 2:1219–30.

Mildenberg, Leo. 1979. "Yehud: A Preliminary Study of the Provincial Coinage of Judaea." Pp. 183–96 in *Greek Numismatics and Archaeology: Essays in Honor of Margaret Thompson*, edited by Otto Mørkholm and Nancy M. Waggoner. Wetteren: Editions NR.

Milgrom, Jacob. 1976. *Cult and Conscience: The Asham and the Priestly Doctrine of Repentance*. SJLA 18. Leiden: Brill.

———. 1991. *Leviticus 1–16: A New Translation with Introduction and Commentary*. AB 3. New York: Doubleday.

———. 2001. *Leviticus 23–27.* AB 3B. New York: Doubleday.

Millard, Alan R. 1980. "Methods of Studying the Patriarchal Narratives as Ancient Texts." Pp. 43–58 in *Essays on the Patriarchal Narratives,* edited by Alan R. Millard and D. J. Wiseman. Reprint, Eugene, OR: Wipf & Stock.

———. 1989. "Does the Bible Exaggerate King Solomon's Golden Wealth?" *BAR* 15:3:20–34.

———. 1999a. "The Knowledge of Writing in Late Bronze Age Palestine." Pp. 317–26 in *Languages and Cultures in Contact: At the Crossroads of Civilizations in the Syro-Mesopotamian Realm; Proceedings of the 42nd RAI, 1995,* edited by K. van Lerberghe and G. Voet. OLA 96. Leuven: Peeters.

———. 1999b. "Oral Proclamation and Written Record: Spreading and Preserving Information in Ancient Israel." Pp. 237–41 in *Michael: Historical, Epigraphical, and Biblical Studies in Honor of Prof. Michael Heltzer,* edited by Yitzhak Avishur and Robert Deutsch. Tel Aviv: Archaeological Center Publications.

———. 2005a. "Only Fragments from the Past: The Role of Accident in Our Knowledge of the Ancient Near East." Pp. 301–19 in *Writing and Ancient Near Eastern Society: Papers in Honour of Alan R. Millard,* edited by Piotr Bienkowski, Christopher Mee, and Elizabeth Slater. LHB/OTS 426. London: T&T Clark.

———. 2005b. "Writing, Writing Materials and Literacy in the Ancient Near East." Pp. 1003–11 in *Dictionary of the Old Testament: Historical Books,* edited by Bill T. Arnold and H. G. M. Williamson. Downers Grove, IL: InterVarsity.

———. 2007. "King Solomon in His Ancient Context." Pp. 30–35 in *The Age of Solomon: Scholarship at the Turn of the Millennium,* edited by Lowell K. Handy. SHANE 11. Leiden: Brill.

———. 2012. "From Woe to Weal: Completing A Pattern in the Bible and the Ancient Near East." Pp. 193–201 in *Let Us Go Up to Zion: Essays in Honour of H. G. M. Williamson on the Occasion of His Sixty-Fifth Birthday,* edited by Ian Provan and Mark J. Boda. VTSup 153. Leiden: Brill.

Miller, Jared L. 2013. *Royal Hittite Instructions and Related Administrative Texts.* WAW. Atlanta: Society of Biblical Literature.

Miller, J. Maxwell. 1989. "Moab and the Moabites." Pp. 1–40 in *Studies in the Mesha Inscription and Moab,* edited by J. Andrew Dearman. ABS 2. Atlanta: Scholars Press.

Miller, J. Maxwell, and John H. Hayes. 2006. *A History of Ancient Israel and Judah.* Louisville: Westminster John Knox.

Miller, Marvin Lloyd. 2010. "Nehemiah 5: A Response to Philippe Guillaume." *Journal of Hebrew Scriptures* 10, article 13. http://www.jhsonline.org/Articles/article_141.pdf.

———. 2015. "Cultivating Curiosity: Methods and Models for Understanding Ancient Economies." Pp. 3–23 in *The Economy of Ancient Judah in Its Historical Context,* edited by Marvin L. Miller, Ehud Ben Zvi, and Gary N. Knoppers. Winona Lake, IN: Eisenbrauns.

Mills, Barbara J. 2007. "Performing the Feast: Visual Display and Suprahousehold Commensalism in the Puebloan Southwest." *American Antiquity* 72 (2): 210–39.

Milviski, Chaim. 1997. "Notions of Exile, Subjugation and Return in Rabbinic Literature." Pp. 265–98 in *Exile: Old Testament, Jewish, and Christian Conceptions,* edited by James M. Scott. JSJSup 56. Leiden: Brill.

Mirelman, S. 2014. "The Ala-Instrument: Its Identification and Role." Pp. 148–71 in *Music in Antiquity: The Near East and the Mediterranean,* edited by Joan Goodnick Westenholz, Yossi Maurey, and Edwin Seroussi. Yuval 8. Berlin: de Gruyter; Jerusalem: Magnes.

Mitchell, William J. T. 1994. *Picture Theory: Essays on Verbal and Visual Representation.* Chicago: University of Chicago Press.

———. 2005. *What Do Pictures Want? The Lives and Loves of Images.* Chicago: University of Chicago Press.

Mittmann, Siegfried. 2000. "Tobia, Sanballat und die persische Provinz Juda." *JNSL* 26:1–50.

Moberly, R. Walter L. 1992. *Genesis 12–50.* Old Testament Guides. Sheffield: JSOT Press.

Monroe, Christopher M. 2009. *Scales of Fate: Trade, Tradition, and Transformation in the Eastern Mediterranean ca. 1350–1175 BCE.* AOAT 357. Münster: Ugarit-Verlag.

———. 2010. "Sunk Costs at Late Bronze Age Uluburun." *BASOR* 357:19–33.

Monson, James M. 2014. *Regional Study Maps (Set of 7).* Marion, OH: Biblical Backgrounds.

Monson, James M., with Steven P. Lancaster. 2009. *Regions on the Run: Introductory Map Studies in the Land of the Bible.* Marion, OH: Biblical Backgrounds.

Monson, John M. 2004. "The Temple of Solomon: Heart of Jerusalem." Pp. 1–22 in *Zion: City of Our God,* edited by Richard Hess and Gordon Wenham. Grand Rapids: Eerdmans.

Montet, Pierre. 1936. "Avaris, Pi-Ramsès, Tanis." *Syria* 17:200–202.

Montserrat, Dominic. 2003. *Akhenaten: History, Fantasy, and Ancient Egypt.* London: Routledge; New York: Taylor & Francis.

Moore, Megan Bishop, and Brad E. Kelle. 2011. *Biblical History and Israel's Past: The Changing Study of the Bible and History*. Grand Rapids: Eerdmans.

Moorey, P. R. S. 1991. *A Century of Biblical Archaeology*. Cambridge: Lutterworth.

Moran, William L. 1992. *The Amarna Letters*. Baltimore: Johns Hopkins University Press.

Morentz, Siegfried. 1973. *Egyptian Religion*. Translated by Ann Keep. Ithaca, NY: Cornell University Press.

Morenz, Ludwig D., and Lutz Popko. 2010. "The Second Intermediate Period and the New Kingdom." Pp. 101–19 in *A Companion to Ancient Egypt*, edited by Alan B. Lloyd. Blackwell Companions to the Ancient World. Malden, MA: Wiley-Blackwell.

Morgan, David. 1998. *Visual Piety: A History and Theory of Popular Religious Images*. Berkeley: University of California Press.

———. 2005. *The Sacred Gaze: Religious Visual Culture in Theory and Practice*. Berkeley: University of California Press.

Morris, Ellen Fowles. 2005. *The Architecture of Imperialism: Military Bases and the Evolution of Foreign Policy in Egypt's New Kingdom*. PÄ 22. Leiden: Brill.

———. 2013. "Propaganda and Performance at the Dawn of the State." Pp. 33–64 in *Experiencing Power, Generating Authority: Cosmos, Politics, and the Ideology of Kingship in Ancient Egypt and Mesopotamia*, edited by Jane A. Hill, Philip Jones, and Antonio Morales. Penn Museum International Research Conferences 6. Philadelphia: University of Pennsylvania Museum of Archaeology and Anthropology.

Morris, Ian. 1986. "Gift and Commodity in Archaic Greece." *Man* 21:1–17.

———. 2005. "Archaeology, Standards of Living, and Greek Economic History." Pp. 91–126 in *The Ancient Economy: Evidence and Models*, edited by J. G. Manning and Ian Morris. Stanford, CA: Stanford University Press.

Moshier, Stephen O., and James K. Hoffmeier. 2015. "Which Way Out of Egypt? Physical Geography Related to the Exodus Itinerary." Pp. 101–8 in *Israel's Exodus in Transdisciplinary Perspective: Text, Archaeology, Culture, and Geoscience*, edited by Thomas E. Levy, Thomas Schneider, and William H. C. Propp. New York: Springer.

Mosser Carl. 2013. "Torah Instruction, Discussion, and Prophecy in First-Century Synagogues." Pp. 523–51 in *Christian Origins and Hellenistic Judaism: Social and Literary Contexts for the New Testament*, edited by Stanley E. Porter and Andrew W. Pitts. Texts and Editions for New Testament Study 10. Leiden: Brill.

Mourad, Anna-Latifa. 2015. *Rise of the Hyksos: Egypt and the Levant from the Middle Kingdom to the Early Second Intermediate Period*. Oxford: Archaeopress.

Moyal, Y., and A. Faust. 2015. "Jerusalem's Hinterland in the Eighth-Seventh Centuries BCE: Towns, Villages, Farmsteads and Royal Estates." *PEQ* 147:283–98.

Muhly, James D. 1987. "Solomon, the Copper King: A Twentieth Century Myth." *Expedition* 29:38–47.

Mulder, Martin J. 1998. *1 Kings*, vol. 1, *1 Kings 1–11*. Historical Commentary on the Old Testament. Leuven: Peeters.

Müller, Hans-Peter. 1995. "Chemosh." Pp. 356–62 in *Dictionary of Deities and Demons in the Bible*, edited by Karel van der Toorn, Bob Becking, and Pieter W. van der Horst. Leiden: Brill.

Mullins, R. 2002. "Beth Shean during the Eighteenth Dynasty: From Canaanite Settlement to Egyptian Garrison." PhD dissertation, Hebrew University.

Mumford, Gregory. 1998. "International Relations between Egypt, Sinai, and Syria-Palestine during the Late Bronze Age to Early Persian Period (Dynasties 18–26: c. 1550–525 B.C.)." PhD dissertation, University of Toronto. http://www.nlc-bnc.ca/obj/s4/f2/dsk1/tape10/PQDD_0020/NQ45825.pdf.

———. 2001a. "Mediterranean Area." *OEAE* 2:358–67.

———. 2001b. "Syria-Palestine." *OEAE* 3:335–43.

———. 2007. "Egypto-Levantine Relations during the Iron Age to Early Persian Periods (Dynasties Late 20 to 26)." Pp. 225–88 in *Egyptian Stories: A British Egyptological Tribute to Alan B. Lloyd on the Occasion of His Retirement*, edited by Thomas Schneider and Kasia M. Szpakowska. AOAT 347. Münster: Ugarit-Verlag.

———. 2014. "Egypt and the Levant." Pp. 69–89 in *The Oxford Handbook of the Archaeology of the Levant: C. 8000–332 BCE*, edited by Margreet L. Steiner and Ann E. Killebrew. Oxford: Oxford University Press.

Münger, S. 2005. "Stamp-Seal Amulets and Early Iron Age Chronology: An Update." Pp. 381–404 in *The Bible and Radiocarbon Dating: Archaeology, Text and Science*, edited by Thomas E. Levy and Thomas Higham. London: Equinox.

Munro, Natalie D. 2004. "Zooarchaeological Measures of Hunting Pressure and Occupation Intensity in the Natufian." *Current Anthropology* 45:S5–S34.

Murnane, William J. 1980. *United with Eternity: A Concise Guide to the Monuments of Medinet Habu*. Cairo: American University in Cairo Press.

———. 1995. *Texts from the Amarna Period in Egypt*. WAW. Atlanta: Scholars Press.

———. 1999. "Observations on Pre-Amarna Theology during the Earliest Reign of Amenhotep IV." Pp.

303–16 in *Gold of Praise: Studies on Ancient Egypt in Honor of Edward F. Wente*, edited by Emily Teeter and John A. Larson. SAOC 58. Chicago: Oriental Institute of the University of Chicago.

———. 2000. "Imperial Egypt and the Limits of Power." Pp. 101–11 in *Amarna Diplomacy: The Beginnings of International Relations*, edited by Raymond Cohen and Raymond Westbrook. Baltimore: Johns Hopkins University Press.

Murnane, William J., and Charles Van Siclen. 1993. *The Boundary Stelae of Akhenaten*. London: Kegan Paul.

Mysliwiec, Karol. 2000. *The Twilight of Ancient Egypt: First Millennium B.C.E.* Ithaca, NY: Cornell University Press.

Na'aman, Nadav. 1976. "Two Notes on the Monolith Inscription of Shalmaneser III from Kurkh." *TA* 3:89–106.

———. 1991. "The Kingdom of Judah under Josiah." *TA* 18:3–71.

———. 1992. "Israel, Edom and Egypt in the 10th Century B.C.E." *TA* 19:71–93.

———. 1994. "The Hurrians and the End of the Middle Bronze Age in Palestine." *Levant* 26:175–87.

———. 1995. "Hazael of 'Amqi and Hadadezer of Beth-Rehob." *UF* 27:381–94.

———. 1997a. "Historical and Literary Notes on the Excavations of Tel Jezreel." *TA* 24:122–28.

———. 1997b. "King Mesha and the Foundation of the Moabite Monarchy." *IEJ* 47:83–92.

———. 1999. "The Contribution of Royal Inscriptions for a Re-Evaluation of the Book of Kings as a Historical Source." *JSOT* 82:3–17.

———. 2001. "An Assyrian Residence at Ramat Rahel?" *TA* 28:260–80.

———. 2002. "In Search of Reality behind the Account of David's Wars with Israel's Neighbours." *IEJ* 52:200–224.

———. 2004a. "The Boundary System and Political Status of Gaza under the Assyrian Empire." *ZDPV* 120:55–72.

———. 2004b. "Death Formulae and the Burial Place of the Kings of the House of David." *Bib* 85:245–54.

———. 2005. *Canaan in the Second Millennium B.C.E.* Winona Lake, IN: Eisenbrauns.

Nadali, Davide. 2005a. "Assyrians to War: Positions, Patterns and Canons in the Tactics of the Assyrian Armies in the VII Century B.C." Pp. 167–207 in *Studi in onore di Paolo Matthiae presentati in occasione del suo sessantacinquesimo compleanno*, edited by Alessandro Di Ludovico and Davide Nadali. Contributi e materiali di archeologia orientale 10. Rome: Università degli studi di Roma "La Sapienza."

———. 2005b. "The Representation of Foreign Soldiers and Their Employment in the Assyrian Army." Pp. 222–44 in *Ethnicity in Ancient Mesopotamia: Papers read at the 48th RAI, Leiden, 1–4 July, 2002*, edited by W. H. van Soldt, R. Kalvelagen, and D. Katz. Leiden: Nederlands Instituut voor het Nabije Oosten.

———. 2010. "Assyrian Open Field Battles: An Attempt at Reconstruction and Analysis." Pp. 117–52 in *Studies on War in the Ancient Near East: Collected Essays on Military History*, edited by Jordi Vidal. AOAT 372. Münster: Ugarit-Verlag.

Nadali, Davide, and Jordi Vidal. 2014. *The Other Face of the Battle: The Impact of War on Civilians in the Ancient Near East*. AOAT 413. Münster: Ugarit-Verlag.

Nadel, Dani, Dolores R. Piperno, Irene Holst, Ainit Snir, and Ehud Weiss. 2012. "New Evidence for the Processing of Wild Cereal Grains at Ohalo II, a 23,000-Year Old Campsite on the Shore of the Sea of Galilee, Israel." *Antiquity* 86:990–1003.

Nadel, Dani, Alexander Tsatskin, Miriam Belmaker, Elisabetta Boaretto, Mordechai E. Kislev, Henk Mienis, Rivka Rabinovich, Orit Simchoni, Tal Simmons, Ehud Weiss, and Irit Zohar. 2004. "On the Shore of a Fluctuating Lake: Environmental Evidence from Ohalo II (19,500 B.P.)." *Israel Journal of Earth Sciences* 53:207–23.

Nakhai, Beth Alpert. 2015. "Where to Worship? Religion in Iron Age Israel and Judah." Pp. 90–101 in *Defining the Sacred: Approaches to the Archaeology of Religion and the Ancient Near East*, edited by Nicola Laneri. Oxford: Oxbow Books.

Nam, Roger. 2012. *Portrayals of Economic Exchange in the Book of Kings*. Biblical Interpretation Series 112. Leiden: Brill.

Nardoni, Enrique. 2004. *Rise Up, O Judge: A Study of Justice in the Biblical World*. Translated by Seán Charles Martin. Peabody, MA: Hendrickson.

Naveh, Joseph. 1982. *Early History of the Alphabet: An Introduction to West Semitic Epigraphy and Paleography*. Jerusalem: Magnes.

Naveh, Joseph, and Shaul Shaked. 2012. *Aramaic Documents from Ancient Bactria (Fourth Century B.C.E.) from the Khalili Collections*. Studies in the Khalili Collection. London: Khalili Family Trust.

Negbi, Ora. 1976. *Canaanite Gods in Metal: An Archaeological Study of Ancient Syro-Palestinian Figurines*. Tel Aviv: Tel Aviv University.

Negueruela, I., J. Pinedo, M. Gomez, A. Minano, I. Arellano, and J. S. Barba. 1995. "Seventh-Century BC Phoenician Vessel Discovered at Playa de La Isla, Mazarron, Spain." *International Journal of Nautical Archaeology* 24:189–97.

Nemet-Nejat, Karen Rhea. 1998. *Daily Life in Ancient Mesopotamia*. Daily Life through History Series. London: Greenwood.

Nestor, D. A. 2010. *Cognitive Perspectives on Israelite Identity*. LHB/OTS 519. London: T&T Clark.

Neu, Erich. 1996. *Das hurritische Epos der Freilassung: Untersuchungen zu einem hurritisch-hethitischen Textensemble aus Ḫattuša*. Studien zu den Boğazköy-Texten 32. Wiesbaden: Harrassowitz.

The Neubauer Expedition to Zincirli: Inscriptions. https://zincirli.uchicago.edu/page/inscriptions.

Neufeld, E. 1960. "The Emergence of a Royal Urban Society in Ancient Israel." *HUCA* 31:31–53.

Neujahr, Matthew. 2012. *Predicting the Past in the Ancient Near East: Mantic Historiography in Ancient Mesopotamia, Judah, and the Mediterranean World*. BJS 354. Providence: Brown University Press.

Neumann, Hans. 2011. "Slavery in Private Households toward the End of the Third Millennium B.C." Pp. 21–32 in *Slaves and Households in the Near East*, edited by Laura Culbertson. OIS 7. Chicago: University of Chicago Press.

Neville, Ann. 2007. *Mountains of Silver and Rivers of Gold: The Phoenicians in Iberia*. Oxford: Oxbow Books.

Newsom, Carol A., with Brennan W. Breed. 2014. *Daniel*. OTL. Louisville: Westminster John Knox.

Niditch, Susan. 1995. *War in the Hebrew Bible: A Study in the Ethics of Violence*. Oxford: Oxford University Press.

———. 1996. *Oral World and Written Word: Ancient Israelite Literature*. Louisville: Westminster John Knox.

———. 2007. "War and Reconciliation in the Traditions of Ancient Israel: Historical, Literary, and Ideological Considerations." Pp. 141–60 in *War and Peace in the Ancient World*, edited by Kurt A. Raaflaub. Malden, MA: Blackwell.

Niehr, Herbert. 2010. "'Israelite' Religion and 'Canaanite' Religion." Pp. 23–36 in *Religious Diversity in Ancient Israel and Judah*, edited by Francesca Stavrakopoulou and John Barton. London: T&T Clark.

———. 2011. "König Hazael von Damaskus im Licht neuer Funde und Interpretationen." Pp. 339–56 in *"Ich werde meinen Bund mit euch niemals brechen!" (Ri 2, 1): Festschrift für Walter Groß zum 70. Geburtstag*, edited by Erasmus Gass and Hermann-Josef Stipp. Herders Biblische Studien 62. Freiburg im Breisgau: Herder.

Niemann, Hermann Michael. 1997. "The Socio-Political Shadow Cast by the Biblical Solomon." Pp. 252–99 in *The Age of Solomon: Scholarship at the Turn of the Millennium*, edited by Lowell K. Handy. SHANE 11. Leiden: Brill.

Niemeyer, Hans Georg. 2000. "The Early Phoenician City-States on the Mediterranean: Archaeological Elements for Their Description." Pp. 89–116 in *A Comparative Study of Thirty City-State Cultures: An Investigation Conducted by the Copenhagen Polis Centre*, edited by Mogens Herman Hansen. Copenhagen: Royal Danish Academy of Sciences and Letters.

———. 2006. "The Phoenicians in the Mediterranean: Between Expansion and Colonisation; A Non-Greek Model of Oversees Settlement and Presence." Pp. 143–68 in *Greek Colonisation: An Account of Greek Colonies and Other Settlements Overseas*, vol. 1, edited by Gocha R. Tsetskhladze. Mnemosyne, bibliotheca classica Batava, Supplementum 193. Leiden: Brill.

Nir, Yaacov, and Iris Eldar-Nir. 1988. "Construction Techniques and Building Materials Used in Ancient Water Wells along the Coastal Plain of Israel." Pp. 1765–74 in *The Engineering Geology of Ancient Works, Monuments and Historical Sites: Preservation and Protection*, vol. 3, edited by Paul G. Marinos and George C. Koukis. Netherlands: Balkema.

Nissinen, Martti. 2000. "The Socioreligious Role of the Neo-Assyrian Prophets." Pp. 89–114 in *Prophecy in Its Ancient Near Eastern Context: Mesopotamian, Biblical, and Arabian Perspectives*, edited by Martti Nissinen. SymS 13. Atlanta: Society of Biblical Literature.

———. 2003. "Neither Prophecies nor Apocalypses: The Akkadian Literary Predictive Texts." Pp. 134–48 in *Knowing the End from the Beginning: The Prophetic, The Apocalyptic, and Their Relationship*, edited by Lester L. Grabbe and Robert D. Haak. Journal for the Study of the Pseudepigrapha Supplement Series 46. London: T&T Clark.

———. 2004. "What Is Prophecy? An Ancient Near Eastern Perspective." Pp. 17–37 in *Inspired Speech: Prophecy in the Ancient Near East; Essays in Honour of Herbert B. Huffmon*, edited by John Kaltner and Louis Stulman. JSOTSup 378. London: T&T Clark.

———. 2010. "Biblical Prophecy from a Near Eastern Perspective: The Cases of Kingship and Divine Possession." Pp. 441–68 in *Congress Volume, Ljubljana 2007*, edited by André Lemaire. VTSup 133. Leiden: Brill.

———. 2014. "Since When Do Prophets Write?" Pp. 585–606 in *In the Footsteps of Sherlock Holmes: Studies in the Biblical Text in Honour of Anneli Aejmelaeus*, edited by Kristin de Troyer, T. Michael Law, and Marketta Liljeström. CBET 72. Leuven: Peeters.

———. 2017. *Ancient Prophecy: Near Eastern, Biblical, and Greek Pespectives*. Oxford: Oxford University Press.

Nissinen, Martti, with contributions by C. L. Seow and Robert K. Ritner. 2003. *Prophets and Prophecy in the Ancient Near East*. WAW 12. Atlanta: Society of Biblical Literature.

Nissinen, Martti, and Risto Uro, eds. 2008. *Sacred Marriages: The Divine-Human Sexual Metaphor from Sumer to Early Christianity.* Winona Lake, IN: Eisenbrauns.

Nocquet, Dany. 2004. *Le "livret noir de Baal": La polémique contre le dieu Baal dans la Bible hébraïque et l'ancien Israël.* Actes et Recherches. Geneva: Labor et Fides.

Nolan, Patrick, and Gerhard Lenski. 2015. *Human Societies: An Introduction to Macrosociology.* 12th ed. Oxford: Oxford University Press.

Noonan, Benjamin J. 2011. "Did Nehemiah Own Tyrian Goods? Trade between Judea and Phoenicia during the Achaemenid Period." *JBL* 130:281–98.

North, Douglass. 1990. *Institutions, Institutional Change and Economic Performance.* Cambridge: Cambridge University Press.

Nossov, Konstantin. 2005. *Ancient and Medieval Siege Weapons: A Fully Illustrated Guide to Siege Weapons and Tactics.* Guilford, CT: Lyons.

Noth, Martin. 1928. *Die israelitischen Personennamen im Rahmen der gemeinsemitischen Namengebung.* BWANT 46. Stuttgart: Kolhammer.

———. 1938. "Die Wege der Pharaonenheere in Palästina und Syrien, IV: Die Schoschenkliste." *ZDPV* 61:277–304.

———. 1960. *The History of Israel.* 2nd rev. ed. Translated by P. R. Ackroyd. New York: Harper & Brothers.

———. 1991. *The Deuteronomistic History.* 2nd ed. JSOTSup 15. Sheffield: Sheffield Academic Press. German original: *Überlieferungsgeschichtliche Studien I.* Halle: M. Niemeyer, 1943.

Notley, R. Steven, and Ze'ev Safrai, trans. 2005. *Eusebius, Onomasticon: The Place Names of Divine Scripture.* Jewish and Christian Perspective Series 9. Leiden: Brill.

Noy, David. 2010. "Alexander the Great." Pp. 316–18 in *The Eerdmans Dictionary of Early Judaism,* edited by John J. Collins and Daniel C. Harlow. Grand Rapids: Eerdmans.

Nur, Amos. 2008. *Apocalypse: Earthquakes, Archaeology, and the Wrath of God.* Princeton: Princeton University Press.

Nutkowicz, Hélène. 2006. *L'Homme face à la mort au royaume de Juda: Rites, pratiques, et représentations.* Paris: Cerf.

Oates, David. 1968. *Studies in the Ancient History of Northern Iraq.* London: British Academy. Reprint, London: British School of Archaeology in Iraq, 2005.

———. 2005. *Studies in the Ancient History of Northern Iraq.* London: British School of Archaeology in Iraq.

O'Brien, John Maxwell. 1992. *Alexander the Great: The Invisible Enemy; A Biography.* London: Routledge.

O'Connor, David. 1997. "The Hyksos Period in Egypt." Pp. 45–67 in *The Hyksos: New Historical and Archaeological Perspectives,* edited by Eliezer D. Oren. UMM 96. Philadelphia: University Museum of the University of Pennsylvania.

———. 2000. "The Sea Peoples and the Egyptian Sources." Pp. 85–101 in *The Sea Peoples and Their World: A Reassessment,* edited by Eliezer D. Oren. UMM 108. Philadelphia: University Museum of the University of Pennsylvania.

O'Connor, David, and Eric H. Cline. 1998. *Amenhotep III: Perspectives on His Reign.* Ann Arbor: University of Michigan Press.

Oded, Bustenay. 1979. *Mass Deportation and Deportees in the Neo-Assyrian Empire.* Wiesbaden: Reichert.

Ofer, A. 1994. "All the Hill Country of Judah: From a Settlement to a Prosperous Monarchy." Pp. 92–122 in *From Nomadism to Monarchy,* edited by Israel Finkelstein and Nadav Na'aman. Jerusalem: Israel Exploration Society.

Oliver-Smith, Anthony. 2002. "Theorizing Disasters: Nature, Power, and Culture." Pp. 23–47 in *Catastrophe and Culture: The Anthropology of Disaster,* edited by Susanna M. Hoffman and Anthony Oliver-Smith. Santa Fe: School of American Research.

Olley, John W. 1999. "'Trust in the Lord': Hezekiah, Kings and Isaiah." *Tyndale Bulletin* 50:59–77.

Olsvig-Whittaker, Linda, Aren M. Maeir, Ehud Weiss, Suembikya Frumin, Oren Ackerman, and Liora Kolska-Horwitz. 2015. "Ecology of the Past: Late Bronze and Iron Age Landscapes, People and Climate Change in Philistia (the Southern Coastal Plain and Shephelah), Israel." *Journal of Mediterranean Ecology* 13:57–75.

Olyan, Saul M. 1988. *Asherah and the Cult of Yahweh in Israel.* Society of Biblical Literature Monograph Series 34. Atlanta: Scholars Press.

———. 2004. *Biblical Mourning: Ritual and Social Dimensions.* Oxford: Oxford University Press.

———. 2005. "Some Neglected Aspects of Israelite Interment Ideology." *JBL* 124:601–16.

———. 2008. "Family Religion in Israel and the Wider Levant of the First Millennium BCE." Pp. 113–26 in *Household and Family Religion in Antiquity,* edited by John Bodel and Saul M. Olyan. Malden, MA: Blackwell.

Oppenheim, A. Leo. 1955. "'Siege-Documents' from Nippur." *Iraq* 17:69–89.

———. 1964. *Ancient Mesopotamia: Portrait of a Dead Civiliztion.* Chicago: University of Chicago Press.

Oren, Eliezer D. 1984. "Migdol: A New Fortress on the Edge of the Eastern Nile Delta." *BASOR* 256:7–44.

———, ed. 2000. *The Sea Peoples and Their World: A Reassessment.* UMM 108. Philadelphia: University Museum of the University of Pennsylvania.

Oriental Institute, Epigraphic Survey. 1932. *Medinet Habu*, vol. 2, *Plates 55–130: Later Historical Records of Ramses III*. OIP. Chicago: University of Chicago Press.

———. 1986. *Reliefs and Inscriptions at Karnak*, vol. 4, *The Battle Reliefs of King Sety I*. OIP. Chicago: University of Chicago Press.

Ornan, Tallay. 2010. "Humbaba, the Bull of Heaven and the Contribution of Images to the Reconstruction of the Gilgameš Epic." Pp. 229–60, 411–24 in *Gilgamesch—Bilder eines Helden: Ikonographie und Überlieferung von Motiven im Gilgameš-Epos*, edited by Hans Ulrich Steymans. OBO 245. Fribourg: Academic Press; Göttingen: Vandenhoeck & Ruprecht.

———. 2016. "Sketches and Final Works of Art: The Drawings and Paintings of Kuntiller ʿAjrud revisited." *TA* 43:3–26.

Ornan, Tallay, et al. 2012. "'The Lord Will Roar from Zion' (Amos 1:2): The Lion as a Divine Attribute on a Jerusalem Seal and Other Hebrew Glyptic Finds from the Western Wall Plaza Excavations." *ʿAtiqot* 72:1–13.

Orthmann, Winfried. 1971. *Untersuchungen zur späthethitischen Kunst*. Bonn: Habelt.

Ortlund, E. N. 2010. *Theophany and Chaoskampf: The Interpretation of Theophanic Imagery in the Baal Epic, Isaiah and the Twelve*. Gorgias Ugaritic Studies 5. Piscataway, NJ: Gorgias.

Ortner, Sherry. 1996. *Making Gender: The Politics and Erotics of Culture*. Boston: Beacon.

Osborne, James F. 2011. "Secondary Mortuary Practice and the Bench Tomb: Structure and Practice in Iron Age Judah." *JNES* 70:35–53.

Otto, Eckart. 1993. "Town and Rural Countryside in Ancient Israelite Law: Reception and Redaction in Cuneiform and Israelite Law." *JSOT* 57:3–22.

———. 2012. *Deuteronomium 1, 1–4, 43*. Herders Theologischer Kommentar zum Alten Testament. Freiburg im Breisgau: Herder.

Otto, S. 2001. *Jehu, Elia und Elisa: Die Erzählung von der Jehu-Revolution und die Komposition der Elia-Elisa-Erzählungen*. BWANT 152. Stuttgart: Kohlhammer.

Overland, Paul. 1996. "Structure in the Wisdom of Amenemope and Proverbs." Pp. 279–95 in *"Go to the Land I Will Show You": Studies in Honor of Dwight W. Young*, edited by Joseph Coleson and Victor Matthews. Winona Lake, IN: Eisenbrauns.

———. 2008. "Chiasm." Pp. 54–57 in *Dictionary of the Old Testament: Wisdom, Poetry and Writings*, edited by Tremper Longman III and Peter Enns. Downers Grove, IL: InterVarsity.

Owen, David I. 1981. "Ugarit, Canaan and Egypt: Some New Epigraphic Evidence from Tel Aphek in Israel." Pp. 49–53 in *Ugarit in Retrospect: Fifty Years of Ugarit and Ugaritic*, edited by G. Douglas Young. Winona Lake, IN: Eisenbrauns.

Pace, Leann. 2014. "Feasting and Everyday Meals in the World of the Hebrew Bible: The Relationship Reexamined through Material Culture and Texts." Pp. 179–98 in *Feasting in the Archaeology and Texts of the Hebrew Bible and Ancient Near East*, edited by Peter Altmann and Janling Fu. Winona Lake, IN: Eisenbrauns.

Palestine Exploration Fund. 1923. "Notes and News: A New Chronological Classification of Palestinian Archaeology." *Palestine Exploration Fund Quarterly Statement* April:54–55.

Panitz-Cohen, N. 2006. "Processes of Ceramic Change and Continuity: Tel Batash in the Second Millennium BCE as a Test Case." PhD dissertation, Hebrew University.

Panofsky, Erwin. 1970. *Meaning in the Visual Arts*. Harmondsworth: Penguin.

Pappa, Eleftheria. 2013. *Early Iron Age Exchange in the West: Phoenicians in the Mediterranean and the Atlantic*. ANESSup 43. Leuven: Peeters.

Pappe, Ilan. 2004. *A History of Modern Palestine: One Land, Two Peoples*. Cambridge: Cambridge University Press.

Pardee, Dennis. 1985. Review of *Scripture in Context: Essays on the Comparative Method*, edited by Carl D. Evans, William W. Hallo, and John B. White. *JNES* 44:221–22.

———. 1988a. "An Evaluation of the Proper Names from Ebla from a West Semitic Perspective: Pantheon Distribution according to Genre." Pp. 119–51 in *Eblaite Personal Names and Semitic Name-Giving: Papers of a Symposium in Rome, July 15–17 1985*, edited by Alfonso Archi. Archivi reali di Ebla Studi 1. Rome: Missione archaeologica italiana in Siria.

———. 1988b. *Les textes paramythologiques de la 24ᵉ campagne (1961)*. Ras Shamra-Ougarit 4. Paris: Éditions Recherche sur les civilisations.

———. 2000. *Les Textes Rituels*. 2 vols. Ras Shamra-Ougarit 12. Paris: Éditions Recherche sur les civilisations.

———. 2002. *Ritual and Cult at Ugarit*. WAW 10. Atlanta: Society of Biblical Literature.

———. 2009. "A New Aramaic Inscription from Zincirli." *BASOR* 356:51–71.

———. 2013. "A Brief Case for the Language of the 'Gezer Calendar' as Phoenician." Pp. 226–46 in *Linguistic Studies in Phoenician in Memory of J. Brian Peckham*, edited by Robert D. Holmstedt and Aaron Schade. Winona Lake, IN: Eisenbrauns.

Park, Song-Mi Suzie. 2015. "Israel in Its Neighboring Context," Pp. 28–46 in *The Wiley Blackwell Companion to Ancient Israel*. Malden, MA: John Wiley & Sons.

Parker, Bradley J. 2001. *The Mechanics of Empire: The Northern Frontier of Assyria as a Case Study in*

Imperial Dynamics. Helsinki: The Neo-Assyrian Text Corpus Project.

———. 2003. "Archaeological Manifestations of Empire: Assyria's Imprint on Southeastern Anatolia." *AJA* 107:525–57.

———. 2011. "Bread Ovens, Social Networks and Gendered Space: An Ethnoarchaeological Study of *Tandir* Ovens in Southeastern Anatolia." *American Antiquity* 76:603–27.

———. 2013. "Geographies of Power: Territoriality and Empire during the Mesopotamian Iron Age." *Archaeological Papers of the American Anthropological Association* 22:126–44.

Parker, Simon B. 1989. *The Pre-Biblical Narrative Tradition: Essays on the Ugaritic Poems Keret and Aqhat.* RBS 24. Atlanta: Scholars Press.

———. 1997. *Stories in Scripture and Inscriptions: Comparative Studies on Narratives in Northwest Semitic Inscriptions and the Hebrew Bible.* Oxford: Oxford University Press.

———. 2000. "Ugaritic Literature and the Bible." *NEA* 63:228–31.

Parker Pearson, Michael. 1999. *The Archaeology of Death and Burial.* College Station: Texas A&M University Press.

Parkinson, Richard B. 1991a. "Teachings, Discourses and Tales from the Middle Kingdom." Pp. 91–122 in *Middle Kingdom Studies,* edited by Stephen Quirke. New Malden, Surrey: SIA.

———. 1991b. *Voices from Ancient Egypt: An Anthology of Middle Kingdom Writings.* Norman: University of Oklahoma Press.

———. 2002. *Poetry and Culture in Middle Kingdom Egypt: A Dark Side to Perfection.* London: Continuum.

Parpola, Asko. 1996. "A Sumerian Motif in Late Indus Seals?" Pp. 227–34 in *The Indian Ocean in Antiquity,* edited by Julian Reade. London: Kegan Paul International and the British Museum.

Parpola, Simo. 2003. "Assyria's Expansion in the 8th and 7th Centuries and Its Long-Term Repercussions in the West." Pp. 99–111 in *Symbiosis, Symbolism, and the Power of the Past: Canaan, Ancient Israel, and Their Neighbors from the Late Bronze Age through Roman Palaestina,* edited by William G. Dever and Seymour Gitin. Winona Lake, IN: Eisenbrauns.

———. 2010. "Neo-Assyrian Concepts of Kingship and Their Heritage in Mediterranean Antiquity." Pp. 35–44 in *Concepts of Kingship in Antiquity,* edited by Giovanni B. Lanfranchi and Robert Rollinger. Padova: S.A.R.G.O.N.

Parrot, André. 1937a. "Les fouilles de Mari, troisième campagne (hiver 1935–36)." *Syria* 18:54–84.

———. 1937b. "Les peintures du palais de Mari." *Syria* 18:325–54.

———. 1951. "Cylindre hittite nouvellement acquis (AO 20.138)." *Syria* 28:180–90.

———. 1957. *Le Musée du Louvre et la Bible.* Neuchâtel: Delachaux & Niestlé.

Parrot, André, and Georges Dossin. 1950. *Correspondance des gouverneurs de Qaṭṭunân.* Archives royales de Mari 27. Paris: Éditions Recherche de civilisations.

Payne, Sebastian. 1973. "Kill-Off Patterns in Sheep and Goats: The Mandibles from Asvan Kale." *Anatolian Studies* 23:281–303.

Pearce, Laurie E. 1995. "The Scribes and Scholars of Ancient Mesopotamia." *CANE* 4:2265–78.

———. 2006. "New Evidence for Judeans in Babylonia." Pp. 399–411 in *Judah and the Judeans in the Persian Period,* edited by Oded Lipschits and Manfred Oeming. Winona Lake, IN: Eisenbrauns.

———. 2011. "'Judean': A Special Status in Neo-Babylonian and Achemenid Babylonia?" Pp. 267–77 in *Judah and the Judeans in the Achaemenid Period: Negotiating Identity in an International Context,* edited by Oded Lipschits, Gary N. Knoppers, and Manfred Oeming. Winona Lake, IN: Eisenbrauns.

Pearce, Laurie E., and Cornelia Wunsch. 2014. *Documents of Judean Exiles and West Semites in Babylonia in the Collection of David Sofer.* CUSAS 28. Bethesda, MD: CDL Press.

Pearsall, Deborah M. 2000. *Paleoethnobotany: A Handbook of Procedures.* 2nd ed. San Diego: Academic Press.

Peckham, J. Brian. 1968. *The Development of Late Phoenician Scripts.* HSS 20. Cambridge, MA: Harvard University Press.

Peden, Alexander J. 2001. *The Graffiti of Pharaonic Egypt: Scope and Roles of Informal Writings (c. 3100–332 BC).* PÄ 17. Leiden: Brill.

Peek-Asa, C., M. Ramirez, H. Seligson, and K. Shoaf. 2003. "Seismic, Structural, and Individual Factors Associated with Earthquake Related Injury." *Injury Prevention* 9:62–66.

Peleg-Barkat, Orit. 2013. "The Architectural Decoration from the Hasmonean and Herodian Palaces at Jericho and Cypros." Pp. 235–69 in *Hasmonean and Herodian Palaces at Jericho: Final Reports of the 1973–1987 Excavations,* vol. 5, *The Finds From Jericho and Cypros,* edited by Rachel Bar-Nathan and Judit Gärtner. Jerusalem: Israel Exploration Society.

Perdu, Olivier. 2002. *Recueil des inscriptions royales saïtes.* Paris: Cybèle.

Perdue, Leo G. 2007. *Wisdom Literature: A Theological History.* Louisville: Westminster John Knox.

———. 2008. "Scribes, Sages, and Seers: An Introduction." Pp. 1–34 in *Scribes, Sages, and Seers: The Sage in the Eastern Mediterranean World,* edited by

Leo G. Perdue. FRLANT 219. Göttingen: Vanden-hoeck & Ruprecht.

Perdue, Leo G., Warren Carter, and Coleman A. Baker, eds. 2015. *Israel and Empire: A Postcolonial History of Israel and Early Judaism*. London: Bloomsbury.

Pernigotti, Sergio. 1997. "Priests." Pp. 121–50 in *The Egyptians*, edited by Sergio Donadoni. Translated by Robert Bianchi et al. Chicago: University of Chicago Press.

Perry-Gal, Lee, Adi Erlich, Ayelet Gilboa, and Guy Bar-Oz. 2015. "Earliest Economic Exploitation of Chicken outside East Asia: Evidence from the Hellenistic Southern Levant." *Proceedings of the National Academy of Sciences* 112 (32): 9849–54. http://www.pnas.org/content/112/32/9849.full.

Person, Raymond F., and Robert Rezetko. 2016. *Empirical Models Challenging Biblical Criticism*. AIL 25. Atlanta: Society of Biblical Literature.

Peters, F. E. 1970. *The Harvest of Hellenism: A History of the Near East from Alexander the Great to the Triumph of Christianity*. New York: Simon & Schuster.

Petrie, William M. Flinders. 1891. *Tell el Hesy*. London: Palestine Exploration Fund.

———. 1904. *Methods and Aims in Archaeology*. London: Macmillan.

———. 1906. *Hyksos and Israelite Cities*. London: Bernard Quaritch.

———. 1909. *Memphis I*. British School of Archaeology in Egypt 15. London: School of Archaeology in Egypt.

Petter, Thomas D. 2014. *The Land between the Two Rivers: Early Israelite Identities in Central Transjordan*. Winona Lake, IN: Eisenbrauns.

Pettinato, Giovanni. 1991. *Ebla: A New Look at History*. Translated by C. Faith Richardson. Baltimore: Johns Hopkins University Press.

Piccirillo, Michele, and Eugenio Alliata, eds. 1999. *The Madaba Map Centenary*. Jerusalem: Studium Biblicum Franciscanum.

Piperno, Dolores R., Ehud Weiss, Irene Holst, and Dani Nadel. 2004. "Processing of Wild Cereal Grains in the Upper Paleolithic Revealed by Starch Grain Analysis." *Nature* 430:670–73.

Pitard, Wayne T. 1987. *Ancient Damascus: A Historical Study of the Syrian City-State from Earliest Times until Its Fall to the Assyrians in 732 B.C.E.* Winona Lake, IN: Eisenbrauns.

———. 2002. "Tombs and Offerings: Archaeological Data and Comparative Methodology in the Study of Death in Israel." Pp. 145–68 in *Sacred Time, Sacred Place: Archaeology and the Religion of Israel*, edited by Barry M. Gittlen. Winona Lake, IN: Eisenbrauns.

Pitkänen, Pekka. 2010. *Joshua*. Apollos Old Testament Commentary 6. Leicester: Inter-Varsity.

———. 2014. "Pentateuch-Joshua: A Settler-Colonial Document of a Supplanting Society." *Settler Colonial Studies* 4 (3): 227–44.

———. 2015. "Reading Genesis–Joshua as a Unified Document from an Early Date: A Settler Colonial Perspective." *Biblical Theology Bulletin* 45:3–31.

———. 2016a. "The Ecological-Evolutionary Theory, Migration, Settler Colonialism, Sociology of Violence and the Origins of Ancient Israel." *Cogent Social Sciences* 2:1210717. https://doi.org/10.1080/23311886.2016.1210717.

———. 2016b. "P/H and D in Joshua 22:9–34." *Biblische Notizen* 171:27–35.

———. 2017a. "Ancient Israelite Population Economy: Ger, Toshav, Nakhri and Karat as Settler Colonial Categories." *JSOT* 42:139–53.

———. 2017b. *A Commentary on Numbers: Narrative, Ritual and Colonialism*. London: Routledge.

Pleiner, Radomir, and Judith K. Bjorkman. 1974. "The Assyrian Iron Age: The History of Iron in the Assyrian Civilization." *Proceedings of the American Philosophical Society* 118 (3):283–313.

Poché, Christian. 2002. "Les lyres de la péninsule arabique selon l'archéologie, les sources écrites et la transission orale." Pp. 23–29 in *Archéologie et musique: Actes du colloque des 9 et 10 fevrier 2001*, edited by Christine Laloue et al. Paris: Cité de la Musique.

Polak, Frank H. 2006. "Sociolinguistics and the Judean Speech Community in the Achaemenid Empire." Pp. 589–628 in *Judah and the Judeans in the Persian Period*, edited by Oded Lipschits and Manfred Oeming. Winona Lake, IN: Eisenbrauns.

Polanyi, Karl. 1957. "The Economy as Instituted Process." Pp. 243–69 in *Trade and Market in the Early Empires*, edited by Karl Polanyi, Conrad Arensberg, and Harry Pearson. Glencoe, IL: Free Press.

Pongratz-Leisten, Beate. 2012. "Sacrifice in the Ancient Near East: Offering and Ritual Killing." Pp. 291–304 in *Sacred Killing: The Archaeology of Sacrifice in the Ancient Near East*, edited by Anne M. Porter and Glenn M. Schwartz. Winona Lake, IN: Eisenbrauns.

———. 2013. "All the King's Men: Authority, Kingship and the Rise of the Elites in Assyria." Pp. 285–309 in *Experiencing Power, Generating Authority: Cosmos, Politics, and the Ideology of Kingship in Ancient Egypt and Mesopotamia*, edited by Jane A. Hill, Philip Jones, and Antonio Morales. Penn Museum International Research Conferences 6. Philadelphia: University of Pennsylvania Museum of Archaeology and Anthropology.

Pope, Marvin H. 1955. *El in the Ugaritic Texts*. VTSup 2. Leiden: Brill.

Porada, Edith. 1948. *Corpus of Ancient Near Eastern Seals in North American Collections I: The Collection of the Pierpont Morgan Library*. Bollingen Series 14; Washington DC: Bollingen Foundation.

Porten, Bezalel. 1968. *Archives from Elephantine: The Life of an Ancient Jewish Military Colony*. Berkeley: University of California Press.

———. 1981. "The Identity of King Adon." *BA* 44:36–52.

———. 1996. *The Elephantine Papyri in English: Three Millennia of Cross-Cultural Continuity and Change*. DMOA 22. Leiden: Brill.

Porten, Bezalel, and Ada Yardeni. 1986. *Textbook of Aramaic Documents from Ancient Egypt*, vol. 1, *Letters*. Jerusalem: Hebrew University.

———. 1989. *Textbook of Aramaic Documents from Ancient Egypt*, vol. 2, *Contracts*. Jerusalem: Hebrew University.

———. 1993. *Textbook of Aramaic Documents from Ancient Egypt*, vol. 3, *Literature, Accounts, Lists*. Jerusalem: Hebrew University.

———. 1999. *Textbook of Aramaic Documents from Ancient Egypt*, vol. 4, *Ostraca and Assorted Inscriptions*. Jerusalem: Hebrew University.

Porter, B. N. 2009. "Blessings from a Crown, Offerings to a Drum: Were There Non-Anthropomorphic Deities in Ancient Mesopotamia?" Pp. 153–94 in *What Is a God? Anthropomorpic and Non-Anthropomorphic Aspects of Deity in Ancient Mesopotamia*, edited by B. N. Porter. Winona Lake, IN: Eisenbrauns.

Porter, Benjamin W. 2013. *Complex Communities: The Archaeology of Early Iron Age West-Central Jordan*. Tucson: University of Arizona.

———. 2016. "Assembling the Iron Age Levant: The Archaeology of Communities, Polities, and Imperial Peripheries." *Journal of Archaeological Research* 24:373–420.

Porter, Bertha, and Rosalind L. B. Moss. 1934. *Topographical Bibliography of Ancient Egyptian Hieroglyphic Texts, Reliefs, and Paintings*. Vol. 4. Oxford: Clarendon.

Porter, N. Barbara. 2003. *Trees, Kings, and Politics: Studies in Assyrian Iconography*. OBO 197. Fribourg: Academic Press; Göttingen: Vandenhoeck & Ruprecht.

Posener, Georges. 1951. "Les richesses inconnues de la littérature égyptienne (Recherches littéraires I)." *Revue d'égyptologie* 6:27–48.

———. 1952. "Compléments aux 'Richesses inconnues.'" *Revue d'égyptologie* 9:117–20.

Postgate, John Nicholas. 1972. "The Role of the Temple in the Mesopotamian Secular Community." Pp. 811–25 in *Man, Settlement, and Urbanism*, edited by Peter J. Ucko, Ruth Tringham, and G. W. Dimbleby. Cambridge, MA: Schenkman.

———. 1974. "Some Remarks on Conditions in the Assyrian Countryside." *JESHO* 17:225–43.

———. 1992. "The Land of Assur and the Yoke of Assur." *World Archaeology* 23 (3): 247–63.

———. 2007. "Introduction." Pp. 1–3 in *Languages of Iraq, Ancient and Modern*, edited by J. N. Postgate. Cambridge: Cambridge University Press.

———. 2013. *Bronze Age Bureaucracy: Writing and the Practice of Government in Assyria*. Cambridge: Cambridge University Press.

Powell, Marvin. 1996. "Money in Mesopotamia." *JESHO* 39:224–42.

Preiser, Wolfgang. 1972. "Vergeltung und Sühne im altisraelitischen Strafrecht." Pp. 236–77 in *Um das Prinzip der Vergeltung in Religion und Recht des Alten Testaments*, edited by K. Koch. Wege der Forschung 125. Darmstadt: Wissenshaftliche Buchgesellschaft.

Price, Simon. 1988. "The History of the Hellenistic Period." Pp. 315–37 in *The Oxford History of Greece and the Hellenistic World*, edited by John Boardman, Jasper Griffin, and Oswyn Murray. Oxford: Oxford University Press.

Pritchard, James B. 1943. *Palestinian Figurines in Relation to Certain Goddesses Known through Literature*. AOS 24. New Haven: American Oriental Society.

———, ed. 1969a. *Ancient Near Eastern Texts Relating to the Old Testament*. 3rd ed. Princeton: Princeton University Press.

———. 1969b. *The Ancient Near East in Pictures Relating to the Old Testament*. 2nd ed. Princeton: Princeton University Press.

———. 1969c. *The Ancient Near East: Supplementary Texts and Pictures Relating to the Old Testament*. Princeton: Princeton University Press.

———, ed. 2011. *The Ancient Near East: An Anthology of Texts and Pictures*. Princeton: Princeton University Press.

Provan, Iain, V. Philips Long, and Tremper Longman III. 2015. *A Biblical History of Israel*. 2nd ed. Louisville: Westminster John Knox.

Pruzsinszky, Regine. 2009. *Mesopotamian Chronology of the 2nd Millennium B.C.: An Introduction to the Textual Evidence and Related Chronological Issues*. Contributions to the Chronology of the Eastern Mediterranean 22. Vienna: Österreichische Akademie der Wissenschaften.

———. 2016. "Musicians and Monkeys: Ancient Near Eastern Clay Plaques Displaying Musicians and their Socio-Cultural Role." Pp. 23–34 in *Musicians in the Coroplastic Art of the Ancient World: Iconography, Ritual Contexts and Functions*, edited by Angela Bellia and Clemente Marconi. Rome: Fabrizio Serra Editore.

Pucci Ben Zeev, Miriam. 2010. "Jews among Greeks and Romans." Pp. 237–55 in *The Eerdmans Dictionary of Early Judaism*, edited by John J. Collins and Daniel C. Harlow. Grand Rapids: Eerdmans.

Pulak, Cemal. 1997. "The Uluburun Shipwreck." Pp. 233–62 in *Res Maritimae: Cyprus and the Eastern Mediterranean from Prehistory to Late Antiquity*, edited by Stuart Swiny, Robert Hohlfelder, and Helena Wylde Swiny. American Schools of Oriental Research Archaeological Reports 4. Atlanta: Scholars Press.

———. 1998. "The Uluburun Shipwreck: An Overview." *International Journal of Nautical Archaeology* 27:188–224.

———. 2008. "The Uluburun Shipwreck and Late Bronze Age Trade." Pp. 289–310 in *Beyond Babylon: Art, Trade, and Diplomacy in the Second Millennium B.C.*, edited by Joan Aruz, Kim Benzel, and Jean M. Evans. New York: Metropolitan Museum of Art.

Quack, Joachim Friedrich. 2003. *Einführung in die altägyptische Literaturgeschichte III: Die demotische und gräko-ägyptische Literatur*. Einführungen und Quellentexte zur Ägyptologie 3. Münster: Lit.

Quirke, Stephen. 2004. *Egyptian Literature 1800 B.C.: Questions and Readings*. London: Golden House.

Rabinowitz, Isaac. 1956. "Aramaic Inscriptions of the Fifth Century B.C.E. from a North-Arab Shrine in Egypt." *JNES* 15:1–9.

Radner, Ellen. 2005. *Die Macht der Namen: Altorientalische Strategien zur Selbsterhaltung*. Arbeiten und Untersuchungen zur Keilschriftkunde 8. Wiesbaden: Harrassowitz.

Radner, Karen. 1999. "Money in the Neo-Assyrian Empire." Pp. 127–57 in *Trade and Finance in Ancient Mesopotamia*, edited by J. G. Dercksen. Mos Studies 1. Leiden: Nederlands Historisch-Archaeologisch Instituut te Istanbul.

———. 2007. "Hired Labour in the Neo-Assyrian Empire." *SAAB* 16:185–226.

———. 2010. "Assyrian and Non-Assyrian Kingship in the First Millennium BC." Pp. 25–34 in *Concepts of Kingship in Antiquity*, edited by Giovanni B. Lanfranchi and Robert Rollinger. Padova: S.A.R.G.O.N.

Rahmani, L. Y. 1981a. "Ancient Jerusalem's Funerary Customs and Tombs, Part One." *BA* 44:171–77.

———. 1981b. "Ancient Jerusalem's Funerary Customs and Tombs, Part Two." *BA* 44:229–35.

Rainey, Anson F. 1963. "Business Agents at Ugarit." *IEJ* 13:313–21.

———. 1978. "The Toponymics of Eretz-Israel." *BASOR* 231:1–17.

———. 1983. "The Biblical Shephelah of Judah." *BASOR* 251:1–10.

———. 1984. "The Early Historical Geography of the Negeb." Pp. 88–104 in *Beer-Sheba II: The Early Iron Age Settlements*, edited by Ze'ev Herzog. Tel Aviv: Institute of Archaeology.

———. 1987. Review of *Habiru-Hebräer: Eine sozio-linguistische Studie über die Herkunft des Gentiliziums ibrî zum Appellativum ḫabiru*, by Oswald Loretz. *JAOS* 107:539–41.

———. 2001a. "Mesha and Syntax." Pp. 287–307 *in The Land That I Will Show You: Essays on the History and Archaeology of the Ancient Near East in Honour of J. Maxwell Miller*, edited by J. Andrew Dearman and M. Patrick Graham. Sheffield: Sheffield Academic Press.

———. 2001b. "Stones for Bread: Archaeology versus History." *NEA* 64:140–49.

———. 2006. "Excursus 11.2: The Solomonic Districts." Pp. 174–78 in *The Sacred Bridge: Carta's Atlas of the Biblical World*, by Anson F. Rainey and Steven Notley. Jerusalem: Carta.

———. 2007. "Whence Came the Israelites and Their Language?" *IEJ* 57:41–64.

———. 2008. "Shasu or Habiru: Who Were the Israelites?" *BAR* 34:51–55.

Rainey, Anson F., and R. Steven Notley. 2006 and 2014. *The Sacred Bridge: Carta's Atlas of the Biblical World*. 1st and 2nd editions. Jerusalem: Carta.

Rajak, Tessa. 2009. *Translation and Survival: The Greek Bible of the Ancient Jewish Diaspora*. Oxford: Oxford University Press.

Ramos, Melissa. 2015. "Making the Cut: Covenant, Curse and Oath in Deuteronomy 27–29 and the Incantation Plaques of Arslan Tash." Paper presented at the Annual Meeting of the Society of Biblical Literature, Atlanta.

Random House Webster's College Dictionary. 1991. New York: Random House.

Rasmussen, Carl G. 2010. *Zondervan Atlas of the Bible*. Rev. ed. Grand Rapids: Zondervan.

Ratner, Robert, and Bruce Zuckerman. 1986. "'A Kid in Milk?' New Photographs of KTU 1.23, Line 14." *HUCA* 57:15–60.

Ray, J. D. 1995. "Egyptian Wisdom Literature." Pp. 17–29 in *Wisdom in Ancient Israel: Essays in Honour of J. A. Emerton*, edited by John Day, Robert P. Gordon, and H. G. M. Williamson. Cambridge: Cambridge University Press.

Ray, Paul. 2014. Review of *Judah in the Neo-Babylonian Period: The Archaeology of Desolation*, by Avraham Faust. *NEASB* 59:40–43.

Reade, Julian. 1979. "Ideology and Propaganda in Assyrian Art." Pp. 329–43 in *Power and Propaganda: A Symposium on Ancient Empires*, edited by Mogens Trolle Larsen. Mesopotamia 7. Copenhagen: Akademisk Forlag.

Reali, Chiara. 2014. "The Seal Impressions from ᶜEzbet Rushdi, Area R/III of Tell el-Dabᶜa: Preliminary Report." *ÄL* 22/23:67–73.

Redding, Richard W. 1984. "Theoretical Determinations of a Herder's Decisions: Modeling Variations in the Sheep/Goat Ratio." Pp. 223–41 in *Animals in Archaeology*, vol. 3, *Early Herders and Their Flocks*, edited by Juliet Clutton-Brock and Caroline Grigson. British Archaeological Reports International Series. Oxford: Archaeopress.

Redford, Donald B. 1967. *History and Chronology of the Eighteenth Dynasty of Egypt: Seven Studies.* Toronto: Toronto University Press.

———. 1973. "Studies of Akhenaten at Thebes 1: A Report of the Work of the Akhenaten Temple Project of the University Museum, The University of Pennsylvania." *JARCE* 10:77–94.

———. 1975. "Studies of Akhenaten at Thebes 2: A Report of the Work of the Akhenaten Temple Project of the University Museum, The University of Pennsylvania." *JARCE* 12:9–14.

———. 1976. "The Sun-Disc in Akhenaten's Program: Its Worship and Antecedents, Part 1." *JARCE* 13:47–61.

———. 1982. "Pithom." Pp. 1054–58 in *Lexikon der Ägyptologie*, vol. 4, edited by Wolfgang Helck and Eberhard Otto. Wiesbaden: Harrassowitz.

———. 1984. *Akhenaten: The Heretic King.* Princeton: Princeton University Press.

———. 1987. "An Egyptological Perspective on the Exodus Narrative." Pp. 137–61 in *Egypt, Israel, Sinai: Archaeological and Historical Relationships in the Biblical Period*, edited by Anson F. Rainey. Tel Aviv: Tel Aviv University Press.

———. 1988. *The Akhenaten Temple Project.* Vol. 2. Toronto: Akhenaten Temple Project/University of Toronto Press.

———. 1992a. *Egypt, Canaan, and Israel in Ancient Times.* Princeton: Princeton University Press.

———. 1992b. "Pi-Hahiroth." *ABD* 5:371.

———. 2000. "New Light on Egypt's Stance toward Asia, 610–586 BCE." Pp. 183–96 in *Rethinking the Foundations: Historiography in the Ancient World and in the Bible; Essays in Honour of John Van Seters*, edited by Steven L. McKenzie and Thomas Römer. New York: de Gruyter.

———. 2003. *The Wars in Syria and Palestine of Thutmose III.* CHANE 16. Leiden: Brill.

———. 2006. *A History of Ancient Egypt: Egyptian Civilization in Context.* Dubuque, IA: Kendall/Hunt.

———. 2013. "Akhenaten: New Theories and Old Facts." *BASOR* 369:9–34.

Redford, Donald B., and Ray W. Smith. 1976. *The Akhenaten Temple Project.* Vol 1. Warminster, UK: Aris & Phillips.

Redford, Susan. 2002. *The Harem Conspiracy: The Murder of Ramesses III.* Dekalb: Northern Illinois University Press.

Redmount, Carol. 1995. "Ethnicity, Pottery, and the Hyksos at Tell El-Maskhuta in the Egyptian Delta." *BA* 58:181–90.

Reeves, Nicholas. 2001. *Akhenaten: Egypt's False Prophet.* London: Thames & Hudson.

Regev, Eyal. 2013. *The Hasmoneans: Ideology, Archaeology, Identity.* Journal of Ancient Judaism Supplements 10. Göttingen: Vandenhoeck & Ruprecht.

Reifenberg, Adolf. 1955. *The Struggle between the Desert and the Sown: Rise and Fall of Agriculture in the Levant.* Jerusalem: Publishing Department of the Jewish Agency.

Reiner, Erica. 1960. "Plague Amulets and House Blessings." *JNES* 9:148–55.

Reisner, G. 1924. *Harvard Excavation at Samaria 1908–1910.* Cambridge, MA: Harvard University Press.

Reitz, E. J., and E. S. Wing. 1999. *Zooarchaeology.* Cambridge: Cambridge University Press.

Rendsburg, Gary. 1992. "The Date of the Exodus and Conquest/Settlement: The Case for the 1100s." *VT* 42:510–27.

Renfrew, Colin. 1975. "Trade as Action at a Distance: Questions of Integration and Communication." Pp. 3–59 in *Ancient Civilization and Trade*, edited by Jeremy Sabloff and C. C. Lamberg-Karlovsky. Albuquerque: University of New Mexico Press.

Renfrew, Colin, and Paul Bahn. 2016. *Archaeology: Theories, Methods and Practice.* 7th ed. London: Thames & Hudson.

Renger, Johannes. 1966. "Untersuchungen zum Priestertum in der altbabylonischen Zeit (1. Teil)." *Zeitschrift für Assyriologie* 58:110–88.

———. 1969. "Untersuchungen zum Priestertum in der altbabylonischen Zeit (2. Teil)." *Zeitschrift für Assyriologie* 59:104–230.

Revell, Ernest J. 1996. *The Designation of the Individual: Expressive Usage in Biblical Narrative.* CBET 14. Kampen: Kok Pharos.

Ribar, J. W. 1973. "Death Cult Practices in Ancient Palestine." PhD dissertation, University of Michigan.

Richardson, M. E. J. 2000. *Hammurabi's Laws: Text, Translation and Glossary.* Biblical Seminar 73; Semitic Texts and Studies 2. Sheffield: Sheffield Academic Press.

Richardson, Peter. 2003. "An Architectural Case for Synagogues as Associations." Pp. 90–117 in *The Ancient Synagogue from Its Origins until 200 C.E.: Papers Presented at an International Conference at Lund University, October 14–17, 2001*, edited by Birger Olsson and Magnus Zetterholm. Coniectanea Biblica: New Testament Series 39. Stockholm: Almqvist & Wiksell.

Richardson, Seth. 2010a. "Introduction: The Fields of Rebellion and Periphery." Pp. xvii–xxxii in *Rebellions and Peripheries in the Cuneiform World*, edited by Seth Richardson. AOS 91. New Haven: American Oriental Society.

———. 2010b. "Writing Rebellion Back into the Record: A Methodologies Toolkit." Pp. 1–27 in *Rebellions and Peripheries in the Cuneiform World*, edited by Seth Richardson. AOS 91. New Haven: American Oriental Society.

———. 2011. "Mesopotamia and the 'New' Military History." Pp. 11–51 in *Recent Directions in the Military History of the Ancient World*, edited by Lee L. Brice and Jennifer T. Roberts. Claremont, CA: Regina.

———. 2015. "Insurgency and Terror in Mesopotamia." P. 31 in *Brill's Companion to Insurgency and Terrorism in the Ancient Mediterranean*, edited by Timothy Howe and Lee L. Brice. Warfare in the Ancient Mediterranean World 1. Leiden: Brill.

Richter, Thomas, and Sarah Lange. 2012. *Das Archiv des Idadda: Die Keilschrifttexte aus den deutsch-syrischen Ausgrabungen 2001–2003 im Königspalast von Qaṭna*. Qaṭna Studien 3. Wiesbaden: Harrassowitz.

Ristau, Kenneth A. 2016. *Reconstructing Jerusalem: Persian-Period Prophetic Perspectives*. Winona Lake, IN: Eisenbrauns.

Ritmeyer, Leen. 2015. "Was One of Jerusalem's Greatest Archaeological Mysteries Solved?" http://www.ritmeyer.com/2015/11/03/was-one-of-jerusalems-greatest-archaeological-mysteries-solved/.

Roberts, J. J. M. 1971. "The Hand of Yahweh." *VT* 21:244–51.

———. 2003. "Solomon's Jerusalem and the Zion Tradition." Pp. 163–70 in *Jerusalem in Bible and Archaeology: The First Temple Period*, edited by Andrew G. Vaughan and Ann E. Killebrew. SymS 18. Atlanta: Society of Biblical Literature.

Roberts, J. J. M., et al. 2003. *Hebrew Inscriptions: Texts from the Period of the Monarchy*. New Haven: Yale University Press.

Roberts, N., W. J. Eastwood, C. Kuzucuoğlu, G. Fiorentino, and V. Caracuta. 2011. "Climatic, Vegetation and Cultural Change in the Eastern Mediterranean during the Mid-Holocene Environmental Transition. *The Holocene* 21:147–62.

Roberts, Ryan N. 2012. "Terra Terror: An Interdisciplinary Study of Earthquakes in Ancient Near Eastern Texts and the Hebrew Bible." PhD dissertation, University of California, Los Angeles.

———. 2015. "Is Anyone Home? Amos 6.8–11 in Light of Post-Earthquake Housing." Pp. 186–200 in *Methods, Theories, Imagination: Social Scientific Approaches in Biblical Studies*, edited by David J. Chalcraft, Frauke Uhlenbruch, and Rebecca S. Watson. The Bible and Social Science 1. Sheffield: Sheffield Phoenix Press.

Robertson, Warren C. 2010. *Drought, Famine, Plague, and Pestilence: Ancient Israel's Understandings of and Responses to Natural Catastrophes*. Gorgias Dissertations 45. Piscataway, NJ: Gorgias.

Robins, Gay. 1993. "The Representation of Sexual Characteristics in Amarna Art." *JSSEA* 23:29–41.

———. 1997. *The Art of Ancient Egypt*. Cambridge, MA: Harvard University Press.

Robinson, Edward, and Eli Smith. 1841. *Biblical Researches in Palestine, Mount Sinai and Arabia Petraea: A Journal of Travels in the Year 1838*. 2 vols. Boston: Crocker & Brewster.

———. 1856a. *Biblical Researches in Palestine and the Adjacent Regions: A Journal of Travels in the Years 1838 and 1852*. Boston: Crocker & Brewster.

———. 1856b. *Later Biblical Researches in Palestine and in the Adjacent Regions: A Journal of Travels in the Year 1852*. Boston: Crocker & Brewster.

Robinson, Joseph. 1972. *The First Book of Kings*. Cambridge Bible Commentary. Cambridge: Cambridge University Press.

Rocca, Samuel. 2012. *The Fortifications of Ancient Israel and Judah 1200–586 BC*. London: Bloomsbury.

Rochberg, Francesca. 1984. "Canonicity in Cuneiform Texts." *JCS* 36:127–44.

———. 2004. *The Heavenly Writing: Divination, Horoscopy, and Astronomy in Mesopotamian Culture*. Cambridge: Cambridge University Press.

Rofe, Alexander. 1985. "The Laws of Warfare in the Book of Deuteronomy: Their Origins, Intent and Positivity." *JSOT* 10:23–44.

Roisman, Joseph, ed. 2002. *Brill's Companion to Alexander the Great*. Leiden: Brill.

Rollston, Christopher A. 2006. "Epigraphic Essays: An Introduction." *BASOR* 344:1–3.

———. 2010. *Writing and Literacy in the World of Ancient Israel: Epigraphic Evidence from the Iron Age*. ABS 11. Atlanta: Society of Biblical Literature.

———. 2013. "The Ninth Century 'Moabite Pedestal Inscription' from King Mesha's Ataruz: Preliminary Synopsis of an Excavated Epigraphic Text and its Biblical Connections." http://www.rollstonepigraphy.com/?s=Ataruz.

———. 2016. "Intellectual Infrastructure and the Writing of the Pentateuch: Empirical Models from Iron Age Inscriptions." Pp. 15–45 in *Formation of the Pentateuch: Bridging the Academic Cultures of Europe, Israel, and North America*, edited by Jan C. Gertz, Bernard M. Levinson, Dalit Rom-Shiloni, and Konrad Schmid. FAT 111. Tübingen: Mohr Siebeck.

Rom-Shiloni, Dalit. 2013. *Exclusive Inclusivity: Identity Conflict between the Exiles and the People Who Remained (6th-5th Centuries BCE)*. LHB/OTS 543. London: T&T Clark.

Ron, Z. 1966. "Agricultural Terraces in the Judean Mountains." *IEJ* 16:33–49, 111–22.

Root, Bradley W. 2005. "Coinage, War, and Peace in Fourth-Century Yehud." *NEA* 68:131–34.

Rosen, Arlene M. 2007. *Civilizing Climate: Social Responses to Climate Change in the Ancient Near East*. Lanham, MD: Altamira.

Rosen, Arlene M., and Steven Rosen. 2001. "Determinist or Not Determinist? Climate, Environment, and Archaeological Explanation in the Levant." Pp. 535–54 in *Studies in the Archaeology of Israel and Neighboring Lands in Memory of Douglas L. Esse*, edited by Samuel R. Wolff. SAOC 59. Chicago: Oriental Institute of the University of Chicago.

Rosen, Steven. 2009. "History Does Not Repeat Itself: Cyclicity and Particularism in Nomad-Sedentary Relations in the Negev in the Long Term." Pp. 57–86 in *Nomads, Tribes, and the State in the Ancient Near East*, edited by Jeffrey Szuchman. OIS 5. Chicago: University of Chicago Press.

———. 2016. "Basic Instabilities? Climate and Culture in the Negev over the Long Term." *Geoarchaeology* 10:1–17. http://onlinelibrary.wiley.com/doi/10.1002/gea.21572/epdf.

Rostovtzeff, M. 1941. *The Social and Economic History of the Hellenistic World*. 3 vols. Oxford: Oxford University Press.

Roth, Ann Macy. 2001a. "Funerary Ritual." *OEAE* 1:575–80.

———. 2001b. "Opening of the Mouth." *OEAE* 2:605–9.

Roth, Martha T. 1997. *Law Collections from Mesopotamia and Asia Minor*. 2nd ed. WAW 6. Atlanta: Scholars Press.

Routledge, Bruce. 2004. *Moab in the Iron Age: Hegemony, Polity, Archaeology*. Philadelphia: University of Pennsylvania Press.

———. 2008. "Thinking 'Globally' and Analysing 'Locally': South-Central Jordan in the Early Iron Age." Pp. 144–76 in *Israel in Transition: From Late Bronze II to Iron IIa (c. 1250–850 B.C.E.)*, vol. 1, *The Archaeology*, edited by Lester L. Grabbe. LHB/OTS 491. London: T&T Clark.

Rowe, Ignacio Márquez. 2008. "Scribes, Sages, and Seers in Ugarit." Pp. 95–108 in *Scribes, Sages, and Seers: The Sage in the Eastern Mediterranean World*, edited by Leo G. Perdue. FRLANT 219. Göttingen: Vandenhoeck & Ruprecht.

Rowlett, Lori L. 1996. *Joshua and the Rhetoric of Violence: A New Historicist Analysis*. London: A&C Black.

Rowton, Michael B. 1967. "The Physical Environment and the Problem of Nomads." Pp. 109–21 in *Actes de la 15e RAI*, edited by A. Finet. Liège: Les Belles Lettres.

———. 1973. "Urban Autonomy in a Nomadic Environment." *JNES* 32:201–15.

———. 1974. "Enclosed Nomadism." *JESHO* 17:1–30.

Rubin, Aaron. 2008. "The Subgrouping of the Semitic Languages." *Language and Linguistics Compass* 2:61–84.

Runesson, Anders. 2001. *The Origins of the Synagogue: A Socio-Historical Study*. Coniectanea Biblica: New Testament Series 37. Stockholm: Almqvist & Wiksell.

———. 2003. "Persian Imperial Politics, the Beginnings of Public Torah Reading, and the Origins of the Synagogue." Pp. 63–89 in *The Ancient Synagogue from Its Origins until 200 C.E.: Papers Presented at an International Conference at Lund University October 14–17, 2001*, edited by Birger Olsson and Magnus Zetterholm. Stockholm: Almqvist & Wiksell.

Runesson, Anders, Donald D. Binder, and Birger Olsson. 2008. *The Ancient Synagogue from Its Origins to 200 C.E.: A Source Book*. Ancient Judaism and Early Christianity 72. Leiden: Brill.

Russell, James R. 1990. "The Sage in Ancient Iranian Literature." Pp. 81–92 in *The Sage in Israel and the Ancient Near East*, edited by John G. Gammie and Leo G. Perdue. Winona Lake, IN: Eisenbrauns.

Russell, John Malcolm. 1991. *Sennacherib's Palace without Rival at Nineveh*. Chicago: University of Chicago Press.

Russell, Stephen C. 2009. *Images of Egypt in Early Biblical Literature: Cisjordan-Israelite, Transjordan-Israelite, and Judahite Portrayals*. BZAW 403. Berlin: de Gruyter.

———. 2014. "The Hierarchy of Estates in Land and Naboth's Vineyard." *JSOT* 34:453–69.

Russmann, Edna R. 1989. *Egyptian Sculpture: Cairo and Luxor*. London: British Museum.

Ryan, Jordan J. 2017. "Jesus and Synagogue Disputes: Recovering the Institutional Context of Luke 13:10–17." *CBQ* 79:41–59.

Rzepka, Slawomir, Mustafa Nour el-Din, Anna Wodzińska, and Łukasz Jarmużek. 2013. "Egyptian Mission Rescue Excavations in Tell el-Retaba, Part I: New Kingdom Remains." *ÄL* 22/23:253–87.

Sacchi, Paolo. 2000. *The History of the Second Temple Period*. JSOTSup 285. Sheffield: Sheffield Academic Press.

Sader, Hélène. 2014. "The Northern Levant during the Iron Age I Period." Pp. 607–23 in *The Oxford Handbook of the Archaeology of the Levant: C. 8000–332 BCE*, edited by Margreet L. Steiner and Ann E. Killebrew. Oxford: Oxford University Press.

Sadman, Maj. 1938. *Texts from the Time of Akhenaton*. Bibliotheca Aegyptiaca 8. Brussels: Fondation Égyptologique Reine Élisabeth.

Saggs, H. W. F. 1962. *The Greatness That Was Babylon*. Great Civilization Series. London: Sidgwick & Jackson.

———. 1974. "'External Souls' in the Old Testament." *Journal of Semitic Studies* 19:1–12.

Sagona, Antonio, and Paul Zimansky. 2009. *Ancient Turkey*. Routledge World Archaeology. London: Routledge.

Sagrillo, Troy Leiland. 2012. "Šîšaq's Army: 2 Chronicles 12:2–3 from an Egyptological Perspective." Pp. 425–50 in *The Ancient Near East in the 12th–10th Centuries BCE: Culture and History; Proceedings of the International Conference Held at the University of Haifa, 2–5 May, 2010*, edited by Gershon Galil, Ayelet Gilboa, Aren M. Maeir, and Dan'el Kahn. AOAT 392. Münster: Ugarit-Verlag.

Sakenfeld, Katherine D. 1988. "Zelophehad's Daughters." *Perspectives in Religious Studies* 15:37–47.

———. 2002. *The Meaning of* Hesed *in the Hebrew Bible*. Eugene OR: Wipf & Stock.

Salzman, Carl P., ed. 1980. *When Nomads Settle: Processes of Sedentarization as Adaptation and Response*. New York: Praeger.

Samuel, Alan E. 1989. *The Shifting Sands of History: Interpretations of Ptolemaic Egypt*. Publications of the Association of Ancient Historians 2. Lanham, MD: University Press of America.

Sandars, N. K. 1985. *The Sea Peoples: Warriors of the Ancient Mediterranean*. London: Thames & Hudson.

Sanders, Paul. 2007. "*Argumenta ad deum* in the Plague Prayers of Mursili II and in the Book of Psalms." Pp. 181–217 in *Psalms and Prayers: Papers Read at the Joint Meeting of the Society of Old Testament Study and Het Oudtestamentische Werkgezelschap in Nederland en België, Apeldoorn August 2006*, edited by Bob Becking and Eric Peels. OtSt 55. Leiden: Brill.

Sanders, Seth L. 2004. "What Was the Alphabet for? The Rise of Written Vernaculars and the Making of Israelite National Literature." *Maarav* 11:25–56.

———. 2013. "The Appetites of the Dead: West Semitic Linguistic and Ritual Aspects of the Katumuwa Stele." *BASOR* 369:35–55.

———. 2015a. "Introduction: How to Build a Sacred Text in the Ancient Near East." *JANER* 15:113–20.

———. 2015b. "When the Personal Became Political: An Onomastic Perspective on the Rise of Yahwism." *Hebrew Bible and Ancient Israel* 4:59–86.

Sandman, Maj. 1938. *Texts from the Time of Akhenaten*. Brussels: Queen Elizabeth Foundation of Egyptology.

Sandmel, Samuel. 1962. "Parallelomania." *JBL* 81:1–13.

Sandy, D. Brent. 2000. "Hellenistic Egypt." Pp. 473–77 in *Dictionary of New Testament Background*, edited by Craig A. Evans and Stanley E. Porter. Downers Grove, IL: InterVarsity.

———. 2002. *Plowshares and Pruning Hooks: Rethinking the Language of Biblical Prophecy and Apocalyptic*. Downers Grove, IL: InterVarsity.

Sapir-Hen, Lidar, Guy Bar-Oz, Yuval Gadot, and Israel Finkelstein. 2013. "Pig Husbandry in Iron Age Israel and Judah: New Insights regarding the Origin of the 'Taboo.'" *ZDPV* 129:1–20.

Sapir-Hen, Lidar, Meirav Meiri, and Israel Finkelstein. 2015. "Iron Age Pigs: New Evidence on Their Origin and Role in Forming Identity Boundaries." *Radiocarbon* 57:307–15.

Sass, B. 1988. *The Genesis of the Alphabet and Its Development in the Second Millennium B.C.* Wiesbaden: Harrassowitz.

———. 2005. "The Genesis of the Alphabet and Its Development in the Second Millennium B.C.—Twenty Years Later." *De Kemi à Birit Nari* 2:137–56.

Sass, B., and I. Finkelstein. 2016. "The Swan-Song of Proto-Canaanite in the Ninth Century BCE in Light of an Alphabetic Inscription from Megiddo." *Semitica et Classica* 9:19–42.

Sasson, Jack M. 1993. "Albright as an Orientalist." *BA* 56:3–7.

———. 2015. *From the Mari Archives: An Anthology of Old Babylonian Letters*. Winona Lake, IN: Eisenbrauns.

Sasson, Victor. 1982. "The Siloam Tunnel Inscription." *PEQ* 114:111–17.

Sauer, Carl Ortwin. 1963a. "The Education of a Geographer." Pp. 389–404 in *Land and Life: A Selection from the Writings of Carl Ortwin Sauer*, edited by John Leighly. Berkeley: University of California Press.

———. 1963b. "Forward to Historical Geography." Pp. 351–79 in *Land and Life: A Selection from the Writings of Carl Ortwin Sauer*, edited by John Leighly. Berkeley: University of California Press.

Saur, Markus. 2015. "Where Can Wisdom Be Found? New Perspectives on the Wisdom Psalms." Pp. 181–204 in *Was There a Wisdom Tradition? New Prospects in Israelite Wisdom Studies*, edited by Mark R. Sneed. AIL 23. Atlanta: Society of Biblical Literature.

Schäfer, Heinrich. 1986. *Principles of Egyptian Art*. Oxford: Oxford University Press.

Schaper, Joachim. 1995. "The Jerusalem Temple as an Instrument of the Achaemenid Fiscal Administration." *VT* 45:528–39.

———. 1997. "The Temple Treasury Committee in the Times of Nehemiah and Ezra." *VT* 47:200–206.

Schep, Leo. 2009. "The Death of Alexander the Great: Reconsidering Poison." Pp. 227–36 in *Alexander and His Successors: Essays from the Antipodes*, edited by Pat Wheatley and Robert Hannah. Claremont, CA: Regina.

Schipper, Bernd U. 1999. *Israel und Ägypten in der Königszeit: Die kulturellen Kontakte von Salomo bis zum Fall Jerusalems.* OBO 170. Göttingen: Vandenhoeck & Ruprecht.

———. 2010. "Egypt and the Kingdom of Judah under Josiah and Jehoiakim." *TA* 37:200–226.

Schloen, J. David. 2001. *The House of the Father as Fact and Symbol: Patrimonialism in Ugarit and the Ancient Near East.* Studies in the Archaeology and History of the Levant 2. Winona Lake, IN: Eisenbrauns.

Schmidt, Brian B. 1994. *Israel's Beneficent Dead: Ancestor Cult and Necromancy in Ancient Israelite Religion and Tradition.* FAT 11. Tübingen: Mohr Siebeck.

———. 2002. "The Iron Age Pithoi Drawings from Horvat Teman or Kuntillet Ajrud: Some New Proposals." *JANER* 2:91–125.

Schmidt, Werner H. 1965. "Die Deuteronomistische Redaktion des Amosbuches." *ZAW* 77:168–93.

Schmitz, Philip C. 2010. "The Phoenician Contingent in the Campaign of Psammetichus II against Kush." *Journal of Egyptian History* 3:321–37.

Schneider, Tammi. 1993. *Form and Context in the Royal Inscriptions of Shalmaneser III.* Claremont, CA: Institute for Antiquity and Christianity.

Schneider, Thomas. 2008. "Knowledge and Knowledgeable Persons in Ancient Egypt: Queries and Arguments about an Unsettled Issue." Pp. 35–46 in *Scribes, Sages, and Seers: The Sage in the Eastern Mediterranean World*, edited by Leo G. Perdue. FRLANT 219. Göttingen: Vandenhoeck & Ruprecht.

———. 2010. "Contributions to the Chronology of the New Kingdom and the Third Intermediate Period." *ÄL* 20:373–403.

Schniedewind, William M. 1996. "Tel Dan Stela: New Light on Aramaic and Jehu's Revolt." *BASOR* 302:75–90.

———. 2004. *How the Bible Became a Book.* Cambridge: Cambridge University Press.

———. 2010. "Excavating the Text of 1 Kings 9: In Search of the Gates of Solomon." Pp. 241–49 in *Historical Biblical Archaeology and the Future: The New Pragmatism*, edited by Thomas E. Levy. London: Equinox.

———. 2013. *A Social History of Hebrew: Its Origins through the Rabbinic Period.* New Haven: Yale University Press.

Schroer, Silvia. 1987. *In Israel gab es Bilder: Nachrichten von darstellender Kunst im Alten Testament.* OBO 74. Fribourg: Universitätverlag; Göttingen: Vandenhoeck & Ruprecht.

———. 2008, 2011. *Die Ikonographie Palästinas/Israels und der Alte Orient: Eine Religionsgeschichte in Bildern.* Vols. 2 and 3. Fribourg: Universitätsverlag.

Schroer, Silvia, and Othmar Keel. 2005. *Die Ikonographie Palästinas/Israels und der Alte Orient: Eine Religionsgeschichte in Bildern.* Vol. 1. Fribourg: Universitätsverlag.

Schroer, Silvia, and Thomas Staubli. 2001. *Body Symbolism in the Bible.* Collegeville, MN: Liturgical.

Schürer, E. 1973. *The History of the Jewish People in the Age of Jesus Christ (175 B.C.–A.D. 135).* Vol. 1. Edinburgh: T&T Clark.

Schwarcz, Henry P. 1989. "Uranium Series Dating of Quaternary Deposits." *Quaternary International* 1:7–17.

Schwemer, Daniel. 1995. "Das alttestamentliche Doppelritual *'lwt wšlmym* im Horizont der hurritischen Opfertermini *ambašši* und *keldi*." Pp. 81–116 in *Edith Porada Memorial Volume*, edited by David I. Owen and Wilhelm Gernot. Studies on the Civilization and Culture of Nuzi and the Hurrians 7. Bethesda, MD: CDL Press.

Scurlock, JoAnn. 1997. "Neo-Assyrian Battle Tactics." Pp. 491–517 in *Crossing Boundaries and Linking Horizons: Studies in Honor of Michael C. Astour on His 80th Birthday*, edited by Gordon Douglas Young, Mark William Chavalas, Richard E. Averbeck, and Kevin L. Danti. Bethesda, MD: CDL Press.

Scurlock, JoAnn, and Richard Beal, eds. 2013. *Creation and Chaos: A Reconsideration of Herman Gunkel's Chaoskampf Hypothesis.* Winona Lake, IN: Eisenbrauns.

Seeher, Jürgen. 2011a. *Gods Carved in Stone: The Hittite Rock Sanctuary of Yazilikaya.* Istanbul: Ege Yayinlari.

———. 2011b. "The Plateau: The Hittites." Pp. 376–92 in *The Oxford Handbook of Ancient Anatolia*, edited by Sharon R. Steadman and Gregory McMahon. Oxford: Oxford University Press.

Seevers, Boyd. 2013. *Warfare in the Old Testament: The Organization, Weapons, and Tactics of Ancient Near Eastern Armies.* Grand Rapids: Kregel Academic.

Segal, Arthur, and Michael Eisenberg. 2011. "Hercules in Galilee." *BAR* 37 (6): 50–51.

Seger, Karen, ed. 1981. *Portrait of a Palestinian Village: The Photographs of Hilma Granqvist.* London: The Third World Center for Research and Publishing.

Sekunda, Nicholas V. 1985. "Achaemenid Colonization in Lydia." *Revue des Études anciennes* 87:7–29.

———. 1988. "Persian Settlement in Hellespontine Phrygia." Pp. 175–95 in *Method and Theory: Proceedings of the London 1985 Achaemenid History Workshop*, edited by Heleen Sancisi-Weerdenburg and Amélie Kuhrt. Achaemenid History 3. Leiden: Nederlands Instituut voor het Nabije Oosten.

———. 1991. "Achaemenid Settlement in Caria, Lycia, and Greater Phrygia." Pp. 83–143 in *Asia Minor and Egypt: Old Cultures in a New Empire: Proceedings of the Groningen 1988 Achaemenid History Workshop*, edited by Heleen Sancisi-Weerdenburg and Amélie Kuhrt. Achaemenid History 6. Leiden: Nederlands Instituut voor het Nabije Oosten.

Sellin, E. 1904. *Tell Taʿannek*. Vol. 1. Vienna: Buchhändler der Kaiserlichen Akademie der Wissenschaften.

Selman, Martin J. 1980. "Comparative Customs and the Patriarchal Age." Pp. 91–139 in *Essays on the Patriarchal Narratives*, edited by Alan R. Millard and Donald J. Wiseman. Winona Lake, IN: Eisenbrauns.

———. 1995. "Sacrifice in the Ancient Near East." Pp. 88–104 in *Sacrifice in the Bible*, edited by Roger Beckwith and Martin Selman. Grand Rapids: Baker.

———. 2003. "Law." Pp. 497–515 in *Dictionary of the Old Testament: Pentateuch*, edited by T. Desmond Alexander and David W. Baker. Downers Grove, IL: InterVarsity.

Sergi, Omer, Manfred Oeming, and Izaak J. de Hulster, eds. 2016. *In Search for Aram and Israel: Politics, Culture, and Identity*. Orientalische Religionen in der Antike 20. Tübingen: Mohr Siebeck.

Seri, Andrea. 2011. "Domestic Female Slaves during the Old Babylonian Period." Pp. 49–67 in *Slaves and Households in the Near East*, edited by Laura Culbertson. OIS 7. Chicago: University of Chicago Press.

Serpico, M., J. Bourriau, L. Smith, Y. Goren, B. Stern, and C. Heron. 2003. "Commodities and Containers: A Project to Study Canaanite Amphorae Imported into Egypt during the New Kingdom." Pp. 365–75 in *The Synchronisation of Civilisations in the Eastern Mediterranean in the Second Millennium BC II: Proceedings of the SCIEM 2000 Euro-Conference, Haindorf, 2nd of May–7th of May 2001*, edited by Manfred Bietak. Contributions to the Chronology of the Eastern Mediterannean 4. Vienna: Österreichische Akademie der Wissenschaften.

Shafer, Byron E., ed. 1997. *Temples of Ancient Egypt*. Ithaca, NY: Cornell University Press.

Shafer-Elliott, Cynthia. 2013a. "Cooking." *OEBA* 1:218–24.

———. 2013b. *Food in Ancient Judah: Domestic Cooking in the Time of the Hebrew Bible*. Sheffield: Equinox.

———. 2014. "Economics—Hebrew Bible." Pp. 119–25 in *The Oxford Encyclopedia of the Bible and Gender Studies*, vol. 1, edited by Julia M. O'Brien. Oxford: Oxford University Press.

Shahack-Gross, Ruth, Elisabetta Boaretto, Dan Cabanes, Ofir Katz, and Israel Finkelstein. 2014. "Subsistence Economy in the Negev Highlands: The Iron Age and the Byzantine/Early Islamic Period." *Levant* 46:98–117. http://www.tandfonline.com/doi/full/10.1179/0075891413Z.00000000034.

Shahack-Gross, Ruth, and Israel Finkelstein. 2015. "Settlement Oscillations in the Negev Highlands Revisited: The Impact of Microarchaeological Methods." *Radiocarbon* 57:253–64. https://journals.uair.arizona.edu/index.php/radiocarbon/article/download/18561/18209.

Shai, I. 2011. "Philistia and the Philistines in the Iron Age IIA." *ZDPV* 127:119–34.

Shai, I., and J. Uziel. 2010. "The Whys and Why Nots of Writing: Literacy and Illiteracy in the Southern Levant during the Bronze Ages." *Kaskal* 7:67–84.

Shanks, H. 1990. "Celebrating at the Annual Meeting." *BAR* 16 (2): 26–31.

———. 1997. "Face to Face: Biblical Minimalists Meet Their Challengers." *BAR* 23 (4): 26–43, 66.

Sharon, D. 1965. "Variability of Rainfall in Israel: A Map of the Relative Standard Deviation of the Annual Amounts." *IEJ* 15:169–76.

Shaw, Ian, ed. 2000. *The Oxford History of Ancient Egypt*. Oxford: Oxford University Press.

Sheldon, Rose Mary. 2005. "The Military History of Ancient Israel." *Journal of Military History* 69:197–204.

Shelmerdine, Cynthia W., ed. 2008. *The Cambridge Companion to the Aegean Bronze Age*. Cambridge: Cambridge University Press.

Sherwin, Simon. 2008. "Did the Israelites Really Learn Their Monotheism in Babylon?" Pp. 257–81 in *Israel: Ancient Kingdom or Late Invention?*, edited by Daniel I. Block. Nashville: B&H Academic.

Shryock, Andrew. 1997. *Nationalism and the Genealogical Imagination: Oral History and Textual Authority in Tribal Jordan*. Berkeley: University of California Press.

Shupak, Nili. 1989–90. "Egyptian 'Prophecy' and Biblical Prophecy: Did the Phenomenon of Prophecy, in the Biblical Sense, Exist in Ancient Egypt?" *Jahrbericht van det Vooraziatisch-Egyptisch Gezelschap "Ex oriente lux"* 31:5–40.

———. 1993. *Where Can Wisdom Be Found? The Sage's Language in the Bible and in Ancient Egyptian Literature*. OBO 130. Fribourg: University Press; Göttingen: Vandenhoeck & Ruprecht.

———. 1999. "Animal Drawings in Ancient Egypt: The World's First 'Mickey Mouse.'" Pp. 19*–23*, 15–19 in *"Couched as a Lion . . . Who Shall Rouse Him Up?" (Genesis 49:9): Depictions of Animals from the Leo Mildenberg Collection*, edited by Ofra Rimon and Rachel Shchori. Haifa: Reuben and Edith Hecht Museum, University of Haifa [In Hebrew and English.]

———. 2001. "'Canon' and 'Canonization' in Ancient Egypt." *BO* 58:535–47.

———. 2006. "A Fresh Look at the Dreams of the Officials and of Pharaoh in the Story of Joseph (Genesis 40–41) in the Light of Egyptian Dreams." *JANES* 30:103–38.

———. 2006–7. "'He Hath Subdued the Water Monster Crocodile': God's Battle with the Sea in Egyptian Sources." *Jahrbericht van det Voorazitatisch-Egyptisch Gezelschap "Ex oriente lux"* 40:77–89.

———. 2011. "Ancient Egyptian Literature." Pp. 605–56 in *The Literature of the Hebrew Bible: Introductions and Studies*, edited by Zipora Talshir. 2 vols. Jerusalem: Yad Ben Zvi. [In Hebrew.]

———. 2014. "Straightening the Crooked Stick: The Boundaries of Education in the Ancient Egyptian Tradition." Pp. 251–70 in *"And Inscribe the Name of Aaron": Studies in Bible Epigraphy, Literacy and History Presented to Aaron Demsky*, edited by Yigal Levin and Ber Kotlerman. Rolling Hills Estates, CA: Western Academic Press.

———. 2015. "The Contribution of Egyptian Wisdom to the Study of the Biblical Wisdom Literature." Pp. 265–304 in *Was There a Wisdom Tradition? New Prospects in Israelite Wisdom Studies*, edited by Mark R. Sneed. AIL 23. Atlanta: Society of Biblical Literature.

———. 2016. *"No Man Is Born Wise": Ancient Egyptian Wisdom Literature and Its Contact with Biblical Literature*. Jerusalem: Bialik Institute. [In Hebrew.]

Sievers, J. 1990. *The Hasmoneans and Their Supporters: From Mattathias to the Death of John Hyrcanus I*. South Florida Studies in the History of Judaism 6. Atlanta: Scholars Press.

Silberman, Neil Asher. 1982. *Digging for God and Country: Exploration, Archaeology, and the Secret Struggle for the Holy Land, 1799–1917*. New York: Anchor Books.

Silverman, David P. 1991. "Divinity and Deities in Ancient Egypt." Pp. 4–75 in *Religion in Ancient Egypt: Gods, Myths, and Personal Practice*, edited by Byron E. Shafer. Ithaca, NY: Cornell University Press.

Silverman, David P., Josef W. Wegner, and Jennifer Houser Wegner, eds. 2006. *Akhenaten and Tutankhamun: Revolution and Restoration*. Philadelphia: University of Pennsylvania Museum of Archaeology and Anthropology.

Simpson, Beryl B., and Molly C. Ogorzaly. 2001. *Economic Botany: Plants in our World*. 3rd ed. New York: McGraw-Hill.

Simpson, William Kelly. 1973. "The Hymns to Aten." Pp. 289–95 in *The Literature of Ancient Egypt: An Anthology of Stories, Instructions, and Poetry*, edited by William Kelly Simpson, Raymond O.

Faulkner, and Edward F. Wente. 2nd ed. New Haven: Yale University Press.

———, ed. 2003. *The Literature of Ancient Egypt: An Anthology of Stories, Instructions, Stelae, Autobiographies, and Poetry*. 3rd ed. New Haven: Yale University Press.

Singer, Itamar. 1988. "The Origin of the Sea Peoples and Their Settlement on the Coast of Canaan." Pp. 239–50 in *Society and Economy in the Eastern Mediterranean (c. 1500–1000 BC)*, edited by Michael Heltzer and Edward Lipinski. OLA 23. Leuven: Peeters.

———. 1994. "Egyptians, Canaanites, and Philistines in the Period of the Emergence of Israel." Pp. 282–338 in *From Nomadism to Monarchy: Archaeological and Historical Aspects of Early Israel*, edited by Israel Finkelstein and Nadav Na'aman. Jerusalem: Israel Exploration Society.

———. 1995. "Some Thoughts on Translated and Original Hittite Literature." Pp. 123–28 in *Language and Culture in the Near East*, edited by Shlomo Izre'el and Rina Drory. Israel Oriental Studies 15. Leiden: Brill.

———. 1999. "A Political History of Ugarit." Pp. 603–733 in *Handbook of Ugaritic Studies*, edited by W. G. E. Watson and Nicolas Wyatt. HdO 1/39. Leiden: Brill.

Skoglund, Pontus, et al. 2015. "Ancient Wolf Genome Reveals an Early Divergence of Domestic Dog Ancestors and Admixture into High-Latitude Breeds." *Current Biology* 25 (11): 1515–19.

Smelik, Klaas A. D. 1992. *Converting the Past: Studies in Ancient Israelite and Moabite Historiography*. OtSt 28. Leiden: Brill.

Smith, Bruce D. 2007. "Niche Construction and the Behavioral Context of Plant and Animal Domestication." *Evolutionary Anthropology: Issues, News, and Reviews* 16 (5): 188–99.

———. 2011a. "A Cultural Niche Construction Theory of Initial Domestication." *Biological Theory* 6 (3): 260–71.

———. 2011b. "General Patterns of Niche Construction and the Management of 'Wild' Plant and Animal Resources by Small-Scale Pre-Industrial Societies." *Philosophical Transactions of the Royal Society B: Biological Sciences* 366 (1566): 836–48.

———. 2016. "Neo-Darwinism, Niche Construction Theory, and the Initial Domestication of Plants and Animals." *Evolutionary Ecology* 30:307–24.

Smith, Christopher. 2008. "Gideon at Thermopylae: Mapping War in Biblical Narratives." Pp. 197–212 in *Writing and Reading War: Rhetoric, Gender, and Ethics in Biblical and Modern Contexts*, edited by Brad E. Kelle and Frank Ritchel Ames. SymS 42. Atlanta: Society of Biblical Literature.

Smith, Cyril S. 1974. "Metallurgy as a Human Experience." *Metallurgical Transactions A* 6 (4): 603–23.

Smith, George Adam. 1894. *The Historical Geography of the Holy Land*. London: Hodder & Stoughton.

Smith, Harry. 1994. "Ma'et and Isfet." *Bulletin of the Australian Centre for Egyptology* 5:67–88.

Smith, Mark S. 1990. *The Early History of God: Yahweh and the Other Deities in Ancient Israel*. San Francisco: Harper & Row.

———. 2001a. *The Origins of Biblical Monotheism: Israel's Polytheistic Background and the Ugaritic Texts*. Oxford: Oxford University Press.

———. 2001b. *Untold Stories: The Bible and Ugaritic Studies in the Twentieth Century*. Peabody, MA: Hendrickson.

———. 2002. *The Early History of God: Yahweh and the Other Deities in Ancient Israel*. 2nd ed. Grand Rapids: Eerdmans.

———. 2004. "The Polemic of Biblical Monotheism: Outsider Context and Insider Referentiality in Second Isaiah." Pp. 201–34 in *Religious Polemics in Context: Papers Presented to the Second International Conference of the Leider Institute for the Study of Religions (LISOR) Held at Leiden, 27–28 April 2000*, edited by T. L. Hettema and A. van der Kooij. Studies in Theology and Religion 11. Assen: Van Gorcum.

———. 2007. "Biblical Narrative between Ugaritic and Akkadian Literature, Part I: Ugarit and the Hebrew Bible: Consideration of Comparative Research." *RB* 114:5–29.

———. 2008. *God in Translation: Deities in Cross-Cultural Discourse in the Biblical World*. FAT 57. Tübingen: Mohr Siebeck.

———. 2010. *The Priestly Vision of Genesis 1*. Minneapolis: Fortress.

———. 2016. "Monotheism and the Redefinition of Divinity in Ancient Israel." Pp. 278–93 in *The Wiley Blackwell Companion to Ancient Israel*, edited by Susan Niditch. Chichester: Wiley.

Smith, Mark S., and Elizabeth Bloch-Smith. 1988. "Death and Afterlife in Ugarit and Israel." *JAOS* 108:277–84.

Smith, Michael E. 1987. "Household Possessions and Wealth in Agrarian States: Implications for Archaeology." *Journal of Anthropological Archaeology* 6:297–335.

———. 1994. "Social Complexity in the Aztec Countryside." Pp. 143–59 in *Archaeological Views from the Countryside*, edited by Glenn M. Schwartz and Steven E. Falconer. Washington: Smithsonian Institution Press.

———. 2015. "Quality of Life and Prosperity in Ancient Households and Communities." In *The Oxford Handbook of Historical Ecology and Applied Archaeology*, edited by Christian Isendahl and Daryl Stump. doi/10.1093/oxfordhb/9780199672691.013.4.

Smith, Michael E., Patricia Aguirre, Cynthia Heath-Smith, Kathryn Hirst, Scott O'Mack, and Jeffrey Price. 1989. "Architectural Patterns at Three Aztec-Period Sites in Morelos, Mexico." *Journal of Field Archaeology* 16:185–203.

Smith, Michael E., Timothy Dennehy, April Kamp-Whittaker, Emily Colon, and Rebecca Harkness. 2014. "Quantitative Measures of Wealth Inequality in Ancient Central Mexican Communities." *Advances in Archaeological Practice* 2:311–23.

Smith, Monica L. 2005. "Networks, Territories, and the Cartography of Ancient States." *Annals of the Association of American Geographers* 95:832–49.

———. 2015. "Feasts and Their Failures." *Journal of Archaeological Method and Theory* 22:1215–37.

Smith-Christopher, Daniel. 1997. "Reassessing the Historical and Sociological Impact of the Babylonian Exile (597/587–539 BCE)." Pp. 7–36 in *Exile: Old Testament, Jewish, and Christian Conceptions*, edited by James M. Scott. JSJSup 56. Leiden: Brill.

———. 2002. *A Biblical Theology of Exile*. Minneapolis: Fortress.

Smoak, Jeremy D. 2016. *The Priestly Blessing in Inscription and Scripture: The Early History of Numbers 6:24–26*. Oxford: Oxford University Press.

Sneed, Mark. 2011. "Is the 'Wisdom Tradition' a Tradition?" *CBQ* 73:50–71.

———. 2015a. "'Grasping after the Wind': The Elusive Attempt to Define and Delimit Wisdom." Pp. 39–68 in *Was There a Wisdom Tradition? New Prospects in Israelite Wisdom Studies*, edited by Mark R. Sneed. AIL 23. Atlanta: Society of Biblical Literature.

———. 2015b. *The Social World of the Sages: An Introduction to the Israelite and Jewish Wisdom Literature*. Minneapolis: Fortress.

Snir, Ainit, Dani Nadel, Iris Groman-Yaroslavski, Yoel Melamed, Marcelo Sternberg, Ofer Bar-Yosef, and Ehud Weiss. 2015. "The Origin of Cultivation and Proto-Weeds, Long before Neolithic Farming." *PLOS ONE* 10 (7). https://doi.org/10.1371/journal.pone.0131422.

Snir, Ainit, Dani Nadel, and Ehud Weiss. 2015. "Plant-Food Preparation on Two Consecutive Floors at Upper Paleolithic Ohalo II, Israel." *JAS* 53:61–67.

Snodgrass, A. M. 1999. *Arms and Armour of the Greeks*. Ithaca, NY: Cornell University Press.

Sommer, Michael. 2007. "Networks of Commerce and Knowledge in the Iron Age: The Case of the Phoenicians." *Mediterranean Historical Review* 22:97–111.

Spalinger, Anthony J. 1977. "Egypt and Babylonia: A Survey (c. 620 BCE–550 BC)." *Studien zur Altägyptischen Kultur* 5:221–44.

———. 1998. "The Limitations of Formal Ancient Egyptian Religion." *JNES* 57:241–60.

———. 2005. *War in Ancient Egypt*. Oxford: Blackwell.

Sparks, Kenton, L. 1998. *Ethnicity and Identity in Ancient Israel*. Winona Lake, IN: Eisenbrauns.

———. 2005. *Ancient Texts for the Study of the Hebrew Bible: A Guide to the Background Literature*. Peabody, MA: Hendrickson.

Spencer, F. Scott. 2007. "Earthquake." Pp. 174–75 in *The New Interpreter's Dictionary of the Bible*, vol. 2, edited by Katharine Doob Sakenfeld. Nashville: Abingdon.

Spencer, Neal. 2014. *Kom Firin II: The Urban Fabric and Landscape*. British Museum Reseach Publication 192. London: British Museum Press.

Spronk, Klaas. 1986. *Beatific Afterlife in Ancient Israel and in the Ancient Near East*. AOAT 219. Kevelaer: Butzon & Bercker; Neukirchen-Vluyn: Neukirchener Verlag.

Spycket, Agnès. 1945–46. "Illustration d'un texte hépatoscopique concernant Sargon d'Agade (?)." *Revue d'Assyriologie* 40:151–56.

———. 1981. *La statuaire du Proche-Orient ancien*. HdO 7/1. Leiden: Brill.

———. 2000. *The Human Form Divine: From the Collection of Elie Borowski*. Jerusalem: Bible Lands Museum.

Srebro, Haim, and Tamar Soffer. 2011. *The New Atlas of Israel: The National Atlas*. Jerusalem: Survey of Israel and Hebrew University.

Stager, Lawrence E. 1976. "Farming in the Judean Desert in the Iron Age." *BASOR* 121:145–58.

———. 1985. "The Archaeology of the Family in Ancient Israel." *BASOR* 260:1–35.

———. 1995. "The Impact of the Sea Peoples in Canaan (1185–1050 BCE)." Pp. 332–48 in *The Archaeology of Society in the Holy Land*, edited by Thomas E. Levy. New York: Facts on File.

———. 1996a. "Ashkelon and the Archaeology of Destruction: Kislev 604 B.C.E." *ErIsr* 25:61*–74*.

———. 1996b. "The Fury of Babylon: The Archaeology of Destruction." *BAR* 22:56–66, 76–77.

———. 1998. "Forging an Identity: The Emergence of Ancient Israel." Pp. 123–75 in *The Oxford History of the Biblical World*, edited by Michael D. Coogan. New York: Oxford University Press.

———. 2003a. "The Patrimonial Kingdom of Solomon." Pp. 63–74 in *Symbiosis, Symbolism, and the Power of the Past: Canaan, Ancient Israel, and Their Neighbors from the Late Bronze Age through Roman Palaestina*, edited by William G. Dever and Seymour Gitin. Winona Lake, IN: Eisenbrauns.

———. 2003b. "Phoenician Shipwrecks in the Deep Sea." Pp. 233–47 in *Sea Routes: Interconnections in the Mediterranean 16th–6th C. BC, Proceedings of the International Symposium Held at Rethymnon, Crete, September 29th–October 2nd 2002*, edited by Nicholas Stampolidis and Vassos Karageorghis. Athens: University of Crete and the A. G. Leventis Foundation.

———. 2006. "Biblical Philistines: A Hellenistic Literary Creation?" Pp. 375–84 in *"I Will Speak the Riddles of Ancient Times": Archaeological and Historical Studies in Honor of Amihai Mazar*, vol. 1, edited by Aren. M. Maeir and Pierre de Miroschedji. Winona Lake, IN: Eisenbrauns.

———. 2011. "Ashkelon on the Eve of Destruction in 604 B.C." Pp. 3–11 in *Ashkelon 3: The Seventh Century*, edited by Lawrence E. Stager, Daniel M. Master, and J. David Schloen. Winona Lake, IN: Eisenbrauns.

Stager, Lawrence E., and Daniel M. Master. 2011. "Conclusions." Pp. 737–40 in *Ashkelon 3: The Seventh Century*, edited by Lawrence E. Stager, Daniel M. Master, and J. David Schloen. Winona Lake, IN: Eisenbrauns.

Stager, Lawrence E., Daniel. M. Master, and J. David Schloen, eds. 2011. *Ashkelon 3: The Seventh Century*. Winona Lake, IN: Eisenbrauns.

Starr, Ivan, Jussi Aro, and Simo Parpola. 1990. *Queries to the Sungod: Divination and Politics in Sargonid Assyria*. SAA 4. Helsinki: Helsinki University Press.

Staubli, Thomas. 1991. *Das Image der Nomaden im Alten Israel und in der Ikonographie seiner sesshaften Nachbarn*. OBO 107. Freiburg: Universitätsverlag; Göttingen: Vandenhoeck & Ruprecht.

———. 2009. "Bull Leaping and Other Images and Rites of the Southern Levant in the Sign of Scorpius." *UF* 41:611–30.

Stavi, Boaz. 2015. *The Reign of Tudhaliya II and Šuppiluliuma I: The Contribution of the Hittite Documentation to a Reconstruction of the Amarna Age*. Texte der Hethiter, Philologische und Historische Studien zur Altanatolisk 31. Heidelberg: Universitätsverlag Winter.

Stavrakopoulou, Francesca. 2006. "Exploring the Garden of Uzza: Death, Burial and Ideologies of Kingship." *Bib* 87:1–21.

———. 2010a. *Land of Our Fathers: The Roles of Ancestor Veneration in Biblical Land Claims*. LHB/OTS 473. London: T&T Clark.

———. 2010b. "'Popular' Religion and 'Official' Religion: Practice, Perception, Portrayal." Pp. 37–58 in *Religious Diversity in Ancient Israel and Judah*, edited by Francesca Stavrakopoulou and John Barton. London: T&T Clark.

Steinberg, Naomi. 1991. "Alliance or Descent? The Function of Marriage in Genesis." *JSOT* 51:45–55.

———. 1993. *Kinship and Marriage in Genesis: A Household Economics Perspective*. Minneapolis: Fortress.

Steindorff, George, and Keith C. Seele. 1957. *When Egypt Ruled the East*. Chicago: University of Chicago Press.

Steiner, Margreet L. 2014. "Moab during the Iron Age II Period." Pp. 770–81 in *The Oxford Handbook of the Archaeology of the Levant: C. 8000–332 BCE*, edited by Margreet L. Steiner and Ann E. Killebrew. Oxford: Oxford University Press.

Steiner, Margreet L., and Ann E. Killebrew, eds. 2014. *The Oxford Handbook of the Archaeology of the Levant: C. 8000–332 BCE*. Oxford: Oxford University Press.

Steiner, Richard C. 1991. "The Aramaic Text in Demotic Script: The Liturgy of a New Year's Festival Imported from Bethel to Syene by Exiles from Rash." *JAOS* 111:362–63.

———. 2015. *Disembodied Souls: The Nefesh in Israel and Kindred Spirits in the Ancient Near East, with an Appendix on the Katumuwa Inscription*. ANEM 11. Atlanta: Society of Biblical Literature.

Stern, Ephraim. 1976. "Bes Vases from Palestine and Syria." *IEJ* 26:183–87.

———. 1982. *Material Culture of the Land of the Bible in the Persian Period, 538–332 B.C.* Warminster: Aris & Phillips; Jerusalem: Israel Exploration Society.

———, ed. 1993a. *The New Encyclopedia of Archaeological Excavations in the Holy Land*, vols. 1–4. Jerusalem: Israel Exploration Society and Carta.

———. 1993b. "The Renewal of Trade in the Eastern Mediterranean in Iron Age I." Pp. 325–34 in *Biblical Archaeology Today, 1990: Proceedings of the Second International Congress on Biblical Archaeology (Jerusalem)*, edited by Avraham Biran and Joseph Aviram. Jerusalem: Israel Exploration Society.

———. 2001. *Archaeology of the Land of the Bible*, vol. 2, *The Assyrian, Babylonian, and Persian Periods (732–332 BCE)*. Anchor Bible Reference Library. New York: Doubleday.

———, ed. 2008. *The New Encyclopedia of Archaeological Excavations in the Holy Land*, vol. 5. Jerusalem: Israel Exploration Society and Biblical Archaeological Society.

Stern, Philip D. 1991. *The Biblical Ḥerem: A Window on Israel's Religious Experience*. BJS 211. Missoula, MT: Scholars Press.

———. 1993. "Of Kings and Moabites: History and Theology in 2 Kings 3 and the Mesha Inscription." *HUCA* 64:1–14.

Stevens, Anna. 2011. "Egypt." Pp. 722–44 in *The Oxford Handbook of the Archaeology of Ritual and Religion*, edited by Timothy Insoll. Oxford: Oxford University Press.

———. 2012. "Private Religion in the Amarna Suburbs." Pp. 92–97 in *In the Light of Amarna: 100 years of the Nefertiti Discovery*, edited by Friederike Seyfried. Berlin: Michael Imhof.

Stewart, Andrew, and Rebecca S. Martin. 2003. "Hellenistic Discoveries at Tel Dor." *Hesperia* 72:121–45.

Stiebing, William H., Jr. 2009. *Ancient Near Eastern History and Culture*. New York: Pearson.

Stillman, Nigel, and Nigel Tallis. 1984. *Armies of the Ancient Near East, 3000 B.C. to 539 B.C.: Organisation, Tactics, Dress and Equipment*. Cambridge: Wargames Research Group.

Stiner, Mary C., Natalie D. Munro, and Todd A. Surovell. 2000. "The Tortoise and the Hare: Small Game Use, the Broad Spectrum Revolution, and Paleolithic Demography." *Current Anthropology* 41:39–73.

Stiros, Stathis C. 1996. "Identification of Earthquakes from Archaeological Data: Methodology, Criteria and Limitations." Pp. 129–52 in *Archaeoseismology*, edited by Stathis Stiros and R. E. Jones. Fitch Laboratory Occasional Papers 7. Athens: British School at Athens.

Stith, D. M. 2008. *The Coups of Hazael and Jehu: Building an Historical Narrative*. Gorgias Dissertations 37. Piscataway, NJ: Gorgias.

Stökl, Jonathan. 2012. *Prophecy in the Ancient Near East: A Philological and Sociological Comparison*. CHANE 56. Leiden: Brill.

Stolper, Matthew W. 1985. *Entrepreneurs and Empire: The Murašû Archive, the Murašû Firm, and Persian Rule in Babylonia*. Uitgaven van het Nederlands Historisch-Archaeologisch Instituut te Istanbul 54. Leiden: Nederlands Instituut voor het Nabije Oosten.

———. 1988. "The Kasr Archive." *AJA* 92:587–88.

———. 1989. "The Governor of Babylon and Across-the-River in 486 B.C." *JNES* 48:283–305.

———. 1990. "The Kasr Archive." Pp. 195–205 in *Centre and Periphery: Proceedings of the Groningen 1986 Achaemenid History Workshop*, edited by Heleen Sancisi-Weerdenburg and Amélie Kuhrt. Achaemenid History 4. Leiden: Nederlands Instituut voor het Nabije Oosten.

———. 1992. "Murashû, Archive of." *ABD* 4:927–28.

Strawn, Brent A. 2005. *What Is Stronger than a Lion? Leonine Image and Metaphor in the Hebrew Bible and the Ancient Near East*. OBO 212. Fribourg: Academic Press; Göttingen: Vandenhoeck & Ruprecht.

———. 2015. "'With a Strong Hand and an Outstretched Arm': On the Meaning(s) of the Exodus Tradition(s)." Pp. 19–42 in *Iconographic Exegesis of the Hebrew Bible/Old Testament: An Introduction to Its Method and Practice*, edited by Izaak J. de Hulster, Brent A. Strawn, and Ryan P. Bonfiglio. Göttingen: Vandenhoeck & Ruprecht.

———. 2016. "Material Culture, Iconography, and the Prophets." Pp. 87–116 in *The Oxford Handbook to the Prophets*, edited by Carolyn J. Sharp. Oxford: Oxford University Press.

Strawn, Brent A., and Joel M. LeMon. Forthcoming. "Religion in Eighth-Century Judah: The Case of Kuntillet ʿAjrud (and Beyond)." In *Oded Borowski Festschrift*, edited by Zev Farber and Jacob Wright. Atlanta: Society of Biblical Literature.

Struble, Eudora, and Virginia Herrmann. 2009. "An Eternal Feast at Samʾal: The New Iron Age Mortuary Stele from Zincirli in Context." *BASOR* 356:15–49.

Suriano, Matthew J. 2007. "The Apology of Hazael: A Literary and Historical Analysis of the Tel Dan Inscription." *JNES* 66:163–76.

———. 2010. *The Politics of Dead Kings: Dynastic Ancestors in the Book of Kings and Ancient Israel.* FAT 2/48. Tübingen: Mohr Siebeck.

———. 2014. "Breaking Bread with the Dead: Katumuwa's Stele, Hosea 9:4, and the Early History of the Soul." *JAOS* 134:385–405.

Suter, Claudia E. 2000. *Gudea's Temple Building: The Representation of an Early Mesopotamian Ruler in Text and Image.* Cuneiform Monographs 17. Leiden: Brill.

Suter, Claudia E., and Christoph Uehlinger, eds. 2005. Crafts *and Images in Contact: Studies on Eastern Mediterranean Art of the First Millennium BCE.* OBO 210. Freiburg: Universitätsverlag; Göttingen: Vandenhoeck & Ruprecht.

Sutton, David. 2001. *Remembrance of Repasts: An Anthropology of Food and Memory.* Oxford: Berg.

———. 2013. "Cooking Skills, the Senses, and Memory: The Fate of Practical Knowledge." Pp. 299–319 in *Food and Culture: A Reader*, edited by Carole Counihan and Penny Van Esterik. 3rd ed. New York: Routledge.

Sweet, Ronald F. G. 1990a. "The Sage in Akkadian Literature: A Philological Study." Pp. 45–65 in *The Sage in Israel and the Ancient Near East*, edited by John G. Gammie and Leo G. Perdue. Winona Lake, IN: Eisenbrauns.

———. 1990b. "The Sage in Mesopotamian Palaces and Royal Courts." Pp. 99–107 in *The Sage in Israel and the Ancient Near East*, edited by John G. Gammie and Leo G. Perdue. Winona Lake, IN: Eisenbrauns.

Tadmor, Hayim. 1975. "Assyria and the West: The Ninth Century and Its Aftermath." Pp. 36–48 in *Unity and Diversity: Essays in the History, Literature and Religion of the Ancient Near East*, edited by Hans Goedicke and J. J. M. Roberts. Baltimore: Johns Hopkins University Press.

Tadmor, M. 1982. "Female Cult Figurines in Late Canaan and Early Israel: Archaeological Evidence." Pp. 139–73 in *Studies in the Period of David and Solomon and Other Essays: Papers Read at the International Symposium for Biblical Studies, Tokyo, 5–7 December, 1979*, edited by Tomoo Ishida. Winona Lake, IN: Eisenbrauns.

Taggar-Cohen, Ada. 2006. "The NIN.DINGIR in the Hittite Kingdom: A Mesopotamian Priestly Office in Ḫatti?" *AoF* 33:313–27.

Tal, Oren. 2003. "On the Origin and Concept of the Loculi Tombs of Hellenistic Palestine." *Ancient West and East* 2:288–307.

———. 2005. "Some Remarks on the Coastal Plain of Palestine under Achaemenid Rule—An Archaeological Synopsis." Pp. 71–96 in *L'archéologie de l'empire achéménide: Nouvelles recherches*, edited by Pierre Briant and Rémy Boucharlat. Persika 6. Paris: Éditions de Boccard.

———. 2011. "Negotiating Identity in an International Context under Achaemenid Rule: The Indigenous Coinages of Persian-Period Palestine as an Allegory." Pp. 445–59 in *Judah and the Judeans in the Achaemenid Period: Negotiating Identity in an International Context*, edited by Oded Lipschits, Gary N. Knoppers, and Manfred Oeming. Winona Lake, IN: Eisenbrauns.

Tappy, Ron E., P. Kyle McCarter, Marilyn J. Lundberg, and Bruce Zuckerman. 2006. "An Abecedary of the Mid-Tenth Century B.C.E. from the Judaean Shephelah." *BASOR* 344:5–46.

Tartaron, Thomas F. 2013. *Maritime Networks in the Mycenaean World.* Cambridge: Cambridge University Press.

Tatton-Brown, Veronica. 1987. *Ancient Cyprus.* British Museum Publications for the Trustees of the British Museum. Cambridge, MA: Harvard University Press.

Tchernov, Eitan. 1991. "Biological Evidence for Human Sedentism in Southwest Asia during the Natufian." Pp. 315–40 in *The Natufian Culture in the Levant*, edited by Ofer Bar-Yosef and François R. Valla. Ann Arbor, MI: International Monographs in Prehistory.

Tebes, Juan Manuel. 2006. "Trade and Nomads: The Commercial Relations between the Negev, Edom, and the Mediterranean in the Late Iron Age." *Journal of the Serbian Archaeological Society* 22:45–62.

———. 2014. "Socio-Economic Fluctuations and Chiefdom Formation in Edom, the Negev and the Hejaz during the First Millennium BCE." Pp. 1–30 in *Unearthing the Wilderness: Studies on the History and Archaeology of the Negev and Edom in the Iron Age*, edited by Juan M. Tebes. ANESSup 45. Leuven: Peeters.

Teissier, Beatrice. 1990. "The Seal Impression Alalakh 194: A New Aspect of Egypto-Levantine Relations in the Middle Kingdom." *Levant* 22:65–73.

Tenney, Jonathan S. 2011. "Household Structure and Population Dynamics in the Middle Babylonian

Province 'Slave' Population." Pp. 135–46 in *Slaves and Households in the Near East*, edited by Laura Culbertson. OIS 7. Chicago: University of Chicago Press.

Tepper, Yotam. 2007. "Soil Improvement and Agricultural Pesticides in Antiquity: Examples from Archaeological Research in Israel." Pp. 41–52 in *Middle East Garden Traditions: Unity and Diversity; Colloquium on the History of Landscape Architecture XXXI*, edited by Michel Conan. Washington, DC: Dumbarton Oaks.

te Velde, Herman. 1995. "Theology, Priests, and Worship in Ancient Egypt." *CANE* 3:1731–49.

Thareani, Yifat. 2007. "The 'Archaeology of the Days of Manasseh' Reconsidered in the Light of Evidence from the Beersheba Valley." *PEQ* 139:69–77.

———. 2009. "In the Service of the Empire: Local Elites and 'Pax Assyriaca' in the Negev." *ErIsr* 29:184–91. [In Hebrew.]

———. 2016. "The Empire and the 'Upper Sea': Assyrian Control Strategies along the Southern Levantine Coast." *BASOR* 375:77–102.

Thiele, Edwin R. 1965. *The Mysterious Numbers of the Hebrew Kings: A Reconstruction of the Chronology of the Kingdoms of Israel and Judah*. 2nd ed. Grand Rapids: Eerdmans.

Thomas, David Hurst, and Robert L. Kelly. 2006. *Archaeology: Down to Earth*. 4th ed. Belmont, CA: Thomson/Wadsworth.

Thompson, Thomas L. 1974. *The Historicity of the Patriarchal Narratives: The Quest for the Historical Abraham*. BZAW 133. Berlin: de Gruyter.

———. 1992. *Early History of the Israelite People: From the Written and Archaeological Sources*. Leiden: Brill.

———. 1999. *The Mythic Past: Biblical Archaeology and the Myth of Israel*. London: Basic Books.

Tigay, Jeffrey H. 1982. *The Evolution of the Gilgamesh Epic*. Philadelphia: University of Pennsylvania Press.

———. 1985. *Empirical Models for Biblical Criticism*. Philadelphia: University of Pennsylvania Press.

———. 1987a. "Israelite Religion: The Onomastic and Epigraphic Evidence." Pp. 157–94 in *Ancient Israelite Religion: Essays in Honor of Frank Moore Cross*, edited by Patrick D. Miller, Paul Hanson, and Dean McBride. Philadelphia: Fortress.

———. 1987b. *You Shall Have No Other Gods: Israelite Religion in the Light of Hebrew Inscriptions*. HSS 31. Atlanta: Scholars Press.

Tiradritti, Francesco. 2008. *Egyptian Wall Painting*. New York: Abeville.

Tobin, Vincent A. 1985. "The Amarna Period and Biblical Religion." Pp. 231–77 in *Pharaonic Egypt, the Bible, and Christianity*, edited by Sarah Israelit Groll. Jerusalem: Magnes.

———. 2001. "Myths: Creation Myths." *OEAE* 2:469–72.

Traunecker, Claude. 1984. "Données nouvelles sur le début au règne d'Aménophis IV et son oeuvre à Karnak." *JSSEA* 14:60–69.

Trigger, B. G. 2004. "Writing Systems: A Case Study in Cultural Evolution." Pp. 39–68 in *The First Writing: Script Invention as History and Process*, edited by Stephen D. Houston. Cambridge: Cambridge University Press.

Trimm, Charles. 2012. "Recent Research on Warfare in the Old Testament." *Currents in Biblical Research* 10 (2): 171–216.

Tromp, Nicholas J. 1969. *Primitive Conceptions of Death and the Nether World in the Old Testament*. BibOr 21. Rome: Pontifical Biblical Institute.

Tropper, Josef. 1989. *Nekromantie: Totenbefragung im Alten Orient und im Alten Testament*. AOAT 223. Kevelaer: Butzon & Bercker; Neukirchen-Vluyn: Neukirchener Verlag.

Trotter, J. M. 2001. "Was the Second Jerusalem Temple Project a Primarily Persian Project?" *Scandinavian Journal of the Old Testament* 21:276–94.

Tsahar, Ella, Ido Izhaki, Simcha Lev-Yadun, and Guy Bar-Oz. 2009. "Distribution and Extinction of Ungulates during the Holocene of the Southern Levant." *PLOS ONE* 4. https://doi.org/10.1371/journal.pone.0005316.

Tsetskhladze, Gocha R. 2006. "Introduction: Revisiting Ancient Greek Colonisation." Pp. xxiii–lxiii in *Greek Colonisation: An Account of Greek Colonies and Other Settlements Overseas*, vol. 1, edited by Gocha R. Tsetskhladze. Mnemosyne, bibliotheca classica Batava, Supplementum 193. Leiden: Brill.

Tsukimoto, Akio. 1999. "'By the Hand of Madi-Dagan, the Scribe and *Apkallu*-Priest': A Medical Text from the Middle Euphrates Region." Pp. 187–200 in *Priest and Officials in the Ancient Near East: Papers of the Second Colloquium on the Ancient Near East*, edited by Kazuko Watanabe. Heidelberg: Universitätsverlag C. Winter.

Tsumura, David Toshio. 1999. "Kings and Cults in Ancient Ugarit." Pp. 215–38 in *Priest and Officials in the Ancient Near East: Papers of the Second Colloquium on the Ancient Near East*, edited by Kazuko Watanabe. Heidelberg: Universitätsverlag C. Winter.

———. 2005. *Creation and Destruction: A Reappraisal of Chaoskampf Theory in the Old Testament*. Winona Lake, IN: Eisenbrauns.

———. 2015. "The Creation Motif in Psalm 74:12–14? A Reappraisal of the Theory of the Dragon Myth." *JBL* 134:547–55.

Tubb, Jonathan N. 2000. "Sea Peoples in the Jordan Valley." Pp. 181–96 in *The Sea Peoples and Their*

World: A Reassessment, edited by Eliezer D. Oren. UMM 108. Philadelphia: University Museum of the University of Pennsylvania.

Tucker, Gene M. 1977. "Prophetic Inscriptions and the Growth of the Canon." Pp. 56–70 in *Canon and Authority: Essays in Old Testament Religion and Theology*, edited by George W. Coats and Burke O'Connor Long. Philadelphia: Fortress.

Tufnell, O. 1958. *Lachish*, vol. 4, *The Bronze Age*. Oxford: Oxford University Press.

Tuplin, C. 1991. "Darius' Suez Canal and Persian Imperialism." Pp. 237–83 in *Asia Minor and Egypt: Old Cultures in a New Empire; Proceedings of the Groningen 1988 Achaemenid History Workshop*, edited by Heleen Sancisi-Weerdenburg and Amélie Kuhrt. Achaemenid History 6. Leiden: Nederlands Instituut voor het Nabije Oosten.

Tyson, Craig W. 2014. *The Ammonites: Elites, Empires, and Sociopolitical Change (1000–500 BCE)*. LHB/OTS 585. London: T&T Clark.

Uehlinger, Christoph. 1993. "Northwest Semitic Inscribed Seals, Iconography, and Syro-Palestinian Religions of Iron Age II: Some Afterthoughts and Conclusions." Pp. 257–89 in *Studies in the Iconography of Northwest Semitic Inscribed Seals*, edited by Benjamin Sass and Christoph Uehlinger. OBO 125. Göttingen: Vandenhoeck & Ruprecht.

———, ed. 2000. *Images as Media: Sources for the Cultural History of the Near East and the Eastern Mediterranean, 1st Millennium BCE*. OBO 175. Freiburg: Universitätsverlag; Göttingen: Vandenhoeck & Ruprecht.

———. 2007. "Neither Eyewitnesses, Nor Windows to the Past, but Valuable Testimony in Its Own Right: Remarks on Iconography, Source Criticism and Ancient Data-Processing." Pp. 230–59 in *Understanding the History of Ancient Israel*, edited by H. G. M. Williamson. Oxford: Oxford University Press.

Uerpmann, Margarethe, and Hans-Peter Uerpmann. 2012. "Archeozoology of Camels in South-Eastern Arabia." Pp. 109–22 in *Camels in Asia and North Africa: Interdisciplinary Perspectives on Their Past and Present Significance*, edited by Eva-Maria Knoll and Pamela Burger. Österreichische Akademie Der Wissenschaft, Philosophisch-Historische Klasse Denkschriften 451. Vienna: Österreichische Akademie der Wissenschaften.

Uffenheimer, B. 1968. "Urbanization as a Religious and Social Problem for the Prophets." Pp. 207–26 in *Town and Community: Proceedings of the 12th Conference of the Israeli Historical Society*. Jerusalem: Israeli Historical Society. [In Hebrew.]

Urciuoli, G. M. 1995. "Šeš-Il-ib Priests at Ebla." *Aula Orientalis* 13:107–26.

Ussishkin, David. 1970. "The Necropolis from the Time of the Kingdom of Judah at Silwan, Jerusalem." *BA* 33:33–46.

———. 1980. "The 'Lachish Reliefs' and the City of Lachish." *IEJ* 30:174–95.

———. 1982. *The Conquest of Lachish by Sennacherib*. Tel Aviv: Tel Aviv University, Institute of Archaeology.

———. 1995. "The Destruction of Megiddo at the End of the Late Bronze Age and Its Historical Significance." *TA* 22:240–67.

———. 2008. "The Chronology of the Iron Age in Israel: The Current State of Research." *Ancient Near Eastern Studies* 45:218–34.

———. 2014a. *Biblical Lachish: A Tale of Construction, Destruction, Excavation and Restoration*. Jerusalem: Israel Exploration Society.

———. 2014b. "Sennacherib's Campaign to Judah: The Archaeological Perspective with an Emphasis on Lachish and Jerusalem." Pp. 75–103 in *Sennacherib at the Gates of Jerusalem: Story, History and Historiography*, edited by Isaac Kalimi and Seth Richardson. CHANE 71. Leiden: Brill.

Uziel, Joe. 2010. "Middle Bronze Age Ramparts: Functional and Symbolic Structures." *PEQ* 142:24–30.

———. 2011a. "Figurines and the Way in Which They Reflect Cultic Practice in the Middle and Late Bronze Age: A Comparative Study." *ErIsr* 30:352–56. [In Hebrew.]

———. 2011b. "Technology and Ideology in Middle Bronze Age Canaan." *Rosetta* 10:49–75.

Uziel, Joe, and Yuval Gadot. 2010. "The 'Cup-and-Saucer' Vessel: Function, Chronology, Distribution and Symbolism." *IEJ* 60:41–57.

Uziel, Joe, and A. M. Maeir. 2005. "Scratching the Surface at Gath: Implications of the Tell es-Safi/Gath Surface Survey." *TA* 32:50–75.

Uziel, Joe, and Itzhaq Shai. 2007. "Iron Age Jerusalem: Temple-Palace, Capital City." *JAOS* 127:161–70.

Van Beek, Gus W. 1989. "William Foxwell Albright: A Short Biography." Pp. 7–16 in *The Scholarship of William Foxwell Albright: An Appraisal*, edited by Gus W. Van Beek. HSS 33. Atlanta: Scholars Press.

———. 1993. "Tell Jemmeh." Pp. 667–74 in *The New Encyclopedia of Archaeological Excavations in the Holy Land*, edited by E. Stern, A. Lewinson-Gilboa, and J. Aviram. Jerusalem: Israel Exploration Society.

———. 2003. "Jemmeh, Tell." *NEAEHL* 2:667–74.

van Buren, Elizabeth Douglas. 1933. *The Flowing Vase and the God with Streams*. Berlin: H. Schoetz.

Van Dam, C. 2012. "Divination, Magic." Pp. 159–62 in *Dictionary of the Old Testament: Prophets*, edited by Mark J. Boda and J. G. McConville. Downers Grove, IL: InterVarsity.

van de Mieroop, Marc. 2011. *A History of Ancient Egypt*. Chichester: Wiley-Blackwell.

—————. 2016. *Philosophy before the Greeks: The Pursuit of Truth in Ancient Babylonia*. Princeton: Princeton University Press.

van den Hout, Theo P. J. 2002. "Another View of Hittite Literature." Pp. 857–78 in *Anatolia antica: Studi in memoria di Fiorella Imparati*, edited by Stefano de Martino and Franca Pecchioli Daddi. Eothen 11. Florence: LoGisma.

—————. 2013. "A Short History of the Hittite Kingdom and Empire." Pp. 22–45 in *Hititler: Bir Anadolu Imparatorlugu / Hittites: An Anatolian Empire*, edited by Meltem Dogan-Alparslan and Metin Alparslan, translated by Mary Işin and Gürkan Ergin. Istanbul: Yapi Kredi Yayinlari.

Vanderhooft, David S. 1999. *The Neo-Babylonian Empire and Babylon in the Latter Prophets*. HSM 59. Atlanta: Scholars Press.

—————. 2003. "Babylonian Strategies of Imperial Control in the West: Royal Practice and Rhetoric." Pp. 235–62 in *Judah and the Judeans in the Neo-Babylonian Period*, edited by Oded Lipschits and Joseph Blenkinsopp. Winona Lake, IN: Eisenbrauns.

Vanderhooft, David S, and Wayne Horowitz. 2002. "The Cuneiform Inscription from Tell en-Nasbeh: The Demise of an Unknown King!" *TA* 29:318–27.

VanderKam, James C. 2004. *From Joshua to Caiaphas: High Priests after the Exile*. Minneapolis: Fortress; Assen: Van Gorcum.

—————. 2010. *The Dead Sea Scrolls Today*. 2nd ed. Grand Rapids: Eerdmans.

Van der Merwe, N. J. 1982. "Carbon Isotopes, Photosynthesis, and Archaeology: Different Pathways of Photosynthesis Cause Characteristic Changes in Carbon Isotope Ratios That Make Possible the Study of Prehistoric Human Diets." *American Scientist* 70 (6): 596–606.

van der Steen, Eveline J. 2004. *Tribes and Territories in Transition: The Central East Jordan Valley in Late Bronze Age and Early Iron Ages; A Study of the Sources*. OLA 130. Leuven: Peeters.

van der Steen, Eveline J., and Klaas A. D. Smelik. 2007. "King Mesha and the Tribe of Dibon." *JSOT* 32:139–62.

van der Toorn, Karel. 1985. *Sin and Sanction in Israel and Mesopotamia*. Studia Semitica Neerlandica 22. Assen: Van Gorcum.

—————. 1988. "Echoes of Judean Necromancy in Isaiah 28,7–22." *ZAW* 100:199–217.

—————. 1991a. "Form and Function of the New Year Festival in Babylonia and Israel." Pp. 1–25 in *Congress Volume: Leuven 1989*, edited by John A. Emerton. VTSup 43. Leiden: Brill.

—————. 1991b. "Funerary Rituals and Beatific Afterlife in Ugaritic Texts and the Bible." *BO* 48:40–66.

—————. 1995a. "The Domestic Cult at Emar." *JCS* 47:35–49.

—————. 1995b. "Yahweh." Pp. 1711–30 in *Dictionary of Deities and Demons in the Bible*, edited by Karel van der Toorn, Bob Becking, and Pieter W. van der Horst. Leiden: Brill.

—————. 1996. *Family Religion in Babylonia, Syria, and Israel: Continuity and Changes in the Forms of Religious Life*. SHANE 7. Leiden: Brill.

—————, ed. 1997. *The Image and the Book: Iconic Cults, Aniconism, and the Rise of Book Religion in Israel and the Ancient Near East*. CBET 21. Leuven: Peeters.

—————. 2000a. "Israelite Figurines: A View from the Texts." Pp. 45–62 in *Sacred Time, Sacred Place: Archaeology and the Religion of Israel*, edited by Barry M. Gittlen. Winona Lake, IN: Eisenbrauns.

—————. 2000b. "Mesopotamian Prophecy between Immanence and Transcendence: A Comparison of Old Babylonian and Neo-Assyrian Prophecy." Pp. 71–87 in *Prophecy in Its Ancient Near Eastern Context: Mesopotamian, Biblical, and Arabian Perspectives*, edited by Martti Nissinen. SymS 13. Atlanta: Society of Biblical Literature.

—————. 2007. *Scribal Culture and the Making of the Hebrew Bible*. Cambridge, MA: Harvard University Press.

van Dijk, Jacobus. 2000. "The Amarna Period and the Later New Kingdom." Pp. 272–329 in *The Oxford History of Ancient Egypt*, edited by Ian Shaw. Oxford: Oxford University Press.

—————. 2004. "The Amarna Period and the Later New Kingdom." Pp. 265–307 in *The Oxford History of Ancient Egypt*, edited by Ian Shaw. Oxford: Oxford University Press.

Van Seters, John. 1975. *Abraham in History and Tradition*. New Haven: Yale University Press.

—————. 1997. "Solomon's Temple: Fact and Ideology in Biblical and Near Eastern Historiography." *CBQ* 59:45–57.

—————. 2003. *A Law Book for the Diaspora: Revision in the Study of the Covenant Code*. New York: Oxford University Press.

Vanstiphout, Herman. 2003. *Epics of Sumerian Kings: The Matter of Aratta*. WAW. Atlanta: Society of Biblical Literature.

Vaughn, Andrew G. 1999. *Theology, History, and Archaeology in the Chronicler's Account of Hezekiah*. Atlanta: Scholars Press.

Veenhof, Klaas R. 1972. *Aspects of Old Assyrian Trade and Its Terminology*. Studia et documenta ad iura Orientis antiqui pertinentia 10. Leiden: Brill.

—————. 2003. "Fatherhood Is a Matter of Opinion: An Old Babylonian Trial on Filiation and Service Duties." Pp. 313–25 in *Literature, Politik und Recht in*

Mesopotamien: Festschrift für C. Wilcke, edited by W. Sallaberger et al. Wiesbaden: Harrassowitz.

———. 2013. "New Mesopotamian Treaties from the Early Second Millennium BC from *Kārum* Kanesh and Tell Leilan (Šehna)" *Zeitshrift für Altorientalische und Biblische Rechtsgeschichte* 19:23–57.

Veracini, Lorenzo. 2010. *Settler Colonialism: A Theoretical Overview*. Basingstoke: Palgrave MacMillan.

Vermes, Geza. 1997. *The Complete Dead Sea Scrolls in English*. New York: Penguin.

Vernus, Pascal. 2003. *Affairs and Scandals in Ancient Egypt*. Translated by David Lorton. Ithaca, NY: Cornell University Press.

———. 2010. *Sagesses de l'Égypte pharaonique*. 2nd ed. Paris: Actes Sudes.

Vickers, M., and D. Gill. 1994. *Artful Crafts: Ancient Greek Silverware and Pottery*. Oxford: Clarendon.

Visicato, Guiseppe. 1995. *The Bureaucracy of Šuruppak: Administrative Centres, Central Offices, Intermediate Structures and Hierarchies in the Economic Documentation of Fara*. Münster: Ugarit-Verlag.

Vitale, R. 1982. "La Musique suméro-akkadienne: Gamme et notation musicale." *UF* 14:241–63.

Vogel, J. C. 1978. "Isotopic Assessment of the Dietary Habits of Ungulates." *South African Journal of Science* 74 (8): 298–301.

Von Beckerath, J. 1999. *Handbuch der ägyptischen Königsnamen*. 2nd ed. Münchner ägyptologische Studien 49. Mainz: Zabern.

Von Rad, Gerhard. 1952. "Typologische Auslegung des Alten Testaments." *Evangelische Theologie* 12:17–33.

Wachsmann, Shelly. 2000. "To the Sea of the Philistines." Pp. 103–43 in *The Sea Peoples and Their World: A Reassessment*, edited by Eliezer D. Oren. UMM 108. Philadelphia: University Museum of the University of Pennsylvania.

Waerzeggers, Caroline. 2011. "The Pious King: Royal Patronage of Temples." Pp. 725–51 in *The Oxford Handbook of Cuneiform Culture*, edited by Karen Radner and Eleanor Robson. Oxford: Oxford University Press.

Waiman-Barak, P., A. Gilboa, and Y. Goren. 2014. "A Stratified Sequence of Early Iron Age Egyptian Ceramics at Tel Dor, Israel." *ÄL* 24:317–41.

Wakeman, Mary K. 1973. *God's Battle with the Monster: A Study in Biblical Imagery*. Leiden: Brill.

Walbank, F. W. 1993. *The Hellenistic World*. Rev. ed. Cambridge, MA: Harvard University Press.

Waldbaum, Jane. 1994. "Early Greek Contacts with the Southern Levant, ca. 1000–600 B.C.: The Eastern Perspective." *BASOR* 293:53–66.

———. 1997. "Greeks in the East or Greeks and the East? Problems in the Definition and Recognition of Presence." *BASOR* 305:1–17.

———. 2011. "Greek Pottery." Pp. 701–36 in *Ashkelon 3: The Seventh Century*, edited by Lawrence E. Stager, Daniel M. Master, and J. David Schloen. Winona Lake, IN: Eisenbrauns.

Walker, Christopher, and Michael Dick. 2001. *The Induction of the Cult Image in Ancient Mesopotamia: The Mesopotamian Mis Pî Ritual*. SAA Literary Texts 1. Helsinki: Neo-Assyrian Text Corpus Project.

Walsh, C. E. 2000. *The Fruit of the Vine: Viticulture in Ancient Israel*. Winona Lake, IN: Eisenbrauns.

Walsh, Peter. 2014. *The Archaeology of Mediterranean Landscapes: Human-Environment Interaction from the Neolithic to the Roman Period*. Cambridge: Cambridge University Press.

Walton, John H. 1986. "The Four Kingdoms of Daniel." *Journal of the Evangelical Theological Society* 29:25–36.

———. 1989. *Ancient Israelite Literature in Its Cultural Context*. Grand Rapids: Zondervan.

———. 1995. "The Mesopotamian Background of the Tower of Babel Account and Its Implications." *BBR* 5:155–75.

———. 2003. "Exodus, Date of." Pp. 258–72 in *Dictionary of the Old Testament: Pentateuch*, edited by T. Desmond Alexander and David W. Baker. Downers Grove, IL: InterVarsity.

———. 2008. "Creation in Genesis 1:1–2:3 and the Ancient Near East: Order Out of Disorder after Chaoskampf." *Calvin Theological Journal* 43:48–63.

———. 2009a. *The Lost World of Genesis One: Ancient Cosmology and the Origins Debate*. Downers Grove, IL: InterVarsity.

———, ed. 2009b. *Zondervan Illustrated Bible Background Commentaries: Old Testament*. 5 vols. Grand Rapids: Zondervan.

Walton, John H., and J. Harvey Walton. 2017. *The Lost World of the Israelite Conquest: Covenant, Retribution, and the Fate of the Canaanites*. Downers Grove, IL: InterVarsity.

Ward, William A., and Martha S. Joukowsky, eds. 1992. *The Crisis Years: The 12th Century B.C. from beyond the Danube to the Tigris*. Dubuque, IA: Kendall/Hunt.

Wason, P. K. 1994. *The Archaeology of Rank*. Cambridge: Cambridge University Press.

Watson, Patty Jo. 1979. *Archaeological Ethnography in Western Iran*. Viking Fund Publications in Anthropology 57. Tucson: University of Arizona Press.

Watson, R. S. 2005. *Chaos Uncreated: The Reassessment of the Theme of "Chaos" in the Hebrew Bible*. BZAW 431. Berlin: de Gruyter.

Watson, W. G. E. 1984. *Classical Hebrew Poetry: A Guide to Its Techniques*. JSOTSup 26. Sheffield: JSOT Press.

Watterson, Barbara. 1991. *Women in Ancient Egypt*. New York: St. Martin's Press.

Watts, James W. 2013. "The Political and Legal Uses of Scripture." Pp. 345–64 in *The New Cambridge History of the Bible: From the Beginnings to 600*, edited by James Carleton Paget and Joachim Schaper. Cambridge: Cambridge University Press.

Weber, Max. 1976. *The Agrarian Sociology of Ancient Civilizations*. New York: Knopf.

Weidner, E. F. 1939. "Jojachin, König von Juda, in Babylonischen Keilschrifttexten." Pp. 923–35 in *Mélanges syriens offerts à Monsieur René Dussaud*. Academie des inscriptions et belles-lettres 2. Paris: Geuthner.

Weinfeld, Moshe. 1972. *Deuteronomy and the Deuteronomic School*. Oxford: Oxford University Press.

Weinstein, J. 1981. "The Egyptian Empire in Palestine: A Reassessment." *BASOR* 241:1–28.

———. 1991. "Egypt and the Middle Bronze IIC / Late Bronze IA Transition in Palestine." *Levant* 23:105–15.

Weippert, Manfred. 1972. "Heiliger Krieg in Israel und Assyrien: Kritische Anmerkungen zu Gerhard von Rads Konzept des Heiligen Krieges im alten Israel." *ZAW* 84:460–93.

———. 1997. *Israelites, Araméens et Assyriens dans la Transjordanie septentrionale*. Wiesbaden: Harrassowitz.

Weisgerber, G. 2003. "Spatial Organisation of Mining and Smelting at Feinan, Jordan: Mining Archaeology beyond the History of Technology." Pp. 76–89 in *Mining and Metal Production through the Ages*, edited by Paul Craddock and Janet Lang. London: British Museum Press.

Weiss, B. 1982. "The Decline of Late Bronze Age Civilization as a Possible Response to Climatic Change." *Climatic Change* 4:173–98.

Weiss, Ehud. 2015. "'Beginnings of Fruit Growing in the Old World'—Two Generations Later." *Israel Journal of Plant Sciences* 62:75–85. https://doi.org/10.1080/07929978.2015.1007718.

Weiss, Ehud, Mordechai E. Kislev, and Anat Hartmann. 2008. "Autonomous Cultivation before Domestication." *Science* 312:1608–10.

Weiss, Ehud, Mordechai E. Kislev, Orit Simhoni, and Hartmut Tschauner. 2008. "Plant-Food Preparation Area on an Upper Paleolithic Brush Hut Floor at Ohalo II, Israel." *JAS* 35 (8): 2400–14.

Weiss, Ehud, Wilma Wetterstrom, Dani Nadel, and Ofer Bar-Yosef. 2004. "The Broad Spectrum Revisited: Evidence from Plant Remains." *Proceedings of the National Academy of Sciences* 101 (26): 9551–55.

Weissbrod, Lior, Guy Bar-Oz, Reuven Yeshurun, and Mina Weinstein-Evron. 2012. "Beyond Fast and Slow: The Mole Rat *Spalax ehrenbergi* (Order Rodentia) as a Test Case for Subsistence Intensification of Complex Natufian Foragers in Southwest Asia." *Quaternary International* 264:4–16.

Weissenrieder, Annette, and Friederike Wendt. 2005. "Images as Communication: The Methods of Iconography." Pp. 1–49 in *Picturing the New Testament: Studies in Ancient Visual Images*, edited by Annette Weissenrieder, Friederike Wendt, and Petra von Gemünden. Wissenschaftliche Untersuchungen zum Neuen Testament 2/193. Tübingen: Mohr Siebeck.

Welles, C. Bradford. 1970. *Alexander and the Hellenistic World*. Toronto: Hakkert.

Wellhausen, Julius. 1927. *Prolegomena zur Geschichte Israels*. 6th ed. Berlin: de Gruyter.

Wells, Bruce. 2006. "The Covenant Code and Ancient Near Eastern Legal Traditions: A Response to David P. Wright." *Maarav* 13:85–118.

Wenham, Gordon J. 1981. *Numbers: An Introduction and Commentary*. Tyndale Old Testament Commentaries. Downers Grove, IL: InterVarsity.

———. 1986. "Sanctuary Symbolism in the Garden of Eden Story." Pp. 19–25 in *Proceedings of the Ninth World Congress of Jewish Studies, Jerusalem, August 4–12, 1985: Division A: The Period of the Bible*, edited by David Assaf. Jerusalem: World Union of Jewish Studies. Reprint, pp. 399–404 in *I Studied Inscriptions from before the Flood: Ancient Near Eastern, Literary, and Linguistic Approaches to Genesis 1–11*, edited by Richard S. Hess and David Toshio Tsumura. Sources for Biblical and Theological Study 4. Winona Lake, IN: Eisenbrauns.

———. 2002. *Exploring the Old Testament: The Pentateuch*. Downers Grove, IL: InterVarsity.

Wente, Edward F. 1995. "The Scribes of Ancient Egypt." *CANE* 4:2211–21.

Wente, Edward F., and Edmund S. Meltzer, eds. 1990. *Letters from Ancient Egypt*. WAW 1. Atlanta: Scholars Press.

Westbrook, Raymond. 1988a. *Old Babylonian Marriage Law*. Archiv für Orientforschung Beiheft 23. Horn: F. Berger.

———. 1988b. *Studies in Biblical and Cuneiform Law*. Cahiers de la Revue Biblique 26. Paris: Gabalda.

———. 1989. "Cuneiform Law Codes and the Origins of Legislation." *Zeitschrift für Assyriologie* 79:201–22.

———, ed. 2003a. *A History of Ancient Near Eastern Law*. 2 vols. Handbook of Oriental Studies: Section One: The Near and Middle East. Leiden: Brill.

———. 2003b. "Introduction: The Character of Ancient Near Eastern Law." Pp. 1–90 in *A History of Ancient Near Eastern Law*, edited by Raymond Westbrook. Handbook of Oriental Studies: Section One: The Near and Middle East. Leiden: Brill.

———. 2009a. "The Female Slave." Pp. 149–74 in *Law from the Tigris to the Tiber: The Writings* of *Raymond Westbrook; Cuneiform and Biblical Sources*, vol. 2, edited by Bruce Wells and Rachel Magdalene. Winona Lake, IN: Eisenbrauns. First published as pp. 214–38 in *Gender and Law in the Hebrew Bible and the Ancient Near East*, edited by Victor H. Matthews, Bernard M. Levinson, and Tikva Frymer-Kensky. JSOTSup 62. Sheffield: Sheffield Academic Press, 1998.

———. 2009b. "Slave and Master in Ancient Near Eastern Law." Pp. 161–216 in *Law from the Tigris to the Tiber: The Writings of Raymond Westbrook; Cuneiform and Biblical Sources* vol. 1, edited by Bruce Wells and Rachel Magdalene. Winona Lake, IN: Eisenbrauns. First published in *Chicago-Kent Law Review* 70 (1995): 1631–76.

———. 2009c. "Social Justice in the Ancient Near East." Pp. 144–60 in *Law from the Tigris to the Tiber: The Writings of Raymond Westbrook; Cuneiform and Biblical Sources*, vol. 1, edited by Bruce Wells and Rachel Magdalene. Winona Lake, IN: Eisenbrauns. First published as pp. 149–63 in *Social Justice in the Ancient World*, edited by K. D. Irani and Morris Silver. Westport, CT: Greenwood, 1995.

Westbrook, Raymond, and Bruce Wells. 2009. *Everyday Law in Biblical Israel: An Introduction*. Louisville: Westminster John Knox.

Westermann, W. L. 1928. "On Inland Transportation and Communication in Antiquity." *Political Science Quarterly* 43:375–76.

Whitelam, K. W. 1996. *The Invention of Ancient Israel: The Silencing of Palestinian History*. Abingdon: Routledge, 1996.

Whitt, W. D. 1995. "The Story of the Semitic Alphabet." *CANE* 4:2379–97.

Whybray, R. N. 1990. "The Sage in the Israelite Royal Court." Pp. 133–39 in *The Sage in Israel and the Ancient Near East*, edited by John G. Gammie and Leo G. Perdue. Winona Lake, IN: Eisenbrauns.

Widengren, Geo. 1951. *The King and the Tree of Life in Ancient Near Eastern Religion*. Acta Universitatis Upsaliensis 4. Uppsala: Lundequist; Wiesbaden: Harrassowitz.

Wiggermann, F. A. M. 1995. "Theologies, Priests, and Worship in Ancient Mesopotamia." *CANE* 3:1857–70.

Wikander, Ola. 2013. "Ungrateful Grazers: A Parallel to Deut 32:15 from the Hurrian/Hittite *Epic of Liberation*." *Svensk exegetisk årsbok* 78:137–46.

Wilcke, Claus. 2007. *Early Ancient Near Eastern Law: A History of Its Beginnings; The Early Dynastic and Sargonid Periods*. Winona Lake, IN: Eisenbrauns.

Wilcox, George. 2012. "Searching for the Origins of Arable Weeds in the Near East." *Vegetation History and Archaeobotany* 21:163–67.

Wilkin, Robert L. 1992. *The Land Called Holy: Palestine in Christian History and Thought*. New Haven: Yale University Press.

Wilkinson, Tony J., Jason Ur, Eleanor Barbanes Wilkinson, and Mark Altaweel. 2005. "Landscape and Settlement in the Neo-Assyrian Empire." *BASOR* 340:23–56.

Willems, Harco. 2004. "Sacrifice, Offerings, and Votives: Egypt." Pp. 326–30 in *Religions of the Ancient World: A Guide*, edited by Sarah Iles Johnston. Religions of the Ancient World, Harvard University Press Reference Library. Cambridge, MA: Belknap Press of Harvard University Press.

Willet, Elizabeth. 2001. "Women and House Religion." *The Bible and Interpretation*. http://www.bibleinterp.com/articles/HouseReligion.shtml.

Williams, Margaret H. 1998. *The Jews among Greeks and Romans: A Diasporan Sourcebook*. Baltimore: Johns Hopkins University Press.

Williams, Michael J. 2012. *Basics of Ancient Ugaritic: A Concise Grammar, Workbook, and Lexicon*. Grand Rapids: Zondervan.

Williams, Peter J. 2011. "'Slaves' in Biblical Narrative and in Translation." Pp. 441–52 in *On Stone and Scroll: Essays in Honour of Graham Ivor Davies*, edited by James K. Aitken, Katherine J. Dell, and Brian A. Mastin. BZAW 420. Berlin: de Gruyter.

Williams, Roland J. 1958. "The Hymn to Aton." Pp. 142–50 in *Documents from Old Testament Times*, edited by D. Winton Thomas. New York: Harper & Row.

Williams, Ronald J. 1990a. "The Functions of the Sage in the Egyptian Royal Court." Pp. 95–98 in *The Sage in Israel and the Ancient Near East*, edited by John G. Gammie and Leo G. Perdue. Winona Lake, IN: Eisenbrauns.

———. 1990b. "The Sage in Egyptian Literature." Pp. 19–30 in *The Sage in Israel and the Ancient Near East*, edited by John G. Gammie and Leo G. Perdue. Winona Lake, IN: Eisenbrauns.

Williamson, Jacquelyn. 2015. "Amarna Period." In *UCLA Encyclopedia of Egyptology*, edited by Wolfram Grajetzki and Willeke Wendric. http://digital2.library.ucla.edu/viewItem.do?ark=21198/zz002k2h3t.

Wilson, John. 1951. *The Culture of Ancient Egypt*. Chicago: University of Chicago Press.

Wilson, Kevin A. 2005. *The Campaign of Pharaoh Shoshenq I into Palestine*. FAT 2/9. Tübingen: Mohr Siebeck.

Winnett, Frederick V. 1937. *A Study of the Lihyanite and Thamudic Inscriptions*. Toronto: University of Toronto Press.

Winter, Irene J. 1986. "The King and the Cup: Iconography of the Royal Presentation Scene on Ur III Seals." Pp. 253–68 in *Insight through Images: Studies in Honor of Edith Porada*, edited by Marilyn Kelly-Buccellati, Paolo Matthiae, and Maurits Van Loon. Bibliotheca Mesopotamica 21. Malibu, CA: Undena.

———. 2007. "Representing Abundance: A Visual Dimension of the Agrarian State." Pp. 117–38 in *Settlement and Society: Essays Dedicated to Robert McCormick Adams*, edited by Elizabeth C. Stone. Los Angeles: Cotsen Institute of Archaeology, University of California; Chicago: Oriental Institute of the University of Chicago.

———. 2010. *On Art in the Ancient Near East*. 2 vols. CHANE 34/1–2. Leiden: Brill.

Winter, Urs. 1987. *Frau und Göttin: Exegetische und ikonographische Studien zum weiblichen Gottesbild im Alten Israel und in desen Umwelt*. 2nd ed. OBO 53. Fribourg: Universitätsverlag; Göttingen: Vandenhoeck & Ruprecht.

Wiseman, Donald J. 1952. "A New Stele of Assurnasir-pal." *Iraq* 14:24–44.

———. 1956. *Chronicles of Chaldean Kings in the British Museum*. London: Trustees of the British Museum.

———. 1958. "Abban and Alalah." *JCS* 12:124–29.

———. 1980. "Abraham Reassessed." Pp. 139–56 in *Essays on the Patriarchal Narratives*, edited by A. R. Millard and D. J. Wiseman. Eugene, OR: Wipf & Stock.

———. 1993. *1 and 2 Kings: An Introduction and Commentary*. Tyndale Old Testament Commentaries. Downers Grove, IL: InterVarsity.

Wolfe, Patrick. 1999. *Settler Colonialism and the Transformation of Anthropology: The Politics and Poetics of an Ethnographic Event*. Writing Past Colonialism. London: Cassell.

———. 2006. "Settler Colonialism and the Elimination of the Native." *Journal of Genocide Research* 8:387–409.

———. 2008. "Structure and Event: Settler Colonialism, Time and the Question of Genocide." Pp. 102–32 in *Empire, Colony, Genocide: Conquest, Occupation and Subaltern Resistance in World History*, edited by A. Dirk Moses. New York: Berghahn Books.

Wolff, S. 1998. "An Iron Age I Site at ʿEn Haggit (northern Ramat Manashe)." Pp. 449–54 in *Mediterranean Peoples in Transition: Thirteenth to Early Tenth Centuries BCE*, edited by Seymour Gitin, Amihai Mazar, and Ephraim Stern. Jerusalem: Israel Exploration Society.

Wong, Gordon C. I. 2001. "Faith in the Present Form of Isaiah vii 1–17." *VT* 51:535–47.

Wood, B. G. 2009. "The Search for Joshua's Ai." Pp. 205–40 in *Critical Issues in Early Israelite History*, edited by Richard S. Hess, Gerald A. Klingbeil, and Paul J. Ray Jr. BBRSup 3. Winona Lake, IN: Eisenbrauns.

Woods, Christopher E. 2004. "The Sun-God Tablet of Nabû-apla-iddina Revisited." *JCS* 56:23–103.

Woolley, C. Leonard. 1921. *Carchemish: Report on the Excavations at Djerabis on Behalf of the British Museum, Part 2: The Town Defenses*. London: British Museum.

Worthington, Ian. 2010. *Philip II of Macedonia*. New Haven: Yale University Press.

———. 2014. *By the Spear: Philip II, Alexander the Great, and the Rise and Fall of the Macedonian Empire*. Oxford: Oxford University Press.

Wright, David P. 1986. "The Gesture of Hand Placement in the Hebrew Bible and in Hittite Literature." *JAOS* 106:433–46.

———. 1987. *The Disposal of Impurity: Elimination Rites in the Bible and in Hittite and Mesopotamian Literature*. Society of Biblical Literature Dissertation Series 101. Atlanta: Scholars Press.

———. 1993. "Analogy in Biblical and Hittite Ritual." Pp. 473–506 in *Religionsgeschichtliche Beziehungen zwischen Kleinasien, Nordsyrien und dem Alten Testament*, edited by Bernd Janowski, Klaus Koch, and Wilhelm Gernot. OBO 129. Fribourg: Universitätsverlag.

———. 2003. "The Laws of Hammurabi as a Source for the Covenant Collection (Exodus 20:23–23:19)." *Maarav* 10:211–60.

———. 2009. *Inventing God's Law: How the Covenant Code of the Bible Used and Revised the Laws of Hammurabi*. Oxford: Oxford University Press.

Wright, G. E. 1959. "Is Glueck's Aim to Prove That the Bible Is True?" *BA* 22:101–8.

———. 1965. *Shechem: The Biography of a Biblical City*. New York: McGraw-Hill.

———. 1969. Archaeological Method in Palestine—An American Interpretation. *ErIsr* 9:120–33.

Wright, Jacob L. 2008. "Military Valor and Kingship: A Book-Oriented Approach to the Study of a Major War Theme." Pp. 33–56 in *Writing and Reading War: Rhetoric, Gender, and Ethics in Biblical and Modern Contexts*, edited by Brad E. Kelle and Frank Ritchel Ames. SymS 42. Atlanta: Society of Biblical Literature.

Wright, L. 2016. "Glyptic Art under and after Empire: Late Bronze IIB and Iron I Scarabs and Stamp Seals from the Southern Levant." PhD dissertation, Johns Hopkins University.

Wyssmann, Patrick. 2014. "The Coinage Imagery of Samaria and Judah in the Late Persian Period." Pp. 221–66 in *A "Religious Revolution" in Yehûd? The Material Culture of the Persian Period as a Test Case*, edited by Christian Frevel, Katharina Pyschny, and Izak Cornelius. OBO 267. Fribourg: Academic Press; Göttingen: Vandenhoeck & Ruprecht.

Xella, Paolo. 1995. "Le dieu et 'sa' déesse: l'utilization des suffixes pronominaux avec des théonymes d'Ebla à Ugarit et à Kuntillet ʿAjrud." *UF* 27:599–610.

———. 2001. "Yhwh e la sua *ʾšrh*: La dea o il suo simbolo? (Una riposta a J. A. Emerton)." *Studi epigrafici e linguistici sul Vicino Oriente antico* 18:71–81.

Yadin, Yigael. 1963. *The Art of Warfare in Biblical Lands: In the Light of Archaeological Study.* Vol. 2. Translated by M. Pearlman. New York: McGraw-Hill.

Yahalom-Mack, Naama, et al. 2014. "New Insights into Levantine Copper Trade: Analysis of Ingots from the Bronze and Iron Ages in Israel." *JAS* 45:159–77.

Yamada, Sigeo. 1995. "Aram-Israel Relations as Reflected in the Aramaic Inscription from Tel Dan." *UF* 27:611–25.

———. 1998. "The Manipulative Counting of the Euphrates Crossings in the Later Inscriptions of Shalmaneser III." *JCS* 50:87–94.

———. 2000. *The Construction of the Assyrian Empire: A Historical Study of the Inscriptions of Shalmaneser III (859–824 BC) Relating to His Campaigns to the West.* SHANE 3. Leiden: Brill.

Yamauchi, Edwin. 2010. "Akhenaten, Moses, and Monotheism." *Near East Archaeological Society Bulletin* 55:1–15.

Yasur-Landau, Assaf. 2010. *The Philistines and Aegean Migration at the End of the Late Bronze Age.* Cambridge: Cambridge University Press.

Yee, Gale A. 1992. *Composition and Tradition in the Book of Hosea: A Redaction Critical Investigation.* Society of Biblical Literature Dissertation Series 102. Atlanta: Scholars Press.

Yisraeli, Yael. 1993. "Far'ah, Tell El- (South)." *NEAEHL* 2:441–44.

Yom-Tov, Yoram. 2013. *Faunistics of Terrestrial Vertebrates: An Israeli View,* vol. 1, *Introduction.* Ra'anana: Open University of Israel Press.

Yon, Marguerite. 1991. *Arts et industries de la pierre: Ras Shamra-Ougarit VI.* Paris: Éditions Recherches sur les civilisations.

———. 2006. *The City of Ugarit at Tell Ras Shamra.* Winona Lake, IN: Eisenbrauns.

Young, Robb Andrew. 2012. *Hezekiah in History and Tradition.* VTSup 155. Leiden: Brill.

Younger, K. Lawson, Jr. 1990. *Ancient Conquest Accounts: A Study in Ancient Near Eastern and Biblical History Writing.* JSOTSup 98. Sheffield: JSOT Press.

———. 2003. "Assyrian Involvement in the Southern Levant at the End of the Eighth Century BCE." Pp. 235–63 in *Jerusalem in Bible and Archaeology: The First Temple Period,* edited by Andrew G. Vaughan and Ann E. Killebrew. SymS 18. Atlanta: Society of Biblical Literature.

———. 2005. "'Haza'el, Son of a Nobody': Some Reflections in Light of Recent Study." Pp. 245–70 in *Writing and Ancient Near Eastern Society: Papers in Honour of Alan R. Millard,* edited by Piotr

Bienkowski, Christopher Mee, and Elizabeth Slater. LHB/OTS 426. London: T&T Clark.

———. 2007. "The Late Bronze Age/Iron Age Transition and the Origins of the Arameans." Pp. 131–74 in *Ugarit at Seventy-Five,* edited by K. Lawson Younger Jr. Winona Lake, IN: Eisenbrauns.

———. 2016. *A Political History of the Arameans: From Their Origins to the End of Their Polities.* ABS 13. Atlanta: Society of Biblical Literature.

Younker, Randall W. 1999. "The Emergence of the Ammonites." Pp. 189–218 in *Ancient Ammon,* edited by Burton MacDonald and Randall W. Younker. SHANE 17. Leiden: Brill.

———. 2003. "The Iron Age in the Southern Levant." Pp. 367–82 in *Near Eastern Archaeology: A Reader,* edited by Suzanne Richard. Winona Lake, IN: Eisenbrauns.

———. 2014. "Ammon during the Iron Age II Period." Pp. 757–69 in *The Oxford Handbook of the Archaeology of the Levant: C. 8000–332 BCE,* edited by Margreet L. Steiner and Ann E. Killebrew. Oxford: Oxford University Press.

Zabkar, Louis. 1954. "The Theocracy of Amarna and the Doctrine of the Ba." *JNES* 13:87–101.

Zaccagnini, C. 2000. "The Interdependence of the Great Powers." Pp. 141–53 in *Amarna Diplomacy: The Beginning of International Relations,* edited by Raymond Cohen. Baltimore: Johns Hopkins University Press.

Zadok, Ran. 1979. *The Jews in Babylonia during the Chaldean and Achaemenian Periods according to the Babylonian Sources.* Studies in the History of the Jewish People and the Land of Israel 3. Haifa: University of Haifa Press.

———. 1996. "Notes on Syro-Palestinian History, Toponymy and Anthroponymy." *UF* 28:721–49.

Zaouali, L. 2007. *Medieval Cuisine of the Islamic World: A Concise History with 174 Recipes.* Translated by M. B. DeBevoise. Berkeley: University of California Press.

Zayadine, Fawzi. 1991. "Sculpture in Ancient Jordan." Pp. 31–61 in *The Art of Jordan: Treasures from an Ancient Land,* edited by Piotr Bienkowski. Stroud: Sutton.

Zeder, Melinda A. 1998. "Pigs and Emergent Complexity in the Ancient Near East." Pp. 109–22 in *Ancestors for the Pigs: Pigs in Prehistory,* edited by Sarah M. Nelson. MASCA Research Papers in Science and Archaeology 15. Philadelphia: University of Pennsylvania Museum of Archaeology and Anthropology.

———. 2011. "The Origins of Agriculture in the Near East." *Current Anthropology* 52:S221–35.

———. 2016. "Domestication as a Model System for Niche Construction Theory." *Evolutionary Ecology* 30:325–48.

Zertal, Adam. 1986–87. "An Early Iron Age Cultic Site on Mount Ebal: Excavation Seasons 1982–1987; Preliminary Report." *TA* 13–14:105–65.

———. 1990. "The *Paḥwāh* of Samaria (Northern Israel) during the Persian Period: Types of Settlement, Economy, History and New Discoveries." *Transeuphratène* 3:9–30.

———. 2001. "The Heart of the Monarchy: Pattern of Settlement and Historical Considerations of the Israelite Kingdom of Samaria." Pp. 38–64 in *Studies in the Archaeology of the Iron Age in Israel and Jordan*, edited by Amihai Mazar. JSOTSup 331. Sheffield: Sheffield Academic Press.

———. 2003. "The Province of Samaria (Assyrian *Samerina*) in the Late Iron Age (Iron Age III)." Pp. 377–412 in *Judah and the Judeans in the Neo-Babylonian Period*, edited by Oded Lipschits and Joseph Blenkinsopp. Winona Lake, IN: Eisenbrauns.

———. 2004. *A People Is Born: The Mt. Ebal Altar and Israel's Beginnings*. Judaism Here and Now. Tel Aviv: Yediot Ahronot. [In Hebrew.]

———. 2012. *El-Ahwat: A Fortified Site from the Early Iron Age near Nahal 'Iron, Israel*. Leiden: Brill.

Zertal, Adam, and D. Ben-Yosef. 2009. "Bedhat Esh-Sha'ab: An Iron Age I Enclosure in the Jordan Valley." Pp. 517–29 in *Exploring the Longue Durée: Essays in Honor of Lawrence E. Stager*, edited by J. David Schloen. Winona Lake, IN: Eisenbrauns.

Zevit, Ziony. 1977. "A Phoenician Inscription and Biblical Covenant Theology." *IEJ* 27:110–18.

———. 2001. *The Religions of Ancient Israel: A Synthesis of Parallactic Approaches*. New York: Continuum.

Ziegler, C. 1979. *Les instruments de musique égyptiens*. Paris: Réunion des Musées Nationaux.

Ziegler, N. 1999. *La population féminine des Palais d'aprè les archives royales de Mari: Le Harem de Zimrî-Lîm*. Florilegium marianum 4. Mémoires de NABU 5. Paris: SEPOA.

———. 2007. *Les musiciens et la musique d'après les archives de Mari*. Florilegium marianum 9. Mémoires de NABU 10. Paris: SEPOA.

Ziffer, Irit. 2005. "From Acemhöyük to Megiddo: The Banquet Scene in the Art of the Levant in the Second Millennium BCE." *TA* 32:133–67.

Zohary, Daniel, Maria Hopf, and Ehud Weiss. 2012. *Domestication of Plants in the Old World*. 4th ed. Oxford: Oxford University Press.

Zohary, Daniel, and Pinhas Spiegel-Roy. 1975. "Beginnings of Fruit Growing in the Old World." *Science* 187:319–27.

Zohary, Michael. 1962. *Plant Life of Palestine (Israel and Jordan)*. New York: Ronald.

———. 1971. "Pista, Pistim." Pp. 635–36 in *Encyclopaedia Biblica*, edited by B. Mazar and H. Tadmor. Jerusalem: Bialik.

———. 1973. *Geobotanical Foundations of the Middle East*. Stuttgart: Fischer.

———. 1982a. *Plants of the Bible*. Cambridge: Cambridge University Press.

———. 1982b. *Vegetation of Israel and Adjacent Areas*. Wiesbaden: Reichert.

Zorn, Jeffrey R. 1993. "Tell en-Naṣbeh: A Re-evaluation of the Architecture and Stratigraphy of the Early Bronze Age, Iron Age and Later Periods." PhD dissertation, University of California, Berkeley.

———. 1994. "Estimating the Population Size of Ancient Settlements: Methods, Problems, Solutions and a Case Study." *BASOR* 295:31–48.

———. 2003. "Tell en-Naṣbeh and the Problem of the Material Culture of the Sixth Century." Pp. 413–47 in *Judah and the Judeans in the Neo-Babylonian Period*, edited by Oded Lipschits and Joseph Blenkinsopp. Winona Lake, IN: Eisenbrauns.

———. 2006. "The Burials of the Judean Kings: Sociohistorical Considerations and Suggestions." Pp. 801–20 in *"I Will Speak of the Riddles of Ancient Times": Archaeological and Historical Studies in Honor of Amihai Mazar on the Occasion of His Sixtieth Birthday*, vol. 1, edited by Aren. M. Maeir and Pierre de Miroschedji. Winona Lake, IN: Eisenbrauns.

———. 2014a. "The Levant during the Babylonian Period." Pp. 825–40 in *The Oxford Handbook of the Archaeology of the Levant: C. 8000–332 BCE*, edited by Margreet L. Steiner and Ann E. Killebrew. Oxford: Oxford University Press.

———. 2014b. "War and Its Effects on Civilians in Ancient Israel and Its Neighbors." Pp. 79–100 in *The Other Face of the Battle: The Impact of War on Civilians in the Ancient Near East*, edited by Davide Nadali and Jordi Vidal. AOAT 413. Münster: Ugarit-Verlag.

Scripture Index

Old Testament

Genesis

1 96, 105, 106, 335–36, 337, 346, 346n12
1–3 338
1:1–24 335
1:1–2:3 334
1:2 335–36, 346
1:16 334
1:21 336
1:26 131
2 108, 110
2–3 96
2:4 392
3 106, 124, 157, 352
4:1–8 492
4:9 393
4:21 468
5:3 131
6–9 93
6:5–7 106
7:23 106
8:21–22 106
8:22 21
9:18–28 205n6
11 338
11:3 451
12–50 187, 189, 191, 193
12:1–3 201
12:7 201
12:10–13:1 392
12:13 191
12:16 428
12:19 191
14 189, 192–93, 192n19
14:4–5 192
14:5 386
14:18–22 124

15 191, 192
15:2–3 405
15:4 392
15:7 393
15:9–11 191
15:13 187
15:17–18 191
15:18 129
15:20 386
16 428–29
16:1–2 191, 405
17:1 134
17:12–13 436
17:17–22 429
17:23 428
17:27 428
18:6 461
18:6–8 364
18:7 462
18:8 457
19:3 465
19:24–29 307
20:2 191
20:5 191
20:12 191
21:8 465
21:22 190n14
21:25 413
21:30 413
21:32 190n14
23 383, 421n17
24:10 12, 190n11
24:30 434
24:34–60 404
24:53 434
25:29 462
25:29–34 414, 461
25:34 462
26:2–5 201

26:7 191
26:9 191
26:19 428
26:20–22 497
26:26 190n14
26:30 465
27:3–4 462
27:28 414
27:41 385
28:10–15 201
28:20 457
29:1–12 414
29:14 191
29:21–22 462
30:1 405
30:43 428
31 175
31:19 375, 398
31:19–35 386
33:20 124
35:11 134
35:17 401
35:20 383
37 188, 192
37–50 392
37:8 393
37:19–20 393
37:34 385
38:8–9 407
38:12–19 407
38:24–26 404
38:27–30 407
39–50 192
39:14 195
40:16 453
40:20 465
41 108
41:45 356
41:53–57 392

42:1–2 194
42:38 386
44:29–31 386
45:10 194
46:28 492
47:11 196
49:1–28 404
49:29–33 405
50:2–3 383
50:7–12 385
50:10 385
50:21 393
50:26 383

Exodus

1–14 195n2
1:11 197, 202n1
1:14 197
1:15–19 195
2:1–10 198
2:3 453
2:20 457
3:8 411, 462
3:17 462
5:7 197
5:7–8 197
5:13–14 197
7–8 107
8:3 459
9:16–17 343
9:29 343
10:9 465
12 367
12:1–30 494
12:3–7 401n11
12:3–9 462
12:14 465
12:25 7

12:34 199
12:37 197, 198, 199
12:38 205
13:5 462
13:19 198
13:20 199
14:2 199
14:21–31 107
15:3 512
15:20 470
15:20–21 401
15:22 200
15:25 492
16:1 200
16:3 459
16:4–5 462
18:13–26 496
18:25–26 496
20 153
20–24 496
20:1 495
20:1–21 494
20:2–17 498
20:3 342
20:4–6 172
20:8–10 401
20:12 398, 405
20:14–17 408
20:16 497
20:22 495
20:22–23:19 494
21 427
21–23 426
21:1–11 498
21:2 425, 427
21:2–11 426, 427
21:4 425
21:5–6 424, 427
21:6 425
21:7 404
21:12 498
21:12–36 398
21:14 498
21:16 498
21:17 493
21:20–21 426, 429
21:22 498
21:26–27 426, 429
21:28–32 497
21:32 426, 429
21:35–36 497
22:1–15 498
22:3 426
22:16–17 498
22:18 370
22:19 498
22:21 513
22:22–24 498
22:22–23:19 495

22:25–26 494
22:25–27 435
22:29 406
23:2–3 497
23:6 498
23:8 497
23:9 498
23:19 455
23:27–33 205
23:29 513
24:12 495
25 200
25–40 206
25:23–30 462
25:29–30 363
26–36 439
27:20–21 362, 494
28:1–43 494
28:30 370
29 364
29:3 453
29:23 453
30:7–8 362, 364
31:2–3 439
32:3–4 439
32:4 175n3
33:3 462
34:7 132
34:11–16 205
34:18–22 406
34:26 455
35:13 462
35:25–26 401
38:8 401
38:26 198
40:34–35 364

Leviticus

1 363, 365
1–7 364, 435, 498
1:3 363
1:3–17 494
1:4 363
1:9 361
1:14–17 494
2 361, 364, 366
2:4 459
3 363
3:16 457
4:1–5:13 365
4:16 365
5:10 494
5:14–6:7 365
6:12–16 MT 364
6:19–23 364, 366
7:9 459, 461
7:11–36 363
7:12–15 366
7:12–16 364

7:20–21 365
8 359, 364
8–9 364
8:2 453
8:26 453
8:31 453
10:1–11 494
10:10–11 496
11 498
11:31 385
11:35 459
12:6–8 365
13:47–48 453
13:52 453
13:59 453
14:4 454
14:19 365
14:40–44 454
15:31 365
16 364, 367, 494
16:6–14 376
16:12–16 361
16:16 365
16:19 365
16:29 363
16:29–31 365
17 498
17–27 426
17:11 363
18 498
18:1–5 201
18:12 359
18:21 364, 387
18:24–30 205
19 498
19:13 495
19:19 415
19:26 370
19:28 385
19:31 386
19:32 405
19:33–34 513
19:35–36 494
19:36 418
20:1–5 364
20:2–5 387
20:6 386
20:10–21 493
20:24 462
20:27 386
21–22:16 498
21:1–2 385
21:10–11 385
22:16–23:44 498
22:17–25 363
23 367
23:3 361
23:4–25 462
23:33–43 494

24:5–8 363
24:5–9 462
24:7–9 363
24:10–23 494
25 433, 435, 498
25:29–30 433n2
25:39–43 426, 427, 428, 429
25:39–55 423
25:44–46 424, 428, 429
25:53 429
26:26 459, 461
27 366
27:5 193n23
27:29 513

Numbers

1:18 404
5:12–31 496
6:1–21 366, 498
6:15 453
6:17 453
6:19 453
6:22–27 95
6:24–26 137
9:9–14 494
10:10 406
11 494
11:5 414
11:8 459
11:16 496
13:19 395n11
13:27 462
14:8 462
15:1–16 364
15:1–31 498
15:19 457
15:19–21 400
15:28–29 498
15:30–31 365
16:13–14 462
16:31–33 307
19 365
19:11–16 385
19:22 385
20:16 441
20:17 210
20:29 385
21 201
21:2 513
21:9 439
21:11–24:25 288
21:13 290, 291
21:17 392
21:22 210
21:27–30 392n6
21:29 292
21:30 290

22–24 133
22:5 373
25:7–13 246
26:29 206n7
27 201, 433
27:1 206n7
27:1–8 398
27:1–11 407, 494
27:2 496
27:5 496
27:36 494
28–29 364, 367
28:1–8 362, 364
28:2 364
28:7 363, 364
28:11–15 462
30 498
31–34 201
31:19 385
31:19–24 512
32 201
32:3 290, 291
32:34 290, 291
32:38 291
33:3 197, 198, 199
33:5 197
33:7 199
33:8 200
33:45–46 290
34:3 441
34:5 15
35:1–8 212
35:30 497
36 201, 494
36:1–2 497
36:1–12 407, 494
36:2 496
36:6 496

Deuteronomy

1:8 201
1:15 496
1:15–16 481
1:30–31 405
2:8 441
2:8–36 288
2:11 386
3:11 124, 386
4 343
4:9–10 399, 406
4:20 440
4:34 163
4:35 340, 343
4:39 340, 341, 343
5:1–22 194
5:2 129
5:6–21 498
5:8–10 172

5:9 132
5:20 497
6:1–2 406
6:3 462
6:3–9 408
6:4 138
6:6–9 129
7 205
7:1–5 514
7:5 124
7:9 137
7:12–13 457
7:21 512
7:24 513
8:7–8 107
8:7–9 411, 439
8:7–10 432
8:15 163
9:3 512
10:17–18 498
11 22
11:9 462
11:13–14 457
11:14 412
11:19 406
12–26 426, 494
12:1 201
13:15 513
14:1 385
14:1–21 498
14:21 455
14:22–27 462
14:24–26 436
14:28–29 434, 408, 498
15 427
15:12 425, 427
15:12–18 426–27, 498
15:16–17 424–25, 427
15:18 426
16:1–8 465
16:1–17 462, 498
16:9–17 465
16:11 376
16:18 496
16:19 497
16:19–20 481
16:21 124
16:21–17:7 498
17:5 85
17:6 497
17:7 498
17:8–13 496
17:14–20 476, 496
18:9–12 370
18:9–14 498
18:9–22 368
18:10 364
18:11 386
19:12 496

19:14 408
19:16–21 497
19:17 497
20 498
20:4 512
20:10 513
20:11 513
20:16–18 513
20:19–20 513
21:2 496
21:7–8 362
21:10 428
21:10–11 513
21:10–14 429, 498
21:12–14 513
21:14 428
21:15–17 406, 498
21:18–21 404, 498
21:19 85
21:22–23 383
22:11 453
22:13–19 404
22:15 85
22:24 85
23:7–8 513
23:10–14 512
23:15–16 428, 429
23:17 401
23:20 435
24:10–13 435
24:12–15 494
24:14 495
24:14–15 435
24:17 435, 494
24:17–21 498
24:19–21 408
25:1 497
25:1–3 496, 497
25:2 498
25:5 407
25:5–6 407
25:7–10 407
25:13–15 418, 494
25:27 85
26:1–11 434
26:5 190n11
26:9 462
26:15 462
27 134
27:3 462
27:15–26 493
27:17 408
27:19 498
28 132
28:4 392
28:11–12 392
28:12 412
28:26 384
28:38–40 406

30:19 129
31:3 512
31:6 512
31:8 512
31:20 462
32 343
32:5 118n5
32:8–9 341
32:14 457
32:22 386
32:39 343, 387
32:49 291
33:2 343n5
34:1 291
34:5–6 383
34:8 385

Joshua

1:7 494
2 393
4:21–22 399
5:6 462
5:13–15 364
6 393
6–11 11
6:17 394
6:20–21 307
6:21 513
6:22–25 206
6:25 394
7 353n6, 394n9
7:10 394
7:11 394n8
7:12 394n8
7:16–19 394
7:25 394
8:33 496
9 206
9:1 412
10:9 512
10:14 512
10:42 512
11:2 412
11:10–11 206
11:12–13 206, 394n8
11:21 412
12:7 206
12:8 412
13–19 10, 404
13:1–7 206
13:9 291
13:16 291
13:17 290
13:18 291
15:1 441
15:20–32 278
16:2 291
16:7 291
17:15 412

17:17–18 413
19 124
19:1–8 278
19:26 412
20:4 497
21 124, 212
23:3 512
23:10 512
24:1 496
24:2 393

Judges

1–2 201
1:16 278
3 124
3:12–30 288
4 480n5
4–5 393
4:4 496
4:19 457
5 469
5:4–5 306
5:25 397
5:29–30 436
6 124
6:6 436
6:19 459, 461, 462
6:25 124
6:28 124
6:30–31 124
6:37 453
8:1 497
8:2 497
8:2–3 497
8:30 405
9:27 406
9:30 496
11:24 292, 342
11:26 202
11:39–40 385
13–16 11
14 465
14:8 463
16 269
17–18 379
17:5 386
17:5–6 375
18:14–20 386
20:14 393
20:27–28 512
20:29–48 512
20:38 139
20:40 139
21:6 393
21:11 393

Ruth

1:6 457
2:14 414, 458

1 Samuel

3:1–13 407
4:1–6 404
4:1–12 85
4:6 434
4:13–17 408
4:14–17 399

1 Samuel

1–2 380
1:2 405
1:4–8 405
2:1–5 405
2:6 387
2:13–16 435
2:14 459
2:22 401
2:28 370
8:5 475
8:10–18 204
8:12–13 436
8:13 401
8:15 436
8:16–17 436
8:17 436
9 421
10:5 401
13:19–22 270
13:21 44
14:3 370
14:27 463
14:50 480
14:50–51 479
15 477
15:8 513
15:23 386
15:25 497
16:13 393
17:45 512
18:13 480
19:11–17 386
19:13 375
20 465
20:5–6 462
20:5–29 401
21:7 480
21:9 370
23 512
23:6 370
23:9 370
25:1 385
25:36 466
25:39 497
26:22 481
27:10 278
28 386, 401
28:6 370
28:24 461, 462
29:1 413

30:7–8 370
30:14 278
30:22–25 494
30:23–25 496
31:8–10 124
31:10 384

2 Samuel

1:11 385
1:19 393
1:21 412
2:12–4:12 211
2:14 481
3:1 393
3:10 224
3:13 211
3:20 465
3:32 384
4:12 384
5:11 322n13
5:13 405
5:17–25 211
6 211
6:14 470
6:23 405
7 211, 217, 305, 477
7:22 346
8:2 288
8:6 211
8:14 211
8:16 479
8:16–18 478
8:18 481
9 211
9:10 457
11:1 408
12:1–15 496
12:7–12 497
12:13 497
12:23 385
13:6 461
13:8 461
13:10 461
13:29 415
13:37 385
14:1–20 401
14:2 385, 504
14:4–11 498
15:2 85
15:3–4 481
17:23 384
17:27–29 457
18:33 393
19:35 401
19:37 384
20:7 212
20:14–22 504
20:15 508

20:16–20 401
20:23–26 478, 481
21:14 383
22:8–16 307
23:1–5 305
23:8–39 212
24:10 497
24:11–17 497
24:24 417

1 Kings

1–11 209
1:33 415
1:50–51 139
2:10 384
2:28 139
2:34 384
3:1 211
3:16–18 497
3:16–28 496
4 479
4:1–19 478
4:2–19 479
4:7–19 10, 210, 212
4:20–25 466
4:21 213
4:25 213, 224
4:30 499
4:33 7
5:1–12 322n13
5:8–9 422
6:1 198, 198n9, 202
6:21 214
7:8 211
7:13–14 439
7:23–26 124
7:48–51 214
8:42 163
8:46 392, 439
8:51 440
8:60 346
9 420, 421
9:11 214
9:15 211, 276
9:15–17 10, 64
9:16 211
9:19 213
9:20–22 201, 204
9:24 211
9:28 214
10 201, 421, 465
10:2 214, 420
10:10 214
10:14 214
10:23–24 209
10:24–25 421
10:25 415
10:26 213

10:28 211, 421
10:29 279, 418
11 272
11–12 477
11:1 211
11:1–13 217
11:3 405
11:7 292
11:29–39 217
11:40 272, 273n2, 274
11:43 384
12 393, 480
12:1–4 204
12:1–15 217
12:16 395
12:26–33 217
12:28–29 175
13–14 217
13:22 384
13:31 386
14 272
14:11–13 384
14:14 217
14:18 385
14:21–15:24 225
14:25 10, 273n2
14:25–26 217, 225, 272, 436
14:26 214
15 421n8
15:13 124
15:16–22 218
15:19 421n8
15:27 218
15:33 218
15:34 477
15:34–16:4 218
16 124, 279
16–18 124
16:9 477, 480, 481
16:11 218
16:13–14 218
16:15–20 218
16:16 480
16:16–28 290
16:21–22 218
16:24 417
16:28 384
16:29–22:40 290
16:30 219
16:31 219
16:33 219
18 124, 392
18–19 124
18:19–29 471
19:6 458
20:1–4 284
20:7–8 497
20:23 6

20:23–34 282
20:30–34 297
20:31 513
20:34 219, 305
21 436
21:1–16 219
21:2 414
21:2–3 406
21:8–9 401
21:11–16 496, 497
21:17–24 219
22 219, 283
22:4 218, 282
22:26 481, 496
22:29–40 219
22:47 288
22:48 422
22:51–54 291
22:52 219

2 Kings

1–10 279
1:2 219
1:18 291
2 219
3 130, 219, 225, 288, 289, 291
3:2–3 219
3:4 394
3:4–27 289, 394n7
3:7 282
3:13–14 219
3:15 471
3:18–27 508
3:25 290
3:27 364, 387
4:38–40 462
4:38–41 459, 462
5 219
5:17 415
6–7 219
6:25 418
6:25–30 507
7:12 512
7:16 418
8 295, 296
8:7–15 220, 283, 294n6, 295n10, 297
8:19 305
8:25–29 283
8:28–29 219, 284
9 297, 477
9–10 297n22
9:10 384
9:14–15 219
9:14–24 291
9:14–28 220, 297
9:25 481

9:28 384
9:33–37 384
10–11 124
10:5 480
10:11–28 220
10:32 220
10:32–33 284
11–12 481
11:2 401
12:11 480
12:17 67, 224
13:1–9 220
13:7 282
13:21 386
13:22 220
13:24–25 220
13:25 131
14:7 225
14:13–14 225
14:25 131, 220
15:8–12 221
15:17–22 221
15:19–20 436
15:19–21 221
15:25 481
15:29 221
15:30 221
15:35 225
15:37 221
16:8 421n8
16:9 221
17:3–4 221
17:34 494
17:37 494
18–19 293n1, 301, 480
18:4 227, 245, 384
18:5 227
18:13–14 11
18:13–19:37 301
18:14 300
18:17 30
18:17–19:9 301
18:17–19:37 301
18:18 480
18:22 384
18:37 480
19:2 480
19:8 300
19:9–35 301
19:29–36 304
19:34 305
19:36–37 301
19:37 301
20:6 305
20:13 303n4
20:20 136, 226, 511
21–23 481
21:1 228
21:6 386

21:7 124
21:18 384
21:26 384
22 228
22–23:30 228
22:3 479
22:12 497
23:4 124
23:6 382
23:7 124, 313, 379, 398
23:8 496
23:10 387
23:13 292
23:24 386
23:25 494
23:30 384
24–25 230
24:1 317, 318
24:7 317, 318
24:10–12 231
24:12 231n1
24:14 232
24:15 231n1
24:17 231
25 234
25:4 384
25:11–12 232
25:20–21 231
25:22 232, 479
25:27–30 231, 433n1

1 Chronicles

1–8 10
1–9 392
4:21–23 434
4:28–33 278
6:54–81 212
7:22 385
10:13–14 386
11:11 212
11:19 212
16:4–7 362
18:1 211
23:4 496
27:29 16
27:33 479

2 Chronicles

1:16 211
2:3–16 322n13
2:16 20
5:12–13 362
8:1 225
8:11 211
9 201
9:24 415
9:28 211

10:1–15 217
11:5–10 10, 212
12 225, 273n2
12:1–12 10
12:5 496
16:6 511
16:14 384
17:14–18 480
19:4–7 496
19:5–11 481
20:35–37 225
21:1–3 481
21:6 225
21:12 496
21:20 384
22:1–9 297
22:5–6 284
22:7 297n26
22:9 297n26
23:1 480
25:15 496
26:2 225
26:6 224, 225
26:9–15 511
26:11 480, 481
28:1–4 227
28:9 512
28:22–25 227
29:3 227
30 228
31:5–10 457
32 293n1, 301
32:1–22 301
32:4 136, 511
32:5 226, 511
32:6 303n4
32:27–29 303n4
32:30 511
33:13 148
34:8 481, 496
34:8–13 480
34:24–25 385
35:25 385
36 230
36:22–23 237

Ezra

1:1–4 237
2 241, 392
2:59 233, 243
2:68–69 74
3:4 494
6:1–13 238
6:2–5 237
8:17 233, 243, 433
10:3 494

Nehemiah

1:5 137
1:9 137
2:10 73, 80
2:19–20 394
3:15 384
4:2 75
5 435
5:1–13 435
5:4–5 73
5:14–18 73n9
6:10 139
7 241, 392, 395
7:70–71 74
8:1–8 85
9 392n5
9:6 341
9:36 394
10 124
10:32 73
11 241, 395
11:18 394
11:25–28 278
13:4–9 435
13:12 457
13:15–22 436

Job

2:8 385
3:8 124
10:10 457
11:7 386
17:13 386
17:16 386
18:12–13 124
21:20 134
22:9 498
24:3 498
24:19–20 386
24:21 498
26:5 386
26:6 387
26:13 124
27:15 385
28:2 439
28:4 439
28:9–10 439
28:22 387
29:2–3 400
31:6 387
31:12 387
36:22 492
38:17 386
39:13–18 181
41 124
42:11 457

Psalms

2:6 305
16:10 387
18:1 11
18:8–16 307
18:31 346
22:15 386
22:29 386, 387
23 467
23:4 386
24:1 393
28:1 387
29 336
29:10 124
30:9 386
30:19 386
31:2 11
31:12 386
34:11–14 405
35:13 363, 385
48:1–2 124
48:2 305, 394
49:14 387
50 352
50:5 352
50:12–13 363
50:12–16 352
67:1 137
68:5 124, 498
68:7–10 307
68:24–25 401
69:28 129
71:3 11
71:20 387
72:10 421
74 336–37
74:13 122
74:13–14 124
74:13–15 124
78 195n2
78:12 195n2
78:43 195n2, 197
78:64 385
78:67–70 305
78:68–69 305
78:69 352
79:3 384
82 341
88:5 386
88:6 386
88:10 386
88:11 387
89 305
89:48 386
104 258, 343
104:3 124
113:9 405
114:1–5 124

115:17 386
125 305
127:3–5 405
132 305
132:13–14 305
132:15 457
143:3 386
150 362

Proverbs

1:8 399, 405
2:18 386
5:7 406
6:20 399, 405
7:1 406
9:3–4 401
10:1 405
10:5 406
11:1 418, 494
13:1 406
15:11 387
16:11 418
17:18 435
19:13 406
19:14 398
20:16 435
20:23 418, 494
21:2 387
22:6 405
22:15 405
22:26 435
23:27 401
27:13 435
27:20 124
30:8 461
31:13 453
31:15 461
31:19 398
31:22 398
31:23 497
31:24 398
31:27 462

Ecclesiastes

3:1–8 412
6:3 384
7:2 385
7:4 385
8:8 386
9:5 386
9:10 386
9:13–16 504
10:19 406
11:1 462
12:5–6 122

Song of Songs

4:11 462
5:1 462

Isaiah

1–33 216
1:11–17 110
1:18 412
1:23 498
1:25 440
2 467
2:3 305
3:4–5 405
5:1–3 397
5:8–10 434, 490
5:14 387
6 163
7–8 221
7:22 462
8:18 305
9:1 16
10:1–2 498
10:28–32 300n1
13:6 134
14:9 124, 386
14:19–20 384
14:29 163
15:2 290, 291
15:4 291
15:5 291
16:2 290
19:25 393
23:1–18 322n13
24–27 123, 337–38
24:17–25:8 337
24:21–23 124
25 467
25:6–8 124, 337
26:13–19 124
27:1 94, 124, 337
28:25 114
28:27 414
29:5–6 307
30:6 163, 420
30:14 413, 413n5
30:33 384
32:1 496
33:9 412
36–37 293n1, 301
36–39 301
40–55 346, 348
40–66 241
40:9 401
40:22 6
43–47 346
44 334
44:16 462
44:19 458, 461, 462

46:9 345
47:2 397
48:10 440
49 243
51:8 453
51:17 467
56:5 131
57:9 387
58:1–59:8 243
60:6 420
60:20 385
65:20 398
66:1 352

Jeremiah

1:13 459
2:6 319
2:22 454
4:8 385
5:15 512
5:24 22, 412
5:27 490
6:1 139
6:9 453
6:26 385
6:28–29 440
7 305
7:1–8:3 304
7:14–15 392
7:18 379, 398
7:21–26 319
7:33 384
8:1–2 384
9:17–18 385
9:17–20 401
9:21 387
9:22 384
10 334
11:1–8 319
11:4 440
11:5 462
14:16 384
16:4 384, 385
16:5–8 385, 465
16:14 319
17:13 387
18 434
19:7 384
22:3 490
22:18–19 384
23:7 319
23:18 368
23:22 368
24:1 453
25:15 467
25:31 497
25:33 385
26 496, 497

26:1–6 497
26:17 497
26:23 382, 384
26:24 497
27 318, 319
27–28 231
28n2 319
29:1 433
29:2 231n1
29:25 433
31:31–32 319
31:40 382
32:6–8 407
32:9–10 418
32:12 479
32:20–22 319
32:21 163
32:35 387
34:7 139
34:13 319
36:10 141
36:11 479
36:30 384
37:3 141
37:5 318
37:11 318
37:13–14 319
38:1 141
38:4 319
39–43 230
39:4 384
39:14 497
40:5–6 72, 232
40:14 73
41:3 232
43:2–3 319
43:7 234
43:7–44:30 234
44:1 233, 234
44:17–19 379
46 315, 317, 319
46:2–12 315
46:10 313
46:14 317
46:19 317
47:1 314n4
47:4 269
48 393
48:1 291
48:3 291
48:5 291
48:7 292
48:13 292
48:18 290
48:21 291
48:22 290, 291
48:34 291
48:46 292
49:3 385

51:59 479
52 394
52:7 384
52:28–30 232
52:30 231

Lamentations

3:6 386

Ezekiel

1 165, 171
3:15 233, 243
6:5 385
10 165
10:1 171
11:3 459
11:7 459
11:11 459
12:13 167
14 124
14:14 124
14:20 124
16:20–21 387
16:45 196
17:11–15 318
17:13–15 231
17:20 167
18:18 495
19:8 167
19:9 167
20:6 462
20:15 462
21:1–32 326
21:21 386
22:7 498
22:29 495
23:37–39 387
26–28 322n13
27 419
27:20–22 420
27:31 385
28 124
28:2 124
28:3 124
28:28 386
29:5 384
31 334n1
32:3 167
34:3 453
37:19–22 393
43 384
44:25 385
44:30 400
45:10 494
46:17 493
47:1–12 167, 168
47:2 167

47:9 168
47:9–10 170
47:11 413n5
47:12 168

Daniel

2:27–45 326
3 146
4 334n1
5 234, 467, 472
6 146
7–8 117
7–12 146, 147
7:1–27 326
8:1–14 326
8:20–21 327
8:27 327
9:4 137
10:2–3 363
10:12 363
11:2–45 327
12:2 386
12:2–3 327
12:10 327

Hosea

2:9 453
3:2 418
4:1 497
7:4 459
7:6–7 459
8:5–6 221
10:14 284, 304
11:1 394, 405
12:2 497
12:7–8 494
13:4 346
13:14 387

Joel

1:8 385
2:8 104n13
2:10 307
2:13 385

Amos

1:1 307
1:2 181
1:5 281
2:1 384
2:6 418
2:6–7 311
2:6–8 434
2:13 307
3:12 181
3:14–15 307
3:15 221
4:1 495
5:15 85
5:16 385
5:21–25 110
6:3–6 311
6:7 385
6:11 307
8:5 141, 418, 494
8:10 385
9:1 307
9:1–2 387
9:5 315
9:7 369

Jonah

2:6 387

Micah

1 300
2:2 434, 490, 495
3:3 459, 462
3:12 497
4 467
4:5 342
6:2 497
6:6–8 110
6:11 418, 494

Nahum

1:5 307
1:8 304

1:13 304
2:11–13 304

Habakkuk

2:5 124, 387
3:3 343n5
3:3–15 138, 307

Zephaniah

2:15 345

Haggai

2:12 462
2:13–14 386

Zechariah

1:8–17 243
3:2 137
7:3–5 385
7:10 495, 498
8:16 85
9–14 243
9:14 138
10:2 386
12:12 385
14:4 307
14:5 307
14:20–21 459

Malachi

3:5 495, 498
4:2 343

New Testament

Matthew

5:17 493
6:26 7
7:12 493
11:13 493
16:18 11

22:40 493
24:7 307
24:41 397

Mark

7:24 322n13
13:8 307

Luke

16:16 496
21:11 307
24:44 493

John

1:45 493
2:14 435

Acts

13:15 493

Galatians

4:7 395

Revelation

6:12 307
8:5 307
11:13 307
12:3 124
16:18–19 307
21:1–2 6

Ancient Text Index

Page numbers in italics refer to figures.

Ancient Near Eastern Texts

Admonitions of Ipuwer, 502
Admonitions of the Egyptian Sage
    (or *Admonitions of Ipuwer*), 110
Advice of Shupe-awilum, 503
Advice to a Prince, 501
Ahiram Coffin, 128, 129, 129n1
Alalakh texts
    54:16–18 192
    54:39b–42 191–92
Apology of Hattušili III, 114
Arad ostraca, 46
Arslan Tash Inscription
    5–8 129
    9–11 129
    22–26 130
Assyrian annals, 441
Astarte and the Insatiable Sea, 106
Ataruz pillar, 130

Ba'al Cycle, 123–24, 337
Babylonian Chronicle 1
    iv.23–28 313
Babylonian Chronicle 3
    10–11 314
    61–69 314
Babylonian Chronicle 4
    16–26 314
Babylonian Chronicle 5
    1–8 315
    5–7 318
    15–20 316
    15–23 316
Babylonian Theodicy, 502–3
Balaam Son of Beor Inscription,
    133–34

Ballad of Early Rulers, 503, 505
Black Obelisk, 39, 220, 283, 290n2
BM (cuneiform tablet), 318n14
    18–20 316n9
Book of Caverns, 105
Book of the Dead, 104
Book of Gates, 105
boundary stele K, 257n12
boundary stele L, 257n12
boundary stele X, 257n12
Bubastite Portal Inscription, 273

Carlsberg Papyri XIII, 105
Carlsberg Papyri XIV, 105
Chicago Prism, 301
Complaints of Khakheperre-Sonb,
    111
cuneiform alphabetic texts from
    Ugarit, Ras Ibn Hani, and Other
    Places
    ix–x 121
    1.5 I 1–3 124, 337
*Cycle of Kumarbi (Song of Emer-
    gence)*, 116–17

Demotic Chronicle, 105
Destruction of Mankind, 106
Dialogue of a Man with His Soul,
    110
*Disputations between Silver and
    Mighty Copper*, 502
*Dispute between the Head and Stom-
    ach*, 108
Doomed Prince, 108
*Dream of the Ethiopian Prince Tanu-
    tamun*, 108

Ekron Royal Dedicatory Inscription,
    44
Eloquent Peasant
    80 501
    B1 92–99 111
    B1 247–50 111
Emar texts, 358, 359
Enlil and Namzitarra, 502
Enki and Ninmach, 103
Enmerkar and the Lord of Aratta,
    339
Enuma Elish, 98, 103, 334–36, 338,
    345, 346n12
Epic of Aqhat, 123, 405n1
Epic of Atra-Hasis, 103, 115, 500, 503
Epic of Gilgamesh, 93, 95, 99–100,
    103, 115, 118, 333, 504
Eridu Genesis, 103
Erra and Ishum, 334

Gezer Calendar, 23, 93
Great Hymn to Aten, 109, 343

Hittite Laws, 424, 426, 494
Hymn to Shamash, 295n2

Idumean ostraca, 241
Instruction Addressed to Merikare,
    108, 110
Instruction of a Man to His Son, 110
Instruction of Amenemhat I, 110
Instruction of Amenemope, 110,
    494n2, 501–4
Instruction of Any, 110
Instruction of Khety, 111
Instruction of Prince Hardjedef, 500

Instruction of the Loyalist, 110
Instruction of Onchsheshonqy, 110, 501
Instruction of Ptahhotep, 109
Instructions of Shuruppak, 501–2
Iran Stela, 221

Kahun papyrus, 109
Karnak list, 278
Kemit (*The Complete*), 111
Ketef Hinnom Silver Scrolls, 137
Khirbet el-Qom Tomb Inscriptions, 137
King Cheops and the Magicians, 107
Kuntillet ʿAjrud Inscriptions
　Pithos A, 138, 177–80
　Pithos B, 178–80
Kuttamuwa Stele, 133

Lachish Letters, 46
　3 318
　4 139–40
　4.10 139
　4.11 139
　4.11–12 139
　6 374
Law Code of Hammurabi, 424–26, 428–29, 434n4, 493, 495
Laws of Eshnunna, 424, 428, 493
Laws of Lipit-Ishtar, 424, 429, 493
Laws of Ur-Namma, 424, 428
Laws of Ur-Nammu, 493
Legend of King Kirta, 123
Ludlul bēl Nēmeqi, 502–3

Mari texts, 188, 190
　ARM X 167
　ARM XIII 167
Maxims of Ptahhotep, 502
Middle Assyrian Laws, 424, 493
Moabite Stone (Mesha Inscription), 46, 130, 286–92, 287, 393n7
　1 289
　1–4 289
　3 290
　5 290
　5–21a 289
　6 290
　7 290
　7–8 291
　10 393

　10–11 291
　12–13 291
　14–21a 292
　17–18 291
　21b–31a 289
　26 290
　31 292
　31b–34 289
Murashu archives, 71n3
Myth of Illuyanka, 115
Myth of Telepinu, 116

Neo-Babylonian Laws, 424, 493
Nergal and Ereshkigal, 339

Ox and the Horse, The, 502

Panammu Inscriptions, 132
Pap. Anastasi I, 111
Pap. Anastasi III, 197, 199, 199n12
Pap. Chester Beatty IV, 111
Pap. Chester Beatty VII, 105
Pap. Rylands 9, 318
Pap. Sallier IV, 105
Pap. Salt, 105
Poor Man of Nippur, 95, 103
Potter's Prophecy, 105
Prayer of Prince Kantuzzili, 119
Prayer of the Righteous Sufferer, 372
Prophecies of Neferti, 110, 502

Rassam Cylinder, 300
Ritual of Ishtar, 471

SAA 4 (Starr 1990)
　156 370
　281 512
　287–89 512
SAA 8 (Hunger 1992)
　110 369
SAA 9 (Parpola 1997)
　1.1 372
SAA 16 (Luukko 2002)
　127 422
　128 422
Samaria ostraca, 46
Satire of the Trades, 111
Sayings of Ahiqar, 503
Sefire Inscriptions, 132
Sennacherib Cylinder C, 301

Shipwrecked Sailor, 107
Siloam Tunnel Inscription, 46, 136
Šimâ milka, 502
Song of Kešši, 117–8
Song of Release, 118
Stele of King Piye, 107
Stele of Merneptah, 107
Story of Ahiqar, 110
Story of Sinuhe, 109, 411
　B1 81–84 107
šumma alu, 339
Sumerian Gudea Cylinder, 168

Tale of Two Brothers, 108
Tale of Wenamun, 372, 419, 421, 421n9
Tale of Zalpa, 114
Tamarisk and the Palm, The, 502
Taylor Prism, 301
Tel Arad ostraca, 139
Tel Dan Inscription, 45, 64, 131–32, 208, 293–98, 477
　2 294, 294n5
　3 294, 296n17
　3–5 296
　3b–4a 293n18
　4 194
　4–7 296n16
　5 297
　7–9 297n20
　9 132
Tell Fekheriya Inscription
　1 131
　12 131
　12–16 131
　15 131
　16 131
That Which Is in the Underworld, 105
Truth and Falsehood, 108

Yehaumilk Inscription, 130

Zakkur Stele
　A.4–9 131
　A.11 131
　A.12 131
　B.14–17 131, 373
　B.15 131
　C.2 131
Zeno papyri
　1.11 238n4

Other Ancient Texts

Deuterocanonical Books

Additions to Daniel

Bel and the Dragon
in toto, 146

Susanna
in toto, 146
62 86

2 Esdras

143

Judith

in toto, 143
3 146

1 Maccabees

in toto, 143, 146
1:1 78
1:11–15 326
1:14 245
1:29–33 245
1:35–38 84
1:41 246
1:43 246
1:50 246
1:60–61 246
1:62–63 246
2:4 244
2:19–30 246
2:26 246
2:34–41 86
3:1 246
3:48 86
4:36–59 246
5:1–8 82
5:65–66 82
8 246
9 246
9:20 385
9:56–57 246
10:20 247
11:74 247
12:1–23 247
12:39–13:24 247
13:26 385
13:27–30 80
13:49–51 247
13:49–52 84
14:41–45 248

2 Maccabees

in toto, 143, 146
3–4 245
4:7–17 245
5 245
6–7 246
8:1 246
10:1–8 246

Sirach (Ecclesiasticus)

in toto, 143, 147
Prologue 1 493
22:12 385
38:17 385
38:24–39:15 111

Tobit

in toto, 143, 146
1:8 86
7:12–13 86

Wisdom

in toto, 143
12:24–25 405

Pseudepigrapha

Apocalypse of Abraham
in toto, 146

Biblical Antiquities
in toto, 147

1 Enoch
17–36 146
85–90 146

Genesis Apocryphon
in toto, 147

Jubilees
in toto, 147

Letter of Aristeas
in toto, 145

Psalms of Solomon
in toto, 148

Reworked Pentateuch
in toto, 147

Dead Sea Scrolls

Cairo Damascus

in toto, 147

4QNahum Pesher

in toto, 3–4
1:3 249
1:6–8 249

4QSongs of the Sabbath Sacrifice

fragment 1, column 1, 30–37 341

Thanksgiving Hymns

in toto, 148

Josephus

Against Apion
1.73–91 195

Antiquities
10.1–23 301
12.160 238n4
12.230–33 80
12.237–41 245
12.246 245
12.248–52 245
12.252 84
12.253–56 246
12.285 246
12.316–22 246
12.414–19 246
12.426–34 246
13.22 247
13.163 247
13.181–83 247
13.171–72 247
13.187–93 247
13.214 247
13.259–66 248
13.288–98 248
13.299–300 248
13.304–10 249
13.372–73 249
13.376 249
13.377–87 249
13.398 249
13.401–4 249
13.407 249
13.422–29 249
13.432 249
15.37–45 249
15.56 244

Jewish War
1.32 245
1.34–35 246
1.36–37 246
1.38 246
1.39 246
1.47 246
1.49 247
1.53 247
1.70 248
1.77 249
1.91 249
1.92–98 249
1.109 249
1.112 249
1.118–19 249
1.123–26 249
1.153–57 250
3.51–56 10

Life of Josephus
277–303 87

Ancient Jewish Writings

Corpus inscriptionum judaicarum
2:1440 85

Corpus papyrorum judaicarum
1:129 85
3:1532a 85

Rabbinic Works

Tosefta Sukkah
3:10 168

Early Christian Writings

Eusebius

Onomasticon
7 9n2

Jerome

Preface to Chronicles
in toto, 6

Greco-Roman Literature
Against Ctesiphon
132 327

Arrian

History of Alexander
1.2.3 322n9
1.12.6–1.16.7 322n10

2.8.5–2.11.10 322n11
2.12.3–8 322n12
2.21.1–2.24.6 323n14
3.9.1–3.15.6 323n18

Diodorus

Library of History
16.89.2 322
16.91.1–16.95.1 321
16.95.2 322
17.17.3–4 322n17
17.19.1–17.21.7 322n10
17.32.1–17.38.7 322n11
17.37.3–7 322n12
17.40.2–17.46.6 323n14

17.49.1 323n15
17.53.1–2 323n17
17.53.1–17.61.3 323n18
17.64.4 323

Herodotus

Histories
in toto, 13, 91, 235, 314n4, 432
2.141–42 301
2.157 314n4

Hesiod

Theogony
in toto, 117

Pliny

Natural History
36.30 81

Polybius

Histories
29.21.1–6 327n36

Quintus Curtius Rufus

History of Alexander the Great
4.9.5 323n17

Author Index

Page numbers in italics refer to figures.

Abel, F.-M., 9
Achenbach, Reinhard, 205n3, 512
Ackerman, Susan, 166, 379
Ackermann, Oren, 30, 30n2, 31, 35
Adam, Klaus-Peter, 467
Adams, Colin, 418n4
Adams, Russell, 442
Adams, Samuel L., 434
Agnon, Amotz, 308, 308n3, 309
Aharoni, Yohanan, 9, 20n3, 43, *43*,
    55, 139, 274, 274n6, 413, 507
Ahituv, Shmuel, 67, 73n8, 129n1, 139,
    140, 141
Ahlström, Gösta W., 187, 189, 189n7,
    193n24, 194, 274n6
Aitken, James K., 326n32
Albertz, Rainer, 63, 230, 231, 344,
    355n1, 376–78, 376n1, 380, 400n9
Albright, William F., 9, 40–45, 40n2,
    41, 41n4, 55, 125, 188, 190,
    199n12, 203, 231, 232, 232n2,
    238n5, 274n5, 344, 414, 440
Aldred, Cyril, 258n15, 259
Alexander, David, 309
Allam, S., 424, 426, 429
Alliata, Eugenio, 7
Almogi-Labin, A., 21
Alster, Bendt, 500–501, 503
Alt, Albrecht, 9–10, 55, 203, 492–93
Altmann, Peter, 74, 431, 456–57,
    464–67
Ambraseys, Nicholas, 308n3, 309
Ambrose, S. H., 24
Ames, K. M., 483
Amiet, Pierre, 165, 471
Amiran, R., 49
Amiry, Suad, 397
Amit, Yairah, 242n14
Amzallag, Nissim, 439–40

Anbar, Moshe, 193
Anderson, James S., 344
Andrae, E. Walter, 169
Angier, Natalie, 396
Anson, Edward M., 321n6, 324n24
Appadurai, Arjun, 464n2, 465
Archi, Alfonso, 112, 114, 358
Ardzinba, Vladislav, 366
Arnold, Bill T., 99, 102, 188, 478n1
Arnold, Elizabeth, 21
Aro, Jussi, 370n2, 512
Ash, Paul S., 211n8
Ashton, David, 196
Assmann, Jan, 104n3, 108n8, 257–59
Aster, Shawn Zelig, 345
Astour, Michael C., 279, 343n5
Athas, G., 293n2
Aubet, Maria, 419
Austin, M. M., 325n29
Austin, Steven A., 309
Averbeck, Richard E., 349n1, 423,
    426n1, 427–28
Aviam, Mordechai, 82–83
Avigad, Nahman, 43, 73, 73n8, 181,
    496
Avishur, Yitzhak, 336
Avi-Yonah, Michael, 7, 9, 173
Avruch, Kevin, 421
Ayalon, A., 23, 26

Baadsgaard, Aubrey, 397, 459
Bachhuber, Christoph, 260, 260n1,
    263
Badian, Ernst, 321n6
Badre, Leila, 50
Bagg, Ariel M., 101
Bahn, Paul, 262
Bahrani, Zainab, 156, 172n1
Baines, John, 104n2

Baker, Coleman A., 302, 304
Baker, David W., 302, 304, 492, 494
Balasse, M., 24
Ballentine, D. S., 336–37
Balter, M., 45
Baly, Denis, 6, 20n3
Barber, Elizabeth Wayland, 398, 453
Barber, Keith, 32
Barclay, John M. G., 195
Barjamovic, Gojko, 420
Barkay, Gabriel, 63, 137, 157, 487, 496
Barker, Graeme, 442
Barker, William D., 120, 122–23, 337
Bar-Matthews, M., 21, 23–24, 26
Barnett, Richard D., 155
Bar-Oz, Guy, 33
Barrelet, Marie-Thérèse, 170, 471
Barron, Amy E., 508
Barstad, Hans M., 73, 232n3, 292
Barta, Winfried, 156
Baruch, Yuval, 76n14
Bar-Yosef, O., 33
Batto, B. F., 337
Bauckham, Richard, 82
Baudains, Peter, 302
Bawanypeck, Daliah, 360
Bayer, Bathja, 468–69
Baynham, 320n2, 321n6
Beal, Richard H., 337, 370
Beale, G. K., 349n1
Beaulieu, Paul-Alain, 234, 236, 420,
    434, 500–501, 503
Beck, John A., 11
Beck, Pirhiya, 156, 178–80, 178n4
Becking, Bob, 222n5, 345
Beckman, Gary, 101, 112, 266, 363,
    366
Beitzel, Barry J., 20n3
Bellow, Saul, 375

Bellwood, Peter, 205
Ben-Arieh, S., 160
Ben-Arieh, Yehoshua, 8, 10
Bendor, S., 482, 490
Ben-Dor Evian, Shirly, 273n4
Benjamin, Don C., 405–6
Bennett, Crystal M., 441
Ben-Shlomo, David, 49, 160n2, 271, 303, 460–61
Ben-Tor, Amnon, 55, 193n25
Ben-Tor, D., 159–60, 163
Ben-Yehoshua, Shimshon, 74
Ben-Yosef, D., 56
Ben-Yosef, Erez, 60, 268, 438, 440n3, 442, 445
Ben Zion, Ilan, 76n14
Berger, John, 181
Berlejung, Angelika, 157
Berlin, Andrea M., 80–82, 347n13
Berman, Joshua, 204, 426
Berman, Lawrence, 254
Bernand, A., 317
Bernett, Monika, 154
Bernhardt, C. E., 26
Berquist, Jon L., 74
Betlyon, John W., 75, 77, 232, 242n16
Beyer, Dominique, 165
Bianchi, Francesco, 237
Bidmead, Julye, 367
Bienkowski, Piotr, 71, 268, 287, 442
Bietak, Manfred, 196–98, 267
Billows, Richard A., 324n25
Bimson, J. J., 276n9
Binder, Donald D., 84, 86
Binford, L. R., 487
Biran, Avraham, 75, 293, 293n3, 347n14
Bjorkman, Judith K., 507
Black, Jeremy, 99
Blanton, R. E., 483
Blasius, Andreas, 105
Blenkinsopp, Joseph, 238n1, 242n14, 404
Bliss, F. J., 49
Bloch, M., 490
Bloch, Yigal, 433
Bloch-Smith, Elizabeth M., 63, 228, 300–301, 303n4, 345, 349n1, 382, 384
Block, Daniel I., 403–4
Blum, Erhard, 293n2, 294nn5–6, 297n22
Bober, P. B., 454
Boda, Mark J., 307, 349n1
Bodi, Daniel, 165, 167, 169, 334
Boecker, Hans J., 495
Boer, Roland, 431
Boertien, Jeannette H., 152
Bohmbach, Karla G., 396

Bolin, Thomas M., 510, 512–13
Bonatz, Dominik, 156, 466
Bonfiglio, Ryan P., 153, 156, 158, 163, 173, 180
Bongenaar, A. C. V. M., 421
Borger, Rykle, 313
Borghouts, J. F., 369
Borowitz, Carole, 74
Borowski, Oded, 22, 34, 157, 303n4, 411n1, 412–15, 412n2, 413n6, 414n7, 414n9, 457–58, 461
Borza, Eugene, 324n25
Bosworth, A. B., 320n2, 321n6, 324nn22–24
Bottéro, Jean, 98, 357, 461–62, 494
Bourdieu, Pierre, 465, 483
Bovati, Pietro, 497, 497n5
Boyer, Georges, 188
Braje, Todd J., 33
Brandl, Baruch, 161, *181*
Braudel, Fernand, 159, 418
Braun, Joachim, 362, 468, 470
Breasted, James Henry, 41n4, 258n19, 259, 317
Brenner, Athalya, 401n12
Bresciani, Eddia, 238n1
Briant, Pierre, 235, 237–38, 238n1, 239n8, 323n19, 324n23
Brichto, Herbert Chanan, 129
Bright, John, *41*, 42n5, 347
Brinkman, J. A., 417n2
Broodbank, Cyprian, 262, 418
Broshi, Magen, 310
Brosius, Maria, 98
Brown, Brian B., 156
Brueggemann, Walter, 496
Bruins, Hendrik J., 35
Brunner, Hellmut, 104, 109
Brunner-Traut, Emma, 153
Bryan, Betsy M., 160, 254nn4–5, 262n3
Bryce, Trevor, 195, 266–67
Buccellati, Georgio, 188
Bugh, Glenn, 325n29
Bunimovitz, Shlomo, 48, 53, 56, 60, 508
Bürge, T., 60
Burkard, Günter, 104n3
Burke, A. A., 48, 509
Burridge, Alwyn, 255n10
Burstein, Stanley M., 320n1, 324n22, 325nn28–29
Byrne, Ryan, 176, 420

Cameron, George G., 239
Caminos, Ricardo A., 104n3, 111, 197, 254n7, 270
Camp, Claudia, 399
Campbell, Duncan B., 510

Campbell Thompson, Reginald, 168
Cantrell, Deborah O., 213, 507
Capomacchia, Anna Maria G., 512
Carile, Maria C., 152
Carpenter, R., 26
Carroll, John T., 405–6
Carroll, Robert, 373n15, 512
Carter, Charles E., 73–74, 74n10, 232, 242
Carter, Tristan, 466
Carter, Warren, 302, 304
Cassuto, Deborah, 402
Cassuto, M. D., 414
Cassuto, Umberto, 122
Castillo, Luis J., 466
Cathcart, Kevin, 505
Catto, Stephen K., 85
Caubet, Annie F., 468, 470–71
Cavanagh, Edward, 207
Cavillier, Giacoma, 199
Chadwick, Christie Goulart, 73
Chaney, M. L., 490
Chapman III, Rupert L., 6–7
Charlesworth, James H., 144n5
Charpin, Dominique, 93n1, 169, 493
Chavalas, Mark W., 118, 279, 281
Chevereau, Pierre-Marie, 317n12
Chiera, E., 191
Childs, Brevard S., 514
Childs, William A. P., 471
Chirichigno, Gregory C., 426
Cho, Paul Kang-Kul, 467
Christiansen, Birgit, 119
Civil, M., 100
Clancy, Frank, 276
Clark, Douglas R., 73, 310, 452
Clarke, Lee, 310
Clements, R. E., 505
Clifford, Richard J., 103, 500, 504
Cline, Eric H., 54, 260n1, 262n3, 266, 419, 506
Clines, David J. A., 376, 376n2
Coben, Lawrence S., 466
Cochavi-Rainey, Zippora, 421
Cogan, Mordechai, 303, 507–8, 511
Cohen, Margaret E., 126
Cohen, Mark E., 76, 76n17, 366
Cohen, Raymond, 262n3
Cohen, Yoram, 100, 355, 500, 502–4
Colijn, Brenda B., 405
Collins, Billie Jean, 360
Collins, John J., 142n1, 147n8, 148n11, 326n30, 512–13
Collins, Paul, 153
Collon, Dominique, 154, 355, 357–58, 360, 471
Conder, C. R., 8
Connerton, Paul, 399
Coogan, Michael D., 23, 174

Cook, Stephen L., 258
Coombes, Paul, 32
Copan, Paul, 513
Corduan, Winfried, 259
Cornelius, Izak, 50, 151–53, 157–58, 176
Counihan, Carole, 399
Cowley, Arthur E., 240
Crabtree, P., 453–54
Craigie, Peter C., 120, 513
Craven, Toni, 401n12
Crawford, Sidnie White, 147n10
Crenshaw, James L., 502–3, 505
Cribb, Roger, 34
Crisostomo, C. Jay, 99n1, 100
Crocker, P. T., 483
Cross, Frank Moore, 40, 42n5, 238n2, 306, 336n2, 417
Crouch, C. L., 339, 512–13
Culbertson, Laura, 423–24
Currid, John D., 273n3, 276n9, 334
Curtis, Adrian, 123, 174, 412, 412n3
Curtis, John, 508

Dabrowa, E., 247–48
Dagan, Yehudah, 227
Dahood, Mitchell, 121
Dalley, Stephanie, 507
D'Amato, Raffaele, 260n1
Damrosch, D., 100
Dandamaev, Muhammad A., 238n1, 241n12
Danin, Avinoam, 29–32
Dansgaard, W., 24
Darby, Erin D., 67, 76n16, 155, 175–77, 347, 378, 378n3
Darnell, John, 254
Davey, Christopher J., 349n1
Davies, Eryl W., 513–14
Davies, Graham I., 135–36, 139–41, 197, 505
Davies, Norman de Garis, 197, 254n8, 256, 258n19 259, 419
Davies, Philip R., 194, 203, 208n2, 292
Davis, Andrew R., 375–76, 380
Davis, Simon J., 33
Day, David, 205
Day, John, 337, 346n12, 349n1, 387, 505
Dearman, J. Andrew, 287–88, 289n1, 290–91, 408
De Backer, Fabrice, 508–9
Deetz, J., 483
Deger-Jalkotzy, Sigrid, 262, 264
De Geus, V. J. K., 490
de Hulster, Izaak J., 60, 76n16, 153, 157–58, 163, 166, 173, 347, 495
Delitzsch, F., 94, 162

Dell, Katharine, 505
del Olmo Lete, G., 359n7
De Luca, Stefano, 82
DeMarrais, Elizabeth, 466
DeNiro, M. J., 24
Derks, Ton, 392
Der Manuelian, Peter, 262n3
de Roos, Johan, 114
des Gagniers, Jean, 472
Deuel, David C., 97, 100–101
De Vaux, R., 490
Dever, William G., 9, 44–45, 47, 56, 76, 137, 173, 176, 195, 204, 270, 364, 490, 509–11
Dezső, Tamás, 508
Dick, Michael B., 172
Dietler, Michael, 465
Dietrich, Manfred, 349n1, 359
Dincauze, D. F., 23, 25
Dines, Jennifer M., 326n32
Dion, P.-E., 281, 294, 296n19
Doak, Brian R., 345, 345n11, 354n9
Dobbs-Allsopp, F. W., 135–36, 138–39, 141
Dodson, Aidan, 253n1, 254n6, 260n2, 262–63, 262n3, 276n9
Dornemann, Rudolph H., 282
Dorsey, David A., 20
Dossin, Georges, 188, 192n20
Dothan, Moshe, 268, 270
Dothan, Trude, 58, 210, 268–69, 269n4
Douglas, Mary, 386
Doxey, Denise M., 356
Dozeman, Thomas B., 258n17
Drabsch, Bernadette A., 154
Draffkorn, A., 191
Drake, B. L., 27
Drews, R., 260n1, 507
Driver, Godfrey R., 240
Dubovský, Peter, 511
Dumbrell, William J., 238n5
Dunand, Françoise, 356
Dunn, Jacob E., 312
Durand, Jean-Marie, 167, 190, 192n20, 471
Dusinberre, Elspeth R. M., 237
Dyrness, William A., 172

Earl, Douglas S., 513
Earle, Timothy, 416–17, 466
Ebeling, Jennie R., 398, 448, 458–59, 461
Edelman, Diana V., 238, 238n6, 241, 242n14, 274
Edelstein, G., 412n4
Efron, J., 244
Egberts, Arno, 421n9
Eggler, Jürg, 173n2, 181

Eichler, B. L., 191
Eisenberg, Michael, 82
Eitam, David, 227
Elat, M., 210, 281
Elayi, Josette, 238n3
Eldar-Nir, Iris, 310
Elitzur, Yoel, 9n2
Ellis, Maria de Jong, 374n16
Ellis, Walter M., 324n26
El-Rishi, 32, 35
Emerton, J. A., 138, 178
Eph'al, Israel, 318, 420, 509
Epstein, C., 24, 49
Erlandson, Jon M., 33
Ermidoro, Stefania, 467
Erskine, Andrew, 325n29
Eshel, H., 247
Eskenazi, Tamara, 396n1
Espak, P., 339
Evans, Paul S., 301
Evenari, Michael, 31, 35, 413

Fagan, Garrett G., 507
Fales, Frederick M., 417
Falk, David A., 194
Fantalkin, Alexander, 316nn9–10, 317n11, 510
Farber, Walter, 370
Faulkner, Raymond O., 104–5, 419
Faust, Avraham, 10, 56–57, 70–73, 76, 202, 212–14, 212n10, 217, 228, 232, 232n3, 267, 270, 315–16, 420, 482–85, 487–88, 490–91, 511
Feder, Yitzhaq, 354n7, 360, 363, 400
Feldman, Louis H., 326n30
Feldman, Marian, 156
Fensham, F. Charles, 112n1
Fernández Marcos, Natalio, 326n32
Finkelstein, Israel, 27, 35–36, 35n5, 44–45, 47, 51, 55–56, 56n4, 59, 62n1, 64, 64n2, 173, 188, 188n3, 192, 202, 208n3, 210n5, 213, 232, 276–77, 310, 312, 391, 445, 506, 510
Fischer, David Hackett, 196
Fischer, P. M., 60
Fischer-Elfert, Hans-Werner, 111
Fitzmyer, Joseph A., 132, 314
Fleming, Daniel E., 55n2, 101, 188, 188n5, 190, 190n10, 192n21, 216, 345n9, 358–59, 364, 366, 394n10
Fokaefs, Anna, 312
Fontaine, Carole R., 504
Forstner-Müller, Irene, 197–98
Forti, Tova, 505
Foster, John L., 258n19
Fourrier, S., 469, 470, 472
Fowler, Jeaneane D., 377

Fowler, M. D., 50
Fox, Michael V., 109n9, 502n3, 505
Fox, Nili Sacher, 475, 478–79
Frahm, Eckart, 334, 338
Francfort, Henri-Paul, 471
Francia, Rita, 118
Franken, Hendricus J., 49, 241
Franz, Gordon W., 309
Freed, Rita, 255
Freedberg, David, 173
Freedman, David Noel, 40–42, 42n5, 173, 307
Freedman, S. M., 339
Freeman-Grenville, G. S. P., 6–7
Frerichs, Ernest S., 267
Fretheim, Terence E., 310
Freud, Sigmund, 358n16
Frevel, Christian, 153
Fried, Lisbeth S., 73
Friedman, Florence Dunn, 199n12
Friedman, J., 465
Fritz, Volkmar, 195
Frost, Eric G., 309
Frumin, Suembikya, 36
Frye, Northrop, 165
Frymer-Kensky, Tikva, 493, 196n3
Fu, Janling, 456, 464–67
Fuks, Daniel, 28
Fulton, Deirdre N., 230

Gabbay, U., 470
Gabolde, Marc, 256–57
Gabriel, Richard A., 321, 506–7, 511–12
Gachet-Bizollon, J., 470
Gadot, Yuval, 49–50, 60, 226, 240, 242n15, 303
Gafney, Wilda C., 401n10
Galil, Gershon, 214, 293n2
Gallagher, William R., 301n3
Gane, Constance E., 70, 72
Gane, Roy E., 117n4, 361, 363, 365, 367
Ganor, Saar, 212n9
García Martínez, Florentino, 144n6
Gardiner, Alan H., 104n3, 111, 199 199n12, 262, 269
Garfinkel, Yosef, 64n2, 212n9, 470, 510
Garr, W. Randall, *128*, 129, 132–33
Garroway, Kristine H., 405, 424, 427
Gaspa, Salvatore, 417
Gass, E., 60
Gat, Y., 412n4
Gates, Marie-Henriette, 266
Geisler, Hans, 126
Gelb, Ignace J., 187
Geller, J. Mark, 168
Gentry, Peter J., 395
George, Andrew, 103, 339, 349

Geraty, Lawrence T., 194n1
Gernot, Wilhelm, 112n1
Ghantous, H., 293n2, 295, 295n13
Gianto, A., 51–52
Gibson, John, 129, 129n1, 130–31
Gibson, S., 412n4
Gilbertson, David D., 32, 35, 442
Gilboa, Ayelet, 59, 268, 270
Gilibert, Alessandra, 154, 466–67
Gill, D., 483
Gitin, Seymour, 39–40, 43n8, 49, 63, 317, 317n11, 419
Giveon, Raphael, 123, 160, 343n5
Glass, Roger I., 310,
Glassner, Jean-Jacques, 102, 168
Glueck, Nelson, 9, *41*, 42, *42*, 42n6, 393, 440–41, 445
Goelet, Ogden, 263
Goldwasser, Orly, 52, 258
Golub, Mitka, 344, 344n8, 376–77
Gonen, Rivka, 48, 53, 508
González-Ruibal, Alfredo, 71
Goodenough, E. R., 173
Goodfriend, G. A., 24
Gordin, Shai, 98
Gordon, Cyrus H., *41*, 120–21, 191
Gordon, Robert P., 505
Goren, Yuval, 47, 51, 59
Görke, Susanne, 360
Gorman, Frank H., 364
Gottwald, Norman K., 55, 203
Grabbe, Lester L., 74–75, 299, 326n31, 359, 368, 370, 511
Grainger, John D., 324n27
Gray, John, 198
Grayson, A. Kirk, 231, 235, 280–81, 300–301, 313–16, 318
Green, Alberto R., 336, 360
Green, Douglas J., 466
Green, John D. M., 160
Green, Peter, 321n6
Greenberg, Moshe, 362, 514
Greene, Elizabeth, 419
Greene, Jennifer, 76n14
Greenfield, Jonas, 131
Greengus, Samuel, 191, 425–26
Greenspahn, Frederick E., 406
Greenstein, Edward L., 122
Greenwood, Kyle, 219n3, 220n4
Greer, Jonathan S., 217–18
Gressmann, Hugo, 151, 157, 166, *166*
Groom, Nigel, 420
Gropp, Douglas M., 131, 238n2
Gruen, Erich S., 326n31, 326n33
Guillaume, Philippe, 431, 436
Guinan, Ann K., 368
Gunkel, Hermann, 162, 202, 337
Gur-Arieh, Shira, 460, 509
Güterbock, Hans Gustav, 112

Haas, G. H., 428
Haas, Volkert, 112, 360
Habichi, Labib, 195
Hadley, Judith M., 135–38, 505
Hafþórsson, S., 293n2
Haider, Peter W., 260n1, 264
Hairman, Moti, 213
Hall, M., 483
Hallo, William W., 163, 279
Hallock, Richard T., 239
Hallote, Rachel S.,
Halpern, Baruch, 132, 193, 202, 208n2, 227–28, 304, 345
Halstead, Paul, 34, 421
Hamilton, G. J., 51–52
Hamilton, Mark W., 504n4
Hamori, Esther J., 368–69, 401
Hancock, Jim F., 33
Hanuš, Lumír Ondřej, 74
Haran, Menahem, 362
Har-El, M., 22
Harlow, Daniel, 142
Harrington, D. J., 245–47
Harris, David R., 33, 199n12, 262
Harrison, Timothy P., 392
Hartman, G., 22
Hartmann, Anat, 33
Hartmann, Benedikt, 346
Hartmann-Shenkman, Anat, 33–34
Hartwig, Melinda K., 156
Harvey, Paul B., 202
Hasel, G., 335
Hasel, M., 212n9, 262, 513
Hauptmann, Andreas, 442, 444, *444*
Hausleiter, Arnulf, 420
Hawass, Zahi, 255n10
Hawkins, Ralph K., 55n3, 56, 56n4, 201, 203, 206
Hayden, Roy, E., 101
Hays, Christopher B., 381, 383, 386
Heckel, Waldemar, 323n17, 323n21, 324nn23–24
Heide, Martin, 192
Heider, George C., 387
Heimpel, Wolfgang, 192n20
Heintz, Jean-Georges, 167
Heltzer, Michael, 418, 421
Hendel, Ronald S., 189, 189n6, 190, 192n19, 193n23
Hengel, Martin, 238n4, 325–26n30
Herodotus, 13, 235, 237, 301, 314n4, 432
Herr, Larry G., 63, 67, 73, 268, 310, 404, 452
Herrmann, Christian, 155, 162, 378
Herrmann, Siegfried, 274n6
Herrmann, Virginia, 133
Herzog, Chaim, 511–12

Herzog, Ze'ev, 48, 63, 210, 212, 276, *485*, 508
Hess, Richard S., 53, 135, 175, 187, 190–92, 211, 215, 343–44, 344n7, 513
Hesse, Brian, 35n5
Hestrin, Ruth, 140
Hetzron, Robert, 126
Heuzey, A. Léon, 170
Higginbotham, Carolyn R., 160n1
Higham, Thomas, 441
Hilber, John W., 105n5, 368, 372, 372n10, 373–74, 374n16
Hincks, E., 39
Hitchcock, L. A., 58, 60
Hixson, Walter L., 207
Hodge, Carleton, 255n11
Hoffman, Sara L., 313
Hoffman, Yair, 514
Hoffmeier, James K., 47, 163, 194, 199, 202n1, 253–59, 253n1, 253nn3–4, 254n6, 254nn8–9, 255nn10–11, 258nn17–19, 263, 267, 335, 343
Hoffner, Harry A., 114, 115n2, 116n3, 119, 195, 262, 360, 363, 426
Hoftijzer, Jacob, 129n1, 133
Hoglund, Kenneth G., 239n7
Holl, Augustin F. C., 395
Holladay, John S., 214, 214n12, 224, 269n4, 270, 304, 394, 420–21, 487, 490
Holland, Gary, 114
Holloway, S. W., 302
Hom, Mary Katherine Yem Hing, 511
Homan, Michael M., 398
Hong, S., 23
Hopf, Maria, 33
Hopkins, D. C., 22
Horden, Peregrine, 418
Hornung, Erik, 255, 255n11, 257, 258n15
Horowitz, Wayne, 51, 53, 72n5, 100, 193n25
Horton, B. P., 26
Houston, Walter J., 311, 432, 482, 490
Huddlestun, John R., 315n8
Hudson, Michael, 435
Huehnergard, John, 120, 122–23, 133
Huffmon, Herbert B., 358n5, 371
Hulin, Linda, 421
Hummel, Bradford S., 439
Hundley, Michael B., 102, 349, 349n1, 353n5, 362–63
Hunger, Hermann, 369n1
Hunt, Chris O., 32, 35
Huntington, Richard, 487

Hurowitz, Victor, 102, 349n1, 500, 503
Hutter, Manfred, 112

Ikeda, Yutaka, 281
Ikram, Salima, 257
Ilan, D., 47
Inomata, Takeshi, 466
Irvine, S. A., 297n21
Israel Antiquities Authority, 84, *180*
Issar, A., 22
Isserlin, B. S. J., 506–7, 511

Jackson, Kent P., 289n1, 292
Jacobsen, Thorkild, 168, 346, 349n1, 351n3
James, Frances W., 160
Jamison-Drake, David W., 213
Janeway, Brian, 57n5
Janowski, Bernd, 112n1, 349n1
Janzen, Mark D., 253
Jepsen, A., 295n10
Joannès, Francis, 239n10
Jobes, Karen H., 326
Joffe, Alexander H., 210nn5–6, 465
Johnson, Raymond W., 255n11, 257n14
Johnston, Philip S., 305
Johnston, Sarah, 130
Jones, A. H. M., 418
Jones, Sian, 393
Joukowsky, Martha S., 260n1
Jursa, Michael, 357, 435

Kagen, Elisa, 308
Kahn, Dan'el, 318
Kamlah, Jens, 349n1
Kang, Sa-Moon, 394n8, 512–13
Kaniastry, Krzysztof, 310
Kaniewski, D., 26–27
Kaplan, Philip, 317
Karageorghis, Vassos, 198n11, 266, 472
Katz, J., 50
Kaufmann, Yehezkel, 10, 340, 344
Keefer, Donald K., 310
Keel, Othmar, 50–51, 123, 138, 151n1, 154, 156, 158–63, 166, 170–71, *171*, 173n2, 174, *174*, *175*, 176, 178–79, 178n4, 181, *181*
Keimer, Kyle H., 299, 303
Kelle, Brad E., 71n3, 72n6, 282
Kelly, Robert L., 25
Kelly, Thomas, 238n3
Kemp, Barry J., 197, 253n3, 256–57, 483
Kempinsky, Aharon, 63
Ken-Tor, Revital, 308
Kern, Paul Bentley, 508–11

Khazanov, Anatoly, 34
Kilchör, Benjamin, 207
Killebrew, Ann E., 57, 63, 201, 261–63, 267–69, 460–61
King, Philip J., 22–23, 39, 365, 478, 496, 506
Kirch, Patrick V., 464n1
Kislev, Mordechai E., 33, 36, 412n4
Kitchen, Kenneth A., 104n3, 107, 187n1, 189, 189n6, 190–92, 192n19, 193n23, 196, 198n9, 203, 205–7, 208n1, 211, 211n8, 218n1, 258nn17–19, 262–63, 273n3, 274n6, 276n8, 494
Kitchener, H. H., 8
Kleber, Kristin, 424
Kleiman, S., 60
Klein, Nancy L., 79
Kletter, Raz, 57, 67, 141, 210n5, 488
Klingbeil, Gerald A., 355, 359
Klingbeil, Martin, 158
Klinger, Jörg, 114
Kloos, Carola, 336–37
Knabb, Kyle, 444–45
Knapp, A. Bernard, 266, 268
Knapp, Andrew, 114, 295n12, 296, 297n24, 298
Knauf, Ernst Axel, 276
Knight, Douglas A., 497
Knoppers, Gary N., 240, 242n14, 243n18
Koch, Klaus, 112n1
Koch, Ulla Susanne, 358
Kochavi, Moshe, 270
Köckert, Matthias, 123
Koepf-Taylor, Laurel W., 398
Kofoed, Jens Bruun, 216
Kogan-Zehavi, Elena, 315n6
Korpel, Marjo C. A., 173–74
Kotsonas, Antonis, 260n2
Kottmeier, Christoph, 308
Kottsieper, Ingo, 500
Kozloff, Arielle P., 254n5, 255
Kraemer, Ross S., 401n12
Kramer, Samuel Noah, 340, 500, 502
Kreps, Gary A., 311
Kreimerman, I., 64
Kruchten, Jean-Marie, 370
Kuemmerlin-McLean, Joanne K., 370
Kuhn, Thomas S., 206
Kuhrt, Amélie, 72, 237, 323n15, 323n19
Kutsko, John F., 346
Kynes, Will, 504

LaBianca, Øystein S., 392
Laboury, Dimitri, 254, 256–57
Lambert, David, 398n8

Lambert, Wilfried G., 100, 102, 280, 358, 499n2, 500–502, 505
Lancaster, Steven P., 20nn2–3
Lang, Bernhard, 482, 490
Lange, Sarah, 358n4
Langgut, Dafna, 26–27, 36, 242n15, 312
Lapp, Nancy L., 79–80
Lapp, Paul W., 79–80
Larsen, Mogens Trolle, 94, 420, 424
Latour, Bruno, 172
Lauffrey, Jean, 254
Lawergren, Bo, 469
Lawrence, Paul J. A., 203, 205, 207, 210, 494
Layard, Austen Henry, 39, 165–66
Leahy, Anthony, 260n1, 317, 318n14
Lederman, Z., 56, 60
Lehmann, Gunnar, 57, 71, 73–76, 213, 269
Leichty, Erle, 102, 313
Leidwanger, Justin, 419
Lemaire, André, 73, 141, 237, 241, 291, 295–96, 297n23, 347, 495, 505
Lemche, Niels Peter, 43, 193n22, 208n2
LeMon, Joel M., 157–58, 173, *177*, *178*, *178*, 178n4, *179*, 180, *180*
Lemos, T. M., 404
Lenski, Gerhard, 203–4, 206n8
Lesko, Leonard H., 267
Levenson, Jon D., 349n1, 387
Levin, Yigal, 272, 278n10
Levine, Lee I., 86, 173, 325n30
Levine, Louis D., 304
Levinson, Bernard M., 496
Lévi-Strauss, Claude, 168
Lev-Tov, Justin, 35n5
Levy, Thomas E., 60, 203, 210, 267–68, 270, 395, 438, 441–45
Lev-Yadun, Simcha, 33
Lewis, Theodore J., 131
Lichtheim, Miriam, 104n3, 106, 106n7, 108–9, 111, 258n19, 421n9, 500–501
Lieberman, Saul, 168
Liebner, Uzi, 82
Liebowitz, H., 160
Lipiński, Edward, 60, 221, 269, 283, 295n10
Lipschits, Oded, 60, 71, 231n1, 232–33, 232n3, 240–42, 242n15, 315, 317n13
Liss, Brady, 438
List, Johann-Mattis, 126
Litt, Thomas, 26–27, 36, 312
Liverani, Mario, 98, 187, 189n7, 281, 301–2, 421, 506–7

Loewenstamm, Samuel E., 306
London, Gloria, 49, 446, 447, *447*, *448*, *449*, *450*, 451, *451*, 455, 461
Long, B. O., 41
Loprieno, Antonio, 104n3
Loren, D. D., 483
Loud, G., 160
Lucas, E. C., 326n34
Ludlum, Ruth, 511
Lukonin, Vladimir, 238n1, 241n12
Lundquist, John M., 349n1
Luukko, Mikko, 422
Lynch, Matthew J., 340, 341, *342*, 345, 347

Macabuag, J., 310
Macalister, R. A. S., 49
Maccoby, Hyam, 365
MacDonald, Burton, 442
MacDonald, Nathan, 22–23, 34n4, 341, 345–46, 457
Machinist, Peter, 40–41, 242n16, 304
Mack-Fisher, Loren R., 499
Macqueen, J. G., 360n8
Maeir, Aren M., 46n11, 48–51, 54, 55nn1–3, 56–60, 67, 75, 270–71, 460, *460*, 464n1, 509
Magdalene, F. Rachel, 424
Magen, Yitzhak, 232
Magness, Jodi, 81, 247, 467
Mahler-Slasky, Yael, 36
Maidman, Maynard P., 100–101
Malamat, Abraham, 190, 192, 192n17, 193n25, 211n8, 358n5, 511
Malešević, Siniša, 206
Manassa, Colleen, 254
Mann, R., 483
Manniche, Lisa, 255
Manning, Patrick, 205
Manning, Stuart W., 421
Marchetti, N., 50
Marcus, Michelle I., 467
Marcuson, Hannah, 100, 372n11
Marfoe, Leon, 391
Markoe, G. E., 59
Marinatos, Nannó, 197–98
Marom, Nimrod, 28, 33
Marquand, Allan, 79
Martens, Elmer A., 513
Martin, Geoffrey Thorndike, 253n2
Martin, Mario A. S., 160n1, 445
Martin, Rebecca S., 81
Marx, Emanuel, 22
Masson, Frédéric, 308
Masson, O., 317
Master, Daniel M., 63, 160, 210n5, 214n12, 316, 394, 418–19, 433, 466

Math, Nicola, 198
Matney, Timothy, 508
Matoušova-Rajmova, M., 470
Matthews, Victor H., 112n1, 403–4, 405n1, 407–8
Matthiae, Paolo, 358
Mattingly, David, 442
Mattingly, Gerald L., 289, 292, 442
Mauss, Marcel, 465
Mays, James Luther, 307
Mazar, Amihai, 43n8, 45, 48, 50–51, 53, 55–56, 56n4, 59, 62–64, 62n1, 64n2, 161–62, 174, *174*, 188n4, 213, 216–18, 261, 269–70, 463
Mazar, Benjamin, 238n4, 274n6
Mazar, Eilat, 66, 141, 212n10
McCarter, P. Kyle, Jr., 134, 188, 192n18
McCown, C. C., 238n4
McGeough, Kevin, 421
McGovern, Patrick E., 160n1
McKenzie, J. S., 42n6
McKenzie, Steven L., 208n3, 297n27
McNutt, Paula M., 440, 440n2
McQuitty, Alison, 398
Mee, Christopher, 266, 269
Meier, Samuel A., 101
Meiggs, Russell, 239n8
Meiri, Meirav, 35
Meltzer, Edmund S., 262
Melville, Sarah C., 507, 512
Mendelsohn, Isaac, 423
Mendelssohn, Heinrich, 29
Mendenhall, G. E., 55, 203
Merlo, Paolo, 176
Meshel, Ze'ev, 138, 154, 177, *177*, *178*, 178n4, 179, *179*, 180, *180*, 471
Meshorer, Ya'akov, 242nn16–17
Metcalf, Christopher, 119
Metcalf, Peter, 487
Mettinger, Tryggve N. D., 173, 175n3, 342, 345, 349n1, 354n9
Meyers, Carol, 76n15, 187, 378–79, 378n3, 396–98, 396n2, 397nn3–4, 398n7, 400n9, 401n12, 402n14, 404, 456, 466
Michalowski, Piotr, 97, 99, 339n6, 503
Mierse, William E., 214, 349n1
Miglio, Adam E., 91, 394n10
Migowski, Claudia, 308
Milano, Lucio, 358
Mildenberg, Leo, 242n16
Milgrom, Jacob, 365, 394n8
Millard, Alan R., 51–53, 99–100, 136, 198n10, 214, 214n11
Miller, J. Maxwell, 224, 270, 288
Miller, Jared L., 350n2, 353n4
Miller, Marvin Lloyd, 434n3

Mills, Barbara J., 466
Milviski, Chaim, 232
Mirelman, S., 470, 472
Mitchell, William J. T., 121, 156
Mittmann, Siegfried, 238n2, 238n4
Moberly, R. Walter L., 193
Monroe, Christopher M., 417, 421
Monson, James M., 20nn2–3
Monson, John M., 214
Montet, Pierre, 197
Montserrat, Dominic, 253, 253n3, 259
Moore, Megan Bishop, 71n3, 72n6
Moorey, P. R. S., 201, 203
Moran, William L., 259, 262, 476
Morentz, Siegfried, 257
Morgan, David, 180
Morris, Ellen Fowles, 98, 160, 262, 483
Morris, Ian, 417n1
Moshier, Stephen O., 199
Mosser, Carl, 86
Mourad, Anna-Latifa, 195
Mouton, Alice, 112
Moyal, Y., 490
Muhly, James D., 441
Mulder, Martin J., 420
Müller, Hans-Peter, 292
Müller, Vera, 198
Mullins, R., 160n1
Mumford, Gregory, 260–62, 268–69
Münger, S., 161
Munro, Natalie D., 33
Murnane, William J., 253n1, 256–57, 257n12, 258n19, 259, 262
Mysliwiec, Karol, 211

Na'aman, Nadav, 45, 47, 51, 56n4, 193, 219, 274, 274n6, 280, 284, 291, 295, 297n21, 303, 314n2, 314n5, 384, 508
Nadali, Davide, 507, 509–11
Nadel, Dani, 33
Nagelsmit, Eelco, 152
Nahmias-Lotan, Tamar, 269n4
Najjar, Mohammed, 60, 67, 268, 438, 442, 445
Nam, Roger, 417
Nardoni, Enrique, 311
Naveh, Joseph, 51, 240, 293, 293n3, 507
Negbi, Ora, 50, 115
Nemet-Nejat, Karen Rhea, 357n2
Nestor, D. A., 57
Neu, Erich, 118
Neufeld, E., 482, 490
Neujahr, Matthew, 374n16
Neumann, Hans, 423–26
Neville, Ann, 419

Newsom, Carol A., 326n33
Niditch, Susan, 395, 513
Niehr, Herbert, 294n6, 295, 344
Niemann, Hermann Michael, 276
Niemeyer, Hans Georg, 419
Nigro, L., 50
Nir, Yaacov, 310
Nissinen, Martti, 357n3, 368, 371nn4–6, 371n8, 372nn9–10, 372nn12–14, 374, 374nn16–18, 471
Nocquet, Dany, 123
Nolan, Patrick, 204, 206n8
Noonan, Benjamin J., 75, 75n12
Norris, Fran H., 310
North, Douglass, 417
Nossov, Konstantin, 509, 512
Noth, Martin, 202–3, 274, 295n10
Notley, R. Steven, 7, 9–10, 15–16, 16n1, 20n3, 73, 188–89, 278, 392, 506
Novotny, Jamie, 300–301, 349n1
Noy, David, 323n16
Nur, Amos, 311

Oates, David, 510
O'Brien, John Maxwell, 321n6, 324n22
O'Connor, David, 262n3, 264
Oded, Bustenay, 302, 510
Oeming, Manfred, 60
Ofer, A., 213
Oliver-Smith, Anthony, 310–11
Olsson, Birger, 84
Olsvig-Whittaker, Linda, 36
Olyan, Saul M., 258n17, 380, 384
Oppenheim, A. Leo, 363, 435
Oren, Eliezer D., 260n1, 317
Oriental Institute, Epigraphic Survey, 199
Ornan, Tallay, 77, 156, 180
Orshan, Gideon, 30
Orthmann, Winfried, 154
Ortiz, Steven M., 208
Ortner, Sherry, 400
Oshima, Takayoshi, 51, 53, 193n25
Otto, Eckart, 203, 494
Otto, S., 297n22
Overland, Paul, 499, 505
Owen, David I., 123
Ozdas, Harun, 419

Pace, Leann, 457, 464n2
Palestine Exploration Fund, 8, 39–40
Palivou, Clairy, 197–98
Panitz-Cohen, N., 49, 463
Panofsky, Erwin, 156
Papadopoulos, Gerassimos A., 312
Pappa, Eleftheria, 419

Pappe, Ilan, 207
Pardee, Dennis, 93, 133, 163, 344n7, 359n7, 363, 370, 381, 471
Park, Song-Mi Suzie, 506
Parker, Bradley J., 301–3, 397, 399, 459
Parker, Simon B., 122, 163, 512
Parker Pearson, Michael, 487–88
Parkinson, Richard B., 104n3
Parpola, Simo, 301–2, 370n2, 512
Parrot, André, 167, 167, 169, 169, 170, 170, 192n20
Payne, Sebastian, 34
Pearce, Laurie E., 71, 99, 233–34, 433, 502
Pearsall, Deborah M., 25
Peckham, J. Brian, 238n3
Peden, Alexander J., 262
Peek-Asa, C., 310
Peleg-Barkat, Orit, 83
Perdu, Olivier, 314n3
Perdue, Leo G., 302, 304, 503–4
Pernigotti, Sergio, 356
Perry-Gal, Lee, 35
Person, Raymond F., 100
Peters, F. E., 320n1
Petrie, William M. Flinders, 39, 40, 161, 197
Petter, Thomas D., 391, 393–94
Pettinato, Giovanni, 358
Piasetzky, Eli, 55, 62n1
Piccirillo, Michele, 7
Piperno, Dolores R., 33
Pitard, Wayne T., 295, 295n9
Pitkänen, Pekka, 201, 203–4, 205n4, 206–7, 207n9
Pleiner, Radomir, 507
Plitmann, Uzi, 30
Polak, Frank H., 72, 72n7
Polanyi, Karl, 416
Pongratz-Leisten, Beate, 101, 350n2
Ponting, Matthew, 508
Pope, Marvin H., 174–75
Porada, Edith, 171
Porten, Bezalel, 239–40, 242, 314, 347
Porter, B. N., 353n5
Porter, Benjamin W., 60, 70–72, 70n1, 210n6, 287
Porter, Bertha, 197
Posener, Georges, 104n3
Postgate, John Nicholas, 97–98, 296n15, 349n1, 506
Powell, Marvin, 417
Preiser, Wolfgang, 495
Price, Simon, 325n28
Pritchard, James B., 50, 151n1, 157, 166, 175, 191n15, 289n1, 290, 362, 364, 411, 457, 476, 493–94, 507
Propp, W. H. C., 267, 270

Provan, Iain, 55
Pruzsinszky, Regine, 196, 196n5, 471
Pucci Ben Zeev, Miriam, 326n33
Pulak, Cemal, 418, 421
Purcell, Nicholas, 418
Pyschny, Katharina, 153

Qedar, Shraga, 242n17
Quack, Joachim Friedrich, 104n3
Quirke, Stephen, 104n3

Rabinowitz, Isaac, 238n5
Radner, Ellen, 360
Radner, Karen, 302, 417, 434
Rainey, Anson F., 7–10, 15–16, 16n1,
    20n3, 47, 73, 188–90, 195n3, 211,
    278, 292, 392, 421, 506
Rajak, Tessa, 326n32
Ramos, Melissa, 129
Rasmussen, Carl G., 20n3
Ratner, Robert, 121
Ray, J. D., 501
Ray, Paul, 70, 72, 76
Reade, Julian, 510
Reali, Chiara, 194
Redding, Richard W., 34
Redford, Donald B., 195, 195n2,
    197, 199n12, 254–59, 267, 273n3,
    276n9, 314n4
Redford, Susan, 267
Redmount, Carol, 193
Reeves, Nicholas, 254n6, 255, 255n11,
    257, 257n12, 257n14
Regev, Eyal, 245–47
Reich, Ronny, 63
Reifenberg, Adolf, 34
Reiner, Erica, 95
Reisner, George A., 39–40
Reitz, E. J., 24
Rendsburg, Gary, 258n18
Renfrew, Colin, 262, 416
Renger, Johannes, 356
Revell, Ernest J., 395
Rezetko, Robert, 100
Richardson, M. E. J., 493
Richardson, Peter, 85–86
Richardson, Seth, 101, 510
Richter, Thomas, 358n4
Ristau, Kenneth A., 236, 240, 243
Ritmeyer, Leen, 84
Rivaroli, Marta, 512
Roberts, J. J. M., 163, 305, 383
Roberts, N., 24
Roberts, R. Gareth, 260n1, 307, 310
Roberts, Ryan N., 306
Robertson, Warren C., 310, 345n11
Robins, Gay, 153–54, 255
Robinson, Edward, 7–8, 39
Robinson, Joseph, 198

Rocca, Samuel, 507, 510
Rochberg, Francesca, 98, 369
Rofe, Alexander, 513
Rogel, M., 458–59
Roisman, Joseph, 321n6
Rollston, Christopher A., 67, 98, 128,
    135–36
Rom-Shiloni, Dalit, 319n18
Ron, Z., 412
Root, Bradley W., 74n11
Rosen, Arlene M., 32
Rosen, Steven, 32, 35
Rostovtzeff, M., 320n1
Roth, Ann Macy, 356
Roth, Martha T., 425–26, 428–29, 493
Routledge, Bruce, 60, 287, 289–90,
    289n1
Rowan, York, 461
Rowe, Ignacio Márquez, 503
Rowlands, M. J., 465
Rowlett, Lori L., 513
Rowton, Michael B., 34, 188
Rubin, Aaron, 127, 133
Ruiz-Gálvez, Luisa, 71
Runesson, Anders, 84–85, 85
Russell, James R., 500
Russell, John Malcolm, 301, 510
Russell, Stephen C., 406
Russmann, Edna R., 154
Ryan, Jordan J., 78, 81, 82, 83, 86, 86
Rzepka, Slawomir, 197

Sacchi, Paolo, 238n6
Sader, Hélène, 268
Safrai, Ze'ev, 7, 484, 488
Saggs, H. W. F., 357
Sagona, Antonio, 266, 268
Sagrillo, Troy Leiland, 273n1
Sakenfeld, Katherine D., 392, 407
Salimbeti, Andrea, 260n1
Salzman, Carl P., 34
Samuel, Alan E., 324n26
Sandars, N. K., 260n1
Sanders, Paul, 118
Sanders, Seth L., 51–53, 98–100,
    344–45, 344n7
Sandman, Maj, 104n3, 109, 254n7,
    258n19
Sandmel, Samuel, 121, 163
Sandy, D. Brent, 320, 324n24, 324n26,
    327n35
Sanmartín, J., 359n7
Sapir-Hen, Lidar, 35n5, 57
Sass, Benjamin, 51–53, 51n1, 59, 180,
    181
Sasson, Jack M., 40, 196
Sasson, Victor, 136
Sauer, Carl Ortwin, 6–7
Saur, Markus, 505

Schäfer, Heinrich, 156
Schaper, Joachim, 238n1
Schep, Leo, 323n21
Schipper, Bernd U., 105, 314n5,
    315n7, 318, 318n15
Schloen, J. David, 316, 376, 394, 418,
    465, 482, 490
Schmidt, Konrad, 258n17
Schmidt, Werner H., 307
Schmitt, Rüdiger, 63, 166, 344, 376–
    78, 376n1, 380, 400n9
Schmitz, Philip C., 317
Schneider, Tammi, 281
Schneider, Thomas, 196, 267, 270,
    501–2
Schniedewind, William M., 51,
    72, 211n7, 293n3, 297nn23–24,
    297n27
Schroer, Silvia, 151n1, 153, 158, 166,
    172, 173n2, 174, 174
Schürer, E., 248
Schwarcz, Henry P., 25
Schwartz, Mark, 506
Schwemer, Daniel, 112n1
Scurlock, JoAnn, 337, 507, 509
Seeher, Jürgen, 154, 266
Seele, Keith C., 256
Seevers, Boyd, 511
Segal, Arthur, 82
Sekunda, Nicholas V., 237
Sellin, E., 160
Selman, Martin J., 191, 363, 365, 493
Sergi, Omer, 60
Seri, Andrea, 428
Serpico, M., 49
Shafer, Byron E., 349n1
Shafer-Elliott, Cynthia, 456–59,
    461–62
Shaffer, Aaron, 131, 193n25
Shafiq, Rula, 442
Shahack-Gross, Ruth, 35, 460
Shai, Itzhaq, 52, 212
Shaked, Shaul, 240
Shanan, Leslie, 31, 35, 413
Shanks, H., 42–43
Shaw, Ian, 253n1, 261
Sheldon, Rose Mary, 511
Shelmerdine, Cynthia W., 261
Sherman, Tina M., 496
Sherwin, Simon, 258n17
Shryock, Andrew, 393
Shupak, Nili, 104, 104n1, 105, 105n5,
    106, 108–11, 372, 501, 505
Sievers, J., 245–48
Silberman, Neil Asher, 8, 45, 64n2,
    192, 208n3, 445
Silva, Moisés, 326n32
Silverman, David P., 173, 257
Simpson, Beryl B., 33

Simpson, William Kelly, 104n3, 258n19, 262, 269
Singer, Itamar, 114, 123, 210, 269
Skoglund, Pontus, 33
Smelik, Klaas A. D., 290, 512
Smith, Bruce D., 32–33
Smith, Christopher, 511–12
Smith, Cyril S., 438
Smith, Eli, 7–8, 39
Smith, George Adam, 8, 10, 92–93
Smith, Harry, 254
Smith, Mark S., 120–21, 258n17, 304, 340, 343–46, 346n12
Smith, Michael E., 483, 485
Smith, Monica L., 301, 464n1
Smith, Ray W., 254
Smith-Christopher, Daniel, 232, 234, 235n6
Smoak, Jeremy D., 95, 137
Sneed, Mark, 499nn1–2, 500, 504–5, 504n4
Snir, Ainit, 33
Snodgrass, A. M., 321n4
Soffer, Tamar, 29
Sommer, Michael, 417
Spalinger, Anthony J., 262, 267, 318n14, 367
Sparks, Kenton, L., 392, 493–94
Spencer, F. Scott, 307
Spencer, Neal, 263
Spiegel-Roy, Pinhas, 34
Spycket, Agnès, 50, 154, 167, 167
Srebro, Haim, 29
Stager, Lawrence E., 22–23, 43–44, 44n9, 210, 228, 230, 260n1, 316, 362, 365, 391, 396n2, 398, 418–19, 466, 478, 496, 506
Stanley, J. D., 26
Starr, Ivan, 370n2, 512
Staubli, Thomas, 158, 166, 471
Stavi, Boaz, 262
Stavrakopoulou, Francesca, 376, 380
Steinberg, Naomi, 191n16
Steindorff, George, 256
Steiner, Margreet L., 63, 71, 152, 201, 261–62
Steiner, Richard C., 133, 347n15
Sterling, Gregory E., 326n30
Stern, Ephraim, 62n1, 63, 68–71, 73–77, 73n8, 75nn12–13, 237, 242n16, 346–47, 419
Stern, Philip D., 288, 513
Stevens, Anna, 257, 365
Stewart, Andrew, 81
Stiebing, William H., Jr., 476
Stillman, Nigel, 508
Stiner, Mary C., 33
Stiros, Stathis C., 309
Stith, D. M., 294n6, 297n24

Stokes, Ryan, 142
Stökl, Jonathan, 358n5, 371n7
Stolper, Matthew W., 238–39, 241n12, 433
Strawn, Brent A., 153, 157–58, 163, 166, 172–74, 177, 178, 178, 178n4, 179, 180–81, 180, 181
Struble, Eudora, 133
Suriano, Matthew J., 295–96, 296n17
Surovell, Todd A., 33
Suter, Claudia E., 153, 157
Sutton, David, 399, 466
Sweet, Ronald F. G., 500

Tadmor, Hayim, 212, 284, 508, 511
Tadmor, M., 50
Tadmor, Naphtali, 31, 35, 413
Taggar-Cohen, Ada, 360
Tal, Oren, 74, 76–77, 77nn18–19, 240, 347
Tallis, Nigel, 508
Tamari, Vera, 397
Tappy, Ron E., 135
Tartaron, Thomas F., 264
Tatton-Brown, Veronica, 266
Taylor, Joan E., 6–7
Tchernov, Eitan, 33
Tebes, Juan Manuel, 286–87, 289, 420
Teissier, Beatrice, 123
Tenney, Jonathan S., 424
Tepper, Yotam, 35
te Velde, Herman, 355–56
Thareani, Yifat, 301–3
Thiele, Edwin R., 198
Thissen, Heinz J., 104n3
Thomas, David Hurst, 25
Thompson, Thomas L., 43, 168, 188, 188n2, 191, 194, 208n2
Tigay, Jeffrey H., 100, 161–62, 344, 344n8, 377
Tiradritti, Francesco, 154
Tobin, Vincent A., 106n6, 257, 258n19
Trigger, B. G., 51
Trimm, Charles, 513
Trotter, J. M., 238n1
Tsahar, Ella, 32
Tsetskhladze, Gocha R., 419
Tsukimoto, Akio, 358
Tsumura, David Toshio, 337, 359
Tubb, Jonathan N., 268–69
Tucker, Gene M., 307
Tufnell, O., 160
Tuplin, C., 238n1
Tyson, Craig W., 60

Uehlinger, Christoph, 50–51, 123, 138, 151n1, 153, 157–58, 166,

173n2, 174, 174, 175, 178, 178n4, 179, 181, 181, 343
Uerpmann, Margarethe, 420
Uerpmann, Hans-Peter, 420
Uffenheimer, B., 490
Urciuoli, G. M., 358
Uro, Risto, 357n3
Ussishkin, David, 277, 506, 508–11
Uziel, David J., 49
Uziel, Joe, 47–50, 52–53, 212

Valla, François, 33
Van Beek, Gus W., 41, 315n6
van Buren, Elizabeth Douglas, 170
Van Buylaere, Greta, 422
Van Dam, C., 371
van de Mieroop, Marc, 369, 475
van den Hout, Theo P. J., 100, 112, 266
Vanderhooft, David S., 72, 72n5, 230, 232–34, 233n4, 236, 240, 242, 314n2
VanderKam, James C., 144n7, 245–50
van der Kooij, G., 133
Van der Merwe, N. J., 24
van der Plicht, Johannes, 35
van der Steen, Eveline J., 60, 290, 391–93
van der Toorn, Karel, 98, 292, 292n3, 354n9, 355, 365–66, 371, 376
van Dijk, Jacobus, 255n11, 256, 267
Van Seters, John, 188, 191–92, 194, 349
Van Siclen, Charles, 257, 257n12
Vanstiphout, Herman, 339, 339n8, 354n7
Vaughn, Andrew G., 141, 227
Veenhof, Klaas R., 112n1, 167, 420
Veracini, Lorenzo, 205, 205n4, 206–7
Vermes, Geza, 144n6
Vernus, Pascal, 109, 267
Vickers, M., 483
Vidal, Jordi, 510–11
Visicato, Guiseppe, 99
Vitale, R., 469
Vogel, J. C., 24
Von Beckerath, J., 255
Von Rad, Gerhard, 512

Wachsmann, Shelly, 264
Waerzeggers, Caroline, 357
Waiman-Barak, P., 59
Wakeman, Mary K., 337
Walbank, F. W., 325n39
Waldbaum, Jane, 316n10, 419
Walker, Christopher, 172n1
Walsh, C. E., 414
Walsh, Peter, 262
Walton, J. Harvey, 394, 394n8

Walton, John H., 96n3, 151n1, 158, 191, 196n4, 326n34, 333, 337, 349, 349n1, 394, 394n8
Walton, Joshua T., 416
Wapnish, Paula, 35n5
Ward, William A., 260
Wason, P. K., 483
Watson, Patty Jo, 462
Watson, R. S., 337
Watson, W. G. E., 122
Watterson, Barbara, 198
Watts, James W., 86
Weber, Max, 418, 465
Weibel, Peter, 172
Weidner, E. F., 231
Weinfeld, Moshe, 505
Weinstein, J., 47, 160, 260n1
Weippert, Manfred, 393, 512
Weisgerber, G., 444–45
Weiss, B., 23, 26
Weiss, Ehud, 33–34, 228, 316, 420
Weissenrieder, Annette, 156
Welch, Andrew, 307
Welch, Eric L., 223
Welles, C. Bradford, 325n29
Wellhausen, Julius, 40–41, 202
Wells, Bruce, 492, 494–95
Wellum, Stephen J., 395
Wendt, Friederike, 156
Wenham, Gordon J., 202, 205n3, 349n1
Wente, Edward F., 262, 500, 504
Westbrook, Raymond, 262n3, 404, 424–28, 492, 494
Westermann, W. L., 101
Whitelam, K. W., 203
Whitt, W. D., 135
Whybray, R. N., 504
Widengren, Geo, 168
Wiggermann, F. A. M., 357

Wikander, Ola, 118n5
Wilcke, Claus, 101
Wilcox, George, 34
Wilkin, Robert L., 7
Wilkinson, Tony J., 510
Willekes, Carolyn, 323n17
Willems, Harco, 363
Williams, Margaret H., 326n33
Williams, Michael J., 124
Williams, Peter J., 424
Williams, Roland J., 258n19
Williams, Ronald, 500, 504
Williamson, Jacquelyn, 253n3, 254, 254n7, 256, 257n12, 259, 478n1
Willitts, Joel, 244
Wilson, John, 256–57, 258n19
Wilson, Kevin A., 273n3, 274n6
Wing, E. S., 24
Winnett, Frederick V., 238n5
Winter, Irene J., 156–57, 166, 466–67
Winter, Urs, 166, 173n2, 176
Wiseman, Donald J., 191, 195, 195n3, 229, 231, 420, 467
Wolfe, Patrick, 205
Wolff, S., 160
Wong, Gordon C., 305
Wood, B. G., 55n1
Woods, Christopher E., 349n1
Woolley, C. Leonard, 315
Worthington, Ian, 321n4, 322n8
Wright, David P., 360, 363, 366, 495
Wright, G. E., 40, 42
Wright, Jacob L., 507, 513
Wright, Laura, 159–61
Wright, Paul, 5
Wrightson, Graham, 323n17
Wunsch, Cornelia, 233–34
Wyssmann, Patrick, 155

Xella, Paolo, 178

Yadin, Yigael, 43, *43*, 55, 507–8, 510
Yahalom-Mack, Naama, 445
Yamada, Sigeo, 281–82, 294n6, 295
Yamauchi, Edwin, 257n13
Yardeni, Ada, 239, 347
Yasur-Landau, Assaf, 36, 49, 58, 270
Yee, Gale A., 304
Yisraeli, Yael, 270
Yom-Tov, Yoram, 29, 32
Yon, Marguerite, 154, 262, 468, 471
Young, Robb Andrew, 301
Younger, K. Lawson, Jr., 58n5, 60, 190, 206, 240, 293, 293n1, 294n4, 294nn6–7, 295nn8–9, 296n14–15, 297n20, 297n23, 297n25
Younker, Randall W., 71–73, 75–76, 210n6, 270, 391–92

Zabkar, Louis, 258
Zaccagnini, C., 421, 421n6
Zadok, Ran, 233, 233n4, 234, 281
Zaouali, L., 454
Zayadine, Fawzi, 154,
Zeder, Melinda A., 32–33, 35n5
Zertal, Adam, 56, 160, 213, 240
Zevit, Ziony, 63, 67, 129, 174, 176, 178, 365, 378, 401
Ziegler, Nele, 169, 469–71
Ziffer, Irit, 467
Zilberg, P., 64n2
Zimansky, Paul, 266, 268
Zivie-Coche, Christiane, 356
Zohar, M., 22
Zohary, Daniel, 29, 29, 30
Zohary, Michael, 33–34, 414, 414n8
Zorman, Marina, 114
Zorn, Jeffrey R., 48, 71–73, 73n8, 76–77, 232, 507, 509, 511
Zuckerman, Bruce, 121
Zuckerman, S., 50